W9-AON-040

The Oxford English Minidictionary

The Oxford English Minidictionary

Compiled by
JOYCE M. HAWKINS

Revised Third Edition

Clarendon Press · Oxford

Oxford University Press, Walton Street, Oxford OX2 6DP

Oxford New York

Athens Auckland Bangkok Bombay
Calcutta Cape Town Dar es Salaam Delhi
Florence Hong Kong Istanbul Karachi
Kuala Lumpur Madras Madrid Melbourne
Mexico City Nairobi Paris Singapore
Taipei Tokyo Toronto

and associated companies in
Berlin Ibadan

Oxford is a trade mark of Oxford University Press

Published in the United States by
Oxford University Press Inc., New York

© Oxford University Press 1981, 1988, 1991, 1994

First edition 1981
Second edition 1988
Third edition 1991
Revised edition 1994

All rights reserved. No part of this publication may be reproduced,
stored in a retrieval system, or transmitted, in any form or by any means,
without the prior permission in writing of Oxford University Press. Within
the UK, exceptions are allowed in respect of any fair dealing for the purpose
of research or private study, or criticism or review, as permitted under the
Copyright, Designs and Patents Act, 1988, or in the case of reprographic
reproduction in accordance with the terms of the licences issued by the
Copyright Licensing Agency. Enquiries concerning reproduction outside
these terms and in other countries should be sent to the Rights Department,
Oxford University Press, at the address above

This book is sold subject to the condition that it shall not, by way
of trade or otherwise, be lent, re-sold, hired out or otherwise circulated
without the publisher's prior consent in any form of binding or cover
other than that in which it is published and without a similar condition
including this condition being imposed on the subsequent purchaser

British Library Cataloguing in Publication Data

Data available

Library of Congress Cataloging in Publication Data

Data available

ISBN 0–19–861310–5

10 9 8 7 6 5 4 3 2

Printed in Great Britain by
Charles Letts (Scotland) Ltd.

Contents

Preface

This is the smallest member of the Oxford family of dictionaries, and is written for those who need a compact guide to the spelling and meaning of the commonest words of the English language of today.

In spite of its small format the dictionary gives many derivative words (e.g. *basically*, *happiness*, *sedately*, *swimmer*) comparatives and superlatives in *-er*, *-est* are indicated, plurals of nouns and inflexions of verbs are given if there might be doubt about their formation or spelling (e.g. *potatoes*, *stimuli* p.t. *shook*, p.p. *shaken*; p.t. *referred*; the past participle is given separately unless it is the same as the past tense in form).

For international convenience, pronunciation is given by means of the International Phonetic Alphabet (see p. viii).

A new feature included in this third edition is the special Supplement of short words of kinds likely to be sought by players of word-games; letters received, and our knowledge of the purposes for which dictionaries are actually used, has led us to believe that this will be welcome. Many of these words are rare or obsolete or are found only in dialectal use, and would normally fall outside the scope of a small dictionary. No book of this size could hope to provide a complete list of every possible item, but we hope that the selections assembled here will be useful. I am grateful to Peter Newby, expert in word-games, for advice and generous help in the preparation of this Supplement.

February 1991

J.M.H.

Note to Revised Third Edition

For the 1994 revised impression a large number of corrections and improvements have been made to the text. In addition, many topical new words and phrases have been added, e.g. *bhaji*, *body piercing*, *council tax*, *gene therapy*, *hospital trust*, *keyhole surgery*, *national curriculum*, *ram-raid*, and *repetitive train injury*, reflecting some of the most recent social and political changes and scientific advancements.

March 1994   D.J.T.

Pronunciation

A guide to this is given, by means of the International Phonetic Alphabet, for a word or part of a word that is difficult to pronounce, or is spelt the same as another word but pronounced differently. The stressed syllable in words of two or more syllables is shown by the mark ' placed immediately before it.

The pronunciation indicated represents the standard speech of southern England.

Key to phonetic symbols

Consonants

The following consonants have their usual English sound values:

b, d, f, h, k, l, m, n, p, r, t, v, w, z.

g as in go	ʃ as in ship	x (Scottish) as in loch
ŋ as in sing	ʒ as in vision	(in general use
θ as in thin	j as in yet	often pronounced
ð as in then		as k)
s as in hiss		tʃ as in chin
		dʒ as in jam

Vowels

æ as in fat	ʌ as in dug	aɪə(r) as in fire
ɑ: as in cart	ʊ as in book	aʊə(r) as in sour
e as in met	u: as in boot	eɪ as in fate
ɪ as in bit	ɜ:(r) as in fur	eə(r) as in fair
i: as in meet	ə as in ago	ɔɪ as in boil
ɒ as in got	aɪ as in bite	ʊə(r) as in poor
ɔ: as in port	aʊ as in brow	əʊ as in goat

The symbol ˜ over a vowel indicates nasalization as in French *vin blanc* (vã blã).

Abbreviations

a. adjective	*N.Engl*. northern	*S.Afr*. South
abbr. abbreviation	England	African
adjs. adjectives	*n.fem*. noun	*Sc*. Scottish
adv. adverb	feminine	Sept. September
advs. adverbs	Nov. November	*sing*. singular
attrib. attributively	*n.pl*. noun plural	*sl*. slang
Austr. Australian	*ns*. nouns	US United States
colloq. colloquial	orig. originally	usu. usually
conj. conjunction	[P.] proprietary	*v*. verb
Dec. December	term	*v.aux*. auxiliary
dial. dialect	*pl*. plural	verb
esp. especially	*poss*. possessive	*v.i*. intransitive
Feb. February	*p.p*. past participle	verb
fem. feminine	*pr*. pronounced	*v.imper*. imperative
imper. imperative	*pref*. prefix	verb
Ind. Indian	*prep*. preposition	*v.refl*. reflexive
int. interjection	*preps*. prepositions	verb
ints. interjections	*pres*. present	*v.t*. transitive
iron. ironically	*pres.p*. present	verb
Ir. Irish	participle	*v.t./i*. transitive
Jan. January	*pron*. pronoun	and intransitive
joc. jocularly	*p.t*. past tense	verb
n. noun	*rel.pron*. relative	*vulg*. vulgar
	pronoun	

Abbreviations that are in general use (such as ft., RC) appear in the dictionary itself.

Proprietary Terms

This dictionary includes some words which are, or are asserted to be, proprietary terms or trade marks. Their inclusion does not mean that they have acquired for legal purposes a non-proprietary or general significance, nor is any other judgement implied concerning their legal status. In cases where the editor has some evidence that a word is used as a proprietary name or trade mark this is indicated by the letter [P.], but no judgement concerning the legal status of such words is made or implied thereby.

A

a *a.* one, any; in, to, or for each.

aback *adv.* **taken aback** disconcerted.

abacus *n.* (*pl.* **-cuses**) frame with balls sliding on rods, used for counting.

abaft *adv.* & *prep.* nearer to the stern (than).

abandon *v.t.* leave without intending to return; give up. —*n.* careless freedom of manner. **abandonment** *n.*

abandoned *a.* (of manner etc.) showing abandon; depraved.

abase *v.t.* humiliate, degrade. **abasement** *n.*

abashed *a.* embarrassed, ashamed.

abate *v.t./i.* make or become less intense. **abatement** *n.*

abattoir /-twɑ:(r)/ *n.* slaughterhouse.

abbey *n.* building occupied by a community of monks or nuns; church belonging to this.

abbot *n.* head of a community of monks. **abbess** *n.fem.*

abbreviate *v.t.* shorten.

abbreviation *n.* shortened form of word(s).

ABC *n.* alphabet; alphabetical guide; rudiments (of a subject).

abdicate *v.t./i.* renounce (a throne or right etc.). **abdication** *n.*

abdomen /'æ-/ *n.* part of the body containing the digestive organs. **abdominal** /-'dɒm-/ *a.*

abduct *v.t.* kidnap. **abduction** *n.*, **abductor** *n.*

aberrant /æ'ber-/ *a.* showing aberration. **aberrance** *n.*

aberration /-'reɪ-/ *n.* deviation from what is normal; mental or moral lapse; distortion.

abet *v.t.* (*p.t.* ꜰbetted) encourage or assist in wrongdoing. **abettor** *n.*

abeyance *n.* **in abeyance** not being used or dealt with for a time.

abhor *v.t.* (*p.t.* abhorred) detest. **abhorrence** /-'hɒ-/ *n.*

abhorrent /-'hɒ-/ *a.* detestable.

abide *v.t./i.* (*old use; p.t.* abode) remain, dwell; (*p.t.* abided) tolerate. **abide by** keep (a promise); accept (consequences etc.).

abiding *a.* lasting, permanent.

ability *n.* quality that makes an action or process possible, power to do something; cleverness.

abject /'æ-/ *a.* wretched; lacking all pride. **abjectly** *adv.*

ablaze *a.* blazing.

able *a.* (-**er**, -**est**) having enough power; having ability. **ably** *adv.*

ablutions *n.pl.* process of washing oneself; place for this.

abnegate /'æ-/ *v.t.* renounce. **abnegation** *n.*

abnormal *a.* not normal, not usual. **abnormally** *adv.*, **abnormality** *n.*

aboard *adv.* & *prep.* on board.

abode *see* abide. —*n.* (*old use*) dwelling-place.

abolish *v.t.* put an end to. **abolition** *n.*, **abolitionist** *n.*

abominable *a.* detestable; very bad or unpleasant. **abominably** *adv.*

abominate *v.t.* detest. **abomination** *n.*

aboriginal *a.* existing in a country from its earliest times. —*n.* aboriginal inhabitant.

aborigines /-niːz/ *n.pl.* aboriginal inhabitants. **aborigine** /-niː/ *n.* (*colloq.*) one of these.

abort v.t./i. (cause to) expel a foetus prematurely; end prematurely and unsuccessfully; (cause to) remain undeveloped.

abortion n. premature expulsion of a foetus from the womb; operation to cause this; misshapen creature.

abortionist n. person who performs abortions.

abortive a. producing abortion; unsuccessful. **abortively** adv.

abound v.i. be plentiful. **abound in** be rich in.

about adv. & prep. all round; near; here and there; (in circulation; approximately; in connection with; so as to face in the opposite direction; in rotation. **about-face**, **about-turn** ns. reversal of direction or policy. **be about to** be on the point of (doing).

above adv. & prep. at or to a higher point (than); over; beyond the level or understanding etc. of. **above-board** without deception.

abracadabra n. magic formula.

abrade v.t. scrape or wear away by rubbing.

abrasion n. rubbing or scraping away; injury caused by this.

abrasive a. causing abrasion; harsh. —n. substance used for grinding or polishing surfaces. **abrasively** adv.

abreast adv. side by side. **abreast** of level with, not behind; up to date with.

abridge v.t. shorten by using fewer words. **abridgement** n.

abroad adv. away from one's country; over a wide area.

abrogate v.t. repeal, cancel. **abrogation** n.

abrupt a. sudden; curt; steep. **abruptly** adv., **abruptness** n.

abscess n. collection of pus formed in the body.

abscond v.i. go away secretl

abseil /ˈæbseɪl/ v.i. descend by using a rope fixed at a higher point. —n. such a descent.

absence n. being absent; lack.

absent¹ /ˈæ-/ a. not present; lacking, non-existent; absentminded. **absent-minded** a. with one's mind on other things; forgetful. **absently** adv.

absent² /-ˈsent/ v.refl. **absent oneself** stay away.

absentee n. person who is absent from work etc. **absenteeism** n.

absinthe n. a green liqueur.

absolute a. complete; unrestricted; independent. **absolutely** adv.

absolution n. priest's formal declaration of forgiveness of sins.

absolutism n. principle of government with unrestricted powers. **absolutist** n.

absolve v.t. clear of blame or guilt; free from an obligation.

absorb v.t. take in, combine into itself or oneself; reduce the intensity of; occupy the attention or interest of. **absorber** n., **absorption** n., **absorptive** a.

absorbent a. able to absorb moisture etc. **absorbency** n.

abstain v.i. refrain, esp. from drinking alcohol; decline to use one's vote. **abstainer** n., **abstention** n.

abstemious /-ˈstiː-/ a. not self-indulgent. **abstemiously** adv., **abstemiousness** n.

abstinence n. abstaining esp. from food or alcohol. **abstinent** a., **abstinently** adv.

abstract¹ /ˈæ-/ a. having no material existence; theoretical; (of art) not representing things pictorially; summary. —n. abstract quality or idea; summary; piece of abstract art.

abstract² /-ˈstrækt/ v.t. take out, remove; make a summary of. **abstracted** a. with one's mind on other things. **abstraction** n.

abstruse /-'stru:s/ a. hard to understand, profound. **abstrusely** adv.

absurd a. not in accordance with common sense, ridiculous. **absurdly** adv., **absurdity** n.

abundant a. plentiful; having plenty of something. **abundantly** adv., **abundance** n.

abuse v.t. make bad use of; ill-treat; attack with abusive language. —n. abusing; abusive language.

abusive a. using harsh words or insults. **abusively** adv., **abusiveness** n.

abut v.t./i. (p.t. abutted) border (upon), end or lean (against); have a common boundary. **abutment** n.

abysmal a. very bad or deplorable. **abysmally** adv.

abyss /-'bɪs/ n. bottomless chasm.

acacia n. a kind of flowering tree or shrub.

academic a. of a college or university; scholarly; of theoretical interest only. —n. academic person. **academically** adv.

academician n. member of an Academy.

Academy n. society of scholars or artists. **academy** n. school, esp. for specialized training.

acanthus /-'kæ-/ n. plant with large thistle-like leaves.

accede /-'si:d/ v.i. accede to agree to; enter upon (office).

accelerate v.t./i. increase the speed (of). **acceleration** n.

accelerator n. device (esp. a pedal of a vehicle) for increasing speed.

accent¹ /'æ-/ n. emphasis; mark showing the emphasis or quality of a vowel; national or local etc. way of pronouncing words. **accentual** /-'sen-/ a.

accent² /-'sent/ v.t. pronounce with an accent; emphasize.

accentuate v.t. emphasize; make prominent. **accentuation** n.

accept v.t./i. take willingly, say yes to an offer or invitation; agree to; take as true. **acceptance** n.

acceptable a. worth accepting; tolerable. **acceptably** adv., **acceptability** n.

access n. way in; right or means of approaching or entering; attack of emotion. —v.t. obtain (data) from a computer etc.

accessible a. able to be reached or obtained. **accessibly** adv., **accessibility** n.

accession n. reaching a rank or position; thing added.

accessory n. additional. —n. accessory fitment or decoration etc.; person who helps in a crime.

accidence n. part of grammar dealing with inflexions.

accident n. unexpected event, esp. one causing damage; chance.

accidental a. happening by accident. —n. sign attached to a note in music, showing temporary departure from the key signature. **accidentally** adv.

acclaim v.t. welcome or applaud enthusiastically. —n. shout of welcome, applause. **acclamation** n.

acclimatize v.t./i. make or become used to a new climate. **acclimatization** n.

accolade n. bestowal of a knighthood or other honour; praise.

accommodate v.t. provide lodging or room for; supply; adapt, make harmonize.

accommodating a. willing to do as asked.

accommodation n. process of accommodating; living-premises. **accommodation address** one to which letters may be sent for a person not living there.

accompany v.t. go with; be present with; provide in addition; play an instrumental part supporting (singer(s) or instrument). **accompaniment** n., **accompanist** n.

accomplice n. partner in crime.

accomplish v.t. succeed in doing or achieving.

accomplished a. skilled; having many accomplishments.

accomplishment n. accomplishing; useful ability.

accord v.t./i. be consistent; grant. —n. consent, agreement. **of one's own accord** without being asked or compelled.

accordance n. conformity.

according adv. **according as** in proportion as. **according to** as stated by; in proportion to. **accordingly** adv.

accordion n. portable musical instrument with bellows and a keyboard.

accost v.t. approach and speak to.

account n. statement of money paid or owed; credit arrangement with a bank or firm; importance; description, report. —v.t. regard as. **account for** give a reckoning of; explain the cause of; kill, overcome. **on account of** because of.

accountable a. obliged to account for one's actions. **accountability** n.

accountant n. person who keeps or inspects business accounts. **accountancy** n.

accoutrements /-'ku:trə-/ n.pl. equipment, trappings.

accredited a. holding credentials.

accretion n. growth; matter added.

accrue v.i. accumulate. **accrual** n.

accumulate v.t./i. acquire more and more of; increase in amount. **accumulation** n., **accumulative** a.

accumulator n. rechargeable electric battery; bet on a series of events with winnings restaked; storage register in a computer.

accurate a. free from error. **accurately** adv., **accuracy** n.

accusative n. grammatical case indicating the object of an action.

accuse v.t. state that one lays the blame for a crime or fault etc. upon. **accusation** n., **accuser** n.

accustom v.t. make used (to).

accustomed a. used, usual; customary.

ace n. playing-card with one spot; expert; unreturnable stroke in tennis.

acerbity /-'sɜ:-/ n. sharpness of manner.

acetate n. synthetic textile fibre.

acetic acid /-'si:-/ ethanoic acid essential ingredient of vinegar.

acetone /'æsɪ-/ n. colourless liquid used as a solvent.

acetylene /-'set-/ n. colourless gas burning with a bright flame.

ache n. dull continuous pain —v.i. suffer an ache. **achy** a.

achieve v.t. accomplish; reach or gain by effort. **achievable** a. **achiever** n., **achievement** n.

Achilles heel /ə'kɪli:z/ vulnerable point. **Achilles tendon** tendon attaching the calf muscles to the heel.

acid a. sour. —n. any of a class of substances that contain hydrogen and neutralize alkalis. **acid house** type of synthesized music with a simple repetitive beat. **acidly** adv., **acidity** n.

acidify /'-sɪd-/ v.t./i. make or become acid.

acidulated /-'sɪd-/ a. made somewhat acid.

acknowledge v.t. admit the truth of; show recognition of; announce the receipt of. **acknowledgement** n.

acme /-mɪ/ n. peak (of perfection).

acne /-nɪ/ n. eruption of pimples.

acolyte n. person assisting priest in a church service.

aconite n. plant with a poisonous root.

acorn n. oval nut of the oak-tree.

acoustic /-'ku:-/ a. of sound; of acoustics. **acoustics** n.pl. qualities of a room etc. that affect the way sound carries in it; (n.) study of sound. **acoustical** a.

acquaint *v.t.* make known to. **be acquainted with** know slightly.

acquaintance *n.* slight knowledge; person one knows slightly.

acquaintance rape rape of a girl or woman by a person known to her.

acquiesce /-'es/ *v.i.* assent. **acquiescent** *a.*, **acquiescence** *n.*

acquire *v.t.* get possession of. **acquirement** *n.*

acquisition *n.* acquiring; thing acquired.

acquisitive *a.* eager to acquire things. **acquisitiveness** *n.*

acquit *v.t.* (*p.t.* **acquitted**) declare to be not guilty. **acquit oneself** perform one's part. **acquittal** *n.*

acre *n.* measure of land, 4,840 sq. yds.

acreage /'eɪkərɪdʒ/ *n.* number of acres.

acrid *a.* bitter. **acridity** *n.*

acrimonious /-'məʊ-/ *a.* angry and bitter. **acrimoniously** *adv.*, **acrimony** /'æ-/ *n.*

acrobat *n.* performer of acrobatics.

acrobatic *a.* involving spectacular gymnastic feats. **acrobatics** *n.pl.* acrobatic feats.

acronym *n.* word formed from the initial letters of others.

acropolis /-'krɒp-/ *n.* citadel or upper fortified part of an ancient Greek city.

across *prep.* & *adv.* from side to side (of); to or on the other side (of); crosswise.

acrostic *n.* poem etc. in which the first and/or last letters of lines form word(s).

acrylic *a.* & *n.* (synthetic fibre) made from an organic substance.

act *n.* thing done; law made by parliament; section of a play; item in a circus or variety show. —*v.t./i.* perform actions, behave; play the part of; be an actor.

action *n.* process of doing something or functioning; thing done; lawsuit; battle.

actionable *a.* giving cause for a lawsuit.

activate *v.t.* make active. **activation** *n.*, **activator** *n.*

active *a.* doing things; energetic; in operation. —*n.* form of a verb indicating that the subject performs the action (e.g. he *saw* it). **actively** *adv.*

activist *n.* person adopting a policy of vigorous action in politics etc. **activism** *n.*

activity *n.* being active; action, occupation.

actor *n.* performer in stage play(s) or film(s). **actress** *n.fem.*

actual *a.* existing in fact, current.

actuality /-'æl-/ *n.* reality.

actually *adv.* in fact, really.

actuary *n.* insurance expert who calculates risks and premiums. **actuarial** /-'eər-/ *a.*

actuate *v.t.* activate; be a motive for. **actuation** *n.*

acuity /-'kju:-/ *n.* sharpness.

acumen /'ækjʊmən/ *n.* shrewdness.

acupressure *n.* pressing the body at specific points to relieve pain.

acupuncture *n.* pricking the body with needles to relieve pain etc. **acupuncturist** *n.*

acute *a.* sharp; intense, (of illness) severe for a time; quick at understanding. **acute accent** the accent ˊ. **acutely** *adv.*, **acuteness** *n.*

AD *abbr.* (Latin *anno domini*) of the Christian era.

ad *n.* (colloq.) advertisement.

adage /'ædɪdʒ/ *n.* proverb, saying.

adamant *a.* not yielding to requests.

Adam's apple prominent cartilage at the front of the neck.

adapt *v.t./i.* make or become suitable for new use or conditions. **adaptation** *n.*, **adaptor** *n.*

adaptable *a.* able to be adapted or to adapt oneself. **adaptability** *n.*

add v.t./i. join as an increase or supplement; say further; put together to get a total.

addendum n. (pl. **-da**) thing to be added to a book etc.; (pl.) appendix.

adder n. small poisonous snake.

addict n. one who is addicted, esp. to drug(s).

addicted a. doing or using something as a habit or compulsively; devoted (to a hobby or interest). **addiction** n.

addictive a. causing addiction.

addition n. adding; thing added. **in addition** as an added thing. **additional** a. added, extra. **additionally** adv.

additive n. substance added.

addle v.t./i. make (an egg) rotten and with no chick after being brooded; become rotten thus; muddle, confuse.

address n. particulars of where a person lives or a firm is situated, or where mail should be delivered; location in a computer memory; a speech. —v.t. write the address on; speak to; apply (oneself) to a task; locate by means of an address. **addressable** a.

addressee n. person to whom a letter etc. is addressed.

adduce v.t. cite as an example or proof.

adenoids n.pl. enlarged tissue at the back of the throat. **adenoidal** a.

adept /'æ-/ a. & n. very skilful (person). **adeptly** adv., **adeptness** n.

adequate a. enough; satisfactory but not excellent. **adequately** adv., **adequacy** n.

adhere v.i. stick; continue to give one's support. **adherence** n., **adherent** a. & n.

adhesion n. adhering; abnormal union of inflamed tissue.

adhesive a. sticking, sticky. —n. adhesive substance.

ad hoc for a specific purpose.

adieu /ə'dju:/ int. & n. goodbye.

ad infinitum /-'naɪ-/ for ever.

adipose a. of fat, fatty.

adjacent a. lying near; adjoining.

adjective n. descriptive word. **adjectival** a., **adjectivally** adv.

adjoin v.t. be next to.

adjourn /ə'dʒɜːn/ v.t./i. move (a meeting etc.) to another place or time. **adjournment** n.

adjudge v.t. decide or award judicially. **adjudgement** n.

adjudicate v.t./i. act as judge (of); adjudge. **adjudication** n., **adjudicator** n.

adjunct n. thing that is subordinate or incidental to another.

adjure v.t. command or urge strongly.

adjust v.t./i. alter slightly so as to be correct or in the proper position; adapt (oneself) to new conditions; assess (loss or damages). **adjuster** n., **adjustment** n.

adjustable a. able to be adjusted.

adjutant /'ædʒu-/ n. army officer assisting in administrative work.

ad lib as one pleases; (colloq.) improvise(d).

administer v.t./i. manage (business affairs); formally give or hand out.

administrate v.t./i. act as administrator (of).

administration n. administering; management of public or business affairs. **administrative** a.

administrator n. person responsible for administration.

admirable a. worthy of admiration. **admirably** adv.

admiral n. naval officer of the highest rank. **red admiral**, **white admiral** kinds of butterfly.

Admiralty n. former name for the government department superintending the Royal Navy.

admire v.t. regard with pleasure; think highly of; compliment a person on. **admiration** n., **admirer** n.

dmissible a. able to be admitted or allowed. **admissibility** n.

dmission n. admitting; statement admitting something.

dmit v.t. (p.t. **admitted**) allow to enter; accept as valid; state reluctantly. **admit** of leave room for (doubt, improvement, etc.).

dmittance n. admitting, esp. to a private place.

dmittedly adv. as an acknowledged fact.

dmixture n. thing added as an ingredient; adding of this.

dmonish v.t. exhort; reprove. **admonition** n., **admonitory** -'mon-/ a.

d nauseam /'nɔːzɪæm/ to a sickening extent.

do n. fuss, trouble.

dobe /ə'dəʊbɪ/ n. sun-dried brick.

dolescent a. & n. (person) between childhood and maturity. **adolescence** n.

dopt v.t. take as one's own; accept responsibility for maintenance of (a road etc.); accept, approve (a report etc.). **adoption** n.

doptive a. related by adoption.

dorable a. very lovable. **adorably** adv.

dore v.t. love deeply; worship as divine; (colloq.) like very much. **adoration** n.

dorn v.t. decorate with ornaments; be an ornament to. **adornment** n.

drenal /-'driː-/ a. close to the kidneys.

drenalin /-'dren-/ n. stimulant hormone produced by the adrenal glands.

drift adj. & adv. drifting; loose.

droit a. skilful, ingenious. **adroitly** adv.

dsorb v.t./i. attract and hold (a gas or liquid) to a surface; be held thus. **adsorption** n.

dulation n. excessive flattery.

dult /'æ-/ a. & n. fully grown (person etc.). **adulthood** n.

adulterate v.t. make impure by adding substance(s). **adulteration** n.

adulterer n. person who commits adultery. **adulteress** n.fem.

adultery n. infidelity to one's wife or husband by voluntarily having sexual intercourse with someone else. **adulterous** a.

adumbrate v.t. indicate faintly; foreshadow. **adumbration** n.

advance v.t./i. move or put forward; make progress; lend (money). —n. forward movement; progress; increase in price or amount; loan; attempt to establish a friendly relationship. —a. going or done in advance. **in advance** ahead. **advancement** n.

advanced a. far on in time or progress etc.; not elementary.

advantage n. favourable circumstance; benefit; next point won after deuce in tennis. **take advantage of** make use of; exploit.

advantageous a. profitable, beneficial. **advantageously** adv.

Advent n. coming of Christ; season before Christmas. **advent** n. arrival of an important development etc.

Adventist n. member of a sect believing that Christ's second coming is very near.

adventitious /-'tɪʃəs/ a. accidental, casual; occurring in an unusual place.

adventure n. exciting or dangerous experience. **adventurous** a.

adventurer n. person who seeks adventures; one living by his wits. **adventuress** n.fem.

adverb n. word qualifying a verb, adjective, or other adverb. **adverbial** a., **adverbially** adv.

adversary /'æ-/ n. opponent, enemy. **adversarial** /-'seər-/ a.

adverse /'æ-/ a. unfavourable, bringing harm. **adversely** adv., **adversity** n.

advert[1] /'æ-/ n. (colloq.) advertisement.

advert[2] /-'vɜːt/ v.i. refer, allude.

advertise *v.t./i.* make publicly known, esp. to encourage sales; seek by public notice. **advertiser** *n.*

advertisement *n.* advertising; public notice advertising something.

advice *n.* opinion given about what should be done; piece of information.

advisable *a.* worth recommending as a course of action. **advisability** *n.*

advise *v.t./i.* give advice to; recommend; inform. **adviser** *n.*

advisory *a.* giving advice.

advocacy *n.* pleading in support; advocate's function.

advocate[1] /-kət/ *n.* person who pleads on behalf of another.

advocate[2] /-keɪt/ *v.t.* recommend.

adze *n.* axe with an arched blade used for trimming wood.

aegis /ˈiːdʒɪs/ *n.* protection, sponsorship.

aeon /ˈiːən/ *n.* immense time.

aerate *v.t.* expose to the action of air; add carbon dioxide to. **aeration** *n.*, **aerator** *n.*

aerial *a.* of or like air; existing or moving in the air; by or from aircraft. —*n.* wire or rod for transmitting or receiving radio waves. **aerially** *adv.*

aerobatics *n.pl.* spectacular feats by aircraft in flight. **aerobatic** *a.*

aerobics /-ˈrəʊ-/ *n.pl.* vigorous exercises designed to increase oxygen intake. **aerobic** *a.*

aerodrome *n.* airfield.

aerodynamic *a.* of the interaction between air-flow and the movement of solid bodies through air. **aerodynamics** *n.* study of this. **aerodynamically** *adv.*

aerofoil *n.* aircraft wing, fin, or tailplane giving lift in flight.

aeronautics *n.* study of the flight of aircraft. **aeronautical** *a.*

aeroplane *n.* mechanically driven aircraft with wings.

aerosol *n.* container holding substance sealed into it for release as a fine spray; its contents.

aerospace *n.* earth's atmosphere and space beyond this.

aesthete /ˈiːsθiːt/ *n.* person claiming to understand and appreciate beauty, esp. in the arts.

aesthetic /ɪsˈθeɪ-/ *a.* of or showing appreciation of beauty; artistic; tasteful. **aesthetically** *adv.*

aetiology /iːtɪ-/ *n.* study of causation; study of the causes of disease. **aetiological** *a.*

afar *adv.* far off, far away.

affable *a.* polite and friendly. **affably** *adv.*, **affability** *n.*

affair *n.* thing to be done, matter, business; temporary sexual relationship.

affect *v.t.* pretend to have or feel; or be; use for show; have an effect on.

affectation *n.* pretence, esp. in behaviour.

affected *a.* full of affectation.

affection *n.* love, liking; disease.

affectionate *a.* loving. **affectionately** *adv.*

affiance /-ˈfaɪ-/ *v.t.* betroth.

affidavit /-ˈdeɪ-/ *n.* written statement sworn on oath to be true.

affiliate *v.t.* connect as a subordinate member or branch. **affiliation** *n.*

affinity *n.* close resemblance or connection; strong liking, attraction; tendency to combine.

affirm *v.t./i.* state as a fact; declare formally and solemnly instead of on oath. **affirmation** *n.*

affirmative *a. & n.* saying 'yes'. **affirmatively** *adv.*

affix /-ˈfɪks/ *v.t.* attach; add (a signature etc.). —/-/ *n.* thing affixed; prefix, suffix.

afflict *v.t.* distress physically or mentally.

affliction *n.* distress; thing causing this.

affluence *n.* wealth.

affluent *a.* wealthy. **affluently** *adv.*

fford v.t. have enough money or time etc. for; provide.

forest v.t. convert into forest; plant with trees. **afforestation** n.

fray n. public fight or riot.

front v.t. & n. insult.

fghan hound large dog with long silky hair.

field adv. at or to a distance.

float adv. & a. floating; on the sea.

foot adv. & a. going on.

foresaid a. mentioned previously.

forethought a. premeditated.

fraid a. frightened; regretful.

fresh adv. anew, with a fresh start.

frican a. of Africa. —n. African (esp. dark-skinned) person.

frikaans /-'kɑːns/ n. language of South Africa, developed from Dutch.

frikaner /-'kɑː-/ n. Afrikaans-speaking White person in South Africa.

fro a. (of hair) bushy and fuzzy.

fro- pref. African.

ft adv. at or towards the rear of a ship or aircraft.

fter prep., adv., & a. behind; later (than); in pursuit of; concerning; according to. —conj. at a time later than. **after-effect** n. effect persisting after its cause has gone.

fterbirth n. placenta discharged from the womb after childbirth.

fterlife n. life after death.

ftermath n. after-effects.

fternoon n. time between morning and evening after 6 p.m. or sunset.

ftershave n. lotion for use after shaving.

fterthought n. thing thought of or added later.

fterwards adv. at a later time.

gain adv. another time, once more; besides.

against prep. in opposition or contrast to; in preparation or return for; into collision or contact with.

agape a. gaping, open-mouthed.

agate /'ægət/ n. hard stone with patches or bands of colour.

agave /ə'gɑːvɪ/ n. spiny-leaved plant.

age n. length of life or existence; later part of life; historical period; (colloq., usu. pl.) very long time. —v.t./i. (pres.p. ageing) grow old, show signs of age; cause to do this.

aged /eɪdʒd/ a. of the age of; /'eɪdʒɪd/ old.

ageism /'eɪdʒɪz(ə)m/ n. prejudice on grounds of age. **ageist** a.

ageless a. not growing old; not seeming old.

agency n. business or office of an agent; means of action by which something is done.

agenda n. list of things to be dealt with, esp. at a meeting.

agent n. person who does something; thing producing an effect; one who acts on behalf of another.

agent provocateur /aː'ʒɑ̃ prɒvɒ kaˈtɜː(r)/ person employed to tempt suspected offenders into overt action.

agglomeration n. mass.

agglutination n. sticking or fusing together. **agglutinative** a.

aggrandize v.t. increase the power, rank, or wealth of; make seem greater. **aggrandizement** n.

aggravate v.t. make worse; (colloq.) annoy. **aggravation** n.

aggregate[1] /-ət/ a. combined, total. —n. total; collected mass; broken stone etc. used in making concrete.

aggregate[2] /-eɪt/ v.t./i. collect into an aggregate, unite; (colloq.) amount to. **aggregation** n.

aggression n. unprovoked attacking; hostile act(s) or behaviour.

aggressive *a.* showing aggression; forceful. **aggressively** *adv.*, **aggressiveness** *n.*

aggressor *n.* one who begins hostilities.

aggrieved *a.* having a grievance.

aggro *n. (sl.)* aggravation, deliberate trouble-making.

aghast *a.* filled with consternation.

agile *a.* nimble, quick-moving. **agilely** *adv.*, **agility** *n.*

agitate *v.t.* shake briskly; cause anxiety to; stir up interest or concern. **agitation** *n.*, **agitator** *n.*

aglow *a.* glowing.

agnail *n.* torn skin at the root of a finger-nail.

agnostic *a. & n.* (person) holding that nothing can be known about the existence of God. **agnosticism** *n.*

ago *adv.* in the past.

agog *a.* eager, expectant.

agonize *v.t./i.* cause agony to; suffer agony, worry intensely.

agony *n.* extreme suffering.

agoraphobia *n.* abnormal fear of crossing open spaces.

agrarian *a.* of land or agriculture.

agree *v.t./i.* consent; approve as correct or acceptable; hold or reach a similar opinion; get on well together; be consistent. **agree with** suit the health or digestion of.

agreeable *a.* pleasing; willing to agree. **agreeably** *adv.*

agreement *n.* agreeing; arrangement agreed between people.

agriculture *n.* large-scale cultivation of land. **agricultural** *a.*

agronomy /-grə-/ *n.* soil management and crop production.

aground *adv. & a.* (of a ship) on the bottom of shallow water.

ague /ˈeɪɡjuː/ *n. (old use)* fever with shivering.

ah, aha *ints.* exclamations of surprise, triumph, etc.

ahead *adv.* further forward in position or time.

ahoy *int.* seaman's shout to ca attention.

aid *v.t. & n.* help.

aide *n.* aide-de-camp; assistant.

aide-de-camp /ˈkɑ̃/ *n. (pl.* **aides de-camp,** *pr.* edz-) officer assis ing a senior officer.

Aids or AIDS *n.* acquire immune deficiency syndrome, condition that breaks down a per son's natural defences agains illness.

ail *v.t./i.* make or become ill.

aileron *n.* hinged flap on an air craft wing.

ailment *n.* slight illness.

aim *v.t./i.* point, send, or direc towards a target; attempt; hav ambition. —*n.* aiming; intention

aimless *a.* without a purpose **aimlessly** *adv.*, **aimlessness** *n.*

ain't *(colloq.)* am not, has not, etc

air *n.* mixture of oxygen, nitrogen etc., surrounding the earth; atmosphere overhead, aircraft operating there; light wind; im pression given; impressive man ner; melody. —*v.t./i.* expose to air; dry off; express publicly **air-bed** *n.* inflatable mattress **air-brick** *n.* perforated brick fo ventilation. **air-conditioned** *a* supplied with **air-conditioning,** system controlling the humidity and temperature of air. **air force** branch of the armed forces using aircraft in attack and defence. **air raid** attack by aircraft dropping bombs. **in the air** prevalent; not yet decided. **on the air** broadcast(ing) by radio or television.

airborne *a.* carried by air or aircraft; (of aircraft) in flight.

aircraft *n. (pl.* same) machine or structure capable of flight in air.

Airedale *n.* large rough-coated terrier.

airfield *n.* area with runways etc. for aircraft.

airgun *n.* gun with a missile propelled by compressed air.

airlift *n.* large-scale transport of supplies etc. by aircraft, esp. in an emergency. —*v.t.* transport thus.

irline *n.* public air transport service; company providing this.

irliner *n.* large passenger aircraft.

irlock *n.* stoppage of the flow in a pump or pipe, caused by an airbubble; airtight compartment giving access to a pressurized chamber.

irmail *n.* mail carried by aircraft. —*v.t.* send by airmail.

irman *n.* (*pl.* -**men**) member of an air force, esp. below the rank of officer.

irport *n.* airfield with facilities for passengers and goods.

irship *n.* power-driven lighter-than-air aircraft.

irstrip *n.* strip of ground for take-off and landing of aircraft.

irtight *a.* not allowing air to enter or escape.

irworthy *a.* (of aircraft) fit to fly. **airworthiness** *n.*

iry *a.* (-**ier**, -**iest**) well-ventilated; light as air; careless and light-hearted. **airily** *adv.*, **airiness** *n.*

aisle /aɪl/ *n.* side part of a church; gangway between rows of seats.

ajar *adv.* & *a.* slightly open.

akimbo *adv.* with hands on hips and elbows pointed outwards.

akin *a.* related, similar.

alabaster *n.* translucent usu. white form of gypsum.

à la carte (of a meal) ordered as separate items from a menu.

alacrity *n.* eager readiness.

alarm *n.* warning sound or signal; device giving this; alarm-clock; fear caused by expectation of danger. —*v.t.* cause alarm to. **alarm clock** clock with a device that rings at a set time.

alarmist *n.* person who raises unnecessary or excessive alarm.

alas *int.* exclamation of sorrow.

albatross *n.* sea-bird with long wings.

albino /-'biː-/ *n.* (*pl.* -**os**) person or animal with no natural colouring-matter in the hair or skin.

album *n.* blank book for holding photographs, postage-stamps, etc.; set of recordings, holder for these.

albumen *n.* white of egg.

albumin *n.* protein found in egg-white, milk, blood, etc.

alchemy *n.* medieval form of chemistry, seeking to turn other metals into gold. **alchemist** *n.*

alcohol *n.* colourless inflammable liquid, intoxicant present in wine, beer, etc.; liquor containing this; compound of this type.

alcoholic *a.* of alcohol. —*n.* person addicted to continual heavy drinking of alcohol. **alcoholism** *n.*

alcove *n.* recess in a wall or room.

al dente *a.* & *adv.* cooked so as to be still firm when bitten.

alder *n.* tree related to birch.

ale *n.* beer.

alert *a.* watchful, observant. —*n.* warning to be ready for action or danger. —*v.t.* rouse to be alert. **on the alert** watchful. **alertly** *adv.*, **alertness** *n.*

alfresco *adv.* & *a.* in the open air.

alga *n.* (*pl.* -**gae**, *pr.* -dʒiː) water plant with no true stems or leaves.

algebra *n.* branch of mathematics using letters etc. to represent quantities. **algebraic** *a.*, **algebraically** *adv.*

algorithm *n.* step-by-step procedure for (esp. machine-)calculation etc.

alias *n.* (*pl.* -**ases**) false name. —*adv.* also falsely called.

alibi *n.* (*pl.* -**is**) evidence that an accused person was elsewhere when a crime was committed; (*loosely*) excuse. —*v.t.* (*p.t.* alibied, *pres.p.* alibiing) provide an alibi for.

alien *n.* person who is not a subject of the country where he or she lives; a being from another world. —*a.* foreign; unfamiliar.

alienate *v.t.* cause to become unfriendly. **alienation** *n.*

alight[1] *v.i.* get down from (a vehicle etc.); descend and settle.

alight[2] *a.* on fire.

align *v.t.* place or bring into line; join as an ally. **alignment** *n.*

alike *adj.* like one another. —*adv.* in the same way.

alimentary *a.* of nourishment. **alimentary canal** tubular passage by which food passes through the body.

alimony *n.* former term for maintenance paid to spouse.

aliquot *n.* divisor or part contained an exact number of times.

alive *a.* living; alert; lively.

alkali /-lai/ *n.* (*pl.* -**is**) any of a class of substances that neutralize acids. **alkaline** *a.*, **alkalinity** /-'lɪn-/ *n.*

alkaloid *n.* a kind of organic compound containing nitrogen.

all *a.* whole amount or number or extent of. —*n.* all those concerned, everything. —*adv.* entirely, quite. **all but** almost. **all-clear** *n.* signal that danger is over. **all in** exhausted; including everything. **all out** using maximum effort. **all over** in or on all parts of; excessively attentive to (a person); being very characteristic. **all right** satisfactory, satisfactorily; in good condition etc.; I consent. **all round** in all respects; for each person. **all-round** *a.* general, not specialized. **all-rounder** *n.* person with all-round abilities. **all there** mentally alert; sane. **all the same** in spite of that. **all up** (*colloq.*) ended.

Allah *n.* Muslim name of God.

allay *v.t.* lessen (fears).

allegation *n.* thing alleged.

allege *v.t.* declare without proof.

allegedly /-ɪdlɪ/ *adv.* according to allegation.

allegiance *n.* support given to government, sovereign, or caus[e]

allegorize *v.t.* represent in all[e]gory. **allegorization** *n.*

allegory /'ælɪ-/ *n.* story symbol[is]ing an underlying meaning. **all[e]gorical** *a.*, **allegorically** *adv.*

allegro /ə'leɪgrəʊ/ *adv.* & *n.* (*pl.* -o[s]) (passage to be played) briskly.

alleluia *int.* & *n.* praise to God.

allergen *n.* substance causing a[n] allergic reaction. **allergenic** *a.*

allergic *a.* having or caused by a allergy; having a strong dislike.

allergy *n.* condition causing a unfavourable reaction to certai[n] foods, pollens, etc.

alleviate *v.t.* lessen (pain or dis[-] tress etc.). **alleviation** *n.*

alley *n.* (*pl.* -**eys**) narrow stree[t] passage; long enclosure for ten[-] pin bowling etc.

alliance *n.* union or associatio[n] formed for mutual benefit.

allied *a.* of allies; of the same ge[-] neral kind.

alligator *n.* reptile of the croco[-] dile family.

alliteration *n.* occurrence of th[e] same sound at the start of adjac[ent] words. **alliterative** /-'lɪtərə-/ *a.*

allocate *v.t.* allot. **allocation** *n.*

allot *v.t.* (*p.t.* **allotted**) distribut[e] officially, give as a share.

allotment *n.* allotting; share al[-] lotted; small area of public lan[d] let for cultivation.

allow *v.t./i.* permit; give a limite[d] quantity or sum; add or deduct i[n] estimating; admit, agree.

allowable *a.* able to be allowed.

allowance *n.* allowing; amoun[t] or sum allowed. **make allow[-] ances for** be lenient towards o[r] because of.

alloy *n.* mixture of metals. —*v.t.* mix (with another metal); spoil or weaken (pleasure etc.).

allspice *n.* pimento berry; spice[s] from this.

allude *v.i.* refer briefly or indi[-] rectly.

...lure v.t. entice, attract. —n. attractiveness. **allurement** n.

...lusion n. statement alluding to something. **allusive** a.

...luvium n. deposit left by a flood. **alluvial** a.

...ly[1] /'æ-/ n. country or person in alliance with another.

...ly[2] /-'laɪ/ v.t. join as an ally.

...manac /'ɔ:l-/ n. calendar with astronomical or other data.

...mighty a. all-powerful; (colloq.) very great; **the Almighty** God.

...mond n. kernel of a fruit related to the peach; tree bearing this.

...most adv. very little short of, as the nearest thing to.

...ms /ɑ:mz/ n. (old use) money etc. given to the poor.

...mshouse /'ɑ:m-/ n. house built by charity for poor (usu. elderly) people.

...oe n. plant with bitter juice.

...oft adv. high up; upwards.

...one a. not with others; without company or help. —adv. only.

...ong adv. through part or the whole of a thing's length; on-ward; in company with oneself or others. —prep. beside the length of. **along with** in company with; in addition to.

...ongside adv. close to the side of a ship or wharf etc. —prep. beside.

...oof adv. apart. —a. showing no interest, unfriendly. **aloofly** adv., **aloofness** n.

...oud adv. in a voice that can be heard, not in a whisper.

...paca n. llama with long wool; its wool; cloth made from this.

...pha n. first letter of the Greek alphabet, = a.

...phabet n. letters used in writing a language; signs indicating these. **alphabetical** a., **alphabetically** adv.

...phabetize v.t. put into alphabetical order. **alphabetization** n.

...pine a. of the Alps.

alpine a. of high mountains. plant growing on mountains or in rock gardens.

already adv. before this time; as early as this.

Alsatian n. dog of a large strong smooth-haired breed.

also adv. in addition, besides.

also-ran n. horse or dog not in the first three to finish a race.

altar n. structure on which offerings are made to a god; table used in a religious service.

alter v.t./i. make or become different. **alteration** n.

altercation n. noisy dispute.

alternate[1] /-nət/ a. first one then the other successively. **alternately** adv.

alternate[2] /-neɪt/ v.t./i. place or occur etc. alternately. **alternation** n.

alternative a. usable instead of another; different, unconventional. —n. alternative thing. **alternatively** adv.

alternator n. dynamo producing alternating current.

although conj. though.

altimeter /'æ-/ n. instrument (esp. in an aircraft) showing altitude.

altitude n. height above sea level or above the horizon.

alto n. (pl. -os) highest adult male voice; contralto; musical instrument with the second-highest pitch in its group.

altogether adv. entirely; on the whole.

altruism /'æl-/ n. unselfishness. **altruist** /'æl-/ n. unselfish person. **altruistic** a., **altruistically** adv.

aluminium n. lightweight silvery metal.

always adv. at all times; whatever the circumstances.

alyssum /'æli-/ n. plant with small usu. yellow or white flowers.

am see be.

a.m. abbr. (Latin ante meridiem) before noon.

amalgam n. alloy of mercury; soft pliable mixture.

amalgamate v.t./i. mix, combine. **amalgamation** n.

amanuensis /-'en-/ n. (pl. **-enses**) person who writes from dictation.

amaryllis n. lily-like plant.

amass v.t. heap up, collect.

amateur n. person who does something as a pastime not as a profession.

amateurish a. lacking professional skill. **amateurishly** adv.

amatory a. of or showing (esp. sexual) love.

amaze v.t. overwhelm with wonder. **amazement** n.

amazon n. fierce strong woman. **amazonian** /-'zəʊ-/ a.

ambassador n. highest-ranking diplomat representing his country in another. **ambassadorial** a.

amber n. hardened brownish-yellow resin; its colour; yellow traffic-light used as a cautionary signal.

ambergris n. waxy substance found in tropical seas, used in perfumery.

ambidextrous a. able to use either hand equally well.

ambience n. surroundings.

ambient a. surrounding.

ambiguous a. having two or more possible meanings; uncertain. **ambiguously** adv., **ambiguity** n.

ambit n. bounds, scope.

ambition n. strong desire to achieve something; object of this.

ambitious a. full of ambition. **ambitiously** adv.

ambivalent /-'brv-/ a. with mixed feelings towards something. **ambivalence** n., **ambivalently** adv.

amble v.i. & n. walk at a leisurely pace. **ambler** n.

ambrosia n. something delicious.

ambulance n. vehicle equippe to carry sick or injured persons

ambulatory a. of or for walking —n. place for walking in.

ambuscade v.t. & n. ambush.

ambush n. troops etc. lying con cealed to make a surprise attack this attack. —v.t. attack thus.

ameliorate /-'mi:-/ v.t./i. make o become better. **amelioration** n.

amen /ɑ:- or eɪ-/ int. so be it.

amenable /-'mi:-/ a. responsive **amenably** adv., **amenability** n.

amend v.t. make minor altera tion(s) in. **make amends** com pensate for something. **amend ment** n.

amenity /-'mi:- or -'me-/ n. pleasant feature of a place etc.

American a. of America; of the USA. —n. American person form of English used in the USA **Americanism** n. American wor or phrase.

Americanize v.t. make Amer ican in character. **Americaniza tion** n.

amethyst n. precious stone, pur ple or violet quartz; its colour.

amiable a. likeable; friendly **amiably** adv., **amiability** n.

amicable /'æ-/ a. friendly. **ami cably** adv.

amid, **amidst** preps. in th middle of, during.

amino acid /-'mi:-/ organic aci found in proteins.

amiss a. & adv. wrong(ly), badly

amity n. friendship.

ammonia n. strong-smelling ga solution of this in water.

ammonite n. fossil of a spira shell.

ammunition n. bullets, shell etc.; facts used in argument.

amnesia n. loss of memory **amnesiac** a. & n.

amnesty n. general pardon.

amniocentesis /-'ti:-/ n. samplin of amniotic fluid.

amniotic fluid fluid surroundin the foetus in the womb.

moeba n. (pl. **-bae** or **-bas**) simple microscopic organism changing shape constantly.

mok adv. **run amok** be out of control and do much damage.

mong, amongst preps. surrounded by; in the number of; between.

moral /er'mɒ-/ a. not based on moral standards.

morous a. showing or readily feeling sexual love. **amorously** adv., **amorousness** n.

morphous a. shapeless.

mortize v.t. pay off (a debt) gradually from a sinking fund. **amortization** n.

mount n. total of anything; quantity. —v.i. **amount to** add up to; be equivalent to.

mp n. (colloq.) ampere; amplifier.

mpere /-peə(r)/ n. unit of electric current.

mpersand n. the sign & (= and).

mphetamine /-mɪn/ n. stimulant drug.

mphibian n. animal with an aquatic larval and air-breathing adult stage; amphibious vehicle.

mphibious a. able to live or operate both on land and in water; using both sea and land forces. **amphibiously** adv.

mphitheatre n. semicircular unroofed building with tiers of seats round a central arena.

mphora n. (pl. **-ae**) ancient two-handled jar.

mple a. (**-er, -est**) plentiful, quite enough; large. **amply** adv.

mplify v.t. increase the strength of, make louder; add details to (a statement). **amplification** n., **amplifier** n.

mplitude n. breadth; abundance.

mpoule /-puːl/ n. small sealed container holding liquid for injection.

mputate v.t. cut off by surgical operation. **amputation** n.

mulet n. thing worn as a charm against evil.

amuse v.t. cause to laugh or smile; make time pass pleasantly for. **amusement** n., **amusing** a.

an a. form of a used before vowel sounds other than long 'u'.

anachronism /-'næk-/ n. thing that does not belong in the period in which it is placed. **anachronistic** a.

anaconda n. large tropical snake of South America.

anaemia /-'niː-/ n. lack of haemoglobin in blood.

anaemic /-'niː-/ a. suffering from anaemia; lacking strong colour or characteristics.

anaesthesia n. loss of sensation, esp. induced by anaesthetics.

anaesthetic a. & n. (substance) causing loss of sensation.

anaesthetist /-'niː-/ n. person trained to administer anaesthetics.

anagram n. word formed from the rearranged letters of another.

anal a. of the anus.

analgesic /-'dʒiː-/ a. & n. (drug) relieving pain. **analgesia** n.

analogous a. similar in certain respects. **analogously** adv.

analogue /-lɒg/ n. analogous thing.

analogy n. partial likeness between things that are compared.

analyse v.t. make an analysis of; psychoanalyse. **analyst** n.

analysis n. (pl. **-lyses**) separation of a substance into parts for study and interpretation; detailed examination.

analytic, analytical adjs. of or using analysis. **analytically** adv.

anarchist n. person who believes that government is undesirable and should be abolished. **anarchistic** adj., **anarchism** n.

anarchy n. total lack of organized control, resulting in disorder or lawlessness; this disorder. **anarchical** a., **anarchically** adv.

anathema /-'næθə-/ n. formal curse; detested thing.

anathematize /-ˈnæ-/ v.t. put under an anathema.

anatomist n. expert in anatomy.

anatomize v.t. examine the anatomy or structure of.

anatomy n. bodily structure; study of this. **anatomical** a., **anatomically** adv.

ancestor n. person from whom one's father or mother is descended; prototype. **ancestral** a., **ancestress** n.fem.

ancestry n. line of ancestors.

anchor n. heavy metal structure for mooring a ship to the seabottom. —v.t./i. moor with an anchor; fix firmly.

anchorage n. place where ships may anchor; lying at anchor.

anchorite n. hermit, recluse.

anchovy n. small rich-flavoured fish.

ancient a. belonging to times long past; very old.

ancillary a. helping in a subsidiary way.

and conj. connecting words, phrases, or sentences.

andiron n. stand for supporting logs in a hearth.

anecdote n. short amusing or interesting usu. true story. **anecdotal** a.

anemone n. plant with white, red, or purple flowers.

aneroid barometer barometer measuring air-pressure by the action of this on the lid of a box containing a vacuum.

aneurysm /ˈænjʊərɪz(ə)m/ n. excessive enlargement of an artery.

anew adv. again; in a new way.

angel n. attendant or messenger of God; very kind person. **angelic(al)** a., **angelically** adv.

angelica n. candied stalks of a fragrant plant; this plant.

angelus n. RC devotional exercise at morning, noon, and sunset; bell rung for this.

anger n. extreme displeasure. —v.t. make angry.

angina n. constricting pain. a gina pectoris sharp pain in th chest, brought on by exertion.

angle¹ n. space between two line or surfaces that meet; point view. —v.t. place obliquely; pr sent from a particular point view.

angle² v.i. fish with hook and line try to obtain by hinting. **angler**

Anglican a. & n. (member) the Church of England or Church in communion with i **Anglicanism** n.

Anglicism n. English idiom.

anglicize v.t. make English i character. **anglicization** n.

Anglo- pref. English, British.

Anglo-Saxon n. English perso or language of the period befor the Norman Conquest; person c English descent. —a. of Angl Saxon(s).

angora n. long-haired variety c cat, goat, or rabbit; yarn or fabri made from the hair of such goat or rabbits.

angostura n. aromatic bitte bark of a South American tree.

angry a. (-ier, -iest) feelin or showing anger; inflamed **angrily** adv.

angstrom /ˈæŋstrəm/ n. unit c measurement for wavelengths.

anguish n. severe physical o mental pain. **anguished** a.

angular a. having angles or shar corners; measured by angle.

aniline /-liːn/ n. oily liquid used in making dyes and plastics.

animadvert v.i. make hostile comments. **animadversion** n.

animal n. living thing that ca move voluntarily, esp. other thar man; quadruped. —a. of animals or their nature.

animate¹ /-ət/ a. living.

animate² /-ett/ v.t. give life or movement to; make lively; moti vate. **animated cartoon** film made by photographing a series f drawings. **animation** *n.*, **animator** *n.*

animosity *n.* hostility.

animus *n.* animosity.

anion *n.* negatively charged ion.

anionic *a.*

aniseed *n.* fragrant seed of a plant **anise**, used for flavouring.

ankle *n.* joint connecting the foot with the leg; part of the leg below the calf.

anklet *n.* chain or band worn round the ankle.

annals *n.pl.* narrative of events year by year; historical records.

anneal *v.t.* toughen (metal or glass) by heat and slow cooling.

annex *v.t.* take possession of; add as a subordinate part. **annexation** *n.*

annexe *n.* additional building.

annihilate *v.t.* destroy completely. **annihilation** *n.*

anniversary *n.* yearly return of the date of an event.

anno Domini in the year of the Christian era; (*colloq.*) advancing age.

annotate *v.t.* add explanatory notes to. **annotation** *n.*

announce *v.t.* make known publicly; make known the presence or arrival of. **announcement** *n.*

announcer *n.* person who announces items in a broadcast.

annoy *v.t.* cause slight anger to; be troublesome to. **annoyance** *n.*

annoyed *a.* slightly angry.

annual *a.* yearly. —*n.* plant that lives for one year or one season; book etc. published in yearly issues. **annually** *adv.*

annuity *n.* yearly allowance, esp. provided by a form of investment. **annuitant** *n.*

annul *v.t.* (*p.t.* **annulled**) make null and void. **annulment** *n.*

annular *a.* ring-shaped.

Annunciation *n.* announcement by the angel Gabriel to the Virgin Mary that she was to be the mother of Christ.

anode *n.* electrode by which current enters a device.

anodize *v.t.* coat (metal) with a protective layer by electrolysis.

anodyne *n.* something that relieves pain or distress.

anoint *v.t.* apply ointment or oil etc. to, esp. in religious consecration.

anomaly *n.* something irregular or inconsistent. **anomalous** *a.*

anon *adv.* (*old use*) soon, presently.

anon. *abbr.* anonymous.

anonymous *a.* of unknown or undisclosed name or authorship. **anonymously** *adv.*, **anonymity** /-'nım-/ *n.*

anorak *n.* waterproof jacket with hood attached.

anorexia *n.* loss of appetite for food; reluctance to eat. **anorexic** *a.* & *n.*, **anorectic** *a.* & *n.*

another *a.* one more; a different; any other. —*pron.* another one.

answer *n.* thing said, written, needed, or done to deal with a question, problem, etc.; figure etc. produced by calculation. —*v.t./i.* make or be an answer (to); act in response to; take responsibility; correspond (to a description etc.).

answerable *a.* able to be answered; having to account for something.

ant *n.* small insect living in highly organized groups.

antacid *n.* & *a.* (substance) preventing or correcting acidity.

antagonism *n.* active opposition, hostility. **antagonistic** *a.*

antagonist *n.* opponent.

antagonize *v.t.* rouse antagonism in.

Antarctic *a.* & *n.* (of) regions round the South Pole.

ante *n.* stake put up by a poker-player before drawing new cards.

ante- *pref.* before.

anteater *n.* mammal that eats ants.

antecedent n. preceding thing or circumstance. —a. previous.

antedate v.t. put an earlier date on; precede in time.

antediluvian a. of the time before Noah's Flood; antiquated.

antelope n. (pl. antelope) animal resembling a deer.

antenatal a. before birth; or during pregnancy.

antenna n. (pl. -ae) insect's feeler; (US, pl. -as) radio or TV aerial.

anterior a. coming before in position or time.

ante-room n. room leading to a more important one.

anthem n. piece of music to be sung in a religious service.

anther n. part of a flower's stamen containing pollen.

anthill n. mound over an ants' nest.

anthology n. collection of passages from literature, esp. poems.

anthracite n. form of coal burning with little flame or smoke.

anthrax n. disease of sheep and cattle, transmissible to people.

anthropoid a. & n. human-like (ape).

anthropology n. study of the origin and customs of mankind. **anthropological** a., **anthropologist** n.

anthropomorphic a. attributing human form or personality to a god, animal, etc. **anthropomorphism** n.

anti- pref. opposed to; counteracting. **anti-aircraft** a. used against enemy aircraft.

antibiotic n. substance that destroys bacteria or prevents their growth.

antibody n. protein formed in the blood in reaction to a substance which it then destroys.

antic n. (usu. pl.) absurd movement or behaviour.

anticipate v.t. deal with or use etc. in advance; forestall; look forward to; (loosely) expect. **anticipation** n., **anticipatory** a.

anticlimax n. dull ending whe a climax was expected.

anticlockwise a. & adv. in t direction opposite to clockwise

anticyclone n. outward flow air from an area of high atm spheric pressure, producing fi weather. **anticyclonic** a.

antidote n. substance that cou teracts the effects of poison etc

antifreeze n. substance added water to prevent freezing.

antigen n. foreign substan stimulating the production antibodies.

antihistamine /-mɪn/ n. su stance counteracting the effe of histamine.

antimacassar n. protective c vering for a chair-back.

antimony /ˈæ-/ n. brittle silver metallic element.

antipathy /-ˈtɪp-/ n. strong settle dislike; object of this.

antiperspirant n. substance tha prevents or reduces sweating.

antiphon n. composition i which verses are sung by tw bodies of singers alternatel **antiphonal** a.

antipodes /-ˈtɪpədiːz/ n.pl. place on opposite sides of the earth esp. Australia and New Zealan (opposite Europe). **antipodea** /-ˈdiːən/ a. & n.

antiquarian a. of the study o antiques. —n. person who studie antiques.

antiquated a. very old; very old fashioned.

antique a. belonging to the dis tant past. —n. antique interestin or valuable object.

antiquity n. ancient times; grea age; object dating from ancien times.

antirrhinum /-ˈraɪ-/ n. snapdra gon.

anti-Semitic a. hostile to Jews.

antiseptic a. & n. (substance) pre venting things from becomin septic. **antiseptically** adv.

atisocial *a.* destructive of or ostile to other members of so‑iety; not sociable.

atistatic *a.* counteracting the ffects of static electricity.

atithesis /-'tɪθə-/ *n.* (*pl.* **-eses**) ontrast. **antithetical** /-'θet-/ *a.*

atitoxin *n.* substance that neut‑alizes a toxin. **antitoxic** *a.*

ativivisectionist *n.* person pposed to making experiments n live animals.

atler *n.* branched horn of a deer tc.

atonym *n.* word opposite to nother in meaning.

aus *n.* opening at the excretory nd of the alimentary canal.

avil *n.* iron block on which a mith hammers metal into shape.

axiety *n.* state of being anxious; ause of this.

axious *a.* troubled and uneasy n mind; eager. **anxiously** *adv.*

ay *a.* one or some from three or nore or from a quantity; every; n a significant amount. —*pron.* n any one, some. —*adv.* at all.

aybody *n.* & *pron.* any person; erson of importance.

ayhow *adv.* anyway; not in an rderly manner.

ayone *n.* & *pron.* anybody.

aything *n.* & *pron.* any item. nything but far from being.

ayway *adv.* in any way, in any ase.

aywhere *adv.* & *pron.* (in or to) ny place.

nzac *n.* member of the Austra‑.an and New Zealand Army orps (1914–18); Australian or New Zealander.

rta /erˈɔːtə/ *n.* great artery arrying blood from the heart.

ace *adv.* swiftly.

art *adv.* separately, so as to be‑ome separated; to or at a dis‑ance; into pieces.

artheid /-heɪt/ *n.* former policy f racial segregation in South Africa.

artment *n.* set of rooms; (*US*) .at.

apathy *n.* lack of interest. **apa‑thetic** *a.*, **apathetically** *adv.*

ape *n.* tailless monkey. —*v.t.* imi‑tate, mimic.

aperient /əˈpɪər-/ *a.* & *n.* laxative.

aperitif /əˈperɪtɪf/ *n.* alcoholic drink taken as an appetizer.

aperture *n.* opening, esp. one that admits light.

apex *n.* tip, highest point; pointed end.

aphelion /əˈfiː-/ *n.* (*pl.* **-ia**) point nearest to the sun in the orbit of a comet or planet.

aphid /ˈeɪfɪd/ *n.* small insect de‑structive to plants.

aphis /ˈeɪfɪs/ *n.* (*pl.* **-ides**, pr. -ɪdiːz) aphid.

aphorism /ˈæf-/ *n.* pithy saying.

aphrodisiac *a.* & *n.* (substance) arousing sexual desire.

apiary /ˈeɪ-/ *n.* place where bees are kept. **apiarist** *n.*

apiece *adv.* to or for or by each.

aplomb /əˈplɒm/ *n.* self‑con‑fidence.

apocalypse /-ˈlɪp-/ *n.* prophesy‑ing great and dramatic events like those in the **Apocalypse** (last book of the New Testament).

Apocrypha /əˈpɒkrɪfə/ *n.* books of the Old Testament not accepted as part of the Hebrew scriptures.

apocryphal *a.* untrue, invented.

apogee /ˈæ-/ *n.* highest point; orbital point furthest from the earth.

apologetic *a.* making an apology. **apologetically** *adv.*

apologize *v.i.* make an apology.

apology *n.* statement of regret for having done wrong or hurt; ex‑planation of one's beliefs; poor specimen.

apoplectic /-ˈplek-/ *a.* of or liable to suffer apoplexy; liable to fits of red‑faced rage.

apoplexy /ˈæ-/ *n.* sudden loss of ability to feel and move, caused by rupture or blockage of the brain artery; a stroke.

apostasy /-ˈpɒ-/ *n.* abandonment of a former (esp. religious) belief.

apostate /-'pɒs-/ n. person who is guilty of apostasy. **apostatize** v.i.

Apostle n. any of the twelve men sent forth by Christ to preach the gospel. **apostolic** /-'stɒl-/ a.

apostrophe /ə'pɒstrəfɪ/ n. the sign' used esp. to show the possessive case or omission of a letter; passage (in a speech) pointedly addressing someone. **apostrophize** v.t. address in this way.

apothecary /-'pɒθ-/ n. (old use) pharmaceutical chemist.

apotheosis /-θɪ'əʊ-/ n. (pl. **-oses**) deification; highest development.

appal v.t. (p.t. **appalled**) fill with horror or dismay. **appalling** a.

apparatus /-'reɪ-/ n. equipment for scientific or other work.

apparel n. clothing.

apparent /-'pæ-/ a. clearly seen or understood; seeming but not real. **apparently** adv.

apparition n. appearance, thing appearing, esp. of a startling or remarkable kind; ghost.

appeal v.t./i. make an earnest or formal request; refer to a higher court for reversal of a lower court's decision; seem attractive. —n. act of appealing; attractiveness.

appear v.i. be or become visible; present oneself; be published; seem. **appearance** n.

appease v.t. soothe or conciliate, esp. by giving what was asked. **appeasement** n.

appellant n. person who appeals to a higher court.

appellation n. name, title.

append v.t. attach, add at the end.

appendage n. thing appended.

appendicitis n. inflammation of the intestinal appendix.

appendix n. (pl. **-ices**) section at the end of a book, giving extra information; (pl. **-ixes**) small blind tube of tissue attached to the intestine.

appertain v.i. belong; be relevant.

appetite n. desire, esp. for food.

appetizer n. thing eaten or dru to stimulate the appetite.

appetizing a. stimulating the petite. **appetizingly** adv.

applaud v.t./i. express approv (of), esp. by clapping; prai **applause** n.

apple n. round fruit with fi flesh. **apple-pie order** perf order.

appliance n. device, instrumen

applicable /'æ-/ a. able to be plied, appropriate; relevant. **plicability** n.

applicant n. person who appli esp. for a job.

application n. applying; th applied; ability to work hard.

applicator n. device for applyi something.

applied a. put to practical use.

appliqué /æ'pli:keɪ/ n. piece fabric attached ornamental **appliquéd** a.

apply v.t./i. make a formal quest; put into contact w another thing; bring into use action; be relevant. **apply o self** give one's attention a energy.

appoint v.t. fix or decide by au ority; choose (a person or p sons) for a job, committee, etc

appointee n. person appointed

appointment n. arrangement meet or visit at a specified tir appointing a person to a job, job itself; (pl.) equipment.

apportion v.t. divide into shar allot. **apportionment** n.

apposite /-zɪt/ a. appropriate. **positely** adv.

apposition n. relationship words that are syntactica parallel.

appraise v.t. estimate the val or quality of. **appraisal** n.

appreciable a. perceptible; considerable. **appreciably** adv.

appreciate v.t./i. value greatly, grateful for; enjoy intelligen understand; increase in val

‣ppreciation n., **appreciative**

‣prehend v.t. seize, arrest; grasp the meaning of; expect with fear or anxiety. **apprehension** n.

‣prehensive a. feeling apprehension, anxious. **apprehensively** adv.

‣rentice n. person learning a craft and formerly bound to an employer by a legal agreement. —v.t. bind as an apprentice. **ppprenticeship** n.

‣prise v.t. inform.

‣proach v.t./i. come nearer (to); set about doing; go to with a request or offer. —n. approaching; way or means of this.

‣proachable a. able to be approached; easy to talk to.

‣probation n. approval.

‣propriate[1] /-ət/ a. suitable, proper. **appropriately** adv.

‣propriate[2] /-ert/ v.t. take and use; set aside for a special purpose. **appropriation** n.

‣proval n. approving. **on approval** (of goods) supplied without obligation to buy if not satisfactory.

‣prove v.t./i. say or feel that (a thing) is good or suitable; agree

‣proximate[1] /-ət/ a. almost but not quite exact. **approximately** adv.

‣proximate[2] /-ert/ v.t./i. be almost the same; make approximate. **approximation** n.

‣purtenance n. minor thing that goes with a more important one.

rès-ski /æprer'ski:/ a. & n. (for) the evening period of relaxation and partying after skiing.

ricot n. stone-fruit related to the peach; its orange-pink colour.

ril n. fourth month of the year. **pril fool** person hoaxed on April Fool's Day (1 April).

ron n. garment worn over the front of the body to protect clothes; hard-surfaced area on an airfield, where aircraft are manoeuvred, loaded, etc.

apropos /æprə'pəʊ/ adv. & a. appropriate(ly). **apropos of** concerning.

apse n. recess usu. with an arched or domed roof, esp. in a church.

apt a. suitable; having a certain tendency; quick at learning. **aptly** adv., **aptness** n.

aptitude n. natural ability.

aqualung n. portable underwater breathing-apparatus.

aquamarine /-'ri:n/ n. bluish-green beryl; its colour.

aquarium n. (pl. **-ums**) tank for keeping living fish etc.; building containing such tanks.

aquatic a. living in or near water; taking place in or on water.

aquatint n. a kind of etching.

aqueduct n. artificial channel on a raised structure, carrying water across country.

aqueous /'eɪ-/ a. of or like water.

aquifer n. water-bearing rock or soil.

aquilegia /-'li:-/ n. columbine.

aquiline /-lam/ a. like an eagle; (of a nose) hooked.

Arab n. member of a Semitic people of the Middle East. —a. of Arabs.

arabesque /-'besk/ n. dancer's posture with the body bent forward and leg and arm extended in line; decoration with intertwined lines etc.

Arabian a. of Arabia.

Arabic /'æ-/ a. & n. (of) the language of the Arabs. **arabic numerals** the symbols 1, 2, 3, etc.

arable /'æ-/ a. & n. (land) suitable for growing crops.

arachnid /-'ræk-/ n. member of the class to which spiders belong.

arachnophobia /-ræk-/ n. fear of spiders.

Aran a. knitted in patterns traditional to the Aran Islands, usu. in unbleached wool.

arbiter n. person with power to decide what shall be done or accepted; arbitrator.

arbitrary a. based on random choice. **arbitrarily** adv.

arbitrate v.i. act as arbitrator. **arbitration** n.

arbitrator n. impartial person chosen to settle a dispute.

arboreal /-'bɔːr-/ a. of or living in trees.

arboretum /-'riː-/ n. (pl. **-ta** or **tums**) place where trees are grown for study and display.

arbour n. shady shelter under trees or a framework with climbing plants.

arc n. part of a curve; luminous electric current crossing a gap between terminals. **arc lamp, light, welding** that using an electric arc.

arcade n. covered walk between shops; series of arches. **amusement arcade** area with pintables, gambling machines, etc.

arcane /-'kem/ a. mysterious.

arch[1] n. curved structure, esp. as a support. —v.t./i. form (into) an arch. **archway** n.

arch[2] a. consciously or affectedly playful. **archly** adv., **archness** n.

archaeology n. study of civilizations through their material remains. **archaeological** a., **archaeologist** n.

archaic a. belonging to former or ancient times. **archaically** adv.

archaism n. (use of) an archaic word or phrase.

archangel n. angel of the highest rank. **archangelic** a.

archbishop n. chief bishop.

archdeacon n. priest ranking next below bishop. **archdeaconry** n.

arch-enemy n. chief enemy.

archer n. person who shoots with bow and arrows. **archery** n. sport of shooting thus.

archetype /-kɪ-/ n. prototype; typical specimen. **archetypal** a.

archipelago /-kɪ'pel-/ n. (pl. -o(group of islands; sea round thi

architect n. designer of buil ings.

architecture n. designing buildings; style of building(**architectural** a.

architrave n. moulded fram round a doorway or window.

archive /-kaɪv/ n. (usu. pl.) hi torical documents. **archival** a.

archivist /-kɪv-/ n. person traine to deal with archives.

archway n. arched entrance (passage.

Arctic a. & n. (of) regions rour the North Pole. **arctic** a. ver cold.

ardent a. full of ardour, enthus astic. **ardently** adv., **ardency** r

ardour n. great warmth of fee ing, enthusiasm.

arduous a. needing much effor **arduously** adv., **arduousness** r

are see **be**.

area n. extent or measure of surface; region; range of a subjec etc.; sunken courtyard.

areca /-'riː-/ n. a kind of palm tre

arena n. level area in the centre (an amphitheatre or sports sta dium; scene of conflict.

aren't (colloq.) = are not.

argon n. an inert gas.

argot n. jargon.

arguable a. able to be asserted not certain. **arguably** adv.

argue v.t./i. express disagree ment; exchange angry word give as reason(s); indicate.

argument n. discussion involv ing disagreement, quarre reason put forward; chain c reasoning.

argumentation n. arguing.

argumentative a. fond of argu ing.

aria /'ɑːr-/ n. solo in opera.

arid /'æ-/ a. dry, parched. **aridl** adv., **aridness** n., **aridity** /-'rɪd n.

aright adv. rightly.

arise v.i. (p.t. **arose**, p.p. **arisen**) come into existence or to people's notice; (old use) rise.

aristocracy n. hereditary upper classes; form of government in which these rule. **aristocratic** a.

aristocrat /æ/ n. member of the aristocracy.

arithmetic n. calculating by means of numbers. **arithmetical** a., **arithmetically** adv.

ark n. Noah's boat in which he and his family and animals were saved from the Flood; wooden chest in which the writings of Jewish Law were kept.

arm[1] n. upper limb of the human body; similar projection; raised side part of a chair.

arm[2] v.t. equip with weapon(s); make (a bomb etc.) ready to explode. —n.pl. weapons. See also **coat of arms**.

armada n. fleet of warships.

armadillo n. (pl. **-os**) burrowing animal of South America with a body encased in bony plates.

Armageddon n. final disastrous conflict.

armament n. military weapons; process of equipping for war.

armature n. rotating coil or coils of a dynamo etc.; bar of soft iron placed on the poles of a magnet; internal framework of a piece of sculpture.

armchair n. chair with raised sides.

armful n. as much as an arm can hold.

armistice n. agreement to stop fighting temporarily.

armlet n. band worn round an arm or sleeve.

armorial a. of heraldic arms.

armour n. protective metal covering, esp. that formerly worn in fighting.

armoured a. protected by armour; equipped with armoured vehicles.

armourer n. maker, repairer, or keeper of weapons.

armoury n. place where weapons are kept.

armpit n. hollow under the arm at the shoulder.

army n. organized force for fighting on land; vast group; body of people organized for a purpose.

aroma n. smell, esp. a pleasant one. **aromatic** a.

aromatherapy n. use of fragrant oils etc. in massage.

arose see **arise**.

around adv. & prep. all round, on every side (of); near at hand; (US) approximately.

arouse v.t. rouse.

arpeggio n. (pl. **-os**) notes of a musical chord played in succession.

arraign /-'rem/ v.t. indict, accuse; find fault with. **arraignment** n.

arrange v.t. put into order; form plans, settle the details of; adapt. **arrangement** n.

arrant /'æ/ a. downright. **arrantly** adv.

array v.t. arrange in order; dress, adorn. —n. imposing series, display.

arrears n.pl. money owed and overdue for repayment; work overdue for being finished.

arrest v.t. stop (a movement or moving thing); catch and hold (attention); seize by authority of law. —n. stoppage; seizure, legal seizure of an offender. **arrester** n., **arrestor** n.

arrestable a. (of an offence) such that the offender may be arrested.

arrival n. arriving; person or thing that has arrived.

arrive v.i. reach a destination or other point on a journey; (of time) come; (colloq., of a baby) be born; be recognized as having achieved success.

arrogant a. proud and overbearing. **arrogantly** adv., **arrogance** n.

arrow *n.* straight shaft with a sharp point to be shot from a bow; line with an outward-pointing V at the end, indicating direction etc.

arrowroot *n.* edible starch made from the root of a West Indian plant.

arsenal *n.* place where weapons and ammunition are stored or made.

arsenic *n.* semi-metallic element; strongly poisonous compound of this. **arsenical** /-'sen-/ *a.*

arson *n.* intentional and unlawful setting on fire of a building.

arsonist *n.* person guilty of arson.

art[1] *n.* production of something beautiful; skill or ability; paintings or sculptures etc.; (*pl.*) subjects other than sciences, requiring sensitive understanding rather than use of measurement; (*pl.*) creative activities (e.g. painting, music, writing).

art[2] *(old use, with thou)* = are.

artefact *n.* man-made object, simple prehistoric tool or weapon.

arterial /-'tiər-/ *a.* of an artery. **arterial road** main trunk road.

artery *n.* large blood-vessel conveying blood away from the heart.

artesian well /-'ti:ʒən/ a well that is bored vertically into oblique strata so that water rises naturally with little or no pumping.

artful *a.* crafty. **artfully** *adv.*, **artfulness** *n.*

arthritis *n.* condition in which there is pain and stiffness in the joints. **arthritic** /-'rɪt-/ *a. & n.*

arthropod *n.* animal with a segmented body and jointed limbs (e.g. an insect or crustacean).

artichoke *n.* plant with a flower of leaf-like scales used as a vegetable. **Jerusalem artichoke** sunflower with an edible root.

article *n.* particular or separate thing; piece of writing in a newspaper or magazine; clause in an agreement. —*v.t.* bind by articles

of apprenticeship. **definite article** the word 'the'. **indefinite article** 'a' or 'an'.

articulate[1] /-ət/ *a.* spoken distinctly; able to express idea clearly.

articulate[2] /-ert/ *v.t./i.* say o speak distinctly; form a joint connect by joints. **articulated lorry** one with sections connected by a flexible joint **articulation** *n.*

artifice *n.* trickery; device.

artificer /-'tɪf-/ *n.* craftsman.

artificial *a.* not originating naturally; man-made. **artificially** *adv.*, **artificiality** *n.*

artillery *n.* large guns used in fighting on land; branch of an army using these.

artisan /-'zæn or 'ɑ:-/ *n.* skilled workman.

artist *n.* person who produces works of art, esp. paintings; one who does something with exceptional skill; professional entertainer. **artistry** *n.*

artiste /-'ti:st/ *n.* professional entertainer.

artistic *a.* of art or artists; showing or done with good taste. **artistically** *adv.*

artistry *n.* artistic skill.

artless *a.* free from artfulness, simple and natural. **artlessly** *adv.*, **artlessness** *n.*

arty *a.* (**-ier, -iest**) (*colloq.*) with an exaggerated or affected display of artistic style or interests.

arum /'eər-/ *n.* plant with arrow-shaped leaves.

Aryan *a.* of the original Indo-European language; of its speakers or their descendants. —*n.* Aryan person.

as *adv. & conj.* in the same degree, similarly; in the form or function of; while; when; because. —*rel. pron.* that, who, which. **as for, as** to with regard to. **as well in** addition; desirable, desirably.

safoetida /-'fi:-/ n. resinous gum with a strong smell.

sbestos n. soft fibrous mineral substance; fireproof material made from this.

sbestosis n. lung disease caused by inhaling asbestos particles.

scend v.t./i. go or come up.

ascend the throne become king or queen.

scendancy n. being dominant.

scendant a. rising. **in the ascendant** rising in power or influence.

scension n. ascent, esp. (**Ascension**) that of Christ to heaven.

scent n. ascending; way up, upward slope or path.

scertain v.t. find out by enquiring.

scertainable a. able to be ascertained.

scetic /-'set-/ a. not allowing oneself pleasures and luxuries. —n. person who is ascetic esp. for religious reasons. **ascetically** adv., **asceticism** n.

scorbic acid vitamin C.

scribe v.t. attribute. **ascription** n.

sepsis /er-/ n. aseptic condition. **septic** /er-/ a. free from harmful bacteria. **aseptically** adv.

sexual /er-/ a. without sex. **asexually** adv.

sh¹ n. tree with silver-grey bark.

sh² n. powder that remains after something has burnt. **Ash Wednesday** first day of Lent.

shamed a. feeling shame.

shen a. pale as ashes.

shlar n. square-cut stones; masonry made of these.

shore adv. to or on shore.

shram n. (orig. in India) retreat for religious meditation.

shtray n. receptacle for tobacco ash.

shy a. (-ier, -iest) ashen; covered with ash.

Asian a. of Asia or its people. —n. Asian person.

Asiatic a. of Asia.

aside adv. to or on one side, away from the main part or group. —n. words spoken so that only certain people will hear. **aside from** (US) apart from.

asinine /'æsɪnaɪn/ a. silly.

ask v.t./i. call for an answer to or about; address a question to; seek to obtain; invite.

askance adv. **look askance at** look at with distrust or displeasure.

askew adv. & a. crooked(ly).

asleep adv. & a. in or into a state of sleep; numbed.

asp n. small poisonous snake.

asparagus n. plant whose shoots are used as a vegetable; these shoots.

aspect n. look or appearance; feature of a complex matter; direction a thing faces, side facing this way.

aspen n. a kind of poplar.

asperity /-'spe-/ n. harshness.

aspersion n. derogatory remark.

asphalt /'æsfælt/ n. black substance like coal-tar; mixture of this with gravel etc. for paving. —v.t. surface with asphalt.

asphyxia n. suffocation.

asphyxiate v.t. suffocate. **asphyxiation** n.

aspic n. savoury jelly for coating cooked meat, eggs, etc.

aspidistra n. ornamental plant with broad tapering leaves.

aspirant /'æ-/ n. person who aspires to something.

aspirate¹ /-ət/ n. sound of h.

aspirate² /-eɪt/ v.t. pronounce with an h.

aspiration n. aspirating; aspiring; earnest desire or ambition.

aspire v.i. feel an earnest ambition.

aspirin n. drug that relieves pain and reduces fever; tablet of this.

ass n. donkey; (colloq.) stupid person.

assail v.t. attack violently.

assailant n. attacker.

assassin n. person who assassinates another.

assassinate v.t. kill (an important person) by violent means. assassination n., assassinator n.

assault n. & v.t. attack.

assay /-'set/ n. test of metal for quality. —v.t. make an assay of.

assegai /'æsɪgaɪ/ n. throwing-spear of South African peoples.

assemblage n. assembly.

assemble v.t./i. bring or come together; put or fit together.

assembly n. assembling; assembled group.

assent v.i. consent; express agreement. —n. consent, permission.

assert v.t. state, declare to be true; use (power etc.) effectively. assertion n., assertive a, assertiveness n.

assess v.t. decide the amount or value of; estimate the worth or likelihood etc. of. assessment n., assessor n.

asset n. property with money value, esp. as available to meet debts; useful quality, person or thing having this.

assiduous a. diligent and persevering. assiduously adv., assiduousness n., assiduity n.

assign v.t. allot; designate to perform a task etc.; ascribe.

assignation n. assigning; arrangement to meet.

assignment n. assigning; task assigned.

assimilate v.t./i. absorb or be absorbed into the body or a group etc., or into the mind as knowledge. assimilation n.

assist v.t./i. help. assistance n.

assistant n. helper; person who serves customers in a shop. —a. assisting, esp. as a subordinate.

assizes n.pl. former periodical session for the administration of justice.

associate¹ /-ert/ v.t./i. join as a companion or supporter etc.; mix socially; connect in one's mind.

associate² /-ət/ n. companion, partner; subordinate member. —a. associated; having subordinate membership.

association n. associating; group organized for a common purpose; mental connection between ideas. Association football that played with a spherical ball not to be handled in play except by the goalkeeper. associative a.

assonance /'æ-/ n. resemblance o sound in syllables; rhyme o vowel-sounds. assonant a.

assorted a. of different sorts put together.

assortment n. collection composed of several sorts.

assuage /-'sweɪdʒ/ v.t. soothe allay.

assume v.t. take as true, without proof; take or put upon oneself.

assumption n. assuming; thing assumed to be true. Assumption reception of the Virgin Mary in bodily form into heaven.

assurance n. positive assertion; self-confidence; life insurance.

assure v.t. tell confidently, promise; make certain.

assured a. sure, confident; insured.

assuredly /-ɪdlɪ/ adv. certainly.

aster n. garden plant with daisy-like flowers.

asterisk n. star-shaped symbol *.

astern adv. at or towards the stern; backwards.

asteroid n. any of the small planets revolving round the sun.

asthma /-sm-/ n. chronic condition causing difficulty in breathing. asthmatic /-s'mæ-/ a. & n.

astigmatism /-'stɪg-/ n. defect in an eye or lens, preventing proper focusing. astigmatic /-'mæ-/ a.

astonish v.t. surprise very greatly. astonishment n.

astound v.t. shock with surprise.

astrakhan /-'kæn/ n. dark curly fleece of lambs from Astrakhan in Russia; fabric imitating this.

astral *a.* of stars; of the spirit world.

astray *adv.* & *a.* away from the proper path. **go astray** be mislaid.

astride *adv.* with legs wide apart; with one leg on each side of something. —*prep.* astride of; extending across.

astringent *a.* causing tissue to contract; harsh, severe. —*n.* astringent substance. **astringently** *adv.*, **astringency** *n.*

astrolabe *n.* device for measuring the altitudes of stars etc.

astrology *n.* study of the supposed influence of stars on human affairs. **astrologer** *n.*, **astrological** *a.*

astronaut *n.* person trained to travel in a spacecraft.

astronautics *n.* study of space travel and its technology.

astronomer *n.* person skilled in astronomy.

astronomical *a.* of astronomy; enormous in amount. **astronomically** *adv.*

astronomy *n.* study of stars and planets and their movements.

astute *a.* shrewd, quick at seeing how to gain an advantage. **astutely** *adv.*, **astuteness** *n.*

asunder *adv.* apart, into pieces.

asylum *n.* refuge; (*old use*) mental institution.

asymmetrical *a.* not symmetrical. **asymmetrically** *adv.*, **asymmetry** *n.*

at *prep.* having as position, time of day, condition, or price. **at all** in any way; of any kind. **at once** immediately; simultaneously.

atavism /'æ-/ *n.* resemblance to remote ancestors. **atavistic** *a.*

ate *see* **eat.**

atheist /'eɪθɪ-/ *n.* person who does not believe in the existence of God or god(s). **atheism** *n.*

athlete *n.* person who is good at athletics.

athletic *a.* of athletes; muscular and physically active. **athletically** *adv.*, **athleticism** *n.*

athletics *n.pl.* or *sing.* sports, esp. running, jumping, and throwing.

Atlantic *a.* & *n.* (of) the **Atlantic Ocean** (east of the American continent).

atlas *n.* book of maps.

atmosphere *n.* mixture of gases surrounding the earth or other planet; air in any place; feeling conveyed by an environment or group of people etc.; unit of pressure. **atmospheric** *a.*

atmospherics *n.pl.* electrical disturbances in the air, causing interference in telecommunications.

atoll /'æ-/ *n.* ring-shaped coral reef enclosing a lagoon.

atom *n.* smallest particle of a chemical element; very small quantity or thing. **atom bomb** atomic bomb.

atomic *a.* of atom(s). **atomic bomb** bomb deriving its power from atomic energy. **atomic energy** that obtained from nuclear fission.

atomize *v.t.* reduce to atoms or fine particles. **atomization** *n.*, **atomizer** *n.*

atonal /eɪˈtəʊnəl/ *a.* (of music) not written in any key. **atonality** *n.*

atone *v.i.* make amends for an error or wrong. **atonement** *n.*

atrocious *a.* extremely wicked; very bad. **atrociously** *adv.*

atrocity *n.* wickedness; wicked or cruel act etc.

atrophy /'æ-/ *n.* wasting away through lack of nourishment or of use. —*v.t./i.* cause atrophy in; suffer atrophy.

attach *v.t./i.* fix to something else; join; attribute, be attributable. **attached** *a.* bound by affection or loyalty. **attachment** *n.*

attaché /-ˈʃeɪ/ *n.* person attached to an ambassador's staff. **attaché**

case small rectangular case for carrying documents etc.

attack *n.* violent attempt to hurt, overcome, or defeat; strong criticism; sudden onset of illness. —*v.t./i.* make an attack (on); act harmfully on. **attacker** *n.*

attain *v.t.* achieve. **attainment** *n.*

attainable *a.* able to be attained.

attar *n.* a fragrant oil.

attempt *v.t.* make an effort to accomplish or overcome. —*n.* such an effort.

attend *v.t./i.* give attention to; be present at; accompany as an attendant. **attendance** *n.*

attendant *a.* accompanying. —*n.* person present as a companion or to provide service.

attention *n.* applying one's mind; awareness; consideration; care; erect attitude in military drill.

attentive *a.* giving attention. **attentively** *adv.*, **attentiveness** *n.*

attenuate *v.t.* make slender, thin, or weaker. **attenuation** *n.*

attest *v.t./i.* provide proof of; declare true or genuine. **attestation** *n.*

attic *n.* room in the top storey of a house.

attire *n.* clothes. —*v.t.* clothe.

attitude *n.* position of the body; way of thinking or behaving.

attorney /-ˈtɜː-/ *n.* (*pl.* -eys) person appointed to act for another in legal or business matters; (*US*) lawyer.

attract *v.t.* draw towards itself by unseen force; arouse the interest or pleasure of. **attraction** *n.*

attractive *a.* attracting; pleasing in appearance. **attractively** *adv.*, **attractiveness** *n.*

attributable *a.* that may be attributed.

attribute[1] /-ˈtrɪb-/ *v.t.* **attribute to** regard as belonging to or caused by. **attribution** *n.*

attribute[2] /ˈæ-/ *n.* characteristic quality; object regularly associated with a person or thing.

attributive *a.* qualifying a noun and placed before it. **attributively** *adv.*

attrition *n.* wearing away.

attune *v.t.* adapt; tune.

atypical /eɪ-/ *a.* not typical. **atypically** *adv.*

aubergine /ˈəʊbəʒiːn/ *n.* deep purple vegetable; its colour.

aubrietia /-ˈbriːʃə/ *n.* perennial rock-plant flowering in spring.

auburn *a.* (of hair) reddish brown.

auction *n.* public sale where articles are sold to the highest bidder. —*v.t.* sell by auction.

auctioneer *n.* person who conducts an auction.

audacious *a.* bold, daring. **audaciously** *adv.*, **audacity** *n.*

audible *a.* loud enough to be heard. **audibly** *adv.*, **audibility** *n.*

audience *n.* group of listeners or spectators; formal interview.

audio *n.* sound reproduced mechanically; its reproduction. **audio typist** one who types from a recording.

audiovisual *a.* using both sight and sound.

audit *n.* official examination of accounts. —*v.t.* make an audit of.

audition *n.* test of a prospective performer's ability. —*v.t./i.* test or be tested in an audition.

auditor *n.* one who audits accounts.

auditorium *n.* part of a building where the audience sits.

auditory *a.* of hearing.

au fait /əʊ ˈfeɪ/ well acquainted.

auger *n.* boring-tool.

aught *a.* (*old use*) anything.

augment /-ˈment/ *v.t.* increase. **augmentation** *n.*, **augmentative** *a.*

augur *v.i.* bode.

augury *n.* divination; omen.

August *n.* eighth month of the year.

august /-'gʌst/ a. majestic, imposing. **augustly** adv., **augustness** n.

auk n. northern sea bird.

aunt n. sister or sister-in-law of one's father or mother. **Aunt Sally** target in a throwing-game; target of general abuse.

aunty n. (colloq.) aunt.

au pair /əʊ/ young person (esp. a woman) from overseas helping with housework in return for board and lodging.

aura n. atmosphere surrounding a person or thing.

aural a. of the ear. **aurally** adv.

aureole /'ɔːrɪəʊl/ n. halo.

au revoir /əʊ rə'vwɑː(r)/ goodbye for the moment.

auricular a. of the ear.

aurora n. luminous electrical radiation. **aurora australis** from the southern magnetic pole, **aurora borealis** from the northern.

auscultation n. listening to the sound of the heart etc. for diagnosis.

auspice n. omen; (pl.) patronage.

auspicious a. showing signs that promise success. **auspiciously** adv., **auspiciousness** n.

austere a. severely simple and plain. **austerely** adv., **austerity** /-'ste-/ n.

Australasian a. & n. (native or inhabitant) of Australia, New Zealand, and neighbouring islands.

Australian a. & n. (native or inhabitant) of Australia.

autarchy n. absolute sovereignty. **autarchic(al)** a.

authentic a. genuine, known to be true. **authentically** adv., **authenticity** n.

authenticate v.t. prove the truth or authenticity of. **authentication** n.

author n. writer of a book etc.; originator. **authoress** n.fem., **authorship** n.

authoritarian a. favouring complete obedience to authority. **authoritarianism** n.

authoritative a. having or using authority. **authoritatively** adv.

authority n. power to enforce obedience; person(s) with this; person with specialized knowledge.

authorize v.t. give authority to or permission for. **authorization** n.

autistic a. suffering from a mental disorder that prevents proper response to one's environment. **autism** n. this disorder.

auto- pref. self-.

autobiography n. story of a person's life written by himself or herself. **autobiographical** a.

autocracy /-'tɒk-/ n. despotism.

autocrat n. person with unrestricted power; dictatorial person. **autocratic** a., **autocratically** adv.

autocross n. motor-racing on dirt tracks.

autogenic a. (of training) using self-produced management of stress. **autogenics** n.

autogiro n. (pl. -os) early form of helicopter.

autograph n. person's signature; manuscript in the author's handwriting. —v.t. write one's name in or on.

automate v.t. control by automation.

automatic a. mechanical, self-regulating; done without thinking. —n. automatic machine or firearm etc. **automatically** adv.

automation n. use of automatic equipment in industry etc.

automaton /-'tɒm-/ n. (pl. -tons, -ta) robot.

automobile n. (US) car.

automotive a. concerned with motor vehicles.

autonomous a. self-governing. **autonomy** n. self-government. **autonomously** adv.

autopilot n. device for keeping an aircraft on a set course automatically.

autopsy n. post-mortem.

autumn n. season between summer and winter. **autumnal** a.

auxiliary a. giving help or support. —n. helper; (pl.) foreign troops employed by a country at war. **auxiliary verb** one used in forming tenses etc. of other verbs.

avail v.t./i. be of use or help (to). —n. effectiveness, advantage. **avail oneself of** make use of.

available a. ready to be used; obtainable. **availability** n.

avalanche n. mass of snow pouring down a mountain; great onrush.

avant-garde /ævã'gɑ:d/ n. group of innovators. —a. novel, progressive.

avarice n. greed for gain. **avaricious** a., **avariciously** adv.

avenge v.t. take vengeance for. **avenger** n.

avenue n. wide street or road; way of approach.

aver /-'vɜ:(r)/ v.t. (p.t. **averred**) assert, affirm.

average n. value arrived at by adding several quantities together and dividing by the number of these; standard regarded as usual. —a. found by making an average; of ordinary standard. —v.t./i. calculate the average of; amount to or produce as an average.

averse a. unwilling, disinclined.

aversion n. strong dislike.

avert v.t. turn away; ward off.

aviary n. large cage or building for keeping birds.

aviation n. flying an aircraft.

aviator n. (old use) pilot or member of an aircraft crew.

avid a. eager, greedy. **avidly** adv., **avidity** n.

avocado /-'kɑ:-/ n. (pl. **-os**) pear-shaped tropical fruit.

avocation n. activity, occupation.

avocet /'æv əsɛt/ n. wading bird with a long upturned bill.

avoid v.t. keep oneself away from; refrain from. **avoidance** n.

avoidable a. able to be avoided.

avoirdupois /ævədə'pɔɪz/ n. system of weights based on the pound of 16 ounces.

avow v.t. declare. **avowal** n.

avuncular a. of or like a kindly uncle.

await v.t. wait for.

awake v.t./i. (p.t. **awoke**, p.p. **awoken**) wake. —a. not asleep; alert.

awaken v.t./i. awake.

award v.t. give by official decision as a prize or penalty etc. —n. awarding; thing awarded.

aware a. having knowledge or realization. **awareness** n.

awash a. washed over by water.

away adv. to or at a distance; into non-existence; persistently. —a. played on an opponent's ground. —n. away match or win.

awe n. respect combined with fear or wonder. —v.t. fill with awe.

aweigh adv. (of anchor) raised just clear of the sea bottom.

awesome a. causing awe.

awestricken, **awestruck** adjs. suddenly filled with awe.

awful a. extremely bad or unpleasant; (colloq.) very great. **awfully** adv.

awhile adv. for a short time.

awkward a. difficult to use or handle; clumsy; inconvenient; embarrassed. **awkwardly** adv., **awkwardness** n.

awl n. small pricking-tool.

awning n. roof-like canvas shelter.

awoke, **awoken** see **awake**.

awry /ə'raɪ/ adv. & a. twisted to one side; amiss.

axe n. chopping-tool. —v.t. (pres.p. **axing**) remove by abolishing or dismissing.

axil n. angle where a leaf joins a stem.

axiom *n.* accepted general truth or principle. **axiomatic** /-ˈmæ-/ *a.*

axis *n.* (*pl.* **axes**) line through the centre of an object, round which it rotates if spinning. **axial** *a.*

axle *n.* rod on which wheels turn.

ay /aɪ/ *adv.* & *n.* (*pl.* **ayes**) aye.

ayatollah /aɪəˈtɒlə/ *n.* senior Muslim religious leader in Iran.

aye[1] /aɪ/ *adv.* yes. —*n.* vote in favour of a proposal.

aye[2] /aɪ/ *adv.* (*old use*) always.

azalea *n.* shrub-like flowering plant.

azimuth *n.* arc of the sky from zenith to horizon; angle between this and the meridian.

Aztec *n.* member of a former Indian people of Mexico.

azure *a.* & *n.* sky-blue.

B

BA *abbr.* Bachelor of Arts.

baa *n.* & *v.i.* bleat.

baba *n.* sponge-cake soaked in rum syrup.

babble *v.i.* chatter indistinctly or foolishly; (of a stream) murmur. —*n.* babbling talk or sound.

babe *n.* baby.

babel /ˈbeɪ-/ *n.* confused noise.

baboon *n.* a kind of large monkey.

baby *n.* very young child or animal; thing small of its kind; (*US sl.*) person, esp. a man's girlfriend. **baby-sit** *v.i.* act as **babysitter**, person employed to look after a child while its parents are out.

babyish *a.* like a baby.

baccarat /-rɑː/ *n.* gambling card-game.

bachelor *n.* unmarried man. **Bachelor of Arts** etc., person with the lowest university degree.

bacillus /-ˈsɪl-/ *n.* (*pl.* **-li**) rod-like bacterium.

back *n.* surface or part furthest from the front; rear part of the

human body from shoulders to hips; corresponding part of an animal's body; defensive player positioned near the goal in football etc. —*a.* situated behind; of or for past time. —*adv.* at or towards the rear; in check; in or into a previous time, position, or state; in return. —*v.t./i.* move backwards; help, support; lay a bet on; cover the back of. **back-bencher** *n.* MP not entitled to sit on the front benches. **back down** withdraw a claim or argument. **back of beyond** very remote place. **back out** withdraw from an agreement. **back-pedal** *v.i.* reverse one's previous action or opinion. **back seat** inferior position or status. **back up** support by subordinate action. **backup** *n.* such support. **backer** *n.*

backache *n.* pain in one's back.

backbiting *n.* spiteful talk.

backbone *n.* column of small bones down the centre of the back.

backchat *n.* answering back.

backcloth *n.* painted cloth at the back of a stage or scene.

backdate *v.t.* regard as valid from an earlier date.

backdrop *n.* backcloth.

backfire *v.i.* make an abnormal explosion, e.g. in an exhaust pipe; produce an undesired effect.

backgammon *n.* game played on a board with draughts and dice.

background *n.* back part of a scene or picture; conditions surrounding and influencing something.

backhand *n.* backhanded stroke. —*a.* of or made with this stroke.

backhanded *a.* performed with the back of the hand turned forwards; said with underlying sarcasm.

backhander *n.* backhanded stroke; (*sl.*) bribe, reward for services.

backlash n. violent hostile reaction.

backlog n. arrears of work.

backpack n. rucksack.

backside n. (colloq.) buttocks.

backslide v.i. slip back from good behaviour into bad.

backstage a. & adv. behind a theatre stage.

backstroke n. stroke used in swimming on one's back.

backtrack v.i. retrace one's route; reverse one's opinion.

backward a. directed backwards; having made less than normal progress; diffident. —adv. backwards.

backwards adv. towards the back; with the back foremost; in a reverse direction or order. **backwards and forwards** each way alternately.

backwash n. receding waves created by a ship etc.; reaction.

backwater n. stagnant water joining a stream; place unaffected by new ideas or progress.

backwoods n.pl. remote region.

backyard n. yard behind a house; (colloq.) area near one's home.

bacon n. salted or smoked meat from a pig.

bacteriology n. study of bacteria. **bacteriological** a., **bacteriologist** n.

bacterium n. (pl. -ia) microscopic organism. **bacterial** a.

bad a. (worse, worst) having undesirable qualities; wicked; evil; unpleasant; harmful; serious; of poor quality; diseased, decayed. —adv. (US) badly. **bad lang.age** swear-words. **badly** adv., **badness** n.

bade see bid[2].

badge n. thing worn to show membership, rank, etc.

badger n. burrowing animal of the weasel family. —v.t. pester.

badinage /-a:ʒ/ n. banter.

badminton n. game like tennis played with a shuttle-cock.

baffle v.t. be too difficult for; frustrate. —n. screen. **bafflement** n.

bag n. flexible container; handbag; amount of game shot by a sportsman; (pl., sl.) large amount. —v.t./i. (p.t. **bagged**) put into bag(s); hang loosely; (colloq.) take for oneself.

bagatelle n. game played with small balls on a board with holes.

baggage n. luggage.

baggy a. (-ier, -iest) hanging in loose folds.

bagpipes n.pl. wind instrument with air stored in a bag connected to pipes. **bagpiper** n.

bail[1] n. money pledged as security that an accused person will return for trial. —v.t. (esp. with out) obtain or allow the release of (a person) on bail; relieve by financial help. **bailable** a.

bail[2] n. each of two cross-pieces resting on the stumps in cricket.

bail[3] v.t. scoop water out of. **bail out** = bale out (bale[1]).

bailey n. outer wall of a castle; area enclosed by this.

bailie n. Scottish municipal councillor serving as a magistrate.

bailiff n. law officer empowered to seize goods for non-payment of fines or debts, serve writs and summonses, etc.

bailiwick n. district of a bailie; area of authority.

bairn n. (Sc.) child.

bait n. food etc. placed to attract prey, esp. fish. —v.t. place bait on or in; torment by jeers.

baize n. thick woollen green cloth used for covering billiard tables, card tables, etc.

bake v.t./i. cook or harden by dry heat.

bakelite n. a kind of plastic.

baker n. person who bakes and sells bread. **baker's dozen** thirteen.

bakery *n.* place where bread is baked for sale.

baking-powder *n.* mixture of powders used to make cakes etc. rise.

Balaclava (helmet) woollen cap covering the head and neck.

balalaika /-'laɪ-/ *n.* Russian guitar-like instrument with a triangular body.

balance *n.* weighing apparatus with hanging pans; regulating apparatus of a clock; even distribution of weight or amount; difference between credits and debits; remainder. —*v.t./i.* consider by comparing; be, put, or keep in a state of balance; equalize.

balcony *n.* projecting platform with a rail or parapet; upper floor of seats in a cinema etc.

bald *a.* (-er, -est) with scalp wholly or partly hairless; without details; (of tyres) with the tread worn away. **baldly** *adv.*, **baldness** *n.*

balderdash *n.* nonsense.

balding *a.* becoming bald.

bale[1] *n.* large bound bundle of straw etc.; large package of goods. —*v.t.* make into a bale or bales. **bale out** make an emergency parachute jump from an aircraft etc.

bale[2] *v.t.* =bail[3].

baleful *a.* menacing, destructive. **balefully** *adv.*

balk *v.t./i.* shirk; frustrate. —*n.* hindrance.

ball[1] *n.* spherical object, esp. used in a game; rounded part or mass; single delivery of a ball by a bowler. —*v.t./i.* form into a ball. **ball-bearing** *n.* bearing using small steel balls; one such ball. **ball-point** *n.* pen with a tiny ball as its writing-point.

ball[2] *n.* social assembly for dancing.

ballad *n.* simple song or poem telling a story. **balladry** *n.*

ballade /-'lɑːd/ *n.* type of poem with set(s) of three verses; short lyrical piece of music.

ballast *n.* heavy material placed in a ship's hold to steady it.

ballcock *n.* device with a floating ball controlling the water-level in a cistern.

ballerina *n.* female ballet-dancer.

ballet /-leɪ/ *n.* performance of dancing and mime to music.

ballistic *a.* of projectiles. **ballistic missile** one that is powered and guided at first but falls to its target by gravity.

ballistics *n.pl.* study of projectiles.

balloon *n.* bag inflated with air or lighter gas. —*v.i.* swell like this.

balloonist *n.* person who travels by balloon.

ballot *n.* vote recorded on a slip of paper; voting by this. —*v.t./i.* (*p.t.* **balloted**) vote by ballot; cause to do this.

ballroom *n.* large room where dances are held.

bally *a.* & *adv.* (*sl.*) cursed.

ballyhoo *n.* fuss; extravagant publicity.

balm *n.* soothing influence; fragrant herb; (*old use*) ointment.

balmy *a.* (-ier, -iest) fragrant; (of air) soft and warm; (*sl.*) crazy.

baloney *n.* =boloney.

balsa *n.* tropical American tree; its lightweight wood.

balsam *n.* soothing oil; a kind of flowering plant.

Balti *n.* type of Pakistani curry.

baluster *n.* short stone pillar in a balustrade.

balustrade *n.* row of short pillars supporting a rail or coping.

bamboo *n.* giant tropical grass with hollow stems.

bamboozle *v.t.* (*sl.*) cheat, trick.

ban *v.t.* (*p.t.* **banned**) forbid officially. —*n.* order banning something.

banal /-'nɑːl/ *a.* commonplace, uninteresting. **banality** /-'næ-/ *n.*

banana n. finger-shaped fruit; tropical tree bearing this.

band[1] n. strip, hoop, loop; range of values or wavelengths etc.; organized group of people; set of musicians, esp. one playing wind or percussion instruments. —v.t./i. put a band on; form an organized group. **bandmaster** n., **bandsman** n.

bandage n. strip of material for binding a wound. —v.t. bind with this.

bandanna n. large coloured handkerchief.

bandeau /-dəʊ/ n. (pl. -eaux) head-band.

bandit n. member of a band of robbers. **banditry** n.

bandoleer n. (also **bandolier**) belt worn across the chest, holding ammunition.

bandstand n. covered outdoor platform for a band playing music.

bandwagon n. **climb on the bandwagon** join a movement heading for success.

bandy[1] v.t. pass to and fro.

bandy[2] a. (-ier, -iest) curving apart at the knees. **bandiness** n.

bane n. cause of trouble or anxiety. **baneful** a., **banefully** adv.

bang n. noise of or like an explosion; sharp blow. —v.t./i. make this noise; strike; shut noisily. —adv. abruptly; exactly.

banger n. firework that explodes noisily; (sl.) noisy old car; (sl.) sausage.

bangle n. bracelet of rigid material.

banian n. Indian fig-tree with branches that root.

banish v.t. condemn to exile; dismiss from one's presence or thoughts. **banishment** n.

banisters n.pl. uprights and handrail of a staircase.

banjo n. (pl. -os) guitar-like musical instrument with a circular body. **banjoist** n.

bank[1] n. slope, esp. at the side of a river; raised mass of earth etc.; row of lights, switches, etc. —v.t./i. form or build up into a bank; tilt sideways in rounding a curve.

bank[2] n. establishment for safe keeping of money which it pays out on a customer's order; money held by the keeper of a gaming-table; place storing a reserve supply. —v.t./i. place money in a bank; base one's hopes. **bank holiday** public holiday when banks are officially closed.

banking n. business of running a financial bank. **banker** n.

banknote n. printed strip of paper issued by a bank as currency.

bankrupt a. unable to pay one's debts. —n. bankrupt person. —v.t. make bankrupt. **bankruptcy** n.

banner n. a kind of flag carried in processions; any flag.

banns n.pl. announcement in church about a forthcoming marriage.

banquet n. elaborate ceremonial public meal. **banqueting** n. taking part in a banquet.

banquette /-'ket/ n. long upholstered seat attached to a wall.

banshee n. (Ir. & Sc.) spirit whose wail is said to foretell a death.

bantam n. small kind of fowl.

bantamweight n. boxing weight (54 kg).

banter n. good-humoured joking. —v.i. joke thus.

Bantu /-'tu:/ a. & n. (pl. -u or -us) (member) of a group of African Negroid peoples or their languages.

baobab /'beɪə-/ n. African tree with a very thick trunk and edible fruit.

bap n. large soft bread roll.

baptism n. religious rite of sprinkling with water as a sign of purification and admission to a

Christian Church, usu. with name-giving. **baptismal** a.

Baptist n. member of a Protestant sect believing that baptism should be by immersion.

baptistery n. place where baptism is performed.

baptize v.t. perform baptism on; name, nickname.

bar[1] n. long piece of solid material; strip; barrier; sandbank; counter where alcohol or refreshments are served, room containing this; vertical line dividing music into units; this unit; barristers, their profession. —v.t. (p.t. **barred**) fasten or keep in or out with bar(s); obstruct; prohibit. —prep. except.

bar[2] n. unit of atmospheric pressure.

barathea /-'θiːə/ n. fine wool cloth.

barb n. backward-pointing part of an arrow etc.; wounding remark.

barbarian n. uncivilized person.

barbaric a. of or like barbarians, rough and wild. **barbarically** adv.

barbarity n. savage cruelty.

barbarous a. uncivilized, cruel. **barbarously** adv., **barbarism** n.

barbecue n. frame for grilling food above an open fire; this food; open-air party where such food is served. —v.t. cook on a barbecue.

barbed a. having barbs. **barbed wire** wire with many short sharp points.

barber n. men's hairdresser.

barbican n. outer defence to a city or castle; double tower over a gate or bridge.

barbiturate n. sedative drug.

bar-code n. pattern of printed stripes as a machine-readable code identifying a commodity etc.

bard n. Celtic minstrel; poet. **bardic** a.

bare a. (-er, -est) not clothed or covered; not adorned; scanty. —v.t. uncover, reveal. **barely** adv., **bareness** n.

bareback adv. on horseback without a saddle.

barefaced a. shameless, undisguised.

bareheaded a. not wearing a hat.

bargain n. agreement with obligations on both or all sides; thing obtained cheaply. —v.i. discuss the terms of an agreement; expect. **bargainer** n.

barge n. large flat-bottomed boat used on rivers and canals. —v.i. move clumsily. **barge in** intrude.

bargee n. person in charge of a barge.

baritone n. male voice between tenor and bass.

barium n. white metallic element.

bark[1] n. outer layer of a tree. —v.t. scrape skin off accidentally.

bark[2] n. sharp harsh sound made by a dog. —v.t./i. make this sound; utter in a sharp commanding voice.

barker n. tout at an auction or side-show etc.

barley n. a kind of cereal plant; its grain. **barley sugar** sweet made of boiled sugar. **barley water** drink made from pearl barley.

barm n. froth on fermenting malt liquor.

barmaid n. female attendant at a bar serving alcohol.

barman n. (pl. **-men**) male attendant at a bar serving alcohol.

barmy a. (-ier, -iest) (sl.) crazy.

barn n. simple roofed farm building for storing grain or hay etc.

barnacle n. shellfish that attaches itself to objects under water.

barney n. (colloq.) noisy quarrel.

barograph n. barometer that records its measurings.

barometer n. instrument measuring atmospheric pressure, used in forecasting weather. **barometric** a.

baron n. member of the lowest rank of nobility; magnate. **baroness** n.fem., **baronial** /-'rəʊ-/ a.

baronet n. the lowest hereditary title; man holding this. **baronetage** n., **baronetcy** n.

baroque /bəˈrɒk/ a. of the ornate architectural style of the 17th-18th centuries. —n. this style.

barque n., **barquentine** n. kinds of old sailing-ship.

barrack v.t./i. shout protests; jeer at.

barracks n.pl. building(s) for soldiers to live in.

barracuda n. large voracious West Indian fish.

barrage n. heavy bombardment; artificial barrier.

barrel n. large round container with flat ends; tube-like part esp. of a gun. **barrel-organ** n. mechanical instrument producing music by a pin-studded cylinder acting on pipes or keys.

barren a. not fertile, unable to bear fruit or young. **barrenness** n.

barricade n. barrier. —v.t. block or defend with a barricade.

barrier n. thing that prevents or controls advance or access.

barrister n. lawyer entitled to represent clients in the higher courts.

barrow[1] n. wheelbarrow; cart pushed or pulled by hand.

barrow[2] n. prehistoric burial mound.

barter n. & v.t./i. trade by exchange of goods for other goods.

basal a. of a base; fundamental.

basalt /ˈbæsɔːlt/ n. dark rock of volcanic origin. **basaltic** a.

bascule bridge type of bridge raised and lowered by counter-weights.

base n. lowest part; part on which a thing rests or is supported; starting-point; basis; headquarters; main ingredients of a mixture; substance capable of combining with an acid to form a salt; each of four stations to be reached by a batter in baseball. —v.t. use as a base or foundation

or evidence for a forecast etc. —a. dishonourable; of inferior value. **basely** adv., **baseness** n.

baseball n. American team game in which the batter hits the ball and runs round a circuit.

baseless a. without foundation. **baselessly** adv.

basement n. storey below ground level.

bash v.t. strike violently; attack. —n. violent blow or knock; (sl.) attempt.

bashful a. shy and self-conscious. **bashfully** adv., **bashfulness** n.

BASIC n. computer language using familiar English words.

basic a. forming a basis; fundamental. **basically** adv.

basil n. sweet-smelling herb.

basilica n. oblong hall or church with an apse at one end.

basilisk n. small American lizard; mythical reptile with lethal breath and look.

basin n. deep round open container; wash-basin; sunken place, area drained by a river; almost land-locked harbour. **basinful** n. (pl. **-fuls**)

basis n. (pl. **bases**) foundation or support; main principle.

bask v.i. sit or lie comfortably exposed to pleasant warmth.

basket n. container made of interwoven cane or wire etc.

basketball n. team game in which the aim is to throw the ball through a high hoop.

basketwork n. structure of baskets; art of making this.

Basque n. & a. (member) of a people living in the western Pyrenees; (of) their language.

bas-relief /ˈbæs-/ n. sculpture or carving in low relief.

bass[1] /bæs/ n. (pl. **bass**) fish of the perch family.

bass[2] /beɪs/ a. deep-sounding, of the lowest pitch in music. —n. (pl. **basses**) lowest male voice; bass pitch; double-bass.

bass³ /bæs/ n. inner bark of the lime tree; similar fibre.

basset n. short-legged hound used for hunting hares etc.

bassinet n. baby's hooded wicker cradle or pram.

bassoon /-'su:n/ n. woodwind instrument with a deep tone.

bastard n. illegitimate child; (sl.) unpleasant or difficult person or thing. **bastardy** n.

baste¹ v.t. stitch with tacks.

baste² v.t. moisten with fat during cooking; thrash.

bastinado /-'net-/ n. caning on the soles of the feet.

bastion n. projecting part of a fortified place; stronghold.

bat¹ n. wooden implement for striking a ball in games; batsman. —v.t./i. (p.t. **batted**) perform or strike with the bat in cricket etc.

bat² n. flying animal with a mouse-like body.

bat³ v.t. (p.t. **batted**) flutter.

batch n. set of people or things dealt with as a group.

bated a. **with bated breath** with breath held anxiously.

bath n. washing (esp. of the whole body) by immersion; container used for this; (pl.) public swimming-pool. —v.t./i. wash in a bath.

Bath bun sugared currant bun.

Bath chair a kind of wheelchair.

bathe v.t./i. apply liquid to, immerse in liquid; make wet or bright all over; swim for pleasure. —n. swim. **bather** n.

bathos /'beɪθɒs/ n. anticlimax, descent from an important thing to a trivial one.

bathroom n. room with a bath.

bathyscaphe, bathysphere ns. vessel for deep-sea diving and observation.

batik n. method of printing designs on textiles by waxing parts not to be dyed; fabric printed thus.

batman n. (pl. **-men**) soldier acting as an officer's personal servant.

baton n. short stick, esp. used by a conductor; truncheon.

batrachian /-'treɪk-/ a. & n. (amphibian) that discards gills and tail when fully developed.

batsman n. (pl. **-men**) player batting in cricket.

battalion n. army unit of several companies.

batten¹ n. bar of wood or metal, esp. holding something in place. —v.t. fasten with batten(s).

batten² v.i. feed greedily, thrive at the expense of others.

batter¹ v.t. hit hard and often. —n. beaten mixture of flour, eggs, and milk, used in cooking.

batter² n. player batting in baseball.

battering-ram n. iron-headed beam formerly used in war for breaking through walls or gates; device used similarly.

battery n. group of big guns; artillery unit; set of similar or connected units of equipment, poultry cages, etc.; electric cell(s) supplying current; unlawful blow or touch.

battle n. fight between large organized forces; contest. —v.i. engage in battle, struggle.

battleaxe n. heavy axe used as a weapon in ancient times; (colloq.) formidable woman.

battlefield n. scene of battle.

battlements n.pl. parapet with gaps at intervals, orig. for firing from.

battleship n. warship of the most heavily armed kind.

batty a. (**-ier, -iest**) (sl.) crazy.

bauble n. showy valueless ornament.

baulk n. ridge between furrows; timber beam; starting-area on a billiard table.

bauxite n. mineral from which aluminium is obtained.

bawdy a. (-ier, -iest) humorously indecent. **bawdiness** n.

bawl v.t./i. shout; weep noisily. **bawl out** (colloq.) reprimand.

bay¹ n. a kind of laurel. **bay-leaf** n.

bay² n. part of a sea or lake within a wide curve of the shore.

bay³ n. recess, compartment. **bay window** one projecting from an outside wall.

bay⁴ n. deep cry of a large dog or of hounds. —v.i. make this sound. **at bay** forced to face attackers. **keep at bay** ward off.

bay⁵ a. & n. reddish-brown (horse).

bayonet n. stabbing-blade that can be fixed to the muzzle of a rifle. —v.t. stab with this.

bazaar n. series of shops or stalls in an Oriental country; large shop selling a variety of cheap goods; sale of goods to raise funds.

bazooka n. portable weapon for firing anti-tank rockets.

BBC abbr. British Broadcasting Corporation.

BC abbr. British Columbia.

BC abbr. Before Christ.

be v.i. (pres. tense **am, are, is**; p.t. **was, were**; p.p. **been**) exist, occur; have a certain position or quality or condition; become. —v.aux. (used to form tenses of other verbs). **have been to** have visited.

beach n. shore between high and low water marks. —v.t. bring on shore from water.

beachcomber n. person who salvages stray articles along a beach.

beachhead n. fortified position set up on a beach by an invading army.

beacon n. signal-fire on a hill; large light used as a signal or warning.

bead n. small shaped piece of hard material pierced for threading with others on a string; drop or bubble of liquid; small knob in the front sight of a gun; (pl.) necklace, rosary.

beading n. moulding or carving like beads; strip of trimming for wood.

beadle n. ceremonial officer of a church or college etc.

beady a. (-ier, -iest) (of eyes) small and bright.

beagle n. small hound used for hunting hares.

beak n. bird's horny projecting jaws; any similar projection; (sl.) magistrate. **beaked** a.

beaker n. tall drinking-cup; glass vessel with a lip, used in laboratories.

beam n. long piece of timber or metal carrying the weight of part of a house etc.; ship's breadth; ray of light or other radiation; radio signal; bright look, smile. —v.i. send out light etc.; look or smile radiantly. **on one's beam-ends** near the end of one's resources.

bean n. plant with kidney-shaped seeds in long pods; seed of this or of coffee etc. **full of beans** (colloq.) lively, in high spirits.

beano n. (pl. **-os**) jolly party.

bear¹ n. large heavy animal with thick fur; child's toy like this; person who sells stocks and shares for future delivery hoping to buy them cheaper before then.

bear² v.t./i. (p.t. **bore**, p.p. **borne**) carry, support; have in one's heart or mind; endure; be fit for; produce, give birth to; take (a specified direction); exert pressure. **bear on** be relevant to. **bear out** confirm. **bearer** n.

bearable a. endurable.

beard n. hair on and round a man's chin; similar growth on an animal or plant. —v.t. confront boldly.

beargarden n. scene of uproar.

bearing n. deportment, behaviour; relevance; compass

direction; device reducing friction where a part turns; heraldic emblem.

bearskin n. guardsman's tall furry cap.

beast n. large four-footed animal; unpleasant person or thing. **beast of burden** animal that carries packs on its back.

beastly a. (-ier, -iest) (colloq.) very unpleasant. **beastliness** n.

beat v.t./i. (p.t. beat, p.p. beaten) hit repeatedly, strike strongly; mix vigorously; (of the heart) pump rhythmically; (do) better than, defeat. —n. regular repeated stroke; its sound; recurring emphasis marking rhythm; appointed course of a policeman or sentinel. **beat a retreat** go away defeated. **beat time** mark the rhythm of music with a baton or by tapping. **beat up** assault violently. **beater** n.

beatific a. showing great happiness. **beatifically** adv.

beatify v.t. (RC Church) declare blessed, as first step in canonization. **beatification** n.

beatitude n. blessedness.

Beaufort scale /'bəʊ-/ scale of wind speeds.

beauteous a. (poetic) beautiful.

beautician n. person whose job is to give beautifying treatment.

beautiful a. having beauty; very satisfactory. **beautifully** adv.

beautify v.t. make beautiful. **beautification** n.

beauty n. combination of qualities giving pleasure to the sight or other senses or to the mind; beautiful person or thing.

beaver n. small amphibious rodent; its brown fur; **Beaver** member of the junior branch of the Scout Association. —v.i. work hard.

becalmed a. unable to move because there is no wind.

became see become.

because conj. for the reason that. —adv. **because of** by reason of.

beck[1] n. **at the beck and call of** always ready and waiting to obey.

beck[2] n. brook, mountain stream.

beckon v.t. summon by a gesture.

become v.t./i. (p.t. became, p.p. become) come or grow to be, begin to be; give a pleasing appearance or effect upon; befit.

bed n. thing to sleep or rest on; framework with a mattress and coverings; flat base, foundation; bottom of a sea or river etc.; layer; garden plot. —v.t./i. (p.t. bedded) provide with a bed; put or go into a bed.

bedbug n. bug infesting beds.

bedclothes n.pl. sheets, blankets, etc.

bedding n. beds and bedclothes.

bedevil v.t. (p.t. bedevilled) afflict with difficulties. **bedevilment** n.

bedfellow n. person sharing one's bed; associate.

bedlam n. scene of uproar.

Bedouin /'beduɪn/ n. (pl. **Bedouin**) member of an Arab people living in tents in the desert.

bedpan n. pan for use as a lavatory by a person confined to bed.

bedpost n. upright support of a bed.

bedraggled a. limp and untidy.

bedridden a. permanently confined to bed through illness or weakness.

bedrock n. solid rock beneath loose soil; basic facts.

bedroom n. room for sleeping in.

bedside n. position by a bed.

bedsitting room room used for both living and sleeping in. **bedsit**, **bedsitter** n. (colloq.)

bedsore n. sore developed by lying in bed for a long time.

bedspread n. covering spread over a bed during the day.

bedstead n. framework of a bed.

bedtime n. hour for going to bed.

bee n. insect that produces wax and honey.

beech n. tree with smooth bark and glossy leaves. **beechmast** n. its fruit.

beef n. meat from ox, bull, or cow; muscular strength; (sl.) grumble. —v.i. (sl.) grumble.

beefburger n. hamburger.

beefeater n. warder in the Tower of London, wearing Tudor dress.

beefsteak n. slice of beef.

beefy a. (-ier, -iest) having a solid muscular body. **beefiness** n.

beehive n. hive.

beeline n. **make a beeline for** go straight or rapidly towards.

been see **be**.

beep n. & v.i. bleep. **beeper** n.

beer n. alcoholic drink made from malt and hops. **beery** a.

beeswax n. yellow substance secreted by bees, used as polish.

beet n. plant with a fleshy root used as a vegetable or for making sugar; (US) beetroot.

beetle[1] n. insect with hard wing-covers.

beetle[2] n. tool for ramming or crushing things.

beetle[3] v.i. overhang, project.

beetroot n. (pl. beetroot) root of beet as a vegetable.

befall v.t./i. (p.t. befell, p.p. befallen) happen; happen to.

befit v.t. (p.t. befitted) be suitable for.

before adv., prep., & conj. at an earlier time (than); ahead, in front of; in preference to.

beforehand adv. in advance.

befriend v.t. show kindness towards.

beg v.t./i. (p.t. begged) ask for as a gift or charity; obtain a living thus; request earnestly or humbly; ask for formally; (of a dog) sit up expectantly with forepaws off the ground. **beg the question** use circular reasoning. **go begging** be available but unwanted.

began see **begin**.

beget v.t. (p.t. begot, p.p. begotten, pres.p. begetting) be the father of; give rise to.

beggar n. person who lives by begging; very poor person; (sl.) person. —v.t. reduce to poverty. **beggary** n.

beggarly a. mean and insufficient. **beggarliness** n.

begin v.t./i. (p.t. began, p.p. begun, pres.p. beginning) perform the first or earliest part of (an activity etc.); be the first to do a thing; come into existence; have its first element or starting-point.

beginner n. person just beginning to learn a skill.

beginning n. first part; starting-point, source or origin.

begone int. go away.

begonia n. garden plant with bright leaves and flowers.

begot, begotten see **beget**.

begrudge v.t. grudge.

beguile v.t. deceive; entertain pleasantly. **beguilement** n.

begum /'bei-/ n. title of a Muslim married woman in India and Pakistan.

begun see **begin**.

behalf n. **on behalf of** in aid of; as the representative of.

behave v.i. act or react in a specified way; (also **behave oneself**) show good manners.

behaviour n. way of behaving.

behead v.t. cut the head from; execute (a person) thus.

beheld see **behold**.

behind adv. & prep. in or to the rear (of); behindhand; remaining after others' departure. —n. buttocks.

behindhand adv. & a. in arrears; late; out of date.

behold v.t. (p.t. beheld) (old use) see, observe. **beholder** n.

beholden a. owing thanks.

behove v.t. be incumbent on, befit.

beige a. & n. light fawn (colour).

being n. existence; thing that exists and has life, person.

belabour v.t. beat; attack verbally.

belated a. coming very late or too late. **belatedly** adv.

belch v.t./i. send out wind noisily from the stomach through the mouth; send out from an opening or funnel, gush. —n. act or sound of belching.

beleaguer v.t. besiege.

belfry n. bell tower; space for bells in a tower.

belie v.t. contradict, fail to confirm.

belief n. believing; thing believed.

believe v.t./i. accept as true or as speaking or conveying truth; think, suppose. **believe in** have faith in the existence of; feel sure of the worth of. **believer** n.

Belisha beacon /-'li:-/ flashing orange ball on a striped post marking a pedestrian crossing.

belittle v.t. disparage. **belittlement** n.

bell n. cup-shaped metal instrument that makes a ringing sound when struck; its sound, esp. as a signal; bell-shaped thing; (*informal*) telephone call.

belladonna n. deadly nightshade; drug obtained from this.

belle n. beautiful woman.

belles-lettres /bel'letr/ n.pl. literary studies.

bellicose a. eager to fight. **bellicosity** n.

belligerent a. & n. (person or country) waging war; aggressive. **belligerently** adv., **belligerence** n., **belligerency** n.

bellow n. loud deep sound made by a bull; deep shout. —v.t./i. make this sound.

bellows n.pl. apparatus for driving air into something; part that expands or flattens in a series of folds.

belly n. abdomen; stomach; bulging or rounded part. —v.t./i. swell out.

bellyful n. (*colloq.*) as much as one wants or rather more.

belong v.i. be rightly assigned as property, part, duty, etc.; have

a rightful place; (with *to*) be a member of.

belongings n.pl. personal possessions.

beloved /-'lʌvɪd/ a. & n. dearly loved (person).

below adv. & prep. at or to a lower position or amount (than).

belt n. strip of cloth or leather etc., esp. worn round the waist; long narrow region. —v.t./i. put a belt round; (sl.) hit; (sl.) rush.

bemoan v.t. lament; complain about.

bemused a. bewildered; lost in thought. **bemusement** n.

bench n. long seat of wood or stone; long working-table; judges or magistrates hearing a case.

benchmark n. surveyor's fixed point; standard or point of reference.

bend v.t./i. (p.t. & p.p. **bent**) make or become curved or angular; turn downwards, stoop; turn in a new direction. —n. curve, turn.

bender n. (sl.) drinking-spree.

beneath adv. & prep. below, underneath; not worthy of.

Benedictine /-tɪn/ n. monk or nun following the rule of St Benedict. —/-tɪːn/ n. [P.] liqueur originally made by Benedictines.

benediction n. spoken blessing.

benefactor n. one who gives financial or other help. **benefaction** n., **benefactress** n.fem.

benefice n. position providing a clergyman with a livelihood.

beneficent /-'nef-/ a. doing good; actively kind. **beneficence** n.

beneficial a. having a helpful or useful effect. **beneficially** adv.

beneficiary n. one who receives a benefit or legacy.

benefit n. something helpful or favourable or profitable; allowance payable in accordance with an insurance plan. —v.t./i. (p.t. **benefited**, pres.p. **benefiting**) do good to; receive benefit.

benevolent a. kindly and helpful.
benevolently adv., **benevolence** n.
benighted a. in darkness; intellectually ignorant.
benign a. kindly; mild and gentle; not malignant.
benignant a. kindly, beneficial. **benignantly** adv., **benignancy** n.
bent see **bend**. —n. natural skill or liking. —a. (sl.) dishonest.
bent on seeking or determined to do.
benzene n. liquid obtained from petroleum and coal-tar, used as a solvent, fuel, etc.
benzine /-zi:n/ n. liquid mixture of hydrocarbons used in dry-cleaning.
benzol n. (unrefined) benzene.
bequeath v.t. leave as a legacy.
bequest n. legacy.
berate v.i. scold.
bereave v.t. deprive, esp. of a relative, by death. **bereavement** n.
bereft a. deprived.
beret /'berei/ n. round flat cap.
bergamot n. a citrus tree; perfume obtained from its fruit; an aromatic herb.
beriberi n. disease caused by lack of vitamin B.
berry n. small round juicy fruit with no stone. **berried** a.
berserk n. **go berserk** go into an uncontrollable destructive rage.
berth n. bunk or sleeping-place in a ship or train; place for a ship to anchor or tie up at a wharf. —v.t. moor at a berth. **give a wide berth** to keep away from.
beryl n. transparent usu. green precious stone.
beseech v.t. (p.t. **besought**) implore.
beset v.t. (p.t. **beset**, pres.p. **besetting**) hem in, surround; habitually affect or trouble.
beside prep. at the side of, close to; compared with. **be beside oneself** be at the end of one's self-control. **beside the point**

irrelevant.
besides prep. in addition to, other than. —adv. also.
besiege v.t. lay siege to; crowd round. **besieger** n.
besom n. broom made of twigs tied to a long handle.
besotted a. infatuated.
besought see **beseech**.
bespeak v.t. (p.t. **-spoke**, p.p. **-spoken**) engage beforehand; be evidence of.
bespectacled a. wearing spectacles.
bespoke a. making or (of clothes) made to a customer's order.
best a. of the most excellent kind. —adv. in the best way; most usefully. —n. best thing; victory. **best man** bridegroom's chief attendant. **best part of** most of.
bestial /'bes-/ a. of or like a beast, savage. **bestiality** n.
bestir v.refl. (p.t. **bestirred**) **bestir oneself** exert oneself.
bestow v.t. confer as a gift. **bestowal** n.
bestride v.t. (p.t. **-strode**, p.p. **-stridden**) sit or stand astride over.
bet n. agreement pledging a thing that will be forfeited if one's forecast is wrong; money etc. pledged. —v.t./i. (p.t. **bet** or **betted**) make a bet; (colloq.) predict.
beta n. second letter of the Greek alphabet, = b.
betake v.refl. (p.t. **betook**, p.p. **betaken**) **betake oneself** go.
betel /'bi:-/ n. tropical Asian plant whose leaf is chewed with the **betel nut** (areca nut).
bête noire /bet 'nwɑ:(r)/ person or thing one most dislikes.
betide v.t. happen to.
betimes adv. in good time, early.
betoken v.t. be a sign of.
betray v.t. give up or reveal disloyally to an enemy; be disloyal to; reveal unintentionally. **betrayal** n. **betrayer** n.
betroth v.t. cause to be engaged to marry. **betrothal** n.

better[1] a. of a more excellent kind; recovered from illness. —adv. in a better manner; more usefully. —n. better thing; (pl.) persons of higher status than oneself. —v.t. improve; do better than. **better half** (joc.) one's wife or husband. **better part** more than half. **get the better of** overcome; outwit. **betterment** n.

better[2] n. person who bets.

betting-shop n. bookmaker's office.

between prep. in the space or time or quality etc. bounded by (two limits); separating; to and from; connecting; shared by; taking one and rejecting the other of. —adv. between points or limits etc.

betwixt prep. & adv. between.

bevel n. sloping edge. —v.t. (p.t. **bevelled**) give a sloping edge to.

beverage n. any drink.

bevy n. company, large group.

bewail v.t. wail over.

beware v.i. be on one's guard.

bewilder v.t. puzzle, confuse. **bewilderment** n.

bewitch v.t. put under a magic spell; delight very much.

beyond adv. & prep. at or to the further side (of); outside the range of; besides. **beyond doubt** certain.

bhaji n. small cake of vegetables fried in batter.

biannual a. happening twice a year. **biannually** adv.

bias n. influence favouring one of a group; diagonal across threads of woven fabric; tendency of a bowl to swerve because of its lopsided form. —v.t. (p.t. **biased**) give a bias to, influence.

bib n. covering put under a young child's chin to protect its clothes while feeding; front part of an apron, above the waist.

Bible n. Christian or Jewish scriptures; copy of these.

biblical a. of or in the Bible.

bibliography n. list of books about a subject or by a specified author; study of the history of books. **bibliographer** n., **bibliographical** a.

bibliophile n. book-lover.

bibulous a. fond of drinking.

bicarbonate n. a kind of carbonate.

bicentenary /-'ti:-/ n. 200th anniversary.

bicentennial /-'ten'-/ a. happening every 200 years. —n. bicentenary.

biceps /'baɪs-/ n. large muscle at the front of the upper arm.

bicker v.i. quarrel constantly about unimportant things.

bicuspid a. & n. (tooth) having two cusps.

bicycle n. two-wheeled vehicle driven by pedals. —v.i. ride a bicycle.

bid[1] n. offer of a price, esp. at an auction; statement of the number of tricks a player proposes to win in a card-game; attempt. —v.t./i. (p.t. **bid**, pres.p. **bidding**) make a bid (of), offer. **bidder** n.

bid[2] v.t. (p.t. **bid** (old use **bade**, pr. **bæd**), p.p. **bidden**, pres.p. **bidding**) command; say as a greeting etc.

biddable a. willing to obey.

bidding n. command.

bide v.t. await (one's time).

bidet /'bi:deɪ/ n. low washbasin that one can sit astride to wash the genital and anal regions.

biennial a. lasting for two years; happening every second year. —n. plant that flowers and dies in its second year. **biennially** adv.

bier n. movable stand for a coffin.

biff v.t. & n. (sl.) hit.

bifocals n.pl. spectacles with lenses that have two segments, assisting both distant and close focusing.

bifurcate v.i. fork. **bifurcation** n.

big a. (**bigger**, **biggest**) large in size, amount, or intensity; elder;

important; boastful; (sl.) generous. —adv. (US sl.) on a large scale.

bigamist n. person guilty of bigamy.

bigamy n. crime of going through a form of marriage while a previous marriage is still valid. **bigamous** a.

bight n. loop of rope; recess of a coast, bay.

bigot n. person who holds an opinion obstinately and is intolerant towards those who disagree. **bigoted** a., **bigotry** n.

bigwig n. (colloq.) important person.

bijou /'biːʒuː/ a. small and elegant.

bike n. (colloq.) bicycle, motor cycle. —v.i. (colloq.) ride a bicycle or motor cycle. **biker** n.

bikini n. (pl. -is) woman's scanty two-piece beach garment.

bilateral a. having two sides; existing between two groups. **bilaterally** adv.

bilberry n. small round dark blue fruit; shrub producing this.

bile n. bitter yellowish liquid produced by the liver.

bilge n. ship's bottom; water collecting there; (sl.) worthless talk.

bilharzia n. disease caused by a tropical parasitic flatworm.

bilingual a. written in or able to speak two languages.

bilious a. sick, esp. from trouble with bile or liver. **biliousness** n.

bilk v.t. defraud of payment.

bill[1] n. written statement of charges to be paid; poster; programme; certificate; draft of a proposed law; (US) banknote. —v.t. announce, advertise; send a bill to. **bill of exchange** written order to pay a sum of money on a specified date.

bill[2] n. bird's beak. —v.i. **bill and coo** exchange caresses.

billabong n. (Austr.) backwater.

billet n. lodging for troops. —v.t. (p.t. **billeted**) place in a billet.

billet-doux /biːleɪˈduː/ n. (pl. -s-doux, pr. -duːz) love-letter.

billhook n. pruning-instrument with a concave edge.

billiards n. game played with cues and three balls on a table.

billion n. one thousand million; one million million.

billow n. great wave. —v.t./i. rise or move like waves; swell out.

billy n. can used by campers etc. as a kettle or cooking-pot. **billycan** n.

billy-goat n. male goat.

bimbo n. (pl. -os) (sl.) person; (empty-headed) young woman.

bin n. large rigid container or receptacle.

binary a. dual, of two. **binary digit** either of the two digits (0 and 1) used in the **binary scale**, system of numbers using only these.

bind v.t./i. (p.t. **bound**) tie, fasten together; cover the edge of so as to strengthen or decorate; fasten into a cover; place under an obligation or legal agreement; (sl.) grumble. —n. (sl.) bore, nuisance. **binder** n.

bindery n. workshop where books are bound.

binding n. book-cover; braid etc. used to bind an edge.

bindweed n. wild convolvulus.

bine n. flexible stem of a climbing plant, esp. the hop.

binge n. (sl.) spree, eating and drinking and making merry. —v.i. (pres. p. **bingeing**) (sl.) go on a binge.

bingo n. gambling game using cards marked with numbered squares.

binocular a. using two eyes.

binoculars n.pl. instrument with lenses for both eyes, making distant objects seem larger.

binomial a. & n. (expression or name) consisting of two terms.

biochemistry n. chemistry of living organisms. **biochemical** a., **biochemist** n.

biodegradable *a.* able to be decomposed by bacteria.

biodiversity *n.* diversity of plant and animal life.

biographer *n.* writer of a biography.

biography *n.* story of a person's life. **biographical** *a.*

biology *n.* study of the life and structure of living things. **biological** *a.*, **biologically** *adv.*, **biologist** *n.*

bionic *a.* (of a person or faculties) operated electronically. **bionically** *adv.*

biopsy *n.* examination of tissue cut from a living body.

biorhythm *n.* any of the recurring cycles of activity said to occur in a person's life.

bipartite *a.* consisting of two parts; involving two groups.

biped /'barped/ *n.* two-footed animal. **bipedal** *a.*

biplane *n.* aeroplane with two pairs of wings.

birch *n.* tree with smooth bark; bundle of birch twigs for flogging delinquents. —*v.t.* flog with this.

bird *n.* feathered animal; (*colloq.*) person; (*sl.*) young woman.

birdie *n.* (*children's use*) bird; (in golf) score of one under par for a hole.

birdseed *n.* special seeds used as food for caged birds.

biretta *n.* priest's square cap.

Biro *n.* (*pl.* **-os**) [P.] ball-point pen.

birth *n.* emergence of young from the mother's body; parentage. **birth control** prevention of unwanted pregnancy. **give birth to** produce as young from the body.

birthday *n.* anniversary of the day of one's birth.

birthmark *n.* unusual coloured mark on the skin at birth.

birthright *n.* thing that is one's right through being born into a certain family or country.

biscuit *n.* small flat thin piece of pastry baked crisp.

bisect *v.t.* divide into two equal parts. **bisection** *n.*, **bisector** *n.*

bisexual *a.* sexually attracted to members of both sexes; having both sexes in one individual. **bisexuality** *n.*

bishop *n.* clergyman of high rank; mitre-shaped chess piece.

bishopric *n.* diocese of a bishop.

bismuth *n.* metallic element; compound of this used in medicines.

bison *n.* (*pl.* **bison**) wild ox.

bisque *n.* free point or stroke awarded to a player.

bistro *n.* (*pl.* **-os**) small bar or restaurant.

bit[1] *n.* small piece or quantity; short time or distance; mouthpiece of a bridle; part of a tool that cuts or bores or grips when twisted.

bit[2] *n.* (in computers) unit of information expressed as a choice between two possibilities, binary digit.

bit[3] *see* bite.

bitch *n.* female dog; (*colloq.*) spiteful woman, difficult thing. —*v.i.* (*colloq.*) speak spitefully or sourly. **bitchy** *a.*, **bitchiness** *n.*

bite *v.t./i.* (*p.t.* **bit**, *p.p.* **bitten**) cut with the teeth; penetrate; grip or act effectively. —*n.* act of biting; wound made by this; small meal.

biting *a.* causing a smarting pain; sharply critical.

bitter *a.* tasting sharp, not sweet or mild; with mental pain or resentment; piercingly cold. —*n.* bitter beer or (*pl.*) liquor. **bitterly** *adv.*, **bitterness** *n.*

bittern *n.* a kind of marsh bird.

bitty *a.* (-**ier**, -**iest**) made up of unrelated bits. **bittiness** *n.*

bitumen *n.* black substance made from petroleum. **bituminous** *a.*

bivalve *n.* shellfish with a hinged double shell.

bivouac /'brvuæk/ *n.* temporary camp without tents. —*v.i.* (*p.t.* **bivouacked**) camp thus.

bizarre *a.* strikingly odd in appearance or effect.

blab *v.i.* (*p.t.* **blabbed**) talk indiscreetly. **blabber** *n.*

black *a.* (**-er**, **-est**) of the very darkest colour, like coal or soot; having a black skin; dismal, gloomy; hostile; evil; not to be handled by trade unionists. —*n.* black colour or thing; **Black Negro.** —*v.t.* make black; declare (goods etc.) 'black'. **black coffee** coffee without milk. **black economy** unofficial economic activity. **black eye** bruised eye. **black hole** region in outer space from which matter and radiation cannot escape. **black list** list of persons who are disapproved of. **black market** illegal buying and selling. **black out** cover windows etc. so that no light can penetrate; suffer a blackout. **black pudding** sausage of blood, suet, etc. **black sheep** scoundrel. **black spot** place of danger or difficulty. **in the black** with a credit balance, not in debt.

blackball *v.t.* reject as a member.

blackberry *n.* bramble; its edible dark berry.

blackbird *n.* European songbird, male of which is black.

blackboard *n.* board for writing on with chalk in front of a class.

blackcock *n.* male black grouse.

blacken *v.t./i.* make or become black; say evil things about.

blackfly *n.* insect infesting plants.

blackguard /ˈblægɑːd/ *n.* scoundrel. **blackguardly** *adv.*

blackhead *n.* small dark lump blocking a pore in the skin.

blacking *n.* black polish.

blackleg *n.* person who works while fellow workers are on strike. —*v.i.* (*p.t.* **blacklegged**) work thus.

blacklist *v.t.* enter in a black list.

blackmail *v.t.* demand payment or action from (a person) by threats. —*n.* this demand; money demanded thus. **blackmailer** *n.*

blackout *n.* being blacked out; temporary loss of consciousness or memory; suspension of radio reception; temporary suppression of news.

blacksmith *n.* smith who works in iron.

blackthorn *n.* thorny shrub bearing white flowers and sloes.

bladder *n.* sac in which urine collects in the body; inflatable bag.

blade *n.* flattened cutting-part of a knife or sword etc.; flat part of an oar, propeller, etc.; flat narrow leaf esp. of grass; broad bone.

blame *v.t.* hold responsible and criticize for a fault. —*n.* responsibility or criticism for a fault. **blameless** *a.* not subject to blame. **blameworthy** *a.* deserving blame.

blanch *v.t./i.* make or become white or pale; immerse in boiling water.

blancmange /bləˈmɒnʒ/ *n.* flavoured jelly-like pudding made with milk.

bland *a.* (**-er**, **-est**) mild; gentle and casual, not irritating or stimulating. **blandly** *adv.*, **blandness** *n.*

blandishments *n.pl.* flattering or coaxing words.

blank *a.* not written or printed on; without interest or expression, without result. —*n.* blank space or paper; blank cartridge. **blank cartridge** one containing no bullet. **blank cheque** one with the amount left blank for the payee to fill in. **blank verse** verse without rhyme, usu. in lines of ten syllables. **blankly** *adv.*, **blankness** *n.*

blanket *n.* warm covering made of woollen or similar material; thick covering mass. —*v.t.* (*p.t.* **blanketed**) cover with a blanket.

blare *v.t./i.* sound loudly and harshly. —*n.* this sound.

blarney *n.* smooth talk that flatters and deceives. —*v.t./i.*

blasé /'blɑːzeɪ/ *a.* bored or unimpressed by things.

blaspheme *v.t./i.* utter blasphemies (about). **blasphemer** *n.*

blasphemy *n.* irreverent talk about sacred things. **blasphemous** *a.*, **blasphemously** *adv.*

blast *n.* strong gust; wave of air from an explosion; sound of a wind instrument or whistle or car horn etc.; severe reprimand. —*v.t.* blow up with explosives; cause to wither, destroy; (*colloq.*) reprimand severely. **blast-furnace** *n.* furnace for smelting ore, with compressed hot air driven in. **blast off** be launched by firing of rockets. **blast-off** *n.*

blatant /'bleɪt-/ *a.* very obvious; shameless. **blatantly** *adv.*, **blatancy** *n.*

blather *v.i.* talk foolishly. —*n.* foolish talk.

blaze¹ *n.* bright flame or fire; bright light or display; outburst; (*pl.*, *sl.*) hell. —*v.i.* burn or shine brightly; have an intense outburst of feeling.

blaze² *n.* white mark on an animal's face; mark chipped in the bark of a tree to mark a route. —*v.t.* mark (a tree or route) with blazes. **blaze a trail** make such marks; pioneer.

blaze³ *v.t.* proclaim (news).

blazer *n.* loose-fitting jacket, esp. in the colours or bearing the badge of a school, team, etc.

blazon *n.* heraldic shield, coat of arms. —*v.t.* proclaim; ornament with heraldic or other devices; describe (a coat of arms) in technical terms.

bleach *v.t./i.* whiten by sunlight or chemicals. —*n.* bleaching substance or process. **bleacher** *n.*

bleak *a.* (**-er, -est**) cold and cheerless. **bleakly** *adv.*, **bleakness** *n.*

bleary *a.* (**-ier, -iest**) (of eyes) watery and seeing indistinctly. **blearily** *adv.*, **bleariness** *n.*

bleat *n.* cry of a sheep, goat, or calf. —*v.t./i.* utter this cry; speak or say plaintively.

bleed *v.t./i.* (*p.t.* **bled**) leak blood or other fluid; draw blood or fluid from; extort money from.

bleep *n.* short high-pitched sound. —*v.i.* make this sound. **bleeper** *n.*

blemish *n.* flaw or defect that spoils the perfection of a thing. —*v.t.* spoil with a blemish.

blench *v.i.* flinch.

blend *v.t./i.* mix into a uniform or harmonious compound or combination. —*n.* mixture. **blender** *n.*

blenny *n.* sea-fish with spiny fins.

bless *v.t.* call God's favour upon; make sacred or holy; praise (God). **be blessed with** be fortunate in having.

blessed /-stɪd/ *a.* holy, sacred; in paradise; (*colloq.*) damned. **blessedly** *adv.*, **blessedness** *n.*

blessing *n.* God's favour; prayer for this; something one is glad of.

blest *a.* (*old use*) blessed.

blether *v.i.* & *n.* = blather.

blew see **blow**¹.

blight *n.* disease, fungus, or insect that withers plants; malignant influence. —*v.t.* affect with blight; spoil.

blighter *n.* (*sl.*) person or thing, esp. an annoying one.

blimey *int.* (*sl.*) exclamation of surprise.

blimp *n.* small non-rigid airship.

blind *a.* without sight; without foresight or understanding or adequate information; failing to flower; (in cookery) without filling. —*adv.* blindly. —*v.t./i.* make blind; take away power of judgement from; (*sl.*) go along recklessly. —*n.* screen, esp. on a roller, for a window; pretext. **blind alley** alley closed at one end; job with no prospects of advancement. **blindly** *adv.*, **blindness** *n.*

blindfold *a.* & *adv.* with eyes covered with a cloth to block one's sight. —*n.* cloth used for this. —*v.t.* cover the eyes of (a person) thus.

blindworm *n.* slow-worm.

blink *v.t./i.* open and shut one's eyes rapidly; shine unsteadily; shirk facing (facts). —*n.* act of blinking; quick gleam.

blinker *n.* leather piece fixed to a bridle to prevent a horse from seeing sideways. —*v.t.* obstruct the sight or understanding of.

blinking *a.* & *adv.* (*sl.*) annoying(ly).

blip *n.* quick sound or movement; temporary rise; small image on a radar screen. —*v.t./i.* make a blip; strike briskly.

bliss *n.* perfect happiness. **blissful** *a.*, **blissfully** *adv.*

blister *n.* bubble-like swelling on skin; raised swelling on a surface. —*v.t./i.* cause blister(s) on; be affected with blister(s).

blithe *a.* casual and carefree. **blithely** *adv.*

blithering *a.* (*colloq.*) contemptible.

blitz *n.* violent attack, esp. from aircraft. —*v.t.* attack in a blitz.

blizzard *n.* severe snowstorm.

bloat *v.t./i.* swell with fat, gas, or liquid.

bloater *n.* salted smoked herring.

blob *n.* drop of liquid; round mass.

bloc *n.* group of parties or countries who combine for a purpose.

block *n.* solid piece of hard substance; log of wood; (*sl.*) head; pulley(s) mounted in a case; compact mass of buildings; large building divided into flats or offices; large quantity treated as a unit; pad of paper for drawing or writing on; obstruction. —*v.t.* obstruct, prevent the movement or use of. **block in** sketch in roughly. **block letters** plain capital letters. **block vote** vote proportional to the number of persons represented. **blocker** *n.*

blockade *n.* blocking of access to a place, to prevent entry of goods etc. —*v.t.* set up a blockade of.

blockage *n.* blocking; thing that blocks.

blockhead *n.* stupid person.

bloke *n.* (*sl.*) man.

blond *a.* & *n.* fair-haired (man).

blonde *a.* & *n.* fair-haired (woman).

blood *n.* red liquid circulating in the bodies of animals; bloodshed; temper, courage; race, descent, parentage; kindred. —*v.t.* give a first taste of blood to (a hound); initiate (a person). **blood bath** massacre. **blood-curdling** *a.* horrifying. **blood sports** *n.* involving killing. **blood-vessel** *n.* tubular structure conveying blood within the body.

bloodhound *n.* large keen-scented dog, formerly used in tracking.

bloodless *a.* without blood; drained of blood; without bloodshed. **bloodlessly** *adv.*

bloodshed *n.* killing or wounding.

bloodshot *a.* (of eyes) red from dilated veins.

bloodstock *n.* thoroughbred horses.

bloodstream *n.* blood circulating in the body.

bloodsucker *n.* creature that sucks blood; person who extorts money.

bloodthirsty *a.* eager for bloodshed.

bloody *a.* (-ier, -iest) bloodstained; with much bloodshed; cursed. —*adv.* (*sl.*) extremely. —*v.t.* stain with blood. **bloody-minded** *a.* (*colloq.*) deliberately uncooperative. **bloodily** *adv.*, **bloodiness** *n.*

bloom *n.* flower; beauty, perfection; fine powder on grapes etc. —*v.i.* bear flowers; be in full beauty.

bloomer *n.* (*sl.*) blunder.

bloomers *n.pl.* (*colloq.*) knickers.

blossom n. flower(s), esp. of a fruit-tree. —v.i. open into flowers; develop and flourish.

blot n. spot of ink etc.; something ugly or disgraceful. —v.t. (p.t. **blotted**) make blot(s) on; dry with blotting-paper, soak up; obscure.

blotch n. large irregular mark. **blotched** a., **blotchy** a.

blotter n. pad of blotting-paper; device holding this.

blotting-paper n. absorbent paper for drying ink writing.

blotto a. (sl.) very drunk.

blouse n. shirt-like garment worn by women and children; waistlength coat forming part of military uniform. —v.t./i. hang loosely like a blouse.

blow[1] v.t./i. (p.t. **blew**, p.p. **blown**) send out a current of air or breath; move or flow as a current of air does; propel, shape, or sound by this; be moved or carried by air; puff and pant; (of a fuse) melt; cause (a fuse) to melt; break with explosives; (sl.) reveal; (sl.) spend recklessly. —n. blowing. **blow-dry** v.t dry and style (hair) with a hand-held drier. **blow in** (colloq.) arrive casually or unexpectedly. **blow-out** n. burst tyre; melted fuse; (sl.) large meal. **blow over** die down. **blow up** explode, shatter by an explosion; inflate; exaggerate; enlarge (a photograph); lose one's temper; reprimand severely; become a crisis.

blow[2] n. hard stroke with a hand, tool, or weapon; shock, disaster.

blower n. (colloq.) telephone.

blowfly n. fly that lays its eggs on meat.

blowlamp n. portable burner for directing a very hot flame.

blown see **blow**[1]. —a. breathless.

blowpipe n. tube through which air etc. is blown, e.g. to heat a flame or send out a missile.

blowy a. (-ier, -iest) windy.

blowzy /-ou-/ a. (-ier, -iest) red-faced and coarse-looking.

blub v.i. (p.t. **blubbed**) (sl.) weep.

blubber[1] n. whale fat.

blubber[2] v.i. weep noisily.

bludgeon n. heavy stick used as a weapon. —v.t. strike with a bludgeon; compel forcefully.

blue a. (-er, -est) of a colour like the cloudless sky; unhappy; indecent. —n. blue colour or thing; (pl.) melancholy jazz melodies, state of depression. (sl. pres.p.) **blueing**) make blue; (sl.) spend recklessly. **blue-blooded** a. of aristocratic descent. **blue cheese** cheese with veins of blue mould. **blue-pencil** v.t. censor. **out of the blue** unexpectedly.

bluebell n. plant with blue bell-shaped flowers.

blueberry n. edible blue berry; shrub bearing this.

bluebottle n. large bluish fly.

blueprint n. blue photographic print of building plans; detailed scheme.

bluff[1] a. with a broad steep front; abrupt, frank, and hearty. —n. bluff cliff etc. **bluffly** adv., **bluffness** n.

bluff[2] v.t./i. deceive by a pretence esp. of strength. —n. bluffing.

bluish a. rather blue.

blunder v.i. move clumsily and uncertainly; make a blunder. —n. mistake. **blunderer** n.

blunderbuss n. old type of gun firing many balls at one shot.

blunt a. without a sharp edge or point; speaking or expressed plainly. —v.t./i. make or become blunt. **bluntly** adv., **bluntness** n.

blur n. smear; indistinct appearance. —v.t./i. (p.t. **blurred**) smear; make or become indistinct.

blurb n. written description praising something.

blurt v.t. utter abruptly or tactlessly.

blush v.i. become red-faced from shame or embarrassment. —n. blushing; pink tinge.

blusher n. rouge.

bluster v.i. blow in gusts; talk aggressively, with empty threats. —n. blustering talk. **blustery** a.

BMX n. bicycle-racing on a dirt track; bicycle for this.

boa /'bəʊə/ n. large South American snake that crushes its prey.

boar n. male pig.

board n. long piece of sawn wood; flat piece of wood or stiff material; notice-board; thick stiff card used for book covers; daily meals supplied in return for payment or services; committee. —v.t./i. cover or block with boards; enter (a ship, aircraft, or vehicle); provide with or receive meals and accommodation for payment. **go by the board** be ignored or rejected. **on board** on or in a ship, aircraft, or vehicle.

boarder n. person who boards with someone; resident pupil.

boarding-house n., **boarding-school** n. one taking boarders.

boardroom n. room where a board of directors meets.

boast v.t./i. speak with great pride, trying to impress people; be the proud possessor of. —n. boastful statement; thing one is proud of. **boaster** n.

boastful a. boasting frequently. **boastfully** adv., **boastfulness** n.

boat n. vessel for travelling on water; boat-shaped serving-dish for sauce etc. **in the same boat** suffering the same troubles.

boater n. flat-topped straw hat.

boathouse n. shed at the water's edge for boats.

boating n. going out in a rowing-boat for pleasure.

boatman n. (pl. -men) man who rows or sails or rents out boats.

boatswain /'bəʊs(ə)n/ n. ship's officer in charge of rigging etc.

bob[1] v.t./i. (p.t. **bobbed**) move quickly up and down; cut (hair) short to hang loosely. —n. bobbing movement; bobbed hair.

bob[2] n. (pl. bob) (sl.) shilling, 5p.

bobbin n. small spool holding thread or wire in a machine.

bobble n. small woolly ball as an ornament.

bobby n. (colloq.) policeman.

bob-sled, bob-sleigh ns. sledge with two sets of runners in tandem. —v.i. race in this.

bobtail n. docked tail.

bode v.t./i. be a sign of, promise.

bodice n. part of a dress from shoulder to waist; undergarment for this part of the body.

bodily a. of the human body or physical nature. —adv. in person, physically; as a whole.

bodkin n. thick blunt needle with a large eye for threading tape etc.

body n. structure of bones and flesh etc. of man or an animal; corpse; main part; group regarded as a unit; separate piece of matter; strong texture or quality. **body-blow** n. severe blow. **body-piercing** the piercing of holes in parts of the body other than the ear lobes.

bodyguard n. escort or personal guard of an important person.

bodysuit n. close-fitting garment for the whole body, worn by women esp. for sports.

Boer /'bəʊə(r)/ n. Afrikaner; (old use) early Dutch inhabitant of South Africa.

boffin n. (colloq.) person engaged in technical research.

bog n. permanently wet spongy ground. —v.t. (p.t. **bogged**) make or become stuck and unable to progress. **bogginess** n.

bogey[1] n. (pl. -eys) (in golf) one stroke above par at a hole.

bogey[2] n. (pl. -eys or -ies) evil spirit; thing causing fear.

boggle v.i. be startled or bewildered, hesitate; raise objections.

bogie *n.* undercarriage on wheels, pivoted at each end.

bogus *a.* false.

bogy *n.* = bogey².

bohemian *a.* socially unconventional.

boil¹ *n.* inflamed swelling producing pus.

boil² *v.t./i.* bubble up with heat; heat so that liquid does this.

boiler *n.* container in which water is heated. **boiler suit** one-piece suit for rough work.

boisterous *a.* windy; noisy and cheerful. **boisterously** *adv.*

bold *a.* (-er, -est) confident and courageous; (of colours) strong and vivid. **boldly** *adv.*, **boldness** *n.*

bole *n.* trunk of a tree.

bolero /-'lear-/ *n.* (*pl.* -os) Spanish dance; /'bɔlə-/ woman's short jacket with no fastening.

boll *n.* round seed-vessel of cotton, flax, etc.

bollard *n.* short thick post.

boloney *n.* (*sl.*) nonsense.

Bolshie *a.* & *n.* (*sl.*) Communist; rebellious (person).

bolster *n.* long pad placed under a pillow. —*v.t.* support, prop.

bolt *n.* sliding bar for fastening a door; strong metal pin; sliding part of a rifle-breech; shaft of lightning; roll of cloth; arrow from a crossbow; act of bolting. —*v.t./i.* fasten with bolts; run away; gulp (food) hastily. **bolt-hole** *n.* place into which one can escape. **bolt upright** quite upright. **bolter** *n.*

bomb *n.* case of explosive or incendiary material to be set off by impact or a timing device; (*sl.*) large sum of money; the **bomb** atomic or hydrogen bomb. —*v.t./i.* attack with bombs.

bombard *v.t.* attack with artillery; send a stream of particles against; attack with questions etc. **bombardment** *n.*

bombardier *n.* artillery NCO.

bombastic *a.* using pompous words.

Bombay duck dried fish served as a relish, esp. with curry.

bombazine /-zi:n/ *n.* twilled worsted dress material.

bomber *n.* aircraft that carries and drops bombs; person who throws or places bombs.

bombshell *n.* great shock.

bona fide /bəʊnə 'faɪdɪ/ genuine.

bona fides /bəʊnə 'faɪdi:z/ honest intention, sincerity.

bonanza *n.* sudden great wealth or luck.

bond *n.* thing that unites or restrains; binding agreement; document issued by a government or public company acknowledging that money has been lent to it and will be repaid; emotional link; high-quality writing-paper. —*v.t./i.* unite with a bond. **in bond** stored in a Customs warehouse until duties are paid.

bondage *n.* slavery, captivity.

bonded *a.* stored or (of a warehouse) storing goods in bond.

bone *n.* each of the hard parts making up the vertebrate skeleton; substance of this. —*v.t.* remove bones from. **bone china** made of clay and bone ash. **bone-dry** *a.* quite dry. **bone idle** very lazy. **bone-meal** *n.* powdered bones used as a fertilizer.

bonehead *n.* (*sl.*) stupid person.

bonfire *n.* fire built in the open air to destroy rubbish or in celebration.

bongo *n.* (*pl.* -os) each of a pair of small drums played with the fingers.

bonhomie /'bɒnəmɪ/ *n.* geniality.

bonk *v.t./i.* make an abrupt thudding sound; bump; (*sl.*) have sexual intercourse (with). —*n.* thudding sound.

bonnet *n.* hat with strings that tie under the chin; Scotch cap; hinged cover over the engine etc. of a motor vehicle.

bonny *a.* (-ier, -iest) healthy-looking; (Sc.) good-looking.

bonsai *n.* miniature tree or shrub; art of growing these.

bonus *n.* extra payment or benefit.

bony *a.* (-ier, -iest) like bones; having bones with little flesh; full of bones. **boniness** *n.*

boo *int.* exclamation of disapproval. —*v.t./i.* shout 'boo' (at).

boob *n. & v.i.* (sl.) blunder.

booby *n.* foolish person. **booby prize** one given as a joke to the competitor with the lowest score. **booby trap** hidden trap rigged up as a practical joke; hidden bomb. **booby-trap** *v.t.* place a booby trap in or on.

boogie *n.* (in full **boogie-woogie**) jazz piano music with a persistent bass rhythm. —*v.i.* dance to this.

book *n.* set of sheets of paper bound in a cover; literary work filling this; main division of a literary work or of the Bible; record of bets made. —*v.t./i.* enter in a book or list; reserve; buy a ticket in advance.

bookable *a.* able to be booked.

bookcase *n.* piece of furniture with shelves for books.

bookie *n.* (colloq.) bookmaker.

bookkeeping *n.* systematic recording of business transactions.

booklet *n.* small thin book.

bookmaker *n.* person whose business is the taking of bets.

bookmark *n.* strip of paper etc. to mark a place in a book.

book-plate *n.* label for pasting in a book, bearing the owner's name.

bookworm *n.* grub that eats holes in books; person fond of reading.

boom[1] *v.i.* make a deep resonant sound; have a period of prosperity. —*n.* booming sound; prosperity. **boomer** *n.*, **boomlet** *n.*

boom[2] *n.* long pole; floating barrier.

boomerang *n.* Australian missile of curved wood that can be thrown so as to return to the thrower. —*v.i.* (of a scheme etc.) cause harm to the originator.

boon[1] *n.* benefit.

boon[2] *a.* **boon companion** pleasant companion.

boor *n.* ill-mannered person. **boorish** *a.*, **boorishness** *n.*

boost *v.t.* push upwards; increase the strength or reputation of. —*n.* upward thrust; increase. **booster** *n.*

boot *n.* covering of leather etc. for the foot and ankle or leg; covered luggage-compartment in a car; (sl.) dismissal. —*v.t.* kick.

bootee *n.* baby's woollen boot.

booth *n.* small shelter.

bootleg *a.* smuggled, illicit. **bootlegger** *n.*, **bootlegging** *n.*

booty *n.* loot.

booze *v.i.* (colloq.) drink alcohol. —*n.* (colloq.) alcoholic drink; drinking spree. **boozer** *n.*, **boozy** *a.*, **boozily** *adv.*, **booziness** *n.*

boracic /-'ræs-/ *a.* boric.

borage *n.* blue-flowered plant.

borax *n.* compound of boron used in detergents etc.

border *n.* edge, boundary; part near this; edging; flower-bed round part of a garden. —*v.t./i.* put or be a border to. **border on** be next to; come close to being.

borderline *n.* line of demarcation.

bore[1] *see* **bear**[2].

bore[2] *v.t./i.* make (a hole) with a revolving tool or by digging; pierce thus; thrust one's way. —*n.* hole bored; hollow inside of a cylinder; its diameter. **borer** *n.*

bore[3] *v.t.* weary by dullness. —*n.* boring person or thing. **boredom** *n.*

bore[4] *n.* tidal wave in an estuary.

boric *a.* **boric acid** substance derived from boron, used as an antiseptic.

born a. brought forth by birth; having a specified natural quality. **born-again** a. reconverted, esp. to religion.

borne see **bear**².

boron n. chemical element very resistant to high temperatures.

borough /'bʌrə/ n. town or district with certain rights of self-government; administrative area of London.

borrow v.t./i. get temporary use of (a thing or money); use (an idea etc.) without being the inventor. **borrowed time** extension of one's life. **borrower** n.

Borstal n. former name of an institution for reformative training of young offenders.

bortsch /bɔ:ʃ/ n. Russian beetroot soup.

borzoi n. Russian wolfhound.

bosh int. & n. (sl.) nonsense.

bo's'n /'bəʊs(ə)n/ n. boatswain.

bosom n. breast. **bosom friend** very dear friend. **bosomy** a.

boss¹ n. (colloq.) master, manager, overseer. —v.t. (colloq.) be the boss of; give orders to.

boss² n. projecting knob.

boss-shot n. (sl.) bad shot; failed attempt.

bossy a. (-ier, -iest) fond of giving orders to people. **bossily** adv., **bossiness** n.

botany n. study of plants. **botanical** a., **botanist** n.

botch v.t. spoil by poor work.

both a., pron., & adv. the two, not only the one.

bother v.t./i. cause trouble, worry, or annoyance to; pester; take trouble, feel concern. —int. exclamation of annoyance. —n. worry, minor trouble. **bothersome** a.

bottle n. narrow-necked glass or plastic container for liquid. —v.t. store in bottles; preserve in jars.

bottleneck n. narrow place where traffic cannot flow freely; obstruction to an even flow of work etc.

bottom n. lowest part or place; buttocks; ground under a stretch of water; basic cause. —a. lowest in position, rank, or degree. —v.t./i. put a bottom to; reach the bottom (of). **bottom line** (colloq.) underlying or ultimate truth; ultimate financial criterion.

bottomless a. extremely deep.

botulism n. poisoning by bacteria in food.

bouclé /'bu:kleɪ/ n. yarn or fabric with thread looped at intervals.

boudoir /'bu:dwɑ:(r)/ n. woman's small private room.

bougainvillaea /bu:gən'vɪlɪə/ n. tropical shrub with red or purple bracts.

bough n. large branch coming from the trunk of a tree.

bought see **buy**.

boulder n. large rounded stone.

boulevard /'bu:ləvɑ:d/ n. wide street.

bounce v.t./i. rebound; cause to do this; (sl., of a cheque) be sent back by a bank as worthless; move in a lively manner. —n. bouncing movement or power; lively manner.

bouncer n. bouncing ball; (sl.) person employed to eject trouble-makers.

bouncing a. big and healthy.

bound¹ v.t. limit, be a boundary of. —n. (usu. pl.) limit. **out of bounds** beyond the permitted area.

bound² v.i. spring, run with a jumping movement. —n. bounding movement.

bound³ see **bind**. —a. obstructed by a specified thing (snowbound). **bound to** certain to. **I'll be bound** I feel certain.

bound⁴ a. going in a specified direction.

boundary n. line that marks a limit; hit to the boundary in cricket.

bounden a. **bounden duty** duty dictated by conscience.

bounder n. (colloq.) cad; ill-bred person.

boundless a. without limits.

bountiful a. giving generously; abundant. **bountifully** adv.

bounty n. generosity; generous gift; gratuity, reward. **bounteous** a., **bounteously** adv.

bouquet /bu'keɪ/ n. bunch of flowers for carrying; perfume of wine.

bouquet garni bunch of herbs for flavouring.

bourbon /'bɜːbən/ n. whisky made mainly from maize.

bourgeois /'buǝʒwɑː/ a. (derog.) middle-class, conventional.

bourgeoisie /buǝʒwɑːˈzɪ/ n. bourgeois society.

bout n. period of exercise or work or illness; boxing contest.

boutique /buːˈtiːk/ n. small shop selling fashionable clothes etc.

bovine a. of oxen; dull and stupid.

bow[1] /bǝʊ/ n. strip of wood curved by a tight string joining its ends, for shooting arrows; rod with horse-hair stretched between its ends, for playing a violin etc.; knot with loop(s), ribbon etc. tied in this way. **bow-legged** a. bandy. **bow-tie** n. necktie tied in a bow. **bow-window** n. curved bay window.

bow[2] /baʊ/ n. bending of the head or body in greeting, respect, agreement, etc. —v.t./i. bend thus; bend downwards under weight; submit.

bow[3] /baʊ/ n. front end of a boat or ship; oarsman nearest the bow.

bowdlerize /'baʊdlǝraɪz/ v.t. expurgate. **bowdlerization** n.

bowel n. intestine; (pl.) intestines, innermost parts.

bower n. leafy shelter. **bowery** a.

bowie knife /'bǝʊɪ/ hunting-knife with a long curved blade.

bowl[1] n. basin; hollow rounded part of a spoon, tobacco-pipe, etc.

bowl[2] n. heavy ball weighted to roll in a curve; (pl.) game played with such balls; ball used in skittles etc. —v.t./i. send rolling along the ground; go fast and smoothly; send a ball to a batsman, dismiss by knocking balls off with this.

bowl over knock down; overwhelm with surprise or emotion.

bowler[1] n. person who bowls in cricket; one who plays at bowls.

bowler[2] n. **bowler hat** hard felt hat with a rounded top.

bowling n. playing bowls or skittles or a similar game.

bowsprit n. spar projecting forward from a ship's bow.

box[1] n. container or receptacle with a flat base; numbered receptacle at a newspaper office for holding replies to an advertisement; compartment in a theatre, stable, etc.; small shelter. —v.t. put into a box. **box in** shut into a small space. **box office** office for booking seats at a theatre etc. **box pleat** two parallel pleats folded to form a raised band.

box[2] v.t./i. slap (a person's ears); fight with fists as a sport, usu. in padded gloves. —n. slap. **boxing** n.

box[3] n. small evergreen shrub; its wood. **boxwood** n.

boxer n. person who engages in the sport of boxing; dog of a breed resembling a bulldog.

Boxing Day first weekday after Christmas Day.

boxroom n. room for storing empty boxes etc.

boy n. male child; young man; male native servant. **boyhood** n., **boyish** a.

boycott v.t. refuse to deal with or trade with. —n. boycotting.

boyfriend n. person's regular male companion or lover.

bra n. woman's undergarment worn to support the breasts.

brace n. device that holds things together or in position; pair; (pl.) straps to keep trousers up, passing over the shoulders. —v.t. give support or firmness to.

bracelet *n.* ornamental band worn on the arm.

bracing *n.* invigorating.

bracken *n.* large fern that grows on waste land; mass of such ferns.

bracket *n.* support projecting from an upright surface; any of the marks used in pairs for enclosing words or figures, (), [], {}; group bracketed together as similar. —*v.t.* (*p.t.* **bracketed**) enclose by brackets; put together as similar.

brackish *a.* slightly salt.

bract *n.* leaf-like part of a plant.

brad *n.* thin flat nail.

bradawl *n.* small boring-tool.

brae *n.* (*Sc.*) hillside.

brag *v.i.* (*p.t.* **bragged**) boast.

braggart *n.* person who brags.

brahmin *n.* member of the Hindu priestly caste.

braid *n.* woven ornamental trimming; plait of hair. —*v.t.* trim with braid; plait.

Braille *n.* system of representing letters etc. by raised dots which blind people read by touch.

brain *n.* mass of soft grey matter in the skull, centre of the nervous system in animals; (also *pl.*) mind, intelligence. —*v.t.* kill by a heavy blow on the head.

brainchild *n.* person's invention or plan.

brainstorm *n.* violent mental disturbance; (*US*) bright idea.

brainwash *v.t.* force (a person) to change his views by subjecting him to great mental pressure.

brainwave *n.* bright idea.

brainy *a.* (**-ier, -iest**) clever.

braise *v.t.* cook slowly with little liquid in a closed container.

brake[1] *n.* device for reducing speed or stopping motion. —*v.t./i.* slow by use of this.

brake[2] *n.* thicket, brushwood.

bramble *n.* shrub with long prickly shoots, blackberry.

bran *n.* ground inner husks of grain, sifted from flour.

branch *n.* arm-like part of a tree; similar part of a road, river, etc.; subdivision of a family or subject; local shop or office belonging to a large organization. —*v.i.* send out or divide into branches. **branch off** leave a main route. **branch out** begin a new line of activity.

brand *n.* trade mark; goods of a particular make; mark of identification made with hot metal; piece of burning or charred wood. —*v.t.* mark with a brand; give a bad name to. **brand-new** *a.* new, unused.

brandish *v.t.* wave, flourish.

brandy *n.* strong alcoholic spirit distilled from wine or fermented fruit-juice. **brandy-snap** *n.* crisp curled gingerbread wafer.

brash *a.* vulgarly self-assertive. **brashly** *adv.*, **brashness** *n.*

brass *n.* yellow alloy of copper and zinc; thing(s) made of this; (*sl.*) money. —*a.* made of brass. **brass tacks** (*sl.*) basic facts, practical details. **top brass** (*collog.*) important officers.

brasserie *n.* restaurant (orig. one serving beer with food).

brassière /-stea(r)/ *n.* bra.

brassy *a.* (**-ier, -iest**) like brass; bold and vulgar. **brassiness** *n.*

brat *n.* (*derog.*) child.

bravado /-'vɑ:-/ *n.* show of boldness.

brave *a.* (**-er, -est**) able to face and endure danger or pain; spectacular. —*n.* American Indian warrior. —*v.t.* face and endure bravely. **bravely** *adv.*, **bravery** *n.*

bravo *int.* well done!

brawl *n.* noisy quarrel or fight. —*v.i.* take part in a brawl. **brawler** *n.*

brawn *n.* muscular strength; pressed meat from a pig's or calf's head.

brawny *a.* (**-ier, -iest**) muscular.

bray *n.* donkey's cry; similar sound. —*v.i.* make this cry or sound.

braze v.t. solder with an alloy of brass.

brazen a. like or made of brass; shameless, impudent. —v.t. **brazen it out** behave (after doing wrong) as if one has no need to be ashamed. **brazenly** adv.

brazier n. basket-like stand for holding burning coals.

breach n. breaking or neglect of a rule or contract; estrangement; broken place, gap. —v.t. break through, make a breach in.

bread n. food made of baked dough of flour and liquid, usu. leavened by yeast; (sl.) money.

breadcrumbs n.pl. bread crumbled for use in cooking.

breadfruit n. tropical fruit with bread-like pulp.

breadline n. **on the breadline** living in extreme poverty.

breadth n. width, broadness.

breadwinner n. member of a family who earns money to support the other(s).

break v.t./i. (p.t. **broke**, p.p. **broken**) divide or separate otherwise than by cutting; fall into pieces, come apart; cause to do this; damage; become unusable; fail to keep (a promise or law); make or become discontinuous; make a way suddenly or violently; appear suddenly; reveal (news); surpass (a record); subdue; weaken, destroy; (of a boy's voice) become suddenly deeper at puberty; (of a ball) change direction after touching the ground; decipher (a code). —n. breaking; sudden dash; gap; interval; points scored continuously in billiards; (colloq.) opportunity, piece of luck. **break down** fail, collapse; give way to emotion; analyse. **break even** make gains and losses that balance exactly. **break service** win a game at tennis when one's opponent is serving. **break up** bring or come to an end; become weaker; begin holidays at the end of school term.

break with give up; end one's friendship with.

breakable a. able to be broken.

breakage n. breaking.

break-dancing n. a kind of energetic street-dancing.

breakdown n. mechanical failure; weakening; collapse of health or mental stability; analysis.

breaker n. heavy ocean wave that breaks on a coast.

breakfast n. first meal of the day. —v.i. eat breakfast.

breakneck a. dangerously fast.

breakthrough n. breaking through; major advance in knowledge or negotiation.

breakwater n. wall built out into the sea to break the force of waves.

bream n. fish of the carp family.

breast n. upper front part of the body; either of the two milk-producing organs on a woman's chest. —v.t. face and advance.

breast-stroke n. swimming-stroke performed face downwards.

breastbone n. bone down the centre of the upper front of the body.

breastplate n. armour covering the breast.

breath n. air drawn into and sent out of the lungs in breathing; breathing in; gentle blowing. **out of breath** panting after exercise. **under one's breath** in a whisper. **breathy** a.

breathalyse v.t. test by a breathalyser.

breathalyser n. device measuring the alcohol in a person's breath.

breathe v.t./i. draw (air etc.) into the lungs or body or tissues and send it out again; utter.

breather n. pause for rest; short period in fresh air.

breathless a. out of breath.

breathtaking a. amazing.

bred see **breed**.

breech *n.* back part of a gun barrel; buttocks. **breech birth** birth in which a baby's buttocks emerge first.

breeches *n.pl.* trousers reaching to just below the knees.

breed *v.t./i.* (*p.t.* **bred**) produce offspring; train, bring up; give rise to. —*n.* variety of animals etc. within a species; sort.

breeder *n.* one who breeds. **breeder reactor** nuclear reactor that produces fissile material.

breeding *n.* good manners resulting from training or background.

breeze *n.* light wind. **breezy** *a.*

breeze-blocks *n.pl.* lightweight building blocks.

brent *n.* smallest kind of wild goose.

brethren *n.pl.* (*old use*) brothers.

Breton *a.* & *n.* (native) of Brittany.

breve *n.* mark (˘) over a short or unstressed vowel; (in music) note equal to two semibreves.

breviary /'briːvjəri/ *n.* book of prayers to be said by RC priests.

brevity *n.* briefness.

brew *v.t./i.* make (beer) by boiling and fermentation; make (tea) by infusion; bring about, develop. —*n.* liquid or amount brewed.

brewer *n.* person whose trade is brewing beer.

brewery *n.* building where beer is brewed commercially.

briar *n.* = **brier**.

bribe *n.* thing offered to influence a person to act in favour of the giver. —*v.t.* persuade by this. **bribery** *n.*

bric-à-brac *n.* odd items of ornaments, furniture, etc.

brick *n.* block of baked or dried clay used to build walls; rectangular block; (*sl.*) kind-hearted person. —*v.t.* block with a brick structure. **brick-red** *a.* reddish.

brickbat *n.* piece of brick, esp. as a missile.

bricklayer *n.* workman who builds with bricks.

brickwork *n.* bricks in a building.

bridal *a.* of a bride or wedding.

bride *n.* woman on her wedding-day or when newly married.

bridegroom *n.* man on his wedding-day or when newly married.

bridesmaid *n.* girl or unmarried woman attending a bride.

bridge[1] *n.* structure providing a way across or joining something; captain's platform on a ship; bony upper part of the nose. —*v.t.* make or be a bridge over, span as if with a bridge.

bridge[2] *n.* card-game developed from whist.

bridgehead *n.* fortified area established in enemy territory, esp. on the far side of a river.

bridle *n.* harness on a horse's head. —*v.t./i.* put a bridle on; restrain; draw up one's head in pride or scorn. **bridle-path** *n.* path suitable for horse-riding but not for vehicles.

brief[1] *a.* (-er, -est) lasting only for a short time; concise; short. **briefly** *adv.*, **briefness** *n.*

brief[2] *n.* set of instructions and information, esp. to a barrister about a case. —*v.t.* employ (a barrister); inform or instruct in advance.

briefcase *n.* case for carrying documents.

briefs *n.pl.* very short pants or underpants.

brier *n.* thorny bush, wild rose; bush with a woody root, pipe made of this.

brig *n.* two-masted sailing-vessel.

brigade *n.* army unit forming part of a division; organized group.

brigadier *n.* officer commanding a brigade or of similar status.

brigand *n.* member of a band of robbers. **brigandage** *n.*

bright *a.* (-er, -est) giving out or reflecting much light, shining; cheerful; quick-witted, clever. **brightly** *adv.*, **brightness** *n.*

brighten *v.t./i.* make or become brighter.

brill *n.* flat-fish like turbot.

brilliant *a.* very bright, sparkling; very clever. —*n.* cut diamond with many facets. **brilliantly** *adv.*, **brilliance** *n.*

brilliantine /-ti:n/ *n.* substance used to make hair glossy.

brim *n.* edge of a cup or hollow or channel; projecting edge of a hat. —*v.i.* (*p.t.* **brimmed**) be full to the brim.

brimstone *n.* (old use) sulphur.

brindled *a.* brown with streaks of another colour.

brine *n.* salt water; sea-water.

bring *v.t.* (*p.t.* **brought**) convey; cause to come; put forward (charges etc.) in a lawcourt. **bring about** cause to happen. **bring off** do successfully. **bring out** show clearly; publish. **bring up** look after and train (growing children); vomit; cause to stop suddenly. **bring up the rear** come last in a line. **bringer** *n.*

brink *n.* edge of a steep place or of a stretch of water; point just before a change.

brinkmanship *n.* policy of pursuing a dangerous course to the brink of catastrophe.

briny *a.* of brine or sea water. —*n.* (*sl.*) the sea.

briquette /-'ket/ *n.* block of compressed coal-dust.

brisk *a.* (-er, -est) lively, moving quickly. **briskly** *adv.*, **briskness** *n.*

brisket *n.* joint of beef from the breast.

brisling *n.* small herring or sprat.

bristle *n.* short stiff hair; one of the stiff pieces of hair or wire etc. in a brush. —*v.i.* raise bristles in anger or fear; show indignation; be thickly set with bristles. **bristle with** be full of. **bristly** *a.*

Brit *n.* (*colloq.*) British person.

Britannia *n.* British gold bullion coin first issued in 1987.

Britannic *a.* of Britain.

British *a.* of Britain or its people.

Briton *n.* British person.

brittle *a.* hard but easily broken. **brittly** *adv.*, **brittleness** *n.*

broach *v.t.* open and start using; begin discussion of.

broad *a.* (-er, -est) large across, wide; measuring from side to side; full and complete; in general terms; (of an accent) strong; (of humour) rather coarse. —*n.* broad part. **broad bean** edible bean with flat seeds. **broad-minded** *a.* having tolerant views. **broadly** *adv.*, **broadness** *n.*

broadcast *v.t./i.* (*p.t.* **broadcast**) send out by radio or television; speak on radio or television; make generally known; sow (seed) by scattering. —*n.* broadcast programme. **broadcaster** *n.*

broaden *v.t./i.* make or become broader.

broadsheet *n.* large sheet of paper printed on one side only.

broadside *n.* firing of all guns on one side of a ship. **broadside on** sideways on.

broadsword *n.* sword with a broad blade, used for slashing.

brocade *n.* fabric woven with raised patterns. **brocaded** *a.*

broccoli /-lɪ/ *n.* (*pl.* -li) hardy kind of cauliflower.

brochure /'brəʊʃə/ *n.* booklet or leaflet giving information.

broderie anglaise /brəʊdərɪ ɑ̃gleɪz/ fabric with openwork embroidery.

brogue *n.* strong shoe with ornamental perforated bands; dialectal esp. Irish accent.

broil *v.t./i.* grill esp. on a fire or gridiron; make or become very hot.

broiler *n.* chicken suitable for broiling.

broke see **break**. —*a.* (*sl.*) having spent all one's money; bankrupt.

broken see **break.** —a. **broken English** English spoken imperfectly by a foreigner. **brokenhearted** a. crushed by grief.

broker n. agent who buys and sells on behalf of others; member of the Stock Exchange dealing in stocks and shares; official licensed to sell the goods of persons unable to pay their debts.

brolly n. (colloq.) umbrella.

bromide n. chemical compound used to calm nerves.

bromine n. poisonous liquid element.

bronchial a. of the branched tubes into which the windpipe divides.

bronchitis n. inflammation of the bronchial tubes.

bronco n. (pl. -os) wild or half-tamed horse of western North America.

brontosaurus n. large plant-eating dinosaur.

bronze n. brown alloy of copper and tin; thing made of this; its colour. —a. made of bronze, bronze-coloured. —v.t./i. make or become suntanned. **bronzy** a.

brooch n. ornamental hinged pin fastened with a clasp.

brood n. young produced at one hatching or birth; (joc.) family of children.—v.t./i. sit on (eggs) and hatch them; think long and deeply or resentfully. **broody** a. (of a hen) wanting to brood; thoughtful and depressed.

brook[1] n. small stream.

brook[2] v.t. tolerate, allow.

broom n. long-handled brush for sweeping floors; shrub with white, yellow, or red flowers. **broomstick** n. broom-handle.

broth n. thin meat or fish soup.

brothel n. house where women work as prostitutes.

brother n. son of the same parents as another person; man who is a fellow member of a group or Church etc.; monk who is not a priest. **brother-in-law** n. (pl.

brothers-in-law) brother of one's husband or wife; husband of one's sister. **brotherly** a.

brotherhood n. relationship of brothers; comradeship; association of men.

brought see **bring.**

brow n. eyebrow; forehead; projecting or overhanging part.

browbeat v.t. (p.t. -beat, p.p. -beaten) intimidate.

brown a. (-er, -est) of a colour between orange and black; dark-skinned. —n. brown colour or thing. —v.t./i. make or become brown. **browned off** (sl.) bored, fed up. **brownish** a.

Brownie n. member of the junior branch of the Guides.

browse v.i. feed on leaves or grass etc.; read or look around casually.

bruise n. injury that discolours skin without breaking it. —v.t./i. cause bruise(s) on; become bruised.

bruiser n. tough brutal person.

bruit /bru:t/ v.t. (old use) spread (news etc.).

brunch n. (colloq.) meal combining breakfast and lunch.

brunette n. woman with brown hair.

brunt n. chief stress or strain.

brush n. implement with bristles; fox's tail; skirmish; brushing; undergrowth.—v.t./i. use a brush on; touch lightly in passing. **brush off** reject curtly; snub. **brush up** smarten; study and revive one's knowledge of.

brushwood n. undergrowth; cut or broken twigs.

brusque /brusk/ a. curt and offhand. **brusquely** adv., **brusqueness** n.

Brussels sprout edible bud of a kind of cabbage.

brutal a. very cruel, without mercy. **brutally** adv., **brutality** n.

brutalize v.t. make brutal; treat brutally. **brutalization** n.

brute n. animal other than man; brutal person; (*colloq.*) unpleasant person or thing. —a. unable to reason; unreasoning. **brutish** a.

bryony n. climbing hedge-plant.

B.Sc. *abbrev.* Bachelor of Science.

BSE *abbrev.* bovine spongiform encephalopathy (disease of cattle).

Bt. *abbrev.* Baronet.

bubble n. thin ball of liquid enclosing air or gas; air-filled cavity; transparent domed cover. —v.t./i. send up or rise in bubbles; show great liveliness. **bubbly** a.

bubonic a. (of plague) characterized by swellings (**buboes**).

buccaneer n. pirate; adventurer.

buck[1] n. male of deer, hare, or rabbit. —v.i. (of a horse) jump with the back arched. **buck up** (*sl.*) make haste; make or become more cheerful.

buck[2] n. article placed before the dealer in a game of poker. **pass the buck** shift the responsibility (and possible blame). **buck-passing** n.

buck[3] n. (*US & Austr. sl.*) dollar.

bucked a. (*sl.*) cheered and encouraged.

bucket n. round open container with a handle, for carrying or holding liquid. —v.i. move fast and bumpily; pour heavily. **bucketful** n.

buckle n. device through which a belt or strap is threaded to secure it. —v.t./i. fasten with a buckle; crumple under pressure. **buckle down** to set about doing.

buckler n. small round shield.

buckram n. coarse stiffened fabric.

buckshee a. & *adv.* free, gratis.

buckwheat n. cereal plant; its seed.

bucolic a. rustic.

bud n. leaf or flower not fully open. —v.i. (*p.t.* **budded**) put forth buds.

Buddhism n. Asian religion based on the teachings of Buddha. **Buddhist** a. & n.

budding a. beginning to develop.

buddleia /-lɪə/ n. tree or shrub with purple or yellow flowers.

buddy n. (*colloq.*) friend. —v.i. become friendly.

budge v.t./i. move slightly.

budgerigar n. a kind of Australian parakeet.

budget n. plan of income and expenditure, esp. of a country; amount allowed. —v.t./i. (*p.t.* **budgeted**) allow or arrange in a budget.

buff n. fawn colour; bare skin; (*US colloq.*) enthusiast. —v.t. polish with soft material.

buffalo n. (*pl.* **-oes** or **-o**) a kind of ox.

buffer n. thing that lessens the effect of impact; (*sl.*) man. —v.t. act as a buffer to. **buffer zone** region between hostile areas, preventing direct conflict.

buffet[1] /'bufeɪ/ n. counter where food and drink are served; meal where guests serve themselves.

buffet[2] /'bʌfɪt/ n. blow, esp. with a hand. —v.t. (*p.t.* **buffeted**) deal blows to.

buffoon n. person who plays the fool. **buffoonery** n.

bug n. small unpleasant insect; (*sl.*) microbe; (*sl.*) secret microphone; (*sl.*) defect. —v.t. (*p.t.* **bugged**) (*sl.*) install a secret microphone in; (*US sl.*) annoy.

bugbear n. thing feared or disliked.

buggy n. light carriage; small sturdy vehicle.

bugle[1] n. brass instrument like a small trumpet. **bugler** n.

bugle[2] n. tube-shaped glass bead.

build v.t./i. (*p.t.* **built**) construct by putting parts or material together. —n. bodily shape. **build on** rely on. **build up** establish gradually; increase in height or thickness; boost with praise.

build-up n. this process. **builder** n.

building n. house or similar structure. **building society** organization that accepts deposits of money and lends to people buying houses.

built see **build**. **built-in** a. forming part of a structure. **built-up** a. covered with buildings.

bulb n. rounded base of the stem of certain plants, from which roots grow downwards; thing (esp. an electric lamp) shaped like this. **bulbous** a.

bulge n. rounded swelling; outward curve. —v.t./i. form a bulge, swell. **bulgy** a.

bulk n. size, esp. when great; greater part; bulky thing. —v.t. increase the size or thickness of. **bulk large** seem important. **in bulk** in large amounts; in a mass, not packaged.

bulkhead n. partition in a ship etc.

bulky a. (-ier, -iest) taking up much space. **bulkiness** n.

bull[1] n. male of ox, whale, elephant, etc.; bull's-eye of a target; person who buys stocks hoping to sell at a higher price shortly. **bull's-eye** n. centre of a target; hard round peppermint sweet. **bull-terrier** n. terrier resembling a bulldog.

bull[2] n. pope's official edict.

bull[3] n. (sl.) absurd statement; unnecessary routine tasks.

bulldog n. powerful dog with a short thick neck.

bulldoze v.t. clear with a bulldozer.

bulldozer n. powerful tractor with a device for clearing ground.

bullet n. small missile used in a rifle or revolver.

bulletin n. short official statement of news.

bulletproof a. able to keep out bullets.

bullfight n. sport of baiting and killing bulls as an entertainment.

bullfinch n. songbird with a strong beak and pinkish breast.

bullion n. gold or silver in bulk or bars, before manufacture.

bullock n. castrated bull.

bullring n. arena for bullfights.

bully[1] n. one who uses his strength or power to hurt or intimidate others. —v.t. behave as a bully towards.

bully[2] v.i. **bully off** put the ball into play in hockey by two opponents striking sticks together.

bulrush n. a kind of tall rush.

bulwark n. wall of earth built as a defence; ship's side above the deck.

bum[1] n. (sl.) buttocks.

bum[2] n. (US sl.) beggar, loafer.

bumble v.i. move or act in a blundering way. **bumbler** n.

bumble-bee n. large bee.

bump v.t./i. knock with a dull-sounding blow; travel with a jolting movement. —n. bumping sound or knock; swelling, esp. left by a blow. **bumpy** a., **bumpily** adv.

bumper n. something unusually large; horizontal bar at the front and back of a motor vehicle to lessen the effect of collision; brim-full glass.

bumpkin n. country person with awkward manners.

bumptious a. conceited. **bumptiously** adv., **bumptiousness** n.

bun n. small round sweet cake; hair twisted into a bun shape at the back of the head.

bunch n. cluster; number of small things fastened together; (sl.) group. —v.t./i. make into bunch(es); form a group. **bunchy** a.

bundle n. collection of things loosely fastened or wrapped together; (sl.) much money. —v.t. make into a bundle; push hurriedly.

bung n. stopper for closing the hole in a barrel or jar. —v.t. close with a bung; block; (sl.) throw.

bungee n. an elasticated cord, used for securing baggage and in **bungee jumping**, the sport of jumping from a height secured by a bungee from the ankles, or a harness.

bungalow n. one-storeyed house.

bungle v.t. spoil by lack of skill, mismanage. —n. bungled attempt. **bungler** n.

bunion n. swelling at the base of the big toe, with thickened skin.

bunk¹ n. shelf-like bed.

bunk² v. (sl.) run away. —n. **do a bunk** (sl.) run away.

bunk³ n. (sl.) bunkum.

bunker n. container for fuel; sandy hollow forming a hazard on a golf-course; reinforced underground shelter.

bunkum n. nonsense, humbug.

bunny n. (children's use) rabbit.

Bunsen burner device burning mixed air and gas in a single very hot flame.

bunt v.t. & n. push with the head.

bunting¹ n. bird related to the finches.

bunting² n. decorative flags.

buoy n. anchored floating object serving as a navigation mark; lifebuoy. —v.t. mark with buoy(s). **buoy up** keep afloat; sustain, hearten.

buoyant a. able to float; cheerful. **buoyancy** n.

bur n. plant's seed-case or flower that clings to clothing etc.

burble v.i. make a gentle murmuring sound; speak lengthily.

burden n. thing carried; heavy load or obligation; trouble; theme. —v.t. put a burden on. **burdensome** a.

bureau /ˈbjʊərəʊ/ n. (pl. **-eaux**, pr. -əʊz) writing-desk with drawers; office, department.

bureaucracy /-ˈrɒk-/ n. government by (esp. unaccountable) State officials; excessive official routine. **bureaucratic** a.

bureaucrat n. official in a government office.

burgee n. sailing-club's triangular or swallow-tailed flag.

burgeon v.i. grow rapidly.

burgess n. citizen of a borough.

burgh /ˈbʌrə/ n. Scottish borough.

burglar n. person who breaks into a building, esp. in order to steal. **burglary** n.

burglarize v.t. (US) burgle.

burgle v.t. rob as a burglar.

burgomaster n. Dutch or Flemish mayor.

burgundy n. red or white wine from Burgundy; similar wine.

burial n. burying.

burlesque n. mocking imitation. —v.t. imitate mockingly.

burly a. (-ier, -iest) with a strong heavy body. **burliness** n.

Burmese a. & n. (native, language) of Burma.

burn¹ v.t./i. (p.t. **burned** or **burnt**) be on fire; damage, destroy, or mark by fire, heat, or acid; be damaged or destroyed thus; use as fuel; produce heat or light; feel a sensation (as) of heat. —n. mark or sore made by burning; firing of a spacecraft's rockets.

burn² n. (Sc.) brook.

burner n. part that shapes the flame in a lamp or cooker etc.

burning a. intense; hotly discussed.

burnish v.t. polish by rubbing.

burnt see burn¹.

burp n. & v.i. (colloq.) belch.

burr n. whirring sound; rough pronunciation of 'r'; country accent using this; small drill; bur. —v.i. make a whirring sound.

burrow n. hole dug by a fox or rabbit etc. as a dwelling. —v.t./i. dig a burrow, tunnel; form by tunnelling; search deeply, delve.

bursar n. person who manages the finances of a college etc.; holder of a bursary.

bursary n. scholarship or grant given to a student; bursar's office.

burst v.t./i. (p.t. burst) force or be forced open; fly violently apart; begin or appear or come suddenly. —n. bursting; outbreak; brief violent effort, spurt.

burton n. go for a burton (sl.) be lost, destroyed, or killed.

bury v.t. place (a dead body) in the earth or a tomb or the sea; put or hide underground; cover up; involve (oneself) deeply.

bus n. (pl. buses) long-bodied passenger vehicle. —v.t./i. (p.t. bussed) travel by bus; transport by bus.

busby n. tall fur cap worn as part of military ceremonial uniform.

bush[1] n. shrub; thick growth; wild uncultivated land. **bush-baby** n. small African tree-climbing lemur. **bush telegraph** way news is spread unofficially.

bush[2] n. perforated plug; metal-lined hole.

bushel n. measure for grain and fruit (8 gallons).

bushy a. (-ier, -iest) covered with bushes; growing thickly. **bushily** adv., **bushiness** n.

business n. occupation, trade; task, duty; thing to be dealt with; process, affair, structure; buying and selling, trade; commercial establishment. **have no business** to have no right to (do).

businesslike a. practical, systematic.

businessman n. (pl. -men) man engaged in trade or commerce. **businesswoman** n.fem. (pl. -women)

busk v.i. perform as a busker.

busker n. entertainer performing in the street.

busman n. (pl. -men) driver of a bus. **busman's holiday** leisure time spent in something similar to one's work.

bust[1] n. sculptured head, shoulders, and chest; bosom;

measurement round a woman's body there.

bust[2] v.t./i. (p.t. busted or bust) (sl.) burst, break. —n. (sl.) failure; spree. **bust-up** n. (sl.) quarrel, break up. **go bust** (sl.) become bankrupt. **buster** n.

bustard n. large swift-running bird.

bustier /'bʌstɪeɪ/ n. strapless usu. boned bodice.

bustle[1] v.t./i. make a show of activity; cause to hurry. —n. excited activity. **bustler** n.

bustle[2] n. padding used to puff out the top of a skirt at the back.

busy a. (-ier, -iest) working, occupied; having much to do; full of activity. **busily** adv.

busybody n. meddlesome person.

but adv. only. —prep. & conj. however; except.

butane n. inflammable liquid used as fuel.

butch a. (sl.) strongly masculine.

butcher n. person who cuts up and sells animal flesh for food; one who butchers people. —v.t. kill needlessly or brutally. **butchery** n.

butler n. chief manservant, in charge of the wine-cellar.

butt[1] n. large cask or barrel.

butt[2] n. thicker end of a tool or weapon; short remnant, stub.

butt[3] n. mound behind a target, (pl.) shooting-range; target for ridicule or teasing.

butt[4] v.t./i. push with the head; meet or place edge to edge. **butt in** interrupt; meddle.

butter n. fatty food substance made from cream. —v.t. spread with butter. **butter-bean** n. dried haricot bean. **butter-fingers** n. person likely to drop things. **butter muslin** thin loosely woven fabric. **butter up** (colloq.) flatter.

buttercup n. wild plant with yellow cup-shaped flowers.

butterfly n. insect with four large often brightly coloured wings. **butterfly stroke** swimming-stroke with both arms lifted at the same time.

buttermilk *n.* liquid left after butter is churned from milk.

butterscotch *n.* hard toffee-like sweet.

buttery[1] *a.* like butter.

buttery[2] *n.* place where provisions are kept in a college etc.

buttock *n.* either of the two fleshy rounded parts at the lower end of the back of the body.

button *n.* disc or knob sewn to a garment as a fastener or ornament; small rounded object; knob etc. pressed to operate a device. —*v.t.* fasten with button(s).

buttonhole *n.* slit through which a button is passed to fasten clothing; flower worn in the buttonhole of a lapel. —*v.t.* accost and talk to.

buttress *n.* support built against a wall; thing that supports or reinforces. —*v.t.* reinforce, prop up.

buxom *a.* plump and healthy.

buy *v.t.* (*p.t.* **bought**) obtain in exchange for money or by sacrifice; bribe; (*sl.*) accept, believe. —*n.* purchase. **buyer** *n.*

buzz *n.* vibrating humming sound; rumour; thrill. —*v.t./i.* make or be filled with a buzz; go about busily; threaten (an aircraft) by flying close to it. **buzzword** *n.* (*sl.*) piece of fashionable jargon.

buzzard *n.* a kind of hawk.

buzzer *n.* device that produces a buzzing sound as a signal.

by *prep. & adv.* near, beside, in reserve; along, via, past; during; through the agency or means of; having as another dimension; not later than; according to; after, succeeding; to the extent of; in respect of; (of an animal) having as its sire. **by and by** before long. **by and large** on the whole. **by-election** *n.* election of an MP to replace one who has died or resigned. **by-law** *n.* regulation

made by a local authority or corporation. **by oneself** alone, without help. **by-product** *n.* thing produced while making something else. **by the by** by the way (*see* way).

bye *n.* run scored by a ball not hit by the batsman; state of having no opponent for one round of a tournament.

bye-bye *int.* (*colloq.*) goodbye.

bygone *a.* belonging to the past.

bygones *n.pl.* bygone things.

bypass *n.* road taking traffic round a congested area; secondary channel for use when the main route is blocked. —*v.t.* provide with a bypass; use a bypass round; avoid.

bypath *n.* minor or secluded path.

byplay *n.* minor action in a drama etc.

byre *n.* cow-shed.

byroad *n.* minor road.

bystander *n.* person standing near when something happens.

byte *n.* (in computers) group of bits.

byway *n.* minor road.

byword *n.* notable example; familiar saying.

Byzantine /baɪ-/ *a.* of Byzantium or the eastern Roman Empire; complicated, underhand.

C

C *abbr.* Celsius; centigrade.

cab *n.* taxi; compartment for the driver of a train, lorry, etc.

cabaret /-reɪ/ *n.* entertainment provided in a night-club etc.

cabbage *n.* vegetable with a round head of green or purple leaves.

cabby *n.* (*colloq.*) taxi-driver.

caber *n.* trimmed tree-trunk used in the sport of *tossing the caber*.

cabin *n.* small hut; compartment in a ship or aircraft.

cabinet *n.* cupboard or case with drawers or shelves; **Cabinet** central group of a government, formed from the most important ministers. **cabinet-maker** n. skilled joiner.

cable n. thick rope of fibre or wire; set of insulated wires for carrying electricity or telegraph messages; telegram sent abroad. —v.t./i. telegraph by cable. **cable-car** n. car of a cable railway drawn on an endless cable by a stationary engine. **cable television** transmission by cable to subscribers.

caboodle n. (sl.) lot.

cacao n. (pl. **-os**) seed from which cocoa and chocolate are made; tree producing this.

cache /kæʃ/ n. hiding-place for treasure or stores; things in this. —v.t. put into a cache.

cachet /ˈkæʃeɪ/ n. prestige; distinctive mark or characteristic.

cackle n. clucking of hens etc.; chattering talk; loud silly laugh. —v.i. utter a cackle.

cacophony /-ˈkɒf-/ n. harsh discordant sound. **cacophonous** a.

cactus n. (pl. **-ti** or **-tuses**) fleshy plant, often with prickles, from a hot dry climate.

cad n. man who behaves dishonourably. **caddish** a.

cadaver /-ˈdeɪ-/ n. corpse.

cadaverous /-ˈdæ-/ a. gaunt and pale.

caddie n. golfer's attendant carrying clubs. —v.i. act as caddie.

caddis-fly n. four-winged insect living near water.

caddy n. small box for tea.

cadence /ˈkeɪ-/ n. rhythm in sound; rise and fall of the voice in speech; end of a musical phrase.

cadenza n. elaborate passage for a solo instrument or singer.

cadet n. young trainee in the armed forces or police.

cadge v.t./i. ask for as a gift, beg things. **cadger** n.

cadmium n. metallic element.

cadre /ˈkɑːdə(r)/ n. small group forming a nucleus that can be expanded.

caecum /ˈsiː-/ n. (pl. **-ca**) blind tube at the first part of the large intestine.

Caesarean section /-ˈzeər-/ operation to deliver a child by an incision through the walls of the mother's abdomen and womb.

café n. shop selling refreshments, informal restaurant.

cafeteria n. self-service restaurant.

caffeine /-ˈfiːn/ n. stimulant found in tea and coffee.

caftan n. long loose robe or dress.

cage n. enclosure of wire or with bars, esp. for birds or animals; enclosed platform carrying people in a lift or mine-shaft. —v.t. place or keep in a cage.

cagey a. (**-ier, -iest**) (colloq.) secretive; shrewd; wary. **cagily** adv., **caginess** n.

cagoule /-ˈguː-/ n. light hooded waterproof jacket.

cagy a. = cagey.

cahoots /-ˈhuːts/ n. (sl.) partnership.

cairn n. mound of stones as a memorial or landmark etc. **cairn terrier** small shaggy short-legged terrier.

cairngorm n. yellow or wine-coloured gem-stone.

caisson n. watertight chamber used in underwater construction work.

cajole /-ˈdʒəʊl/ v.t. coax. **cajolery** n.

Cajun n. descendent of French Canadians living in Louisiana. —a. of the Cajuns.

cake n. baked sweet bread-like food; small flattened mass. —v.t./i. form into a compact mass; encrust.

calabash n. a kind of gourd.

calamine /-mam/ n. lotion containing zinc carbonate.

calamity n. disaster. **calamitous** a., **calamitously** adv.

calcify v.t./i. harden by a deposit of calcium salts. **calcification** n.

calcium n. whitish metallic element.

calculable a. able to be calculated. **calculably** adv., **calculability** n.

calculate v.t./i. reckon mathematically; estimate; plan deliberately; (US) suppose. **calculation** n.

calculator n. electronic device for making mathematical calculations.

calculus n. (pl. -li) method of calculating in mathematics; stone formed in the body.

Caledonian a. of Scotland. —n. Scottish person.

calendar n. chart showing dates of days of the year; method of fixing these; device displaying the date; register or list (e.g. of events).

calender n. machine for smoothing paper etc. —v.t. press in this.

calf[1] n. (pl. **calves**) young of cattle, also of elephant, whale, and seal; leather from calf-skin.

calf-love n. immature romantic affection.

calf[2] n. (pl. **calves**) fleshy hind part of the human leg below the knee.

calibrate v.t. mark or correct the units of measurement on (a gauge); find the calibre of. **calibration** n.

calibre n. diameter of a gun or tube or bullet etc.; level of ability or importance.

calico n. a kind of cotton cloth.

caliph /ˈkæ- or ˈkeɪ-/ n. Muslim ruler.

call v.t./i. shout to attract attention; utter a characteristic cry; read (a list) aloud for checking; summon; demand, invite; rouse from sleep; communicate (with) by telephone or radio; name; describe or address as; make a brief visit. —n. shout; bird's cry; signal on a bugle etc.; vocation; invitation, demand; need; telephone communication; short visit. **callbox** n. telephone kiosk. **call for** demand; need. **call off** cancel. **call up** summon to join the armed forces. **caller** n.

calligraphy n. (beautiful) handwriting. **calligraphic** a.

calliper n. splint for a weak leg; (pl.) compasses for measuring cavities.

callisthenics n.pl. exercises to develop strength and grace.

callosity n. callus.

callous a. feeling no pity or sympathy. **callously** adv., **callousness** n.

callow /-əʊ/ a. (-er, -est) immature and inexperienced. **callowness** n.

callus n. patch of hardened skin.

calm /kɑːm/a. (-er, -est) still, not windy; not excited or agitated. —n. calm condition. —v.t./i. make calm. **calmly** adv., **calmness** n.

calorie n. unit of heat; unit of the energy-producing value of food.

calorific a. heat-producing.

calumniate v.t. slander. **calumniation** n., **calumniator** n.

calumny n. slander.

calve v.i. give birth to a calf.

Calvinism n. teachings of the Protestant reformer John Calvin or his followers. **Calvinist** n., **Calvinistic** a.

calypso n. (pl. -os) topical West Indian song.

calyx /ˈkeɪ-/ n. ring of sepals covering a flower-bud.

cam n. device changing rotary to-and-fro motion. **camshaft** n.

camaraderie n. comradeship.

camber n. slight convex curve given to a surface esp. of a road.

cambric n. thin linen or cotton cloth.

camcorder n. combined video camera and sound-recorder.

came see **come**.

camel *n.* quadruped with one hump or two; fawn colour.

camellia /-'mi:l- *or* -'mel-/ *n.* evergreen flowering shrub.

Camembert /-bea(r)/ *n.* a kind of soft rich cheese.

cameo *n.* (*pl.* **-os**) stone with coloured layers carved in a raised design; short well-executed description or part in a play etc.

camera *n.* apparatus for taking photographs or film etc. pictures. **in camera** in private. **cameraman** *n.* (*pl.* **-men**)

camiknickers *n.* woman's undergarment combining camisole and knickers.

camisole *n.* woman's cotton bodice-like garment or undergarment.

camomile *n.* aromatic herb.

camouflage *n.* disguise, concealment, esp. by colouring or covering. —*v.t.* disguise or conceal thus.

camp[1] *n.* temporary accommodation for travellers etc., esp. in tents; place where troops are lodged or trained; fortified site. —*v.i.* encamp, be in a camp. **camp-bed** *n.* portable folding bed. **camper** *n.*

camp[2] *n.* affected, exaggerated, bizarre; homosexual. —*n.* camp behaviour. —*v.t./i.* act or behave in a camp way.

campaign *n.* series of military operations; organized course of action. —*v.i.* conduct or take part in a campaign. **campaigner** *n.*

campanology *n.* study of bells, bell-ringing. **campanologist** *n.*

campanula /-'pæn-/ *n.* plant with bell-shaped flowers.

camphor *n.* strong-smelling white substance used in medicine and moth-balls. **camphorated** *a.*

campion *n.* wild plant with pink or white flowers.

campus *n.* (*pl.* **-puses**) grounds of a university or college.

can[1] *n.* metal vessel for liquids; tinplate container in which food

etc. is hermetically sealed. —*v.t.* (*p.t.* **canned**) put or preserve in a can. **canned music** music recorded for reproduction.

can[2] *v.aux.* is or are able or allowed to.

Canadian *a. & n.* (native, inhabitant) of Canada.

canal *n.* artificial watercourse; duct.

canalize /'kæ-/ *v.t.* convert into a canal; channel. **canalization** *n.*

canapé /'kænəpeɪ/ *n.* small piece of bread etc. with savoury topping.

canary *n.* small yellow songbird.

canasta *n.* card-game like rummy.

cancan *n.* lively high-kicking dance performed by women.

cancel *v.t./i.* (*p.t.* **cancelled**) cross out; mark to prevent re-use; declare that (something arranged) will not take place; order to be discontinued. **cancel out** neutralize. **cancellation** *n.*

cancer *n.* malignant tumour; spreading evil. **cancerous** *a.*

candela *n.* unit of luminous intensity.

candelabrum *n.* (*pl.* **-bra**) large branched candlestick or stand for a lamp.

candid *a.* frank. **candidly** *adv.*, **candidness** *n.*

candidate *n.* person applying for a job etc., or taking an examination. **candidacy** *n.*, **candidature** *n.*

candied *a.* encrusted or preserved in sugar.

candle *n.* stick of wax enclosing a wick which is burnt to give light. **candlestick** *n.* holder for a candle.

candlewick *n.* fabric with a tufted pattern.

candour *n.* frankness.

candy *n.* (US) sweets, a sweet.

candyfloss *n.* fluffy mass of spun sugar.

candystripe *n.* alternate stripes of white and colour. **candy-striped** *a.*

candytuft n. garden plant with flowers in flat clusters.

cane n. stem of a tall reed or grass or slender palm; light walking-stick; rod with which children are struck as a punishment. —v.t. strike with a cane.

canine /'keməm/ a. of dog(s). —n. a **canine tooth**, a pointed tooth between incisors and molars.

canister n. small metal container.

canker n. disease of animals or plants; influence that corrupts.

cannabis n. hemp plant; drug made from this.

canned see **can**[1].

cannibal n. person who eats human flesh; animal that eats others of its own kind. **cannibalism** n.

cannibalize v.t. use parts from (a machine) to repair another. **cannibalization** n.

cannon n. large mounted gun (pl. **cannon**); hitting of two balls in one shot in billiards. —v.i. bump heavily (into an obstacle).

cannonade n. continuous gunfire. —v.t. bombard with this.

cannot negative form of **can**[2].

canny a. (-ier, -iest) shrewd. **cannily** adv.

canoe n. light boat propelled by paddle(s). —v.i. go in a canoe. **canoeist** n.

canon n. member of cathedral clergy; general rule or principle; set of writings etc. accepted as genuine. **canonical** a.

canonize v.t. declare officially to be a saint. **canonization** n.

canopy n. covering hung or held up over a throne, bed, person, etc.; spreading fabric of a parachute. —v.t. provide or be a canopy to.

cant[1] v.t./i. tilt, slope.

cant[2] n. insincere talk; jargon.

can't (colloq.) = cannot.

cantaloup n. small ribbed melon.

cantankerous a. perverse, peevish. **cantankerously** adv., **cantankerousness** n.

cantata /-'tɑː-/ n. choral composition.

canteen n. restaurant for employees in a factory etc.; case of cutlery.

canter n. gentle gallop. —v.t./i. go or cause to go at a canter.

canticle n. song or chant with words from the Bible.

cantilever n. projecting beam or girder supporting a structure.

canto n. (pl. -os) division of a long poem.

canton n. division of Switzerland.

canvas n. strong coarse cloth; a painting on this.

canvass v.t./i. ask for political support, orders, etc.; propose (a plan).

canyon n. deep gorge.

cap n. soft brimless hat, often with a peak; head-dress worn as part of uniform etc.; cap-like cover or top; limit; explosive device for a toy pistol. —v.t. (p.t. **capped**) put or confer a cap on; cover or form the top or end of; surpass; impose a limit on.

capable a. having a certain ability or capacity; competent. **capably** adv., **capability** n.

capacious a. roomy. **capaciously** adv., **capaciousness** n.

capacitance n. ability to store an electric charge.

capacitor n. device storing a charge of electricity.

capacity n. ability to contain or accommodate; amount that can be contained or produced; mental power; function or character.

caparison v.t. deck out.

cape[1] n. cloak; short similar part.

cape[2] n. coastal promontory.

caper[1] v. move friskily. —n. frisky movement; (sl.) activity.

caper[2] n. bramble-like shrub; one of its buds, pickled for use in sauces.

capercaillie *n.* (also **capercailzie**) largest kind of grouse.

capillary *n.* very fine hair-like tube or blood-vessel.

capital *a.* chief, very important; (*colloq.*) excellent; involving the death penalty; (of a letter of the alphabet) of the kind used to begin a name or sentence etc. —*n.* chief town of a country etc.; capital letter; accumulated wealth; money with which a business is started; top part of a pillar.

capitalism /ˈkæp/ *n.* system in which trade and industry are controlled by private owners.

capitalist /ˈkæp/ *n.* rich person, one who has much capital invested.

capitalize *v.t.* convert into or provide with capital; write as or with a capital letter. **capitalize on** make advantageous use of. **capitalization** *n.*

capitulate *v.i.* surrender, yield. **capitulation** *n.*

capon /ˈkeɪ-/ *n.* domestic cock castrated and fattened.

caprice /-ˈpriːs/ *n.* whim; piece of music in a lively fanciful style.

capricious *a.* guided by caprice, impulsive; unpredictable. **capriciously** *adv.*, **capriciousness** *n.*

capsicum *n.* tropical plant with pungent seeds.

capsize *v.t./i.* overturn.

capstan *n.* revolving post or spindle on which a cable etc. winds.

capsule *n.* gelatine case enclosing medicine for swallowing; detachable compartment of a spacecraft; plant's seed-case.

captain *n.* leader of a group or sports team; person commanding a ship or civil aircraft; naval officer next below rear admiral; army officer next below major. —*v.t.* be captain of. **captaincy** *n.*

caption *n.* short title or heading; description or explanation on an illustration etc. —*v.t.* provide with a caption.

captious *a.* fond of finding fault, esp. about trivial matters. **captiously** *adv.*, **captiousness** *n.*

captivate *v.t.* capture the fancy of, charm. **captivation** *n.*

captive *a.* taken prisoner, unable to escape. —*n.* captive person or animal. **captivity** *n.*

captor *n.* one who takes a captive.

capture *v.t.* take prisoner; take or obtain by force or skill or attraction; cause (data) to be stored in a computer. —*n.* capturing; person or thing captured.

Capuchin /ˈkæp-/ *n.* friar of a branch of the Franciscan order.

car *n.* motor car; (*US*) railway carriage; passenger compartment of a cable railway.

carafe /-ˈræf/ *n.* glass bottle for serving wine or water.

caramel *n.* brown syrup made from heated sugar; toffee tasting like this.

caramelize *v.t./i.* make into or become caramel. **caramelization** *n.*

carapace /ˈkæ-/ *n.* upper shell of a tortoise or crustacean.

carat *n.* unit of purity of gold or of weight of precious stones.

caravan *n.* dwelling on wheels, able to be towed by a horse or car; company travelling together across desert. **caravanning** *n.*

caraway *n.* plant with spicy seeds that are used for flavouring cakes.

carbine /-baɪn/ *n.* automatic rifle.

carbohydrate *n.* energy-producing compound (e.g. starch) in food.

carbolic *n.* a kind of disinfectant.

carbon *n.* non-metallic element occurring as diamond, graphite, and charcoal, and in all living matter; sheet of carbon paper; carbon copy. **carbon copy** copy made with carbon paper; exact copy. **carbon paper** paper coated with pigment for making a copy as something is typed or written.

carbonate n. compound releasing carbon dioxide when mixed with acid. —v.t. impregnate with carbon dioxide.

carboniferous a. producing coal.

carbonize v.t. reduce to charcoal or coke by burning; coat with carbon. **carbonization** n.

carborundum n. compound of carbon and silicon used for grinding and polishing things.

carboy n. large round bottle with a protective framework, for transporting liquids.

carbuncle n. severe abscess; garnet cut in a round knob shape.

carburettor n. apparatus mixing air and petrol vapour in a motor engine.

carcass n. dead body of an animal; bony part of the body of a bird before or after cooking; framework.

carcinogen n. cancer-producing substance. **carcinogenic** a.

carcinoma n. cancerous tumour.

card[1] n. piece of cardboard or thick paper; this printed with a greeting or invitation etc.; postcard; playing-card; list of races etc.; piece of plastic issued by a bank etc., holding personal data; (colloq.) odd or amusing person; (pl.) card-game(s); (pl., colloq.) employee's official documents, held by the employer. **card index** index on cards. **card-sharper** n. professional swindler at card-games.

card[2] v.t. clean or comb (wool) with a wire brush or toothed instrument. **carder** n.

cardboard n. stiff substance made by pasting together sheets of paper.

cardiac a. of the heart.

cardigan n. knitted jacket.

cardinal n. chief, most important. —n. member of the Sacred College of the RC Church, which elects the pope; deep scarlet. **cardinal numbers** whole numbers 1, 2, 3, etc.

cardiogram n. record of heart movements. **cardiograph** n. instrument producing this.

cardiology n. study of diseases etc. of the heart. **cardiological** a., **cardiologist** n.

cardphone n. public telephone operated by a plastic machine-readable card.

care n. serious attention and thought; caution to avoid damage or loss; protection, supervision; worry, anxiety. —v.i. feel concern, interest, affection, or liking. **take care of** take charge of; see to the safety or well-being of; deal with.

careen v.t./i. tilt or keel over; (US) swerve.

career n. way of making one's living; profession; course through life; swift course. —v.i. go swiftly or wildly.

careerist n. person intent on advancement in a career.

carefree a. light-hearted through being free from anxieties.

careful a. acting or done with care. **carefully** adv., **carefulness** n.

careless a. not careful. **carelessly** adv., **carelessness** n.

carer n. person who looks after a sick or disabled person at home.

caress n. loving touch, kiss. —v.t. give a caress to.

caret /ˈkærət/ n. omission-mark.

caretaker n. person employed to look after a building.

careworn a. showing signs of prolonged worry.

cargo n. (pl. -oes) goods carried by ship or aircraft.

Caribbean a. of the West Indies or their inhabitants.

caribou /ˈbuː/ n. (pl. **caribou**) North American reindeer.

caricature n. exaggerated portrayal of a person etc., esp. for comic effect. —v.t. make a caricature of.

caries /ˈkɛəriːz/ n. (pl. **caries**) decay of tooth or bone.

carillon /-'rɪljən/ *n.* set of bells sounded mechanically; tune played on these.

Carmelite *n.* member of an order of white-cloaked friars or nuns.

carmine /-maɪn/ *a.* & *n.* vivid crimson.

carnage *n.* great slaughter.

carnal *a.* of the body or flesh, not spiritual. **carnally** *adv.*, **carnality** *n.*

carnation *n.* cultivated clove-scented pink.

carnet /-neɪ/ *n.* permit allowing a vehicle to cross a frontier or enter a camping site.

carnival *n.* public festivities, usu. with a procession.

carnivore *n.* carnivorous animal.

carnivorous *a.* feeding on flesh.

carol *n.* Christmas hymn. —*v.i.* (*p.t.* carolled) sing carols; sing joyfully.

carotid /-'rɒ-/ *a.* & *n.* (artery) carrying blood to the head.

carouse /-'raʊz/ *v.i.* drink and be merry. **carousal** *n.*, **carouser** *n.*

carousel /kæru'sel/ *n.* (*US*) merry-go-round; rotating conveyor.

carp[1] *n.* (*pl.* carp) freshwater fish.

carp[2] *v.i.* keep finding fault.

carpenter *n.* person who makes or repairs wooden objects or structures. **carpentry** *n.*

carpet *n.* textile fabric for covering a floor. —*v.t.* (*p.t.* carpeted) cover with a carpet. **carpet slippers** slippers with cloth uppers. **carpet-sweeper** *n.* household device with revolving brushes for sweeping carpets. **on the carpet** (*colloq.*) being reprimanded.

carport *n.* roofed open-sided shelter for a car.

carpus *n.* set of small bones forming the wrist joint.

carriage *n.* wheeled vehicle or support; moving part carrying or holding something in a machine; conveying of goods etc., cost of this. **carriage clock** small portable clock with a handle on top.

carriageway *n.* that part of the road on which vehicles travel.

carrier *n.* person or thing carrying something; paper or plastic bag with handles, for holding shopping. **carrier pigeon** homing pigeon transporting messages.

carrion *n.* dead decaying flesh.

carrot *n.* tapering orange-red root vegetable; incentive.

carry *v.t./i.* transport, convey; support; be the bearer of; involve, entail; take (a process etc.) to a specified point; get the support of; win acceptance for (a motion etc.); capture (a fortress etc.); stock (goods for sale); be audible at a distance. **carry away** arouse great emotion in. **carry-cot** *n.* baby's portable cot. **carry off** remove by force; win; manage well. **carry on** continue; (*colloq.*) behave excitedly; flirt. **carry out** put into practice.

cart *n.* wheeled structure for carrying loads. —*v.t.* carry, transport. **cart-horse** *n.* horse of heavy build. **cart-track** *n.* track suitable for carts.

carte blanche /kɑːt blɑ̃ʃ/ full power to do as one thinks best.

cartel *n.* manufacturer's or producer's union to control prices.

cartilage *n.* firm elastic tissue in skeletons of vertebrates, gristle.

cartography /-'tɒg-/ *n.* map-drawing. **cartographer** *n.*, **cartographic** *a.*

carton *n.* cardboard or plastic container.

cartoon *n.* humorous drawing in a newspaper etc.; sequence of these; animated cartoon; sketch for a painting etc. —*v.t.* draw a cartoon of. **cartoonist** *n.*

cartridge *n.* case containing explosive for firearms; sealed cassette; head of the pick-up on a record-player. **cartridge paper** thick strong paper.

cartwheel n. handspring with limbs spread like spokes of a wheel.

carve v.t./i. make or inscribe or decorate by cutting; cut (meat) into slices for eating.

carvel-built a. made with planks flush with the side.

caryatid n. supporting pillar sculpted as a female figure.

Casanova n. man noted for seducing women.

cascade n. waterfall; thing falling or hanging like this. —v.i. fall thus.

cascara n. a purgative tree-bark.

case[1] n. instance of a thing's occurring; situation; crime being investigated; lawsuit; set of facts or arguments supporting something; form of a noun, adjective, or pronoun showing its relationship to another word. **in case** lest.

case[2] n. container or protective covering; this with its contents; suitcase. —v.t. enclose in a case; (sl.) examine (a house etc.) in preparation for a crime. **case-harden** v.t. harden the surface of (esp. steel); make callous.

casement n. window opening on vertical hinges.

cash n. money in the form of coins or banknotes. —v.t. give or obtain cash for (a cheque etc.). **cash dispenser** machine from which customers of a bank etc. can withdraw cash. **cash in (on)** get profit or advantage (from).

cashcard n. plastic card for drawing money from a cash dispenser.

cashew n. a kind of edible nut.

cashier[1] n. person employed to receive and pay out money in a bank or receive payments in a shop.

cashier[2] v.t. dismiss from military service in disgrace.

cashmere n. very fine soft wool; fabric made from this.

cashpoint n. cash dispenser.

casing n. enclosing material or framework.

casino n. (pl. -os) public building or room for gambling.

cask n. barrel for liquids.

casket n. small usu. ornamental box for valuables; (US) coffin.

cassava /-'saː-/ n. tropical plant; flour made from its roots.

casserole n. covered dish in which meat etc. is cooked and served; food cooked in this. —v.t. cook in a casserole.

cassette n. small case containing a reel of film or magnetic tape.

cassock n. long robe worn by clergy and choristers.

cassowary n. large flightless bird related to the emu.

cast v.t./i. (p.t. **cast**) throw; shed; direct (a glance etc.); register (one's vote); shape (molten metal) in a mould; calculate; select actors for a play or film, assign a role to. —n. throw of dice, fishing-line. etc.; moulded mass of solidified material; set of actors in a play etc.; type, quality; slight squint; worm-cast. **cast-iron** a. made of cast iron; very strong. **cast-off** a. & n. discarded (thing).

castanets n.pl. pair of shell-shaped pieces of wood etc. clicked in the hand to accompany dancing.

castaway n. shipwrecked person.

caste n. exclusive social class, esp. in the Hindu system.

castellated a. having battlements.

caster n. = castor.

castigate v.t. punish or rebuke or criticize severely. **castigation** n.

casting vote deciding vote when those on each side are equal.

castle n. large fortified residence; rook in chess. —v.i. make a special move with a chess king and rook.

castor n. small swivelling wheel on a leg of furniture; small container with a perforated top for sprinkling sugar etc. **castor**

sugar finely granulated white sugar.

castor oil purgative and lubricant oil from seeds of a tropical plant.

castrate v.t. remove the testicles of. **castration** n.

casual a. happening by chance; not serious or formal or methodical; not permanent. **casually** adv., **casualness** n.

casualty n. person killed or injured; thing lost or destroyed.

casuist n. theologian etc. who studies and resolves moral problems; sophist, quibbler. **casuistic** a., **casuistry** n.

cat[1] n. small furry domesticated animal; wild animal related to this; (colloq.) spiteful or malicious woman; whip with knotted lashes formerly used for flogging people. **cat's cradle** child's game with string. **cat's-paw** n. person used as a tool by another.

cat[2] n. catalytic converter.

cataclysm n. violent upheaval or disaster. **cataclysmic** a.

catacomb n. underground gallery with recesses for tombs.

catafalque n. platform for the coffin of a distinguished person before or during a funeral.

catalepsy n. seizure or trance with rigidity of the body. **cataleptic** a.

catalogue n. systematic list of items. —v.t. list in a catalogue.

catalyse v.t. subject to the action of a catalyst. **catalysis** n.

catalyst n. substance that aids a chemical reaction while remaining unchanged.

catalytic a. using catalysis. **catalytic converter** device for reducing toxic exhaust fumes.

catamaran n. boat with twin hulls.

catapult n. device with elastic for shooting small stones. —v.t./i. hurl from or as if from a catapult; rush violently.

cataract n. large waterfall; opaque area clouding the lens of the eye.

catarrh n. inflammation of mucous membrane, esp. of the nose, with a watery discharge. **catarrhal** a.

catastrophe /-əfi/ n. sudden great disaster. **catastrophic** a., **catastrophically** adv.

catcall n. whistle of disapproval.

catch v.t./i. (p.t. **caught**) capture, seize; come unexpectedly upon, detect; surprise, trick; overtake; be in time for; grasp and hold; make or become fixed, check suddenly; become infected with; hit. —n. act of catching; thing caught or worth catching; concealed difficulty; fastener. **catch crop** crop grown between two staple crops. **catch fire** begin to burn. **catch it** (sl.) be scolded or punished. **catch on** (colloq.) become popular; understand what is meant. **catch out** detect in a mistake etc. **catch-phrase** n. phrase in frequent current use, slogan. **catch-22** n. dilemma where the victim is bound to suffer. **catch up** come abreast with; do arrears of work.

catching a. infectious.

catchment area area from which rainfall drains into a river etc.; area from which a hospital draws patients or a school draws pupils.

catchword n. catch-phrase.

catchy a. (-ier, -iest) (of a tune) pleasant and easy to remember.

catechism n. series of questions; **Catechism** summary of the principles of a religion in the form of questions and answers. **catechist** n.

catechize /ˈkætɪkaɪz/ v.t. put a series of questions to.

catechumen /-ˈkjuː-/ n. person being instructed before baptism.

categorical a. unconditional, absolute. **categorically** adv.

categorize v.t. place in a category. **categorization** n.

category n. class of things.

cater v.i. supply food; provide what is needed or wanted. **caterer** n.

caterpillar n. larva of butterfly or moth. **Caterpillar track** [P.] steel band with treads, passing round a vehicle's wheels.

caterwaul v.i. make a cat's howling cry.

catgut n. gut as thread.

catharsis n. purgation; emotional release. **cathartic** a.

cathedral n. principal church of a diocese.

Catherine wheel rotating firework.

catheter /'kæθ-/ n. tube inserted into the bladder to extract urine.

catheterize v.t. insert a catheter into.

cathode n. electrode by which current leaves a device. **cathode ray** beam of electrons from the cathode of a vacuum tube.

catholic a. universal, including many or most things; **Catholic** of all Churches or all Christians. **Catholic** a. & n. Roman Catholic.

catholicism n. being catholic; adherence to the Catholic Church.

cation /'kæt-/ n. positively charged ion. **cationic** a.

catkin n. hanging flower of willow, hazel, etc.

catmint n. strong-smelling plant attractive to cats.

catnap n. short nap.

catnip n. catmint.

Catseye n. [P.] reflector stud on a road.

cattle n.pl. large ruminant animals with horns and cloven hoofs.

catty a. (-ier, -iest) slightly spiteful. **cattily** adv., **cattiness** n.

catwalk n. narrow strip for walking on as pathway or platform.

Caucasian a. & n. (person) of the light-skinned division of mankind.

caucus n. (usu. derog.) local committee of a political party; (US) meeting of party leaders.

caudal a. of or at the tail.

caudate a. having a tail.

caught see catch.

caul n. membrane sometimes found on a child's head at birth.

cauldron n. large deep pot for boiling things in.

cauliflower n. cabbage with a white flower-head.

caulk v.t. stop up (a ship's seams) with waterproof material or by driving edges of plating together.

causal a. of or forming a cause; of cause and effect. **causality** n.

causation n. causality.

cause n. what produces an effect; reason or motive for action etc.; lawsuit, party's case in this; movement or principle supported. —v.t. be the cause of, make happen.

cause célèbre /se'lebr/ lawsuit etc. exciting much interest.

causeway n. raised road across low or wet ground.

caustic a. burning by chemical action; sarcastic. —n. caustic substance. **caustically** adv.

cauterize v.t. burn the surface of (tissue) to destroy infection or stop bleeding. **cauterization** n.

caution n. avoidance of rashness; attention to safety; warning; (colloq.) amusing person or thing. —v.t. warn; reprimand with a warning not to repeat an offence.

cautionary a. conveying a warning.

cautious a. having or showing caution. **cautiously** adv.

cavalcade n. procession, esp. on horseback or in cars.

Cavalier n. supporter of Charles I in the English Civil War.

cavalier a. arrogant, offhand.

cavalry n. troops who fight on horseback.

cave n. natural hollow in a hill. —v.t./i. **cave** in collapse; yield.

caveat /'kæviæt/ n. warning.

caveman n. (pl. -men) person of prehistoric times living in caves.

cavern n. large cave; hollow part.

cavernous a. like a cavern.

caviare n. pickled roe of sturgeon or other large fish.

cavil v.i. (p.t. cavilled) raise petty objections. —n. petty objection.

caving n. sport of exploring caves.

cavity n. hollow within a solid body.

cavort v.i. caper excitedly.

cavy n. small rodent of the kind that includes guinea pigs.

caw n. harsh cry of a rook etc. —v.i. utter a caw.

cayenne n. hot red pepper.

cayman n. South American alligator.

CB abbr. citizens' band.

CBI abbr. Confederation of British Industry.

cc abbr. cubic centimetre(s).

CD abbr. compact disc.

cease v.t./i. come to an end, discontinue, stop. **cease-fire** n. signal to stop firing guns. **without cease** not ceasing.

ceaseless a. not ceasing.

cedar n. evergreen tree; its hard fragrant wood. **cedarwood** n.

cede v.t. surrender (territory etc.).

cedilla n. mark written under c (ç) to show that it is pronounced as s.

ceilidh /'keɪlɪ/ n. (Sc. & Ir.) informal gathering for music and dancing.

ceiling n. interior surface of the top of a room; upper limit or level.

celandine /-daɪn/ n. small wild plant with yellow flowers.

celebrate v.t./i. mark or honour with festivities; engage in festivities; officiate at (a religious ceremony). **celebrant** n., **celebration** n.

celebrated a. famous.

celebrity n. famous person; fame.

celeriac /sɪˈlɛr-/ n. celery with a turnip-like root.

celerity /sɪˈlɛr-/ n. swiftness.

celery n. plant with edible crisp juicy stems.

celestial a. of the sky; of heaven.

celibate a. remaining unmarried, esp. for religious reasons. **celibacy** n.

cell n. small room for a monk or prisoner; compartment in a honeycomb; device for producing electric current chemically; microscopic unit of living matter; small group as a nucleus of political activities.

cellar n. underground room; stock of wine, place where this is stored.

cello /'tʃe-/ n. (pl. -os) bass instrument of the violin family. **cellist** n. its player.

Cellophane n. [P.] thin transparent wrapping material.

cellular a. of or consisting of cells; woven with open mesh; (of a radio-telephone) operating within linked small areas or 'cells' each with its own transmitter.

celluloid n. plastic made from cellulose nitrate and camphor.

cellulose n. organic substance in plant tissues, used in making plastics; paint made from this.

Celsius a. of a centigrade scale with 0° as the freezing-point and 100° as the boiling-point of water.

Celt /k-/ n. member of an ancient European people or their descendants. **Celtic** a.

cement n. substance of lime and clay setting like stone; similar material used as an adhesive; substance for filling cavities in teeth. —v.t. put cement on; join with cement; unite firmly.

cemetery n. burial ground other than a churchyard.

cenotaph n. tomb-like monument to persons buried elsewhere.

cense v.t. perfume with incense from a censer.

censer n. container for burning incense, swung on chains.

censor n. person authorized to examine letters, books, films, etc., and remove or ban anything regarded as harmful. —v.t. remove or ban thus. **censorial** a., **censorship** n.

censorious a. severely critical. **censoriously** adv., **censoriousness** n.

censure n. severe criticism and rebuke. —v.t. criticize and rebuke severely.

census n. official counting of population or traffic etc.

cent n. 100th part of a dollar or other currency; coin worth this.

centaur n. mythical creature half man, half horse.

centenarian /-'near-/ n. person 100 years old or more.

centenary /-'ti:n-/ n. 100th anniversary.

centennial /-'ten-/ a. of a centenary. —n. (US) centenary.

centigrade a. using a temperature scale of 100°; = Celsius.

centigram n. 100th of a gram.

centilitre n. 100th of a litre.

centimetre n. 100th of a metre.

centipede n. small segmented crawling creature with many legs.

central a. of, at, or forming a centre; most important. **central heating** heating of a building from one source. **centrally** adv., **centrality** n.

centralize v.t. bring under the control of a central authority. **centralization** n.

centre n. middle point or part; point or place where things are concentrated or from which they are dispersed; holders of moderate political views; centreforward. —a. at or of the centre. —v.t./i. (p.t. **centred**, pres.p. **centring**) place in or at a centre; concentrate at one point.

centrifugal /-'trɪf-or-'fu:-/a. moving away from the centre.

centrifuge n. machine using centrifugal force for separating substances. —v.t. separate by this.

centripetal /-'trɪp-or-'pe-/a. moving towards the centre.

centrist n. person or party holding moderate views. **centrism** n.

centurion n. commander of a company in the ancient Roman army.

century n. period of 100 years; 100 runs at cricket.

cephalic /-'fæ-/ a. of or in the head.

cephalopod n. mollusc with tentacles on its head (e.g. an octopus).

ceramic a. of pottery or a similar substance. **ceramics** n. art of making pottery.

cereal n. grass-plant with edible grain; this grain, breakfast food made from it.

cerebral a. of the brain; intellectual. **cerebrally** adv.

cerebration n. working of the brain. **cerebrate** v.i.

cerebrum n. main part of the brain.

ceremonial a. of or used in ceremonies, formal. —n. ceremony; rules for this. **ceremonially** adv.

ceremonious a. full of ceremony. **ceremoniously** adv.

ceremony n. set of formal acts.

cerise /sə'ri:z/ a. & n. light red.

certain a. feeling sure; believed firmly; able to be relied on to happen or be effective; specific but not named; some. **make certain** make sure.

certainly adv. without doubt; yes.

certainty n. being certain; thing that is certain.

certifiable a. able to be certified; (sl.) mad. **certifiably** adv.

certificate n. official document attesting certain facts. **certificated** a., **certification** n.

certify v.t. declare formally, show on a certificate or other document.

certitude n. feeling of certainty.

cerulean /-'ru:-/ a. sky-blue.

cervix n. neck; neck-like structure, esp. of the womb. **cervical** /'sɜ:vɪk(ə)l or-'vaɪ-/ a.

cessation n. ceasing.

cession n. ceding.

cesspit, cesspool ns. covered pit to receive liquid waste or sewage.

cetacean /sɪ'teɪʃ(ə)n/ a. & n. (member) of the whale family.

cf. abbr. compare.

CFC abbr. chlorofluorocarbon, (usu. gaseous) compound thought to harm the earth's atmosphere.

chafe v.t./i. warm by rubbing; make or become sore by rubbing; become irritated or impatient.

chafer n. large beetle.

chaff n. corn-husks separated from seed; chopped hay and straw; banter. —v.t./i. banter, tease.

chaffer v.i. bargain, haggle.

chaffinch n. European finch.

chafing-dish n. heated pan for cooking or keeping food warm at the table.

chagrin /'ʃægrɪn/ n. annoyance and embarrassment or disappointment. **chagrined** a.

chain n. series of connected metal links; connected series or sequence; measure of length (22 yds.). —v.t. fasten with chain(s).

chain reaction change causing further changes. **chain-smoke** v.t./i. smoke continuously. **chain-smoker** n. person who chain-smokes. **chain store** any of a set of similar shops owned by one firm.

chair n. movable seat, with a back, for one person; (position of) chairman; position of a professor. —v.t. seat in the chair of honour; carry in triumph on the shoulders of a group; act as chairman of. **chair-lift** n. series of chairs on a cable for carrying people up a mountain.

chairman n. (pl. -men) person who presides over a meeting or committee. **chairwoman** n.fem. (pl. -women), **chairperson** n.

chaise longue /ʃeɪz 'lɒŋ/ chair with a very long seat to support a sitter's legs.

chalcedony n. type of quartz.

chalet /'ʃæleɪ/ n. Swiss hut or cottage; small villa; small hut in a holiday camp etc.

chalice n. large goblet.

chalk n. white soft limestone; piece of this or similar coloured substance used for drawing. —v.t. rub, mark, or draw with chalk. **chalk-striped** a. patterned with thin white stripes. **chalky** a.

challenge n. call to try one's skill or strength; demand to respond or identify oneself; formal objection; demanding task. —v.t. make a challenge to; question the truth or rightness of. **challenger** n.

chamber n. hall used for meetings of an assembly, the assembly itself; (old use) room, bedroom; (pl.) set of rooms; chamber-pot; cavity or compartment. **chamber music** music for performance in a room rather than a hall. **chamber-pot** n. bedroom receptacle for urine.

chamberlain n. official managing a sovereign's or noble's household.

chambermaid n. woman cleaner of hotel bedrooms.

chameleon /kə'mi:ljən/ n. small lizard that changes colour according to its surroundings.

chamfer v.t. (p.t. **chamfered**) bevel the edge of.

chamois /'ʃæmwɑ:/ n. small mountain antelope; /'ʃæmɪ/ a kind of soft leather, a piece of this.

champ v.t./i. munch noisily, make a chewing action; show impatience.

champagne *n.* sparkling white wine; its pale straw colour.

champion *n.* person or thing that defeats all others in a competition; person who fights or speaks in support of another or of a cause. —*a. & adv.* (*colloq.* or *dial.*) splendid, splendidly. —*v.t.* support as champion. **championship** *n.*

chance *n.* way things happen through no known cause or agency, luck; likelihood; opportunity. —*a.* happening by chance. —*v.t./i.* happen; risk.

chancel *n.* part of a church near the altar.

chancellery *n.* chancellor's office; office attached to an embassy.

chancellor *n.* State or law official of various kinds; non-resident head of a university. **chancellorship** *n.*

Chancery *n.* division of the High Court of Justice.

chancy *a.* (**-ier, -iest**) risky, uncertain. **chanciness** *n.*

chandelier /ʃændəˈlɪə(r)/ *n.* hanging support for several lights.

chandler *n.* dealer in ropes, canvas, etc., for ships.

change *v.t./i.* make or become different; interchange, exchange, substitute; put fresh clothes or coverings etc. on; go from one of two (sides, trains, etc.) to another; get or give small money or different currency for. —*n.* changing; money in small units or returned as balance of that offered in payment; menopause. **changeable** *a.*, **changer** *n.*

changeling *n.* child or thing believed to have been substituted secretly for another.

channel *n.* sunken bed of a stream; stretch of water connecting two seas; course in which anything moves; passage for liquid; medium of communication; band of broadcasting frequencies. —*v.t.* (*p.t.* **channelled**) form

channel(s) in; direct through a channel.

chant *n.* melody for psalms; monotonous singing; rhythmic shout. —*v.t./i.* sing, esp. to a chant; shout rhythmically.

chanter *n.* melody-pipe of bagpipes.

chantry *n.* chapel founded for priests to sing masses for the founder's soul.

chaos *n.* great disorder. **chaotic** *a.*, **chaotically** *adv.*

chap¹ *n.* (*colloq.*) man.

chap² *n.* crack in skin. —*v.t./i.* (*p.t.* **chapped**) cause chaps in; suffer chaps.

chap³ *n.* lower jaw or half of cheek, esp. of a pig, as food.

chaparral /ˈræl/ *n.* (*US*) dense tangled brushwood.

chapatti *n.* (*pl.* -is) small flat cake of unleavened bread.

chapel *n.* place used for Christian worship, other than a cathedral or parish church; religious service in this; place with a separate altar within a church; section of a trade union in a printing works.

chaperon /ˈʃæp/ *n.* older woman in charge of a young unmarried woman on social occasions. —*v.t.* act as chaperon to. **chaperonage** *n.*

chaplain *n.* clergyman of an institution, private chapel, ship, regiment, etc. **chaplaincy** *n.*

chaplet *n.* wreath or circlet for the head; short rosary.

chapter *n.* division of a book; canons of a cathedral; members of a monastic order. **chapter house** building used for meetings of a cathedral chapter.

char¹ *n.* charwoman. —*v.i.* (*p.t.* **charred**) work as a charwoman.

char² *v.t./i.* (*p.t.* **charred**) make or become black by burning.

charabanc /ˈʃæ/ *n.* early form of motor bus used for outings.

character *n.* qualities making a person or thing what he or it is;

moral strength; noticeable or ec-centric person; person in a novel or play etc.; reputation; testi-monial; biological characteristic; letter or sign used in writing, printing, etc.

characteristic a. & n. (feature) forming part of the character of a person or thing. **characteristically** adv.

characterize v.t. describe the character of; be a characteristic of. **characterization** n.

charade /ʃəˈrɑːd/ n. scene acted as a clue to a word in the game of charades; absurd pretence.

charcoal n. black substance made by burning wood slowly in an oven.

charge n. price asked for goods or services; appropriate quantity of material put into a receptacle etc. at one time, esp. of an explosive; electricity contained in a sub-stance; task, duty; custody; per-son or thing entrusted; formal in-structions about one's responsi-bility; accusation; rushing at-tack; heraldic device. —v.t./i. ask as a price or from (a person); re-cord as a debt; load or fill with a charge of explosive etc.; give an electric charge to, store energy in (a battery etc.); give as a task or duty, entrust; accuse formally; rush forward in attack. **in charge** in command. **take charge** take control.

chargeable a. able to be charged.

chargé d'affaires /ʃɑːʒeɪ dæˈfeə(r)/ (pl. **-gés**, pr. **-ʒeɪ**-) ambassa-dor's deputy; envoy to a minor country.

chariot n. two-wheeled horse-drawn vehicle used in ancient times in battle and in racing.

charioteer n. driver of a chariot.

charisma /kəˈrɪzmə/ n. power to inspire devotion and enthusiasm.

charismatic /kærɪzˈmæ-/ a. hav-ing charisma; (of worship) char-acterized by spontaneity and re-ligious ecstasy. **charismatically** adv.

charitable a. full of charity; of or belonging to charities. **charit-ably** adv., **charitableness** n.

charity n. loving kindness; un-willingness to think badly of others; institution or fund for helping the needy, help so given.

charlady n. charwoman.

charlatan /ˈʃɑːlət(ə)n/ n. person falsely claiming to be an expert, esp. in medicine.

charlotte n. pudding of cooked fruit with a covering of bread-crumbs.

charm n. attractiveness, power of arousing love or admiration; act, object, or words believed to have magic power; small ornament worn on a bracelet etc. —v.t. give pleasure to; influence by per-sonal charm; influence as if by magic. **charmer** n.

charming a. delightful.

charnel-house n. place contain-ing corpses or bones.

chart n. map for navigators; table, diagram, or outline map showing special information; list of re-cordings that are currently most popular. —v.t. make a chart of.

charter n. official document granting rights or defining the form of an institution; chartering of aircraft etc. —v.t. grant a charter to; let or hire (an aircraft, ship, or vehicle). **chartered accountant** etc., one qualified according to the rules of an asso-ciation holding a royal charter. **charter flight** flight by a char-tered aircraft.

chartreuse /ʃɑːˈtrɜːz/ n. fragrant green or yellow liqueur.

charwoman n. (pl. **-women**) wo-man employed to clean a house etc.

chary /ˈtʃeərɪ/ a. (**-ier, -iest**) cau-tious. **charily** adv., **chariness** n.

chase[1] v.t./i. go quickly after in order to capture, overtake, or drive away; hurry; (colloq.) try to obtain. —n. chasing, pursuit; hunting; steeplechase; unenclosed hunting-land.

chase[2] v.t. engrave, emboss.

chaser n. horse for steeplechasing; (colloq.) drink taken after another of a different kind.

chasm n. deep cleft.

chassis /ˈʃæsɪ/ n. (pl. chassis, pr. -siːz) base-frame, frame of a vehicle.

chaste a. virgin, celibate; not sexually immoral; simple in style, not ornate. **chastely** adv.

chasten v.t. discipline by punishment; subdue the pride of.

chastise v.t. punish, esp. by beating. **chastisement** n.

chastity n. being chaste.

chasuble n. loose garment worn over other vestments by a priest celebrating the Eucharist.

chat n. informal conversation. —v.i. (p.t. chatted) have a chat.

château /ˈʃætəʊ/ n. (pl. -eaux, pr. -əʊz) French castle or large country house.

chatelaine /ˈʃætəleɪn/ n. mistress of a large house.

chattel n. movable possession.

chatter v.i. talk quickly and continuously about unimportant matters; (of teeth) rattle together. —n. chattering talk. **chatterer** n.

chatterbox n. talkative person.

chatty a. (-ier, -iest) fond of chatting; resembling chat. **chattily** adv., **chattiness** n.

chauffeur n. person employed to drive a car. **chauffeuse** n.fem.

chauvinism /ˈʃəʊvɪn-/ n. exaggerated patriotism. **male chauvinism** some men's prejudiced belief in their superiority over women. **chauvinist** n., **chauvinistic** a.

cheap a. (-er, -est) low in cost or value; poor in quality. —adv. cheaply. **cheaply** adv., **cheapness** n.

cheapen v.t./i. make or become cheap; degrade.

cheapjack a. of poor quality, shoddy.

cheat v.t./i. act dishonestly or unfairly to win profit or advantage; trick, deprive by deceit. —n. person who cheats; deception.

check[1] v.t./i. stop, slow the mo... tion (of); test or examine for correctness etc.; (US) correspond when compared. —n. process or means of checking; pause; restraint; exposure of a chess king to capture; receipt; bill in a restaurant; (US) cheque. **check in** register on arrival. **check out** register on departure or dispatch (US) test for correctness etc.

check-out n. desk where goods are paid for in a supermarket. **checker** n.

check[2] n. pattern of squares or crossing lines. **checked** a.

checkmate n. situation in chess where capture of a king is inevitable; complete defeat, deadlock. —v.t. put into checkmate; defeat, foil.

Cheddar n. firm cheese of a kind orig. made at Cheddar in England.

cheek n. side of the face below the eye; impudent speech, quiet arrogance. —v.t. speak cheekily to. **cheek by jowl** close together.

cheeky a. (-ier, -iest) showing bold or cheerful lack of respect, coquettish. **cheekily** adv. **cheekiness** n.

cheep n. weak shrill cry like that of a young bird. —v.i. make this cry.

cheer n. shout of applause; cheerfulness. —v.t./i. utter a cheer, applaud with a cheer; gladden. **cheer up** make or become more cheerful.

cheerful a. happy, contented, pleasantly bright. **cheerfully** adv., **cheerfulness** n.

cheerio int. (colloq.) goodbye.

cheerless a. gloomy, dreary.

cheery a. (-ier, -iest) cheerful. **cheerily** adv., **cheeriness** n.

cheese *n.* food made from pressed milk curds; shaped mass of this. **cheesed off** (*sl.*) bored, fed up. **cheese-paring** *a.* stingy, (*n.*) stinginess. **cheesy** *a.*

cheeseburger *n.* hamburger with cheese in or on it.

cheesecake *n.* open tart filled with sweetened curds; (*sl.*) display of a woman's shapely body in an advertisement etc.

cheesecloth *n.* thin loosely-woven cotton fabric.

cheetah *n.* a kind of leopard.

chef *n.* professional cook.

chef-d'œuvre /ʃeɪˈdɜːvr/ *n.* (*pl.* **chefs-d'œuvre**) masterpiece.

chemical *a.* of or made by chemistry. —*n.* substance obtained by or used in a chemical process. **chemically** *adv.*

chemise /ʃəˈmiːz/ *n.* woman's loose-fitting undergarment or dress.

chemist *n.* person skilled in chemistry; dealer in medicinal drugs.

chemistry *n.* study of substances and their reactions; structure and properties of a substance.

chemotherapy *n.* treatment of disease by drugs etc.

chenille /ʃəˈniːl/ *n.* fabric with velvety pile, used for furnishings.

cheque *n.* written order to a bank to pay out money from an account; printed form for this. **cheque card** guaranteeing payment of a bank customer's cheques.

chequer *n.* pattern of squares, esp. of alternating colours.

chequered *a.* marked with a chequer pattern; having frequent changes of fortune.

cherish *v.t.* take loving care of; be fond of; cling to (hopes etc.).

cheroot /ʃəˈruːt/ *n.* cigar with both ends open.

cherry *n.* small soft round fruit with a stone; tree bearing this or grown for its ornamental flowers; deep red. —*a.* deep red.

cherub *n.* angelic being (*pl.* **cherubim**); (in art) representation of a chubby infant with wings; angelic child. **cherubic** /-ˈruː-/ *a.*

chervil *n.* herb with aniseed flavour.

chess *n.* game for two players using 32 **chess-men** on a chequered board (**chess-board**) with 64 squares.

chest *n.* large strong box for storing or shipping things in; upper front surface of the body, part containing the heart and lungs. **chest of drawers** piece of furniture with drawers for clothes etc.

chesterfield *n.* sofa with a padded back, seat, and ends.

chestnut *n.* tree with a hard brown nut; this nut; reddish-brown, horse of this colour; old joke or anecdote. —*a.* reddish-brown.

cheval-glass /ʃə'væl-/ *n.* tall mirror swung on an upright frame.

chevron /'ʃev-/ *n.* V-shaped symbol.

chew *v.t./i.* work or grind between the teeth; make this movement. **chewing-gum** *n.* flavoured gum used for prolonged chewing. **chewy** *a.* (-ier, -iest) suitable for chewing. **chewiness** *n.*

Chianti /kɪ-/ *n.* dry usu. red Italian wine.

chiaroscuro /kɪɑːrəˈskʊərəʊ/ *n.* light and shade effects; use of contrast.

chic /ʃiːk/ *a.* (-er, -est) stylish and elegant. —*n.* stylishness, elegance.

chicane /ʃɪˈkeɪn/ *n.* chicanery; artificial barrier or obstacle on a motor-racing course. —*v.t./i.* use chicanery, cheat.

chicanery /ʃɪˈkeɪnərɪ/ *n.* trickery.

chick *n.* young bird before or after hatching.

chicken *n.* young domestic fowl; its flesh as food; (*sl.*) game testing courage. —*a.* (*sl.*) cowardly. —*v.i.* **chicken out** (*sl.*) withdraw through cowardice. **chicken-feed** n. (colloq.) insignificant amount of money. **chicken-pox** n. disease with a rash of small red blisters.

chickweed n. weed with small white flowers.

chicory n. blue-flowered plant used for salad; its root, roasted and ground for use with coffee.

chide v.t./i. (p.t. chided or chid, p.p. chidden) (old use) rebuke.

chief n. leader, ruler; person with the highest rank etc. —a. highest in rank etc.; most important.

chiefly adv. mainly.

chieftain n. chief of a clan or tribe.

chiffon /'ʃɪ-/ n. thin almost transparent fabric.

chignon /'ʃiːnjɔ̃/ n. coil of hair worn at the back of the head.

chihuahua /tʃɪˈwaːwə/ n. very small smooth-haired dog.

chilblain n. painful swelling caused by exposure to cold.

child n. (pl. children) young human being; son or daughter. **child's play** very easy task.

childhood n.

childbirth n. process of giving birth to a child.

childish a. like a child, unsuitable for a grown person.

childless a. having no children.

childlike a. simple and innocent.

chill n. unpleasant coldness; illness with feverish shivering. —a. chilly. —v.t./i. make or become chilly; preserve at a low temperature without freezing.

chilli n. (pl. -ies) dried pod of red pepper.

chilly a. (-ier, -iest) rather cold, unpleasantly cold; cold and unfriendly in manner. **chilliness** n.

chime n. tuned set of bells; series of notes from these. —v.t./i. ring as a chime; show (the hour) by chiming. **chime in** be in agreement; put in a remark.

chimera /kɪˈmɪərə/ n. legendary monster with a lion's head, goat's body, and serpent's tail; hybrid thing.

chimney n. (pl. -eys) structure for carrying off smoke or gases

chimney-pot n. pipe at the top of a chimney. **chimney-sweep** n. person whose trade is to remove soot from inside chimneys.

chimp n. (colloq.) chimpanzee.

chimpanzee n. African ape.

chin n. front of the lower jaw.

chin-wag n. & v.i. (colloq.) chat.

china n. fine earthenware, porcelain; things made of this.

chinchilla n. small squirrel-like South American animal; its grey fur.

chine n. animal's backbone; ravine in southern England. —v.t. cut or slit (meat) along the chine.

Chinese a. & n. (native, language) of China.

chink[1] n. narrow opening, slit.

chink[2] n. sound like glasses or coins striking together. —v.t./i. make or cause to make this sound.

chintz n. cotton usu. glazed cloth used for furnishings.

chip n. small piece cut or broken off something hard; microchip; fried oblong strip of potato; basket made of thin strips of wood; counter used in a gambling game. —v.t./i. (p.t. chipped) break or cut the edge or surface of; shape thus; make (potato) into chips; (colloq.) tease. **chip in** (colloq.) interrupt; contribute money. **chip on one's shoulder** feeling of resentment.

chipboard n. board made of compressed wood chips.

chipmunk n. striped squirrel-like animal of North America.

chipolata /-'laː-/ n. small thin sausage.

chiropody /kɪ-/ n. treatment of minor ailments of the feet. **chiropodist** n.

chiropractic /kaɪər-/ n. treatment of physical disorders by manipulation of the spinal column. **chiropractor** n.

chirp n. short sharp sound made by a small bird or grasshopper. —v.i. make this sound.

chirpy a. (-ier, -iest) lively and cheerful. **chirpily** adv., **chirpiness** n.

chisel n. tool with a sharp bevelled end for shaping wood or stone etc. —v.t. (p.t. **chiselled**) cut with this.

chit[1] n. young child; small young woman.

chit[2] n. short written note.

chit-chat n. chat, gossip.

chitterlings n.pl. pig's small intestines, cooked as food.

chivalry n. courtesy and considerate behaviour, inclination to help weaker persons. **chivalrous** a.

chive n. small herb with onion-flavoured leaves.

chivvy v.t. (colloq.) urge to hurry.

chloride n. compound of chlorine and another element.

chlorinate v.t. treat or sterilize with chlorine. **chlorination** n.

chlorine n. chemical element, heavy yellowish-green gas.

chloroform /'klɔ-/ n. liquid giving off vapour that causes unconsciousness when inhaled. —v.t. make unconscious with this.

chlorophyll /'klɒ-/ n. green colouring-matter in plants.

choc n. (colloq.) chocolate. **choc-ice** n. bar of ice-cream coated with chocolate.

chock n. block or wedge for preventing something from moving. —v.t. wedge with chock(s). **chock-a-block** a. & adv. crammed, crowded together. **chock-full** a. crammed full.

chocolate n. edible substance from cacao seeds; drink made with this, sweet made of

or coated with this; dark brown colour.

choice n. choosing, right of choosing; variety from which to choose; person or thing chosen. —a. of especially good quality. **choicely** adv., **choiceness** n.

choir n. organized band of singers, esp. in church; part of a church where these sit, chancel.

choirboy n. boy singer in a church choir.

choke v.t./i. stop (a person) breathing, esp. by squeezing or blocking the windpipe; be unable to breathe; clog, smother. —n. valve controlling the flow of air into a petrol engine. **choke off** (colloq.) silence, discourage, esp. by a snub.

choker n. high stiff collar; close-fitting necklace.

choler /'kɒl-/ n. (old use) anger.

cholera n. serious often fatal disease caused by bacteria.

choleric /'kɒl-/ a. easily angered. **cholerically** adv.

cholesterol /kə'les-/ n. fatty animal substance thought to cause hardening of arteries.

choose v.t./i. (p.t. **chose**, p.p. **chosen**) select out of a greater number of things; decide, prefer. **chooser** n.

choosy a. (-ier, -iest) (colloq.) careful in choosing, hard to please. **choosiness** n.

chop[1] v.t./i. (p.t. **chopped**) cut by a blow with an axe or knife; hit with a short downward movement. —n. chopping stroke; thick slice of meat, usu. including a rib.

chop[2] n. = chap[3].

chopper n. chopping tool; (sl.) helicopter.

choppy a. (-ier, -iest) full of short broken waves; jerky. **choppily** adv., **choppiness** n.

chopstick n. each of a pair of sticks used in China to lift food to the mouth.

chopsuey n. Chinese dish of meat or fish fried with vegetables.

choral a. of or for or sung etc. by a chorus. **chorally** adv.

chorale /kɒˈrɑːl/ n. choral composition using the words of a hymn.

chord[1] n. string of a harp etc.; straight line joining two points on a curve.

chord[2] n. combination of notes sounded together.

chore /tʃɔː(r)/ n. routine task.

choreography /kɒrɪ-/ n. composition of stage dances. **choreographer** n, **choreographic** a.

chorister /ˈkɒr-/ n. member of a choir.

chortle n. loud chuckle. —v.i. utter a chortle.

chorus n. group of singers; thing spoken or sung by many together; refrain of a song; group of singing dancers in a musical comedy etc. —v.t./i. speak or sing as a group. **in chorus** speaking or singing together.

chose, chosen see **choose**.

chough /tʃʌf/ n. red-legged crow.

choux pastry /ʃuː/ light pastry for making small cakes.

chow n. long-haired dog of a Chinese breed; (sl.) food.

chowder n. stew of fish with bacon and onions etc.

chow mein /mein/ Chinese dish of fried noodles and shredded meat etc.

christen v.t. admit to the Christian Church by baptism; name.

Christendom n. all Christians or Christian countries.

christening n. baptism.

Christian a. of or believing in Christianity; kindly, humane. —n. believer in Christianity. **Christian name** personal name given at a christening. **Christian Science** religious system by which health and healing are sought by Christian faith, without medical treatment.

Christianity n. religion based on the teachings of Christ.

Christianize v.t. make Christian.

Christmas n. festival (25 Dec. commemorating Christ's birth.

Christmas-box n. Christmas present. **Christmas Day** 25 Dec. **Christmas Eve** 24 Dec. **Christmas tree** evergreen or artificial tree decorated at Christmas. **Christmassy** a.

chromatic a. of colour, in colours. **chromatic scale** music scale proceeding by semitones. **chromatically** adv.

chromatography n. separation of substances by slow passage through or over an absorbing material. **chromatograph** n.

chrome n. chromium; yellow pigment from a compound of this.

chromium n. metallic element that does not rust.

chromosome /ˈkrəʊ-/ n. threadlike structure carrying genes in animal and plant cells.

chronic a. constantly present or recurring; having a chronic disease or habit; (colloq.) bad. **chronically** adv.

chronicle n. record of events in order of their occurrence. —v.t. record in a chronicle. **chronicler** n.

chronological a. arranged in the order in which things occurred. **chronologically** adv.

chronology n. arrangement of events in order of occurrence.

chronometer n. time-measuring instrument, esp. one unaffected by temperature changes.

chrysalis n. form of an insect in the stage between grub and adult insect; case enclosing it.

chrysanthemum n. garden plant flowering in autumn.

chub n. (pl. **chub**) river fish with a thick body.

chubby a. (-ier, -iest) round and plump. **chubbiness** n.

chuck[1] v.t. (colloq.) throw carelessly or casually; touch playfully under the chin. **chuck out** (colloq.) expel.

chuck ^{2} *n.* part of a lathe holding the drill; part of a drill holding the bit; cut of beef from neck to ribs.

chuckle *n.* quiet laugh. —*v.i.* utter a chuckle.

chuffed *a.* (*sl.*) pleased.

chug *v.i.* (*p.t.* chugged) make or move with a dull short repeated sound. —*n.* this sound.

chukker *n.* period of play in a polo game.

chum *n.* (*colloq.*) close friend. —*v.i.* (*p.t.* chummed) chum up form a close friendship. **chummy** *a.* & *n.*

chump *n.* (*sl.*) head; foolish person. **chump chop** chop from the thick end of a loin of mutton.

chunk *n.* thick piece; substantial amount.

chunky *a.* (-ier, -iest) short and thick; in chunks, containing chunks. **chunkiness** *n.*

chupatty *n.* = chapatti.

church *n.* building for public Christian worship; religious service in this; **Church** Christians collectively; particular group of these; clergy, clerical profession. —*v.t.* perform the church service of thanksgiving for (a woman after childbirth). **churchgoer** *n.*

churchwarden *n.* representative of a parish, assisting with church business.

churchyard *n.* enclosed land round a church, often used for burials.

churlish *a.* ill-mannered, surly. **churlishly** *adv.*, **churlishness** *n.*

churn *n.* machine in which milk is beaten to make butter; very large milk-can. —*v.t./i.* beat (milk) or make (butter) in a churn; stir or swirl violently. **churn out** produce.

chute *n.* sloping channel down which things can be slid or dropped.

chutney *n.* (*pl.* -eys) seasoned mixture of fruit, vinegar, spices, etc., eaten with meat or cheese.

ciao /tʃaʊ/ *int.* (*colloq.*) goodbye; hallo.

cicada /sɪˈkɑːdə/ *n.* chirping insect resembling a grasshopper.

cicatrice /ˈsɪk-/ *n.* scar.

CID *abbr.* Criminal Investigation Department.

cider *n.* fermented drink made from apples.

cigar *n.* roll of tobacco-leaf for smoking.

cigarette *n.* roll of shredded tobacco in thin paper for smoking.

cinch /sɪntʃ/ *n.* (*US sl.*) certainty, easy task.

cincture /ˈsɪŋk-/ *n.* girdle, belt; border.

cinder *n.* piece of partly burnt coal or wood.

cine-camera /ˈsɪnɪ-/ *n.* cinematographic camera.

cinema *n.* theatre where films are shown; films as an art form or industry.

cinematography *n.* process of making and projecting moving pictures. **cinematographic** *a.*

cineraria /-ˈreər-/ *n.* plant with downy leaves.

cinerary urn urn for holding ashes after cremation.

cinnamon *n.* spice made from the bark of a south-east Asian tree.

cinquefoil /ˈsɪŋk-/ *n.* plant with a compound flower of five leaflets.

cipher *n.* symbol for nought or zero; any Arabic numeral; person or thing of no importance; system of letters or numbers used to represent others for secrecy.

circa /ˈsɜːkə/ *prep.* about.

circle *n.* perfectly round plane figure, line, or shape; curved tier of seats at a theatre etc.; group with similar interests. —*v.t./i.* move in a circle; form a circle round.

circlet *n.* small circle; circular band worn as an ornament.

circuit /'sɜːkɪt/ n. line, route, or distance round a place; judge's journey through a district to hold courts, this district; path of an electric current; apparatus through which a current passes.

circuitous /sə'kjuːɪtəs/ a. roundabout, indirect. **circuitously** adv.

circuitry /'sɜːkɪtrɪ/ n. circuits.

circular a. shaped like or moving round a circle. —n. letter or leaflet etc. sent to a great no. of people. **circularity** n.

circularize v.t. send circular(s) to. **circularization** n.

circulate v.t./i. go or send round.

circulation n. circulating; movement of blood round the body; number of copies sold, esp. of a newspaper. **circulatory** a.

circumcise v.t. cut off the foreskin of. **circumcision** n.

circumference n. boundary of a circle, distance round this.

circumflex accent the accent ˆ.

circumlocution n. roundabout, verbose, or evasive expression. **circumlocutory** /-'lɒk-/ a.

circumnavigate v.t. sail completely round. **circumnavigation** n., **circumnavigator** n.

circumscribe v.t. draw a line round; restrict. **circumscription** n.

circumspect a. cautious and watchful, wary. **circumspection** n., **circumspectly** adv.

circumstance n. occurrence or fact connected with an event or person.

circumstantial a. detailed; consisting of facts that strongly suggest something but do not prove it. **circumstantially** adv.

circumvent v.t. evade (a difficulty etc.). **circumvention** n.

circus n. travelling show with performing animals, acrobats, etc.; group performing in a series of sports matches etc.

cirrhosis /sɪ'rəʊsɪs/ n. disease of the liver.

cirrus n. (pl. **cirri**) high wisp white cloud.

Cistercian a. & n. (monk or nun of a very strict Benedictine order

cistern n. tank for storing water

citadel n. fortress overlooking city.

cite v.t. quote or mention as an example etc. **citation** n.

citizen n. inhabitant of a city; person with full rights in a country or Commonwealth. **citizens band** system of local intercom munication by radio **citizenship** n.

citric acid acid in the juice o lemons, limes, etc.

citrus n. tree of a group including lemon, orange, etc.

city n. important town; town with special rights given by charter **the City** oldest part of London now a centre of finance.

civet /'sɪvɪt/ n. cat-like animal o central Africa; musky substance obtained from its glands.

civic a. of a city or citizenship.

civics n. study of municipa government and of citizens rights and duties.

civil a. of citizens; not of the armed forces or the Church; po lite and obliging. **civil engineer ing** designing and constructio of roads, bridges, etc. **civil list** annual allowance for the sover eign's household expenses. **civil servant** employee of the civil **service**, government depart ments other than the armed forces. **civil war** war between citizens of the same country **civilly** adv.

civilian n. person not in the armed forces. —a. of or for civi lians.

civility n. politeness.

civilization n. making or be coming civilized; stage in the evolution of society; civilized conditions.

civilize v.t. cause to improve from a primitive to a developed stage of society; improve the behaviour of.

civvies *n.pl.* (*sl.*) civilian clothes.

cl *abbr.* centilitre(s).

clack *n.* short sharp sound; noise of chatter. —*v.i.* make this sound.

clad *see* **clothe**.

cladding *n.* boards or metal plates applied as a protective covering.

claim *v.t.* demand as one's right; assert. —*n.* demand; assertion; right or title.

claimant *n.* person making a claim.

clairvoyance *n.* power of seeing in the mind events etc. that are in the future or out of sight. **clairvoyant** *n.* person thought to have this.

clam *n.* shellfish with a hinged shell. —*v.i.* (*p.t.* **clammed**) **clam up** (*US sl.*) refuse to talk.

clamber *v.i.* climb with difficulty.

clammy *a.* (-ier, -iest) unpleasantly moist and sticky. **clammily** *adv.*, **clamminess** *n.*

clamour *n.* loud confused noise; loud protest etc. **clamorous** *a.*

clamp[1] *n.* device for holding things tightly; device for immobilizing an illegally parked car. —*v.t.* grip with a clamp, fix firmly. **clamp down on** become firmer about, put a stop to.

clamp[2] *n.* pile of bricks for burning; pile of potatoes etc. stored under straw and earth.

clan *n.* group of families with a common ancestor; large family forming a close group.

clandestine /-'destin/ *a.* kept secret, done secretly. **clandestinely** *adv.*

clang *n.* loud ringing sound. —*v.i.* make this sound.

clanger *n.* (*sl.*) blunder.

clangour *n.* clanging noise. **clangorous** *a.*

clank *n.* sound like metal striking metal. —*v.t./i.* make or cause to make this sound.

clannish *a.* united in a close group. **clannishness** *n.*

clap *v.t./i.* (*p.t.* **clapped**) strike palms loudly together, esp. in applause; strike or put quickly or vigorously. —*n.* act or sound of clapping; sharp noise of thunder. **clapped out** (*sl.*) worn out.

clapper *n.* tongue or striker of a bell.

clapperboard *n.* device in filmmaking for making a sharp clap for synchronizing picture and sound.

claptrap *n.* insincere talk.

claret *n.* a dry red wine.

clarify *v.t./i.* make or become clear. **clarification** *n.*

clarinet *n.* wood-wind instrument with finger-holes and keys. **clarinettist** *n.* its player.

clarion *a.* loud, rousing.

clarity *n.* clearness.

clash *n.* loud harsh sound as of cymbals; conflict; discordant effect of colours. —*v.t./i.* make or cause to make a clash; conflict.

clasp *n.* device for fastening things, with interlocking parts; grasp, hand-shake. —*v.t./i.* fasten, join with a clasp; grasp, embrace closely. **clasp-knife** *n.* folding knife with a catch for fixing it open. **clasper** *n.*

class *n.* set of people or things with characteristics in common; standard of quality; rank of society; set of students taught together. —*v.t.* place in a class.

classic *a.* of recognized high quality; typical; simple in style. —*n.* classic author or work etc.; (*pl.*) study of ancient Greek and Roman literature, history, etc. **classicism** *n.*, **classicist** *n.*

classical *a.* a classic; of the ancient Greeks and Romans; traditional and standard. **classically** *adv.*

classifiable *a.* able to be classified.

classify *v.t.* arrange systematically, class; designate as officially secret. **classification** *n.*

classless a. without distinctions of social class. **classlessness** n.

classroom n. room where a class of students is taught.

classy a. (sl.) of high quality.

clatter n. rattling sound. —v.t./i. make or cause to make this sound.

clause n. single part in a treaty, law, or contract; distinct part of a sentence, with its own verb.

claustrophobia n. abnormal fear of being in an enclosed space.

claustrophobic a. causing or suffering from claustrophobia.

clavichord n. early small keyboard instrument.

clavicle n. collar-bone.

claw n. pointed nail on an animal's or bird's foot; claw-like device for grappling or holding things. —v.t. scratch or pull with a claw or hand.

clay n. stiff sticky earth, used for making bricks and pottery. **clay pigeon** breakable disc thrown up as a target for shooting. **clayey** a.

claymore n. Scottish two-edged broadsword; broadsword with a basket-like structure over the hilt.

clean a. (-er, -est) free from dirt or impurities; not soiled or used; without projections; free from indecency; complete. —adv. completely. —v.t. make clean; dryclean; gut (fish etc.). **cleaner** n.

cleanly[1] /'kli:-/ adv. in a clean way.

cleanly[2] /'kle-/ a. attentive to cleanliness. **cleanliness** n.

cleanse /klenz/ v.t. clean. **cleanser** n.

clear a. (-er, -est) transparent; free from doubt, difficulties, obstacles, etc.; easily seen or heard or understood; complete; net. —adv. completely; apart. —v.t./i. make or become clear; prove innocent; get past or over; make as net profit. **clear off** get rid of; (colloq.) go away. **clear out**

empty; remove; (colloq.) go away.

clearly adv., **clearness** n.

clearance n. clearing; permission; space allowed for one object to pass or move within another.

clearing n. space cleared of trees in a forest.

clearway n. road where vehicles must not stop on the carriageway.

cleat n. projecting piece to provide a footing or for fastening ropes to; wedge.

cleavage n. split, separation; hollow between full breasts.

cleave[1] v.t./i. (p.t. cleaved, clove, or cleft) (p.p. cloven or cleft) split.

cleave[2] v. (old use) stick, cling.

cleaver n. butcher's chopper.

clef n. symbol on a stave in music, showing the pitch of notes.

cleft see **cleave**[1]. —n. split, cleavage. **in a cleft stick** unable to evade difficulties.

clematis /'klemə- or klɪr'mer-/ n. climbing plant with showy flowers.

clemency n. mildness, esp. of weather; mercy. **clement** a.

clementine n. a kind of small orange.

clench v.t. close (teeth or fingers) tightly; grasp firmly; clinch (a nail etc.). —n. clenching, clenched state.

clerestory /'klɪəstərɪ/ n. upper row of windows in a large church.

clergy n. persons ordained to religious duties. **clergyman** n. (pl. -men).

cleric /'klerɪk/ n. member of the clergy.

clerical a. of clerks; of the clergy.

clerihew n. witty verse in four lines of unequal length.

clerk /klɑːk/ n. person employed to do written work in an office.

clever a. (-er, -est) quick at learning and understanding things;

showing skill. **cleverly** adv., **cleverness** n.

clew n. lower corner of a sail.

cliché /'kliːʃeɪ/ n. hackneyed phrase or idea.

click n. short sharp sound. —v.t./i. make or cause to make a click; (sl.) be a success, be understood.

client n. person using the services of a professional person; customer.

clientele /kliːɒn'tel/ n. clients.

cliff n. steep rock-face, esp. on a coast. **cliff-hanger** n. story or contest full of suspense.

climacteric /klaɪ'mæktərɪk/ n. period of life when physical powers begin to decline.

climate n. regular weather conditions of an area.

climax n. point of greatest interest or intensity —v.i. reach a climax. **climactic** a.

climb v.t./i. go up or over. —n. ascent made by climbing. **climber** n.

clime n. climate, region.

clinch v.t./i. fasten securely; secure (a nail etc.) by driving the point sideways when through; settle conclusively; (of boxers) be too close together for strong blows. —n. clinching. **clincher** n.

cling v.i. (p.t. **clung**) hold on tightly; stick. **cling film** n. thin polythene wrapping.

clinic n. place or session at which medical treatment is given to visiting persons; private or specialized hospital.

clinical a. of or used in treatment of patients. **clinically** adv.

clink n. thin sharp sound. —v.t./i. make or cause to make this sound.

clinker n. fused ash of coal etc., piece of this.

clinker-built a. (of a boat) made with planks overlapping downwards.

clip¹ n. device for holding things tightly or together. —v.t. (p.t. **clipped**) fix or fasten with clip(s).

clip² v.t. cut, esp. with shears or scissors; (colloq.) hit sharply. —n. act of clipping; piece clipped from something; (colloq.) sharp blow.

clipper n. fast sailing-ship; (pl.) instrument for clipping things.

clipping n. piece clipped off; newspaper cutting.

clique /kliːk/ n. small exclusive group.

clitoris /'klɪ-/ n. small erectile part of female genitals.

cloak n. loose sleeveless outer garment. —v.t. cover, conceal.

cloakroom n. room where outer garments and packages etc. can be left, often containing a lavatory.

clobber n. (sl.) equipment. —v.t. (sl.) hit repeatedly; defeat heavily.

cloche /klɒʃ or -əʊʃ/ n. translucent cover for protecting plants; woman's small bell-shaped hat.

clock¹ n. instrument indicating time; clock-like measuring device. —v.t. time; (colloq.) achieve as speed. **clock in** or **on**, **out** or **off** register one's time of arrival or departure. **clock up** achieve.

clock² n. ornamental pattern on the side of a stocking or sock.

clockwise adv. & a. moving in the direction of the hands of a clock.

clockwork n. mechanism with wheels and springs.

clod n. lump of earth.

clog n. wooden-soled shoe. —v.t./i. (p.t. **clogged**) cause an obstruction in; become blocked.

cloister n. covered walk along the side of a church etc.; life in a monastery or convent.

cloistered a. shut away, secluded.

clone n. group of plants or organisms produced asexually from one ancestor. —v.t./i. grow thus.

clop n. (p.t. **clopped**) move with the sound of horses' hooves. —n.

close¹ /kləʊs/ a. (-er, -est) near; near together; dear to each other;

dense; concentrated; secretive; stingy; stuffy. —*adv.* closely; in a near position. —*n.* street closed at one end; grounds round a cathedral or abbey. **close season** period when killing of game is forbidden by law. **close-up** *n.* photograph etc. showing a subject as at close range. **closely** *adv.*, **closeness** *n.*

close² /kləʊz/ *v.t./i.* shut; bring or come to an end; bring or come nearer together. —*n.* conclusion, end. **closed shop** system whereby employees must be members of a specified trade union.

closet *n.* (US) cupboard; store room. —*v.t.* (*p.t.* **closeted**) shut away in private conference or study.

closure *n.* closing, closed condition.

clot *n.* thickened mass of liquid; (*sl.*) stupid person. —*v.i.* (*p.t.* **clotted**) form clot(s). **clotted cream** thick cream formed by slow scalding.

cloth *n.* woven or felted material; piece of this; table-cloth.

clothe *v.t.* (*p.t.* **clothed** or **clad**) put clothes on, provide with clothes.

clothes *n.pl.* things worn to cover the body; bedclothes.

clothier *n.* person who deals in cloth and men's clothes.

clothing *n.* clothes for the body.

cloud *n.* visible mass of watery vapour floating in the sky; mass of smoke or dust etc.; state of gloom. —*v.t./i.* make or become covered with clouds or gloom.

cloudburst *n.* violent storm of rain.

cloudy *a.* (**-ier**, **-iest**) covered with clouds; (of liquid) not transparent. **cloudiness** *n.*

clout *n.* blow; (*colloq.*) power of effective action. —*v.t.* hit.

clove¹ *n.* dried bud of a tropical tree, used as spice.

clove² *n.* one division of a compound bulb such as garlic.

clove³, cloven see **cleave¹**. —*a.* **clove hitch** knot used to fasten a rope round a pole etc. **cloven hoof** divided hoof like that of sheep etc.

clover *n.* plant with three-lobed leaves. **in clover** in ease and luxury.

clown *n.* person who does comical tricks. —*v.i.* perform or behave as a clown.

cloy *v.t.* sicken by glutting with sweetness or pleasure.

club *n.* heavy stick used as a weapon; stick with a wooden or metal head, used in golf; playing-card of the suit marked with black clover-leaves; group who meet for social or sports etc. purposes, their premises; organization offering benefit to subscribers. —*v.t./i.* (*p.t.* **clubbed**) strike with a club. **club foot** congenitally deformed foot. **club together** join in subscribing.

clubbable *a.* sociable.

cluck *n.* throaty cry of hen. —*v.i.* utter a cluck.

clue *n.* fact or idea giving a guide to the solution of a problem.

clump *n.* cluster, mass. —*v.t./i.* tread heavily; form into a clump; (*colloq.*) hit.

clumsy *a.* (**-ier**, **-iest**) large and ungraceful or difficult to handle; not skilful. **clumsily** *adv.*, **clumsiness** *n.*

clung see **cling**.

cluster *n.* small close group. —*v.t./i.* make into or form a cluster.

clutch¹ *v.t./i.* grasp tightly; try to grasp. —*n.* tight grasp; clutching movement; device for connecting and disconnecting moving parts.

clutch² *n.* set of eggs for hatching; chickens hatched from these.

clutter *n.* things lying about untidily. —*v.t.* fill with clutter.

cm *abbr.* centimetre(s).

Co. *abbr.* Company; County.

c/o *abbr.* care of.

co- *pref.* joint, jointly.

coach n. private or long-distance bus; railway carriage; large horse-drawn carriage; private tutor; instructor in sports. —v.t. train, teach.

coagulate v.t./i. change from liquid to semi-solid, clot. **coagulant** n., **coagulation** n.

coal n. hard black mineral used esp. for burning as fuel; piece of this. **coalmine** n., **coalminer** n.

coalesce v.i. combine. **coalescence** n.

coalfield n. area where coal occurs.

coalition n. union, esp. temporary union of political parties.

coarse a. (-er, -est) composed of large particles; rough or loose in texture; rough or crude in manner, vulgar. **coarse fish** freshwater fish other than salmon and trout. **coarsely** adv., **coarseness** n.

coarsen v.t./i. make or become coarse.

coast n. sea-shore and land near it. —v.i. sail along a coast; ride a bicycle or drive a motor vehicle without using power. **coastal** a.

coaster n. ship trading along a coast; tray for bottle(s); mat for a glass.

coastguard n. public organization that keeps watch on the coast to report passing ships, prevent smuggling, etc.; member of this.

coastline n. line of a coast.

coat n. outdoor garment with sleeves; fur or hair covering an animal's body; covering layer. —v.t. cover with a layer. **coat of arms** design on a shield as the emblem of a family or institution.

coatee n. woman's short coat.

coating n. covering layer.

coax v.t. persuade gently; manipulate carefully or slowly.

coaxial /-ˈæks-/ a. (of cable) in which a central conductor is surrounded by an insulated tubular conductor. **coaxially** adv.

cob n. sturdy short-legged horse for riding; a kind of hazel-nut; stalk of an ear of maize; small round loaf.

cobalt n. metallic element; deep-blue pigment made from it.

cobber n. (Austr. & NZ colloq.) friend, mate.

cobble[1] n. rounded stone formerly used for paving roads.

cobble[2] v.t. mend roughly.

cobbler n. (old use) shoe-mender.

cobra /ˈkəʊ- or ˈkɒ-/ n. poisonous snake of India and Africa.

cobweb n. network spun by a spider.

cocaine n. drug used as a local anaesthetic or as a stimulant.

coccyx /ˈkɒksɪks/ n. bone at the base of the spinal column.

cochineal n. red colouring-matter used in food.

cochlea n. (pl. -leae) spiral cavity of the internal ear.

cock n. male bird; tap or valve controlling a flow; lever in a gun. —v.t. tilt or turn upwards; set the cock of (a gun) for firing, set (a camera shutter) ready for release. **cock-a-hoop** a. pleased and triumphant. **cock-and-bull story** foolish story that no one should believe. **cocked hat** triangular hat worn as part of a uniform. **cock-eyed** a. (sl.) askew; absurd.

cockade n. rosette etc. worn on a hat as a badge.

cockatoo n. (pl. -oos) crested parrot.

cockatrice n. basilisk; fabled cock with a serpent's tail.

cockchafer n. flying beetle.

cocker n. breed of spaniel.

cockerel n. young male fowl.

cockle n. edible shellfish. —v.t./i. make or become puckered.

cockney n. (pl. -eys) native or dialect of the East End of London.

cockpit n. compartment for the pilot and crew in an aircraft, or for the driver in a racing-car; pit for cock-fighting.

cockroach *n.* beetle-like insect.

cockscomb *n.* cock's crest.

cocksure *a.* very self-confident.

cocktail *n.* mixed alcoholic drink; appetizer containing shellfish. **fruit cocktail** mixed chopped fruit.

cocky *a.* (-ier, -iest) conceited and arrogant. **cockily** *adv.*, **cockiness** *n.*

cocoa *n.* powder of crushed cacao seeds; drink made from this.

coconut *n.* nut of a tropical palm; its edible lining. **coconut matting** that made from the fibre of its husk.

cocoon *n.* silky sheath round a chrysalis; protective wrapping. —*v.t.* wrap completely.

cod *n.* (*pl.* **cod**) large edible seafish. **cod-liver oil** rich oil from its liver.

coda *n.* final part of a musical composition etc.

coddle *v.t.* cherish and protect; cook (an egg) slowly in hot water.

code *n.* set of laws, rules, or signals; pre-arranged word or phrase used to represent a message, esp. for secrecy; cipher. —*v.t.* put into code.

codeine *n.* substance made from opium, used to relieve pain.

codfish *n.* cod.

codger *n.* (*colloq.*) fellow, person.

codicil /ˈkɒd-/ *n.* appendix to a will.

codify /ˈkəʊd-/ *v.t.* arrange (laws etc.) into a code. **codification** *n.*

codling *n.* a kind of cooking apple; moth whose larva feeds on apples.

coeducation *n.* education of boys and girls in the same classes. **coeducational** *a.*

coefficient *n.* multiplier; mathematical factor.

coelacanth /ˈsiːl-/ *n.* a kind of fish extinct except for one species.

coeliac disease /ˈsiːl-/ disease causing inability to digest fats.

coerce *v.t.* compel by threats or force. **coercion** *n.*, **coercive** *a.*

coeval *a.* of the same age or epoch.

coexist *v.i.* exist together harmoniously. **coexistence** *n.*, **coexistent** *a.*

coextensive *a.* extending over same space or time.

coffee *n.* bean-like seeds of a tropical shrub, roasted and ground for making a drink; this drink; light-brown colour. **coffee bar** place serving coffee and light refreshments from a counter. **coffee-table** *n.* small low table.

coffer *n.* large strong box for holding money and valuables; (*pl.*) financial resources; sunk panel. **coffer-dam** *n.* enclosure pumped dry to enable construction work to be done within it.

coffin *n.* box in which a corpse is placed for burial or cremation.

cog *n.* one of a series of projections on the edge of a wheel, engaging with those of another. **cog-wheel** *n.*

cogent /ˈkəʊ-/ *a.* convincing. **cogently** *adv.*, **cogency** *n.*

cogitate *v.i.* think deeply. **cogitation** *n.*, **cogitative** *a.*

cognac /ˈkɒnjæk/ *n.* French brandy.

cognate *a.* akin, related. —*n.* relative; cognate word.

cognition *n.* knowing, perceiving. **cognitive** *a.*

cognizant *a.* aware, having knowledge. **cognizance** *n.*

cognomen *n.* nickname; surname.

cohabit *v.i.* live together as man and wife. **cohabitation** *n.*

cohere *v.i.* stick together.

coherent *a.* cohering; connected logically, not rambling. **coherently** *adv.*, **coherence** *n.*

cohesion *n.* tendency to cohere. **cohesive** *a.* cohering.

cohort *n.* tenth part of a Roman legion; persons banded or grouped together.

coiffure /kwɑː-/ *n.* hair-style.

coil v.t./i. wind into rings or a spiral. —n. something coiled; one ring or turn in this.

coin n. metal money; piece of this. —v.t. make (coins) by stamping metal; get (money) in large quantities as profit; invent (a word or phrase). **coiner** n.

coinage n. coining; coins, system of these; coined word or phrase.

coincide v.i. occupy the same portion of time or space; be in agreement or identical.

coincidence n. coinciding; remarkable occurrence of similar or corresponding events at the same time by chance. **coincident, coincidental** adjs., **coincidentally** adv.

coir n. coconut husk fibre.

coition n. sexual intercourse.

coitus n. coition.

coke[1] n. solid substance left after gas and tar have been extracted from coal, used as fuel.

coke[2] n. (sl.) cocaine.

col n. depression in a range of mountains.

colander n. bowl-shaped perforated vessel for draining food.

cold a. (-er, -est) at or having a low temperature; not affectionate, not enthusiastic; (of scent in hunting) grown faint; (colloq.) at one's mercy; (sl.) unconscious. —n. low temperature; cold condition; illness causing catarrh and sneezing. **cold-blooded** a. having a blood temperature varying with that of the surroundings; unfeeling, ruthless. **cold calling** making unsolicited calls to try and sell goods etc. **cold cream** ointment for softening the skin. **cold feet** fear. **cold-shoulder** v.t. treat with deliberate unfriendliness. **cold war** intense hostility between nations without fighting. **coldly** adv., **coldness** n.

coleopterous a. having hard wing-covers.

coleslaw n. salad of shredded raw cabbage coated in dressing.

coley n. cod-like fish.

colic n. severe abdominal pain. **colicky** a.

colitis /ka'laɪ-/ n. inflammation of the colon.

collaborate v.i. work in partnership. **collaboration** n., **collaborator** n., **collaborative** a.

collage /kɒ'lɑːʒ/ n. artistic composition in which objects are glued to a backing to form a picture.

collapse v.t./i. fall down or in suddenly; lose strength suddenly; fold; cause to collapse. —n. collapsing; breakdown.

collapsible a. made so as to fold up.

collar n. upright or turned-over band round the neck of a garment; strap put round an animal's neck; band holding part of a machine; cut of bacon from near the head. —v.t. (colloq.) seize, take for oneself. **collar-bone** n. bone joining breast-bone and shoulder-blade.

collate v.t. compare in detail; collect and arrange systematically. **collator** n.

collateral a. parallel; additional but subordinate. —n. collateral security, additional security pledged. **collaterally** adv.

collation n. collating; light meal.

colleague n. fellow worker esp. in a business or profession.

collect[1] /-'lekt/ v.t./i. bring or come together; seek and obtain from a number of sources; obtain specimens of, esp. as a hobby; fetch. **collectable** a. & n., **collectible** a. & n.

collect[2] /'kɒ-/ n. short prayer for use on an appointed day.

collected a. calm and controlled.

collection n. collecting; objects or money collected.

collective a. of a group taken or working as a unit. —n. collective farm; collective noun. **collective farm** group of smallholdings

run jointly by their workers.
collective noun noun (singular in form) denoting a group (e.g. *army*, *herd*). **collectively** adv.
collectivize v.t. organize as a collective farm. **collectivization** n.
collector n. one who collects things.
colleen n. (Ir.) girl.
college n. educational establishment for higher or professional education; organized body of professional people. **collegiate** a.
collegian n. member of a college.
collide v.i. come into collision.
collie n. dog with a pointed muzzle and shaggy hair.
collier n. coalminer; coal-ship.
colliery n. coalmine.
collision n. violent striking of one body against another; clash of interests; disagreement.
collocate v.t. place (esp. words) together; arrange. **collocation** n.
colloid n. gluey substance.
collop n. escalope.
colloquial a. suitable for informal speech or writing. **colloquially** adv., **colloquialism** n.
colloquy n. talk, discussion.
collusion n. agreement made for a deceitful or fraudulent purpose.
collywobbles n.pl. (colloq.) aching or rumbling in the belly; nervousness.
cologne /-'ləʊn/ n. eau-de-Cologne or similar scented liquid.
colon[1] n. lower part of the large intestine. **colonic** /-'lɒn-/ a.
colon[2] n. punctuation-mark.
colonel /'kɜːn(ə)l/ n. army officer next below brigadier. **colonelcy** n.
colonial a. of a colony or colonies. —n. inhabitant of a colony.
colonialism n. policy of acquiring or maintaining colonies.
colonize v.t. establish a colony in. **colonization** n., **colonist** n.
colonnade n. row of columns.
colony n. settlement or settlers in new territory, remaining subject

to the parent State; people of one nationality or occupation etc. living in a particular area; birds etc. congregated similarly.
colophon n. publisher's device, esp. tailpiece.
Colorado beetle beetle with larvae destructive to potato plants.
coloration n. colouring.
colossal a. immense. **colossally** adv.
colossus n. (pl. colossi) immense statue.
colostomy /-'lɒs-/ n. opening made surgically in the surface of the abdomen, through which the bowel can empty.
colour n. sensation produced by rays of light of different wavelengths; one or more varieties of this; ruddiness of complexion; pigmentation of skin, esp. if dark; pigment, paint; (usu. pl.) flag of a ship or regiment; (pl.) award to a regular member of a sports team. —v.t./i. put colour on; paint, stain, dye; change colour, blush; give a special character or bias to. **colour-blind** a. unable to distinguish between certain colours. **lend colour to** give an appearance of truth to.
colourant n. colouring-matter.
coloured a. & n. (person) wholly or partly of non-White descent.
colourful a. full of colour; with vivid details. **colourfully** adv.
colourless a. without colour; lacking vividness.
colt n. young male horse.
coltsfoot n. wild plant with yellow flowers.
columbine n. garden flower with pointed projections on its petals.
column n. round pillar; thing shaped like this; vertical division of a page, printed matter in this; long narrow formation of troops, vehicles, etc.
columnar a. of or in columns.

columnist *n.* journalist who regularly writes a column of comments.

coma *n.* deep unconsciousness.

comatose *a.* in a coma; drowsy.

comb *n.* toothed strip of stiff material for tidying hair, separating strands, etc.; fowl's fleshy crest; honeycomb. —*v.t.* tidy or separate with a comb; search thoroughly.

combat *n.* battle, contest. —*v.t.* (*p.t.* **combated**) counter. **combative** *a.*

combatant *a.* & *n.* (person etc.) engaged in fighting.

combination *n.* combining; set of people or things combined; (*pl.*) undergarment covering body and legs. **combination lock** lock controlled by a sequence of dial(s).

combine[1] /-'bam/ *v.t./i.* join into a group or set or mixture.

combine[2] /'kom-/ *n.* combination of people or firms acting together in business. **combine harvester** combined reaping and threshing machine.

combustible *a.* capable of catching fire. **combustibility** *n.*

combustion *n.* burning; process in which substances combine with oxygen and produce heat.

come *v.i.* (*p.t.* **came**, *p.p.* **come**) move towards a speaker or place or point; begin to develop; arrive, reach a point or condition; occupy a specified position; occur; originate from; (*sl.*) behave as; (*imper.*) exclamation of mild protest or of encouragement. **come about** happen. **come across** meet or find unexpectedly. **comeback** *n.* return to a former successful position; retort. **come by** obtain. **come-down** *n.* fall in status. **come into** inherit. **come off** fare; be successful. **come out** become visible or revealed or known etc. **come out with** utter. **come round** recover from fainting; be converted to the speaker's

opinion. **come to** amount to; regain consciousness. **come to pass** happen. **come up** arise for discussion etc. **come up with** contribute (a suggestion etc.). **comer** *n.*

comedian *n.* humorous entertainer or actor. **comedienne** /-'en/ *n.fem.*

comedy *n.* light amusing drama; amusing incident.

comely *a.* (**-ier, -iest**) (*old use*) good-looking. **comeliness** *n.*

comestibles /-'mest-/ *n.pl.* things to eat.

comet *n.* heavenly body with a luminous 'tail'.

comeuppance *n.* (*colloq.*) deserved punishment or rebuke.

comfit *n.* sugar-coated nut etc.

comfort *n.* state of ease and contentment; relief of suffering or grief; person or thing giving this. —*v.t.* give comfort to. **comforter** *n.*

comfortable *a.* providing or having ease and contentment; not close or restricted. **comfortably** *adv.*

comfrey *n.* tall bell-flowered plant.

comfy *a.* (*colloq.*) comfortable.

comic *a.* causing amusement; of comedy. —*n.* comedian; children's periodical with a series of strip cartoons. **comical** *a.*, **comically** *adv.*, **comicality** *n.*

coming *n.* arrival. —*a.* approaching, next. **coming man** one likely to be important in the near future.

comity *n.* courtesy.

comma *n.* punctuation-mark , .

command *n.* statement, given with authority, that an action must be performed; tenure of authority; mastery; forces or district under a commander. —*v.t.* give a command to; have authority over; deserve and get; dominate from a strategic position, look down over.

commandant /'kɒ-/ n. officer in command of a fortress etc.

commandeer v.t. seize for use.

commander n. person in command; naval officer next below captain; police officer next below commissioner. **commander-in-chief** n. supreme commander.

commandment n. divine command.

commando n. (pl. -os) member of a military unit specially trained for making raids and assaults.

commemorate v.t. keep in the memory by a celebration or memorial. **commemoration** n., **commemorative** a.

commence v.t./i. begin. **commencement** n.

commend v.t. praise; recommend; entrust. **commendation** n.

commendable a. worthy of praise. **commendably** adv.

commensurable a. measurable by the same standard. **commensurably** adv., **commensurability** n.

commensurate a. of the same size; proportionate.

comment n. opinion given; explanatory note. —v.i. make comment(s) on.

commentary n. series of comments.

commentate v.i. act as commentator.

commentator n. person who writes or speaks a commentary.

commerce n. all forms of trade and the services (e.g. banking, insurance) that assist trading.

commercial a. of or engaged in commerce; (of broadcasting) financed by firms whose advertisements are included. **commercially** adv.

commercialize v.t. make commercial, alter so as to make profitable. **commercialization** n.

commingle v.t./i. mix.

comminute v.t. reduce to small portions or fragments. **comminution** n.

commiserate v.t./i. express pity for; sympathize. **commiseration** n.

commissariat /-'seər-/ n. stock of food; department supplying this.

commission n. committing; giving of authority to perform a task; task given; body of people given such authority; warrant conferring authority, esp. on officers in the armed forces; payment to an agent selling goods or services. —v.t. give commission to; place an order for. **commission-agent** n. bookmaker. **in commission** ready for service. **out of commission** not in commission; not in working order.

commissionaire n. uniformed attendant at the door of a theatre, business premises, etc.

commissioner n. member of a commission; head of Scotland Yard; government official in charge of a district abroad.

commit v.t. (p.t. **committed**) do, perform; entrust, consign; pledge or bind to a course of action etc. **commit to memory** memorize. **committal** n.

commitment n. committing; obligation or pledge, state of being involved in this.

committee n. group of people appointed to attend to special business or manage the affairs of a club etc.

commode n. chest of drawers; chamber-pot mounted in a chair or box, with a cover.

commodious a. roomy.

commodity n. article of trade, product.

commodore n. naval officer next below rear admiral; commander of a division of a fleet; president of a yacht-club.

common a. (-er, -est) of or affecting all; occurring often; ordinary; of inferior quality; ill-bred. —n.

area of unfenced grassland for all to use; (*pl.*) common people; (*pl.*) shared provisions. (**House of**) **Commons** lower house of the British Parliament. **common law** unwritten law based on custom and former court decisions. **Common Market** European Economic Community, association of countries with internal free trade. **common-room** *n.* room shared by students or teachers for social purposes. **common sense** normal good sense in practical matters. **common time** 4 crotchets in the bar in music. **commonness** *n.*

commonalty *n.* general community; common people.

commoner *n.* one of the common people, not a noble.

commonly *adv.* usually, frequently.

commonplace *a.* ordinary; lacking originality. —*n.* commonplace thing.

commonwealth *n.* independent State; republic; federation of States.

commotion *n.* fuss and disturbance.

communal /'kɒm-/ *a.* shared among a group. **communally** *adv.*

commune[1] /-'mjuːn/ *v.i.* communicate mentally or spiritually.

commune[2] /'kɒm-/ *n.* group (not all of one family) sharing accommodation and goods; district of local government in France etc.

communicable *a.* able to be communicated.

communicant *n.* person who receives Holy Communion; one who communicates information.

communicate *v.t./i.* make known; transmit; pass news and information to and fro, have social dealings with; have or be a means of access; receive Holy Communion. **communicator** *n.*

communication *n.* communicating; letter or message; means of access.

communicative *a.* talkative, willing to give information.

communion *n.* fellowship; social dealings; branch of the Christian Church; (**Holy**) **Communion** sacrament in which bread and wine are consumed.

communiqué /-keɪ/ *n.* official communication giving a report.

communism *n.* social system based on common ownership of property, means of production, etc. **Communism** political doctrine or movement seeking a form of this, such a system in the USSR etc. **Communist** *n.*, **communistic** *a.*

community *n.* body of people living in one district etc. or having common interests or origins; state of being shared or alike. **community service** work, esp. voluntary, in the community.

commutable *a.* exchangeable.

commute *v.t./i.* exchange or change for something else; travel regularly by train or car etc. to and from one's work. **commuter** *n.*

compact[1] /'kɒm-/ *n.* pact, contract.

compact[2] /-'pækt/ *a.* closely or neatly packed together; concise. —*v.t.* make compact. —/'kɒm-/ *n.* small flat case for face-powder. **compact disc** small disc from which sound etc. is reproduced by laser action.

companion *n.* one who accompanies another; member of certain orders of knighthood; thing that matches or accompanies another. **companion-way** *n.* staircase from a ship's deck to cabins etc. **companionship** *n.*

companionable *a.* sociable.

company *n.* being with another or others; people assembled;

guests; associate(s); people working together or united for business purposes, firm; subdivision of an infantry battalion.

comparable /'kɒm-/ *a.* suitable to be compared, similar. **comparably** *adv.*, **comparability** *n.*

comparative *a.* involving comparison; of the grammatical form expressing 'more'. —*n.* comparative form of a word. **comparatively** *adv.*

compare *v.t./i.* estimate the similarity of; liken; declare to be similar; be worthy of comparison; form the comparative and superlative of. **compare notes** exchange ideas.

comparison *n.* comparing.

compartment *n.* partitioned space. **compartmental** *a.*

compass *n.* device showing the direction of the magnetic or true north; range, scope; (*pl.*) hinged instrument for drawing circles. —*v.t.* encompass.

compassion *n.* feeling of pity. **compassionate** *a.*, **compassionately** *adv.*

compatible *a.* able to exist or be used together; consistent; able to be together harmoniously. **compatibly** *adv.*, **compatibility** *n.*

compatriot /-'pæ-/ *n.* fellow-countryman.

compeer *n.* equal, comrade.

compel *v.t.* (*p.t.* **compelled**) force; arouse (a feeling) irresistibly.

compendious *a.* giving much information concisely. **compendiously** *adv.*, **compendiousness** *n.*

compendium *n.* (*pl.* **-dia** *or* **-s**) summary; package of table-games or writing-paper.

compensate *v.t./i.* make payment to (a person) in return for loss or damage; counterbalance. **compensation** *n.*, **compensatory** *a.*

compère /-pɛə(r)/ *n.* person who introduces performers in a variety show etc. —*v.t.* act as compère to.

compete *v.i.* take part in a competition or other contest.

competence *n.* ability, authority; adequate income. **competency** *n.*

competent *a.* having ability or authority to do what is required; adequate. **competently** *adv.*

competition *n.* friendly contest; competing; those who compete.

competitive *a.* involving competition. **competitively** *adv.*, **competitiveness** *n.*

competitor *n.* one who competes.

compile *v.t.* collect and arrange into a list or book etc.; make (a book) thus. **compilation** *n.*, **compiler** *n.*

complacent /-'pleɪ-/ *a.* self-satisfied. **complacently** *adv.*, **complacency** *n.*

complain *v.i.* say one is dissatisfied; say one is suffering from pain etc. **complainant** *n.*

complaint *n.* statement that one is dissatisfied; illness.

complaisant /-'pleɪz-/ *a.* willing to please others. **complaisance** *n.*

complement *n.* that which completes or fills something; degrees required to make up a given angle to 90°. —*v.t.* form a complement to. **complementary** *a.*

complete *a.* having all its parts; finished; thorough, in every way. —*v.t.* make complete; fill in (a form etc.). **completely** *adv.*, **completeness** *n.*, **completion** *n.*

complex *a.* made up of parts; complicated. —*n.* complex whole; set of feelings that influence behaviour; set of buildings. **complexity** *n.*

complexion *n.* colour and texture of the skin of the face; general character of things.

compliant /-'plaɪ-/ *a.* complying, obedient. **compliance** *n.*

complicate *v.t.* make complicated. **complicated** *a.* complex; difficult because of this. **complication** *n.*

complicity *n.* involvement in wrongdoing.

compliment *n.* polite expression of praise; (*pl.*) formal greetings in a message. —*v.t.* pay compliment to.

complimentary *a.* expressing a compliment; given free of charge.

compline *n.* last service of the day in the RC Church.

comply *v.i.* comply with act in accordance with (a command etc.).

component *n.* any of the parts of which a thing is composed. —*a.* being a component.

comport *v.t./i.* agree, accord. **comport oneself** behave.

compose *v.t.* form, make up; create in music or literature; arrange in good order; calm. **composer** *n.*

composite /-zɪt/ *a.* made up of parts.

composition *n.* composing; thing composed; compound artificial substance.

compositor *n.* typesetter.

compos mentis sane.

compost *n.* decayed matter used as a fertilizer; mixture of soil or peat for growing seedlings etc.

composure *n.* calmness.

compote *n.* fruit in syrup.

compound[1] /'kɒm-/ *a.* made up of two or more parts or ingredients. —*n.* compound thing or substance.

compound[2] /'paʊ-/ *v.t./i.* combine; add to; settle by agreement; condone (a felony etc.).

compound[3] /'kɒm-/ *n.* (in India, China, etc.) fenced enclosure.

comprehend *v.t.* understand; include.

comprehensible *a.* intelligible. **comprehensibly** *adv.*, **comprehensibility** *n.*

comprehension *n.* understanding.

comprehensive *a.* including much or all. —*n.* comprehensive school. **comprehensive school** one providing secondary education for children of all abilities.

comprehensively *adv.*, **comprehensiveness** *n.*

compress[1] /-'pres/ *v.t.* squeeze, force into less space. **compressible** *a.*, **compression** *n.*, **compressor** *n.*

compress[2] /'kɒm-/ *n.* pad to stop bleeding or to cool inflammation.

comprise *v.t.* include; consist of; form, make up.

compromise /'kɒm-/ *n.* settlement reached by making concessions on each side. —*v.t./i.* make a settlement thus; expose to suspicion or commit to a policy etc. unwisely.

compulsion *n.* compelling, being compelled; irresistible urge.

compulsive *a.*, **compulsively** *adv.*

compulsory *a.* that must be done, required by rules etc. **compulsorily** *adv.*

compunction *n.* regret, scruple.

compute *v.t./i.* calculate; use a computer. **computation** *n.*

computer *n.* electronic apparatus for analysing or storing data, making calculations, controlling machinery, etc.

computerize *v.t.* equip with or perform or operate by computer. **computerization** *n.*

comrade *n.* companion, associate; fellow socialist. **comradeship** *n.*

con[1] *v.t.* (*p.t.* **conned**) (*colloq.*) persuade or swindle after winning confidence. —*n.* (*sl.*) confidence trick.

con[2] *v.t.* (*p.t.* **conned**) direct the steering of (a ship).

con[3] *see* pro and con.

concatenation *n.* combination.

concave *a.* curved like the inner surface of a ball. **concavity** *n.*

conceal *v.t.* hide, keep secret. **concealer** *n.*, **concealment** *n.*

concede *v.t.* admit to be true; grant (a privilege etc.); admit defeat in (a contest).

conceit *n.* too much pride in oneself; affectation of style. **conceited** *a.*

conceivable *a.* able to be imagined or believed true. **conceivably** *adv.*

conceive *v.t./i.* become pregnant; form (an idea etc.) in the mind, think.

concentrate *v.t./i.* employ all one's thought or effort; bring or come together; make less dilute. —*n.* concentrated substance.

concentration *n.* concentrating; concentrated thing. **concentration camp** camp for detention of internees or political prisoners, esp. in Nazi Germany.

concentric *a.* having the same centre. **concentrically** *adv.*, **concentricity** *n.*

concept *n.* idea, general notion.

conception *n.* conceiving; idea.

conceptual *a.* of concepts. **conceptualize** *v.t.* form a concept of. **conceptualization** *n.*

concern *v.t.* be about; be relevant or important to; involve. —*n.* thing that concerns one; anxiety; business or firm; (*colloq.*) thing. **concerned** *a.* anxious.

concerning *prep.* with reference to.

concert *n.* musical entertainment. **in concert** in combination. **concerted** *a.* done in concert.

concertina *n.* portable musical instrument with bellows and keys. —*v.t./i.* fold like bellows.

concerto /-'tʃeə-/ *n.* (*pl.* **-os**) musical composition for solo instrument(s) and orchestra.

concession *n.* conceding; thing conceded; special privilege; right granted. **concessionary** *a.*, **concessive** *a.*

conch *n.* spiral shell.

conciliate *v.t.* soothe the hostility of; reconcile. **conciliation** *n.*, **conciliatory** /-'sɪlɪə-/ *a.*

concise *a.* brief and comprehensive. **concisely** *adv.*, **conciseness** *n.*

conclave *n.* assembly for discussion.

conclude *v.t./i.* end; settle finally; reach an opinion by reasoning.

conclusion *n.* concluding; ending; opinion reached.

conclusive *a.* ending doubt, convincing. **conclusively** *adv.*

concoct *v.t.* prepare from ingredients; invent. **concoction** *n.*

concomitant /-'kɒm-/ *a.* accompanying. **concomitantly** *adv.*, **concomitance** *n.*

concord *n.* agreement, harmony.

concordance *n.* agreement; index of words.

concordant *a.* being in concord.

concourse *n.* crowd, gathering; open area at a railway terminus etc.

concrete *n.* mixture of gravel and cement etc. used for building. —*a.* existing in material form; definite. —*v.t./i.* cover with or embed in concrete; solidify.

concretion *n.* solidified mass.

concubine *n.* woman who cohabits with a man without marriage; (in polygamy) secondary wife. **concubinage** *n.*

concupiscence /-'pɪs-/ *n.* sexual desire. **concupiscent** *a.*

concur *v.i.* (*p.t.* **concurred**) agree in opinion; coincide. **concurrence** *n.*, **concurrent** *a.*, **concurrently** *adv.*

concuss *v.t.* affect with concussion.

concussion *n.* injury to the brain caused by a hard blow.

condemn *v.t.* express strong disapproval of; convict; sentence; doom; declare unfit for use. **condemnation** *n.*, **condemnatory** *a.*

condense *v.t./i.* make denser or briefer; change from gas or vapour to liquid. **condensation** *n.*

condenser *n.* capacitor.

condescend *v.i.* consent to do something less dignified or fitting than is usual. **condescension** *n.*

condiment *n.* seasoning for food.

condition n. thing that must exist if something else is to exist or occur; state of being; (pl.) circumstances. —v.t. bring to the desired or good condition; have a strong effect on; accustom. **on condition that** with the stipulation that. **conditioner** n.

conditional a. subject to specified conditions. **conditionally** adv.

condole v.i. express sympathy. **condolence** n.

condom n. contraceptive sheath.

condominium n. joint control of a State's affairs by other States; (US) building in which flats are individually owned.

condone v.t. forgive or overlook (a fault etc.). **condonation** n.

conduce v.t. help to cause or produce. **conducive** a.

conduct[1] /'dʌkt/ v.t. lead, guide; be the conductor of; manage; transmit (heat, electricity, etc.).

conduct[2] /'kɒn-/ n. behaviour; way of conducting business etc.

conduction n. conducting of heat etc. **conductive** a., **conductivity** n.

conductor n. person who controls an orchestra's or choir's performance by gestures; one who collects fares in a bus etc. (fem. **conductress**); thing that conducts heat etc.

conduit /'kʌndɪt/ n. pipe or channel for liquid; tube protecting wires.

cone n. tapering object with a circular base; cone-shaped thing; dry scaly fruit of pine or fir.

coney n. = cony.

confab n. (colloq.) chat.

confabulate v.i. talk together. **confabulation** n.

confection n. prepared dish or delicacy; ornate hat.

confectioner n. maker or seller of confectionery.

confectionery n. sweets, cakes, and pastries.

confederacy n. league of States.

confederate a. joined by treaty or agreement. —n. member of a confederacy; accomplice.

confederation n. union of States or people or organizations.

confer v.t./i. (p.t. **conferred**) grant; hold a discussion. **conferment** n.

conference n. meeting for discussion.

confess v.t./i. acknowledge, admit; declare one's sins, esp. to a priest; hear the confession of. **confessedly** adv.

confession n. acknowledgement of a fact, sin, guilt, etc.; statement of one's principles.

confessional n. enclosed stall in a church, for hearing of confessions.

confessor n. priest who hears confessions and gives counsel.

confetti n. bits of coloured paper thrown at a bride and bridegroom.

confidant /'kɒn-/ n. person one confides in. **confidante** n.fem.

confide v.t./i. tell confidentially; entrust. **confide in** talk confidentially to.

confidence n. firm trust; feeling of certainty, boldness; thing told confidentially. **confidence trick** swindle worked by gaining a person's trust. **in confidence** confidentially.

confident a. feeling confidence. **confidently** adv.

confidential a. to be kept secret; entrusted with secrets. **confidentially** adv., **confidentiality** n.

configuration n. shape, outline.

confine /-'faɪn/ v.t. keep within limits; keep shut up.

confinement n. confining, being confined; time of childbirth.

confines /'kɒn-/ n.pl. boundaries.

confirm v.t. make firmer or definite; corroborate; administer the rite of confirmation to. **confirmatory** /-'fɜː-/ a.

confirmation n. confirming; thing that confirms; rite in which a person confirms the vows made for him at baptism.

confiscate *v.t.* take or seize by authority. **confiscation** *n.*

conflagration *n.* great fire.

conflate *v.t.* blend or fuse together. **conflation** *n.*

conflict[1] /'kɒn-/ *n.* fight, struggle; disagreement.

conflict[2] /-'flɪkt/ *v.i.* have a conflict.

confluence *n.* place where two rivers unite. **confluent** *a.*

conform *v.t./i.* make similar; act or be in accordance, keep to rules or custom. **conformity** *n.*

conformable *a.* consistent; adaptable. **conformably** *adv.*

conformation *n.* conforming; structure.

conformist *n.* person who conforms to rules or custom. **conformism** *n.*

confound *v.t.* astonish and perplex; confuse.

confront *v.t.* be or come or bring face to face with; face boldly. **confrontation** *n.*

confuse *v.t.* throw into disorder; make unclear; bewilder; destroy the composure of. **confusion** *n.*

confute *v.t.* prove wrong. **confutation** *n.*

conga *n.* dance in which people form a long winding line.

congeal *v.t./i.* coagulate, solidify. **congelation** *n.*

congenial *a.* pleasant, agreeable to oneself. **congenially** *adv.*, **congeniality** *n.*

congenital /-'dʒen-/ *a.* being so from birth. **congenitally** *adv.*

conger *n.* large sea eel.

congeries /-'dʒɪərɪːz/ *n.* disorderly collection; mass.

congest *v.t.* make too full; make abnormally full of blood. **congestion** *n.*

conglomerate *a.* gathered into a mass. —*n.* coherent mass. —*v.t.* collect into a coherent mass. **conglomeration** *n.*

congratulate *v.t.* tell (a person) that one admires his success. **congratulation** *n.*, **congratulatory** *a.*

congregate *v.i.* flock together.

congregation *n.* people assembled esp. at a church service. **congregational** *a.*

Congregationalism *n.* system of self-governing churches. **Congregational** *a.*, **Congregationalist** *n.*

congress *n.* formal meeting of delegates for discussion. **Congress** law-making assembly, esp. of the USA. **congressional** *a.*

congruent *a.* suitable, consistent; having exactly the same shape and size. **congruently** *adv.*, **congruence** *n.*

conic *a.* of a cone.

conical *a.* cone-shaped.

conifer /'kəʊ-/ *n.* tree bearing cones. **coniferous** *a.*

conjecture *n.* & *v.t./i.* guess. **conjectural** *a.*, **conjecturally** *adv.*

conjoin *v.t./i.* join, combine. **conjoint** *a.*

conjugal /'kɒn-/ *a.* of marriage.

conjugate *v.t.* inflect (a verb). **conjugation** *n.*

conjunct *a.* combined, associated.

conjunction *n.* word that connects others; combination.

conjunctivitis *n.* inflammation of the membrane (**conjunctiva**) connecting eyeball and eyelid.

conjure *v.t./i.* do sleight-of-hand tricks; produce. **conjuror** *n.*

conk *n.* (*sl.*) nose, head. —*v.t.* (*sl.*) hit. **conk out** (*sl.*) break down; become unconscious, die.

conker *n.* fruit of the horse-chestnut.

connect *v.t./i.* join, be joined; associate mentally; (of a train etc.) arrive so that passengers are in time for another conveyance. **connection** *n.*, **connective** *a.*

conning tower raised structure on a submarine.

connive *v.i.* **connive at** tacitly consent to. **connivance** *n.*

connoisseur /kɒnə'sɜ:(r)/ *n.* person with expert understanding esp. of artistic subjects.

connote *v.t.* imply in addition to its basic meaning. **connotation** *n.*, **connotative** *a.*

connubial *a.* of marriage.

conquer *v.t.* overcome in war or by effort. **conqueror** *n.*

conquest *n.* conquering; thing won by conquering.

consanguineous *a.* related by descent. **consanguinity** *n.*

conscience *n.* person's sense of right and wrong; feeling of remorse.

conscientious *a.* showing careful attention. **conscientiously** *adv.*, **conscientiousness** *n.*

conscious *a.* with mental faculties awake; aware; intentional. **consciously** *adv.*, **consciousness** *n.*

conscript[1] /'kɒnskrɪpt/ *v.t.* summon for compulsory military service. **conscription** *n.*

conscript[2] /kɒn-/ *n.* conscripted person.

consecrate *v.t.* make sacred; dedicate to the service of God. **consecration** *n.*

consecutive *a.* following continuously. **consecutively** *adv.*

consensus *n.* general agreement.

consent *v.i.* say one is willing to do or allow what is asked. —*n.* willingness; permission. **consentient** *a.*

consequence *n.* result; importance.

consequent *a.* resulting.

consequential *a.* consequent; self-important. **consequentially** *adv.*

consequently *adv.* as a result.

conservancy *n.* commission controlling a river etc.; conservation.

conservation *n.* conserving.

conservationist *n.* one who seeks to preserve the natural environment.

Conservative *a. & n.* (member) of the UK political party favouring freedom from State control.

conservative *a.* opposed to great change; avoiding extremes; (of an estimate) purposely low. —*n.* conservative person. **conservatively** *adv.*, **conservatism** *n.*

conservatory *n.* greenhouse, esp. forming an extension of a house.

conserve[1] /-'sɜ:v/ *v.t.* keep from harm, decay, or loss.

conserve[2] /'kɒn-/ *n.* jam made from fresh fruit and sugar.

consider *v.t.* think about, esp. in order to decide; allow for; be of the opinion.

considerable *a.* fairly great in amount etc. **considerably** *adv.*

considerate *a.* careful not to hurt or inconvenience others. **considerately** *adv.*

consideration *n.* considering; careful thought; being considerate; fact that must be kept in mind; payment given as a reward.

considering *prep.* taking into account.

consign *v.t.* deposit, entrust; send (goods etc.). **consignor** *n.*

consignee *n.* person to whom goods are sent.

consignment *n.* consigning; batch of goods etc.

consist *v.i.* **consist in** have as its essential feature. **consist of** be composed of.

consistency *n.* being consistent; degree of thickness or solidity.

consistent *a.* unchanging; not contradictory. **consistently** *adv.*

consistory *n.* ecclesiastical council, esp. of cardinals.

consolation *n.* consoling; thing that consoles. **consolation prize** one given to a runner-up.

console[1] /-'səʊl/ *v.t.* comfort in time of sorrow.

console[2] /'kɒn-/ *n.* bracket supporting a shelf; frame or panel holding the controls of equipment; cabinet for a television set etc.

consolidate *v.t./i.* make or become secure and strong; combine. **consolidation** *n.*

consols *n.pl.* government securities.

consommé /-meɪ/ *n.* clear meat soup.

consonant *n.* letter other than a vowel; sound it represents. —*a.* consistent, harmonious. **consonantly** *adv.*, **consonance** *n.*

consort¹ /ˈkɒn-/ *n.* husband or wife, esp. of a monarch; ship sailing with another.

consort² /-ˈsɔːt/ *v.i.* keep company.

consortium *n.* (*pl. -tia*) combination of firms etc. acting together.

conspectus *n.* general view; synopsis.

conspicuous *a.* easily seen, attracting attention. **conspicuously** *adv.*, **conspicuousness** *n.*

conspiracy *n.* conspiring; plan made by conspiring.

conspirator *n.* one who conspires. **conspiratorial** *a.*, **conspiratorially** *adv.*

conspire *v.i.* plan secretly and usu. unlawfully against others; (of events) seem to combine.

constable *n.* policeman or policewoman of the lowest rank.

constabulary *n.* police force.

constancy *n.* quality of being unchanging; faithfulness.

constant *a.* continuous; occurring repeatedly; unchanging; faithful. —*n.* unvarying quantity. **constantly** *adv.*

constellation *n.* group of stars.

consternation *n.* great surprise and anxiety or dismay.

constipate *v.t.* affect with constipation. **constipation** *n.* difficulty in emptying the bowels.

constituency *n.* body of voters who elect a representative; area represented thus.

constituent *a.* forming part of a whole. —*n.* constituent part; member of a constituency.

constitute *v.t.* be the parts of, form; establish, be; appoint.

constitution *n.* constituting; composition; principles by which a State is organized; bodily condition.

constitutional *a.* of or in accordance with a constitution. —*n.* walk as exercise. **constitutionally** *adv.*, **constitutionality** *n.*

constrain *v.t.* compel, oblige.

constraint *n.* constraining; restriction; strained manner.

constrict *v.t.* tighten by making narrower, squeeze. **constriction** *n.*, **constrictor** *n.*

constrictive *a.* constricting.

construct *v.t.* make by placing parts together. **constructor** *n.*

construction *n.* constructing; thing constructed; words put together to form a phrase etc.; interpretation. **constructional** *a.*

constructive *a.* constructing; making useful suggestions. **constructively** *adv.*

construe *v.t.* interpret; analyse or combine grammatically; translate word for word.

consubstantiation *n.* presence of Christ's body and blood together with the elements in the Eucharist.

consul *n.* official appointed by a State to live in a foreign city to protect its subjects there and assist commerce. **consular** *a.*

consulate *n.* consul's position or premises.

consult *v.t./i.* seek information or advice from. **consultation** *n.*

consultant *n.* specialist consulted for professional advice. **consultancy** *n.*

consultative *a.* of or for consultation; advisory.

consume *v.t.* use up; eat or drink up; destroy (by fire); dominate by a feeling.

consumer *n.* person who buys or uses goods or services.

consumerism *n.* protection of consumers' interests.

consummate[1] /-'sʌm-/ *a.* perfect.

consummate[2] /'kɒn-/ *v.t.* accomplish, complete (esp. marriage by sexual intercourse). **consummation** *n.*

consumption *n.* consuming; (*old use*) tuberculosis.

consumptive *a. & n.* (person) suffering from tuberculosis.

contact *n.* touching, meeting, communicating; electrical connection; one who has been near an infected person; one who may be contacted for information or help. —*v.t.* get in touch with. **contact lens** very small lens worn in contact with the eye.

contagion *n.* spreading of disease by contact; disease etc. spread thus. **contagious** *a.*, **contagiousness** *n.*

contain *v.t.* have within itself; include; control, restrain.

container *n.* receptacle, esp. of standard design to transport goods.

containerize *v.t.* use containers for transporting (goods). **containerization** *n.*

containment *n.* prevention of hostile expansion.

contaminate *v.t.* pollute. **contaminant** *n.*, **contamination** *n.*

contemplate /-'tem-/ *v.t./i.* gaze at; consider as a possibility, intend; meditate. **contemplation** *n.*

contemplative /-'tem-/ *a.* meditative; of religious meditation. **contemplatively** *adv.*

contemporaneous *a.* existing or occurring at the same time. **contemporaneously** *adv.*

contemporary *a.* of the same period or age; modern in style. —*n.* person of the same age.

contempt *n.* despising, being despised; disrespect.

contemptible *a.* deserving contempt.

contemptuous *a.* showing contempt. **contemptuously** *adv.*

contend *v.t./i.* strive, compete; assert. **contender** *n.*

content[1] /-'ten-/ *a.* satisfied with what one has. —*n.* being content. —*v.t.* make content. **contented** *a.*, **contentment** *n.*

content[2] /'kɒn-/ *n.* what is contained in something.

contention *n.* contending; assertion made in argument.

contentious *a.* quarrelsome; likely to cause contention. **contentiously** *adv.*, **contentiousness** *n.*

contest[1] /'kɒn-/ *n.* struggle for victory; competition.

contest[2] /-'test/ *v.t./i.* compete for or in; dispute. **contestant** *n.*

context *n.* what precedes or follows a word or statement and fixes its meaning; circumstances. **contextual** *a.*

contiguous *a.* adjacent, next. **contiguously** *adv.*, **contiguity** *n.*

continent *n.* one of the main land masses of the earth; **the Continent** Europe as distinct from the British Isles. —*a.* able to control one's excretions. **continence** *n.*

continental *a.* of a continent; **Continental** of Europe. **Continental breakfast** light breakfast of coffee and rolls etc.

contingency *n.* something unforeseen; thing that may occur.

contingent *a.* happening by chance; possible but not certain; conditional. —*n.* body of troops or ships etc. contributed to a larger group.

continual *a.* never ending. **continually** *adv.*

continuance *n.* continuing.

continue *v.t./i.* not cease; remain in a place or condition; resume. **continuation** *n.*

continuous *a.* without interval. **continuously** *adv.*, **continuity** *n.*

continuum n. (pl. **-tinua**) continuous thing.

contort v.t. force or twist out of normal shape. **contortion** n.

contortionist n. performer who can twist his body dramatically.

contour n. outline; line on a map joining points of the same altitude.

contra- pref. against.

contraband n. smuggled goods.

contraception n. prevention of conception.

contraceptive a. & n. (drug or device) preventing conception.

contract[1] /'kɒn-/ n. formal agreement. **contractual** a.

contract[2] /-'trækt/ v.t./i. make a contract; arrange (work) to be done by contract; catch (an illness); acquire (a habit, debt, etc.); make or become smaller or shorter. **contraction** n., **contractor** n.

contractile a. able to contract.

contradict v.t. say that (a statement) is untrue or (a person) is wrong; be contrary to. **contradiction** n., **contradictory** a.

contradistinction n. distinguishing by contrast.

contraflow n. flow (esp. of traffic) in a direction opposite to and alongside the usual flow.

contralto n. (pl. **-os**) lowest female voice.

contraption n. (colloq.) strange device or machine.

contrapuntal a. of or in counterpoint.

contrariwise adv. on the other hand; in the opposite way.

contrary[1] /'kɒn-/ a. opposite in nature or tendency or direction. —n. the opposite. —adv. in opposition. **on the contrary** as the opposite of what was just stated.

contrary[2] /-'treə-/ a. perverse. **contrarily** adv., **contrariness** n.

contrast[1] /'kɒn-/ n. difference shown by comparison; thing showing this.

contrast[2] /-'trɑː-/ v.t./i. show contrast; compare so as to do this. **contrastive** a.

contravene v.t. break (a rule etc.). **contravention** n.

contretemps /'kɒntrətã/ n. unfortunate happening.

contribute v.t./i. give to a common fund or effort etc. **contribute** to help to bring about. **contribution** n., **contributor** n., **contributory** a.

contrite /'kɒn-/ a. penitent. **contritely** adv., **contrition** n.

contrivance /-'traɪ-/ n. contriving; contrived thing, device.

contrive v.t./i. plan, make, or do something resourcefully. **contriver** n.

control n. power to give orders or restrain something; means of restraining or regulating; check. —v.t. (p.t. **controlled**) have control of; regulate; restrain. **controllable** a., **controller** n.

controversial a. causing controversy. **controversially** adv.

controversy /'kɒn- or -'trɒv-/ n. prolonged dispute.

controvert v.t. deny the truth of. **controvertible** a.

contumacy /'kɒn-/ n. stubborn disobedience. **contumacious** a.

contumely /'kɒn-/ n. insult; disgrace. **contumelious** /-'miː-/ a.

contuse v.t. bruise. **contusion** n.

conundrum n. riddle, puzzle.

conurbation n. large urban area formed where towns have spread and merged.

convalesce v.i. regain health after illness. **convalescence** n., **convalescent** a. & n.

convection n. transmission of heat within a liquid or gas by movement of heated particles.

convector n. heating appliance that circulates warmed air.

convene v.t./i. assemble. **convener** n.

convenience n. being convenient; convenient thing; lavatory.

convenient a. easy to use or deal with; with easy access. **conveniently** adv.

convent n. residence of a community of nuns.

convention n. assembly; formal agreement; accepted custom. **conventional** a., **conventionally** adv.

converge v.i. come to or towards the same point. **convergence** n., **convergent** a.

conversant a. **conversant with** having knowledge of.

conversation n. informal talk between people. **conversational** a., **conversationally** adv.

conversationalist n. person who is good at conversation.

converse[1] /-'vɜːs/ v.i. hold a conversation. —n. (old use) conversation.

converse[2] /'kɒn-/ a. opposite, contrary. —n. converse idea or statement. **conversely** adv.

convert[1] /-'vɜːt/ v.t./i. change from one form or use etc. to another; cause to change an attitude or belief. **conversion** n., **converter** n.

convert[2] /'kɒn-/ n. person converted, esp. to a religious faith.

convertible a. able to be converted. —n. car with a folding or detachable roof. **convertibility** a.

convex a. curved like the outer surface of a ball. **convexity** n.

convey v.t. carry, transport, transmit; communicate as an idea. **conveyable** a.

conveyance n. conveying; means of transport, vehicle.

conveyancing n. business of transferring legal ownership of land.

conveyor n. person or thing that conveys; continuous moving belt conveying objects.

convict[1] /-'vɪkt/ v.t. prove or declare guilty.

convict[2] /'kɒn-/ n. convicted person in prison.

conviction n. convicting; firm opinion. **carry conviction** be convincing.

convince v.t. make (a person) feel certain that something is true.

convivial a. sociable and lively. **convivially** adv., **conviviality** n.

convocation n. convoking; assembly convoked.

convoke v.t. summon to assemble.

convoluted a. coiled, twisted.

convolution n. coil, twist.

convolvulus n. twining plant with trumpet-shaped flowers.

convoy n. ships or vehicles travelling under escort or together. —v.t. escort in a convoy.

convulse v.t. cause violent movement or a fit of laughter in.

convulsion n. violent involuntary movement of the body; upheaval.

convulsive a. like or causing convulsion. **convulsively** adv.

cony n. rabbit; (shop term) rabbit-fur.

coo v.i. make a soft murmuring sound like a dove. —n. this sound. —int. (sl.) exclamation of surprise.

cooee int. cry to attract attention.

cook v.t./i. prepare (food) by heating; undergo this process; (colloq.) falsify (accounts etc.). —n. person who cooks, esp. as a job. **cook-chill** a. cooked and refrigerated ready for later reheating. **cook up** (colloq.) concoct.

cooker n. stove for cooking food; apple suitable for cooking.

cookery n. art and practice of cooking.

cookie n. (US) sweet biscuit.

cool a. (-er, -est) fairly cold; providing coolness; calm, unexcited; not enthusiastic; (of a large sum of money) no less than. —n. coolness; (sl.) calmness. —v.t./i. make or become cool. **cooler** n., **coolly** adv., **coolness** n.

coolant n. fluid for cooling machinery etc.

coolie n. unskilled native labourer in eastern countries.

coomb n. valley on the side of a hill.

coon n. racoon.

coop n. cage for poultry. —v.t. confine, shut in.

co-op n. (colloq.) cooperative society; shop etc. run by this.

cooper n. person who makes or repairs casks and barrels.

cooperate v.i. work or act together. **cooperation** n.

cooperative a. cooperating; willing to help; based on economic cooperation. —n. farm or firm etc. run on this basis.

co-opt v.t. appoint to a committee etc. by invitation of existing members. **co-option** n., **co-optive** a.

coordinate[1] /-ət/ a. equal in importance. —n. any of the magnitudes used to give the position of a point.

coordinate[2] /-ert/ v.t. bring into a proper relation; cause to function together efficiently. **coordination** n., **coordinative** a., **coordinator** n.

coot n. a kind of water-bird.

cop v.t. (p.t. **copped**) (sl.) catch. —n. (sl.) capture; police officer.

cope[1] v.i. (colloq.) manage successfully. **cope with** deal successfully with.

cope[2] n. long loose cloak worn by clergy in certain ceremonies.

copier n. copying machine.

coping n. top (usu. sloping) row of masonry in a wall. **copingstone** n.

copious a. plentiful. **copiously** adv., **copiousness** n.

copper[1] n. reddish-brown metallic element; coin containing this; its colour. —a. made of copper.

copper[2] n. (sl.) policeman.

copperplate n. neat handwriting.

coppice, copse ns. group of small trees and undergrowth.

Coptic a. of the Egyptian branch of the Christian Church.

copula n. part of the verb be connecting subject and predicate.

copulate v.i. come together sexually as in mating. **copulation** n., **copulatory** a.

copy n. thing made to look like another; specimen of a book etc.; material for printing. —v.t. make a copy of; imitate. **copyist** n.

copyright n. sole right to print, publish, perform, etc., a work. —a. protected by copyright. —v.t. secure copyright for.

coquette /-'ket/ n. woman who flirts. **coquettish** a., **coquetry** n.

coracle n. small wicker boat.

coral n. hard red, pink, or white substance built by tiny sea creatures; reddish-pink colour.

cor anglais /'ɑ̃ɡlei/ n. musical instrument like the oboe but lower in pitch.

corbel n. stone or wooden support projecting from a wall. **corbelled** a.

cord n. long thin flexible material made from twisted strands; piece of this; similar structure in the body; corduroy.

corded a. with raised ridges.

cordial a. warm and friendly. —n. fruit-flavoured essence diluted to make a drink. **cordially** adv., **cordiality** n.

cordite n. smokeless explosive used as a propellant.

cordon n. line of police, soldiers, etc., enclosing something; cord or braid worn as a badge; fruit tree pruned to grow as a single stem. —v.t. enclose by a cordon.

cordon bleu /kɔːdɔ̃ 'blɜː/ of the highest degree of excellence in cookery.

corduroy n. cloth with velvety ridges; (pl.) trousers made of this.

core n. central or most important part; horny central part of an apple etc., containing seeds; unit storing one bit of data in a computer. —v.t. remove the core from. **corer** n.

co-respondent n. person with whom the respondent in a divorce suit is said to have committed adultery.

corgi n. (pl. -is) dog of a small Welsh breed with short legs.

coriander n. plant with seeds used for flavouring.

Corinthian a. of the most ornate style in Greek architecture.

cork n. light tough bark of a South European oak; piece of this used as a float; bottle-stopper. —v.t. stop up with a cork.

corkage n. restaurant's charge for serving wine.

corker n. (sl.) excellent person or thing.

corkscrew n. tool for extracting corks from bottles; spiral thing.

corm n. bulb-like underground stem from which buds grow.

cormorant n. large black sea-bird.

corn[1] n. wheat, oats, or maize; its grain; (sl.) something corny.

corn[2] n. small area of horny hardened skin, esp. on the foot.

corncrake n. bird with a harsh cry.

cornea n. transparent outer covering of the eyeball. **corneal** a.

corned a. preserved in salt.

cornelian /-'ni:-/ n. reddish or white semi-precious stone.

corner n. angle or area where two lines, sides, or streets meet; remote place; free kick or hit from the corner of the field in football or hockey; monopoly. —v.t./i. drive into a position from which there is no escape; move round a corner; obtain a monopoly of.

cornerstone n. basis; vital foundation.

cornet n. brass instrument like a small trumpet; cone-shaped wafer holding ice-cream.

cornflakes n.pl. breakfast cereal of toasted maize flakes.

cornflour n. flour made from maize.

cornflower n. plant (esp. blue-flowered) that grows among corn.

cornice n. ornamental moulding round the top of an indoor wall.

Cornish a. of Cornwall. —n. Celtic language of Cornwall.

cornucopia n. horn-shaped container overflowing with fruit and flowers, symbol of abundance.

corny a. (-ier, -iest) (colloq.) hackneyed. **corniness** n.

corolla n. proposition that follows logically from another.

corona n. (pl. -nae) ring of light round something.

coronary a. one of the arteries supplying blood to the heart; thrombosis in this.

coronation n. ceremony of crowning a monarch or consort.

coroner n. officer holding inquests.

coronet n. small crown.

corporal[1] n. non-commissioned officer next below sergeant.

corporal[2] a. of the body. **corporal punishment** whipping or beating.

corporate a. shared by members of a group; united in a group.

corporation n. group constituted to act as an individual or elected to govern a town; (colloq.) protruding abdomen.

corporeal a. having a body, tangible. **corporeally** adv., **corporeality** n.

corps /kɔ:(r)/ n. (pl. **corps**, pr. kɔ:z) military unit; organized body of people.

corpse n. dead body.

corpulent a. having a bulky body, fat. **corpulence** n.

corpus n. (pl. **corpora**) set of writings.

corpuscle n. blood-cell.

corral /-'rɑ:l/ n. (US) enclosure for cattle etc. —v.t. (p.t. **corralled**) put or keep in a corral.

correct *a.* true, accurate; in accordance with an approved way of behaving or working. —*v.t.* make correct; mark errors in; reprove; punish. **correctly** *adv.*, **correctness** *n.*, **corrector** *n.*

correction *n.* correcting; alteration correcting something.

corrective *a.* & *n.* (thing) correcting what is bad or harmful.

correlate *v.t./i.* compare or connect or be connected systematically. **correlation** *n.*, **correlative** *a.*

correspond *v.i.* be similar or equivalent or in harmony; write letters to each other.

correspondence *n.* similarity; writing letters; letters written.

correspondent *n.* person who writes letters; person employed by a newspaper etc. to gather news and send reports.

corridor *n.* passage in a building or train; strip of territory or air space giving access to a point or area.

corrigendum *n.* (*pl.* -**da**) thing to be corrected.

corroborate *v.t.* get or give supporting evidence. **corroboration** *n.*, **corroborative** *a.*, **corroboratory** *a.*

corrode *v.t.* destroy (metal etc.) gradually by chemical action. **corrosion** *n.*, **corrosive** *a.*

corrugated *a.* shaped into alternate ridges and grooves. **corrugation** *n.*

corrupt *a.* dishonest, accepting bribes; immoral, wicked; decaying. —*v.t.* make corrupt; spoil, taint. **corruption** *n.*, **corruptible** *a.*

corsage /-'sɑːʒ/ *n.* (*US*) flowers worn by a woman.

corsair *n.* (*old use*) pirate (ship).

corset *n.* close-fitting undergarment worn to shape or support the body.

corslet *n.* piece of armour covering the trunk.

cortège /-'teɪʒ/ *n.* funeral procession.

cortex *n.* (*pl.* -**ices**) outer part of the kidney or brain.

cortisone *n.* hormone produced by adrenal glands or synthetically.

coruscate *v.i.* sparkle. **coruscation** *n.*

corvette *n.* small fast gunboat.

cos[1] *n.* long-leaved lettuce.

cos[2] *abbr.* cosine.

cosh *n.* weighted weapon for hitting people. —*v.t.* hit with a cosh.

cosine *n.* sine of the complement of a given angle.

cosmetic *n.* substance for beautifying the complexion etc. —*a.* improving the appearance.

cosmic *a.* of the universe. **cosmic rays** radiation from outer space.

cosmogony /-'mɒg-/ *n.* (theory) of the origin of the universe.

cosmology *n.* science or theory of the universe. **cosmological** *a.*

cosmonaut *n.* Soviet astronaut.

cosmopolitan *a.* of or from all parts of the world; free from national prejudices. —*n.* cosmopolitan person.

cosmos *n.* universe.

Cossack *n.* member of a people of south Russia, famous as horsemen.

cosset *v.t.* (*p.t.* cosseted) pamper.

cost *v.t.* (*p.t.* cost) have as its price; involve the sacrifice or loss of; (*p.t.* costed) fix or estimate the cost of. —*n.* what a thing costs; (*pl.*) expenses of a lawsuit.

costal *a.* of the ribs.

costermonger *n.* person selling fruit etc. from a barrow in the street.

costly *a.* (-**ier**, -**iest**) costing much, expensive. **costliness** *n.*

costume *n.* style of clothes, esp. that of a historical period; garment(s) for a specified activity.

costumier *n.* person who makes or sells costumes.

cosy *a.* (-ier, -iest) warm and comfortable. —*n.* cover to keep a teapot hot. **cosily** *adv.*, **cosiness** *n.*

cot *n.* child's bed with high sides; light bed. **cot-death** *n.* unexplained death of a sleeping baby.

cote *n.* shelter for birds or animals.

coterie /ˈkəʊtərɪ/ *n.* select group.

cotoneaster /kəˈtəʊnɪˈæstə/ *n.* shrub or tree with red berries.

cottage *n.* small simple house in the country. **cottage cheese** that made from curds without pressing. **cottage hospital** one without resident doctors. **cottage industry** one carried on at home. **cottage loaf** loaf with a small round mass on top of a larger one. **cottage pie** dish of minced meat topped with mashed potato.

cottager *n.* country person living in a cottage.

cotter pin bolt or wedge securing machine parts.

cotton *n.* soft white substance round the seeds of a tropical plant; this plant; thread or fabric made from cotton. —*v.i.* **cotton on** (*sl.*) understand. **cotton wool** raw cotton prepared as wadding. **cottony** *a.*

cotyledon *n.* first leaf growing from a seed.

couch¹ *n.* long piece of furniture for lying or sitting on, usu. with a head-rest at one end. —*v.t.* express in a specified way. **couch potato** (*sl.*) person who likes lazing at home.

couch² *n.* (also **couch-grass**) weed with long creeping roots.

couchette /kuːˈʃet/ *n.* railway sleeping-berth convertible to seats.

cougar /ˈkuːgə(r)/ *n.* (*US*) puma.

cough *v.t./i.* expel air etc. from lungs with a sudden sharp sound. —*n.* act or sound of coughing; illness causing coughing.

could *p.t.* of **can**²; feel inclined to.

couldn't (*colloq.*) = could not.

coulomb /ˈkuːlɒm/ *n.* unit of electric charge.

coulter /ˈkəʊlt-/ *n.* blade in front of a ploughshare.

council *n.* assembly to advise on, discuss, or organize something. **council house** etc. one owned and let by a municipal council. **council tax** tax replacing domestic rates.

councillor *n.* member of a council.

counsel *n.* advice, suggestions; barrister(s). —*v.t.* (*p.t.* **counselled**) advise. **keep one's own counsel** not confide in others.

counsellor *n.*

count¹ *v.t./i.* find the total of; say numbers in order; include or be included in a reckoning; be important; regard as. —*n.* counting, number reached by this; point being considered. **count on** rely on; expect confidently.

count² *n.* foreign nobleman.

countdown *n.* counting seconds backwards to zero.

countenance *n.* expression of the face; appearance of approval. —*v.t.* give approval to.

counter¹ *n.* flat-topped fitment over which goods are sold or business transacted with customers; apparatus for counting things; small disc etc. used for keeping account in table-games.

counter² *adv.* in the opposite direction. —*a.* opposed. —*v.t./i.* hinder or defeat by an opposing action. —*n.* return action or blow.

counter- *pref.* rival; retaliatory; reversed; opposite.

counteract *v.t.* reduce or prevent the effects of. **counteraction** *n.*

counter-attack *n.* & *v.t./i.* attack in reply to an opponent's attack.

counterbalance *n.* weight or influence balancing another. —*v.t.* act as a counterbalance to.

counterblast *n.* powerful retort.

counter-espionage n. action against an enemy's spy system.

counterfeit a., n., & v.t. fake.

counterfoil n. section of a cheque or receipt kept as a record.

counter-intelligence n. counter-espionage.

countermand v.t. cancel.

countermeasure n. action taken to counteract danger etc.

counterpane n. bedspread.

counterpart n. person or thing corresponding to another.

counterpoint n. method of combining melodies.

counterpoise n. & v.t. counterbalance.

counter-productive a. having the opposite of the desired effect.

countersign n. password. —v.t. add a confirming signature to.

countersink v.t. (p.t. -sunk) sink (a screw-head) into a shaped cavity so that the surface is level.

counter-tenor n. male alto.

countervail v.t. counterbalance; avail against.

counterweight n. & v.t. counterbalance.

countess n. count's or earl's wife or widow; woman with the rank of count or earl.

countless a. too many to be counted.

countrified a. like the countryside or country life.

country n. nation's or State's land; people of this; State of which one is a member; region; land consisting of fields etc. with few buildings. **country dance** folk-dance. **go to the country** hold a general election.

countryman n. (pl. -men) man living in the country; man of one's own country. **countrywoman** n.fem. (pl. -women)

countryside n. country district(s).

county n. major administrative division of a country; its residents; families of high social level long established in a county.

coup /ku:/ n. sudden action taken to obtain power etc.

coup de grâce /ku: də 'grɑːs/ finishing-stroke.

coup d'état /ku: der'tɑ:/ sudden overthrow of a government by force or illegal means.

coupé /'ku:peɪ/ n. closed two-door car with a sloping back.

couple n. two people or things; married or engaged pair; partners in a dance. —v.t./i. fasten or link together; join by coupling; copulate. **coupler** n.

couplet n. two successive rhyming lines of verse.

coupling n. device connecting railway carriages or machine parts.

coupon n. form or ticket entitling the holder to something; entry-form for a football pool etc.

courage n. ability to control fear when facing danger or pain. **courageous** a., **courageously** adv.

courgette /kʊə'ʒet/ n. a kind of small vegetable marrow.

courier n. messenger carrying documents; person employed to guide and assist tourists.

course n. onward progress; direction taken or intended; series of lessons or treatments etc.; area on which golf is played or a race takes place; layer of stone etc. in a building; one part of a meal. —v.t./i. hunt with hounds that follow game by sight not scent; move or flow freely. **of course** without doubt.

courser n. (poetic) swift horse.

court n. courtyard; area marked out for certain games; sovereign's establishment with attendants; lawcourt. —v.t. try to win the favour or support or love of; invite (danger etc.). **court martial** (pl. **courts martial**) court trying offences against military law; trial by this. **court-martial** v.t. (p.t. -martialled) try by court martial. **pay court to** court.

courteous *a.* polite. **courteously** *adv.*, **courteousness** *n.*

courtesan /kɔːtɪˈzan/ *n.* (old use) prostitute with upper-class clients.

courtesy *n.* courteous behaviour or act. **by courtesy of** by permission of.

courtier *n.* (old use) one of a sovereign's companions at court.

courtly *a.* dignified and polite. **courtliness** *n.*

courtship *n.* courting, esp. of an intended wife or mate.

courtyard *n.* space enclosed by walls or buildings.

cousin *n.* (also **first cousin**) child of one's uncle or aunt. **second cousin** child of one's parent's cousin. **cousinly** *adv.*

couture /kuːˈtjʊə(r)/ *n.* design and making of fashionable clothes.

couturier /kuːˈtjʊərɪeɪ/ *n.* designer of fashionable clothes.

cove *n.* small bay; curved moulding.

coven *n.* assembly esp. of witches.

covenant *n.* formal agreement, contract. —*v.i.* make a covenant.

Coventry *n.* **send to Coventry** refuse to speak to or associate with.

cover *v.t.* place or be or spread over; conceal or protect thus; travel over (a distance); have within range of gun's; protect by insurance or a guarantee; be enough to pay for; deal with (a subject etc.); report for a newspaper etc. —*n.* thing that covers; wrapper, envelope, binding of a book; screen, shelter, protection; place laid at a meal. **cover up** conceal (a thing or fact). **cover-up** *n.*

coverage *n.* process of covering; area or risk etc. covered.

coverlet *n.* cover lying over other bedclothes.

covert *n.* thick undergrowth where animals hide; feather covering the base of another. —*a.* concealed, done secretly. **covertly** *adv.*, **covertness** *n.*

covet *v.t.* (*p.t.* **coveted**) desire eagerly (esp. a thing belonging to another person). **covetous** *a.*, **covetously** *adv.*, **covetousness** *n.*

covey (*pl.* **-eys**) group of partridges.

cow[1] *n.* fully grown female of cattle or other large animals, esp. one that has had young.

cow[2] *v.t.* intimidate.

coward *n.* person who lacks courage. **cowardly** *a.*, **cowardliness** *n.*

cowardice *n.* lack of courage.

cowboy *n.* man in charge of grazing cattle on a ranch; (colloq.) person with reckless or unscrupulous methods in business.

cower *v.i.* crouch or shrink in fear.

cowl *n.* monk's hood or hooded robe; hood-shaped covering.

cowling *n.* removable metal cover on an engine.

cowrie *n.* a kind of sea shell.

cowshed *n.* shed for cattle.

cowslip *n.* wild plant with small fragrant yellow flowers.

cox *n.* coxswain. —*v.t.* act as cox of (a racing-boat).

coxswain /ˈkɒksweɪn, *nautical* ˈkɒks(ə)n/ *n.* steersman.

coy *a.* (**-er, -est**) pretending to be shy or embarrassed. **coyly** *adv.*, **coyness** *n.*

coyote /ˈkɔɪəʊtɪ/ *n.* prairie-wolf.

coypu *n.* beaver-like water animal.

cozen *v.t./i.* cheat, defraud.

crab *n.* ten-legged shellfish. —*v.t./i.* (*p.t.* **crabbed**) find fault with; grumble. **crab-apple** *n.* a kind of small sour apple. **crabby** *a.*

crabbed /-bɪd/ *a.* bad-tempered; (of handwriting) hard to read.

crack *n.* sudden sharp noise; sharp blow; line where a thing is broken but not separated; (sl.) joke; (sl.) potent form of cocaine. —*a.* (colloq.) first-rate. —*v.t./i.* make or cause to make the sound of a crack; break without parting completely; knock sharply; break into or through; find a solution to (a problem); tell (a joke); (of the voice) become harsh; give way under strain; break down (heavy oils) to produce lighter ones. **crack-brained** a. (colloq.) crazy. **crack down on** (colloq.) take severe measures against. **crack up** (colloq.) have a physical or mental breakdown; praise. **get cracking** (colloq.) start working.

crackdown n. (colloq.) severe measures against something.

cracked a. (sl.) crazy.

cracker n. small explosive firework; toy paper tube made to give an explosive crack when pulled apart; thin dry biscuit.

crackers a. (sl.) crazy.

cracking a. (sl.) very good.

crackle v.t./i. make or cause to make a series of light cracking sounds. —n. these sounds.

crackling n. crisp skin on roast pork.

crackpot n. (sl.) eccentric or impractical person. —a. (sl.) crazy; unworkable.

cradle n. baby's bed usu. on rockers; place where something originates; supporting structure. —v.t. hold or support gently.

craft n. skill, technique; occupation requiring this; cunning, deceit; (pl. **craft**) ship, boat, raft, aircraft, or spacecraft.

craftsman n. (pl. **-men**) worker skilled in a craft. **craftsmanship** n.

crafty a. (**-ier**, **-iest**) cunning, using underhand methods. **craftily** adv., **craftiness** n.

crag n. steep or rugged rock.

craggy a. (**-ier**, **-iest**) rugged. **craggily** adv., **cragginess** n.

cram v.t. (p.t. **crammed**) force into too small a space; overfill thus; study intensively for an examination. **crammer** n.

cramp n. painful involuntary tightening of a muscle etc.; metal bar with bent ends for holding masonry etc. together. —v.t. keep within too narrow limits.

crampon n. spiked plate worn on boots for climbing on ice.

cranberry n. small red acid berry; shrub bearing this.

crane n. large wading bird; apparatus for lifting and moving heavy objects. —v.t./i. stretch (one's neck) to see something. **crane-fly** n. long-legged flying insect.

cranium n. (pl. **-ia**) skull. **cranial** a.

crank[1] n. L-shaped part for converting to-and-fro into circular motion. —v.t. turn with a crank. **crankshaft** n. shaft turned thus.

crank[2] n. person with very strange ideas. **cranky** a.

cranny n. crevice.

crape n. (esp. black) crêpe.

craps n.pl. (US) gambling game played with a pair of dice.

crash n. loud noise of breakage; violent collision or fall; financial collapse. —v.t./i. make a crash; move or go with a crash; be or cause to be involved in a crash; (colloq.) gatecrash. —a. involving intense effort to achieve something rapidly. **crash-helmet** n. padded helmet worn to protect the head in a crash. **crash-land** v.t./i. land (an aircraft) in emergency, esp. with damage to it. **crash-landing** n.

crass a. very stupid.

crate n. packing-case made of wooden slats; (sl.) old aircraft or car. —v.t. pack in crate(s).

crater n. bowl-shaped cavity.

cravat n. short scarf; neck-tie.

crave v.t./i. feel an intense longing (for); ask earnestly for.

craven a. cowardly. **cravenly** adv.

craving n. intense longing.

craw n. bird's crop.

crawfish n. large spiny sea lobster.

crawl *v.i.* move on hands and knees or with the body on the ground; move very slowly; (*colloq.*) seek favour by servile behaviour; be covered or feel as if covered with crawling things. —*n.* crawling movement or pace; overarm swimming-stroke. **crawler** *n.*

crayfish *n.* freshwater shellfish like a small lobster; crawfish.

crayon *n.* stick of coloured wax etc. —*v.t.* draw or colour with crayon(s).

craze *n.* temporary enthusiasm; its object.

crazed *a.* driven insane.

crazy *a.* (-ier, -iest) insane; very foolish; (*colloq.*) madly eager. **crazy paving** paving made of irregular pieces. **crazily** *adv.*, **craziness** *n.*

creak *n.* harsh squeak. —*v.i.* make this sound. **creaky** *a.*, **creakily** *adv.*

cream *n.* fatty part of milk; its colour, yellowish-white; cream-like substance; best part. —*a.* cream-coloured. —*v.t.* remove the cream from; beat to a creamy consistency; apply cosmetic cream to. **cream cheese** soft rich cheese. **cream cracker** crisp unsweetened biscuit. **creamy** *a.*

crease *n.* line made by crushing or pressing; line marking the limit of the bowler's or batsman's position in cricket. —*v.t./i.* make a crease in; develop creases.

create *v.t./i.* bring into existence; produce by what one does; give a new rank to; (*sl.*) make a fuss. **creation** *n.*, **creative** *a.*, **creativity** *n.*, **creator** *n.*

creature *n.* animal, person.

crèche /kreʃ/ *n.* day nursery.

cred *n.* (*sl.*) (*colloq.*) credibility, reputation.

credence /ˈkriː-/ *n.* belief; small table for the elements of the Eucharist.

credentials *n.pl.* documents showing that a person is who or what he or she claims to be.

credible *a.* believable. **credibly** *adv.*, **credibility** *n.*

credit *n.* belief that a thing is true; honour for an achievement etc., good reputation; source of this; system of allowing payment to be deferred; sum at a person's disposal in a bank; entry in an account for a sum paid; acknowledgement of services to a book or film etc. —*v.t.* (*p.t.* credited) believe; attribute; enter as credit. **credit card** card authorizing a person to buy on credit. **creditworthy** *a.*

creditable *a.* deserving praise. **creditably** *adv.*

creditor *n.* person to whom money is owed.

credulous *a.* too ready to believe things. **credulously** *adv.*, **credulousness** *n.*, **credulity** *n.*

creed *n.* set of beliefs or principles.

creek *n.* narrow inlet of water, esp. on a coast; (*US*) tributary. **up the creek** (*sl.*) in difficulties.

creel *n.* fisherman's wicker basket for carrying fish.

creep *v.i.* (*p.t.* crept) move with the body close to the ground; move timidly, slowly, or stealthily; develop gradually; (of a plant) grow along the ground or a wall etc.; feel creepy. —*n.* creeping; (*sl.*) person one dislikes; (*pl.*) nervous sensation.

creeper *n.* creeping plant.

creepy *a.* (-ier, -iest) feeling or causing a nervous shivering sensation. **creepiness** *n.*

cremate *v.t.* burn (a corpse) to ashes. **cremation** *n.*

crematorium /krem-/ *n.* (*pl.* -ia) place where corpses are cremated.

crème de menthe /krem də mãt/ *n.* peppermint-flavoured liqueur.

crenellated *a.* having battlements. **crenellation** *n.*

Creole /'kri:əʊl/ n. descendant of European settlers in the West Indies or in Central or South America; their dialect; hybrid (European and other) language.

creosote n. brown oily liquid distilled from coal tar, used as a preservative for wood; colourless antiseptic liquid distilled from wood tar. —v.t. treat with this.

crêpe n. fabric with a wrinkled surface; rubber with a wrinkled texture, used for shoe-soles. **crêpe paper** thin crêpe-like paper. **crêpey** a., **crêpy** a.

crept see **creep**.

crepuscular a. active at twilight.

crescendo adv. & n. (pl. -os) increasing in loudness.

crescent n. narrow curved shape tapering to a point at each end; curved street of houses.

cress n. plant with hot-tasting leaves used in salads.

crest n. tuft or outgrowth on a bird's or animal's head; plume on a helmet; top of a slope or hill, white top of a large wave; design above a shield on a coat of arms or used separately. **crested** a.

crestfallen a. disappointed at failure.

cretaceous /-'teɪʃəs/ a. chalky.

cretin /'kre-/ n. person who is deformed and mentally defective through lack of thyroid hormone. **cretinous** a., **cretinism** n.

cretonne /kre'tɒn/ n. heavy cotton cloth used in furnishings.

crevasse n. deep open crack esp. in a glacier.

crevice n. narrow gap in a surface.

crew[1] see **crow**.

crew[2] n. people working a ship or aircraft; group working together; gang. —v.t./i. act as crew (of). **crew cut** man's closely cropped haircut.

crewel n. thin worsted yarn for embroidery. **crewel needle** blunt needle used in embroidery.

crib n. rack for fodder; model of the manger-scene at Bethlehem; cot; (colloq.) cribbage; (colloq.) piece of cribbing; translation for students' use. —v.t. (p.t. **cribbed**) copy unfairly.

cribbage n. a card-game.

crick n. painful stiffness in the neck or back. —v.t. cause this to.

cricket[1] n. outdoor game for two teams of 11 players with ball, bats, and wickets. **not cricket** (colloq.) not fair play. **cricketer** n.

cricket[2] n. brown insect resembling a grasshopper.

crier n. official making public announcements in streets etc.

crikey int. (sl.) exclamation of surprise.

crime n. serious offence, act that breaks a law; illegal acts.

criminal n. person guilty of a crime. —a. of or involving crime. **criminally** adv., **criminality** n.

criminalize v.t. treat as criminal. **criminalization** n.

criminology n. study of crime. **criminologist** n.

crimson a. & n. deep red.

cringe v.i. cower; behave obsequiously.

crinkle n. & v.t./i. wrinkle.

crinoline n. light framework formerly worn to make a long skirt stand out.

cripple n. lame person. —v.t. make lame; weaken seriously.

crisis n. (pl. **crises**) decisive moment; time of acute difficulty.

crisp a. (-er, -est) brittle; slightly stiff; cold and bracing; brisk and decisive. —n. thin slice of potato fried crisp. —v.t./i. make or become crisp. **crisply** adv., **crispness** n., **crispy** a.

crispbread n. thin crisp biscuit of crushed rye etc.

criss-cross n. pattern of crossing lines. —a. & adv. in this pattern.

—*v.t./i.* mark, form, or move thus, intersect.

criterion *n.* (pl. **-ia**) standard of judgement.

critic *n.* person who points out faults; one skilled in criticism.

critical *a.* looking for faults; expressing criticism; of or at a crisis. **critically** *adv.* **criticality** *n.*

criticism *n.* pointing out of faults; judging of merit, esp. of literary or artistic work.

criticize *v.t.* express criticism of.

critique /'ti:k/ *n.* critical essay.

croak *n.* deep hoarse cry or sound like that of a frog. —*v.t./i.* utter or speak with a croak; (*sl.*) die, kill. **croaker** *n.*, **croaky** *a.*

crochet /'krəʊʃeɪ/ *n.* handiwork done with a thread and a hooked needle. —*v.t./i.* make by or do such work.

crock[1] *n.* earthenware pot; broken piece of this.

crock[2] *n.* (*colloq.*) person who is disabled or often ill; worn-out vehicle etc. —*v.i.* (*colloq.*) disable. **crock up** become a crock.

crockery *n.* household china.

crocodile *n.* large amphibious tropical reptile; its skin; (*colloq.*) line of children walking in pairs. **crocodile tears** pretence of sorrow. **crocodilian** *a.* & *n.*

crocus *n.* (pl. **-uses**) spring-flowering plant growing from a corm.

croft *n.* small enclosed field or rented farm in Scotland.

crofter *n.* tenant of a croft.

croissant /'krwæsɑ̃/ *n.* rich crescent-shaped roll.

cromlech /'krɒmlek/ *n.* dolmen.

crone *n.* withered old woman.

crony *n.* close friend or companion.

crook *n.* hooked stick; bent thing; (*colloq.*) criminal. —*v.t.* bend.

crooked /-ɪd/ *a.* not straight; dishonest. **crookedly** *adv.*

croon *v.t./i.* sing softly. **crooner** *n.*

crop *n.* batch of plants grown for their produce; harvest from this; group or amount produced at one time; pouch in a bird's gullet where food is broken up for digestion; whip-handle; very short haircut. —*v.t./i.* (*p.t.* **cropped**) cut or bite off; produce or gather as harvest. **crop up** occur unexpectedly.

cropper *n.* (*sl.*) heavy fall.

croquet /'krəʊkeɪ/ *n.* game played on a lawn with balls and mallets.

croquette /-'ket/ *n.* fried ball or roll of potato, meat, or fish.

crosier *n.* bishop's hooked staff.

cross *n.* mark made by drawing one line intersecting another; thing shaped like this; stake with a transverse bar used in crucifixion (**the Cross** that on which Christ was crucified); affliction to be borne with Christian patience; hybrid animal or plant; mixture of or compromise between two things; crossing shot in football etc. —*v.t./i.* go or extend across; place crosswise; draw line(s) across, mark (a cheque) thus so that it must be paid into a bank; make the sign of the Cross on or over; oppose the wishes of; cause to interbreed; cross-fertilize. —*a.* passing from side to side; reciprocal; showing bad temper. **at cross purposes** misunderstanding or conflicting. **cross off** or **out** draw a line through (an item) to make it invalid. **on the cross** diagonally. **crossly** *adv.*, **crossness** *n.*

crossbar *n.* horizontal bar.

crossbill *n.* finch with crossing mandibles.

crossbow *n.* mechanical bow fixed across a wooden stock.

cross-bred *a.* produced by interbreeding. **cross-breed** *n.* cross-bred animal. **cross-breeding** *n.*

cross-check *v.t./i.* check again by a different method.

crosse *n.* netted crook used in lacrosse.

cross-examine v.t. cross-question, esp. in a lawcourt. **cross-examination** n.

cross-eyed a. squinting.

cross-fertilize v.t. fertilize (a plant) from one of a different kind. **cross-fertilization** n.

crossfire n. gunfire crossing other line(s) of fire.

cross-grained a. bad-tempered.

crossing n. journey across water; place where things cross; place for pedestrians to cross a road.

crosspatch n. bad-tempered person.

crossply a. (of a tyre) having fabric layers with cords lying crosswise.

cross-question v.t. question closely so as to test earlier answers.

cross-reference n. reference to another place in the same book etc.

crossroads n. place where roads intersect.

cross-section n. diagram showing internal structure; representative sample.

crosswise adv. in the form of a cross.

crossword n. puzzle in which intersecting words have to be inserted into a diagram.

crotch n. place where things fork, esp. where legs join the trunk.

crotchet n. note in music, half a minim.

crotchety a. peevish. **crotchetiness** n.

crouch v.i. stoop low with legs tightly bent. —n. this position.

croup[1] /kru:p/ n. laryngitis in children, with a hard cough.

croup[2] /kru:p/ n. rump, esp. of a horse.

croupier /ˈkru:pɪə(r)/ n. person who rakes in stakes and pays out winnings at a gaming-table.

croûton /ˈkru:tɔ̃/ n. small piece of fried or toasted bread.

crow n. large black bird; crowing cry or sound. —v.i. utter a cock's cry (p.t. **crew**); (of a baby) make sounds of pleasure; exult. **as the crow flies** in a straight line.

crow's-feet n.pl. wrinkles beside the eyes. **crow's-nest** n. protected platform on a ship's mast.

crowbar n. bar of iron, usually with a bent end, used as a lever.

crowd n. large group. —v.t./i. come together in a crowd; fill or occupy fully.

crown n. monarch's ceremonial headdress, usu. a circlet of gold etc.; **the Crown** supreme governing power in a monarchy; crown-shaped object or ornament; top part of a head, hat, or arched thing. —v.t. place a crown on; form or cover or ornament the top part of; be a climax to; (sl.) hit on the head. **Crown Court** court where criminal cases are tried in England and Wales. **Crown prince** or **princess** heir to a throne.

crucial a. very important, decisive. **crucially** adv. **cruciality** n.

crucible n. pot in which metals are melted.

crucifix n. model of the Cross or of Christ on this.

crucifixion n. crucifying; **the Crucifixion** that of Christ.

cruciform a. cross-shaped.

crucify v.t. put to death by nailing or binding to a transverse bar; cause extreme mental pain to.

crude a. (-er, -est) in a natural or raw state; not well finished: lacking good manners, vulgar. **crudely** adv., **crudity** n.

cruel a. (crueller, cruellest) feeling pleasure in another's suffering; hard-hearted; causing suffering. **cruelly** adv., **cruelty** n.

cruet n. set of containers for oil, vinegar, or salt etc. at the table; stand holding these.

cruise v.i. sail for pleasure or on patrol; travel at a moderate economical speed. —n. cruising voyage. **cruise missile** missile guiding itself at low altitudes by reference to ground features.

cruiser *n.* fast warship; motor boat with a cabin.

crumb *n.* small fragment, esp. of bread or similar food. **crumby** *a.*

crumble *v.t./i.* break into small fragments. —*n.* pudding of fruit with crumbly topping.

crumbly *a.* easily crumbled.

crummy *a.* (-ier, -iest) (*sl.*) dirty, squalid; inferior. **crumminess** *n.*

crump *n.* dull thud of an explosion. —*v.i.* make this sound.

crumpet *n.* flat soft yeast cake eaten toasted.

crumple *v.t./i.* crush or become crushed into creases; collapse.

crunch *v.t.* crush noisily with the teeth; make this sound. —*n.* sound of crunching; decisive event.

crunchy *a.* able to be crunched.

crupper *n.* strap looped under a horse's tail from the back of a saddle.

crusade *n.* medieval Christian military expedition to recover the Holy Land from Muslims; campaign against an evil. —*v.i.* take part in a crusade. **crusader** *n.*

crush *v.t./i.* press so as to break or injure or wrinkle; pound into fragments; become crushed; defeat or subdue completely. —*n.* crowded mass of people; drink made from crushed fruit; (*sl.*) infatuation.

crust *n.* hard outer layer, esp. of bread.

crustacean *n.* animal with a hard shell (e.g. lobster).

crusty *a.* (-ier, -iest) with a crisp crust; having a harsh manner.

crutch *n.* support for a lame person; crotch.

crux *n.* (*pl.* **cruces**) vital part of a problem; difficult point.

cry *n.* loud wordless sound uttered; appeal; rallying call; spell of weeping. —*v.t./i.* shed tears; call loudly; appeal for help etc.

cry-baby *n.* person who weeps easily. **cry off** withdraw from a promise.

cryogenics *n.* branch of physics dealing with very low temperatures. **cryogenic** *a.*

crypt *n.* room below the floor of a church.

cryptic *a.* concealing its meaning in a puzzling way. **cryptically** *adv.*

cryptogam *n.* non-flowering plant such as a fern, moss, or fungus.

cryptogram *n.* thing written in cipher.

cryptography *n.* study of ciphers. **cryptographer** *n.*

crystal *a.* glass-like mineral; piece of this; high-quality glass; symmetrical piece of a solidified substance.

crystalline /-am/ *a.* like or made of crystal; clear.

crystallize *v.t./i.* form into crystals; make or become definite in form. **crystallized fruit** fruit preserved in sugar. **crystallization** *n.*

cub *n.* young of certain animals. **Cub** (*Scout*) member of the junior branch of the Scout Association.

cubby-hole *n.* small compartment.

cube *n.* solid object with six equal square sides; product of a number multiplied by itself twice. —*v.t.* cut into small cubes; find the cube of. **cube root** number which produces a given number when cubed.

cubic *a.* of three dimensions. **cubic centimetre** volume of a cube with sides 1 cm long, used as a unit.

cubical *a.* cube-shaped.

cubicle *n.* small division of a large room, screened for privacy.

cubism *n.* style of painting in which objects are shown as geometrical shapes. **cubist** *n.*

cuckold n. man whose wife has committed adultery. —v.t. make a cuckold of.

cuckoo n. bird with a call that is like its name.

cucumber n. long green-skinned fruit eaten as salad; plant producing this.

cud n. food that cattle bring back from the stomach into the mouth and chew again.

cuddle v.t./i. hug lovingly; nestle. —n. gentle hug. **cuddlesome**, **cuddly** adjs. pleasant to cuddle.

cudgel n. short thick stick used as a weapon. —v.t. (p.t. **cudgelled**) beat with a cudgel. **cudgel one's brains** think hard about a problem.

cue[1] n. & v.t. (pres.p. **cueing**) signal to do something. —v.t. strike with a cue.

cue[2] n. long rod for striking balls in billiards etc.

cuff n. band of cloth round the edge of a sleeve; cuffing blow. —v.t. strike with the open hand. **cuff-link** n. device of two linked discs etc. to hold cuff edges together. **off the cuff** without preparation.

cui bono? /kwiː ˈbəʊnəʊ/ who gains?

cuirass /kwɪˈræs/ n. armour breastplate and back-plate fastened together.

cuisine /kwɪˈziːn/ n. style of cooking.

cul-de-sac n. (pl. **culs-de-sac**) street closed at one end.

culinary /ˈkʌl-/ a. of, for, or used in cooking.

cull v.t. pick (flowers); select; select and kill (surplus animals). —n. culling; thing(s) culled.

culminate v.i. reach its highest point or degree. **culmination** n.

culotte /kjuːˈlɒt/ n.pl. women's trousers styled to resemble a skirt.

culpable a. deserving blame. **culpably** adv., **culpability** n.

culprit n. person who has committed a slight offence.

cult n. system of religious worship; worship of a person or thing. **cultic** a.

cultivar n. variety of plant produced by cultivation.

cultivate v.t. prepare and use (land) for crops; produce (crops) by tending them; develop by practice; further one's acquaintance with (a person). **cultivation** n., **cultivator** n.

culture n. developed understanding of literature, art, music, etc.; type of civilization; artificial rearing of bees, bacteria, etc.; bacteria grown for study. —v.t. grow in artificial conditions. **cultural** a., **culturally** adv.

cultured a. exhibiting culture. **cultured pearl** pearl artificially induced in an oyster.

culvert n. drain under a road etc.

cumber v.t. hamper, burden.

cumbersome a. clumsy to carry or use.

cumin n. plant with aromatic seed.

cummerbund n. sash for the waist worn by men with evening dress.

cumulative /ˈkjuː-/ a. increasing by additions. **cumulatively** adv.

cumulus n. (pl. **-li**) cloud in heaped-up rounded masses.

cuneiform /ˈkjuːnɪfɔːm/ n. ancient writing done in wedge-shaped strokes cut into stone etc.

cunning a. skilled at deception, crafty; ingenious; (US) attractive. —n. craftiness, ingenuity. **cunningly** adv.

cup n. drinking-vessel usu. with a handle at the side; amount it holds; ornamental goblet as a prize; rounded cavity; wine or fruit-juice with added flavourings. —v.t. (p.t. **cupped**) form into a cup-like shape; hold as if in a cup. **cupful** n. (pl. **cupfuls**).

cupboard *n.* recess or piece of furniture with a door, in which things may be stored.

cupidity *n.* greed for gain.

cupola /'kju:-/ *n.* small dome.

cupreous *a.* of or like copper.

cupric *a.* of copper.

cur *n.* worthless dog.

curable *a.* able to be cured.

curaçao /'kjʊərəsəʊ/ *n.* orange-flavoured liqueur.

curacy *n.* position of curate.

curare /-'rɑːrɪ/ *n.* vegetable poison that induces paralysis.

curate *n.* member of the clergy who assists a parish priest.

curative *a.* curing illness.

curator *n.* person in charge of a museum or other collection.

curb *n.* means of restraint. —*v.t.* restrain.

curd *n.* thick soft substance, esp. (*pl.*) that formed when milk turns sour.

curdle *v.t./i.* form or cause to form curds.

cure *v.t.* restore to health; get rid of (a disease or trouble etc.); preserve by salting, drying, etc. —*n.* curing; substance or treatment that cures disease etc.

curette /-'ret/ *n.* surgical scraping-instrument. —*v.t.* scrape with this. **curettage** *n.*

curfew *n.* signal or time after which people must stay indoors.

curio *n.* (*pl.* -os) unusual and therefore interesting object.

curiosity *n.* desire to find out and know things; curio.

curious *a.* eager to learn or know something; strange, unusual. **curiously** *adv.*, **curiousness** *n.*

curium *n.* artificial radioactive element.

curl *v.t./i.* curve, esp. in a spiral shape or course. —*n.* coiled thing or shape; coiled lock of hair.

curler *n.* device for curling hair.

curlew *n.* wading bird with a long curved bill.

curling *n.* game like bowls played on ice.

curly *a.* (-ier, -iest) curling, full of curls. **curliness** *n.*

curmudgeon /kə'mʌdʒ(ə)n/ *n.* badtempered person.

currant *n.* dried grape used in cookery; small round edible berry, shrub producing this.

currency *n.* money in use; state of being widely known.

current *a.* belonging to the present time; in general use. —*n.* body of water or air moving in one direction; flow of electricity. **currently** *adv.*

curriculum *n.* (*pl.* -la) course of study. **curriculum vitae** /'viːtaɪ/ brief account of one's career.

curry[1] *n.* seasoning made with hot-tasting spices; dish flavoured with this. —*v.t.* flavour with curry.

curry[2] *v.t.* groom with a **currycomb**, a pad with rubber or plastic projections. **curry favour** win favour by flattery.

curse *n.* call for evil to come on a person or thing; a great evil; violent exclamation of anger. —*v.t./i.* utter a curse (against); afflict **cursed** /-std/ *a.*

cursive *a.* & *n.* (writing) done with joined letters.

cursor *n.* movable indicator on a VDU screen; transparent slide on a slide-rule.

cursory *a.* hasty and not thorough. **cursorily** *adv.*, **cursoriness** *n.*

curt *a.* noticeably or rudely brief. **curtly** *adv.*, **curtness** *n.*

curtail *v.t.* cut short, reduce. **curtailment** *n.*

curtain *n.* piece of cloth etc. hung as a screen, esp. at a window; fall of a stage-curtain at the end of an act or scene. —*v.t.* provide or shut off with curtain(s).

curtsy *n.* movement of respect made by bending the knees. —*v.i.* make a curtsy.

curvaceous *a.* (*colloq.*) having a shapely curved figure.

curvature *n.* curving; curved form.

curve *n.* line or surface with no part straight or flat. —*v.t./i.* form (into) a curve.

curvet /-'vet/ *n.* horse's frisky leap. —*v.i.* (*p.t.* **curvetted**) make this.

curvilinear *a.* using curved lines.

cushion *n.* stuffed bag used as a pad, esp. for leaning against; padded part; body of air supporting a hovercraft. —*v.t.* protect with a pad; lessen the impact of; protect thus.

cushy *a.* (**-ier, -iest**) (*colloq.*) pleasant and easy. **cushily** *adv.*, **cushiness** *n.*

cusp *n.* pointed part where curves meet. **cuspid** *a.*, **cuspidal** *a.*

cuss *n.* (*colloq.*) curse; perverse person. **cussed** /-ɪd/ *a.* perverse.

custard *n.* dish or sauce made with milk and eggs or flavoured cornflour.

custodian *n.* guardian, keeper.

custody *n.* safe-keeping; imprisonment.

custom *n.* usual way of behaving or acting; regular dealing by customer(s); (*pl.*) duty on imported goods, officials dealing with these.

customary *a.* usual. **customarily** *adv.*

customer *n.* person buying goods or services from a shop etc.

cut *v.t./i.* (*p.t.* **cut**, *pres.p.* **cutting**) divide, wound, or shape etc. by pressure of an edge; reduce; intersect; divide (a pack of cards); switch off (an engine etc.); ignore, absent oneself from; (*sl.*) go quickly; (*US*) dilute; have (a tooth) coming through the gum. —*n.* cutting, wound etc. made by this; piece cut off; stroke of a whip etc.; style of cutting; hurtful remark; reduction; (*sl.*) share. **cut in** interpose a remark etc.;

intrude; obstruct the path of a vehicle in overtaking it.

cutaneous *a.* of the skin.

cute *a.* (**-er, -est**) (*colloq.*) sharp-witted; ingenious; (*US*) quaint. **cutely** *adv.*, **cuteness** *n.*

cuticle *n.* skin at the base of a nail.

cutlass *n.* short curved sword.

cutler *n.* maker of cutlery.

cutlery *n.* table knives, forks, and spoons.

cutlet *n.* neck-chop; mince cooked in this shape; thin piece of veal.

cutter *n.* person or thing that cuts; a kind of small boat.

cutthroat *a.* merciless. —*n.* murderer. **cutthroat razor** razor with a long blade set in a handle.

cutting *a.* (of remarks) hurtful. —*n.* piece cut from something; passage cut through high ground for a road etc.; piece of a plant for replanting.

cuttlefish *n.* sea creature that ejects black fluid when attacked.

cutwater *n.* forward edge of a ship's prow; wedge-shaped projection from a pier of a bridge.

cyanide *n.* a strong poison.

cyanosis *n.* blue discoloration of the skin. **cyanosed** *a.*

cybernetics /sar-/ *n.* science of systems of control and communication in animals and machines.

cyclamen /'stk-/ *n.* plant with petals that turn back.

cycle *n.* recurring series of events; bicycle, motor cycle. —*v.i.* ride a bicycle. **cyclist** *n.*

cyclic, cyclical /'sar-/ *adjs.* happening in cycles. **cyclically** *adv.*

cyclone *n.* violent wind rotating round a central area. **cyclonic** *a.*

cyclostyle *n.* device printing copies from a stencil. —*v.t.* print thus.

cyclotron /'sar-/ *n.* apparatus for accelerating charged particles in a spiral path.

cygnet /'stg-/ *n.* young swan.

cylinder *n.* object with straight sides and circular ends. **cylindrical** *a.*, **cylindrically** *adv.*

cymbal n. brass plate struck with another or with a stick as a percussion instrument.

cynic n. person who believes motives are bad or selfish. **cynical** a., **cynically** adv., **cynicism** n.

cynosure /'saməzjʊ(r)/ n. centre of attention.

cypress n. evergreen tree with dark feathery leaves.

cyst /sɪst/ n. sac of fluid or soft matter on or in the body.

cystic /'sɪs-/ a. of the bladder or gall-bladder. **cystic fibrosis** disease affecting the exocrine glands, usu. resulting in respiratory infections.

cystitis /sɪs-/ n. inflammation of the bladder.

cytology n. study of biological cells. **cytological** a.

czar n. = tsar.

D

dab[1] n. quick light blow or pressure; small lump of a soft substance. —v.t./i. (p.t. **dabbed**) strike or press lightly or feebly.

dab[2] n. a kind of small flat-fish.

dab[3] n. & a. adept.

dabble v.t./i. move (feet etc.) lightly in water or mud; splash; work at something in an amateur way.

dabchick n. little grebe.

dace n. (pl. **dace**) small freshwater fish.

dachshund /'dæks-/ n. small dog with a long body and short legs.

dad n. (colloq.) father.

daddy n. (children's use) father.

daddy-long-legs n. crane-fly.

dado /'deɪdəʊ/ n. (pl. **-os**) lower part of a wall decorated differently from the upper part.

daffodil n. yellow flower with a trumpet-shaped central part.

daft a. (-er, -est) silly, crazy.

dagger n. short pointed two-edged weapon used for stabbing.

dago n. (pl. **-oes**) (sl., offensive) foreigner, esp. from southern Europe.

daguerrotype /də'ge-/ n. early kind of photograph.

dahlia n. garden plant with bright flowers.

Dáil (Eirann) /dɔɪl 'eɪrən/ lower house of parliament in the Republic of Ireland.

daily a. happening or appearing on every day or every weekday. —adv. once a day. —n. daily newspaper; (colloq.) charwoman.

dainty a. (-ier, -iest) small and pretty; fastidious. —n. choice food, delicacy. **daintily** adv., **daintiness** n.

daiquiri /'daɪ-/ n. cocktail of rum and lime-juice.

dairy n. place where milk and its products are processed or sold. **dairy farm** one producing chiefly milk.

dais /'deɪs/ n. low platform, esp. at the end of a hall.

daisy n. flower with many petal-like rays. **daisy wheel** printing device with radiating spokes.

dale n. valley.

dally v.i. idle, dawdle; flirt. **dalliance** n.

Dalmatian n. large white dog with dark spots.

dam[1] n. barrier built across a river to hold back water. —v.t. (p.t. **dammed**) hold back with a dam; obstruct (a flow).

dam[2] n. mother of an animal.

damage n. something done that reduces the value or usefulness of the thing affected or spoils its appearance; (pl.) money as compensation for injury. —v.t. cause damage to.

damascene v.t. decorate (metal) with inlaid gold or silver.

damask n. fabric woven with a pattern visible on either side. **damask rose** old fragrant variety of rose.

dame n. (old use or US sl.) woman; comic female pantomime character usu. played by a man; **Dame** title of a woman with an order of knighthood.

damn v.t. condemn to hell; condemn as a failure; swear at. —int. & n. uttered curse. —a. & adv. damned.

damnable a. hateful, annoying. **damnably** adv.

damnation n. eternal punishment in hell. —int. exclamation of annoyance.

damp n. moisture in air or in or on a thing. —a. (-er, -est) slightly wet. —v.t. make damp; discourage; stop the vibration of. **damp course** layer of damp-proof material in a wall, to keep damp from rising. **dampness** n.

dampen v.t. make or become damp. **dampener** n.

damper n. metal plate controlling the flow of air into a flue; depressing influence; pad that damps the vibration of a piano string.

damsel n. (old use) young woman.

damson n. small dark-purple plum.

dance v.t./i. move with rhythmical steps and gestures, usu. to music; move in a quick or lively way. —n. piece of dancing; music for this; social gathering for dancing. **dance attendance on** follow about and help dutifully. **dancer** n.

dandelion n. wild plant with bright yellow flowers.

dander n. temper, fighting spirit.

dandified a. like a dandy.

dandle v.t. dance or nurse (a child) in one's arms.

dandruff n. scurf from the scalp.

dandy n. man who pays excessive attention to the smartness of his appearance. —a. (colloq.) very good. **dandyism** n.

Dane n. native of Denmark; Norse invader of England (9th–11th centuries).

danger n. liability or exposure to harm or death; thing causing this.

dangerous a. causing danger, not safe. **dangerously** adv.

dangle v.t./i. hang or swing loosely; hold out (hopes) temptingly. **dangler** n., **dangly** a.

Danish a. & n. (language) of Denmark.

dank a. (-er, -est) damp and cold. **dankly** adv., **dankness** n.

daphne n. flowering shrub.

dapper a. neat and smart.

dapple v.t. mark with patches of colour or shade. **dapple-grey** a. grey with darker markings.

Darby and Joan devoted old married couple.

dare v.t. be bold enough (to do something); challenge to do something risky. —n. this challenge. **I dare say** I am prepared to believe.

daredevil n. recklessly daring person.

daring a. bold. —n. boldness.

dark a. (-er, -est) with little or no light; of deep shade or colour, closer to black than to white; having dark hair or dark skin; gloomy; secret; mysterious. —n. absence of light; time of darkness, nightfall; dark colour. **Dark Ages** early Middle Ages in Europe. **dark horse** competitor etc. of whose abilities little is known. **darkly** adv., **darkness** n.

darken v.t./i. make or become dark.

darkroom n. room with daylight excluded, for processing photographs.

darling n. & a. dearly loved or lovable (person or thing); favourite.

darn[1] v.t. mend by weaving thread across a hole. —n. place darned.

darn[2] int. & v.t. (sl.) damn.

dart n. small pointed missile, esp. for throwing at the target in the game of **darts**; darting movement; tapering tuck. —*v.t./i.* run suddenly; send out (a glance etc.) rapidly. **darter** *n.*

dartboard *n.* target in the game of darts.

dash *v.t./i.* run rapidly, rush; knock or throw forcefully against something; destroy (hopes); write hastily. —*n.* rapid run; rush; small amount of liquid or flavouring added; dashboard; vigour; punctuation mark — showing a break in the sense; longer signal in the Morse code.

dashboard *n.* board below the windscreen of a motor vehicle, carrying various instruments and controls.

dashing *a.* spirited, showy.

dastardly *a.* contemptible.

data /'deɪ-/ *n.pl.* facts on which a decision is to be based; facts prepared for being processed by computer.

databank *n.* large store of computerized data.

database *n.* organized store of computerized data.

datable *a.* able to be dated.

date[1] *n.* day, month, or year of a thing's occurrence; period to which a thing belongs; (*colloq.*) appointment to meet socially; (*colloq.*) person to be met thus. —*v.t./i.* mark with a date; assign a date to; originate from a particular date; become out of date; (*colloq.*) make a social appointment (with). **date-line** *n.* north-to-south line in the Pacific, east and west of which the date differs. **date rape** rape of a girl or woman by person with whom she is on a date. **to date** until now.

date[2] *n.* small brown edible fruit. **date-palm** *n.* palm tree bearing this.

dative *n.* grammatical case indicating the indirect object of a verb.

datum *n.* (*pl.* **data**) item of data; (*pl.* **data**) fixed starting-point of a scale etc.

daub *v.t.* smear roughly. —*n.* clumsily painted picture; smear; clay coating for walls.

daughter *n.* female in relation to her parents. **daughter-in-law** *n.* (*pl.* **-s-in-law**) son's wife.

daunt *v.t.* make afraid or discouraged.

dauntless *a.* brave, not daunted.

dauphin *n.* title of the eldest son of former kings of France.

davenport *n.* a kind of writing-desk; (*US*) large sofa.

davit /'dæ-/ *n.* small crane on a ship.

dawdle *v.i.* walk slowly and idly, take one's time. **dawdler** *n.*

dawn *n.* first light of day; beginning. —*v.i.* begin to grow light; begin to appear. **dawning** *n.*

day *n.* time while the sun is above the horizon; period of 24 hours; hours given to work during a day; specified day; time, period.

daybreak *n.* first light of day.

day-dream *n.* pleasant idle thoughts. —*v.i.* have day-dreams.

daylight *n.* light of day.

daytime *n.* time of daylight.

daze *v.t.* cause to feel stunned or bewildered. —*n.* dazed state.

dazzle *v.t.* make unable to see because of too much light; impress by a splendid display. **dazzlement** *n.*

de- *pref.* implying removal or reversal.

deacon *n.* member of the clergy ranking below priest; layman attending to church business in Nonconformist churches.

dead *a.* no longer alive; numb; no longer used; without brightness or resonance or warmth; not functioning; dull; exact; (of the ball in games) out of play. —*adv.* completely, exactly. —*n.* dead person; inactive or silent time. **dead beat** tired out. **dead end** blind alley. **dead heat** race in which two or more competitors finish exactly even. **dead letter** letter that cannot be delivered; law or rule no longer observed. **dead march** funeral march. **dead-nettle** n. nettle-like plant that does not sting. **dead reckoning** calculating a ship's position by log and compass etc. **dead weight** heavy inert weight.

deaden v.t./i. deprive of or lose vitality, loudness, feeling, etc.

deadline n. time limit.

deadlock n. state when no progress can be made. —v.i. reach this.

deadly a. (-ier, -iest) causing death or serious damage; death-like; very dreary. —adv. as if dead; extremely. **deadly nightshade** plant with poisonous black berries. **deadliness** n.

deadpan a. expressionless.

deaf a. (-er, -est) wholly or partly unable to hear; refusing to listen. **deaf-aid** n. hearing-aid. **deafness** n.

deafen v.t. make unable to hear by a very loud noise.

deal[1] n. fir or pine timber.

deal[2] v.t./i. (p.t. **dealt**) distribute; hand out (cards) to players in a card-game; give, inflict; do business; trade. —n. dealing; player's turn to deal; business transaction; treatment; (colloq.) large amount. **deal with** take action about; treat (a subject) in a book or speech etc.

dealer n. person who deals; trader.

dean n. cleric who is head of a cathedral chapter; university official. **rural dean** cleric in charge of a group of parishes.

deanery n. dean's position or residence; rural dean's parishes.

dear a. (-er, -est) much loved, cherished; costing more than it is worth. —n. dear person. —adv.

dearly. —int. exclamation of surprise or distress. **dearly** adv. **dearness** n.

dearth /dɜːθ/ n. scarcity, lack.

death n. process of dying, end of life; state of being dead; ending of something, destruction. **death duty** tax levied on property after the owner's death. **death's head** picture of a skull as a symbol of death. **death-trap** n. very dangerous place. **death-watch beetle** beetle whose larvae bore into wood and make a ticking sound.

deathly a. (-ier, -iest) like death.

deb n. (colloq.) débutante.

débâcle /deɪˈbɑːkl/ n. general collapse.

debar v.t. (p.t. **debarred**) exclude.

debark v.t./i. disembark. **debarkation** n.

debase v.t. lower in quality or value. **debasement** n.

debatable a. questionable.

debate n. formal discussion. —v.t. hold a debate about, consider.

debauch /-ˈbɔːtʃ/ v.t. make dissolute, lead into over-indulgence in harmful or immoral pleasures. **debauchery** n.

debenture n. bond acknowledging a debt on which fixed interest is being paid.

debilitate v.t. weaken. **debilitation** n.

debility n. weakness of health.

debit n. entry in an account for a sum owing. —v.t. (p.t. **debited**) enter as a debit, charge.

debonair /-ˈneə(r)/ a. having a carefree self-confident manner.

debouch v.i. come out from a narrow into an open area.

debrief v.t. question to obtain facts about a completed mission.

debris /ˈdebriː/ n. scattered broken pieces or rubbish.

debt n. something owed. **in debt** owing something.

debtor n. person who owes money.

debug v.t. (p.t. **debugged**) remove bugs from.

debunk v.t. (colloq.) show up as exaggerated or false.

début /'deɪbjuː/ n. first public appearance.

débutante /'debjuːtɑːnt/ n. (old use) young woman making her first appearance in society.

deca- pref. ten.

decade /'dek-/ n. ten-year period.

decadent a. deteriorating in standard. **decadence** n.

decaffeinated a. with caffeine removed or reduced.

decagon n. geometric figure with ten sides. **decagonal** a.

Decalogue n. the Ten Commandments.

decamp v.i. go away suddenly or secretly.

decanal /-'keɪ-/ a. of a dean; of the south (dean's) side of the choir.

decant /-'kæ-/ v.t. pour (liquid) into another container, leaving sediment behind; (colloq.) transfer.

decanter n. stoppered bottle into which wine etc. may be decanted before serving.

decapitate v.t. behead. **decapitation** n.

decarbonize v.t. remove carbon deposit from (an engine). **decarbonization** n.

decathlon /dɪ'kæθ-/ n. athletic contest involving ten events.

decay v.t./i. rot; lose quality or strength. —n. decaying, rot.

decease n. death.

deceased a. dead.

deceit n. deceiving, deception.

deceitful a. deceiving people. **deceitfully** adv.

deceive v.t. cause to believe something that is not true; be sexually unfaithful to. **deceiver** n.

decelerate v.t./i. reduce the speed (of). **deceleration** n.

December n. twelfth month of the year.

decennial /-'sen-/ a. happening every tenth year; lasting ten years. **decennially** adv.

decent a. conforming to accepted standards of what is proper; respectable; (colloq.) quite good; (colloq.) kind, obliging. **decently** adv., **decency** n.

decentralize v.t. transfer from central to local control. **decentralization** n.

deception n. deceiving.

deceptive a. deceiving; misleading. **deceptively** adv.

deci- pref. one-tenth.

decibel /'des-/ n. unit for measuring the relative loudness of sound.

decide v.t./i. think about and make a choice or judgement; settle by giving victory to one side; cause to reach a decision.

decided a. having firm opinions; clear, definite. **decidedly** adv.

deciduous /-'sɪd-/ a. shedding its leaves annually; periodically shed. **deciduousness** n.

decimal a. reckoned in tens or tenths. —n. decimal fraction. **decimal currency** that with each unit 10 or 100 times the value of the one next below it. **decimal fraction** fraction with 10 as denominator, expressed in figures after a dot. **decimal point** this dot.

decimalize v.t. convert into a decimal fraction or system. **decimalization** n.

decimate v.t. destroy one-tenth of; (loosely) destroy a large proportion of. **decimation** n.

decipher v.t. make out the meaning of (a coded message, bad handwriting, etc.). **decipherment** n.

decision n. deciding, judgement reached by this; ability to form firm opinions and act on them.

decisive a. conclusive; showing decision and firmness. **decisively** adv., **decisiveness** n.

deck[1] n. horizontal floor in a ship; similar floor or platform, esp. one of two or more. **deck-chair** n.

folding canvas chair for outdoors.

deck[2] *v.t.* decorate, dress up.

declaim *v.t./i.* speak or say impressively. **declamation** *n.*, **declamatory** *a.*

declare *v.t./i.* make known, announce openly or formally; state firmly; end one's side's innings at cricket before ten wickets have fallen. **declaration** *n.*, **declaratory** /'klæ-/ *a.*

declassify *v.t.* cease to classify as officially secret. **declassification** *n.*

declension *n.* class of nouns and adjectives having the same inflectional forms.

declination *n.* downward slope; deviation.

decline *v.t./i.* refuse; slope downwards; decrease, lose strength or vigour. —*n.* gradual decrease or loss of strength.

declivity *n.* downward slope.

declutch *v.i.* disengage the clutch.

decoct *v.t.* make a decoction of.

decoction *n.* boiling to extract essence; the essence itself.

decode *v.t.* put (a coded message) into plain language.

decoder *n.* person or machine that decodes; device analysing and distributing stereophonic signals etc.

decoke *v.t.* (*colloq.*) decarbonize. —*n.* (*colloq.*) decarbonization.

decolletage /deɪkɒl'tɑːʒ/ *n.* low-cut neckline. **décolleté** /-'kɒlteɪ/ *a.* having this.

decompose *v.t./i.* separate (a substance) into its parts; rot. **decomposition** *n.*

decompress *v.t.* release from compression; reduce air pressure in. **decompression** *n.*

decongestant *n.* medicinal substance that relieves congestion.

decontaminate *v.t.* rid of (esp. radioactive) contamination. **decontamination** *n.*

décor /'deɪ-/ *n.* style of decoration used in a room etc.

decorate *v.t.* make look attractive by adding objects or details; paint or paper the walls of; confer a medal or award on. **decoration** *n.*

decorative *a.* ornamental, pleasant to look at. **decoratively** *adv.*, **decorativeness** *n.*

decorator *n.* tradesman who paints and papers rooms etc.

decorous *a.* polite and well-behaved, decent. **decorously** *adv.*

decorum /-'kɔːr-/ *n.* correctness and dignity of behaviour.

decoy[1] /'diː-/ *n.* thing used to lure a person or animal into a trap etc.

decoy[2] /-'kɔɪ/ *v.t.* lure by a decoy.

decrease *v.t./i.* make or become smaller or fewer. —*n.* decreasing; amount of this.

decree *n.* order given by a government or other authority. —*v.t.* (*p.t.* **decreed**) order by decree.

decrepit *a.* made weak by old age or use; dilapidated. **decrepitude** *n.*

decretal *n.* papal decree.

decry *v.t.* disparage.

dedicate *v.t.* devote to a sacred person or use, or to a purpose. **dedication** *n.*, **dedicatory** *a.*

deduce *v.t.* arrive at (knowledge) by reasoning. **deducible** *a.*

deduct *v.t.* subtract. **deductible** *a.*

deduction *n.* deducting; thing deducted; deducing; conclusion deduced.

deductive *a.* based on reasoning.

deed *n.* thing done, act; written or printed legal agreement. **deed poll** deed made by one party only, as a formal declaration.

deem *v.t.* believe, consider to be.

deep *a.* (**-er, -est**) going or situated far down or in; intense; low-pitched; absorbed; profound. **deep-freeze** *n.* freezer; (*v.t.*) store in this. **deeply** *adv.*, **deepness** *n.*

deepen *v.t./i.* make or become deeper.

deer n. (pl. **deer**) ruminant swift-footed animal, male of which usu. has antlers.

deerstalker n. cloth cap with a peak in front and at the back.

def a. (sl.) very good.

deface v.t. spoil or damage the surface of. **defacement** n.

de facto existing in fact.

defalcate v.i. misappropriate money. **defalcation** n.

defamatory /-'fæm-/ a. defaming.

defame v.t. attack the good reputation of. **defamation** n.

default v.i. fail to fulfil one's obligations or to appear. —n. this failure. **defaulter** n.

defeat v.t. win victory over; cause to fail, frustrate; baffle. —n. defeating others; being defeated.

defeatist n. person who pessimistically expects or accepts defeat. **defeatism** n.

defecate /'di:fi-, 'defi-/ v.i. discharge faeces from the body. **defecation** n.

defect¹ /'di:- or dɪ'fekt/ n. deficiency, imperfection.

defect² /-'fekt/ v.i. desert one's country, abandon one's allegiance to a cause. **defection** n., **defector** n.

defective a. having defect(s); incomplete. **defectively** adv., **defectiveness** n.

defence n. defending; protection; justification put forward against an accusation; defendant's case.

defenceless a. having no defences. **defencelessness** n.

defend v.t. protect, esp. by warding off an attack; uphold by argument; represent (the defendant) in a lawsuit. **defender** n.

defendant n. person accused or sued in a lawsuit.

defensible a. able to be defended. **defensibly** adv., **defensibility** n.

defensive a. used or done for defence. **on the defensive** in an attitude of defence. **defensively** adv., **defensiveness** n.

defer¹ v.t. (p.t. **deferred**) postpone. **deferment** n., **deferral** n.

defer² v.i. (p.t. **deferred**) yield to a person's wishes or authority. **deference** n. polite respect. **deferential** a., **deferentially** adv.

defiance n. defying; open disobedience. **defiant** a., **defiantly** adv.

deficiency n. lack, shortage; thing or amount lacking.

deficient a. not having enough; insufficient, lacking.

deficit n. amount by which a total falls short of what is required; excess of liabilities over assets.

defile¹ v.t. make dirty, pollute. **defilement** n.

defile² n. narrow pass or gorge.

define v.t. give a definition of; state precisely; outline, mark the boundary of. **definable** a.

definite a. having exact limits; clear and unmistakable, not vague; certain. **definitely** adv.

definition n. statement of a thing's precise meaning; making or being distinct, clearness of outline.

definitive a. finally fixing or settling something; most authoritative. **definitively** adv.

deflate v.t./i. let out air from; counteract inflation in; become deflated. **deflation** n., **deflationary** a.

deflect v.t./i. turn aside. **deflection** n., **deflector** n.

deflower v.t. deprive of virginity; strip of flowers.

defoliate v.t. remove or destroy the leaves of. **defoliant** n., **defoliation** n.

deforest v.t. clear of trees. **deforestation** n.

deform v.t. spoil the shape of. **deformation** n.

deformity n. abnormality of shape, esp. of a part of the body.

defraud v.t. deprive by fraud.

defray v.t. provide money to pay (costs). **defrayal** n.

defrost v.t./i. remove frost from; thaw. **defroster** n.

deft *a.* (-er, -est) skilful, handling things neatly. **deftly** *adv.*, **deftness** *n.*

defunct *a.* dead; no longer existing or functioning.

defuse *v.t.* remove the fuse from (an explosive); reduce the dangerous tension in (a situation).

defy *v.t.* resist; refuse to obey; challenge to do something.

degenerate[1] /-ət/ *v.i.* become worse. **degeneration** *n.*

degenerate[2] /-ət/ *a.* having degenerated. **degeneracy** *n.*

degrade *v.t./i.* reduce to a lower rank; bring disgrace or humiliation on; decompose. **degradation** *n.*

degree *n.* stage in a series or of intensity; academic rank given for proficiency or as an honour; unit of measurement for angles or temperature.

dehumanize *v.t.* remove human qualities from; make impersonal. **dehumanization** *n.*

dehydrate *v.t./i.* remove moisture from; lose moisture. **dehydration** *n.*, **dehydrator** *n.*

de-ice *v.t.* remove or prevent formation of ice on. **de-icer** *n.*

deify /'di:ɪ-/ *v.t.* treat as a god. **deification** *n.*

deign *v.i.* condescend.

deism /'di:ɪz(ə)m/ *n.* belief in the existence of a divine being, without accepting revelation. **deist** *n.*, **deistic** *a.*

deity /'di:ɪtɪ/ *n.* god, goddess.

déjà vu /deɪʒɑː'vuː/ feeling of having experienced the present situation before.

dejected *a.* in low spirits.

dejection *n.* lowness of spirits.

de jure /di: 'dʒʊərɪ/ rightful(ly).

delay *v.t./i.* make or be late; postpone. —*n.* delaying.

delectable *a.* delightful. **delectably** *adv.*

delectation *n.* enjoyment.

delegacy /'del-/ *n.* body of delegates.

delegate[1] /-gət/ *n.* representative.

delegate[2] /-geɪt/ *v.t.* entrust (a task or power) to an agent.

delegation *n.* delegating; delegacy.

delete *v.t.* strike out (a word etc.). **deletion** *n.*

deleterious *a.* harmful.

delft *n.* a kind of earthenware.

deliberate[1] /-ət/ *a.* intentional; slow and careful. **deliberately** *adv.*

deliberate[2] /-eɪt/ *n.t./i.* think over or discuss carefully.

deliberation *n.* deliberating; being deliberate.

deliberative *a.* for the purpose of deliberating or discussing.

delicacy *n.* being delicate; choice food.

delicate *a.* fine, slender; not intense; easily harmed, liable to illness; requiring or using carefulness or tact; not coarse. **delicately** *adv.*

delicatessen *n.* shop selling prepared delicacies.

delicious *a.* delightful, esp. to taste or smell. **deliciously** *adv.*

delight *n.* great pleasure; thing giving this. —*v.t./i.* please greatly; feel delight. **delightful** *a.*, **delightfully** *adv.*

delimit *v.t.* determine the limits or boundaries of. **delimitation** *n.*

delineate *v.t.* outline. **delineation** *n.*, **delineator** *n.*

delinquent *a.* & *n.* (person) guilty of an offence or neglect of duty. **delinquency** *n.*

deliquesce *v.i.* become liquid. **deliquescence** *n.*, **deliquescent** *a.*

delirium *n.* disordered state of mind, esp. during fever; wild excitement. **delirious** *a.*, **deliriously** *adv.*

deliver *v.t.* take to an addressee or purchaser; transfer, hand over; utter; aim (a blow or attack); bowl; rescue, set free; assist in the birth (of); give birth to. **deliverer** *n.*, **delivery** *n.*

deliverance *n.* rescue, freeing.

dell *n.* small wooded hollow.

delphinium n. tall garden plant with usu. blue flowers.

delta n. Greek letter D, written Δ; triangular patch of alluvial land at the mouth of a river.

delude v.t. deceive.

deluge n. & v.t. flood.

delusion n. false belief or impression; this as a symptom of madness. **delusional** a.

delusive a. deceptive, raising false hopes. **delusively** adv., **delusiveness** n.

de luxe /də lʌks/ of superior quality; luxurious.

delve v.i. search deeply.

demagogue n. person who wins support by appealing to popular feelings and prejudices. **demagogic** a., **demagogy** n.

demand n. request made imperiously or by authority; customers' desire for goods or services; claim. —v.t. make a demand for; need.

demanding a. making many demands; requiring great skill or effort.

demarcation n. marking of a boundary or limits, esp. of work for different trades.

demean v.t. lower the dignity of.

demeanour n. way a person behaves.

demented a. driven mad, crazy.

dementia n. a type of insanity.

demerara /-'reərə/ n. brown raw cane sugar.

demerit n. fault, defect.

demesne /dɪ'miːn/ n. domain; landed estate.

demi- pref. half.

demilitarize v.t. remove military forces and installations from. **demilitarization** n.

demi-monde n. class of women of immoral repute; group behaving with doubtful legality etc.

demise /-'maɪz/ n. death.

demisemiquaver n. note equal to half a semiquaver.

demist v.t. clear mist from (a windscreen etc.). **demister** n.

demo n. (pl. -os) (colloq.) demonstration.

demob v.t. (p.t. demobbed) (colloq.) demobilize. —n. (colloq.) demobilization.

demobilize v.t. release from military service. **demobilization** n.

democracy n. government by all the people, usu. through elected representatives; country governed thus.

democrat n. person favouring democracy; **Democrat** member of the Democratic Party in the USA.

democratic a. of or according to democracy. **Democratic Party** one of the two main US political parties. **democratically** adv.

democratize v.t. make democratic. **democratization** n.

demography n. statistical study of life in human communities. **demographic** a.

demolish v.t. pull or knock down; destroy. **demolition** n.

demon n. devil, evil spirit; cruel or forceful person. **demonic** /-'mɒn-/ a., **demoniac** a., **demoniacal** /-'naɪ-/ a.

demonstrable /'dem-/ a. able to be demonstrated. **demonstrably** adv., **demonstrability** n.

demonstrate v.t./i. show evidence of, prove; show the working of; take part in a procession etc. to express a group's opinion publicly. **demonstration** n., **demonstrator** n.

demonstrative /-'mɒnstrə-/ a. showing, proving; showing one's feelings. **demonstratively** adv.

demoralize v.t. weaken the morale of, dishearten. **demoralization** n.

demote v.t. reduce to a lower rank or category. **demotion** n.

demur v.i. (p.t. demurred) raise objections. —n. objection raised.

demure a. quiet and serious or pretending to be so. **demurely** adv., **demureness** n.

demurrer n. legal objection to an opponent's point.

den n. wild animal's lair; person's small private room.

denary a. of ten; decimal.

denationalize v.t. privatize. **denationalization** n.

denature v.t. change the properties of; make (alcohol) unfit for drinking.

deniable a. able to be denied. **deniability** n.

denial n. denying; statement that a thing is not true.

denier /'denjə(r)/ n. unit of weight by which the fineness of yarn is measured.

denigrate v.t. blacken the reputation of. **denigration** n.

denim n. strong twilled fabric; (pl.) trousers made of this.

denizen n. person or plant living in a specified place.

denominate v.t. give a name to; describe as.

denomination n. name, title; specified Church or sect; class of units of measurement or money.

denominational a. of a particular religious denomination.

denominator n. number below the line in a vulgar fraction.

denote v.t. be the sign, symbol, or name of; indicate. **denotation** n.

denouement /der'nu:mã/ n. clearing up of a plot's complications, at the end of a play or story.

denounce v.t. speak against; inform against; announce one's withdrawal from (a treaty etc.).

dense a. (-er, -est) thick; closely massed; stupid. **densely** adv., **denseness** n.

density n. denseness; relation of weight to volume.

dent n. depression left by a blow or pressure. —v.t./i. make a dent in; become dented.

dental a. of or for teeth; of dentistry.

dentate a. toothed; notched.

dentifrice n. substance for cleaning teeth.

dentine n. hard dense tissue forming the teeth.

dentist n. person qualified to treat decay and malformations of teeth.

dentistry n. dentist's work.

dentition n. arrangement of the teeth.

denture n. set of artificial teeth.

denude v.t. strip of covering or property. **denudation** n.

denunciation n. denouncing. **denunciatory** a.

deny v.t. say that (a thing) is untrue or does not exist; disown; prevent from having. **deny oneself** restrict one's food, drink, or pleasure.

deodorant /di'əʊ-/ n. substance that removes or conceals unwanted odours. —a. deodorizing.

deodorize /di'əʊ-/ v.t. destroy the odour of. **deodorization** n.

deoxyribonucleic acid substance storing genetic information in chromosomes.

depart v.t./i. go away, leave.

department n. section of an organization. **department store** large shop with departments each selling a separate type of goods.

departmental a. of a department. **departmentally** adv.

departure n. departing; setting out on a new course of action.

depend v.i. **depend on** be controlled or determined by; be unable to do without; trust confidently.

dependable a. reliable.

dependant n. one who depends on another for support.

dependence n. depending.

dependency n. dependent State.

dependent a. depending; controlled by another.

depict v.t. represent in a picture or in words. **depiction** n.

depilatory /-'pɪlə-/ a. & n. (substance) removing hair.

deplete v.t. reduce by using quantities of. **depletion** n.

deplorable a. regrettable; very bad. **deplorably** adv.

deplore v.t. find or call deplorable.

deploy v.t./i. spread out, organize for effective use. **deployment** n.

depopulate v.t. reduce the population of. **depopulation** n.

deport v.t. remove (an unwanted person) from a country. **deport oneself** behave. **deportation** n.

deportment n. behaviour, bearing.

depose v.t./i. remove from power; testify, state on oath.

deposit v.t. (p.t. **deposited**) put down; leave as a layer of matter; entrust for keeping; pay as a deposit. —n. thing or substance deposited; sum paid into a bank or as a guarantee or first instalment. **depositor** n.

depositary n. person to whom a thing is entrusted.

deposition n. deposing from power; sworn statement; depositing.

depository n. storehouse.

depot /'depəʊ/ n. storehouse; headquarters; (US) bus or railway station.

deprave v.t. make morally bad, corrupt. **depravation** n.

depravity /-'præ-/ n. moral corruption, wickedness.

deprecate v.t. express disapproval of; disclaim politely. **deprecation** n., **deprecatory** a.

depreciate v.t./i. make or become lower in value; disparage. **depreciation** n.

depreciatory /-'pri:ʃə-/ a. disparaging.

depredation /deprɪ-/ n. plundering, destruction.

depress v.t. press down; reduce (trade etc.); make sad. **depressant** a. & n.

depression n. pressing down; state of sadness; long period of inactivity in trading; area of low

atmospheric pressure; sunken place. **depressive** a.

deprive v.t. take a thing away from; prevent from using or enjoying something. **deprival** n., **deprivation** n.

depth n. deepness, measure of this; deepest or most central part. **depth charge** bomb that will explode under water. **in depth** thoroughly. **out of one's depth** in water too deep to stand in; attempting something beyond one's ability.

deputation n. body of people sent to represent others.

depute /-'pju:t/ v.t. delegate; appoint to act as one's representative.

deputize v.i. act as deputy.

deputy n. person appointed to act as a substitute or representative.

derail v.t. cause (a train) to leave the rails. **derailment** n.

derange v.t. disrupt; make insane. **derangement** n.

Derby n. annual horse-race at Epsom; important race or contest.

derelict a. abandoned; left to fall into ruin.

dereliction n. abandonment; neglect (of duty).

deride v.t. scoff at.

derision n. scorn, ridicule.

derisive a. scornful, showing derision. **derisively** adv.

derisory a. showing derision; deserving derision.

derivative a. & n. derived (thing).

derive v.t./i. obtain from a source; have its origin. **derivation** n.

dermatitis n. inflammation of the skin.

dermatology n. study of the skin and its diseases. **dermatologist** n., **dermatological** a.

derogate v.i. detract. **derogation** n.

derogatory a. disparaging. **derogatorily** adv.

derrick n. crane with an arm pivoted to the floor or base; framework holding drilling machinery over an oil-well etc.

derris n. an insecticide.

derv n. fuel for diesel engines.

dervish n. member of a Muslim religious order vowed to poverty.

desalinate v.t. remove salt from (esp. sea water). **desalination** n.

descant n. treble accompaniment to a main melody. —v.i. talk lengthily.

descend v.t./i. go or come down; stoop to unworthy behaviour. **be descended from** have origin from (an ancestor, family, etc.). **descendant** n. person etc. descended from another.

descent n. descending; downward route or slope; sudden attack; lineage, family origin.

describe v.t. give a description of; mark the outline of, move in (a specified pattern).

description n. statement of what a person or thing is like; sort.

descriptive a. describing.

descry v.t. catch sight of, discern.

desecrate /'desɪ-/ v.t. treat (a sacred thing) irreverently. **desecration** n., **desecrator** n.

desegregate v.t. abolish segregation in or of. **desegregation** n.

deselect v.t. vote to reject (an already selected candidate). **deselection** n.

desert[1] /'dez-/ n. & a. barren uninhabited often sandy (area).

desert[2] /-'zɜ:t/ v.t./i. abandon; leave one's service in the armed forces without permission. **deserter** n., **desertion** n.

deserts /-'zɜ:ts/ n.pl. what one deserves.

deserve v.t. be worthy of or entitled to, because of actions or qualities. **deservedly** /-vɪdlɪ/ adv.

déshabillé /deɪzæ'bi:eɪ/ n. state of being only partly dressed.

desiccate v.t. dry out moisture from. **desiccation** n.

desideratum n. (pl. **-ta**) thing required.

design n. drawing that shows how a thing is to be made; general form or arrangement; lines or shapes forming a decoration; mental plan. —v.t. prepare a design for; plan, intend. **designedly** /-ɪdlɪ/ adv., **designer** n.

designate[1] /-ət/ a. appointed but not yet installed.

designate[2] /-eɪt/ v.t. describe or name as; specify; appoint to a position. **designation** n.

designing a. scheming.

desirable a. arousing desire, worth desiring. **desirability** n.

desire n. unsatisfied longing; thing desired. —v.t. feel a desire for; ask for.

desirous a. desiring.

desist v.i. cease.

desk n. piece of furniture for reading or writing at; counter; section of a newspaper office etc.

deskill v.t. render (a worker or job) unskilled.

desktop a. (esp. of a microcomputer) suitable for use at a desk.

desolate a. solitary, lonely; deserted, uninhabited. **desolated** a. very distressed. **desolation** n.

despair n. complete lack of hope; cause of this. —v.i. feel despair.

desperado /-'rɑ:-/ n. (pl. **-oes**) reckless criminal.

desperate a. hopelessly bad; reckless through despair. **desperately** adv., **desperation** n.

despicable /'des-or-'spɪk-/ a. contemptible. **despicably** adv.

despise v.t. regard as inferior or worthless.

despite prep. in spite of.

despoil v.t. plunder. **despoilment** n., **despoliation** n.

despondent a. dejected. **despondently** adv., **despondency** n.

despot n. tyrant, ruler with unrestricted power. **despotic** a., **despotically** adv.

despotism n. tyranny.

dessert /-'zɜːt/ n. sweet course of a meal; fruit etc. at the end of dinner.

dessertspoon n. medium-sized spoon for eating puddings etc.

destination n. place to which a person or thing is going.

destine v.t. settle the future of, set apart for a purpose.

destiny n. fate considered as a power; what is destined by fate to happen to a person or thing.

destitute a. penniless, without the necessaries of life; devoid. **destitution** n.

destroy v.t. pull or break down; make useless, spoil completely; kill (an animal) deliberately. **destruction** n., **destructive** a.

destroyer n. one who destroys; fast warship.

destruct v.t. (US) destroy deliberately.

destructible a. able to be destroyed.

desuetude /'deswɪ-/ n. disuse.

desultory /'des-/ a. going from one subject to another, not systematic. **desultorily** adv.

detach v.t. release or remove from something else or from a group.

detachable a. able to be detached.

detached a. not joined to another; free from bias or emotion.

detachment n. detaching; being detached; group detached from a larger one for special duty.

detail n. small fact or item; such items collectively; small military detachment. —v.t. relate in detail; assign to special duty.

detain v.t. keep in confinement; cause delay to. **detainment** n.

detainee n. person detained in custody.

detect v.t. discover the presence or activity of. **detection** n., **detector** n.

detective n. person whose job is to investigate crimes.

détente /'dertãt/ n. easing of strained relations between States.

detention n. detaining; imprisonment.

deter v.t. (p.t. deterred) discourage from action. **determent** n.

detergent a. & n. cleansing (substance, esp. other than soap).

deteriorate v.i. become worse. **deterioration** n.

determinable a. able to be determined.

determinant n. decisive factor.

determination n. firmness of purpose; process of deciding.

determine v.t. decide; calculate precisely; resolve firmly.

determined a. full of determination.

determinism n. theory that actions are determined by forces independent of the will. **determinist** n., **deterministic** a.

deterrent /-'te-/ n. thing that deters; nuclear weapon deterring attack. **deterrence** n.

detest v.t. dislike intensely. **detestable** a., **detestation** n.

dethrone v.t. remove from a throne. **dethronement** n.

detonate v.t./i. explode. **detonation** n., **detonator** n.

detour /'diːtʊə(r)/ n. deviation from a direct or intended course.

detoxify v.t. remove the poison from. **detoxification** n.

detract v.t./i. detract from reduce the credit that is due to; lessen. **detraction** n.

detractor n. person who criticizes a thing unfavourably.

detriment n. harm; cause of this.

detrimental a. harmful. **detrimentally** adv.

de trop /də 'trəʊ/ not wanted.

deuce[1] n. score of 40-all in tennis.

deuce[2] n. (in exclamations of annoyance) the Devil. **deuced** a.

deuterium n. heavy form of hydrogen.

Deutschmark /ˈdɔɪtʃ-/ n. unit of money in Germany.

devalue v.t. reduce the value of. **devaluation** n.

devastate v.t. cause great destruction to. **devastation** n.

devastating a. overwhelming.

develop v.t./i. (p.t. **developed**) make or become larger or more mature or organized; bring or come into existence; make usable or profitable, build on (land); treat (a film etc.) so as to make a picture visible. **developer** n., **development** n.

deviant a. & n. (person or thing) deviating from normal behaviour.

deviate v.t. turn aside from a course of action, truth, etc. **deviation** n.

device n. thing made or used for a purpose; scheme; design used as a decoration or emblem.

devil n. evil spirit (**the Devil** supreme spirit of evil); cruel or annoying person; person of mischievous energy or cleverness; (colloq.) difficult person or problem. —v.t.i. (p.t. **devilled**) cook (food) with hot seasoning; do research for an author or barrister. **devil's advocate** person who tests a proposition by arguing against it. **devilish** a.

devilment n. mischief.

devilry n. wickedness; devilment.

devious a. roundabout; not straightforward, underhand. **deviously** adv., **deviousness** n.

devise v.t. plan; invent. **devisor** n.

devoid a. devoid of lacking, free from.

devolution n. devolving; delegation of power from central to local or regional administration.

devolve v.t.i. pass or be passed to a deputy or successor. **devolvement** n.

devote v.t. give or use for a particular purpose.

devoted a. showing devotion.

devotee n. enthusiast.

devotion n. great love or loyalty; zeal; worship; (esp. pl.) prayer(s).

devotional a. used in worship.

devour v.t. eat hungrily or greedily; consume; take in greedily with the eyes or ears. **devourer** n.

devout a. earnestly religious; earnest, sincere. **devoutly** adv.

dew n. drops of moisture on a surface, esp. condensed during the night from water vapour in air.

dew-claw n. small claw on the inner side of a dog's leg.

dewdrop n. drop of dew.

dewlap n. fold of loose skin at the throat of cattle etc.

dewy a. wet with dew. **dewy-eyed** a. innocently trusting or sentimental. **dewily** adv., **dewiness** n.

dexter a. (in heraldry) on or of the right-hand side of a shield.

dexterity n. skill.

dexterous a. (also **dextrous**) skilful. **dexterously** adv.

diabetes n. disease in which sugar and starch are not properly absorbed by the body. **diabetic** /-ˈbet-/ a. & n.

diabolic a. of the Devil.

diabolical a. very cruel, wicked, or cunning. **diabolically** adv.

diabolism n. worship of the Devil.

diaconal a. of a deacon.

diaconate n. office of deacon; body of deacons.

diacritic, diacritical adjs. & ns. (of) a distinguishing mark placed on a letter to show its sound.

diadem n. crown.

diaeresis /daɪˈɪərɪsɪs/ n. mark over a vowel sounded separately.

diagnose v.t. make a diagnosis of.

diagnosis n. (pl. **-oses**) identification of a disease or condition after observing its signs. **diagnostic** a., **diagnostician** n.

diagonal *a. & n.* (line) crossing from corner to corner. **diagonally** *adv.*

diagram *n.* drawing that shows the parts of a thing or how it works, or represents the operation of a process etc. **diagrammatic** *a.*, **diagrammatically** *adv.*

dial *n.* face of a clock or watch; similar plate or disc with a movable pointer; movable disc manipulated to connect one telephone with another; (*sl.*) face. —*v.t./i.* (*p.t.* dialled) select or operate by using a dial or numbered buttons.

dialect *n.* words and pronunciation peculiar to a district. **dialectal** *a.*

dialectic *n.* investigation of truths in philosophy etc. by systematic reasoning. **dialectical** *a.*

dialogue *n.* talk between people.

dialysis /daɪˈælɪ-/ *n.* purification of blood by causing it to flow through a suitable membrane.

diamanté /dɪəˈmɒnteɪ/ *a.* decorated with sparkling fragments of crystal etc.

diameter *n.* straight line from side to side through the centre of a circle or sphere; its length.

diametrical *a.* of or along a diameter; (of opposition) direct. **diametrically** *adv.*

diamond *n.* very hard brilliant precious stone; four-sided figure with equal sides and with angles that are not right angles; thing shaped thus, playing-card of the suit marked with such shapes. **diamond wedding** etc., 60th (or 75th) anniversary.

diapason /-ˈpeɪ-/ *n.* whole compass of a voice or instrument; organ-stop extending through the whole compass.

diaper *n.* (*US*) baby's nappy.

diaphanous *a.* almost transparent. **diaphanously** *adv.*

diaphragm *n.* a kind of partition, esp. that between chest and abdomen; vibrating disc in a microphone etc.; device for varying the aperture of a lens; contraceptive cap fitting over the cervix.

diarrhoea *n.* condition with frequent fluid faeces.

diary *n.* daily record of events; book for noting these. **diarist** *n.*

diastole /daɪˈæstəlɪ/ *n.* rhythmic dilatation of chambers of the heart. **diastolic** /-ˈstɒl-/ *a.*

diathermy *n.* medical heat-treatment by electric currents.

diatom *n.* microscopic alga.

diatonic *a.* using notes of the major and minor (not chromatic) scales.

diatribe *n.* violent verbal attack.

dibber *n.* tool to make holes in ground for young plants.

dice *n.* (*pl.* of die², but often as *sing.* with *pl.* **dice**) small cube marked on each side with 1–6 spots, used in games of chance; game played with these. —*v.i.* gamble using dice; take great risks; cut into small cubes.

dicey *a.* (*sl.*) risky; unreliable.

dichotomy /daɪˈkɒt-/ *n.* division into two parts or kinds.

dickens *n.* (*colloq.*, in exclamations) the deuce, the Devil.

dicker *v.i.* (*colloq.*) haggle; hesitate.

dicky *a.* (**-ier**, **-iest**) (*sl.*) shaky, unsound.

dicotyledon *n.* plant with two cotyledons.

dictate *v.t./i.* say (words) aloud to be written by a person or recorded by a machine; state or order authoritatively; give orders officiously. **dictation** *n.*

dictates /ˈdɪk-/ *n.pl.* commands.

dictator *n.* ruler with unrestricted authority; domineering person. **dictatorship** *n.*

dictatorial *a.* of or like a dictator. **dictatorially** *adv.*

diction *n.* manner of uttering or pronouncing words.

dictionary n. book that lists and explains the words of a language or the topics of a subject.

dictum n. (pl. -ta) formal saying.

did see do.

didactic a. meant or meaning to instruct. **didactically** adv.

diddle v.t. (sl.) cheat, swindle.

didn't (colloq.) = did not.

die[1] v.i. (pres.p. dying) cease to be alive; cease to exist or function; fade away. **be dying to** or **for** feel an intense longing to or for.

die[2] n. see **dice**; device that stamps a design or that cuts or moulds material into shape. **die-cast** a. made by casting metal in a mould.

die-hard n. very conservative or stubborn person.

diesel n. diesel engine; vehicle driven by this. **diesel-electric** a. using an electric generator driven by a diesel engine. **diesel engine** oil-burning engine in which ignition is produced by the heat of compressed air.

diet[1] n. habitual food; restricted selection of food. —v.t./i. keep to a restricted diet. **dietary** a., **dieter** n.

diet[2] n. congress, parliamentary assembly in certain countries.

dietetic /-'tet-/ a. of diet and nutrition. **dietetics** n. study of diet and nutrition.

dietitian n. expert in dietetics.

differ v.i. be unlike; disagree.

difference n. being different; amount of this; remainder after subtraction; disagreement.

different a. unlike, not the same; separate; unusual. **differently** adv.

differential a. of, showing, or depending on a difference. —n. agreed difference in wage-rates; arrangement of gears allowing a vehicle's wheels to revolve at different speeds when cornering.

differentiate v.t./i. be a difference between; distinguish between; develop differences. **differentiation** n.

difficult a. needing much effort or skill to do, deal with, or understand; troublesome. **difficulty** n.

diffident a. lacking self-confidence. **diffidently** adv., **diffidence** n.

diffract v.t. break up a beam of light into a series of coloured or dark-and-light bands. **diffraction** n., **diffractive** a.

diffuse[1] /-'fju:s/ a. diffused, not concentrated; wordy. **diffusely** adv., **diffuseness** n.

diffuse[2] /-'fju:z/ v.t./i. spread widely or thinly; mix slowly. **diffuser** n., **diffusion** n., **diffusive** a.

diffusable a. able to be diffused.

dig v.t./i. (p.t. **dug**, pres.p. **digging**) break up and move soil; make (a way or hole) thus; remove by digging; excavate; seek or discover by investigation; thrust, poke. —n. piece of digging; excavation; thrust, poke; cutting remark; (pl., colloq.) lodgings.

digest[1] /-'dʒe-/ v.t. dissolve (food) in the stomach etc. for absorption by the body; absorb into the mind. **digester** n.

digest[2] /'daɪ-/ n. methodical summary; publication giving excerpts of news, writings, etc.

digestible a. able to be digested. **digestibility** n.

digestion n. process or power of digesting food.

digestive a. of or aiding digestion. **digestive biscuit** wholemeal biscuit.

digger n. one who digs; mechanical excavator.

digit n. any numeral from 0 to 9; finger or toe.

digital a. of or using digits. **digital clock** one that shows the time as a row of figures. **digitally** adv.

digitalis /-'ter-/ n. heart stimulant prepared from foxglove leaves.

digitate a. having separate fingers or toes.

dignified a. showing dignity.

dignify v.t. give dignity to.

dignitary n. person holding high rank or position.

dignity n. calm and serious manner or style; worthiness; high rank or position.

digress v.i. depart from the main subject temporarily. **digression** n., **digressive** a.

dike n. dyke.

dilapidated a. in disrepair.

dilapidation n. dilapidated state.

dilate v.t./i. make or become wider. **dilation, dilatation** ns., **dilator** n.

dilatory /'dɪlə-/ a. delaying, not prompt. **dilatorily** adv., **dilatoriness** n.

dilemma n. situation in which a choice must be made between unwelcome alternatives.

dilettante /dɪlɪ'tænti/ n. person who dabbles in a subject for pleasure.

diligent a. working or done with care and effort. **diligently** adv., **diligence** n.

dill n. herb with spicy seeds.

dilly-dally v.i. (colloq.) dawdle; waste time by indecision.

dilute v.t. reduce the strength of (fluid) by adding water etc.; reduce the forcefulness of. **diluent** a. & n., **diluter** n., **dilution** n.

dim a. (**dimmer, dimmest**) lit faintly; indistinct; (colloq.) stupid. —v.t./i. (p.t. **dimmed**) make or become dim. **dimly** adv., **dimness** n.

dime n. 10-cent coin of the USA.

dimension n. measurable extent; scope. **dimensional** a.

diminish v.t./i. make or become less.

diminuendo adv. & n. (pl. -os)

decreasing in loudness.

diminution n. decrease.

diminutive a. tiny. —n. word for a small specimen of a thing; affectionate form of a name.

dimple n. small dent, esp. in the skin. —v.t./i. show dimple(s); produce dimples in.

din n. loud annoying noise. —v.t./i. (p.t. **dinned**) make a din; force (information) into a person by constant repetition.

dinar /'di:-/ n. unit of money in countries of former Yugoslavia and various other countries esp. in the Middle East.

dine v.t./i. eat dinner; entertain to dinner.

diner n. one who dines; dining-room.

ding-dong n. sound of clapper bell(s). —a. & adv. with vigorous action; with success alternating between contestants.

dinghy n. small open boat or inflatable rubber boat.

dingle n. deep dell.

dingo n. (pl. -oes) Australian wild dog.

dingy a. (-ier, -iest) dirty-looking. **dingily** adv., **dinginess** n.

dining-room n. room in which meals are eaten.

dinkum a. (Austr. & NZ sl.) true, real.

dinky a. (-ier, -iest) (colloq.) attractively small and neat.

dinner n. chief meal of the day; formal evening meal. **dinner-jacket** n. man's usu. black jacket for evening wear.

dinosaur n. extinct lizard-like creature.

dint n. dent. **by dint of** by means of.

diocese n. district under the care of a bishop. **diocesan** /-'ɒs-/ a.

diode n. thermionic valve with two electrodes; semiconductor rectifier with two terminals.

dioptre n. unit of refractive power of a lens.

dioxide n. oxide with two atoms of oxygen to one of a metal or other element.

dip v.t./i. (p.t. **dipped**) put into liquid; go under water and emerge quickly; lower, go downwards. —n. dipping; short bathe; liquid or mixture into which something is dipped; downward slope. **dip into** read briefly from (a book).

diphtheria /dɪf-/ n. infectious disease with inflammation of the throat.

diphthong n. compound vowelsound (as *ou* in *loud*).

diploma n. certificate awarded by a college etc. to a person completing a course of study.

diplomacy n. handling of international relations; tact.

diplomat n. member of the diplomatic service; tactful person.

diplomatic a. of or engaged in diplomacy; tactful. **diplomatically** adv.

dipper n. diving bird; ladle.

dipsomania n. uncontrollable craving for alcohol. **dipsomaniac** n. person suffering from this.

diptych n. pair of pictures or carvings on two panels hinged together.

dire a. (-er, -est) dreadful; ominous; extreme and urgent. **direly** adv., **direness** n.

direct a. straight, not crooked or roundabout; with nothing or no one between; straightforward, frank. —adv. by a direct route. —v.t. tell or show how to do something or reach a place; address (a letter etc.); cause to have a specified direction or target; control; command. **directness** n.

direction n. directing; line along which a thing moves or faces; instruction.

directional a. of direction; operating in one direction only.

directive n. general instruction issued by authority.

directly adv. in a direct line; in a direct manner; very soon. —conj. (colloq.) as soon as.

director n. supervisor; member of a board directing a business company's affairs; one who supervises acting and filming. **directorship** n.

directorate n. office of director; board of directors.

directory n. list of telephone subscribers, inhabitants, members, etc.

dirge n. song of mourning.

dirigible a. able to be steered. —n. dirigible balloon or airship.

dirk n. a kind of dagger.

dirndl n. full skirt gathered into a tight waistband.

dirt n. unclean matter; soil; anything worthless; foul words, scandal. **dirt-track** n. racing track made of earth or cinders etc.

dirty a. (-ier, -iest) soiled, not clean; producing impurities or much fall-out; dishonourable; stormy; lewd, obscene. —v.t./i. make or become dirty. **dirtily** adv., **dirtiness** n.

disability n. thing that disables or disqualifies a person.

disable v.t. deprive of some ability, make unfit. **disabled** a. having a physical disability. **disablement** n.

disabuse v.t. disillusion.

disadvantage n. unfavourable condition. **disadvantaged** a., **disadvantageous** a.

disaffected a. discontented, having lost one's feelings of loyalty. **disaffection** n.

disagree v.i. have a different opinion; fail to agree; quarrel. **disagreement** n.

disagreeable a. unpleasant; bad-tempered. **disagreeably** adv.

disallow v.t. refuse to sanction.

disappear v.i. pass from sight or existence. **disappearance** n.

disappoint v.t. fail to do what was desired or expected by. **disappointment** n.

disapprobation n. disapproval.

disapprove v.i. have or express an unfavourable opinion. **disapproval** n.

disarm v.t./i. deprive of weapon(s); disband or reduce armed forces; defuse (a bomb); make less hostile.

disarmament n. reduction of a country's forces or weapons.

disarrange v.t. put into disorder. **disarrangement** n.

disarray n. & v.t. disorder.

disaster n. sudden great misfortune; great failure. **disastrous** a., **disastrously** adv.

disavow v.t. disclaim. **disavowal** n.

disband v.t./i. separate, disperse. **disbandment** n.

disbar v.t. (p.t. **disbarred**) deprive of the status of barrister.

disbelieve v.t./i. refuse or be unable to believe. **disbelief** n.

disbud v.t. (p.t. **disbudded**) remove unwanted buds from.

disburden v.t. relieve of a burden.

disburse v.t. pay out (money). **disbursement** n.

disc n. thin circular plate or layer; thing shaped thus; record bearing recorded sound; non-magnetic circular storage-device for data; magnetic disk (see *magnetic*). **disc jockey** compère of a broadcast programme of recorded light music.

discard[1] /'-'ka:d/ v.t. throw away, put aside as useless or unwanted.

discard[2] /'dɪs-/ n. discarded thing.

discern v.t. perceive with the mind or senses. **discernment** n.

discernible a. able to be discerned. **discernibly** adv.

discerning a. perceptive, showing sensitive understanding.

discharge v.t./i. send or flow out; unload; release the electric

charge (of); allow to leave; dismiss; pay (a debt), perform (a duty etc.). —n. discharging; substance discharged.

disciple n. one of the original followers of Christ; person accepting the teachings of another.

disciplinarian n. person who enforces strict discipline.

disciplinary /'dɪs-/ a. of or for discipline.

discipline n. orderly or controlled behaviour; training or control producing this; branch of learning. —v.t. train to be orderly; punish.

disclaim v.t. disown.

disclaimer n. statement disclaiming something.

disclose v.t. reveal. **disclosure** n.

disco n. (pl. -os) (colloq.) discothèque.

discolour v.t./i. spoil the colour of; become discoloured or changed in colour. **discoloration** n.

discomfit v.t. (p.t. **discomfited**) disconcert. **discomfiture** n.

discomfort n. being uncomfortable; thing causing this.

discommode v.t. inconvenience.

disconcert v.t. upset the self-confidence of, fluster.

disconnect v.t. break the connection of; put out of action by disconnecting parts. **disconnection** n.

disconsolate a. unhappy, disappointed. **disconsolately** adv.

discontent n. dissatisfaction.

discontented a. feeling discontent.

discontinue v.t./i. put an end to; cease. **discontinuance** n.

discontinuous a. not continuous. **discontinuity** n.

discord n. disagreement, quarrelling; harsh sound. **discordant** a., **discordance** n., **discordancy** n.

discothèque /'dɪskətek/ n. club or party where amplified recorded music is played for dancing; equipment for playing this.

discount[1] /'dıs-/ n. amount of money taken off the full price.

discount[2] /-'kaʊnt/ v.t. disregard partly or wholly; purchase (a bill of exchange) for less than its value will be when matured.

discourage v.t. dishearten; dissuade (from). **discouragement** n.

discourse[1] /'dıs-/ n. speech, lecture; treatise.

discourse[2] /-'kɔːs/ v.i. utter or write a discourse.

discourteous a. lacking courtesy. **discourteously** adv., **discourtesy** n.

discover v.t. obtain sight or knowledge of. **discovery** n.

discredit v.t. (p.t. **discredited**) damage the reputation of; refuse to believe; cause to be disbelieved. —n. damage to a reputation; thing causing this; doubt. **discreditable** a. bringing discredit.

discreet a. cautious and prudent; not giving away secrets; unobtrusive, not showy. **discreetly** adv.

discrepancy n. failure to tally. **discrepant** a.

discrete a. separate, not continuous. **discretely** adv.

discretion n. being discreet; freedom to decide something.

discretionary a. done or used at a person's discretion.

discriminate v.t./i. make a distinction (between). **discriminate against** treat unfairly. **discriminating** a. having good judgement. **discrimination** n., **discriminatory** a.

discursive a. rambling, not keeping to the main subject.

discus n. heavy disc thrown in contests of strength.

discuss v.t. examine by argument, talk or write about. **discussion** n.

disdain v.t. & n. scorn.

disdainful a. showing disdain. **disdainfully** adv.

disease n. unhealthy condition; specific illness. **diseased** a.

disembark v.t./i. put or go ashore. **disembarkation** n.

disembarrass v.t. free from embarrassment; rid, relieve.

disembodied a. (of a spirit) freed from the body; (of a voice) whose owner cannot be seen.

disembowel v.t. (p.t. **disembowelled**) take out the bowels of. **disembowelment** n.

disenchant v.t. free from enchantment, disillusion. **disenchantment** n.

disencumber v.t. free from an encumbrance.

disenfranchise v.t. deprive of the right to vote. **disenfranchisement** n.

disengage v.t. free from engagement; detach. **disengagement** n.

disentangle v.t. free from tangles or confusion; separate. **disentanglement** n.

disfavour n. dislike, disapproval.

disfigure v.t. spoil the appearance of. **disfigurement** n.

disgorge v.t./i. eject, pour forth; (colloq.) hand over. **disgorgement** n.

disgrace n. loss of favour or respect; thing causing this. —v.t. bring disgrace upon. **disgraceful** a., **disgracefully** adv.

disgruntled a. discontented, resentful. **disgruntlement** n.

disguise v.t. conceal the identity of; conceal. —n. disguising, disguised condition; thing that disguises.

disgust n. strong dislike. —v.t. cause disgust in. **disgusting** a.

dish n. shallow flat-bottomed object for holding food; food prepared for the table; shallow concave object or feature. —v.t. (colloq.) ruin (hopes etc.). **dish out** (colloq.) distribute. **dish up** put food into dishes for serving.

disharmony n. lack of harmony.

dishcloth n. cloth for washing dishes.

dishearten v.t. cause to lose hope or confidence.

dished a. concave.

dishevelled a. ruffled and untidy. **dishevelment** n.

dishonest a. not honest. **dishonestly** adv., **dishonesty** n.

dishonour v.t. & n. disgrace.

dishonourable a. not honourable, shameful. **dishonourably** adv.

dishwasher n. machine for washing dishes etc. automatically.

dishwater n. water in which dishes etc. have been washed.

disillusion v.t. free from pleasant but mistaken beliefs. **disillusionment** n.

disincentive n. thing that discourages an action or effort.

disinclination n. unwillingness.

disincline v.t. cause to feel reluctant or unwilling.

disinfect v.t. cleanse by destroying harmful bacteria. **disinfection** n.

disinfectant n. substance used for disinfecting things.

disinflation n. reduction of inflation.

disinformation n. deliberately misleading information.

disingenuous a. insincere.

disinherit v.t. reject from being one's heir. **disinheritance** n.

disintegrate v.t./i. break into small parts or pieces. **disintegration** n.

disinter v.t. (p.t. **disinterred**) dig up, unearth. **disinterment** n.

disinterested a. unbiased.

disjoin v.t. separate.

disjointed a. (of talk) lacking orderly connection.

disjunction n. disjoining, separation.

disjunctive a. involving separation.

disk n. = disc; = magnetic disk (see *magnetic*).

dislike n. feeling of not liking something. —v.t. feel dislike for.

dislocate v.t. displace from its position; disrupt. **dislocation** n.

dislodge v.t. move or force from an established position. **dislodgement** n.

disloyal a. not loyal. **disloyally** adv., **disloyalty** n.

dismal a. gloomy; (colloq.) feeble. **dismally** adv.

dismantle v.t. take away equipment from; take to pieces.

dismay n. feeling of surprise and discouragement. —v.t. cause dismay to.

dismember v.t. remove the limbs of; partition (a country etc.). **dismemberment** n.

dismiss v.t. send away from one's presence or employment; reject; put (a batsman or side) out in cricket. **dismissal** n., **dismissive** a.

dismount v.i. get off or down from a thing on which one is riding.

disobedient a. not obedient. **disobediently** adv., **disobedience** n.

disobey v.t./i. disregard orders, fail to obey.

disoblige v.t. disregard the wishes or convenience of. **disobliging** a.

disorder n. lack of order or of discipline; ailment. —v.t. throw into disorder; upset. **disorderly** a., **disorderliness** n.

disorganize v.t. upset the orderly system or arrangement of. **disorganization** n.

disorientate v.t. cause (a person) to lose his bearings. **disorientation** n.

disown v.t. refuse to acknowledge as one's own; reject all connection with.

disparage v.t. speak slightingly of. **disparagement** n.

disparate /ˈdis-/ a. different in kind. **disparately** adv.

disparity /-'pæ-/ n. inequality, difference.

dispassionate a. free from emotion; impartial. **dispassionately** adv.

dispatch v.t. send off to a destination or for a purpose; kill; complete (a task etc.) quickly. —n. dispatching; promptness; official message; news report. **dispatch-box** n. container for carrying official documents. **dispatch-rider** n. messenger who travels by motor cycle.

dispel v.t. (p.t. dispelled) drive away. **dispeller** n.

dispensable a. not essential.

dispensary n. place where medicines are dispensed.

dispensation n. dispensing; distributing; management, esp. of the world by Providence; exemption.

dispense v.t./i. distribute, deal out; prepare and give out (medicine etc.). **dispense with** do without; make unnecessary. **dispenser** n.

disperse v.t./i. go or send in different directions, scatter. **dispersal** n., **dispersion** n.

dispirited a. dejected. **dispiriting** a.

displace v.t. shift from its place; take the place of; oust. **displacement** n.

display v.t. show, arrange conspicuously. —n. displaying; thing(s) displayed. **displayer** n.

displease v.t. arouse displeasure of.

displeasure n. disapproval.

disport v.refl. **disport oneself** frolic.

disposable a. able to be disposed of; at one's disposal; designed to be thrown away after use. **disposability** n.

disposal n. disposing. **at one's disposal** available for one's use.

dispose v.t./i. place, arrange; make willing or ready to do something. **dispose of** get rid of; finish

off. **be well disposed** be friendly or favourable.

disposition n. arrangement; person's character; tendency.

dispossess v.t. deprive of the possession of. **dispossession** n.

disproof n. disproving, refutation.

disproportion n. disproportionate condition.

disproportionate a. relatively too large or too small. **disproportionately** adv.

disprove v.t. show to be wrong.

disputable /-'pju:-/ a. questionable. **disputably** adv.

disputant /-'pju-/ n. person engaged in a dispute.

disputation n. argument, debate.

disputatious a. fond of arguing.

dispute /-'pju:t/ v.t./i. argue, debate; quarrel; question the truth or validity of. —n. argument, debate; quarrel; quarrel. **in dispute** being disputed.

disqualify v.t. make ineligible or unsuitable. **disqualification** n.

disquiet n. uneasiness, anxiety. —v.t. cause disquiet to.

disquisition n. long discourse.

disregard v.t. pay no attention to. —n. lack of attention.

disrepair n. bad condition caused by lack of repair.

disreputable a. not respectable. **disreputably** adv.

disrepute n. discredit.

disrespect n. lack of respect. **disrespectful** a., **disrespectfully** adv.

disrobe v.t./i. undress.

disrupt v.t. cause to break up; interrupt the flow or continuity of. **disruption** n., **disruptive** a.

dissatisfaction n. lack of satisfaction or of contentment.

dissatisfied a. not satisfied.

dissect /dɪs-/ v.t. cut apart so as to examine the internal structure. **dissection** n., **dissector** n.

dissemble v.t./i. conceal (feelings). **dissemblance** n.

disseminate v.t. spread widely. **dissemination** n., **disseminator** n.

dissension n. disagreement that gives rise to strife.

dissent v.i. have or express a different opinion. —n. difference in opinion. **dissenter** n., **dissentient** a. & n.

dissertation n. detailed discourse.

disservice n. harmful action done by a person intending to help.

dissident a. disagreeing. —n. person who disagrees; one who opposes the authorities. **dissidence** n.

dissimilar a. unlike. **dissimilarity** n., **dissimilitude** n.

dissimulate v.t. dissemble. **dissimulation** n.

dissipate v.t./i. dispel; fritter away. **dissipated** a. living a dissolute life. **dissipation** n.

dissociate v.t. separate, esp. in one's thoughts; declare to be unconnected. **dissociation** n.

dissolute a. lacking moral restraint or self-discipline.

dissolution n. dissolving of an assembly or partnership.

dissolve v.t./i. make or become liquid or dispersed in liquid; disappear gradually; disperse (an assembly); end (a partnership, esp. marriage); give way to emotion. **dissolvable** a.

dissonant a. discordant. **dissonantly** adv., **dissonance** n.

dissuade v.t. persuade against a course of action. **dissuasion** n., **dissuasive** a.

distaff n. cleft stick holding wool etc. in spinning. **distaff side** maternal side; female line of descent.

distance n. length of space between two points; distant part; remoteness. —v.t. place or cause to seem far off; outdistance.

distant a. at a specified or considerable distance away; aloof. **distantly** adv.

distaste n. dislike.

distasteful a. arousing distaste. **distastefully** adv.

distemper n. disease of dogs and certain other animals; a kind of paint for use on plaster etc. —v.t. paint with distemper.

distend v.t./i. swell from pressure within. **distensible** a., **distension** n.

distil v.t./i. (p.t. **distilled**) treat or make by distillation; undergo distillation.

distillation n. process of vaporizing, condensing, and re-collecting a liquid so as to purify it or to extract elements; something distilled.

distiller n. one who makes alcoholic liquor by distillation.

distillery n. place where alcohol is distilled.

distinct a. clearly perceptible; different in kind. **distinctly** adv.

distinction n. distinguishing; difference; thing that differentiates; mark of honour; excellence.

distinctive a. distinguishing, characteristic. **distinctively** adv., **distinctiveness** n.

distinguish v.t./i. be or see or point out a difference between; discern; make notable. **distinguishable** a.

distinguished a. having distinction; famous for great achievements.

distort v.t. pull or twist out of shape; misrepresent. **distortion** n.

distract v.t. draw away the attention of.

distracted a. distraught.

distraction n. distracting; thing that distracts the attention; entertainment; distraught state, frenzy.

distrain v.i. **distrain upon** seize (goods) to enforce payment of a debt etc.; subject (a person) to this. **distraint** n.

distrait /-'treɪ/ a. (fem. **distraite**) inattentive; distraught.

distraught a. nearly crazy with grief or worry.

distress n. suffering, unhappiness. —v.t. cause distress to. **in distress** in danger and needing help.

distribute v.t. divide and share out; scatter, place at different points. **distribution** n.

distributive a. of or concerned with distribution.

distributor n. one who distributes things; device for passing electric current to sparking-plugs.

district n. part (of a country, county, or city) with a particular feature or regarded as a unit.

distrust n. lack of trust, suspicion. —v.t. feel distrust in. **distrustful** a., **distrustfully** adv.

disturb v.t. break the quiet or rest or calm of; cause to move from a settled position. **disturbance** n.

disturbed a. mentally or emotionally unstable or abnormal.

disunity n. lack of unity.

disuse n. state of not being used.

disused a. no longer used.

ditch n. long narrow trench for drainage or as a boundary. —v.t./i. make or repair ditches; (sl.) abandon; (sl.) make a forced landing of (an aircraft) on the sea.

dither v.i. tremble; hesitate indecisively. —n. state of dithering.

ditsy a. (US colloq.) fussy; scatterbrained.

ditto n. (in lists) the same again.

ditty n. short simple song.

diuretic a. & n. (substance) causing more urine to be excreted.

diurnal a. of or in the day; occupying one day.

diva /'diːvə/ n. famous woman singer.

divan n. low couch without a raised back or ends; bed resembling this.

dive v.t./i. plunge head first into water; plunge or move quickly downwards; go under water; rush headlong. —n. diving; sharp downward movement or fall; (sl.) disreputable place.

diver n. one who dives; person who works underwater in a special suit with an air supply.

diverge v.i. go in different directions from a point or each other; depart from a path etc. **divergence** n., **divergent** a.

divers /-vɜːz/ a. (old use) various.

diverse /-'vɜːs/ a. of differing kinds.

diversify v.t. introduce variety into; vary. **diversification** n.

diversion n. diverting; thing that diverts attention; entertainment; route round a closed road.

diversity n. variety.

divert v.t. turn from a course or route; entertain, amuse.

divest v.t. **divest of** strip of.

divide v.t./i. separate into parts or groups or from something else; cause to disagree; find how many times one number contains another; be able to be divided. —n. dividing line; watershed.

dividend n. number to be divided; share of profits payable esp. as interest; benefit from an action.

divider n. thing that divides; (pl.) measuring-compasses.

divination n. divining.

divine a. (-er, -est) of, from, or like God or a god; (colloq.) excellent, very beautiful. —v.t. discover by intuition or allegedly magical means. **divinely** adv., **diviner** n.

divining-rod n. dowser's forked stick.

divinity n. being divine; god.

divisible a. able to be divided. **divisibility** n.

division n. dividing; separation of MPs into two sections for counting votes in parliament; dividing line, partition; one of the parts into which a thing is divided. **divisional** a.

divisive /-'vaɪ-/ a. tending to cause disagreement.

divisor n. number by which another is to be divided.

divorce n. legal termination of a marriage; separation. —v.t. end the marriage of (a person) by divorce; separate.

divorcee n. divorced person.

divot n. piece of turf dislodged by a club-head in golf.

divulge v.t. reveal (information). **divulgation** n.

divvy n. (colloq.) dividend. —v.t./i. **divvy up** (colloq.) share out.

Diwali /di:'wɑːlɪ/ n. Hindu festival at which lamps are lit, held between September and November.

dixie n. large iron cooking-pot.

DIY abbr. do-it-yourself.

dizzy a. (-**ier**, -**iest**) giddy, feeling confused; causing giddiness.- **dizzily** adv., **dizziness** n.

DJ abbr. disc jockey.

djellaba /'dʒe-/ n. Arab cloak.

DNA abbr. deoxyribonucleic acid.

do v.t./i. (3 sing. pres. tense **does**, p.t. **did**, p.p. **done**) perform, complete; deal with; cover (a distance) in travelling; undergo; provide food etc. for; act, proceed; fare; be suitable or acceptable; (sl.) swindle, rob, attack. —v.aux. (used to form present or past tense, for emphasis, or to avoid repeating a verb just used.) —n. (pl. **dos** or **do's**) entertainment, party; dealing. **do away with** abolish, get rid of. **do down** (colloq.) swindle. **do for** (colloq.) ruin, destroy. **do-gooder** n. well-meaning but unrealistic promoter of social work or reform. **do in** (sl.) ruin, kill; tire out. **do-it-yourself** a. for use by an amateur handyman. **do out** clean, redecorate. **do up** fasten, wrap; repair, redecorate; tire out. **do with** tolerate; need, want. **do without** manage without.

Dobermann pinscher dog of a large smooth-coated breed.

doc n. (colloq.) doctor.

docile /'dəʊ-/ a. willing to obey. **docilely** adv., **docility** n.

dock[1] n. enclosed body of water where ships are admitted for loading, unloading, or repair. —v.t./i. bring or come into dock; join (spacecraft) together in space, be joined thus.

dock[2] n. enclosure for the prisoner in a criminal court.

dock[3] v.t. cut short; reduce, take away part of.

dock[4] n. tall weed with broad leaves.

docker n. labourer who loads and unloads ships in a dockyard.

docket n. document or label listing goods delivered; voucher. —v.t. (p.t. **docketed**) enter on a docket; label with a docket.

dockyard n. area and buildings round a shipping dock.

doctor n. person qualified to give medical treatment; person holding a doctorate. —v.t. treat medically; castrate; patch up; tamper with, falsify. **doctoral** a.

doctorate n. highest degree at a university.

doctrinaire a. applying theories or principles rigidly.

doctrine n. principle(s) of a religious, political, or other group. **doctrinal** /-'traɪ-/ a., **doctrinally** adv.

docudrama n. television film dramatization of real events.

document n. piece of paper giving information or evidence. —v.t. provide or prove with documents. **documentation** n.

documentary a. consisting of documents; giving a factual filmed report. —n. documentary film.

dodder v.i. totter because of age or frailty. **dodderer** n., **doddery** a.

dodecagon n. geometric figure with twelve sides. **dodecagonal** a.

dodge v.t./i. move quickly to one side so as to avoid (a thing); evade. —n. dodging movement; (colloq.) clever trick, ingenious action. **dodger** n.

dodgem n. one of the small cars in an enclosure at a fun-fair, driven so as to bump or dodge others.

dodgy a. (-ier, -iest) (colloq.) untrustworthy, unsafe, tricky.

dodo n. (pl. -os) large extinct bird.

doe n. female of deer, hare, or rabbit.

does see do.

doesn't (colloq.) = does not.

doff v.t. (colloq.) take off (one's hat).

dog n. four-legged carnivorous wild or domesticated animal; male of this or of fox or wolf; (colloq.) person; mechanical device for gripping things; (pl.) greyhound racing. —v.t. (p.t. dogged) follow persistently. **dog-collar** n. (colloq.) clerical collar fastening at the back of the neck. **dog-eared** a. with page-corners crumpled through use. **dog-star** n. the star Sirius.

dogcart n. two-wheeled cart with back-to-back seats.

doge /dəʊʒ/ n. former ruler of Venice.

dogfish n. a kind of small shark.

dogged /ˈdɒgɪd/ a. determined. **doggedly** adv.

doggerel n. bad verse.

doggo adv. lie doggo (sl.) remain motionless or making no sign.

doggy a. & n. (of) a dog. **doggy bag** bag for carrying away leftovers.

doghouse n. (US) kennel. **in the doghouse** (sl.) in disgrace.

dogma n. doctrine(s) put forward by authority.

dogmatic a. of or like dogmas; stating things in an authoritative way. **dogmatically** adv., **dogmatism** n.

dogmatize v.i. make dogmatic statement(s).

dogrose n. wild hedge-rose.

dogsbody n. (colloq.) drudge.

dogwatch n. half-watch of two hours.

dogwood n. shrub with dark-red branches and whitish flowers.

doh n. name for the keynote of a scale in music, or the note C.

doily n. small ornamental mat.

doldrums n.pl. ocean regions near the equator, with little or no wind. **in the doldrums** in low spirits.

dole v.t. distribute. —n. (colloq.) unemployment benefit.

doleful a. mournful. **dolefully** adv., **dolefulness** n.

doll n. small model of a human figure, esp. as a child's toy. —v.t. **doll up** (colloq.) dress smartly.

dollar n. unit of money in the USA and various other countries.

dollop n. (colloq.) mass of a soft substance.

dolly n. (children's use) doll; movable platform for a cine camera.

dolman sleeve loose sleeve cut in one piece with the body of a garment.

dolmen n. megalithic structure of a large flat stone laid on two upright ones.

dolomite n. a type of limestone rock. **dolomitic** a.

dolour n. sorrow. **dolorous** a.

dolphin n. sea animal like a large porpoise, with a beak-like snout.

dolt n. stupid person. **doltish** a.

Dom n. title of some RC dignitaries and monks.

domain n. area under a person's control; field of thought or activity.

dome n. rounded roof with a circular base; thing shaped like this. **domed** a.

domestic a. of home or household; of one's own country; domesticated. —n. servant in a household. **domestic science**

study of household management. **domestically** *adv.*

domesticate *v.t.* train (an animal) to live with humans; accustom to household work and home life. **domestication** *n.*

domesticity *n.* domestic life.

domicile *n.* place of residence. **domiciled** *a.* dwelling.

domiciliary *a.* of or relating to a dwelling-place.

dominant *a.* dominating. **dominance** *n.*

dominate *v.t./i.* have a commanding influence over; be the most influential or conspicuous person or thing; tower over. **domination** *n.*

domineer *v.i.* behave forcefully, making others obey.

Dominican *n.* friar or nun of the order founded by St Dominic.

dominion *n.* authority to rule, control; ruler's territory.

domino *n.* (*pl.* -oes) small oblong piece marked with pips, used in the game of **dominoes**.

don[1] *v.t.* (*p.t.* **donned**) put on.

don[2] *n.* head, fellow, or tutor of a college; **Don** Spanish title put before a man's Christian name. **donnish** *a.*

donate *v.t.* give as a donation.

donation *n.* gift (esp. of money) to a fund or institution.

done *see* do. —*a.* (*colloq.*) socially acceptable.

donjon *n.* castle keep.

donkey *n.* animal of the horse family, with long ears. **donkey engine** small auxiliary engine. **donkey jacket** thick weatherproof jacket. **donkey's years** (*colloq.*) a very long time. **donkey-work** *n.* drudgery.

donor *n.* one who gives or donates something.

don't (*colloq.*) = do not.

doodle *v.i.* scribble idly. —*n.* drawing or marks made thus.

doom *n.* grim fate; death or ruin. —*v.t.* destine to a grim fate.

doomsday *n.* day of the Last Judgement.

door *n.* hinged, sliding, or revolving barrier closing an opening; doorway.

doormat *n.* mat placed at a doorway, for wiping dirt from shoes.

doorstep *n.* step or ground just outside a door.

doorway *n.* opening filled by a door.

dope *n.* (*sl.*) medicine, drug; information; stupid person. —*v.t./i.* (*sl.*) drug.

dopey *a.* (*colloq.*) half asleep, stupid.

Doric *a.* of the simplest style in Greek architecture.

dormant *a.* sleeping; temporarily inactive. **dormancy** *n.*

dormer *n.* upright window under a small gable on a sloping roof.

dormitory *n.* room with several beds, esp. in a school. **dormitory town** one from which most residents travel to work elsewhere.

dormouse *n.* (*pl.* -mice) mouse-like animal that hibernates.

dormy *a.* (in golf) leading by as many holes as there are holes left to play.

dorsal *a.* of or on the back.

dory *n.* edible sea-fish.

dosage *n.* giving of medicine; size of a dose.

dose *n.* amount of medicine to be taken at one time; amount of radiation received. —*v.t.* give dose(s) of medicine to.

dosh *n.* (*sl.*) money.

doss *v.i.* (*sl.*) sleep in a doss-house or on a makeshift bed etc. **doss-house** *n.* cheap hostel. **dosser** *n.*

dossier /'dɒsɪə(r)/ *n.* set of documents about a person or event.

dot *n.* small round mark; shorter signal in the Morse code. —*v.t.* (*p.t.* **dotted**) mark with dot(s); scatter here and there; (*sl.*) hit. **on the dot** exactly on time.

dotage *n.* senility with mental weakness.

dotard *n.* person in his dotage.

dote v.i. **dote on** feel great fondness for. **doting** a.

dottle n. unburnt tobacco left in a pipe.

dotty a. (**-ier, -iest**) (colloq.) feeble-minded; eccentric; silly. **dottily** adv., **dottiness** n.

double a. consisting of two things or parts; twice as much or as many; designed for two persons or things; having two or more circles of petals. —adv. twice as much; in twos. —n. double quantity or thing; person or thing very like another; (pl.) game with two players on each side. —v.t./i. make or become twice as much or as many; fold in two; turn back sharply from a course; act two parts in the same play etc. **at the double** running, hurrying. **double-bass** n. lowest-pitched instrument of the violin family. **double-breasted** a. (of a coat) with fronts overlapping. **double chin** chin with a roll of fat below. **double cream** thick cream. **double-cross** v.t. cheat, deceive. **double-dealing** n. deceit, esp. in business. **double-decker** n. bus with two decks. **double Dutch** unintelligible talk. **double figures** numbers from 10 to 99. **double glazing** two sheets of glass in a window. **double-jointed** a. have unusually flexible joints. **double take** delayed reaction just after one's first reaction. **double-talk** n. talk that means something very different from its apparent meaning. **doubly** adv.

double entendre /du:bl ã'tãdr/ phrase with two meanings, one of which is usu. indecent.

doublet n. each of a pair of similar things; (old use) man's close-fitting jacket.

doubloon n. former Spanish coin.

doubt n. feeling of uncertainty or disbelief; being undecided. —v.t./i. feel doubt about, hesitate to believe. **doubter** n.

doubtful a. feeling or causing doubt; unreliable. **doubtfully** adv.

doubtless a. certainly.

douche /du:ʃ/ n. jet of water applied to the body; device for applying this. —v.t./i. use a douche (on).

dough n. thick mixture of flour etc. and liquid, for baking; (sl.) money. **doughy** a.

doughnut n. small cake of fried sweetened dough.

doughty a. (old use) valiant.

dour /duə(r)/ a. stern, gloomy-looking. **dourly** adv., **dourness** n.

douse /daus/ v.t. extinguish (a light); throw water on, put into water.

dove n. bird with a thick body and short legs; person favouring a policy of peace and negotiation rather than violence.

dovecot, dovecote n. shelter for domesticated pigeons.

dovetail n. wedge-shaped joint interlocking two pieces of wood. —v.t./i. join by this; combine neatly.

dowager n. woman holding a title or property from her dead husband.

dowdy a. (**-ier, -iest**) unattractively dull, not stylish; dressed in dowdy clothes. **dowdily** adv., **dowdiness** n.

dowel n. headless wooden or metal pin holding pieces of wood or stone together. **dowelling** n. rod for cutting into dowels.

dower n. widow's share of her husband's estate. **dower house** small house near a larger one, forming part of a dower.

down[1] n. area of open undulating land, esp. (pl.) chalk uplands.

down[2] n. very fine soft furry feathers or short hairs.

down[3] adv. to, in, or at a lower place or state etc.; to a smaller size; from an earlier to a later time; recorded in writing etc.; to the source or place where a thing is; as (partial) payment at the time of purchase. —*prep.* downwards along or through or into; at a lower part of. —*a.* directed downwards; travelling away from a central place. —*v.t.* (*colloq.*) knock or bring or put down; swallow. **down-and-out** *n.* destitute person. **down on** hostile to. **have a down on** (*colloq.*) show hostility towards. **down-to-earth** *a.* sensible and practical. **down under** in Australia or other countries of the antipodes.

downbeat *n.* accented beat. —*a.* (*colloq.*) gloomy; relaxed.

downcast *a.* dejected; (of eyes) looking downwards.

downfall *n.* fall from prosperity or power; thing causing this.

downgrade *v.t.* reduce to a lower grade.

downhearted *a.* in low spirits.

downhill *a.* & *adv.* going or sloping downwards.

download *v.t.* transfer (data) from one computer storage device etc. to another.

downpour *n.* great fall of rain.

downright *a.* frank, straightforward; thorough. —*adv.* thoroughly.

downside *n.* negative aspect; downward movement of share prices etc.

Down's syndrome abnormal congenital condition causing a broad face and mental retardation.

downstairs *adv.* & *a.* to or on a lower floor.

downstream *a.* & *adv.* in the direction in which a stream flows.

downtown *a.* & *n.* (*US*) (of) the lower or more central part of a city.

downtrodden *a.* oppressed.

downward *a.* moving or leading down. —*adv.* downwards.

downwards *adv.* towards a lower place etc.

downy *a.* (**-ier, -iest**) of like, or covered with soft down. **downily** *adv.*, **downiness** *n.*

dowry *n.* property or money brought by a bride to her husband.

dowse /dauz/ *v.i.* search for underground water or minerals by using a forked stick which dips when these are present. **dowser** *n.*

doxology *n.* formula of praise to God.

doyen /'dɔɪən/ *n.* senior member of a staff or profession. **doyenne** *n,fem.*

doze *v.i.* sleep lightly. —*n.* short light sleep.

dozen *n.* set of twelve; (*pl.*, *colloq.*) very many.

Dr *abbr.* Doctor; debtor.

drab *a.* dull, uninteresting.

drachm /dræm/ *n.* one-eighth of an ounce or of a fluid ounce.

drachma *n.* (*pl.* **-as** *or* **-ae**) unit of money in Greece.

draconian *a.* (of laws) harsh.

draft[1] *n.* rough preliminary written version; written order to a bank to pay money; group detached for special duty, selection of these; (*US*) conscription. —*v.t.* prepare a draft of; select; (*US*) conscript.

draft[2] *n.* (*US*) draught.

drag *v.t./i.* (*p.t.* **dragged**) pull along; trail on the ground; bring or proceed with effort; search (the bottom of water) with grapnels, nets, etc.; draw at a cigarette or pipe. —*n.* heavy harrow; net for dragging water; thing that slows progress; (*sl.*) draw at a cigarette etc.; (*sl.*) women's clothes worn by men. **drag race** acceleration race between cars over a short distance.

dragon *n.* mythical reptile able to breathe out fire; fierce person.

dragonfly *n.* long-bodied insect with gauzy wings.

dragoon *n.* cavalryman or (formerly) mounted infantryman. —*v.t.* force into action.

drain *v.t./i.* draw off (liquid) by channels or pipes etc.; flow away; deprive gradually of (strength or resources); drink all of. —*n.* channel or pipe carrying away water or sewage; thing that drains one's strength etc.

drainage *n.* draining; system of drains; what is drained off.

drake *n.* male duck.

dram *n.* drachm; small drink of spirits.

drama *n.* play(s) for acting on the stage or broadcasting; dramatic quality or series of events.

dramatic *a.* of drama; thrilling, impressive. **dramatics** *n.pl.* performance of plays. **dramatically** *adv.*

dramatist *n.* writer of plays.

dramatize *v.t.* make into a drama. **dramatization** *n.*

drank *see* **drink.**

drape *v.t.* cover or arrange loosely. —*n.* (US) curtain.

draper *n.* (old use) retailer of cloth or clothing.

drapery *n.* draper's trade or fabrics; fabric draped in folds.

drastic *a.* having a strong or violent effect. **drastically** *adv.*

drat *v.t.* (*p.t.* **dratted**) (*colloq.*) curse.

draught *n.* current of air; pulling; fish caught in a net; depth of water needed to float a ship; drawing of liquor from a cask etc.; one continuous act of swallowing, amount swallowed; (*pl.*) game played with 24 round pieces on a chess-board. **draught beer** beer drawn from a cask.

draughtsman *n.* (*pl.* -**men**) one who draws plans or sketches.

draughty *a.* (-ier, -iest) letting in sharp currents of air. **draughtily** *adv.*, **draughtiness** *n.*

draw *v.t./i.* (*p.t.* **drew**, *p.p.* **drawn**) pull; attract; take in (breath etc.); take from or out;

draw lots, obtain by a lottery; seek to get information from (a person); finish a contest with scores equal; require (a specified depth) in which to float; produce (a picture or diagram) by making marks; formulate; write out (a cheque) for encashment; search (a covert) for game; promote or allow a draught of air (in); make one's way, come; infuse. —*n.* act of drawing; thing that draws custom or attention; drawing of lots; drawn game. **draw at** suck in smoke from (a pipe etc.). **draw in** (of days) become shorter. **draw out** prolong; (of days) become longer. **draw-sheet** *n.* sheet that can be taken from under a patient without re-making the bed. **draw-string** *n.* string that can be pulled to tighten an opening. **draw the line** at refuse to do or tolerate. **draw up** halt; compose (a contract etc.); make (oneself) stiffly erect.

drawback *n.* disadvantage.

drawbridge *n.* bridge over a moat, hinged for raising.

drawer *n.* person who draws; one who writes a cheque; horizontal sliding compartment; (*pl.*) knickers, underpants.

drawing *n.* picture etc. drawn but not coloured. **drawing-pin** *n.* pin with a broad flat head, for fastening paper etc. to a surface. **drawing-room** *n.* formal sitting-room.

drawl *v.t./i.* speak lazily or with drawn-out vowel sounds. —*n.* drawling manner of speaking.

drawn *see* **draw.** —*a.* looking strained from tiredness or worry.

dray *n.* strong low cart for heavy loads. **drayman** *n.*

dread *n.* great fear. —*v.t.* fear greatly. —*a.* dreaded.

dreadful *a.* very bad. **dreadfully** *adv.*

dream *n.* series of pictures or events in a sleeping person's mind; day-dream; beautiful person or thing. —v.t./i. (p.t. dreamed or dreamt) have dream(s); have an ambition; think of as a possibility. **dream up** imagine; invent. **dreamer** n., **dreamless** a.

dreamy a. (-ier, -iest) day-dreaming. **dreamily** adv., **dreaminess** n.

dreary a. (-ier, -iest) dull, boring; gloomy. **drearily** adv., **dreariness** n.

dredge[1] n. apparatus for scooping things from the bottom of a river or sea. —v.t./i. bring up or clean with a dredge. **dredger**[1] n. boat that dredges.

dredge[2] v.t. sprinkle with flour or sugar. **dredger**[2] n. container with a perforated lid for sprinkling flour etc.

dregs n.pl. bits of worthless matter that sink to the bottom of liquid; worst and useless part.

drench v.t. wet all through; force (an animal) to swallow medicine. —n. this medicine; thorough wetting.

dress n. outer clothing; woman's or girl's garment with a bodice and skirt. —v.t./i. put clothes on; clothe oneself; arrange, decorate, trim; put a dressing on. **dress circle** first gallery in a theatre. **dress rehearsal** final one, in costume. **dress-shirt** n. shirt for wearing with evening dress.

dressage /-ɑːʒ/ n. management of a horse to show its obedience and deportment.

dresser[1] n. one who dresses a person or thing.

dresser[2] n. kitchen sideboard with shelves for dishes etc.

dressing n. sauce or stuffing for food; fertilizer etc. spread over land; bandage or ointment etc. for a wound; substance for stiffening fabric in manufacture. **dressing-case** n. case for brushes, cosmetics, etc., while travelling. **dressing down** scolding. **dressing-gown** n. loose gown worn when one is not fully dressed. **dressing-table** n. table with a mirror, for use while dressing.

dressmaker n. woman who makes women's clothes. **dressmaking** n.

dressy a. (-ier, -iest) wearing stylish clothes; elegant, elaborate. **dressiness** n.

drew see **draw**.

drey n. squirrel's nest.

dribble v.t./i. have saliva flowing from the mouth; flow or let flow in drops; (in football etc.) move the ball forward with slight touches. —n. act or flow of dribbling.

driblet n. small amount.

dried a. (of food) preserved by removal of moisture.

drier n. device for drying things.

drift v.t./i. be carried by a current of water or air; go casually or aimlessly; pile or be piled into drifts. —n. drifting movement; mass of snow piled up by the wind; deviation from a set course; general meaning of a speech etc.

drifter n. aimless person.

driftwood n. wood floating on the sea or washed ashore.

drill[1] n. tool or machine for boring holes or sinking wells; training; (colloq.) routine procedure. —v.t./i. use a drill, make (a hole) with a drill; train, be trained.

drill[2] n. furrow; machine for making this or sowing seeds in furrows. —v.t. plant in drills.

drill[3] n. strong twilled fabric.

drill[4] n. a kind of baboon.

drily adv. in a dry way.

drink v.t./i. (p.t. **drank**, p.p. **drunk**) swallow (liquid); take alcoholic drink, esp. in excess; pledge good wishes (to) by drinking. —n. liquid for drinking; alcoholic liquors. **drink in** watch or listen to eagerly. **drinker** n.

drip *v.t./i. (p.t.* **dripped)** fall or let fall in drops. —*n.* liquid falling in drops; sound of this; device administering a liquid at a very slow rate, esp. intravenously; *(sl.)* weak or dull person. **dripdry** *v.i.* & *a.* (able to) dry easily without ironing. **drip-feed** *n.* & *v.t.* feed(ing) by a drip.

dripping *n.* fat melted from roast meat.

drive *v.t./i. (p.t.* **drove,** *p.p.* **driven)** send or urge onwards; propel; force to penetrate; operate (a vehicle) and direct its course; travel or convey in a private vehicle; keep (machinery) going; cause, compel; make (a bargain). —*n.* journey in a private vehicle; stroke hitting a ball strongly; transmission of power to machinery; energy, urge; organized effort; road; track for a car, leading to a private house. **drive at** intend to convey as a meaning. **drive-in** *a.* (of a cinema etc.) able to be used without getting out of one's car.

drivel *n.* silly talk, nonsense.

driver *n.* person who drives; golf-club for driving from a tee.

drizzle *n.* & *v.i.* rain in very fine drops.

drogue *n.* funnel-shaped piece of fabric used as a wind-sock, brake, target, etc.

droll *a.* (**-er, -est)** amusing in an odd way. **drolly** *adv.,* **drollery** *n.*

dromedary *n.* camel with one hump, bred for riding.

drone *n.* male honey-bee; idler; deep humming sound. —*v.i.* make this sound; speak monotonously.

drool *v.i.* slaver, dribble; show gushing appreciation.

droop *v.t./i.* bend or hang down limply. —*n.* drooping attitude. **droopy** *a.*

drop *n.* small rounded mass of liquid; thing shaped like this; *(pl.)* medicine measured by drops; very small quantity; fall; steep descent, distance of this; painted curtain or scenery let down on to a stage. —*v.t./i. (p.t.* **dropped)** fall; shed, let fall; sink from exhaustion; make or become lower; utter or send casually; omit; reject, give up. **drop in** pay a casual visit. **drop-kick** *n.* kicking of a football as it falls when dropped from one's hands. **drop off** fall asleep. **drop out** cease to participate. **drop-out** *n.* one who drops out from a course of study or from conventional society.

droplet *n.* small drop of liquid.

dropper *n.* device for releasing liquid in drops.

droppings *n.pl.* fallen drops; animal dung.

dropsy *n.* disease in which fluid collects in the body. **dropsical** *a.*

dross *n.* scum on molten metal; impurities, rubbish.

drought *n.* long spell of dry weather.

drove *see* **drive.** —*n.* moving herd or flock or crowd.

drover *n.* person who drives cattle.

drown *v.t./i.* kill or be killed by suffocating in water or other liquid; flood, drench; deaden (grief etc.) with drink; overpower (sound) with greater loudness.

drowse *v.i.* be lightly asleep. **drowsy** *a.,* **drowsily** *adv.,* **drowsiness** *n.*

drub *v.t. (p.t.* **drubbed)** thrash; defeat.

drudge *n.* person who does laborious or menial work. —*v.i.* do such work. **drudgery** *n.*

drug *n.* substance used in medicine or as a stimulant or narcotic. —*v.t./i. (p.t.* **drugged)** add or give a drug to; take drugs as an addict.

drugget *n.* coarse woven fabric for covering floors etc.

drugstore *n. (US)* chemist's shop also selling various goods.

Druid *n.* priest of an ancient Celtic religion. **Druidical** *a.,* **Druidism** *n.*

drum *n.* percussion instrument, a round frame with skin or plastic etc. stretched across; cylindrical object; eardrum. —*v.t./i.* (*p.t.* **drummed**) tap or thump continually; din. **drum up** obtain by vigorous effort.

drummer *n.* person who plays drum(s).

drumstick *n.* stick for beating a drum; lower part of a cooked fowl's leg.

drunk *see* **drink**. —*a.* excited or stupefied by alcoholic drink. —*n.* drunken person; (*sl.*) drinking-bout.

drunkard *n.* person who is often drunk.

drunken *a.* intoxicated, frequently in this condition. **drunkenly** *adv.*, **drunkenness** *n.*

drupe *n.* fruit with juicy flesh round a kernel (e.g. peach).

dry *a.* (**drier**, **driest**) without water, moisture, or rainfall; thirsty; uninteresting; not allowing the sale of alcohol; expressed with pretended seriousness; (of wine) not sweet. —*v.t./i.* make or become dry; preserve (food) by removing its moisture. **dry-clean** *v.t.* clean by solvent that evaporates quickly. **dry rot** decay of wood that is not ventilated. **dry run** (*colloq.*) dummy run. **dry up** dry washed dishes; (*colloq.*) cease talking. **dryness** *n.*

dryad *n.* wood-nymph.

dual *a.* composed of two parts, double. **dual carriageway** road with a dividing strip between traffic travelling in opposite directions. **duality** *n.*

dub[1] *v.t.* (*p.t.* **dubbed**) make into a knight by touching on the shoulders with a sword; nickname.

dub[2] *v.t.* (*p.t.* **dubbed**) replace or add to the sound-track of a film etc.; copy (a recording).

dubbin *n.* thick grease for softening and waterproofing leather.

dubiety *n.* feeling of doubt.

dubious *a.* doubtful. **dubiously** *adv.*

ducal *a.* of a duke.

ducat *n.* former gold coin of various European countries.

duchess *n.* duke's wife or widow; woman with the rank of duke.

duchy *n.* territory of a duke.

duck[1] *n.* swimming-bird of various kinds; female of this; (*colloq.*) dear; batsman's score of 0; ducking movement. —*v.t./i.* push (a person) or dip one's head under water; bob down, esp. to avoid being seen or hit; dodge (a task etc.).

duck[2] *n.* strong linen or cotton cloth; (*pl.*) trousers made of this.

duckboards *n.pl.* boards forming a narrow path, esp. over mud.

duckling *n.* young duck.

duckweed *n.* plant forming on the surface of ponds etc.

duct *n.* channel or tube conveying liquid or air etc. —*v.t.* convey through a duct. **ductless** *a.*

ductile *a.* (of metal) able to be drawn into fine strands.

dud *n.* & *a.* (*sl.*) (thing) that is useless or counterfeit or fails to work.

dude *n.* (*US*) dandy. **dude ranch** ranch used as a holiday centre.

dudgeon *n.* indignation.

due *a.* owed; payable immediately; merited; scheduled to do something or to arrive. —*adv.* exactly. —*n.* a person's right, what is owed to him or her; (*pl.*) fees. **be due to** be attributable to.

duel *n.* fight or contest between two persons or sides. **duelling** *n.*, **duellist** *n.*

duenna *n.* chaperon.

duet *n.* musical composition for two performers.

duff *a.* (*sl.*) dud.

duffel *n.* = **duffle**.

duffer *n.* inefficient or stupid person.

duffle *n.* heavy woollen cloth with thick nap.

dug[1] *see* **dig**. **dug-out** *n.* underground shelter; canoe made from a hollowed tree-trunk.

dug[2] *n.* udder, teat.

dugong *n.* Asian sea-mammal.

duke *n.* nobleman of the highest hereditary rank; ruler of certain small States. **dukedom** *n.*

dulcet *a.* sounding sweet.

dulcimer *n.* musical instrument with strings struck by two hammers.

dull *a.* (**-er, -est**) not bright; lacking intelligence or liveliness; stupid; not sharp; not resonant. —*v.t./i.* make or become dull. **dully** *adv.*, **dullness** *n.*

dullard *n.* stupid person.

duly *adv.* in a correct or suitable way.

dumb *a.* (**-er, -est**) unable to speak; silent; (*colloq.*) stupid. **dumb-bell** *n.* short bar with weighted ends, lifted to exercise muscles. **dumb show** gestures without speech. **dumbly** *adv.*, **dumbness** *n.*

dumbfound *v.t.* astonish, strike dumb with surprise.

dumdum bullet soft-nosed bullet that expands on impact.

dummy *n.* sham article; model of the human figure, used to display clothes; rubber teat for a baby to suck; card-player whose cards are exposed and played by his partner. —*a.* sham. **dummy run** trial attempt; rehearsal.

dump *v.t./i.* deposit as rubbish; put down carelessly; (*colloq.*) abandon; market abroad at a lower price than at home. —*n.* rubbish-heap; temporary store; (*colloq.*) dull place.

dumpling *n.* ball of dough cooked in stew or with fruit inside.

dumps *n.pl.* (*colloq.*) low spirits.

dumpy *a.* (**-ier, -iest**) short and fat. **dumpiness** *n.*

dun[1] *a. & n.* greyish-brown.

dun[2] *v.t.* (*p.t.* dunned) ask persistently for payment of a debt.

dunce *n.* person slow at learning.

dunderhead *n.* stupid person.

dune *n.* mound of drifted sand.

dung *n.* animal excrement.

dungarees *n.pl.* overalls of coarse cotton cloth.

dungeon *n.* strong underground cell for prisoners.

dunk *v.t.* dip into liquid.

dunlin *n.* red-backed sandpiper.

dunnock *n.* hedge-sparrow.

duo *n.* (*pl.* **-os**) pair of performers.

duodecimal *a.* reckoned in twelves or twelfths.

duodenum *n.* part of the intestine next to the stomach. **duodenal** *a.*

dupe *v.t.* deceive, trick. —*n.* duped person.

duple *a.* having two parts; (in music) having two beats to the bar.

duplex *a.* having two elements.

duplicate[1] /-kət/ *n.* one of two or more things that are exactly alike; exact copy. —*a.* exactly like another or others.

duplicate[2] /-kert/ *v.t.* make or be a duplicate; do twice. **duplication** *n.*

duplicator *n.* machine for copying documents.

duplicity *n.* deceitfulness.

durable *a.* likely to last. **durables** *n.pl.* durable goods. **durably** *adv.*, **durability** *n.*

duration *n.* time during which a thing continues.

duress *n.* use of force or threats.

during *prep.* throughout; at a point in the continuance of.

dusk *n.* darker stage of twilight.

dusky *a.* (**-ier, -iest**) shadowy, dim; dark-coloured. **duskiness** *n.*

dust *n.* fine particles of earth or other matter. —*v.t./i.* sprinkle with dust or powder; clear of dust by wiping, clean a room etc. thus. **dust bowl** area denuded of vegetation and reduced to desert.

dust cover paper jacket on a book.

dustbin *n.* bin for household rubbish.

duster *n.* cloth for dusting things.

dustman *n.* (*pl.* **-men**) man employed to empty dustbins and cart away rubbish.

dustpan *n.* pan into which dust is brushed from a floor.

dusty *a.* (**-ier, -iest**) like dust; covered with dust. **dusty answer** sharp rejection. **dustily** *adv.*, **dustiness** *n.*

Dutch *a.* & *n.* (language) of the Netherlands. **Dutch courage** that obtained by drinking alcohol. **Dutch treat** outing in which each person pays his own expenses. **go Dutch** share expenses thus. **Dutchman** *n.* (*pl.* **-men**), **Dutchwoman** *n. fem.* (*pl.* **-women**).

dutch *n.* (*costermongers' sl.*) wife.

duteous *a.* dutiful. **duteously** *adv.*, **duteousness** *n.*

dutiable *a.* on which customs or other duties must be paid.

dutiful *a.* doing one's duty, showing due obedience. **dutifully** *adv.*

duty *n.* moral or legal obligation; task etc. that must be done; tax on certain goods or imports. **on duty** actually engaged in one's regular work.

duvet /'du:vei/ *n.* thick soft quilt used as bedclothes.

dwarf *n.* (*pl.* **-fs**) person or thing much below the usual size; (in fairy-tales) small being with magic powers. —*a.* very small. —*v.t.* stunt; make seem small.

dwell *v.i.* (*p.t.* **dwelt**) live as an inhabitant. **dwell on** write or speak or think lengthily about. **dweller** *n.*

dwelling *n.* house etc. to live in.

dwindle *v.i.* become less or smaller.

dye *v.t./i.* (*pres.p.* **dyeing**) colour, esp. by dipping in liquid. —*n.* substance used for dyeing things; colour given by dyeing. **dyer** *n.*

dying *see* **die**[1].

dyke *n.* long wall or embankment to prevent flooding; drainage ditch.

dynamic *a.* of force producing motion; energetic, forceful. **dynamically** *adv.*

dynamics *n.* branch of physics dealing with matter in motion.

dynamism *n.* energizing power.

dynamite *n.* powerful explosive made of nitroglycerine. —*v.t.* fit or blow up with dynamite.

dynamo *n.* (*pl.* **-os**) small generator producing electric current.

dynasty /'dm-/ *n.* line of hereditary rulers. **dynast** *n.*, **dynastic** /-'næ-/ *a.*

dysentery *n.* disease causing severe diarrhoea.

dysfunction *n.* malfunction.

dyslexia *n.* abnormal difficulty in reading and spelling. **dyslexic** *a.* & *n.*

dyspepsia *n.* indigestion. **dyspeptic** *a.* & *n.*

dystrophy *n.* progressive weakness of muscles.

E

E. *abbr.* east; eastern.

each *a.* & *pron.* every one of two or more. **each way** (of a bet) backing a horse to win or be placed.

eager *a.* full of desire, enthusiastic. **eagerly** *adv.*, **eagerness** *n.*

eagle *n.* large bird of prey; score of two under par for a hole in golf.

eaglet *n.* young eagle.

ear[1] *n.* organ of hearing; external part of this; ability to distinguish sounds accurately; listening, attention; ear-shaped thing.

ear[2] *n.* seed-bearing part of corn.

earache *n.* pain in the eardrum.

eardrum *n.* membrane inside the ear, vibrating when sound waves strike it.

earl n. British nobleman ranking between marquess and viscount. **earldom** n.

early a. (-ier, -iest) a. & adv. before the usual or expected time; not far on in development or in a series.

earmark n. distinguishing mark. —v.t. put such mark on; set aside for a particular purpose.

earn v.t. get or deserve as a reward for one's work or merit; (of money) gain as interest.

earnest[1] a. showing serious feeling or intention. **in earnest** seriously. **earnestly** adv., **earnestness** n.

earnest[2] n. money paid to confirm a contract; foretaste.

earnings n.pl. money earned.

earphone n. headphone.

earring n. ornament worn on the ear-lobe.

earshot n. range of hearing.

earth n. the planet we live on; its surface, dry land; soil; hole of a fox or badger; connection to ground as completion of an electrical circuit. —v.t. heap earth over (roots etc.); connect an electrical circuit to earth. **run to earth** find after a long search.

earthen a. made of earth or of baked clay.

earthenware n. pottery made of coarse baked clay.

earthly a. of this earth, of man's life on it. **no earthly use** etc., (colloq.) no use etc. at all.

earthquake n. violent movement of part of the earth's crust.

earthwork n. bank built of earth.

earthworm n. worm living in the soil.

earthy a. like earth or soil; (of humour etc.) gross, coarse.

earwig n. small insect with pincers at the end of its body.

ease n. freedom from pain, trouble, or anxiety; absence of painful effort. —v.t./i. relieve from pain etc.; make or become less tight or forceful or burdensome; move gently or gradually.

easel n. frame to support a painting or blackboard etc.

easement n. right of way over another's property.

east n. point on the horizon where the sun rises; direction in which this lies; eastern part. —a. in the east; (of wind) from the east. —adv. towards the east.

Easter n. festival commemorating Christ's resurrection. **Easter egg** artificial usu. chocolate egg given as a gift at Easter.

easterly a. towards or blowing from the east.

eastern a. of or in the east.

easternmost a. furthest east.

eastward a. towards the east. **eastwards** adv.

easy a. (-ier, -iest) done or got without great effort; free from pain, trouble, or anxiety. —adv. in an easy way. **easy chair** large comfortable chair. **go easy with** (colloq.) do not use too much of. **easily** adv., **easiness** n.

easygoing a. relaxed in manner, not strict.

eat v.t./i. (p.t. **ate**, p.p. **eaten**) chew and swallow (food); have a meal; destroy gradually. **eater** n.

eatable a. fit to be eaten.

eatables n.pl. food.

eau-de-Cologne /əʊdəkə'ləʊn/ n. delicate perfume originally made at Cologne.

eaves n.pl. overhanging edge of a roof.

eavesdrop v.i. (p.t. **-dropped**) listen secretly to a private conversation. **eavesdropper** n.

ebb n. outward movement of the tide, away from the land; decline. —v.i. flow away; decline. **ebb-tide** n. retreating tide.

ebonite n. vulcanite.

ebony n. hard black wood of a tropical tree. —a. black as ebony.

ebullient a. full of high spirits. **ebulliently** adv., **ebullience** n.

EC *abbr.* European Community; European Commission.

eccentric *a.* unconventional; not concentric; not placed centrally; (of an orbit) not circular. —*n.* eccentric person. **eccentrically** *adv.*, **eccentricity** *n.*

ecclesiastic *n.* clergyman.

ecclesiastical *a.* of the Church or clergy.

echelon /'eʃəl-/ *n.* staggered formation of troops etc.; level of rank or authority.

echidna /ɪ'kɪd-/ *n.* Australian egg-laying burrowing mammal.

echo *n.* (*pl.* **-oes**) repetition of sound by reflection of sound-waves; close imitation. —*v.t./i.* (*p.t.* **echoed**, *pres.p.* **echoing**) repeat by an echo; imitate. **echoic** *a.*

éclair /eɪ-/ *n.* finger-shaped cake of choux pastry with cream filling.

éclat /eɪ'klɑ:/ *n.* splendour; renown.

eclectic *a.* choosing or accepting from various sources.

eclipse *n.* blocking of light from one heavenly body by another; loss of brilliance or power etc. —*v.t.* cause an eclipse of; outshine.

ecliptic *n.* sun's apparent path among the stars.

eclogue *n.* short pastoral poem.

ecology *n.* study of living things in relation to their environment; this relationship; protection of the natural environment. **ecological** *a.*, **ecologically** *adv.*, **ecologist** *n.*

economic /i:- *or* e-/ *a.* of economics; enough to give a good return for money or effort outlaid. **economics** *n.* science of the production and consumption or use of goods or services; (as *pl.*) financial aspects.

economical /i:- *or* e-/ *a.* thrifty, avoiding waste. **economically** *adv.*

economist *n.* expert in economics.

economize *v.i.* use or spend less.

economy *n.* being economical; community's system of using its resources to produce wealth; state of a country's prosperity.

ecru /'eɪkru:/ *n.* light fawn colour.

ecstasy *n.* intense delight. **ecstatic** *a.*, **ecstatically** *adv.*

ectoplasm *n.* substance supposed to be exuded from a spiritualist medium in a trance.

ecu /'eɪkju:/ *n.* European currency unit.

ecumenical /i:kju:'men-/ *a.* of the whole Christian Church; seeking world-wide Christian unity.

eczema *n.* skin disease causing scaly itching patches.

eddy *n.* swirling patch of water or air etc. —*v.i.* swirl in eddies.

edelweiss /'eɪdlvaɪs/ *n.* alpine plant with woolly white bracts.

edge *n.* sharpened side of a blade; sharpness; line where two surfaces meet at an angle; rim, narrow surface of a thin or flat object; outer limit of an area. —*v.t./i.* border; move gradually. **have the edge on** (*colloq.*) have an advantage over. **on edge** tense and irritable.

edgeways, edgewise *advs.* with the edge forwards or outwards.

edging *n.* something placed round an edge to define or decorate it.

edgy *a.* tense and irritable. **edgily** *adv.*, **edginess** *n.*

edible *a.* suitable for eating. **edibility** *n.*

edict *n.* order proclaimed by authority.

edifice *n.* large building.

edify *v.t.* be an uplifting influence on the mind of. **edification** *n.*

edit *v.t.* (*p.t.* **edited**) be the editor of; prepare for publication; prepare (a film or recording) by arranging sections in sequence.

edition *n.* form in which something is edited or published;

number of objects issued at one time.

editor *n.* person responsible for the contents of a newspaper etc. or a section of this; one who edits.

editorial *a.* of an editor. —*n.* newspaper article giving the editor's comments.

educable *a.* able to be educated.

educate *v.t.* train the mind and abilities of; provide such training for. **education** *n.*, **educational** *a.*

educationist *n.* expert in educational methods.

educative *a.* educating.

educe *v.t.* elicit. **eduction** *n.*

Edwardian /-'wɔ:-/ *a.* & *n.* (person) of the reign of Edward VII (1901–10).

EEC *abbr.* European Economic Community.

eel *n.* snake-like fish.

eerie *a.* (**-ier, -iest**) causing a feeling of mystery and fear. **eerily** *adv.*, **eeriness** *n.*

efface *v.t.* rub out, obliterate; make inconspicuous. **effacement** *n.*

effect *n.* change produced by an action or cause; impression; state of being operative; (*pl.*) property. —*v.t.* cause to occur.

effective *a.* producing an effect; striking; operative. **effectively** *adv.*, **effectiveness** *n.*

effectual *a.* answering its purpose. **effectually** *adv.*

effectuate *v.t.* cause to happen.

effeminate *a.* not manly, womanish. **effeminately** *adv.*, **effeminacy** *n.*

effervesce *v.i.* give off bubbles. **effervescence** *n.*, **effervescent** *a.*

effete /-'fi:t/ *a.* having lost its vitality. **effeteness** *n.*

efficacious *a.* producing the desired result. **efficaciously** *adv.*, **efficacy** *n.*

efficient *a.* producing results with little waste of effort. **efficiently** *adv.*, **efficiency** *n.*

effigy *n.* model of person.

effloresce *v.i.* flower. **efflorescence** *n.*

effluent *n.* outflow, sewage.

effluvium *n.* (*pl.* **-ia**) outflow, esp. unpleasant or harmful.

effort *n.* use of energy; thing produced.

effortless *a.* done without effort.

effrontery *n.* shameless insolence.

effusion *n.* outpouring.

effusive *a.* expressing emotion in an unrestrained way. **effusively** *adv.*, **effusiveness** *n.*

e.g. *abbr.* (Latin *exempli gratia*) for example.

egalitarian *a.* & *n.* (person) holding the principle of equal rights for all. **egalitarianism** *n.*

egg[1] *n.* hard-shelled oval body produced by the female of birds, esp. that of the domestic hen; ovum. **eggshell** *n.*

egg[2] *v.t.* **egg on** (*colloq.*) urge on.

egghead *n.* (*colloq.*) intellectual person.

eggplant *n.* aubergine.

eglantine *n.* sweet-brier.

ego /'i:- *or* 'e-/ *n.* self; self-esteem.

egocentric /eg-/ *a.* self-centred.

egoism /'eg-/ *n.* self-centredness.

egoist /'eg-/ *n.* self-centred person. **egoistic** *a.*

egotism /'eg-/ *n.* practice of talking too much about oneself, conceit.

egotist /'eg-/ *n.* conceited person. **egotistic** *a.*, **egotistical** *a.*

egregious /ɪ'gri:dʒəs/ *a.* shocking; (*old use*) remarkable.

egress *n.* departure; way out.

egret /'i:grɪt/ *n.* a kind of heron.

Egyptian *a.* & *n.* (native) of Egypt.

Egyptology *n.* study of Egyptian antiquities. **Egyptologist** *n.*

eh /eɪ/ *int.* (*colloq.*) exclamation of enquiry.

Eid /i:d/ *n.* Muslim week-long festival at the end of Ramadan.

eider *n.* northern species of duck.

eiderdown *n.* quilt stuffed with soft material.

eight a. & n. one more than seven (8, VIII); crew of eight. **eighth** a. & n.

eighteen a. & n. one more than seventeen (18, XVIII). **eighteenth** a. & n.

eighty a. & n. ten times eight (80, LXXX). **eightieth** a. & n.

eisteddfod /aıs'teðvɒd/ n. Welsh congress of bards; gathering of poets and musicians for competitions.

either /'aı- or 'i:-/ a. & pron. one or other of two; each of two. —adv. & conj. as the first alternative; likewise.

ejaculate v.t./i. utter suddenly; eject fluid (esp. semen) from the body. **ejaculation** n.

eject v.t. send out forcefully; expel. **ejection** n., **ejectment** n., **ejector** n.

eke v.t. **eke out** supplement; make (a living) laboriously.

elaborate[1] /-ət/a. with many parts or details. **elaborately** adv.

elaborate[2] /-əɪt/ v.t./i. work out or describe in detail. **elaboration** n.

élan /eɪˈlɑ̃/ n. vivacity, vigour.

eland /'iː-/ n. large African antelope.

elapse v.i. (of time) pass away.

elastic a. going back to its original length or shape after being stretched or squeezed; adaptable. —n. cord or material made elastic by interweaving strands of rubber etc. **elasticity** n.

elate v.t. cause to feel very pleased or proud. **elated** a., **elation** n.

elbow n. joint between the forearm and upper arm; part of a sleeve covering this; sharp bend. —v.t. thrust with one's elbow. **elbow-grease** n. (joc.) vigorous polishing; hard work. **elbow-room** n. enough space to move or work in.

elder[1] a. older. —n. older person; official in certain Churches.

elder[2] n. tree with dark berries. **elderberry** n. its berry.

elderly a. old.

eldest a. oldest; first-born.

eldorado n. (pl. **-os**) fictitious region rich in gold.

elect v.t. choose by vote; choose as a course. —a. chosen.

election n. electing; process of electing representative(s), esp. as MP(s).

electioneer v.i. busy oneself in an election campaign.

elective a. chosen by election; entitled to elect; optional.

elector n. person entitled to vote in an election. **electoral** a.

electorate n. whole body of electors.

electric a. of, producing, or worked by electricity; startling. **electric chair** chair used to electrocute condemned criminals.

electrical a. of electricity; startling. **electrically** adv.

electrician n. person whose job is to deal with electrical equipment.

electricity n. form of energy occurring in certain particles and in bodies containing these; supply of electric current.

electrics n.pl. electrical fittings.

electrify v.t. charge with electricity; convert to the use of electric power; startle. **electrification** n.

electrocardiogram n. record of the electric current generated by heartbeats. **electrocardiograph** n. instrument producing this.

electroconvulsive therapy therapy using convulsions produced by electric shock.

electrocute v.t. kill by electricity. **electrocution** n.

electrode n. solid conductor through which electricity enters or leaves a vacuum tube etc.

electroencephalogram n. record of the electrical activity of the brain. **electroencephalograph** n. instrument producing this.

electrolysis /-ˈtrɒlɪ-/ n. decomposition or breaking up (e.g. of hair-roots) by electric current. **electrolytic** a.

electrolyte n. solution that conducts electric current, esp. in an electric cell or battery.

electromagnet n. magnet consisting of a metal core magnetized by a current-carrying coil round it.

electromagnetic a. having both electrical and magnetic properties. **electromagnetism** n., **electromagnetically** adv.

electromotive a. producing electric current.

electron n. particle with a negative electric charge. **electron microscope** very powerful one using a focused beam of electrons instead of light.

electronic a. produced or worked by a flow of electrons; of electronics. **electronically** adv. **electronic tagging** the attaching of electronic markers to people or goods enabling them to be traced.

electronics n. use of electronic devices; (as pl.) electronic circuits.

electroplate v.t. coat with a thin layer of silver etc. by electrolysis. —n. objects plated thus.

elegant a. tasteful and dignified. **elegantly** adv., **elegance** n.

elegiac a. suited to elegies.

elegy n. sad poem or song.

element n. component part; any of about 100 substances composed of atoms with the same number of protons in the nucleus; trace; wire that gives out heat in an electrical appliance; (pl.) atmospheric forces, basic principles, bread and wine in the Eucharist. **in one's element** in one's preferred occupation etc. **elemental** a.

elementary a. dealing with the simplest facts of a subject. **elementary particle** one not consisting of simpler particles.

elephant n. very large animal with a trunk and ivory tusks.

elephantiasis n. disease in which the legs become grossly enlarged.

elephantine /-ˈfæn-/ a. of or like elephants; very large, clumsy.

elevate v.t. raise to a higher position or level.

elevation n. elevating; altitude; hill; drawing showing one side of a structure.

elevator n. thing that hoists something; (US) lift.

eleven a. & n. one more than ten (11, XI); team of eleven players. **eleventh** a. & n.

elevenses n.pl. refreshments about 11 a.m.

elf n. (pl. **elves**) imaginary small being with magic powers. **elfin** a.

elicit v.t. draw out (information or a response).

elide v.t. omit in pronunciation.

eligible a. qualifying, entitled; desirable. **eligibility** n.

eliminate v.t. get rid of; exclude. **elimination** n., **eliminator** n.

elision n. omission of part of a word in pronouncing it.

élite /erˈliːt/ n. group regarded as superior and favoured; size of letters in typewriting.

élitism /erˈliː-/ n. favouring of or dominance by a selected group. **élitist** n.

elixir n. fragrant liquid used as medicine or flavouring.

Elizabethan a. & n. (person of) of Elizabeth I's reign (1558-1603).

elk n. large deer.

ell n. (old use) measure of length (45 in.).

ellipse n. regular oval.

ellipsis n. (pl. **-pses**) omission of words.

elliptical a. shaped like an ellipse; containing an ellipsis, having omissions. **elliptically** adv.

elm n. tree with rough serrated leaves; its wood.

elocution n. style or art of speaking. **elocutionary** a.

elongate v.t. lengthen. **elongation** n.

elope v.i. run away secretly with a lover. **elopement** n.

eloquence n. fluent speaking. **eloquent** a., **eloquently** adv.

else adv. besides; otherwise.

elsewhere adv. somewhere else.

elucidate v.t. throw light on (a problem), explain. **elucidation** n.

elude v.t. escape skilfully from; avoid; escape the memory or understanding of. **elusion** n.

elusive a. eluding, escaping.

elver n. young eel.

emaciated a. thin from illness or starvation. **emaciation** n.

email n. electronic mail, messages distributed electronically.

emanate v.i. issue, originate from a source. **emanation** n.

emancipate v.t. liberate, free from restraint. **emancipation** n.

emasculate v.t. deprive of force, weaken. **emasculation** n.

embalm v.t. preserve (a corpse) by using spices or chemicals. **embalmment** n.

embankment n. bank or stone structure to keep a river from spreading or to carry a railway etc.

embargo n. (pl. **-oes**) order forbidding commerce or other activity.

embark v.t./i. put or go on board ship; begin an undertaking. **embarkation** n. embarking on a ship.

embarrass v.t. cause to feel awkward or ashamed. **embarrassment** n.

embassy n. ambassador and his staff; their headquarters.

embattled a. prepared for battle; fortified.

embed v.t. (p.t. **embedded**) fix firmly in a surrounding mass.

embellish v.t. ornament; improve (a story) with invented details. **embellishment** n.

ember days days appointed by the Church for fasting and prayer in each of the four seasons.

embers n.pl. small pieces of live coal or wood in a dying fire.

embezzle v.t. take (money etc.) fraudulently for one's own use. **embezzlement** n., **embezzler** n.

embitter v.t. rouse bitter feelings in. **embitterment** n.

emblazon v.t. ornament with heraldic or other devices.

emblem n. symbol, design used as a badge etc.

emblematic a. serving as an emblem, symbolic. **emblematically** adv.

embody v.t. express (principles or ideas) in visible form; incorporate. **embodiment** n.

embolden v.t. make bold, encourage.

embolism n. obstruction of a blood-vessel by a clot or air-bubble.

emboss v.t. decorate by a raised design; mould in relief. **embossment** n.

embrace v.t./i. hold closely and lovingly, hold each other thus; accept, adopt; include. —n. act of embracing, hug.

embrasure n. splaying of the sides of a window or door so that the opening is larger from within; similar opening in a parapet for a gun etc.

embrocation n. liquid for rubbing on the body to relieve aches.

embroider v.t. ornament with needlework; embellish (a story). **embroidery** n.

embroil v.t. involve in an argument or quarrel etc.

embryo n. (pl. **-os**) animal developing in a womb or egg; thing in a rudimentary stage. **embryonic** a.

embryology n. study of embryos.

emend v.t. alter to remove errors. **emendation** n., **emendatory** a.

emerald n. bright green precious stone; its colour.

emerge v.i. come up or out into view; become known. **emergence** n., **emergent** a.

emergency n. serious situation needing prompt attention.

emeritus a. retired and holding an honorary title.

emery n. coarse abrasive for smoothing wood etc. **emeryboard** n. strip of cardboard coated with emery, used for filing the nails.

emetic n. medicine used to cause vomiting.

emigrate v.i. leave one country and go to settle in another. **emigration** n., **emigrant** n.

eminence n. state of being eminent; piece of rising ground; **His Eminence** title of a cardinal.

eminent a. famous, distinguished; outstanding. **eminently** adv.

emir /e'mɪə(r)/ n. Muslim ruler. **emirate** n. his territory.

emissary n. person sent to conduct negotiations.

emit v.t. (p.t. **emitted**) send out (light, heat, fumes, etc.); utter. **emission** n., **emitter** n.

emollient a. softening, soothing. —n. emollient substance.

emolument n. fee; salary.

emotion n. intense mental feeling.

emotional a. of emotion(s); showing great emotion. **emotionally** adv., **emotionalism** n.

emotive a. rousing emotion.

empanel v.t. (p.t. **empanelled**) enter (a jury) on a panel.

empathize v.t./i. show empathy; treat with empathy.

empathy n. ability to identify oneself mentally with, and so understand, a person or thing.

emperor n. male ruler of an empire.

emphasis n. (pl. **-ases**) special importance; vigour of expression etc.; stress on a sound or word.

emphasize v.t. lay emphasis on.

emphatic a. using or showing emphasis. **emphatically** adv.

emphysema n. abnormal distension of body tissue with air.

empire n. group of countries ruled by a supreme authority; controlling power; large organization controlled by one person or group.

empirical a. based on observation or experiment, not on theory. **empirically** adv., **empiricism** n., **empiricist** n.

emplacement n. place or platform for a gun or battery of guns.

employ v.t. give work to; use the services of; make use of. **employment** n., **employer** n.

employee n. person employed by another in return for wages.

emporium n. (pl. **-ia**) centre of commerce; shop.

empower v.t. authorize, enable.

empress n. female ruler of an empire; wife or widow of an emperor.

empty a. (**-ier, -iest**) containing nothing; without occupant(s); lacking good sense; (colloq.) hungry. —v.t./i. make or become empty; transfer the contents of, empties; **empties** n.pl. emptied boxes or bottles etc. **emptiness** n.

emu n. large Australian bird resembling an ostrich.

emulate v.t. try to do as well as, imitate. **emulation** n., **emulator** n.

emulative a. emulating.

emulsify v.t./i. convert or be converted into emulsion. **emulsifier** n., **emulsification** n.

emulsion n. creamy liquid; light-sensitive coating on photographic film.

enable v.t. give the means or authority to do something.

enact v.t. decree, make into a law; perform (a play etc.). **enactment** n.

enamel n. glass-like substance for coating metal or pottery; paint that dries hard and glossy; hard outer covering of teeth. —*v.t.* (*p.t.* **enamelled**) coat with enamel.

enamoured *a.* fond.

en bloc /ã 'blɒk/ in a block.

encamp *v.t./i.* settle in a camp.

encampment *n.* camp.

encapsulate *v.t.* enclose (as) in a capsule; summarize. **encapsulation** *n.*

encase *v.t.* enclose in a case.

encash *v.t.* cash. **encashment** *n.*

encaustic *a.* with colours burnt in.

encephalitis *n.* inflammation of the brain.

enchain *v.t.* chain up. **enchainment** *n.*

enchant *v.t.* bewitch. **enchanter** *n.,* **enchantment** *n.,* **enchantress** *n.fem.*

encircle *v.t.* surround. **encirclement** *n.*

enclave *n.* small territory wholly within the boundaries of another.

enclose *v.t.* put a fence etc. round, shut in on all sides, seclude; shut up in a receptacle; put into an envelope or parcel along with other contents.

enclosure *n.* enclosing; enclosed area; thing enclosed.

encomium /-'kəʊ-/ *n.* formal praise.

encompass *v.t.* surround, encircle. **encompassment** *n.*

encore /'ɒŋk-/ *int.* & *v.* call for repetition of a performance. —*n.* this call; thing performed in response to it.

encounter *v.t.* meet, esp. by chance; find oneself faced with. —*n.* unexpected meeting; battle.

encourage *v.t.* give hope or confidence or stimulus to; urge. **encouragement** *n.*

encroach *v.i.* intrude on someone's territory or rights etc.; advance beyond proper limits. **encroachment** *n.*

encrust *v.t.* cover with a crust of hard material; ornament with jewels etc. **encrustation** *n.*

encumber *v.t.* be a burden to, hamper.

encumbrance *n.* thing that encumbers.

encyclical /-'sɪk-/ *n.* pope's letter for circulation to churches.

encyclopaedia *n.* book of information on all branches of knowledge or on one subject. **encyclopaedic** *a.*

encyclopaedist *n.* person who writes an encyclopaedia.

end *n.* limit; furthest point or part; final part; destruction, death; purpose. —*v.t./i.* bring or come to an end. **make ends meet** keep expenditure within income. **no end of** (*colloq.*) much, many.

endanger *v.t.* cause danger to.

endear *v.t.* cause to be loved.

endearment *n.* word(s) expressing love.

endeavour *v.t.* & *n.* attempt.

endemic *a.* commonly found in a specified area or people. **endemically** *adv.*

ending *n.* final part.

endive /-drɪv/ *n.* curly-leaved plant used as salad; (*US*) chicory.

endless *a.* without end, continual. **endlessly** *adv.*

endocrine gland /-kraɪn-/gland pouring secretions straight into the blood, not through a duct.

endogenous /-'dɒdʒ-/ *a.* originating from within.

endorse *v.t.* sign or write comment on (a document); sign the back of (a cheque); enter particulars of an offence on (a driving-licence etc.); confirm, declare approval of. **endorsable** *a.,* **endorsement** *n.*

endow *v.t.* provide with a permanent income; provide with an ability or quality. **endowment** *n.*

endue *v.t.* provide with a quality etc.

endurable *a.* able to be endured.

endurance *n.* power of enduring.

endure *v.t./i.* experience and survive (pain or hardship); tolerate; last.

enema /'en-/ n. liquid injected into the rectum through the anus by a syringe; injecting of this.

enemy n. one who is hostile to and seeks to harm another.

energetic a. full of energy; done with energy. **energetically** adv.

energize v.t. give energy to; cause electricity to flow into.

energy n. capacity for vigorous activity; ability of matter or radiation to do work; oil etc. as fuel.

enervate v.t. cause to lose vitality. **enervation** n.

enfant terrible /äfä te'ri:bl/ person whose behaviour is embarrassing or irresponsible.

enfeeble v.t. make feeble. **enfeeblement** n.

enfilade n. gunfire raking a line. —v.t. rake with gunfire.

enfold v.t. wrap up; clasp.

enforce v.t. compel obedience to. **enforceable** a., **enforcement** n.

enfranchise v.t. give the right to vote. **enfranchisement** n.

engage v.t./i. take as an employee; reserve; promise; take part; occupy the attention of; begin a battle against; interlock.

engaged a. having promised to marry a specified person; occupied; in use.

engagement n. engaging something; promise to marry a specified person; appointment; battle.

engaging a. attractive.

engender v.t. give rise to.

engine n. mechanical contrivance using fuel and supplying power; part of a railway train containing this; fire-engine.

engineer n. person skilled in engineering; one in charge of machines and engines. —v.t. contrive; bring about.

engineering n. application of science for the use of power in machines, road-building, etc.

English a. & n. (language) of England. **Englishman** n. (pl. -men), **Englishwoman** n. (pl. -women).

engraft v.t. graft on or into.

engrave v.t. cut (a design) into a hard surface; ornament thus. **engraver** n.

engraving n. print made from an engraved metal plate.

engross /-'grəus/ v.t. occupy fully by absorbing the attention; write in large letters; write in legal form. **engrossment** n.

engulf v.t. swamp.

enhance v.t. increase the quality or power etc. of. **enhancement** n.

enigma n. enigmatic person or thing.

enigmatic a. mysterious and puzzling. **enigmatically** adv.

enjoin v.t. command, order.

enjoy v.t. get pleasure from; have as an advantage or benefit. **enjoy oneself** experience pleasure from what one is doing. **enjoyment** n.

enjoyable a. giving enjoyment.

enlarge v.t./i. make or become larger; reproduce on a larger scale. **enlarge upon** say more about. **enlargement** n., **enlarger** n.

enlighten v.t. inform; free from ignorance etc. **enlightenment** n.

enlist v.t. enrol for military service; get the support of. **enlistment** n.

enliven v.t. make more lively. **enlivenment** n.

en masse /ä 'mæs/ all together.

enmesh v.t. entangle.

enmity n. hostility of enemies.

ennoble v.t. make noble. **ennoblement** n.

ennui /'ɒnwi/ n. boredom.

enormity n. great wickedness or crime.

enormous a. very large.

enough a., adv., & n. as much or as many as necessary.

en passant /ä 'pæsä/ by the way.

enquire v.t./i. ask. **enquiry** n.

enrage v.t. make furious. **enragement** n.

enrapture v.t. delight intensely.

enrich v.t. make richer. **enrichment** n.

enrol v.t./i. (p.t. **enrolled**) admit as or become a member. **enrolment** n.

en route /ä 'ru:t/ on the way.

ensconce v.t. establish securely or comfortably.

ensemble /ä'sämbl/ n. thing viewed as a whole; set of performers; outfit.

enshrine v.t. set in a shrine. **enshrinement** n.

enshroud v.t. shroud.

ensign n. military or naval flag.

ensilage n. silage.

enslave v.t. make slave(s) of. **enslavement** n.

ensnare v.t. snare, trap as if in a snare.

ensue v.i. happen afterwards or as a result.

en suite /ä 'swi:t/ forming a single unit.

ensure v.t. make safe or certain.

entail v.t. make necessary; leave (land) to a line of heirs so that none can give away or sell it. —n. entailing; entailed land. **entailment** n.

entangle v.t. tangle; entwine and trap. **entanglement** n.

entente /ä'tät/ n. friendly understanding between countries.

enter v.t./i. go or come in or into; put on a list or into a record etc.; register as a competitor.

enteric a. of the intestines.

enteritis n. inflammation of the intestines.

enterprise n. bold undertaking; initiative; business activity.

enterprising a. full of initiative.

entertain v.t. amuse, occupy pleasantly; receive with hospitality; have in one's mind; consider favourably. **entertainer** n., **entertainment** n.

enthral v.t. (p.t. **enthralled**) hold spellbound. **enthralment** n.

enthrone v.t. place on a throne. **enthronement** n.

enthuse v.t./i. fill with or show enthusiasm.

enthusiasm n. eager liking or interest. **enthusiastic** a., **enthusiastically** adv.

enthusiast n. person who is full of enthusiasm for something.

entice v.t. attract by offering something pleasant. **enticement** n.

entire a. complete. **entirely** adv.

entirety n. in its entirety as a whole.

entitle v.t. give a title to (a book etc.); give (a person) a right or claim. **entitlement** n.

entity n. something that exists as a separate thing.

entomb v.t. place in a tomb.

entomology n. study of insects. **entomological** a., **entomologist** n.

entourage /ɒntʊ'rɑːʒ/ n. people accompanying an important person.

entr'acte /'ɒn-/ n. performance in the interval of a play etc.

entrails n.pl. intestines.

entrance[1] /'en-/ n. entering; door or passage by which one enters; right of admission, fee for this.

entrance[2] /'trɑːns/ v.t. fill with intense delight.

entrant n. one who enters.

entreat v.t. request earnestly or emotionally. **entreaty** n.

entrée /'ɒntreɪ/ n. right or privilege of admission; dish served between the fish and meat courses.

entrench v.t. establish firmly. **entrenchment** n.

entrepreneur /ɒntrəprə'nɜː(r)/ n. person who organizes a commercial undertaking, esp. involving risk. **entrepreneurial** a.

entropy n. measure of the amount of a system's thermal energy not available for conversion into mechanical work.

entrust v.t. give as a responsibility, place in a person's care.

entry n. entering; entrance; alley; item entered in a list etc. or for a competition; entrant.

entwine v.t. twine round.

enumerate *v.t.* count, mention (items) one by one. **enumeration** *n.*

enunciate *v.t.* pronounce (words); state clearly. **enunciation** *n.*

envelop /-'vel-/ *v.t.* (*p.t.* **enveloped**) wrap, cover on all sides. **envelopment** *n.*

envelope /'en-/ *n.* folded gummed cover for a letter.

envenom *v.t.* put poison or bitterness into.

enviable *a.* desirable enough to arouse envy. **enviably** *adv.*

envious *a.* full of envy. **enviously** *adv.*

environment *n.* surroundings; natural world. **environmental** *a.,* **environmentally** *adv.*

environmentalist *n.* & *a.* (person) seeking to protect the natural environment.

environs /-'vaɪər-/ *n.pl.* surrounding districts, esp. of a town.

envisage *v.t.* imagine; foresee.

envoy *n.* messenger; diplomatic minister ranking below ambassador.

envy *n.* discontent aroused by another's possession of a thing one would like to have; object of this. —*v.t.* feel envy of.

enzyme *n.* protein formed in living cells (or produced synthetically) and assisting chemical processes.

epaulette *n.* ornamental shoulder-piece.

ephemera /ɪ'fiː-/ *n.pl.* things of only short-lived use.

ephemeral /ɪ'fiː-/ *a.* lasting only a very short time. **ephemerally** *adv.*

epic *n.* long poem, story, or film about heroic deeds or history. —*a.* of or like an epic.

epicene /-siːn/ *a.* having the characteristics of both sexes.

epicentre *n.* point where an earthquake reaches the earth's surface.

epicure *n.* person who enjoys delicate food and drink. **epicurean** *a.* & *n.,* **epicureanism** *n.*

epidemic *n.* outbreak of a disease etc. spreading through a community.

epidemiology *n.* study of epidemics.

epidermis *n.* outer layer of the skin.

epidural /-'djʊər-/ *a.* & *n.* (injection of anaesthetic) round the nerves of the spine, anaesthetizing the lower part of the body.

epiglottis *n.* cartilage that covers the larynx in swallowing.

epigram *n.* short witty saying. **epigrammatic** *a.,* **epigrammatist** *n.*

epigraphy *n.* study of inscriptions. **epigraphic** *a.*

epilepsy *n.* disorder of the nervous system, causing fits. **epileptic** *a.* & *n.*

epilogue *n.* short concluding part.

Epiphany *n.* festival (6 Jan.) commemorating the showing of Christ to the Magi.

episcopal /ɪ'pɪsk-/ *a.* of or governed by bishop(s). **episcopacy** *n.*

episcopalian *a.* & *n.* (member) of an episcopal Church.

episcopate *n.* position of a bishop; bishops collectively.

episiotomy *n.* cut made at opening of vagina to aid delivery of child.

episode *n.* event forming one part of a sequence; one part of a serial. **episodic** *a.,* **episodically** *adv.*

epistle *n.* letter. **epistolary** *a.*

epitaph *n.* words inscribed on a tomb or describing a dead person.

epithet *n.* descriptive word(s).

epitome /ɪ'pɪtəmɪ/ *n.* perfect model or example.

epitomize *v.t.* be an epitome of. **epitomization** *n.*

epoch /'iːpɒk/ *n.* particular period. **epoch-making** *a.* important.

eponymous /-'pɒn-/ *a.* after whom something is named.

equable /'ek-/ a. (of a climate) even, free from extremes; even-tempered. **equably** adv.

equal a. same in size, amount, value, etc.; having the same rights or status. —n. person or thing equal to another. —v.t. (p.t. **equalled**) be the same in size etc. as; do something equal to. be **equal to** have the strength or ability for (a task). **equally** adv., **equality** n.

equalize v.t./i. make or become equal; equal an opponent's score. **equalization** n.

equalizer n. equalizing goal etc.

equanimity /ek-/ n. calmness of mind or temper.

equate v.t. consider to be equal or equivalent.

equation /-ʒ(ə)n/ n. mathematical statement that two expressions are equal; equating, making equal.

equator n. imaginary line round the earth at an equal distance from the North and South Poles. **equatorial** a.

equerry /'ekwərɪ/ n. official of the British royal household, attending members of the royal family.

equestrian a. of horse-riding; on horseback.

equidistant /iː-/ a. at an equal distance.

equilateral /iː-/ a. having all sides equal.

equilibrium /iː-/ n. state of balance.

equine /'ekwam/ a. of or like a horse.

equinox /'ekwɪ-/ n. time of year when night and day are of equal length. **equinoctial** a.

equip v.t. (p.t. **equipped**) supply with what is needed.

equipage /'ek-/ n. outfit; carriage and horses with attendants.

equipment n. equipping; tools or outfit etc. needed for a job or expedition.

equipoise n. equilibrium; counterbalance.

equitable /'ek-/ a. fair and just. **equitably** adv.

equitation n. horse-riding.

equity n. fairness, impartiality; (pl.) stocks and shares not bearing fixed interest.

equivalent a. equal in amount, value, or meaning etc. —n. equivalent thing. **equivalence** n.

equivocal a. ambiguous; questionable. **equivocally** adv.

equivocate v.i. use words ambiguously, esp. to conceal truth. **equivocation** n.

era n. period of history.

eradicate v.t. get rid of completely, wipe out. **eradication** n., **eradicator** n.

erase v.t. rub or wipe out. **eraser** n., **erasure** n.

erect a. upright; rigid from sexual excitement. —v.t. set up, build. **erector** n.

erectile a. able to become rigid from sexual excitement.

erection n. erecting; becoming erect; thing erected, building.

ergonomics n. study of work and its environment in order to achieve maximum efficiency. **ergonomic** a., **ergonomically** adv.

ergot n. fungal disease of rye etc.

ermine /-mɪn/ n. stoat; its white winter fur.

erode v.t. wear away gradually. **erosion** n., **erosive** a.

erogenous /ɪ'dʒɪːn-/ a. arousing sexual excitement.

erotic a. of or arousing sexual desire. **erotically** adv., **eroticism** n.

err /ɜː(r)/ v.i. (p.t. **erred**) make a mistake; be incorrect; sin.

errand n. short journey to take or fetch something; its purpose.

errant /'e-/ a. misbehaving; travelling in search of adventure.

erratic a. irregular, uneven. **erratically** adv.

erratum /e'rɑː-/ n. (pl. **-ta**) error in printing or writing.

erroneous *a.* incorrect. **erroneously** *adv.*

error *n.* mistake; being wrong; amount of inaccuracy.

erstwhile *a.* former. —*adv.* (*old use*) formerly.

eructation *n.* belch.

erudite *a.* learned. **erudition** *n.*

erupt *v.i.* break out or through; eject lava. **eruption** *n.*

eruptive *a.* erupting, liable to erupt.

escalate *v.t./i.* increase in intensity or extent. **escalation** *n.*

escalator *n.* staircase with a line of steps moving up or down.

escalope /'eskǝlǝʊp/ *n.* slice of boneless meat, esp. veal.

escapade *n.* piece of reckless or mischievous conduct.

escape *v.t./i.* get free; get out of its container; avoid; be forgotten or unnoticed by; be uttered unintentionally. —*n.* act or means of escaping; temporary distraction from reality or worry.

escapee *n.* one who escapes.

escapement *n.* mechanism regulating the movement of a watch or clock.

escapism *n.* escape from the realities of life. **escapist** *n.* & *a.*

escapologist *n.* person who entertains by escaping from confinement.

escarpment *n.* steep slope at the edge of a plateau etc.

eschatology /eskǝ-/ *n.* doctrine of death and afterlife.

eschew *v.t.* abstain from.

escort[1] /'esˈ-/ *n.* person(s) or ship(s) accompanying another as a protection or honour; person accompanying a person of the opposite sex socially.

escort[2] /-'kɔːt/ *v.t.* act as escort to.

escritoire /-'twɑː(r)/ *n.* writing-desk with drawers etc.

escudo /-'kjuː-/ *n.* (*pl.* **-os**) unit of money in Portugal.

escutcheon /ɪ'skʌtʃ(ǝ)n/ *n.* shield bearing a coat of arms; pivoted cover over a keyhole.

Eskimo *n.* (*pl.* **-os** *or* **-o**) member or language of a people living in Arctic regions.

esoteric /esǝ'te-/ *a.* intended only for people with special knowledge or interest.

espadrille /'esˈ-/ *n.* canvas shoe with a sole of plaited fibre.

espalier /ɪ'spæljǝ(r)/ *n.* trellis; shrub or tree trained on this.

esparto *n.* a kind of grass used in making paper.

especial *a.* special, outstanding. **especially** *adv.*

Esperanto /espǝ'ræntǝʊ/ *n.* artificial language designed for international use.

espionage /'espɪǝnɑːʒ/ *n.* spying.

esplanade /-'neɪd/ *n.* level area, promenade.

espouse *v.t.* support (a cause); marry. **espousal** *n.*

espresso *n.* (*pl.* **-os**) coffee made by forcing steam through powdered coffee-beans.

esprit de corps /espri: dǝ 'kɔː(r)/ loyalty uniting a group.

espy *v.t.* catch sight of.

Esq. *abbr.* Esquire, courtesy title placed after a man's surname.

essay[1] /'e-/ *n.* short literary composition in prose.

essay[2] /-'seɪ/ *v.t.* attempt.

essayist *n.* writer of essays.

essence *n.* thing's nature; indispensable quality or element; concentrated extract; liquid perfume.

essential *a.* unable to be dispensed with; of a thing's essence. —*n.* essential thing. **essentially** *adv.*

establish *v.t.* set up; settle; cause people to accept (a custom, belief, etc.); prove.

establishment *n.* establishing; staff of employees; firm or institution; **the Establishment** people established in authority and resisting change.

estate *n.* landed property; residential or industrial district planned as a unit; all a person owns, esp. that left at his death;

(old use) state. **estate car** car that can carry passengers and goods in one compartment.

esteem v.t. think highly of. —n. favourable opinion, respect.

ester n. a kind of chemical compound.

estimable a. worthy of esteem.

estimate[1] /-ət/ n. judgement of a thing's approximate value or amount or cost etc.

estimate[2] /-eɪt/ v.t. form an estimate of. **estimation** n.

estrange v.t. cause to be no longer friendly or loving. **estrangement** n.

estuary n. mouth of a large river, affected by tides. **estuarine** a.

etc. abbr. = et cetera /-'set-/, and other things of the same kind.

etch v.t. engrave with acids. **etcher** n., **etching** n.

eternal a. existing always; unchanging. **eternally** adv.

eternity n. infinite time; endless life after death. **eternity ring** finger-ring with gems set all round it, symbolizing eternity.

ethanoic acid essential ingredient of vinegar.

ether n. upper air; liquid used as an anaesthetic and solvent.

ethereal /-'θɪər-/ a. light and delicate; heavenly. **ethereally** adv., **ethereality** n.

ethic n. moral principle. **ethics** n. moral philosophy.

ethical a. of ethics; morally correct, honourable; (of medicines) not advertised to the public. **ethically** adv., **ethicality** n.

ethnic a. of a racial group; influenced by the culture of a particular people. **ethnic cleansing** mass expulsion or killing of people opposing ethnic or religious group. **ethnically** adv., **ethnicity** n.

ethnology n. study of human races and their characteristics. **ethnological** a., **ethnologist** n.

ethos /'iː.θɒs/ n. characteristic

spirit and beliefs.

etiolate /'iː-/ v.t. make pale through lack of light.

etiquette n. rules of correct behaviour.

étude /'eɪ-/ n. short musical composition or exercise.

etymology n. account of a word's origin and development. **etymological** a., **etymologically** adv., **etymologist** n.

eucalypt n., **eucalyptus** n. evergreen tree with leaves that yield a strong-smelling oil.

Eucharist n. Christian sacrament in which bread and wine are consumed; this bread and wine. **Eucharistic** a.

euchre /'juː.kə(r)/ n. American card-game.

eugenics n. science of improving the population by control of inherited characteristics. **eugenic** a.

eulogize v.t. write or utter a eulogy of.

eulogy n. piece of spoken or written praise. **eulogistic** a.

eunuch n. castrated man.

euphemism n. mild word(s) substituted for improper or blunt one(s). **euphemistic** a., **euphemistically** adv.

euphonium n. tenor tuba.

euphony n. pleasantness of sounds, esp. in words.

euphoria n. feeling of happiness. **euphoric** a., **euphorically** adv.

Eurasia a. of Europe and Asia; of mixed European and Asian parentage. —n. Eurasian person.

eureka /jʊə'riː.kə/ int. I have found it.

eurhythmics n.pl. harmony of movement developed with music and dance.

Euro- prefix European (as in Eurofanatic).

Eurocrat n. bureaucrat of the EC.

European a. of Europe or its people. —n. European person.

Eustachian tube /juːˈsteɪʃ(ə)n/ passage between the ear and the throat.

euthanasia n. bringing about a gentle and easy death, esp. to end suffering.

evacuate v.t. send away from a place considered dangerous; empty of contents or occupants. **evacuation** n.

evacuee n. evacuated person.

evade v.t. avoid by cleverness or trickery.

evaluate v.t. find out or state the value of; assess. **evaluation** n.

evanesce /evəˈnes/ v.i. fade from sight. **evanescence** n., **evanescent** a.

evangelical a. of or preaching the gospel. **evangelicalism** n.

evangelist n. author of a Gospel; person who preaches the gospel. **evangelism** n., **evangelistic** a.

evangelize v.t. preach the gospel to. **evangelization** n.

evaporate v.t./i. turn into vapour; cease to exist. **evaporated milk** milk thickened by partial evaporation and tinned. **evaporation** n.

evasion n. evading; evasive answer or excuse.

evasive a. evading; not frank. **evasively** adv., **evasiveness** n.

eve n. evening or day just before a festival; time just before an event.

even[1] a. level, smooth; uniform; calm; equal; (of an amount) not involving fractions; (of a number) divisible by two without remainder. —v.t./i. make or become even. —adv. (used for emphasis or in comparing things). **evenly** adv., **evenness** n.

even[2] n. (poetic) evening.

evening n. latter part of the day, before nightfall.

evensong n. service of evening prayer in the Church of England.

event n. something that happens, esp. something important; item in a sports programme.

eventful a. full of incidents.

eventide n. (old use) evening.

eventual a. coming at last, ultimate. **eventually** adv.

eventuality n. possible event.

ever adv. always; at any time; in any possible way. **ever since** through the period since (then). **ever so** (colloq.) very (much).

evergreen a. having green leaves throughout the year. —n. evergreen tree or shrub.

everlasting a. lasting for ever or for a very long time.

evermore adv. for ever, always.

every a. each one without exception; each in a series; all possible. **every other** with one between each two selected.

everybody pron. every person.

everyday a. worn or used on ordinary days; usual, commonplace.

everyone pron. everybody.

everything pron. all things; all that is important.

everywhere adv. in every place.

evict v.t. expel (a tenant) by legal process. **eviction** n., **evictor** n.

evidence n. anything that establishes a fact or gives reason for believing something; statements made in a lawcourt to support a case. —v.t. be evidence of. **be in evidence** be conspicuous. **evidential** a.

evident a. obvious to the eye or mind. **evidently** adv.

evil a. morally bad; harmful; very unpleasant. —n. evil thing, sin, harm. **evilly** adv., **evildoer** n.

evince v.t. show, indicate.

eviscerate v.t. disembowel. **evisceration** n.

evoke v.t. bring to one's mind, produce. **evocation** n., **evocative** a.

evolution n. process of developing into a different form; origination of living things by

development from earlier forms.
evolutionary a.

evolutionism n. theory of the evolution of species. **evolutionist** n.

evolve v.t./i. develop or work out gradually. **evolvement** n.

ewe n. female sheep.

ewer n. pitcher, water-jug.

ex[1] prep. excluding; (of goods) as sold from.

ex[2] n. (colloq.) former spouse.

ex- pref. former.

exacerbate /-'sæs-/ v.t. make worse; irritate. **exacerbation** n.

exact[1] a. accurate; giving all details. **exactness** n.

exact[2] v.t. insist on and obtain. **exaction** n.

exacting a. making great demands, requiring great effort.

exactitude n. exactness.

exactly adv. in an exact manner; quite so, as you say.

exaggerate v.t. make seem larger, better, or worse etc. than it really is. **exaggeration** n., **exaggerator** n.

exaggerated a. exaggerating.

exalt v.t. raise in rank or power etc.; praise highly; make joyful. **exaltation** n.

exam n. (colloq.) examination.

examination n. examining; testing of knowledge etc. by this.

examine v.t. look at closely, esp. in order to learn about or from; put questions or exercises to (a person) to test his knowledge or ability; question formally. **examiner** n.

examinee n. person being tested in an examination.

example n. fact illustrating a general rule; thing showing what others of the same kind are like; person or thing worthy of imitation. **make an example of** punish as a warning to others.

exasperate v.t. annoy greatly. **exasperation** n.

excavate v.t. make (a hole) by digging, dig out; reveal by digging. **excavation** n., **excavator** n.

exceed v.t. be greater than; go beyond the limit of.

exceedingly adv. very.

excel v.t./i. (p.t. **excelled**) be or do better than; be very good at something.

Excellency n. title of an ambassador or governor etc.

excellent a. extremely good. **excellently** adv., **excellence** n.

except prep. not including. —v.t. exclude from a statement etc.

excepting prep. except.

exception n. excepting; thing that does not follow the general rule. **take exception to** object to.

exceptionable a. open to objection.

exceptional a. very unusual; outstandingly good. **exceptionally** adv.

excerpt[1] /'ek-/ n. extract from a book or film or piece of music etc.

excerpt[2] /-'sɜːpt/ v.t. select excerpts from. **excerption** n.

excess n. exceeding of due limits; amount by which one quantity etc. exceeds another; agreed amount deductible by an insurer from the total claimed by the insured person; (pl.) immoderation in eating or drinking. —a. exceeding a limit.

excessive a. too much. **excessively** adv.

exchange v.t./i. give or receive in place of another thing or from another person. —n. exchanging; price at which one currency is exchanged for another; place where merchants, brokers, or dealers assemble to do business; central telephone office where connections are made between lines involved in calls. **exchangeable** a.

exchequer n. country's or person's supply of money.

excise[1] /'eksaɪz/ n. duty or tax on certain goods and licences.

excise[2] /-'saɪz/ *v.t.* cut out or away. **excision** *n.*

excitable *a.* easily excited. **excitably** *adv.*, **excitability** *n.*

excitation *n.* exciting, arousing; stimulation.

excite *v.t.* rouse the emotions of, make eager; cause (a feeling or reaction); stimulate to activity. **excitement** *n.*

exclaim *v.t./i.* cry out or utter suddenly from pain, pleasure, etc.

exclamation *n.* exclaiming; word(s) exclaimed. **exclamation mark** punctuation mark ! placed after an exclamation. **exclamatory** *a.*

exclude *v.t.* keep out from a place or group or privilege etc.; omit, ignore as irrelevant; make impossible. **exclusion** *n.*

exclusive *a.* excluding others; selective; catering only for the wealthy; not obtainable elsewhere. **exclusive** of not including. **exclusively** *adv.*, **exclusiveness** *n.*

excommunicate *v.t.* cut off from participation in a Church or its sacraments. **excommunication** *n.*

excoriate *v.t.* abrade or strip skin from; criticize severely. **excoriation** *n.*

excrement /'ekskrɪ-/ *n.* faeces.

excrescence /ɪks'kres-/ *n.* outgrowth on an animal body or plant; ugly addition.

excreta /-'kri:-/ *n.pl.* matter (esp. faeces) excreted from the body.

excrete *v.t.* expel (waste matter) from the body or tissues. **excretion** *n.*, **excretory** *a.*

excruciating *a.* intensely painful.

exculpate /'eks-/ *v.t.* free from blame. **exculpation** *n.*, **exculpatory** *a.*

excursion *n.* short journey or outing, returning afterwards to the starting-point.

excursus *n.* digression. **excursive** *a.*

excusable *a.* able to be excused. **excusably** *adv.*

excuse[1] /-'kju:z/ *v.t.* pardon, overlook (a slight offence); be a justification of (a fault or error); release from an obligation.

excuse[2] /-'kju:s/ *n.* reason put forward for excusing a fault etc.

ex-directory *a.* deliberately not listed in a telephone directory.

execrable /'eksɪ-/ *a.* abominable. **execrably** *adv.*

execrate *v.t./i.* express loathing for; utter curses. **execration** *n.*

execute *v.t.* carry out (an order); perform; produce (a work of art); put (a condemned person) to death. **execution** *n.*, **executant** /ɪg'zek-/*n.*

executioner *n.* one who executes condemned person(s).

executive /ɪg'zek-/*n.* person or group with managerial powers, or with authority to put government decisions into effect. —*a.* having such power or authority.

executor /ɪg'zek-/ *n.* person appointed by a testator to carry out the terms of his will. **executrix** *n.fem.*

exegesis /-'dʒi:sɪs/ *n.* explanation, esp. of Scripture. **exegetic** *a.*, **exegetical** *a.*

exemplar *n.* model, type.

exemplary *a.* fit to be imitated; serving as a warning to others.

exemplify *v.t.* serve as an example of. **exemplification** *n.*

exempt *a.* free from a customary obligation or payment etc. —*v.t.* make exempt. **exemption** *n.*

exequies /'eksɪkwɪz/ *n.pl.* funeral rites.

exercise *n.* use of one's powers or rights; activity, esp. designed to train the body or mind, or requiring physical exertion. —*v.t.* use (powers etc.); take or cause to take exercise, train by exercises; perplex, worry. **exercise book**

book for writing in, with limp covers.

exert *v.t.* bring into use. **exert oneself** make an effort.

exertion *n.* exerting; great effort.

exeunt /'eksɪənt/ (*stage direction*) they leave the stage.

exfoliate *v.i.* come off in scales or layers. **exfoliation** *n.*

ex gratia /eks 'greɪʃə/ done or given as a concession, without legal obligation.

exhale *v.t./i.* breathe out; give off in vapour. **exhalation** *n.*

exhaust *v.t.* use up completely; tire out. —*n.* expulsion of waste gases from an engine etc.; these gases; device through which they are expelled. **exhaustible** *a.*

exhaustion *n.* exhausting; being tired out.

exhaustive *a.* thorough, trying all possibilities. **exhaustively** *adv.*

exhibit *v.t.* display, present for the public to see. —*n.* thing exhibited. **exhibitor** *n.*

exhibition *n.* exhibiting; public display; grant to a student from college funds etc.

exhibitioner *n.* student receiving an exhibition.

exhibitionism *n.* tendency to behave in a way designed to attract attention. **exhibitionist** *n.*

exhilarate *v.t.* make joyful or lively. **exhilaration** *n.*

exhort *v.t.* urge or advise earnestly. **exhortation** *n.*, **exhortative** *a.*

exhume /ɪg'zjuːm/ *v.t.* dig up (a buried corpse etc.). **exhumation** *n.*

exigency, exigence /'eks-/ *ns.* urgent need; emergency.

exigent /'eks-/ *a.* urgent; requiring much, exacting.

exiguous /eg'zɪg-/ *a.* very small. **exiguously** *adv.*, **exiguousness** *n.*

exile *n.* being sent away from one's country as a punishment; long absence from one's country

or home; exiled person. —*v.t.* send into exile.

exist *v.i.* have place as part of what is real; occur in specified conditions; continue living. **existence** *n.*, **existent** *a.*

existentialism *n.* philosophical theory emphasizing that people are free to choose their actions. **existentialist** *n.*

exit (*stage direction*) he or she leaves the stage. —*n.* departure from a stage or place; way out.

Exocet *n.* [P.] guided missile used esp. in sea warfare.

exodus *n.* departure of many people from a place.

ex officio /eks ə'fɪʃɪəʊ/ because of his or her official position.

exogenous /-'ɒdʒ-/ *a.* originating from outside.

exonerate *v.t.* declare or show to be blameless. **exoneration** *n.*

exorbitant *a.* (of a price or demand) much too great. **exorbitantly** *adv.*, **exorbitance** *n.*

exorcize *v.t.* drive out (an evil spirit) by prayer; free (a person or place) of an evil spirit. **exorcism** *n.*, **exorcist** *n.*

exordium *n.* introductory part of a speech or treatise.

exotic *a.* introduced from abroad; colourful, unusual. **exotically** *adv.*

expand *v.t./i.* make or become larger; spread out; give a fuller account of, write out in full; become genial. **expandable** *a.*, **expander** *n.*, **expansion** *n.*

expanse *n.* wide area or extent.

expansive *a.* able to expand; genial, communicative. **expansiveness** *n.*

expatiate /-'peɪʃɪeɪt/ *v.i.* speak or write at length about a subject.

expatriate /-'pætrɪət/ *a.* living abroad. —*n.* expatriate person.

expect *v.t.* think or believe that (a person or thing) will come or (a thing) will happen; wish for and be confident of receiving; think, suppose. **expecting a baby** pregnant.

expectant *a.* filled with expectation. **expectant mother** pregnant woman. **expectantly** *adv.*, **expectancy** *n.*

expectation *n.* expecting; thing expected; probability.

expectorant *n.* medicine for causing a person to expectorate. **expectorate** *v.i.* cough and spit phlegm; spit. **expectoration** *n.*

expedient *a.* suitable, advisable; advantageous rather than right or just. **expediency** *n.*

expedite /'eks-/ *v.t.* help or hurry the progress of.

expedition *n.* journey or voyage for a purpose; people or ships etc. making this; promptness, speed. **expeditionary** *a.* of or used in an expedition.

expeditious *a.* speedy and efficient. **expeditiously** *adv.*

expel *v.t.* (*p.t.* **expelled**) send or drive out; compel to leave.

expend *v.t.* spend; use up.

expendable *a.* able to be expended; not worth saving.

expenditure *n.* expending of money etc.; amount expended.

expense *n.* cost; cause of spending money; (*pl.*) reimbursement.

expensive *a.* involving great expenditure; costing or charging more than average. **expensively** *adv.*, **expensiveness** *n.*

experience *n.* observation of fact(s) or event(s), practice in doing something; knowledge or skill gained by this. —*v.t.* feel or have an experience of.

experienced *a.* having had much experience.

experiment *n.* & *v.i.* test to discover how a thing works or what happens, or to demonstrate a known fact. **experimentation** *n.*

experimental *a.* of or used in experiments; still being tested. **experimentally** *adv.*

expert *n.* person with great knowledge or skill in a particular

thing. —*a.* having great knowledge or skill. **expertly** *adv.*

expertise /-'ti:z/ *n.* expert knowledge or skill.

expiable *a.* able to be expiated.

expiate *v.t.* make amends for (wrongdoing). **expiation** *n.*, **expiatory** *a.*

expire *v.t./i.* breathe out (air); die; come to the end of a period of validity. **expiration** *n.*

expiry *n.* termination of validity.

explain *v.t.* make clear, show the meaning of; account for. **explanation** *n.*, **explanatory** *a.*

expletive /-'pli:tiv/ *n.* violent exclamation, oath.

explicable /'eks-* or *-'plɪ-/ *a.* able to be explained. **explicability** *n.*

explicit /-'splɪs-/ *a.* stated plainly. **explicitly** *adv.*, **explicitness** *n.*

explode *v.t./i.* expand and break with a loud noise; cause to do this; burst out, show sudden violent emotion; increase suddenly; destroy (a theory) by showing it to be false. **explosion** *n.*

exploit[1] /'eks-/ *n.* bold or notable deed.

exploit[2] /-'splɔɪt/ *v.t.* make good use of; use selfishly. **exploitable** *a.*, **exploiter** *n.*, **exploitation** *n.*

explore *v.t.* travel into (a country etc.) in order to learn about it; examine. **exploration** *n.*, **exploratory** /-'plɒ-/ *a.*, **explorer** *n.*

explosive *a.* & *n.* (substance) able or liable to explode.

exponent /-'pəʊ-/ *n.* person who expounds something; one who favours a specified theory etc.; symbol showing what power of a mathematical factor is to be taken.

exponential *a.* (of an increase) more and more rapid.

export *v.t.* send (goods etc.) to another country for sale. —*n.* exporting; thing exported. **exportation** *n.*, **exporter** *n.*

expose *v.t.* leave uncovered or unprotected; subject to a risk etc.;

allow light to reach (film etc.); reveal. **exposure** n.

exposé /-zeɪ/ n. statement of facts; disclosure.

exposition n. expounding; explanation; large exhibition.

expositor n. person who expounds. **expository** a.

expostulate v.i. protest, remonstrate. **expostulation** n., **expostulatory** a.

expound v.t. set forth or explain in detail.

express[1] a. definitely stated; travelling rapidly, designed for high speed. —adv. at high speed. —n. train or bus travelling rapidly to its destination with few or no stops. —v.t. send by express service.

express[2] v.t. make (feelings or qualities) known; put into words; represent by symbols; press or squeeze out. **expressible** a.

expression n. expressing; word or phrase; look or manner that expresses feeling; mathematical symbols expressing a quantity.

expressionism n. style of painting, drama, or music seeking to express feelings rather than to represent objects realistically. **expressionist** n.

expressive a. expressing something; full of expression. **expressively** adv.

expressly adv. explicitly; for a particular purpose.

expropriate v.t. seize (property); dispossess. **expropriation** n.

expulsion n. expelling; being expelled. **expulsive** a.

expunge v.t. wipe out.

expurgate /'eks-/ v.t. remove (objectionable matter) from (a book etc.). **expurgation** n., **expurgator** n., **expurgatory** a.

exquisite /'eks-/ a. having exceptional beauty; acute, keenly felt. **exquisitely** adv.

ex-service a. formerly a member of the armed services. **exserviceman** n. (pl. -men).

extant /-'stæ-/ a. still existing.

extempore /-'stempərɪ/ a. & adv. impromptu, without preparation. **extemporaneous**, a., **temporary** a.

extemporize v.t./i. speak, perform, or produce extempore. **extemporization** n.

extend v.t./i. make longer; stretch; reach, be continuous; enlarge; offer, grant.

extendible, extensible adjs. able to be extended.

extension n. extending; extent, range; additional part or period; subsidiary telephone, its number; extramural instruction.

extensive a. extending far, large in area or scope. **extensively** adv.

extensor n. muscle that extends a part of the body.

extent n. space over which a thing extends; scope; large area.

extenuate v.t. make (an offence) seem less great by providing a partial excuse. **extenuation** n.

exterior a. on or coming from the outside. —n. exterior surface or appearance.

exterminate v.t. destroy all members or examples of. **extermination** n., **exterminator** n.

external a. of or on the outside; from an independent source. **externally** adv.

extinct a. no longer burning or active or existing in living form.

extinction n. extinguishing; making or becoming extinct.

extinguish v.t. put out (a light or flame); end the existence of.

extinguisher n. device for discharging liquid chemicals or foam to extinguish a fire.

extirpate v.t. root out, destroy. **extirpation** n.

extol v.t. (p.t. **extolled**) praise enthusiastically.

extort *v.t.* obtain by force or threats. **extortion** *n.*, **extortioner** *n.*

extortionate *a.* excessively high in price, exorbitant. **extortionately** *adv.*

extra *a.* additional, more than is usual or expected. —*adv.* more than usually; in addition. —*n.* extra thing; person employed as one of a crowd in a cinema film.

extra- *pref.* outside, beyond.

extract[1] /-'stræ-/ *v.t.* take out or obtain by force or effort; obtain (juice etc.) by suction or pressure or chemical treatment. **extractor** *n.*

extract[2] /'eks-/ *n.* substance extracted from another; passage from a book, play, film, or music.

extraction *n.* extracting; lineage.

extractive *a.* extracting minerals from the ground.

extraditable *a.* liable to or warranting extradition.

extradite *v.t.* hand over or obtain (an accused person) for trial or punishment in the country where a crime was committed. **extradition** *n.*

extramarital *a.* of sexual relationships outside marriage.

extramural *a.* for students who are non-resident or not members of a university.

extraneous *a.* of external origin; not belonging to the subject being discussed. **extraneously** *adv.*

extraordinary *a.* very unusual or remarkable; beyond what is usual. **extraordinarily** *adv.*

extrapolate /-'træ-/ *v.t./i.* estimate on the basis of available data. **extrapolation** *n.*

extrasensory *a.* achieved by some means other than the known senses.

extraterrestrial *a.* of or from outside the earth or its atmosphere.

extravagant *a.* spending or using much more than is necessary; going beyond what is reasonable. **extravagantly** *adv.*, **extravagance** *n.*

extravaganza /-'gæn-/ *n.* fanciful composition; lavish spectacular film or theatrical production.

extreme *a.* very great or intense; at the end(s), outermost; going to great lengths in actions or views. —*n.* end; extreme degree or act or condition. **extremely** *adv.*

extremist *n.* person holding extreme views, esp. in politics. **extremism** *n.*

extremity /-'strem-/ *n.* extreme point, end; extreme degree of need or danger etc.; (*pl.*) hands and feet.

extricable /'eks-/ *a.* able to be extricated.

extricate *v.t.* take out or release from an entanglement or difficulty etc. **extrication** *n.*

extrinsic *a.* not intrinsic; extraneous. **extrinsically** *adv.*

extrovert *n.* lively sociable person. **extroversion** *n.*

extrude *v.t.* thrust or squeeze out. **extrusion** *n.*, **extrusive** *a.*

exuberant *a.* full of high spirits; growing profusely. **exuberantly** *adv.*, **exuberance** *n.*

exude *v.t./i.* ooze; give off like sweat or a smell. **exudation** *n.*

exult *v.i.* rejoice greatly. **exultant** *a.* exulting. **exultation** *n.*

eye *n.* organ of sight; iris of this; region round it; power of seeing; thing like an eye, spot, hole. —*v.t.* (*p.t.* eyed, *pres.p.* eyeing) look at, watch. **eye-liner** *n.* cosmetic applied as a line round the eye. **eye-opener** *n.* thing that brings enlightenment or great surprise. **eye-shade** *n.* device to protect the eyes from strong light. **eye-shadow** *n.* cosmetic applied to the skin round the eyes. **eye-**

tooth n. canine tooth in the upper jaw, below the eye.

eyeball n. whole of the eye within the eyelids.

eyebrow n. fringe of hair on the ridge above the eye-socket.

eyeful n. something thrown or blown into one's eye; (colloq.) thorough look, remarkable or attractive sight.

eyelash n. one of the hairs fringing the eyelids.

eyeless a. without eyes.

eyelet n. small hole; ring strengthening this.

eyelid n. either of the two folds of skin that can be moved together to cover the eye.

eyepiece n. lens(es) to which the eye is applied in a telescope or microscope etc.

eyesight n. ability to see; range of vision.

eyesore n. ugly object.

eyewash n. (sl.) talk or behaviour intended to give a misleadingly good impression.

eyewitness n. person who actually saw something happen.

eyrie /'aɪrɪ/ n. eagle's nest; house etc. perched high up.

F

F abbr. Fahrenheit.

fable n. story not based on fact, often conveying a moral. **fabled** a.

fabric n. cloth or knitted material; plastic used similarly; walls etc. of a building.

fabricate v.t. construct, manufacture; invent (a story etc.). **fabrication** n., **fabricator** n.

fabulous a. incredibly great; (colloq.) marvellous. **fabulously** adv., **fabulosity** n.

façade /fə'sɑːd/ n. principal (esp. front) face of a building; outward appearance.

face n. front of the head; expression shown by its features; grimace; outward aspect; front or right side; dial-plate of a clock; coal-face. —v.t./i. have or turn the face towards; meet firmly; meet as an opponent; put a facing on.

face-flannel n. cloth for washing one's face. **face-lift** n. operation for tightening the skin of the face; alteration that improves the appearance. **face-pack** n. paste for improving the skin of the face.

faceless a. without identity; purposely not identifiable.

facer n. sudden great difficulty.

facet /'fæsɪt/ n. one of many sides of a cut stone or jewel; one aspect.

facetious a. intended or intending to be amusing. **facetiously** adv., **facetiousness** n.

facia /'feɪʃə/ n. dashboard; plate over a shop front bearing its name etc.

facial a. of the face. —n. beauty treatment for the face.

facile /'fæsaɪl/ a. done or doing something easily; superficial.

facilitate v.t. make easy or easier. **facilitation** n.

facility n. ease, absence of difficulty; means for doing something.

facing n. covering made of different material.

facsimile n. a reproduction of a document etc.

fact n. thing known to have happened or to be true or to exist. **in fact** in reality, indeed.

faction n. small united group within a larger one.

factitious a. made for a special purpose; artificial.

factor n. circumstance that contributes towards a result; number by which a given number can be divided exactly; (Sc.) land-agent. **factorial** a.

factorize v.t. resolve (a number) into factors. **factorization** n.

factory n. building(s) in which goods are manufactured.

factotum /-'taʊt-/ n. servant or assistant doing all kinds of work.

factual a. based on or containing facts. **factually** adv.

faculty n. any of the powers of the body or mind; department teaching a specified subject in a university or college; authorization given by Church authorities.

fad n. person's particular like or dislike; craze. **faddish** a.

faddy a. having petty likes and dislikes, esp. about food. **faddiness** n.

fade v.t./i. lose or cause to lose colour, freshness, or vigour; disappear gradually; cause (a cinema picture or sound) to decrease or increase gradually. **fadeless** a.

faeces /'fiːsiːz/ n.pl. waste matter discharged from the bowels. **faecal** a.

fag v.t./i. toil; make tired; be a fag for a senior pupil. —n. (colloq.) tiring work, drudgery; exhaustion; pupil who does services for a senior in certain schools; (sl.) cigarette.

fagged a. tired.

faggot n. tied bundle of sticks or twigs; ball of chopped seasoned liver, baked or fried.

Fahrenheit a. of a temperature scale with the freezing-point of water at 32° and boiling-point at 212°.

faience /faɪ'ɑːns/ n. painted glazed earthenware.

fail v.t./i. be unsuccessful; become weak, cease functioning; neglect or be unable; disappoint; become bankrupt; declare to be unsuccessful. —n. failure.

failing n. weakness or fault. —prep. in default of.

failure n. failing, lack of success; person or thing that fails.

fain adv. (old use) gladly.

faint a. (-er, -est) indistinct; not intense; weak, feeble; about to faint. —v.i. collapse unconscious. —n. act or state of fainting. **faint-**

hearted a. timid. **faintly** adv. **faintness** n.

fair¹ n. fun-fair; gathering for a sale of goods, exhibition of commercial goods. **fair-ground** n. open space where a fair is held.

fair² a. (-er, -est) light in colour, having light-coloured hair; (old use) beautiful; (of weather) fine, (of wind) favourable; just, unbiased; of moderate quality or amount. —adv. fairly. **fair play** equal opportunities etc. for all.

fairing n. streamlining structure.

Fair Isle knitted or knitwear in a pattern of coloured wools.

fairly adv. in a fair manner; moderately; actually.

fairway n. navigable channel; smooth part of a golf-course between tee and green.

fairy n. imaginary small being with magical powers. **fairy godmother** benefactress. **fairy lights** strings of small coloured lights used as decorations. **fairy story, fairy tale** tale about fairies or magic; falsehood.

fairyland n. world of fairies; very beautiful place.

fait accompli /feɪt ə'kɒmpliː/ thing already done and not reversible.

faith n. reliance, trust; belief in religious doctrine; loyalty, sincerity. **faith-cure** n., **faith-healing** n. cure etc. depending on faith. **faith-healer** n.

faithful a. loyal, trustworthy; true, accurate. **faithfully** adv. **faithfulness** n.

faithless a. disloyal.

fake n. thing that looks genuine but is not, a forgery; person pretending to be something he or she is not. —a. faked. —v.t. make an imitation of; pretend. **faker** n.

fakir /'feɪkɪə(r)/ n. Muslim or Hindu religious mendicant or ascetic.

falcon /'fɔːlkən/ n. a kind of small hawk. **falconry** n. breeding and training of hawks. **falconer** n.

fall *v.i.* (*p.t.* **fell**, *p.p.* **fallen**) come or go down freely; lose one's position or office; decrease; die in battle; pass into a specified state; occur; (of the face) show dismay; be captured or conquered. —*n.* falling; amount of this; (*US*) autumn; (*pl.*) waterfall; **the Fall (of man)** Adam's sin and its results. **fall back on** retreat or have recourse to. **fall for** (*colloq.*) fall in love with; be deceived by. **fall in take** one's place in a military formation, order to do this; (of a lease) end. **fall in with** meet by chance; agree to. **fall off** decrease, degenerate. **fall out** quarrel; happen; leave one's place in a military formation, order to do this. **fall short** be inadequate. **fall through** (of a plan) fail to be achieved. **fall to** begin working, fighting, or eating.

fallacious /-ˈleɪʃəs/ *a.* containing a fallacy.

fallacy *n.* false belief or reasoning.

fallible *a.* liable to make mistakes. **fallibility** *n.*

Fallopian tube either of the two tubes from the ovary to the womb.

fallout *n.* airborne radioactive debris.

fallow[1] *a.* (of land) left unplanted for a time. —*n.* such land.

fallow[2] *a.* **fallow deer** deer of pale brownish-yellow colour.

false *a.* incorrect; deceitful, unfaithful; not genuine, sham. **falsely** *adv.*, **falseness** *n.*

falsehood *n.* lie(s).

falsetto *n.* (*pl.* **-os**) voice above one's natural range.

falsify *v.t.* alter fraudulently; misrepresent. **falsification** *n.*

falsity *n.* falseness; falsehood.

falter *v.i.* go or function unsteadily; become weaker; speak hesitantly.

fame *n.* condition of being known to many people; good reputation.

famed *a.* famous.

familial *a.* of a family.

familiar *a.* well known; well acquainted; too informal. **familiarly** *adv.*, **familiarity** *n.*

familiarize *v.t.* make familiar. **familiarization** *n.*

family *n.* parents and their children; a person's children; set of relatives; group of related plants or animals, or of things that are alike.

famine *n.* extreme scarcity (esp. of food) in a region.

famished, famishing *adjs.* suffering from extreme hunger.

famous *a.* known to very many people; (*colloq.*) excellent. **famously** *adv.*

fan[1] *n.* device waved in the hand or operated mechanically to create a current of air. —*v.t.* (*p.t.* **fanned**) drive a current of air upon; spread from a central point. **fan belt** belt driving a fan that cools a car engine.

fan[2] *n.* enthusiastic admirer or supporter. **fan mail** letters from fans.

fanatic *n.* person filled with excessive enthusiasm. **fanatical** *a.*, **fanatically** *adv.*

fanaticism *n.* excessive enthusiasm.

fancier *n.* person who likes animals or plants, or who breeds or grows these as a hobby.

fanciful *a.* imaginative; imaginary. **fancifully** *adv.*

fancy *n.* imagination; thing imagined, unfounded idea; desire; liking. —*a.* ornamental, elaborate; arbitrary. —*v.t.* imagine; suppose; (*colloq.*) like, find attractive. **fancy dress** costume representing an animal, historical character, etc., worn for a party.

fandango *n.* (*pl.* **-oes**) lively Spanish dance.

fanfare n. short showy or ceremonious sounding of trumpets.

fang n. long sharp tooth; snake's tooth that injects venom.

fanlight n. small window above a door or larger window.

fantail n. pigeon with a semicircular tail.

fantasia /-'teɪz-/ n. imaginative musical or other composition.

fantasize v.i. day-dream.

fantastic a. absurdly fanciful; (colloq.) excellent. **fantastically** adv.

fantasy n. imagination; thing(s) imagined; fanciful design, fantasia.

far adv. at or to or by a great distance. —a. distant, remote. **Far East** countries of east and south-east Asia. **far-fetched** a. not obvious, very unlikely.

farad n. unit of capacitance.

farce n. light comedy; absurd and useless proceedings, pretence. **farcical** a., **farcically** adv.

fare n. price charged for a passenger to travel; passenger paying this; food provided. —v.i. have good or bad treatment etc., progress.

farewell int. & n. goodbye.

farinaceous a. starchy.

farm n. unit of land used for raising crops or livestock; farmhouse. —v.t./i. grow crops, raise livestock; use (land) for this. **farm out** delegate (work).

farmer n. owner or manager of a farm.

farmhouse n. farmer's house on a farm.

farmstead /-sted/ n. farm and its buildings.

farmyard n. enclosed area round farm buildings.

faro n. gambling card-game.

farrago /-'rɑːgəʊ/ n. (pl. -os) hotchpotch.

farrier n. smith who shoes horses.

farrow v.i. give birth to young pigs. —n. farrowing; litter of pigs.

farther adv. & a. at or to a greater distance, more remote.

farthest adv. & a. at or to the greatest distance, most remote.

farthing n. former British coin worth one-quarter of a penny.

farthingale n. hooped petticoat.

fascicle /'fæsɪk(ə)l/ n. one section of a book that is issued in sections.

fascinate v.t. attract and hold the interest of; charm greatly; make (a victim) powerless by a fixed look. **fascination** n., **fascinator** n.

fascism n. system of extreme right-wing dictatorship. **fascist** n.

fashion n. manner or way of doing something; style popular at a given time. —v.t. shape, make.

fashionable a. in or using a currently popular style; used by stylish people. **fashionably** adv.

fast[1] a. (-er, -est) moving or done quickly; allowing quick movement; showing a time ahead of the correct one; pleasure-seeking and immoral; firmly fixed. —adv. quickly; firmly, tightly. **fast food** prepared food needing a minimum of further cooking etc.

fast[2] v.i. go without food or without certain kinds of food. —n. fasting; day or season appointed for this.

fasten v.t./i. fix firmly, tie or join together; become fastened.

fastener, fastening ns. device used for fastening something.

fastidious a. choosing only what is good; easily disgusted. **fastidiously** adv., **fastidiousness** n.

fastness n. stronghold, fortress; being fast or firmly fixed.

fat n. white or yellow substance found in animal bodies and certain seeds. —a. (fatter, fattest) excessively plump; containing much fat; fattened; thick; profitable. **fat-head** n. (sl.) stupid person. **a fat lot** (sl.) very little. **fatness** n.

fatal *a.* causing or ending in death or disaster; fateful. **fatally** *adv.*

fatalist *n.* person who submits to what happens, regarding it as inevitable. **fatalism** *n.*, **fatalistic** *a.*, **fatalistically** *adv.*

fatality /fə'tæl-/ *n.* death caused by accident or in war etc.

fate *n.* power thought to control all events; person's destiny.

fated *a.* destined by fate; doomed.

fateful *a.* bringing great usu. unpleasant events. **fatefully** *adv.*

father *n.* male parent or ancestor; founder, originator; title of certain priests; the **Father** God, first person of the Trinity. —*v.t.* beget; originate; fix the paternity of (a child) on a person. **father-in-law** *n.* (*pl.* **-in-law**) father of one's wife or husband. **fatherhood** *n.*, **fatherly** *adj.*

fatherland *n.* one's native country.

fatherless *a.* without a living or known father.

fathom *n.* measure (6 ft.) of the depth of water. —*v.t.* measure the depth of; find the cause of, understand. **fathomable** *a.*

fathomless *a.* too deep to fathom; incomprehensible.

fatigue *n.* tiredness; weakness in metal etc., caused by stress; soldier's non-military task. —*v.t.* cause fatigue to.

fatstock *n.* livestock fattened for slaughter as food.

fatten *v.t./i.* make or become fat.

fatty *a.* like fat, containing fat. —*n.* (*colloq.*) fat person.

fatuity *n.* being fatuous; fatuous remark etc.

fatuous *a.* foolish, silly. **fatuously** *adv.*, **fatuousness** *n.*

fatwa *n.* Islamic decree.

faucet *n.* tap.

fault *n.* defect, imperfection; offence; responsibility for something wrong; break in layers of rock; incorrect serve in tennis.

—*v.t.* find fault(s) in; make imperfect. **at fault** responsible for a mistake etc.

faultless *a.* without fault. **faultlessly** *adv.*, **faultlessnes** *n.*

faulty *a.* (-**ier**, -**iest**) having fault(s). **faultily** *adv.*, **faultiness** *n.*

faun *n.* Latin rural deity with a goat's legs and horns.

fauna *n.pl.* animals of an area or period.

faux pas /fəu 'pɑː/ (*pl.* **faux pas**, *pr.* -'pɑːz) embarrassing blunder.

favour *n.* liking, approval; kindly or helpful act beyond what is due; favouritism; badge or ornament worn to show that one supports a certain party. —*v.t.* regard or treat with favour; oblige; resemble (one parent etc.).

favourable *a.* giving or showing approval; pleasing, satisfactory; advantageous. **favourably** *adv.*

favourite *a.* liked above others. —*n.* favoured person or thing; competitor generally expected to win.

favouritism *n.* unfair favouring of one at the expense of others.

fawn[1] *n.* fallow deer in its first year; light yellowish brown. —*a.* fawn-coloured.

fawn[2] *v.i.* (of a dog) show affection; try to win favour by obsequiousness.

fax *n.* facsimile transmission by electronic scanning; document produced thus. —*v.t.* transmit by this process.

fay *n.* (*poetic*) fairy.

faze *v.t.* (*colloq.*) daze and confuse.

fealty /'fiːltɪ/ *n.* loyalty.

fear *n.* unpleasant sensation caused by nearness of danger or pain; awe felt for God. —*v.t./i.* feel fear of; be afraid; revere (God).

fearful *a.* terrible; feeling fear; (*colloq.*) extreme. **fearfully** *adv.*

fearless *a.* feeling no fear. **fearlessly** *adv.*, **fearlessness** *n.*

fearsome *a.* frightening, alarming.

feasible *a.* able to be done; plausible. **feasibly** *adv.*, **feasibility** *n.*

feast *n.* large elaborate meal; joyful festival; treat. —*v.t./i.* eat heartily; give a feast to.

feat *n.* remarkable achievement.

feather *n.* each of the structures with a central shaft and fringe of fine strands, growing from a bird's skin; long silky hair on a dog's or horse's legs. —*v.t.* cover or fit with feathers; turn (an oar-blade etc.) to pass through the air edgeways. **feather-bed** *v.t.* make things financially easy for. **feather-brained** *a.* silly. **feather one's nest** enrich oneself. **feathery** *a.*

featherweight *n.* boxing-weight (57 kg); very lightweight thing or person.

feature *n.* one of the named parts of the face; noticeable quality; prominent article in a newspaper etc.; full-length cinema film; documentary broadcast. —*v.t.* give prominence to; be a feature of or in.

febrile /'fi:-/ *a.* of fever.

February *n.* second month of the year.

feckless *a.* incompetent and irresponsible. **fecklessness** *n.*

fecund /'fi:-/ *a.* fertile. **fecundity** /fr'kʌnd-/ *n.*

fecundate /'fi:-/ *v.t.* make fecund; fertilize. **fecundation** *n.*

fed *see* **feed**. —*a.* **fed up** (*colloq.*) discontented, displeased.

federal *a.* of a system in which States unite under a central authority but are independent in internal affairs. **federally** *adv.*, **federalism** *n.*, **federalist** *n.*

federalize *v.t.* make federal. **federalization** *n.*

federate *v.t./i.* unite on a federal basis or for a common purpose. —*a.* united thus. **federative** *a.*

federation *n.* federating; federated society or group of States.

fedora *n.* soft felt hat.

fee *n.* sum payable for a person's advice or services, or for a privilege or instruction etc.

feeble *a.* (**-er, -est**) weak; ineffective. **feeble-minded** *a.* mentally deficient. **feebly** *adv.*, **feebleness** *n.*

feed *v.t./i.* (*p.t.* **fed**) give food to; give as food; (of animals) take food; nourish; supply; send passes to (a player) in football etc. —*n.* meal; food for animals; pipe or channel carrying material to a machine; this material.

feedback *n.* return of part of a system's output to its source; return of information about a product etc. to its supplier.

feeder *n.* one that feeds; bottle with a teat for feeding babies; baby's bib; feeding-apparatus in a machine; branch road or railway line etc. linking outlying areas to a central system.

feel *v.t./i.* (*p.t.* **felt**) explore or perceive by touch; be conscious of (being); give a sensation; have a vague conviction or impression; have as an opinion. —*n.* sense of touch; act of feeling; sensation produced by a thing touched. **feel like** be in the mood for.

feeler *n.* long slender part in certain animals, used for testing things by touch; tentative suggestion. **feeler gauge** set of blades used for measuring narrow gaps.

feeling *n.* power to feel things; mental or physical awareness; (*pl.*) emotional susceptibilities; idea or belief not based on reasoning; opinion; readiness to feel, sympathy.

feet *see* **foot**.

feign /feɪn/ *v.t.* pretend.

feint /feɪnt/ *n.* sham attack made to divert attention. —*v.i.* make a feint. —*a.* (of ruled lines) faint.

feldspar *n.* white or red mineral containing silicates.

felicitate *v.t.* congratulate. **felicitation** *n.*

felicitous a. well-chosen, apt. **felicitously** adv., **felicitousness** n.

felicity n. happiness; pleasing manner or style.

feline /'fi:lain/ a. of cats, cat-like. —n. animal of the cat family.

fell[1] n. stretch of moor or hilly land, especially in north England.

fell[2] a. ruthless. **at one fell swoop** in a single deadly action.

fell[3] v.t. strike down; cut down (a tree); stitch down (a seam).

fell[4] see **fall**.

felloe n. outer circle of a wheel, attached by spokes.

fellow n. associate, comrade; (colloq.) man, boy; thing like another; member of a learned society or governing body of a college. **fellow traveller** non-Communist who sympathizes with Communist aims.

fellowship n. friendly association with others; society, membership of this; position of a college fellow.

felon n. person who has committed a felony.

felony n. (old use) serious crime. **felonious** a.

felt[1] n. cloth made by matting and pressing fibres. —v.t./i. make or become matted; cover with felt.

felt[2] see **feel**.

female a. of the sex that can bear offspring or produce eggs; (of plants) fruit-bearing; (of a socket etc.) hollow. —n. female animal or plant.

feminine a. of, like, or considered suitable for women; of the grammatical form suitable for names of females. —n. feminine word.

femininity n.

feminist n. supporter of women's claims to be given rights equal to those of men. **feminism** n.

femur /'fi:mə(r)/ n. thigh-bone.

femoral a.

fen n. low-lying marshy or flooded tract of land. **fenny** a.

fence n. barrier round the boundary of a field or garden etc.; person who knowingly buys and resells stolen goods. —v.t./i. surround with a fence; act as a fence for (stolen goods); engage in the sport of fencing. **fencer** n.

fencing n. fences, their material; sport of fighting with foils.

fend v.t./i. **fend for** provide a livelihood for, look after. **fend off** ward off.

fender n. low frame bordering a fireplace; pad hung over a moored vessel's side to prevent bumping.

fennel n. fragrant herb.

feral /'fɪər(ə)l/ a. wild.

ferment[1] /-'ment/ v.t./i. undergo fermentation; cause fermentation in; seethe with excitement.

ferment[2] /'fə-/ n. fermentation; thing causing this; excitement.

fermentation n. chemical change caused by an organic substance, producing effervescence and heat.

fern n. flowerless plant with feathery green leaves. **ferny** a.

ferocious a. fierce, savage. **ferociously** adv., **ferocity** n.

ferret n. small animal of the weasel family. —v.t./i. (p.t. **ferreted**) search, rummage. **ferret out** discover by searching. **ferrety** a.

ferric, **ferrous** adjs. of or containing iron.

Ferris wheel large vertical wheel with seats for people to ride in at fun-fairs etc.

ferroconcrete n. reinforced concrete.

ferrule /'feru:l/ n. metal ring or cap on the end of a stick or tube.

ferry v.t. convey (esp. in a boat) across water; transport. —n. boat etc. used for ferrying; place where it operates; service it provides.

fertile a. able to produce vegetation, fruit, or young; capable of developing into a new plant or animal; inventive. **fertility** n.

fertilize v.t. make fertile; introduce pollen or sperm into. **fertilization** n.

fertilizer n. material added to soil to make it more fertile.

fervent a. showing fervour. **fervently** adv., **fervency** n.

fervid a. fervent. **fervidly** adv.

fervour n. intensity of feeling.

fescue n. a kind of pasture grass.

festal a. of a feast; merry.

fester v.t./i. make or become septic; cause continuing resentment.

festival n. day or period of celebration; series of performances of music or drama etc.

festive a. of or suitable for a festival, gaily decorated. **festively** adv., **festiveness** n.

festivity n. festive proceedings.

festoon n. hanging chain of flowers or ribbons etc. —v.t. decorate with hanging ornaments.

fetch v.t. go for and bring back; cause to come out; be sold for (a price); (colloq.) deal (a blow). **fetch up** end up.

fetching a. attractive.

fête /feɪt/ n. festival; outdoor entertainment or sale, esp. in aid of charity. —v.t. entertain in celebration of an achievement.

fetid /ˈfetɪ/ a. stinking.

fetish /ˈfetɪ/ n. object worshipped as having magical powers; thing given foolishly excessive respect.

fetlock n. part of a horse's leg above and behind the hoof.

fetter n. & v.t. shackle.

fettle n. condition, trim.

feu n. (Sc.) perpetual lease; land so held. —v.t. (Sc.) grant (land) thus.

feud n. lasting hostility. —v.i. conduct a feud.

feudal a. of or like the feudal system. **feudal system** medieval system of holding land by giving one's services to the owner. **feudalism** n., **feudalistic** a.

fever n. abnormally high body-temperature; disease causing it; nervous excitement. **fevered** a., **feverish** a., **feverishly** adv.

few a. & n. (-er, -est) not many. **a few** some. **a good few, quite a few** (colloq.) a fairly large number. **fewness** n.

fey a. strange, other-worldly; (Sc.) clairvoyant. **feyness** n.

fez n. (pl. fezzes) Muslim man's high flat-topped red cap.

fiancé n., **fiancée** /fɪˈɒnseɪ/ n.fem. person one is engaged to marry.

fiasco n. (pl. -os) ludicrous failure.

fiat /ˈfaɪæt/ n. order, decree.

fib n. unimportant lie. **fibbing** n. telling fibs. **fibber** n.

fibre n. thread-like strand; substance formed of fibres; indigestible material in food plants etc. that stimulates the action of the intestines; strength of character. **fibre optics** transmission of information by infra-red signals along thin glass fibre. **fibrous** a.

fibreboard n. board made of compressed fibres.

fibreglass n. textile fabric made of glass fibres; plastic containing glass fibres.

fibril /ˈfaɪ-/ n. small fibre.

fibroid /ˈfaɪ-/ a. consisting of fibrous tissue. —n. benign fibroid tumour.

fibrositis n. rheumatic pain in tissue other than bones and joints.

fibula n. (pl. -lae) bone on the outer side of the shin.

fiche /fiːʃ/ n. microfiche.

fickle a. often changing, not loyal. **fickleness** n.

fiction n. invented story; class of literature consisting of books containing such stories. **fictional** a.

fictitious a. imaginary, not true.

fiddle n. (colloq.) violin; (sl.) piece of cheating, swindle. —v.t./i. fidget with something; (sl.) cheat, falsify; (colloq.) play the violin. **fiddler** n.

fiddlesticks n. nonsense.

fiddling a. petty, trivial.

fiddly a. (colloq.) awkward to do or use.

fidelity n. faithfulness, loyalty; accuracy.

fidget v.t./i. (p.t. **fidgeted**) make small restless movements; make or be uneasy. —n. one who fidgets; (in pl.) restless mood. **fidgety** a.

fiduciary a. held or given etc. in trust. —n. trustee.

fie int. exclamation of disgust.

fief n. land held under the feudal system; domain.

field n. piece of open ground, esp. for pasture or cultivation; sports ground; area from in a natural product; area or sphere of action, operation, or interest etc.; all competitors in an outdoor contest or sport; fielders; (in computers) part of a record, representing a unit of information. —v.t./i. be a fielder, stop and return (a ball); put (a team) into the field. **field-day** n. day of much activity. **field events** athletic contests other than races. **field-glasses** n.pl. binoculars. **Field Marshal** army officer of the highest rank.

fielder n. person who fields a ball; member of the side not batting.

fieldsman n. (pl. **-men**) fielder.

fieldwork n. practical work done by surveyors, social workers, etc. **fieldworker** n.

fiend /fi:nd/ n. evil spirit; wicked, mischievous, or annoying person; devotee. **fiendish** a.

fierce a. (-er, -est) violent in manner or action; eager, intense. **fiercely** adv., **fierceness** n.

fiery a. (-ier, -iest) consisting of fire, flaming; bright red; intensely hot; intense, spirited. **fierily** adv., **fieriness** n.

fiesta /fi'e-/ n. festival in Spanish-speaking countries.

fife n. small shrill flute.

fifteen a. & n. one more than fourteen (15, XV); team of fifteen players. **fifteenth** a. & n.

fifth a. & n. next after fourth. **fifth column** organized body working

for the enemy in a country at war. **fifthly** adv.

fifty a. & n. five times ten (50, L). **fifty-fifty** a. & adv. half-and-half, equally. **fiftieth** a. & n.

fig n. tree with broad leaves and soft pear-shaped fruit; this fruit.

fight v.t./i. (p.t. **fought**) struggle against, esp. in physical combat or war; contend; strive to obtain or accomplish something or to overcome. —n. fighting; battle, contest, struggle; boxing-match. **fight shy of** avoid.

fighter n. one who fights; aircraft designed for attacking others.

figment n. thing that does not exist except in the imagination.

figurative a. metaphorical. **figuratively** adv.

figure n. written symbol of a number; bodily shape; representation of a person or animal; value, amount of money; (pl.) arithmetic; diagram; geometric shape. —v.t./i. appear or be mentioned; represent in a diagram or picture; imagine; form part of a plan etc.; work out by arithmetic or logic; (US) understand; (US colloq.) make sense. **figure of speech** word(s) used for effect and not literally.

figured a. with a woven pattern.

figurehead n. carved image at the prow of a ship; leader with only nominal power.

figurine /'figjuəri:n/ n. statuette.

filament n. strand; fine wire giving off light in an electric lamp.

filbert n. nut of cultivated hazel.

filch v.t. pilfer, steal.

file[1] n. tool with a rough surface for smoothing things. —v.t. shape or smooth with a file.

file[2] n. cover or box etc. for keeping papers for reference; its contents; set of data in a computer; line of people or things one behind another. —v.t./i. place in a file; place on record; march in a file.

filial *a.* of or due from a son or daughter. **filially** *adv.*

filibuster *v.i.* delay or prevent the passing of a law by making a long speech. —*n.* this process; person using it.

filigree *n.* lace-like work in metal.

filings *n.pl.* particles filed off.

fill *v.t./i.* make or become full; spread over or through; block; occupy; appoint a person to (a vacant post). —*n.* enough to fill a thing; enough to satisfy a person. **fill in** complete; (*colloq.*) inform; act as substitute. **fill out** enlarge; become enlarged or plumper. **fill up** fill completely.

filler *n.* thing or material used to fill a gap or increase bulk.

fillet *n.* piece of boneless meat or fish. —*v.t.* (*p.t.* **filleted**) remove bones from. **filleter** *n.*

filling *n.* substance used to fill a cavity etc. **filling-station** place selling petrol to motorists.

fillip *n.* quick blow with a finger; boost. —*v.t.* (*p.t.* **filliped**) give a fillip to.

filly *n.* young female horse.

film *n.* thin layer; sheet or rolled strip of light-sensitive material for taking photographs; motion picture. —*v.t./i.* make a film of; cover or become covered with a thin layer. **film star** star actor or actress in films. **film-strip** *n.* series of transparencies in a strip for projection.

filmy *a.* (**-ier, -iest**) thin and almost transparent.

filo *n.* pastry in thin leaves.

filter *n.* device or substance for holding back impurities in liquid or gas passing through it; screen for absorbing or modifying light or electrical or sound waves; arrangement for filtering traffic. —*v.t./i.* pass through a filter, remove impurities from; make a way in or out gradually; (of traffic) be allowed to pass while other traffic is held up. **filter-bed** *n.*

tank or reservoir for filtering liquid. **filter tip** (cigarette with) a filter at the mouth end.

filth *n.* disgusting dirt; obscenity. **filthy** *a.*, **filthily** *adv.*, **filthiness** *n.*

filtrate *n.* filtered liquid. —*v.t./i.* filter. **filtration** *n.*

fin *n.* thin projection from a fish's body, used for propelling and steering itself; similar projection to improve the stability of aircraft etc.

finagle /fɪˈneɪ-/ *v.t./i.* (*colloq.*) behave or obtain dishonestly.

final *a.* at the end, coming last; conclusive. —*n.* last contest in a series; last edition of a day's newspaper; (*pl.*) final examinations. **finally** *adv.*

finale /fɪˈnɑːli/ *n.* final section of a drama or musical composition.

finalist *n.* competitor in a final.

finality /faɪˈnæ-/ *n.* quality or fact of being final.

finalize *v.t.* bring to an end; put in final form. **finalization** *n.*

finance /faɪ-/ *n.* management of money; money resources. —*v.t.* provide money for. **financial** *a.*, **financially** *adv.*

financier /faɪ-/ *n.* person engaged in financing businesses.

finch *n.* a kind of small bird.

find *v.t./i.* (*p.t.* **found**) discover; obtain; supply; (of a jury etc.) decide and declare. —*n.* discovery; thing found. **find out** get information about; detect, discover. **finder** *n.*

fine[1] *n.* sum of money to be paid as a penalty. —*v.t.* punish by a fine.

fine[2] *a.* (**-er, -est**) of high quality or merit; bright, free from rain; slender, in small particles; delicate, subtle; excellent. —*adv.* finely. —*v.t./i.* make or become finer. **fine arts** painting, sculpture, and architecture. **finely** *adv.*, **fineness** *n.*

finery *n.* showy clothes etc.

finesse /fɪˈnes/ *n.* delicate manipulation; tact.

finger *n.* each of the five parts extending from each hand; any of these other than the thumb; finger-like object or part; measure (about ¾ inch) of alcohol in a glass. —*v.t.* touch or feel with the fingers. **finger-stall** *n.* sheath to cover an injured finger.

fingerprint *n.* impression of ridges on the pad of a finger.

fingertip *n.* tip of a finger.

finial *n.* ornament at the apex of a gable, pinnacle, etc.

finicking *a.* & *n.* giving or needing extreme care about details. **finical** *a.*, **finicky** *a.*

finish *v.t./i.* bring or come to an end, complete; reach the end of a task or race etc.; consume all of; put final touches to. —*n.* last stage; point where a race etc. ends; completed state. **finisher** *n.*

finite /'faɪnaɪt/ *a.* limited.

finnan *n.* smoked cured haddock.

fiord /fjɔːd/ *n.* narrow inlet of the sea between cliffs esp. in Norway.

fir *n.* evergreen cone-bearing tree.

fire *n.* combustion; flame; burning fuel; heating device with a flame or glow; destructive burning; firing of guns; angry or excited feeling. —*v.t.* send a bullet or shell from (a gun), detonate; discharge (a missile); dismiss from a job; set fire to; catch fire; bake (pottery etc.); excite. **fire away** (*colloq.*) begin. **fire-break** *n.* open space as an obstacle to the spread of fire. **fire brigade** organized body of people trained and employed to extinguish fires. **fire-engine** *n.* vehicle fitted with equipment for putting out large fires. **fire-escape** *n.* special staircase or apparatus for escape from a burning building. **fire-irons** *n.pl.* poker, tongs, and shovel for tending a domestic fire.

firearm *n.* gun, pistol, etc.

firebrand *n.* person who stirs up trouble.

firedamp *n.* explosive mixture of methane and air in mines.

firefly *n.* phosphorescent beetle.

firelight *n.* light from a fire.

fireman *n.* (*pl.* **-men**) member of a fire brigade; man employed to tend a furnace.

fireplace *n.* recess with a chimney for a domestic fire.

fireside *n.* space round a fireplace.

firewood *n.* wood for use as fuel.

firework *n.* device containing chemicals that burn or explode spectacularly.

firing-squad *n.* group detailed to fire rifles as a salute during a military funeral, or to shoot a condemned man.

firkin *n.* small barrel.

firm[1] *n.* business company.

firm[2] *a.* (**-er**, **-est**) not yielding when pressed or pushed; steady, not shaking; securely established; resolute. —*adv.* firmly. —*v.t./i.* make or become firm.

firmament *n.* sky with its clouds and stars, regarded as a vault.

first *a.* coming before all others in time or order or importance. —*n.* first thing or occurrence; first day of a month. —*adv.* before all others or another; in preference; first-class. **at first** at the beginning. **first aid** treatment given for an injury etc. before a doctor arrives. **first-class** *a.* & *adv.* of the best quality; in the best category or accommodation. **first cousin** (*see* **cousin**). **at first hand** directly from the original source. **first name** personal or Christian name. **first-rate** *a.* excellent.

firstly *adv.* first.

firth *n.* estuary or narrow inlet of the sea in Scotland.

fiscal *a.* of public revenue.

fish[1] *n.* (*pl. usu.* **fish**) cold-blooded vertebrate living wholly in water; its flesh as food. —*v.t./i.* try to catch fish (from); make a search by reaching into something, (*colloq.*) bring out; try to obtain something by hints or indirect questioning.

fish[2] *n.* strengthening piece of wood or iron.

fishery *n.* area of sea where fishing is done; business of fishing.

fishmeal *n.* dried ground fish used as a fertilizer.

fishmonger *n.* shopkeeper who sells fish.

fishwife *n.* woman selling fish.

fishy *a.* (-**ier**, -**iest**) like fish; causing disbelief or suspicion. **fishily** *adv.*, **fishiness** *n.*

fissile *a.* tending to split; capable of undergoing nuclear fission.

fission *n.* splitting (esp. of an atomic nucleus, with release of energy). —*v.t./i.* (cause to) undergo fission.

fissionable *a.* fissile.

fissure *n.* cleft.

fist *n.* hand when tightly closed.

fisticuffs *n.* fighting with fists.

fistula *n.* pipe-like ulcer; pipe-like passage in the body.

fit[1] *n.* sudden attack of illness or its symptoms, or of convulsions or loss of consciousness; short period of a feeling or activity.

fit[2] *a.* (**fitter**, **fittest**) suitable, good enough; right and proper; in good physical condition or health. —*v.t./i.* (*p.t.* **fitted**) be or adjust to be the right shape and size for; put into place; make or be suitable or competent. —*n.* way a thing fits. **fit out fit up** supply, equip. **fitly** *adv.*, **fitness** *n.*

fitful *a.* occurring in short periods not steadily. **fitfully** *adv.*

fitment *n.* piece of fixed furniture.

fitter *n.* person who supervises the fitting of clothes; mechanic.

fitting *a.* right and proper.

fittings *n.pl.* fixtures and fitments.

five *a.* & *n.* one more than four (5, V).

fiver *n.* (*colloq.*) £5; five-pound note.

fives *n.* ball game played with hands or bat against the wall of a court.

fix *v.t./i.* make firm, stable, or permanent; direct steadily; establish, specify; repair; (*sl.*) deal with, arrange or influence fraudulently; (*sl.*) inject oneself with a narcotic. —*n.* awkward situation; position determined by taking bearings; (*sl.*) addict's dose of a narcotic. **fix up** organize; provide for. **fixer** *n.*

fixated *a.* having an obsession.

fixation *n.* fixing; obsession.

fixative *n.* & *a.* (substance) for keeping things in position, or preventing fading or evaporation.

fixedly /-idli/ *adv.* intently.

fixity *n.* fixed state, stability, permanence.

fixture *n.* thing fixed in position; firmly established person or thing; match, race; date fixed for this.

fizz *v.i.* hiss or splutter, esp. when gas escapes in bubbles from a liquid. —*n.* this sound; fizzing drink. **fizzy** *a.*, **fizziness** *n.*

fizzle *v.i.* fizz feebly. **fizzle out** end feebly or unsuccessfully.

flab *n.* (*colloq.*) flabbiness, fat.

flabbergast *v.t.* (*colloq.*) astound.

flabby *a.* (-**ier**, -**iest**) fat and limp, not firm. **flabbiness** *n.*

flaccid /'flæksid/ *a.* hanging loose or wrinkled, not firm. **flaccidly** *adv.*, **flaccidity** *n.*

flag[1] *n.* piece of cloth attached by one edge to a staff or rope, used as a signal or symbol; similarly shaped device. —*v.t.* (*p.t.* **flagged**) mark or signal (as) with a flag. **flag-day** *n.* day on which small emblems are sold for a charity.

flag[2] *v.i.* (*p.t.* **flagged**) droop; lose vigour.

flag[3] *n.* flagstone. **flagged** *a.* paved with flagstones.

flagellate *v.t.* whip, flog. **flagellant** *n.*, **flagellation** *n.*

flageolet /-dʒə'let/ *n.* small wind instrument resembling a recorder.

flagon *n.* large bottle in which wine or cider is sold; vessel with a handle, lip, and lid for serving wine.

flagrant /'fleɪɡr-/ *a.* (of an offence or offender) very bad and obvious. **flagrantly** *adv.*, **flagrance** *n.*

flagship *n.* ship carrying an admiral and flying his flag; principal vessel, shop, product, etc.

flagstone *n.* large paving-stone.

flail *n.* strong stick hinged on a long handle, formerly used for threshing grain. —*v.t./i.* beat with or as if with a flail; swing about wildly.

flair *n.* natural ability.

flak *n.* anti-aircraft shells; (*colloq.*) barrage of criticism.

flake *n.* small thin piece, esp. of snow. —*v.t./i.* make or come off in flakes; fall or sprinkle in flakes. **flake out** (*colloq.*) faint, fall asleep from exhaustion. **flaky** *a.*, **flakiness** *n.*

flambé /'flɑ̃beɪ/ *a.* (of food) covered with spirit and served alight.

flamboyant *a.* showy in appearance or manner. **flamboyantly** *adv.*, **flamboyance** *n.*

flame *n.* bright tongue-shaped portion of gas burning visibly; bright red. —*v.i.* burn with flames; become bright red. **old flame** (*colloq.*) former sweetheart.

flamenco *n.* (*pl.* -**os**) Spanish gypsy style of singing and dancing.

flamingo *n.* (*pl.* -**os**) wading bird with long legs and pink feathers.

flammable *a.* able to be set on fire. **flammability** *n.*

flan *n.* open pastry or sponge case with filling.

flange *n.* projecting rim. **flanged** *a.*

flank *n.* side, esp. of the body between ribs and hip. —*v.t.* place or be at the side of.

flannel *n.* a kind of woollen fabric; face-flannel; (*pl.*) trousers of flannel or similar fabric; (*sl.*) nonsense, flattery. —*v.t.* (*p.t.* **flannelled**) (*sl.*) flatter.

flannelette *n.* cotton fabric made to look and feel like flannel.

flap *v.t./i.* (*p.t.* **flapped**) sway or move up and down with a sharp sound; strike lightly with something flat; (*colloq.*) show agitation. —*n.* act or sound of flapping; hanging or hinged piece; (*colloq.*) agitation.

flare *v.i.* blaze suddenly; burst into sudden activity or anger; widen outwards. —*n.* sudden blaze; device producing a flaring light as a signal or illumination; flared shape. **flare off** burn off (unwanted gas).

flash *v.t./i.* give out a sudden bright light; show suddenly or ostentatiously; come suddenly into sight or mind; move rapidly; cause to shine briefly; signal with light(s); send (news etc.) by radio or telegraph; (*sl.*) briefly expose oneself indecently. —*n.* sudden burst of flame or light; sudden show of wit or feeling; very brief time; brief news item; device producing a brief bright light in photography; coloured patch of cloth as an emblem. —*a.* (*colloq.*) flashy. **flash-flood** *n.* sudden destructive flood.

flashback *n.* change of scene in a story or film to an earlier period.

flashing *n.* strip of metal covering a joint in a roof etc.

flashlight *n.* electric torch.

flashpoint *n.* temperature at which a vapour ignites; point at which anger etc. breaks out.

flashy *a.* (-**ier**, -**iest**) showy, gaudy. **flashily** *adv.*, **flashiness** *n.*

flask *n.* narrow-necked bottle; vacuum flask.

flat *a.* (**flatter, flattest**) horizontal, level; spread out, lying at full length; absolute; dull, monotonous; dejected; having lost its effervescence or its power to generate electric current; below the correct pitch in music. —*adv.* in a flat manner; (*colloq.*) completely, exactly. —*n.* flat thing or part, level ground; set of rooms on one floor, used as a residence; music note a semitone lower than the corresponding one of natural pitch, sign indicating this. **flatfish** *n.* fish with a flattened body, swimming on its side. **flat out** at top speed; with maximum effort. **flat rate** rate that is the same in all cases, not proportional.

flatlet *n.* small flat.

flatten *v.t./i.* make or become flat.

flatter *v.t.* compliment, esp. in order to win favour; cause to feel honoured; exaggerate the good looks of. **flatterer** *n.*, **flattery** *n.*

flatulent *a.* causing or suffering from formation of gas in the digestive tract. **flatulence** *n.*

flatworm *n.* type of worm with a flattened body.

flaunt *v.t./i.* display proudly or ostentatiously.

flautist *n.* flute-player.

flavour *n.* distinctive taste; special characteristic. —*v.t.* give flavour to. **flavourful** *a.*

flavouring *n.* substance used to give flavour to food.

flaw *n.* imperfection. —*v.t.* spoil with a flaw.

flawless *a.* without a flaw. **flawlessly** *adv.*, **flawlessness** *n.*

flax *n.* blue-flowered plant; textile fibre from its stem.

flaxen *a.* made of flax; pale yellow like dressed flax.

flay *v.t.* strip off the skin or hide of; criticize severely.

flea *n.* small jumping bloodsucking insect. **flea market** (*joc.*) street market.

fleck *n.* very small patch of colour; speck. —*v.t.* mark with flecks.

fled *see* flee.

fledged *a.* (of a young bird) with fully grown wing-feathers, able to fly; (of a person) fully trained.

fledgling *n.* bird just fledged.

flee *v.t./i.* (*p.t.* **fled**) run or hurry away (from).

fleece *n.* sheep's woolly hair; soft fabric used for linings. —*v.t.* defraud, rob by trickery. **fleecy** *a.*

fleet[1] *n.* navy; ships sailing together; vehicles or aircraft under one command or ownership.

fleet[2] *a.* (**-er, -est**) moving swiftly, nimble. **fleetly** *adv.*, **fleetness** *n.*

fleeting *a.* passing quickly, brief.

Flemish *a.* & *n.* (language) of Flanders in north-west Belgium.

flesh *n.* soft substance of animal bodies; body as opposed to mind or soul; pulpy part of fruits and vegetables. **flesh and blood** human nature; one's relatives.

flesh-wound *n.* wound not reaching a vital organ.

fleshly *a.* worldly, carnal.

fleshy *a.* of or like flesh; having much flesh, plump, pulpy.

fleur-de-lis /flɑ:də'li:/ *n.* (*pl.* **fleurs-de-lis**, *pr.* flɑ:d-) heraldic design of three petal-like parts.

flew *see* fly[2].

flex[1] *v.t.* bend; move (a muscle) so that it bends a joint. **flexion** *n.*

flex[2] *n.* flexible insulated wire for carrying electric current.

flexible *a.* able to bend easily; adaptable, able to be changed. **flexibly** *adv.*, **flexibility** *n.*

flexitime *n.* system of flexible working hours.

flibbertigibbet *n.* flighty person.

flick *n.* quick light blow or stroke; (*colloq.*) film, (*pl.*) cinema performance. —*v.t./i.* move or strike or remove with a flick. **flickknife** *n.* knife with a blade that springs out.

flicker *v.i.* burn or shine unsteadily; occur briefly; quiver. —*n.*

flickering light or movement; brief occurrence.

flier n. =flyer.

flight[1] n. flying; movement or path of a thing through the air; journey in or of an aircraft; flock of birds or insects; series of aircraft; series of stairs; feathers etc. on a dart or arrow. **flight-deck** n. cockpit of a large aircraft; deck of an aircraft-carrier. **flight-recorder** n. electronic device in an aircraft recording technical details of its flight.

flight[2] n. fleeing. **put to flight** cause to flee. **take flight, take to flight** flee.

flightless a. non-flying.

flighty a. (-ier, -iest) frivolous. **flightily** adv., **flightiness** n.

flimsy a. (-ier, -iest) light and thin; fragile; unconvincing. **flimsily** adv., **flimsiness** n.

flinch v.i. draw back in fear, wince; shrink from one's duty etc.

fling v.t./i. (p.t. flung) throw violently or hurriedly; rush, go angrily. —n. act or movement of flinging; spell of indulgence in pleasure.

flint n. very hard stone producing sparks when struck with steel; piece of hard alloy used to produce a spark. **flinty** a.

flintlock n. old type of gun discharged by a spark from a flint.

flip v.t./i. (p.t. flipped) flick; toss with a sharp movement. —n. action of flipping; (colloq.) short flight, quick tour. —a. (colloq.) glib, flippant. **flip side** reverse side of a gramophone record.

flippant a. not showing proper seriousness. **flippantly** adv., **flippancy** n.

flipper n. sea animal's limb used in swimming; large flat rubber attachment to the foot for underwater swimming.

flirt v.t./i. pretend lightheartedly to court a person; toy; move (a thing) rapidly to and fro. —n. person who flirts. **flirtation** n.

flirtatious a. flirting; fond of flirting. **flirtatiously** adv.

flit v.i. (p.t. flitted) fly or move lightly and quickly; decamp stealthily. —n. act of flitting.

flitch n. a side of bacon.

flitter v.i. flit about.

float v.t./i. rest or drift on the surface of liquid; be held up freely in gas or air; have or allow (currency) to have a variable rate of exchange; start (a company or scheme). —n. thing designed to float on liquid; low cart; money for minor expenditure or giving change; (also n.) footlights. **floating voter** one not attached to any political party.

flocculent a. like tufts of wool.

flock[1] n. number of animals or birds together; large number of people, congregation. —v.i. gather or go in a flock.

flock[2] n. tuft of wool or cotton; wool or cotton waste as stuffing.

floe n. sheet of floating ice.

flog v.t. (p.t. flogged) beat severely; (sl.) sell. **flogging** n.

flood n. great quantity of water coming over a place usually dry; great outpouring; inflow of the tide. —v.t./i. cover or fill with a flood; overflow; come in great quantities. **flood-tide** n. advancing tide.

floodgate n. gate controlling a flow of water.

floodlight n. lamp producing a broad bright beam to light up a stage or building. —v.t. (p.t. floodlit) illuminate with this.

floor n. lower surface of a room, part on which one stands; part of a legislative assembly hall where members sit; storey. —v.t. provide with a floor; knock down; baffle. **floor show** cabaret.

flooring n. material for a floor.

flop v.i. (p.t. flopped) hang or fall heavily and loosely; (sl.) be a failure. —n. flopping movement or sound; (sl.) failure.

floppy a. (-ier, -iest) tending to flop. **floppy disc** flexible disc for storing machine-readable data.

flora n. plants of an area or period.

floral a. of flowers.

floret n. each of the small flowers of a composite flower.

floribunda n. flower (esp. rose) bearing dense clusters of flowers.

florid /ˈflɒ-/ a. ornate; ruddy. **floridity** n.

florin n. guilder; former British coin worth two shillings (10p).

florist /ˈflɒɪ-/ n. person who sells or grows flowers as a business.

floruit /ˈflɒrʊɪt/ n. date when a person lived or worked.

floss n. mass of silky fibres; silk thread with little twist. **flossy** a.

flotation n. floating, esp. of a commercial venture.

flotilla n. small fleet; fleet of small ships.

flotsam n. floating wreckage. **flotsam and jetsam** odds and ends.

flounce[1] v.i. go in an impatient annoyed manner. —n. flouncing movement.

flounce[2] n. deep frill attached by its upper edge. **flounced** a.

flounder[1] n. small flat-fish.

flounder[2] v.i. move or struggle clumsily, as in mud; become confused when trying to do something.

flour n. fine powder made from grain, used in cooking. —v.t. cover with flour. **floury** a., **flouriness** n.

flourish v.t./i. grow vigorously; prosper, be successful; be alive and active; wave dramatically. —n. dramatic gesture; ornamental curve; fanfare.

flout v.t. disobey openly.

flow v.i. glide along as a stream; proceed evenly; hang loosely; curve smoothly; gush forth. —n.

flowing movement or mass; amount flowing; outpouring; inflow of the tide. **flow chart** or **diagram** diagram showing a sequence of processes.

flower n. part of a plant where fruit or seed develops; this and its stem; best part. —v.t./i. produce or allow to produce flowers. **in flower** with flowers opened.

flowered a. ornamented with a design of flowers.

flowerless a. non-flowering.

flowerpot n. pot in which a plant may be grown.

flowery a. full of flowers; full of ornamental phrases.

flown see **fly**[2].

flu n. (colloq.) influenza.

fluctuate v.i. vary irregularly. **fluctuation** n.

flue n. smoke-duct in a chimney; channel for conveying heat.

fluent a. speaking or spoken smoothly and readily. **fluently** adv., **fluency** n.

fluff n. soft mass of fibres or down. —v.t./i. shake into a soft mass; (sl.) bungle. **fluffy** a. (-ier, -iest) **fluffily** adv., **fluffiness** n.

fluid a. consisting of particles that move freely among themselves; not stable. —n. fluid substance. **fluidity** n.

fluke[1] n. success due to luck.

fluke[2] n. barbed arm of an anchor etc.; lobe of a whale's tail.

fluke[3] n. a kind of flat-fish; flat parasitic worm.

flummery n. sweet milk pudding; empty talk.

flummox v.i. (colloq.) baffle.

flung see **fling**.

flunk v.t./i. (US colloq.) fail.

flunkey n. (pl. -eys) (colloq.) servant wearing livery.

fluoresce v.i. be or become fluorescent.

fluorescent a. taking in radiations and sending them out as light. **fluorescence** n.

fluoridate *v.t.* add fluoride to (a water-supply) to reduce tooth-decay. **fluoridation** *n.*

fluoride *n.* compound of fluorine with metal.

fluorine *n.* pungent corrosive gas.

fluorspar *n.* calcium fluoride as a mineral.

flurry *n.* short rush of wind, rain, or snow; commotion; nervous agitation. —*v.t.* fluster.

flush[1] *v.t./i.* become red in the face; fill with pride; cleanse or dispose of with a flow of water; rush out in a flood. —*n.* flushing of the face, blush; rush of emotion; rush of water; fresh growth of vegetation. —*a.* level, in the same plane; (*colloq.*) well supplied with money.

flush[2] *n.* (in poker) hand of cards all of one suit.

flush[3] *v.t.* drive out, esp. from cover.

fluster *v.t.* make nervous or confused. —*n.* flustered state.

flute *n.* wind instrument, pipe with a mouth-hole at the side; ornamental groove. —*v.t./i.* speak or utter in flute-like tones; make ornamental grooves in. **fluting** *n.*

flutter *v.t./i.* move wings hurriedly; wave or flap quickly; (of the heart) beat irregularly. —*n.* fluttering movement or beat; nervous excitement; stir.

fluvial *a.* of or found in rivers.

flux *n.* flow; continuous succession of changes; substance mixed with metal etc. to assist fusion.

fly[1] *n.* two-winged insect. **fly-blown** *a.* tainted by flies' eggs.

fly[2] *v.t./i.* (*p.t.* flew, *p.p.* flown) move through the air, esp. on wings or in an aircraft; control the flight of; wave, mount (a flag) to wave; go quickly; pass suddenly; flee. —*n.* flying; flap covering an opening or containing a fastening, (*pl.*, *colloq.*) fastening down the front of trousers; speed-regulating device in machinery;

(*pl.*) space over a proscenium.

fly-post *v.t.* display (posters etc.) in unauthorized places. **fly-tip** *v.t.* dump (waste) illegally.

fly[3] *a.* (*sl.*) astute, knowing.

flycatcher *n.* bird that catches insects in the air.

flyer *n.* one that flies; airman; fast animal or vehicle.

flying *a.* able to fly. **flying boat** seaplane with a boat-like fuselage. **flying buttress** one based on separate structure, usu. forming an arch. **flying colours** great credit. **flying fox** fruit-eating bat. **flying saucer** unidentified object reported as seen in the sky. **flying squad** detachment of police etc. organized for rapid movement. **flying start** vigorous start giving an initial advantage.

flyleaf *n.* blank leaf at the beginning or end of a book.

flyover *n.* bridge carrying one road or railway over another.

flysheet *n.* leaflet of two or four pages; canvas cover for protecting a tent.

flyweight *n.* boxing-weight (51 kg).

flywheel *n.* heavy wheel revolving on a shaft to regulate machinery.

foal *n.* young of the horse or a related animal. —*v.i.* give birth to a foal.

foam *n.* collection of small bubbles; spongy rubber or plastic. —*v.i.* form foam. **foamy** *a.*

fob[1] *n.* ornament worn hanging from a key or watch-chain etc.

fob[2] *v.t.* (*p.t.* fobbed) **fob off** palm off; get (a person) to accept something inferior.

focal *a.* of or at a focus.

fo'c's'le /ˈfəʊks(ə)l/ *n.* forecastle.

focus *n.* (*pl.* -cuses or -ci, *pr.* -saɪ) point where rays meet; distance at which an object is most clearly seen; adjustment on a lens to produce a clear image; centre of activity or interest. —*v.t./i.* (*p.t.* focused) adjust the focus of; bring into focus; concentrate.

fodder n. dried food, hay, etc. for horses or other animals. —v.t. give fodder to.

foe n. enemy. **foeman** n.

foetal /'fiː-/ a. of a foetus.

foetus /'fiː-/ n. (pl. **-tuses**) developed embryo in a womb or egg.

fog n. thick mist that is difficult to see through. —v.t./i. (p.t. **fogged**) cover or become covered with fog or condensed vapour; perplex. **foggy** a., **fogginess** n.

foghorn n. sounding-instrument for warning ships in fog.

fogy n. (pl. **-gies**) person with old-fashioned ideas.

foible n. harmless peculiarity in a person's character.

foil[1] n. paper-thin sheet of metal; person or thing emphasizing another's qualities by contrast.

foil[2] v.t. thwart, frustrate.

foil[3] n. long thin sword with a button on the point.

foist v.t. cause a person to accept (an inferior or unwelcome thing).

fold[1] v.t./i. bend or turn (a flexible thing) so that one part lies on another; close by pressing parts together; become folded; clasp; envelop; cease to function. —n. folded part; hollow between thicknesses; line made by folding.

fold[2] n. enclosure for sheep. —v.t. enclose (sheep) in a fold.

folder n. folding cover for loose papers; leaflet.

foliaceous a. of or like leaves.

foliage n. leaves.

foliate[1] /-at/ a. leaf-like; having leaves.

foliate[2] /-ert/ v.t. split into thin layers. **foliation** n.

folio n. (pl. **-os**) largest-sized book; page-number.

folk n. people; one's relatives. **folk-dance**, **folk-song** nn., dance, song, etc., in the traditional style of a country. **folky** a.

folklore n. traditional beliefs and tales of a community.

folksy a. informal and friendly.

folkweave n. loosely woven fabric used chiefly for furnishings.

follicle n. very small cavity containing a hair-root. **follicular** a.

follow v.t./i. go or come after; go along (a road etc.); use as a guide or leader, conform to; take an interest in the progress of; grasp the meaning of; result from; be true in consequence of something else. **follow suit** play a card of the suit led; follow a person's example. **follow up** pursue; develop, supplement. **follow-up** n. this process. **follower** n.

following n. body of believers or supporters. —a. now to be mentioned. —prep. as a sequel to.

folly n. foolishness, foolish act; ornamental building serving no practical purpose.

foment v.t. stir up (trouble).

fomentation n. fomenting; hot lotion used to bathe a painful or inflamed part.

fond a. (**-er**, **-est**) affectionate; doting; (of hope) cherished but unlikely to be fulfilled; (old use) foolish. **fond of** having a liking for; much inclined to. **fondly** adv., **fondness** n.

fondant n. soft sugary sweet.

fondle v.t. touch or stroke lovingly.

fondue n. dish of flavoured melted cheese.

font n. basin in a church, holding water for baptism.

fontanelle /-'nel/ n. soft spot on an infant's head where the bones of the skull have not yet grown together.

food n. substance (esp. solid) that can be taken into the body of an animal or plant to maintain its life. **food processor** electric machine for chopping and mixing etc. food.

foodie n. (colloq.) gourmet.

foodstuff n. substance used as food.

fool n. foolish person; jester in a medieval household; creamy fruit-flavoured pudding. —v.t./i. joke, tease; play about idly; trick.

foolery n. foolish acts.

foolhardy a. taking foolish risks.

foolish a. lacking good sense or judgement; ridiculous. **foolishly** adv., **foolishness** n.

foolproof a. simple and easy to use, unable to go wrong.

foolscap n. size of paper ($17 \times 13\frac{1}{4}$ in.).

foot n. (pl. **feet**) end part of the leg below the ankle; similar part in animals; lower part or end; measure of length, = 12 inches (30.48 cm); unit of rhythm in a line of verse; (old use) infantry. —v.t. walk; be the one to pay (a bill). **foot-and-mouth disease** contagious virus disease of cattle etc. **on foot** walking. **to one's feet** to a standing position. **under one's feet** in danger of being trodden on, in the way.

footage n. length measured in feet.

football n. large round or elliptical inflated ball; game played with this. **football pool** form of gambling on the results of football matches. **footballer** n., **footballing** n.

footbridge n. bridge for pedestrians.

footfall n. sound of footsteps.

foothills n.pl. low hills near the bottom of a mountain or range.

foothold n. place just wide enough to put a foot on when climbing; small but secure position gained.

footing n. foothold; balance; status, conditions.

footlights n.pl. row of lights along the front of a stage floor.

footling /ˈfuː-/ a. (sl.) trivial.

footloose a. independent, without responsibilities.

footman n. (pl. **-men**) manservant, usu. in livery.

footmark n. footprint.

footnote n. note printed at the bottom of a page.

footpath n. path for pedestrians, pavement.

footplate n. platform for the crew operating a locomotive.

footprint n. impression left by a foot or shoe.

footslog v.i. (p.t. **-slogged**) walk laboriously. —n. such a walk.

footsore a. with feet sore from walking.

footstep n. step; sound of this.

footstool n. stool for resting the feet on while sitting.

footwear n. shoes and stockings.

footwork n. manner of moving or using the feet in sports etc.

fop n. dandy.

for prep. in place of; as the price or penalty of; in defence or favour of; with a view to; in the direction of; intended to be received or used by; because of; so as to happen at (a time); during. —conj. because. **be for it** (colloq.) be about to meet with punishment or trouble.

forage /ˈfɒ-/ v.i. go searching, rummage. —n. foraging; food for horses and cattle.

foray /ˈfɒ-/ n. sudden attack, raid. —v.i. make a foray.

forbade see **forbid**.

forbear v.t./i. (p.t. **forbore**, p.p. **forborne**) refrain (from).

forbearance n. patience, tolerance.

forbearing a. patient, tolerant.

forbid v.t. (p.t. **forbade** /-ˈbæd/, p.p. **forbidden**) order not to; refuse to allow.

forbidding a. having an uninviting appearance, stern.

force n. strength; intense effort; influence tending to cause movement; body of troops or police; organized or available group; compulsion; effectiveness. —v.t. use force upon, esp. in order to get or do something; break open by force; strain to the utmost, overstrain; impose; produce by effort; cause (plants etc.) to reach maturity early. **forced landing** emergency landing. **forced march** lengthy march requiring special effort. —*v.t.* (*p.t.* **-fed**) feed (a prisoner etc.) against his will.

forceful *a.* powerful and vigorous. **forcefully** *adv.*, **forcefulness** *n.*

forcemeat *n.* finely chopped seasoned meat used as stuffing.

forceps *n.* (*pl.* **forceps**) small tongs.

forcible *a.* done by force. **forcibly** *adv.*

ford *n.* shallow place where a stream may be crossed by wading or driving through. —*v.t.* cross thus.

fordable *a.* able to be forded.

fore *a.* & *adv.* in, at, or towards the front. —*n.* fore part. **fore-and-aft** *a.* (of sails) set lengthways, not on yards. **to the fore** in front, conspicuous.

forearm[1] *n.* arm from the elbow downwards.

forearm[2] *v.t.* arm or prepare in advance against possible danger.

forebears *n.pl.* ancestors.

foreboding *n.* feeling that trouble is coming.

forecast *v.t.* (*p.t.* **forecast**) tell in advance (what is likely to happen). —*n.* statement that does this. **forecaster** *n.*

forecastle /ˈfəʊks(ə)l/ *n.* forward part of certain ships.

foreclose *v.t.* take possession of property and prevent (a mortgage) from being redeemed when a loan is not duly repaid. **foreclosure** *n.*

forecourt *n.* enclosed space in front of a building; outer courtyard.

forefathers *n.pl.* ancestors.

forefinger *n.* finger next to the thumb.

forefoot *n.* (*pl.* **-feet**) animal's front foot.

forefront *n.* the very front.

foregoing *a.* preceding.

foregone *a.* **foregone conclusion** result that can be foreseen easily.

foreground *n.* part of a scene etc. that is nearest to the observer.

forehand *n.* stroke played with the palm of the hand turned forwards. —*a.* of or made with this stroke. **forehanded** *a.*

forehead /ˈfɒrɪd or ˈfɔːhed/ *n.* part of the face above the eyes.

foreign *a.* of, from, or dealing with a country that is not one's own; not belonging naturally.

foreigner *n.* person born in or coming from another country.

foreknow *v.t.* (*p.t.* **-knew**, *p.p.* **-known**) have foreknowledge of.

foreknowledge *n.* knowledge of a thing before it occurs.

foreland *n.* cape, promontory.

foreleg *n.* animal's front leg.

forelock *n.* lock of hair just above the forehead.

foreman *n.* (*pl.* **-men**) workman superintending others; president and spokesman of a jury.

foremast *n.* mast nearest a ship's bow.

foremost *a.* most advanced in position or rank; most important. —*adv.* in the foremost position etc.

forename *n.* first name.

forenoon *n.* (*old use*) day until noon.

forensic /fəˈren-/ *a.* of or used in lawcourts. **forensic medicine** medical knowledge used in police investigations etc.

foreordain *v.t.* destine beforehand.

foreplay *n.* stimulation preceding sexual intercourse.

forerunner *n.* person or thing that comes in advance of another which it foreshadows.

foresail *n.* principal sail on a foremast.

foresee v.t. (p.t. **-saw**, p.p. **-seen**) be aware of or realize beforehand.

foreseeable a. able to be foreseen.

foreshadow v.t. be an advance sign of (a future event etc.)

foreshore n. shore that the tide flows over; empty land near a shore.

foreshorten v.t. show or portray with apparent shortening giving an effect of distance.

foresight n. ability to foresee and prepare for future needs.

foreskin n. loose skin at the end of the penis.

forest n. trees and undergrowth covering a large area; dense concentration of things. **forested** a.

forestall v.t. prevent or foil by taking action first.

forester n. officer in charge of a forest or of growing timber.

forestry n. science of planting and caring for forests.

foretaste n. experience in advance of what is to come.

foretell v.t. (p.t. **foretold**) forecast.

forethought n. careful thought and planning for the future.

forewarn v.t. warn beforehand.

forewoman n. (pl. **-women**) woman equivalent of a foreman.

foreword n. introductory remarks at the beginning of a book, usu. by a person other than the author.

forfeit /-fit/ n. thing that has to be paid or given up as a penalty. —v.t. give or lose as a forfeit. —a. forfeited. **forfeiture** n.

forfend v.t. (old use) avert.

forgather v.i. assemble.

forgave see **forgive**.

forge[1] v.i. advance by effort.

forge[2] n. blacksmith's workshop; furnace where metal is heated. —v.t. shape (metal) by heating and hammering; make a fraudulent copy of. **forger** n.

forgery n. forging; thing forged.

forget v.t./i. (p.t. **forgot**, p.p. **forgotten**) lose remembrance (of); stop thinking about. **forget-me-not** n. plant with small blue flowers. **forget oneself** behave without suitable dignity.

forgetful a. tending to forget. **forgetfully** adv., **forgetfulness** n.

forgive v.t. (p.t. **forgave**, p.p. **forgiven**) cease to feel angry or bitter towards or about. **forgivable** a., **forgiveness** n.

forgo v.t. (p.t. **forwent**, p.p. **forgone**) give up, go without.

fork n. pronged instrument or tool; thing or part divided like this; each of its divisions. —v.t./i. lift or dig with a fork; separate into two branches; follow one of these branches. **fork-lift truck** truck with a forked device for lifting and carrying loads. **fork out** (sl.) pay.

forlorn a. left alone and unhappy. **forlorn hope** the only faint hope left. **forlornly** adv.

form n. shape, appearance; way in which a thing exists; class in a school; usual method, formality, ritual; document with blank spaces to be filled in with information; condition, style; bench; hare's lair. —v.t./i. shape, produce; bring into existence, constitute; take shape; develop; arrange in a formation.

formal a. conforming to accepted rules or customs; of form; regular in design. **formally** adv.

formaldehyde n. colourless gas used in solution as a preservative and disinfectant.

formalin n. solution of formaldehyde.

formality n. being formal; formal act, esp. one required by rules.

formalize v.t. make formal or official. **formalization** n.

format n. shape and size of a book etc.; style of arrangement. —v.t. (p.t. **formatted**) arrange in a format.

formation n. forming; thing formed; particular arrangement.

formative a. forming; of formation.

former a. of an earlier period; mentioned first of two.

formerly adv. in former times.

formic acid irritant acid in fluid emitted by ants.

formidable /'fɔː-/ a. inspiring fear or awe; difficult to do. **formidably** adv.

formless a. without regular form.

formula n. (pl. **-ae** or **-as**) symbols showing chemical constituents or a mathematical statement; fixed series of words for use on social or ceremonial occasions; list of ingredients; classification of a racing car. **formulaic** a.

formulate v.t. express systematically. **formulation** n.

fornicate v.i. have sexual intercourse while unmarried. **fornication** n., **fornicator** n.

forsake v.t. (p.t. **forsook**, p.p. **forsaken**) renounce; withdraw one's help or companionship etc. from.

forsooth adv. (old use) indeed.

forswear v.t. (p.t. **forswore**, p.p. **forsworn**) renounce.

forsythia n. shrub bearing yellow flowers in spring.

fort n. fortified place or building.

forte /-tɪ/ n. person's strong point.

forth adv. out; onwards. **back and forth** to and fro.

forthcoming a. about to occur or appear; available; communicative, responsive.

forthright a. frank, outspoken.

forthwith adv. immediately.

fortification n. fortifying; defensive wall or building etc.

fortify v.t. strengthen, esp. against attack; increase the vigour of.

fortissimo adv. very loudly.

fortitude n. courage in bearing pain or trouble.

fortnight n. period of two weeks.

fortnightly a. & adv. (happening or appearing) once a fortnight.

Fortran n. computer language used esp. for scientific calculations.

fortress n. fortified building or town.

fortuitous /-'tjuː-/ a. happening by chance. **fortuitously** adv.

fortunate a. lucky. **fortunately** adv.

fortune n. chance as a power in mankind's affairs; events it brings; destiny; prosperity, success; much wealth. **fortune-teller** n. person who claims to foretell future events in people's lives.

forty a. & n. four times ten (40, XL). **forty winks** a nap. **fortieth** a. & n.

forum n. place or meeting where a public discussion is held.

forward a. directed towards the front or its line of motion; having made more than normal progress; presumptuous. —n. attacking player (= striker) in football or hockey. —adv. forwards; towards the future; in advance, ahead. —v.t. send on (a letter etc.) to a new address or (goods) to a customer; help to advance (interests). **forwardness** n.

forwards adv. towards the front; with forward motion; so as to make progress; with the front foremost.

fosse n. ditch as a fortification.

fossil n. hardened remains or traces of a prehistoric animal or plant. —a. of or like a fossil; (of fuel) extracted from the ground.

fossilize v.t. turn or be turned into a fossil. **fossilization** n.

foster v.t. promote the growth of; rear (a child that is not one's own). **foster-child** n. child reared thus. **foster home** home in which a foster-child is reared.

foster-mother n. woman who fosters a child.

fought see **fight**.

foul a. (-er, -est) causing disgust; clogged; entangled, in collision; unfair, against the rules of a game. —adv. unfairly. —n. stroke or blow etc. that breaks rules. —v.t./i. make or become foul; entangle or collide with; obstruct; commit a foul against. **foulmouthed** a. using foul language. **foully** adv., **foulness** n.

foulard /fuːˈlɑːd/ n. thin soft silky fabric.

found[1] see **find**.

found[2] v.t. establish; provide money for starting (an institution etc.); base. **founder**[1] n., **foundress** n.fem.

found[3] v.t. melt or mould (metal), fuse (materials for glass); make (an object) in this way. **founder**[2] n.

foundation n. founding; institution or fund founded; base, first layer; underlying principle.

founder[1, 2] see **found**[2, 3].

founder[3] v.i. stumble or fall; (of a ship) fill with water and sink; fail completely.

foundling n. deserted child of unknown parents.

foundry n. workshop where metal or glass founding is done.

fount n. fountain, source; one size and style of printing-type.

fountain n. spring or jet of water; structure provided for this; source. **fountain-head** n. source. **fountain-pen** n. pen that can be filled with a supply of ink.

four a. & n. one more than three (4, IV); four-oared boat or its crew. **four-in-hand** n. carriage with four horses driven by one person. **four-poster** n. bed with four posts that support a canopy. **four-wheel drive** motive power acting on all four wheels of a vehicle.

fourfold a. & adv. four times as much or as many.

foursome n. party of four people.

fourteen a. & n. one more than thirteen (14, XIV). **fourteenth** a. & n.

fourth a. next after the third. —n. fourth thing, class, etc.; quarter, one of four equal parts. **fourthly** adv.

fowl n. kind of bird kept to supply eggs and flesh for food.

fowling n. catching or shooting wildfowl. **fowler** n.

fox n. wild animal of the dog family with a bushy tail; its fur; crafty person. —v.t. deceive or puzzle by acting craftily. **fox-terrier** n. short-haired terrier. **foxy** a.

foxglove n. tall plant with flowers like glove-fingers.

foxhole n. small trench as a military shelter.

foxhound n. hound bred to hunt foxes.

foxtrot n. dance with slow and quick steps; music for this.

foyer /ˈfɔɪeɪ/ n. entrance hall of a theatre, cinema, or hotel.

fracas /-kɑː/ n. (pl. **-cas**, pr. -kɑːz) noisy quarrel or disturbance.

fraction n. number that is not a whole number; small part or amount; portion obtained by distillation. **fractional** a., **fractionally** adv.

fractious a. irritable, peevish. **fractiously** adv., **fractiousness** n.

fracture n. break, esp. of bone. —v.t./i. break.

fragile a. easily broken or damaged; not strong. **fragility** n.

fragment[1] /ˈfræ-/ n. piece broken off something; isolated part.

fragment[2] /-ˈment/ v.t./i. break into fragments. **fragmentation** n.

fragmentary /ˈfræ-/ a. consisting of fragments.

fragrance n. being fragrant; perfume.

fragrant a. having a pleasant smell.

frail a. (-er, -est) not strong; physically weak. **frailty** n.

frame n. rigid structure supporting other parts; open case or border enclosing a picture or pane of glass etc.; single exposure on cine film; box-like structure for protecting plants. —v.t. put or form a frame round; construct; express in words; (sl.) arrange false evidence against. **frame of mind** temporary state of mind. **frame-up** n. (colloq.) arrangement of false evidence.

framework n. supporting frame.

franc n. unit of money in France, Belgium, and Switzerland.

franchise n. right to vote in public elections; authorization to sell a company's goods or services in a certain area. —v.t. grant a franchise to.

Franciscan n. friar or nun of the order founded by St Francis.

Franco- pref. French.

frangipani /-'pɑ:-/ n. fragrant tropical shrub or tree; its perfume.

frank[1] a. (-er, -est) showing one's thoughts and feelings unmistakably. **frankly** adv., **frankness** n.

frank[2] v.t. mark (a letter etc.) to show that postage has been paid.

frankfurter n. highly seasoned smoked sausage.

frankincense n. sweet-smelling gum burnt as incense.

frantic a. wildly excited or agitated. **frantically** adv.

fraternal a. of a brother or brothers. **fraternally** adv.

fraternity n. brotherhood; (US) male students' society in a university etc.

fraternize v.i. associate with others in a friendly way. **fraternization** n.

fratricide n. killing or killer of own brother or sister etc. **fratricidal** a.

Frau /frau/ n. (pl. **Frauen**) title of a German-speaking married woman.

fraud n. criminal deception; dishonest trick; person or thing that is not what he or it seems or pretends to be. **fraudulence** n., **fraudulent** a., **fraudulently** adv.

fraught a. (colloq.) causing or suffering anxiety. **fraught with** filled with, involving.

Fraulein /'frɔɪlɑn/ n. title of a German-speaking unmarried woman.

fray[1] n. fight, conflict.

fray[2] v.t./i. make or become worn so that there are loose threads; strain or upset (nerves or temper).

frazzle n. exhausted state.

freak n. person or thing that is abnormal in form; something very unusual; person who dresses absurdly. —v.t./i. **freak out** (sl.) (cause to) hallucinate or become wildly excited; adopt an unconventional life-style. **freakish** a., **freaky** a.

freckle n. light brown spot on the skin. —v.t./i. spot or become spotted with freckles. **freckled** a.

free a. (freer, freest) not in the power of another, not a slave; having freedom; not fixed, able to move; without, not subject to; costing nothing to the recipient; not occupied, not in use; lavish. —v.t./i. (p.t. freed) make free; rid of; clear, disentangle. **free fall** unrestricted fall under the force of gravity; movement of a spacecraft in space without thrust from the engines. **free from** not containing. **free hand** right of taking what action one chooses. **free-hand** a. (of drawing) done without ruler or compasses etc. **free house** inn or public house not controlled by one brewery. **free lance** person who sells his services to various employers. **free-range** a. (of hens) allowed to range freely in search of food; (of eggs) from such hens. **free-**

wheel v.i. ride a bicycle without pedalling.

freebie n. (US colloq.) thing provided free of charge.

freebooter n. pirate.

freedom n. being free; independence; frankness; unrestricted use; membership, honorary citizenship.

freefone, freephone n. system of making business telephone calls paid for by the recipient.

freehold n. holding of land or a house etc. in absolute ownership. —a. owned thus. **freeholder** n.

Freemason n. member of a fraternity with elaborate ritual and secret signs. **Freemasonry** n. their system and institutions.

freemasonry n. sympathy and mutual help between people of similar interests.

freepost n. system of conveying replies to business communications with postage paid by the issuing firm.

freesia n. a kind of fragrant flower.

freeway n. express highway.

freeze v.t./i. (p.t. **froze**, p.p. **frozen**) change from liquid to solid by extreme cold; be so cold that water turns to ice; chill or be chilled by extreme cold or fear; preserve by refrigeration; make (assets) unable to be realized; hold (prices or wages) at a fixed level; stop, stand very still. —n. period of freezing weather; freezing of prices etc. **freeze-dry** v.t. freeze and dry by evaporation of ice in a vacuum. **freeze-frame** n. arrest of movement in a filmshot. **freeze on to** (sl.) take or keep tight hold of.

freezer n. refrigerated container for preserving and storing food.

freight n. cargo; transport of goods in containers or by water or air (in USA also by land). —v.t. load with freight; transport as freight.

freighter n. ship or aircraft carrying mainly freight.

freightliner n. train carrying goods in containers.

French a. & n. (language) of France. **French chalk** powdered talc. **French horn** brass wind instrument with a coiled tube. **French leave** absence without permission. **French-polish** v.t. polish (wood) with shellac polish. **French window** one reaching to the ground, used also as a door. **Frenchman** n. (pl. **-men**), **Frenchwoman** n. (pl. **-women**).

frenetic a. frenzied. **frenetically** adv.

frenzied a. in a state of frenzy. **frenziedly** adv.

frenzy n. violent excitement or agitation.

frequency n. frequent occurrence; rate of repetition; number of cycles of a carrier wave per second, band or group of these.

frequent[1] /'fri:-/ a. happening or appearing often. **frequently** adv.

frequent[2] /-'kwe-/ v.t. go frequently to, be often in (a place).

fresco n. (pl. **-os**) picture painted on a wall or ceiling before the plaster is dry.

fresh a. (**-er**, **-est**) new, not stale or faded; not preserved by tinning or freezing etc.; not salty; refreshing; vigorous; (US) presumptuous. **freshly** adv., **freshness** n.

freshen v.t./i. make or become fresh. **freshener** n.

freshet n. freshwater stream flowing into the sea; river's flood.

freshman n. (pl. **-men**) first-year university student.

freshwater adj. of rivers or lakes, not of the sea.

fret[1] v.t./i. (p.t. **fretted**) worry; vex; wear away by rubbing or gnawing.

fret[2] n. each of the ridges on the finger-board of a guitar etc.

fretful a. constantly worrying or crying. **fretfully** adv.

fretsaw *n.* very narrow saw used for fretwork.

fretwork *n.* woodwork cut in decorative patterns.

Freudian /ˈfrɔɪ-/ *a.* of Freud or his theories of psychoanalysis.

friable /ˈfraɪ-/ *a.* easily crumbled. **friability** *n.*

friar *n.* member of certain religious orders of men.

friary *n.* monastery of friars.

fricassee *n.* dish of pieces of meat served in a thick sauce. —*v.t.* make a fricassee of.

friction *n.* rubbing; resistance of one surface to another that moves over it; conflict of people who disagree. **frictional** *a.*

Friday *n.* day after Thursday.

fridge *n.* (*colloq.*) refrigerator.

fried *see* **fry**[1].

friend *n.* person (other than a relative or lover) with whom one is on terms of mutual affection; helper, sympathizer; **Friend** member of the Society of Friends, a Christian sect with no written creed or ordained ministers. **friendship** *n.*

friendly *a.* (-ier, -iest) like a friend; favourable. **Friendly Society** one providing benefits for its members e.g. during illness or old age. **friendliness** *n.*

Friesian /ˈfriːʒ(ə)n/ *n.* one of a breed of black-and-white dairy cattle.

frieze *n.* band of sculpture or decoration round the top of a wall.

frigate *n.* small fast naval ship.

fright *n.* sudden great fear; ridiculous-looking person or thing.

frighten *v.t./i.* cause fright to; feel fright; drive or compel by fright.

frightened *a.* afraid.

frightful *a.* causing horror; ugly; (*colloq.*) extremely great or bad. **frightfully** *adv.*, **frightfulness** *n.*

frigid *a.* intensely cold; very cold in manner; unresponsive sexually. **frigidly** *adv.*, **frigidity** *n.*

frill *n.* gathered or pleated strip of trimming attached at one edge; unnecessary extra. **frilled** *a.*, **frilly** *a.*

fringe *n.* ornamental edging of hanging threads or cords; front hair cut short to hang over the forehead; edge of an area or group etc. —*v.t.* edge. **fringe benefit** one provided by an employer in addition to wages or salary.

frippery *n.* showy unnecessary finery or ornament.

frisk *v.t./i.* leap or skip playfully; (*sl.*) pass hands over (a person) to search for concealed weapons etc. —*n.* playful leap or skip; (*sl.*) search.

frisky *a.* (-ier, -iest) lively, playful. **friskily** *adv.*, **friskiness** *n.*

fritillary /-ˈtɪl-/ *n.* plant with speckled flowers; spotted butterfly.

fritter[1] *n.* fried batter-coated slice of fruit or meat etc.

fritter[2] *v.t.* waste little by little on trivial things.

frivol *v.i.* (*p.t.* **frivolled**) spend time frivolously.

frivolous *a.* lacking a serious purpose, pleasure-loving. **frivolously** *adv.*, **frivolity** *n.*

frizz *v.t./i.* curl into a wiry mass. **frizzy** *a.*, **frizziness** *n.*

frizzle *v.t./i.* fry crisp.

fro *see* **to and fro.**

frock *n.* woman's or girl's dress. **frock-coat** *n.* man's long-skirted coat not cut away in front.

frog *n.* small amphibian with long web-footed hind legs; horny substance in the sole of a horse's foot; looped cord and button as a fastener. **frog in one's throat** hoarseness.

frogman *n.* (*pl.* -men) swimmer with a rubber suit and oxygen supply for use under water.

frogmarch *v.t.* hustle (a person) forcibly, holding the arms.

frolic v.i. (p.t. **frolicked**) play about in a lively way. —n. such play.

frolicsome a. inclined to frolic.

from prep. having as the starting-point, source, or cause; as separated, distinguished, or unlike. **from time to time** at intervals of time.

frond n. leaf-like part of a fern or palm-tree etc.

front n. side or part normally nearer or towards the spectator or line of motion; area where fighting takes place in a war; outward appearance; cover for secret activities; promenade of a seaside resort; boundary between warm and cold air-masses; auditorium of a theatre. —a. of the front; situated in front. —v.t./i. face, have the front towards; (sl.) serve as a cover for in secret activities. **front bench** seats for leading members of each party in Parliament. **front-runner** n. leading contestant. **in front** at the front.

frontage n. front of a building; land bordering this.

frontal a. of or on the front.

frontier n. boundary between countries.

frontispiece n. illustration opposite the title-page of a book.

frost n. freezing weather-condition; white frozen dew or vapour. —v.t./i. injure with frost; cover with frost or frosting; make (glass) opaque by roughening its surface. **frosty** a., **frostily** adv.

frostbite n. injury to body-tissue from freezing. **frostbitten** a.

frosting n. sugar icing.

froth n. & v.t./i. foam. **frothy** a., **frothiness** n.

frown v.i. wrinkle one's brow in thought or disapproval. —n. frowning movement or look. **frown on** disapprove of.

frowsty a. (-ier, -iest) fusty, stuffy. **frowstiness** n.

frowzy a. (-ier, -iest) fusty; dingy. **frowziness** n.

froze, frozen see **freeze**.

fructify v.t./i. bear fruit; make fruitful. **fructification** n.

frugal a. careful and economical; scanty, costing little. **frugally** adv., **frugality** n.

fruit n. seed-containing part of a plant; this used as food; (usu. pl.) vegetable products; product of labour; currants etc. used in food. —v.t./i. produce or allow to produce fruit. **fruit machine** coin-operated gambling machine. **fruit salad** fruits cut up and mixed.

fruiterer n. shopkeeper selling fruit.

fruitful a. producing much fruit or good results. **fruitfully** adv., **fruitfulness** n.

fruition /fru'ɪʃ(ə)n/ n. fulfilment of hopes; results of work.

fruitless a. producing little or no result. **fruitlessly** adv., **fruitlessness** n.

fruity a. (-ier, -iest) like fruit in smell or taste; (colloq.) of full rich quality. **fruitiness** n.

frump n. dowdy woman. **frumpish** a., **frumpy** a.

frustrate v.t. prevent from achieving something or from being achieved. **frustration** n.

fry[1] v.t./i. (p.t. **fried**) cook or be cooked in very hot fat. —n. internal parts of animals, usu. eaten fried; fried food.

fry[2] n. (pl. **fry**) young fishes. **small fry** people of little importance.

frying-pan n. shallow pan used in frying.

ft. abbr. foot or feet (as a measure).

fuchsia /'fjuːʃə/ n. ornamental shrub with drooping flowers.

fuddle v.t. stupefy, esp. with drink.

fuddy-duddy a. & n. (sl.) (person who is) out of date and unable to accept new ideas.

fudge n. soft sweet made of milk, sugar, and butter. —v.t. put together in a makeshift or dishonest way, fake.

fuel n. material burnt as a source of warmth, light, or energy, or used as a source of nuclear energy; thing that increases anger etc. —v.t. (p.t. **fuelled**) supply with fuel.

fug n. (colloq.) stuffy atmosphere in a room etc. **fuggy** a., **fugginess** n.

fugitive n. person who is fleeing or escaping. —a. fleeing, escaping; transient.

fugue /fjuːg/ n. musical composition with theme(s) repeated in a complex pattern. **fugal** a.

fulcrum n. (pl. **-cra**) point of support on which a lever pivots.

fulfil v.t. (p.t. **fulfilled**) accomplish, carry out (a task); satisfy, do what is required by (a contract etc.); make (a prophecy) come true. **fulfil oneself** develop and use one's abilities fully. **fulfilment** n.

full[1] a. (**-er, -est**) holding or having as much as the limits will allow; copious; complete; plump; made with material hanging in folds; (of tone) deep and mellow. —adv. completely; exactly. **full-blooded** a. vigorous, hearty. **full-blown** a. fully developed. **full moon** moon with the whole disc illuminated. **full-scale** a. of actual size, not reduced. **full stop** dot used as a punctuation-mark at the end of a sentence or abbreviation; complete stop. **fully** adv., **fullness** n.

full[2] v.t. clean and thicken (cloth). **fuller** n.

fuller's earth clay used in fulling.

fulmar n. Arctic sea bird.

fulminate v.i. protest loudly and bitterly. **fulminant** a., **fulmination** n.

fulsome a. praising excessively and sickeningly. **fulsomeness** n.

fumble v.t./i. touch or handle (a thing) awkwardly; grope about.

fume n. strong-smelling smoke or gas or vapour. —v.t./i. emit fumes; seethe with anger; subject to fumes; darken (oak) thus.

fumigate v.t. disinfect by fumes. **fumigation** n., **fumigator** n.

fun n. light-hearted amusement; source of this. **fun run** non-competitive run, esp. with sponsorship for a charity. **make fun of** cause people to laugh at.

function n. special activity or purpose of a person or thing; important ceremony; (in mathematics) quantity whose value depends on varying values of others. —v.i. perform a function; be in action.

functional a. of function(s); practical and not decorative or luxurious; able to function. **functionally** adv.

functionary n. official.

fund n. sum of money for a special purpose; stock, supply; (pl.) money resources. —v.t. provide with money.

fundament n. foundation; buttocks.

fundamental a. of the basis or foundation of a subject etc.; essential. —n. fundamental fact or principle. **fundamentally** adv.

fundamentalist n. person who upholds a strict or literal interpretation of traditional religious beliefs. **fundamentalism** n.

funeral n. ceremony of burial or cremation; procession to this.

funerary a. of or used for a burial or funeral.

funereal /-ˈnɪər-/ a. suitable for a funeral, dismal, dark. **funereally** adv.

funfair n. fair consisting of amusements and sideshows.

fungicide /-dʒɪ-/ n. substance that kills fungus. **fungicidal** a.

fungoid a. like a fungus.

fungus n. (pl. -**gi**, pr. -gar) plant without green colouring-matter (e.g. mushroom, mould). **fungal** a., **fungous** a.

funicular /fjʊ'nɪk-/ n. cable railway with ascending and descending cars counterbalancing each other.

funk n. (sl.) fear; coward. —v.t./i. (sl.) show fear; fear and shirk.

funky a. (sl.) (of jazz etc.) uncomplicated, emotional; having a strong smell. **funkiness** n.

funnel n. tube with a wide top for pouring liquid etc. into small openings; metal chimney on a steam engine or ship. —v.t./i. (p.t. **funnelled**) move through a funnel or narrowing space.

funny a. (-**ier**, -**iest**) causing amusement; puzzling, odd. **funny-bone** n. part of the elbow where a very sensitive nerve passes. **funny business** trickery. **funnily** adv.

fur n. short fine hair covering the bodies of certain animals; skin with this, or fabric imitating it, used for clothing; coating, incrustation. —v.t./i. (p.t. **furred**) cover or become covered with fur.

furbelows n.pl. showy trimmings.

furbish v.t. polish, clean, renovate.

furcate v.t./i. fork, divide. —a. forked, branched. **furcation** n.

furious a. full of anger; violent, intense. **furiously** adv.

furl v.t. roll up and fasten.

furlong n. one-eighth of a mile.

furlough /-loʊ/ n. leave of absence.

furnace n. closed fireplace for central heating; enclosed space for heating metals etc.

furnish v.t. equip with furniture; provide, supply. **furnishings** n.pl. furniture and fitments etc.

furniture n. movable articles (e.g. chairs, beds) for use in a room.

furore /fjʊ'rɔːrɪ/ n. uproar of enthusiastic admiration or fury.

furrier /'fʌ-/ n. person who deals in furs or fur clothes.

furrow n. long cut in the ground; groove. —v.t. make furrows in.

furry a. like fur; covered with fur. **furriness** n.

further adv. & a. more distant; to a greater extent; additional(ly). —v.t. help the progress of. **further education** that provided for persons above school age. **furtherance** n.

furthermore adv. moreover.

furthermost a. most distant.

furthest a. most distant. —adv. at or to the greatest distance.

furtive a. sly, stealthy. **furtively** adv., **furtiveness** n.

fury n. wild anger, rage; violence; avenging spirit; violently angry person.

furze n. gorse.

fuse[1] v.t./i. blend (metals etc.), become blended; unite; fit with a fuse; stop functioning through melting of a fuse. —n. strip of wire placed in an electric circuit to melt and interrupt the current when the circuit is overloaded.

fuse[2] n. length of easily burnt material for igniting a bomb or explosive. —v.t. fit a fuse to.

fuselage /-lɑːʒ/ n. body of an aeroplane.

fusible a. able to be fused. **fusibility** n.

fusilier n. soldier of some regiments formerly armed with light muskets.

fusillade /-'leɪd/ n. continuous firing of guns; outburst of questions etc.

fusion n. fusing; union of atomic nuclei, with release of energy.

fuss n. unnecessary excitement or activity; vigorous protest. —v.t./i. make a fuss; agitate. **make a fuss of** treat with a great display of attention or affection.

fussy a. (-ier, -iest) often fussing; fastidious; with much unnecessary detail or decoration. **fussily** adv., **fussiness** n.

fusty a. (-ier, -iest) smelling stale and stuffy; old-fashioned in ideas etc. **fustiness** n.

futile a. producing no result. **futilely** adv., **futility** n.

futon /'fuːtɒn/ n. light orig. Japanese kind of mattress.

future a. belonging to the time after the present. —n. future time, events, or condition; prospect of success etc. **in future** from now on.

futuristic a. looking suitable for the distant future, not traditional. **futuristically** adv.

futurity /-'tjʊər-/ n. future time.

fuzz n. fluff, fluffy or frizzy thing; (sl.) police.

fuzzy a. (-ier, -iest) like or covered with fuzz; frizzy; blurred, indistinct. **fuzzily** adv., **fuzziness** n.

G

g abbr. gram(s).

gab n. (colloq.) chatter. **gabby** a.

gabardine n. strong twilled fabric.

gabble v.t./i. talk or utter quickly and indistinctly. —n. gabbled talk.

gable n. triangular part of an outside wall, between sloping roofs. **gabled** a.

gad v.i. (p.t. **gadded**) **gad about** travel constantly for pleasure.

gadabout n. person who gads about.

gadfly n. fly that bites cattle.

gadget n. small mechanical device or tool. **gadgetry** n. gadgets.

Gael n. Scottish or Irish Celt.

Gaelic /'gæ- or 'geɪ-/ n. Celtic language of Scots or Irish.

gaff[1] n. stick with a hook for landing large fish. —v.t. seize with gaff.

gaff[2] n. **blow the gaff** (sl.) divulge a secret.

gaffe n. blunder.

gaffer n. (colloq.) elderly man; boss, foreman.

gag n. thing put in or over a person's mouth to silence him; surgical device to hold the mouth open; joke. —v.t./i. (p.t. **gagged**) put a gag on; deprive of freedom of speech; tell jokes; retch.

gaga a. (sl.) senile.

gage[1] n. pledge, security; challenge.

gage[2] n. greengage.

gaggle n. flock (of geese); disorderly group.

gaiety n. cheerfulness, bright appearance; merrymaking.

gaily adv. with gaiety.

gain v.t./i. obtain, secure; acquire gradually; profit; get nearer in racing or pursuit; reach; (of a clock) become fast. —n. increase in wealth or possessions etc.

gainful a. profitable. **gainfully** adv.

gainsay v.t. (p.t. **gainsaid**) (formal) deny, contradict.

gait n. manner of walking or running.

gaiter n. cloth or leather covering for the lower part of the leg.

gala /'gaː-/ n. festive occasion; fête.

galantine n. cold dish of meat in jelly.

galaxy n. system of stars; brilliant company; **the Galaxy** the Milky Way. **galactic** a.

gale n. very strong wind; noisy outburst.

gall[1] n. bile; bitterness of feeling; (sl.) impudence. **gall-bladder** n. organ storing bile.

gall[2] n. sore made by rubbing. —v.t. rub and make sore; vex, humiliate.

gall[3] n. abnormal growth on a plant, esp. on an oak-tree.

gallant /'gæ-/ *a.* brave, chivalrous; /*also* gə'lænt/attentive to women. —*n.* /*also* gə'lænt/ ladies' man. **gallantly** *adv.*, **gallantry** *n.*

galleon *n.* large Spanish sailing-ship in the 15th–17th centuries.

gallery *n.* balcony in a hall or theatre etc.; long room or passage, esp. used for special purpose; room or building for showing works of art.

galley *n.* (*pl.* **-eys**) ancient ship, esp. propelled by oars; kitchen in a ship or aircraft; oblong tray holding type for printing; (also **galley proof**) printer's proof in a long narrow form.

Gallic *a.* of ancient Gaul; French.

Gallicism *n.* French idiom.

gallivant *v.i.* (*colloq.*) gad about.

gallon *n.* measure for liquids, = 4 quarts (4.546 litres).

gallop *n.* horse's fastest pace; ride at this. —*v.t./i.* (*p.t.* **galloped**) go or ride at a gallop; progress rapidly.

gallows *n.* framework with a noose for hanging criminals.

gallstone *n.* small hard mass formed in the gall-bladder.

Gallup poll public opinion poll.

galore *adv.* in plenty.

galosh *n.* rubber overshoe.

galumph *v.i.* more noisily or clumsily.

galvanic /-'væn-/ *a.* producing electric current by chemical action; stimulating people into activity. **galvanically** *adv.*

galvanize *v.t.* stimulate into activity; coat with zinc. **galvanization** *n.*

galvanometer *n.* instrument for measuring small electric currents.

gambit *n.* opening move or remark.

gamble *v.t./i.* play games of chance for money; risk in hope of gain. —*n.* gambling; risky undertaking. **gamble on** act in the hope of. **gambler** *n.*

gamboge /-'bu:dʒ *or* -'bəʊ-/ *n.* gum-resin used as a yellow pigment.

gambol *v.i.* (*p.t.* **gambolled**) jump about in play. —*n.* gambolling movement.

game[1] *n.* play or sport, esp. with rules; section of this as a scoring unit; scheme; wild animals hunted for sport or food; their flesh as food. —*v.i.* gamble for money stakes. —*a.* brave; willing. **gamely** *adv.*, **gameness** *n.*

game[2] *a.* lame.

gamekeeper *n.* person employed to protect and breed game.

gamesmanship *n.* art of winning games by upsetting the confidence of one's opponent.

gamete *n.* sexual cell.

gamin /-mɪn/ *n.* street urchin; impudent child.

gamine /-'mi:n/ *n.* girl with mischievous charm.

gamma *n.* third letter of the Greek alphabet, = g.

gammon *n.* bottom piece of a flitch of bacon, including a hind leg; cured or smoked ham.

gammy *a.* (*sl.*) = game[2].

gamut *n.* whole range of notes used in music; whole series or scope.

gamy *a.* smelling or tasting like high game. **gaminess** *n.*

gander *n.* male goose.

gang *n.* group of people working or going about together. —*v.i.* **gang up** combine in a gang.

ganger *n.* foreman of a gang of workmen.

gangling *a.* tall and awkward.

ganglion *n.* (*pl.* **-ia**) group of nerve-cells from which nerve-fibres radiate; cyst on the sheath of a tendon.

gangplank *n.* plank placed for walking into or out of a boat.

gangrene *n.* decay of body tissue. **gangrenous** *a.*

gangster *n.* member of a gang of violent criminals.

gangway *n.* gap left for people to pass, esp. between rows of seats;

passageway, esp. on a ship; movable bridge from a ship to land.

ganja n. marijuana.

gannet n. large sea bird.

gantry n. overhead bridge-like framework supporting railway signals or a travelling crane etc.

gaol n. & v.t. = jail. **gaoler** n.

gap n. opening, space, interval; deficiency; wide difference. **gappy** a.

gape v.i. open the mouth wide; stare in surprise; be wide open. —n. yawn; stare.

garage /'gæraːʒ or -rɪdʒ/ n. building for storing motor vehicle(s); commercial establishment where motor vehicles are repaired and serviced, or selling petrol and oil. —v.t. put or keep in a garage.

garb n. clothing. —v.t. clothe.

garbage n. domestic waste; rubbish.

garble v.t. distort or confuse (a message or story etc.).

garden n. piece of cultivated ground, esp. attached to a house; (pl.) ornamental public grounds. —v.i. tend a garden. **gardener** n.

gardenia n. fragrant white or yellow flower; tree or shrub bearing this.

gargantuan /-'gæn-/ a. gigantic.

gargle v.i. wash the inside of the throat with liquid held there by the breath. —n. liquid used for this.

gargoyle n. grotesque carved face or figure on a building.

garish /'geər-/ a. gaudy. **garishly** adv., **garishness** n.

garland n. wreath of flowers etc. as a decoration. —v.t. deck with garland(s).

garlic n. onion-like plant. **garlicky** a.

garment n. article of clothing.

garner v.t. store up, collect. —n. storehouse, granary.

garnet n. red semi-precious stone.

garnish v.t. decorate (esp. food. —n. thing used for garnishing.

garret n. attic, esp. a poor one.

garrison n. troops stationed in a town or fort to defend it; building they occupy. —v.t. place a garrison in; occupy thus.

garrotte /-'rɒt/ n. cord, wire, or a metal collar used to strangle a victim. —v.t. strangle or (in Spain) execute with this.

garrulous a. talkative. **garrulously** adv., **garrulousness** n., **garrulity** n.

garter n. band worn round the leg to keep a stocking up. **garter stitch** pattern made by knitting all rows plain.

gas n. (pl. **gases**) substance with particles that can move freely; such a substance used as a fuel or anaesthetic; (colloq.) empty talk; (US colloq.) gasoline, petrol. —v.t./i. (p.t. **gassed**) kill or overcome by poisonous gas; (colloq.) talk lengthily. **gas chamber** room that can be filled with poisonous gas to kill animals or prisoners. **gas mask** device worn over face as a protection against poisonous gas. **gas ring** hollow perforated ring through which gas flows for cooking on. **gassy** a.

gasbag n. (sl.) empty talker.

gaseous /'gæ-/ a. of or like a gas.

gash n. long deep cut. —v.t. make a gash in.

gasholder n. gasometer.

gasify v.t./i. convert or be converted into gas. **gasification** n.

gasket n. sheet or ring of rubber, asbestos, etc., sealing a joint between metal surfaces.

gasoline /-liːn/ n. (US) petrol.

gasometer /-'sɒmɪ-/ n. large round storage tank from which gas is piped to a district.

gasp v.t./i. draw breath in sharply in exhaustion or surprise; speak breathlessly. —n. breath drawn in thus.

gastric a. of the stomach.

gastro-enteritis n. inflammation of the stomach and intestines.

gastronomy n. science of good eating and drinking. **gastronomic** a., **gastronomically** adv.

gastropod n. mollusc that moves by means of a ventral organ.

gasworks n. place where fuel gas is made.

gate n. hinged movable barrier in a wall or fence etc.; gateway; slots controlling movement of a gear lever; number of spectators entering by payment to see a football match etc., amount of money taken.

gateau /ˈgætəʊ/ n. (pl. -eaux pr. -əʊz) large rich cream cake.

gatecrash v.t./i. go to (a private party) uninvited. **gatecrasher** n.

gated a. fitted with gates.

gatelegged a. (of a table) with legs in a frame that can be moved to support leaves.

gateway n. opening or structure framing a gate; entrance.

gather v.t./i. bring or come together; collect; obtain gradually; understand, conclude; draw together in folds; swell and form pus. **gathers** n.pl. gathered folds of fabric.

gathering n. people assembled; inflamed swelling containing pus.

gauche /gəʊʃ/ a. lacking ease and grace of manner. **gaucherie** /-rɪ/ n.

gaucho /ˈgaʊtʃəʊ/ n. (pl. -os) mounted herdsman in the South American pampas.

gaudy a. (-ier, -iest) showy or bright in a tasteless way. **gaudily** adv., **gaudiness** n.

gauge /geɪdʒ/ n. standard measure esp. of contents or thickness; device for measuring things; distance between pairs of rails or wheels. —v.t. measure; estimate.

gaunt a. lean and haggard; grim, desolate. **gauntness** n.

gauntlet[1] n. glove with a long wide cuff; this cuff.

gauntlet[2] n. **run the gauntlet** be exposed to continuous criticism or risk.

gauze n. thin transparent fabric; fine wire mesh. **gauzy** a.

gave see **give**.

gavel n. mallet used by an auctioneer or chairman etc. to call for attention or order.

gavotte n. old French dance.

gawk v.i. (colloq.) stare stupidly.

gawky a. (-ier, -iest) awkward and ungainly. **gawkiness** n.

gawp v.i. (colloq.) stare stupidly.

gay a. (-er, -est) happy and full of fun; brightly coloured; (colloq.) homosexual. —n. (colloq.) homosexual person. **gayness** n.

gaze v.i. look long and steadily. —n. long steady look.

gazebo /-ˈziː-/ n. (pl. -os) turret or summer-house with a wide view.

gazelle n. small antelope.

gazette n. title of certain newspapers or of official journals containing public notices.

gazetteer /-ˈtɪə(r)/ n. index of places, rivers, mountains, etc.

gazump v.t. disappoint (an intended purchaser) by raising the price after accepting his offer.

GB abbr. Great Britain.

gear n. equipment; apparatus; set of toothed wheels working together in machinery. —v.t. provide with gear(s); adapt (to a purpose). **in gear** with gear mechanism engaged. **out of gear** with it disengaged.

gearbox, **gearcase** ns. case enclosing gear mechanism.

gecko n. (pl. -os) tropical lizard.

gee int. exclamation of surprise.

geese see **goose**.

gee-up int. command to a horse to move on or go faster.

geezer n. (sl.) person, old man.

Geiger counter /ˈgaɪ-/ device for detecting and measuring radioactivity.

geisha /ˈgeɪ-/ n. Japanese woman trained to entertain men.

gel /dʒel/ n. jelly-like substance.

gelatine n. clear substance made by boiling bones. **gelatinous** a.

geld v.t. castrate, spay.

gelding n. gelded horse.

gelignite /ˈdʒel-/ n. explosive containing nitro-glycerine.

gem n. precious stone; thing of great beauty or excellence.

gen n. (sl.) information.

gender n. grammatical classification corresponding roughly to the two sexes and sexlessness; one's sex.

gene n. unit of heredity containing DNA or RNA. **gene therapy** introduction of normal genes into cells in place of missing or defective ones, to correct genetic disorders.

genealogy /-nɪˈæl-/ n. list of ancestors; study of family pedigrees. **genealogical** a., **genealogist** n.

genera see **genus**.

general a. of or involving all or most parts, things, or people; involving main features only, not detailed or specific; (in titles) chief. —n. army officer next below field marshal; commander of an army. **general election** election of parliamentary representatives from the whole country. **general practitioner** doctor treating cases of all kinds in a section of the community. **general staff** army officers assisting a commander at headquarters. **in general** as a general rule, usually; for the most part. **generally** adv.

generality n. being general; general statement without details.

generalize v.t./i. draw a general conclusion; speak in general terms; bring into general use. **generalization** n.

generate v.t. bring into existence, produce.

generation n. generating; single stage in descent or pedigree; all persons born at about the same time; period of about 30 years.

generator n. machine converting mechanical energy into electricity.

generic /dʒɪˈne-/ a. of a whole genus or group. **generically** adv.

generous a. giving or giving freely; noble-minded; plentiful. **generously** adv., **generosity** n.

genesis n. origin.

genetic a. of genes or genetics. **genetic fingerprinting** analysis of DNA patterns in body fluids to identify people. **genetically** adv.

genetics n. science of heredity.

genial a. kindly and cheerful; pleasantly warm. **genially** adv., **geniality** n.

genie /ˈdʒiːnɪ/ n. (pl. **genii**) spirit or goblin in Arabian tales.

genital /ˈdʒenɪ-/ a. of animal reproduction; of genitals. **genitals** n.pl. external sex organs.

genitive n. grammatical case showing source or possession.

genius n. (pl. **-uses**) exceptionally great natural ability; person having this; (pl. **-ii**) guardian spirit.

genocide /ˈdʒen-/ n. deliberate extermination of a race of people.

genre /ˈʒɑr/ n. kind, esp. of art or literature; portrayal of scenes from everyday life.

gent n. (colloq.) gentleman.

genteel a. affectedly polite and refined. **genteelly** adv.

gentian n. alpine plant with usu. deep-blue flowers. **gentian violet** dye used as an antiseptic.

gentile n. non-Jewish person.

gentility n. good manners and elegance.

gentle a. (**-er**, **-est**) mild, moderate, not rough; of good family. —v.t. coax. —n. maggot used as bait. **gently** adv., **gentleness** n.

gentlefolk n.pl. people of good family.

gentleman n. (pl. **-men**) man, esp. of good social position; well-mannered man. **gentlemanly** a.

gentlewoman n. (pl. **-women**) woman of good family.

gentrify v.t. alter (an area) socially by arrival of middle-class residents. **gentrification** n.

gentry n.pl. people ranking next below nobility; (derog.) people.

genuflect v.i. bend the knee and lower the body, esp. in worship. **genuflexion** n.

genuine a. really what it is said to be. **genuinely** adv., **genuineness** n.

genus /'dʒi:-/ n. (pl. **genera**, pr. 'dʒen-) group of animals or plants, usu. containing several species; kind.

geocentric a. having the earth as a centre; as viewed from the earth's centre.

geode n. cavity lined with crystals; rock containing this.

geodesic /-'de- or -'di:-/ a. (also **geodetic**) of geodesy. **geodesic dome** dome built of flat pieces forming a rough hemisphere.

geodesy /-'ɒdɪ-/ n. study of earth's shape and area.

geography n. study of earth's surface and its physical features, climate, etc.; features and arrangement of a place. **geographical** a., **geographically** adv., **geographer** n.

geology n. study of earth's crust; features of earth's crust. **geological** a., **geologically** adv., **geologist** n.

geometry n. branch of mathematics dealing with properties and relations of lines, angles, surfaces, and solids. **geometric** a., **geometrical** a., **geometrically** adv., **geometrician** n.

georgette n. thin silky fabric.

Georgian a. & n. (person) of the time of the Georges, kings of England, esp. 1714–1830.

geranium n. garden plant with red, pink, or white flowers.

gerbil /'dʒɜː-/ n. rodent with long hind legs.

geriatrics /dʒerɪ'æ-/ n. branch of medicine dealing with the diseases and care of old people. **geriatric** a.

germ n. micro-organism, esp. one capable of causing disease; portion (of an organism) capable of developing into a new organism; basis from which a thing may develop.

German a. & n. (native, language) of Germany. **German measles** disease like mild measles.

germane /-'meɪn/ a. relevant.

Germanic /-'mæ-/ a. having German characteristics.

germicide n. substance that kills germs. **germicidal** a.

germinate v.t./i. begin or cause to develop and grow. **germination** n.

gerontology /dʒe-/ n. study of ageing and of old people's problems. **gerontologist** n.

gerrymander /-'mæn-/ v.t./i. arrange boundaries of (a constituency etc.) so as to gain unfair electoral advantage.

gerund /'dʒe-/ n. English verbal noun ending in -ing.

Gestapo n. German secret police of the Nazi regime.

gestation n. carrying in the womb between conception and birth; period of this.

gesticulate /dʒes-/ v.i. make expressive movements with the hands and arms. **gesticulation** n.

gesture n. expressive movement or action —v.i. make a gesture.

get v.t./i. (p.t. **got**, pres.p. **getting**) come into possession of; earn; win; fetch; capture, catch; establish communication with by radio or telephone; prepare (a meal); bring or come into a certain state; succeed in coming or going or bringing; persuade; (colloq.) understand; (colloq.) annoy. **get at** reach; (colloq.) imply; (sl.) imply criticism of; (sl.) tamper with, bribe. **get away** escape. **get**

by (colloq.) pass; manage to survive. **get off** be acquitted; obtain an acquittal for. **get on** manage; make progress; be on harmonious terms; advance in age. **get out of** evade. **get-out** n. means of evading something. **get over** recover from. **get round** influence in one's favour; evade (a law or rule). **get-together** n. (colloq.) social gathering. **get up** stand after sitting, kneeling, or lying down; get out of bed; prepare, organize; dress. **get-up** n. outfit.

getaway n. escape after a crime.

gewgaw n. gaudy ornament etc.

geyser /'gaɪz- or 'giːz-/ n. natural spring that spouts hot water or steam; /'giːz-/ a kind of waterheater.

ghastly a. (-ier, -iest) causing horror; (colloq.) very bad; pale and ill-looking. **ghastliness** n.

ghat /gæt/ n. (in India) steps down to a river; landing-place.

ghee n. Indian clarified butter.

gherkin /'gɜː-/ n. small cucumber used for pickling.

ghetto n. (pl. -os) slum area occupied by a particular group. **ghetto-blaster** n. (sl.) large loud-playing portable radio.

ghost n. person's spirit appearing after his death. —v.t./i. write as a ghost-writer. **ghost-writer** n. person who writes a book etc. for another to pass off as his own. **ghostly** a., **ghostliness** n.

ghoul /guːl/ n. person who enjoys gruesome things; (in Muslim stories) spirit that robs and devours corpses. **ghoulish** a., **ghoulishly** adv., **ghoulishness** n.

giant n. (in fairy-tales) a being of superhuman size; abnormally large person, animal, or thing; person of outstanding ability. —a. very large. **giantess** n.fem.

gibber v.i. make meaningless sounds, esp. in shock or terror.

gibberish n. unintelligible talk, nonsense.

gibbet n. gallows; post with an arm from which an executed criminal was hung.

gibbon n. long-armed ape.

gibbous a. convex, humped; (of the moon) having more than half but less than the whole of its disc illuminated.

gibe /dʒaɪb/ n. & v.t./i. jeer.

giblets n.pl. edible organs from a bird.

giddy a. (-ier, -iest) having or causing the feeling that everything is spinning round; excitable, flighty. **giddily** adv., **giddiness** n.

gift n. thing given or received without payment; natural ability; easy task. —v.t. bestow. **gift-wrap** v.t. (p.t. -wrapped) wrap attractively as a gift.

gifted a. having great natural ability.

gig[1] /g-/ n. light two-wheeled horse-drawn carriage.

gig[2] /g-/ n. (colloq.) engagement to play jazz etc. —v.i. (p.t. gigged) (colloq.) perform a gig.

giga- /gaɪgə-/ prefix multiplied by 10^9 (as in gigametre).

gigantic a. very large.

giggle v.i. give small bursts of half-suppressed laughter. —n. this laughter.

gigolo /'dʒɪ-/ n. (pl. -os) man paid by a woman to be her escort or lover.

gild[1] v.t. (p.t. & p.p. gilded) cover with a thin layer of gold or gold paint.

gild[2] n. old spelling of **guild**.

gilet /dʒɪˈleɪ/ n. waistcoat for a woman's garment.

gill[1] /g-/ n. (usu. pl.) respiratory opening on the body of a fish etc.; each of the vertical plates on the under side of a mushroom cap.

gill[2] /dʒ-/ n. one-quarter of a pint.

gillie /'gɪ-/ n. man or boy attending a person hunting or fishing in Scotland.

gilt[1] a. gilded, gold-coloured. —n. substance used in gilding; gilt-edged investment. **gilt-edged** *a.* (of an investment etc.) very safe.

gilt[2] *n.* young sow.

gimbals /'gɪ-/ *n.pl.* contrivance of rings to keep instruments horizontal in a moving ship etc.

gimcrack /'dʒɪ-/ *a.* cheap and flimsy.

gimlet /'gɪ-/ *n.* small tool with a screw-like tip for boring holes.

gimmick /'gɪ-/ *n.* trick or device to attract attention or publicity. **gimmicky** *a.*

gin[1] *n.* trap, snare; machine for separating raw cotton from its seeds. —*v.t.* (*p.t.* **ginned**) treat (cotton) in a gin.

gin[2] *n.* alcoholic spirit flavoured with juniper berries.

ginger *n.* hot-tasting root of a tropical plant; liveliness; reddish yellow. —*v.t.* make more lively. **ginger ale**, **ginger beer** ginger-flavoured fizzy drinks. **ginger group** group urging a more active policy. **gingery** *a.*

gingerbread *n.* ginger-flavoured cake or biscuit.

gingerly *a.* & *adv.* cautious(ly).

gingham *n.* cotton fabric, often with a checked or striped pattern.

gingivitis /-'vaɪ-/ *n.* inflammation of the gums.

gingko *n.* (*pl.* **-os**) Chinese and Japanese tree with yellow flowers.

ginseng *n.* plant with a fragrant root used in medicine.

gipsy *n.* = gypsy.

giraffe *n.* long-necked African animal.

gird *v.t.* encircle, attach with a belt or band.

girder *n.* metal beam supporting part of a building or bridge.

girdle[1] *n.* belt or cord worn round the waist; elastic corset; ring of bones in the body. —*v.t.* surround.

girdle[2] *n.* round iron plate for cooking things over heat.

girl *n.* female child; young woman; female assistant or employee; man's girlfriend. **girlhood** *n.* **girlish** *a.*

girlie *n.* (*colloq.*) girl. **girlie magazines** those containing erotic pictures of young women.

girlfriend *n.* female friend, esp. man's usual companion.

giro /'dʒaɪ-/ *n.* (*pl.* **-os**) banking system by which payment can be made by transferring credit from one account to another; cheque or payment made by this.

girt *a.* (*poet.*) girded.

girth *n.* distance round something; band under a horse's belly, holding a saddle in place.

gist /dʒɪ-/ *n.* essential points or general sense of a speech etc.

give *v.t./i.* (*p.t.* **gave**, *p.p.* **given**) cause to receive or have, supply; provide; utter; pledge; make over in exchange or payment; present (a play etc.) in public; yield as a product or result; permit a view or access; declare (judgement) authoritatively; be flexible. —*n.* springiness, elasticity. **give and take** exchange of talk or ideas; willingness to make reciprocal concessions. **give away** give as a gift; hand over (a bride) to a bridegroom; reveal (a secret etc.) unintentionally. **give-away** *n.* (*colloq.*) unintentional disclosure. **give in** acknowledge that one is defeated. **give off** emit. **give out** announce; become exhausted or used up. **give over** devote; (*colloq.*) cease. **give tongue** speak; (of hounds) bark. **give up** cease; part with, hand over; abandon hope or an attempt. **give way** yield; allow other traffic to go first; collapse. **giver** *n.*

given *see* give. —*a.* specified; having a tendency. **given name** Christian name, first name (given in addition to the family name).

gizzard *n.* bird's second stomach, in which food is ground.

glacé /'glæseɪ/ a. iced with sugar; preserved in sugar.

glacial /'gleɪʃ(ə)l/ a. icy; of or from glaciers or other ice. **glacially** adv.

glaciated /'gleɪ-/ a. covered with or affected by a glacier. **glaciation** n.

glacier /'glæ-/ n. mass or river of ice moving very slowly.

glad a. pleased, joyful. **gladly** adv., **gladness** n.

gladden v.t. make glad.

glade n. open space in a forest.

gladiator n. man trained to fight at public shows in ancient Rome. **gladiatorial** a.

gladiolus n. (pl. **-li**) garden plant with spikes of flowers.

glair n. white of egg; similar viscous substance.

glamorize v.t. make glamorous. **glamorization** n.

glamour n. alluring beauty; attractive exciting qualities. **glamorous** a., **glamorously** adv.

glance v.i. look briefly; strike and glide off. —n. brief look.

gland n. organ that extracts from the blood substances to be used or expelled by the body. **glandular** a.

glanders n. contagious disease of horses.

glare v.i. shine with a harsh dazzling light; stare angrily or fiercely. —n. glaring light or stare. **glaring** a. conspicuous.

glasnost /-z-/ n. (in the USSR) openness in information etc.

glass n. hard brittle usu. transparent substance; things made of this; mirror; glass drinking-vessel; barometer; (pl.) spectacles, binoculars. —v.t. fit or cover with glass. **glassy** a., **glassily** adv., **glassiness** n.

glasshouse n. greenhouse; (sl.) military prison.

glaucoma n. condition caused by increased pressure of fluid within the eyeball.

glaze v.t./i. fit or cover with glass; coat with a glossy surface; become glassy. —n. shiny surface or coating.

glazier n. person whose trade is to fit glass in windows etc.

gleam n. beam or ray of soft light; brief show of a quality. —v.i. send out gleams.

glean v.t./i. pick up (grain left by harvesters); gather scraps of. **gleaner** n., **gleanings** n.pl.

glee n. lively or triumphant joy; part-song. **glee club** type of choral society. **gleeful** a., **gleefully** adv.

glen n. narrow valley.

glengarry n. Scotch cap with a pointed front.

glib a. ready with words but insincere or superficial.

glide v.i. move smoothly; fly in a glider or aircraft without engine power. —n. gliding movement.

glider n. aeroplane with no engine.

glimmer n. faint gleam. —v.i. gleam faintly.

glimpse n. brief view. —v.t. catch a glimpse of.

glint n. very brief flash of light. —v.i. send out a glint.

glissade /-'seɪd/ v.i. slide skilfully. —n. glissading movement.

glisten v.i. shine like something wet.

glitch n. (colloq.) malfunction; hitch.

glitter v.i. & n. sparkle.

glitz n. (sl.) extravagant showiness, esp. in show business. **glitzy** a.

gloaming n. evening twilight.

gloat v.i. be full of greedy or malicious delight.

global a. worldwide; of a whole group of items. **global warming** worldwide rise in temperature. **globally** adv.

globe n. ball-shaped object, esp. with a map of the earth on it; the world; hollow round glass object.

globe-trotting n. travelling widely as a tourist. **globose** a.

globular a. shaped like a globe.

globule n. small rounded drop.

globulin n. a kind of protein found in animal and plant tissue.

glockenspiel n. musical instrument of tuned steel bars or tubes struck by hammers.

gloom n. semi-darkness; feeling of sadness and depression. **gloomy** a. (-ier, -iest), **gloomily** adv.

glorify v.t. praise highly; worship; make seem grander than it is. **glorification** n.

glorious a. possessing or bringing glory; splendid. **gloriously** adv.

glory n. fame and honour won by great deeds; adoration and praise in worship; beauty, magnificence; thing deserving praise and honour. —v.i. rejoice, pride oneself. **glory-hole** n. (colloq.) untidy room or cupboard etc.

gloss[1] n. shine on a smooth surface. —v.t. make glossy. **gloss over** cover up (a mistake etc.).

gloss[2] n. explanatory comment. —v.t. add such a comment to.

glossary n. list of technical or special words, with definitions.

glossy a. (-ier, -iest) shiny. **glossily** adv., **glossiness** n.

glottis n. opening at the upper end of the windpipe between the vocal cords. **glottal** a.

glove n. covering for the hand, usu. with separate divisions for fingers and thumb. **gloved** a. wearing a glove. **glover** n. maker of gloves.

glow v.i. send out light and heat without flame; have a warm or flushed look, colour, or feeling. —n. glowing state, look, or feeling. **glow-worm** n. beetle that can give out a greenish light.

glower /'glau-/ v.i. scowl.

glowing a. (of a description etc.) very enthusiastic or favourable.

gloxinia n. tropical plant with bell-shaped flowers.

glucose n. form of sugar found in fruit-juice.

glue n. sticky substance used for joining things together. —v.t. (pres.p. gluing) fasten with glue; attach closely. **glue ear** blocking of Eustachian tube by mucus, esp. in children. **gluey** a.

glum a. (**glummer, glummest**) sad and gloomy. **glumly** adv., **glumness** n.

glut n. (p.t. glutted) supply with more than is needed; satisfy fully with food. —n. excessive supply.

gluten /'glu:-/ n. sticky protein substance left when starch is washed out of flour.

glutinous a. glue-like, sticky. **glutinously** adv.

glutton n. one who eats far too much; one who is eager for something; wolverine. **gluttonous** a., **gluttony** n.

glycerine /-m/ n. thick sweet liquid used in medicines etc.

GMT abbr. Greenwich Mean Time.

gnarled a. knobbly; twisted.

gnash v.t./i. (of teeth) strike together; grind (one's teeth).

gnat n. small biting fly.

gnaw v.t./i. bite persistently.

gnome n. dwarf in fairy-tales.

gnomic /'nəʊ-/ a. sententious.

gnomon /'nəʊ-/ n. rod etc. of a sundial, showing the time by its shadow.

gnu /nu:/ n. ox-like antelope.

go v.i. (p.t. went, p.p. gone) move; depart; extend; be in a specified state; be functioning; make (a specified movement or sound); (of time) pass; be allowable or successful; belong in a specified place; be, on average; become; proceed; be sold; be spent or used up; be abolished or lost; collapse, fail, die; be able to be put; be given or allotted; be guided or directed; contribute, serve (to show etc.). —n. (pl. goes) energy; turn, try; success; (colloq.) state of affairs;

attack of illness. **be going to** be about or likely to (do something). **go-ahead** *n.* signal to proceed; (*a.*) enterprising. **go back on** fail to keep (a promise). **go-between** *n.* one who acts as messenger or negotiator. **go-cart** *n.* simple four-wheeled structure for a child to play on. **go for** (*sl.*) attack. **go-getter** *n.* (*colloq.*) pushful enterprising person. **go-go** *a.* (*colloq.*) very active or energetic. **go-kart** *n.* miniature racing-car. **go-karting** *n.* racing in this. **go off** explode. **go out** be extinguished. **go round** be enough for everyone. **go slow** work at a deliberately slow pace as a form of industrial protest. **go-slow** *n.* this procedure. **go under** succumb; fail. **go up** rise in price; explode; burn rapidly. **go with** match, harmonize with. **it's no go** (*colloq.*) nothing can be done. **on the go** in constant motion, active.

goad *n.* pointed stick for prodding cattle to move; stimulus to activity. —*v.t.* stimulate by annoying.

goal *n.* structure or area into which players try to send the ball in certain games; point scored thus; objective.

goalie *n.* (*colloq.*) goalkeeper.

goalkeeper *n.* player whose task is to keep the ball out of the goal.

goalpost *n.* either of the posts marking the limit of a goal.

goat *n.* small horned animal.

goatee *n.* short pointed beard.

gobble *v.t./i.* eat quickly and greedily; make a throaty sound like a turkey-cock. **gobbler** *n.*

gobbledegook *n.* (*sl.*) pompous language used by officials.

goblet *n.* drinking-glass with a stem and foot; container for the liquid in a liquidizer.

goblin *n.* mischievous ugly elf.

goby *n.* fish with ventral fins forming a sucker.

God *n.* creator and ruler of the universe in Christian, Jewish, and Muslim teaching. **god** *n.* superhuman being worshipped as having power over nature and human affairs; person or thing that is greatly admired or adored. **God-fearing** *a.* sincerely religious. **God-forsaken** *a.* wretched, dismal.

godchild *n.* (*pl.* **-children**) child in relation to its godparent(s).

god-daughter *n.* female godchild.

goddess *n.* female god.

godetia /gəˈdiːʃə/ *n.* hardy annual plant with showy flowers.

godfather *n.* male godparent; (*US*) mastermind of an illegal organization.

godhead *n.* divine nature; deity.

godlike *a.* like God or a god.

godly *a.* sincerely religious. **godliness** *n.*

godmother *n.* female godparent.

godparent *n.* person who undertakes, when a child is baptized, to see that it is brought up as a Christian.

godsend *n.* piece of unexpected good fortune.

godson *n.* male godchild.

goggle *v.i.* stare with wide-open eyes.

goggles *n.pl.* spectacles for protecting the eyes from wind, water, etc.

going *pres.p.* of **go.**

goitre *n.* enlarged thyroid gland.

gold *n.* yellow metal of high value; coins or articles made of this; its colour. —*a.* made of or coloured like gold. **gold-digger** *n.* (*sl.*) woman who uses her attractions to obtain money from men. **goldfield** *n.* area where gold is found. **gold-mine** *n.* place where gold is mined; source of great wealth. **gold-rush** *n.* rush to a newly discovered gold-field.

golden *a.* gold; precious, excellent. **golden handshake** generous cash payment to a person dismissed or forced to retire. **golden**

jubilee, golden wedding 50th anniversary.

goldfinch n. songbird with a band of yellow across each wing.

goldfish n. (pl. **goldfish**) small reddish Chinese carp kept in a bowl or pond.

goldsmith n. person whose trade is making articles in gold.

golf n. game in which a ball is struck with clubs towards and into a series of holes. —v.i. play golf. **golf ball** ball used in golf; (colloq.) spherical unit carrying type in some typewriters. **golf-course, golf-links** ns. area of land on which golf is played. **golfer** n.

golliwog n. a kind of black male doll with fuzzy hair.

golosh n. = galosh.

gonad /'gəʊ-/ n. animal organ producing gametes.

gondola n. boat with high pointed ends, used on canals in Venice; structure slung beneath a balloon, for carrying passengers etc.

gondolier n. man who propels a gondola by means of a pole.

gone see go.

goner n. (sl.) doomed or irrevocably lost person or thing.

gong n. metal plate that resounds when struck, esp. as a signal for meals; (sl.) medal.

gonorrhoea /-'rɪə/ n. venereal disease with a discharge from the genitals.

goo n. (sl.) sticky wet substance.

good a. (**better, best**) having the right or desirable qualities; proper, expedient; morally correct, kindly; well-behaved; enjoyable, beneficial; efficient; thorough; considerable, full; valid. —n. morally right thing; profit, benefit; (pl.) movable property, articles of trade, things to be carried by road or rail. **as good as** practically, almost. **good-for-nothing** a. & n. worthless (person). **Good Friday** Friday before

Easter, commemorating the Crucifixion. **good name** good reputation. **good will** intention that good shall result.

goodbye int. & n. expression used when parting.

goodish a. fairly good; rather large or great.

goodness n. quality of being good; good element; (in exclamations) God.

goodwill n. friendly feeling; established popularity of a business, treated as a saleable asset.

goody n. (colloq.) something good or attractive, esp. to eat. **goody-goody** a. & n. smugly virtuous (person).

gooey a. (sl.) wet and sticky.

goof n. (sl.) stupid person or mistake. —v.t./i. (sl.) blunder, bungle. **goofy** a.

googly n. ball bowled to break in an unexpected direction.

goon n. (sl.) stupid person; hired ruffian.

goose n. (pl. **geese**) web-footed bird larger than a duck; female of this. **goose-flesh, goose-pimples** ns. bristling skin caused by cold or fear. **goose-step** n. way of marching without bending the knees.

gooseberry n. thorny shrub; its edible (usu. green) berry.

gopher n. burrowing rodent.

gore¹ n. clotted blood from a wound.

gore² v.t. pierce with a horn or tusk.

gore³ n. triangular or tapering section of a skirt or sail. **gored** a.

gorge n. narrow steep-sided valley. —v.t./i. eat greedily; fill full, choke up. **one's gorge rises** one is sickened or disgusted.

gorgeous a. richly coloured, magnificent; (colloq.) very pleasant, beautiful. **gorgeously** adv.

gorgon n. terrifying woman.

Gorgonzola n. rich strong blue-veined Italian cheese.

gorilla n. large powerful ape.

gormandize v.i. eat greedily.

gormless a. (colloq.) stupid.

gorse n. wild evergreen thorny shrub with yellow flowers.

gory a. (-ier, -iest) covered with blood; involving bloodshed.

gosh int. (sl.) exclamation of surprise.

gosling n. young goose.

Gospel n. book(s) of the New Testament recording Christ's life and teachings. **gospel** n. teachings of Christ; thing one may safely believe; set of principles believed in.

gossamer n. fine filmy piece of cobweb; flimsy delicate material.

gossip n. casual talk, esp. about other people's affairs; person fond of gossiping. —v.i. (p.t. **gossiped**) engage in gossip. **gossipy** a.

got see **get**. — **have got** possess. **have got to do it** must do it.

Goth n. any of the Germanic invaders of the Roman Empire in the 3rd-5th centuries.

Gothic a. of an architectural style of the 12th-16th centuries, with pointed arches; (of a novel etc.) in a horrific style popular in the 18th-19th centuries.

gouge n. chisel with a concave blade. —v.t. cut out with a gouge; scoop or force out.

goulash n. stew of meat and vegetables, seasoned with paprika.

gourd n. fleshy fruit of a climbing plant; container made from its dried rind.

gourmand /ˈgʊə-/ n. glutton.

gourmet /ˈgʊə-/ n. connoisseur of good food and drink.

gout n. disease causing inflammation of the joints. **gouty** a.

govern v.t./i. rule with authority; conduct the affairs of a country or organization; keep under control; influence, direct. **governor** n.

governable a. able to be governed.

governance n. governing, control.

governess n. woman employed to teach children in a private household.

government n. governing; group or organization governing a country; State as an agent. **governmental** a.

gown n. loose flowing garment; woman's long dress; official robe.

GP abbr. general practitioner.

grab v.t./i. (p.t. **grabbed**) grasp suddenly; take greedily; operate harshly; (sl.) impress. —n. sudden clutch or attempt to seize; mechanical device for gripping things.

grace n. attractiveness and elegance, esp. of manner or design or ease of movement; favour; mercy; short prayer of thanks said at a meal; title of a duke, duchess, or archbishop. —v.t. confer honour or dignity on, be an ornament to. **grace-note** n. note embellishing a melody.

graceful a. having or showing grace. **gracefully** adv., **gracefulness** n.

graceless a. inelegant; ungracious. **gracelessly** adv.

gracious a. kind and pleasant towards inferiors; merciful; elegant. **graciously** adv., **graciousness** n.

grackle n. a kind of oriole; a kind of mina.

gradation n. stage in a process of gradual change; this process.

grade n. level of rank, quality, or value; class of people or things of the same grade; mark given to a student for his standard of work; slope. —v.t. arrange in grades; assign a grade to; adjust the slope of (a road). **make the grade** be successful.

gradient n. slope, amount of this.

gradual *a.* taking place by degrees, not sudden. **gradually** *adv.*

graduate[1] /-ət/ *n.* person who holds a university degree.

graduate[2] /-ert/ *v.t./i.* take a university degree; divide into graded sections; mark into regular divisions. **graduation** *n.*

graffito *n.* (*pl.* **-ti**) word(s) or a drawing scribbled or scratched on a wall etc.

graft[1] *n.* shoot fixed into a cut in a tree to form a new growth; living tissue transplanted surgically; (*sl.*) hard work. —*v.t./i.* put a graft in or on; join inseparably; (*sl.*) work hard.

graft[2] *n.* obtaining an advantage by bribery or unfair means; this bribe or bribery; the advantage gained.

Grail *n.* Holy Grail cup or platter used by Christ at the Last Supper.

grain *n.* small hard seed(s) of a food plant such as wheat or rice; these plants; small hard particle; unit of weight (about 65 mg); texture produced by particles in stone etc.; pattern of lines made by fibres or layers. **grainy** *a.*

gram *n.* one-thousandth of a kilogram.

grammar *n.* use of words in their correct forms and relationships. **grammar school** secondary school for pupils with academic ability.

grammarian *n.* expert in grammar.

grammatical *a.* according to the rules of grammar. **grammatically** *adv.*

gramophone *n.* record-player.

grampus *n.* dolphin-like sea animal.

gran *n.* (*colloq.*) grandmother.

granary *n.* storehouse for grain.

grand *a.* (**-er**, **-est**) great; splendid; imposing; (*colloq.*) very good. —*n.* grand piano; (*sl.*) one thousand pounds or dollars. **grand piano** large full-toned piano with

horizontal strings. **Grand Prix** /grã 'pri:/ important international motor race. **grandly** *adv.*, **grandness** *n.*

grandad *n.* (*colloq.*) grandfather.

grandchild *n.* (*pl.* **-children**) child of one's son or daughter.

granddaughter *n.* female grandchild.

grandee *n.* person of high rank.

grandeur *n.* splendour, grandness.

grandfather *n.* male grandparent. **grandfather clock** clock in a tall wooden case.

grandiloquent /-'dil-/ *a.* using pompous language. **grandiloquently** *adv.*, **grandiloquence** *n.*

grandiose *a.* imposing; planned on a large scale; pompous. **grandiosely** *adv.*, **grandiosity** *n.*

grandma *n.* (*colloq.*) grandmother.

grandmother *n.* female grandparent. **grandmother clock** clock like a grandfather clock but in a smaller case.

grandpa *n.* (*colloq.*) grandfather.

grandparent *n.* parent of one's father or mother.

grandson *n.* male grandchild.

grandstand *n.* principal stand for spectators at races and sports.

grange *n.* country house with farm-buildings that belong to it.

granite *n.* hard grey stone.

granny *n.* (*colloq.*) grandmother. **granny flat** self-contained accommodation in one's house for a relative. **granny knot** reef-knot with threads wrongly crossed.

grant *v.t.* give or allow as a privilege; admit to be true. —*n.* thing granted; student's allowance from public funds; granting. **take for granted** assume to be true or sure to happen or continue.

granular *a.* like grains.

granulate *v.t./i.* form into grains; roughen the surface of. **granulation** *n.*

granule *n.* small grain.

grape n. green or purple berry used for making wine.

grapefruit n. large round yellow citrus fruit.

grapevine n. vine bearing grapes; way news spreads unofficially.

graph n. diagram of line(s) showing the relationship between quantities. —v.t. draw a graph of.

graphic a. of drawing, painting, or engraving; giving a vivid description. **graphic equalizer** device for separate control of radio frequency bands. **graphics** n.pl. diagrams etc. used in calculation and design. **graphically** adv.

graphical a. using diagrams or graphs. **graphically** adv.

graphite n. a form of carbon.

graphology n. study of handwriting. **graphologist** n.

grapnel n. small anchor with several hooks; hooked device for dragging a river-bed.

grapple v.t./i. seize, hold firmly; struggle. **grappling-iron** n. grapnel.

grasp v.t./i. seize and hold; understand. —n. firm hold or grip; understanding. **grasp at** snatch at.

grasping a. greedy for money or possessions.

grass n. wild low-growing plant with green blades eaten by animals; species of this (e.g. a cereal plant); ground covered with grass; (sl.) person who grasses, betrayal. —v.t. cover with grass; (sl.) betray a conspiracy etc. **grass roots** fundamental level or source; rank-and-file members. **grass widow** wife whose husband is absent for some time. **grassy** a.

grasshopper n. jumping insect that makes a chirping noise.

grassland n. wide grass-covered area with few trees.

grate¹ n. metal framework keeping fuel in a fireplace; hearth.

grate² v.t./i. shred finely by rubbing against a jagged surface;

make a harsh noise by rubbing; sound harshly; have an irritating effect.

grateful a. feeling that one values a kindness or benefit received. **gratefully** adv.

grater n. device for grating food.

gratify v.t. give pleasure to; satisfy (wishes). **gratification** n.

grating n. screen of spaced bars placed across an opening.

gratis /'grei- or 'grɑː-/ a. & adv. free of charge.

gratitude n. being grateful.

gratuitous a. given or done free of charge; uncalled for. **gratuitously** adv.

gratuity n. money given as a present for services rendered.

gravamen /-'vei-/ n. essence or worst part of an accusation.

grave¹ n. hole dug to bury a corpse.

grave² a. (-er, -est) serious, causing great anxiety; solemn. **grave accent** /grɑːv/ the accent `. **gravely** adv.

grave³ v.t. clean (a ship's bottom).

graving dock dry dock.

gravel n. coarse sand with small stones, used for paths.

gravelly a. of or like gravel; rough-sounding.

graven a. carved.

gravestone n. stone placed over a grave.

graveyard n. burial ground.

gravid a. pregnant.

gravitate v.i. move or be attracted towards something.

gravitation n. gravitating; force of gravity. **gravitational** a.

gravity n. seriousness; solemnity; force that attracts bodies towards the centre of the earth.

gravy n. juice from cooked meat; sauce made from this. **gravy train** (sl.) source of easy money.

gray a. & n.=grey.

grayling n. grey freshwater fish.

graze¹ v.t./i. feed on growing grass; pasture animals in (a field).

graze[2] *v.t./i.* injure by scraping the skin; touch or scrape lightly in passing. —*n.* grazed place on the skin.

grazier *n.* person who feeds cattle for market; (*Austr.*) sheep-farmer.

grease *n.* fatty or oily matter, esp. as a lubricant; animal fat melted soft. —*v.t.* put grease on. **greaser** *n.*, **greasy** *a.*

greasepaint *n.* make-up used by actors.

great *a.* (-**er**, -**est**) much above average in size, amount, or intensity; of remarkable ability or character, important; (*colloq.*) very good. **greatness** *n.*

great- *pref.* (of a family relationship) one generation removed in ancestry or descent.

greatcoat *n.* heavy overcoat.

greatly *adv.* very much.

greave *n.* piece of armour worn on the shin.

grebe *n.* a diving bird.

Grecian *a.* Greek.

greed *n.* excessive desire, esp. for food or wealth. **greedy** *a.* (-**ier**, -**iest**), **greedily** *adv.*, **greediness** *n.*

Greek *a. & n.* (native, language) of Greece.

green *a.* (-**er**, -**est**) of the colour between blue and yellow, coloured like grass; unripe, not seasoned, (of bacon) not smoked; (of wood) not seasoned; concerned with protecting the environment; immature, inexperienced, easily deceived. —*n.* green colour or thing; piece of grassy public land; grassy area; environmentalist; (*pl.*) green vegetables. **green belt** area of open land round a town. **green fingers** skill in making plants grow. **green light** signal or (*colloq.*) permission to proceed. **Green Paper** government report of proposals being considered. **green pound** agreed value of the £ used for reckoning payments to EEC agricultural producers.

green-room *n.* room in a theatre for the use of actors when off stage. **greenness** *n.*

greenery *n.* green foliage or plants.

greenfinch *n.* finch with green and yellow feathers.

greenfly *n.* (*pl.* -**fly**) small green insect that sucks juices from plants.

greengage *n.* round plum with a greenish skin.

greengrocer *n.* shopkeeper selling vegetables and fruit.

greengrocery *n.* greengrocer's shop or goods.

greenhorn *n.* inexperienced person.

greenhouse *n.* building with glass sides and roof, for rearing plants. **greenhouse effect** trapping of the sun's radiation by the atmosphere. **greenhouse gas** gas causing this.

greenish *a.* rather green.

greenstick fracture bone-fracture in which the bone is partly broken and partly bent.

greenstone *n.* a kind of jade.

greet *v.t.* address politely on meeting or arrival; react to; present itself to (sight or hearing). **greetings card** decorative card for conveying a goodwill message.

gregarious *a.* living in flocks or communities; fond of company. **gregariousness** *n.*

gremlin *n.* (*sl.*) mischievous spirit said to cause mishaps to machinery.

grenade *n.* small bomb thrown by hand or fired from a rifle.

grenadier *n.* soldier of some regiments formerly armed with grenades.

grenadine *n.* flavouring syrup made from pomegranates etc.

grew *see* grow.

grey *a.* (-**er**, -**est**) of the colour between black and white, coloured like ashes. —*n.* grey colour or thing. —*v.t./i.* make or become grey. **greyness** *n.*

greyhound n. slender smooth-haired dog noted for its swiftness.

greyish a. rather grey.

greylag n. grey wild goose.

grid n. grating; system of numbered squares for map references; network of lines, power-cables, etc.; gridiron. **gridded** a.

griddle n. = girdle².

gridiron n. framework of metal bars for cooking on; field for American football, marked with parallel lines.

gridlock n. (US) urban traffic jam with intersecting lines of traffic.

grief n. deep sorrow. **come to grief** meet with disaster; fail; fall.

grievance n. ground of complaint.

grieve v.t./i. cause grief to; feel grief.

grievous a. causing grief; serious. **grievously** adv.

griffin n. mythological creature with an eagle's head and wings on a lion's body.

griffon n. small terrier-like dog; a kind of vulture; griffin.

grill n. metal grid, grating; device on a cooker for radiating heat downwards; grilled food; grill-room. —v.t./i. cook under a grill or on a gridiron; question closely and severely. **grill room** restaurant or room where grills and other foods are served.

grille n. grating, esp. in a door or window.

grilse n. young salmon returning from the sea to fresh water for the first time.

grim a. (grimmer, grimmest) stern, severe; without cheerfulness, unattractive. **grimly** adv., **grimness** n.

grimace n. contortion of the face in pain or disgust, or done to cause amusement. —v.i. make a grimace.

grime n. ingrained dirt. —v.t. blacken with grime. **grimy** a., **grimily** adv., **griminess** n.

grin v.i. (p.t. grinned) smile broadly, showing the teeth. —n. broad smile.

grind v.t./i. (p.t. ground) crush into grains or powder; produce thus; crush or oppress by cruelty; sharpen or smooth by friction; rub harshly together; make a grating sound; produce with effort; study hard, toil. —n. grinding process; hard monotonous work. **grinder** n.

grindstone n. thick revolving disc for sharpening or grinding things.

grip v.t./i. (p.t. gripped) take or keep firm hold of; hold the attention of. —n. firm grasp or hold; way of or thing for gripping; understanding, mental hold or control; (US) suitcase, travelling-bag.

gripe v.t./i. cause colic; (sl.) grumble. —n. colic pain; (sl.) grumble.

grisly a. (-ier, -iest) causing fear, horror, or disgust. **grisliness** n.

grist n. grain to be ground or already ground.

gristle n. tough flexible tissue of animal bodies, esp. in meat. **gristly** a.

grit n. particles of stone or sand; (colloq.) courage and endurance. —v.t./i. (p.t. gritted) make a grating sound; clench; spread grit on. **gritty** a., **grittiness** n.

grits n.pl. coarsely ground grain; oats husked but not ground.

grizzle v.i. & n. whimper, whine.

grizzled a. grey; grey-haired.

grizzly a. grizzled. **grizzly bear** large brown bear of North America.

groan v.i. make a long deep sound in pain, grief, or disapproval; make a deep creaking sound. —n. sound made by groaning.

groat n. former silver fourpenny piece.

groats n.pl. crushed oats.

grocer n. shopkeeper selling foods and household stores.

grocery n. grocer's shop or goods.

grog n. drink of spirits mixed with water.

groggy a. (-ier, -iest) weak and unsteady, esp. after illness. **groggily** adv., **grogginess** n.

groin n. groove where each thigh joins the trunk; curved edge where two vaults meet; arch supporting a vault. **groined** a.

grommet n. insulating washer; tube placed through the eardrum.

groom n. person employed to look after horses; official of the royal household; bridegroom. —v.t. clean and brush (an animal); make neat and trim; prepare (a person) for a career or position.

groove n. long narrow channel. —v.t. make groove(s) in.

groovy a. (-ier, -iest) (sl.) enjoyable; excellent. **grooviness** n.

grope v.i. feel about as one does in the dark.

grosgrain /'grəʊ-/ n. silky corded fabric used for ribbons etc.

gross a. (-er, -est) thick, large-bodied; vulgar; outrageous; total, without deductions. —n. (pl. **gross**) twelve dozen. —v.t. produce or earn as total profit. **gross up** work out the gross amount by re-adding to the net amount the tax etc. deducted. **grossly** adv.

grotesque a. very odd or ugly. —n. comically distorted figure; design using fantastic forms. **grotesquely** adv., **grotesqueness** n.

grotto n. (pl. -oes) picturesque cave.

grouch v.i. & n. (colloq.) grumble.

ground[1] n. solid surface of earth; area, position, or distance on this, (pl.) enclosed land of a large house or institution; foundation for a theory, reason for action; underlying part; (pl.) solid particles (e.g. of coffee) that do not dissolve. —v.t./i. run aground; prevent (an aircraft or airman) from flying; base; give basic training to. **ground-rent** n. rent

paid for land leased for building. **ground swell** slow heavy waves.

ground[2] see **grind**. —a. **ground glass** glass made opaque by grinding.

grounding n. basic training.

groundless a. without foundation.

groundnut n. peanut.

groundsel n. weed with yellow flowers.

groundsheet n. waterproof sheet for spreading on the ground.

groundsman n. (pl. -men) man employed to look after a sports ground.

groundwork n. preliminary or basic work.

group n. number of persons or things near, belonging, classed, or working together. —v.t./i. form or gather into group(s).

grouper n. sea fish used as food.

grouse[1] n. a kind of game-bird.

grouse[2] v.i. & n. (colloq.) grumble. **grouser** n.

grout n. thin fluid mortar. —v.t. fill with grout.

grove n. small wood; group of trees.

grovel v.i. (p.t. grovelled) lie or crawl face downwards; humble oneself.

grow v.t./i. (p.t. grew, p.p. grown) increase in size or amount; develop or exist as a living plant; become; allow to grow; produce by cultivation. **grow up** become adult or mature. **grower** n.

growl v.i. make a low threatening sound as a dog does. —n. this sound.

grown see **grow**. —a. adult; covered with a growth. **grown-up** a. & n. adult.

growth n. process of growing; thing that grows or has grown; tumour. **growth industry** one developing faster than others.

groyne n. solid structure projecting towards the sea to prevent sand and pebbles from being washed away.

grub n. worm-like larva of certain insects; (sl.) food. —v.t./i. (p.t. grubbed) dig the surface of soil; dig up by the roots; rummage. **grub-screw** n. headless screw.

grubby a. (-ier, -iest) dirty; infested with grubs. **grubbiness** n.

grudge v.t. resent having to give or allow. —n. feeling of resentment or ill will.

gruel n. thin oatmeal porridge.

gruelling a. very tiring.

gruesome a. filling one with horror or disgust.

gruff a. (-er, -est) (of the voice) low and hoarse; having a gruff voice; surly. **gruffly** adv., **gruffness** n.

grumble v.i. complain in a bad-tempered way; rumble. —n. complaint, esp. a bad-tempered one; rumble. **grumbler** n.

grumpy a. (-ier, -iest) bad-tempered. **grumpily** adv., **grumpiness** n.

grunge n. laid-back style of rock music with raucous guitar sound; US dirt, grime.

grunt n. gruff snorting sound made by a pig. —v.t./i. make this sound; speak or utter with such a sound.

Gruyère /'gru:jeə(r)/ n. a kind of orig. Swiss cheese with holes.

gryphon n. = griffin.

G-string n. strip of cloth etc. covering the genitals, attached to a string round the waist.

guano /'gwɑ:nəʊ/ n. dung of sea-birds, used as manure; artificial manure esp. made from fish.

guarantee n. formal promise to do something or that a thing is of specified quality; thing offered as security; guarantor. —v.t. give or be a guarantee of or to.

guarantor n. giver of a guarantee.

guard v.t./i. watch over and protect or supervise; restrain; take precautions. —n. state of watchfulness for danger; defensive attitude in boxing, cricket, etc.;

person(s) guarding something; railway official in charge of a train; protecting part or device; **Guards** household troops.

guarded a. cautious, discreet.

guardian n. one who guards or protects; person undertaking legal responsibility for an orphan. **guardianship** n.

guardsman n. (pl. -men) soldier acting as guard.

guava /'gwɑ:-/ n. orange-coloured fruit of a tropical American tree.

gudgeon[1] n. small freshwater fish.

gudgeon[2] n. a kind of pivot; socket for a rudder; metal pin.

guelder rose /'gel-/ shrub with round white flowers.

guerrilla n. person who takes part in **guerrilla warfare**, fighting or harassment by small groups acting independently.

guess v.t./i. form an opinion or state without definite knowledge or without measuring; think likely; (US) suppose. —n. opinion formed by guessing. **guesser** n.

guesstimate n. (colloq.) estimate formed by guesswork.

guesswork n. guessing.

guest n. person entertained at another's house or table etc., or lodging at a hotel; visiting performer. **guest-house** n. superior boarding-house.

guff n. (sl.) empty talk.

guffaw n. coarse noisy laugh. —v.i. utter a guffaw.

guidance n. guiding; advising or advice on problems.

Guide n. member of a girls' association similar to the Scout Association.

guide n. person who shows others the way; one employed to point out interesting sights to travellers; guidebook, book of information about a subject; directing principle; thing marking a position or steering moving parts. —v.t. act as guide to.

guidebook n. book of information about a place, for visitors.

Guider n. adult leader of Guides.

guild n. society for mutual aid or with a common purpose; association of craftsmen or merchants.

guilder n. unit of money of the Netherlands.

guildhall n. town hall.

guile n. treacherous cunning, craftiness. **guileful** a., **guileless** a.

guillemot /'gɪlɪmɒt/ n. a kind of auk.

guillotine n. machine used in France for beheading criminals; machine with a long blade for cutting paper or metal; fixing of times for voting in Parliament, to prevent a lengthy debate. —v.t. use a guillotine on.

guilt n. fact of having committed an offence; feeling that one is to blame. **guiltless** a.

guilty a. (-ier, -iest) having done wrong; feeling or showing guilt. **guiltily** adv., **guiltiness** n.

guinea n. former British coin worth 21 shillings (£1.05); this amount. **guinea-fowl** n. bird of the pheasant family. **guinea-pig** n. rat-like animal kept as a pet or for biological experiments; person or thing used as a subject for an experiment.

guipure /'giːpʊə(r)/ n. heavy lace of linen pieces joined by embroidery.

guise n. false outward manner or appearance; pretence.

guitar n. a kind of stringed musical instrument. **guitarist** n.

gulf n. large area of sea partly surrounded by land; deep hollow; wide difference in opinion.

gull n. sea bird with long wings.

gullet n. passage by which food goes from mouth to stomach.

gullible a. easily deceived. **gullibility** n.

gully n. narrow channel cut by water or carrying rainwater from a building; fielding position in cricket.

gulp v.t./i. swallow (food etc.) hastily or greedily; make a gulping movement. —n. act of gulping; large mouthful of liquid gulped.

gum[1] n. firm flesh in which teeth are rooted.

gum[2] n. sticky substance exuded by certain trees, made into adhesives; chewing-gum; gumdrop; gum-tree. —v.t. (p.t. **gummed**) smear or stick together with gum. **gum-tree** n. tree that exudes gum; eucalyptus. **gummy** a.

gum[3] n. **by gum** (sl.) by God.

gumboil n. small abscess on the gum.

gumboot n. rubber boot, wellington.

gumdrop n. hard gelatine sweet.

gumption n. (colloq.) common sense.

gumshoe n. (US) galosh.

gun n. weapon that sends shells or bullets from a metal tube; device operating similarly; member of a shooting party. —v.t./i. (p.t. **gunned**) shoot with a gun.

gunboat n. small armed vessel with heavy guns.

gunfire n. firing of guns.

gunman n. (pl. -men) man armed with a gun.

gunner n. artillery soldier, esp. a private; naval warrant officer in charge of a battery of guns; member of an aircraft crew who operates a gun.

gunnery n. construction and operating of large guns.

gunny n. coarse material for making sacks; sack made of this.

gunpowder n. explosive of saltpetre, sulphur, and charcoal.

gunroom n. room where sporting guns are kept; room for junior officers in a warship.

gunrunning n. smuggling of fire-arms. **gunrunner** n.

gunshot n. shot fired from a gun.

gunsmith n. maker and repairer of small firearms.

gunwale /ˈɡʌn(ə)l/ n. upper edge of a small ship's or boat's side.

guppy n. very small brightly coloured tropical fish.

gurgle n. low bubbling sound. —v.t./i. make or utter with this sound.

Gurkha n. member of a Hindu people in Nepal, forming regiments in the British army.

gurnard n. sea-fish with a large spiny head.

guru n. (pl. **-us**) Hindu spiritual teacher; revered teacher.

gush v.t./i. flow or pour suddenly or in great quantities; talk effusively. —n. sudden or great outflow; effusiveness. **gushy** a.

gusher n. oil-well emitting oil without pumping; person who gushes.

gusset n. triangular or diamond-shaped piece of cloth inserted to strengthen or enlarge a garment etc. **gusseted** a.

gust n. sudden rush of wind, rain, smoke, or sound. —v.i. blow in gusts. **gusty** a., **gustily** adv.

gustatory a. of the sense of taste.

gusto n. zest.

gut n. intestine; thread made from animal intestines; (pl.) abdominal organs; (pl., colloq.) courage and determination. —a. fundamental; instinctive. —v.t. (p.t. **gutted**) remove guts from (fish); remove or destroy internal fittings or parts of.

gutsy a. (colloq.) courageous, greedy. **gutsily** adv., **gutsiness** n.

gutta-percha n. rubbery substance made from the juice of Malayan trees.

gutter n. trough round a roof, or channel at a roadside, for carrying away rain-water; slum environment. —v.i. (of a candle) burn unsteadily so that melted wax runs freely down the sides.

guttering n. material for gutter(s).

guttersnipe n. dirty child who plays in slum streets.

guttural a. throaty, harsh-sounding. **gutturally** adv.

guy[1] n. effigy of Guy Fawkes burnt on 5 Nov.; oddly dressed person; (colloq.) man. —v.t. ridicule, esp. by comic imitation.

guy[2] n. rope or chain used to keep a thing steady or secured.

guzzle v.t./i. eat or drink greedily.

gybe v.t./i. (of a sail or boom) swing across; (of a boat) change course thus. —n. this change.

gym n. (colloq.) gymnasium, gymnastics.

gymkhana n. public display of sports competitions, esp. horseriding.

gymnasium n. room equipped for physical training and gymnastics.

gymnast n. expert in gymnastics.

gymnastics n. & n.pl. exercises to develop the muscles or demonstrate agility. **gymnastic** a.

gymslip, gym-tunic ns. sleeveless tunic worn as part of a girl's school uniform.

gynaecology /ɡaɪ-/ n. study of the physiological functions and diseases of women. **gynaecological** a., **gynaecologist** n.

gypsophila n. garden plant with many small white flowers.

gypsum n. chalk-like substance.

gypsy n. member of a wandering people of Europe.

gyrate /dʒaɪˈ-/ v.i. move in circles or spirals, revolve. **gyration** n.

gyratory /ˈdʒaɪ-/ a. gyrating, following a circular or spiral path.

gyro /ˈdʒaɪ-/ n. (pl. **-os**) (colloq.) gyroscope.

gyrocompass /ˈdʒaɪ-/ n. navigation compass using a gyroscope.

gyroscope /ˈdʒaɪ-/ n. rotating device used to keep navigation instruments steady. **gyroscopic** a.

H

ha int. exclamation of triumph.

habeas corpus /ˈheɪbɪəs/ order requiring a person to be brought before a judge or into court, esp. to investigate the authorities' right to keep him imprisoned.

haberdasher n. dealer in haberdashery.

haberdashery n. small articles of dress, sewing-goods, etc.

habiliments /-'bɪl-/ n.pl. clothing.

habit n. settled way of behaving; monk's or nun's long dress; woman's riding-dress.

habitable a. suitable for living in.

habitat n. animal's or plant's natural environment.

habitation n. place to live in.

habitual a. done or doing something constantly, esp. as a habit; usual. **habitually** adv.

habituate v.t. accustom. **habituation** n.

habitué /-'tju:eɪ/ n. one who visits a place frequently or lives there.

hacienda /-sɪ'en-/ n. ranch or large estate in South America.

hack[1] n. horse for ordinary riding; person doing routine work, esp. as a writer. —v.i. ride on horseback at an ordinary pace.

hack[2] v.t./i. cut, chop, or hit roughly. —n. blow given thus.

hacker n. (colloq.) computer enthusiast, esp. one gaining unauthorized access to files.

hacking a. (of a cough) dry and frequent.

hackles n.pl. long feathers on a cock's neck. **with his hackles up** angry.

hackney carriage taxi.

hackneyed a. (of sayings) overused and therefore lacking impact.

hacksaw n. saw for metal.

had see **have**.

haddock n. (pl. **haddock**) sea-fish like a cod, used as food.

hadji n. = hajji.

haematology n. study of blood. **haematologist** n.

haemoglobin n. red oxygen-carrying substance in blood.

haemophilia n. tendency to bleed excessively. **haemophiliac** n.

haemorrhage n. profuse bleeding. —v.i. bleed profusely.

haemorrhoids n.pl. varicose veins at or near the anus.

haft n. handle of a knife or dagger.

hag n. ugly old woman.

haggard a. looking ugly from exhaustion. **haggardness** n.

haggis n. Scottish dish made from sheep's heart, lungs, and liver.

haggle v.i. argue about price or terms when settling a bargain.

hagiography /-'ɒg-/ n. writing the lives of saints. **hagiographer** n.

hagridden a. afflicted by worries.

ha-ha n. sunk fence.

haiku /'haɪkʊ/ n. (pl. **haiku**) three-line poem of 17 syllables.

hail[1] v.t./i. greet; call to; signal to and summon. **hail from** originate from, have come from.

hail[2] n. pellets of frozen rain falling in a shower; shower of blows, questions, etc. —v.t./i. pour down as or like hail. **hailstone** n.

hailstorm n. storm of hail.

hair n. fine thread-like strand growing from the skin; mass of these, esp. on the head. **hair-raising** a. terrifying. **hair-trigger** n. trigger operated by the slightest pressure.

hairbrush n. brush for grooming the hair.

haircut n. shortening hair by cutting it; style of this.

hairdo n. (pl. **-dos**) arrangement of the hair.

hairdresser n. person whose job is to cut and arrange hair. **hairdressing** n.

hairgrip n. springy hairpin.

hairless a. without hair.

hairline n. edge of the hair on the forehead etc.; very narrow crack or line.

hairpin n. U-shaped pin for keeping hair in place. **hairpin bend** sharp U-shaped bend in a road.

hairspring n. very fine spring in a watch.

hairy a. (-ier, -iest) covered with hair; (sl.) hair-raising, unpleasant, difficult. **hairiness** n.

Haitian /'haɪ-/ a. & n. (native) of Haiti.

hajji n. Muslim who has been to Mecca on pilgrimage.

hake n. (pl. **hake**) sea-fish of the cod family, used as food.

halal v.t. kill (animals for meat) according to Muslim law. —n. meat prepared thus.

halberd n. combined spear and battleaxe.

halcyon a. calm and peaceful; (of a period) happy and prosperous.

hale[1] a. strong and healthy.

hale[2] v.t. (old use) drag, haul.

half n. (pl. **halves**) each of two equal parts; this amount; (colloq.) half-back, half-pint, etc. —a. amounting to a half. —adv. to the extent of a half, partly. **half a dozen** six. **half-and-half** a. half one thing and half another. **half-back** n. player between forwards and full back(s). **half-baked** a. (colloq.) not competently planned; foolish. **half-breed** n. **half-caste**. **half-brother** n. brother with only one parent in common with another. **half-caste** n. person of mixed race. **half-crown** n. former British coin worth 2s. 6d. (12½p). **half-hearted** a. not very enthusiastic. **half-life** n. time after which radioactivity etc. is half its original level. **at half-mast** (of a flag) lowered in mourning. **half nelson** a kind of wrestling hold. **half-term** n. short holiday half-way through a school term. **half-timbered** a. built with a timber frame with brick or plaster filling. **half-time** n. interval between two halves of a game. **half-tone** n. illustration with light and dark shades represented by means of small and large dots.

halfpenny n. (pl. **-pennies** for single coins, **-pence** for a sum of money) coin worth half a penny.

halfway a. & adv. at a point equidistant between two others.

halfwit n. halfwitted person.

halfwitted a. mentally retarded; stupid.

halibut n. (pl. **halibut**) large flatfish used as food.

halitosis n. breath that smells unpleasant.

hall n. large room or building for meetings, concerts, etc.; large country house; space inside the front entrance of a house.

hallelujah int. & n. = alleluia.

hallmark n. official mark put on gold, silver, and platinum to indicate its standard; distinguishing characteristic. **hallmarked** a.

hallo int. & n. = hello.

halloo int. & v.i. shout to urge on hounds or call attention.

hallow v.t. make holy; honour as holy.

Hallowe'en n. 31 Oct., eve of All Saints' Day.

hallucinate v.i. experience hallucinations.

hallucination n. illusion of seeing or hearing something not actually present. **hallucinatory** a.

hallucinogenic /-'dʒen-/ a. causing hallucinations.

halo n. (pl. **-oes**) circle or disc of light shown round the head of a sacred figure; corona. —v.t. surround with a halo.

halogen n. any of a group of certain non-metallic elements.

halt n. & v.t./i. stop.

halter n. strap round the head of a horse for leading or fastening it.

halting a. slow and hesitant, limping.

halve v.t. divide or share equally between two; reduce by half.

halyard n. rope for raising or lowering a sail or flag.

ham n. upper part of a pig's leg, dried and salted or smoked; meat from this; back of thigh; (*sl.*) poor actor or performer; (*sl.*) operator of an amateur radio station. —*v.t./i.* (*p.t.* **hammed**) (*sl.*) overact. **ham-fisted** *a.*, **ham-handed** *a.* (*sl.*) clumsy.

hamburger *n.* flat round cake of minced beef.

hamlet *n.* small village.

hammer *n.* tool with a heavy metal head for breaking things or driving nails in; thing shaped or used like this; metal ball attached to a wire for throwing as an athletic contest. —*v.t./i.* hit or beat with a hammer; strike loudly. **hammer and tongs** with great energy and noise. **hammer-toe** *n.* toe permanently bent downwards.

hammock *n.* hanging bed of canvas or netting.

hamper[1] *n.* basketwork packing-case; selection of food packed as a gift.

hamper[2] *v.t.* prevent free movement or activity of, hinder.

hamster *n.* small rodent with cheek-pouches for carrying grain.

hamstring *n.* tendon at the back of a knee or hock. —*v.t.* (*p.t.* **hamstrung**) crippled by cutting hamstring(s); cripple the activity of.

hand *n.* end part of the arm, below the wrist; control, influence, or help in doing something; pledge of marriage; manual worker, member of a ship's crew; style of handwriting; signature; pointer on a dial etc.; (right or left) side; unit of 4 inches as a measure of a horse's height; round of a card-game, player's cards; (*colloq.*) applause. —*v.t.* give or pass by hand or otherwise. **at hand** close by. **hand-out** *n.* thing distributed free of charge. **hands down** easily. **hands on** requiring manual operation of controls etc. **on**

hand available. **on one's hands** resting on one as a responsibility. **out of hand** out of control; without delay. **to hand** within reach.

handbag *n.* bag to hold a purse and small personal articles; travelling-bag.

handbill *n.* printed notice circulated by hand.

handbook *n.* small book giving useful facts.

handcuff *n.* metal ring linked to another, for securing a prisoner's wrists. —*v.t.* put handcuffs on.

handful *n.* quantity that fills the hand; a few; (*colloq.*) person difficult to control, difficult task.

handicap *n.* disadvantage imposed on a superior competitor to equalize chances; race etc. in which handicaps are imposed; thing that makes progress difficult or lessens the chance of success; physical or mental disability. —*v.t.* (*p.t.* **handicapped**) impose or be a handicap on. **handicapped** *a.* suffering from a physical or mental disability. **handicapper** *n.*

handicraft *n.* work needing skill with the hands and artistic design.

handiwork *n.* thing made or done by the hands or by a named person.

handkerchief *n.* (*pl.* -**fs**) small square of cloth for wiping the nose etc.

handle *n.* part by which a thing is to be held, carried, or controlled. —*v.t.* touch or move with the hands; deal with; manage; deal in.

handlebar *n.* steering-bar of a bicycle etc.

handler *n.* person in charge of a trained dog etc.

handmaid, handmaiden *ns.* (*old use*) female servant.

handrail *n.* rail beside stairs etc.

handshake n. act of shaking hands as a greeting etc.

handsome a. good-looking; generous; (of a price etc.) very large.

handspring n. somersault involving a handstand.

handstand n. balancing on one's hands with feet in the air.

handwriting n. writing by hand with pen or pencil; style of this.

handy a. (-ier, -iest) convenient; clever with one's hands. **handily** adv., **handiness** n.

handyman n. (pl. -men) person who does odd jobs.

hang v.t./i. (p.t. hung) support or be supported from above with the lower end free; rest on hinges; stick (wallpaper) to a wall; kill or be killed by suspension from a rope that tightens round the neck (p.t. hanged); droop; remain. —n. way a thing hangs. **get the hang of** (colloq.) get the knack of, understand. **hang about** loiter. **hang back** hesitate. **hang fire** be slow in developing. **hang-glider** n. frame used in **hang-gliding**, sport of being suspended in an airborne frame controlled by one's own movements. **hang on** hold tightly; depend on; pay close attention to; remain; (sl.) wait. **hang out** (sl.) have one's home; often be present. **hang-up** n. (sl.) difficulty, inhibition.

hangar n. shed for aircraft.

hangdog a. shamefaced.

hanger n. loop or hook by which a thing is hung; shaped piece of wood etc. to hang a garment on. **hanger-on** n. person who attaches himself or herself to another for personal gain.

hangings n.pl. draperies hung on walls.

hangman n. (pl. -men) man whose job is to hang persons condemned to death.

hangnail n. agnail.

hangover n. unpleasant after-effects from drinking much alcohol; thing left from an earlier time.

hank n. coil or length of thread.

hanker v.i. crave, feel a longing.

hanky n. (colloq.) handkerchief.

hanky-panky n. (sl.) trickery.

Hansard n. official printed report of proceedings in Parliament.

hansom n. **hansom cab** (old use) two-wheeled horse-drawn carriage for hire.

Hanukkah /'hɑː-/ n. Jewish festival of lights, beginning in December.

haphazard a. done or chosen at random. **haphazardly** adv.

hapless a. unlucky.

happen v.i. occur; chance. **happen to** be the fate or experience of.

happening a. (colloq.) fashionable, exciting.

happy a. (-ier, -iest) contented, pleased; fortunate; pleasing. **happy-go-lucky** a. taking events cheerfully. **happily** adv., **happiness** n.

hara-kiri n. suicide as formerly practised by Japanese military officers.

harangue n. lengthy earnest speech. —v.t. make a harangue to.

harass /'hæ-/ v.t. worry or annoy continually; make repeated attacks on. **harassment** /'hæ-/ n.

harbinger /-dʒə/ n. person or thing whose presence announces the approach of another.

harbour n. place of shelter for ships. —v.t. give shelter or refuge to; keep (evil thoughts) in one's mind.

hard a. (-er, -est) firm, not easily cut; difficult; not easy to bear; harsh; strenuous; (of drugs) strong and addictive; (of currency) not likely to drop suddenly in value; (of drinks) strongly alcoholic; (of water) containing mineral salts that prevent soap from lathering freely. —*adv.* intensively; with difficulty; so as to be hard. **hard-boiled** *a.* (of eggs) boiled until yolk and white are set; callous. **hard by** close by. **hard copy** material produced in printed form by a computer. **hard disk** rigid usu. magnetic large-capacity storage disk. **hard-headed** *a.* shrewd and practical. **hard-hearted** *a.* unfeeling. **hard lines** worse luck than is deserved. **hard of hearing** slightly deaf. **hard sell** aggressive salesmanship. **hard shoulder** extra strip of road beside a motorway, for use in an emergency. **hard up** short of money. **hardness** *n.*

hardbitten *a.* tough and cynical.

hardboard *n.* stiff board made of compressed wood-pulp.

harden *v.t./i.* make or become hard or hardy.

hardihood *n.* boldness.

hardly *adv.* only with difficulty; scarcely.

hardship *n.* harsh circumstance.

hardware *n.* tools and household implements sold by a shop; weapons; machinery; mechanical and electronic components of a computer.

hardwood *n.* hard heavy wood of deciduous trees.

hardy *a.* (-ier, -iest) capable of enduring cold or harsh conditions. **hardiness** *n.*

hare *n.* field animal like a large rabbit. —*v.i.* run rapidly. **harebrained** *a.* wild and foolish, rash.

harebell *n.* wild plant with blue bell-shaped flowers.

harelip *n.* deformed lip with a vertical slit like that of a hare.

harem /ˈhɑːriːm/ *n.* women of a Muslim household; their apartments.

haricot bean white dried seed of a kind of bean.

hark *v.i.* listen. **hark back** return to an earlier subject.

harlequin *a.* in varied colours.

harlot *n.* (*old use*) prostitute.

harm *n.* damage, injury. —*v.t.* cause harm to. **harmful** *a.*, **harmless** *a.*

harmonic *a.* full of harmony.

harmonica *n.* mouth-organ.

harmonious *a.* forming a pleasing or consistent whole; free from disagreement or ill-feeling; sweet-sounding. **harmoniously** *adv.*

harmonium *n.* musical instrument like a small organ.

harmonize *v.t./i.* make or be harmonious; add notes to (a melody) to form chords. **harmonization** *n.*

harmony *n.* being harmonious; combination of musical notes to form chords; melodious sound.

harness *n.* straps and fittings by which a horse is controlled; similar fastenings. —*v.t.* put harness on, attach by this; control and use.

harp *n.* musical instrument with strings in a roughly triangular frame. —*v.i.* **harp on** talk tiresomely about. **harpist** *n.*

harpoon *n.* spear-like missile with a rope attached. —*v.t.* spear with a harpoon. **harpooner** *n.*

harpsichord *n.* piano-like instrument with strings sounded by mechanism that plucks them.

harpy *n.* mythical monster with a woman's head and body and bird's wings and claws; grasping unscrupulous person.

harridan *n.* bad-tempered old woman.

harrier *n.* hound used for hunting hares; a kind of falcon; (*pl.*) cross-country runners.

harrow *n.* heavy frame with metal spikes or discs for breaking up clods. —*v.t.* draw a harrow over (soil); distress greatly.

harry *v.t.* harass.

harsh *a.* (**-er, -est**) rough and dis-agreeable; severe, cruel. **harshly** *adv.*, **harshness** *n.*

hart *n.* adult male deer.

hartebeest *n.* large African antelope.

harum-scarum *a.* & *n.* wild and reckless (person).

harvest *n.* gathering of crop(s); season for this; season's yield of a natural product; product of action. —*v.t./i.* gather a crop; reap. **harvester** *n.*

has *see* **have**.

hash *n.* dish of chopped re-cooked meat; jumble. —*v.t.* make into hash. **make a hash of** (*colloq.*) make a mess of, bungle. **settle a person's hash** (*colloq.*) deal with and subdue him or her.

hashish *n.* hemp dried for chewing or smoking as a narcotic.

hasp *n.* clasp fitting over a staple, secured by a pin or padlock.

hassle *n.* & *v.i.* (*colloq.*) quarrel, struggle.

hassock *n.* thick firm cushion for kneeling on in church.

hast (*old use*, with *thou*) = **have**.

haste *n.* hurry. **make haste** hurry.

hasten *v.t./i.* hurry.

hasty *a.* (**-ier, -iest**) hurried; acting or done too quickly. **hastily** *adv.*, **hastiness** *n.*

hat *n.* covering for the head, worn out of doors. **hat trick** three successes in a row, esp. taking of three wickets by three successive balls.

hatband *n.* band of ribbon round a hat.

hatch[1] *n.* opening in a door, floor, ship's deck, etc.; its cover.

hatch[2] *v.t./i.* emerge or produce (young) from an egg; devise (a plot). —*n.* brood hatched.

hatch[3] *v.t.* mark with close parallel lines. **hatching** *n.* these marks.

hatchback *n.* sloping back of a car, hinged at the top so that it can be opened; car with this.

hatchery *n.* place for hatching eggs.

hatchet *n.* small axe. **bury the hatchet** cease quarrelling and become friendly. **hatchet-faced** *a.* having a narrow face with sharp features. **hatchet man** person employed to attack and destroy reputations.

hatchway *n.* = **hatch**[1].

hate *n.* hatred. —*v.t.* feel hatred towards; dislike greatly. **hater** *n.*

hateful *a.* arousing hatred.

hatless *a.* not wearing a hat.

hatred *n.* violent dislike or enmity.

hatter *n.* maker or seller of hats.

haughty *a.* (**-ier, -iest**) proud of oneself and looking down on others. **haughtily** *adv.*, **haughtiness** *n.*

haul *v.t.* pull or drag forcibly; transport by truck etc. —*n.* process of hauling; amount gained by effort, booty; distance to be traversed.

haulage *n.* transport of goods.

haulier *n.* person or firm whose trade is the transporting of goods by road.

haunch *n.* fleshy part of the buttock and thigh; leg and loin of meat.

haunt *v.t.* be persistently in (a place); linger in the mind of; (of a ghost) manifest its presence in (a place). —*n.* place often visited by person(s) named. **haunted** *a.*

haute couture /əʊˈts kuːˈtjʊə(r)/ high fashion.

hauteur /əʊˈtɜː(r)/ *n.* haughtiness.

have *v.t.* (3 *sing. pres.* **has**; *p.t.* **had**) possess; contain; experience, undergo; give birth to; cause to be or do or be done; engage in; allow; be under the obligation of; show (a quality); receive, accept; (*colloq.*) cheat, deceive. —*v.aux.* (used with *p.p.* to form past tenses). **have it out** settle a problem by frank discussion. **have up** bring (a person) before a court of justice. **haves**

and have-nots people with and without wealth or privilege.

haven n. refuge; harbour.

haver /'her-/ v.i. hesitate; talk foolishly.

haversack n. strong bag carried on the back or slung from a shoulder.

havoc n. great destruction or disorder.

haw[1] n. hawthorn berry.

haw[2] see **hum**[2].

hawk[1] n. bird of prey; person who favours an aggressive policy.

hawk-eyed a. having very keen sight.

hawk[2] v.i. clear one's throat of phlegm noisily.

hawk[3] v.t. carry (goods) about for sale. **hawker** n.

hawser n. heavy rope or cable for mooring or towing a ship.

hawthorn n. thorny tree or shrub with small red berries.

hay n. grass mown and dried for fodder. **hay fever** catarrh caused by pollen or dust. **make hay** seize opportunities for profit or fun.

haymaking n. mowing grass and spreading it to dry.

haystack n. regular pile of hay firmly packed for storing.

haywire a. badly disorganized.

hazard n. risk, danger; source of this; obstacle. —v.t. risk. **hazardous** a.

haze n. thin mist; mental obscurity.

hazel n. bush with small edible nuts; light brown. **hazel-nut** n.

hazy a. (-ier, -iest) misty; indistinct; vague. **hazily** adv., **haziness** n.

H-bomb n. hydrogen bomb.

he pron. male previously mentioned; person of unspecified sex. —n. male animal.

head n. part of the body containing the eyes, nose, mouth, and brain; intellect; individual person or animal; (colloq.) headache; thing like the head in form or position, top or leading part or position; signal-converting device on a tape recorder etc.; foam on beer etc.; chief person; headmaster, headmistress; body of water or steam confined for exerting pressure; **heads** side of a coin showing a head, turned upwards after being tossed. —v.t./i. be at the head or top of; strike (a ball) with one's head in football; direct one's course. **head-dress** n. ornamental covering or band worn on the head. **head-hunt** v.t. seek to recruit (senior staff) from another firm etc. **head off** force to turn by getting in front. **head-on** a. & adv. with head or front foremost. **head over heels** in a somersault. **head wind** wind blowing directly from in front.

headache n. continuous pain in the head; worrying problem.

header n. dive with the head first; heading of the ball in football.

headgear n. hat or head-dress.

heading n. word(s) at the top of printed or written matter as a title etc.; passage in a mine.

headlamp n. headlight.

headland n. promontory.

headless a. having no head.

headlight n. powerful light on the front of a vehicle etc.; its beam.

headline n. heading in a newspaper; (pl.) summary of broadcast news.

headlong a. & adv. falling or plunging with the head first; in a hasty and rash way.

headmaster, headmistress ns. principal teacher in a school, responsible for organizing it.

headphone n. receiver held over the ear(s) by a band over the head.

headquarters n.pl. place from which an organization is controlled.

headstone n. stone set up at the head of a grave.

headstrong a. self-willed and obstinate.

headway n. progress.

headword *n.* word forming a heading.

heady *a.* (**-ier**, **-iest**) likely to cause intoxication. **headiness** *n.*

heal *v.t./i.* form healthy flesh again, unite after being cut or broken; cause to do this; (*old use*) cure. **healer** *n.*

health *n.* state of being well and free from illness; condition of the body.

healthful *a.* health-giving.

healthy *a.* (**-ier**, **-iest**) having or showing or producing good health; beneficial; functioning well. **healthily** *adv.*, **healthiness** *n.*

heap *n.* a number of things or particles lying one on top of another; (usu. *pl.*, *colloq.*) plenty. —*v.t./i.* pile or become piled in a heap; load with large quantities.

hear *v.t./i.* (*p.t.* **heard**) perceive (sounds) with the ear; listen, pay attention to; listen to and try (a lawsuit); receive information or a letter etc. **hear! hear!** I agree. **not hear of** refuse to allow. **hearer** *n.*

hearing *n.* ability to hear; opportunity of being heard, trial of a lawsuit. **hearing-aid** *n.* small sound-amplifier worn by a deaf person to improve the hearing.

hearken *v.i.* (*old use*) listen.

hearsay *n.* things heard in rumour.

hearse *n.* vehicle for carrying the coffin at a funeral.

heart *n.* muscular organ that keeps blood circulating by contracting rhythmically; centre of a person's emotions, affections, or inmost thoughts; courage; enthusiasm; central part; symmetrical figure representing a heart; playing-card of the suit marked with these. **break the heart of** cause overwhelming grief to. **by heart** memorized thoroughly. **heart attack** sudden failure of the heart to function normally. **heart-searching** *n.* examination

of one's own feelings and motives. **heart-to-heart** *a.* frank and personal. **heart-warming** *a.* emotionally moving and encouraging.

heartache *n.* mental pain, sorrow.

heartbeat *n.* pulsation of the heart.

heartbreak *n.* overwhelming grief.

heartbroken *a.* broken-hearted.

heartburn *n.* burning sensation in the lower part of the chest.

heartburning *n.* jealousy.

hearten *v.t.* cause to feel encouraged.

heartfelt *a.* felt deeply, sincere.

hearth *n.* floor of a fireplace; fireside.

hearthrug *n.* rug laid in front of a fireplace.

heartless *a.* not feeling pity or sympathy. **heartlessly** *adv.*

heartsick *a.* despondent.

heartstrings *n.pl.* one's deepest feelings of love or pity.

heartthrob *n.* (*colloq.*) object of romantic affection.

hearty *a.* (**-ier**, **-iest**) vigorous; showing warmth of feeling, enthusiastic; (of meals) large. **heartily** *adv.*, **heartiness** *n.*

heat *n.* form of energy produced by movement of molecules; sensation produced by this, hotness; intense feeling, anger; preliminary contest. —*v.t./i.* make or become hot. **heat wave** period of very hot weather.

heated *a.* (of a person or discussion) angry. **heatedly** *adv.*

heater *n.* device supplying heat.

heath *n.* flat uncultivated land with low shrubs; small shrubby plant of the heather kind.

heathen *n.* person who is neither Christian, Jewish, Muslim, nor Buddhist. **heathenish** *a.*

heather *n.* evergreen plant with purple, pink, or white flowers.

heatstroke *n.* illness caused by overexposure to sun.

heave v.t./i. lift or haul with great effort; utter (a sigh); (colloq.) throw; rise and fall like waves at sea; pant, retch. —n. act of heaving. **heave in sight** (p.t. **hove**) come into view. **heave to** (p.t. **hove**) come or bring (a ship) to a standstill with head to wind.

heaven n. abode of God; place or state of supreme bliss; **the heavens** the sky as seen from the earth.

heavenly a. of heaven, divine; of or in the heavens; (colloq.) very pleasing.

heavy a. (-ier, -iest) having great weight; of more than average weight or force or intensity; dense; stodgy; serious in tone, dull and tedious. **heavy-hearted** a. sad. **heavy industry** that producing metal or heavy machines etc. **heavy metal** (colloq.) a kind of loud rock music. **heavy water** deuterium oxide. **heavily** adv., **heaviness** n.

heavyweight n. a having great weight or influence. —n. heavyweight person; heaviest boxing-weight.

Hebrew n. & a. (member) of a Semitic people in ancient Palestine; (of) their language or a modern form of this. **Hebraic** a.

heckle v.t. interrupt (a public speaker) with aggressive questions and abuse. **heckler** n.

hectare /-tea:(r)/ n. unit of area, 10,000 sq. metres (about 2¼ acres).

hectic a. with feverish activity. **hectically** adv.

hectogram n. 100 grams.

hector v.t. intimidate by bullying.

hedge n. fence of bushes or shrubs; barrier. —v.t./i. surround with a hedge; make or trim hedges; protect oneself against loss on (a bet etc.); avoid giving a direct answer or commitment.

hedgehog n. small animal with a back covered in stiff spines.

hedgerow n. bushes etc. forming a hedge.

hedonist /'hi:-/ n. person who believes pleasure is the chief good. **hedonism** n., **hedonistic** a.

heed v.t. pay attention to. —n. careful attention. **heedful** a., **heedless** a., **heedlessly** adv.

hee-haw n. & v.i. bray.

heel[1] n. back part of the human foot; part of a stocking or shoe covering or supporting this; (sl.) dishonourable man. —v.t. make or repair the heel(s) of; kick (a ball) with the heel. **down at heel** shabby. **take to one's heels** run away.

heel[2] v.t./i. tilt (a ship) or become tilted to one side. —n. this tilt.

hefty a. (-ier, -iest) large and heavy. **heftily** adv., **heftiness** n.

hegemony /hɪ'ge-/ n. leadership, esp. by one country.

Hegira /'hedʒ-/ n. Muhammad's flight from Mecca (AD 622), from which the Muslim era is reckoned.

heifer /'hef-/ n. female calf.

height n. measurement from base to top or head to foot; distance above ground or sea level; high place; highest degree of something.

heighten v.t./i. make or become higher or more intense.

heinous /'heɪ-/ a. very wicked.

heir /eə(r)/ n. person entitled to inherit property or a rank etc. **heir apparent** legal heir whose claim cannot be set aside by the birth of another heir. **heir presumptive** 'one whose claim may be set aside thus.

heiress /'eər-/ n. female heir, esp. to great wealth.

heirloom /'eər-/ n. possession handed down in a family for several generations.

heist n. (US sl.) robbery. —v.t. (US sl.) rob.

held see **hold**[1].

helical /'hel-/ a. like a helix.

helicopter n. aircraft with blades that revolve horizontally.

heliograph /'hi:-/ n. signalling apparatus reflecting flashes of sunlight. —v.t. send (a message) by this.

heliotrope /'hi:-/ n. plant with small purple flowers; light purple.

heliport n. helicopter station.

helium /'hi:-/ n. light colourless gas that does not burn.

helix /'hi:-/ n. (pl. **-ices**) spiral.

hell n. place of punishment for the wicked after death; place or state of supreme misery. **hell-bent** a. recklessly determined. **hell for leather** at great speed.

hellebore /'hel-/ n. plant with white or greenish flowers.

Hellene /'hel-/ n. Greek person.

Hellenistic a. of Greece in the 4th–1st centuries BC.

hello int. & n. exclamation used in greeting or to call attention.

helm n. tiller or wheel by which a ship's rudder is controlled.

helmet n. protective head-covering.

helmsman n. (pl. **-men**) person controlling a ship's helm.

helot n. serf.

help v.t./i. do part of another's work; be useful (to); make easier; prevent; serve with food. —n. act of helping; person or thing that helps. **help oneself** to take without seeking assistance or permission. **helper** n.

helpful a. giving help, useful. **helpfully** adv., **helpfulness** n.

helping n. portion of food served.

helpless a. unable to manage without help; powerless. **helplessly** adv., **helplessness** n.

helpline n. telephone service providing help with problems.

helpmate n. helper.

helter-skelter adv. in disorderly haste. —n. spiral slide at a fun-fair.

hem n. edge of (cloth) turned under and sewn down or fixed down. —v.t. (p.t. **hemmed**) sew thus.

hem in or **round** surround and restrict.

hemisphere n. half a sphere; half the earth, esp. as divided by the equator or a line through the poles. **hemispherical** a.

hemlock n. poisonous plant.

hemp n. plant with coarse fibres used in making rope and cloth; narcotic drug made from it.

hempen a. made of hemp.

hemstitch v.t. & n. (sew a hem with) a kind of ornamental stitching.

hen n. female bird, esp. of the domestic fowl. **hen-party** n. (colloq.) party of women only.

hence adv. from this time; for this reason; (old use) from here.

henceforth, **henceforward** advs. from this time on, in future.

henchman n. (pl. **-men**) trusty supporter.

henna n. reddish dye used esp. on the hair; tropical plant from which it is obtained. **hennaed** a.

henpecked a. nagged by his wife.

henry n. unit of inductance.

hepatic a. of the liver.

hepatitis n. inflammation of the liver.

heptagon n. geometric figure with seven sides. **heptagonal** a.

heptathlon n. athletic contest involving seven events.

her pron. objective case of she. —a. belonging to her.

herald n. officer in former times who made State proclamations; person or thing heralding something; official of the corporation (**Heralds' College**) concerned with pedigrees and coats of arms. —v.t. proclaim the approach of.

heraldic /-'ræl-/ a. of heralds or heraldry.

heraldry n. study of armorial bearings.

herb n. plant with a soft stem that dies down to the ground after flowering; one used in making medicines or flavourings.

herbaceous a. of or like herbs.
 herbaceous border border containing esp. perennial plants.
herbage n. herbs; pasturage.
herbal a. of herbs. —n. book about herbs.
herbalist n. dealer in medicinal herbs.
herbarium n. collection of plants.
herbicide n. substance used to destroy unwanted vegetation. **herbicidal** a.
herbivore n. herbivorous animal.
herbivorous /-'brv-/ a. feeding on plants.
herculean /-'li:-/ a. needing or showing great strength or effort.
herd n. group of animals feeding or staying together; mob. —v.t./i. gather, stay, or drive as a group; tend (a herd). **herdsman** n.
here adv. in, at, or to this place; at this point. —n. this place.
hereabouts adv. near here.
hereafter adv. from now on. —n. the future; the next world.
hereby adv. by this act or decree etc.
hereditable a. able to be inherited.
hereditary a. inherited; holding a position by inheritance.
heredity n. inheritance of characteristics from parents.
herein adv. in this place or book etc.
heresy n. opinion contrary to accepted beliefs; holding of this.
heretic n. person who holds a heresy. **heretical** /-'ret-/ a., **heretically** adv.
hereto adv. to this
herewith adv. with this.
heritable a. able to be inherited or inherit.
heritage n. thing(s) inherited.
hermaphrodite /-'mæ-/ n. creature with male and female sexual organs.
hermetic a. with airtight closure. **hermetically** adv.
hermit n. person living in solitude.
hermitage n. hermit's dwelling.

hernia n. abnormal protrusion of part of an organ through the wall of the cavity (esp. the abdomen) containing it.
hero n. (pl. **-oes**) man admired for his brave deeds; chief male character in a story etc.
heroic a. very brave. **heroics** n.pl. over-dramatic behaviour. **heroically** adv.
heroin n. powerful drug prepared from morphine.
heroine n. female hero.
heroism n. heroic conduct.
heron n. long-legged wading-bird.
heronry n. place where herons breed.
herpes /'h3:pi:z/ n. virus disease causing blisters.
Herr /heə(r)/ n. (pl. **Herren**) title of a German-speaking man.
herring n. North Atlantic fish much used for food. **herringbone** n. zigzag pattern or arrangement.
hers poss.pron. belonging to her.
herself pron. emphatic and reflexive form of she and her.
hertz n. (pl. **hertz**) unit of frequency of electromagnetic waves.
hesitant a. hesitating. **hesitantly** adv., **hesitancy** n.
hesitate v.i. pause in doubt; be reluctant, scruple. **hesitation** n.
hessian n. strong coarse cloth of hemp or jute.
het a. **het up** (colloq.) excited, agitated.
heterodox a. not orthodox.
heterogeneous a. made up of people or things of various sorts. **heterogeneity** n.
heterosexual a. & n. (person) sexually attracted to people of the opposite sex. **heterosexuality** n.
heuristic a. finding out, investigating. **heuristically** adv.
hew v.t. (p.p. **hewn**) chop or cut with an axe etc.; cut into shape.
hexagon n. geometric figure with six sides. **hexagonal** a.
hexameter /-'sæm-/ n. line of verse with six metrical feet.

hey *int.* exclamation of surprise or inquiry, or calling attention. **hey presto!** conjuror's formula, calling attention.

heyday *n.* time of greatest success.

hi *int.* exclamation calling attention or (*US*) greeting.

hiatus *n.* (*pl.* **-tuses**) break or gap in a sequence or series.

hibernate *v.i.* spend the winter in sleep-like state. **hibernation** *n.*

Hibernian *a.* & *n.* (native) of Ireland.

hibiscus *n.* shrub or tree with trumpet-shaped flowers.

hiccup *n.* cough-like stopping of breath. —*v.i.* (*p.t.* **hiccuped**) make this sound.

hick *n.* (*US*) yokel.

hickory *n.* tree related to the walnut; its wood.

hide[1] *v.t./i.* (*p.t.* **hid**, *p.p.* **hidden**) put or keep out of sight; keep secret; conceal oneself. —*n.* camouflaged shelter. **hidden agenda** ulterior motive. **hide-out** *n.* (*colloq.*) hiding-place.

hide[2] *n.* animal's skin.

hidebound *a.* rigidly conventional.

hideous *a.* very ugly. **hideously** *adv.*, **hideousness** *n.*

hiding *n.* (*colloq.*) thrashing.

hie *v.i.* & *refl.* go quickly.

hierarchy /ˈhaɪ-/ *n.* system with grades of status. **hierarchical** *a.*

hieroglyph /ˈhaɪ-/ *n.* pictorial symbol used in ancient Egyptian and other writing. **hieroglyphic** *a.*, **hieroglyphics** *n.pl.*

hi-fi *a.* & *n.* (*colloq.*) high fidelity, (equipment) reproducing sound with little or no distortion.

higgledy-piggledy *a.* & *adv.* in complete confusion.

high *a.* (**-er, -est**) extending far or a specified distance upwards; far above ground or sea level; ranking above others; extreme, greater than normal; (of sound or a voice) with rapid vibrations, not deep or low; (of meat) slightly decomposed; (*sl.*) intoxicated, esp. by drugs. —*n.* high level; area of high pressure. —*adv.* in, at, or to a high level. **High Church** section of the Church of England giving an important place to ritual and the authority of priests. **High Commission** embassy from one Commonwealth country to another. **higher education** education above the level given in schools. **high explosive** that with a violently shattering effect. **high-handed** *a.* using authority arrogantly. **high priest** chief priest. **high-rise** *a.* with many storeys. **high road** main road. **high school** secondary (*usu.* grammar) school. **high sea(s)** sea outside territorial waters. **high season** busiest season. **high-speed** *a.* operating at great speed. **high-spirited** *a.* lively. **high spot** (*sl.*) important place or feature. **high street** principal shopping-street. **high tea** evening meal with tea and cooked food. **high tech, high technology** advanced technology, esp. in electronics. **high-water mark** level reached by the tide at its highest level.

highball *n.* (*US*) drink of spirits and soda served in a tall glass.

highbrow *a.* very intellectual, cultured. —*n.* highbrow person.

highfalutin *a.* (*colloq.*) pompous.

highlands *n.pl.* mountainous region. **highland** *a.*, **highlander** *n.*

highlight *n.* bright or light area in a picture; best or most outstanding feature; bright tint in hair. —*v.t.* emphasize.

highly *adv.* in a high degree, extremely; very favourably. **highly-strung** *a.* (of a person) easily upset.

Highness *n.* title of a prince or princess.

highway *n.* public road; main route.

highwayman *n.* (*pl.* **-men**) man

(usu. on horseback) who formerly robbed passing travellers.

hijack *v.t.* seize control illegally of (a vehicle or aircraft in transit). —*n.* hijacking. **hijacker** *n.*

hike *n.* long walk. —*v.i.* go for a hike. **hiker** *n.*

hilarious /-'leər-/ *a.* noisily merry; extremely funny. **hilariously** *adv.*, **hilarity** /-'læ-/ *n.*

hill *n.* raised part of earth's surface, less high than a mountain; slope in a road etc.; mound. **hillbilly** *n.* (*US*) rustic person; folk music like that of the southern USA.

hillock *n.* small hill, mound.

hillside *n.* sloping side of a hill.

hilly *a.* full of hills.

hilt *n.* handle of a sword or dagger. **to the hilt** completely.

him *pron.* objective case of *he.*

Himalayan /-'leɪ-/ *a.* of the Himalaya Mountains.

himself *pron.* emphatic and reflexive form of *he* and *him.*

hind[1] *n.* female deer.

hind[2] *a.* situated at the back.

hinder[1] /'hɪn-/ *v.t.* delay progress of.

hinder[2] /'haɪ-/ *a.* = hind[2].

Hindi *n.* a form of Hindustani; group of spoken languages of northern India.

hindmost *a.* furthest behind.

hindrance *n.* thing that hinders; hindering, being hindered.

hindsight *n.* wisdom about an event after it has occurred.

Hindu *n.* person whose religion is Hinduism. —*a.* of Hindus.

Hinduism *n.* a religion and philosophy of India.

Hindustani *n.* language of much of northern India and Pakistan.

hinge *n.* movable joint such as that on which a door or lid turns. —*v.t./i.* attach or be attached to hinge(s). **hinge on** depend on.

hint *n.* slight indication, suggestion made indirectly; small piece of practical information. —*v.i.* make a hint.

hinterland *n.* district behind a coast etc. or served by a port or other centre.

hip[1] *n.* projection of the pelvis on each side of body. **hipped** *a.*

hip[2] *n.* fruit of wild rose.

hip[3] *int.* introducing a cheer.

hip[4] *a.* (*sl.*) stylish; well-informed.

hip hop type of Black youth culture and pop music.

hippie *n.* young person who adopts an unconventional style of dress and living-habits.

hippopotamus *n.* (*pl.* **-muses**) large African river-animal with tusks and a thick skin.

hire *v.t.* engage or grant temporary use of, for payment. —*n.* hiring. **hire purchase** system by which a thing becomes the hirer's after a number of payments. **hirer** *n.*

hireling *n.* (*derog.*) hired helper.

hirsute /'hɜ:-/ *a.* hairy, shaggy.

his *a.* & *poss.pron.* belonging to him.

Hispanic *a.* & *n.* (native) of Spain or a Spanish-speaking country.

hiss *n.* sound like 's'. —*v.t./i.* make this sound; utter with a hiss; express disapproval in this way.

histamine /-mɪn/ *n.* substance present in the body and causing some allergic reactions.

histology *n.* study of organic tissues. **histological** *a.*

historian *n.* expert in or writer of history.

historic *a.* famous in history.

historical *a.* of or concerned with history. **historically** *adv.*

historicity *n.* historical truth or authenticity.

historiography *n.* writing of history; study of this. **historiographer** *n.*

history *n.* past events; methodical record of these; study of past events; story. **make history** do something memorable.

histrionic *a.* of acting; theatrical in manner. **histrionics** *n.pl.* theatricals; theatrical behaviour.

hit v.t./i. (p.t. **hit**, pres.p. **hitting**) strike with a blow or missile, come forcefully against; have a bad effect upon (a person etc.); come to, find, encounter. —n. blow, stroke; shot that hits its target; success. **hit it off** get on well with a person. **hit list** (sl.) list of prospective victims. **hit off** represent exactly. **hit on** discover. **hit-or-miss** a. aimed or done carelessly. **hitter** n.

hitch v.t./i. move (a thing) with a slight jerk; fasten or be fastened with a loop or hook etc.; hitchhike, obtain (a lift) in this way. —n. slight jerk; noose or knot of various kinds; temporary stoppage, snag. **get hitched** (sl.) get married.

hitchhike v.i. travel by begging lifts in vehicles. **hitchhiker** n.

hi-tech n. high tech(nology).

hither adv. to or towards this place. **hither and thither** to and fro.

hitherto adv. until this time.

HIV abbr. human immunodeficiency virus (causing Aids).

hive n. container for bees to live in; bees living in this. —v.t./i. **hive off** separate from a larger group. **hive of industry** place full of people working busily.

hives n.pl. skin eruption, esp. nettle-rash.

ho int. exclamation of triumph or scorn, or calling attention.

hoard v.t. save and store away. —n. things hoarded. **hoarder** n.

hoarding n. fence of boards, often bearing advertisements.

hoar-frost n. white frost.

hoarse a. (-er, -est) (of a voice) sounding rough as if from a dry throat; having such a voice. **hoarsely** adv., **hoarseness** n.

hoary a. (-ier, -iest) grey with age; (of a joke etc.) old.

hoax v.t. deceive jokingly. —n. joking deception. **hoaxer** n.

hob n. metal shelf on the side of a grate, where a pan can be kept

hot; top of a cooker, with hotplates.

hobble v.t./i. walk lamely; fasten the legs of (a horse) to limit its movement. —n. hobbling walk; rope etc. for hobbling a horse.

hobby n. thing done often and for pleasure in one's spare time.

hobby-horse n. figure of a horse used in a morris dance; stick with a horse's head, as a toy; rocking-horse; favourite topic.

hobgoblin n. mischievous or evil spirit.

hobnail n. heavy-headed nail for boot-soles. **hobnailed** a.

hobnob v.i. (p.t. **-nobbed**) spend time together in a friendly way.

hock[1] n. middle joint of an animal's hind leg.

hock[2] n. German white wine.

hock[3] v.t. (US sl.) pawn. **in hock** in pawn; in debt; in prison.

hockey n. field-game played with curved sticks and a small hard ball; ice hockey.

hocus-pocus n. trickery.

hod n. trough on a pole for carrying mortar or bricks; container for shovelling and holding coal.

hoe n. tool for loosening soil or scraping up weeds. —v.t./i. (pres.p. **hoeing**) dig or scrape with a hoe.

hog n. castrated male pig reared for meat; (colloq.) greedy person. —v.t. (p.p. **hogged**) (colloq.) take greedily; hoard selfishly.

hogmanay n. (Sc.) New Year's Eve.

hogshead n. large cask; measure of beer (usu. about 50 gallons).

hoick v.t. (colloq.) lift or bring out, esp. with a jerk. —n.

hoi polloi /-ˈlɔɪ/ ordinary people.

hoist v.t. raise or haul up. —n. apparatus for hoisting things; pull or haul.

hoity-toity a. haughty.

hokey-pokey n. (sl.) trickery.

hokum n. (sl.) bunkum.

hold[1] v.t./i. (p.t. **held**) keep in one's arms or hands etc. or in one's possession or control; keep in a position or condition; contain; bear the weight of; remain unbroken under strain; continue; occupy; cause to take place; believe. —*n.* act, manner, or means of holding; means of exerting influence. **get hold of** acquire; make contact with. **hold forth** speak lengthily. **hold one's tongue** be or keep silent. **hold out** offer; last; continue to make a demand. **hold over** postpone. **hold up** hinder; stop and rob by use of threats or force. **hold-up** *n.* delay; stoppage and robbery. **hold water** (of reasoning) be sound. **hold with** (*colloq.*) approve of. **holder** *n.*

hold² *n.* storage cavity below a ship's deck.

holdall *n.* large soft travel-bag.

holding *n.* something held or owned; land held by an owner or tenant.

hole *n.* hollow place; burrow; aperture; wretched place; (*sl.*) awkward situation. —*v.t.* make hole(s) in; send (a golf-ball) into the hole. **hole-and-corner** *a.* underhand. **hole up** (*US colloq.*) hide oneself.

holey *a.* full of holes.

holiday *n.* day(s) of recreation. —*v.i.* spend a holiday.

holiness *n.* being holy; **His Holiness** title of the pope.

holistic *a.* (of treatment) involving the mind, body, social factors, etc.

holland *n.* a kind of (esp. unbleached) linen.

hollandaise /-'deɪz/ *n.* creamy sauce of butter, egg-yolks, and vinegar.

hollow *a.* empty within, not solid; sunken; echoing as if in something hollow; worthless. —*n.* hollow or sunken place; valley. —*adv.* completely. —*v.t.* make hollow. **hollowly** *adv.*, **hollowness** *n.*

holly *n.* evergreen shrub with prickly leaves and red berries.

hollyhock *n.* plant with large flowers on a tall stem.

holm-oak /'həʊm-/ *n.* evergreen oak.

holocaust *n.* large-scale destruction, esp. by fire.

hologram *n.* photographic pattern giving a three-dimensional image when projected.

holograph¹ *v.t.* record as a hologram. **holography** *n.*

holograph² *a.* & *n.* (document) written wholly in the handwriting of the person in whose name it appears.

holster *n.* leather case holding a pistol or revolver.

holy *a.* (-ier, -iest) belonging or devoted to God and reverenced; consecrated. **holy of holies** most sacred place. **Holy Ghost, Holy Spirit** third person of the Trinity. **Holy Week** week before Easter Sunday. **Holy Writ** the Bible.

homage *n.* things said or done as a mark of respect or loyalty.

Homburg *n.* man's stiff felt hat with a narrow curved brim.

home *n.* place where one lives; dwelling-house; institution where those needing care may live; place to be reached by a runner or in certain games. —*a.* of one's home or country; played on one's own ground. —*adv.* at or to one's home; to the point aimed at. —*v.i.* make its way home or to a target. **Home Counties** those nearest London. **Home Office** British government department dealing with law and order in England and Wales. **Home Secretary** minister in charge of this. **home truth** unpleasant truth about oneself.

homeland *n.* native land.

homeless *a.* lacking a dwelling. **homelessness** *n.*

homely a. (-ier, -iest) simple and informal; (US) plain, not beautiful. **homeliness** n.

homer n. homing pigeon.

Homeric a. of or in the style of the Greek poet Homer.

homesick a. longing for home.

homespun a. & n. (fabric) made of yarn spun at home.

homestead n. house (esp. a farmhouse) with surrounding land and buildings. **homesteader** n.

homeward a. & adv. going towards home. **homewards** adv.

homework n. work set for a pupil to do away from school.

homicide n. killing of one person by another. **homicidal** a.

homily n. moralizing lecture. **homiletic** a., **homiletics** n.pl.

homing a. (of a pigeon) trained to fly home from a distance.

hominid a. & n. (member) of the family of existing and fossil man.

homoeopathy /həʊmɪ'ɒp-/ n. treatment of a disease by very small doses that in a healthy person would produce its symptoms. **homoeopathic** /-'pæ-/ a.

homogeneous /-'dʒiːn-/ a. of the same kind, uniform. **homogeneously** adv., **homogeneity** /-'niːɪ-/ n.

homogenize /-'mɒdʒ-/ v.t. treat (milk) so that cream does not separate and rise to top. **homogenization** n.

homologous /-'mɒ-/ a. having the same relation or value, corresponding. **homology** n.

homonym /'hɒm-/ n. word with the same spelling as another.

homophobia n. fear of homosexuals.

homophone /'hɒm-/ n. word with the same sound as another.

homosexual a. & n. (person) sexually attracted only to people of the same sex. **homosexuality** n.

Hon. abbr. Honourable; Honorary.

hone v.t. sharpen on a whetstone.

honest a. truthful, trustworthy; fairly earned. **honest-to-goodness** a. (colloq.) real, straightforward. **honestly** adv., **honesty** n.

honey n. (pl. **-eys**) sweet substance made by bees from nectar; its yellowish colour; sweetness, pleasantness; darling. **honeybee** n. common bee living in a hive. **honeyed** a.

honeycomb n. bees' wax structure for holding their honey and eggs; pattern of six-sided sections. —v.t. fill with holes or tunnels.

honeydew melon melon with pale skin and sweet green flesh.

honeymoon n. holiday spent together by a newly married couple; initial period of goodwill. —v.i. spend a honeymoon.

honeysuckle n. climbing shrub with fragrant pink and yellow flowers.

honk n. noise like the cry of a wild goose or the sound of an old-style motor horn. —v.i. make this noise.

honorarium /ɒnə'reər-/ n. (pl. **-ums**) voluntary payment for services where no fee is legally required.

honorary a. given as an honour; unpaid.

honorific a. & n. (title) implying respect. **honorifically** adv.

honour n. great respect or public regard; mark of this, privilege; good personal character or reputation; title of respect, esp. given to certain judges. —v.t. feel honour for; confer honour on; acknowledge and pay (a cheque) or fulfil (a promise etc.).

honourable a. deserving, possessing, or showing honour; **Honourable** a courtesy title. **honourably** adv.

hood[1] n. covering for the head and neck, esp. forming part of a garment; hood-like thing over a car, folding roof over a car. **hooded** a.

hood[2] n. (US) gangster, gunman.

hoodlum *n.* hooligan, young thug.

hoodwink *v.t.* deceive.

hoof *n.* (*pl.* **hoofs** *or* **hooves**) horny part of a quadruped's foot.

hook *n.* bent or curved piece of metal etc. for catching hold or hanging things on; thing shaped like this; curved cutting-tool; hooking movement, short blow made with the elbow bent. —*v.t./i.* grasp, catch, or fasten with hook(s); scoop or propel with a curving movement. **by hook or by crook by** some means no matter what. **hook it** (*sl.*) run away. **hook-up** *n.* interconnection. **off the hook** freed from a difficulty. **hooker** *n.*

hookah *n.* oriental tobacco-pipe with a long tube passing through water.

hooked *a.* hook-shaped. **hooked on** (*sl.*) addicted to.

hookey *n.* **play hookey** (*US sl.*) play truant.

hookworm *n.* parasitic worm, male of which has hook-like spines.

hooligan *n.* young ruffian. **hooliganism** *n.*

hoop *n.* circular band; metal arch used in croquet. **go or be put through the hoops** undergo a test or ordeal. **hooped** *a.*

hoop-la *n.* game in which rings are thrown to encircle a prize.

hoopoe *n.* bird with a crest and striped plumage.

hooray *int.* & *n.* =hurrah.

hoot *n.* owl's cry; sound of a hooter; cry of scorn or disapproval; (*colloq.*) laughter, cause of this. —*v.t./i.* make or cause to make a hoot.

hooter *n.* siren or steam-whistle used as a signal; car horn.

Hoover *n.* [P.] a kind of vacuum cleaner. **hoover** *v.t.* clean with a vacuum cleaner.

hop[1] *v.t./i.* (*p.t.* **hopped**) jump on one foot or (of an animal) from both or all feet; (*colloq.*) make a quick short trip. —*n.* hopping movement; informal dance; short flight. **hop in** *or* **out** (*colloq.*) get into or out of a car. **hop it** (*sl.*) go away. **on the hop** (*colloq.*) unprepared.

hop[2] *n.* plant cultivated for its cones (**hops**) which are used to give a bitter flavour to beer.

hope *n.* feeling of expectation and desire; person or thing giving cause for this; what one hopes for.—*v.t./i.* feel hope. **hopeful** *a.*, **hopefully** *adv.*

hopeless *a.* without hope; inadequate, incompetent. **hopelessly** *adv.*, **hopelessness** *n.*

hopper *n.* one who hops; container with an opening at its base through which its contents can be discharged.

hopsack *n.* a kind of coarsely woven fabric.

hopscotch *n.* game involving hopping over marked squares.

horde *n.* large group or crowd.

horizon *n.* line at which earth and sky appear to meet; limit of knowledge or interests.

horizontal *a.* parallel to the horizon, going straight across. **horizontally** *adv.*

hormone *n.* secretion (or synthetic substance) that stimulates an organ or growth. **hormone replacement therapy** treatment with oestrogens to alleviate menopausal symptoms. **hormonal** *a.*

horn *n.* hard pointed growth on the heads of certain animals; substance of this; similar projection; wind instrument with a trumpet-shaped end; device for sounding a warning signal. —*v.t.* cut off the horns of; gore with horn(s). **horn in** (*sl.*) intrude, interfere. **horn-rimmed** *a.* with frames of material like horn or tortoiseshell.

hornbeam *n.* hedgerow tree with tough wood.

hornblende n. dark mineral constituent of granite etc.

horned a. having horns.

hornet n. a kind of large wasp.

hornpipe n. lively solo dance esp. associated with sailors.

horny a. (-**ier**, -**iest**) of or like horn; hardened and calloused. **horniness** n.

horology n. art of making clocks etc. **horologist** n.

horoscope n. astrologer's diagram of relative positions of stars; forecast of events, based on this.

horrendous a. horrifying. **horrendously** adv.

horrible a. causing horror; (colloq.) unpleasant. **horribly** adv.

horrid a. horrible.

horrific a. horrifying. **horrifically** adv.

horrify v.t. arouse horror in, shock.

horror n. loathing and fear; intense dislike or dismay; person or thing causing horror. **horror-stricken**, **horror-struck** adjs. horrified.

hors-d'œuvre /ɔː'dɜːvr/ n. food served as an appetizer.

horse n. quadruped with a mane and tail; frame for hanging things on; padded structure for vaulting over in a gymnasium. —v.i. (colloq.) fool, play. **horse chestnut** brown shiny nut; tree bearing this. **horse sense** (colloq.) common sense.

horseback n. **on horseback** riding on a horse.

horsebox n. closed vehicle for transporting a horse.

horsehair n. hair from a horse's mane or tail, used for padding furniture.

horseman n. (pl. -**men**) rider on horseback. **horsewoman** n.fem. (pl. -**women**), **horsemanship** n.

horseplay n. boisterous play.

horsepower n. unit for measuring the power of an engine.

horseradish n. plant with a hot-tasting root used to make sauce.

horseshoe n. U-shaped strip of metal nailed to a horse's hoof.

horsy a. of or like a horse; interested in horses and horse-racing.

hortatory /'hɔː-/ adj. exhorting.

horticulture n. art of garden cultivation. **horticultural** a., **horticulturist** n.

hosanna int. & n. cry of adoration to God and the Messiah.

hose n. hose-pipe; stockings and socks. —v.t. water or spray with a hose-pipe. **hose-pipe** n. flexible tube for conveying water.

hosiery n. stockings, socks, etc.

hospice n. lodging for travellers; home for destitute or sick people.

hospitable /'hɒs- or -'pɪt-/ a. giving hospitality. **hospitably** adv.

hospital n. institution for treatment of sick or injured people. **hospital trust** hospital that has opted to withdraw from local authority control.

hospitality n. friendly and generous entertainment of guests.

hospitalize v.t. send or admit to a hospital. **hospitalization** n.

host[1] n. large number of people or things; (old use) army.

host[2] n. person who entertains another as his guest; organism on which another lives as a parasite. —v.t. act as host to.

host[3] n. bread consecrated for the Eucharist.

hostage n. person held as security that the holder's demands will be satisfied.

hostel n. lodging-house for students or other special group.

hostelry n. (old use) inn.

hostess n. woman host.

hostile a. of an enemy; unfriendly. **hostilely** a.

hostility n. being hostile, enmity; (pl.) acts of warfare.

hot a. (**hotter**, **hottest**) at or having a high temperature; producing a burning sensation to the taste; eager, angry; excited, excitable; (of scent in hunting) fresh and strong; (of news) fresh; (*colloq.*) very skilful; (of jazz) strongly rhythmical and emotional; (*sl.*) radioactive; (*sl.*, of goods) recently stolen and risky to handle. —*v.t./i.* (*p.t.* hotted) (*collog.*) make or become hot or exciting. **hot air** (*sl.*) excited or boastful talk. **hot dog** hot sausage in a bread roll. **hot line** direct line of communication. **hot-water bottle** container filled with hot water for warmth in bed. **in hot water** (*colloq.*) in trouble.

hotbed *n.* place favourable to the growth of something evil.

hotchpotch *n.* jumble.

hotel *n.* building where meals and rooms are provided for travellers.

hotelier *n.* hotel-keeper.

hotfoot *adv.* in eager haste.

hothead *n.* impetuous person.

hotheaded *a.* impetuous.

hothouse *n.* heated greenhouse.

hotplate *n.* heated surface on which food is heated or kept hot.

hotpot *n.* stew of meat, potatoes, and vegetables.

Hottentot *n.* member of a negroid people of South Africa.

hotting *n.* practice of driving recklessly in a stolen car.

hound *n.* dog used in hunting. —*v.t.* pursue, harass; urge, incite.

hour *n.* one twenty-fourth part of a day and night; point of time; occasion; (*pl.*) period for daily work; (*pl.*) prayers said at any of seven fixed times of day.

hourglass *n.* glass containing sand that takes one hour to trickle from upper to lower section through a narrow opening.

houri /'hʊərɪ/ *n.* (*pl.* -is) beautiful young woman of the Muslim paradise.

hourly *a.* done or occurring once an hour; continual. —*adv.* every hour.

house[1] /-s/ *n.* building for people (usu. one family) to live in, or for a particular purpose; household; legislative assembly; business firm; theatre audience or performance; family, dynasty; each of twelve astrological divisions of the heavens. **house arrest** detention in one's own home. **house-proud** *a.* giving great attention to the appearance of one's home. **house-sit** *v.i.* live in and look after house in owner's absence. **house surgeon** surgeon resident at a hospital. **house-trained** *a.* trained to be clean in the house. **house-warming** *n.* party to celebrate occupation of a new home.

house[2] /-z/ *v.t.* provide accommodation or storage-space for; encase.

houseboat *n.* barge-like boat fitted up as a dwelling.

housebound *a.* unable to leave one's house through illness etc.

housebreaker *n.* burglar; person employed in demolition of houses. **housebreaking** *n.*

housecoat *n.* woman's long dress-like garment for informal wear.

household *n.* occupants of a house living as a family. **household troops** those nominally employed to guard the sovereign. **household word** familiar saying or name.

householder *n.* person owning or renting a house or flat.

housekeeper *n.* person employed to look after a household.

housekeeping *n.* management of household affairs; money to be used for this.

housemaid *n.* woman servant in a house, esp. one who cleans rooms.

housemaster, housemistress *ns.* teacher in charge of a school boarding-house.

housewife *n.* woman managing a household. **housewifely** *adv.*

housewifery /-wɪf-/ *n.* housekeeping.

housework n. cleaning and cooking etc. done in housekeeping.

housing n. accommodation; rigid case enclosing machinery.

hove see **heave**.

hovel n. small miserable dwelling.

hover v.i. (of a bird etc.) remain in one place in the air; linger, wait close at hand. **hover-fly** n. wasplike insect that hovers.

hovercraft n. (pl. **-craft**) vehicle supported by air thrust downwards from its engines.

how adv. by what means, in what way; to what extent or amount etc.; in what condition. **how about** what is your feeling about (this thing). **how do you do** formal greeting. **how-d'ye-do** n. (colloq.) awkward state of affairs. **how many** what total. **how much** what amount or price.

howdah n. seat, usu. with a canopy, on an elephant's back.

however adv. in whatever way, to whatever extent; nevertheless.

howitzer n. short gun firing shells at high elevation.

howl n. long loud wailing cry or sound. —v.t./i. make or utter with a howl; weep loudly.

howler n. one that howls; (colloq.) stupid mistake.

hoyden n. girl who behaves boisterously. **hoydenish** a.

h.p. abbr. hire-purchase; horsepower.

HRH abbr. His or Her Royal Highness.

hub n. central part of a wheel; central point of activity. **hub-cap** n. cover for the hub of a car wheel.

hubble-bubble n. hookah.

hubbub n. confused noise of voices.

hubby n. (colloq.) husband.

hubris /'hju:-/ n. arrogant pride.

huckaback n. rough-surfaced fabric for towels etc.

huckleberry n. low shrub common in North America; its fruit.

huckster n. hawker; mercenary person. —v.i. haggle; be a hawker.

huddle v.t./i. crowd into a small place. —n. close mass.

hue¹ n. colour.

hue² n. **hue and cry** outcry.

huff n. fit of annoyance. —v.i. blow. **huffy** a. **huffily** adv.

hug v.t. (p.t. **hugged**) squeeze tightly in one's arms; keep close to. —n. hugging movement.

huge a. extremely large. **hugely** adv., **hugeness** n.

hugger-mugger n. & adv. full of secrecy; in disorder.

hula n. Hawaiian women's dance. **hula hoop** large hoop for spinning round the body.

hulk n. body of an old ship; large clumsy-looking person or thing.

hulking a. (colloq.) large and clumsy.

hull¹ n. framework of a ship.

hull² n. pod of a pea or bean; cluster of leaves on a strawberry. —v.t. remove the hull of.

hullabaloo n. uproar.

hullo int. = hello.

hum v.t./i. (p.t. **hummed**) sing with closed lips; make a similar sound; (colloq.) be in state of activity; (sl.) smell bad. —n. humming sound; (sl.) bad smell. **hum and ha** or **haw** hesitate.

human a. of mankind; of persons. —n. human being. **humanly** adv.

humane /-'mem/ a. kind-hearted, merciful. **humanely** adv.

humanism n. system of thought concerned with human affairs and ethics (not theology); promotion of human welfare. **humanist** n., **humanistic** a.

humanitarian a. promoting human welfare and reduction of suffering. **humanitarianism** n.

humanity n. human nature or qualities; kindness; human race; (pl.) arts subjects.

humanize v.t. make human; make humane. **humanization** n.

humble a. (**-er**, **-est**) having or showing a modest estimate of one's own importance; of low rank; not large or expensive. —v.t. lower the rank or self-importance of. **eat humble pie** make a humble apology. **humbly** adv., **humbleness** n.

humbug n. misleading behaviour or talk to win support or sympathy; person behaving thus; hard usu. peppermint-flavoured boiled sweet. —v.t. (p.t. **humbugged**) delude.

humdinger n. (sl.) remarkable person or thing.

humdrum n. dull, commonplace.

humerus n. (pl. **-ri**) bone of the upper arm. **humeral** a.

humid a. (of air) damp. **humidity** n.

humidify v.t. keep (air) moist in a room etc. **humidifier** n.

humiliate v.t. cause to feel disgraced. **humiliation** n.

humility n. humble condition or attitude of mind.

hummock n. hump in the ground.

humoresque n. light and lively musical composition.

humorist n. person noted for his humour.

humour n. quality of being amusing; ability to perceive and enjoy this; state of mind. —v.t. keep (a person) contented by doing as he or she wishes. **humorous** a., **humorously** adv.

hump n. rounded projecting part; curved deformity of the spine; **the hump** (sl.) fit of depression or annoyance. —v.t. form into a hump; hoist and carry. **humped** a.

humpback n. hunchback. **humpback bridge** small steeply arched bridge.

humus /ˈhjuː-/ n. soil-fertilizing substance formed by decay of dead leaves and plants etc.

hunch v.t./i. bend into a hump. —n. hump; hunk; intuitive feeling.

hunchback n. person with a hump back.

hundred n. ten times ten (100, C). **hundredth** a. & n.

hundredfold a. & adv. 100 times as much or as many.

hundredweight n. measure of weight, 112 lb or (**metric hundredweight**) 50 kg (110.25 lb).

hung see **hang**. —**hung-over** a. (colloq.) having a hangover.

Hungarian a. & n. (native, language) of Hungary.

hunger n. uneasy sensation felt when one has not eaten for some time; strong desire. —v.i. feel hunger. **hunger strike** refusal of food as a form of protest.

hungry a. (**-ier**, **-iest**) feeling hunger. **hungrily** adv.

hunk n. large or clumsy piece.

hunt v.t./i. pursue (wild animals) for food or sport; pursue with hostility; use (a horse or hounds) in hunting; seek; search; (of an engine) run fast and slow alternately. —n. process of hunting; hunting district or group.

hunter n. one who hunts; horse used for hunting; watch with a hinged cover over the dial. **huntress** n.fem.

huntsman n. (pl. **-men**) hunter.

hurdle n. portable frame with bars, used as a temporary fence; frame to be jumped over in a race; obstacle, difficulty. **hurdler** n.

hurdy-gurdy n. musical instrument with a droning sound, played by turning a handle; (colloq.) barrel-organ.

hurl v.t. throw violently. —n. violent throw.

hurley n. Irish game resembling hockey.

hurly-burly n. rough bustle.

hurrah, hurray int. & n. exclamation of joy or approval.

hurricane n. violent storm-wind. **hurricane lamp** lamp with the flame protected from the wind.

hurried a. done with great haste. **hurriedly** adv.

hurry *v.t./i.* act or move with eagerness or too quickly; cause to do this. —*n.* hurrying.

hurt *v.t./i.* (*p.t.* **hurt**) cause pain, harm, or injury to; cause or feel pain. —*n.* injury, harm. **hurtful** *a.*

hurtle *v.t./i.* move or hurl rapidly.

husband *n.* married man in relation to his wife. —*v.t.* use economically, try to save.

husbandry *n.* farming; management of resources.

hush *v.t./i.* make or become silent or quiet. —*n.* silence. **hush-hush** *a.* (*colloq.*) kept very secret. **hush up** suppress information about.

husk *n.* dry outer covering of certain seeds and fruits. —*v.t.* remove the husk from.

husky[1] *a.* (**-ier, -iest**) dry; hoarse; burly. **huskily** *adv.*, **huskiness** *n.*

husky[2] *n.* Eskimo dog.

hussar /-'zɑ:(r)/ *n.* light-cavalry soldier.

hussy *n.* cheeky young woman.

hustings *n.* parliamentary election proceedings.

hustle *v.t./i.* push roughly; hurry. —*n.* hustling. **hustler** *n.*

hut *n.* small simple or roughly made house or shelter.

hutch *n.* box-like pen for rabbits.

hyacinth *n.* plant with fragrant bell-shaped flowers.

hybrid *n.* offspring of two different species or varieties; thing made by combining different elements. —*a.* produced in this way. **hybridism** *n.*

hybridize *v.t./i.* cross-breed; produce hybrids; interbreed. **hybridization** *n.*

hydra *n.* thing hard to get rid of; water-snake; freshwater polyp.

hydrangea *n.* shrub with pink, blue, or white flowers in clusters.

hydrant *n.* pipe from a water-main (esp. in a street) to which a hose can be attached.

hydrate *n.* chemical compound of water with another substance.

hydraulic *a.* of water etc. conveyed through pipes or channels; involving water-power; hardening under water. **hydraulics** *n.* science of hydraulic operations. **hydraulically** *adv.*

hydro *n.* (*pl.* **-os**) hotel etc. providing hydrotherapy; hydroelectric power-plant.

hydrocarbon *n.* compound of hydrogen and carbon.

hydrochloric acid /-'klɔ:r-/ corrosive acid containing hydrogen and chlorine.

hydrodynamic *a.* of the forces exerted by liquids in motion. **hydrodynamics** *n.* science of these forces.

hydroelectric *a.* using water-power to produce electricity.

hydrofoil *n.* boat with a structure that raises its hull out of the water when the boat is in motion; this structure.

hydrogen *n.* odourless gas, the lightest element. **hydrogen bomb** powerful bomb releasing energy by fusion of hydrogen nuclei.

hydrolysis /-'drɒl-/ *n.* decomposition by chemical reaction with water. **hydrolytic** /-'lɪt-/ *a.*

hydrometer /-'drɒm-/ *n.* instrument measuring the density of liquids.

hydropathy /-'drɒp-/ *n.* hydrotherapy. **hydropathic** *a.*

hydrophobia *n.* abnormal fear of water, esp. as a symptom of rabies; rabies.

hydroponics /-'pɒn-/ *n.* art of growing plants in water impregnated with chemicals.

hydrostatic *a.* of the pressure and other characteristics of liquid at rest. **hydrostatics** *n.* science of this.

hydrotherapy *n.* use of water to treat diseases etc.

hydrous *a.* containing water.

hyena *n.* wolf-like animal with a howl that sounds like laughter.

hygiene *n.* cleanliness as a means of preventing disease. **hygienic**

a., **hygienically** *adv.*, **hygienist** *n.*

hygrometer /-'grɒm-/ *n.* instrument measuring humidity.

hygroscopic *a.* absorbing moisture from the air.

hymen *n.* membrane partly closing the opening of the vagina of a virgin girl or woman.

hymenopterous *a.* of the group of insects with four membranous wings.

hymn *n.* song of praise to God or a sacred being. **hymn-book** *n.* book of hymns.

hymnal *n.* hymn-book.

hyoscine /-si:n/ *n.* alkaloid used as a sedative etc.

hyper- *pref.* excessively.

hyperactive *a.* abnormally active. **hyperactivity** *n.*

hyperbola /-'pɜ:-/ *n.* a kind of curve. **hyperbolic** /-'bɒl-/ *a.*

hyperbole /-'pɜ:bəlɪ/ *n.* rhetorical exaggeration. **hyperbolical** /-'bɒl-/ *a.*

hypermarket *n.* very large self-service store selling a wide variety of goods and services.

hypersonic *a.* of speeds more than five times that of sound.

hypertension *n.* abnormally high blood-pressure; extreme tension.

hypertrophy *n.* abnormal enlargement due to excessive nutrition. **hypertrophic** *a.*

hyphen *n.* the sign - used to join words together or divide a word into parts. —*v.t.* hyphenate.

hyphenate *v.t.* join or divide with a hyphen. **hyphenation** *n.*

hypnosis *n.* sleep-like condition produced in a person who then obeys suggestions; production of this.

hypnotic *a.* of or producing hypnosis or a similar condition; producing sleep. —*n.* drug producing sleep. **hypnotically** *adv.*

hypnotism *n.* hypnosis.

hypnotize *v.t.* produce hypnosis in; fascinate, dominate the mind or will of. **hypnotist** *n.*

hypocaust /'haɪ-/ *n.* ancient Roman system of under-floor heating by hot air.

hypochondria /-'kɒn-/ *n.* state of constantly imagining that one is ill. **hypochondriac** *n.* person suffering from this.

hypocrisy *n.* falsely pretending to be virtuous; insincerity.

hypocrite *n.* person guilty of hypocrisy. **hypocritical** *a.*, **hypocritically** *adv.*

hypodermic *a.* injected beneath the skin; used for such injections. —*n.* hypodermic syringe.

hypotenuse /-'pɒt-/ *n.* longest side of a right-angled triangle.

hypothermia *n.* condition of having an abnormally low body-temperature.

hypothesis /-'pɒθ-/ *n.* (*pl.* **-theses**) supposition put forward as a basis for reasoning or investigation.

hypothesize *v.t./i.* form (as) a hypothesis.

hypothetical *a.* supposed but not necessarily true. **hypothetically** *adv.*

hyssop *n.* small bushy fragrant herb.

hysterectomy *n.* surgical removal of the womb.

hysteria *n.* wild uncontrollable emotion. **hysterical** *a.*, **hysterically** *adv.*

hysterics *n.pl.* hysterical outburst.

Hz *abbr.* hertz.

I

I *pron.* person speaking or writing and referring to himself or herself.

iambic *a.* & *n.* (verse) using iambuses, metrical feet of one long and one short syllable.

iatrogenic *a.* (of disease) caused unintentionally by medical treatment etc.

Iberian *a.* of the peninsula comprising Spain and Portugal.

ibex *n.* (*pl.* **ibex** or **ibexes**) mountain goat with curving horns.

ibis /'aɪ-/ *n.* wading bird found in warm climates.

ice *n.* frozen water, brittle transparent solid; portion of icecream. —*v.t./i.* become frozen; make very cold; decorate with icing. **ice-cream** *n.* sweet creamy frozen food. **ice dancing** iceskating to choreographed dance moves, esp. in pairs. **ice hockey** game like hockey played on ice by skaters. **ice lolly** water-ice or icecream on a stick.

iceberg *n.* mass of ice floating in the sea.

Icelandic *a.* & *n.* (language) of Iceland.

ichneumon /'ɪknju-/ *n.* mongoose of North Africa etc. **ichneumon fly** insect parasitic on others.

ichthyology /ɪkθɪ-/ *n.* study of fishes. **ichthyologist** *n.*

icicle *n.* hanging ice formed when dripping water freezes.

icing *n.* mixture of powdered sugar etc. used to decorate food.

icon /'aɪkɒn/ *n.* (in the Eastern Church) sacred painting or mosaic; (in computing) graphic symbol on a computer screen.

iconoclast /aɪ'kɒn-/ *n.* person who attacks cherished beliefs. **iconoclasm** *n.,* **iconoclastic** *a.*

iconography /-'nɒg-/ *n.* representation of a subject etc. in pictures; study of this.

icy *a.* (**-ier, -iest**) very cold; covered with ice; very unfriendly. **icily** *adv.,* **iciness** *n.*

id *n.* mind's instinctive impulses.

idea *n.* plan etc. formed in the mind by thinking; opinion; mental impression; vague belief.

ideal *a.* satisfying one's idea of what is perfect. —*n.* person or thing regarded as perfect or as a standard to aim at. **ideally** *adv.*

idealist *n.* person with high ideals. **idealism** *n.,* **idealistic** *a.*

idealize *v.t.* regard or represent as perfect. **idealization** *n.*

identical *a.* the same; exactly alike. **identically** *adv.*

identify *v.t./i.* recognize as being a specified person or thing; consider to be identical; associate (oneself) closely in feeling or interest. **identifiable** *a.,* **identification** *n.*

identikit *n.* set of pictures of features that can be put together to form a likeness.

identity *n.* who or what a person or thing is; sameness.

ideogram, ideograph /'ɪdɪ-/ *ns.* symbol indicating the idea of a thing.

ideology /aɪdɪ-/ *n.* ideas that form the basis of a political or economic theory. **ideological** *a.*

idiocy *n.* state of being an idiot; extreme foolishness.

idiom *n.* phrase or usage peculiar to a language; characteristic expression in art or music.

idiomatic *a.* in accordance with or full of idioms. **idiomatically** *adv.*

idiosyncrasy /-'sɪŋk-/ *n.* person's own characteristic way of behaving. **idiosyncratic** /-'kræt-/ *a.*

idiot *n.* very stupid person.

idiotic *a.* very stupid. **idiotically** *adv.*

idle *a.* (**-er, -est**) doing no work; not employed or in use; lazy; having no special purpose. —*v.t./i.* be idle, pass (time) without working; (of an engine) run slowly in neutral gear. **idly** *adv.,* **idleness** *n.,* **idler** *n.*

idol *n.* image worshipped as a god; idolized person or thing.

idolatry /-'dɒl-/ *n.* worship of idols. **idolater** *n.,* **idolatrous** *a.*

idolize *v.t.* love or admire excessively. **idolization** *n.*

idyll /'ɪdɪl/ *n.* peaceful or romantic scene or incident; description of this, usu. in verse. **idyllic** /-'dɪl-/ *a.*, **idyllically** *adv.*

i.e. *abbr.* (Latin *id est*) that is.

if *conj.* on condition that; supposing that; whether; used in exclamations of wish or surprise. —*n.* condition, supposition.

igloo *n.* Eskimo's snow hut.

igneous *a.* (of rock) formed by volcanic action.

ignite *v.t./i.* set fire to; catch fire.

ignition *n.* igniting; mechanism producing a spark to ignite the fuel in an engine.

ignoble *a.* not noble in character, aims, or purpose. **ignobly** *adv.*

ignominy /'ɪg-/ *n.* disgrace, humiliation. **ignominious** /-'mɪn-/ *a.*, **ignominiously** *adv.*

ignoramus /-'reɪ-/ *n.* (*pl.* -**muses**) ignorant person.

ignorant *a.* lacking knowledge; behaving rudely through not knowing good manners. **ignorantly** *adv.*, **ignorance** *n.*

ignore *v.t.* take no notice of.

iguana /ɪ'gwɑː-/ *n.* tropical tree-climbing lizard.

iguanodon *n.* large herbivorous dinosaur.

il -*pref.* see **in-**.

ileostomy /ɪlɪ'ɒs-/ *n.* opening made surgically in the surface of the abdomen, through which the small intestine can empty.

ileum *n.* part of the small intestine.

ilk *a.* (Sc.) same. —*n.* (*colloq.*) kind. **of that ilk** of the ancestral estate with the same name.

ill *a.* unwell; bad; harmful; hostile, unkind. —*adv.* badly. —*n.* evil, harm, injury. **ill-advised** *a.* unwise. **ill at ease** uncomfortable, embarrassed. **ill-bred** *a.* ill-mannered. **ill-gotten** *a.* gained by evil or unlawful means. **ill-mannered** *a.* having bad manners. **ill-natured** *a.* unkind. **ill-starred** *a.* unlucky. **ill-treat** *v.t.* treat badly or cruelly. **ill will** hostility, unkind feeling.

illegal *a.* against the law. **illegally** *adv.*, **illegality** *n.*

illegible *a.* not legible. **illegibly** *adv.*, **illegibility** *n.*

illegitimate *a.* born of parents not married to each other; contrary to a law or rule. **illegitimately** *adv.*, **illegitimacy** *n.*

illicit /-'lɪs-/ *a.* unlawful, not allowed. **illicitly** *adv.*

illiterate *a.* unable to read and write; uneducated. **illiteracy** *n.*

illness *n.* state of being ill; particular form of ill health.

illogical *a.* not logical. **illogically** *adv.*, **illogicality** *n.*

illuminate *v.t.* light up; throw light on (a subject); decorate with lights; decorate (a manuscript) with coloured designs. **illuminant** *n.*, **illumination** *n.*, **illuminator** *n.*

illumine *v.t.* light up; enlighten.

illusion *n.* false belief; thing wrongly supposed to exist. **illusive** *a.*

illusionist *n.* conjuror.

illusory *a.* based on illusion, not real.

illustrate *v.t.* supply (a book etc.) with drawings or pictures; make clear by example(s) or picture(s) etc.; serve as an example of. **illustration** *n.*, **illustrator** *n.*

illustrative /'ɪl-/ *a.* serving as an illustration or example.

illustrious *a.* distinguished.

im- *pref.* see **in-**.

image *n.* statue; optical appearance of a thing produced in a mirror or through a lens; likeness; mental picture; general reputation. —*v.t.* picture.

imagery *n.* images; metaphorical language evoking mental pictures.

imaginable *a.* able to be imagined.

imaginary *a.* existing only in the imagination, not real.

imagination *n.* imagining; ability to imagine or to plan creatively. **imaginative** a., **imaginatively** adv.

imagine v.t. form a mental image of; think, suppose; guess.

imago /-'meɪ-/ n. (pl. **-gines**) insect in its fully developed adult stage.

imam /ɪ'mɑːm/ n. Muslim spiritual leader.

imbalance n. lack of balance.

imbecile /-siːl/ n. stupid person. —a. idiotic. **imbecilic** a., **imbecility** n.

imbibe v.t. drink; absorb into the mind.

imbroglio /-'brəʊ-/ n. (pl. **-os**) confused situation, usu. with disagreement.

imbue v.t. fill with feelings, qualities, or emotions.

imitable a. able to be imitated.

imitate v.t. try to act or be like; copy. **imitation** n., **imitator** n.

imitative a. imitating.

immaculate a. free from stain, blemish, or fault. **immaculately** adv., **immaculacy** n.

immanent a. having no physical substance; of no importance.

immaterial a. having no physical substance; of no importance.

immature a. not mature. **immaturity** n.

immeasurable a. not measurable, immense. **immeasurably** adv., **immeasurability** n.

immediate a. with no delay; nearest, with nothing between. **immediately** adv. & conj., **immediacy** n.

immemorial a. existing from before what can be remembered.

immense a. extremely great. **immensely** adv., **immensity** n.

immerse v.t. put completely into liquid; absorb deeply in thought or business etc.

immersion n. immersing. **immersion heater** electric heating element designed to be placed in the liquid to be heated.

immigrate v.i. come into a foreign country as a permanent resident. **immigrant** a. & n., **immigration** n.

imminent a. about to occur. **imminently** adv., **imminence** n.

immobile a. immovable; not moving. **immobility** n.

immobilize v.t. make or keep immobile. **immobilization** n.

immoderate a. excessive, lacking moderation. **immoderately** adv., **immoderation** n.

immodest a. not modest. **immodestly** adv., **immodesty** n.

immolate v.t. kill as a sacrifice. **immolation** n.

immoral a. morally wrong. **immorally** adv., **immorality** n.

immortal a. living for ever, not mortal; famous for all time. —n. immortal being. **immortality** n.

immortalize v.t. make immortal. **immortalization** n.

immovable a. unable to be moved; unyielding. **immovably** adv., **immovability** n.

immune a. having immunity.

immunity n. ability to resist infection; special exemption.

immunize v.t. make immune to infection. **immunization** n.

immunodeficiency n. reduction in normal resistance to infection.

immunology n. study of resistance to infection. **immunological** a., **immunologist** n.

immure v.t. imprison, shut in.

immutable a. unchangeable. **immutably** adv., **immutability** n.

imp n. small devil; mischievous child.

impact[1] /'ɪm-/ n. collision, force of this; strong effect.

impact[2] /-'pæ-/ v.t. press or wedge firmly. **impaction** n.

impair v.t. damage, weaken. **impairment** n.

impala /-'pɑː-/ n. (pl. **impala**) small antelope.

impale v.t. fix or pierce with a pointed object. **impalement** n.

impalpable a. intangible. **impalpably** adv.

impart *v.t.* give; make (informa-tion etc.) known.

impartial *a.* not favouring one more than another. **impartially** *adv.*, **impartiality** *n.*

impassable *a.* impossible to tra-vel on or over.

impasse /'æmpɑːs/ *n.* deadlock.

impassioned *a.* passionate.

impassive *a.* not feeling or show-ing emotion. **impassively** *adv.*

impatient *a.* feeling or showing lack of patience; intolerant. **im-patiently** *adv.*, **impatience** *n.*

impeach *v.t.* accuse of a serious crime against the State and bring for trial; disparage. **impeach-ment** *n.*

impeccable *a.* faultless. **impec-cably** *adv.*, **impeccability** *n.*

impecunious *a.* having little or no money. **impecuniosity** *n.*

impedance *n.* resistance of an electric circuit to the flow of cur-rent.

impede *v.t.* hinder.

impediment *n.* hindrance, ob-struction; lisp or stammer.

impedimenta *n.pl.* encum-brances, baggage.

impel *v.t.* (*p.t.* **impelled**) urge; drive forward.

impending *a.* imminent.

impenetrable *a.* unable to be penetrated. **impenetrably** *adv.*, **impenetrability** *n.*

impenitent *a.* not penitent. **im-penitently** *adv.*, **impenitence** *n.*

imperative *a.* expressing a com-mand; essential. —*n.* command; essential thing. **imperatively** *adv.*

imperceptible *a.* not perceptible; too slight to be noticed. **imper-ceptibly** *adv.*

imperfect *a.* not perfect; (of a tense) implying action going on but not completed. **imperfectly** *adv.*, **imperfection** *n.*

imperial *a.* of an empire or em-peror or empress; majestic; (of measures) belonging to the Brit-ish official non-metric system. **imperially** *adv.*

imperialism *n.* policy of having or extending an empire. **imperi-alist** *n.*, **imperialistic** *a.*

imperil *v.t.* (*p.t.* **imperilled**) en-danger.

imperious *a.* commanding, bossy. **imperiously** *adv.*, **imper-iousness** *n.*

impermanent *a.* not permanent.

impermeable *a.* not permeable. **impermeability** *n.*

impersonal *a.* not showing or in-fluenced by personal feeling; not involving a person. **impersonally** *adv.*, **imperson-ality** *n.*

impersonate *v.t.* pretend to be (another person). **impersona-tion** *n.*, **impersonator** *n.*

impertinent *a.* not showing proper respect. **impertinently** *adv.*, **impertinence** *n.*

imperturbable *a.* not excitable, calm. **imperturbably** *adv.*, **im-perturbability** *n.*

impervious *a.* **impervious to** not able to be penetrated or in-fluenced by. **imperviousness** *n.*

impetigo /-'taɪ-/ *n.* contagious skin disease causing spots.

impetuous *a.* acting or done on impulse or with sudden energy. **impetuously** *adv.*, **impetuosity** *n.*

impetus *n.* moving force.

impiety *n.* lack of reverence.

impinge *v.i.* make an impact; en-croach. **impingement** *n.*

impious /'ɪmpɪ-/ *a.* not reverent, wicked. **impiously** *adv.*

impish *a.* of or like an imp.

implacable *a.* not able to be pla-cated, relentless. **implacably** *adv.*, **implacability** *n.*

implant[1] /-'plɑː-/ *v.t.* plant, insert, insert (tissue) in a living thing. **implantation** *n.*

implant[2] /'ɪm-/ *n.* implanted tis-sue.

implausible *a.* not plausible. **im-plausibly** *adv.*, **implausibility** *n.*

implement[1] *n.* tool.

implement² *v.t.* put into effect. **implementation** *n.*

implicate *v.t.* show or cause to be concerned in a crime etc.

implication *n.* implicating; implying; thing implied.

implicit *a.* implied but not made explicit; absolute. **implicitly** *adv.*

implode *v.t./i.* burst or cause to burst inwards. **implosion** *n.*, **implosive** *a.*

implore *v.t.* request earnestly.

imply *v.t.* suggest without stating directly; mean; involve the existence or truth of.

impolite *a.* not polite. **impolitely** *adv.*, **impoliteness** *n.*

impolitic *a.* unwise; inexpedient.

imponderable *a.* not able to be estimated. —*n.* imponderable thing. **imponderably** *adv.*, **imponderability** *n.*

import¹ /-'pɔ:-/ *v.t.* bring in from abroad or from an outside source; imply. **importation** *n.*, **importer** *n.*

import² /'im-/ *n.* importing; thing imported; meaning; importance.

important *a.* having a great effect; having great authority or influence; pompous. **importance** *n.*

importunate *a.* making persistent requests. **importunity** *n.*

importune /'im-/ *v.t.* solicit.

impose *v.t./i.* put (a tax, obligation, etc.); inflict; force acceptance of. **impose on** take unfair advantage of.

imposing *a.* impressive.

imposition *n.* act of imposing something; thing imposed; burden imposed unfairly.

impossible *a.* not possible; unendurable. **impossibly** *adv.*, **impossibility** *n.*

impost /'impəʊst/ *n.* tax, duty.

impostor *n.* person who fraudulently pretends to be someone else.

imposture *n.* fraudulent deception.

impotent *a.* powerless, unable to take action; (of a male) unable to copulate successfully or to procreate. **impotently** *adv.*, **impotence** *n.*

impound *v.t.* take (property) into legal custody; confiscate.

impoverish *v.t.* cause to become poor; exhaust the natural strength or fertility of. **impoverishment** *n.*

impracticable *a.* not practicable. **impracticability** *n.*

impractical *a.* not practical.

imprecation *n.* spoken curse.

imprecise *a.* not precise. **imprecisely** *adv.*, **imprecision** *n.*

impregnable *a.* safe against attack. **impregnability** *n.*

impregnate *v.t.* introduce sperm or pollen into and fertilize; penetrate all parts of. **impregnation** *n.*

impresario /-'sɑːr-/ *n.* (*pl.* **-os**) manager of an operatic or concert company.

impress *v.t.* cause to form a strong (usu. favourable) opinion; fix in the mind; press a mark into.

impression *n.* effect produced on the mind; uncertain idea; imitation done for entertainment; impressed mark; making of this; reprint.

impressionable *a.* easily influenced. **impressionability** *n.*

impressionism *n.* style of painting etc. giving a general impression without detail. **impressionist** *n.*, **impressionistic** *a.*

impressive *a.* making a strong favourable impression. **impressively** *adv.*, **impressiveness** *n.*

imprimatur /-'met-/ *n.* licence to print, usu. from the RC Church.

imprint¹ /'im-/ *n.* mark made by pressing on a surface; publisher's name etc. on a title-page.

imprint² /-'prınt/ *v.t.* impress or stamp a mark etc. on.

imprison *v.t.* put into prison; keep in confinement. **imprisonment** *n.*

improbable *a.* not likely to be true or to happen. **improbably** *adv.*, **improbability** *n.*

impromptu *a. & adv.* without preparation or rehearsal. —*n.* impromptu musical composition.

improper *a.* unsuitable; incorrect; not conforming to social conventions; indecent. **improper fraction** fraction greater than unity, with the numerator greater than the denominator. **improperly** *adv.*

impropriety /-'prai-/ *n.* being improper; improper act, remark, etc.

improve *v.t./i.* make or become better. **improvement** *n.*

improver *n.* person working at a trade for a low wage to improve his or her skill.

improvident *a.* not providing for future needs. **improvidently** *adv.*, **improvidence** *n.*

improvise *v.t.* compose impromptu; provide from whatever materials are at hand. **improvisation** *n.*

imprudent *a.* unwise, rash. **imprudently** *adv.*, **imprudence** *n.*

impudent *a.* impertinent, cheeky. **impudently** *adv.*, **impudence** *n.*

impugn /-'pju:n/ *v.t.* express doubts about the truth or honesty of.

impulse *n.* push, thrust; impetus; stimulating force in a nerve; sudden inclination to act, without thought for the consequences.

impulsion *n.* impelling; impulse; impetus.

impulsive *a.* acting or done on impulse. **impulsively** *adv.*, **impulsiveness** *n.*

impunity *n.* freedom from punishment or injury.

impure *a.* not pure.

impurity *n.* being impure; substance that makes another impure.

impute *v.t.* attribute (a fault etc.). **imputation** *n.*

in *prep.* having as a position or state within (limits of space, time, surroundings, etc.); having as a state or manner; into, towards. —*adv.* in a position bounded by limits, or to a point enclosed by these; inside; in fashion, season, or office; batting; (of a fire) burning; having arrived or been gathered or received. —*a.* internal; living etc. inside; fashionable. **in for** about to experience; competing in. **ins and outs** details of activity or procedure; passages. **in so far** to such an extent.

in- *pref.* (**il-** before *l*; **im-** before *b, m, p*; **ir-** before *r*) not; without, lacking.

in. *abbr.* inch(es).

inability *n.* being unable.

inaccessible *a.* not accessible.

inaccurate *a.* not accurate. **inaccurately** *adv.*, **inaccuracy** *n.*

inaction *n.* lack of action.

inactive *a.* not active. **inactivity** *n.*

inadequate *a.* not adequate; not sufficiently able. **inadequately** *adv.*, **inadequacy** *n.*

inadmissible *a.* not allowable.

inadvertent *a.* unintentional.

inadvisable *a.* not advisable.

inalienable *a.* not able to be given away or taken away. **inalienably** *adv.*, **inalienability** *n.*

inane *a.* silly, lacking sense. **inanely** *adv.*, **inanity** *n.*

inanimate *a.* lacking animal life; showing no sign of being alive.

inanition *n.* loss or lack of vitality.

inapplicable *a.* not applicable.

inapposite *a.* not apposite.

inappropriate *a.* unsuitable.

inarticulate *a.* not expressed in words; unable to speak distinctly; unable to express ideas clearly.

inartistic *a.* not artistic.

inasmuch *adv.* **inasmuch as** seeing that, because.

inattention *n.* lack of attention.

inattentive *a.* not paying attention. **inattentiveness** *n.*

inaudible *a.* not audible. **inaudibly** *adv.*, **inaudibility** *n.*

inaugural *a.* of an inauguration.

inaugurate *v.t.* admit to office ceremonially; begin (an undertaking), open (a building etc.) formally; be the beginning of. **inauguration** *n.*, **inaugurator** *n.*

inauspicious *a.* not auspicious.

inborn *a.* existing in a person or animal from birth, natural.

inbred *a.* produced by inbreeding; inborn.

inbreeding *n.* breeding from closely related individuals.

Inc. *abbr.* (US) Incorporated.

Inca *n.* member of a former American Indian people in Peru.

incalculable *a.* unable to be calculated. **incalculably** *adv.*

incandesce *v.t./i.* glow or cause to glow with heat, shine. **incandescence** *n.*, **incandescent** *a.*

incantation *n.* words or sounds uttered as a magic spell.

incapable *a.* not capable; helpless. **incapability** *n.*

incapacitate *v.t.* disable; make ineligible. **incapacitation** *n.*

incapacity *n.* inability, lack of sufficient strength or power.

incarcerate *v.t.* imprison. **incarceration** *n.*

incarnate *a.* embodied, esp. in human form.

incarnation *n.* embodiment, esp. in human form; **the Incarnation** that of God as Christ.

incautious *a.* rash. **incautiously** *adv.*

incendiary *a.* designed to cause fire. —*n.* incendiary bomb; arsonist. **incendiarism** *n.*

incense[1] /'m-/ *n.* substance burnt to produce fragrant smoke, esp. in religious ceremonies; this smoke.

incense[2] /-'sens/ *v.t.* make angry.

incentive *n.* thing that encourages an action or effort. —*a.* inciting.

inception *n.* beginning.

incertitude *n.* uncertainty.

incessant *a.* not ceasing. **incessantly** *adv.*

incest *n.* sexual intercourse between very closely related people. **incestuous** *a.*

inch *n.* measure of length (= 2.54 cm). —*v.t./i.* move gradually.

inchoate /'mkəʊət/ *a.* just begun; undeveloped.

incidence *n.* rate at which a thing occurs; falling.

incident *n.* event, esp. one causing trouble. —*a.* liable to happen; falling.

incidental *a.* occurring in connection with something; casual.

incidentally *adv.* in an incidental way; by the way.

incinerate *v.t.* burn to ashes. **incineration** *n.*, **incinerator** *n.*

incipient *a.* beginning to exist.

incise *v.t.* make a cut in; engrave. **incision** *n.*

incisive *a.* clear and decisive. **incisively** *adv.*, **incisiveness** *n.*

incisor *n.* any of the front teeth.

incite *v.t.* urge on to action; stir up. **incitement** *n.*

incivility *n.* impoliteness.

inclement *a.* (of weather) cold, wet. **inclemency** *n.*

inclination *n.* slope; bending; tendency; liking, preference.

incline[1] /-'klain/ *v.t./i.* slope; bend; have or cause to have a certain tendency, influence.

incline[2] /'m-/ *n.* slope.

include *v.t.* have or treat as part of a whole; put into a specified category. **inclusion** *n.*

inclusive *a. & adv.* including what is mentioned; including everything. **inclusively** *adv.*, **inclusiveness** *n.*

incognito /-'kɒgni-/ *a. & adv.* with one's identity kept secret. —*n.* (*pl.* -os) pretended identity.

incoherent a. rambling in speech or reasoning. **incoherently** adv., **incoherence** n.

incombustible a. not able to be burnt. **incombustibility** n.

income n. money received during a period as wages, interest, etc.

incoming a. coming in.

incommode v.t. inconvenience.

incommunicado /-'ka:-/ a. not allowed or not wishing to communicate with others.

incomparable /-'kɒm-/ a. beyond comparison, without an equal.

incompatible a. not compatible. **incompatibility** n.

incompetent a. not competent. **incompetently** adv., **incompetence** n.

incomplete a. not complete. **incompletely** adv.

incomprehensible a. not able to be understood. **incomprehension** n.

inconceivable a. unable to be imagined; (colloq.) most unlikely.

inconclusive a. not fully convincing. **inconclusively** adv.

incongruous a. unsuitable, not harmonious. **incongruously** adv., **incongruity** n.

inconsequent a. irrelevant; disconnected; not following logically. **inconsequently** adv.

inconsequential a. unimportant; inconsequent. **inconsequentially** adv.

inconsiderable a. negligible.

inconsiderate a. not considerate. **inconsiderately** adv.

inconsistent a. not consistent. **inconsistently** adv., **inconsistency** n.

inconsolable a. not able to be consoled. **inconsolably** adv.

inconspicuous a. not conspicuous. **inconspicuously** adv.

inconstant a. fickle; variable; irregular. **inconstantly** adv., **inconstancy** n.

incontestable a. indisputable. **incontestably** adv., **incontestability** n.

incontinent a. unable to control one's excretion of urine and faeces; lacking self-restraint. **incontinence** n.

incontrovertible a. indisputable. **incontrovertibly** adv., **incontrovertibility** n.

inconvenience n. lack of convenience; thing causing this. —v.t. cause inconvenience to.

inconvenient a. not convenient, slightly troublesome. **inconveniently** adv.

incorporate v.t. include as a part; form into a corporation. **incorporation** n.

incorporeal a. having no material existence.

incorrect a. not correct. **incorrectly** adv., **incorrectness** n.

incorrigible /-'kɒr-/ a. not able to be reformed. **incorrigibly** adv.

incorruptible a. not liable to decay; not corruptible morally. **incorruptibility** n.

increase[1] /-'kri:s/ v.t./i. make or become greater.

increase[2] /'ın-/ n. increasing; amount by which a thing increases.

increasingly adv. more and more.

incredible a. unbelievable. **incredibly** adv., **incredibility** n.

incredulous a. unbelieving, showing disbelief. **incredulously** adv., **incredulity** n.

increment n. increase, added amount. **incremental** a.

incriminate v.t. indicate as involved in wrongdoing. **incrimination** n., **incriminatory** a.

incrustation n. encrusting; crust or deposit formed on a surface.

incubate v.t. hatch (eggs) by warmth; cause (bacteria etc.) to develop. **incubation** n.

incubator n. apparatus for incubating eggs or bacteria; enclosed heated compartment in which a baby born prematurely can be kept.

incubus *n.* (*pl.* -**uses**) burdensome person or thing.

inculcate *v.t.* implant (a habit etc.) by constant urging. **inculcation** *n.*

inculpate *v.t.* incriminate.

incumbent *a.* forming an obligation or duty. —*n.* holder of an office; rector, vicar.

incunabula *n.pl.* early printed books, esp. from before 1501.

incur *v.t.* (*p.t.* **incurred**) bring upon oneself.

incurable *a.* unable to be cured. **incurably** *adv.*, **incurability** *n.*

incurious *a.* feeling or showing no curiosity. **incuriously** *adv.*

incursion *n.* brief invasion, raid.

indebted *a.* owing a debt.

indecent *a.* offending against standards of decency; unseemly. **indecently** *adv.*, **indecency** *n.*

indecipherable *a.* unable to be deciphered. **indecipherably** *adv.*

indecision *n.* inability to decide something, hesitation.

indecisive *a.* not decisive.

indecorous /-'dek-/ *a.* unseemly.

indeed *adv.* in truth, really.

indefatigable *a.* untiring. **indefatigably** *adv.*

indefeasible *a.* unable to be forfeited or annulled.

indefensible *a.* unable to be defended; not justifiable.

indefinable *a.* unable to be defined or described clearly. **indefinably** *adv.*

indefinite *a.* not clearly stated or fixed, vague. **indefinite article** the word 'a' or 'an'.

indefinitely *adv.* in an indefinite way; for an unlimited period.

indelible *a.* (of a mark) unable to be removed or washed away; making such a mark. **indelibly** *adv.*, **indelibility** *n.*

indelicate *a.* slightly indecent; tactless. **indelicately** *adv.*, **indelicacy** *n.*

indemnify *v.t.* provide indemnity to. **indemnification** *n.*

indemnity *n.* protection against penalties incurred by one's actions; compensation for injury.

indent[1] /-'dent/ *v.t./i.* make notches or recesses in; start inwards from a margin; place an official order (for goods etc.). **indentation** *n.*

indent[2] /'in-/ *n.* official order for goods etc.; indentation.

indenture *n.* written contract, esp. of apprenticeship. —*v.t.* bind by this.

independent *a.* not dependent on or not controlled by another person or thing; (of broadcasting) not financed by licence-fees. **independently** *adv.*, **independence** *n.*

indescribable *a.* unable to be described. **indescribably** *adv.*

indestructible *a.* unable to be destroyed. **indestructibly** *adv.*

indeterminable *a.* impossible to discover or decide.

indeterminate *a.* not fixed in extent or character.

index *n.* (*pl.* **indexes** *or* (in mathematics etc.) **indices**) list (usu. alphabetical) of names, subjects, etc., with references; figure indicating the current level of prices etc. compared with a previous level; (in mathematics) exponent. —*v.t.* make an index to; enter in an index; adjust (wages etc.) according to a price-index. **index finger** forefinger. **indexation** *n.*

Indian *a.* of India or Indians. —*n.* native of India; any of the original inhabitants of the American continent or their descendants. **Indian club** bottle-shaped club used in physical training. **Indian corn** maize. **Indian file** single file. **Indian ink** a black pigment. **Indian summer** dry sunny weather in autumn.

indiarubber *n.* rubber for rubbing out pencil or ink marks.

indicate *v.t.* point out; be a sign of; show the need of; state briefly. **indication** *n.*

indicative *a.* giving an indication; (of a form of a verb) used in statements. —*n.* this form of a verb.

indicator *n.* thing that indicates something; pointer; device on a vehicle showing that it is about to change direction.

indict /-'dart/ *v.t.* make a formal accusation against. **indictment** *n.*

indictable /-'dart-/ *a.* making or being liable to indictment.

indie *a.* colloq. independent. —*n.* independent record company etc.

indifferent *a.* showing no interest or sympathy; neither good nor bad; not very good. **indifferently** *adv.*, **indifference** *n.*

indigenous /-'dɪdʒ-/ *a.* native.

indigent /'ɪn-/ *a.* needy.

indigestible *a.* difficult or impossible to digest.

indigestion *n.* pain caused by difficulty in digesting food.

indignant *a.* feeling or showing indignation. **indignantly** *adv.*

indignation *n.* anger aroused by something unjust or wicked.

indignity *n.* unworthy treatment, humiliation.

indigo *n.* deep-blue dye or colour.

indirect *a.* not direct. **indirectly** *adv.*

indiscernible *a.* unable to be discerned. **indiscernibly** *adv.*

indiscreet *a.* revealing secrets; not cautious. **indiscreetly** *adv.*, **indiscretion** *n.*

indiscriminate *a.* not discriminating, not making a careful choice. **indiscriminately** *adv.*

indispensable *a.* essential.

indisposed *a.* slightly ill; unwilling. **indisposition** *n.*

indisputable /-'pjuː-/ *a.* undeniable. **indisputably** *adv.*

indissoluble *a.* firm and lasting, not able to be destroyed.

indistinct *a.* not distinct. **indistinctly** *adv.*, **indistinctness** *n.*

indistinguishable *a.* not distinguishable.

indite *v.t.* compose (a poem, speech, etc.); (*old use*) dictate.

individual *a.* single, separate; characteristic of one particular person or thing. —*n.* one person or animal or plant considered separately; (*colloq.*) person. **individually** *adv.*, **individuality** *n.*

individualist *n.* person who is very independent in thought or action. **individualism** *n.*

indivisible *a.* not divisible.

indoctrinate *v.t.* fill (a person's mind) with particular ideas or doctrines. **indoctrination** *n.*

Indo-European *a.* & *n.* (of) the family of languages spoken over most of Europe and in Asia as far as northern India.

indolent *a.* lazy. **indolently** *adv.*

indomitable *a.* unyielding, untiringly persistent. **indomitably** *adv.*

indoor *a.* situated, used, or done inside a building. **indoors** *adv.* inside a building.

indubitable *a.* that cannot reasonably be doubted. **indubitably** *adv.*

induce *v.t.* persuade; produce, cause; bring on (labour) artificially; infer.

inducement *n.* inducing; incentive.

induct *v.t.* install (a clergyman) ceremonially into a benefice.

inductance *n.* amount of induction of electric current.

induction *n.* inducting; inducing; reasoning (from observed examples) that a general law exists; production of an electric or magnetic state by proximity of an electrified or magnetic object; drawing of a fuel mixture into the cylinder(s) of an engine; formal introduction to a new job. **inductive** *a.*

indulge *v.t./i.* allow (a person) to have what he wishes; gratify. **indulgence** *n.*

indulgent *a.* indulging a person's wishes too freely; kind, lenient. **indulgently** *adv.*

industrial *a.* of, for, or full of industries. **industrially** *adv.*

industrialist *n.* owner or manager of an industrial business. **industrialism** *n.*

industrialized *a.* full of highly developed industries.

industrious *a.* hard-working. **industriously** *adv.*

industry *n.* manufacture or production of goods; business activity; being industrious.

inebriated /-'ni:-/ *a.* drunken. **inebriation** *n.*

inedible *a.* not edible.

ineducable *a.* incapable of being educated.

ineffable *a.* too great to be described. **ineffably** *adv.*

ineffective *a.* not effective.

ineffectual *a.* not effectual.

inefficient *a.* not efficient. **inefficiently** *adv.*, **inefficiency** *n.*

inelegant *a.* not elegant.

ineligible *a.* not eligible.

ineluctable *a.* against which it is useless to struggle.

inept *a.* unsuitable, absurd; unskilful. **ineptly** *adv.*, **ineptitude** *n.*, **ineptness** *n.*

inequality *n.* lack of equality.

inequitable /-'nek-/ *a.* unfair, unjust. **inequitably** *adv.*

ineradicable *a.* not able to be eradicated. **ineradicably** *adv.*

inert *a.* without the power of moving; without active properties; not moving or taking action. **inertly** *adv.*, **inertness** *n.*

inertia *n.* being inert; property by which matter continues in its state of rest or line of motion.

inescapable *a.* unavoidable. **inescapably** *adv.*

inessential *a.* not essential. —*n.* inessential thing.

inestimable *a.* too great or intense to be estimated. **inestimably** *adv.*

inevitable *a.* not able to be prevented, sure to happen or appear. **inevitably** *adv.*, **inevitability** *n.*

inexact *a.* not exact. **inexactly** *adv.*, **inexactitude** *n.*

inexcusable *a.* not able to be excused. **inexcusably** *adv.*

inexhaustible *a.* available in unlimited quantity.

inexorable /-'neks-/ *a.* relentless. **inexorably** *adv.*, **inexorability** *n.*

inexpedient *a.* not expedient.

inexpensive *a.* not expensive. **inexpensively** *adv.*

inexperience *n.* lack of experience. **inexperienced** *a.*

inexpert *a.* not expert, unskilful. **inexpertly** *adv.*

inexplicable /-'neks-/ *a.* unable to be explained. **inexplicably** *adv.*, **inexplicability** *n.*

in extremis /-'stri:-/ *a.* at the point of death; in great difficulties.

inextricable /-'neks-/ *a.* unable to be extricated or disentangled. **inextricably** *adv.*

infallible *a.* incapable of being wrong; never failing. **infallibly** *adv.*, **infallibility** *n.*

infamous /'mfə-/ *a.* having a bad reputation. **infamously** *adv.*, **infamy** *n.*

infancy *n.* early childhood, babyhood; early stage of development.

infant *n.* child during the earliest stage of its life.

infanta *n.* (formerly) daughter of the king of Spain or Portugal.

infanticide /-'fæ-/ *n.* killing or killer of an infant soon after its birth. **infanticidal** *a.*

infantile *a.* of infants or infancy; very childish.

infantry *n.* troops who fight on foot.

infatuated *a.* filled with intense unreasoning love. **infatuation** *n.*

infect v.t. affect or contaminate with a disease or its germs; affect with one's feeling.

infection n. infecting, being infected; disease or diseased condition.

infectious a. (of disease) able to spread by air or water; infecting others. **infectiousness** n.

infelicity n. unhappiness; inappropriate expression etc. **infelicitous** a., **infelicitously** adv.

infer v.t. (p.t. inferred) reach (an opinion) from facts or reasoning. **inference** n.

inferior a. low or lower in rank, importance, quality, or ability. —n. person inferior to another, esp. in rank. **inferiority** n.

infernal a. of hell; (colloq.) detestable, tiresome. **infernally** adv.

inferno n. (pl. -os) hell; intensely hot place; raging fire.

infertile a. not fertile. **infertility** n.

infest v.t. be numerous or troublesome in (a place). **infestation** n.

infidel /'m-/ n. person with no religious faith; opponent of a religion, esp. Christianity. **infidelity** n. unfaithfulness.

infighting n. boxing closer than at arm's length; hidden conflict within an organization.

infiltrate v.t. enter gradually and unperceived; pass or permeate by filtration. **infiltration** n., **infiltrator** n.

infinite a. having no limit; too great or too many to be measured. **infinitely** adv.

infinitesimal a. extremely small. **infinitesimally** adv.

infinitive n. form of a verb not indicating tense, number, or person (e.g. to go).

infinitude n. infinity; being infinite.

infinity n. infinite number, extent, or time.

infirm a. weak from age or illness. **infirmity** n.

infirmary n. hospital.

inflame v.t. arouse strong feeling in; cause inflammation in.

inflammable a. able to be set on fire. **inflammability** n.

inflammation n. redness and heat produced in a part of the body.

inflammatory a. arousing strong feeling or anger.

inflatable a. able to be inflated.

inflate v.t./i. fill with air or gas so as to swell; increase artificially.

inflation n. inflating; general increase in prices and fall in the purchasing power of money. **inflationary** a. causing inflation.

inflect v.t. change the pitch of (a voice) in speaking; change the ending or form of (a word) grammatically. **inflection** n., **inflectional** a.

inflexible a. not flexible; unyielding. **inflexibly** adv., **inflexibility** n.

inflexion n. = inflection. **inflexional** a.

inflict v.t. cause (a blow, penalty, etc.) to be suffered. **infliction** n.

inflow n. inward flow.

influence n. ability to produce an effect or to affect character, beliefs, or actions; person or thing with this. —v.t. exert influence on.

influential a. having great influence. **influentially** adv.

influenza n. virus disease causing fever, muscular pain, and catarrh.

influx n. inflow.

inform v.t./i. give information to; reveal secret or criminal activities to police etc. **informer** n.

informal a. not formal, without formality or ceremony. **informally** adv., **informality** n.

informant n. giver of information.

information *n.* facts told or heard or discovered.

informative *a.* giving information. **informatively** *adv.*

infra dig. (*colloq.*) beneath one's dignity.

infrared *a.* of or using radiation with a wavelength just greater than that of the red end of the visible spectrum.

infrastructure *n.* parts forming the basis of an enterprise.

infrequent *a.* not frequent. **infrequently** *adv.*, **infrequency** *n.*

infringe *v.t.* break (a rule or agreement); encroach. **infringement** *n.*

infuriate *v.t.* make very angry.

infuse *v.t.* imbue, instil; steep (tea or herbs etc.) in liquid, (of tea etc.) undergo this.

infusion *n.* infusing; liquid made by this; thing added to a stock.

ingenious *a.* clever at inventing things; cleverly contrived. **ingeniously** *adv.*, **ingenuity** *n.*

ingenuous *a.* without artfulness, unsophisticated. **ingenuously** *adv.*, **ingenuousness** *n.*

ingest *v.t.* take in as food.

inglenook *n.* nook beside a deeply recessed fireplace.

inglorious *a.* not bringing glory.

ingoing *a.* going in.

ingot *n.* oblong lump of cast metal.

ingrained *a.* deeply fixed in a surface or character.

ingratiate *v.refl.* bring (oneself) into a person's favour, esp. to gain advantage. **ingratiation** *n.*

ingratitude *n.* lack of gratitude.

ingredient *n.* one element in a mixture or combination.

ingress *n.* going in; right of entry.

ingrowing *a.* growing abnormally into the flesh.

inhabit *v.t.* live in as one's home or dwelling-place. **inhabitable** *a.*, **inhabitant** *n.*

inhalant /-'her-/ *n.* medicinal substance to be inhaled.

inhale *v.t./i.* breathe in; draw tobacco-smoke into the lungs. **inhalation** *n.*

inhaler *n.* device producing a medicinal vapour to be inhaled.

inhere *v.i.* be inherent.

inherent /-'hɪər-/ *a.* existing in a thing as a permanent quality. **inherently** *adv.*

inherit *v.t.* receive by legal right from its former owner; receive from a predecessor; derive from parents etc. **inheritance** *n.*

inhibit *v.t.* restrain, prevent; cause inhibitions in. **inhibitor** *n.*, **inhibitive** *a.*

inhibition *n.* inhibiting; resistance to an instinct, impulse, or feeling.

inhospitable /-'hɒs- *or* -'pɪt-/ *a.* not hospitable.

inhuman *a.* brutal, lacking qualities of kindness etc. **inhumanly** *adv.*, **inhumanity** *n.*

inhumane *a.* not humane. **inhumanely** *adv.*, **inhumanity** *n.*

inimical *a.* hostile. **inimically** *adv.*

inimitable *a.* impossible to imitate. **inimitably** *adv.*

iniquitous *a.* very unjust.

iniquity *n.* great injustice; wickedness.

initial *n.* first letter of a word or name. —*v.t.* (*p.t.* **initialled**) mark or sign with initials. —*a.* of the beginning. **initially** *adv.*

initiate *v.t.* cause to begin; admit into membership; give basic instruction to. —*n.* initiated person. **initiation** *n.*, **initiator** *n.*, **initiatory** *a.*

initiative *n.* first step in a process; right or power to take this; readiness to initiate things.

inject *v.t.* force or drive (a liquid etc.) into something, esp. by a syringe. **injection** *n.*

injudicious *a.* unwise. **injudiciously** *adv.*, **injudiciousness** *n.*

injunction *n.* command.

injure *v.t.* cause injury to.

injurious *a.* causing injury.

injury *n.* damage, harm; form of this; wrong or unjust act.

injustice *n.* lack of justice; unjust action or treatment.

ink *n.* coloured liquid or paste used in writing with a pen, printing, etc. —*v.t.* apply ink to. **inky** *a.*

inkling *n.* hint, slight knowledge or suspicion.

inlaid *see* **inlay**[1].

inland *a. & adv.* in or towards the interior of a country. **Inland Revenue** government department assessing and collecting taxes.

in-laws *n.pl.* (*colloq.*) one's relatives by marriage.

inlay[1] /-'leɪ/ *v.t.* (*p.t.* **inlaid**) set (one thing in another) so that the surfaces are flush and form a design.

inlay[2] /'m-/ *n.* inlaid material or design.

inlet *n.* strip of water extending into land; piece inserted; way in (e.g. for water into a tank).

inmate *n.* inhabitant, esp. of an institution.

in memoriam in memory of one who has died.

inmost *a.* furthest inward.

inn *n.* hotel, esp. in the country; public house. **Inns of Court** four law societies with exclusive right of admitting people to practise as barristers in England.

innards *n.pl.* (*colloq.*) entrails; inner parts.

innate *a.* inborn. **innately** *adv.*

inner *a.* nearer to the centre or inside; interior, internal. **inner city** central densely populated urban area.

innermost *a.* furthest inward.

innings *n.* (*pl.* **innings**) turn at batting; period of power or opportunity.

innkeeper *n.* keeper of an inn.

innocent *a.* not guilty, free of evil or wrongdoing; harmless; foolishly trustful. —*n.* innocent person. **innocently** *adv.*, **innocence** *n.*

innocuous *a.* harmless. **innocuously** *adv.* **innocuousness** *n.*

innovate *v.i.* introduce something new. **innovation** *n.*, **innovator** *n.*

innovative *a.* making innovations.

innuendo *n.* (*pl.* **-oes**) insinuation.

innumerable *a.* too many to be counted.

innumerate *a.* without knowledge of basic mathematics and science. **innumeracy** *n.*

inoculate *v.t.* protect (against disease) with vaccines or serums. **inoculation** *n.*

inoffensive *a.* not offensive.

inoperable *a.* unable to be cured by surgical operation.

inoperative *a.* not functioning.

inopportune *a.* happening at an unsuitable time. **inopportunely** *adv.*

inordinate *a.* excessive. **inordinately** *adv.*

inorganic *a.* of mineral origin, not organic. **inorganically** *adv.*

in-patient *n.* patient residing in a hospital during treatment.

input *n.* what is put in. —*v.t.* (*p.t.* **-put** *or* **-putted**) put in; supply (data etc.) to a computer.

inquest *n.* judicial investigation to establish facts esp. about a sudden death; (*colloq.*) detailed discussion of a thing that is over.

inquietude *n.* uneasiness.

inquire *v.i.* make an inquiry. **inquirer** *n.*

inquiry *n.* investigation.

inquisition *n.* detailed questioning; **the Inquisition** tribunal of the medieval RC Church, esp. in Spain, to discover heretics.

inquisitive *a.* eagerly seeking knowledge; prying. **inquisitively** *adv.*, **inquisitiveness** *n.*

inquisitor *n.* person who questions another searchingly. **inquisitorial** *a.*

inroad *n.* incursion.

inrush *n.* violent influx.

insalubrious *a.* unhealthy.

insane *a.* not sane, mad; extremely foolish. **insanely** *adv.*, **insanity** *n.*

insanitary *a.* unhygienic.

insatiable /-'seɪʃ-/ *a.* unable to be satisfied. **insatiably** *adv.*, **insatiability** *n.*

inscribe *v.t.* write or engrave.

inscription *n.* words or names inscribed on a coin, stone, etc.

inscrutable *a.* baffling, impossible to interpret. **inscrutably** *adv.*, **inscrutability** *n.*

insect *n.* small creature with six legs, no backbone, and a segmented body.

insecticide *n.* substance for killing insects.

insectivorous *a.* feeding on insects.

insecure *a.* not secure. **insecurely** *adv.*, **insecurity** *n.*

inseminate *v.t.* insert semen into. **insemination** *n.*

insensate *a.* unfeeling; stupid.

insensible *a.* unconscious; unaware; callous; imperceptible. **insensibly** *adv.*

insensitive *a.* not sensitive.

insentient *a.* inanimate.

inseparable *a.* unable to be separated or kept apart. **inseparably** *adv.*, **inseparability** *n.*

insert[1] /-'sɜːt/ *v.t.* put into or between or among. **insertion** *n.*

insert[2] /'m-/ *n.* thing inserted.

inset[1] /-'set/ *v.t.* (*p.t.* **inset**, *pres.p.* **insetting**) set or place in; decorate with an inset.

inset[2] /'m-/ *n.* thing set into a larger thing.

inshore *a.* & *adv.* near or nearer to the shore.

inside *n.* inner side, surface, or part. —*a.* of or from the inside. —*adv.* on, in, or to the inside. —*prep.* on or to the inside of; within. **inside out** with the inner side turned outwards; thoroughly.

insider *n.* person who is within an organization etc., person privy to a secret, esp. when using it to gain advantage.

insidious *a.* proceeding inconspicuously but with harmful effect. **insidiously** *adv.*, **insidiousness** *n.*

insight *n.* perception and understanding of a thing's nature.

insignia *n.pl.* symbols of authority or office; identifying badge.

insignificant *a.* unimportant. **insignificantly** *adv.*, **insignificance** *n.*

insincere *a.* not sincere. **insincerely** *adv.*, **insincerity** *n.*

insinuate *v.t.* insert gradually or craftily; hint artfully. **insinuation** *n.*, **insinuator** *n.*

insipid *a.* lacking flavour, interest, or liveliness. **insipidity** *n.*

insist *v.t./i.* declare or demand emphatically.

insistent *a.* insisting; forcing itself on one's attention. **insistently** *adv.*, **insistence** *n.*

in situ /-'sɪtjuː/ in its (original) place.

insobriety *n.* intemperance; intoxication.

insole *n.* inner sole of a boot or shoe; loose piece of material laid in the bottom of a shoe.

insolent *a.* insulting, arrogant. **insolently** *adv.*, **insolence** *n.*

insoluble *a.* unable to be dissolved; unable to be solved.

insolvent *a.* unable to pay one's debts. **insolvency** *n.*

insomnia *n.* inability to sleep sufficiently.

insomniac *n.* sufferer from insomnia.

insouciant /-'su:s-/ a. carefree, unconcerned. **insouciantly** adv., **insouciance** n.

inspect v.t. examine critically or officially. **inspection** n.

inspector n. person whose job is to inspect or supervise; police officer next above sergeant.

inspectorate n. body of inspectors.

inspiration n. inspiring; inspiring influence; sudden brilliant idea. **inspirational** a.

inspire v.t. stimulate to creative or other activity; instil (a feeling or idea) into; breathe in; animate.

inspirit v.t. animate, encourage.

instability n. lack of stability.

install v.t. place (a person) in office ceremonially; set in position and ready for use; establish.

installation n. process of installing; apparatus etc. installed.

instalment n. one of the parts in which a thing is presented or a debt paid over a period of time.

instance n. example; particular case. —v.t. mention as an instance. **in the first instance** firstly.

instant a. immediate; (of food) designed to be prepared quickly and easily. —n. exact point of time; moment. **instantly** adv.

instantaneous a. occurring or done instantly. **instantaneously** adv., **instantaneousness** n.

instead adv. as an alternative or substitute.

instep n. inner arch of foot between toes and ankle; part of a shoe etc. covering this.

instigate v.t. incite; initiate. **instigation** n., **instigator** n.

instil v.t. (p.t. **instilled**) implant (ideas etc.) gradually.

instinct n. inborn impulse; natural tendency or ability. **instinctive** a., **instinctively** adv., **instinctual** a.

institute n. society or organization for promotion of a specified activity; its premises. —v.t.

establish; cause to be started. **institutor** n.

institution n. process of instituting; institute, esp. for a charitable or social activity; established rule or custom. **institutional** a.

institutionalize v.t. accustom to living in an institution. **institutionalization** n.

instruct v.t. give instruction to (a person) in a subject or skill; inform; give instructions to. **instructor** n., **instructress** n.fem.

instruction n. process of teaching; knowledge or teaching imparted; (pl.) statements telling a person what to do.

instructive a. giving instruction, enlightening. **instructively** adv.

instrument n. tool or implement for delicate work; measuring-device used in operation of an engine or aircraft etc.; device for producing musical sounds; person used and controlled by another; formal document.

instrumental a. serving as a means; performed on musical instruments. **instrumentally** adv., **instrumentality** n.

instrumentalist n. player of a musical instrument.

insubordinate a. disobedient, rebellious. **insubordination** n.

insubstantial a. lacking reality or solidity. **insubstantiality** n.

insufferable a. unbearable. **insufferably** adv.

insufficient a. not sufficient. **insufficiently** adv., **insufficiency** n.

insular a. of an island; of islanders, narrow-minded. **insularity** n.

insulate v.t. cover with a substance that prevents the passage of electricity, sound, or heat; isolate from influences. **insulation** n., **insulator** n.

insulin n. hormone controlling the body's absorption of sugar.

insult[1] /-'sʌlt/ v.t. speak or act so as to hurt the feelings and rouse the anger of.

insult[2] /'ɪn-/ n. insulting remark or action. **insulting** a.

insuperable a. unable to be overcome. **insuperably** adv., **insuperability** n.

insupportable a. unbearable.

insurance n. contract to provide compensation for loss, damage, or death; sum payable as a premium for this, or in compensation; safeguard against loss or failure.

insure v.t. protect by insurance; (US) ensure. **insurer** n.

insurgent a. rebellious, rising in revolt. —n. rebel. **insurgency** n.

insurmountable a. insuperable.

insurrection n. rebellion. **insurrectionist** n.

insusceptible a. not susceptible. **insusceptibility** n.

intact a. undamaged, complete.

intaglio /-'tɑːli-/ n. (pl. **-os**) engraved design; gem with this.

intake n. process of taking thing(s) in; place or amount of this.

intangible a. not tangible. **intangibly** adv., **intangibility** n.

integer n. whole number.

integral /'ɪn-/ a. forming or necessary to form a whole; of an integer. **integrally** adv.

integrate v.t./i. combine (parts) into a whole; bring or come into full membership of a community. **integration** n.

integrity n. honesty.

integument n. skin, husk, rind.

intellect n. mind's power of reasoning and acquiring knowledge.

intellectual a. of or using the intellect; having a strong intellect. —n. intellectual person. **intellectually** adv., **intellectuality** n.

intelligence n. mental ability to learn and understand things; information, esp. that of military value; people collecting this.

intelligence quotient ratio of a person's intelligence to the norm or average.

intelligent a. having mental ability. **intelligently** adv.

intelligentsia /-'dʒen-/ n. intellectual people regarded as a class.

intelligible a. able to be understood. **intelligibly** adv., **intelligibility** n.

intemperate a. drinking alcohol excessively. **intemperance** n.

intend v.t. have in mind as what one wishes to do or achieve.

intense a. strong in quality or degree; feeling strong emotion. **intensely** adv., **intensity** n.

intensify v.t. make or become more intense. **intensification** n.

intensive a. employing much effort; concentrated. **intensively** adv., **intensiveness** n.

intent n. intention. —a. with concentrated attention. **intent on** concentrating on; having as an intention. **intently** adv., **intentness** n.

intention n. what one intends to do.

intentional a. done on purpose, not accidental. **intentionally** adv.

inter /-'tɜː(r)/ v.t. (p.t. **interred**) bury.

inter- prep. between, among.

interact v.i. have an effect upon each other. **interaction** n., **interactive** a.

interbreed v.t./i. (p.t. **-bred**) breed with each other, crossbreed.

intercalary a. inserted to harmonize the calendar year with the solar year.

intercede v.i. intervene on someone's behalf.

intercept v.t. stop or catch between starting-point and destination. **interception** n., **interceptor** n.

intercession n. interceding.

interchange[1] /-'tʃeɪ-/ v.t./i. put (each of two things) into the other's place; exchange; alternate.

interchange[2] /'m-/ n. process of interchanging; road junction designed so that streams of traffic do not intersect on the same level.

interchangeable a. able to be interchanged.

intercom n. (colloq.) communication system operating like a telephone.

interconnect v.t. connect with each other. **interconnection** n.

intercontinental a. between continents.

intercourse n. dealings between people or countries; copulation.

interdict[1] /-'dıkt/ v.t. prohibit formally. **interdiction** n.

interdict[2] /'m-/ n. formal prohibition.

interest n. feeling of curiosity or concern; quality causing this; object of it; advantage; legal share; financial stake; money paid for use of money borrowed. —v.t. arouse the interest of; cause to take an interest in.

interested a. feeling interest; having a private interest, not impartial.

interesting a. arousing interest.

interface n. surface forming a common boundary between two portions of matter or space; place where interaction occurs.

interfere v.i. take part in dealing with others' affairs without right or invitation; be an obstruction.

interference n. interfering; disturbance of radio signals.

interferon /-'fıar-/ n. protein preventing the development of a virus.

interim n. intervening period. —a. of or in such a period, temporary.

interior a. inner. —n. interior part.

interject v.t. put in (a remark) when someone is speaking.

interjection n. process of interjecting; remark interjected; exclamation.

interlace v.t./i. weave or lace together.

interlard v.t. insert contrasting remarks into.

interleave v.t. insert pages between those of (a book).

interlink v.t./i. link together.

interlock v.t./i. fit into each other. —n. fine machine-knitted fabric.

interlocutor /-'lɒk-/ n. person taking part in a conversation.

interloper n. intruder.

interlude n. interval; thing happening or performed in this.

intermarry v.i. marry members of the same or another group. **intermarriage** n.

intermediary n. mediator, messenger. —a. acting as intermediary; intermediate.

intermediate a. coming between two things in time, place, or order.

interment n. burial.

intermezzo /-'mets-/ n. (pl. -os) a kind of short musical composition.

interminable a. very long and boring. **interminably** adv.

intermingle v.t./i. mingle.

intermission n. interval, pause.

intermittent a. occurring at intervals. **intermittently** adv.

intermix v.t./i. mix together.

intern[1] /-'tɜːn/ v.t. compel (an enemy alien or prisoner) to live in a special area.

intern[2] /'m-/ n. (US) resident physician or surgeon.

internal a. of or in the inside; of a country's domestic affairs. **internal-combustion engine** engine producing motive power from fuel exploded within a cylinder. **internally** adv.

international a. between countries. —n. sports contest between players representing different countries; one of these players. **internationally** *adv.*

internationalize *v.t.* make international.

internecine /-'niːsaɪn/ *a.* mutually destructive.

internee *n.* interned person.

internment *n.* interning.

interpersonal *a.* between persons.

interplanetary *a.* between planets.

interplay *n.* interaction.

interpolate *v.t.* interject; insert (esp. misleadingly). **interpolation** *n.*

interpose *v.t.* insert; intervene. **interposition** *n.*

interpret *v.t./i.* explain the meaning of; act as interpreter. **interpretation** *n.*

interpreter *n.* person who orally translates speech between persons speaking different languages.

interregnum *n.* period between the rule of two successive rulers.

interrelated *a.* related.

interrogate *v.t.* question closely. **interrogation** *n.*, **interrogator** *n.*

interrogative *a.* forming or having the form of a question. **interrogatively** *adv.*

interrupt *v.t.* break the continuity of; break the flow of (speech etc.) by a remark. **interruption** *n.* **interrupter** *n.*, **interruptor** *n.*

intersect *v.t./i.* divide or cross by passing or lying across. **intersection** *n.*

intersperse *v.t.* insert here and there.

interstate *a.* between States, esp. of the USA.

interstice /ɪn'tɜːstɪs/ *n.* small intervening space. **interstitial** *a.*

intertwine *v.t./i.* entwine, be entwined.

interval *n.* time or pause between two events or parts of an action; space between two things; difference in musical pitch. **at intervals** with some time or space between.

intervene *v.i.* occur between events; cause hindrance by occurring; enter a dispute etc. to change its course or resolve it. **intervention** *n.*

interview *n.* formal meeting or conversation with a person to assess his merits or obtain information. —*v.t.* hold an interview with. **interviewer** *n.*, **interviewee** *n.*

interweave *v.t.* (*p.t.* **interwove**, *p.p.* **interwoven**) weave together.

intestate *a.* not having made a valid will. **intestacy** *n.*

intestine *n.* long tubular section of the alimentary canal between stomach and anus. **intestinal** *a.*

intifada *n.* Palestinian uprising.

intimate[1] /-ət/ *a.* closely acquainted or familiar; having a sexual relationship with a person (esp. outside marriage) with a person; private and personal. —*n.* intimate friend. **intimately** *adv.*, **intimacy** *n.*

intimate[2] /-eɪt/ *v.t.* make known, esp. by hinting. **intimation** *n.*

intimidate *v.t.* influence by frightening. **intimidation** *n.*

into *prep.* to the inside of, to a point within; to a particular state or occupation; dividing (a number) mathematically; (*colloq.*) interested and involved in.

intolerable *a.* unbearable. **intolerably** *adv.*, **intolerability** *n.*

intolerant *a.* not tolerant. **intolerantly** *adv.*, **intolerance** *n.*

intonation *n.* intoning; pitch of the voice in speaking; slight accent.

intone *v.t.* chant, esp. on one note.

intoxicant *n.* intoxicating drink.

intoxicate *v.t.* make drunk; excite excessively. **intoxication** *n.*

intra- *pref.* within.

intractable *a.* hard to deal with or control. **intractability** *n.*

intransigent *a.* stubborn. **intransigently** *adv.*, **intransigence** *n.*

intransitive *a.* (of a verb) used without a direct object. **intransitively** *adv.*

intra-uterine *a.* within the uterus.

intravenous /-'vi:-/ *a.* into a vein. **intravenously** *adv.*

in-tray *n.* tray for documents awaiting attention.

intrepid *a.* fearless, brave. **intrepidly** *adv.*, **intrepidity** *n.*

intricate *a.* very complicated. **intricately** *adv.*, **intricacy** *n.*

intrigue *v.t./i.* plot in an underhand way; rouse the interest or curiosity of. —*n.* underhand plot or plotting; secret love affair.

intrinsic *a.* belonging to a person's or thing's basic nature. **intrinsically** *adv.*

introduce *v.t.* make (a person) known to another; present to an audience; bring into use; insert.

introduction *n.* introducing; introductory section or treatise.

introductory *a.* introducing; preliminary.

introspection *n.* examination of one's own thoughts and feelings. **introspective** *a.*, **introspectively** *adv.*

introvert *n.* introspective and shy person. **introverted** *a.*

intrude *v.t./i.* come or join in without being invited or wanted; thrust in. **intruder** *n.*, **intrusion** *n.*

intrusive *a.* intruding.

intuition *n.* power of knowing without reasoning or being taught. **intuitive** *a.*, **intuitively** *adv.*

Inuit /'mju:ɪt/ *n.* (*pl.* same or -s) North American Eskimo.

inundate *v.t.* flood. **inundation** *n.*

inure *v.t.* accustom, esp. to something unpleasant.

invade *v.t.* enter (territory) with hostile intent; crowd into; penetrate harmfully. **invader** *n.*

invalid[1] /'ɪn-/ *n.* person suffering from ill health. —*v.t.* remove from active service because of ill health or injury. **invalidism** *n.*

invalid[2] /-'væl-/ *a.* not valid. **invalidity** /-'lɪ-/ *n.*

invalidate *v.t.* make no longer valid. **invalidation** *n.*

invaluable *a.* having value too great to be measured.

invariable *a.* not variable, always the same. **invariably** *adv.*

invasion *n.* invading.

invasive *a.* tending to encroach.

invective *n.* violent attack in words; abusive language.

inveigh /-'veɪ/ *v.i.* attack violently or bitterly in words.

inveigle /-'veɪg(ə)l/ *v.t.* entice. **inveiglement** *n.*

invent *v.t.* create by thought, make or design (a thing not previously known); construct (a false or fictional story). **inventor** *n.*

inventive *a.* able to invent things. **inventiveness** *n.*

inventory /'m-/ *n.* detailed list of goods or furniture.

inverse *a.* reversed in position, relation, or order. —*n.* inverted thing, opposite. **inversely** *adv.*

invert *v.t.* turn upside down; reverse the position, order, or relationship of. **inverted commas** quotation-marks. **inversion** *n.*

invertebrate /-ət/ *a.* & *n.* (animal) having no backbone.

invest *v.t./i.* use (money) to buy shares or property etc. to earn interest or bring profit; confer rank or power upon; endow with a quality. **invest in** (*colloq.*) spend money or effort etc. on (a useful thing). **investment** *n.*, **investor** *n.*

investigate *v.t.* study (a thing) carefully to discover facts about it. **investigation** *n.*, **investigator** *n.*, **investigative** *a.*

investiture n. formal investing of a person with a rank or office etc.

inveterate a. habitual; firmly established. **inveterately** adv.

invidious a. liable to cause resentment. **invidiously** adv.

invigilate v.i. supervise candidates at an examination. **invigilation** n., **invigilator** n.

invigorate v.t. fill with vigour, give strength or courage to.

invincible a. unconquerable. **invincibly** adv., **invincibility** n.

inviolable a. not to be violated. **inviolably** adv., **inviolability** n.

invisible a. not able to be seen. **invisibly** adv., **invisibility** n.

invite v.t. ask (a person) politely to come or to do something; ask for; attract, tempt. —n. (sl.) invitation. **invitation** n.

inviting a. pleasant and tempting. **invitingly** adv.

in vitro in a test-tube or other laboratory environment.

invocation n. invoking; calling to God in prayer.

invoice n. list of goods or services supplied, with prices. —v.t. make an invoice of; send an invoice to.

invoke v.t. call for the help or protection of; summon (a spirit).

involuntary a. done without intention or without conscious effort. **involuntarily** adv.

involve v.t. have as a consequence; include or affect in its operation; cause to share an experience etc.; implicate. **involvement** n.

involved a. complicated; concerned.

invulnerable a. not vulnerable. **invulnerability** n.

inward a. situated on or going towards the inside; in the mind or spirit. —adv. inwards. **inwardly** adv., **inwards** adv.

iodine /-dm/ n. chemical substance used in solution as an antiseptic.

iodize v.t. impregnate with iodine. **iodization** n.

ion n. electrically charged particle. **ionic** a.

Ionic a. of the order of architecture using scroll-like ornamentation.

ionize v.t./i. convert or be converted into ions. **ionization** n.

ionosphere n. ionized region of the atmosphere. **ionospheric** a.

iota n. Greek letter i; very small amount.

IOU n. signed paper given as a receipt for money borrowed.

ipecacuanha n. dried root used esp. as an emetic.

ipso facto by that very fact.

IQ abbr. intelligence quotient.

ir- see in-.

IRA abbr. Irish Republican Army.

irascible /-'ræs-/ a. irritable, hot-tempered. **irascibly** adv., **irascibility** n.

irate a. angry. **irately** adv.

ire n. anger.

iridescent a. coloured like a rainbow; shimmering. **iridescence** n.

iris n. coloured part of the eyeball, round the pupil; lily-like flower.

Irish a. & n. (language) of Ireland. **Irishman** n. (pl. -men), **Irishwoman** n. (pl. -women).

irk v.t. annoy, be tiresome to.

irksome a. tiresome.

iron n. hard grey metal; tool etc. made of this; implement with a flat base heated for smoothing cloth or clothes; (pl.) fetters. —a. made of iron; strong as iron. —v.t. smooth (clothes etc.) with iron. **Iron Curtain** former notional barrier round the Soviet bloc. **ironing-board** n. narrow folding table etc. for ironing clothes on. **iron-mould** n. brown spot on fabric, caused by iron rust.

ironic, ironical adjs. using irony. **ironically** adv.

ironmonger n. shopkeeper selling tools and household implements. **ironmongery** n. ironmonger's shop or goods.

ironstone *n.* hard iron-ore; a kind of hard white pottery.

ironwork *n.* things made of iron.

ironworks *n.* place where iron is smelted or iron goods made.

irony *n.* expression of meaning by use of words normally conveying the opposite; apparent perversity of fate or circumstances.

irradiate *v.t.* throw light or other radiation on; treat (food) by radiation. **irradiation** *n.*

irrational *a.* not rational. **irrationally** *adv.*, **irrationality** *n.*

irreconcilable *a.* not reconcilable. **irreconcilably** *adv.*, **irreconcilability** *n.*

irrecoverable *a.* unable to be recovered. **irrecoverably** *adv.*

irredeemable *a.* unable to be redeemed. **irredeemably** *adv.*

irreducible *a.* not reducible.

irrefutable /-'ref-/ *a.* unable to be refuted. **irrefutably** *adv.*

irregular *a.* not regular; contrary to rules or custom. **irregularly** *adv.*, **irregularity** *n.*

irrelevant *a.* not relevant. **irrelevantly** *adv.*, **irrelevance** *n.*

irreligious *a.* not religious; irreverent.

irreparable /-'rep-/ *a.* unable to be repaired. **irreparably** *adv.*

irreplaceable *a.* unable to be replaced.

irrepressible *a.* unable to be repressed. **irrepressibly** *adv.*

irreproachable *a.* blameless, faultless. **irreproachably** *adv.*

irresistible *a.* too strong or delightful to be resisted. **irresistibly** *adv.*, **irresistibility** *n.*

irresolute *a.* unable to make up one's mind. **irresolutely** *adv.*, **irresolution** *n.*

irrespective *a.* irrespective of not taking (a thing) into account.

irresponsible *a.* not showing a proper sense of responsibility. **irresponsibly** *adv.*, **irresponsibility** *n.*

irretrievable *a.* not retrievable.

irretrievably *adv.*, **irretrievability** *n.*

irreverent *a.* not respectful. **irreverently** *adv.*, **irreverence** *n.*

irreversible *a.* not reversible, unable to be altered or revoked. **irreversibly** *adv.*, **irreversibility** *n.*

irrevocable /-'rev-/ *a.* unable to be revoked, unalterable. **irrevocably** *adv.*, **irrevocability** *n.*

irrigate *v.t.* supply (land) with water by streams, pipes, etc.; moisten (a wound) constantly. **irrigation** *n.*

irritable *a.* bad-tempered. **irritable bowel syndrome** condition involving abdominal pain and diarrhoea or constipation, related to stress etc. **irritably** *adv.*, **irritability** *n.*

irritant *a.* & *n.* (thing) causing irritation.

irritate *v.t.* annoy; cause itching in. **irritation** *n.*

irrupt *v.i.* make a violent entry. **irruption** *n.*

is *see* be.

isinglass /'aɪz-/ *n.* a kind of gelatine obtained from sturgeon etc.

Islam *n.* Muslim religion; Muslim world. **Islamic** *a.*

island *n.* piece of land surrounded by water. **traffic island** raised area in a road, where people crossing may be safe from traffic.

islander *n.* inhabitant of an island.

isle *n.* island.

islet *n.* small island.

isobar *n.* line on a map, connecting places with the same atmospheric pressure. **isobaric** *a.*

isolate *v.t.* place apart or alone; separate from others or from a compound. **isolation** *n.*

isolationism *n.* policy of holding aloof from other countries or groups. **isolationist** *n.*

isomer *n.* substance whose molecules have the same atoms as another but differently arranged.

isometric *a.* of equal measure; drawing a three-dimensional object so that equal lengths along its three axes are equal; using muscular tension without movement.

isosceles /aɪˈsɒsɪliːz/ *a.* (of a triangle) having two sides equal.

isotherm *n.* line on a map, connecting places with the same temperature.

isotope *n.* each of two or more forms of a chemical element differing in their atomic weight. **isotopic** *a.*

issue *n.* outgoing, outflow; issuing, quantity issued; one publication (e.g. of a magazine) in a series; result, outcome; important topic; offspring. —*v.t./i.* come or flow out; supply for use; publish; send out; result, originate. **at issue** being discussed or disputed or risked. **join** *or* **take issue** proceed to argue.

isthmus *n.* (*pl.* **-muses**) narrow strip of land with water on each side, connecting two masses of land.

it *pron.* thing mentioned or being discussed; impersonal subject of a verb.

Italian *a. & n.* (native, language) of Italy.

italic *a.* (of type) sloping like *this*; of a compact pointed form of writing. **italics** *n.pl.* italic type.

italicize *v.t.* print in italics.

itch *n.* tickling sensation in the skin, causing a desire to scratch; restless desire. —*v.i.* have or feel an itch. **itchy** *a.*

item *n.* single thing in a list or collection; single piece of news.

itemize *v.t.* list, state the individual items of. **itemization** *n.*

iterate *v.t.* repeat. **iteration** *n.*

itinerant /ɪˈtɪn-/ *a.* travelling.

itinerary /aɪ-/ *n.* route, list of places to be visited on a journey.

its *poss.pron.* of it.

it's = it is, it has.

itself *pron.* emphatic and reflexive form of *it*.

ITV *abbr.* Independent Television.

ivory *n.* hard creamy-white substance forming tusks of elephant etc.; object made of this; its colour. —*a.* creamy-white. **ivory tower** seclusion from the harsh realities of life.

ivy *n.* climbing evergreen shrub.

J

jab *v.t.* (*p.t.* **jabbed**) poke roughly. —*n.* rough poke; (*colloq.*) injection.

jabber *v.i.* talk rapidly, often unintelligibly. —*n.* jabbering talk.

jabot /ˈʒæbəʊ/ *n.* frill at the neck or front of a shirt.

jacaranda *n.* tropical tree with hard scented wood.

jacinth *n.* reddish-orange gem.

jack *n.* portable device for raising heavy weights off the ground; playing-card next below queen; ship's small flag showing nationality; electrical connection with a single plug; small ball aimed at in bowls; male donkey. —*v.t.* raise with a jack.

jackal *n.* dog-like wild animal.

jackass *n.* male ass; stupid person. **laughing jackass** kookaburra.

jackboot *n.* large high boot.

jackdaw *n.* bird of the crow family.

jacket *n.* short coat usu. reaching to the hips; outer covering.

jackknife *n.* large folding knife. —*v.i.* fold accidentally.

jackpot *n.* large prize of money that has accumulated until won. **hit the jackpot** (*colloq.*) have a sudden success.

Jacobean *a.* of the reign of James I of England (1603–25).

Jacobite *n. & a.* (of) a supporter of the exiled Stuart kings of England.

jacquard /-kɑːd/ *n.* fabric with an intricate woven pattern.

Jacuzzi *n.* [P.] large bath with underwater jets of water.

jade *n.* hard green, blue, or white stone; its green colour.

jaded *a.* tired and bored.

jag *n.* (*sl.*) drinking-bout, spree.

jagged *a.* having sharp projections.

jaguar *n.* large flesh-eating animal of the cat family.

jail *n.* prison. —*v.t.* put into jail.

jailbird *n.* person who has been in jail, esp. frequently.

jailer *n.* person in charge of a jail or its prisoners.

jalopy /-'lɒp-/ *n.* battered old car.

jam¹ *n.* thick sweet substance made by boiling fruit with sugar; (*colloq.*) something easy or pleasant. —*v.t.* (*p.t.* **jammed**) spread with jam; make into jam.

jam² *v.t./i.* (*p.t.* **jammed**) squeeze or wedge into a space; become wedged; crowd or block (an area); apply forcibly; make (a broadcast) unintelligible by causing interference. —*n.* squeeze, crush; stoppage caused by jamming; crowded mass; (*colloq.*) difficult situation. **jam-packed** *a.* (*colloq.*) very full. **jam session** improvised playing of jazz.

jamb *n.* side-post of a door or window.

jamboree *n.* large party; rally.

jammy *a.* smeared with jam.

jangle *n.* harsh metallic sound. —*v.t./i.* make or cause to make this sound; upset by discord.

janitor *n.* caretaker of a building.

January *n.* first month of the year.

japan *n.* hard usu. black varnish. —*v.t.* (*p.t.* **japanned**) coat (as) with this.

Japanese *a.* & *n.* (native, language) of Japan.

japonica *n.* ornamental shrub with red flowers.

jar¹ *n.* cylindrical glass or earthenware container.

jar² *v.t./i.* (*p.t.* **jarred**) jolt; have a harsh or disagreeable effect (upon). —*n.* jarring movement or effect.

jardinière /-'njeə(r)/ *n.* large ornamental plant-pot.

jargon *n.* words or expressions developed for use within a particular group of people.

jasmine *n.* shrub with white or yellow flowers.

jasper *n.* a kind of quartz.

jaundice *n.* condition in which the skin becomes abnormally yellow.

jaundiced *a.* affected by jaundice; filled with resentment.

jaunt *n.* short trip. —*v.i.* make a jaunt.

jaunty *a.* (-ier, -iest) cheerful, self-confident. **jauntily** *adv.*, **jauntiness** *n.*

javelin *n.* light spear.

jaw *n.* bone(s) forming the framework of the mouth; (*pl.*) gripping-parts; (*colloq.*) lengthy talk. —*v.t./i.* (*sl.*) talk lengthily (to).

jay *n.* bird of the crow family.

jaywalker *n.* person walking carelessly in a road. **jaywalking** *n.*

jazz *n.* type of music with strong rhythm and much syncopation; (*sl.*) pretentiousness. —*v.t.* play or arrange as jazz; liven. **jazzy** *a.*

jealous *a.* resentful towards a rival; taking watchful care. **jealously** *adv.*, **jealousy** *n.*

jeans *n.pl.* denim trousers.

Jeep *n.* [P.] small sturdy motor-vehicle with four-wheel drive.

jeer *v.t./i.* laugh or shout rudely or scornfully (at). —*n.* jeering.

Jehovah *n.* name of God in the Old Testament. **Jehovah's Witness** member of a fundamentalist Christian sect.

jejune /dʒɪ'dʒuːn/ *a.* meagre; poor, barren.

jell *v.i.* (*colloq.*) set as a jelly; take definite form.

jellied *a.* set in jelly.

jelly n. soft solid food made of liquid set with gelatine; substance of similar consistency; jam made of strained fruit-juice; (sl.) gelignite.

jellyfish n. sea animal with a jelly-like body.

jemmy n. burglar's short crow-bar. —v.t. open with this.

jenny n. female donkey.

jeopardize /ˈdʒep-/ v.t. endanger.

jeopardy /ˈdʒep-/ n. danger.

jerboa n. rat-like desert animal with long hind legs.

jeremiad n. long mournful complaint.

jerk[1] n. sudden sharp movement or pull. —v.t./i. move, pull, or stop with jerk(s). **jerky** a., **jerkily** adv., **jerkiness** n.

jerk[2] v.t. cure (esp. beef) by slicing and drying in the sun.

jerkin n. sleeveless jacket.

jerry-built a. built badly and with poor materials. **jerry-builder** n.

jerrycan n. five-gallon can for petrol or water.

jersey n. (pl. **-eys**) knitted woollen pullover with sleeves; machine-knitted fabric.

jessamine n. = jasmin.

jest n. & v.i. joke.

jester n. person who makes jokes; entertainer at a medieval court.

Jesuit n. member of the Society of Jesus (an RC religious order).

jet[1] n. hard black mineral; glossy black. **jet-black** a.

jet[2] n. stream of water, gas, or flame from a small opening; burner on a gas cooker; engine or aircraft using jet propulsion. —v.t. (p.t. **jetted**) travel or send by jet. **jet lag** delayed tiredness etc. after a long flight. **jet-propelled** a. using jet propulsion, propulsion by engines that send out a high-speed jet of gases at the back. **jet set** (colloq.) wealthy much-travelled élite.

jetsam n. goods jettisoned by a ship and washed ashore.

jettison v.t. throw overboard, eject; discard.

jetty n. breakwater; landing-stage.

Jew n. person of Hebrew descent or whose religion is Judaism. **jew's harp** small metal frame held in the teeth for twanging. **Jewess** n.fem.

jewel n. precious stone cut or set as an ornament; person or thing that is highly valued. **jewelled** a.

jeweller n. person who makes or deals in jewels or jewellery.

jewellery n. jewels or similar ornaments to be worn.

Jewish a. of Jews.

Jewry n. the Jewish people.

jib n. triangular sail stretching forward from a mast; projecting arm of a crane. —v.i. (p.t. **jibbed**) refuse to proceed. **jib at** object to.

jiff, **jiffy** ns. (colloq.) moment.

jig n. lively jumping dance; device that holds work and guides tools working on it; template. —v.t./i. (p.t. **jigged**) move quickly up and down.

jigger n. measure of spirits.

jiggery-pokery n. (colloq.) trickery.

jiggle v.t./i. rock or jerk lightly.

jigsaw n. machine fretsaw. **jigsaw puzzle** picture cut into pieces which are then shuffled and reassembled for amusement.

jilt v.t. abandon (a person) after having courted him or her.

jingle v.t./i. make or cause to make a ringing or clinking sound. —n. this sound; simple rhyme.

jingoism n. excessive patriotism and contempt for other countries. **jingoist** n., **jingoistic** a.

jink v.i. dodge by a sudden turn. **high jinks** boisterous fun.

jinnee n. (pl. **jinn**, also used as sing.) (in Muslim mythology) spirit with supernatural influence.

jinx *n.* (*colloq.*) influence causing bad luck. —*v.t.* (*colloq.*) influence thus.

jitter *v.i.* (*colloq.*) be nervous. **jitters** *n.pl.* (*colloq.*) nervousness. **jittery** *a.*

jive *n.* fast lively jazz; dance to this. —*v.i.* dance to or play this music.

job *n.* piece of work; paid position of employment; (*colloq.*) difficult task. **good** or **bad job** fortunate or unfortunate state of affairs. **job lot** miscellaneous articles sold together.

jobber *n.* principal or wholesaler dealing on the Stock Exchange; (*US*) broker.

jobbing *a.* doing single pieces of work for payment.

jobcentre *n.* government office in a town centre, where notices about jobs available are displayed.

jobless *a.* out of work.

jockey *n.* (*pl.* **-eys**) person who rides in horse-races. —*v.t./i.* manœuvre to gain advantage; force by skilful or unfair means.

jocose /-'kəʊs/ *a.* joking. **jocosely** *adv.*, **jocosity** *n.*

jocular *a.* joking. **jocularly** *adv.*, **jocularity** *n.*

jocund *a.* merry, cheerful. **jocundity** *n.*

jodhpurs *n.pl.* riding-breeches fitting closely from knee to ankle.

jog *v.t./i.* (*p.t.* **jogged**) push or shake slightly; stimulate; proceed at a slow regular pace; run thus for exercise. —*n.* jogging movement or pace; nudge. **jogger** *n.*

joggle *v.t./i.* shake slightly. —*n.* slight shake.

jogtrot *n.* slow regular trot.

joie de vivre /ʒwa: də 'viːvr/ exuberant enjoyment of life.

join *v.t./i.* put or come together, unite; connect by a line etc.; come into the company of; take one's place in; become a member of. —*n.* place where things join. **join**

battle begin fighting. **join up** enlist in the forces.

joiner *n.* maker of furniture and light woodwork. **joinery** *n.* this work.

joint *a.* shared or done by two or more people together; sharing. —*n.* join; structure where parts or bones fit together; section of an animal's carcass as food; (*sl.*) place where people meet for gambling or drinking etc.; (*sl.*) marijuana cigarette. —*v.t.* connect by joint(s); divide into joints. **joint stock** capital held jointly. **out of joint** dislocated; in disorder. **jointly** *adv.*

jointure *n.* estate settled on a wife for the period during which she survives her husband.

joist *n.* one of the beams on which floor boards or ceiling laths are fixed.

jojoba /həʊ'həʊbə/ *n.* plant producing seeds containing oil used in cosmetics.

joke *n.* thing said or done to cause laughter; ridiculous person or thing. —*v.i.* make jokes.

joker *n.* person who jokes; (*sl.*) fellow; extra playing-card used as the highest trump.

jollification *n.* merry-making.

jollity *n.* being jolly; merry-making.

jolly *a.* (**-ier**, **-iest**) cheerful, merry; very pleasant. —*adv.* (*colloq.*) very. —*v.t.* keep in good humour.

jolt *v.t./i.* shake or dislodge with a jerk; move jerkily; shock. —*n.* jolting movement; shock.

jonquil *n.* a kind of narcissus.

josh *v.t./i.* (*US sl.*) poke; tease.

joss *n.* Chinese idol. **joss-stick** *n.* thin stick that burns with a smell of incense.

jostle *v.t./i.* push roughly.

jot *n.* very small amount. —*v.t.* (*p.t.* **jotted**) write down briefly.

jotter *n.* note-pad, notebook.

joule /dʒuːl/ *n.* unit of energy.

journal n. daily record of events; newspaper or periodical.

journalese n. style of language used in inferior journalism.

journalist n. person employed in writing for a newspaper or magazine. **journalism** n. this work.

journey n. (pl. **-eys**) continued course of going or travelling. —v.i. make a journey.

journeyman n. (pl. **-men**) workman who has completed his apprenticeship.

joust /dʒaʊst/ v.i. & n. fight on horseback with lances.

jovial a. full of cheerful good humour. **jovially** adv., **joviality** n.

jowl n. jaw, cheek; dewlap, loose skin on the throat.

joy n. deep emotion of pleasure; thing causing delight.

joyful a. full of joy. **joyfully** adv., **joyfulness** n.

joyous a. joyful. **joyously** adv.

joyride n. (colloq.) car ride taken for pleasure, usu. without the owner's permission. **joyriding** n.

joystick n. aircraft's control lever; device for moving a cursor on a VDU screen.

JP abbr. Justice of the Peace.

jubilant a. rejoicing. **jubilantly** adv., **jubilation** n.

jubilee n. special anniversary.

Judaic a. Jewish.

Judaism n. religion of the Jewish people, based on the teachings of the Old Testament and Talmud.

judder v.i. shake noisily or violently. —n. this movement.

judge n. public officer appointed to hear and try cases in law-courts; person appointed to decide who has won a contest; person able to give an authoritative opinion. —v.t. try (a case) in a lawcourt; act as judge of; give an opinion about; estimate.

judgement n. (in law contexts **judgment**) judging; judge's decision. **Judgement Day** judgement by God at the end of the world. **judgemental** a.

judicature n. administration of justice; a body of judges.

judicial a. of the administration of justice; of a judge or judgement. **judicially** adv.

judiciary /-ˈdrɪʃ-/ n. the whole body of judges in a country.

judicious a. judging wisely, showing good sense. **judiciously** adv., **judiciousness** n.

judo n. Japanese system of unarmed combat. **judoist** n.

jug n. vessel with a handle and a shaped lip, for holding and pouring liquids. —v.t. (p.t. **jugged**) stew (hare). **jugful** n.

juggernaut n. very large transport vehicle; very large overwhelmingly powerful object or institution.

juggle v.t./i. toss and catch objects skilfully for entertainment; manipulate skilfully; rearrange (facts etc.), esp. deceitfully. **juggler** n.

jugular vein either of the two great veins in the neck.

juice n. fluid content of fruits, vegetables, or meat; fluid secreted by an organ of the body. **juicy** a.

ju-jitsu n. Japanese system of unarmed combat.

jujube n. jelly-like sweet.

jukebox n. machine that plays a selected record when a coin is inserted.

julep n. drink of spirits and water flavoured esp. with mint.

julienne n. soup containing vegetables in thin strips.

July n. seventh month of the year.

jumble v.t. mix in a confused way. —n. jumbled articles; items for a jumble sale. **jumble sale** sale of miscellaneous second-hand articles to raise money for charity.

jumbo n. (pl. **-os**) very large thing. **jumbo jet** very large jet aircraft.

jump v.t./i. move up off the ground etc. by muscular movement of the legs; make a sudden upward movement; rise suddenly; pass over by jumping; use (a horse) for jumping; pass over to a point beyond; leave (rails or track) accidentally; abscond from; pounce on. —*n.* jumping movement; sudden rise or change; gap in a series; obstacle to be jumped. **jump at** accept eagerly. **jump-lead** *n.* cable for conveying electric current from one battery through another. **jump suit** one-piece garment for the whole body. **jump the gun** act before the permitted time. **jump the queue** obtain something without waiting one's turn. **jump to conclusions** reach them too hastily.

jumper[1] *n.* one who jumps.

jumper[2] *n.* woman's knitted garment for the upper part of the body; upper part of a sailor's uniform; (*US*) pinafore dress.

jumpy *a.* nervous.

junction *n.* join; place where roads or railway lines unite.

juncture *n.* point of time, convergence of events.

June *n.* sixth month of the year.

jungle *n.* land overgrown with tangled vegetation, esp. in the tropics; tangled mass; scene of ruthless struggle.

junior *a.* younger in age; lower in rank or authority; for younger children. —*n.* junior person.

juniper *n.* evergreen shrub with dark berries.

junk[1] *n.* useless or discarded articles, rubbish. **junk food** food with low nutritional value. **junk shop** shop selling miscellaneous second-hand goods.

junk[2] *n.* flat-bottomed ship with sails, used in China seas.

junket *n.* sweet custard-like food made of milk and rennet.

junketing *n.* merry-making.

junkie *n.* (*sl.*) drug addict.

junta *n.* group who combine to rule a country, esp. after a revolution.

juridical *a.* of law or legal proceedings.

jurisdiction *n.* authority to administer justice or exercise power.

jurisprudence *n.* skill in law.

jurist *n.* person skilled in law.

juror *n.* member of a jury.

jury *n.* group of people sworn to give a verdict on a case in a court of law. **juryman** *n.* (*pl.* **-men**), **jurywoman** *n.* (*pl.* **-women**).

jury-rigged *a.* with makeshift rigging.

just *a.* giving proper consideration to the claims of all concerned; right in amount etc.; deserved. —*adv.* exactly; by only a short amount etc.; only a moment ago; (*colloq.*) merely; positively. **just now** at this moment; a short time ago. **justly** *adv.*, **justness** *n.*

justice *n.* just treatment, fairness; legal proceedings; magistrate; judge. **Justice of the Peace** citizen serving as a magistrate.

justiciary *n.* one who administers justice.

justifiable *a.* able to be justified. **justifiably** *adv.*, **justifiability** *n.*

justificatory *a.* providing justification.

justify *v.t.* show to be right or just or reasonable; be sufficient reason for; adjust (a line of type) to fill a space neatly. **justification** *n.*

jut *v.i.* (*p.t.* **jutted**) project.

jute *n.* fibre from the bark of certain tropical plants.

juvenile *a.* youthful, childish; for young people. —*n.* young person. **juvenility** *n.*

juxtapose *v.t.* put (things) side by side. **juxtaposition** *n.*

K

kaiser *n.* title of German and Austrian emperors until 1918.

kale *n.* cabbage with curly leaves.

kaleidoscope /-'laɪ-/ n. toy tube containing mirrors and coloured fragments reflected to produce changing patterns. **kaleidoscopic** a.

kamikaze /-'kɑːzɪ/ n. (in the Second World War) Japanese explosive-laden aircraft deliberately crashed on its target.

kampong n. Malayan enclosure or village.

kangaroo n. Australian marsupial that jumps along on its strong hind legs. **kangaroo court** court formed illegally by a group to settle disputes among themselves.

kaolin n. fine white clay used in porcelain and medicine.

kapok n. fluffy fibre used for padding things.

kaput /-'pʊt/ a. (sl.) ruined, broken.

karate /kə'rɑːtɪ/ n. Japanese system of unarmed combat using the hands and feet as weapons.

karma n. (in Buddhism & Hinduism) person's actions as affecting his or her next reincarnation.

kauri /'kaʊrɪ/ n. coniferous New Zealand tree yielding **kauri-gum**.

kayak /'kaɪ-/ n. small covered canoe, esp. of Eskimos.

kc/s abbr. kilocycle(s) per second.

kebabs /kɪ'bæ-/ n.pl. small pieces of meat cooked on a skewer.

kedge n. small anchor. —v.t./i. move by hauling on a kedge.

kedgeree n. cooked dish of rice and fish or eggs.

keel n. timber or steel structure along the base of a ship. —v.t./i. overturn; become tilted.

keen[1] a. (-er, -est) sharp; penetrating; piercingly cold; intense; very eager. **keen on** (colloq.) liking greatly. **keenly** adv., **keenness** n.

keen[2] n. Irish funeral song with wailing. —v.i. utter this; wail.

keep v.t./i. (p.t. **kept**) retain possession of, have charge of;

remain or cause to remain in a specified state or position; prevent, detain; put aside for a future time; pay due regard to; celebrate; provide with food and other necessities; own and look after (animals); manage (a shop etc.); have in stock or for sale; make regular entries in (a diary, accounts, etc.); continue doing something; remain in good condition. —n. person's food and other necessities; strongly fortified structure in a castle. **for keeps** (colloq.) permanently. **keep house** look after a house or household. **keep up** progress at the same pace as others; continue; maintain.

keeper n. person who keeps or looks after something, custodian.

keeping n. custody, charge. **in keeping with** suited to.

keepsake n. thing kept in memory of the giver.

keg n. small barrel. **keg beer** beer from a pressurized metal container.

kelp n. large brown seaweed.

kelvin n. degree of the **Kelvin scale** of temperature which has zero at absolute zero (−273.15°C).

ken n. range of sight or knowledge. —v.t. (p.t. **kenned**) (Sc.) know.

kendo n. Japanese sport of fencing with bamboo swords.

kennel n. shelter for a dog; pack of dogs; (pl.) boarding place for dogs.

kept see **keep**.

kerb n. stone edging to a pavement.

kerchief n. square scarf worn on the head.

kerfuffle n. (colloq.) fuss, commotion.

kermes n. insect used in making a red dye.

kernel n. softer part inside the shell of a nut or stone of fruit;

seed within a husk; central or important part.

kerosene *n.* paraffin oil.

kestrel *n.* a kind of small falcon.

ketch *n.* two-masted sailing-boat.

ketchup *n.* thick sauce made from tomatoes and vinegar.

kettle *n.* metal or plastic container with a spout and handle, for boiling water in.

kettledrum *n.* drum with parchment stretched over a large metal bowl.

Kevlar *n.* [P.] strong synthetic fibre used to reinforce rubber etc.

key *n.* piece of metal shaped for moving the bolt of a lock, tightening a spring, etc.; thing giving access or control or insight; set of answers to problems; word or system for interpreting a code etc.; system of related notes in music; style; roughness of surface to help adhesion; lever for a finger to press on a piano, typewriter, etc. —*v.t.* link closely; roughen (a surface) to help adhesion. **key-ring** *n.* ring on which keys are threaded. **key up** stimulate, make nervously tense.

keyboard *n.* set of keys on a piano etc., or on a typewriter or computer. —*v.t.* enter (data) by using a keyboard. **keyboarder** *n.*

keyhole *n.* hole by which a key is put into a lock. **keyhole surgery** minimally invasive surgery carried out through a very small incision.

keynote *n.* note on which a key in music is based; prevailing tone.

keypad *n.* small keyboard or set of buttons for operating an electronic device, telephone, etc.

keystone *n.* central stone of an arch, locking others into position.

keyword *n.* key to a cipher etc.

kg *abbr.* kilogram(s).

KGB *abbr.* secret police of the former USSR.

khaki *a.* & *n.* dull brownish-yellow, colour of military uniforms.

kHz *abbr.* kilohertz.

kibbutz /-'buts/ *n.* (*pl.* -im) communal settlement in Israel.

kick *v.t./i.* strike or propel with the foot; score (a goal) by kicking a ball; (of a gun) recoil when fired. —*n.* act of kicking; blow with the foot; (*colloq.*) thrill, interest. **kick-off** *n.* start of a football game. **kick out** (*colloq.*) expel forcibly; dismiss. **kick-start** *n.*, **kick-starter** *n.* lever pressed with the foot to start a motor cycle. **kick up** (*colloq.*) create a fuss or noise).

kickback *n.* recoil; (*colloq.*) reward, bribe.

kid *n.* young goat; leather made from its skin; (*sl.*) child. —*v.t./i.* (*p.t.* **kidded**) (*sl.*) hoax, tease.

kiddy *n.* (*sl.*) child.

kidnap *v.t.* (*p.t.* **kidnapped**) carry off (a person) illegally in order to obtain a ransom. **kidnapper** *n.*

kidney *n.* (*pl.* -eys) either of a pair of organs that remove waste products from the blood and secrete urine. **kidney bean** French bean; runner bean. **kidney dish** oval dish indented at one side.

kill *v.t.* cause the death of; put an end to; spend (time) unprofitably by waiting. —*n.* killing; animal(s) killed by a hunter. **killer** *n.*

killing *a.* (*colloq.*) very amusing.

killjoy *n.* person who spoils the enjoyment of others.

kiln *n.* oven for hardening or drying things (e.g. pottery, hops).

kilo /'ki:ləʊ/ *n.* (*pl.* -os) kilogram.

kilo- *pref.* one thousand.

kilocycle *n.* 1000 cycles as a unit of wave frequency; kilohertz.

kilogram *n.* unit of weight or mass in the metric system (2.205 lb).

kilohertz *n.* unit of frequency of electromagnetic waves, = 1000 cycles per second.

kilometre /'kɪl- or -'lɒm-/ n. 1000 metres (0.62 mile).

kilovolt n. 1000 volts.

kilowatt n. 1000 watts.

kilt n. knee-length pleated skirt of tartan wool, esp. as part of Highland man's dress. —v.t. tuck up (skirts) round the body; arrange in vertical pleats.

kimono n. (pl. -os) loose Japanese robe worn with a sash; dressing-gown resembling this.

kin n. person's relatives.

kind[1] n. class of similar things. **a kind** of thing belonging approximately to a (class named). **in kind** (of payment) in goods etc. not money. **of a kind** similar.

kind[2] a. (-er, -est) gentle and considerate towards others. **kind-hearted** a., **kindness** n.

kindergarten n. school for very young children.

kindle v.t./i. set on fire; arouse, stimulate; become kindled.

kindling n. small pieces of wood for lighting fires.

kindly a. (-ier, -iest) kind. —adv. in a kind way; please. **kindliness** n.

kindred n. kin. —a. related; of similar kind.

kinetic a. of movement.

king n. male ruler of a country by right of birth; man or thing regarded as supreme in some way; chess piece to be protected from checkmate; playing-card next above queen. **king-size, king-sized** adjs. extra large. **kingly** a., **kingship** n.

kingcup n. marsh marigold.

kingdom n. country ruled by a king or queen; division of the natural world. **kingdom come** (sl.) eternity, the next world.

kingfisher n. small blue bird that dives to catch fish.

kingpin n. indispensable person or thing.

kink n. short twist in thread or wire etc.; mental peculiarity.

—v.t./i. form or cause to form kink(s). **kinky** a.

kinsfolk n.pl. kin. **kinsman** n. (pl. -men), **kinswoman** n.fem. (pl. -women).

kiosk n. booth where newspapers or refreshments are sold, or containing a public telephone.

kip n. & v.i. (p.t. kipped) (sl.) sleep.

kipper n. smoked herring.

kirk n. (Sc.) church.

kirsch /kɪəʃ/ n. colourless liqueur made from wild cherries.

kismet n. destiny, fate.

kiss n. & v.t./i. touch or caress with the lips.

kissogram n. novelty telegram or greetings message delivered with a kiss.

kit n. outfit of clothing, tools, etc.; set of parts to be assembled. —v.t. (p.t. kitted) equip with kit.

kitbag n. bag for holding kit.

kitchen n. room where meals are prepared. **kitchen garden** vegetable garden.

kitchenette n. small kitchen.

kite n. large bird of the hawk family; light framework on a string, for flying in the wind as a toy.

Kitemark n. official symbol on articles approved by the British Standards Institution.

kith n. **kith and kin** relatives.

kitsch n. worthless pretentiousness in art; art showing this.

kitten n. young of cat, hare, rabbit, or ferret. **kittenish** a.

kittiwake n. small seagull.

kitty n. communal fund.

kiwi n. (pl. -is) New Zealand bird that does not fly.

kleptomania n. tendency to steal things without desire to use or profit by them. **kleptomaniac** n.

km abbr. kilometre(s).

knack n. ability to do something skilfully.

knacker n. person who buys and slaughters useless horses. —v.t. (sl.) kill; exhaust.

knapsack *n.* bag worn strapped on the back.

knave *n.* (*old use*) rogue; jack in playing-cards. **knavery** *n.*, **knavish** *a.*

knead *v.t./i.* press and stretch (dough) with the hands; massage with similar movements.

knee *n.* joint between the thigh and the lower part of the leg; part of a garment covering this. —*v.t.* (*p.t.* **kneed**) touch or strike with the knee. **knee-jerk** *a.* (of a reaction) automatic and predictable. **knees-up** *n.* (*colloq.*) lively party with dancing.

kneecap *n.* small bone over the front of the knee; covering for the knee. —*v.t.* (*p.t.* **-capped**) shoot in the knee or leg as a punishment.

kneel *v.i.* (*p.t.* **knelt**) lower one's body to rest on the knees with legs bent back, esp. in reverence.

kneeler *n.* mat or pad for kneeling on.

knell *n.* sound of a bell tolled after a death or at a funeral.

knelt *see* **kneel.**

knew *see* **know.**

knickerbockers *n.pl.* loose breeches gathered in at the knee.

knickers *n.pl.* woman's or girl's undergarment for the lower part of the body, with separate legs or leg-holes.

knick-knack *n.* small ornament.

knife *n.* (*pl.* **knives**) cutting instrument with a sharp blade and a handle; cutting blade in a machine. —*v.t.* cut or stab with a knife.

knight *n.* man given a rank below baronet, with the title 'Sir'; chess piece usu. with the form of a horse's head. —*v.t.* confer a knighthood on. **knightly** *a.*

knighthood *n.* rank of knight.

knit *v.t./i.* (*p.t.* **knitted** *or* **knit**) form (yarn) into fabric of interlocking loops; make in this way; grow together so as to unite.

knit one's brow frown. **knitter** *n.*, **knitting** *n.*

knitwear *n.* knitted garments.

knob *n.* rounded projecting part, esp. as a handle; small lump. **knobby** *a.*, **knobbly** *a.*

knock *v.t./i.* strike with an audible sharp blow; strike a door etc. to summon a person or gain admittance; drive or make by knocking; (of an engine) make an abnormal thumping or rattling noise; (*sl.*) criticize insultingly. —*n.* act or sound of knocking; sharp blow. **knock about** treat roughly; wander casually. **knock down** dispose of (an article) at auction. **knock-down** *a.* (of price) very low. **knock-kneed** *a.* having an abnormal inward curvature of the legs at the knees (**knock knees**). **knock off** (*colloq.*) cease work; complete quickly; (*sl.*) steal. **knock-on effect** secondary or cumulative effect. **knock out** make unconscious by a blow on the head; eliminate; exhaust; disable. **knock up** rouse by knocking at a door; make or arrange hastily; score (runs) at cricket; make exhausted or ill. **knock-up** *n.* practice or casual game at tennis etc.

knocker *n.* one who knocks; hinged flap for rapping on a door.

knockout *n.* knocking a person etc. out; (*colloq.*) outstanding or irresistible person or thing.

knoll /nəʊl/ *n.* hillock, mound.

knop *n.* ornamental knob; loop or tuft in yarn.

knot *n.* intertwining of one or more pieces of thread or rope etc. as a fastening; tangle; hard mass esp. where a branch joins a tree-trunk; round spot in timber; cluster; unit of speed used by ships and aircraft; = one nautical mile per hour. —*v.t./i.* (*p.t.* **knotted**) tie or fasten with a knot; entangle.

knotty *a.* (**-ier, -iest**) full of knots; puzzling, difficult.

know *v.t./i.* (*p.t.* **knew**, *p.p.* **known**) have in one's mind or memory; feel certain; recognize, be familiar with; understand. **in the know** (*colloq.*) having inside information. **know-all** *n.* person who behaves as if he knows everything. **know-how** *n.* practical knowledge or skill.

knowable *a.* able to be known.

knowing *a.* aware; cunning. **knowingly** *adv.*

knowledge *n.* knowing about things; all a person knows; all that is known, body of information.

knowledgeable *a.* well-informed.

knuckle *n.* finger-joint; animal's knee-joint or part joining the leg to the foot, esp. as meat. —*v.i.* **knuckle under** yield, submit.

knuckleduster *n.* metal device worn over the knuckles in fighting, esp. to increase the injury done by a blow.

koala /kəʊˈɑː-/ *n.* **koala bear** Australian tree-climbing animal with thick grey fur.

kohl /kəʊl/ *n.* powder used to darken the eyelids.

kohlrabi /-ˈrɑː-/ *n.* cabbage with a turnip-like edible stem.

kookaburra *n.* Australian giant kingfisher with a harsh cry.

kopeck /ˈkəʊ-/ *n.* coin of the USSR, one-hundredth of a rouble.

koppie *n.* (*S.Afr.*) small hill.

Koran /-ˈrɑːn/ *n.* sacred book of Muslims, containing the revelations of Muhammad.

kosher /ˈkəʊ-/ *a.* conforming to Jewish dietary laws. —*n.* kosher food; shop selling this.

kowtow *v.i.* behave with exaggerated respect. —*n.* Chinese custom of touching the ground with the forehead in respect.

k.p.h. *abbr.* kilometres per hour.

kraal /krɑːl/ *n.* (*S.Afr.*) fenced village of huts; enclosure.

Kremlin *n.* government of the USSR.

krill *n.* tiny plankton crustaceans that are food for whales etc.

krugerrand /ˈkruːgərɑːnt/ *n.* South African gold coin bearing a portrait of President Kruger.

kudos *n.* (*colloq.*) honour and glory.

kudu *n.* African antelope with white stripes and spiral horns.

kummel /ˈkʊ-/ *n.* liqueur flavoured with caraway seeds.

kumquat *n.* tiny variety of orange.

kung fu Chinese form of unarmed combat similar to karate.

Kurd *n.* member of a people of SW Asia. **Kurdish** *a.*

kV *abbr.* kilovolt(s).

kW *abbr.* kilowatt(s).

L

L *abbr.* learner.

l *abbr.* litre(s).

lab *n.* (*colloq.*) laboratory.

label *n.* note fixed on or beside an object to show its nature, destination, etc. —*v.t.* (*p.t.* **labelled**) fix a label to; describe as. **labeller** *n.*

labial *a.* of the lips.

laboratory *n.* room or building equipped for scientific work.

laborious *a.* needing or showing much effort. **laboriously** *adv.*

Labour *a. & n.* (of) the UK political party representing the interests of workers. **Labourite** *n.*

labour *n.* work, exertion; contractions of the womb at childbirth; workers. —*v.t./i.* work hard; progress or operate with difficulty; emphasize lengthily.

laboured *a.* showing signs of great effort, not spontaneous.

labourer *n.* person employed to do unskilled work.

Labrador *n.* dog of the retriever breed with a black or golden coat.

laburnum *n.* tree with hanging clusters of yellow flowers.

labyrinth n. maze. **labyrinthine** a.

lace n. ornamental openwork fabric or trimming; cord etc. threaded through holes or hooks to pull opposite edges together. —v.t./i. fasten with lace(s); intertwine; add a dash of spirits to (drink).

lacerate v.t. injure (flesh) by tearing; wound (feelings). **laceration** n.

lachrymal a. of tears.

lachrymose a. tearful.

lack n. state or fact of not having something. —v.t. be without.

lackadaisical a. lacking vigour or determination, unenthusiastic.

lackey n. (pl. **-eys**) footman, servant; servile follower.

lacking a. undesirably absent; without.

lacklustre a. lacking brightness or enthusiasm.

laconic a. terse. **laconically** adv., **laconicism** n.

lacquer n. hard glossy varnish. —v.t. coat with lacquer.

lacrosse n. team game using a netted crook to carry a ball.

lactation n. suckling; secretion of milk.

lacuna n. (pl. **-ae** or **-as**) gap.

lacy a. of or like lace.

lad n. boy, young fellow.

ladder n. set of crossbars between uprights, used as a means of climbing; vertical ladder-like flaw where stitches become undone in a stocking etc. —v.t./i. cause or develop a ladder (in).

lade v.t. (p.p. **laden**) load (a ship); ship (goods). **bill of lading** list of a ship's cargo.

laden a. loaded.

la-di-da a. (colloq.) pretentious, affected.

ladle n. deep long-handled spoon for transferring liquids. —v.t. transfer with a ladle.

lady n. woman, esp. of good social position; well-mannered woman;

Lady title of wives, widows, or daughters of certain noblemen.

Lady chapel chapel (within a church) dedicated to the Virgin Mary. **lady-in-waiting** n. lady attending a queen or princess.

ladybird n. small flying beetle, usu. red with black spots.

ladylike a. polite and appropriate to a lady.

ladyship n. title used of or to a woman with rank of Lady.

lag[1] v.i. (p.t. **lagged**) go too slow, not keep up. —n. lagging, delay.

lag[2] v.t. (p.t. **lagged**) encase in material that prevents loss of heat.

lag[3] n. old lag (sl.) convict.

lager /ˈlɑː-/ n. light beer. **lager lout** (colloq.) youth behaving badly after drinking.

laggard n. person who lags behind.

lagging n. material used to lag a boiler etc.

lagoon n. salt-water lake beside a sea; freshwater lake beside a river or larger lake.

laicize /ˈleɪɪ-/ v.t. make secular. **laicization** n.

laid see **lay**[3].

lain see **lie**[2].

lair n. sheltered place where a wild animal regularly sleeps or rests; person's hiding-place.

laird n. (Sc.) landowner.

laissez-faire /leɪseɪˈfeə(r)/ n. policy of non-interference.

laity /ˈleɪtɪ/ n. laymen.

lake[1] n. large body of water surrounded by land.

lake[2] n. reddish pigment.

lakh n. (in India) one hundred thousand.

lam v.t./i. (p.t. **lammed**) (sl.) hit hard.

lama n. Buddhist priest in Tibet and Mongolia.

lamasery /-ˈmɑː-/ n. monastery of lamas.

lamb n. young sheep; its flesh as food; gentle or endearing person. —v.i. give birth to a lamb.

lambaste /-'ber-/ v.t. (colloq.) thrash; reprimand severely.

lambent a. (of flame etc.) licking; glowing.

lambswool n. soft fine wool.

lame a. (-er, -est) unable to walk normally; weak, unconvincing. —v.t. make lame. **lame duck** person etc. unable to manage without help. **lamely** adv., **lameness** n.

lamé /'lɑːmeɪ/ n. fabric with gold or silver thread interwoven.

lament n. passionate expression of grief; song or poem expressing grief. —v.t./i. feel or express grief or regret. **lamentation** n.

lamentable /'læ-/ a. regrettable, deplorable. **lamentably** adv.

lamented a. mourned for.

laminate n. laminated material.

laminated a. made of layers joined one upon another.

Lammas n. first day of August, formerly a harvest festival.

lamp n. device for giving light.

lampblack n. pigment made from soot.

lamplight n. light from a lamp.

lampoon n. piece of writing that attacks a person by ridiculing him. —v.t. ridicule in a lampoon.

lamppost n. tall post of a street lamp.

lamprey n. (pl. -eys) small eel-like water animal.

lampshade n. shade placed over a lamp to screen its light.

lance n. long spear. —v.t. prick or cut open with a lancet. **lance-corporal** n. NCO ranking below corporal.

lanceolate a. tapering to each end like a spearhead.

lancer n. soldier of a regiment formerly armed with lances.

lancet n. surgeon's pointed two-edged knife; tall narrow pointed arch or window.

land n. part of earth's surface not covered by water; expanse of this; ground, soil; country, State; (pl.) estates. —v.t./i. set or go ashore; come or bring (an aircraft) down to the surface of land or water; bring to or reach a place or situation; deal (a person) a blow; bring (a fish) to land; obtain (a prize, appointment, etc.). **land-locked** a. surrounded by land.

landau /-dɔː/ n. a kind of horse-drawn carriage.

landed a. owning land; consisting of land.

landfall n. approach to land after a journey by sea or air.

landfill n. waste material etc. used in landscaping or reclaiming ground; use of this.

landing n. coming or bringing ashore or to ground; place for this; level area at the top of one or more flights of stairs. **landing-stage** n. platform for landing from a boat.

landlady n. woman who lets rooms to tenants or who keeps an inn or boarding-house.

landlord n. person who lets land or a house or room to a tenant; one who keeps an inn or boarding-house.

landlubber n. person not accustomed to the sea and seamanship.

landmark n. conspicuous feature of a landscape; event marking a stage in a thing's history.

landrail n. corncrake.

landscape n. scenery of a land area; picture of this. —v.t. lay out (an area) attractively with natural-looking features.

landslide n. landslip; overwhelming majority of votes.

landslip n. sliding down of a mass of land on a slope.

landsman n. (pl. -men) person who is not a sailor.

landward a. & adv. towards the land. **landwards** adv.

lane n. narrow road, track, or passage; strip of road for a single line of traffic; track to which ships or aircraft etc. must keep.

language *n.* words and their use; system of this used by a nation or group.

languid *a.* lacking vigour or vitality. **languidly** *adv.*

languish *v.i.* lose or lack vitality; live under miserable conditions.

languishing *a.* putting on a languid look.

languor *n.* state of being languid; tender mood or effect. **languorous** *a.*, **languorously** *adv.*

lank *a.* tall and lean; straight and limp. **lanky** *a.*, **lankiness** *n.*

lanolin *n.* fat extracted from sheep's wool, used in ointments.

lantern *n.* transparent case for holding and shielding a light outdoors. **lantern jaw** long thin jaw. **lantern-jawed** *a.*

lanyard *n.* short rope for securing things on a ship; cord for hanging a whistle etc. round the neck or shoulder.

lap[1] *n.* flat area over the thighs of a seated person; overlap; single circuit; section of a journey. —*v.t./i.* (*p.t.* **lapped**) wrap round; overlap; be lap(s) ahead of (a competitor in a race). **lap-dog** *n.* small pampered dog.

lap[2] *v.t./i.* (*p.t.* **lapped**) take up (liquid) by movements of tongue; flow (against) with ripples.

lapel *n.* flap folded back at the front of a coat etc.

lapidary *a.* of stones.

lapis lazuli blue semi-precious stone.

Laplander *n.* native of Lapland.

Lapp *n.* Laplander; language of Lapland.

lappet *n.* flap, fold.

lapse *v.i.* fail to maintain one's position or standard; become void or no longer valid. —*n.* slight error; lapsing; passage of time.

laptop *n.* portable microcomputer.

lapwing *n.* a kind of plover.

larboard *a.* & *n.* = port[3].

larceny *n.* (*former use*) theft of personal goods.

larch *n.* deciduous tree of the pine family.

lard *n.* white greasy substance prepared from pig-fat, used in cooking. —*v.t.* put strips of fat bacon in or on (meat etc.) before cooking; interlard. **lardy** *a.*

larder *n.* room or cupboard for storing food.

large *a.* (**-er, -est**) of great size or extent. —*adv.* in a large way. **at large** free to roam about; in general. **largeness** *n.*

largely *adv.* to a great extent.

largess *n.* (also **largesse**) money or gifts generously given.

lariat *n.* lasso; rope for tethering a horse etc.

lark[1] *n.* small brown bird, skylark.

lark[2] *n.* lighthearted adventurous action; amusing incident; activity. —*v.i.* play lightheartedly.

larkspur *n.* plant with spurshaped blue or pink flowers.

larrikin *n.* (*Austr.*) hooligan.

larva *n.* (*pl.* **-vae**) insect in the first stage after coming out of the egg. **larval** *a.*

laryngitis *n.* inflammation of the larynx.

larynx *n.* part of the throat containing the vocal cords. **laryngeal** *a.*

lasagne /-'sænje/ *n.pl.* pasta in sheets.

Lascar *n.* seaman from islands south-east of India.

lascivious /-'sɪv-/ *a.* lustful. **lasciviously** *adv.*, **lasciviousness** *n.*

laser /'leɪ-/ *n.* device emitting an intense narrow beam of light.

lash *v.t./i.* move in a whip-like movement; beat with a whip; strike violently; fasten with a cord etc. —*n.* flexible part of a whip; stroke with this; eyelash. **lash out** attack with blows or words; spend lavishly.

lashings *n.pl.* (*colloq.*) a lot.

lass, lassie *ns.* (*Sc.* & *N.Engl.*) girl, young woman.

lassitude *n.* tiredness, listlessness.

lasso *n.* (*pl.* **-oes**) rope with a noose for catching cattle. —*v.t.* (*p.t.* **lassoed**, *pres.p.* **lassoing**) catch with a lasso.

last[1] *n.* foot-shaped block used in making and repairing shoes.

last[2] *a.* & *adv.* coming after all others; most recent(ly). —*n.* last person or thing. **at last, at long last** in the end, after much delay. **last post** military bugle-call sounded at sunset or military funerals. **last straw** slight addition to difficulties, making them unbearable. **Last Supper** meal eaten by Christ and his disciples on the eve of his crucifixion. **last trump** trumpet to wake the dead on Judgement Day. **last word** final statement in a dispute; latest fashion. **on its last legs** near the end of its usefulness.

last[3] *v.t./i.* continue, endure; suffice for a period of time. **lasting** *a.*

lastly *adv.* finally.

latch *n.* bar lifted from its catch by a lever, used to fasten a gate etc.; spring-lock that catches when a door is closed. —*v.t./i.* fasten with a latch.

latchkey *n.* key of an outer door.

late *a.* & *adv.* (**-er, -est**) after the proper or usual time; far on in a day or night or period; recent; no longer living or holding a position. **of late** lately. **lateness** *n.*

lateen sail triangular sail on a long yard at an angle of 45° to the mast. **lateen-rigged** *a.*

lately *adv.* recently.

latent *a.* existing but not active or developed or visible. **latency** *n.*

lateral *a.* of, at, to, or from the side(s). **laterally** *adv.*

latex *n.* milky fluid from certain plants, esp. the rubber-tree; similar synthetic substance.

lath /læθ/ *n.* (*pl.* **laths**) narrow thin strip of wood, e.g. in trellis.

lathe /leɪð/ *n.* machine for holding and turning pieces of wood or metal etc. while they are worked.

lather *n.* froth from soap and water; frothy sweat. —*v.t./i.* cover with or form lather.

Latin *n.* language of the ancient Romans. —*a.* of or in Latin; speaking a language based on Latin. **Latin America** parts of Central and South America where Spanish or Portuguese is the main language.

latitude *n.* distance of a place from the equator, measured in degrees; region; freedom from restrictions. **latitudinal** *a.*

latitudinarian *a.* & *n.* (person) liberal in opinions etc., esp. in religion.

latrine *n.* lavatory in a camp or barracks.

latter *a.* mentioned after another; nearer to the end; recent. **latter-day** *a.* modern, recent.

latterly *adv.* recently; nowadays.

lattice *n.* framework of crossed strips. **lattice window** one with this.

laud *v.t.* & *n.* praise.

laudable *a.* praiseworthy. **laudably** *adv.*, **laudability** *n.*

laudanum /ˈlɔːdnəm/ *n.* opium prepared for use as a sedative.

laudatory /ˈlɔː-/ *a.* praising.

laugh *v.t./i.* make sounds and movements of the face that express lively amusement or amused scorn; have these emotions; treat with a laugh. —*n.* act or manner of laughing; (*colloq.*) amusing incident. **laughing-gas** *n.* nitrous oxide as an anaesthetic. **laughing-stock** *n.* person or thing that is ridiculed.

laughable *a.* ridiculous.

laughter *n.* act or sound of laughing.

launch[1] *v.t./i.* send forth; put or go into action; cause (a ship) to slide into the water. —*n.* process of launching something. **launch**

out spend lavishly; start an ambitious enterprise. **launcher** n.

launch[2] n. large motor boat.

launder v.t. wash and iron (clothes etc.); (colloq.) transfer (funds) to conceal their origin.

launderette n. establishment fitted with washing-machines to be used for a fee.

laundress n. woman whose job is to launder clothes etc.

laundry n. place where clothes etc. are laundered; batch of clothes etc. sent to or from this.

laureate /'lɒ-/ a. wreathed with laurel as an honour. **Poet Laureate** poet appointed to write poems for State occasions.

laurel /'lɒ-/ n. evergreen shrub with smooth glossy leaves; (pl.) victories or honours gained.

lav n. (colloq.) lavatory.

lava n. flowing or hardened molten rock from a volcano.

lavatory n. pan (usu. a fixture) into which urine and faeces are discharged for disposal; room etc. equipped with this.

lave v.t. (literary) wash; flow along.

lavender n. shrub with fragrant purple flowers; light purple. **lavender-water** n. delicate perfume made from lavender.

laver[1] /'leɪ-, 'lɑː-/ n. edible seaweed.

laver[2] /'leɪ-/ n. basin for ritual ablutions in ancient Israel; (old use) font.

lavish a. giving or producing something in large quantities; plentiful. —v.t. bestow lavishly. **lavishly** adv., **lavishness** n.

law n. rule(s) established by authority or custom; their influence or operation; statement of what always happens in certain circumstances. **law-abiding** a. obeying the law. **lawgiver** n.

lawcourt n. room or building where legal cases are heard and judged.

lawful a. permitted or recognized by law. **lawfully** adv., **lawfulness** n.

lawless a. disregarding the law, uncontrolled. **lawlessness** n.

lawn[1] n. fine woven cotton or synthetic fabric.

lawn[2] n. area of closely cut grass. **lawn tennis** (see **tennis**).

lawnmower n. machine for cutting the grass of lawns.

lawsuit n. process of bringing a problem or claim etc. before a court of law for settlement.

lawyer n. person trained and qualified in legal matters.

lax a. slack, not strict or severe. **laxly** adv., **laxity** n.

laxative a. & n. (medicine) stimulating the bowels to empty.

lay[1] n. (old use) poem meant to be sung, ballad.

lay[2] a. not ordained into the clergy; non-professional.

lay[3] v.t./i. (p.t. **laid**) place on a surface; arrange ready for use; cause to be in a certain condition; cause to subside; present for consideration; stake; (of a hen) produce (an egg or eggs) from the body; (incorrect use) = **lie**[2]. —n. way a thing lies. **lay about one** hit out on all sides. **lay bare** expose, reveal. **lay hold of** grasp. **lay into** (sl.) thrash; reprimand harshly. **lay off** discharge (workers) temporarily through lack of work; (colloq.) cease. **lay-off** n. temporary discharge. **lay on** provide. **lay out** arrange according to a plan; prepare (a body) for burial; spend (money) for a purpose; knock unconscious. **lay up** store; cause (a person) to be ill. **lay waste** destroy the crops and buildings of (an area).

lay[4] see **lie**[2].

layabout n. loafer, one who lazily avoids working for a living.

lay-by n. extra strip of road beside a carriageway, where vehicles may stop without obstructing traffic.

layer *n.* one thickness of material laid over a surface; attached shoot fastened down to take root; one who lays something. —*v.t.* arrange in layers; propagate (a plant) by layers.

layette *n.* outfit for a new-born baby.

lay figure artist's jointed model of the human body; person or character lacking individuality.

layman *n.* (*pl.* **-men**) non-professional person.

layout *n.* arrangement of parts etc. according to a plan.

laze *v.i.* spend time idly or in idle relaxation. —*n.* act or period of lazing.

lazy *a.* (**-ier, -iest**) unwilling to work, doing little work; showing lack of energy. **lazy-tongs** *n.* zig-zag levers for picking up distant objects. **lazily** *adv.*, **laziness** *n.*

lazybones *n.* (*colloq.*) lazy person.

lb *abbr.* pound(s) weight.

lea *n.* (*poetic*) piece of meadow etc.

leach *v.t./i.* percolate (liquid) through soil or ore etc.; remove (soluble matter) or be removed in this way.

lead[1] /li:d/ *v.t./i.* (*p.t.* **led**) guide; influence into an action, opinion, or state; be a route or means of access; pass (one's life); be in first place in, be ahead; make one's start; be the first player in card-game, play as one's first card. —*n.* guidance; clue; leading place, amount by which one competitor is in front; wire conveying electric current; strap or cord for leading an animal; act or right of playing the first card in card-game; this card; chief part in a play or other performance; its player. **lead up to** serve as introduction to or preparation for; direct conversation towards. **leading article** newspaper article giving editorial opinions.

leading question one worded to prompt the desired answer.

lead[2] /led/ *n.* heavy grey metal; graphite as the writing-substance in a pencil; lump of lead used for sounding depths; (*pl.*) strips of lead. —*v.t.* cover, weight, or frame with leads.

leaden /'le-/ *a.* made of lead; heavy, slow as if weighted with lead; dark grey.

leader *n.* person or thing that leads; leading article. **leader board** scoreboard showing names of leading players. **leadership** *n.*

leaf *n.* flat (usu. green) organ growing from the stem, branch, or root of a plant; single thickness of paper as a page of a book; very thin sheet of metal; hinged flap or extra section of a table. —*v.i.* **leaf through** turn over the leaves of (a book). **leaf-mould** *n.* soil or compost consisting of decayed leaves.

leafage *n.* leaves of plants.

leafless *a.* having no leaves.

leaflet *n.* small leaf of a plant; printed sheet of paper giving information. —*v.t.* (*p.t.* **leafleted**) distribute leaflets to.

leafy *a.* with many leaves.

league[1] *n.* (*old use*) measure of distance, about 3 miles.

league[2] *n.* union of people or countries; association of sports clubs which compete against each other for a championship; class of contestants. —*v.i.* form a league. **in league with** allied or conspiring with.

leak *n.* hole through which liquid or gas makes its way wrongly; liquid etc. passing through this; process of leaking; similar escape of an electric charge; disclosure of secret information. —*v.t./i.* escape or let out from a container; disclose. **leak out** become known. **leakage** *n.*, **leaky** *a.*

lean[1] *a.* (**-er, -est**) without much flesh; (of meat) with little or no fat; scanty. —*n.* lean part of meat. **leanness** *n.*

lean² *v.t./i.* (*p.t.* **leaned**, *p.p.* **leant**) put or be in a sloping position; rest against for support; have leanings. **lean on** depend on for help; (*colloq.*) seek to influence by intimidating. **lean-to** *n.* shed etc. abutting against the side of a building.

leaning *n.* inclination, preference.

leap *v.t./i.* (*p.t.* **leaped**, *p.p.* **leapt**) jump vigorously. —*n.* vigorous jump. **leap year** year with an extra day (29 Feb.).

leap-frog *n.* game in which each player in turn vaults over another who is bending down. —*v.t./i.* (*p.t.* -**frogged**) perform this vault (over); overtake alternately.

learn *v.t./i.* (*p.t.* **learned** or **learnt**) gain knowledge of or skill in; become aware of; (*joc.* or *incorrect use*) teach. **learner** *n.*

learned /-nid/ *a.* having or showing great learning. **learnedly** *adv.*

learning *n.* knowledge obtained by study.

lease *n.* contract allowing the use of land or a building for a specified time. —*v.t.* allow, obtain, or hold by lease. **leasehold** *n.*, **leaseholder** *n.*

leash *n.* dog's lead; thong for holding hounds under restraint. —*v.t.* put a leash on; restrain.

least *a.* smallest in amount or degree; lowest in importance. —*n.* least amount etc. —*adv.* in the least degree.

leather *n.* material made from animal skins by tanning or a similar process; piece of soft leather for polishing with. —*v.t.* cover or polish with leather; thrash. **leather-jacket** *n.* cranefly grub with tough skin.

leathery *a.* leather-like; tough.

leave *v.t./i.* (*p.t.* **left**) go away (from); go away finally or permanently; let remain; deposit; entrust with; abandon. —*n.* permission; official permission to be absent from duty, period for which this lasts. **leave out** not insert or include. **on leave** absent in this way. **take one's leave** say farewell and go away.

leaven /'le-/ *n.* substance (e.g. yeast) used to produce fermentation in dough; enlivening influence. —*v.t.* add leaven to; enliven.

leavings *n.pl.* what is left.

lecher *n.* lecherous man.

lechery *n.* unrestrained indulgence in sexual lust. **lecherous** *a.*

lectern *n.* stand with a sloping top to hold a Bible etc. to be read from.

lectionary *n.* list of scriptural passages to be read in church.

lecture *n.* speech giving information about a subject; lengthy reproof or warning. —*v.t./i.* give lecture(s); give a lengthy reproof etc. to. **lecturer** *n.*, **lectureship** *n.*

led *see* **lead**¹.

ledge *n.* narrow horizontal projection; narrow shelf.

ledger *n.* book used as an account-book or to record trading transactions.

lee *n.* sheltered side, shelter in this.

leech¹ *n.* small blood-sucking worm.

leech² *n.* vertical or after side of a sail.

leek *n.* plant related to the onion, with a cylindrical white bulb.

leer *v.i.* look slyly or maliciously or lustfully. —*n.* leering look.

leery *a.* (*sl.*) knowing, sly; wary.

lees *n.pl.* sediment in wine.

leeward /'li:-, *nautical pr.* 'lu:-/ *a.* & *n.* (on) the side away from the wind.

leeway *n.* ship's sideways drift from its course; degree of freedom of action; **make up leeway** make up lost time or position.

left[1] see **leave**.

left[2] a. & adv. of, on, or to the side or region opposite right. —n. left side or region; left hand or foot; people supporting a more extreme form of socialism than others in their group. **left-handed** a. using the left hand.

leftist a. & n. (member) of the left wing of a political party.

leftovers n.pl. things remaining when the rest is finished.

leg n. each of the limbs on which an animal stands or moves; part of a garment covering a person's leg; projecting support of piece of furniture; one section of a journey or contest; side of a cricket field opposite the off side and behind the batsman. —v.t. (p.t. **legged**) **leg it** (colloq.) walk or run rapidly, go on foot. **leg-pull** n. (colloq.) hoax.

legacy n. thing left to someone in a will, or handed down by a predecessor.

legal a. of or based on law; authorized or required by law. **legalistic** a., **legally** adv., **legality** n.

legalize v.t. make legal. **legalization** n.

legate /-ət/ n. envoy.

legatee n. recipient of a legacy.

legation n. diplomatic minister and staff; their headquarters.

legend n. story handed down from the past; such stories collectively; inscription on a coin or medal.

legendary a. of or described in legend; (colloq.) famous.

legerdemain /ledʒədə'meɪn/ n. sleight of hand.

leger line /'ledʒ-/ short line added to a musical staff for notes above or below it.

leggings n.pl. protective coverings for the legs from knee to ankle; knitted trousers.

leggy a. long-legged or -stemmed.

leghorn n. fine plaited straw; hat of this.

legible a. clear enough to read. **legibly** adv., **legibility** n.

legion n. division of the ancient Roman army; organized group; multitude.

legionnaire n. member of a legion. **legionnaires' disease** form of bacterial pneumonia.

legislate v.i. make laws. **legislator** n.

legislation n. legislating; law(s) made.

legislative a. making laws.

legislature n. country's legislative assembly.

legitimate a. in accordance with a law or rule; justifiable; born of parents married to each other. **legitimately** adv., **legitimacy** n.

legitimize v.t. make legitimate. **legitimization** n.

legless a. without legs; (sl.) drunk.

legume /'leg-/ n. leguminous plant; pod of this.

leguminous a. of the family of plants bearing seeds in pods.

lei n. Polynesian garland.

leisure n. time free from work, in which one can do what one chooses. **at one's leisure** when one has time. **leisure centre** large public building with sports facilities, bars, etc.

leisured a. having ample leisure.

leisurely a. & adv. without hurry.

leitmotiv /'laɪtməʊtiːf/ n. theme associated with a person or idea, esp. in a piece of music.

lemming n. mouse-like rodent of arctic regions (said to rush headlong into the sea in its migration, and drown).

lemon n. oval fruit with acid juice; tree bearing it; its pale yellow colour; (colloq.) unsatisfactory person or thing. **lemony** a.

lemonade n. lemon-flavoured soft drink.

lemon sole a kind of plaice.

lemur /ˈliːmə(r)/ n. nocturnal monkey-like animal of Madagascar.

lend v.t. (p.t. **lent**) give or allow to use temporarily; provide (money) temporarily in return for payment of interest; contribute as a help or effect. **lend itself to** be suitable for. **lender** n.

length n. measurement or extent from end to end; great extent; piece (of cloth etc.). **at length** after or taking a long time.

lengthen v.t./i. make or become longer.

lengthways adv. in the direction of a thing's length. **lengthwise** adv. & a.

lengthy a. (-ier, -iest) very long; long and boring. **lengthily** adv.

lenient a. merciful, not punishing severely. **leniently** adv., **lenience** n.

lenity /ˈlen-/ n. gentleness; mercifulness.

lens n. piece of glass or similar substance shaped for use in an optical instrument; transparent part of the eye, behind the pupil.

Lent n. Christian period of fasting and repentance, the 40 weekdays before Easter. **Lenten** a.

lent see **lend**.

lentil n. a kind of bean.

leonine a. of or like a lion.

leopard n. large flesh-eating animal of the cat family, with a dark-spotted yellowish or a black coat. **leopardess** n.fem.

leotard /ˈliːə-/ n. close-fitting garment worn by acrobats etc.

leper n. person with leprosy.

lepidopterous a. of the insects (e.g. butterflies) with scale-covered wings. **lepidopterist** n. person who studies such insects.

leprechaun n. (in Irish folklore) elf resembling a little old man.

leprosy n. infectious disease affecting the skin and nerves and causing deformities. **leprous** a.

lesbian n. & a. homosexual (woman). **lesbianism** n.

lese-majesty /liːz-/ n. treason; presumptuous conduct.

lesion n. harmful change in the tissue of an organ of the body.

less a. not so much of; smaller in amount or degree. —adv. to a smaller extent. —n. smaller amount. —prep. minus, deducting.

lessee n. person holding property by lease.

lessen v.t./i. make or become less.

lesser a. not so great as the other.

lesson n. amount of teaching given at one time; thing to be learnt by a pupil; experience by which one can learn; passage from the Bible read aloud in church.

lessor n. person who lets property on lease.

lest conj. for fear that.

let[1] n. stoppage; (in tennis etc.) obstruction requiring the ball to be served again.

let[2] v.t./i. (p.t. **let**, pres.p. **letting**) allow or cause to; allow or cause to come, go, or pass; allow the use of (rooms or land) in return for payment. —v.aux. (used in requests, commands, assumptions, or challenges). —n. letting of property etc. **let alone** refrain from interfering with or doing; not to mention. **let down** let out air from (a balloon, tyre, etc.); fail to support, disappoint; lengthen. **let-down** n. disappointment. **let in** allow to enter; insert. **let in for** involve in. **let off** fire (a gun); cause to explode; ignite (a firework); excuse from; give little or no punishment to. **let on** (sl.) reveal a secret. **let out** allow to go out or escape; make looser. **let up** (colloq.) relax. **let up** n.

lethal a. causing death.

lethargy n. extreme lack of energy or vitality. **lethargic** a., **lethargically** adv.

letter n. symbol representing a speech-sound; written message, usu. sent by post; strict interpretation (of a law etc.); (*pl.*) literature. —*v.t.* inscribe letters (on).

letter-box *n.* slit in a door, with a movable flap, through which letters are delivered; postbox.

letterhead *n.* printed heading on stationery; stationery with this.

lettuce *n.* plant with broad crisp leaves used as salad.

leucocyte *n.* white blood cell.

leukaemia *n.* disease in which white corpuscles multiply uncontrollably.

Levant /lɪˈvæ-/ *n.* countries and islands of the eastern Mediterranean. **Levantine** /ˈlevəntəm/ *a.* & *n.*

levee[1] *n.* formal assembly of visitors.

levee[2] *n.* (*US*) embankment against floods; quay.

level *a.* horizontal; without projections or hollows; on a level with; steady, uniform. —*n.* horizontal line or plane; device for testing this; measured height or value etc.; relative position; level surface or area. —*v.t./i.* (*p.t.* **levelled**) make or become level; knock down (a building); aim (a gun, missile, or accusation etc.). **level crossing** place where a road and railway cross at the same level. **level-headed** *a.* mentally well-balanced, sensible. **level pegging** equality in score or achievements. **on the level** honest(ly). **leveller** *n.*

lever *n.* bar pivoted on a fixed point to lift something; pivoted handle used to operate machinery; means of power or influence. —*v.t./i.* use a lever; lift by this.

leverage *n.* action or power of a lever; power, influence.

leveret /ˈlev-/ *n.* young hare.

leviathan /lɪˈvaɪ-/ *n.* thing of enormous size and power.

levitate *v.t./i.* rise or cause to rise and float in the air. **levitation** *n.*

levity *n.* humorous attitude.

levy *v.t.* impose (payment) or collect (an army etc.) by authority or force. —*n.* levying; payment or (*pl.*) troops levied.

lewd *a.* (**-er, -est**) indecent, treating sexual matters vulgarly; lascivious. **lewdly** *adv.*, **lewdness** *n.*

lexical *a.* of words. **lexically** *adv.*

lexicography *n.* process of compiling a dictionary. **lexicographer** *n.*

lexicon *n.* dictionary.

ley /leɪ/ *n.* land temporarily under grass.

Leyden jar /ˈleɪ-/ a kind of electrical condenser.

liability *n.* being liable; (*colloq.*) disadvantage; (*pl.*) debts, obligations.

liable *a.* held responsible by law, legally obliged to pay a tax or penalty etc.; likely to do or suffer something.

liaise *v.i.* (*colloq.*) act as liaison.

liaison *n.* communication and cooperation; person who acts as a link or go-between; illicit sexual relationship.

liana /-ˈɑːnə/ *n.* climbing plant of tropical forests.

liar *n.* person who tells lies.

libation *n.* drink-offering to a god.

libel *n.* published false statement that damages a person's reputation; act of publishing it. —*v.t.* (*p.t.* **libelled**) publish a libel against. **libellous** *a.*

Liberal *a.* & *n.* (member) of a political party favouring moderate reform. **Liberal Democrat** member of a UK political party including former Liberals. **Liberalism** *n.*

liberal *a.* generous; tolerant. **liberally** *adv.*, **liberality** *n.*

liberalize *v.t.* make less strict. **liberalization** *n.*, **liberalizer** *n.*

liberate *v.t.* set free, esp. from oppression. **liberation** *n.*, **liberator** *n.*

libertine /-tiːn/ *n.* man who lives an irresponsible immoral life.

liberty n. freedom. **take the liberty** venture. **take liberties** behave with undue freedom or familiarity.

libidinous /-'bɪd-/ a. lustful.

libido /-'biːd/ n. (pl. -os) emotional energy or urge, esp. of sexual desire. **libidinal** /-'bɪd-/ a.

librarian n. person in charge of or assisting in a library.

library n. collection of books for consulting or borrowing; room or building containing these; similar collection of records, films, etc.

libretto n. (pl. -ti or -os) words of opera or other long musical work. **librettist** n.

lice see **louse**.

licence n. official permit to own or do something; permission; disregard of rules etc.

license v.t. grant a licence to or for. **licenser** n., **licensor** n.

licensee n. holder of a licence.

licentiate n. holder of a certificate of competence in a profession.

licentious /-'senʃəs/ a. sexually immoral. **licentiousness** n.

lichen /'laɪkən/ n. dry-looking plant that grows on rocks etc.

lich-gate n. roofed gateway to a churchyard.

lick v.t./i. pass the tongue over; (of waves or flame) touch lightly; (sl.) defeat. —n. act of licking; blow with a stick etc.; slight application (of paint etc.); (sl.) fast pace. **lick into shape** make presentable or efficient.

lid n. hinged or removable cover for a box, pot, etc.; eyelid.

lido /'liːd-/ n. (pl. -os) public open-air swimming-pool or beach.

lie[1] n. statement the speaker knows to be untrue. —v.i. (p.t. **lied**, pres.p. **lying**) tell lie(s). **give the lie to** show to be untrue.

lie[2] v.t./i. (p.t. **lay**, p.p. **lain**, pres.p. **lying**) have or put one's body in a flat or resting position; be at rest on something; be in a specified state; be situated; exist; be admissible or able to be upheld as a lawsuit or appeal. —n. way a thing lies. **lie in** lie idly in bed late in the morning. **lie-in** n. such lying. **lie low** conceal oneself or one's intentions.

lief adv. (old use) willingly.

liege n. (old use) vassal, subject; feudal lord. **liegeman** n.

lien /lɪːn/ n. right to hold another's property until a debt on it is paid.

lieu /ljuː/ n. **in lieu** instead.

lieutenant /lef'ten-/ n. army officer next below captain; naval officer next below lieutenant commander; rank just below a specified officer; chief assistant.

life n. (pl. **lives**) animals' and plants' ability to function and grow; being alive; period of this; living things; liveliness; activities or manner of living; biography. **life cycle** series of forms into which a living thing changes. **life-jacket** n. jacket of buoyant material to keep a person afloat. **life-preserver** n. short heavy stick as a defensive weapon; lifebelt, life-jacket. **life-size**, **life-sized** adjs. of the same size etc. as a real person. **life-support** a. (of equipment etc.) enabling the body to function normally in a hostile environment or in cases of physical failure.

lifebelt n. belt of buoyant material to keep a person afloat.

lifeboat n. boat constructed for going to help people in danger on the sea near a coast; ship's boat for emergency use.

lifebuoy n. buoyant device to keep a person afloat.

lifeguard n. expert swimmer employed to rescue bathers who are in danger.

lifeless a. without life; dead; unconscious; lacking liveliness.

lifelike n. exactly like a real person or thing.

lifeline *n.* rope etc. used in rescue; vital means of communication.

lifelong *a.* for all one's life.

lifetime *n.* duration of a person's life.

lift *v.t./i.* raise; take up; rise, (of fog etc.) disperse; remove (restrictions); steal, plagiarize. —*n.* lifting; apparatus for transporting people or goods from one level to another, esp. in a building; free ride in a motor vehicle; feeling of elation. **lift-off** *n.* vertical take-off of a spacecraft etc.

ligament *n.* tough flexible tissue holding bones together.

ligature *n.* thing that ties something, esp. in surgical operations; letters joined in printing. —*v.t.* tie with a ligature.

light[1] *n.* a kind of radiation that stimulates sight; brightness, light part of a picture etc.; source of light, electric lamp; trafficlight; flame or spark; enlightenment; aspect, way a thing appears to the mind; (*pl.*) mental powers; (*pl.*) words to be deduced from a crossword clue. —*a.* full of light, not in darkness; paled. —*v.t./i.* (*p.t.* **lit** or **lighted**) set burning, begin to burn; provide with light; brighten. **bring to light** reveal. **come to light** be revealed. **light-pen** *n.* light-emitting device for reading bar-codes; (also **light-gun**) pen-like or gun-like device for passing information to a computer screen. **light up** put lights on at dusk; brighten; make or become animated; begin to smoke a pipe or cigar or cigarette. **light-year** *n.* distance light travels in one year, about 6 million million miles.

light[2] *a.* (**-er, -est**) having light weight; not heavy, easy to lift or carry or do; of less than average weight or force or intensity; cheerful; not profound or serious; (of food) easy to digest. —*adv.* lightly, with little load.

light-fingered *a.* apt to steal.

light-headed *a.* feeling slightly faint; delirious. **light-hearted** *a.* cheerful. **light industry** manufacture of small or light articles. **make light of** treat as unimportant. **lightly** *adv.*, **lightness** *n.*

light[3] *v.i.* (*p.t.* **lit** or **lighted**) light on find accidentally. **light out** (*sl.*) depart.

lighten[1] *v.t./i.* shed light on; make or become brighter; flash with lightning.

lighten[2] *v.t./i.* make or become less heavy.

lighter[1] *n.* device for lighting cigarettes and cigars.

lighter[2] *n.* flat-bottomed boat for transporting goods between ship and wharf. **lighterman** *n.*

lighthouse *n.* tower with a beacon light to warn or guide ships.

lighting *n.* means of providing light; the light itself.

lightning *n.* flash of bright light produced from cloud by natural electricity. —*a.* very quick. **like lightning** with very great speed.

lights *n.pl.* lungs of certain animals, used as animal food.

lightship *n.* moored or anchored ship with a beacon light, serving as a lighthouse.

lightsome *a.* gracefully light or agile; merry.

lightweight *a.* not having great weight or influence. —*n.* lightweight person; boxing-weight (60 kg.)

lignite *n.* brown coal of woody texture.

like[1] *a.* having the qualities or appearance of; characteristic of; in a suitable state or right mood for. —*prep.* in the manner of, to the same degree as. —*conj.* (*colloq.*) as; (*US*) as if. —*adv.* (*colloq.*) likely. —*n.* person or thing like another. **like-minded** *a.* having similar tastes or opinions.

like[2] *v.t.* find pleasant or satisfactory; wish for. **likes** *n.pl.* things one likes or prefers.

likeable *a.* pleasant, easy to like.

likelihood *n.* probability.

likely *a.* (**-ier, -iest**) such as may reasonably be expected to occur or be true; seeming to be suitable or have a chance of success. —*adv.* probably. **not likely** (*colloq.*) certainly not. **likeliness** *n.*

liken *v.t.* point out the likeness of (one thing to another).

likeness *n.* being like; copy, portrait.

likewise *adv.* also; in the same way.

liking *n.* what one likes; one's feeling that one likes a thing.

lilac *n.* shrub with fragrant purple or white flowers; pale purple. —*a.* pale purple.

liliaceous *a.* of the lily family.

lilliputian /-'pju:-/ *a.* very small.

lilt *n.* light pleasant rhythm; song with this. **lilting** *a.*

lily *n.* plant growing from a bulb, with large white, orange, or reddish flowers.

limb *n.* projecting part of an animal body, used in movement or in grasping things; large branch of a tree; mischievous child. **out on a limb** isolated, stranded.

limber *a.* flexible, supple. —*v.t./i.* **limber up** exercise in preparation for athletic activity.

limbo[1] *n.* intermediate inactive or neglected state.

limbo[2] *n.* (*pl.* **-os**) West Indian dance in which the dancer bends back to pass below a horizontal bar.

lime[1] *n.* white substance used in making cement etc.

lime[2] *n.* round yellowish-green fruit like a lemon; its colour.

lime[3] *n.* tree with heart-shaped leaves. **lime-tree** *n.*

limelight *n.* great publicity.

limerick *n.* a type of humorous poem with five lines.

limestone *n.* a kind of rock from which lime is obtained.

Limey *n.* (*US sl.*) British person.

limit *n.* point beyond which something does not continue; greatest amount allowed. —*v.t./i.* set or serve as a limit, keep within limits. **limitation** *n.*

limousine *n.* large luxurious car.

limp[1] *v.i.* walk or proceed lamely. —*n.* limping walk.

limp[2] *a.* (**-er, -est**) not stiff or firm; wilting. **limply** *adv.*, **limpness** *n.*

limpet *n.* small shellfish that sticks tightly to rocks.

limpid *a.* (of liquids) clear. **limpidly** *adv.*, **limpidity** *n.*

linchpin *n.* pin passed through the end of an axle to secure a wheel; person or thing vital to something.

linctus *n.* soothing cough-medicine.

linden *n.* lime-tree.

line[1] *n.* long narrow mark; outline; boundary; row of people or things; row of words on a page or in a poem, (*pl.*) words of an actor's part; brief letter; service of ships, buses, or aircraft; series, several generations of a family; direction, course; railway track; type of activity, business, or goods; piece of cord for a particular purpose; electrical or telephone cable, connection by this; each of a set of military fieldworks; **the Line** the equator. —*v.t.* mark with lines; arrange in line(s). **get a line on** (*colloq.*) discover information about. **in line with** in accordance with.

line[2] *v.t.* cover the inside surface of. **line one's pockets** make money, esp. in underhand or dishonest ways.

lineage /'lɪnɪɪdʒ/ *n.* line of ancestors or descendants.

lineal *a.* of or in a line.

lineaments *n.pl.* features of the face.

linear *a.* of a line, of length; arranged in a line.

linen *n.* cloth made of flax; household articles (e.g. sheets, table-cloths) formerly made of this.

liner[1] *n.* passenger ship or aircraft of a regular line.

liner[2] *n.* removable lining.

linesman *n.* (*pl.* **-men**) umpire's assistant at the boundary line; worker who tests railway lines or repairs electrical or telephone cables.

ling[1] *n.* a kind of heather.

ling[2] *n.* sea fish of north Europe.

linger *v.i.* stay on as if reluctant to leave; dawdle.

lingerie /ˈlæʒərɪ/ *n.* women's underwear.

lingo *n.* (*pl.* **-oes**) (*joc.* or *derog.*) language.

lingua franca language used between people of an area where several languages are spoken.

lingual *a.* of the tongue; of speech or languages.

linguist *n.* person who knows foreign languages well; expert in linguistics.

linguistic *a.* of language. **linguistics** *n.* study of languages and their structure. **linguistically** *adv.*

liniment *n.* embrocation.

lining *n.* layer of material or substance covering an inner surface.

link *n.* each ring of a chain; person or thing connecting others. —*v.t.* connect; intertwine. **linkage** *n.*

links *n.* or *n.pl.* golf-course.

linnet *n.* a kind of finch.

lino *n.* linoleum.

linocut *n.* design cut in relief on a block of linoleum; print made from this.

linoleum *n.* a kind of smooth covering for floors.

linseed *n.* seed of flax.

lint *n.* soft fabric for dressing wounds; fluff.

lintel *n.* horizontal timber or stone over a doorway etc.

lion *n.* large flesh-eating animal of the cat family. **lion's share** largest part. **lioness** *n.fem.*

lionize *v.t.* treat as a celebrity.

lip *n.* either of the fleshy edges of the mouth-opening; edge of a container or opening; slight projection shaped for pouring from. **lip-read** *v.t./i.* understand (what is said) from movements of a speaker's lips. **pay lip-service** state approval insincerely. **lipped** *a.*

lipsalve *n.* ointment for the lips.

lipstick *n.* cosmetic for colouring the lips; stick of this.

liquefy *v.t./i.* make or become liquid. **liquefaction** *n.*

liqueur /lɪˈkjʊə(r)/ *n.* strong alcoholic spirit with fragrant flavouring.

liquid *n.* flowing substance like water or oil. —*a.* in the form of liquid; (of sound) flowing pleasantly; (of assets) easy to convert into cash. **liquidity** *n.*

liquidate *v.t.* pay and settle (a debt); close down (a business) and divide its assets between creditors; get rid of, esp. by killing. **liquidation** *n.*, **liquidator** *n.*

liquidize *v.t.* reduce to a liquid state.

liquidizer *n.* machine for making purées etc.

liquor *n.* alcoholic drink; juice from cooked food.

liquorice *n.* black substance used in medicine and as a sweet; plant from whose root it is made.

lira *n.* (*pl.* **lire**, *pr.* ˈlɪəreɪ) unit of money in Italy and Turkey.

lisle *n.* fine smooth cotton thread used esp. for stockings.

lisp *n.* speech defect in which *s* and *z* are pronounced like *th*. —*v.t./i.* speak or utter with a lisp.

lissom *a.* lithe.

list[1] *n.* written or printed series of names, items, figures, etc. —*v.t.* make a list of; enter in a list.

enter the lists make or accept a challenge in a controversy etc.

list[2] *v.i.* (of a ship) lean over to one side. *—n.* listing position.

listen *v.i.* make an effort to hear; pay attention; be persuaded by advice or a request. **listen in** overhear a conversation; listen to a broadcast. **listener** *n.*

listeria *n.* bacterium found in contaminated food.

listeriosis /-'əʊ-/ *n.* infection from eating food containing listeria.

listless *a.* without energy or enthusiasm. **listlessly** *adv.*, **listlessness** *n.*

lit *see* **light**[1], **light**[3].

litany *n.* a set form of prayer.

litchi /'liːtʃiː/ *n.* (*pl.* **-is**) fruit with sweet white pulp in a thin brown shell; tree bearing this.

literacy *n.* being literate.

literal *a.* taking the primary meaning of a word or words, not a metaphorical or exaggerated one. **literally** *adv.*, **literalness** *n.*

literary *a.* of literature.

literate *a.* able to read and write.

literature *n.* writings, esp. great novels, poetry, and plays.

lithe *a.* supple, agile.

litho /'laɪ-/ *a.* & *n.* lithographic (process).

lithograph /'lɪθ-/ *n.* picture printed by lithography.

lithography /-'θɒg-/ *n.* printing from a design on a smooth surface. **lithographic** *a.*

litigant *a.* & *n.* (person) involved in or initiating a lawsuit.

litigate *v.t./i.* carry on a lawsuit; contest in law.

litigious *a.* fond of litigation.

litmus *n.* blue colouring-matter that is turned red by acids and restored to blue by alkalis. **litmus-paper** *n.* paper stained with this.

litre *n.* metric unit of capacity (about 1¾ pints) for measuring liquids.

litter *n.* rubbish left lying about; straw etc. put down as bedding for animals; young animals born at one birth; material for filling a receptacle in which a domestic cat etc. may excrete. *—v.t.* scatter as litter; make untidy by litter; give birth to (a litter of young).

little *a.* small in size, amount, or intensity etc. *—n.* small amount, time, or distance. *—adv.* to a small extent; not at all.

littoral *a.* & *n.* (region) of or on the shore.

liturgy *n.* set form of public worship used in churches. **liturgical** *a.*

live[1] /laɪv/ *a.* alive; burning; unexploded; charged with electricity; (of broadcasts) transmitted while actually happening, not recorded; not obsolete. **live wire** energetic forceful person.

live[2] /lɪv/ *v.t./i.* have life, remain alive; have one's dwelling-place; conduct (one's life) in a certain way; enjoy life fully. **live down** live until (scandal etc.) is forgotten. **live it up** live in a lively extravagant way. **live on** keep oneself alive on. **liveable** *a.*

livelihood *n.* means of earning or providing enough food etc. to sustain life.

livelong *a.* **the livelong day** the whole day.

lively *a.* (**-ier**, **-iest**) full of energy or action. **liveliness** *n.*

liven *v.t./i.* make or become lively.

liver *n.* large organ in the abdomen, secreting bile; animal's liver as food; dark reddish-brown.

liveried *a.* wearing livery.

livery *n.* distinctive uniform worn by male servants or by members of the London trade guilds. **livery stable** stable where horses are kept for an owner or let out for hire.

livestock *n.* farm animals.

livid *a.* of the colour of lead, bluish-grey; (*colloq.*) furiously angry.

living a. having life, not dead; (of likeness) exact. —n. being alive; manner of life; livelihood. **living-room** n. room for general day-time use. **living will** written statement of person's desire not to be kept artificially alive in certain circumstances.

lizard n. reptile with four legs and a long tail.

llama n. South American animal related to the camel but with no hump.

lo int. (old use) see.

loach n. small freshwater fish.

load n. thing or quantity carried; amount of electric current supplied by a generating station or carried by a circuit; burden of responsibility or worry; (pl., colloq.) plenty. —v.t./i. put a load in or on; receive a load; fill heavily; weight; put into; put ammunition into (a gun) or film into (a camera); put (data etc.) into (a computer). **loader** n.

loaf[1] n. (pl. **loaves**) mass of bread shaped in one piece; (sl.) head.

loaf[2] v.i. spend time idly, stand or saunter about. **loafer** n.

loam n. rich soil. **loamy** a.

loan n. lending; thing lent, esp. money. —v.t. grant a loan of.

loath a. unwilling.

loathe v.t. feel hatred and disgust for. **loathing** n., **loathsome** a.

lob v.t. (p.t. **lobbed**) send or strike (a ball) slowly in a high arc. —n. lobbed ball.

lobar /ˈləʊ-/ a. of a lobe, esp. of the lung.

lobby n. porch, entrance-hall, ante-room; body of people lobbying an MP or seeking to influence legislation. —v.t. seek support from (an MP etc.).

lobbyist n. person who lobbies.

lobe n. rounded part or projection; lower soft part of the ear.

lobelia n. low-growing garden plant used esp. for edging.

lobotomy n. surgical incision into a lobe of the brain.

lobster n. large shellfish that turns scarlet when boiled; its flesh as food. **lobster-pot** n. basket for trapping lobsters.

local a. of or affecting a particular place or small area. —n. inhabitant of a particular district; (colloq.) public house of a neighbourhood. **local colour** details added to a story etc. to give a realistic background. **local government** administration of a district by elected representatives of people who live there. **locally** adv.

locale /-ˈkɑːl/ n. scene of event.

locality n. thing's position; site, neighbourhood.

localize v.t. assign to a particular place; confine within an area; decentralize. **localization** n.

locate v.t. discover the position of; situate in a particular location.

location n. locating; place where a thing is situated. **on location** (of filming) in a suitable environment, not in a film studio.

loch /lɒx/ n. (Sc.) lake, arm of sea.

lock[1] n. portion of hair that hangs together; (pl.) hair.

lock[2] n. device (able to be opened by a key) for fastening part of a lid etc.; mechanism for exploding a charge in a gun; gated section of a canal where the water-level can be changed; secure hold; interlocking; turning of a vehicle's front wheels by use of the steering-wheel. —v.t./i. fasten with a lock; shut into a locked place; store inaccessibly; make or become rigidly fixed. **lock out** shut out by locking a door. **lock-up** n. lockable premises; room or building where prisoners can be detained temporarily.

lockable a. able to be locked.

locker n. small cupboard or compartment where things can be stowed securely.

locket n. small ornamental case worn on a chain round the neck.

lockjaw *n.* form of tetanus in which the jaws become rigidly closed.

lockout *n.* employer's procedure of locking out employees during a dispute.

locksmith *n.* maker and mender of locks.

locomotion *n.* ability to move from place to place.

locomotive *n.* railway engine. —*a.* of or effecting locomotion.

locomotor *a.* of locomotion.

locum *n.* doctor or member of the clergy deputizing for one who is absent.

locus *n.* (*pl.* -ci, *pr.* -saɪ) thing's exact place; line or curve etc. formed by certain points or by the movement of a point or line.

locust *n.* a kind of grasshopper that devours vegetation.

locution *n.* word or phrase.

lode *n.* vein of metal ore.

lodestar *n.* star (esp. pole star) used as a guide in navigation.

lodestone *n.* oxide of iron used as a magnet.

lodge *n.* small country house, esp. at the entrance to a park etc.; porter's room at the entrance to a building; members or meeting-place of a branch of certain societies; beaver's or otter's lair. —*v.t./i.* provide with sleeping-quarters or temporary accommodation; live as a lodger; deposit; be or become embedded.

lodger *n.* person paying for accommodation in another's house.

lodging *n.* place where one lodges; (*pl.*) room(s) rented for living in.

loft *n.* space under the roof of a house, stable, or barn; gallery in a church etc. —*v.t.* hit, throw, or kick (a ball) in a high arc.

lofty *a.* (-ier, -iest) very tall; noble; haughty. **loftily** *adv.*, **loftiness** *n.*

log[1] *n.* piece cut from a trunk or branch of a tree; device for gauging a ship's speed; log-book, entry in this. —*v.t.* (*p.t.* logged) enter

(facts) in a log-book. **log-book** *n.* book in which details of a voyage or journey are recorded. **log on** or **off** begin or finish operations at a computer terminal. **log-rolling** *n.* unprincipled assistance to each other's progress.

log[2] *n.* logarithm.

loganberry *n.* large dark-red fruit resembling a blackberry.

logarithm *n.* one of a series of numbers set out in tables, used to simplify calculations. **logarithmic** *a.*

loggerheads *n.pl.* **at loggerheads** disagreeing or quarrelling.

loggia /ˈlɒdʒə/ *n.* open-sided gallery or arcade.

logging *n.* (*US*) work of cutting down forest trees for timber.

logic *n.* science or method of reasoning; correct reasoning.

logical *a.* of or according to logic; reasonable; reasoning correctly. **logically** *adv.*, **logicality** *n.*

logician *n.* person skilled in logic.

logistics /-ˈdʒɪ-/ *n.* organization of supplies and services. **logistical** *a.*

logo /ˈləʊ-/ *n.* (*pl.* -os) logotype.

logotype /ˈlɒg-/ *n.* non-heraldic design used as an emblem.

loin *n.* side and back of the body between ribs and hip-bone.

loincloth *n.* cloth worn round the loins, esp. as a man's sole garment.

loiter *v.i.* linger, stand about idly. **loiterer** *n.*

loll *v.i.* stand, sit, or rest lazily; hang loosely.

lollipop *n.* large usu. flat boiled sweet on a small stick. **lollipop lady** or **man** official using a circular sign on a stick to halt traffic for children to cross a road.

lollop *v.i.* (*p.t.* lolloped) (*colloq.*) move in clumsy bounds; flop.

lolly *n.* (*colloq.*) lollipop; (*Austr.*) sweet; (*sl.*) money.

Londoner n. native or inhabitant of London.

lone a. solitary.

lonely a. solitary; sad because lacking friends or companions; not much frequented. **loneliness** n.

loner n. person who prefers not to associate with others.

lonesome a. lonely.

long[1] a. (-er, -est) of great or specified length. —adv. for a long time; throughout a specified time. **as** or **so long as** provided that. **long-distance** a. travelling or operated between distant places. **long face** dismal expression. **long johns** (colloq.) underpants or knickers with long legs. **long-life** a. (of milk etc.) treated to prolong its shelf-life. **long-lived** a. living or lasting for a long time. **long odds** very uneven odds. **long-playing record** one playing for about 20 to 30 minutes on each side. **long-range** a. having a relatively long range; relating to a long period of future time. **long-shore** a. found or employed on the shore. **long shot** wild guess or venture. **long-sighted** a. able to see clearly only what is at a distance; having foresight. **long-standing** a. having existed for a long time. **long-suffering** a. bearing provocation patiently. **long-term** a. of or for a long period. **long ton** (see **ton**); **long wave** radio wave of frequency less than 300 kHz. **long-winded** a. talking or writing at tedious length.

long[2] v.i. feel a longing.

longboat n. sailing-ship's largest boat.

longbow n. bow shooting a long arrow.

longevity /-'dʒev-/ n. long life.

longhand n. ordinary writing, not shorthand or typing etc.

longhorn n. animal of a breed of cattle with long horns.

longing n. intense wish.

longitude /'lɒndʒ-/ n. distance east or west (measured in degrees on a map) from the Greenwich meridian.

longitudinal /lɒndʒɪ-/ a. of longitude; of length, lengthwise. **longitudinally** adv.

loo n. (colloq.) lavatory.

loofah n. dried pod of a gourd, used as a rough sponge.

look v.t./i. use or direct one's eyes in order to see, search, or examine; face; seem. —n. act of looking; inspection, search; appearance. **look after** take care of; attend to. **look down on** despise. **look forward to** await eagerly. **look in** make a short visit. **look-in** n. chance of participation. **look into** investigate. **look on be** a spectator. **look out** be vigilant; select by inspection. **look up** search for information about; improve in prospects; go to visit. **look up to** admire and respect.

looker-on n. (pl. **lookers-on**) mere spectator.

looking-glass n. mirror.

lookout n. watch; watcher(s); observation-post; prospect; person's own concern.

loom[1] n. apparatus for weaving cloth.

loom[2] v.i. appear, esp. close at hand or threateningly.

loon n. a kind of diving-bird.

loony n. (sl.) lunatic. —a. (sl.) crazy. **loony-bin** n. (sl.) mental institution.

loop n. curve that is U-shaped or crosses itself; thing shaped like this, esp. length of cord or wire etc. fastened at the crossing. —v.t./i. form into loop(s); fasten or join with loop(s); enclose in a loop. **loop the loop** fly in a vertical circle, turning upside down between climb and dive.

loophole n. narrow opening in the wall of a fort etc.; means of evading a rule or contract.

loopy a. (sl.) crazy.

loose a. (-er, -est) not tied or restrained; not tightly fixed or held together; not held or packed or contained in something; slack; not closely packed; inexact, approximate; promiscuous. —adv. loosely. —v.t. release; untie, loosen. **at a loose end** without a definite occupation. **loose box** stall in which a horse can move about. **loose-leaf** a. with each page separate and removable. **loosely** adv., **looseness** n.

loosen v.t./i. make or become loose or looser.

loot n. goods taken from an enemy or by theft. —v.t./i. take loot (from); take as loot. **looter** n.

lop v.t. (p.t. **lopped**) cut branches or twigs of; cut off.

lope v.i. run with a long bounding stride. —n. this stride.

lop-eared a. with drooping ears.

lopsided a. with one side lower, smaller, or heavier than the other.

loquacious a. talkative. **loquaciously** adv., **loquacity** n.

lord n. master, ruler; nobleman; title of certain peers or high officials. —v.t. domineer. **the Lord** God; **Our Lord** Christ. **Lord's Supper** Eucharist. **the (House of) Lords** upper house of the British Parliament.

lordly a. suitable for a lord; haughty, imperious.

lordship n. title used of or to a man with the rank of *Lord*.

lore n. body of traditions and knowledge.

lorgnette /-'njet/ n. eye-glasses or opera-glasses held to the eyes on a long handle.

lorn a. (old use) desolate, forlorn.

lorry n. large strong motor vehicle for transporting heavy loads.

lose v.t./i. (p.t. **lost**) cease to have or maintain; become unable to find or follow; fail to obtain or catch; get rid of; be defeated in a contest etc.; suffer loss (of); cause

the loss of; (of a clock) become slow. **loser** n.

loss n. losing; person or thing or amount etc. lost; disadvantage caused by losing something. **be at a loss** be puzzled, not know what to do or say. **loss-leader** n. popular article sold at a loss to attract customers.

lost see lose. —a. strayed or separated from its owner.

lot[1] n. each of a set of objects used in making a selection by methods depending on chance; this method of selecting; choice resulting from it; person's share or destiny; piece of land; item being sold at auction.

lot[2] n. number of people or things of the same kind; (colloq.) large number or amount; much; **the lot** the total quantity. **bad lot** person of bad character.

loth a. = loath.

lotion n. medicinal or cosmetic liquid applied to the skin.

lottery n. system of raising money by selling numbered tickets and giving prizes to holders of numbers drawn at random; thing where the outcome is governed by luck.

lotto n. game like bingo but with numbers drawn instead of called.

lotus n. (pl. **-uses**) tropical waterlily; mythical fruit.

loud a. (-er, -est) producing much noise, easily heard; gaudy. —adv. loudly. **loud hailer** electronically operated megaphone. **out loud** aloud. **loudly** adv., **loudness** n.

loudspeaker n. apparatus (esp. part of a radio) that converts electrical impulses into audible sound.

lough /lɒx/ n. (Ir.) = loch.

lounge v.i. loll; sit or stand about idly. —n. sitting-room; waiting-room at an airport etc. **lounge suit** man's ordinary suit for day wear. **lounger** n.

lour /lavə(r)/ v.i. scowl; (of the sky) look dark and threatening.

louse n. (pl. **lice**) small parasitic insect; (pl. **louses**) contemptible person.

lousy a. (-ier, -iest) infested with lice; (sl.) very bad.

lout n. clumsy ill-mannered young man. **loutish** a.

louvre /'lu:-/ n. each of a set of overlapping slats arranged to admit air but exclude light or rain. **louvred** a.

lovable a. easy to love.

lovage n. herb used for flavouring etc.

love n. warm liking or affection; sexual passion; loved person; (in games) no score, nil. —v.t. feel love for; like greatly. **in love** feeling (esp. sexual) love for another person. **love affair** romantic or sexual relationship between people who are in love. **love-bird** n. small parakeet that shows great affection for its mate. **love-child** n. illegitimate child. **make love** pay amorous attentions; have sexual intercourse.

loveless a. without love.

lovelorn a. pining with love.

lovely a. (-ier, -iest) beautiful, attractive; (colloq.) delightful. **loveliness** n.

lover n. person (esp. man) in love with another or having an illicit love affair; one who likes or enjoys something.

lovesick a. languishing because of love.

loving a. feeling or showing love. **lovingly** adv.

low[1] n. deep sound made by cattle. —v.i. make this sound.

low[2] a. (-er, -est) not high, not extending or lying far up; ranking below others; ignoble, vulgar; less than normal in amount or intensity; with slow vibrations, not loud or shrill; lacking vigour, depressed. —n. low level; area of low pressure. —adv. in, at, or to a low level. **Low Church** section of the Church of England giving a low place to ritual and the authority of priests. **low-class** a. of low quality or social class. **low-down** a. dishonourable; (n., sl.) relevant information. **low-key** a. restrained, not intense or emotional. **low season** season that is least busy. **Low Sunday** next Sunday after Easter.

lowbrow a. not intellectual or cultured. —n. lowbrow person.

lower[1] a. & adv. see low[2]. —v.t. let or haul down; make or become lower; direct (one's gaze) downwards. **lower case** letters (for printing or typing) that are not capitals. **lower deck** petty officers and lower ranks.

lower[2] v.i. = lour.

lowlands n.pl. low-lying land. **lowland** a., **lowlander** n.

lowly a. (-ier, -iest) of humble rank or condition. **lowliness** n.

loyal a. firm in one's allegiance. **loyally** adv., **loyalty** n.

loyalist n. person who is loyal, esp. while others revolt.

lozenge n. four-sided diamond-shaped figure; small tablet to be dissolved in the mouth.

Ltd. abbr. Limited.

lubber n. clumsy fellow; lout. **lubberly** a.

lubricant n. lubricating substance.

lubricate v.t. oil or grease (machinery etc.). **lubrication** n.

lubricious a. slippery; lewd.

lucerne n. clover-like plant.

lucid a. clearly expressed; sane. **lucidly** adv., **lucidity** n.

luck n. good or bad fortune; chance thought of as a force bringing this.

luckless a. unlucky.

lucky a. (-ier, -iest) having, bringing, or resulting from good luck. **lucky dip** tub containing articles from which one takes at random. **luckily** adv.

lucrative *a.* producing much money.

lucre *n.* (*derog.*) money.

ludicrous *a.* ridiculous. **ludicrously** *adv.*, **ludicrousness** *n.*

ludo *n.* simple game played with counters on a special board.

luff *v.i.* bring a ship's head towards the wind.

lug[1] *v.t.* (*p.t.* lugged) drag or carry with great effort.

lug[2] *n.* ear-like projection; (*colloq.*) ear.

luggage *n.* suitcases and bags etc. holding a traveller's possessions.

lugger *n.* small ship with four-cornered fore-and-aft sails (**lugsails**).

lugubrious /-'gu:-/ *a.* dismal, mournful. **lugubriously** *adv.*

lukewarm *a.* only slightly warm; not enthusiastic.

lull *v.t./i.* soothe or send to sleep; calm; become quiet. —*n.* period of quiet or inactivity.

lullaby *n.* soothing song sung to put a child to sleep.

lumbago *n.* rheumatic pain in muscles of the loins.

lumbar *a.* of or in the loins.

lumber *n.* useless or unwanted articles, esp. furniture; (*US*) timber sawn into planks. —*v.t./i.* encumber; fill up (space) inconveniently; move heavily and clumsily.

lumberjack *n.* (*US*) workman cutting or conveying lumber.

lumen *n.* unit of luminous flux.

luminary *n.* natural light-giving body, esp. the sun or moon; eminent person.

luminescent *a.* emitting light without heat. **luminescence** *n.*

luminous *a.* emitting light, glowing in the dark. **luminously** *adv.*, **luminosity** *n.*

lump[1] *n.* hard or compact mass; swelling; heavy dull person; (*sl.*) great quantity. —*v.t.* put or consider together, treat as alike. **lump sum** money paid as a single amount.

lump[2] *v.t.* **lump it** (*colloq.*) put up with a thing one dislikes.

lumpectomy *n.* surgical removal of a lump from the breast.

lumpish *a.* heavy and clumsy or stupid.

lumpy *a.* (**-ier, -iest**) full of lumps; covered in lumps. **lumpiness** *n.*

lunacy *n.* insanity; great folly.

lunar *a.* of the moon. **lunar month** period between new moons (29½ days), four weeks.

lunate *a.* crescent-shaped.

lunatic *n.* person who is insane or very foolish or reckless.

lunation *n.* period between two new moons (about 29½ days).

lunch *n.* midday meal; mid-morning snack. —*v.t./i.* eat lunch; entertain to lunch.

luncheon *n.* lunch. **luncheon meat** tinned cured meat ready for serving. **luncheon voucher** voucher given to an employee, exchangeable for food.

lung *n.* either of the pair of breathing-organs in the chest of man and most vertebrates.

lunge /lʌndʒ/ *n.* sudden forward movement of the body; thrust. —*v.i.* make this movement.

lupin *n.* garden plant with tall spikes of flowers.

lurch[1] *n.* **leave in the lurch** leave (a person) in difficulties.

lurch[2] *v.i.* & *n.* (make) an unsteady swaying movement, stagger.

lurcher *n.* dog of a breed that is a cross between a greyhound or whippet and some other breed.

lure /ljʊə(r)/ *v.t.* entice. —*n.* enticement; bait or decoy to attract wild animals.

lurid *a.* in glaring colours; vivid and sensational or shocking. **luridly** *adv.*, **luridness** *n.*

lurk *v.i.* wait furtively or keeping out of sight; be latent.

luscious *a.* delicious; voluptuously attractive. **lusciously** *adv.*, **lusciousness** *n.*

lush[1] a. (of grass etc.) growing thickly and strongly; luxurious. **lushly** adv., **lushness** n.

lush[2] v.t. **lush up** (sl.) ply with drink or good food etc. —n. (US sl.) drunkard.

lust n. intense sexual desire; any intense desire. —v.i. feel lust. **lustful** a., **lustfully** adv.

lustre n. soft brightness of a surface; glory; metallic glaze on pottery. **lustrous** a.

lusty a. (-ier, -iest) strong and vigorous. **lustily** adv., **lustiness** n.

lute n. guitar-like instrument of the 14th–17th centuries. **lutenist** n.

Lutheran n. of the Protestant reformer Martin Luther or his teachings. **Lutheranism** n.

luxuriant a. growing profusely. **luxuriantly** adv., **luxuriance** n.

luxuriate v.i. feel great enjoyment in something.

luxurious a. supplied with luxuries, very comfortable. **luxuriously** adv., **luxuriousness** n.

luxury n. choice and costly surroundings, food, etc.; self-indulgence; thing that is enjoyable but not essential.

lych-gate /ˈlɪtʃ-/ n. = lich-gate.

lye n. water made alkaline (esp. with wood-ashes) for washing.

lying see **lie**[1], **lie**[2].

lymph /lɪmf/ n. colourless fluid from body tissue or organs. **lymphatic** a.

lynch v.t. execute or punish violently by a mob, without trial.

lynx n. wild animal of the cat family with spotted fur and keen sight.

lyre n. ancient musical instrument with strings in a U-shaped frame. **lyre-bird** n. Australian bird with a lyre-shaped tail.

lyric a. of poetry that expresses the poet's thoughts and feelings. —n. lyric poem; words of a song.

lyrical a. resembling or using language suitable for lyric poetry; (colloq.) expressing oneself enthusiastically. **lyrically** adv.

lyricist n. person who writes lyrics.

M

m. abbr. metre(s); mile(s); million(s).

MA abbr. Master of Arts.

ma n. (colloq.) mother.

ma'am /mæm/ n. madam.

mac n. (colloq.) mackintosh.

macabre /-ˈkɑːbr/ a. gruesome.

macadam n. layers of broken stone used in road-making.

macadamize v.t. pave with macadam.

macaroni n. tube-shaped pasta.

macaroon n. biscuit or small cake made with ground almonds.

macaw n. American parrot.

mace[1] n. ceremonial staff carried or placed before an official.

mace[2] n. spice made from the dried outer covering of nutmeg.

Mach /mɑːk/ n. **Mach number** ratio of the speed of a moving body to the speed of sound.

machete /-ˈtʃeti/ n. broad heavy knife used in Central America and the West Indies.

machiavellian /mæk-/ a. elaborately cunning or deceitful.

machinations /mæʃ-/ n.pl. clever scheming.

machine n. apparatus for applying mechanical power; thing made by this; (a bicycle, aircraft) operated by this; controlling system of an organization etc. —v.t. produce or work on with a machine. **machine-gun** n. mounted mechanically-operated gun that can fire continuously; (v.t.) shoot at with this. **machine-readable** a. in a form that a computer can process.

machinery *n.* machines; mechanism.

machinist *n.* person who makes or works machinery.

machismo /-'tʃɪz-/ *n.* manly courage; show of this.

macho *a.* ostentatiously manly.

mackerel *n.* (*pl.* **mackerel**) edible sea fish.

mackintosh *n.* cloth waterproofed with rubber; raincoat.

macramé /-'krɑːmɪ/ *n.* art of knotting cord in patterns; work done thus.

macrobiotic *a.* of or involving a diet intended to prolong life.

macrocosm *n.* the universe; any great whole.

mad *a.* (**madder, maddest**) having a disordered mind, not sane; extremely foolish; wildly enthusiastic; frenzied; (*colloq.*) very annoyed. **like mad** with great haste or energy or enthusiasm. **mad cow disease** BSE. **madly** *adv.*, **madness** *n.*

madam *n.* polite form of address to a woman.

Madame /mə'dɑːm/ *n.* (*pl.* **Mesdames**, *pr.* mer'dɑːm) title of a French-speaking woman.

madcap *a. & n.* wildly impulsive (person).

madden *v.t.* make mad or angry.

madder *n.* plant with yellowish flowers; its root; red dye made from this or synthetically.

made *see* **make**.

Madeira *n.* fortified wine from Madeira. **Madeira cake** rich plain cake.

Mademoiselle /mædəmwə'zel/ *n.* (*pl.* **Mesdemoiselles**, *pr.* meɪd-) title of an unmarried French-speaking woman.

madhouse *n.* (*colloq.*) mental institution; scene of confused uproar.

madman *n.* (*pl.* **-men**) man who is mad.

madonna *n.* picture or statue of the Virgin Mary.

madrigal *n.* part-song for voices.

madwoman *n.* (*pl.* **-women**) woman who is mad.

maelstrom /'meɪl-/ *n.* great whirlpool.

maestro /'maɪ-/ *n.* (*pl.* **-i**) great conductor or composer of music; master of any art.

Mafia *n.* international criminal organization. **Mafioso** *n.* (*pl.* **-si**) member of this.

magazine *n.* paper-covered illustrated periodical; store for ammunition, explosives, etc.; chamber holding cartridges in a gun, slides in a projector, etc.

magenta *a. & n.* purplish-red.

maggot *n.* larva, esp. of the bluebottle. **maggoty** *a.*

Magi /'meɪdʒaɪ/ *n.pl.* the 'wise men' from the East who brought offerings to Christ at Bethlehem.

magic *n.* supposed art of controlling things by supernatural power. —*a.* using or used in magic. **magical** *a.*, **magically** *adv.*

magician *n.* person skilled in magic.

magisterial /-'tɪər-/ *a.* of a magistrate; imperious. **magisterially** *adv.*

magistrate *n.* official or citizen with authority to hold preliminary hearings and judge minor cases. **magistracy** *n.*

magnanimous /-'næn-/ *a.* noble and generous in conduct, not petty. **magnanimously** *adv.*, **magnanimity** *n.*

magnate *n.* wealthy influential person, esp. in business.

magnesia /-ʃə/ *n.* compound of magnesium used in medicine.

magnesium *n.* white metal that burns with an intensely bright flame.

magnet *n.* piece of iron or steel that can attract iron and point north when suspended; thing exerting powerful attraction.

magnetic *a.* having the properties of a magnet; produced or acting by magnetism. **magnetic**

disk disc-shaped computer storage device formed from circular magnetically coated plates.

magnetic tape strip of plastic with magnetic particles, used in recording, computers, etc. **magnetically** adv.

magnetism n. properties and effects of magnetic substances; great charm and attraction.

magnetize v.t. make magnetic; attract. **magnetization** n.

magneto /-'niː-/ n. (pl. -os) small electric generator using magnets.

magnification n. magnifying.

magnificent a. splendid in appearance etc.; excellent in quality. **magnificently** adv., **magnificence** n.

magnify v.t. make (an object) appear larger by use of a lens; exaggerate; (old use) extol. **magnifier** n.

magnitude n. largeness, size; importance.

magnolia n. tree with large waxlike white or pink flowers.

magnum n. bottle holding two quarts of wine or spirits.

magpie n. noisy bird with black-and-white plumage; person who collects objects at random.

Magyar a. & n. (member, language) of a people now predominant in Hungary.

maharajah n. former title of certain Indian princes. **maharanee** n.fem.

maharishi /-'rɪʃɪ/ n. Hindu man of great wisdom.

mahatma n. (in India etc.) title of a man regarded with reverence.

mah-jong n. Chinese game played with 136 or 144 pieces (tiles).

mahogany n. very hard reddish-brown wood; its colour.

mahout /-'haʊt/ n. elephant-driver.

maid n. woman servant doing indoor work; (old use) maiden.

maiden n. (old use) girl, young unmarried woman, virgin. —a. unmarried; first. **maiden name** woman's family name before she married. **maiden over** over in cricket in which no runs are scored. **maidenly** adj., **maidenhood** n.

maidenhair n. fern with very thin stalks and delicate foliage.

maidservant n. female servant.

mail[1] n. = post[3]. —v.t. send by post. **mail order** purchase of goods by post.

mail[2] n. body-armour made of metal rings or chains. **mailed** a.

mailshot n. material sent to potential customers in an advertising campaign.

maim v.t. wound or injure.

main a. principal, most important, greatest in size or extent. —n. main pipe or channel in a public system for conveying water, gas, or (pl.) electricity. **in the main** for the most part. **mainly** adv.

mainframe n. large computer.

mainland n. country or continent without its adjacent islands.

mainmast n. principal mast.

mainsail n. lowest sail or sail set on the after part of the mainmast.

mainspring n. chief spring of a watch or clock; chief incentive.

mainstay n. strong cable securing the principal mast; chief support.

mainstream n. dominant trend of opinion or style etc.

maintain v.t. cause to continue, keep in existence; keep in repair; bear the expenses of; assert as true.

maintenance n. process of maintaining something; provision of means to support life; allowance paid by a spouse to his or her divorced or separated husband or wife.

maisonette n. small house; part of a house (usu. not all on one floor) used as a separate dwelling.

maize n. tall cereal plant bearing grain on large cobs; its grain.

majestic a. stately and dignified, imposing. **majestically** adv.

majesty n. impressive stateliness; sovereign power; title of a king or queen.

majolica /-'jo-/ n. a kind of ornamented Italian earthenware.

major a. greater; very important; (of a musical scale) with a semitone above the third and seventh notes. —n. army officer next below lieutenant-colonel; officer in charge of a section of band instruments. —v.i. (US) specialize (in a subject) at college. **major-domo** n. (pl. -os) head steward of a great household. **major-general** n. army officer next below lieutenant-general.

majority n. greatest part of a group or class; number by which votes for one party etc. exceed those for the next or for all combined; age when a person legally becomes adult.

make v.t./i. (p.t. made) form, prepare, produce; cause to exist or be or become; succeed in arriving at or achieving; gain, acquire; reckon to be; compel; perform (an action etc.); ensure the success of. —n. making, way a thing is made; manufacture, brand. **make believe** pretend. **make-believe** a. pretended; (n.) pretence. **make do** manage with something not fully satisfactory. **make for** proceed towards, try to reach; tend to bring about. **make good** become successful; fulfil; repair or pay compensation for. **make much of** treat as important; give much flattering attention to. **make off** go away hastily. **make off with** carry away, steal. **make out** write out (a list etc.); manage to see or understand; assert to be. **make over** transfer the ownership of; refashion (a garment etc.). **make shift** = make do.

make up form, constitute; prepare; invent (a story etc.); compensate (for a loss etc.); become reconciled after (a quarrel); complete (an amount) to supply what is lacking; apply cosmetics (to). **make-up** n. cosmetics applied to the skin esp. of the face; way a thing is made; person's character. **make up one's mind** decide. **make up to** curry favour with.

maker n. one who makes something.

makeshift a. & n. (thing) used as a temporary or improvised substitute.

makeweight n. thing or amount added to make up for a deficiency.

making n. **be the making of** be the main factor in the success of. **have the makings of** have the qualities for becoming.

malachite /'mæləkaɪt/ n. green mineral.

maladjusted a. not happily adapted to one's circumstances. **maladjustment** n.

maladminister v.t. manage (business or public affairs) badly or improperly.

maladroit a. bungling, clumsy.

malady n. illness, disease.

malaise /-'leɪz/ n. feeling of illness or uneasiness.

malapropism /'mæl-/ n. comical confusion of words.

malaria n. disease causing a recurring fever. **malarial** a.

Malay a. & n. (member, language) of a people of Malaysia and Indonesia.

malcontent /'mæ-/ n. discontented person.

male a. of the sex that can beget offspring by fertilizing egg-cells produced by a female; (of a plant) having flowers that contain pollen-bearing organs not seeds; (of a screw etc.) for insertion into a corresponding hollow part. —n. male animal or plant.

malediction n. curse.

malefactor /'mælɪ-/ n. wrong-doer.

malevolent /-'lev-/ a. wishing harm to others. **malevolently** adv., **malevolence** n.

malfeasance n. misconduct.

malformation n. faulty formation. **malformed** a.

malfunction n. faulty functioning. —v.i. function faultily.

malice n. desire to harm others or to tease.

malicious a. showing malice. **maliciously** adv.

malign /-'laɪn/ a. harmful; showing malice. —v.t. say unpleasant and untrue things about. **malignity** /-'lɪg-/ n.

malignant a. showing great ill-will; (of a tumour) growing harmfully and uncontrollably. **malignantly** adv., **malignancy** n.

malinger v.i. pretend illness so as to avoid work. **malingerer** n.

mall n. sheltered walk or promenade; shopping precinct.

mallard n. wild duck, male of which has a glossy green head.

malleable a. able to be hammered or pressed into shape; easy to influence. **malleability** n.

mallet n. hammer, usu. of wood; similarly shaped instrument with a long handle for striking the ball in croquet or polo.

mallow n. wild plant with hairy stems and leaves.

malmsey /'mɑːm-/ n. a kind of strong sweet wine.

malnutrition n. insufficient nutrition.

malodorous /-'ləʊ-/ a. stinking.

malpractice n. wrongdoing; improper or negligent treatment of a patient.

malt n. barley or other grain prepared for brewing or distilling; (colloq.) beer or whisky made with this. **malted milk** drink made from dried milk and malt.

maltreat v.t. ill-treat. **maltreatment** n.

mama /-'mɑː/ n. (old use) mother.

mamba /-'mæm-/ n. poisonous South African tree-snake.

mamma /-'mɑː/ n. = mama.

mammal n. member of the class of animals that suckle their young. **mammalian** /-'meɪl-/ a.

mammary a. of the breasts.

mammogram n. image obtained by **mammography**, an X-ray technique of diagnosing tumours etc. of breasts.

Mammon n. wealth personified.

mammoth n. large extinct elephant with tusks. —a. huge.

mammy n. colloq. mother.

man n. (pl. **men**) adult male person; human being, animal with the power of articulate speech and upright posture; mankind; individual person; male servant or employee; ordinary soldier etc., not an officer; one of the small objects used in board-games. —v.t. (p.t. **manned**) supply with people to guard or operate something. **man-hour** n. one hour's work by one person. **man-hunt** n. organized search for a person, esp. a criminal. **man in the street** ordinary person, not an expert. **man-made** a. made by man not by nature, synthetic. **man of the world** man experienced in the ways of society. **man-of-war** n. warship. **man-sized** a. adequate for a man; large. **man to man** with frankness.

manacle n. & v.t. handcuff.

manage v.t./i. have control of; be manager of; operate (a tool etc.) effectively; contrive; deal with (a person) tactfully. **manageable** a.

management n. managing; people engaged in managing a business.

manager n. person in charge of a business etc. **manageress** n.fem., **managerial** /-'dʒɪər-/ a.

manatee n. large tropical aquatic mammal.

Mandarin n. northern variety of the Chinese language.

mandarin n. senior influential official; a kind of small orange.

mandatary n. holder of a mandate.

mandate n. & v.t. (give) authority to perform certain tasks.

mandatory /ˈmæ-/ a. compulsory.

mandible n. jaw or jaw-like part.

mandolin n. guitar-like musical instrument with strings tuned in pairs.

mandrake n. poisonous plant with a large yellow fruit.

mandrel n. shaft holding work in a lathe.

mandrill n. a kind of large baboon.

mane n. long hair on a horse's or lion's neck.

manful a. brave, resolute. **manfully** adv.

manganese n. hard brittle grey metal or its black oxide.

mange n. skin-disease affecting hairy animals.

mangel-wurzel n. large beet used as cattle-food.

manger n. open trough in a stable etc. for horses or cattle to feed from.

mangle[1] n. wringer. —v.t. press (clothes etc.) in a mangle.

mangle[2] v.t. damage by cutting or crushing roughly, mutilate.

mango n. (pl. **-oes**) tropical fruit with juicy flesh; tree bearing it.

mangrove n. tropical tree or shrub growing in shore-mud and swamps.

mangy a. having mange; squalid.

manhandle v.t. move by human effort alone; treat roughly.

manhole n. opening through which a person can enter a drain etc. to inspect it.

manhood n. state of being a man; manly qualities; men of a country.

mania n. violent madness; extreme enthusiasm for something.

maniac n. person with a mania.

maniacal /məˈnaɪ-/ a. of or like a mania or maniac.

manic /ˈmæ-/ a. of or affected by mania.

manicure n. cosmetic treatment of finger-nails. —v.t. apply such treatment to. **manicurist** n.

manifest a. clear and unmistakable. —v.t. show clearly, give signs of. —n. list of cargo or passengers carried by a ship or aircraft. **manifestation** n.

manifesto n. (pl. **-os**) public declaration of principles and policy.

manifold a. of many kinds. —n. (in a machine) pipe or chamber with several openings.

manikin n. little man, dwarf.

manila n. brown paper used for wrapping and for envelopes.

manioc /ˈmæ-/ n. cassava; flour made from this.

manipulate v.t. handle or manage in a skilful or cunning way. **manipulation** n., **manipulator** n.

mankind n. human beings in general.

manly a. brave, strong; considered suitable for a man. **manliness** n.

manna n. (in the Bible) substance miraculously supplied as food to the Israelites in the wilderness.

mannequin /-kɪn/ n. woman who models clothes.

manner n. way a thing is done or happens; person's way of behaving towards others; kind, sort; (pl.) polite social behaviour.

mannered a. having manners of a certain kind; full of mannerisms.

mannerism n. distinctive personal habit or way of doing something.

mannish a. having masculine characteristics.

manœuvrable a. able to be manœuvred. **manœuvrability** n.

manœuvre n. planned movement of vehicle, body of troops, etc.; skilful or crafty proceeding. —v.t./i. perform manœuvre(s); move or guide skilfully or craftily.

manor n. large country house, usu. with landed estate; (colloq.) police station's district. **manorial** a.

manpower n. number of people available for work or service.

mansard roof roof with a steep lower part and less steep upper part.

manse n. church minister's house, esp. in Scotland.

manservant n. (pl. **menservants**) male servant.

mansion n. large stately house.

manslaughter n. act of killing a person unlawfully but not intentionally, or by negligence.

mantelpiece n. shelf above a fireplace.

mantilla n. Spanish lace veil worn over a woman's hair and shoulders.

mantis n. grasshopper-like insect.

mantle n. loose cloak; covering.

manual a. of the hands; done or operated by the hand(s). —n. handbook; organ keyboard played with the hands. **manually** adv.

manufacture v.t. make or produce (goods) on a large scale by machinery; invent. —n. process of manufacturing. **manufacturer** n.

manure n. substance, esp. dung, used as a fertilizer. —v.t. apply manure to.

manuscript n. book or document written by hand or typed, not printed.

Manx a. & n. (language) of the Isle of Man.

many a. numerous. —n. many people or things.

Maori /'maʊ-/ n. & a. (pl. **Maori** or **-is**) (member, language) of the brown aboriginal race in New Zealand.

map n. representation of earth's surface or a part of it, or of the heavens. —v.t. (p.t. **mapped**) make a map of. **map out** plan in detail.

maple n. a kind of tree with broad leaves.

mar v.t. (p.t. **marred**) damage, spoil.

marabou /-buː/ n. large West African stork; its down used as trimming.

maraca /-'ræk-/ n. club-like gourd containing beads etc., shaken as a musical instrument.

maraschino /'ski:-/ n. liqueur made from cherries.

marathon n. long-distance football race; long test of endurance.

marauding a. & n. going about in search of plunder. **marauder** n.

marble n. a kind of limestone that can be polished; piece of sculpture in this; small ball of glass or clay used in children's games. —v.t. give a veined or mottled appearance to.

marcasite /'mɑːkəsart/ n. crystals of a form of iron, used in jewellery.

March n. third month of the year.

march v.t./i. walk in a regular rhythm or an organized column; walk purposefully; cause to march or walk; progress steadily. —n. act of marching; distance covered by marching; music suitable for marching to; progress. **marcher** n.

marches n.pl. boundary regions.

marchioness /-ʃən-/ n. wife or widow of a marquess; woman with the rank of marquess.

mare n. female of the horse or a related animal. **mare's nest** discovery that turns out to be false or worthless.

margarine /-dʒə- or -gə-/ n. substance made from animal or vegetable fat and used like butter.

marge n. (colloq.) margarine.

margin n. edge or border of a surface; blank space round printed or written matter on a page; amount over the essential minimum.

marginal a. of or in a margin; near a limit; only very slight. **marginal constituency** one where an MP's majority is too small for the seat to be regarded as safe. **marginally** adv.

marginalize v.t. make or treat as insignificant. **marginalization** n.

marguerite /-'riːt/ n. large daisy.

marigold n. garden plant with golden daisy-like flowers.

marijuana /-'hwɑːnə/ n. dried hemp, smoked as a hallucinogenic drug.

marimba n. a kind of xylophone, orig. of Africa and Central America.

marina /-'riː-/ n. harbour for yachts and pleasure-boats.

marinade /-'neɪd/ n. seasoned flavoured liquid in which meat or fish is steeped before being cooked. —v.t./i. steep or be steeped in a marinade.

marine a. of the sea; of shipping. —n. member of a body of troops trained to serve on land or sea; a country's shipping.

mariner /'mæ-/ n. sailor, seaman.

marionette /'mæ-/ n. puppet worked by strings.

marital /'mæ-/ a. of marriage, of husband and wife.

maritime a. living or found near the sea; of seafaring.

marjoram n. herb with fragrant leaves.

mark[1] n. thing that visibly breaks the uniformity of a surface; distinguishing feature; thing indicating the presence of a quality or feeling etc.; symbol; unit awarded for merit of a performance or piece of work; target; line or object serving to indicate a position; numbered design of a piece of equipment etc. —v.t./i.

make a mark on; characterize; assign marks of merit to; notice, watch carefully; keep close to and ready to hamper (an opponent in football etc.). **mark down** reduce the price of a thing. **mark time** move the feet as if marching but without advancing.

mark[2] n. unit of money in Germany.

marked a. clearly noticeable. **markedly** /-kɪdlɪ/ adv.

marker n. person or object that marks something.

market n. gathering for the sale of provisions, livestock, etc.; place where this is held; demand (for a commodity etc.). —v.t./i. buy or sell in a market; offer for sale. **market garden** one in which vegetables are grown for market. **market maker** member of the Stock Exchange given certain privileges. **on the market** offered for sale.

marking n. mark(s); colouring of an animal's skin, feathers, or fur.

marksman n. (pl. **-men**) person who is a skilled shot. **marksmanship** n.

marl n. soil composed of clay and lime, used as a fertilizer.

marlinspike n. pointed tool used to separate strands of rope or wire.

marmalade n. a kind of jam made from citrus fruit, esp. oranges.

marmoreal a. of marble.

marmoset n. small bushy-tailed monkey of tropical America.

marmot n. small burrowing animal of the squirrel family.

marocain n. thin crêpey dress-fabric.

maroon[1] n. brownish-red colour; explosive device used as a warning signal. —a. brownish-red.

maroon[2] v.t. put and leave (a person) ashore in a desolate place; leave stranded.

marquee /-'kiː/ n. large tent used for a party or exhibition etc.

marquess *n.* nobleman ranking between duke and earl.

marquetry /-krt-/ *n.* inlaid work.

marquis *n.* rank in some European nobilities; marquess.

marram *n.* shore grass that binds sand.

marriage *n.* state in which a man and woman are formally united for the purpose of living together; act or ceremony of marrying.

marriageable *a.* suitable or old enough for marriage.

marrow *n.* soft fatty substance in the cavities of bones; a type of gourd used as a vegetable.

marry *v.t./i.* unite or give or take in marriage; put (things) together.

Marsala *n.* dark sweet fortified wine.

marsh *n.* low-lying watery ground. **marsh marigold** kind of large buttercup. **marshy** *a.*

marshal *n.* officer of high or the highest rank; official arranging ceremonies, controlling procedure at races, etc. —*v.t.* (*p.t.* **marshalled**) arrange in proper order; assemble; usher.

marshmallow *n.* soft sweet made from sugar, egg-white, and gelatine.

marsupial *n.* mammal that usu. carries its young in a pouch.

mart *n.* market.

Martello tower small circular tower for coastal defence.

marten *n.* weasel-like animal with thick soft fur.

martial *a.* of war, warlike. **martial law** military government suspending ordinary law.

Martian *a.* & *n.* (inhabitant) of the planet Mars.

martin *n.* bird of the swallow family.

martinet *n.* person who demands strict obedience.

martyr *n.* person who undergoes death or suffering for his beliefs. —*v.t.* kill or torment as a martyr.

be a martyr to suffer constantly from. **martyrdom** *n.*

marvel *n.* wonderful thing. —*v.i.* (*p.t.* **marvelled**) feel wonder.

marvellous *a.* wonderful. **marvellously** *adv.*

Marxism *n.* theories of the German socialist writer Karl Marx, on which Communism is based. **Marxist** *a.* & *n.*

marzipan *n.* edible paste made from ground almonds.

mascara *n.* cosmetic for darkening the eyelashes.

mascot *n.* thing believed to bring good luck to its owner; figurine mounted on a car etc.

masculine *a.* of, like, or suitable for men; of the grammatical form suitable for the names of males. —*n.* masculine word. **masculinity** *n.*

mash *n.* soft mixture of grain or bran; (*colloq.*) mashed potatoes. —*v.t.* beat or crush into a soft mixture.

mask *n.* covering worn over the face as a disguise or protection; respirator worn over the face; replica of the face; face or head of a fox. —*v.t.* cover with a mask; disguise, screen, conceal.

masochism /ˈmæsək-/ *n.* pleasure in suffering physical or mental pain. **masochist** *n.*, **masochistic** *a.*

Mason *n.* Freemason. **Masonic** /-ˈsɒn-/ *a.*, **Masonry** *n.*

mason *n.* person who builds or works with stone.

masonry *n.* mason's work; stonework.

masque *n.* amateur dramatic and musical entertainment, esp. in the 16th–17th century.

masquerade *n.* false show or pretence. —*v.i.* pretend to be what one is not.

mass[1] *n.* celebration (esp. in the RC Church) of the Eucharist; form of liturgy used in this.

mass[2] *n.* coherent unit of matter; large quantity or heap or expanse; quantity of matter a body contains (called *weight* in non-technical usage); **the masses** ordinary people. —*v.t./i.* gather or assemble into a mass. **mass-produce** *v.t.* manufacture in large quantities by a standardized process. **mass production.**

massacre *n.* great slaughter. —*v.t.* slaughter in large numbers.

massage *n.* rubbing and kneading the body to reduce pain or stiffness. —*v.t.* treat in this way.

masseur /-'sɜ:(r)/ *n.* man who practises massage professionally. **masseuse** /-'sɜ:z/ *n.fem.*

massif /'mæ-/ *n.* central mass of mountain heights.

massive *a.* large and heavy or solid; huge. **massively** *adv.*, **massiveness** *n.*

mast[1] *n.* tall pole, esp. supporting a ship's sails.

mast[2] *n.* fruit of beech, oak, chestnut, etc., used as food for pigs.

mastectomy *n.* surgical removal of a breast.

master *n.* man who has control of people or things; employer; male teacher; person with very great skill, great artist; captain of a merchant ship; thing from which a series of copies is made; **Master** title of a boy not old enough to be called *Mr.* —*a.* superior; principal; controlling others. —*v.t.* bring under control; acquire knowledge or skill in. **master-key** *n.* key that opens a number of different locks. **Master of Arts** etc., person with a high university degree. **master-stroke** *n.* very skilful act of policy.

masterful *a.* domineering. **masterfully** *adv.*

masterly *a.* very skilful. **masterliness** *n.*

mastermind *n.* person of outstanding mental ability; one directing an enterprise. —*v.t.* plan and direct.

masterpiece *n.* outstanding piece of work.

mastery *n.* complete control, supremacy; thorough knowledge or skill.

mastic *n.* gum or resin from certain trees; a kind of cement.

masticate *v.t.* chew. **mastication** *n.*

mastiff *n.* large strong dog.

mastodon *n.* extinct animal resembling an elephant.

mastoid *n.* part of a bone behind the ear. **mastoiditis** *n.* inflammation of this area.

masturbate *v.t./i.* stimulate the genitals (of) manually. **masturbation** *n.*

mat[1] *n.* piece of material placed on a floor or other surface as an ornament or to protect it from damage. —*v.t./i.* (*p.t.* **matted**) make or become tangled to form a thick mass. **on the mat** (*sl.*) being reprimanded.

matador *n.* bull-fighter.

match[1] *n.* short piece of wood or pasteboard tipped with material that catches fire when rubbed on a rough surface.

match[2] *n.* contest in a game or sport; person or thing exactly like or corresponding or equal to another; matrimonial alliance. —*v.t./i.* set against each other in a contest; equal in ability or achievement; be alike; find a thing similar or corresponding to.

matchboard *n.* boards fitting into each other by tongue and groove.

matchbox *n.* box for holding matches.

matchless *a.* unequalled.

matchmaking *n.* scheming to arrange marriages. **matchmaker** *n.*

matchstick *n.* stick of a match.

matchwood *n.* wood that splinters easily; wood broken into splinters.

mate[1] n. companion or fellow worker, (colloq.) term of address between men; male or female of mated animals; merchant ship's officer next below master. —v.t./i. put or come together as a pair or as corresponding; come or bring (animals) together to breed.

mate[2] n. checkmate.

material n. that from which something is or can be made; cloth, fabric. —a. of matter; of the physical (not spiritual) world; significant. **materially** adv.

materialism n. belief that only the material world exists; excessive concern with material possessions. **materialist** n., **materialistic** a.

materialize v.i. appear, become visible; become a fact, happen. **materialization** n.

maternal a. of a mother; motherly; related through one's mother. **maternally** adv.

maternity n. motherhood; (attrib.) of or for women in pregnancy and childbirth.

matey a. (colloq.) friendly. —n. (colloq.) mate. **mateyness** n.

mathematician n. person skilled in mathematics.

mathematics n. science of numbers, quantities, and measurements; (as pl.) use of this. **mathematical** a., **mathematically** adv.

maths n. & n.pl. (colloq.) mathematics.

matinée /-neɪ/ n. afternoon performance. **matinée coat** baby's jacket.

matins n. (in the Church of England) service of morning prayer.

matriarch /ˈmeɪ-/ n. female head of a family or tribe. **matriarchal** a.

matriarchy /ˈmeɪ-/ n. social organization in which a female is head of the family.

matricide /-mɪ-/ n. killing or killer of own mother. **matricidal** a.

matriculate v.t./i. admit or be admitted to a university. **matriculation** n.

matrimony n. marriage. **matrimonial** a.

matrix /ˈmeɪ-/ n. (pl. matrices, pr. -ɪsiːz) mould in which a thing is cast or shaped; mass of rock etc. enclosing gems; rectangular array of mathematical quantities.

matron n. married woman; woman in charge of domestic affairs or nursing in a school etc.; (former use) senior nursing officer in a hospital.

matronly a. like or suitable for a dignified married woman.

matt a. (of a surface) dull, not shiny.

matter n. that which occupies space in the visible world; specified substance, material, or things; business etc. being discussed; pus. —v.i. be of importance. **matter-of-fact** a. strictly factual, not imaginative or emotional. **no matter** it is of no importance. **what is the matter?** what is amiss?

matting n. mats, material for making these.

mattock n. agricultural tool with a blade at right angles to the handle.

mattress n. fabric case filled with padding or springy material, used on or as a bed.

maturation n. maturing.

mature a. (fully grown or developed; (of a bill of exchange etc.) due for payment. —v.t./i. make or become mature. **maturity** n.

matutinal /-ˈtjuː-/ a. of the morning.

maudlin a. sentimental in a silly or tearful way.

maul v.t. treat roughly, injure by rough handling.

maulstick n. stick used to support the hand in painting.

maunder v.i. talk in a dreamy or rambling way; move idly.

Maundy n. distribution of Maundy money (special silver coins) to the poor on **Maundy Thursday** (Thursday before Easter).

mausoleum n. magnificent tomb.

mauve /məʊv/ a. & n. pale purple.

maverick n. unorthodox or undisciplined person.

maw n. jaws, mouth, or stomach of a voracious animal.

mawkish a. sentimental in a sickly way. **mawkishly** adv., **mawkishness** n.

maxim n. sentence giving a general truth or rule of conduct.

maximize v.t. increase to a maximum. **maximization** n.

maximum n. & n. (pl. **-ima**) greatest (amount) possible. **maximal** a., **maximally** adv.

May n. fifth month of the year. **May Day** 1 May, esp. as a country festival.

may[1] v.aux. (p.t. **might**) used to express a wish, possibility, or permission.

may[2] n. hawthorn blossom.

maybe adv. perhaps.

mayday n. international radio signal of distress.

mayfly n. insect with long hair-like tails, living in spring.

mayhem n. violent action.

mayonnaise /-ˈneɪz/ n. creamy sauce made with eggs and oil.

mayor n. head of the municipal corporation of a city or borough. **mayoral** a., **mayoralty** n.

mayoress n. mayor's wife, or other lady with her ceremonial duties.

maypole n. tall pole for dancing round on May Day.

maze n. complex and baffling network of paths, lines, etc.

mazurka n. lively Polish dance.

ME abbr. myalgic encephalomyelitis (disease characterized by prolonged tiredness).

me pron. objective case of I.

mead n. alcoholic drink made from fermented honey and water.

meadow n. field of grass.

meadowsweet n. meadow plant with fragrant creamy-white flowers.

meagre a. scant in amount.

meal[1] n. occasion when food is eaten; the food itself.

meal[2] n. coarsely ground grain.

mealy a. of or like meal. **mealy-mouthed** a. trying excessively to avoid offending people.

mean[1] a. (-er, -est) miserly; selfish; unkind; poor in quality or appearance; low in rank; (US) vicious. **meanly** adv., **meanness** n.

mean[2] a. & n. (thing) midway between two extremes; average. **mean time** intervening time.

mean[3] v.t. (p.t. **meant**) intend; have as equivalent word(s) in the same or another language; entail, involve, be the likely to result in; be of specified importance.

meander v.i. follow a winding course; wander in a leisurely way. —n. winding course.

meaning n. what is meant. —a. full of a certain meaning, expressive. **meaningful** a., **meaningless** a.

means n. that by which a result is brought about. —n.pl. resources. **by all means** certainly. **by no means** not nearly. **means test** official inquiry to establish neediness before giving help from public funds.

meant see **mean**[3].

meantime adv. meanwhile.

meanwhile adv. in the intervening period; at the same time.

measles n. infectious disease producing small red spots on the body.

measly a. (sl.) meagre.

measurable a. able to be measured. **measurably** adv., **measurability** n.

measure n. size or quantity found by measuring; extent; unit, standard, device, or system used in measuring; rhythm; suitable action taken for a purpose, (proposed) law. —*v.t./i.* find the size etc. of by comparison with a fixed unit or known standard; be of a certain size; mark or deal (a measured amount). **measure one's length** fall flat on the ground. **measure up to** reach the standard required by.

measured *a.* rhythmical; carefully considered.

measurement *n.* measuring; size etc. found by measuring.

meat *n.* animal flesh as food (usu. excluding fish and poultry).

meaty *a.* (-**ier**, -**iest**) like meat; full of meat; full of subject-matter. **meatiness** *n.*

mechanic *n.* skilled workman who uses or repairs machines or tools.

mechanical *a.* of or worked by machinery; done without conscious thought. **mechanically** *adv.*

mechanician *n.* person skilled in constructing machinery.

mechanics *n.* study of motion and force; science of machinery. —*n.pl.* mechanism, way a thing functions.

mechanism *n.* way a machine works; its parts.

mechanize *v.t.* equip with machinery. **mechanized** *a.* (of troops) equipped with armoured vehicles. **mechanization** *n.*

medal *n.* coin-like piece of metal commemorating an event or awarded for an achievement.

medallion /-ˈdæ-/ *n.* large medal; circular ornamental design.

medallist *n.* winner of a medal.

meddle *v.i.* interfere in people's affairs; tinker. **meddler** *n.*

meddlesome *a.* often meddling.

media *see* medium. —*n.pl.* the media newspapers and broadcasting as conveying information to the public.

mediaeval *a.* = medieval.

medial *a.* situated in the middle. **medially** *adv.*

median *a.* in or passing through the middle. —*n.* median point or line.

mediate *v.t./i.* act as peacemaker between disputants; bring about (a settlement) thus. **mediation** *n.*, **mediator** *n.*

medical *a.* of the science of medicine; involving doctors and their work. —*n.* (*colloq.*) medical examination. **medically** *adv.*

medicament /-ˈdɪk-/ *n.* any medicine, ointment, etc.

medicate *v.t.* treat with a medicinal substance. **medication** *n.*

medicinal *a.* having healing properties. **medicinally** *adv.*

medicine *n.* science of the prevention and cure of disease; substance used to treat disease. **medicine man** witch-doctor.

medieval *a.* of the Middle Ages.

mediocre /miː-/ *a.* of medium quality; second-rate. **mediocrity** *n.*

meditate *v.t.* think deeply and quietly; plan. **meditation** *n.*

meditative *a.* meditating, full of meditation. **meditatively** *adv.*

Mediterranean *a.* & *n.* (of) the sea between Europe and North Africa.

medium *n.* (*pl.* media) middle size, quality, etc.; substance or surroundings in which a thing exists or moves or is produced; agency, means; (*pl.* mediums) person who claims ability to communicate with the spirits of the dead. —*a.* intermediate; average; moderate.

medlar *n.* apple-like fruit eaten when decaying; tree bearing this.

medley *n.* (*pl.* -**eys**) assortment; excerpts of music from various sources.

medulla *n.* spinal or bone marrow; hindmost segment of the brain. **medullary** *a.*

meek *a.* (-**er**, -**est**) quiet and obedient, not protesting. **meekly** *adv.*, **meekness** *n.*

meerschaum /-ʃəm/ n. tobacco-pipe with a white clay bowl; this clay.

meet[1] a. (old use) suitable, proper.

meet[2] v.t./i. (p.t. met) come face to face or into contact (with); go to be present at the arrival of; make the acquaintance of; become perceptible to; experience; satisfy (needs etc.). —n. assembly for a hunt etc.

meeting n. coming together; an assembly for discussion or (of Quakers) worship. **meeting-place** n.

mega- pref. large; one million (as in megavolts, megawatts).

megabyte n. one million bytes, esp. as a unit of computer storage.

megahertz n. one million cycles per second, as a unit of frequency of electromagnetic waves.

megalith n. large stone, esp. as a prehistoric monument. **megalithic** a.

megalomania n. excessive self-esteem, esp. as a form of insanity. **megalomaniac** a. & n.

megaphone n. funnel-shaped device for amplifying and directing a speaker's voice.

megaton n. unit of explosive power equal to one million tons of TNT.

meiosis /mai-/ n. ironical understatement.

melamine /-miːn/ n. resilient kind of plastic.

melancholia /-'kəʊ-/ n. mental depression. **melancholic** /-'kɒl-/ a.

melancholy n. mental depression, sadness; gloom. —a. sad, gloomy.

mélange /mer'lɑ̃ʒ/ n. medley.

melanin n. dark pigment in the skin, hair, etc.

mêlée /'meleɪ/ n. confused fight; muddle.

mellifluous a. sweet-sounding.

mellow a. (-er, -est) (of fruit) ripe and sweet; (of sound or colour) soft and rich; (of persons) having become kindly, e.g. with age. —v.t./i. make or become mellow. **mellowly** adv., **mellowness** n.

melodic /-'lɒd-/ a. of melody. **melodically** adv.

melodious a. full of melody. **melodiously** adv.

melodrama n. sensational or emotional drama. **melodramatic** a., **melodramatically** adv.

melody n. sweet music; main part in a piece of harmonized music; song.

melon n. large sweet fruit of various gourds.

melt v.t./i. make into or become liquid, esp. by heat; soften through pity or love; fade away.

meltdown n. melting, esp. of an overheated reactor core.

member n. person or thing belonging to a particular group or society. **Member of Parliament** constituency's elected representative in the House of Commons. **membership** n.

membrane n. thin flexible skin-like tissue. **membranous** a.

memento n. (pl. -oes) souvenir.

memo n. (pl. -os) (colloq.) memorandum.

memoir /-mwɑː(r)/ n. written account of events etc. that one remembers.

memorable a. worth remembering, easy to remember. **memorably** adv., **memorability** n.

memorandum n. (pl. -da) note written for future use as a reminder; (pl. -dums) informal written message from one colleague to another.

memorial n. object or custom established in memory of an event or person(s). —a. serving as a memorial.

memorize v.t. learn (a thing) so as to know it from memory. **memorizer** n., **memorization** n.

memory n. ability to remember things; thing(s) remembered; computer store for data etc. **from memory** remembered without the aid of notes etc. **in memory of** in honour of a person or thing remembered with respect.

memsahib n. (in India) European lady.

men see **man.**

menace n. threat; annoying or troublesome person or thing. —v.t. threaten. **menacingly** adv.

ménage /meɪˈnɑːʒ/ n. household.

menagerie n. collection of wild or strange animals for exhibition.

mend v.t./i. repair; stitch up (torn fabric); make or become better. —n. repaired place. **on the mend** becoming better after illness etc. **mender** n.

mendacious a. untruthful. **mendaciously** adv., **mendacity** /-ˈdæ-/ n.

mendicant a. & n. (person) living by begging or on alms. **mendicancy** n.

menfolk n. men in general; men of one's family.

menhir /ˈmenhɪə(r)/ n. tall stone set up in prehistoric times.

menial /ˈmiː-/ a. lowly, degrading. —n. lowly servant, person who does humble tasks. **menially** adv.

meningitis /-ˈdʒaɪ-/ n. inflammation of the membranes covering the brain and spinal cord.

meniscus n. curved surface of a liquid; lens convex on one side and concave on the other.

menopause /ˈmen-/ n. time of life when a woman finally ceases to menstruate. **menopausal** a.

menorah n. seven-armed candelabrum used in Jewish worship.

menstrual a. of or in menstruation.

menstruate v.i. experience a monthly discharge of blood from the womb. **menstruation** n.

mensurable a. measurable.

mensuration n. measuring; mathematical rules for this.

mental a. of, in, or performed by the mind; (colloq.) mad. **mental handicap** lack of normal intelligence through imperfect mental development. **mental home** or **hospital** establishment for the care of patients suffering from mental illness. **mentally** adv.

mentality n. person's mental ability or characteristic attitude of mind.

menthol n. camphor-like substance.

mentholated a. impregnated with menthol.

mention v.t. speak or write about briefly; refer to by name. —n. act of mentioning, being mentioned.

mentor n. trusted adviser.

menu /ˈmen-/ n. (pl. -us) list of dishes to be served; list of options displayed on a computer screen.

MEP abbr. Member of the European Parliament.

mercantile a. trading, of trade or merchants.

mercenary a. working merely for money or other reward; grasping; (of soldiers) hired to serve a foreign country. —n. professional soldier hired by a foreign country.

mercer n. dealer in textile fabrics.

mercerized a. (of cotton) given a silky lustre.

merchandise n. goods bought and sold or for sale. —v.t./i. trade; promote sales of (goods). **merchandiser** n.

merchant n. wholesale trader; (US & Sc.) retail trader; (sl.) person fond of a certain activity. **merchant bank** one dealing in commercial loans and the financing of businesses. **merchant navy** shipping employed in commerce. **merchant ship** ship carrying merchandise.

merchantable a. saleable.

merchantman n. (pl. -men) merchant ship.

merciful a. showing mercy; giving relief from pain and suffering. **mercifulness** n.

mercifully *adv.* in a merciful way; (*colloq.*) thank goodness.

merciless *a.* showing no mercy. **mercilessly** *adv.*

mercurial *a.* of or caused by mercury; lively in temperament; liable to sudden changes of mood.

mercury *n.* heavy silvery usu. liquid metal, used in thermometers and barometers etc. **mercuric** *a.*

mercy *n.* kindness shown to an offender or enemy etc. who is in one's power; merciful act. **at the mercy of** wholly in the power of or subject to.

mere[1] *a.* no more or no better than what is specified. **merest** *a.* very small or insignificant. **merely** *adv.*

mere[2] *n.* (*poetic*) lake.

merganser *n.* a kind of diving duck.

merge *v.t./i.* combine into a whole; blend gradually.

merger *n.* combining of commercial companies etc. into one.

meridian /-'rɪd-/ *n.* great semicircle on the globe, passing through the North and South Poles.

meringue /-'ræŋ/ *n.* baked mixture of sugar and white of egg; small cake of this.

merino /-'riː-/ *n.* (*pl.* -os) a kind of sheep with fine soft wool; soft woollen fabric.

merit *n.* feature or quality that deserves praise; excellence, worthiness. —*v.t.* (*p.t.* **merited**) deserve.

meritocracy *n.* government by persons selected for merit.

meritorious *a.* deserving praise.

merlin *n.* a kind of falcon.

merlon *n.* solid part between embrasures in a parapet.

mermaid *n.*, **merman** *n.* (*pl.* -men) imaginary half-human sea creature with a fish's tail instead of legs.

merry *a.* (-ier, -iest) cheerful and lively, joyous. **make merry** hold lively festivities. **merry-go-**

round *n.* revolving machine at a fun-fair, with models of horses or cars etc. to ride on. **merry-making** *n.* lively festivities. **merrily** *adv.*, **merriment** *n.*

mescaline *n.* hallucinogenic drug present in the dried tops of a cactus (**mescal**).

mesembryanthemum *n.* low-growing plant with daisy-like flowers.

mesh *n.* space between threads in net or a sieve or wire screen etc.; network fabric. —*v.i.* (of a toothed wheel) engage with another.

mesmerize *v.t.* hypnotize, dominate the attention or will of. **mesmerization** *n.*, **mesmerism** *n.*, **mesmeric** *a.*

mesolithic *a.* of the period between palaeolithic and neolithic.

meson /'miːzɒn/ *n.* particle intermediate in mass between a proton and an electron

mess *n.* dirty or untidy condition; unpleasant or untidy thing(s); something spilt; difficult or confused situation, trouble; (in the armed forces) group who take meals together, their dining-room. —*v.t./i.* make untidy or dirty; muddle, bungle; (in the armed forces) take meals with a group. **make a mess of** bungle. **mess about** potter; fool about. **mess with** tinker with.

message *n.* spoken or written communication; moral or social teaching.

messenger *n.* bearer of a message.

Messiah *n.* deliverer expected by Jews; Christ as this. **Messianic** /-st'æn-/ *a.*

Messrs *see* **Mr.**

messy *a.* (-ier, -iest) untidy or dirty, slovenly. **messily** *adv.*, **messiness** *n.*

met *see* **meet**[2].

metabolism /-'tæ-/ *n.* process by which nutrition takes place.

metabolic a., **metabolically** adv.

metabolize v.t. process (food) in metabolism.

metal n. any of a class of mineral substances such as gold, silver, iron, etc., or an alloy of these. —a. made of metal. —v.t. cover with metal; make or mend (a road) with road-metal (see road).

metallic a. of or like metal.

metallurgy /-'tæl-/ n. science of extracting and working metals. **metallurgical** a., **metallurgist** n.

metamorphose v.t./i. change by metamorphosis.

metamorphosis /-'mɔːf-/ n. (pl. -phoses) change of form or character. **metamorphic** a.

metaphor n. transferred use of a word or phrase, suggesting comparison with its basic meaning (e.g. the evening of one's life, food for thought). **metaphorical** a., **metaphorically** adv.

metaphysics n. branch of philosophy dealing with the nature of existence and of knowledge. **metaphysical** a.

mete v.t. **mete** out deal out.

meteor n. small mass of matter from outer space.

meteoric a. of meteors; swift and brilliant. **meteorically** adv.

meteorite n. meteor fallen to earth.

meteorology n. study of atmospheric conditions esp. in order to forecast weather. **meteorological** a., **meteorologist** n.

meter[1] n. device measuring and indicating the quantity supplied, distance travelled, time elapsed, etc. —v.t. measure by a meter.

meter[2] n. (US) = metre.

methane /'miːθeɪn/ n. colourless inflammable gas.

methinks (past **methought**) (old use) = I think.

method n. procedure or way of doing something; orderliness.

methodical /-'θɒd-/ a. orderly, systematic. **methodically** adv.

Methodist n. member of a Protestant religious denomination based on the teachings of John and Charles Wesley. **Methodism** n.

meths n. (colloq.) methylated spirit.

methylated spirit form of alcohol used as a solvent and for heating.

meticulous a. very careful and exact. **meticulously** adv., **meticulousness** n.

métier /'meɪtjeɪ/ n. one's trade or profession; one's forte.

metonymy /-'tɒn-/ n. substitution of an associated noun, as in 'the Crown' for 'the Queen'.

metre n. metric unit of length (about 39.4 inches); rhythm in poetry.

metric a. of or using the metric system; of poetic metre. **metric system** decimal system of weights and measures, using the metre, litre, and gram as units.

metrical a. of or composed in rhythmic metre, not prose.

metricate v.t. convert to a metric system. **metrication** n.

metronome n. device sounding a click at a regular pre-set interval, used to indicate tempo while practising music.

metropolis /-'trɒp-/ n. chief city of a country or region.

metropolitan a. of a metropolis.

mettle n. courage, strength of character. **on one's mettle** determined to show one's courage or ability.

mettlesome a. spirited, brave.

mew n. cat's characteristic cry. —v.i. make this sound.

mews n. set of former stables now converted into dwellings or garages etc.

mezzanine /'metsaniːn/ n. extra storey set between two others.

mezzo-soprano *n.* (*pl.* -os) singer with a voice between soprano and contralto.

mezzotint *n.* a kind of engraving.

mg *abbr.* milligram(s).

MHz *abbr.* megahertz.

miaow *n. & v.i.* = mew.

miasma /mɪˈæz-/ *n.* unpleasant or unwholesome air.

mica /ˈmaɪ-/ *n.* mineral substance used as an electrical insulator.

mice *see* mouse.

Michaelmas /ˈmɪkəl-/ *n.* feast of St Michael (29 Sept.).

mickey *n.* **take the mickey out of** (*sl.*) tease, ridicule.

micro *n.* (*pl.* -os) (*colloq.*) microcomputer.

micro- *pref.* extremely small; one-millionth part of (as in *microgram*).

microbe *n.* micro-organism.

microbiology *n.* study of micro-organisms.

microchip *n.* tiny piece of a semi-conductor holding a complex electronic circuit.

microcomputer *n.* computer in which the central processor is contained on microchip(s).

microcosm *n.* community or complex resembling something else but on a very small scale.

microfiche /-fiːʃ/ *n.* (*pl.* -fiche) sheet of microfilm that can be filed like an index-card.

microfilm *n.* length of film bearing a photograph of written or printed matter in greatly reduced size. —*v.t.* photograph on this.

microlight *n.* a kind of motorized hang-glider.

micrometer /-ˈkrɒm-/ *n.* instrument for measuring small lengths or angles.

micron *n.* one-millionth of a metre.

micro-organism *n.* organism invisible to the naked eye.

microphone *n.* instrument for picking up sound waves for recording, amplifying, or broadcasting.

microprocessor *n.* data processor contained on microchip(s).

microscope *n.* instrument with lenses that magnify very small things and make them visible.

microscopic *a.* of a microscope; extremely small; too small to be visible without using a microscope. **microscopically** *adv.*, **microscopy** *n.*

microsurgery *n.* surgery using a microscope to see tissues and instruments.

microwave *n.* electromagnetic wave of length between about 50 cm and 1 mm; microwave oven. **microwave oven** oven using such waves to heat food quickly.

micturition *n.* urination.

mid *a.* middle.

midday *n.* middle of the day; noon.

midden *n.* dung-heap, rubbish-heap.

middle *a.* occurring at an equal distance from extremes or outer limits. —*n.* middle point, position, area, etc. **in the middle of** half-way through (an activity). **middle age** part of life between youth and old age. **middle-aged** *a.* of middle age. **Middle Ages** 5th c.–1453, or *c.* 1000–1453. **middle class** class of society between upper and working classes. **Middle East** area from Egypt to Iran inclusive.

middleman *n.* (*pl.* -men) trader handling a commodity between producer and consumer.

middleweight *n.* boxing-weight (75 kg).

middling *a.* moderately good.

midge *n.* small biting insect.

midget *n.* extremely small person or thing. —*a.* extremely small.

Midlands *n.pl.* inland counties of central England. **midland** *a.*

midnight *n.* 12 o'clock at night; time near this.

midriff *n.* front part of the body just above the waist.

midshipman n. (pl. **-men**) naval rank just below sub-lieutenant.

midst n. **in the midst of** in the middle of; among, surrounded by.

midsummer n. middle of the summer, about 21 June. **Midsummer's Day** 24 June.

midway adv. half-way.

midwife n. (pl. **-wives**) person trained to assist at childbirth.

midwifery /-wɪfrɪ/ n. midwife's work.

midwinter n. middle of the winter, about 22 Dec.

mien /miːn/ n. person's manner or bearing.

might[1] n. great strength or power. **with might and main** with all one's power and energy.

might[2] see **may**[1]. —v.aux. (used to request permission or (like may) to express possibility).

mighty a. (**-ier**, **-iest**) very strong or powerful; very great. **mightily** adv.

mignonette /mɪɡjən-/ n. plant with fragrant grey-green leaves.

migraine /ˈmiːɡ-/ n. severe form of headache.

migrant /ˈmaɪ-/ a. & n. migrating (person or animal).

migrate v.i. leave one place and settle in another; (of animals) go from one place to another at each season. **migration** n., **migratory** /ˈmaɪ-/ a.

mihrab n. niche or slab in a mosque, showing the direction of Mecca.

mike n. (colloq.) microphone.

milch cow cow kept for its milk; person or organization as an easy source of money.

mild a. (**-er**, **-est**) moderate in intensity, not harsh or drastic; gentle; not strongly flavoured. **mildly** adv., **mildness** n.

mildew n. tiny fungi forming a coating on things exposed to damp. **mildewed** a.

mile n. measure of length, 1760 yds (about 1.609 km); (colloq.) great distance. **nautical mile** unit used in navigation, 2025 yds (1.852 km).

mileage n. distance in miles; advantage to be gained.

milestone n. stone beside a road, showing the distance in miles to a certain place; significant event or stage reached.

milieu /ˈmiːljɜː/ n. (pl. **-eus**) environment, surroundings.

militant a. & n. (person) prepared to take aggressive action. **militancy** n.

militarism n. military spirit; reliance on military attitudes. **militaristic** a.

military a. of soldiers or the army or all armed forces.

militate v.i. serve as a strong influence.

militia /-ʃə/ n. a military force, esp. of trained civilians available in an emergency.

milk n. white fluid secreted by female mammals as food for their young; cow's milk as food for human beings; milk-like liquid. —v.t. draw milk from; exploit. **milk shake** frothy drink of flavoured milk. **milk teeth** first (temporary) teeth in young mammals. **milker** n.

milkmaid n. (old use) woman who milks cows.

milkman n. (pl. **-men**) man who delivers milk to customers.

milksop n. weakling.

milky a. of or like milk; containing much milk. **Milky Way** broad luminous band of stars.

mill n. machinery for grinding or something or for processing specified material; building containing this. —v.t./i. grind or produce in a mill; produce grooves in (metal); move in a confused mass. **miller** n.

millennium n. (pl. **-ums**) period of 1000 years; future period of great happiness for everyone.

millepede *n.* small crawling creature with many legs.

millet *n.* tall cereal plant; its small seeds.

milli- *pref.* one-thousandth part of (as in *milligram*, *millilitre*, *millimetre*).

milliard *n.* one thousand million.

milliner *n.* person who makes or sells women's hats. **millinery** *n.* milliner's work or goods.

million *n.* one thousand thousand (1,000,000). **millionth** *a.* & *n.*

millionaire *n.* person who possesses a million pounds.

millstone *n.* heavy circular stone used in grinding corn; great burden that impedes progress.

milometer /-'lɒm-/ *n.* instrument measuring the distance in miles travelled by a vehicle.

milt *n.* sperm discharged by a male fish over eggs laid by the female.

mimbar *n.* pulpit in a mosque.

mime *n.* acting with gestures without words. —*v.t./i.* act with mime.

mimic *v.t.* (*p.t.* **mimicked**) imitate, esp. playfully or for entertainment. —*n.* person who is clever at mimicking others. **mimicry** *n.*

mimosa *n.* tropical shrub with small ball-shaped flowers.

mina *n.* = myna.

minaret *n.* tall slender tower on or beside a mosque.

minatory /'mɪn-/ *a.* threatening.

mince *v.t./i.* cut into small pieces in a mincer; walk or speak with affected refinement. —*n.* minced meat. **mince pie** pie containing mincemeat. **not to mince matters** to speak bluntly.

mincemeat *n.* mixture of dried fruit, sugar, etc., used in pies. **make mincemeat of** defeat utterly.

mincer *n.* machine with revolving blades for cutting food into very small pieces.

mind *n.* ability to be aware of things and to think and reason, originating in the brain; a person's attention, remembrance, intention, or opinion; sanity. —*v.t./i.* have charge of; object to; bear in mind, feel concern about; remember and be careful (about).

minded *a.* having inclinations or interests of a certain kind.

minder *n.* person whose job is to have charge of a person or thing; (*sl.*) bodyguard.

mindful *a.* taking thought or care (of something). **mindfulness** *n.*

mindless *a.* without a mind, without intelligence. **mindlessness** *n.*

mine[1] *a.* & *poss.pron.* belonging to me.

mine[2] *n.* excavation for extracting metal or coal etc.; abundant source; receptacle filled with explosive material, laid in or on the ground or in water. —*v.t./i.* dig for minerals, extract in this way; lay explosive mines under or in.

minefield *n.* area where explosive mines have been laid.

miner *n.* person who works in a mine.

mineral *n.* inorganic natural substance; ore etc. obtained by mining; fizzy soft drink. —*a.* of or containing minerals. **mineral water** water naturally containing dissolved mineral salts or gases; fizzy soft drink.

mineralogy /-'ræl-/ *n.* study of minerals. **mineralogist** *n.*

minestrone /mɪnɪ'strəʊnɪ/ *n.* Italian soup containing chopped vegetables and pasta.

minesweeper *n.* ship for clearing away mines laid in the sea.

mineworker *n.* miner.

mingle *v.t./i.* mix, blend; go about among.

mingy *a.* (*colloq.*) mean, stingy.

mini- *pref.* miniature.

miniature *a.* very small, on a small scale. —*n.* small-scale portrait, copy, or model.

miniaturist n. person who paints miniatures.

miniaturize v.t. make miniature, produce in a very small version. **miniaturization** n.

minibus n. small bus-like vehicle with seats for only a few people.

minim n. note in music, lasting half as long as a semibreve; one-sixtieth of a fluid drachm.

minimal a. very small, least possible. **minimally** adv.

minimize v.t. reduce to a minimum; represent as small or unimportant. **minimization** n.

minimum a. & n. (pl. **-ima**) smallest (amount) possible.

minion n. (derog.) assistant.

minister n. head of a government department; member of the clergy, esp. Presbyterian or Non-conformist; senior diplomatic representative. —v.i. minister to attend to the needs of. **ministerial** /-'tɪər-/ a.

ministry n. government department headed by a minister; period of government under one premier; work of a cleric.

mink n. small stoat-like animal; its valuable fur; coat made of this.

minnow n. small fish of the carp family.

Minoan /mɪn-/ a. & n. (person) of the Cretan Bronze-Age civilization.

minor a. lesser; not very important; (of a musical scale) with a semi-tone above the second note. —n. person not yet legally of adult age.

minority n. smallest part of a group or class; small group differing from others; age when a person is not yet legally adult.

Minster n. name given to certain large or important churches.

minstrel n. medieval singer and musician.

mint[1] n. place authorized to make a country's coins; vast amount (of money); —v.t. make (coins) by stamping metal. **in mint condition** new-looking.

mint[2] n. plant with fragrant leaves used for flavouring; peppermint, sweet flavoured with this. **minty** a.

minuet n. slow stately dance.

minus prep. reduced by subtraction of; below zero; (colloq.) without. —a. less than zero; less than the amount indicated.

minuscule /'mɪn-/ a. extremely small.

minute[1] /'mɪnɪt/ n. one-sixtieth of an hour or degree; moment of time; (pl.) official summary of an assembly's proceedings. —v.t. record in the minutes of an assembly; send a minute to.

minute[2] /maɪ'njuːt/ a. extremely small; very precise. **minutely** adv., **minuteness** n.

minutiae /mɪ'njuːʃiː/ n.pl. very small details.

minx n. cheeky or mischievous girl.

miracle n. event so remarkable that it is attributed to a supernatural agency; remarkable occurrence or specimen. **miraculous** a., **miraculously** adv.

mirage /'mɪrɑːʒ/ n. optical illusion caused by atmospheric conditions.

mire n. swampy ground, bog; mud or sticky dirt. —v.t. coat or spatter with mud. **miry** a.

mirror n. piece of glass coated on one side so that reflections can be seen in it. —v.t. reflect in or as if in a mirror.

mirth n. merriment, laughter. **mirthful** a., **mirthless** a.

mis- pref. badly, wrongly.

misadventure n. piece of bad luck.

misanthrope /'mɪs-/ n. misanthropist.

misanthropy /-'sæn-/ n. dislike of people in general. **misanthropist** n., **misanthropic** /-'θrɒp-/ a.

misapprehend v.t. misunderstand. **misapprehension** n.

misappropriate v.t. take dishonestly. **misappropriation** n.

misbegotten a. contemptible; bastard.

misbehave v.i. behave badly. **misbehaviour** n.

miscalculate v.t./i. calculate incorrectly. **miscalculation** n.

miscall v.t. call wrongly.

miscarriage n. abortion occurring naturally; process of miscarrying.

miscarry v.i. have a miscarriage; go wrong or astray, be unsuccessful.

miscegenation /-sɪdʒ-/ n. interbreeding between people of different races.

miscellaneous a. assorted.

miscellany /-'sel-/ n. collection of assorted items.

mischance n. misfortune.

mischief n. children's annoying but not malicious conduct; playful malice; harm, damage.

mischievous a. full of mischief. **mischievously** adv., **mischievousness** n.

miscible a. able to be mixed.

misconception n. wrong interpretation.

misconduct n. bad behaviour; mismanagement.

misconstrue /-'stru:/ v.t. misinterpret. **misconstruction** n.

miscount v.t./i. count wrongly. —n. wrong count.

miscreant /-krɪə-/ n. wrongdoer.

misdeed n. wrongful act.

misdemeanour n. misdeed.

miser n. person who hoards money and spends as little as possible. **miserly** a., **miserliness** n.

miserable a. full of misery; wretchedly poor in quality or surroundings; miserably adv.

misericord /-'ze-/ n. projection under a hinged seat in a choir stall.

misery n. great unhappiness or discomfort; (colloq.) discontented or disagreeable person.

misfire v.i. (of a gun or engine) fail to fire correctly; go wrong.

misfit n. thing that does not fit; person not well suited to his work or environment.

misfortune n. bad luck, unfortunate event.

misgive v.t. (p.t. -gave, p.p. -given) fill with misgivings.

misgiving n. feeling of doubt or slight fear or mistrust.

misguided a. mistaken in one's opinions or actions.

mishap n. unlucky accident.

misinform v.t. give wrong information to. **misinformation** n.

misinterpret v.t. interpret incorrectly. **misinterpretation** n.

misjudge v.t. form a wrong opinion or estimate of. **misjudgement** n.

mislay v.t. (p.t. **mislaid**) lose temporarily.

mislead v.t. (p.t. **misled**) cause to form a wrong impression.

mismanage v.t. manage badly or wrongly. **mismanagement** n.

misnomer n. wrongly applied name or description.

misogynist /-'sɒdʒɪ-/ n. person who hates women. **misogyny** n.

misplace v.t. put in a wrong place; place (confidence etc.) unwisely.

misprint n. error in printing. —v.t. print incorrectly.

misquote v.t. quote incorrectly. **misquotation** n.

misread v.t. (p.t. -**read**) read or interpret incorrectly.

misrepresent v.t. represent in a false way. **misrepresentation** n.

misrule n. bad government.

Miss n. (pl. **Misses**) title of a girl or unmarried woman.

miss v.t./i. fail to hit, catch, see, hear, understand, etc.; lack; notice or regret the absence or loss of; avoid; (of an engine) misfire. —n. failure to hit or attain what is aimed at. **miss out** leave out, not include; (colloq.) be unsuccessful.

missal *n.* book containing prayers used in Mass in the RC Church.

missel-thrush *n.* = mistle-thrush.

misshapen *a.* badly shaped.

missile *n.* object or weapon suitable for projecting at a target.

missing *a.* not present; not in its place, lost.

mission *n.* task that a person or group is sent to perform; this group; missionaries' headquarters.

missionary *n.* person sent to spread Christian faith in a community.

missis *n.* (*sl.*) wife.

missive *n.* written message sent to someone.

misspell *v.t.* (*p.t.* **misspelt**) spell incorrectly. **misspelling** *n.*

misspend *v.t.* (*p.t.* **misspent**) spend badly or unwisely.

mist *n.* water vapour near the ground or clouding a window etc.; thing resembling this. —*v.t./i.* cover or become covered with mist.

mistake *n.* incorrect idea or opinion; thing done incorrectly. —*v.t.* (*p.t.* **mistook**, *p.p.* **mistaken**) misunderstand; choose or identify wrongly.

mistaken *a.* wrong in opinion; unwise. **mistakenly** *adv.*

mistime *v.t.* say or do (a thing) at a wrong time.

mistle-thrush *n.* large thrush.

mistletoe *n.* plant with white berries, growing on trees.

mistral *n.* cold north or north-west wind in southern France.

mistress *n.* woman who has control of people or things; female teacher; man's illicit female lover.

mistrust *v.t.* feel no trust in. —*n.* lack of trust. **mistrustful** *a.*

misty *a.* (*-ier*, *-iest*) full of mist; indistinct. **mistily** *adv.*, **mistiness** *n.*

misunderstand *v.t.* (*p.t.* **-stood**) fail to understand correctly. **misunderstanding** *n.*

misuse[1] /-'ju:z/ *v.t.* use wrongly; treat badly. **misuser** *n.*

misuse[2] /-'ju:s/ *n.* wrong use.

mite *n.* very small spider-like animal; small creature, esp. a child; small contribution.

mitigate *v.t.* make seem less serious or severe. **mitigation** *n.*

mitre /'maitə(r)/ *n.* pointed headdress of bishops and abbots; join with tapered edges that form a right angle. —*v.t.* join in this way.

mitt *n.* mitten.

mitten *n.* glove with no partitions between the fingers, or leaving the fingertips bare.

mix *v.t./i.* put (different things) together so that they are no longer distinct; prepare by doing this; combine, blend; be compatible; be sociable. —*n.* mixture. **mix up** mix thoroughly; confuse. **mixer** *n.*

mixed *a.* composed of various elements, or of people from different races or social classes; of or for both sexes. **mixed-up** *a.* (*colloq.*) muddled; not well adjusted emotionally.

mixture *n.* thing made by mixing; process of mixing things.

mizen-mast *n.* mast next aft the mainmast.

ml *abbr.* millilitre(s).

mm *abbr.* millimetre(s).

mnemonic /nɪ'mɒn-/ *a.* & *n.* (verse etc.) aiding the memory.

moan *n.* low mournful sound; grumble. —*v.t./i.* make or utter with a moan. **moaner** *n.*

moat *n.* deep wide usu. water-filled ditch round a castle or house etc.

moated *a.* surrounded by a moat.

mob *n.* large disorderly crowd; (*sl.*) gang. —*v.t.* (*p.t.* **mobbed**) crowd round in great numbers.

mob-cap *n.* (*old use*) woman's indoor cap covering all the hair.

mobile *a.* able to move or be moved easily. —*n.* artistic structure for hanging so that its parts move in currents of air. **mobility** *n.*

mobilize *v.t./i.* assemble (troops etc.) for active service. **mobilization** *n.*, **mobilizer** *n.*

moccasin /'mɒk-/ *n.* soft leather shoe stitched round the vamp.

mocha /'məʊkə/ *n.* a kind of coffee.

mock *v.t./i.* make fun of by imitating; jeer; defy contemptuously. —*a.* sham, imitation. **mock-up** *n.* model for use in testing or study.

mocker *n.* one who mocks. **put the mockers on** (*sl.*) bring bad luck to; put a stop to.

mockery *n.* mocking, ridicule; absurd or unsatisfactory imitation.

mode *n.* way a thing is done; current fashion; scale system in music; specific state of operation in a computer; value that occurs most frequently in a set of data. **modal** *a.*

model *n.* three-dimensional reproduction, usu. on a smaller scale; design, style; exemplary person or thing; person employed to pose for an artist or display clothes in a shop etc. by wearing them. —*a.* exemplary. —*v.t./i.* (*p.t.* **modelled**) make a model of; shape; design or plan in accordance with a model; work as artist's or fashion model, display (clothes) thus.

modem *n.* device for sending and receiving computer data through a telephone line.

moderate[1] /-ət/ *a.* medium; not extreme or excessive. —*n.* holder of moderate views. **moderately** *adv.*

moderate[2] /-ert/ *v.t./i.* make or become moderate or less intense.

moderation *n.* moderating. **in moderation** in moderate amounts.

moderator *n.* Presbyterian minister presiding over a church assembly; arbitrator, mediator.

modern *a.* of present or recent times; in current style. **modernity** /-'dɜ:-/ *n.*

modernist *n.* person who favours modern ideas or methods. **modernism** *n.*

modernize *v.t.* make modern, adapt to modern ways. **modernization** *n.*, **modernizer** *n.*

modest *a.* not vain or boastful; moderate in size etc., not showy; showing regard for conventional decencies. **modestly** *adv.*, **modesty** *n.*

modicum *n.* small amount.

modify *v.t.* make less severe; make partial changes in; qualify by describing. **modification** *n.*

modish /'məʊ-/ *a.* fashionable. **modishly** *adv.*, **modishness** *n.*

modulate *v.t./i.* regulate, moderate; vary in tone or pitch. **modulation** *n.*

module *n.* standardized part or independent unit, esp. in furniture or a building or spacecraft etc; unit of training or education. **modular** *a.*

mogul /'məʊ-/ *n.* (*colloq.*) important or influential person.

mohair *n.* fine silky hair of the angora goat; yarn or fabric made from this.

Mohammedan *a.* & *n.* Muslim.

moiety *n.* half.

moiré /'mwɑ:reɪ/ *n.* fabric that looks like watered silk.

moist *a.* (**-er**, **-est**) slightly wet. **moistly** *adv.*, **moistness** *n.*

moisten *v.t./i.* make or become moist.

moisture *n.* water or other liquid diffused through a substance or as vapour or condensed on a surface.

moisturize *v.t.* make (skin) less dry. **moisturizer** *n.*

molar *n.* back tooth with a broad top, used in chewing.

molasses *n.* syrup from raw sugar; (*US*) treacle.

mole[1] *n.* small dark spot on human skin.

mole[2] *n.* breakwater or causeway built out into the sea.

mole[3] *n.* small burrowing animal with dark fur; spy established within an organization.

molecule /'mɒlɪ-/ *n.* very small unit (usu. a group of atoms) of a substance. **molecular** /-'lek-/ *a.*

molehill *n.* mound of earth thrown up by a mole.

molest *v.t.* pester in a hostile way or so as to cause injury; attack or interfere with sexually. **molestation** *n.*

moll *n.* (*colloq.*) gangster's female companion; prostitute.

mollify *v.t.* soothe the anger of. **mollification** *n.*

mollusc *n.* animal with a soft body and often a hard shell.

mollycoddle *v.t.* coddle excessively.

molten *a.* liquefied by heat.

molybdenum *n.* metal used in steel for high-speed tools etc.

moment *n.* point or brief portion of time; importance.

momentary /'məʊ-/ *a.* lasting only a moment. **momentarily** *adv.*

momentous /-'men-/ *a.* of great importance. **momentously** *adv.*

momentum *n.* impetus gained by a moving body.

monarch *n.* ruler with the title of king, queen, emperor, or empress. **monarchic** /-'nɑ:k/ *a.*, **monarchical** *a.*

monarchist *n.* supporter of a monarch or system of monarchy. **monarchism** *n.*

monarchy *n.* form of government with a monarch as the supreme ruler; country governed thus.

monastery *n.* residence of a community of monks.

monastic /-'næs-/ *a.* of monks or monasteries. **monasticism** *n.* monks' way of life.

Monday *n.* day after Sunday.

monetarist /'mʌnɪ-/ *n.* person who advocates control of the money supply in order to curb inflation. **monetarism** *n.*

monetary /'mʌnɪ-/ *a.* of money or currency.

money *n.* current coins; coins and banknotes; (*pl.* **-eys**) any form of currency; wealth. **money order** printed order for payment of a specified sum, issued by a bank or Post Office. **money-spinner** *n.* profitable thing.

moneyed /'mʌnɪd/ *a.* wealthy.

Mongol *a. & n.* Mongolian.

mongolism *n.* Down's syndrome.

mongoose *n.* (*pl.* **-gooses**) stoat-like tropical animal that can attack and kill snakes.

mongrel *n.* animal (esp. a dog) of mixed breed. —*a.* of mixed origin or character.

monitor *n.* device used to observe or test the operation of something; pupil with special duties in a school. —*v.t.* keep watch over; record and test or control.

monk *n.* member of a male community living apart from the world under the rules of a religious order. **monkish** *a.*

monkey *n.* (*pl.* **-eys**) animal of a group closely related to man; mischievous person. —*v.i.* (*p.t.* **monkeyed**) tamper mischievously. **monkey-nut** *n.* peanut. **monkey-puzzle** *n.* evergreen tree with narrow stiff leaves on interlaced branches. **monkey wrench** wrench with an adjustable jaw.

mono *a. & n.* (*pl.* **-os**) monophonic (sound or recording).

mono- *pref.* one, alone, single.

monochrome *a.* done in only one colour, black-and-white.

monocle *n.* eye-glass for one eye only.

monocular *a.* with or for one eye.

monody *n.* dirge, elegy.

monogamy *n.* system of being married to only one person at a time. **monogamous** *a.*

monogram *n.* two or more letters (esp. a person's initials).

combined in one design. **monogrammed** *a.*

monograph *n.* scholarly treatise on a subject.

monolith *n.* large single upright block of stone; massive organization etc. **monolithic** *a.*

monologue *n.* long speech.

monomania *n.* obsession with one idea or interest. **monomaniac** *n.*

monophonic /-'fɒn-/ *a.* using only one transmission channel for reproduction of sound.

monoplane *n.* aeroplane with only one set of wings.

monopolize *v.t.* have a monopoly of; not allow others to share in. **monopolization** *n.*

monopoly *n.* sole possession or control of something, esp. of trade in a specified commodity. **monopolist** *n.*

monorail *n.* railway in which the track is a single rail.

monosodium glutamate substance added to food to enhance its flavour.

monosyllable *n.* word of one syllable. **monosyllabic** /-'læ-/ *a.*

monotheism /'mɒnəθi:ɪzm/ *n.* doctrine that there is only one God. **monotheist** *n.*, **monotheistic** *a.*

monotone *n.* level unchanging tone of voice.

monotonous *a.* lacking in variety or variation; dull because of this. **monotonously** *adv.*, **monotony** *n.*

Monseigneur /-sen'jɜ:(r)/ *n.* title of a French cardinal, bishop, etc.

Monsieur /mə'sjɜ:(r)/ *n.* (*pl.* **Messieurs**, *pr.* mes'jɜ:(r)) title of a French-speaking man.

Monsignor /-'si:njɔ:(r)/ *n.* title of certain RC priests and officials.

monsoon *n.* seasonal wind in South Asia; rainy season accompanying the south-west monsoon.

monster *n.* thing that is huge or very abnormal in form; huge ugly or frightening creature; very cruel or wicked person.

monstrance *n.* framed holder used in the RC Church for exposing the Host for veneration.

monstrosity *n.* monstrous thing.

monstrous *a.* like a monster, huge; outrageous, absurd.

montage /-ta:ʒ/ *n.* making of a composite picture from pieces of others; this picture; joining of disconnected shots in a cinema film.

montbretia /mɒn'bri:ʃə/ *n.* plant of the iris family with small orange-coloured flowers.

month *n.* each of the twelve portions into which the year is divided; period of 28 days.

monthly *a.* & *adv.* (produced or occurring) once a month. —*n.* monthly periodical.

monument *n.* thing (esp. a structure) commemorating a person or event etc.; structure of historical importance.

monumental /-'men-/ *a.* of or serving as a monument; massive; extremely great.

moo *n.* cow's low deep cry. —*v.i.* make this sound.

mooch *v.i.* (*sl.*) walk slowly and aimlessly.

mood *n.* temporary state of mind or spirits; fit of bad temper or depression; verb-form showing whether it is a statement, command, etc.

moody *a.* (**-ier, -iest**) gloomy, sullen; liable to become like this. **moodily** *adv.*, **moodiness** *n.*

moon *n.* earth's satellite, made visible by light it reflects from the sun; natural satellite of any planet. —*v.i.* behave dreamily.

moonbeam *n.* ray of moonlight.

moonlight *n.* light from the moon. —*v.i.* (*colloq.*) have two paid jobs, one by day and the other in the evening.

moonlit *a.* lit by the moon.

moonstone *n.* pearly semi-precious stone.

Moor *n.* member of a Muslim people of north-west Africa. **Moorish** *a.*

moor[1] *n.* stretch of open uncultivated land with low shrubs.

moor[2] *v.t.* secure (a boat etc.) to a fixed object by means of cable(s).

moorhen *n.* small water-bird.

moorings *n.pl.* cables or place for mooring a boat.

moose *n.* (*pl.* **moose**) elk of North America.

moot *a.* debatable. —*v.t.* raise (a question) for discussion.

mop *n.* pad or bundle of yarn on a stick, used for cleaning things; thick mass of hair. —*v.t.* (*p.t.* **mopped**) clean with a mop; wipe away. **mop up** wipe up with a mop or cloth etc.; clear an area of the remnants of defeated enemy troops.

mope *v.i.* be unhappy and listless.

moped /'məup̃ed/ *n.* motorized bicycle.

moquette /-'ket/ *n.* upholstery fabric with loops or pile.

moraine *n.* mass of stones etc. carried and deposited by a glacier.

moral *a.* concerned with right and wrong conduct; virtuous. —*n.* moral lesson or principle; (*pl.*) person's moral habits, esp. sexual conduct. **moral certainty** virtual certainty. **moral support** encouragement. **moral victory** a triumph though without concrete gain. **morally** *adv.*

morale /-'rɑːl/ *n.* state of a person's or group's spirits and confidence.

moralist *n.* person who expresses or teaches moral principles.

morality *n.* moral principles or rules; goodness or rightness.

moralize *v.i.* talk or write about the morality of something.

morass /-'ræs/ *n.* marsh; bog; complex entanglement.

moratorium *n.* (*pl.* **-ums**) temporary agreed ban on an activity.

morbid *a.* preoccupied with gloomy or unpleasant things; unhealthy. **morbidly** *adv.*, **morbidness** *n.*, **morbidity** *n.*

mordant *a.* (of wit etc.) caustic.

more *a.* greater in quantity or intensity etc. —*n.* greater amount or number. —*adv.* to a greater extent; again. **more or less** approximately.

morello *n.* (*pl.* **-os**) dark-coloured bitter cherry.

moreover *adv.* besides.

morganatic marriage /-'næ-/ one where a woman of low rank does not take her husband's high rank.

morgue /mɔːg/ *n.* mortuary.

moribund /'mɒ-/ *a.* in a dying state.

Mormon *n.* member of a Christian sect founded in 1830 in the USA.

morn *n.* (*poetic*) morning.

morning *n.* part of the day from dawn to noon or the midday meal. **morning-after pill** contraceptive pill effective when taken some hours after intercourse.

morocco *n.* goatskin leather of the kind originally made in Morocco; imitation of this.

moron *n.* (*colloq.*) very stupid person. **moronic** *a.*

morose /-'rəus/ *a.* gloomy and unsociable, sullen. **morosely** *adv.*, **moroseness** *n.*

morphia *n.* morphine.

morphine /-'fiːn/ *n.* drug made from opium, used to relieve pain.

morphology *n.* study of forms of animals and plants or of words. **morphological** *a.*

morris dance English folk-dance by men in costume.

morrow *n.* (*poetic*) the following day.

Morse *n.* **Morse code** code of signals using short and long sounds or flashes of light.

morsel *n.* small amount; small piece of food.

mortal *a.* subject to death; fatal; deadly. —*n.* person subject to death, human being. **mortally** *adv.*

mortality *n.* being mortal; loss of life on a large scale; death-rate.

mortar *n.* mixture of lime or cement with sand and water, used for joining bricks or stones; hard bowl in which substances are pounded with a pestle; short cannon.

mortarboard *n.* stiff square cap worn as part of academic dress.

mortgage *n.* loan for purchase of property, in which the property itself is pledged as security; agreement effecting this. —*v.t.* pledge (property) as security thus.

mortgagee *n.* creditor in a mortgage.

mortgager *n.* (in law **mortgagor**) debtor in a mortgage.

mortify *v.t./i.* humiliate greatly; (of flesh) become gangrenous. **mortification** *n.*

mortise *n.* hole in one part of a framework shaped to receive the end of another part. **mortise lock** lock set in (not on) a door.

mortuary *n.* place where dead bodies may be kept temporarily.

mosaic *n.* pattern or picture made with small pieces of glass or stone of different colours.

moselle *n.* German dry white wine.

Moslem *a.* & *n.* = **Muslim**.

mosque *n.* Muslim place of worship.

mosquito *n.* (*pl.* -**oes**) a kind of gnat.

moss *n.* small flowerless plant forming a dense growth in moist places. **mossy** *a.*

most *a.* greatest in quantity or intensity etc. —*n.* greatest amount or number. —*adv.* to the greatest extent; very. at most no more than. **for the most part** in most cases; in most of its extent.

make the most of use or represent to the best advantage.

mostly *adv.* for the most part.

motel *n.* roadside hotel providing accommodation for motorists and their vehicles.

motet *n.* short usu. unaccompanied church anthem.

moth *n.* insect like a butterfly but usu. flying at night; similar insect whose larvae feed on cloth or fur.

moth-eaten *a.* damaged by the larvae of moths.

mothball *n.* small ball of pungent substance for keeping moths away from clothes.

mother *n.* female parent; title of the female head of a religious community. —*v.t.* look after in a motherly way. **Mothering Sunday** fourth Sunday in Lent, with the custom of giving a gift to one's mother. **mother-in-law** *n.* (*pl.* **mothers-in-law**) mother of one's wife or husband. **mother-of-pearl** *n.* pearly substance lining shells of oysters and mussels etc. **Mother's Day** Mothering Sunday. **mother tongue** one's native language. **motherhood** *n.*

motherland *n.* one's native country.

motherless *a.* without a living mother.

motherly *a.* showing a mother's kindness. **motherliness** *n.*

motif /-'tiːf/ *n.* recurring design, feature, or melody; ornament sewn on a dress etc.

motion *n.* moving; movement; formal proposal put to a meeting for discussion; emptying of the bowels, faeces. —*v.t./i.* make a gesture directing (a person) to do something. **motion picture** film recording a story or events with movement as in real life.

motionless *a.* not moving.

motivate *v.t.* supply a motive to; cause to feel active interest. **motivation** *n.*

motive *n.* that which induces a person to act in a certain way.

—*a.* producing movement or action.

motley *a.* multi-coloured; assorted. —*n.* (*old use*) jester's particoloured costume.

motor *n.* machine supplying motive power; motor car. —*a.* producing motion; driven by a motor.—*v.t./i.* go or convey in a motor car. **motor bike** (*colloq.*) motor cycle. **motor car** low short-bodied motor vehicle. **motor cycle** motor-driven cycle that cannot be driven by pedals. **motor cyclist** rider of a motor cycle. **motor vehicle** vehicle with a motor engine, for use on ordinary roads.

motorcade *n.* procession or parade of motor vehicles.

motorist *n.* driver of a motor car.

motorize *v.t.* equip with motor(s) or motor vehicles.

motorway *n.* road constructed and controlled for fast motor traffic.

mottled *n.* patterned with irregular patches of colour.

motto *n.* (*pl.* **-oes**) short sentence or phrase expressing an ideal or rule of conduct; maxim, riddle, etc., inside a paper cracker.

mould[1] *n.* hollow container into which a liquid substance is poured to set or cool in a desired shape; pudding etc. made in this. —*v.t.* shape; guide or control the development of.

mould[2] *n.* furry growth of tiny fungi on a damp substance.

mould[3] *n.* soft fine earth rich in organic matter.

moulder[1] *n.* workman who makes moulds for casting metal.

moulder[2] *v.i.* decay and rot away.

moulding *n.* moulded thing, esp. an ornamental strip of plaster etc.

mouldy *a.* (**-ier, -iest**) covered with mould; stale; (*colloq.*) dull, worthless. **mouldiness** *n.*

moult /məʊ/ *v.i.* shed feathers, hair, or skin before new growth. —*n.* process of moulting.

mound *n.* mass of piled-up earth or small stones; small hill. —*v.t.* pile in mound(s).

mount[1] *n.* mountain, hill.

mount[2] *v.t./i.* go up; get or put on a horse etc. for riding; increase; fix on or in support(s) or setting; organize, arrange. —*n.* horse for riding; thing on which something is fixed for support etc.

mountain *n.* mass of land rising to a great height, esp. over 1000 ft.; large heap or pile. **mountain ash** rowan tree. **mountain bicycle** (**or bike**) strong bicycle with multiple gears, suitable for riding on rough hilly ground.

mountaineer *n.* person who climbs mountains. —*v.i.* climb mountains as a recreation.

mountainous *a.* full of mountains; huge.

mountebank *n.* charlatan.

Mountie *n.* member of the Royal Canadian Mounted Police.

mourn *v.t./i.* feel or express sorrow or regret about (a dead person or lost thing). **mourner** *n.*

mournful *a.* sorrowful. **mournfully** *adv.,* **mournfulness** *n.*

mourning *n.* dark clothes worn as a conventional sign of bereavement.

mouse *n.* (*pl.* **mice**) small rodent with a long tail; quiet timid person; small rolling device for moving the cursor on a VDU screen.

mousetrap *n.* trap for mice.

moussaka /muːˈsɑː-/ *n.* Greek dish of minced meat and aubergine.

mousse /muːs/ *n.* frothy creamy dish; substance of similar texture.

moustache /məˈstɑːʃ/ *n.* hair allowed to grow on a man's upper lip.

mousy *a.* dull greyish-brown; quiet and timid. **mousiness** *n.*

mouth[1] /-θ/ *n.* opening in the head through which food is taken in and sounds uttered; opening of a bag, cave, cannon, etc.; place where a river enters the sea.

mouth-organ *n.* small wind instrument played by blowing and sucking.

mouth[2] /-ð/ *v.t./i.* form (words) soundlessly with the lips; declaim pompously or with exaggerated distinctness.

mouthful *n.* amount that fills the mouth.

mouthpiece *n.* part of an instrument placed between or near the lips; person speaking on behalf of others.

mouthwash *n.* liquid for cleansing the mouth.

movable *a.* able to be moved.

move *v.t./i.* change or cause to change in place, position, or attitude; change one's residence; progress; provoke a reaction or emotion in; take action; put to a meeting formally for discussion. —*n.* act of moving; moving of a piece in chess etc.; calculated action. **move house** change one's residence. **on the move** moving. **mover** *n.*

movement *n.* moving; move; moving parts; group's organized actions to achieve a purpose, the group itself; section of a long piece of music.

movie *n.* (*US colloq.*) cinema film.

moving *a.* arousing pity or sympathy. **movingly** *adv.*

mow *v.t.* (*p.p.* **mown**) cut down (grass or grain etc.); cut grass etc. from. **mow down** kill or destroy by a moving force. **mower** *n.*

MP *abbr.* Member of Parliament.

m.p.h. *abbr.* miles per hour.

Mr *n.* (*pl.* **Messrs**) title prefixed to a man's name.

Mrs *n.* (*pl.* **Mrs**) title prefixed to a married woman's name.

Ms /mɪz/ *n.* title prefixed to a woman's name without distinction of married or unmarried status.

Mt. *abbr.* Mount.

much *a.* & *n.* (existing in) great quantity. —*adv.* in a great degree; to a great extent.

mucilage *n.* sticky substance got from plants; adhesive gum.

muck *n.* farmyard manure; (*colloq.*) dirt, a mess. —*v.t.* make dirty; mess. **muck in** (*sl.*) share tasks etc. equally. **muck out** remove muck from. **mucky** *a.*

muckraking *n.* seeking and exposing scandal.

mucous *a.* like or covered with mucus.

mucus *n.* slimy substance coating the inner surface of hollow organs of the body.

mud *n.* wet soft earth. **mud-slinging** *n.* (*sl.*) attacking a reputation.

muddle *v.t./i.* confuse, mix up; progress in a haphazard way. —*n.* muddled condition or things.

muddy *a.* (-ier, -iest) like mud, full of mud; not clear or pure. —*v.t.* make muddy. **muddiness** *n.*

mudguard *n.* curved cover above the wheel of a cycle or other vehicle as a protection against spray thrown up.

mudlark *n.* child who plays in mud; person who scavenges articles from mud.

muesli /'mjuːzlɪ/ *n.* food of mixed crushed cereals, dried fruit, nuts, etc.

muezzin /muː'ez-/ *n.* man who proclaims the hours of prayer for Muslims.

muff[1] *n.* tube-shaped usu. furry covering for the hands.

muff[2] *v.t.* (*colloq.*) bungle.

muffin *n.* light round yeast cake eaten toasted and buttered.

muffle *v.t.* wrap for warmth or protection, or to deaden sound; make less loud or less distinct.

muffler *n.* scarf worn for warmth.

mufti n. plain clothes worn by one who has the right to wear uniform.

mug[1] n. large drinking-vessel with a handle, for use without a saucer; (sl.) face; (sl.) person who is easily outwitted. —v.t. (p.t. mugged) rob (a person) with violence, esp. in a public place. **mugger** n.

mug[2] v.t. (p.t. mugged) mug up (sl.) learn (a subject) by studying hard.

muggins n. (colloq.) person who is easily outwitted.

muggy a. (-ier, -iest) (of weather) oppressively damp and warm. **mugginess** n.

mujahidin n.pl. Muslim (esp. fundamentalist) guerrilla fighters.

mulatto n. (pl. -os) person with one White and one Black parent.

mulberry n. purple or white fruit resembling a blackberry; tree bearing this; dull purplish-red.

mulch n. mixture of wet straw, leaves, etc., spread on ground to protect plants or retain moisture. —v.t. cover with mulch.

mulct v.t. take money from (a person) by a fine, taxation, etc.

mule[1] n. animal that is the offspring of a horse and a donkey, known for its stubbornness.

mule[2] n. backless slipper.

muleteer n. mule-driver.

mulish a. stubborn. **mulishly** adv., **mulishness** n.

mull[1] v.t. heat (wine etc.) with sugar and spices, as a drink.

mull[2] v.t. mull over think over.

mull[3] n. (Sc.) promontory.

mullah n. Muslim learned in Islamic law.

mullein /-lm/ n. herb with spikes of yellow flowers.

mullet n. small edible sea-fish.

mulligatawny n. curry-flavoured soup.

mullion n. upright usu. stone strip between the panes of a tall window.

multi- pref. many.

multicultural a. of or involving several cultural or ethnic groups. **multiculturalism** n.

multifarious /-'fear-/ a. very varied. **multifariously** adv.

multimillionaire n. person with a fortune of several million pounds.

multinational a. & n. (business company) operating in several countries.

multiple a. having or affecting many parts. —n. quantity containing another a number of times without remainder.

multiplex n. having many elements.

multiplication n. multiplying.

multiplicity n. great variety.

multiply v.t./i. take a quantity a specified number of times and find the quantity produced; increase in number. **multiplier** n.

multiracial a. of or involving people of several races.

multitude n. great number of things or people.

multitudinous a. very numerous.

mum[1] a. (colloq.) silent.

mum[2] n. (colloq.) mother.

mumble v.t./i. speak or utter indistinctly. —n. indistinct speech.

mumbo-jumbo n. meaningless ritual; deliberately obscure language.

mummer n. actor in a traditional mime.

mummify v.t. preserve (a corpse) by embalming as in ancient Egypt. **mummification** n.

mummy[1] n. corpse embalmed and wrapped for burial, esp. in ancient Egypt.

mummy[2] n. (colloq.) mother.

mumps n. virus disease with painful swellings in the neck.

munch v.t. chew vigorously.

mundane *a.* dull, routine; worldly.

municipal *a.* of a town or city.

municipality /-'pæl-/ *n.* self-governing town or district.

munificent *a.* splendidly generous. **munificently** *adv.*, **munificence** *n.*

muniments *n.pl.* title-deeds or similar documents.

munitions *n.pl.* weapons, ammunition, etc., used in war.

mural *a.* of or on a wall. —*n.* a painting made on a wall.

murder *n.* intentional unlawful killing. —*v.t.* kill intentionally and unlawfully; (*colloq.*) ruin by bad performance. **murderer** *n.*, **murderess** *n.fem.*

murderous *a.* involving or capable of murder.

murk *n.* darkness, gloom.

murky *a.* (-ier, -iest) dark, gloomy. **murkiness** *n.*

murmur *n.* low continuous sound; softly spoken words. —*v.t./i.* make a murmur; speak or utter softly.

murrain *n.* infectious disease of cattle.

muscat *n.* musk-flavoured grape; wine made from this.

muscatel *n.* muscat; raisin from this.

muscle *n.* strip of fibrous tissue able to contract and relax and so move a part of an animal body; muscular power; strength. —*v.i.* **muscle in** (*colloq.*) force one's way.

muscular *a.* of muscles; having well-developed muscles. **muscularity** *n.*

Muse *n.* any of the nine sister goddesses in Greek and Roman mythology, presiding over branches of learning and the arts.

muse *v.i.* ponder.

museum *n.* place where objects of historical interest are collected and displayed.

mush *n.* soft pulp.

mushroom *n.* edible fungus with a stem and a domed cap, noted for its rapid growth; fawn colour. —*v.i.* spring up in large numbers; rise and spread in a mushroom shape.

mushy *a.* as or like mush; feebly sentimental. **mushiness** *n.*

music *n.* arrangement of sounds of one or more voices or instruments; written form of this. **music centre** combined radio, record-player, tape-recorder, etc. **music-hall** *n.* variety entertainment.

musical *a.* of or involving music; fond of or skilled in music; sweet-sounding. —*n.* light play with songs and dancing. **musically** *adv.*

musician *n.* person skilled in music.

musicology *n.* study of the history and forms of music. **musicologist** *n.*

musk *n.* substance secreted by certain animals or produced synthetically, used in perfumes. **musky** *a.*

musket *n.* long-barrelled gun formerly used by infantry.

musketeer *n.* soldier armed with a musket.

musketry *n.* muskets; use of these.

Muslim *a.* of or believing in Muhammad's teaching. —*n.* believer in this faith.

muslin *n.* a kind of thin cotton cloth.

musquash *n.* rat-like North American water animal; its fur.

mussel *n.* a kind of bivalve mollusc.

must[1] *v.aux.* (used to express necessity or obligation, certainty, or insistence). —*n.* (*colloq.*) thing that must be done or visited etc.

must[2] *n.* grape-juice etc. undergoing fermentation; new wine.

mustang *n.* wild horse of Mexico and California.

mustard *n.* plant with yellow flowers and sharp-tasting seeds; these seeds ground to paste as a condiment; dark yellow.

muster *v.t./i.* assemble, gather. —*n.* gathering of people or things. **pass muster** be accepted as adequate.

musty *a.* (-ier, -iest) smelling mouldy, stale. **mustiness** *n.*

mutable *a.* liable to change, fickle. **mutability** *n.*

mutant *a. & n.* (living thing) differing from its parents as a result of genetic change.

mutate *v.t./i.* change in form.

mutation *n.* change in form; mutant.

mute *a.* silent; dumb. —*n.* dumb person; device deadening the sound of a musical instrument. —*v.t.* deaden or muffle the sound of. **mutely** *adv.*, **muteness** *n.*

mutilate *v.t.* injure or disfigure by cutting off a part. **mutilation** *n.*

mutineer *n.* person who mutinies.

mutinous *a.* rebellious, ready to mutiny. **mutinously** *adv.*

mutiny *n.* open rebellion against authority, esp. by members of the armed forces. —*v.i.* engage in mutiny.

mutt *n.* (*sl.*) stupid person.

mutter *v.t./i.* speak or utter in a low unclear tone; utter subdued grumbles. —*n.* muttering.

mutton *n.* flesh of sheep as food.

mutual *a.* felt or done by each to the other; (*colloq.*) common to two or more. **mutually** *adv.*, **mutuality** *n.*

muzzle *n.* projecting nose and jaws of certain animals; open end of a firearm; strap etc. over an animal's head to prevent it from biting or feeding. —*v.t.* put a muzzle on; prevent from expressing opinions freely.

muzzy *a.* dazed, feeling stupefied. **muzziness** *n.*

my *a.* belonging to me.

myalgia *n.* pain in a muscle. **myalgic** *a.*

mycology *n.* study of fungi.

myna *n.* tall bird of the starling family.

myopia /-'əʊ-/ *n.* short sight.

myopic /-'ɒp-/ *a.* short-sighted.

myriad /'mɪ-/ *n.* vast number.

myrmidon /'mɜː-/ *n.* henchman.

myrrh[1] /mɜː(r)/ *n.* gum resin used in perfumes, medicines, and incense.

myrrh[2] /mɜː(r)/ *n.* white-flowered herb.

myrtle *n.* evergreen shrub.

myself *pron.* emphatic and reflexive form of *I* and *me.*

mysterious *a.* full of mystery, puzzling. **mysteriously** *adv.*

mystery *n.* a matter that remains unexplained or secret; quality of being unexplained or obscure; story dealing with a puzzling crime.

mystic *a.* having a hidden or symbolic meaning, esp. in religion; inspiring a sense of mystery and awe. —*n.* person who seeks to obtain union with God by spiritual contemplation. **mystical** *a.*, **mystically** *adv.*, **mysticism** *n.*

mystify *v.t.* cause to feel puzzled. **mystification** *n.*

mystique /-'tiːk/ *n.* aura of mystery or mystical power.

myth *n.* traditional tale(s) containing beliefs about ancient times or natural events; imaginary person or thing. **mythical** *a.*

mythology *n.* myths; study of myths. **mythological** *a.*

myxomatosis /-'təʊ-/ *n.* fatal virus disease of rabbits.

N

N. *abbr.* north; northern.

nab *v.t.* (*p.t.* **nabbed**) (*sl.*) catch in wrongdoing, arrest; seize.

nadir /'neɪdɪə(r)/ n. lowest point.

naevus n. (pl. **-vi**) red birthmark.

naff a. (sl.) worthless.

nag[1] n. (colloq.) horse.

nag[2] v.t./i. (p.t. **nagged**) find fault or scold continually; (of pain etc.) be felt persistently.

naiad /'naɪæd/ n. water-nymph.

nail n. layer of horny substance over the outer tip of a finger or toe; claw; small metal spike. —v.t. fasten with nail(s); catch, arrest. **on the nail** (esp. of payment) without delay.

naïve /naː'iːv/ a. showing lack of experience or of informed judgement. **naïvely** adv., **naïvety**, **naïveté** /-vteɪ/ ns.

naked a. without clothes on; without coverings or ornamentation. **naked eye** the eye unassisted by a telescope or microscope etc. **nakedly** adv., **nakedness** n.

namby-pamby a. & n. feeble or unmanly (person).

name n. word(s) by which a person, place, or thing is known or indicated; reputation. —v.t. give as a name; nominate, specify.

nameless a. not named.

namely adv. that is to say, specifically.

namesake n. person or thing with the same name as another.

nanny n. child's nurse. **nanny-goat** n. female goat.

nano- pref. one thousand millionth.

nap[1] n. short sleep, esp. during the day. —v.i. (p.t. **napped**) have a nap. **catch a person napping** catch him or her unawares.

nap[2] n. short raised fibres on the surface of cloth or leather.

nap[3] n. a card-game; betting all one's money on one chance, tipster's choice for this. **go nap** stake everything.

napalm /'neɪpɑːm/ n. jelly-like

petrol substance used in incendiary bombs.

nape n. back part of neck.

naphtha /'næf-/ n. inflammable oil.

naphthalene /'næf-/ n. pungent white substance obtained from coal tar.

napkin n. square piece of cloth or paper used to protect clothes or for wiping one's lips at meals; nappy.

nappy n. piece of absorbent material worn by a baby to absorb or retain its excreta.

narcissism n. abnormal self-love or self-admiration. **narcissistic** a.

narcissus n. (pl. **-cissi**) flower of the group including the daffodil.

narcosis n. sleep etc. induced by a narcotic.

narcotic /-'kɒt-/ a. & n. (drug) causing sleep or drowsiness.

nark v.t. (sl.) annoy. —n. (sl.) police spy or informer.

narrate v.t. tell (a story), give an account of. **narration** n., **narrator** n.

narrative /'næ-/ n. spoken or written account of something. —a. in this form.

narrow a. (**-er**, **-est**) small across, not wide; with little margin or scope or variety. —v.t./i. make or become narrower. **narrow-minded** a. having intolerant views. **narrowly** adv., **narrowness** n.

narwhal /-w(ə)l/ n. Arctic whale with a spirally grooved tusk.

nasal a. of the nose; sounding as if breath came out through the nose. **nasally** adv.

nascent a. just coming into existence. **nascence** n.

nasturtium n. trailing garden plant with orange, red, or yellow flowers.

nasty a. (**-ier**, **-iest**) unpleasant; unkind; difficult. **nastily** adv., **nastiness** n.

natal /'neɪ-/ *a.* of one's birth.

nation *n.* people of mainly common descent and history usu. inhabiting a particular country under one government.

national *a.* of a nation; common to a whole nation. —*n.* citizen or subject of a country. **national curriculum** common programme of study for pupils in England and Wales. **national service** service by conscription in the armed forces. **nationally** *adv.*

nationalism *n.* patriotic feeling; policy of national independence. **nationalist** *n.*, **nationalistic** *a.*

nationality *n.* condition of belonging to a particular nation.

nationalize *v.t.* convert from private to State ownership. **nationalization** *n.*

native *a.* natural; belonging to a place by birth or to a person because of his birthplace; grown or produced in a specified place; of natives. —*n.* person born in a specified place; local inhabitant.

nativity *n.* birth; **the Nativity** that of Christ.

natter *v.i. & n. (colloq.)* chat.

natty *a.* (-ier, -iest) neat and trim, dapper. **nattily** *adv.*

natural *a.* of or produced by nature; normal; not seeming artificial or affected; (of a note in music) neither sharp nor flat. —*n.* person or thing that seems naturally suited for something; natural note in music, sign indicating this; pale fawn colour. **natural history** study of animal and plant life. **naturalness** *n.*

naturalism *n.* realism in art and literature. **naturalistic** *a.*

naturalist *n.* expert in natural history.

naturalize *v.t.* admit (a person of foreign birth) to full citizenship of a country; introduce and acclimatize (an animal or plant) into a country; make look natural. **naturalization** *n.*

naturally *adv.* in a natural manner; as might be expected, of course.

nature *n.* the world with all its features and living things; physical power producing these; kind, sort; complex of innate characteristics; all that makes a thing what it is.

-natured *a.* having a nature of a certain kind.

naturist *n.* nudist. **naturism** *n.*

naught *n.* (old use) nothing.

naughty *a.* (-ier, -iest) behaving badly, disobedient; slightly indecent. **naughtily** *adv.*, **naughtiness** *n.*

nausea *n.* feeling of sickness.

nauseate *v.t.* affect with nausea.

nauseous *a.* causing nausea.

nautical *a.* of sailors or seamanship.

nautilus *n.* (*pl.* **-luses**) mollusc with a spiral shell.

naval *a.* of a navy.

nave[1] *n.* body of a church apart from the chancel, aisles, and transepts.

nave[2] *n.* hub of a wheel.

navel *n.* small hollow in the centre of the abdomen.

navigable *a.* suitable for ships to sail in; able to be steered and sailed. **navigability** *n.*

navigate *v.t.* sail in or through (a sea or river etc.); direct the course of (a ship or vehicle etc.). **navigation** *n.*, **navigator** *n.*

navvy *n.* labourer making roads etc. where digging is necessary.

navy *n.* a country's warships; officers and men of these; navy blue. **navy blue** very dark blue.

nay *adv.* (old use) no.

Nazi *n.* (*pl.* **-is**) member of the National Socialist party in Germany, brought to power by Hitler. **Nazism** *n.*

NB *abbr.* (Latin *nota bene*) note well.

NCO *abbr.* non-commissioned officer.

NE *abbr.* north-east; north-eastern.

neap tide tide when there is least rise and fall of water.

Neapolitan *a. & n.* (native or inhabitant) of Naples. **Neapolitan ice** ice cream made in layers of different colours and flavours.

near *adv.* at, to, or within a short distance or interval; nearly. —*prep.* near to. —*a.* with only a short distance or interval between; closely related; with little margin; of the left side of a horse, vehicle, or road; stingy. —*v.t./i.* draw near. **nearness** *n.*

nearby *a. & adv.* near in position.

nearly *adv.* closely; almost.

neat *a.* (-er, -est) clean and orderly in appearance or workmanship; undiluted. **neatly** *adv.*, **neatness** *n.*

neaten *v.t.* make neat.

nebula *n.* (pl. -ae) bright or dark patch in the sky caused by distant stars or a cloud of gas or dust. **nebular** *a.*

nebulous *a.* indistinct. **nebulously** *adv.*, **nebulosity** *n.*

necessarily /'nes-/ *adv.* as a necessary result, inevitably.

necessary *a.* essential in order to achieve something; happening or existing by necessity. **necessaries** *n.pl.* things without which life cannot be maintained or is harsh.

necessitate *v.t.* make necessary; involve as a condition or result.

necessitous *a.* needy.

necessity *n.* compelling power of circumstances; state or fact of being necessary; necessary thing; state of need or hardship.

neck *n.* narrow part connecting the head to the body; part of a garment round this; narrow part of a bottle, cavity, etc. **neck and neck** running level in a race.

necklace *n.* string of precious stones or beads etc. worn round the neck.

necklet *n.* necklace; fur worn round the neck.

neckline *n.* outline formed by the edge of a garment at the neck.

necktie *n.* tie worn at the neck.

necromancy /'nek-/ *n.* art of predicting things by communicating with the dead. **necromancer** *n.*

necropolis /-'krɒp-/ *n.* ancient cemetery.

necrosis /-'krəʊ-/ *n.* death of a piece of bone or tissue. **necrotic** *a.*

nectar *n.* sweet fluid from plants, collected by bees; any delicious drink.

nectarine /-rɪn/ *n.* a kind of peach with no down on the skin.

née /neɪ/ *a.* born (used in stating a married woman's maiden name).

need *n.* requirement; state of great difficulty or misfortune; poverty. —*v.t./i.* be in need of, require; be obliged.

needful *a.* necessary.

needle *n.* small thin pointed piece of steel used in sewing; thing shaped like this; pointer of a compass or gauge. —*v.t.* annoy, provoke.

needlecord *n.* finely ribbed fabric.

needless *a.* unnecessary. **needlessly** *adv.*

needlework *n.* sewing or embroidery.

needy *a.* (-ier, -iest) lacking the necessaries of life, very poor.

ne'er *adv.* (poetic) never. **ne'er-do-well** *n.* good-for-nothing.

nefarious /nɪ'feər-/ *a.* wicked. **nefariously** *adv.*, **nefariousness** *n.*

negate /-'geɪt/ *v.t.* nullify, disprove. **negation** *n.*

negative *a.* expressing or implying denial, refusal, or prohibition; not positive; (of a quantity) less than zero; (of a battery terminal) through which electric current leaves. —*n.* negative statement or word; negative quality or quantity; photograph with lights and shades or colours reversed, from which positive pictures can be obtained. —v.t. veto; contradict; neutralize (an effect). **negatively** adv.

neglect v.t. pay insufficient or no attention to; fail to take proper care of; omit (to do something). —n. neglecting, being neglected. **neglectful** a.

negligee /ˈnegliʒeɪ/ n. woman's light dressing-gown.

negligence n. lack of proper care or attention. **negligent** a., **negligently** adv.

negligible a. too small to be worth taking into account.

negotiable a. able to be negotiated.

negotiate v.t./i. hold a discussion so as to reach agreement; arrange by such discussion; exchange (a cheque or bonds etc.) for money; get past (an obstacle) successfully. **negotiation** n., **negotiator** n.

Negro n. (pl. **-oes**) member of the black-skinned race that originated in Africa. **Negress** n.fem.

Negroid a. & n. (person) having the physical characteristics of Negroes.

negus /ˈniː-/ n. drink of hot sweetened wine and water.

neigh /neɪ/ n. horse's long high-pitched cry. —v.i. make this cry.

neighbour n. person or thing living or situated near or next to another.

neighbourhood n. district. **in the neighbourhood of** near; approximately. **neighbourhood watch** systematic vigilance by residents to deter crime in their area.

neighbouring a. living or situated nearby.

neighbourly a. kind and friendly towards neighbours. **neighbourliness** n.

neither /ˈnaɪ- or ˈniː-/ a. & pron. not either. —adv. & conj. not either; also not.

nelson n. a kind of hold in wrestling.

nemesis /ˈnemɪ-/ n. inevitable retribution.

neo- pref. new.

neolithic a. of the later part of the Stone Age.

neologism n. new word.

neon n. a kind of gas much used in illuminated signs.

neophyte n. new convert; religious novice; beginner.

nephew n. one's brother's or sister's son.

nephritis /nɪ-/ n. inflammation of the kidneys.

nepotism /ˈnepə-/ n. favouritism shown to relatives in appointing them to jobs. **nepotistic** a.

nerd n. (US sl.) foolish or dull person.

nerve n. fibre carrying impulses of sensation or movement between the brain or spinal cord and a part of the body; courage; (colloq.) impudent boldness; (pl.) nervousness, effect of mental stress. —v.t. give courage to. **nerveless** a. not nervous; lacking vigour; without nerves.

nervous a. of the nerves; easily agitated or frightened; slightly afraid. **nervously** adv., **nervousness** n.

nervy a. nervous. **nerviness** n.

nescient /ˈnesɪənt/ a. not having knowledge. **nescience** n.

nest n. structure or place in which a bird lays eggs; breeding-place, lair; snug place, shelter; set of articles (esp. tables) designed to fit inside each other. —v.i. make or have a nest. **nest egg** sum of money saved for future use.

nestle v.i. press oneself into a soft place; lie sheltered.

nestling n. bird too young to leave the nest.

net[1] n. open-work material of thread, cord, or wire etc.; piece of this used for a particular purpose. —v.t. (p.t. **netted**) make by forming threads into a net; place nets in or on; catch (as if) in a net.

net[2] *a.* remaining after all deductions; (of weight) not including wrappings etc. —*v.t.* (*p.t.* **netted**) obtain or yield as net profit.

netball *n.* team game in which a ball has to be thrown into a high net.

nether /'neð-/ *a.* lower.

nethermost /'neð-/ *a.* lowest.

netting *n.* netted fabric.

nettle *n.* wild plant with leaves that sting and redden the skin when touched; similar non-stinging plant. —*v.t.* irritate, provoke.

nettle-rash *n.* eruption on skin like that caused by nettles.

network *n.* arrangement with intersecting lines; complex system; group of interconnected people or things. —*v.t.* broadcast on interconnected stations.

neural *a.* of nerves.

neuralgia *n.* sharp pain along a nerve, esp. in the head or face. **neuralgic** *a.*

neurasthenia *n.* debility of the nerves, causing fatigue etc.

neuritis *n.* inflammation of nerve(s).

neurology *n.* study of nerve systems. **neurological** *a.*, **neurologist** *n.*

neurosis *n.* (*pl.* **-oses**) mental disorder sometimes with physical symptoms but with no evidence of disease.

neurotic *a.* of or caused by a neurosis; subject to abnormal anxieties or obsessive behaviour. —*n.* neurotic person. **neurotically** *adv.*

neuter *a.* (of words) neither masculine nor feminine; (of plants) without male or female parts; (of insects) sexually undeveloped, sterile. —*n.* neuter word, plant, or insect; castrated animal. —*v.t.* castrate.

neutral *a.* not supporting either

side in a conflict; without distinctive or positive characteristics. —*n.* neutral person, country, or colour; neutral gear. **neutral gear** position of gear mechanism in which the engine is disconnected from driven parts. **neutrally** *adv.*, **neutrality** *n.*

neutralize *v.t.* make ineffective. **neutralization** *n.*

neutrino /-'triː-/ *n.* (*pl.* **-os**) particle with zero electric charge and (probably) zero mass.

neutron *n.* nuclear particle with no electric charge. **neutron bomb** nuclear bomb that kills people by intense radiation but does little damage to property.

never *adv.* on no occasion; not; (*colloq.*) surely not. **never mind** do not be troubled. **never-never** *n.* (*colloq.*) hire purchase.

nevermore *adv.* never again.

nevertheless *adv.* & *conj.* in spite of this.

new *a.* (**-er, -est**) not existing before, recently made or discovered or experienced etc.; unfamiliar, unaccustomed. —*adv.* newly, recently. **New Age** set of beliefs with alternative approaches to religion, medicine, lifestyle, etc. **new man** man who rejects sexist attitudes and the traditional male role. **new moon** moon seen as a crescent. **New Testament** (*see* **testament**). **New World** the Americas. **new year** first days of January. **New Year's Day** 1 Jan. **New Year's Eve** 31 Dec.

newcomer *n.* one who has arrived recently.

newel *n.* top or bottom post of the handrail of a stair; central pillar of a winding stair.

newfangled *a.* objectionably new.

newly *adv.* recently, freshly. **newly-wed** *a.* & *n.* recently married (person).

news *n.* new or interesting information about recent events;

broadcast report of this. **newsy** a.

newsagent n. shopkeeper who sells newspapers.

newscast n. broadcast news report.

newscaster n. newsreader.

newsletter n. informal printed report containing news of interest to members of a club etc.

newspaper n. printed usu. daily or weekly publication containing news reports; sheets of paper forming this.

newsprint n. type of paper on which newspapers are printed.

newsreader n. person who reads broadcast news reports.

newsreel n. cinema film showing current items of news.

newsworthy a. worth reporting as news. **newsworthiness** n.

newt n. small lizard-like amphibious creature.

next a. nearest in position or time etc.; soonest come to. —adv. in the next place or degree; on the next occasion. —n. next person or thing. **next best** second best. **next door** in the next house or room. **next door to** almost. **next of kin** one's closest relative. **next world** life after death.

nexus n. (pl. -uses) connected group or series.

nib n. metal point of a pen; (pl.) crushed coffee- or cocoa-beans.

nibble v.t./i. take small quick or gentle bites (at). —n. small quick bite. **nibbler** n.

Nicam /naɪk-/ n. digital system used in British television to provide video signals with high quality stereo sound.

nice a. (-er, -est) pleasant, satisfactory; (iron.) difficult, bad; needing precision and care; fastidious. **nicely** adv., **niceness** n.

nicety /ˈnaɪsɪtɪ/ n. precision; detail. **to a nicety** exactly.

niche /nɪtʃ/ n. shallow recess esp. in a wall; suitable position in life or employment.

nick n. small cut or notch; (sl.) police station, prison. —v.t. make a nick in; (sl.) steal; (sl.) arrest. **in good nick** (colloq.) in good condition. **in the nick of time** only just in time.

nickel n. hard silvery-white metal used in alloys; (US) 5-cent piece.

nickname n. name given humorously to a person or thing. —v.t. give as a nickname.

nicotine /-tiːn/ n. poisonous substance found in tobacco.

niece n. one's brother's or sister's daughter.

niggardly a. stingy. **niggard** n.

niggle v.i. fuss over details.

nigh /naɪ/ adv. & prep. near.

night n. dark hours between sunset and sunrise; nightfall; specified night or evening. **night-life** n. entertainments available in public places at night. **night-light** n. faint light kept burning in a bedroom at night. **night school** instruction provided in the evening. **night-watchman** n. man employed to keep watch at night in a building that is closed; inferior batsman sent in near the close of play to avoid risking dismissal of a better one.

nightcap n. soft cap formerly worn in bed; drink taken just before going to bed.

nightclub n. club open at night, providing refreshment and entertainment.

nightdress n. woman's or child's loose garment for sleeping in.

nightfall n. onset of night.

nightgown n. nightdress.

nightie n. (colloq.) nightdress.

nightingale n. small thrush, male of which sings melodiously.

nightjar n. night-flying bird with a harsh cry.

nightly a. & adv. (happening) at night or every night.

nightmare n. unpleasant dream or (colloq.) experience. **nightmarish** a.

nightshade *n.* plant with poisonous berries.

nightshirt *n.* man's or boy's long shirt for sleeping in.

nihilism *n.* rejection of all religious and moral principles. **nihilist** *n.*, **nihilistic** *a.*

nil *n.* nothing.

nimble *a.* (-er, -est) able to move quickly. **nimbly** *adv.*

nimbus *n.* (*pl.* -bi) halo, aureole.

nimby *abbr.* not in my backyard.

nincompoop *n.* foolish person.

nine *a.* & *n.* one more than eight (9, IX). **ninth** *a.* & *n.*

ninepins *n.* game of skittles played with nine objects.

nineteen *a.* & *n.* one more than eighteen (19, XIX). **nineteenth** *a.* & *n.*

ninety *a.* & *n.* nine times ten (90, XC). **ninetieth** *a.* & *n.*

ninny *n.* foolish person.

nip[1] *v.t./i.* (*p.t.* nipped) pinch or squeeze sharply; bite quickly with the front teeth; pain or harm with biting cold; (*sl.*) go quickly. —*n.* sharp pinch, squeeze, or bite; biting coldness.

nip[2] *n.* small drink of spirits.

nipper *n.* (*colloq.*) young boy or girl; claw of a lobster etc.; (*pl.*) pincers, forceps.

nipple *n.* small projection at the centre of a breast; similar protuberance; teat of a feeding-bottle.

nippy *a.* (-ier, -iest) (*colloq.*) nimble, quick; bitingly cold.

nirvana /nɜ:'vɑ:/ *n.* (in Buddhism and Hinduism) state of perfect bliss achieved by the soul.

nisi /'naɪsaɪ/ *a.* decree nisi conditional order for divorce.

nit *n.* egg of a louse or similar parasite. **nit-picking** *n.* & *a.* (*colloq.*) petty fault-finding.

nitrate *n.* substance formed from nitric acid, esp. used as a fertilizer.

nitre *n.* saltpetre.

nitric /'naɪ-/ *a.* **nitric acid** corrosive acid containing nitrogen.

nitrogen *n.* gas forming about four-fifths of the atmosphere. **nitrogenous** *a.*

nitroglycerine *n.* a kind of powerful explosive.

nitrous oxide gas used as an anaesthetic.

nitty-gritty *n.* (*sl.*) basic facts or realities of a matter.

nitwit *n.* (*colloq.*) stupid or foolish person.

nix *n.* (*sl.*) nothing.

no *a.* not any; not a. —*adv.* (used as a denial or refusal); not at all. —*n.* (*pl.* **noes**) negative reply, vote against a proposal. **no-ball** *n.* unlawfully delivered ball in cricket etc. **no-fly zone** zone in which aircraft are forbidden to fly. **no-go area** area to which entry is forbidden or restricted. **no man's land** area not firmly assigned to anyone, esp. between opposing armies. **no one** nobody. **no way** (*colloq.*) it is impossible.

No. or **no.** *abbr.* number.

nob[1] *n.* (*sl.*) head.

nob[2] *n.* (*sl.*) person of high rank.

nobble *v.t.* (*sl.*) get hold of, tamper with or influence dishonestly.

nobility *n.* nobleness of character, or of rank; titled people.

noble *a.* (-er, -est) aristocratic; possessing excellent qualities, esp. of character, not mean or petty; imposing. —*n.* member of the nobility. **nobly** *adv.*, **nobleness** *n.*

nobleman, noblewoman *ns.* (*pl.* -men, -women) member of the nobility.

nobody *pron.* no person. —*n.* person of no importance.

nocturnal *a.* of or happening in or active in the night. **nocturnally** *adv.*

nocturne *n.* dreamy piece of music.

nod *v.t./i.* (*p.t.* nodded) move the head down and up quickly, indicate (agreement or casual greeting) thus; let the head droop, be drowsy; bend and sway.

—*n.* nodding movement esp. in agreement or greeting.

noddle *n.* (*colloq.*) head.

node *n.* knob-like swelling; point on a stem where a leaf or bud grows out. **nodal** *a.*

nodule /'nɒd-/ *n.* small rounded lump, small node. **nodular** *a.*

Noel /-'el/ *n.* (in carols) Christmas.

noggin *n.* measure of alcohol, usu. one-quarter of a pint.

Noh *n.* traditional Japanese drama.

noise *n.* sound, esp. loud or harsh or undesired. —*v.t.* spread (a rumour etc.). **noiseless** *a.*

noisome *a.* noxious, disgusting.

noisy *a.* (**-ier, -iest**) making much noise. **noisily** *adv.*, **noisiness** *n.*

nomad *n.* member of a tribe that roams seeking pasture for its animals; wanderer. **nomadic** *a.*

nom de plume /nɒm də 'pluːm/ *n.* writer's pseudonym.

nomenclature /-'menklə-/ *n.* system of names, e.g. in a science.

nominal *a.* in name only; (of a fee) very small. **nominal value** face value of a coin etc. **nominally** *adv.*

nominate *v.t.* name as candidate for or future holder of an office; appoint as a place or date. **nomination** *n.*, **nominator** *n.*

nominative /'nɒm-/ *n.* form of a noun used when it is the subject of a verb.

nominee *n.* person nominated.

non- *pref.* not.

nonagenarian *n.* person in his or her nineties.

nonce *n.* present time.

nonchalant /'nɒnʃ-/ *a.* calm and casual. **nonchalantly** *adv.*, **nonchalance** *n.*

non-commissioned *a.* not holding a commission.

noncommittal *a.* not revealing one's opinion.

non compos mentis insane.

nonconformist *n.* person not conforming to established practices; **Nonconformist**, member of a Protestant sect not conforming to Anglican practices.

nondescript *a.* lacking distinctive characteristics and therefore not easy to classify.

none *pron.* not any; no person(s). —*adv.* not at all.

nonentity /-'nen-/ *n.* person of no importance.

non-event *n.* event that was expected to be important but proves disappointing.

non-existent *a.* not existing. **non-existence** *n.*

nonpareil /-'r(ə)l/ *a.* & *n.* unrivalled or unique (person or thing).

nonplussed *a.* completely perplexed.

nonsense *n.* words put together in a way that does not make sense; foolish talk or behaviour. **nonsensical** /-'sen-/ *a.*

non sequitur /nɒn 'sek-/ conclusion that does not follow from the evidence given.

non-starter *n.* horse entered for a race but not running in it; person or idea etc. not worth considering for a purpose.

non-stop *a.* & *adv.* not ceasing; (of a train etc.) not stopping at intermediate places.

nonsuch *n.* unrivalled person or thing; paragon.

noodles *n.pl.* pasta in narrow strips, used in soups etc.

nook *n.* secluded place or corner, recess.

noon *n.* twelve o'clock in the day; midday.

noose *n.* loop of rope etc. with a knot that tightens when pulled.

nor *conj.* & *adv.* and not.

Nordic *a.* of a tall blond blue-eyed racial type.

norm *n.* standard.

normal *a.* conforming to what is standard or usual; free from mental or emotional disorders. **normally** *adv.*, **normality** *n.*

Norman *a.* & *n.* (member) of a former people of Normandy.

Norse *a.* & *n.* (language) of ancient Norway or Scandinavia. **Norseman** *n.* (*pl.* **-men**).

north *n.* point or direction to the left of person facing east; northern part. —*a.* in the north; (of wind) from the north. —*adv.* towards the north. **north-east** *n.* point or direction midway between north and east. **north-easterly** *a.* & *n.*, **north-eastern** *a.* **north-west** *n.* point or direction midway between north and west. **north-westerly** *a.* & *n.*, **north-western** *a.*

northerly *a.* towards or blowing from the north.

northern *a.* of or in the north.

northerner *n.* native of the north.

northernmost *a.* furthest north.

northward *a.* towards the north. **northwards** *adv.*

Norwegian *a.* & *n.* (native, language) of Norway.

Nos. *or* **nos.** *abbr.* numbers.

nose *n.* organ at the front of the head, used in breathing and smelling; sense of smell; open end of a tube; front end or projecting part. —*v.t./i.* detect or search by use of the sense of smell; push one's nose against or into; push one's way cautiously ahead.

nosebag *n.* bag of fodder for hanging on a horse's head.

nosebleed *n.* bleeding from the nose.

nosedive *n.* steep downward plunge, esp. of an aeroplane. —*v.i.* make this plunge.

nosegay *n.* small bunch of flowers.

nosey *a.* = nosy.

nosh *n.* (*sl.*) food. —*v.t./i.* (*sl.*) eat.

nostalgia *n.* sentimental memory of or longing for things of the past. **nostalgic** *a.*, **nostalgically** *adv.*

nostril *n.* either of the two external openings in the nose.

nostrum *n.* (*pl.* **-ums**) quack remedy.

nosy *a.* (**-ier**, **-iest**) (*sl.*) inquisitive. **nosily** *adv.*, **nosiness** *n.*

not *adv.* expressing a negative or denial or refusal.

notability *n.* being notable; notable person.

notable *a.* worthy of notice, remarkable, eminent. —*n.* eminent person. **notably** *adv.*

notary public person authorized to witness the signing of documents and perform other formal transactions. **notarial** *a.*

notation *n.* system of signs or symbols representing numbers, quantities, musical notes, etc.

notch *n.* V-shaped cut or indentation. —*v.t.* make notch(es) in. **notch up** score, achieve.

note *n.* brief record written down to aid memory; short or informal letter; memorandum; formal diplomatic communication; short written comment; written or printed promise to pay money; banknote; musical tone of definite pitch; symbol representing the pitch and duration of a musical sound; each of the keys on a piano etc.; significant sound, indication of feelings etc.; eminence; notice, attention. —*v.t.* notice, pay attention to; write down.

notebook *n.* book with blank pages on which to write memoranda.

notecase *n.* wallet for banknotes.

noted *a.* famous, well known.

notelet *n.* small folded card etc. for a short informal letter.

notepaper *n.* paper for writing letters on.

noteworthy *a.* worthy of notice, remarkable.

nothing *n.* no thing, not anything; no amount, nought; non-existence; person or thing of no importance. —*adv.* not at all.

nothingness *n.* non-existence; worthlessness.

notice *n.* attention, observation; intimation, warning; formal announcement of the termination of an agreement or employment; written or printed information displayed; review in a newspaper. —*v.t.* perceive; take notice of; remark upon. **notice-board** *n.* board on which notices may be displayed. **take notice** show interest. **take no notice (of)** pay no attention (to).

noticeable *a.* easily seen or noticed. **noticeably** *adv.*

notifiable *a.* that must be notified.

notify *v.t.* inform; report, make known. **notification** *n.*

notion *n.* concept; idea; understanding; intention.

notional *a.* hypothetical. **notionally** *adv.*

notorious *a.* well known, esp. unfavourably. **notoriously** *adv.*, **notoriety** /-'raɪətɪ/ *n.*

notwithstanding *prep.* in spite of. —*adv.* nevertheless.

nougat /'nu:ga:/ *n.* chewy sweet.

nought *n.* the figure 0; nothing.

noun *n.* word used as the name of a person, place, or thing.

nourish *v.t.* keep alive and well by food; foster or cherish (a feeling).

nourishment *n.* nourishing; food.

nous /naʊs/ *n.* (*colloq.*) common sense.

nova /'nəʊ-/ *n.* (*pl.* -ae) star that suddenly becomes much brighter for a short time.

novel *n.* book-length story. —*a.* of a new kind.

novelette *n.* short (esp. romantic) novel.

novelist *n.* writer of novels.

novelty *n.* novel thing or quality; small unusual object.

November *n.* eleventh month of the year.

novena *n.* (in the RC Church) special prayers or services on nine successive days.

novice *n.* inexperienced person; probationary member of a religious order. **noviciate** *n.*

now *adv.* at the time when or of which one is writing or speaking; immediately; (without temporal sense) I wonder or am telling you. —*conj.* as a consequence of or simultaneously with the fact that. —*n.* the present time. **now and again, now and then** occasionally.

nowadays *adv.* in present times.

nowhere *adv.* not anywhere.

noxious *a.* unpleasant and harmful.

nozzle *n.* vent or spout of a hose-pipe etc.

nuance /'nju:ɑ:s/ *n.* shade of meaning.

nub *n.* small lump; central point or core of a matter or problem.

nubile *a.* (of women) marriageable; sexually attractive. **nubility** *n.*

nuclear *a.* of a nucleus; of the nuclei of atoms; using energy released or absorbed during reactions in these.

nucleus *n.* (*pl.* **-lei**, *pr.* -lɪaɪ) central part or thing round which others are collected; central portion of an atom, seed, or cell.

nude *a.* not clothed, naked. —*n.* nude human figure in a picture etc. **nudity** *n.*

nudge *v.t.* poke (a person) gently with one's elbow to attract his attention quietly; push slightly or gradually. —*n.* this movement.

nudist *n.* person who believes that going unclothed is good for the health. **nudism** *n.*

nugatory /'nju:-/ *a.* futile, trivial; not valid.

nugget *n.* rough lump of gold or platinum found in the earth.

nuisance *n.* annoying person or thing.

nuke *n.* (*colloq.*) nuclear weapon. —*v.t.* (*colloq.*) destroy with nuclear weapons.

null *a.* having no legal force. **nullity** *n.*

nullify *v.t.* make null; neutralize the effect of. **nullification** *n.*

numb a. deprived of power to feel or move. —v.t. make numb. **numbly** adv., **numbness** n.

number n. symbol or word indicating how many; total; numeral assigned to a person or thing; single issue of a magazine; item; category 'singular' or 'plural' in grammar. —v.t. count; amount to; mark or distinguish with a number. **number one** (colloq.) oneself. **number-plate** n. plate on a motor vehicle, bearing its registration number.

numberless a. innumerable.

numeral n. written symbol of a number.

numerate a. having a good basic understanding of mathematics and science. **numeracy** n.

numeration n. numbering.

numerator n. number written above the line in a vulgar fraction.

numerical a. of number(s). **numerically** adv.

numerous a. great in number.

numismatics /-'mæ-/ n. study of coins. **numismatic** a., **numismatist** /-'mIz-/ n.

nun n. member of a female community living apart from the world under the rules of a religious order.

nuncio n. (pl. **-os**) pope's diplomatic representative.

nunnery n. residence of a community of nuns.

nuptial a. of marriage or a wedding. **nuptials** n.pl. wedding ceremony.

nurse n. person trained to look after sick or injured people; woman employed to take charge of young children. —v.t./i. work as a nurse, act as nurse (to); feed at the breast or udder; hold carefully; give special care to. **nursing home** privately run hospital or home for invalids.

nursemaid n. young woman employed to take charge of young children.

nursery n. room(s) for young children; place where plants are reared, esp. for sale. **nursery rhyme** traditional verse for children. **nursery school** school for children below normal school age. **nursery slopes** slopes suitable for beginners at skiing.

nurseryman n. (pl. **-men**) person growing plants etc. at a nursery.

nurture v.t. nourish, rear; bring up. —n. nurturing.

nut n. fruit with a hard shell round an edible kernel; this kernel; small lump; small threaded metal ring for use with a bolt; (sl.) head; (sl.) crazy person. **nut-case** n. (sl.) crazy person.

nutcrackers n.pl. pincers for cracking nuts.

nuthatch n. small climbing bird.

nutmeg n. hard fragrant tropical seed ground or grated as spice.

nutria n. fur of the coypu.

nutrient /'nju:-/ a. & n. nourishing (substance).

nutriment n. nourishment.

nutrition n. nourishment. **nutritional** a., **nutritionally** adv.

nutritious a. nourishing.

nutritive a. & n. nourishing (substance).

nuts a. (sl.) crazy.

nutshell n. hard shell of a nut. **in a nutshell** expressed very briefly.

nutty a. full of nuts; tasting like nuts; (sl.) crazy.

nuzzle v.t. press or rub gently with the nose.

NW abbr. north-west; north-western.

nylon n. very light strong synthetic fibre; fabric made of this.

nymph n. mythological semi-divine maiden living in the sea or woods; young insect.

nymphomania *n.* excessive sexual desire in a woman. **nymphomaniac** *n.*

NZ *abbr.* New Zealand.

O

oaf *n.* (*pl.* **oafs**) awkward lout.

oak *n.* deciduous forest tree bearing acorns; its hard wood. **oakapple** *n.* = gall³. **oaken** *a.*

OAP *abbr.* old-age pensioner.

oar *n.* pole with a flat blade used to propel a boat by its leverage against water; oarsman. **put one's oar in** interfere.

oarsman *n.* (*pl.* **-men**) rower.

oasis *n.* (*pl.* **oases**) fertile spot in a desert, with a spring or well of water.

oast *n.* kiln for drying hops. **oasthouse** *n.* building containing this.

oatcake *n.* thin cake made of oatmeal.

oaten *a.* of oats.

oath *n.* solemn promise, appealing to God or a revered object as witness; swear-word.

oatmeal *n.* ground oats; greyish-fawn colour.

oats *n.* hardy cereal plant; its grain.

obbligato /-'gɑː-/ *n.* (*pl.* **-os**) important accompanying part in music.

obdurate /'ɒb-/ *a.* stubborn. **obdurately** *adv.*, **obduracy** *n.*

obedient *a.* doing what one is told to do. **obediently** *adv.*, **obedience** *n.*

obeisance /-'beɪ-/ *n.* bow or curtsy.

obelisk /'ɒb-/ *n.* tall pillar set up as a monument.

obelus /'ɒb-/ *n.* (*pl.* **-li**) dagger-shaped mark of reference, †.

obese /-'biːs/ *a.* very fat. **obesity** *n.*

obey *v.t./i.* do what is commanded (by).

obfuscate *v.t.* darken; confuse, bewilder. **obfuscation** *n.*

obituary *n.* printed statement of person's death (esp. in a newspaper), often with a brief biography. **obituarist** *n.* writer of this.

object¹ /'ɒb-/ *n.* something solid that can be seen or touched; person or thing to which an action or feeling is directed; purpose, intention; noun etc. acted upon by a transitive verb or preposition. **no object** not an important or limiting factor. **object lesson** practical illustration of a principle.

object² /-'dʒekt/ *v.t.* state that one is opposed to, protest. **objector** *n.*

objection *n.* disapproval, opposition; statement of this; reason for objecting.

objectionable *a.* open to objection; unpleasant. **objectionably** *adv.*

objective *a.* not influenced by personal feelings or opinions; of the form of a word used when it is the object of a verb or preposition. —*n.* thing one is trying to achieve, reach, or capture. **objectively** *adv.*, **objectiveness** *n.*, **objectivity** *n.*

objet d'art /ɒbʒeɪ 'dɑː(r)/ (*pl.* **objets d'art**) small artistic object.

objurgate *v.t.* reprimand. **objurgation** *n.*

oblation *n.* offering made to God; pious donation.

obligate *v.t.* oblige.

obligation *n.* being obliged to do something; what one must do to comply with an agreement or law etc. **under an obligation** owing gratitude.

obligatory /-'lɪg-/ *a.* compulsory.

oblige *v.t.* compel; help or gratify by a small service.

obliged *a.* indebted.

obliging *a.* polite and helpful. **obligingly** *adv.*

oblique *a.* slanting; indirect. **obliquely** *adv.*, **obliqueness** *n.*, **obliquity** *n.*

obliterate v.t. blot out, destroy. **obliteration** n.

oblivion n. state of being forgotten; state of being oblivious.

oblivious a. unaware. **obliviously** adv., **obliviousness** n.

oblong a. & n. (having) rectangular shape with length greater than breadth.

obloquy n. abuse, being ill spoken of.

obnoxious a. very unpleasant. **obnoxiously** adv., **obnoxiousness** n.

oboe n. woodwind instrument of treble pitch. **oboist** n.

obscene a. indecent in a repulsive or offensive way. **obscenely** adv., **obscenity** /-'sen-/ n.

obscure a. dark, instinct; remote from observation; not famous; not easily understood. —v.t. make obscure, conceal. **obscurely** adv., **obscurity** n.

obsequies /'bsɪkwɪz/ n.pl. funeral rites.

obsequious /-'si:-/ a. excessively respectful. **obsequiously** adv., **obsequiousness** n.

observable a. able to be observed. **observably** adv.

observance n. keeping of a law, custom, or festival.

observant a. quick at noticing. **observantly** adv.

observation n. observing; remark. **observational** a.

observatory n. building equipped for observation of stars or weather.

observe v.t. perceive, watch carefully; pay attention to; keep or celebrate (a festival); remark. **observer** n.

obsess v.t. occupy the thoughts of continually.

obsession n. state of being obsessed; persistent idea. **obsessional** a.

obsessive a. of, causing, or showing obsession. **obsessively** adv.

obsolescent a. becoming obsolete. **obsolescence** n.

obsolete a. no longer used.

obstacle n. thing that obstructs progress. **obstacle race** in which obstacles have to be passed.

obstetrics n. branch of medicine and surgery dealing with childbirth. **obstetric, obstetrical** adjs., **obstetrician** n.

obstinate a. not easily persuaded or influenced or overcome. **obstinately** adv., **obstinacy** n.

obstreperous a. noisy, unruly.

obstruct v.t. prevent or hinder the movement or progress of or along. **obstructor** n.

obstruction n. obstructing; thing that obstructs.

obstructive a. causing obstruction. **obstructiveness** n.

obtain v.t./i. get, come into possession of; be in use as a rule or custom.

obtainable a. able to be obtained.

obtrude v.t. force (ideas or oneself) upon others. **obtrusion** n.

obtrusive a. obtruding oneself, unpleasantly noticeable. **obtrusively** adv., **obtrusiveness** n.

obtuse a. of blunt shape, (of an angle) more than 90° but less than 180°; slow at understanding. **obtusely** adv., **obtuseness** n.

obverse /'bb-/ n. side of a coin bearing a head or the principal design.

obviate v.t. make unnecessary.

obvious a. easy to perceive or understand. **obviously** adv., **obviousness** n.

ocarina n. egg-shaped wind-instrument.

occasion n. time at which a particular event takes place; special event; opportunity; need or cause. —v.t. cause. **on occasion** occasionally.

occasional a. happening sometimes but not frequently; for a special occasion. **occasionally** adv.

Occident *n.* the West, the western world. **occidental** *a.*

Occidental *n.* native of the Occident.

occiput *n.* back of the head.

occlude *v.t.* stop up, obstruct.

occlusion *n.* upward movement of a mass of warm air caused by a cold front overtaking it.

occult /-'kʌ-/ *a.* secret; supernatural.

occupant *n.* person occupying a place or dwelling. **occupancy** *n.*

occupation *n.* occupying; taking or holding possession by force; activity that keeps a person busy; employment.

occupational *a.* of or caused by one's employment. **occupational therapy** creative activities designed to assist recovery from certain illnesses.

occupy *v.t.* dwell in; take possession of (a country or site etc.), esp. by force; fill (a space or position); keep filled with activity. **occupier** *n.*

occur *v.i* (*p.t.* **occurred**) come into being as an event or process; exist in a specified place or conditions. **occur to** come into the mind of.

occurrence *n.* occurring; incident, event.

ocean *n.* sea surrounding the continents of the earth. **oceanic** *a.*

oceanography *n.* study of the ocean.

ocelot /'ɒsɪ-/ *n.* leopard-like animal of Central and South America; its fur.

och /ɒx/ *int.* (Sc. & Ir.) oh, ah.

oche /'ɒkɪ/ *n.* line behind which a player stands to play darts.

ochre *n.* type of clay used as pigment; pale brownish-yellow.

o'clock *adv.* by the clock (used to specify the hour).

octagon *n.* geometric figure with eight sides. **octagonal** /-'tæ-/ *a.*

octahedron *n.* solid with eight sides. **octahedral** *n.*

octane *n.* hydrocarbon occurring in petrol.

octave *n.* note six whole tones above or below a given note; interval or series of notes between these.

octavo *n.* (*pl.* **-os**) size of book or page with sheets folded into eight leaves.

octet *n.* group of eight voices or instruments; music for these.

October *n.* tenth month of the year.

octogenarian /-'neər-/ *n.* person in his or her eighties.

octopus *n.* (*pl.* **-puses**) sea animal with eight tentacles.

ocular *a.* of, for, or by the eyes.

oculist *n.* specialist in the treatment of eye disorders and defects.

odd *a.* (**-er**, **-est**) unusual; occasional, not regular; (of a number) not exactly divisible by 2; from a pair or set of which the other(s) are lacking; exceeding a round number or amount. **oddly** *adv.*, **oddness** *n.*

oddity *n.* strangeness; unusual person or thing.

oddment *n.* thing left over, isolated article.

odds *n.pl.* probability, esp. expressed as a ratio; ratio between amounts staked by parties to a bet. **at odds** with in conflict with. **no odds** no difference. **odds and ends** oddments. **odds-on** *a.* with success more likely than failure.

ode *n.* type of poem addressed to a person or celebrating an event.

odious *a.* hateful. **odiously** *adv.*, **odiousness** *n.*

odium *n.* widespread hatred or disgust towards a person or actions.

odoriferous *a.* diffusing (usu. pleasant) odours.

odour *n.* smell. **odorous** *a.*

odourless *a.* without a smell.

odyssey *n.* (*pl.* **-eys**) long adventurous journey.

oedema /ɪ'diːmə/ n. excess fluid in tissues, causing swelling.

oesophagus /ɪ'sɒf-/ n. gullet.

of prep. belonging to; from; composed or made from; concerning; for, involving; so as to bring separation or relief from; (colloq.) during.

off adv. away; out of position, disconnected; not operating, cancelled; completely; situated as regards money or supplies; (of food) beginning to decay. —prep. away from; below the normal standard of. —a. of the right-hand side of a horse, vehicle, or road etc.; in, from, or towards the side of a cricket field which the batsman faces when playing. —n. the off side in cricket. **off chance** remote possibility. **off colour** not in the best of health. **off-licence** n. licence to sell alcohol for consumption away from the premises; shop with this. **off-line** a. not on-line. **off-putting** a. (colloq.) repellent. **off-stage** a. & adv. beside a stage and not visible to the audience. **off-white** a. not quite pure white.

offal n. edible organs from an animal carcass.

offbeat a. unusual; unconventional.

offence n. illegal act; feeling of annoyance or resentment.

offend v.t./i. cause offence to; do wrong. **offender** n.

offensive a. causing offence, insulting; disgusting; used in attacking, aggressive. —n. aggressive action. **take the offensive** begin hostilities. **offensively** adv., **offensiveness** n.

offer v.t./i. (p.t. **offered**) present for acceptance or refusal; state what one is willing to do or pay or give; show an intention. —n. expression of willingness to do, give, or pay something; amount offered.

offering n. gift, contribution.

offertory n. collection of money at a religious service.

offhand a. without previous thought or preparation; unceremonious, casual. —adv. in an offhand way. **offhanded** a.

office n. room or building used for clerical and similar work; position of authority or trust; service; (pl.) rooms equipped for household work or as bathrooms etc.

officer n. official; person holding authority on a ship or (esp. with a commission) in the armed services; policeman.

official a. of office or officials; authorized. —n. person holding office. **officially** n.

officiate v.i. act in an official capacity, be in charge.

officious a. asserting one's authority, bossy. **officiously** adv.

offing n. **in the offing** not far off in distance or time.

offload v.t. unload.

offset v.t. (p.t. **-set**, pres.p. **-setting**) counterbalance, compensate for. —n. offshoot; method of printing by transferring ink to and from a rubber surface.

offshoot n. side shoot; subsidiary product.

offside a. & adv. in a position where one may not legally play the ball (in football etc.).

offspring n. (pl. **-spring**) person's child or children; animal's young.

oft adv. (old use) often.

often adv. many times, at short intervals; in many instances.

ogee /'əʊ-/ n. S-shaped curve; moulding with such a section.

ogle v.t. eye flirtatiously.

ogre n. cruel or man-eating giant in fairy-tales etc.; terrifying person. **ogreish** a.

oh int. exclamation of delight or pain, or used for emphasis.

ohm /əʊm/ n. unit of electrical resistance.

oik n. (sl.) lout.

oil n. thick slippery liquid that will not dissolve in water; petroleum, a form of this; oil-colour. —v.t. lubricate or treat with oil.

oil-colour, oil-paint ns. paint made by mixing pigment in oil. **oil-painting** n. picture painted in this.

oilfield n. area where oil is found in the ground.

oilskin n. cloth waterproofed by treatment with oil etc.; (pl.) waterproof clothing made of this.

oily a. (-ier, -iest) of or like oil; covered in oil, full of oil; unpleasantly smooth and ingratiating in manner. **oiliness** n.

ointment n. paste for rubbing on skin to heal it.

OK, okay a. & adv. (colloq.) all right.

okapi /-'kɑ:-/ n. (pl. -is) giraffe-like animal of Central Africa.

okra n. tall African plant with seed-pods used as food.

old a. (-er, -est) having lived or existed or been known etc. for a long time; of specified age; shabby from age or wear; former, not recent or modern; (colloq.) regarded with affection. **of old** of or in former times. **old age** later part of life. **old-fashioned** a. in or according to old fashions. **old hat** tediously familiar thing. **old maid** elderly spinster. **old master** (painting by) a great painter of former times. **Old Testament** (see testament). **old-time** a. belonging to former times. **old-timer** n. (US) person with long experience or standing. **old wives' tale** traditional but foolish belief. **Old World** Europe, Asia, and Africa. **oldness** n.

olden a. (old use) former, not recent.

oldie n. (colloq.) old person or thing.

oleaginous a. producing oil; oily.

oleander /əʊliæ-/ n. flowering shrub of Mediterranean regions.

olfactory /-'fæ-/ a. concerned with smelling.

oligarch n. member of an oligarchy.

oligarchy n. form of government where power is in the hands of a small group; country governed thus. **oligarchic** a.

olive n. small oval fruit from which an oil (**olive oil**) is obtained; tree bearing this; greenish colour. —a. of this colour; (of the complexion) yellowish-brown. **olive branch** thing done or offered to show one's desire to make peace.

Olympian a. of Olympus; majestic and imposing in manner.

Olympic a. of the **Olympic Games**, international sports competitions held every fourth year. **Olympics** n.pl. Olympic Games.

ombudsman n. (pl. -men) official appointed to investigate people's complaints about maladministration by public authorities etc.

omega n. last letter of the Greek alphabet, = o.

omelette n. dish of beaten eggs cooked in a frying-pan.

omen n. event regarded as a prophetic sign.

ominous /'ɒm-/ a. seeming as if trouble is imminent. **ominously** adv., **ominousness** n.

omit v.t. (p.t. **omitted**) leave out, not include; leave not done, neglect (to do something). **omission** n.

omnibus n. bus; comprehensive publication containing several items.

omnipotent /ɒm'nɪp-/ a. having unlimited or very great power. **omnipotence** n.

omnipresent a. present everywhere. **omnipresence** n.

omniscient /-'nɪʃənt/ a. knowing everything, having very extensive knowledge. **omniscience** n.

omnivorous /-'nɪv-/ a. feeding on all kinds of food.

on prep. supported by, attached to, covering; using as a basis or reason etc.; close to; towards; (of time) exactly at, during; in the state or process of; concerning; added to. —adv. so as to be on or covering something; further forward, towards something; with continued movement or action; operating, taking place. —a. & n. (in, from, or towards) the side of a cricket field behind the playing batsman. **be or keep on** at (colloq.) nag. **on and off** from time to time. **on-line** a. directly controlled by or connected to a computer.

onager /'ɒnədʒə(r)/ n. wild ass.

onanism /'əʊ-/ n. masturbation.

once adv., conj., & n. on one occasion, one time or occurrence; at all, as soon as; formerly. **once-over** n. (colloq.) rapid inspection. **once upon a time** at some vague time in the past.

oncology n. study of tumours.

oncoming a. approaching.

one a. single, individual, forming a unity. —n. smallest whole number (1, I); single thing or person; (colloq.) blow. —pron. person; any person (esp. used by a speaker or writer of himself as representing people in general). **one another** each other. **one day** at some unspecified date. **one-sided** a. unfair, prejudiced. **one-track mind** mind preoccupied with one subject. **one-upmanship** n. art of maintaining a psychological advantage over others. **one-way street** street where traffic is permitted to move in one direction only.

onerous /'ɒn-/ a. burdensome.

oneself pron. emphatic and reflexive form of **one**.

ongoing a. continuing, in progress.

onion n. vegetable with a bulb that has a strong taste and smell.

onlooker n. spectator.

only a. being the one specimen or all the specimens of a class, sole. —adv. without anything or anyone else; and that is all; no longer ago than. —conj. but then. **only too** extremely.

onomatopoeia /-'pi:ə/ n. formation of words that imitate the sound of what they stand for. **onomatopoeic** a.

onrush n. onward rush.

onset n. beginning; attack.

onslaught n. fierce attack.

onus /'əʊ-/ n. duty or responsibility of doing something.

onward adv. & a. with an advancing motion; further on. **onwards** adv.

onyx /'ɒnɪks/ n. stone like marble with colours in layers.

oodles n.pl. (colloq.) very great amount.

ooh int. exclamation of surprise, pleasure, or pain.

oolite /'əʊə-/ n. granular limestone.

ooze v.t./i. trickle or flow out slowly; exude. —n. wet mud.

op n. (colloq.) operation.

opacity /-'pæs-/ n. being opaque.

opal n. iridescent quartz-like stone often used as a gem. **opaline** a.

opalescent /-'les-/ a. iridescent like an opal. **opalescence** n.

opaque a. not clear, not transparent. **opaqueness** n.

OPEC abbr. Organization of Petroleum Exporting Countries.

open a. able to be entered; not closed or sealed or locked; not covered or concealed or restricted; spread out, unfolded; frank; not yet decided; available; willing to receive; (of a cheque) not crossed. —v.t./i. make or become open or more open; begin, establish. **in the open air** not in a house or building etc. **open-ended** a. with no fixed limit. **open-handed** a. giving generously. **open-heart** a. (of surgery) with the heart exposed and blood circulating through a bypass.

open house hospitality to all comers. **open letter** one addressed to a person by name but printed in a newspaper. **open plan** *a.* without partition walls or fences. **open secret** one known to so many people that it is no longer secret. **open verdict** coroner's verdict not specifying whether a crime is involved. **openness** *n.*

opencast *a.* (of mining) on the surface of the ground.

opener *n.* device for opening tins or bottles etc.

opening *n.* gap, place where a thing opens; beginning; opportunity.

openly *adv.* publicly, frankly.

openwork *n.* pattern with spaces between threads or strips.

opera *see* **opus**. —*n.* play(s) in which words are sung to music. **opera-glasses** *n.pl.* small binoculars.

operable *a.* able to be operated; suitable for treatment by surgery.

operate *v.t./i.* be in action; produce an effect; control the functioning of; perform an operation on.

operatic *a.* of or like opera.

operation *n.* operating; way a thing works; piece of work, transaction; military action; piece of surgery.

operational *a.* of or used in operations; able to function.

operative /'ɒp-/ *a.* working, functioning; of surgical operations. —*n.* worker, esp. in a factory.

operator *n.* person who operates a machine or business; one who connects lines at a telephone exchange; (*colloq.*) person acting in a specified way.

operetta *n.* short or light opera.

ophidian *a.* & *n.* (member) of the snake family.

ophthalmia *n.* inflammation of the eye.

ophthalmic *a.* of or for the eyes.

ophthalmology *n.* study of the eye and its diseases. **ophthalmologist** *n.*

ophthalmoscope *n.* instrument for examining the eye.

opiate /'əʊ-/ *n.* sedative containing opium; thing that soothes feelings.

opine *v.t.* express or hold as an opinion.

opinion *n.* belief or judgement held without actual proof; what one thinks on a particular point.

opinionated *a.* holding strong opinions obstinately.

opium *n.* narcotic drug made from the juice of certain poppies.

opossum *n.* small furry marsupial.

opponent *n.* one who opposes another.

opportune *a.* (of time) favourable; well-timed. **opportunely** *adv.*, **opportuneness** *n.*

opportunist *n.* person who grasps opportunities. **opportunism** *n.*, **opportunistic** *a.*

opportunity *n.* circumstances suitable for a particular purpose.

oppose *v.t.* argue or fight against; place opposite; place or be in opposition to; contrast.

opposite *a.* facing, on the further side; of a contrary kind, as different as possible from. —*n.* opposite thing or person. —*adv.* & *prep.* in an opposite position or direction (to). **one's opposite number** person holding a similar position to oneself in another group.

opposition *n.* antagonism, resistance; placing or being placed opposite; people opposing something; **the Opposition** the chief parliamentary party opposed to that in office.

oppress *v.t.* govern harshly; treat with continual harshness; weigh down with cares or unhappiness. **oppression** *n.*, **oppressor** *n.*

oppressive *a.* oppressing; hard to endure; sultry and tiring.

oppressively *adv.*, **oppressiveness** *n.*

opprobrious /-'prəʊ-/ *a.* abusive.

opprobrium /-'prəʊ-/ *n.* great disgrace from shameful conduct.

oppugn /ə'pjuːn/ *v.t.* controvert.

opt *v.i.* make a choice. **opt out** choose not to participate.

optic *a.* of the eye or sight.

optical *a.* of or aiding sight; visual. **optical illusion** mental misinterpretation caused by a thing's deceptive appearance. **optically** *adv.*

optician *n.* maker or seller of spectacles.

optics *n.* study of sight and of light as its medium.

optimal *a.* optimum. **optimally** *adv.*

optimism *n.* tendency to take a hopeful view of things. **optimist** *n.*, **optimistic** *a.*, **optimistically** *adv.*

optimum *a. & n.* best or most favourable (conditions, amount, etc.).

option *n.* freedom to choose; thing that is or may be chosen; right to buy or sell a thing within a limited time.

optional *a.* not compulsory. **optionally** *adv.*

opulent /'ɒp-/ *a.* wealthy; abundant. **opulently** *adv.*, **opulence** *n.*

opus /'əʊ-/ *n.* (*pl.* **opera**, *pr.* 'ɒp-) numbered musical composition.

or *conj.* as an alternative; because if not; also known as.

oracle *n.* place where the ancient Greeks consulted a god; the reply received; person or thing giving wise guidance. **oracular** /-'ræ-/ *a.*

oral *a.* spoken not written; of the mouth, taken by mouth. —*n.* (*colloq.*) spoken examination. **orally** *adv.*

orange *n.* round juicy citrus fruit with reddish-yellow peel; this colour. —*a.* reddish-yellow. **orange-stick** *n.* small thin stick for manicuring the nails.

orangeade *n.* orange-flavoured soft drink.

orang-utan /uː'tæn/ *n.* large ape of Borneo and Sumatra.

oration *n.* long speech, esp. of a ceremonial kind.

orator *n.* person who makes public speeches, skilful speaker.

oratorio *n.* (*pl.* -os) musical composition for voices and orchestra, usu. with a biblical theme.

oratory[1] *n.* art of public speaking; eloquent speech. **oratorical** *a.*

oratory[2] *n.* small chapel.

orb *n.* sphere, globe.

orbicular *a.* spherical, circular.

orbit *n.* curved path of a planet, satellite, or spacecraft round another; sphere of influence. —*v.t./i.* (*p.t.* **orbited**) move in an orbit (round).

orbital *a.* of orbits; (of a road) round the outside of a city.

orchard *n.* piece of land planted with fruit-trees; these trees.

orchestra *n.* large body of people playing various musical instruments; part of a theatre (between stalls and stage) where these sit. **orchestral** *a.*

orchestrate *v.t.* compose or arrange (music) for an orchestra; coordinate deliberately. **orchestration** *n.*

orchid *n.* a kind of showy often irregularly shaped flower.

orchis *n.* orchid, esp. a wild one.

ordain *v.t.* appoint ceremonially to the Christian ministry; destine; decree authoritatively.

ordeal /-'diːl/ *n.* difficult experience.

order *n.* way things are placed in relation to each other; proper or usual sequence; efficient state; law-abiding state; system of rules or procedure; command; request to supply goods etc., things supplied; written instruction or permission; rank; kind, quality; group of plants or animals classified as similar in many ways; monastic organization; company to which distinguished people are admitted as an honour; its insignia; style of classical architecture; (*pl.*) holy orders. —*v.t.* arrange in order; command; give an order for (goods etc.). **holy orders** status of ordained clergy. **in order to** or **that** with the purpose or intention that.

orderly *a.* methodical; not unruly; of or for military business. —*n.* soldier assisting an officer; hospital attendant. **orderliness** *n.*

ordinal *a.* **ordinal numbers** those defining position in a series (*first, second,* etc.).

ordinance *n.* decree.

ordinand *n.* candidate for ordination.

ordinary *a.* usual, not exceptional. **ordinarily** *adv.*

ordination *n.* ordaining.

ordnance *n.* military materials; department dealing with these. **Ordnance Survey** official survey of the British Isles, preparing maps.

ordure *n.* dung.

ore *n.* solid rock or mineral from which metal is obtained.

organ *n.* musical instrument with pipes supplied with wind by bellows and sounded by keys; distinct part with a specific function in an animal or plant body; medium of communication, esp. a newspaper.

organdie *n.* fine translucent usu. stiff cotton fabric.

organic *a.* of bodily organ(s); of or formed from living things; organized as a system of related parts; produced or carried out without using chemical fertilizers etc. **organically** *adv.*

organism *n.* a living being.

organist *n.* organ-player.

organization *n.* organizing; organized system or body of people. **organizational** *a.*

organize *v.t.* arrange systematically; make arrangements for;

form (people) into an association for a common purpose. **organizer** *n.*

organza *n.* thin stiff transparent dress-fabric.

orgasm *n.* climax of sexual excitement.

orgy *n.* wild revelry; unrestrained activity. **orgiastic** *a.*

oriel *n.* window projecting from a house wall at an upper level.

Orient *n.* the East, the eastern world.

orient *v.t.* place or determine the position of (a thing) with regard to points of the compass. **orient oneself** get one's bearings; become accustomed to a new situation. **orientation** *n.*

Oriental *n.* native of the Orient.

oriental *a.* of the Orient.

orientate *v.t.* orient.

orienteering *n.* sport of finding one's way across country by map and compass.

orifice *n.* opening of a cavity etc.

origami /-'ga:-/ *n.* Japanese art of folding paper into attractive shapes.

origanum *n.* wild marjoram.

origin *n.* point, source, or cause from which a thing begins its existence; ancestry, parentage.

original *a.* existing from the first, earliest; being the first form of something; new in character or design; inventive, creative. —*n.* first form, thing from which another is copied. **original sin** innate sinfulness held to be common to all mankind in consequence of the Fall. **originally** *adv.*, **originality** *n.*

originate *v.t./i.* bring or come into being. **origination** *n.*, **originator** *n.*

oriole /'ɔ:r-/ *n.* bird with black and yellow plumage.

ormolu /'ɔ:m-/ *n.* gilded bronze; gold-coloured alloy of copper; things made of this.

ornament *n.* decorative object or detail; decoration. —*v.t.* decorate with ornament(s). **ornamentation** n.

ornamental a. serving as an ornament. **ornamentally** adv.

ornate a. elaborately ornamented. **ornately** adv., **ornateness** n.

ornithology n. study of birds. **ornithological** a., **ornithologist** n.

orotund a. (of speech) dignified, pompous.

orphan n. child whose parents are dead. —v.t. make (a child) an orphan.

orphanage n. institution where orphans are housed and cared for.

orrery n. clockwork model of the planetary system.

orrisroot n. violet-scented iris root.

orthodontics n. correction of irregularities in teeth. **orthodontic** a., **orthodontist** n.

orthodox a. of or holding conventional or currently accepted beliefs, esp. in religion. **Orthodox Church** Eastern or Greek Church. **orthodoxy** n.

orthopaedics /-'piː-/ n. surgical correction of deformities in bones or muscles. **orthopaedic** a., **orthopaedist** n.

oryx n. large African antelope.

Oscar n. statuette awarded annually for film acting, directing, etc.

oscillate /'ɒs-/ v.t./i. move to and fro; vary. **oscillation** n.

oscilloscope /ə'sɪl-/ n. device for recording oscillations.

osier /'əʊz-/ n. willow with flexible twigs; twig of this.

osmium n. heavy hard metallic element.

osmosis /ɒz'məʊ-/ n. diffusion of fluid through a porous partition into another fluid. **osmotic** a.

osprey n. (pl. **-eys**) large bird preying on fish in inland waters.

osseous a. like bone, bony.

ossify v.t./i. turn into bone, harden; make or become rigid and unprogressive. **ossification** n.

ostensible a. pretended, used as a pretext. **ostensibly** adv.

ostentation n. showy display intended to impress people. **ostentatious** a., **ostentatiously** adv.

osteopath n. practitioner who treats certain diseases and abnormalities by manipulating bones and muscles. **osteopathic** a., **osteopathy** /-'ɒp-/ n.

ostler n. stableman at an inn.

ostracize v.t. refuse to associate with. **ostracism** n.

ostrich n. large swift-running African bird, unable to fly.

other a. alternative, additional, being the remaining one of a set of two or more; not the same. —n. & pron. the other person or thing. —adv. otherwise. **the other day** or **week** a few days or weeks ago. **other world** life after death.

otherwise adv. in a different way; in other respects; if circumstances are or were different.

otiose /'əʊ-/ a. not required, serving no practical purpose.

otter n. fish-eating water animal with thick brown fur.

Ottoman a. & n. (person) of the former Turkish empire.

ottoman n. long cushioned backless seat; storage box with a padded top.

oubliette n. secret dungeon with a trapdoor entrance.

ouch int. exclamation of pain.

ought v.aux. expressing duty, rightness, advisability, or strong probability.

Ouija(-board) n. [P.] board with letters and a movable pointer used to obtain messages in spiritualist seances.

ounce n. unit of weight, one-sixteenth of a pound (about 28 grams). **fluid ounce** one-twentieth (in USA, one-sixteenth) of a pint.

our *a.*, **ours** *poss.pron.* belonging to us.

ourselves *pron.* emphatic and reflexive form of *we* and *us*.

oust /au-/ *v.t.* drive out, eject.

out *adv.* away from or not in a place; not at home; not in effective action, no longer in fashion or office; on strike; no longer burning; in error; no longer visible; not possible; unconscious; into the open, so as to be heard or seen; unfolded; completely; in finished form. —*prep.* out of. —*n.* way of escape. **be out to** be intending to. **out-and-out** *a.* thorough, extreme. **out of** from within or among; beyond the range of; without a supply of; (of an animal) having as its dam. **out of date** no longer fashionable or current or valid. **out of doors** in the open air. **out of the way** no longer an obstacle; remote; unusual.

out- *pref.* more than, so as to exceed.

outback *n.* (*Austr.*) remote inland districts.

outbid *v.t.* (*p.t.* **-bid**, *pres.p.* **-bidding**) bid higher than.

outboard *a.* (of a motor) attached to the outside of a boat.

outbreak *n.* breaking out of anger or war or disease etc.

outbuilding *n.* outhouse.

outburst *n.* explosion of feeling.

outcast *n.* person driven out of a group or by society.

outclass *v.t.* surpass in quality.

outcome *n.* result of an event.

outcrop *n.* part of an underlying layer of rock that projects on the surface of the ground.

outcry *n.* loud cry; strong protest.

outdated *a.* out of date.

outdistance *v.t.* get far ahead of.

outdo *v.t.* (*p.t.* **-did**, *p.p.* **-done**) be or do better than.

outdoor *a.* of or for use in the open air. **outdoors** *adv.*

outer *a.* further from the centre or inside; exterior, external.

outermost *adv.* furthest outward.

outface *v.t.* disconcert by staring or by a confident manner.

outfall *n.* mouth of a river, drain, etc.

outfit *n.* set of clothes or equipment.

outfitter *n.* supplier of equipment or men's clothing.

outflank *v.t.* get round the flank of (an enemy).

outflow *n.* outward flow.

outgoing *a.* going out; sociable.

outgoings *n.pl.* expenditure.

outgrow *v.t.* (*p.t.* **-grew**, *p.p.* **-grown**) grow faster than; grow too large for; leave aside as one develops.

outgrowth *n.* thing growing out of another.

outhouse *n.* shed, barn, etc.

outing *n.* pleasure-trip.

outlandish *a.* looking or sounding strange or foreign.

outlast *v.t.* last longer than.

outlaw *n.* person punished (in the Middle Ages) by being placed outside the protection of the law. —*v.t.* make (a person) an outlaw; declare illegal. **outlawry** *n.*

outlay *n.* money etc. spent.

outlet *n.* way out; means for giving vent to energies or feelings; market for goods.

outline *n.* line(s) showing a thing's shape or boundary; summary. —*v.t.* draw or describe in outline; mark the outline of.

outlive *v.t.* live longer than.

outlook *n.* view, prospect; mental attitude; future prospects.

outlying *a.* remote.

outmanœuvre *v.t.* outdo in manœuvring.

outmoded *a.* no longer fashionable or accepted.

outmost *a.* outermost; uttermost.

outnumber *v.t.* exceed in number.

outpace *v.t.* go faster than.

out-patient n. person visiting a hospital for treatment but not remaining resident there.

outpost n. outlying settlement or detachment of troops.

output n. amount of electrical power etc. produced. —v.t. (p.t. **-put** or **-putted**) (of a computer) supply (results etc.).

outrage n. act that shocks public opinion; violation of rights. —v.t. shock and anger greatly.

outrageous a. greatly exceeding what is moderate or reasonable, shocking. **outrageously** adv.

outrank v.t. be of higher rank than.

outrider n. mounted attendant or motor-cyclist riding as guard.

outrigger n. beam or spar projecting over a ship's side; stabilizing strip of wood fixed outside and parallel to a canoe; boat with either of these.

outright adv. completely, not gradually; frankly. —a. thorough, complete.

outrun v.t. (p.t. **-ran**, p.p. **-run**, pres.p. **-running**) run faster or further than.

outsell v.t. (p.t. **-sold**) sell more than.

outset n. beginning.

outshine v.t. (p.t. **-shone**) surpass in splendour or excellence.

outside n. outer side, surface, or part. —a. of or from the outside; (of price) greatest possible. —adv. on, at, or to the outside. —prep. on, at, or to the outside of; other than.

outsider n. non-member of a group; horse etc. thought to have no chance in a contest.

outsize a. much larger than average.

outskirts n.pl. outer districts.

outsmart v.t. (colloq.) outwit.

outspoken a. very frank.

outspread a. & v.i. spread out.

outstanding a. conspicuous; exceptionally good; not yet paid or settled. **outstandingly** adv.

outstay v.t. stay longer than.

outstretched a. stretched out.

outstrip v.t. (p.t. **-stripped**) run faster or further than; surpass.

out-tray n. tray for documents that are ready for dispatch.

outvote v.t. defeat by a majority of votes.

outward a. on or to the outside. —adv. outwards. **outwardly** adv., **outwards** adv.

outweigh v.t. be of greater weight or importance than.

outwit v.t. (p.t. **-witted**) defeat by one's craftiness.

outwork n. advanced or detached part of a fortification; work done away from factory etc. premises.

outworn a. worn out.

ouzel /'uːzəl/ n. small bird of the thrush family; diving bird.

ouzo /'uːzəʊ/ n. Greek aniseed-flavoured spirits.

ova see **ovum**.

oval n. & a. (of) rounded symmetrical shape longer than it is broad.

ovary n. organ producing egg-cells; that part of a pistil from which fruit is formed. **ovarian** a.

ovation n. enthusiastic applause.

oven n. enclosed chamber in which things are cooked or heated.

over prep. in or to a position higher than; above and across; throughout; during; transmitted by; concerning; more than; in superiority to. —adv. outwards and downwards from the brink or an upright position etc.; from one side or end etc. to the other; across a space or distance; besides; with repetition; at an end. —n. series of 6 (or 8) balls bowled in cricket.

over- pref. above; excessively.

overall n. garment worn to protect other clothing, which it covers; (pl.) one-piece garment of this kind covering the body and legs. —a. total; taking all aspects into account. —adv. taken as a whole.

overarm a. & adv. with the arm brought forward and down from above shoulder level.

overawe v.t. overcome with awe.

overbalance v.t./i. lose balance and fall; cause to do this.

overbearing a. domineering.

overblown a. pretentious; past its prime.

overboard adv. from a ship into the water. **go overboard** (colloq.) show extreme enthusiasm.

overbook v.t. book too many passengers or vehicles for.

overcast a. covered with cloud.

overcharge v.t. charge too much; fill too full.

overcoat n. warm outdoor coat.

overcome v.t./i. win a victory over; succeed in subduing or dealing with; be victorious; make helpless.

overcrowd v.t. fill too full of people or things.

overdo v.t. (p.t. **-did**, p.p. **-done**) do too much; cook too long.

overdose n. too large a dose. —v.t./i. give an overdose to; take an overdose.

overdraft n. overdrawing of a bank account; amount of this.

overdraw v.t. (p.t. **-drew**, p.p. **-drawn**) draw more from (a bank account) than the amount credited.

overdrive n. mechanism providing an extra gear above top gear.

overdue a. not paid or arrived etc. by the due time.

overestimate v.t. form too high an estimate of.

overflow v.t./i. flow over the edge or limits (of). —n. what overflows; outlet for excess liquid.

overgrown a. grown too large; covered with weeds etc.

overhand a. & adv. overarm.

overhang v.t./i. (p.t. **-hung**) jut out over. —n. overhanging part.

overhaul v.t. examine and repair; overtake. —n. examination and repair.

overhead a. & adv. above the level of one's head; in the sky.

overheads n.pl. expenses involved in running a business etc.

overhear v.t. (p.t. **-heard**) hear accidentally or without the speaker's knowledge or intention.

overjoyed a. filled with great joy.

overkill n. surplus of capacity for destruction above what is needed to defeat or destroy an enemy.

overland a. & adv. (travelling) by land. **overlander** n.

overlap v.t./i. (p.t. **-lapped**) extend beyond the edge of; coincide partially. —n. overlapping; part or amount that overlaps.

overlay[1] /-'leɪ/ v.t. (p.t. **-laid**) lay over the surface of or on top of.

overlay[2] /'əʊ-/ n. thing laid over another.

overleaf adv. on the other side of a leaf of a book etc.

overload v.t. put too great a load on or in. —n. load that is too great.

overlook v.t. have a view over; oversee; fail to observe or consider; ignore, not punish.

overlord n. supreme lord.

overly adv. (esp. Sc. & US) excessively.

overman v.t. (p.t. **-manned**) provide with too many people as workmen or crew.

overnight adv. & a. during a night.

overpass n. road crossing another by means of a bridge.

overpay v.t. (p.t. **-paid**) pay too highly.

overpower v.t. overcome by greater strength or numbers.

overpowering a. (of heat or feelings) extremely intense.

overrate v.t. have too high an opinion of.

overreach *v.refl.* **overreach oneself** fail through being too ambitious.

override *v.t.* (*p.t.* **-rode**, *p.p.* **-ridden**) overrule; prevail over; intervene and cancel the operation of.

overrider *n.* vertical attachment on the bumper of a car.

overripe *a.* too ripe.

overrule *v.t.* set aside (a decision etc.) by using one's authority.

overrun *v.t.* (*p.t.* **-ran**, *p.p.* **-run**, *pres.p.* **-running**) spread over and occupy or injure; exceed (a limit).

overseas *a.* & *adv.* across or beyond the sea, abroad.

oversee *v.t.* (*p.t.* **-saw**, *p.p.* **-seen**) superintend. **overseer** *n.*

oversew *v.t.* (*p.p.* **-sewn**) sew (edges) together so that each stitch lies over the edges.

overshadow *v.t.* cast a shadow over; cause to seem unimportant in comparison.

overshoe *n.* shoe worn over another as a protection against wet etc.

overshoot *v.t.* (*p.t.* **-shot**) pass beyond (a target or limit etc.).

overshot *a.* (of a wheel) turned by water falling from above.

oversight *n.* supervision; unintentional omission or mistake.

oversized *a.* of more than the usual size.

oversleep *v.i.* (*p.t.* **-slept**) sleep longer than one intended.

overspill *n.* what spills over; district's surplus population seeking accommodation elsewhere.

overstate *v.t.* exaggerate.

overstay *v.t.* stay longer than (one's welcome, a time limit, etc.).

oversteer *v.i.* (of a car) tend to turn more sharply than was intended. —*n.* this tendency.

overstep *v.t.* (*p.t.* **-stepped**) go beyond (a limit).

overt *a.* done or shown openly. **overtly** *adv.*

overtake *v.t.* (*p.t.* **-took**, *p.p.* **-taken**) come abreast or level with; pass (a moving person or thing).

overtax *v.t.* levy excessive taxes on; put too great a burden on.

overthrow *v.t.* (*p.t.* **-threw**, *p.p.* **-thrown**) cause the downfall of. —*n.* downfall, defeat.

overtime *adv.* in addition to regular working hours. —*n.* time worked thus; payment for this.

overtone *n.* additional quality or implication.

overture *n.* orchestral composition forming a prelude to an opera or ballet etc.; (*pl.*) friendly approach, formal proposal.

overturn *v.t./i.* turn over; fall down or over, cause to fall.

overview *n.* general survey.

overweight *a.* weighing too much.

overwhelm *v.t.* bury beneath a huge mass; overcome completely; make helpless with emotion.

overwhelming *a.* irresistible through force of numbers or amount or influence.

overwork *v.t./i.* work too hard; make excessive use of. —*n.* excessive work causing exhaustion.

overwrought /-'rɔːt/ *a.* in a state of nervous agitation through over-excitement.

oviduct /'əʊ-/ *n.* tube through which ova pass from the ovary.

oviparous /-'vɪp-/ *a.* egg-laying.

ovoid /'əʊ-/ *a.* egg-shaped, oval.

ovulate /'ɒv-/ *v.i.* produce or discharge an egg-cell from an ovary. **ovulation** *n.*

ovule /'əʊ-/ *n.* germ-cell of a plant.

ovum /'əʊ-/ *n.* (*pl.* **ova**) egg-cell, reproductive cell produced by a female.

owe *v.t.* be under an obligation to pay or repay or render; have (a thing) as the result of the action of another person or cause.

owing *a.* owed and not yet paid. **owing to** caused by; because of.

owl *n.* bird of prey with large eyes, usu. flying at night. **owlish** *a.*

owlet *n.* small or young owl.

own[1] *a.* belonging to oneself or itself. **get one's own back** (*colloq.*) have one's revenge. **hold one's own** maintain one's position, not lose strength. **of one's own** belonging to oneself. **on one's own** alone; independently.

own[2] *v.t.* have as one's own; acknowledge ownership of; confess. **own up** confess.

owner *n.* one who owns something. **ownership** *n.*

ox *n.* (*pl.* **oxen**) animal of or related to the kind kept as domestic cattle; fully grown bullock.

oxalic acid sour poisonous acid found in certain plants.

oxidation *n.* process of combining with oxygen.

oxide *n.* compound of oxygen and one other element.

oxidize *v.t./i.* combine with oxygen; coat with an oxide; make or become rusty. **oxidization** *n.*

oxtail *n.* tail of an ox, used to make soup or stew.

oxyacetylene *a.* using a mixture of oxygen and acetylene, esp. in metal-cutting and welding.

oxygen *n.* colourless gas existing in air.

oxymoron *n.* putting together words which seem to contradict each other (e.g. *bitter-sweet*).

oyster *n.* shellfish used as food.

oz. *abbr.* ounce(s).

ozone *n.* form of oxygen; protective layer of this in the stratosphere.

P

pa *n.* (*colloq.*) father.

pace *n.* single step in walking or running; rate of progress. —*v.t./i.* walk steadily or to and fro; measure by pacing; set the pace for.

pacemaker *n.* runner etc. who sets the pace for another; artificial or natural device stimulating heart contractions.

pachyderm /ˈpæk-/ *n.* large thick-skinned mammal such as the elephant. **pachydermatous** *a.*

Pacific *a. & n.* (of) the **Pacific Ocean** (west of the American continent).

pacific *a.* making or loving peace. **pacifically** *adv.*

pacifist *n.* person totally opposed to war. **pacifism** *n.*

pacify *v.t.* calm and soothe; establish peace in. **pacification** *n.*

pack[1] *n.* collection of things wrapped or tied for carrying or selling; set of playing-cards; group of hounds or wolves; set; large amount or collection. —*v.t./i.* put into or fill a container; press or crowd together, fill (a space) thus; cover or protect with something pressed tightly. **pack off** send away. **send packing** dismiss abruptly. **packer** *n.*

pack[2] *v.t.* select (a jury etc.) fraudulently so as to secure a biased decision.

package *n.* parcel; box etc. in which goods are packed; package deal. —*v.t.* put together in a package. **package deal** set of proposals offered or accepted as a whole. **package holiday** one with set arrangements at an inclusive price. **packager** *n.*

packet *n.* small package; (*colloq.*) large sum of money; mail-boat.

pact *n.* agreement, treaty.

pad[1] *n.* piece of padding; set of sheets of paper fastened together at one edge; soft fleshy part under an animal's paw; flat surface for use by helicopters or for launching rockets. —*v.t./i.* (*p.t.* **padded**) put padding on or into; fill out.

pad[2] *v.i.* (*p.t.* **padded**) walk softly or steadily.

padding *n.* soft material used to protect against jarring, add bulk, absorb fluid, etc.

paddle[1] n. short oar used without a rowlock; thing shaped like this; board of a paddle-wheel. —v.t./i. propel by use of paddle(s); row gently. **paddle-steamer** n. one driven by paddle-wheel(s). **paddle-wheel** n. wheel with boards round its rim that drive a boat by pressing against the water as the wheel revolves.

paddle[2] v.t./i. walk with bare feet in shallow water for pleasure; dabble (feet or hands) in water.

paddock n. small field where horses are kept; enclosure for horses or racing-cars at a racecourse.

paddy[1] n. (colloq.) rage, temper.

paddy[2] n. rice-field; growing rice.

padlock n. detachable lock with a U-shaped bar secured through the object fastened. —v.t. fasten with a padlock.

padre /ˈpɑːdreɪ/ n. (colloq.) chaplain in the army etc.

paean /ˈpiːən/ n. song of triumph.

paediatrics /piː-/ n. study of children's diseases. **paediatric** a., **paediatrician** /-ˈtrɪʃ(ə)n/ n.

paella n. Spanish dish of rice, saffron, chicken, seafood, etc.

pagan a. & n. heathen. **paganism** n.

page[1] n. sheet of paper in a book or newspaper etc.; one side of this.

page[2] n. liveried boy or man employed as a door attendant or to go on errands etc.; boy attendant of a bride or person of rank. —v.t. summon by an announcement, messenger, or pager.

pageant /ˈpædʒ-/ n. public show or procession, esp. with people in costume. **pageantry** n.

pager n. radio device with a bleeper for summoning the wearer.

pagoda n. Hindu temple or Buddhist tower in India, China, etc.

paid see **pay**. —a. **put paid to** (colloq.) end (hopes or prospects etc.).

pail n. bucket.

pain n. unpleasant feeling caused by injury or disease of the body; mental suffering; (pl.) careful effort. —v.t. cause pain to.

painful a. causing or suffering pain; laborious. **painfully** adv., **painfulness** n.

painless a. not causing pain. **painlessly** adv.

painstaking a. very careful.

paint n. colouring-matter for applying in liquid form to a surface; (pl.) tubes or cakes of paint. —v.t. coat with paint; portray by using paint(s) or in words; apply (liquid).

paintbox n. box holding paints.

painter[1] n. person who paints as artist or decorator.

painter[2] n. rope attached to a boat's bow for tying it up.

painting n. painted picture.

pair n. set of two things or people, couple; article consisting of two joined corresponding parts; other member of a pair. —v.t./i. arrange or be arranged in pair(s); (of animals) mate.

Paisley n. pattern of curved abstract figures.

pal n. (colloq.) friend.

palace n. official residence of a sovereign, archbishop, or bishop; splendid mansion.

paladin n. peer of Charlemagne's court; knight errant.

palaeography n. study of ancient writing and inscriptions. **palaeographer** n.

palaeolithic /pælɪə-/ a. of the early part of the Stone Age.

palaeontology n. study of life in the geological past. **palaeontologist** n.

palanquin n. oriental covered litter.

palatable a. pleasant to the taste or mind.

palate *n.* roof of the mouth; sense of taste.

palatial /-'leɪʃ-/ *a.* of or like a palace.

palaver /-'lɑː-/ *n.* (*colloq.*) fuss.

pale[1] *a.* (-er, -est) (of face) having less colour than normal; (of colour or light) faint. —*v.t./i.* turn pale. **palely** *adv.*, **paleness** *n.*

pale[2] *n.* stake forming part of a fence; boundary. **beyond the pale** outside the bounds of acceptable behaviour.

Palestinian *a. & n.* (native) of Palestine.

palette *n.* board on which an artist mixes colours. **palette-knife** *n.* blade with a handle, used for spreading paint or for smoothing soft substances in cookery.

palimony *n.* (*sl.*) compensation claimed by one member of an unmarried couple who have separated.

paling *n.* railing(s).

palisade *n.* fence of pointed stakes.

pall /pɔːl/ *n.* cloth spread over a coffin; heavy dark covering. —*v.i.* become uninteresting.

pallbearer *n.* person helping to carry or walking beside the coffin at a funeral.

pallet[1] *n.* straw-stuffed mattress; hard narrow or makeshift bed.

pallet[2] *n.* tray or platform for goods being lifted or stored.

palliasse *n.* straw-stuffed mattress.

palliate /'pæ-/ *v.t.* alleviate; partially excuse. **palliation** *n.*, **palliative** *a.*

pallid *a.* pale, esp. from illness. **pallidness** *n.*, **pallor** *n.*

pally *a.* (*colloq.*) friendly.

palm *n.* inner surface of the hand; part of a glove covering this; tree of warm and tropical climates, with large leaves and no branches; symbol of victory. —*v.t.* conceal in one's hand; get (a thing) accepted by fraud. **palm**

off get (a thing) accepted fraudulently. **Palm Sunday** Sunday before Easter. **palm-tree** *n.*

palmist *n.* person who tells people's fortunes or characters from lines in their palms. **palmistry** *n.*

palmy *a.* (-ier, -iest) flourishing.

palomino *n.* (*pl.* -os) golden or cream-coloured horse with white mane and tail.

palp *n.* arthropod's feeler.

palpable *a.* able to be touched or felt; obvious. **palpably** *adv.*, **palpability** *n.*

palpate *v.t.* examine medically by touch. **palpation** *n.*

palpitate *v.i.* throb rapidly; quiver with fear or excitement. **palpitation** *n.*

palsy *n.* paralysis, esp. with involuntary tremors. **palsied** *a.*

paltry *a.* (-ier, -iest) worthless. **paltriness** *n.*

pampas *n.* vast grassy plains in South America. **pampas-grass** *n.* large ornamental grass.

pamper *v.t.* treat indulgently.

pamphlet *n.* leaflet or paper-covered booklet. **pamphleteer** *n.*

pan[1] *n.* metal or earthenware vessel with a flat base, used in cooking; similar vessel; bowl of a pair of scales; bowl of a water-closet. —*v.t.* (*p.t.* **panned**) wash (gravel) in a pan in searching for gold; (*colloq.*) criticize severely. **pan out** turn out (well). **panful** *n.*

pan[2] *v.t./i.* (*p.t.* **panned**) turn horizontally in filming.

pan- *pref.* all, whole.

panacea /-'sɪːə/ *n.* remedy for all kinds of diseases or troubles.

panache /-'næʃ/ *n.* confident stylish manner.

panama *n.* hat of fine straw-like material; a kind of woven fabric.

panatella *n.* thin cigar.

pancake *n.* thin round cake of fried batter; thing shaped like this.

panchromatic *a.* sensitive to all colours of the visible spectrum.

pancreas n. gland near the stomach, discharging insulin into the blood. **pancreatic** a.

panda n. large bear-like black-and-white animal of south-west China; racoon-like animal of India. **panda car** police patrol car.

pandemic a. (of a disease) occurring country-wide or worldwide.

pandemonium n. uproar.

pander v.i. **pander to** gratify by satisfying a weakness or vulgar taste. —n. go-between in illicit love affairs.

pane n. sheet of glass in a window or door.

panegyric /-'dʒɪr-/ n. piece of written or spoken praise. **panegyrical** a.

panel n. distinct usu. rectangular section; strip of board etc. forming this; group assembled to discuss or decide something; list of jurors, jury. —v.t. (p.t. **panelled**) cover or decorate with panels.

panelling n. series of wooden panels in a wall; wood used for making panels.

panellist n. member of a panel.

pang n. sudden sharp pain.

pangolin n. scaly ant-eater.

panic n. sudden strong fear. —v.t./i. (p.t. **panicked**) affect or be affected with panic. **panic-stricken**, **panic-struck** adjs. **panicky** a.

panicle n. loose branching cluster of flowers.

panjandrum n. mock title for a great personage.

pannier n. large basket carried by a donkey etc.; bag fitted on a motor cycle.

panoply n. splendid array.

panorama n. view of a wide area or set of events. **panoramic** a.

pansy n. garden flower of violet family with broad petals; (derog.) effeminate or homosexual man.

pant v.t./i. breathe with short quick breaths; utter breathlessly; be extremely eager.

pantaloons n.pl. (old use & US) trousers.

pantechnicon /-'tek/- n. large van for transporting furniture.

pantheism n. doctrine that God is everything and everything is God. **pantheist** n., **pantheistic** a.

panther n. leopard.

panties n.pl. short knickers.

pantile n. curved roof-tile.

pantograph n. device for copying a plan etc. on any scale.

pantomime n. Christmas play based on a fairy-tale; mime. —v.t./i. mime.

pantry n. room for storing china, glass, etc.; larder.

pants n.pl. (colloq.) trousers; underpants; knickers.

pap[1] n. soft food suitable for infants or invalids; pulp.

pap[2] n. (old use) nipple.

papa /pə-'pɑː/ n. (old use) father.

papacy n. position or authority of the pope.

papal a. of the pope or papacy.

paper n. substance manufactured in thin sheets from wood fibre, rags, etc., used for writing on, wrapping things, etc.; newspaper; set of examination questions; document; essay, dissertation. —v.t. cover (walls etc.) with wallpaper. **on paper** in writing; when judged from written or printed evidence.

paperback a. & n. (book) bound in flexible paper binding.

paperweight n. small heavy object to hold loose papers down.

papery a. like paper in texture.

papier mâché /ˌpæpjeɪ 'mæʃeɪ/ moulded paper pulp used for making small objects.

papist n. (derog.) Roman Catholic.

papoose n. young North American Indian child.

paprika /'pæ-/ n. red pepper.

papyrus n. reed-like water-plant from which the ancient Egyptians made a kind of paper; this paper; (*pl.* -**ri**) manuscript written on this.

par *n.* average or normal amount or condition etc.; equal footing.

parable *n.* story told to illustrate a moral or spiritual truth.

parabola /-'ræ-/ *n.* curve like the path of an object thrown up and falling back to earth. **parabolic** /-'bɒl-/ *a.*

paracetamol /-'si:-/ *n.* drug that relieves pain and reduces fever; tablet of this.

parachute *n.* oblong or umbrella-shaped device used to slow the descent of a person or object dropping from a great height. —*v.t./i.* descend or drop by parachute. **parachutist** *n.*

parade *n.* formal assembly of troops for inspection etc.; place for this; procession; ostentatious display; public square or promenade. —*v.t./i.* assemble for parade; march or walk with display; make a display of.

paradigm /-daɪm/ *n.* example, model.

paradise *n.* heaven; Eden.

paradox *n.* statement that seems self-contradictory but contains a truth. **paradoxical** *a.*, **paradoxically** *adv.*

paraffin *n.* oil from petroleum or shale, used as fuel. **liquid paraffin** tasteless form of this used as a mild laxative. **paraffin wax** solid paraffin.

paragon *n.* apparently perfect person or thing.

paragraph *n.* one or more sentences on a single theme, beginning on a new (usu. indented) line. —*v.t.* arrange in paragraphs.

parakeet *n.* a kind of small parrot.

parallax *n.* apparent difference in an object's position when viewed from different points. **parallactic** *a.*

parallel *a.* (of lines or planes) going continuously at the same distance from each other; similar, corresponding. *n.* parallel line or thing; line on a map or globe, drawn parallel to the equator; comparison, analogy. —*v.t./i.* (*p.t.* **paralleled**) be parallel to; compare. **parallelism** *n.*

parallelogram *n.* four-sided geometric figure with its opposite sides parallel to each other.

Paralympics *n.pl.* international sports competitions for disabled people.

paralyse *v.t.* affect with paralysis; bring to a standstill.

paralysis *n.* loss of power of movement, inability to move normally. **paralytic** /-'lɪt-/ *a.* & *n.*

paramedic *n.* (*colloq.*) paramedical worker.

paramedical *a.* supplementing and supporting medical work.

parameter /-'ræ-/ *n.* variable quantity or quality that restricts what it characterizes.

paramilitary *a.* organized like a military force.

paramount *a.* chief in importance.

paramour *n.* (*old use*) illicit lover.

parang *n.* heavy Malaysian knife.

paranoia *n.* mental disorder in which a person has delusions of grandeur or persecution; abnormal tendency to mistrust others. **paranoiac** *a.*, **paranoid** *a.*

parapet *n.* low protective wall along the edge of a balcony or bridge.

paraphernalia /-'neɪ-/ *n.* numerous belongings or pieces of equipment.

paraphrase *v.t.* express in other words. —*n.* rewording in this way.

paraplegia /-'pli:-/ *n.* paralysis of the legs and part or all of the trunk. **paraplegic** *a.* & *n.*

parapsychology n. study of mental perceptions that seem outside normal abilities.

paraquat /'pæ-/ n. extremely poisonous weed-killer.

parasite n. animal or plant living on or in another; person living off another or others and giving no useful return. **parasitic** /-'sıt-/ a.

parasol n. light umbrella used to give shade from the sun.

paratrooper n. member of paratroops.

paratroops n.pl. troops trained to descend by parachute.

paratyphoid n. fever like typhoid but milder.

parboil v.t. cook partially by boiling.

parcel n. thing(s) wrapped for carrying or post; piece of land. —v.t. (p.t. **parcelled**) wrap as a parcel; divide into portions.

parch v.t. make hot and dry; make thirsty.

parchment n. heavy paperlike material made from animal skins; paper resembling this.

pardon n. forgiveness. —v.t. (p.t. **pardoned**) forgive. **pardonable** a., **pardonably** adv.

pare /peə(r)/ v.t. trim the edges of; peel; reduce little by little.

parent n. one who has produced offspring; ancestor; source from which other things are derived. **parental** /-'ren-/ a., **parenthood** n.

parentage n. descent from parents.

parenthesis /-'ren-/ n. (pl. **-theses**) word, phrase, or sentence inserted into a passage that is grammatically complete without it; brackets (like these) placed round this. **parenthetic** /-'θet-/ a., **parenthetical** a., **parenthetically** adv.

parenting n. being a parent.

parget v.t. (p.t. **pargeted**) plaster (a wall etc.) with an ornamental pattern; roughcast.

pariah /pə'raıə/ n. outcast.

parietal bone /-'raıə-/ each of a pair of bones forming part of the skull.

paring /'peər-/ n. piece pared off.

parish n. area (within a diocese) with its own church and clergyman; local-government area within a county.

parishioner n. inhabitant of a parish.

Parisian /-'rız-/ a. & n. (native) of Paris.

parity /'pæ-/ n. equality.

park n. public garden or recreation ground; enclosed land attached to a country house or mansion; parking area. —v.t. place and leave (a vehicle etc.) temporarily.

parka n. a type of thick jacket with a hood attached.

parkin n. gingerbread made with oatmeal and treacle.

parky a. (sl.) (of weather) chilly.

parlance n. phraseology.

parley n. (pl. -eys) discussion, esp. between enemies, to settle a dispute. —v.i. (p.t. **parleyed**) hold a parley.

parliament n. assembly that makes a country's laws. **parliamentary** a., **parliamentarian** n.

parlour n. sitting-room.

parlourmaid n. maid who waits on a household at meals.

parlous a. (old use) perilous.

Parmesan /-'zæn/ n. a kind of hard cheese.

parochial /-'rəuk-/ a. of a church parish; interested in a limited area only. **parochially** adv., **parochialism** n.

parody n. comic or grotesque imitation. —v.t. make a parody of.

parole /-'rəul/ n. person's word of honour; release of a prisoner before the end of his sentence on condition of good behaviour. —v.t. release in this way.

paroxysm /ˈpæ-/ n. spasm; outburst of laughter, anger, etc.

parquet /-keɪ/ n. flooring of wooden blocks arranged in a pattern.

parricide n. killing or killer of own parent. **parricidal** a.

parrot n. tropical bird with a short hooked bill; unintelligent imitator. —v.t. (p.t. **parroted**) repeat mechanically.

parry v.t. ward off (a blow); evade (a question) skilfully. —n. parrying.

parse v.t. identify the grammatical form and function of. **parser** n.

parsec n. unit of distance used in astronomy, about 3.25 lightyears.

parsimonious /-ˈməʊ-/ a. stingy, very sparing. **parsimoniously** adv., **parsimony** /ˈpɑː-/ n.

parsley n. herb with crinkled green leaves.

parsnip n. vegetable with a large yellowish tapering root.

parson n. (colloq.) member of the clergy. **parson's nose** fatty lump on the rump of a cooked fowl.

parsonage n. rectory, vicarage.

part n. some but not all; distinct portion; component; portion allotted, share; character assigned to an actor in a play etc.; melody assigned to one voice or instrument in a group; region; side in an agreement or dispute. —adv. partly. —v.t./i. separate, divide. **in good part** without taking offence. **in part** partly. **part of speech** word's grammatical class (noun, verb, adjective, etc.). **part-time** a. for or during only part of the working week. **part with** give up possession of, hand over.

partake v.i. (p.t. **-took**, p.p. **-taken**) participate; take a portion, esp. of food. **partaker** n.

Parthian shot sharp remark made by a person departing.

partial a. in part but not complete or total. **be partial to** have a strong liking for. **partially** adv.

partiality /-ʃɪˈæl-/ n. bias, favouritism; strong liking.

participate v.i. have a share, take part in something. **participation** n., **participator** n.

participle n. word formed from a verb, as a past participle (e.g. burnt, frightened), present participle (e.g. burning, frightening). **participial** a.

particle n. very small portion of matter; minor part of speech.

particoloured a. coloured partly in one colour, partly in another.

particular a. relating to one person or thing and not others; special, exceptional; carefully insisting on certain standards. —n. detail; piece of information. **in particular** particularly, especially; specifically. **particularly** adv., **particularity** n.

particularize v.t./i. specify, name specially or one by one. **particularization** n.

parting n. leave-taking; line from which hair is combed in different directions.

partisan /-ˈzæn or ˈpɑː-/ n. strong supporter; guerrilla. **partisanship** n.

partition n. division into parts; part formed thus; structure dividing a room or space, thin wall. —v.t. divide into parts or by a partition.

partly adv. partially.

partner n. person sharing with another or others in an activity; each of a pair, esp. in dancing or games; husband or wife or member of an unmarried couple. —v.t. be the partner of; put together as partners. **partnership** n.

partridge n. game-bird with brown feathers and a plump body.

parturition n. process of giving birth to young; childbirth.

party n. social gathering; group travelling or working as a unit; group united in support of a cause or policy, esp. in politics; person(s) forming one side in an agreement or dispute; one who shares in an action or plan etc.; (joc.) person. **party line** shared telephone line; set policy of a political party. **party-wall** n. wall common to two buildings or rooms.

parvenu /'pɑːvənuː/ n. upstart.

paschal /-sk-/ a. of the Passover; of Easter. **paschal lamb** lamb eaten then.

pass[1] v.t./i. (p.t. **passed**) move onward or past; go or cause to go to another person or place; send (a ball) to another player in football etc.; discharge from the body as excreta; change from one state into another; happen; occupy (time); be accepted, be currently known; be allowed or tolerated; examine and declare satisfactory; achieve the required standard in a test; go beyond; utter; (in cards) refuse one's turn. —n. passing, movement made with the hands or thing held; permit to enter or leave; critical state of affairs. **make a pass at** (colloq.) try to attract sexually. **pass away** cease; die. **pass out** (colloq.) become unconscious. **pass over** disregard. **pass up** (colloq.) refuse to accept.

pass[2] n. gap in mountains, allowing passage to the other side.

passable a. able to be traversed; just satisfactory. **passably** adv.

passage n. passing; right to pass or be a passenger; way through, esp. with a wall on each side; tube-like structure; section of a literary or musical work. **passage of arms** fight, dispute. **passageway** n.

passbook n. book recording a customer's deposits and withdrawals from a bank etc.

passenger n. person (other than the driver, pilot, or crew) travelling in a vehicle, train, ship, or aircraft; ineffective member of a team.

passer-by n. (pl. **passers-by**) person who happens to be going past.

passerine a. & n. (bird) of the order of perching birds.

passion n. strong emotion; sexual love; great enthusiasm; **the Passion** sufferings of Christ on the Cross. **passion-flower** n. climbing plant with a flower suggesting the instruments of the Passion. **passion-fruit** n. edible fruit of some kinds of this.

passionate a. full of passion, intense. **passionately** adv.

passive a. acted upon and not active; inert; not resisting; lacking initiative or forceful qualities. —n. form of a verb indicating that the subject undergoes the action (e.g. he was seen). **passively** adv., **passiveness** n., **passivity** /-'sɪv-/ n.

passkey n. key to a door or gate; master-key.

Passover n. Jewish festival commemorating the escape of Jews from slavery in Egypt; paschal lamb.

passport n. official document for use by a person travelling abroad.

password n. secret word(s), knowledge of which distinguishes friend from enemy.

past a. belonging to the time before the present, gone by. —n. past time or events; person's past life. —prep. & adv. beyond. **past master** thorough master, expert.

pasta n. dried paste made with flour, produced in various shapes; cooked dish made with this.

paste n. moist fairly stiff mixture; adhesive; edible doughy substance; hard glass-like substance used in imitation gems. —v.t.

fasten or coat with paste; (*sl.*) thrash.

pasteboard *n.* cardboard.

pastel *n.* chalk-like crayon; drawing made with this; light delicate shade of colour.

pastern *n.* part of a horse's foot between fetlock and hoof.

pasteurize *v.t.* sterilize (milk) partially by heating. **pasteurization** *n.*

pastiche /-'tiːʃ/ *n.* musical or other composition made up of selections from various sources.

pastille *n.* small flavoured sweet for sucking; lozenge.

pastime *n.* something done to pass time pleasantly.

pastor *n.* clergyman in charge of a church or congregation.

pastoral *a.* of country life; of a pastor, of spiritual guidance.

pastry *n.* dough made of flour, fat, and water, used for making pies etc.; article(s) made with this.

pasturage *n.* pasture-land.

pasture *n.* land covered with grass etc. suitable for grazing cattle; this grass. —*v.t.* graze, put (animals) to graze.

pasty[1] /'pæ-/ *n.* pastry with sweet or savoury filling, baked without a dish.

pasty[2] /'peɪ-/ *a.* (-ier, -iest) of or like paste; unhealthily pale.

pat *v.t.* (*p.t.* **patted**) tap gently with an open hand or something flat. —*n.* patting movement; sound of this; small mass of a soft substance. —*adv.* & *a.* known and ready. **stand pat** stick firmly to one's decision.

patch *n.* piece put on, esp. in mending; distinct area or period; piece of ground. —*v.t.* put patch(es) on; piece (things) together. **not a patch on** (*colloq.*) not nearly as good as. **patch up** repair; settle (a quarrel etc.).

patchwork *n.* needlework in which small pieces of cloth are joined decoratively; thing made of assorted pieces.

patchy *a.* existing in patches; uneven in quality. **patchily** *adv.*, **patchiness** *n.*

pate *n.* (old use) head.

pâté /'pæteɪ/ *n.* paste of meat etc.

patella *n.* (*pl.* -ae) kneecap.

paten *n.* plate for the bread at the Eucharist.

patent[1] /'peɪ-/ *a.* obvious; patented. —*n.t.* obtain or hold a patent for. **patent leather** leather with glossy varnished surface. **patently** *adv.*

patent[2] /'pæ- or 'peɪ-/ *n.* official right to be the sole maker or user of an invention or process; invention etc. protected by this.

patentee /peɪ- or pæ-/ *n.* holder of a patent.

paternal *a.* of a father; fatherly; related through one's father. **paternally** *adv.*

paternalism *n.* policy of making kindly provision for people's needs but giving them no responsibility. **paternalistic** *a.*

paternity *n.* fatherhood.

path *n.* way by which people pass on foot; line along which a person or thing moves; course of action.

pathetic *a.* arousing pity or sadness; miserably inadequate. **pathetically** *adv.*

pathogenic *a.* causing disease.

pathology *n.* study of disease. **pathological** *a.*, **pathologist** *n.*

pathos /'peɪ-/ *n.* pathetic quality.

patience *n.* calm endurance of annoyance or delay etc.; perseverance; card-game for one player.

patient *a.* showing patience. —*n.* person treated by a doctor or dentist etc. **patiently** *adv.*

patina *n.* attractive green incrustation on old bronze or gloss on old woodwork.

patio /'pæ-/ *n.* (*pl.* -os) paved courtyard.

patois /'pætwɑː/ *n.* dialect.

patriarch /'peɪ-/ *n.* male head of a family or tribe; bishop of high rank in certain Churches. **patriarchal** *a.*, **patriarchate** *n.*

patriarchy /ˈpeɪ-/ n. social organization in which a male is head of the family.

patrician n. member of the aristocracy, esp. in ancient Rome. —a. aristocratic.

patrimony /ˈpæ-/ n. heritage.

patriot /ˈpæ- or ˈpeɪ-/ n. patriotic person.

patriotic /pæ- or peɪ-/ a. loyally supporting one's country. **patriotically** adv., **patriotism** n.

patrol v.t. walk or travel regularly through (an area or building) to see that all is well. —n. patrolling; person(s) patrolling; unit in a Scout or Guide company.

patron /ˈpeɪ-/ n. person giving influential or financial support to a cause; regular customer. **patron saint** saint regarded as a protector. **patroness** n.fem.

patronage /ˈpæ-/ n. patron's support; patronizing behaviour.

patronize /ˈpæ-/ v.t. act as patron to; treat in a condescending way. **patronization** n.

patronymic /ˈpæ-/ n. name derived from that of a father or ancestor.

patten n. (old use) sole mounted on an iron ring etc. to raise the wearer's shoe above wet or mud.

patter[1] v.i. make a series of quick tapping sounds; run with short quick steps. —n. pattering sound.

patter[2] n. rapid glib speech.

pattern n. decorative design; model, design, or instructions showing how a thing is to be made; sample of cloth etc.; excellent example; regular manner in which things occur. **patterned** a.

patty n. small pie or pasty.

paucity n. smallness of quantity.

paunch n. belly; protruding abdomen.

pauper n. very poor person.

pauperize v.t. impoverish greatly. **pauperization** n.

pause n. temporary stop. —v.i. make a pause.

pavane n. slow stately dance.

pave v.t. cover (a road or path etc.) with stones or concrete to make a hard surface. **pave the way** prepare the way for changes etc.

pavement n. paved surface; paved path at the side of a road.

pavilion n. building on a sports ground for use by players and spectators; ornamental building.

pavlova n. meringue cake containing cream and fruit.

paw n. foot of an animal that has claws; (colloq.) hand. —v.t. strike with a paw; scrape (the ground) with a hoof; (colloq.) touch with the hands.

pawky a. (-ier, -iest) drily humorous. **pawkily** adv., **pawkiness** n.

pawl n. lever with a catch that engages with the notches of a ratchet.

pawn[1] n. chess-man of the smallest size and value; person whose actions are controlled by others.

pawn[2] v.t. deposit with a pawnbroker as security for money borrowed. —n. thing deposited as a pledge.

pawnbroker n. person licensed to lend money on the security of personal property deposited.

pawnshop n. pawnbroker's premises.

pawpaw n. edible fruit of a palm-like tropical tree; this tree.

pay v.t./i. (p.t. paid) give (money) in return for goods or services; give what is owed; be profitable or worth while; bestow; suffer (a penalty); let out (a rope) by slackening it. —n. payment; wages. **in the pay of** employed by. **pay-as-you-earn** method of collecting income tax by deducting it at source from wages or interest etc. **pay off** pay in full and be free from (a debt) or discharge (an employee); yield good results. **pay-off** n. (sl.) payment; reward, retribution, climax. **pay out** punish, be revenged on. **pay up** pay in full; pay what is demanded. **payer** n.

payable a. which must or may be paid.

PAYE abbr. pay-as-you-earn.

payee n. person to whom money is paid or is to be paid.

payload n. aircraft's or rocket's total load.

paymaster n. official who pays troops or workmen etc. **Paymaster General** head of the Treasury department through which payments are made.

payment n. paying; money etc. paid.

payola n. bribe or bribery offered in return for dishonest use of influence to promote a commercial product.

payroll n. list of a firm's employees receiving regular pay.

PC abbr. police constable; Privy Counsellor; personal computer.

pea n. plant bearing seeds in pods; its round seed used as a vegetable. **pea-green** a. & n. bright green. **pea-souper** n. (colloq.) thick yellow fog.

peace n. state of freedom from war or disturbance; treaty ending a war.

peaceable a. fond of peace, not quarrelsome; peaceful. **peaceably** adv.

peaceful a. characterized by peace. **peacefully** adv., **peacefulness** n.

peacemaker n. person who brings about peace.

peach n. round juicy fruit with a rough stone; tree bearing this; its yellowish-pink colour; (sl.) greatly admired person or thing.

peacock n. male bird with splendid plumage and a long fan-like tail. **peahen** n.fem., **peafowl** n.

pea-jacket n. sailor's short thick double-breasted overcoat.

peak n. pointed top, esp. of a mountain; projecting part of the edge of a cap; point of highest value or intensity etc. **peaked** a.

peaky a. (-ier, -iest) looking drawn and sickly.

peal n. sound of ringing bell(s); set of bells with different notes; loud burst of thunder or laughter. —v.t./i. sound in a peal.

peanut n. plant bearing underground pods with two edible seeds; this seed; (pl.) very trivial sum of money.

pear n. rounded fruit tapering towards the stalk; tree bearing this.

pearl n. round usu. white gem formed inside the shell of certain oysters; thing resembling this in shape or value or colour. **pearl barley** barley grains ground small. **pearly** a.

peasant n. person working on the land, esp. in the Middle Ages. **peasantry** n. peasants collectively.

pease pudding pudding of dried peas boiled in a cloth.

peat n. decomposed vegetable matter from bogs etc., used in horticulture or as fuel. **peaty** a.

pebble n. small smooth round stone; rock-crystal used for spectacle lenses. **pebbly** a.

pecan /ˈpiː-/ n. smooth pinkish-brown nut; tree bearing this.

peccadillo n. (pl. -oes) trivial offence.

peccary n. small wild pig of Central and South America.

peck[1] n. measure of capacity for dry goods (= 2 gallons); a lot.

peck[2] v.t./i. strike, nip, or pick up with the beak; kiss hastily. —n. pecking movement.

peckish a. (colloq.) hungry.

pectin n. gelatinous substance found in fruits etc., causing jam to set.

pectoral a. of, in, or on the chest or breast. —n. pectoral fin or muscle.

peculate /ˈpek-/ v.t. embezzle. **peculation** n., **peculator** n.

peculiar *a.* strange, eccentric; belonging exclusively to one person or place or thing; special. **peculiarly** *adv.*, **peculiarity** *n.*

pecuniary /-'kju:-/ *a.* of or in money.

pedagogue /-gɒg/ *n.* (*derog.*) person who teaches pedantically.

pedal *n.* lever operated by the foot in a vehicle or machine, or in certain musical instruments. —*v.t./i.* (*p.t. pedalled*) work the pedal(s) of; operate by pedals.

pedalo *n.* (*pl.* -os) pedal-operated pleasure-boat.

pedant /'ped-/ *n.* pedantic person. **pedantry** *n.*

pedantic /-'dæ-/ *a.* insisting on strict observance of rules and details in presenting knowledge; parading one's learning. **pedantically** *adv.*

peddle *v.t.* sell (goods) as a pedlar.

pederasty *n.* sodomy with a boy. **pederast** *n.*

pedestal *n.* base supporting a column or statue etc.

pedestrian *n.* person walking, esp. in a street. —*a.* of or for pedestrians; unimaginative, dull.

pedicure /'ped-/ *n.* care or treatment of the feet and toe-nails.

pedigree *n.* line or list of (esp. distinguished) ancestors. —*a.* (of an animal) of recorded and pure breeding.

pediment *n.* triangular part crowning the front of a building.

pedlar *n.* person who goes from house to house selling small articles.

pedometer *n.* device for estimating the distance travelled on foot.

peduncle *n.* stalk of a flower etc.

pee *v.t./i.* (*colloq.*) urinate. —*n.* (*colloq.*) urine.

peek *v.i.* & *n.* peep, glance.

peel *n.* skin of certain fruits and vegetables etc. —*v.t./i.* remove the peel of; strip off; come off in strips or layers, lose skin or bark etc. thus. **peel off** veer away from

a formation. **peeler** *n.*, **peelings** *n.pl.*

peep[1] *v.i.* look through a narrow opening; look quickly or surreptitiously; show slightly. —*n.* brief or surreptitious look. **peep-hole** *n.* small hole to peep through. **peeping Tom** furtive voyeur. **peep-show** *n.* exhibition of pictures etc. viewed through a lens in a peep-hole.

peep[2] *n.* & *v.t.* cheep.

peer[1] *v.i.* look searchingly or with difficulty or effort.

peer[2] *n.* duke, marquess, earl, viscount, or baron; one who is the equal of another in rank or merit etc. **peeress** *n.fem.*

peerage *n.* peers as a group; rank of peer or peeress.

peerless *a.* without equal, superb.

peeved *a.* (*sl.*) annoyed.

peevish *a.* irritable. **peevishly** *adv.*, **peevishness** *n.*

peewit *n.* = lapwing.

peg *n.* wooden or metal pin or stake; clip for holding clothes on a washing-line; drink or measure of spirits. —*v.t.* (*p.t. pegged*) fix or mark by means of peg(s); keep (wages or prices) at a fixed level. **off the peg** (of clothes) ready-made. **peg away** work diligently. **peg out** (*sl.*) die.

pejorative /-'dʒɒ-/ *a.* derogatory.

peke *n.* Pekingese dog.

Pekingese *n.* dog of a breed with short legs, flat face, and silky hair.

pelargonium *n.* plant with showy flowers.

pelican *n.* water-bird with a pouch in its long bill for storing fish. **pelican crossing** pedestrian crossing with lights operated by pedestrians.

pellagra *n.* deficiency disease causing cracking of the skin.

pellet *n.* small round mass of a substance; small shot. **pelleted** *a.*

pell-mell *a.* & *adv.* in a hurrying disorderly manner, headlong.

pellucid /-'lju:-/ *a.* very clear.

pelmet n. ornamental strip above a window etc.

pelota n. Basque ball-game.

pelt[1] n. an animal skin.

pelt[2] v.t./i. throw missiles at; (of rain etc.) come down fast; run fast. **at full pelt** as fast as possible.

pelvis n. framework of bones round the body below the waist. **pelvic** a.

pen[1] n. small fenced enclosure, esp. for animals. —v.t. (p.t. **penned**) shut in or as if in a pen.

pen[2] n. device with a metal point for writing with ink. —v.t. (p.t. **penned**) write (a letter etc.). **penfriend** n. friend with whom a person corresponds without meeting. **pen-name** n. author's pseudonym.

pen[3] n. female swan.

penal a. of or involving punishment.

penalize v.t. inflict a penalty on; put at a disadvantage. **penalization** n.

penalty n. punishment for breaking a law or rule or contract; disadvantage resulting from an action or quality.

penance n. act performed as an expression of penitence.

pence see **penny**.

penchant /'pãʃã/ n. liking.

pencil n. instrument containing graphite, used for drawing or writing. —v.t. (p.t. **pencilled**) write, draw, or mark with a pencil.

pendant n. ornament hung from a chain round the neck.

pendent a. hanging.

pending a. waiting to be decided or settled. —prep. during; until.

pendulous a. hanging loosely.

pendulum n. weight hung from a cord and swinging freely; rod with a weighted end that regulates a clock's movement.

penetrable a. able to be penetrated. **penetrability** n.

penetrate v.t./i. make a way into or through, pierce; see into or through. **penetration** n.

penetrating a. showing great insight; (of sound) piercing.

penguin n. flightless sea-bird of Antarctic regions, with flippers used for swimming.

penicillin /-'stl-/ n. antibiotic obtained from mould fungi.

peninsula n. piece of land almost surrounded by water. **peninsular** a.

penis /'piː-/ n. organ by which a male animal copulates and urinates.

penitent a. feeling or showing regret that one has done wrong. —n. penitent person. **penitently** adv., **penitence** n.

penitential /-'ten-/ a. of penitence or penance.

penitentiary /-'tenʃ-/ n. (US) federal prison or State prison.

pennant n. ship's long tapering flag.

penniless a. having no money, destitute.

pennon n. flag, esp. a long triangular or forked one; long streamer on a ship.

penny n. (pl. **pennies** for separate coins, **pence** for a sum of money) British bronze coin worth one-hundredth of £1; former coin worth one-twelfth of a shilling.

penny-pinching a. niggardly.

penology /piː-/ n. study of punishment and prison management. **penological** a.

pension[1] n. income consisting of a periodic payment made in consideration of past service or on retirement or widowhood etc. —v.t. pay a pension to. **pension off** dismiss with a pension.

pension[2] /'pãstõ/ n. boarding-house on the Continent.

pensionable a. entitled or (of a job) entitling one to a pension.

pensioner n. person who receives a pension.

pensive a. deep in thought. **pensively** adv., **pensiveness** n.

pent a. shut in a confined space. **pent-up** a.

pentacle n. figure (e.g. a penta-gram) used as a symbol, esp. in magic.

pentagon n. geometric figure with five sides. **pentagonal** /-'tæg-/ a.

pentagram n. five-pointed star.

pentameter /-'tæm-/ n. line of verse with five metrical feet.

Pentateuch /-tju:k/ n. first five books of the Old Testament.

pentathlon n. athletic contest in-volving five events.

Pentecost n. Jewish harvest fest-ival, 50 days after second day of Passover; Whit Sunday.

Pentecostal a. of Pentecost; (of Christian sects) seeking spiritual gifts like those of the Apostles at Pentecost, with religious fervour.

penthouse n. sloping roof sup-ported against the wall of a build-ing; dwelling (usu. with a terrace) on the roof of a tall building.

penultimate a. last but one.

penumbra n. (pl. -ae) area of par-tial shadow, esp. in an eclipse.

penury /'penjʊərɪ/ n. poverty. **penurious** a.

peony n. garden plant with large round red, pink, or white flowers.

people n.pl. human beings; per-sons; subjects of a State; persons without special rank; parents or other relatives. —n. persons composing a race or nation or community. —v.t. fill with people, populate.

PEP abbr. personal equity plan (scheme for limited tax-free in-vestment).

pep n. vigour. —v.t. (p.t. pepped) fill with vigour, enliven. **pep talk** talk urging great effort.

peplum n. short flounce from the waist of a garment.

pepper n. hot-tasting seasoning-powder made from the dried berries of certain plants; capsi-cum. —v.t. sprinkle with pepper; pelt; sprinkle. **pepper-and-salt** a. of mingled dark and light.

peppercorn n. dried black berry from which pepper is made. **peppercorn rent** very low rent.

peppermint n. a kind of mint with strong fragrant oil; this oil; sweet flavoured with this.

peppery a. like pepper; contain-ing much pepper; hot-tempered.

pepsin n. enzyme in gastric juice.

peptic a. of digestion.

per prep. for each; in accordance with; by means of. **per annum** for each year. **per capita** for each person. **per cent** in or for every hundred.

peradventure adv. (old use) per-haps.

perambulate v.t./i. walk through or round (an area). **perambula-tion** n.

perambulator n. child's pram.

perceive v.t. become aware of, see or notice.

percentage n. rate or proportion per hundred; proportion, part.

perceptible a. able to be per-ceived. **perceptibly** adv., **per-ceptibility** n.

perception n. perceiving, ability to perceive.

perceptive a. showing insight and understanding. **percep-tively** adv., **perceptiveness** n., **perceptivity** n.

perch[1] n. bird's resting-place, rod etc. for this; high seat; measure of length (5½ yds.). —v.t./i. rest or place on or as if on a perch.

perch[2] n. (pl. **perch**) edible fresh-water fish with spiny fins.

perchance adv. (old use) perhaps.

percipient a. perceptive. **per-cipience** n.

percolate v.t./i. filter, esp. through small holes; prepare in a percolator. **percolation** n.

percolator n. coffee-pot in which boiling water is circulated repeatedly through ground coffee held in a perforated drum.

percussion n. striking of one object against another. **percussion instrument** musical instrument (e.g. drum, cymbals) played by striking. **percussive** a.

perdition n. eternal damnation.

peregrination n. travelling.

peregrine n. a kind of falcon.

peremptory /-'rem-/ a. imperious. **peremptorily** adv.

perennial a. lasting a long time or for ever; constantly recurring; (of plants) living for several years. —n. perennial plant. **perennially** adv.

perestroika n. (in the USSR) restructuring of the economy etc.

perfect[1] /'pɜː-/ a. complete, entire; faultless, excellent; exact. **perfectly** adv.

perfect[2] /-'fekt/ v.t. make perfect.

perfection n. making or being perfect; person or thing considered perfect. **to perfection** perfectly.

perfectionist n. person who seeks perfection. **perfectionism** n.

perfidious /-'fɪd-/ a. treacherous, disloyal. **perfidy** /'pɜː-/ n.

perforate v.t. make hole(s) through; penetrate. **perforation** n.

perforce adv. by force of circumstances, necessarily.

perform v.t./i. carry into effect; go through (a piece of music, ceremony, etc.); function; act in a play, sing or play an instrument or do tricks etc. before an audience. **performer** n., **performance** n.

perfume n. sweet smell; fragrant liquid for applying to the body. —v.t. give a sweet smell to; apply perfume to.

perfumery /-'fjuː-/ n. perfumes.

perfunctory /-'fʌ-/ a. done or doing things without much care or interest. **perfunctorily** adv.

pergola /-'pɜː-/ n. arch of trellis-work with climbing plants trained over it.

perhaps adv. it may be, possibly.

perianth n. outer part of a flower.

pericardium n. membranous sac enclosing the heart.

perigee n. point nearest to the earth in the moon's orbit.

perihelion n. (pl. -ia) point nearest to the sun in the orbit of a comet or planet.

peril n. serious danger.

perilous a. full of risk, dangerous. **perilously** adv.

perimeter /-'rɪm-/ n. outer edge of an area; length of this.

period n. length or portion of time; occurrence of menstruation; sentence; full stop in punctuation. —a. (of dress or furniture) belonging to a past age.

periodic a. happening at intervals. **periodicity** n.

periodical a. periodic. —n. magazine etc. published at regular intervals. **periodically** adv.

peripatetic /-'tet-/ a. going from place to place.

peripheral /-'rɪf-/ a. of or on the periphery; of minor but not central importance to something.

periphery /-'rɪf-/ n. boundary, edge; fringes of a subject etc.

periphrasis /-'rɪf-/ n. (pl. -ases) circumlocution. **periphrastic** a.

periscope n. tube with mirror(s) by which a person in a trench or submarine etc. can see things otherwise out of sight.

perish v.t./i. suffer destruction, die; rot; distress or wither by cold or exposure. **perishing** a.

perishable a. liable to decay or go bad in a short time.

perisher n. (sl.) annoying person.

peritoneum /-'təʊ-/ n. membrane lining the abdominal cavity.

peritonitis *n.* inflammation of the peritoneum.

periwig *n.* (old use) wig.

periwinkle[1] *n.* trailing plant with blue or white flowers.

periwinkle[2] *n.* winkle.

perjure *v.refl.* **perjure oneself** make a perjured statement. **perjurer** *n.*

perjured *a.* involving perjury.

perjury *n.* deliberate giving of false evidence while under oath; this evidence. **perjurious** *a.*

perk[1] *v.t./i.* **perk up** (colloq.) cheer or brighten or smarten up.

perk[2] *n.* (colloq.) perquisite.

perky *a.* (-ier, -iest) (colloq.) lively and cheerful. **perkily** *adv.*, **perkiness** *n.*

perm[1] *n.* permanent artificial wave in the hair. —*v.t.* give a perm to.

perm[2] *n.* permutation. —*v.t.* make a permutation of.

permafrost *n.* permanently frozen subsoil in arctic regions.

permanent *a.* lasting indefinitely. **permanently** *adv.*, **permanence** *n.*, **permanency** *n.*

permeable *a.* able to be permeated by fluids etc. **permeability** *n.*

permeate *v.t.* pass or flow into every part of. **permeation** *n.*

permissible *a.* allowable.

permission *n.* consent or authorization to do something.

permissive *a.* giving permission; tolerant, esp. in social and sexual matters. **permissiveness** *n.*

permit[1] /-'mɪt/ *v.t.* (p.t. **permitted**) give permission to or for; make possible.

permit[2] /'pɜ:-/ *n.* written permission, esp. for entry to a place.

permutation *n.* variation of the order of or choice from a set of things.

pernicious *a.* harmful.

pernickety *a.* (colloq.) fastidious, scrupulous.

peroration *n.* lengthy speech; last part of this.

peroxide *n.* compound of hydrogen used to bleach hair. —*v.t.* bleach with this.

perpendicular *a.* at an angle of 90° to a line or surface; upright, vertical; **Perpendicular** of or in the style of architecture with vertical tracery (15th–16th century). —*n.* perpendicular line or direction. **perpendicularly** *adv.*

perpetrate *v.t.* commit (a crime), be guilty of (a blunder). **perpetration** *n.*, **perpetrator** *n.*

perpetual *a.* lasting, not ceasing. **perpetually** *adv.*

perpetuate *v.t.* preserve from being forgotten or from going out of use. **perpetuation** *n.*

perpetuity /-'tju:-/ *n.* **in perpetuity** for ever.

perplex *v.t.* bewilder, puzzle.

perplexity *n.* bewilderment.

perquisite *n.* profit or privilege given in addition to wages.

perry *n.* drink resembling cider, made from fermented pears.

persecute *v.t.* treat with hostility esp. because of religious beliefs; harass. **persecution** *n.*, **persecutor** *n.*

persevere *v.i.* continue steadfastly in spite of difficulties. **perseverance** *n.*

Persian *a.* & *n.* (native, language) of Persia.

persiflage /-'fla:ʒ/ *n.* banter.

persimmon *n.* American or East Asian tree; its edible orange plum-like fruit.

persist *v.i.* continue firmly or obstinately; continue to exist. **persistent** *a.*, **persistently** *adv.*, **persistence** *n.*, **persistency** *n.*

person *n.* individual human or divine being; one's body; (in grammar) one of the three classes of personal pronouns and verb-forms, referring to the person(s) speaking, spoken to, or spoken of. **in person** physically present.

persona /-'səʊ-/ *n.* (pl. **-ae**) personality as perceived by others.

personable /'pɜː-/ a. good-looking.

personage n. person, esp. an important one.

persona grata /-səʊnə 'grɑː-/ (pl. **-nae -tae**) acceptable person. **persona non grata** unacceptable person.

personal a. of one's own; of or involving a person's private life; referring to a person; done in person. **personally** adv.

personality n. person's distinctive character; person with distinctive qualities; celebrity; (pl.) personal remarks.

personalize v.t. identify as belonging to a particular person. **personalization** n.

personate v.t. play the part of; pretend to be. **personation** n.

personify v.t. represent in human form or as having human characteristics; embody in one's behaviour. **personification** n.

personnel n. employees, staff.

perspective n. art of drawing so as to give an effect of solidity and relative position; apparent relationship between visible objects as to position, distance, etc. **in perspective** according to the rules of perspective; not distorting a thing's relative importance.

perspicacious a. showing great insight. **perspicaciously** adv., **perspicacity** n.

perspicuous a. expressed or expressing things clearly. **perspicuously** adv., **perspicuity** n.

perspire v.i. sweat. **perspiration** n.

persuade v.t. cause (a person) to believe or do something by reasoning with him or her. **persuader** n.

persuasion n. persuading; persuasiveness; belief.

persuasive a. able or trying to persuade people. **persuasively** adv., **persuasiveness** n.

pert a. cheeky; (US) lively. **pertly** adv., **pertness** n.

pertain v.i. be relevant; belong as a part.

pertinacious a. persistent and determined. **pertinaciously** adv., **pertinacity** n.

pertinent a. pertaining, relevant. **pertinently** adv., **pertinence** n.

perturb v.t. disturb greatly, make uneasy. **perturbation** n.

peruke /-'ruːk/ n. (old use) wig.

peruse /-'ruːz/ v.t. read carefully. **perusal** n.

pervade v.t. spread throughout (a thing). **pervasive** a.

perverse a. obstinately doing something different from what is reasonable or required. **perversely** adv., **perverseness** n., **perversity** n.

pervert [1] /-'vɜːt/ v.t. misapply, lead astray, corrupt. **perversion** n.

pervert [2] /'pɜː-/ n. perverted person.

peseta /-'set-/ n. unit of money in Spain.

peso /'peɪ-/ n. (pl. **-os**) unit of money in several South American countries.

pessary n. device placed in the vagina as a contraceptive or support for the uterus; vaginal suppository.

pessimism n. tendency to take a gloomy view of things. **pessimist** n., **pessimistic** a., **pessimistically** adv.

pest n. troublesome person or thing; insect or animal harmful to plants, stored food, etc.

pester v.t. annoy continually, esp. with requests or questions.

pesticide n. substance used to destroy harmful insects etc.

pestilence n. deadly epidemic disease. **pestilential** a.

pestle n. club-shaped instrument for pounding things to powder.

pesto n. sauce of crushed basil, garlic, pine nuts, olive oil, and served with pasta.

pet n. tame animal treated with affection; darling, favourite. —a. kept as a pet; favourite. —v.t. (p.t.

petted) treat with affection; fondle. **pet name** name used affectionately.

petal n. one of the bright or delicately coloured outer parts of a flower-head.

petard n. (old use) explosive device.

peter v.i. **peter out** dwindle away.

petersham n. strong corded ribbon.

petiole /'pet-/ n. leaf-stalk.

petite /pə'ti:t/ a. small and dainty.

petition n. formal written request, esp. one signed by many people. —v.t. make a petition to. **petitioner** n.

petrel n. a kind of sea bird.

petrify v.t./i. change into a stony mass; paralyse with astonishment or fear. **petrifaction** n.

petrochemical n. chemical substance obtained from petroleum or gas.

petrodollar n. dollar earned by a petroleum-exporting country.

petrol n. inflammable liquid made from petroleum for use as fuel in internal-combustion engines.

petroleum n. mineral oil found underground, refined for use as fuel or in dry-cleaning etc. **petroleum jelly** greasy substance obtained from petroleum, used as a lubricant.

petticoat n. dress-length undergarment worn hanging from the shoulders or waist beneath a dress or skirt.

pettifogging a. trivial; quibbling about unimportant details.

petting n. affectionate treatment; fondling.

pettish a. peevish, irritable. **pettishly** adv., **pettishness** n.

petty a. (-ier, -iest) unimportant; minor, on a small scale; small-minded. **petty cash** money kept by an office etc. for or from small payments. **petty officer** NCO in the Royal Navy. **pettily** adv., **pettiness** n.

petulant a. peevish. **petulantly** adv., **petulance** n.

petunia n. garden plant with funnel-shaped flowers.

pew n. long bench-like seat in a church; (colloq.) seat.

pewter n. grey alloy of tin with lead or other metal; articles made of this.

peyote /-'jəʊtɪ/ n. Mexican cactus; hallocinogenic drug made from this.

phaeton /'feɪt-/ n. old type of open horse-drawn carriage.

phalanger n. Australian tree-dwelling marsupial.

phalanx n. compact mass esp. of people.

phallic /'fæ-/ a. of the penis as symbolizing generative power.

phantasm n. phantom. **phantasmal** a.

phantasmagoria /-'gɔ:-/ n. shifting scene of real or imaginary figures. **phantasmagoric** a.

phantom n. ghost.

Pharaoh /'feərəʊ/ n. title of the king of ancient Egypt.

Pharisee n. member of an ancient Jewish sect; self-righteous person. **pharisaical** /-'seɪ-/ a.

pharmaceutical /-'sju:t-/ a. of or engaged in pharmacy.

pharmacist n. person skilled in pharmacy.

pharmacology n. study of the action of drugs. **pharmacological** a., **pharmacologist** n.

pharmacopoeia /-'pi:ə/ n. list or stock of drugs.

pharmacy n. preparation and dispensing of medicinal drugs; pharmacist's shop, dispensary.

pharyngitis n. inflammation of the pharynx.

pharynx /'fæ-/ n. cavity at the back of the nose and throat. **pharyngeal** a.

phase n. stage of change or development. —v.t. carry out (a programme etc.) in stages. **phase**

in or **out** bring gradually into or out of use.

Ph.D. *abbr.* Doctor of Philosophy.

pheasant *n.* game-bird with bright feathers.

phenobarbitone *n.* sedative drug.

phenomenal *a.* extraordinary, remarkable. **phenomenally** *adv.*

phenomenon *n.* (*pl.* **-ena**) fact, occurrence, or change perceived by the senses or the mind; remarkable person or thing.

phew *int.* exclamation of disgust, relief, etc.

phial /'faɪəl/ *n.* small bottle.

philander *v.i.* (of a man) flirt. **philanderer** *n.*

philanthropy *n.* love of mankind, esp. shown in benevolent acts. **philanthropist** *n.*, **philanthropic** /-'θrɒp-/ *a.*, **philanthropically** *adv.*

philately /-'læta-/ *n.* stamp-collecting. **philatelic** *a.*, **philatelist** *n.*

philharmonic /-lɑːm-/ *a.* (in names of orchestras etc.) devoted to music.

Philippine *a.* of the Philippine Islands.

philistine /-tam/ *a.* & *n.* uncultured (person).

philology *n.* study of languages. **philologist** *n.*, **philological** *a.*

philosopher *n.* person skilled in philosophy; philosophical person.

philosophical *a.* of philosophy; bearing misfortune calmly. **philosophically** *adv.*

philosophize *v.i.* theorize; moralize.

philosophy *n.* system or study of the basic truths and principles of the universe, life, and morals, and of human understanding of these; person's principles.

philtre *n.* magic potion.

phlebitis /flɪ'baɪ-/ *n.* inflammation of the walls of a vein.

phlegm /flem/ *n.* thick mucus in the bronchial passages, ejected by coughing.

phlegmatic /fleg-/ *a.* not easily excited or agitated; sluggish, apathetic. **phlegmatically** *adv.*

phlox /flɒks/ *n.* plant bearing a cluster of red, purple, or white flowers.

phobia *n.* lasting abnormal fear or great dislike. **phobic** *a.* & *n.*

Phoenician /fɪ'nɪʃ-/ *a.* & *n.* (member, language) of an ancient Semitic people of the east Mediterranean.

phoenix /'fiːn-/ *n.* mythical Arabian bird said to burn itself and rise young again from its ashes.

phone *n.* & *v.t./i.* (*colloq.*) telephone. **phone book** telephone directory. **phone-in** *n.* broadcast programme in which listeners participate by telephoning the studio.

phonecard *n.* card with prepaid units for use in a cardphone.

phonetic *a.* of or representing speech-sounds; (of spelling) corresponding to pronunciation. **phonetically** *adv.*

phonetics *n.* study or (as *pl.*) representation of speech-sounds. **phonetician** *n.*

phoney *a.* (**-ier, -iest**) (*sl.*) sham. —*n.* (*sl.*) phoney person or thing.

phonograph *n.* early form of gramophone.

phonology *n.* study of sounds in a language. **phonological** *a.*

phosphate *n.* fertilizer containing phosphorus.

phosphoresce *v.i.* be phosphorescent.

phosphorescent *a.* luminous. **phosphorescence** *n.*

phosphorus *n.* non-metallic chemical element; wax-like form of this appearing luminous in the dark.

photo *n.* (*pl.* **-os**) (*colloq.*) photograph. **photo finish** close finish where the winner is decided by a photograph.

photocopy *n.* photographed copy of a document. —*v.t.* make a photocopy of. **photocopier** *n.*

photoelectric cell electronic device emitting an electric current when light falls on it.

photogenic /-'dʒen-/ *a.* coming out attractively in photographs.

photograph *n.* picture formed by the chemical action of light or other radiation on sensitive material. —*v.t./i.* take a photograph of; come out (well or badly) when photographed. **photographer** *n.*, **photography** *n.*, **photographic** *a.*, **photographically** *adv.*

photolithography *n.* lithographic process with plates made photographically.

photosynthesis /-'sɪn-/ *n.* process by which green plants use sunlight to convert carbon dioxide and water into complex substances.

phrase *n.* group of words forming a unit, esp. within a sentence or clause; unit in a melody. —*v.t.* express in words; divide (music) into phrases. **phrasal** *a.*

phraseology *n.* the way something is worded. **phraseological** *a.*

phut *adv.* **go phut** burst or explode with this sound; (*colloq.*) come to nothing.

phylactery *n.* small box containing Hebrew texts, worn by Jewish men at prayer.

phylum *n.* major division of the plant or animal kingdom.

physic *n.* (*old use*) medicine.

physical *a.* of the body; of matter or the laws of nature; of physics. **physical chemistry** use of physics to study substances and their reactions. **physical geography** study of earth's natural features. **physically** *adv.*

physician *n.* doctor, esp. one specializing in medicine as distinct from surgery.

physicist *n.* expert in physics.

physics *n.* study of the properties and interactions of matter and energy.

physiognomy /-'ɒn-/ *n.* features of a person's face. **physiognomist** *n.*

physiology *n.* study of the bodily functions of living organisms. **physiological** *a.*, **physiologist** *n.*

physiotherapy *n.* treatment of an injury etc. by massage and exercises. **physiotherapist** *n.*

physique /-'ziːk/ *n.* person's physical build and muscular development.

pi /paɪ/ *n.* Greek letter π used as a symbol for the ratio of a circle's circumference to its diameter (about 3.14).

pianist *n.* person who plays the piano.

piano *n.* (*pl.* -os) musical instrument with metal strings struck by hammers operated by pressing the keys of a keyboard.

pianoforte /-'fɔːtɪ/ *n.* piano.

piazza /pɪ'ætsə/ *n.* public square in an Italian town.

pibroch /'piːbrɒk/ *n.* martial or funeral music for bagpipes.

picador *n.* mounted bullfighter with a lance.

picaresque *a.* (of fiction) dealing with the adventures of rogues.

piccalilli *n.* pickle of chopped vegetables and hot spices.

piccaninny *n.* Black child; Australian Aboriginal child.

piccolo *n.* (*pl.* -os) small flute.

pick[1] *n.* pickaxe; plectrum.

pick[2] *v.t./i.* select; use a pointed instrument or the fingers or beak etc. to make (a hole) in or remove bits from (a thing); detach (flower or fruit) from the plant bearing it. —*n.* picking; selection; best part. **pick-a-back** *adv.* piggy-back. **pick a lock** open it with a tool other than a key. **pick a pocket** steal its contents. **pick a quarrel** provoke one deliberately. **pick holes in** find fault with. **pick off** pluck off; shoot or destroy one by one. **pick on** nag, find fault with; select. **pick out** select as a target, esp. for harassment. **pick up** lift or take up; call for and take away; acquire or become acquainted with casually; succeed in seeing or hearing by use of apparatus; recover health, improve; recover (speed). **pick-up** *n.* acquaintance met casually; small open motor truck; stylus-holder in a record-player. **picker** *n.*

pickaxe *n.* heavy tool with a pointed iron bar mounted at right angles to its handle, used for breaking ground etc.

picket *n.* person(s) stationed by trade unionists to dissuade others from entering a building etc. during a strike; party of sentries; pointed stake set in the ground. —*v.t.* (*p.t.* **picketed**) station or act as a picket on (a building etc.); secure or enclose with stakes.

pickings *n.pl.* scraps of good food etc. remaining; odd gains or perquisites.

pickle *n.* vegetables preserved in vinegar or brine; this liquid; (*colloq.*) plight, mess. —*v.t.* preserve in pickle.

pickpocket *n.* thief who picks people's pockets.

picky *a.* (**-ier, -iest**) (*colloq.*) choosy. **pickiness** *n.*

picnic *n.* informal outdoor meal. —*v.i.* (*p.t.* **picnicked**) take part in a picnic. **picnicker** *n.*

picot /'pi:kəʊ/ *n.* small loop of twisted thread in an ornamental edging.

picric acid bitter yellow substance used in dyeing and explosives.

Pict *n.* member of an ancient people of north Britain. **Pictish** *a.*

pictograph *n.* pictorial symbol used as a form of writing.

pictorial *a.* of or in or like a picture or pictures; illustrated. —*n.* newspaper etc. with many pictures. **pictorially** *adv.*

picture *n.* representation of person(s) or object(s) etc. made by painting, drawing, or photography etc.; thing that looks beautiful; scene; description; cinema film. —*v.t.* depict; imagine.

picturesque /-'resk/ *a.* forming a pleasant scene; (of words or description) very expressive.

pidgin *n.* **pidgin English** simplified form of English with elements of a local language.

pie *n.* baked dish of meat, fish, or fruit covered with pastry or other crust. **pie chart** diagram representing quantities as sectors of a circle.

piebald *a.* (of a horse) with irregular patches of white and dark colour.

piece *n.* part, portion; thing regarded as a unit; musical, literary, or artistic composition; coin; small object used in board-games; slice of bread; unit of work. —*v.t.* make by putting pieces together. **of a piece** of the same kind; consistent. **piecework** *n.* work paid according to the quantity done.

pièce de résistance /pies də rer'zīstās/ choicest thing.

piecemeal *a.* & *adv.* done piece by piece, part at a time.

pied /paid/ *a.* particoloured.

pied-à-terre /pjeɪtɑ:'teə(r)/ *n.* (*pl.* **pieds-à-terre**, *pr.* pjeɪt-) small place for use as temporary quarters when needed.

pier *n.* structure built out into the sea, esp. as a promenade; pillar or similar structure supporting an arch or bridge.

pierce *v.t.* go into or through like a sharp-pointed instrument; make (a hole) in; force one's way into or through.

piercing *a.* (of cold or wind) penetrating sharply; (of sound) shrilly audible. **piercingly** *adv.*

piety *n.* piousness.

piffle *n.* (*sl.*) nonsense.

pig n. animal with short legs, cloven hooves, and a blunt snout; (colloq.) greedy or unpleasant person; pig-iron. **pig-iron** n. crude iron from a smelting-furnace.

pigeon n. bird of the dove family; (colloq.) person's business or responsibility.

pigeon-hole n. small compartment in a desk or cabinet. —v.t. put away for future consideration or indefinitely; classify.

piggery n. pig-breeding establishment; pigsty.

piggy a. like a pig. **piggy bank** money box shaped like a pig.

piggyback adv. & n. (ride) on a person's back or on top of a larger object.

pigheaded a. obstinate.

piglet n. young pig.

pigment n. colouring-matter. —v.t. colour (skin or tissue) with natural colouring-matter. **pigmentation** n.

pigskin n. leather made from the skin of pigs.

pigsty n. partly covered pen for pigs.

pigtail n. long hair worn in a plait at the back of the head.

pike n. long wooden shaft with a pointed metal head; peaked summit; (pl. **pike**) large voracious freshwater fish.

pikelet n. crumpet.

pikestaff n. shaft of a pike. **plain as a pikestaff** quite plain or obvious.

pilaff /-ˈlæf/ n. = pilau.

pilaster /-ˈlæ-/ n. rectangular usu. ornamental column.

pilau /-ˈlau/ n. oriental dish of rice with meat, spices, etc.

pilchard n. small sea-fish related to the herring.

pile¹ n. a number of things lying one upon another; heap; pyre; (colloq.) large amount; lofty building. —v.t./i. heap, stack, load; crowd. **pile up** accumulate; run aground; crash (a vehicle).

pile-up n. collision of several vehicles.

pile² n. heavy beam driven vertically into ground as a support for a building or bridge.

pile³ n. cut or uncut loops on the surface of fabric.

pile⁴ n. haemorrhoid.

pilfer v.t./i. steal (small items or in small quantities). **pilferage** n.

pilgrim n. person who travels to a sacred place as an act of religious devotion. **pilgrimage** n.

pill n. small ball or piece of medicinal substance for swallowing whole; **the pill** contraceptive pill.

pillage n. & v.t. plunder.

pillar n. vertical structure used as a support or ornament; thing resembling this. **pillar-box** n. hollow pillar about 5ft. high into which letters may be posted.

pillbox n. small round box for pills; thing shaped like this.

pillion n. saddle for a passenger seated behind the driver of a motor cycle. **ride pillion** ride on this.

pillory n. wooden frame with holes for the head and hands, in which offenders were formerly placed for exposure to public ridicule. —v.t. expose to public ridicule or scorn.

pillow n. cushion used (esp. in bed) for supporting the head. —v.t. rest on or as if on a pillow.

pillowcase, pillowslip ns. cloth cover for a pillow.

pilot n. person who operates an aircraft's flying-controls; person qualified to steer ships into or out of a harbour; guide. —v.t. (p.t. **piloted**) act as pilot of; guide.

pilot-light n. small burning jet of gas which lights a larger burner; electric indicator light.

pimento n. (pl. **-os**) allspice; sweet pepper.

pimp n. man who solicits clients for a prostitute or brothel.

pimpernel /'pɪm-/ n. wild plant with small red, blue, or white flowers.

pimple n. small inflamed spot on the skin. **pimply** a.

PIN abbr. personal identification number (used in withdrawals from a cashpoint etc.).

pin n. short pointed piece of metal usu. with a round broadened head, used for fastening things together; peg or stake of wood or metal. —v.t. (p.t. **pinned**) fasten with pin(s); transfix; hold down and make unable to move; attach, fix. **pin down** establish clearly; bind by a promise. **pins and needles** tingling sensation. **pintable** n. board for pinball. **pintuck** n. narrow ornamental tuck. **pin-up** n. (colloq.) picture of an attractive or famous person.

pinafore n. apron. **pinafore dress** dress without collar or sleeves, worn over a blouse or jumper.

pinball n. game played with a ball on a sloping board set with pins or targets.

pince-nez /'pæs neɪ/ n. (pl. **pince-nez**) glasses that clip on the nose.

pincers n. tool with pivoted jaws for gripping and pulling things; claw-like part of a lobster etc.

pinch v.t./i. squeeze between two surfaces, esp. between finger and thumb; stint; (sl.) steal; (sl.) arrest. —n. pinching; stress of circumstances; small amount. **at a pinch** in time of difficulty or necessity.

pinchbeck n. imitation gold. —a. sham.

pincushion n. small pad for sticking pins in to keep them ready for use.

pine[1] n. evergreen tree with needle-shaped leaves; its wood.

pine[2] v.i. lose strength through grief or yearning; feel an intense longing.

pineal gland conical gland in the brain.

pineapple n. large juicy tropical fruit; plant bearing this.

ping n. short sharp ringing sound. —v.i. make this sound. **pinger** n.

ping-pong n. table tennis.

pinion[1] n. bird's wing. —v.t. restrain by holding or binding the arms or legs.

pinion[2] n. small cog-wheel.

pink[1] a. pale red. —n. pink colour; garden plant with fragrant pink, white, or variegated flowers. **in the pink** (sl.) in very good health. **pinkness** n.

pink[2] v.t. pierce slightly; cut a zig-zag edge on (fabric).

pink[3] v.i. (of an engine) make slight explosive sounds when running imperfectly.

pinnace n. ship's small boat.

pinnacle n. pointed ornament on a roof; peak; highest point.

pinnate a. having leaflets on each side of the leaf-stalk.

pinpoint v.t. locate precisely.

pinprick n. small annoyance.

pinstripe n. very narrow stripe in cloth fabric. **pinstriped** a.

pint n. measure for liquids, one-eighth of a gallon.

pinta n. (colloq.) pint of milk.

pintle n. bolt or pin on which something pivots.

pioneer n. person who is one of the first to explore a new region or subject. —v.t./i. be a pioneer (in).

pious a. devout in religion; ostentatiously virtuous. **piously** adv., **piousness** n.

pip[1] n. small seed in fruit.

pip[2] n. spot on a domino, dice, or playing-card; star on an army officer's uniform.

pip[3] v.t. (p.t. **pipped**) (colloq.) hit with a shot; defeat.

pip[4] n. short high-pitched sound.

pip[5] n. disease of poultry etc.; **the pip** (sl.) fit of disgust or bad temper.

pipe n. tube through which something can flow; tube by which sound is produced, (pl.) bagpipes;

pipeclay narrow tube with a bowl at one end for smoking tobacco. —v.t. convey through pipe(s); transmit (music etc.) by wire or cable; play (music) on pipe(s), lead by sounding pipe(s); utter in a shrill voice; ornament with piping. **pipe down** (colloq.) be quiet.

pipeclay n. fine white clay.

pipedream n. impractical hope or scheme.

pipeline n. long pipe for conveying petroleum etc. to a distance; channel of supply or information. **in the pipeline** on the way, in preparation.

piper n. player of pipe(s).

pipette n. slender tube for transferring or measuring small amounts of liquid.

piping n. length of pipe; pipes; ornamental pipe-like fold or line. **piping hot** very hot.

pipit n. small bird resembling a lark.

pippin n. a kind of apple.

piquant /'piːk-/ a. pleasantly sharp in taste or smell; mentally stimulating. **piquantly** adv., **piquancy** n.

pique /piːk/ v.t. hurt the pride of; stimulate (curiosity etc.). —n. feeling of hurt pride.

piqué /'piːkeɪ/ n. firm usu. cotton fabric with a corded effect.

piquet /-'ket/ n. card-game for two players.

piranha /pɪ'rɑːnə/ n. fierce tropical American freshwater fish.

pirate n. person on a ship who robs another ship at sea or raids a coast; one who infringes copyright or business rights, or broadcasts without due authorization. —v.t. reproduce (a book etc.) without due authorization. **piratical** a., **piracy** /'paɪr-/ n.

pirouette /-rʊ'et/ n. & v.i. spin on the toe in dancing.

piscatorial a. of fishing.

piscina /-'siː-/ n. (pl. **-ae**) basin near the altar in a church.

pistachio /-'tɑːʃ-/ n. (pl. **-os**) a kind of nut.

piste /piːst/ n. ski-track.

pistil n. seed-producing part of a flower.

pistol n. small gun.

piston n. sliding disc or cylinder inside a tube, esp. as part of an engine or pump.

pit n. hole in the ground; coalmine; sunken area; seats on the ground floor of a theatre, behind the stalls; place where race-cars are refuelled etc. during a race. —v.t. (p.t. **pitted**) make pits or depressions in; match or set in competition.

pit-a-pat n. & adv. (with) a sound of light quick steps.

pitch[1] n. dark tarry substance. **pitch-black, pitch-dark** adjs.

pitch[2] v.t./i. throw; erect (a tent or camp); set at a particular slope or level; fall heavily, strike the ground; (of a ship or vehicle) plunge forward and back alternately; (sl.) tell (a yarn or excuse). —n. process of pitching; steepness; intensity; degree of highness or lowness of a music-note or voice; place where a street trader or performer is stationed; playing-field. **pitched battle** one fought from prepared positions. **pitch in** (colloq.) set to work vigorously. **pitch into** (colloq.) attack or reprimand vigorously.

pitchblende n. mineral ore (uranium oxide) yielding radium.

pitcher[1] n. baseball player who delivers the ball to the batter.

pitcher[2] n. large usu. earthenware jug.

pitchfork n. long-handled fork for lifting and tossing hay. —v.t. thrust (a person) into a position or office etc.

piteous a. deserving or arousing pity. **piteously** adv.

pitfall n. unsuspected danger or difficulty.

pith n. spongy tissue in stems or fruits; essential part.

pithy a. (**-ier, -iest**) like pith, containing much pith; brief and full of meaning. **pithily** adv.

pitiable a. pitiful. **pitiably** adv.

pitiful a. deserving or arousing pity or contempt. **pitifully** adv.

pitiless a. showing no pity.

piton /'pi:tɒn/ n. spike or peg used in rock-climbing.

pitta n. a kind of flat bread.

pittance n. very small allowance of money.

pituitary gland /-'tju:-/ gland at the base of the brain, with important influence on bodily growth and functions.

pity n. feeling of sorrow for another's suffering; cause for regret. —v.t. feel pity for. **take pity on** pity and try to help.

pivot n. central point or shaft on which a thing turns or swings. —v.t./i. (p.t. **pivoted**) turn or place to turn on a pivot. **pivotal** a.

pixel n. each minute area of uniform illumination in an image on a VDU screen.

pixie n. a kind of fairy. **pixie hood** woman's or child's pointed hood.

pizza /'pi:tsə/ n. layer of dough baked with a savoury topping.

pizzicato /pɪtsɪ'kɑ:-/ adv. by plucking the strings of a violin etc. instead of using the bow.

placard n. poster or similar notice. —v.t. put up placards on.

placate v.t. conciliate. **placation** n., **placatory** a.

place n. particular part of space or of an area or book etc.; particular town, district, building, etc.; position; duty appropriate to one's rank; step in reasoning. —v.t. put into a place, find a place for; locate, identify; put or give (an order for goods etc.). **be placed** (in a race) be among the first three.

placebo /-'si:-/ n. (pl. **-os**) harmless substance given as medicine, esp. to humour a patient.

placement n. placing.

placenta /-'sen-/ n. (pl. **-ae**) organ that develops in the womb during pregnancy and nourishes the foetus. **placental** a.

placid a. calm and peaceful, not easily upset. **placidly** adv., **placidity** n.

placket n. opening in a skirt to make it easy to put on and take off.

plagiarize /'pleɪdʒ-/ v.t. take and use (another's writings etc.) as one's own. **plagiarizer** n., **plagiarism** n., **plagiarist** n.

plague n. deadly contagious disease; infestation; (colloq.) nuisance. —v.t. (colloq.) annoy, pester.

plaice n. (pl. **plaice**) a kind of flat-fish used as food.

plaid /plæd, Sc. pr. pleɪd/ n. long piece of woollen cloth worn as part of Highland costume; tartan pattern.

plain a. (**-er, -est**) unmistakable, easy to see or hear or understand; not elaborate or luxurious; in exact terms, candid; ordinary, without affectation; not good-looking. —adv. plainly. —n. large area of level country; ordinary stitch in knitting. **plain chocolate** that made without milk. **plain clothes** civilian clothes, not a uniform. **plain sailing** easy course of action. **plainly** adv., **plainness** n.

plainsong n. medieval type of church music for voices, without regular rhythm.

plaintiff n. party that brings an action in a court of law.

plaintive a. sounding sad. **plaintively** adv.

plait /plæt/ v.t. weave (three or more strands) into one rope-like length. —n. something plaited.

plan n. diagram showing the relative position of parts of a building or town etc.; method thought out in advance. —v.t./i. (p.t. **planned**) make a plan (of). **planner** n.

planchette /-ʃet/ *n.* small board on castors, with a pencil, for use in spiritualist seances.

plane[1] *n.* tall spreading tree with broad leaves.

plane[2] *n.* level surface; imaginary surface of this kind; level of thought or existence or development; aeroplane. —*a.* level.

plane[3] *n.* tool for smoothing wood or metal by paring shavings off it. —*v.t.* smooth or pare with this.

planet *n.* any of the heavenly bodies moving round the sun. **planetary** *a.*

planetarium *n.* room with a domed ceiling on which lights are projected to show the positions of the stars and planets.

plangent *a.* resonant, loud and mournful. **plangently** *adv.*, **plangency** *n.*

plank *n.* long flat piece of timber.

plankton *n.* minute forms of organic life floating in the sea or in rivers and lakes.

plant *n.* living organism with neither the power of movement nor special organs of digestion; small plant as distinct from a tree or shrub; factory; its machinery. —*v.t.* place in soil for growing; place in position. **planter** *n.*

plantain[1] *n.* herb whose seed is used as birdseed.

plantain[2] *n.* tropical banana-like fruit; tree bearing this.

plantation *n.* area planted with trees or cultivated plants; estate on which cotton, tobacco, or tea etc. is cultivated.

plaque /-k/ *n.* strip of metal or porcelain fixed on a wall as an ornament or memorial; film forming on teeth and gums.

plasma *n.* colourless fluid part of blood; a kind of gas. **plasmic** *a.*

plaster *n.* soft mixture of lime, sand, and water etc. used for coating walls; plaster of Paris, cast made from this; sticking-plaster. —*v.t.* cover with plaster; coat, daub, make smooth with

a fixative. **plaster of Paris** white paste made from gypsum. **plasterer** *n.*

plasterboard *n.* board with a plaster core.

plastic *a.* able to be moulded; giving form to clay or wax etc.; made of plastic. —*n.* synthetic substance moulded to a permanent shape. **plastic surgery** operation(s) to replace injured or defective external tissue. **plasticity** *n.*

Plasticine *n.* [P.] plastic substance used for modelling.

plate *n.* almost flat usu. circular utensil for holding food; articles of gold, silver, or other metal; flat thin sheet of metal, glass, or other material; illustration on special paper in a book; that part of a denture which fits against the palate or gums; (*colloq.*) denture. —*v.t.* cover or coat with metal. **plate glass** thick glass for windows etc. **plateful** *n.* (*pl.* **-fuls**).

plateau *n.* (*pl.* **-eaux**, *pr.* -əuz) area of level high ground; steady state following an increase.

platelayer *n.* person who fixes and repairs railway tracks.

platen /'plæ-/ *n.* roller of a typewriter or printing press, against which the paper is held.

platform *n.* raised level surface or area, esp. from which a speaker addresses an audience.

platinum *n.* silver-white metal that does not tarnish. **platinum blonde** woman with very light blonde hair.

platitude *n.* commonplace remark. **platitudinous** *a.*

platonic *a.* involving affection but not sexual love between a man and a woman.

platoon *n.* subdivision of a military company.

platter *n.* large plate for food.

platypus *n.* (*pl.* **-puses**) Australian animal with a duck-like beak that lays eggs but suckles its young.

plaudits *n.pl.* applause, expression of approval.

plausible *a.* seeming probable but not proved; persuasive but deceptive. **plausibly** *adv.,* **plausibility** *n.*

play *v.t./i.* occupy oneself in (a game) or in other recreational activity; compete against in a game; move (a piece) or put (a card) or strike (a ball) in a game; act in a drama etc., act the part of; perform (music), perform on (a record-player or recording etc.) to produce sound; move lightly, allow (light or water) to fall on something; allow (a hooked fish) to struggle against the line. —*n.* playing; activity, operation; literary work for stage or broadcast performance; free movement. **play at** perform in a trivial or half-hearted way. **play down** minimize the importance of. **play off** oppose (one person) against another to serve one's own interests. **play on** affect and make use of (a person's sympathy). **play on words** pun. **play-pen** *n.* portable enclosure for a young child to play in. **play safe** not take risks. **play the game** behave honourably. **play up** play vigorously; (*colloq.*) be unruly, annoy by doing this. **play up to** try to encourage or win the favour of by flattery. **playhouse** *n.*

playboy *n.* pleasure-loving usu. rich man.

playfellow *n.* playmate.

playful *a.* full of fun; in a mood for play, not serious. **playfully** *adv.,* **playfulness** *n.*

playground *n.* piece of ground for children to play in.

playgroup *n.* group of preschool children who regularly together under supervision.

playhouse *n.* theatre.

playing-card *n.* one of a pack or set of (usu. 52) pieces of pasteboard used in card-games.

playing-field *n.* field used for outdoor games.

playmate *n.* child's companion in play.

plaything *n.* toy.

playwright *n.* writer of plays.

plc *abbr.* (also **PLC**) Public Limited Company.

plea *n.* defendant's answer (esp. 'guilty' or 'not guilty') to a charge in a lawcourt; appeal, entreaty; excuse.

pleach *v.t.* interlace (esp. branches).

plead *v.t./i.* give as one's plea; put forward (a case) in a lawcourt; make an appeal or entreaty; put forward as an excuse.

pleasant *a.* pleasing; having an agreeable manner. **pleasantly** *adv.,* **pleasantness** *n.*

pleasantry *n.* friendly or humorous remark.

please *v.t./i.* give pleasure to; be so kind as to; think fit. —*adv.* polite word of request. **please oneself** do as one chooses.

pleased *a.* feeling or showing pleasure or satisfaction.

pleasurable *a.* causing pleasure. **pleasurably** *adv.*

pleasure *n.* feeling of satisfaction or joy; source of this; desire.

pleat *n.* flat fold of cloth. —*v.t.* make a pleat or pleats in.

plebeian /pli'bi:ən/ *a.* & *n.* (member) of the lower social classes.

plebiscite /'plebɪsɪt/ *n.* referendum.

plectrum *n.* small piece of metal, bone, or ivory for plucking the strings of a musical instrument.

pledge *n.* thing deposited as a guarantee (e.g. that a debt will be paid) and liable to be forfeited in case of failure; token of something; solemn promise. —*v.t.* deposit as a pledge; promise solemnly; drink a toast to.

plenary /'pli:-/ *a.* entire; attended by all members.

plenipotentiary /-'ten-/ *a.* & *n.* (envoy) with full powers to take action.

plenitude *n.* abundance, completeness.

plentiful *a.* existing in large amounts. **plentifully** *adv.*

plenty *n.* enough and more. —*adv.* (*colloq.*) quite, fully.

plenteous *a.*

pleonasm /'pliːən-/ *n.* expression in which certain words are redundant, as in *a false untruth*. **pleonastic** *a.*

plethora /'pleθ-/ *n.* over-abundance.

pleurisy *n.* inflammation of the membrane round the lungs.

pliable *a.* flexible. **pliability** *n.*

pliant *a.* pliable. **pliancy** *n.*

pliers *n.pl.* pincers with flat surfaces for gripping things.

plight[1] *n.* predicament.

plight[2] *v.t.* (*old use*) pledge, promise.

plimsoll *n.* canvas sports shoe.

Plimsoll line *or* **mark** mark on a ship's side showing the legal water-level when loaded.

plinth *n.* slab forming the base of a column or a support for a vase etc.

PLO *abbr.* Palestine Liberation Organization.

plod *v.i.* (*p.t.* **plodded**) walk doggedly, trudge; work slowly but steadily. —*n.* plodding walk etc. **plodder** *n.*

plonk *n.* (*sl.*) cheap or inferior wine.

plop *n.* & *v.i.* (*p.t.* **plopped**) sound like something small dropping into water with no splash.

plot *n.* small piece of land; story in a play or novel or film; conspiracy, secret plan. —*v.t./i.* (*p.t.* **plotted**) make a map or chart of, mark on this; plan secretly. **plotter** *n.*

plough *n.* implement for cutting furrows in soil and turning it up. —*v.t./i.* cut or turn up (soil etc.)

with a plough; make one's way laboriously. **ploughman** *n.*

ploughshare *n.* cutting-blade of a plough.

plover /'plʌv-/ *n.* a wading bird.

ploy *n.* (*colloq.*) occupation; cunning manoeuvre.

pluck *v.t.* pull at or out or off; pick (a flower etc.); strip (a bird) of its feathers. —*n.* plucking movement; courage. **pluck up courage** summon up one's courage.

plucky *a.* (**-ier, -iest**) showing pluck, brave. **pluckily** *adv.*

plug *n.* thing fitting into and stopping or filling a hole or cavity; device of this kind (usu. with pins) for making an electrical connection. —*v.t./i.* (*p.t.* **plugged**) put a plug into; (*sl.*) shoot, strike; (*colloq.*) work diligently; (*colloq.*) seek to popularize by constant commendation. **plug in** connect electrically by putting a plug into a socket.

plum *n.* fruit with sweet pulp round a pointed stone; tree bearing this; reddish-purple; something desirable, the best. **plum cake, plum pudding** one containing raisins.

plumage /'pluː-/ *n.* bird's feathers.

plumb *n.* lead weight hung on a cord (**plumb-line**), used for testing depths or verticality. —*adv.* exactly; (*US*) completely. —*v.t.* measure or test with a plumb-line; reach (depths); get to the bottom of; work or fit (things) as a plumber.

plumber *n.* person whose job is to fit and repair plumbing.

plumbing *n.* system of water-pipes, cisterns, and drainage-pipes etc. in a building.

plume *n.* feather, esp. as an ornament; thing(s) resembling this. —*v.t./refl.* preen. **plumed** *a.*

plummet *n.* plumb, plumb-line. —*v.i.* (*p.t.* **plummeted**) fall steeply.

plummy a. (colloq.) good, desirable; (of the voice) sounding affectedly rich in tone.

plump[1] a. (-er, -est) having a full rounded shape. —v.t./i. make or become plump. **plumpness** n.

plump[2] v.t./i plunge abruptly. **plump for** choose, decide on.

plunder v.t. rob. —n. plundering; goods etc. acquired by this.

plunge v.t./i. thrust or go forcefully into something; dive; go down suddenly; gamble heavily. —n. plunging, dive.

plunger n. thing that works with a plunging movement.

pluperfect a. & n. (tense) expressing action completed prior to a point of past time.

plural n. form of a noun or verb used in referring to more than one person or thing. —a. of this form; of more than one. **plurality** n.

plus prep. with the addition of; above zero; (colloq.) with. —a. more than zero; more than the amount indicated. —n. the sign +; advantage. **plus-fours** n.pl. knickerbockers worn esp. by golfers.

plush n. cloth with a long soft nap. —a. plush; plushy. **plushy** a. luxurious.

plutocrat n. person who is powerful because of his wealth. **plutocracy** n., **plutocratic** a.

plutonium n. radioactive substance used in nuclear weapons and reactors.

pluvial a. of or caused by rain.

ply[1] n. thickness or layer of wood or cloth etc.; plywood.

ply[2] v.t./i. use or wield (a tool etc.); work (at a trade); keep offering or supplying; go to and fro regularly or looking for custom.

plywood n. board made by gluing layers with the grain crosswise.

PM abbr. Prime Minister.

p.m. abbr. (Latin post meridiem) after noon.

pneumatic /njuː-/ a. filled with or operated by compressed air. **pneumatically** adv.

pneumonia /njuː-/ n. inflammation of one or both lungs.

PO abbr. postal order; Post Office.

poach v.t./i. cook (an egg without its shell) in or over boiling water; simmer in a small amount of liquid; take (game or fish) illegally; trespass, encroach. **poacher** n.

pocket n. small bag-like part in or on a garment; one's resources of money; pouch-like compartment; isolated group or area. —a. suitable for carrying in one's pocket. —v.t. put into one's pocket; appropriate; send (a ball) into a pocket. **in** or **out of pocket** having made a profit or loss. **pocket money** money for small personal expenses; money allowed to children. **pocketful** n. (pl. -fuls).

pocketbook n. notebook; small book-like case for money or papers.

pock-marked a. marked by scars or pits.

pod n. long narrow seed-case.

podgy a. (-ier, -iest) short and fat. **podginess** n.

podium /ˈpəʊdɪ-/ n. (pl. -ia) projecting base; rostrum.

poem n. literary composition in verse.

poesy n. (old use) poems, poetry.

poet n. writer of poems. **poetess** n.fem.

poetic, poetical adjs. of or like poetry. **poetically** adv.

poetry n. poems; poet's work; quality that pleases the mind similarly.

po-faced a. (colloq.) solemn.

pogo stick stilt-like toy with a spring, for jumping about on.

pogrom /ˈpɒg-/ n. organized massacre.

poignant /ˈpɔɪn-/ a. arousing sympathy, moving; keenly felt. **poignantly** adv., **poignancy** n.

poinsettia n. plant with large scarlet bracts.

point n. tapered or sharp end, tip; promontory; dot used as a punctuation mark; particular place, moment, or stage; unit of measurement or value or scoring; item, detail; characteristic; chief or important feature; effectiveness; electrical socket; movable rail for directing a train from one line to another; cricket fielder near the batsman on the off side. —v.t./i. aim, direct (a finger or weapon etc.); have a certain direction; indicate; sharpen; fill in (joints of brickwork) with mortar or cement. **on the point of** on the verge of (an action). **point-blank** a. aimed or fired at very close range; (of a remark) direct; (adv.) in a point-blank manner. **point-duty** n. that of a policeman stationed to regulate traffic. **point of view** way of looking at a matter. **point out** draw attention to. **point-to-point** n. steeplechase over a marked course for horses regularly used in hunting. **point up** emphasize. **to the point** relevant(ly).

pointed a. tapering to a point; (of a remark or manner) emphasized, clearly aimed at a person or thing. **pointedly** adv.

pointer n. thing that points to something; dog that points towards game which it scents.

pointless a. having no purpose or meaning. **pointlessly** adv.

poise v.t./i. balance; hold suspended or supported. —n. balance; dignified self-assured manner. **poised** a.

poison n. substance that can destroy life or harm health. —v.t. give poison to; kill with poison; put poison on or in; corrupt, fill with prejudice. **poison pen letter** anonymous malicious or libellous letter. **poisoner** n., **poisonous** a.

poke[1] v.t./i. thrust with the end of a finger or stick etc.; thrust forward; search, pry. —n. poking movement. **poke fun at** ridicule.

poke[2] n. (dialect) bag, sack. **pig in a poke** thing rashly bought or accepted without inspection.

poker[1] n. stiff metal rod for stirring up a fire.

poker[2] n. gambling card-game. **poker-face** n. one that does not reveal thoughts or feelings.

poky a. (-ier, -iest) small and cramped. **pokiness** n.

polar a. of or near the North or South Pole; of a pole of a magnet. **polar bear** white bear of Arctic regions.

polarize v.t./i. confine similar vibrations of (light-waves) to one direction or plane; give magnetic poles to; set at opposite extremes of opinion. **polarization** n.

Pole[1] n. Polish person.

pole[1] n. long rod or post; measure of length = perch[1]. —v.t. push along by using a pole. **pole position** most favourable starting-position (orig. next to inside fence) in a motor race.

pole[2] n. north (**North Pole**) or south (**South Pole**) end of earth's axis; point in the sky opposite either of these; one of the opposite ends of a magnet or terminals of an electric cell or battery. **pole star** star near the North Pole in the sky.

poleaxe n. battleaxe; implement for slaughtering cattle. —v.t. strike down with this.

polecat n. small animal of the weasel family; (US) skunk.

polemic /-'lem-/ n. verbal attack on a belief or opinion. **polemical** a.

police n. civil force responsible for keeping public order. —v.t. keep order in by means of police. **police state** country where political police supervise and control citizens' activities. **policeman** *n.* (*pl.* **-men**), **policewoman** *n.* (*pl.* **-women**).

policy[1] *n.* course or general plan of action.

policy[2] *n.* insurance contract.

polio /'pəʊ-/ *n.* (*colloq.*) poliomyelitis.

poliomyelitis /pəʊ-/ *n.* infectious disease causing temporary or permanent paralysis.

Polish *a.* & *n.* (language) of Poland.

polish *v.t./i.* make or become smooth and glossy by rubbing; make (work) better by adding improvements. —*n.* smoothness and glossiness; polishing, substance used for this; high degree of elegance. **polish off** finish off. **polisher** *n.*

polished *a.* elegant, perfected.

polite *a.* having good manners, socially correct; refined. **politely** *adv.*, **politeness** *n.*

politic *a.* prudent. **body politic** the State.

political *a.* of or involving politics; of the way a country is governed. **political correctness** avoidance of forms of expression or action that exclude, marginalize, or insult certain groups of people. **politically** *adv.*

politician *n.* person engaged in politics, Member of Parliament.

politicize *v.t.* give a political character to. **politicization** *n.*

politics *n.* science and art of government; political affairs or life. —*n.pl.* political principles.

polka *n.* lively dance for couples. **polka dots** round evenly spaced dots on fabric.

poll *n.* voting or votes at an election; place for this; estimate of public opinion made by questioning people. —*v.t./i.* cast one's vote; receive as votes; cut off the horns of (cattle) or the top of (a tree etc.).

pollack *n.* sea-fish related to cod.

pollard *v.t.* poll (a tree) to produce a close head of young branches. —*n.* pollarded tree; hornless animal.

pollen *n.* fertilizing powder from the anthers of flowers.

pollinate *v.t.* fertilize with pollen. **pollination** *n.*

pollster *n.* person who organizes a public opinion poll.

pollute *v.t.* make dirty or impure. **pollution** *n.*, **pollutant** *n.*

polo *n.* game like hockey played by teams on horseback. **poloneck** *n.* high round turned-over collar.

polonaise /-'neɪz/ *n.* slow processional dance.

poltergeist /-gaɪst/ *n.* spirit that throws things about noisily.

polyandry *n.* polygamy in which a woman has more than one husband. **polyandrous** *a.*

polyanthus *n.* (*pl.* **-thuses** or **-thus**) a cultivated primrose.

polychrome *a.* multicoloured. **polychromatic** *a.*

polyester *n.* synthetic resin or fibre.

polygamy /-'lɪg-/ *n.* system of having more than one spouse at a time. **polygamist** *n.*, **polygamous** *a.*

polyglot *a.* knowing or using several languages. —*n.* polyglot person.

polygon *n.* geometric figure with many sides. **polygonal** *a.*

polygraph *n.* machine recording changes in pulse-rate etc., used as a lie-detector.

polyhedron *n.* (*pl.* **-dra**) solid with many sides. **polyhedral** *a.*

polymath *n.* person with knowledge of many subjects.

polymer *n.* compound whose molecule is formed from a large number of simple molecules.

polymerize *v.t./i.* combine into a polymer. **polymerization** *n.*

polyp *n.* simple organism with a tube-shaped body; abnormal growth projecting from mucous membrane.

polyphony *n.* simultaneous combination of melodies. **polyphonic** *a.*

polystyrene /-'staɪ-/ *n.* a kind of plastic.

polytechnic *n.* institution giving education and training in many subjects at an advanced level.

polytheism *n.* belief in or worship of more than one god. **polytheist** *n.*, **polytheistic** *a.*

polythene *n.* a kind of tough light plastic.

polyunsaturated *a.* (of fat) not associated with the formation of cholesterol in the blood.

polyurethane *n.* synthetic resin or plastic.

polyvinyl chloride /-'vaɪnɪl/ vinyl plastic used as a fabric or for insulation.

pomade /-'mɑːd/ *n.* scented ointment for the hair.

pomander /-'mæn-/ *n.* ball of mixed aromatic substances.

pomegranate /'pɒmɪ-/ *n.* tropical fruit with many seeds; tree bearing this.

Pomeranian *n.* dog of a small silky-haired breed.

pommel /'pʌm-/ *n.* knob on the hilt of a sword; upward projection on a saddle.

pommy *n.* (*Austr. & NZ sl.*) British person, esp. immigrant.

pomp *n.* stately and splendid ceremonial.

pom-pom *n.* = pompon.

pompon *n.* decorative tuft or ball.

pompous *a.* full of ostentatious dignity and self-importance. **pompously** *adv.*, **pomposity** *n.*

ponce *n.* pimp; (*sl.*) effeminate or homosexual man.

poncho *n.* (*pl.* **-os**) cloak like a blanket with a hole for the head.

pond *n.* small area of still water.

ponder *v.t./i.* be deep in thought; think over.

ponderous *a.* heavy, unwieldy; laborious. **ponderously** *adv.*

pong *n. & v.i.* (*sl.*) stink.

poniard *n.* dagger.

pontiff *n.* bishop; chief priest, pope.

pontifical *a.* pompously dogmatic. **pontifically** *adv.*

pontificate *v.i.* speak in a pontifical way.

pontoon[1] *n.* a kind of flat-bottomed boat. **pontoon bridge** temporary bridge supported on boats or hollow cylinders.

pontoon[2] *n.* a kind of card-game.

pony *n.* horse of any small breed. **pony-tail** *n.* long hair drawn back and tied to hang down. **pony-trekking** *n.* riding across country on ponies for pleasure.

poodle *n.* dog with thick curly hair.

pooh *int.* exclamation of contempt. **pooh-pooh** *v.t.* express contempt for.

pool[1] *n.* small area of still water; puddle; swimming-pool.

pool[2] *n.* common fund or supply for sharing; game resembling snooker; (*pl.*) football pools. —*v.t.* put into a common fund or supply.

poop *n.* ship's stern; raised deck at the stern.

pooper scooper *n.* implement for clearing up esp. dog excrement.

poor *a.* (**-er, -est**) having little money or means; not abundant; not very good; pitiable. **poorness** *n.*

poorly *adv.* in a poor way, badly. —*a.* unwell.

pop[1] *n.* small explosive sound; fizzy drink. —*v.t./i.* (*p.t.* **popped**) make or cause to make a pop; put or come or go quickly.

pop[2] *n.* (*colloq.*) father.

pop[3] *a.* in a popular modern style. —*n.* pop record or music.

popcorn *n.* maize heated to burst and form puffy balls.

pope *n.* bishop of Rome, head of the RC Church.

popery *n.* (*derog.*) papal system, Roman Catholicism.

popgun n. child's gun that shoots with a popping sound.

popish a. (derog.) of popery.

poplar n. tall slender tree.

poplin n. plain woven usu. cotton fabric.

poppadam n. large thin crisp savoury Indian biscuit.

poppet n. (colloq.) darling.

popping-crease n. line in front of and parallel to the wicket in cricket.

poppy n. plant with showy flowers and milky juice.

poppycock n. (sl.) nonsense.

populace n. the general public.

popular a. liked or enjoyed or used etc. by many people; or of for the general public. **popularly** adv., **popularity** n.

popularize v.t. make generally liked; present in a popular non-technical form. **popularization** n., **popularizer** n.

populate v.t. fill with a population.

population n. inhabitants of an area.

populous a. thickly populated.

porcelain n. fine china.

porch n. roofed shelter over the entrance of a building.

porcine a. of or like a pig.

porcupine n. small animal covered with protective spines.

pore[1] n. tiny opening on skin or on a leaf, for emitting or taking in moisture.

pore[2] v.i. **pore over** study closely.

pork n. unsalted pig-meat.

porker n. pig raised for pork.

porn n. (colloq.) pornography.

pornography n. writings or pictures intended to stimulate erotic feelings by portraying sexual activity. **pornographer** n., **pornographic** a.

porous a. containing pores; permeable by fluid or air. **porosity** n.

porphyry /-firɪ/ n. rock containing mineral crystals.

porpoise /-pəs/ n. small whale with a blunt rounded snout.

porridge n. food made by boiling oatmeal etc. to a thick paste.

porringer n. small soup-basin.

port[1] n. harbour; town with this; place where goods pass in and out of a country by ship or aircraft.

port[2] n. opening in a ship's side; porthole.

port[3] n. left-hand side of a ship or aircraft. —v.t. turn this way.

port[4] n. strong sweet usu. dark-red wine.

port[5] v.t. hold (a rifle) diagonally in front of the body.

portable a. able to be carried. **portability** n.

portal n. door or entrance, esp. an imposing one.

portcullis n. vertical grating that slides down in grooves to block the gateway to a castle.

portend v.t. foreshadow.

portent /'pɔː-/ n. omen, significant sign. **portentous** /-'ten-/ a.

porter[1] n. doorkeeper of a large building.

porter[2] n. person employed to carry luggage or goods.

porterage n. services of a porter.

portfolio n. (pl. **-os**) case for loose sheets of paper; set of investments; position of a minister of State.

porthole n. window-like structure in the side of a ship or aircraft.

portico n. (pl. **-oes**) columns supporting a roof to form a porch or similar structure.

portion n. part, share; amount of food for one person; one's destiny. —v.t. divide into portions; distribute in portions.

portly a. (-ier, -iest) stout and dignified. **portliness** n.

portmanteau n. (pl. **-eaus**) a kind of trunk for clothes.

portrait n. picture of a person or animal; description.

portray *v.t.* make a picture of; describe; represent in a play etc. **portrayal** *n.*

Portuguese *a.* & *n.* (native, language) of Portugal. **Portuguese man-of-war** a kind of jellyfish.

pose *v.t./i.* put into or take a particular attitude; pretend to be; put forward, present (a problem etc.). —*n.* attitude in which someone is posed; pretence.

poser *n.* puzzling problem; poseur.

poseur /-'zɜ:(r)/ *n.* person who poses or behaves affectedly.

posh *a.* (*colloq.*) very smart, luxurious. **poshly** *adv.*, **poshness** *n.*

posit *v.t.* (*p.t.* posited) postulate.

position *n.* place occupied by or intended for a person or thing; posture; situation; status; job. —*v.t.* place. **positional** *a.*

positive *a.* definite; explicit; constructive; (of a quantity) greater than zero; (of a battery terminal) through which electric current enters; (of a photograph) with lights, shades, or colours as in the subject, not reversed. —*n.* positive quality or quantity or photograph. **positively** *adv.*, **positiveness** *n.*

positivism *n.* philosophical system recognizing only matters of fact and observation. **positivist** *n.*

positron *n.* particle with a positive electric charge.

posse /'pɒsɪ/ *n.* body of constables, strong force or company.

possess *v.t.* hold as belonging to oneself; dominate the mind of. **possess oneself of** take. **possessor** *n.*

possession *n.* possessing; thing possessed. **take possession of** become the owner or possessor of.

possessive *a.* of or indicating possession; desiring to possess things. **possessively** *adv.*, **possessiveness** *n.*

possible *a.* capable of existing or happening or being done etc. **possibly** *adv.*, **possibility** *n.*

possum *n.* (*colloq.*) opossum. **play possum** pretend to be unaware.

post[1] *n.* piece of timber or metal set upright in the ground etc. to support something or mark a position. —*v.t.* display (a notice etc.), announce thus.

post[2] *n.* place of duty; outpost of soldiers; trading-station; job. —*v.t.* place, station. **last post** (see **last**[2]).

post[3] *n.* official conveyance of letters etc.; the letters etc. conveyed. —*v.t.* put into a post-box or post office for transmission; enter in an official ledger. **keep me posted** keep me informed. **post-box** *n.* box into which letters are inserted for transmission. **post-haste** *adv.* with great haste. **Post Office** public authority responsible for postal services. **post office** building or room where postal business is carried on.

post- *pref.* after.

postage *n.* charge for sending something by post.

postal *a.* of the post; by post. **postal order** a kind of money order.

postcard *n.* card for sending messages by post without an envelope.

postcode *n.* group of letters and figures in a postal address to assist sorting.

poster *n.* large sheet of paper announcing or advertising something, for display in a public place.

poste restante /pəʊst 'restɑ̃t/ post office department where letters are kept until called for.

posterior *a.* situated behind or at the back. —*n.* buttocks.

posterity *n.* future generations.

postern /'pɒs-/ *n.* small entrance at the back or side of a fortress etc.

posthumous /-ɒs-/ a. (of a child) born after its father's death; published or awarded after a person's death. **posthumously** adv.

postilion n. rider on the near horse drawing a coach etc. without a coachman.

post-impressionist n. painter using a style that was a reaction against impressionism. **post-impressionism** n.

postman n. (pl. **-men**) person who delivers or collects letters etc.

postmark n. official mark stamped on something sent by post, giving place and date of marking. —v.t. mark with this.

postmaster, postmistress ns. person in charge of certain post offices.

post-mortem a. & n. (examination) made after death.

postnatal a. after birth; after pregnancy.

postpone v.t. keep (an event etc.) from occurring until a later time. **postponement** n.

postprandial a. after lunch or dinner.

postscript n. additional paragraph at the end of a letter etc.

post-traumatic stress disorder persistent mental stress occurring after injury or shock.

postulant n. candidate for admission to a religious order.

postulate¹ /-eɪt/ v.t. assume to be true, esp. as a basis for reasoning. **postulation** n.

postulate² /-ət/ n. thing postulated.

posture n. attitude of the body. —v.i. assume a posture, esp. for effect. **postural** a.

posy n. small bunch of flowers.

pot¹ n. vessel for holding liquids or solids, or for cooking in; (colloq.) large amount. —v.t. (**potted**) put into a pot; send (a ball in billiards etc.) into a pocket; (colloq.) abridge; shoot, kill by a pot-shot. **go to pot** (sl.)

deteriorate, become ruined. **pot-belly** n. protuberant belly. **pot-boiler** n. literary or artistic work produced merely to make a living. **pot luck** whatever is available for a meal. **pot-roast** n. piece of meat cooked whole in a covered dish; (v.t.) cook thus. **pot-shot** n. shot aimed casually.

pot² n. (sl.) marijuana.

potable /ˈpəʊ-/ a. drinkable.

potash n. potassium carbonate.

potassium n. soft silvery-white metallic element.

potation n. drinking; a drink.

potato n. (pl. **-oes**) plant with starchy tubers that are used as food; one of these tubers.

poteen /-ˈtiːn/ n. (Ir.) whisky from an illicit still.

potent /ˈpəʊ-/ a. having great natural power; having a strong effect. **potently** adv., **potency** n.

potentate /ˈpəʊ-/ n. monarch, ruler.

potential a. & n. (ability etc.) capable of being developed or used. **potentially** adv., **potentiality** n.

pothole n. hole formed underground by the action of water; hole in a road surface.

potholing n. exploration of underground potholes. **potholer** n.

potion n. liquid for drinking as a medicine or drug.

pot-pourri n. scented mixture of dried petals and spices; medley.

potsherd n. broken piece of earthenware, esp. in archaeology.

potted see **pot**¹. —a. preserved in a pot. **potted meat** meat paste.

potter¹ n. maker of pottery.

potter² v.i. work on trivial tasks in a leisurely way.

pottery n. vessels and other objects made of baked clay; potter's work or workshop.

potty¹ a. (**-ier, -iest**) (sl.) trivial; crazy. **pottiness** n.

potty² n. (colloq.) child's chamber-pot.

pouch n. small bag or bag-like formation. —v.t./i. put into a pouch; overhang in a pouch-like shape.

pouffe /puːf/ n. padded stool.

poulterer /ˈpəʊ-/ n. dealer in poultry.

poultice /ˈpəʊ-/ n. soft usu. hot dressing applied to a sore or inflamed part. —v.t. put poultice on.

poultry /ˈpəʊ-/ n. domestic fowls.

pounce v.i. swoop down and grasp or attack. —n. pouncing movement.

pound[1] n. measure of weight, 16oz. avoirdupois (0.454kg) or 12oz. troy (0.373kg); unit of money in Britain and certain other countries.

pound[2] n. enclosure where stray animals, or vehicles officially removed, are kept until claimed.

pound[3] v.t./i. beat or crush with heavy strokes; go or run heavily; (of heart) beat heavily.

poundage n. charge or commission per £ or per pound weight.

pour v.t./i. flow, cause to flow; rain heavily; send out freely.

pout[1] v.t./i. push out one's lips, (of lips) be pushed out, esp. in annoyance. —n. pouting expression.

pout[2] n. sea fish related to cod; eel-like freshwater fish.

poverty n. state of being poor; scarcity, lack; inferiority.

powder n. mass of fine dry particles; medicine or cosmetic in this form; gunpowder. —v.t. cover with powder. **powdery** a.

powdered a. made into powder.

power n. ability to do something; vigour, strength; control, authority; influential person or country etc.; product of a number multiplied by itself a given number of times; mechanical or electrical energy; electricity supply. —v.t. supply with (esp. motive) power. **power station** building where electrical power is generated for distribution.

powerful a. having great power or influence. **powerfully** adv.

powerhouse n. power station; person or thing of great energy.

powerless a. without power to take action, wholly unable.

powwow n. meeting for discussion.

practicable a. able to be done. **practicability** n.

practical a. involving activity as distinct from study or theory; suitable for use; clever at doing and making things; virtual. **practical joke** humorous trick played on a person. **practicality** n.

practically adv. in a practical way; virtually, almost.

practice n. action as opposed to theory; habit, custom; repeated exercise to improve skill; professional work, doctor's or lawyer's business. **out of practice** not lately practised in a skill.

practise v.t./i. do something repeatedly to become or remain skilful; carry out in action, do habitually; (of a doctor or lawyer) perform professional work.

practised a. experienced.

practitioner n. professional or practical worker, esp. in medicine.

pragmatic a. treating things from a practical point of view. **pragmatically** adv., **pragmatism** n., **pragmatist** n.

prairie n. large treeless tract of grassland, esp. in North America.

praise v.t. express approval or admiration of; honour (God) in words. —n. praising; approval expressed in words.

praiseworthy a. deserving praise. **praiseworthiness** n.

praline /ˈprɑːliːn/ n. sweet made by browning nuts in syrup.

pram n. four-wheeled carriage for a baby.

prance v.i. move springily.

prank n. piece of mischief.

prankster n. person playing pranks.

prate v.i. chatter foolishly.

prattle v.i. chatter in a childish way. —n. childish chatter.

prawn n. edible shellfish like a large shrimp.

pray v.t./i. say prayers; entreat.

prayer n. solemn request or thanksgiving to God; set form of words used in this; act of praying; entreaty. **prayer-book** n. book of set prayers.

pre- pref. before; beforehand.

preach v.t./i. deliver a sermon; expound (the Gospel etc.); advocate. **preacher** n.

preamble /-æm-/ n. preliminary statement, introductory section.

prearrange v.t. arrange beforehand. **prearrangement** n.

prebendary /'preb-/ n. clergyman receiving a stipend from a cathedral revenue; honorary canon.

precarious /-'keər-/ a. unsafe, not secure. **precariously** adv., **precariousness** n.

precaution n. something done in advance to avoid a risk. **precautionary** a.

precede v.t. come or go or place before in time or order etc.

precedence /'pres-/ n. priority.

precedent /'pres-/ n. previous case serving as an example to be followed.

precentor /-'sen-/ n. clergyman in charge of music at a cathedral.

precept /'priː-/ n. command, rule of conduct.

preceptor n. teacher.

precession n. change by which equinoxes occur earlier in each sidereal year.

precinct n. enclosed area, esp. round a place of worship; district where traffic is prohibited in a town; (pl.) environs; (US) administrative area of a city etc.

precious a. of great value; beloved; affectedly refined. —adv. (colloq.) very. **precious metals** gold, silver, and platinum. **precious stone** small valuable piece of mineral.

precipice n. very steep or vertical face of a cliff or rock.

precipitance n. rash haste. **precipitancy** n.

precipitate[1] /-tert/ v.t. throw headlong; send rapidly into a certain state; cause to happen suddenly or soon; cause (a substance) to be deposited; condense (vapour). **precipitation** n.

precipitate[2] /-tət/ n. substance deposited from a solution etc.; moisture condensed from vapour. —a. headlong, violently hurried; hasty, rash. **precipitately** adv.

precipitous /-'sɪp-/ a. very steep.

précis /'preɪsiː/ n. (pl. **précis**, pr. -siːz) summary. —v.t. make a précis of.

precise a. exact; correct and clearly stated. **precisely** adv., **precision** n.

preclude v.t. exclude the possibility of, prevent.

precocious /-'kəʊʃ-/ a. having developed abilities earlier than is usual; developed thus. **precociously** adv., **precocity** /-'kɒs-/ n.

precognition n. foreknowledge, esp. supernatural.

preconceived a. (of an idea) formed beforehand. **preconception** n.

precondition n. condition to be fulfilled beforehand.

precursor n. forerunner.

predator /'predə-/ n. predatory animal.

predatory /'predə-/ a. preying upon others.

predecease v.t. die earlier than (another person).

predecessor n. former holder of an office or position; ancestor.

predestine v.t. destine beforehand; appoint as if by fate. **predestination** n.

predicament /-'dɪk-/ n. difficult situation.

predicate n. the part of a sentence that says something about the subject (e.g. 'is short' in life is short).

predicative /-'drɪk-/ a. forming the predicate or part of this. **predicatively** adv.

predict v.t. foretell. **prediction** n., **predictive** a., **predictor** n.

predictable a. able to be predicted. **predictably** adv.

predilection n. special liking.

predispose v.t. influence in advance; render liable or inclined. **predisposition** n.

predominate v.i. be greater than others in number or intensity etc.; exert control. **predominant** a., **predominantly** adv., **predominance** n.

pre-eminent a. excelling others, outstanding. **pre-eminently** adv., **pre-eminence** n.

pre-empt v.t. take (a thing) before anyone else can do so. **pre-emption** n., **pre-emptive** a.

preen v.t. smooth (feathers) with the beak. **preen oneself** groom oneself; show self-satisfaction.

pre-exist v.i. exist previously. **pre-existence** n., **pre-existent** a.

prefab n. (colloq.) prefabricated building.

prefabricate v.t. manufacture in sections for assembly on a site. **prefabrication** n.

preface n. introductory statement. —v.t. introduce with a preface; lead up to (an event).

prefect n. senior pupil authorized to maintain discipline in a school; administrative official in certain countries. **prefecture** n.

prefer v.t. (p.t. **preferred**) choose as more desirable, like better; put forward (an accusation); promote (a person).

preferable /'pref-/ a. more desirable. **preferably** adv.

preference n. preferring; thing preferred; prior right; favouring.

preferential a. giving preference. **preferentially** adv.

preferment n. promotion.

prefigure v.t. foreshadow.

prefix n. (pl. **-ixes**) word or syllable placed in front of a word to add to or change its meaning. —v.t. add as a prefix or introduction.

pregnant a. having a child or young developing in the womb; full of meaning. **pregnancy** n.

prehensile /-'hensaɪl/ a. able to grasp things. **prehensility** n.

prehistoric a. of the ancient period before written records were made. **prehistorically** adv.

prehistory n. prehistoric matters or times. **prehistorian** n.

prejudge v.t. form a judgement on before knowing all the facts. **prejudgement** n.

prejudice n. unreasoning opinion or dislike; harm to rights. —v.t. cause to have a prejudice; harm the rights of. **prejudiced** a.

prejudicial a. harmful to rights or interests. **prejudicially** adv.

prelate /'prel-/ n. clergyman of high rank. **prelacy** n.

preliminary a. & n. (action or event etc.) preceding and preparing for a main action or event.

prelude n. action or event preceding and leading up to another; introductory part or piece of music.

premarital a. before marriage.

premature /'prem-/ a. coming or done before the usual or proper time. **prematurely** adv.

premedication n. medication in preparation for an operation.

premeditated a. planned beforehand. **premeditation** n.

premenstrual a. before each menstruation.

premier /'prem-/ a. first in importance or order or time. —n. prime minister. **premiership** n.

première /'premjeə(r)/ n. first public performance. —v.t. give a première of.

premises n.pl. house or other building and its grounds.

premiss n. statement on which reasoning is based.

premium n. amount or instalment paid for an insurance policy; extra sum added to a wage or charge; fee for instruction. **at a premium** above the nominal or usual price; highly esteemed. **Premium (Savings) Bond** government security paying no interest but offering a periodical chance of a cash prize. **put a premium on** provide an incentive to (an action etc.).

premonition /prɪ-/ n. presentiment. **premonitory** a.

prenatal a. before birth; before childbirth. **prenatally** adv.

preoccupation n. being preoccupied; thing that fills one's thoughts.

preoccupied a. mentally engrossed and inattentive to other things; already occupied.

prep n. (see **preparation**). **prep school** preparatory school.

preparation n. preparing; thing done to make ready; substance prepared for use; (also **prep**) work set for a pupil to do outside lessons.

preparatory /-'pæ-/ a. preparing for something. —adv. in a preparatory way. **preparatory school** usu. private school where pupils are prepared for a higher school or (US) for college.

prepare v.t./i. make or get ready. **prepared to** ready and willing to.

prepay v.t. (p.t. **-paid**) pay beforehand. **prepayment** n.

preponderate v.i. be greater in number or intensity etc. **preponderant** a., **preponderantly** adv., **preponderance** n.

preposition n. word used with a noun or pronoun to show position, time, or means (e.g. *at* home, *by* train). **prepositional** a.

prepossessing a. attractive.

preposterous a. utterly absurd, outrageous. **preposterously** adv., **preposterousness** n.

preppy n. & a. (US colloq.) (neat like) person attending an expensive private school.

prepuce n. foreskin.

prerequisite a. & n. (thing) required before something can happen.

prerogative n. right or privilege belonging to a person or group.

presage /'pres-/ n. omen; presentiment. —v.t. portend; foresee.

presbyter n. priest of the Episcopal Church; elder of the Presbyterian Church.

Presbyterian a. & n. (member) of a Church governed by elders all of equal rank. **Presbyterianism** n.

presbytery n. body of presbyters; eastern part of a chancel; RC priest's house.

preschool a. of the time before a child is old enough to attend school.

prescribe v.t. advise the use of (a medicine etc.); lay down as a course or rule to be followed.

prescript /'pri:-/ n. rule, command.

prescription n. prescribing; doctor's written instructions for the preparation and use of a medicine.

prescriptive a. prescribing.

presence n. being present; person's impressive bearing; person or thing that is or seems present. **presence of mind** ability to act sensibly in a crisis.

present[1] /'prez-/ a. being in the place in question; existing or being dealt with now. —n. present time, time now passing. **at present** now. **for the present** for now, temporarily.

present[2] /'prez-/ n. gift.

present[3] /-'zent/ v.t. give as a gift or award; offer for acceptance; introduce; bring to the public; show, reveal; aim (a weapon). **present arms** bring a rifle vertically in front of the body as a salute. **presenter** n.

presentable a. fit to be presented, of good appearance. **presentably** adv.

presentation n. presenting; thing presented.

presentiment /-'zent-/ n. feeling of something about to happen, foreboding.

presently adv. soon; (Sc. & US) now.

preservation n. preserving.

preservative a. preserving. —n. substance that preserves perishable food.

preserve v.t. keep safe, unchanged, or in existence; treat (food) to prevent decay. —n. area where game or fish are preserved for private use; interests etc. regarded as one person's domain; (also pl.) jam. **preserver** n.

preside v.i. be president or chairman; have the position of control.

president n. head of an institution or club etc.; head of a republic. **presidency** n., **presidential** a.

presidium /-'sɪd-/ n. standing committee, esp. in a Communist organization.

press[1] v.t./i. apply weight or force against; squeeze; make by pressing; flatten, smooth; iron (clothes etc.); urge, force; throng closely. —n. process of pressing; throng; instrument for pressing something; printing-press, printing or publishing firm; newspapers and periodicals, people involved in writing or producing these. **be pressed for** have barely enough of. **press conference** interview before a number of reporters. **press cutting** report etc. cut from a newspaper. **press-stud** n. small fastener with two parts that engage when pressed together. **press-up** n. exercise of pressing on the hands to raise the shoulders and trunk while prone.

press[2] v.t. (old use) force to serve in the army or navy; bring into use as a makeshift. **press-gang** n.

body of men employed to press men for the navy; (v.t.) force into service.

pressing a. urgent; urging something strongly. —n. thing made by pressing; gramophone record or series of these made at one time.

pressure n. exertion of force against a thing; this force, that of the atmosphere; compelling or oppressive influence. —v.t. pressurize (a person). **pressure-cooker** n. pan for cooking things quickly by steam under high pressure. **pressure group** organized group seeking to exert influence by intensive concerted action.

pressurize v.t. try to compel into an action; maintain a constant atmospheric pressure in (a compartment). **pressurization** n.

prestige /-'tiːʒ/ n. respect resulting from good reputation or achievements.

prestigious /-'tɪdʒ-/ a. having or giving prestige.

prestressed a. (of concrete) strengthened by stretched wires etc. in it.

presumably adv. it may be presumed.

presume v.t./i. suppose to be true; take the liberty (to do something); be presumptuous. **presume on** take liberties because of. **presumption** n.

presumptive a. giving grounds for presumption.

presumptuous a. behaving with impudent boldness; acting beyond one's authority. **presumptuously** adv., **presumptuousness** n.

presuppose v.t. assume beforehand; involve the existence etc. of. **presupposition** n.

pretence n. pretending, make-believe; claim (e.g. to merit or knowledge).

pretend v.t./i. create a false impression of (in play or deception);

claim falsely that one has or is something; lay claim. **pretender** n.

pretension n. asserting of a claim; pretentiousness.

pretentious a. claiming great merit or importance, showy. **pretentiously** adv., **pretentiousness** n.

preterite a. & n. (tense) expressing past action.

preternatural /priː-/ a. beyond what is natural. **preternaturally** adv.

pretext /ˈpriː-/ n. reason given to conceal one's true reason.

pretty a. (-ier, -iest) attractive in a delicate way. —adv. fairly, moderately. **a pretty penny** much money. **prettily** adv., **prettiness** n.

pretzel n. salted biscuit.

prevail v.i. be victorious, gain the mastery; be the most usual. **prevail on** persuade.

prevalent a. existing generally, widespread. **prevalence** n.

prevaricate v.i. speak evasively or misleadingly. **prevarication** n., **prevaricator** n.

prevent v.t. keep from happening; keep from doing something. **prevention** n., **preventable** a.

preventative a. & n. preventive.

preventive a. & n. (thing) preventing something.

preview n. advance viewing, esp. of a film or exhibition.

previous a. coming before in time or order; done or acting prematurely. **previous** adv. to before. **previously** adv.

prey n. animal hunted or killed by another for food; victim. —v.i. **prey on** seek or take as prey; cause worry to. **bird of prey** one that kills and eats animals.

price n. amount of money for which a thing is bought or sold; what must be given or done etc. to achieve something. —v.t. fix, find, or estimate the price of.

priceless a. invaluable; (sl.) very amusing or absurd.

pricey a. (colloq.) expensive.

prick v.t./i. pierce slightly; feel a pricking sensation; erect (the ears). —n. act of pricking; sensation of being pricked. **prick out** plant (seedlings etc.) in small holes pricked in the soil. **prick up one's ears** listen alertly.

prickle n. small thorn; pointed spine on a hedgehog etc.; pricking sensation. —v.t./i. feel or cause a pricking sensation.

prickly a. having prickles; irritable, touchy. **prickliness** n.

pride n. feeling of pleasure or satisfaction about one's actions or qualities or possessions etc.; source of this; proper sense of one's dignity; group (of lions). —v.refl. **pride oneself on** be proud of. **pride of place** most prominent position.

prie-dieu /priːˈdjɜː/ n. desk for kneeling at in prayer.

priest n. member of the clergy; official of a non-Christian religion. **priestess** n.fem., **priesthood** n., **priestly** a.

prig n. self-righteous person. **priggish** a., **priggishness** n.

prim a. (primmer, primmest) stiffly formal and precise; disliking what is rough or improper. **primly** adv., **primness** n.

prima /ˈpriː-/ a. **prima ballerina** chief ballerina. **prima donna** chief female singer in opera.

prima facie /praɪmə ˈfeɪʃɪ/ at first sight; based on a first impression.

primal /ˈpraɪ-/ a. primitive, primeval; fundamental.

primary a. first in time, order, or importance. —n. primary thing. **primary colours** those not made by mixing others, i.e. red, green, violet, or (for pigments) red, blue, yellow. **primary education**, **primary school** that in which the rudiments of knowledge are taught. **primarily** /ˈpraɪmə-/ adv.

primate /'praɪ-/ n. archbishop; member of the highly developed order of animals that includes man, apes, and monkeys.

prime[1] a. chief; first-rate; fundamental. —n. state of greatest perfection; best portion. **prime minister** chief minister in a government. **prime number** number that can be divided exactly only by itself and unity.

prime[2] v.t. prepare for use or action; provide with information, or with food and drink, in preparation for something.

primer[1] n. substance used to prime a surface for painting or to ignite an explosive.

primer[2] n. elementary textbook.

primeval /-'miːv-/ a. of the earliest times of the world.

primitive a. of or at an early stage of civilization; simple, crude.

primogeniture /praɪmə'dʒen-/ n. system by which an eldest son inherits all his parents' property.

primordial /praɪ-/ a. primeval.

primrose n. pale-yellow spring flower; its colour.

primula n. perennial plant of a kind that includes the primrose.

prince n. male member of a royal family; sovereign's son or grandson; the greatest or best.

princely a. like a prince; splendid, generous.

princess n. female member of a royal family; sovereign's daughter or granddaughter; prince's wife.

principal a. first in rank or importance. —n. head of certain schools or colleges; person with highest authority or playing the leading part; capital sum as distinct from interest or income. **principal boy** leading male part in a pantomime, played by a woman.

principality n. country ruled by a prince; **the Principality** Wales.

principally adv. mainly.

principle n. general truth or doctrine used as a basis of reasoning or a guide to action; general or scientific law shown or used in the working of a machine etc. **in principle** as regards the main elements. **on principle** because of one's principles of conduct.

prink v.t./i. smarten.

print v.t. press (a mark) on a surface, impress (a surface etc.) in this way; produce by applying inked type to paper; write with unjoined letters; produce a positive picture from (a photographic negative etc.) by transmission of light. —n. mark left by pressing; printed lettering or words; printed design or picture or fabric. **in print** available from the publisher. **out of print** no longer in print. **printed circuit** electric circuit with lines of conducting material printed on a flat sheet (instead of wires).

printer n. person who prints books or newspapers etc.

printout n. computer output in printed form.

prior[1] a. coming before in time or order or importance. **prior to** before.

prior[2] n. monk who is head of a religious house or order, or (in an abbey) ranking next below an abbot. **prioress** n.fem.

prioritize v.t. treat as a priority. **prioritization** n.

priority n. being earlier or more important, right to be first; thing that should be treated as most important.

priory n. monastery or nunnery governed by a prior or prioress.

prise v.t. force out or open by leverage.

prism n. solid geometric shape with ends that are equal and parallel; transparent object of this shape with refracting surfaces.

prismatic a. of or like a prism; (of colours) rainbow-like.

prison n. building used to confine people convicted of crimes; place of custody or confinement; imprisonment.

prisoner n. person kept in prison; captive; person in confinement.

prissy a. (-ier, -iest) prim. **prissily** adv., **prissiness** n.

pristine /-ti:n/ a. in its original and unspoilt condition.

privacy /'priv-/ n. being private.

private a. belonging to a person or group, not public; confidential; secluded; not provided or managed by the State. —n. soldier of the lowest rank. **in private** privately. **private eye** (colloq.) private detective. **privately** adv.

privateer /prai-/ n. privately owned warship; its commander.

privation /prai-/ n. loss, lack; hardship. **privative** /'priv-/ a.

privatize v.t. transfer from State to private ownership. **privatization** n.

privet n. bushy evergreen shrub much used for hedges.

privilege n. special right granted to a person etc. **privileged** a.

privy a. (old use) secret, private. —n. (old use & US) lavatory. **be privy to** know about (secret plans etc.). **Privy Council** sovereign's body of advisers. **Privy Counsellor** member of this. **privy purse** allowance to the sovereign from public revenue. **privily** adv.

prize[1] n. award for victory or superiority; thing that can be won. —a. winning a prize; excellent. —v.t. value highly.

prize[2] n. ship or property captured at sea during a war.

prize[3] v.t. = prise.

prizefight n. boxing-match fought for money. **prizefighter** n.

pro[1] n. (pl. -os) (colloq.) professional.

pro[2] prep. pro and con for and

against. —n. **pros and cons** arguments for and against something.

pro- pref. in favour of.

proactive a. taking the initiative. **proactively** adv.

probable a. likely to happen or be true. **probably** adv., **probability** n.

probate /'prəʊ-/ n. official process of proving that a will is valid; certified copy of a will.

probation n. testing of behaviour or abilities; system whereby certain offenders are supervised by an official (**probation officer**) instead of being imprisoned. **probationary** a.

probationer n. person undergoing a probationary period, esp. in training to be a hospital nurse.

probe n. blunt surgical instrument for exploring a wound; device used similarly; unmanned exploratory spacecraft; investigation. —v.t. explore with a probe; investigate.

probity /'prəʊ-/ n. honesty.

problem n. something difficult to deal with or understand; thing to be solved or dealt with. **problematic**, **problematical** /-'mæ-/ adjs.

proboscis /-'bɒsɪs/ n. long flexible snout; insect's elongated mouthpart used for sucking things.

procedure n. series of actions done to accomplish something. **procedural** a.

proceed v.i. go forward or onward; continue; start a lawsuit; come forth, originate.

proceedings n.pl. what takes place, esp. at a formal meeting; published report of a conference; lawsuit.

proceeds /'prəʊ-/ n.pl. profit from a sale or performance etc.

process[1] /'prəʊ-/ n. series of operations used in making or manufacturing something; procedure; series of changes or events; lawsuit; natural projection. —v.t. subject to a process; deal with.

process[2] /-'ses/ *v.i.* go in procession.

procession *n.* number of people or vehicles or boats etc. going along in an orderly line.

processor *n.* machine that processes things; part of a computer that controls other units and performs actions specified in a program.

proclaim *v.t.* announce publicly; make known as being. **proclamation** *n.*

proclivity /-'klɪv-/ *n.* tendency.

procrastinate *v.i.* postpone action. **procrastination** *n.*

procreate *v.t.* beget or generate (offspring). **procreation** *n.*

Procrustean *a.* compelling conformity by drastic means.

proctor *n.* university official with disciplinary powers. **Queen's Proctor** official with the power to intervene in cases of divorce etc.

procurator fiscal (in Scotland) public prosecutor and coroner of a district.

procure *v.t./i.* obtain by care or effort, acquire; act as procurer. **procurement** *n.*

procurer *n.* person who obtains women for prostitution. **procuress** *n.fem.*

prod *v.t./i.* (*p.t.* prodded) poke; stimulate to action. —*n.* prodding action; stimulus; pointed instrument for prodding things.

prodigal *a.* wasteful, extravagant. **prodigally** *adv.*, **prodigality** *n.*

prodigious /-'dɪdʒ-/ *a.* amazing; enormous. **prodigiously** *adv.*

prodigy *n.* person with exceptional qualities or abilities; wonderful thing.

produce[1] /-'djuːs/ *v.t.* bring forward for inspection; bring (a performance etc.) before the public; direct the acting of (a play etc.); bring into existence, cause; manufacture; extend (a line). **producer** *n.*, **production** *n.*

produce[2] /'prɒd-/ *n.* amount or thing(s) produced.

product *n.* thing produced; result obtained by multiplying two quantities together.

productive *a.* producing things, esp. in large quantities.

productivity *n.* efficiency in industrial production.

profane *a.* secular, not sacred; irreverent, blasphemous. —*v.t.* treat irreverently. **profanely** *adv.*, **profanity** /-'fæ-/ *n.*, **profanation** *n.*

profess *v.t.* state that one has (a quality etc.), pretend; affirm one's faith in (a religion).

professed *a.* self-acknowledged; alleged. **professedly** *adv.*

profession *n.* occupation, esp. one that requires advanced learning; people engaged in this; declaration.

professional *a.* of or belonging to a profession; showing the skill of a trained person; doing specified work etc. for payment, not as a pastime. —*n.* professional worker or player etc. **professionalism** *n.*, **professionally** *adv.*

professor *n.* university teacher of the highest rank. **professorial** *a.*

proffer *v.t. & n.* offer.

proficient *a.* competent, skilled. **proficiently** *adv.*, **proficiency** *n.*

profile *n.* side view, esp. of the face; short account of a person's character or career.

profit *n.* advantage, benefit; money gained. —*v.t./i.* (*p.t.* profited) obtain a profit; bring advantage to.

profitable *a.* bringing profit. **profitably** *adv.*, **profitability** *n.*

profiteer *n.* person who makes excessive profits. **profiteering** *n.*

profiterole *n.* small hollow cake of choux pastry with filling.

profligate *a.* wasteful, extravagant; dissolute. —*n.* profligate person. **profligacy** *n.*

pro forma as a matter of form; (invoice) sent to the purchaser in advance; standardized form.

profound *a.* intense; showing or needing great insight. **profoundly** *adv.*, **profundity** *n.*

profuse *a.* lavish; plentiful. **profusely** *adv.*, **profuseness** *n.*

profusion *n.* abundance.

progenitor /-'dʒen-/ *n.* ancestor.

progeny /'prɒdʒ-/ *n.* offspring.

progesterone *n.* sex hormone that maintains pregnancy.

prognosis /-'gnəʊ-/ *n.* (*pl.* -oses) forecast, esp. of the course of a disease. **prognostic** /-'nɒs-/ *a.*

prognosticate *v.t.* forecast. **prognostication** *n.*

program *n.* (*US*) = programme; series of coded instructions for a computer. —*v.t.* (*p.t.* **programmed**) instruct (a computer) or express (a problem) by means of this. **programmer** *n.*

programme *n.* plan of procedure; list of events or of items in an entertainment; these events etc.; broadcast performance.

progress[1] /'prəʊ-/ *n.* forward or onward movement; advance, development. **in progress** taking place.

progress[2] /-'gres/ *v.i.* make progress; develop. **progression** *n.*

progressive *a.* making continuous progress; favouring progress or reform; (of a disease) gradually increasing in its effect. **progressively** *adv.*

prohibit *v.t.* forbid. **prohibition** *n.*

prohibitive *a.* prohibiting; intended to prevent the use or purchase of something.

project[1] /-'dʒe-/ *v.t./i.* extend outwards; cast, throw; imagine (oneself etc.) in another situation or time; plan.

project[2] /'prɒdʒ-/ *n.* plan, undertaking; task involving research.

projectile *n.* missile.

projection *n.* process of projecting something; thing projecting

from a surface; representation on a plane surface of earth's surface; estimate of future situations based on a study of present ones.

projectionist *n.* person who operates a projector.

projector *n.* apparatus for projecting images on to a screen.

prolapse[1] /-'læ-/ *v.i.* slip forward and down out of place.

prolapse[2] /'prəʊ-/ *n.* prolapsing of an organ of the body.

proletariat /prəʊlɪ'teər-/ *n.* working-class people. **proletarian** *a.* & *n.*

proliferate *v.i.* produce new growth or offspring rapidly, multiply. **proliferation** *n.*

prolific *a.* producing things abundantly. **prolifically** *adv.*

prolix /'prəʊ-/ *a.* lengthy. **prolixly** *adv.*, **prolixity** *n.*

prologue /-lɒg/ *n.* introduction to a poem or play etc.

prolong *v.t.* lengthen in extent or duration. **prolongation** *n.*

prolonged *a.* continuing for a long time.

prom *n.* (*colloq.*) promenade along a sea front; promenade concert.

promenade /-'nɑːd/ *n.* leisurely walk in a public place; paved public walk (esp. along a sea front). —*v.t./i.* go or take for a promenade. **promenade concert** one where part of the audience is not seated and can move about.

prominent *a.* projecting; conspicuous; important, well-known. **prominently** *adv.*, **prominence** *n.*

promiscuous *a.* indiscriminate; having sexual relations with many people. **promiscuously** *adv.*, **promiscuity** /-'kjuː-/ *n.*

promise *n.* declaration that one will give or do or not do a certain thing; indication of what will occur or of future good results. —*v.t./i.* make a promise (to); say that one will do or give (a thing);

promising *a.* likely to turn out well or produce good results.

seem likely, produce expectation of. **promise well** offer good prospects.

promissory /'prom-/ *a.* conveying a promise.

promontory *n.* high land jutting out into the sea or a lake.

promote *v.t.* raise to a higher rank or office; help the progress of; publicize in order to sell. **promotion** *n.*, **promotional** *a.*, **promoter** *n.*

prompt *a.* done or doing something without delay; punctual. —*adv.* punctually. —*v.t.* incite; assist (an actor or speaker) by supplying words. **promptly** *adv.*, **promptness** *n.*, **promptitude** *n.*

prompter *n.* person stationed offstage to prompt actors.

promulgate /'prom-/ *v.t.* make known to the public. **promulgation** *n.*, **promulgator** *n.*

prone *a.* lying face downwards; likely to do or suffer something.

prong *n.* each of the projecting pointed parts of a fork. **pronged** *a.*

pronoun *n.* word used as a substitute for a noun (e.g. *I, me, who, which*). **pronominal** *a.*

pronounce *v.t.* utter (a sound or word) distinctly or in a certain way; declare. **pronunciation** *n.*

pronounced *a.* noticeable.

pronouncement *n.* declaration.

pronto *adv.* (sl.) at once.

proof *n.* evidence that something is true or valid or exists; standard of strength for distilled alcoholic liquors; trial impression of printed matter for correction. —*a.* able to resist penetration or damage. —*v.t.* make (fabric) proof against something (e.g. water).

proofread *v.t.* read and correct (printed proofs). **proofreader** *n.*

prop[1] *n.* & *v.t.* (*p.t.* **propped**) support to prevent something from falling or sagging or failing.

prop[2] *n.* (colloq.) a stage property.

prop[3] *n.* (colloq.) aircraft propeller.

propaganda *n.* publicity intended to persuade or convince people.

propagate *v.t.* breed or reproduce from parent stock; spread (news etc.); transmit. **propagation** *n.*, **propagator** *n.*

propane /'prəʊ-/ *n.* hydrocarbon fuel gas.

propel *v.t.* (*p.t.* **propelled**) push forward, give onward movement to.

propellant *n.* thing that propels something. **propellent** *a.*

propeller *n.* revolving device with blades, for propelling a ship or aircraft.

propensity *n.* tendency; inclination.

proper *a.* suitable; correct; conforming to social conventions; (colloq.) thorough. **proper fraction** fraction that is less than unity, with the numerator less than the denominator. **proper name** *or* **noun** name of an individual person or thing.

property *n.* thing(s) owned; real estate, land; movable object used on the stage in a play etc.; quality, characteristic.

prophecy *n.* power of prophesying; statement prophesying something.

prophesy *v.t./i.* foretell (what will happen).

prophet *n.* person who foretells the future; religious teacher inspired by God; **the Prophet** Muhammad. **prophetess** *n.fem.*

prophetic, **prophetical** *adjs.* prophesying. **prophetically** *adv.*

prophylactic *a.* & *n.* (medicine or action etc.) preventing disease or misfortune. **prophylactically** *adv.*, **prophylaxis** *n.*

propinquity *n.* nearness.

propitiate /-'pɪʃ-/ v.t. win the favour of. **propitiation** n., **propitiatory** a.

propitious /-'pɪʃəs/ a. giving a good omen, favourable. **propitiously** adv., **propitiousness** n.

proponent n. person putting forward a proposal.

proportion n. fraction or share of a whole; ratio; correct relation in size or amount or degree; (pl.) dimensions. **proportional** a., **proportionally** adv.

proportionate a. in due proportion. **proportionately** adv.

proposal n. proposing of something; thing proposed; request to marry the person asking.

propose v.t./i. put forward for consideration; have and declare as one's plan; nominate as a candidate; make a proposal of marriage. **proposer** n.

proposition n. statement; proposal, scheme proposed; (colloq.) undertaking. —v.t. (colloq.) put a proposal to.

propound v.t. put forward for consideration.

proprietary a. made and sold by a particular firm, usu. under a patent; of an owner or ownership.

proprietor /-'praɪə-/ n. owner of a business. **proprietress** n.fem., **proprietorial** a.

propriety /-'praɪə-/ n. being proper or suitable; correctness of behaviour.

propulsion n. process of propelling or being propelled. **propulsive** a.

pro rata /'rɑː-/ proportional(ly).

prorogue /-'rəʊg/ v.t./i. discontinue meetings of (a parliament) without dissolving it; be prorogued. **prorogation** n.

prosaic a. plain and ordinary, unimaginative. **prosaically** adv.

proscribe v.t. forbid by law.

prose n. written or spoken language not in verse form.

prosecute v.t. take legal proceedings against (a person) for a

crime; carry on, conduct. **prosecution** n., **prosecutor** n.

proselyte /'prɒsəl-/ n. recent convert to a belief.

proselytize v.t. seek to convert.

prosody /'prɒs-/ n. study of verseforms and poetic metres.

prospect[1] /'prɒs-/ n. view; what one is to expect; chance of success or advancement.

prospect[2] /-'spekt/ v.i. explore in search of something. **prospector** n.

prospective a. expected to be or to occur; future, possible.

prospectus n. printed document advertising the chief features of a school, business enterprise, etc.

prosper v.i. be successful, thrive.

prosperous a. financially successful. **prosperity** n.

prostate gland gland round the neck of the bladder in males. **prostatic** a.

prosthesis /'prɒs-/ n. (pl. -theses) artificial limb or similar appliance. **prosthetic** /-'θet-/ a.

prostitute n. woman who engages in promiscuous sexual intercourse for payment. —v.t. make a prostitute of; put (talent etc.) to an unworthy use. **prostitution** n.

prostrate[1] /'prɒs-/ a. face downwards; lying horizontally; overcome, exhausted.

prostrate[2] /-'treɪt/ v.t. cause to be prostrate. **prostration** n.

prosy a. tedious; commonplace.

protagonist n. one of the chief contenders; (incorrect use) supporter.

protea /'prəʊ-/ n. South African shrub with cone-shaped flowerheads.

protean a. variable; versatile.

protect v.t. keep from harm or injury. **protection** n., **protector** n.

protectionism n. policy of protecting home industries by tariffs etc. **protectionist** n.

protective a. protecting, giving protection. **protectively** adv.

protectorate n. country that is under the official protection and partial control of a stronger one.

protégé /'prɒteʒeɪ/ n. (fem. **protégée**) person under the protection or patronage of another.

protein /-tiːn/ n. organic compound containing nitrogen, forming an essential part of animals' food.

pro tem (colloq.) for the time being (Latin *pro tempore*).

protest[1] /'prəʊ-/ n. statement or action indicating disapproval.

protest[2] /-'test/ v.t./i. express disapproval; declare firmly.

Protestant n. member of one of the western Churches that are separated from the Roman Catholic Church. **Protestantism** n.

protestation n. firm declaration.

protocol n. etiquette applying to rank or status; draft of a treaty.

proton n. particle of matter with a positive electric charge.

protoplasm n. contents of a living cell.

prototype n. original example from which others are developed; trial model (e.g. of an aircraft).

protozoon /-'zəʊɒn/ n. (pl. **-zoa**) one-celled microscopic animal. **protozoan** n. & a.

protract v.t. prolong in duration. **protraction** n.

protractor n. instrument for measuring angles, usu. a semicircle marked off in degrees.

protrude v.t./i. project, stick out. **protrusion** n., **protrusive** a.

protuberance n. bulging part.

protuberant a. bulging outwards.

proud a. (-er, -est) full of pride; imposing; slightly projecting. —adv. **do a person proud** (colloq.) treat him or her lavishly. **proudly** adv.

provable a. able to be proved.

prove v.t./i. give or be proof of; be found to be; (of unbaked dough)

rise. **prove oneself** show that one has the required abilities.

proven a. proved.

provenance n. place of origin.

provender n. fodder; (joc.) food.

proverb n. short well-known saying.

proverbial a. of or mentioned in a proverb; well-known. **proverbially** adv.

provide v.t./i. cause to have possession or use of; supply the necessities of life; make preparations. **provider** n.

provided conj. on condition (that).

providence n. being provident; God's or nature's care and protection; **Providence** God.

provident a. showing wise forethought for future needs, thrifty.

providential a. happening very luckily. **providentially** adv.

providing conj. = provided.

province n. administrative division of a country; district under an archbishop's charge; range of learning or responsibility; (pl.) all parts of a country outside its capital city; **the Province** Northern Ireland.

provincial a. of a province or provinces; having limited interests and narrow-minded views. —n. inhabitant of province(s).

provision n. process of providing things, esp. for future needs; stipulation in a treaty or contract etc.; (pl.) supply of food and drink.

provisional a. arranged temporarily. **provisionally** adv.

proviso /-'vaɪ-/ n. (pl. **-os**) stipulation. **provisory** a.

provoke v.t. make angry; rouse to action; produce as a reaction or effect. **provocation** n., **provocative** /-'vɒk-/ a., **provocatively** adv.

provoking a. annoying.

provost /'prɒv-/ n. head of certain colleges or cathedral chapters;

head of a municipal corporation or burgh in Scotland.

prow /prau/ *n.* projecting front part of a ship or boat.

prowess /'praʊ-/ *n.* great ability or daring.

prowl *v.t./i.* go about stealthily or restlessly. —*n.* act of prowling. **prowler** *n.*

proximate *a.* nearest.

proximity *n.* nearness.

proxy *n.* person authorized to represent or act for another; use of such a person.

prude *n.* person of exaggerated propriety, one who is easily shocked. **prudery** *n.*

prudent *a.* showing carefulness and foresight. **prudently** *adv.*, **prudence** *n.*

prudential *a.* prudent.

prudish *a.* showing prudery. **prudishly** *adv.*, **prudishness** *n.*

prune[1] *n.* dried plum.

prune[2] *v.t.* trim by cutting away dead or unwanted parts; reduce.

prurient *a.* having or arising from lewd thoughts. **pruriently** *adv.*, **prurience** *n.*

prussic acid highly poisonous acid.

pry[1] *v.i.* inquire or peer impertinently (often furtively).

pry[2] *v.t.* (US) prise.

PS *abbr.* postscript.

psalm *n.* sacred song, esp. from the Book of Psalms in the Old Testament.

psalmist *n.* writer of psalms.

psalmody *n.* singing psalms.

psalter *n.* copy of the Book of Psalms.

psaltery *n.* ancient and medieval stringed instrument.

psephology /sef-/ *n.* study of trends in election and voting. **psephological** *a.*, **psephologist** *n.*

pseudo- /sju:-/ *pref.* false.

pseudonym *n.* fictitious name, esp. used by an author. **pseudonymous** /-'dɒn-/ *a.*

psoriasis /sɔː'raɪ-/ *n.* skin disease causing scaly red patches.

psyche /'saɪkɪ/ *n.* soul, self; mind.

psychedelic /-'del-/ *a.* hallucinogenic; vivid, bright.

psychiatry /sɪ'kaɪə-/ *n.* study and treatment of mental disease. **psychiatrist** *n.*, **psychiatric** /-kɪ'æ-/ *a.*

psychic *a.* psychical; able to exercise psychical powers.

psychical *a.* of the soul or mind; of phenomena that seem to be outside physical and natural laws. **psychically** *adv.*

psychoanalyse *v.t.* treat by psychoanalysis. **psychoanalyst** *n.*

psychoanalysis *n.* method of examining and treating mental conditions by investigating the interaction of conscious and unconscious elements.

psychology *n.* study of the mind and how it works; mental characteristics. **psychological** *a.*, **psychologically** *adv.*, **psychologist** *n.*

psychopath *n.* person suffering from a severe mental disorder. **psychopathic** *a.*

psychosis *n.* (*pl.* -oses) severe mental disorder involving a person's whole personality. **psychotic** *a.* & *n.*

psychosomatic /-'mæt-/ *a.* (of illness) caused or aggravated by mental stress.

psychotherapy *n.* treatment of mental disorders by the use of psychological methods. **psychotherapist** *n.*

pt. *abbr.* pint.

ptarmigan /'tɑː-/ *n.* bird of the grouse family with plumage that turns white in winter.

pterodactyl /te-/ *n.* extinct reptile with wings.

ptomaine /'təʊ-/ *n.* compound (esp. toxic) found in putrefying matter.

pub *n.* (*colloq.*) public house.

puberty *n.* stage in life at which a person's reproductive organs

pubic able to function.

pubertal a.

pubic a. of the abdomen at the lower front part of the pelvis.

public a. of, for, or known to people in general. —n. members of a community in general. **in public** openly, not in private. **public house** building (other than a hotel) licensed to sell alcoholic drinks (other with meals). **public school** secondary school for fee-paying pupils; (in Scotland, USA, etc.) school managed by public authorities. **public-spirited** a. showing readiness to do things for the benefit of people in general. **publicly** adv.

publican n. keeper of a public house; (in the Bible) tax-collector.

publication n. publishing; published book or newspaper item.

publicity n. public attention directed upon a person or thing; process of attracting this.

publicize v.t. bring to the attention of the public. **publicist** n.

publish v.t. issue copies of (a book etc.) to the public; make generally known. **publisher** n.

puce a. & n. brownish purple.

puck n. hard rubber disc used in ice hockey.

pucker v.t./i. & n. wrinkle.

puckish a. impish.

pudding n. baked, boiled, or steamed dish containing or enclosed in a mixture of flour and other ingredients; sweet course of a meal; a kind of sausage.

puddle n. small pool of rainwater or of liquid on a surface.

pudenda /-'den-/ n.pl. genitals.

pudgy a. (-ier, -iest) podgy. **pudginess** n.

puerile /'pjʊəraɪl/ a. childish. **puerility** /-'rɪl-/ n.

puerperal /pjuː'ɜː-/ a. of or resulting from childbirth.

puff n. short light blowing of breath, wind, smoke, etc.; round soft mass; soft pad for applying powder to the skin; piece of advertising. —v.t./i. send (air etc.) or come out in puffs; breathe hard, pant; make or become inflated, swell. **puff-ball** n. globular fungus. **puff pastry** very light flaky pastry.

puffin n. sea bird with a short striped bill.

puffy a. puffed out, swollen. **puffiness** n.

pug n. dog of a dwarf breed resembling the bulldog. **pug-nosed** a. having a short fairly flat nose.

pugilist /'pjuːdʒ-/ n. professional boxer. **pugilism** n.

pugnacious a. eager to fight, aggressive. **pugnaciously** adv., **pugnacity** n.

puisne /'pjuːnɪ/ n. judge of a superior court who is inferior in rank to the chief justice.

puissance /'pwiːs-/ n. test of a horse's ability to jump high obstacles.

puke v.t./i. & n. (sl.) vomit.

pull v.t./i. exert force upon (a thing) so as to move it towards oneself or the source of the force; remove or damage or check by pulling; exert a pulling or driving force; attract. —n. act or force of pulling; means of exerting influence; deep drink; draw at a pipe etc. **pull a person's leg** tease him or her. **pull down** demolish; weaken the health of. **pull in** (of a vehicle etc.) move towards the side of the road or into a stopping-place. **pull-in** n. place for doing this. **pull off** succeed in doing or achieving. **pull oneself together** regain one's self-control. **pull one's punches** avoid using full force. **pull one's weight** do one's fair share of work. **pull out** withdraw; (of a vehicle etc.) move away from the side of a road or a stopping-place. **pull through** come or bring successfully through an illness or difficulty. **pull up** stop; reprimand.

pullet n. young hen.

pulley n. (pl. **-eys**) wheel over which a rope etc. passes, used in lifting things or to drive an endless belt.

pullover n. sweater (with or without sleeves) with no fastenings.

pulmonary /'pʌl-/ a. of the lungs.

pulp n. soft moist part (esp. of fruit) or substance. —v.t./i. reduce or become reduced to pulp. **pulpy** a.

pulpit n. raised enclosed platform in a church, for preaching from.

pulsar n. cosmic source of radio pulses.

pulsate v.i. expand and contract rhythmically; vibrate. **pulsation** n.

pulse[1] n. rhythmical throbbing of arteries as blood is propelled along them, esp. as felt in the wrists or temples etc.; single beat, throb, or vibration. —v.i. pulsate.

pulse[2] n. edible seed of beans, peas, lentils, etc.

pulverize v.t./i. crush into powder; become powder; defeat thoroughly. **pulverization** n.

puma n. large brown American animal of the cat family.

pumice /'pʌm-/ n. solidified lava used for rubbing stains from the skin or as powder for polishing things. **pumice-stone** n. piece of this.

pummel v.t. (p.t. **pummelled**) strike repeatedly esp. with the fists.

pump[1] n. machine for raising water, or for moving liquid, gas, or air. —v.t./i. use a pump; move or inflate or empty by using a pump; move vigorously up and down; pour forth; question persistently to obtain information.

pump[2] n. light shoe; plimsoll.

pumpernickel n. wholemeal rye bread.

pumpkin n. large round orange-coloured fruit of a vine.

pun n. humorous use of a word to suggest another that sounds the same. **punning** a. & n., **punster** n.

punch[1] v.t./i. strike with the fist; (US) herd; perforate, cut (a hole etc.) with a device. —n. blow with the fist; (sl.) vigour; device for cutting holes or impressing a design in metal or leather etc. **punch-drunk** a. stupefied by being severely punched. **punch-line** n. words giving the climax of a joke. **punch-up** n. (colloq.) fight with fists, brawl. **punchy** a.

punch[2] n. drink made of wine or spirits mixed with fruit juices etc. **punch-bowl** n.

punctilio n. (pl. **-os**) delicate point of ceremony etc.; petty formality.

punctilious a. very careful about details; conscientious. **punctiliously** adv., **punctiliousness** n.

punctual a. arriving or doing things at the appointed time. **punctually** adv., **punctuality** n.

punctuate v.t. insert the appropriate marks in written material to separate sentences etc.; interrupt at intervals. **punctuation** n.

puncture n. small hole made by something sharp, esp. accidentally in a pneumatic tyre. —v.t./i. make a puncture in; suffer a puncture.

pundit n. learned expert.

pungent /'pʌndʒ-/ a. having a strong sharp taste or smell; (of remarks) biting. **pungently** adv., **pungency** n.

punish v.t. cause (an offender) to suffer for his offence; inflict a penalty for; treat roughly. **punishment** n.

punishable a. liable to be punished.

punitive /'pju-/ a. inflicting or intended to inflict punishment.

punk n. (sl.) worthless stuff, a worthless person; (devotee of) punk rock or bizarre fashions. —a. (sl.) worthless; of punk rock or its devotees. **punk rock** type of pop music involving outrage and shock effects.

punnet *n.* small chip (basket) or similar container for fruit etc.

punt[1] *n.* shallow flat-bottomed boat with broad square ends. —*v.t./i.* propel (a punt) by thrusting with a pole against the bottom of a river; carry or travel in a punt.

punt[2] *v.t.* kick (a dropped football) before it touches the ground. —*n.* this kick.

punt[3] *v.i.* lay a stake against the bank in certain card-games; (*colloq.*) bet on a horse etc.

punter *n.* person who punts (*punt*[3]); (*colloq.*) customer.

puny *a.* (-ier, -iest) undersized; feeble. **puniness** *n.*

pup *n.* young dog; young wolf, rat, or seal. —*v.i.* (*p.t.* **pupped**) give birth to pup(s).

pupa /'pju:-/ *n.* (*pl.* **-ae**) chrysalis. **pupal** *a.*

pupate *v.i.* become a pupa. **pupation** *n.*

pupil *n.* person who is taught by another; opening in the centre of the iris of the eye.

puppet *n.* a kind of doll made to move by various means as an entertainment; person or State whose actions are controlled by another. **puppetry** *n.*

puppy *n.* young dog. **puppy-fat** *n.* temporary fatness of a child or adolescent.

purblind *a.* partially blind; dimsighted; stupid.

purchase *v.t.* buy. —*n.* buying; thing bought; firm hold to pull or raise something, leverage. **purchaser** *n.*

purdah *n.* Muslim or Hindu system of secluding women.

pure *a.* (-er, -est) not mixed with any other substances; mere; free from evil or sin; chaste; (of mathematics or sciences) dealing with theory, not with practical applications. **pureness** *n.*

purée /-rei/ *n.* pulped fruit or vegetables etc. —*v.t.* make into purée.

purely *adv.* in a pure way; entirely; only.

purgative *a.* strongly laxative; purifying. —*n.* purgative substance.

purgatory *n.* place or condition of suffering, esp. (in RC belief) in which souls undergo purification. **purgatorial** *a.*

purge *v.t.* clear the bowels of by a purgative; rid of people or things regarded as undesirable; atone for (an offence). —*n.* process of purging.

purify *v.t.* make pure, cleanse from impurities. **purification** *n.*, **purificatory** *a.*, **purifier** *n.*

purist *n.* stickler for correctness. **purism** *n.*

Puritan *n.* member of those English Protestants (16th–17th centuries) who wanted simpler church ceremonies and gravity in behaviour. **puritan** *n.* person who is strict in morals and regards certain pleasures as sinful. **puritanical** *a.*

purity *n.* pureness.

purl[1] *n.* a kind of knitting-stitch. —*v.t./i.* produce this stitch (in).

purl[2] *v.i.* flow with a gentle babbling sound.

purler *n.* (*colloq.*) headlong fall.

purlieus /-lju:z/ *n.pl.* outskirts.

purlin *n.* horizontal beam along the length of a roof.

purloin *v.t.* steal.

purple *a.* & *n.* (of) a colour made by mixing red and blue.

purport[1] /'pɜ:-/ *n.* meaning.

purport[2] /-'pɔ:t/ *v.t.* have as its purport; pretend, be intended to seem. **purportedly** *adv.*

purpose *n.* intended result of effort; intention to act, determination. —*v.t.* intend. **on purpose** by intention not by chance. **purpose-built** *a.* built for a particular purpose. **to no purpose** with no result.

purposeful a. having or showing a conscious purpose, with determination. **purposefully** adv., **purposefulness** n.

purposely adv. on purpose.

purr n. low vibrant sound that a cat makes when pleased; similar sound. —v.i. make this sound.

purse n. small pouch for carrying money; (US) handbag; money, funds. —v.t. pucker (one's lips).

purser n. ship's officer in charge of accounts.

pursuance n. performance (of duties etc.).

pursuant adv. **pursuant to** in accordance with.

pursue v.t. chase in order to catch or kill; afflict continually; continue, proceed along; engage in. **pursuer** n.

pursuit n. pursuing; activity to which one gives time or effort.

purulent /'pjʊər-/ a. of or containing pus. **purulence** n.

purvey v.t. supply (articles of food) as a trader. **purveyance** n., **purveyor** n.

purview /'pɜː-/ n. range of vision or concern etc.

pus n. thick yellowish matter produced from infected tissue.

push v.t./i. move away by exerting force; thrust forward; make (one's way) forcibly; make a vigorous effort; make demands on the abilities or tolerance of; urge; sell (drugs) illegally. —n. act of pushing; force exerted by this; vigorous effort; self-assertion, determination to get on. **give** *or* **get the push** (sl.) dismiss or be dismissed. **push off** (sl.) go away. **pusher** n.

pushchair n. folding chair on wheels, in which a child can be pushed along.

pushful a. pushy.

pushing a. pushy.

pushy a. (-ier, -iest) (colloq.) self-assertive, determined to get on. **pushiness** n.

pusillanimous /-'læn-/ a. timid, cowardly. **pusillanimity** /-'nɪm-/ n.

puss n. cat.

pussy n. (children's use) cat.

pussy willow willow with furry catkins.

pussyfoot v.i. move stealthily; act cautiously.

pustule n. pimple, blister. **pustular** a.

put v.t./i. (p.t. put, pres.p. putting) cause to occupy or be in a certain place, position, state, or relationship; estimate; express, phrase; impose (as a tax etc.); lay (blame) on; throw (the shot or weight) as an athletic exercise; (of ships) proceed. —n. throw of the shot or weight. **put by** save for future use. **put down** suppress by force or authority; snub; have (an animal) killed; record in writing; reckon, consider. **put in** make (an appearance); (colloq.) spend (time) working. **put in for** apply for. **put off** postpone; dissuade, repel. **put out** disconcert; inconvenience; extinguish; dislocate. **put up** construct, build; raise the price of; provide (money etc.); present as an idea or proposal; give or receive accommodation; attempt or offer (resistance etc.). **put-up job** scheme concocted fraudulently. **put upon** (colloq.) unfairly burdened or deceived. **put up to** instigate (a person) in. **put up with** endure, tolerate.

putative /'pjuː-/ a. reputed, supposed. **putatively** adv.

putrefy v.i. rot. **putrefaction** n.

putrescent a. rotting. **putrescence** n.

putrid a. rotten; stinking.

putsch /pʊtʃ/ n. attempt at revolution.

putt /pʌt/ v.t. strike (a golf-ball) gently to make it roll along the ground. —n. this stroke. **putter** n. club used for this.

puttee *n.* strip of cloth wound spirally from ankle to knee for protection and support.

putty *n.* soft paste that sets hard, used for fixing glass in frames, filling up holes, etc.

puzzle *n.* question that is difficult to answer, problem; problem or toy designed to test knowledge or ingenuity. —*v.t./i.* cause to think hard; use hard thought, solve by this. **puzzlement** *n.*

pygmy *n.* person or thing of unusually small size; **Pygmy** member of a dwarf negroid African people. —*a.* very small.

pyjamas /-'dʒɑ:-/ *n.pl.* loose jacket and trousers esp. for sleeping in.

pylon *n.* tall lattice-work structure used for carrying electricity cables or as a boundary.

pyorrhoea /-'rɪ:ə/ *n.* discharge of pus, esp. from tooth-sockets.

pyramid *n.* structure with sloping sides that meet at the top, esp. built by ancient Egyptians as a tomb or by Aztecs and Mayas as a platform for a temple. **pyramidal** /-'ræm-/ *a.*

pyre *n.* pile of wood etc. for burning a dead body as part of a funeral rite.

Pyrenean /pɪrə'nɪ:ən/ *a.* of the Pyrenees.

pyrethrum /pa'ri:-/ *n.* a kind of chrysanthemum; insecticide made from its dried flowers.

pyrites /-'raɪtɪz/ *n.* mineral sulphide of (copper and) iron.

pyromaniac /paɪrə'meɪ-/ *n.* person with an uncontrollable impulse to set things on fire.

pyrotechnics *n.pl.* firework display. **pyrotechnic** *a.*

Pyrrhic victory /'pɪrɪk/ one gained at too great a cost.

python *n.* large snake that crushes its prey.

pyx *n.* vessel in which bread consecrated for the Eucharist is kept;

box in which specimen coins are deposited at the Royal Mint.

Q

QC *abbr.* Queen's Counsel.

qt. *abbr.* quart(s).

qua /kweɪ/ *conj.* in the capacity of.

quack[1] *n.* duck's harsh cry. —*v.i.* make this sound.

quack[2] *n.* person who falsely claims to have medical skill or remedies.

quad /kwɒd/ *n.* (*colloq.*) quadrangle; quadraphonic; quadruplet.

quadrangle /'kwɒd-/ *n.* four-sided court bordered by large buildings.

quadrant /'kwɒd-/ *n.* one-quarter of a circle or its circumference; graduated instrument for taking angular measurements.

quadraphonic /kwɒd-/ *a. & n.* (sound-reproduction) using four transmission channels. **quadraphony** *n.*

quadratic /kwɒd-/ *a. & n.* (equation) involving the second and no higher power of an unknown quantity or variable.

quadrennial /kwɒd-/ *a.* happening every fourth year; lasting four years. **quadrennially** *adv.*

quadrilateral /kwɒd-/ *n.* geometric figure with four sides.

quadrille /kwɒd'rɪl/ *n.* a kind of square dance.

quadruped /'kwɒd-/ *n.* four-footed animal.

quadruple /'kwɒd-/ *a.* having four parts or members; four times as much. —*v.t./i.* increase by four times its amount.

quadruplet /'kwɒd-/ *n.* one of four children born at one birth.

quaff /kwɒf/ *v.t.* drink in large draughts.

quagmire /'kwæ-/ *n.* bog, marsh.

quail[1] n. bird related to the partridge.

quail[2] v.i. flinch, show fear.

quaint a. (**-er**, **-est**) odd in a pleasing way. **quaintly** adv., **quaintness** n.

quake v.i. shake or tremble, esp. with fear. —n. (colloq.) earthquake.

Quaker n. member of the Society of Friends (see **friend**). **Quakerism** n.

qualification n. qualifying; thing that qualifies a person to do something; thing that limits a meaning.

qualify v.t./i. make or become competent, eligible, or legally entitled to do something; limit the meaning of; attribute a quality to. **qualifier** n.

qualitative /ˈkwɒl-/ a. of or concerned with quality.

quality n. degree or level of excellence; characteristic, something that is special in a person or thing.

qualm /kwɑːm/ n. misgiving, pang of conscience.

quandary /ˈkwɒn-/ n. state of perplexity, difficult situation.

quango n. (pl. **-os**) administrative body (outside the Civil Service) with senior members appointed by the government.

quantify v.t. express as a quantity. **quantifiable** a.

quantitative /ˈkwɒn-/ a. of or concerned with quantity.

quantity n. amount or number of things; ability to be measured; (pl.) large amounts. **in quantity** in large amounts. **quantity surveyor** person who measures and prices building-work.

quantum /ˈkwɒn-/ n. **quantum theory** theory of physics based on the assumption that energy exists in indivisible units.

quarantine /-tiːn/ n. isolation imposed on those who have been exposed to an infection which they could spread. —v.t. put into quarantine.

quark n. component of elementary particles.

quarrel n. angry disagreement. —v.i. (p.t. **quarrelled**) engage in a quarrel.

quarrelsome a. liable to quarrel.

quarry[1] n. intended prey or victim; thing sought or pursued.

quarry[2] n. open excavation from which stone or slate etc. is obtained. —v.t./i. obtain from a quarry; search for information. **quarry tile** unglazed floor-tile.

quart n. quarter of a gallon, two pints.

quarter n. one of four equal parts; this amount; (US & Canada) quarter of a dollar, 25 cents; grain-measure of 8 bushels; fourth part of a year, for which payments are due on **quarter day**; point of time 15 minutes before or after every hour; direction, district; mercy towards an enemy or opponent; (pl.) lodgings, accommodation. —v.t. divide into quarters; place (a symbol) in a coat of arms; put (soldiers etc.) into lodgings; (of a dog) search systematically. **quarter final** n. contest preceding a semi-final. **quarter-light** n. small triangular window in a motor vehicle.

quarterdeck n. part of a ship's upper deck nearest the stern.

quarterly a. & adv. (produced or occurring) once in every quarter of a year. —n. quarterly periodical.

quartermaster n. regimental officer in charge of stores etc.; naval petty officer in charge of steering and signals.

quartet n. group of four instruments or voices; music for these.

quarto n. a size of paper.

quartz n. a kind of hard mineral. **quartz clock** one operated by electric vibrations of a quartz crystal.

quasar /ˈkweɪ-/ n. star-like object that is the source of intense electromagnetic radiation.

quash v.t. annul; suppress.

quasi- /ˈkweɪzaɪ/ pref. seeming to be but not really so.

quassia n. South American tree; its wood, bark, or root; bitter tonic made from this.

quatercentenary /kwæts:sen'ti:-/ n. 400th anniversary.

quatrain /ˈkwɒt-/ n. stanza of four lines.

quatrefoil n. figure with four cusps; leaf or flower with four lobes.

quaver v.t./i. tremble, vibrate; speak or utter in a trembling voice. —n. trembling sound; note in music, half a crochet. **quavery** a.

quay /kiː/ n. landing-place built for ships to load or unload alongside. **quayside** n.

queasy a. feeling or liable to feel slightly sick; squeamish. **queasiness** n.

queen n. female ruler of a country by right of birth; king's wife; woman or thing regarded as supreme in some way; piece in chess; playing-card bearing a picture of a queen; fertile female of bee or ant etc.; (sl.) male homosexual. —v.t./i. convert (a pawn in chess) to a queen; be converted thus. **queen** it behave as if supreme. **queen mother** dowager queen who is the reigning sovereign's mother. **Queen's Bench** division of the high court of justice. **Queen's Counsel** counsel to the Crown. **queenly** a.

queer a. (-er, -est) strange, odd, eccentric; slightly ill or faint; (derog.) homosexual. —n. (derog.) homosexual. —v.t. spoil. **queer a person's pitch** spoil his chances.

quell v.t. suppress.

quench v.t. extinguish (a fire or flame) satisfy (one's thirst) by

drinking something; cool by water.

quern n. hand-mill for grinding corn or pepper.

querulous /ˈkwe-/ a. complaining peevishly. **querulously** adv., **querulousness** n.

query n. question; question mark. —v.t. ask a question or express doubt about.

quest n. seeking, search.

question n. sentence requesting information or an answer; matter for discussion or solution; raising of doubt. —v.t. ask or raise question(s) about. **in question** being referred to or discussed or disputed. **no question of** no possibility of. **out of the question** completely impracticable. **question mark** punctuation mark ? placed after a question.

questionable a. open to doubt.

questionnaire n. list of questions seeking information.

queue n. line or series of people waiting for something. —v.i. (pres.p. **queuing**) wait in a queue.

quibble n. petty objection. —v.i. make petty objections. **quibbler** n.

quiche /kiːʃ/ n. open tart, usu. with a savoury filling.

quick a. (-er, -est) taking only a short time; able to notice or learn or think quickly; (of temper) easily roused; (old use) alive. —n. sensitive flesh below the nails. **quickly** adv., **quickness** n.

quicken v.t./i. make or become quicker or livelier; reach the stage of pregnancy (the **quickening**) when the foetus makes movements that can be felt by the mother.

quickie n. (colloq.) quick one.

quicklime n. = lime¹.

quicksand n. area of loose wet deep sand into which heavy objects will sink.

quickset a. (of a hedge) formed of growing plants.

quicksilver n. mercury.

quid[1] n. (pl. **quid**) (sl.) £1.

quid[2] n. lump of tobacco for chewing.

quid pro quo thing given in return.

quiescent /kwɪˈes- or kwaɪ-/ a. inactive, quiet. **quiescence** n.

quiet a. (-er, -est) with little or no sound; free from disturbance or vigorous activity; silent; subdued. —n. quietness. —v.t./i. quieten. **on the quiet** unobtrusively, secretly. **quietly** adv., **quietness** n.

quieten v.t./i. make or become quiet.

quietude /ˈkwaɪ-/ n. quietness.

quiff n. upright tuft of hair.

quill n. large wing- or tail-feather; thing (esp. old type of pen) made from this; each of a porcupine's spines.

quilt n. padded bed-cover. —v.t. line with padding and fix with cross-lines of stitching.

quin n. (colloq.) quintuplet.

quince n. hard yellowish fruit; tree bearing this.

quincentenary /-ˈtiː-/ n. 500th anniversary.

quinine /-ˈniːn/ n. bitter-tasting medicine.

quinquennial a. happening every fifth year; lasting five years. **quinquennially** adv.

quinsy n. abscess on a tonsil.

quintessence n. essence; perfect example of a quality. **quintessential** a., **quintessentially** adv.

quintet n. group of five instruments or voices; music for these.

quintuple a. having five parts or members; five times as much as. —v.t./i. increase by five times its amount.

quintuplet /-ˈtjuː-/ n. one of five children born at one birth.

quip n. witty or sarcastic remark. —v.t. (p.t. **quipped**) utter as a quip.

quire n. twenty-five or twenty-four sheets of writing-paper.

quirk n. a peculiarity of behaviour; trick of fate.

quisling n. traitor who collaborates with an enemy occupying his country.

quit v.t./i. (p.t. **quitted**) go away from, leave; abandon; (colloq.) cease. —a. rid. **quitter** n.

quite adv. completely; somewhat; really, actually; (as an answer) I agree. **quite a few** a considerable number.

quits a. on even terms after retaliation or repayment.

quiver[1] n. case for holding arrows.

quiver[2] v.i. shake or vibrate with a slight rapid motion. —n. quivering movement or sound.

quixotic /-ˈsɒt-/ a. chivalrous and unselfish. **quixotically** adv.

quiz n. (pl. **quizzes**) series of questions testing knowledge, esp. as an entertainment. —v.t. (p.t. **quizzed**) interrogate; (old use) stare at.

quizzical a. in a questioning way, esp. humorously. **quizzically** adv.

quod n. (sl.) prison.

quoin n. external corner of a building; corner-stone.

quoit /kɔɪt/ n. ring of metal or rubber etc. thrown to encircle a peg in the game of **quoits**.

quorate a. having a quorum present.

quorum n. minimum number of people that must be present to constitute a valid meeting.

quota n. fixed share; maximum number or amount that may be admitted, manufactured, etc.

quotable a. worth quoting.

quotation n. quoting; passage or price quoted. **quotation-marks** n.pl. punctuation marks (' or " ") enclosing words quoted.

quote v.t./i. repeat words from a book or speech; mention in support of a statement; state the price of, estimate.

quoth /kwəʊθ/ (*old use*) said.

quotidian /-'tɪd-/ *a.* daily.

quotient /'kwəʊʃənt/ *n.* result of a division sum.

R

rabbet *n.* step-shaped recess cut along the edge of a piece of wood to receive a matching piece. **rabbet plane** tool for cutting this.

rabbi /-baɪ/ *n.* (*pl.* **-is**) religious leader of a Jewish congregation.

rabbinical /-'bɪn-/ *a.* of rabbis or Jewish doctrines or law.

rabbit *n.* burrowing animal with long ears and a short furry tail.

rabble *n.* disorderly crowd, mob.

rabid /'ræ-/ *a.* furious, fanatical; affected with rabies. **rabidity** *n.*

rabies /'reɪbiːz/ *n.* contagious fatal virus disease of dogs etc., that can be transmitted to man.

race[1] *n.* contest of speed; strong fast current of water; (for balls in a ball-bearing; *pl.*) series of races for horses or dogs. —*v.t./i.* compete in a race (with); engage in horse-racing; move or operate at full or excessive speed. **racer** *n.*

race[2] *n.* one of the great divisions of mankind with certain inherited physical characteristics in common; large group of people related by common descent; genus, species, breed, or variety of animals or plants.

racecourse *n.* ground where horse-races are run.

racehorse *n.* horse bred for racing.

racetrack *n.* racecourse; track for motor-racing.

raceme /-'siːm/ *n.* flower-cluster with flowers attached by short stalks along a central stem.

racial *a.* of or based on race. **racially** *adv.*

racialism *n.* racism. **racialist** *a.* & *n.*

racism *n.* belief in the superiority of a particular race; antagonism between races; theory that human abilities are determined by race. **racist** *a.* & *n.*

rack[1] *n.* framework, usu. with bars or pegs, for keeping or placing things on; bar or rail with teeth or cogs that engage with those of a wheel or gear etc.; instrument of torture on which people were tied and stretched. —*v.t.* inflict great torment on. **rack one's brains** think hard about a problem.

rack[2] *n.* **rack and ruin** destruction.

rack[3] *v.t.* draw (wine or beer) off the lees.

racket[1] *n.* stringed bat used in tennis and similar games; (*pl.*) ball game played with rackets in a four-walled court.

racket[2] *n.* din, noisy fuss; fraudulent business or other activity; (*sl.*) line of business, dodge. **rackety** *a.*

racketeer *n.* person who operates a fraudulent business etc. **racketeering** *n.*

raconteur /-'tɜː(r)/ *n.* person who is good at telling anecdotes.

racoon *n.* small arboreal mammal of North America.

racy *a.* (**-ier, -iest**) spirited and vigorous in style. **racily** *adv.*

radar *n.* system for detecting objects by means of radio waves.

radial *a.* of rays or radii; having spokes or lines etc. that radiate from a central point; (of a tyre; also **radial-ply**) having the fabric layers parallel and the tread strengthened. —*n.* radial-ply tyre. **radially** *adv.*

radiant *a.* emitting rays of light or heat; emitted in rays; looking very bright and happy. **radiantly** *adv.*, **radiance** *n.*

radiate *v.t./i.* spread outwards from a central point: send or be sent out in rays.

radiation *n.* process of radiating; sending out of rays and atomic particles characteristic of radioactive substances; these rays and particles.

radiator *n.* apparatus that radiates heat, esp. a metal case through which steam or hot water circulates; engine-cooling apparatus.

radical *a.* fundamental; drastic, thorough; holding extremist views. —*n.* person desiring radical reforms or holding radical views. **radically** *adv.*

radicle *n.* embryo root.

radio *n.* (*pl.* **-os**) process of sending and receiving messages etc. by electromagnetic waves without a connecting wire; transmitter or receiver for this; sound-broadcasting; station for this. —*a.* of or involving radio. —*v.t.* send, signal, or communicate by radio.

radioactive *a.* sending out radiation that produces electrical and chemical effects. **radioactivity** *n.*

radiocarbon *n.* radioactive form of carbon used in dating ancient organic remains.

radiogram *n.* combined radio and record-player.

radiography /-'ɒg-/ *n.* production of X-ray photographs. **radiographer** *n.*

radiology /-'ɒl-/ *n.* study of X-rays and similar radiation. **radiological** *a.*, **radiologist** *n.*

radiotherapy *n.* treatment of disease by X-rays or similar radiation.

radish *n.* plant with a crisp hot-tasting root that is eaten raw.

radium *n.* radioactive metal obtained from pitchblende.

radius *n.* (*pl.* **-dii**, *pr.* -dɪəɪ) straight line from the centre to the circumference of a circle or

sphere; its length; distance from a centre; thicker long bone of the forearm.

RAF *abbr.* Royal Air Force.

raffia *n.* strips of fibre from the leaves of a kind of palm-tree.

raffish *a.* looking vulgarly flashy or rakish. **raffishness** *n.*

raffle *n.* lottery with object(s) as prize(s). —*v.t.* offer as the prize in a raffle.

raft *n.* flat floating structure of timber etc., used as a boat.

rafter *n.* one of the sloping beams forming the framework of a roof.

rag[1] *n.* torn piece of fabric; (*derog.*) newspaper; (*pl.*) torn clothes.

rag[2] *v.t.* (*p.t.* **ragged**) (*sl.*) tease. —*n.* (*sl.*) prank, piece of fun; students' carnival in aid of charity.

ragamuffin *n.* person in ragged dirty clothes.

rage *n.* violent anger; craze, fashion. —*v.i.* show violent anger; (of a storm or battle) continue furiously.

ragged /-gɪd/ *a.* torn, frayed; in torn clothes; jagged; faulty, uneven.

raglan *n.* type of sleeve joined to a garment by sloping seams.

ragout /'ræguː/ *n.* stew of meat and vegetables.

ragtime *n.* a form of jazz music with much syncopation.

raid *n.* brief attack to destroy or seize or steal something; surprise visit by police etc. to arrest suspected people or seize illicit goods. —*v.t.* make a raid on. **raider** *n.*

rail[1] *n.* horizontal or sloping bar; any of the lines of metal bars on which trains or trams run; railway(s). —*v.t.* fit or protect with a rail.

rail[2] *n.* small wading bird.

rail[3] *v.i.* utter angry reproaches.

railing *n.* fence of rails supported on upright metal bars.

raillery *n.* banter, joking.

railman *n.* (*pl.* **-men**) railwayman.

railroad n. (US) railway. —v.t. force into hasty action.

railway n. set of rails on which trains run; system of transport using these. **railwayman** n. (pl. -men).

raiment n. (old use) clothing.

rain n. atmospheric moisture falling as separate drops; a fall or spell of this; shower of things. —v.t./i. send down or fall as or like rain.

rainbow n. arch of colours formed in rain or spray by the sun's rays.

raincoat n. rain-resistant coat.

raindrop n. single drop of rain.

rainfall n. total amount of rain falling in a given time.

rainforest n. luxuriant tropical forest with heavy rainfall.

rainwater n. water that has fallen as rain.

rainy a. (-ier, -iest) in or on which much rain falls.

raise v.t. bring to or towards a higher level or an upright position; cause, rouse; breed, grow; bring up (a child or family); collect, procure; end (a siege). —n. (US) increase in salary etc. **raising agent** substance that makes bread etc. swell in cooking.

raisin n. dried grape.

raison d'être /reɪzɒ̃ 'detr/ reason for a thing's existence.

raj n. British rule in India.

rajah /'rɑːdʒə/ n. Indian prince.

rake[1] n. tool with prongs for drawing together hay etc. or for smoothing loose soil; implement used similarly. —v.t. gather or smooth with a rake; search; direct (gunfire, a scrutiny, etc.) along. **rake-off** n. (colloq.) commission, share of profits. **rake up** revive the memory of (an unpleasant incident).

rake[2] n. backward slope of an object. —v.t. set at a sloping angle.

rake[3] n. man who lives an irresponsible and immoral life. **rakish** a. like a rake; jaunty.

rally v.t./i. bring or come together for a united effort; reassemble for effort after defeat; rouse, revive; recover strength. —n. act of rallying, recovery; series of strokes in tennis etc.; mass meeting; driving competition over public roads.

RAM abbr. random-access memory.

ram n. uncastrated male sheep; striking or plunging device. —v.t. (p.t. **rammed**) push heavily, crash against. **rammer** n.

Ramadan /-'dɑːn/ n. ninth month of the Muslim year, when Muslims fast during daylight hours.

ramble n. walk taken for pleasure. —v.i. take a ramble; wander, straggle; talk or write disconnectedly. **rambler** n.

ramekin /'ræmɪ-/ n. small mould for individual portion of food.

ramify v.t./i. form branches or subdivisions; become complex. **ramification** n.

ramp n. slope joining two levels; movable set of stairs for entering or leaving an aircraft.

rampage v.i. /-'peɪdʒ/ behave or race about violently. —n. /'ræm-/ violent behaviour. **on the rampage** rampaging.

rampant a. flourishing excessively, unrestrained; (of a heraldic animal) standing on one hind leg with the opposite foreleg raised.

rampart n. broad-topped defensive wall or bank of earth.

ram-raid n. robbery in which a shop window is rammed with a vehicle and looted. **ram-raider** n., **ram-raiding** n.

ramrod n. like a ramrod stiff and straight.

ramshackle n. tumbledown, rickety.

ran see run.

ranch n. cattle-breeding establishment in North America; farm where certain other animals are

bred. —*v.i.* farm on a ranch.
rancher *n.*

rancid *a.* smelling or tasting like
stale fat. **rancidity** *n.*

rancour /-kə:(r)/ *n.* bitter feeling
or ill will. **rancorous** *a.*

rand *n.* unit of money in South
African countries.

random *a.* done or made etc. at
random. —*n.* **at random** without
a particular aim or purpose.
random-access memory etc.
(in a computer) one whose contents can be accessed from any
point, not only sequentially.
randomness *n.*

randy *a.* (-ier, -iest) lustful; (*Sc.*)
boisterous. **randiness** *n.*

ranee *n.* rajah's wife or widow.

rang *see* **ring**².

range *n.* line or series of things;
limits between which something
operates or varies; distance a
thing can travel or be effective;
distance to an objective; large
open area for grazing or hunting;
place with targets for shooting-
practice; fireplace with ovens etc.
for cooking in. —*v.t./i.* arrange in
row(s) etc.; extend, reach; vary
between limits; wander, go about
a place.

rangefinder *n.* device for calculating the distance to a target etc.

ranger *n.* keeper of a royal park
or forest; **Ranger** member of the
senior branch of the Guides.

rangy *a.* (-ier, -iest) tall and thin.

rank¹ *n.* line of people or things;
place in a scale of quality or value
etc.; high social position; (*pl.*)
ordinary soldiers, not officers.
—*v.t./i.* arrange in a rank; assign
a rank to; have a certain rank.
the rank and file the ordinary
people of an organization.

rank² *a.* (-er, -est) growing too
thickly and coarsely; full of
weeds; foul-smelling; unmistakably bad, out-and-out. **rankness**
n.

rankle *v.i.* cause lasting resentment.

ransack *v.t.* search thoroughly or
roughly; rob or pillage (a place).

ransom *n.* price demanded or
paid for the release of a captive.
—*v.t.* demand or pay ransom for.

rant *v.i.* make a violent speech.

rap *n.* quick sharp blow; knocking
sound; rhyming monologue recited to music; rock music with
recited words; (*sl.*) chat; (*sl.*)
blame, punishment. —*v.t./i.* (p.t.
rapped) strike with a rap; make a
knocking sound; (*sl.*) reprimand.
rap out say sharply.

rapacious *a.* grasping, plundering and robbing others. **rapacity**
a.

rape¹ *v.t.* have sexual intercourse
with (esp. a woman) without consent. —*n.* this act or crime.

rape² *n.* plant grown as food for
sheep and for its seed from which
oil is obtained.

rapid *a.* quick, swift. **rapidly**
adv., **rapidity** *n.*

rapids *n.pl.* swift current where a
river-bed slopes steeply.

rapier *n.* thin light double-edged
sword, used for thrusting.

rapist *n.* person who commits
rape.

rapport /-'pɔ:(r)/ *n.* harmonious
understanding relationship.

rapprochement /ræ'prɒʃmɑ̃/ *n.*
reconciliation.

rapscallion *n.* (*old use*) rascal.

rapt *a.* very intent and absorbed,
enraptured. **raptly** *adv.*

raptorial *a.* & *n.* predatory (animal or bird).

rapture *n.* intense delight. **rapturous** *a.*, **rapturously** *adv.*

rare¹ *a.* (-er, -est) very uncommon; exceptionally good; of low
density. **rarely** *adv.*, **rareness** *n.*

rare² *a.* (-er, -est) (of meat)
cooked lightly not thoroughly.

rarebit *n.* see **Welsh rabbit**.

rarefied /'reərifaɪd/ *a.* (of air etc.)
of low density, thin. **rarefaction**
n.

raring *a.* (*colloq.*) eager (to go etc.).

rarity *n.* rareness; rare thing.

rascal *n.* dishonest or mischievous person. **rascally** *adv.*

raschel /rə'ʃel/ *n.* loosely knitted textile fabric.

rash[1] *n.* eruption of spots or patches on the skin.

rash[2] *a.* (**-er**, **-est**) acting or done without due consideration of the risks. **rashly** *adv.*, **rashness** *n.*

rasher *n.* slice of bacon or ham.

rasp *n.* coarse file; rough grating sound. —*v.t./i.* scrape with a rasp; utter with or make a grating sound or effect.

raspberry *n.* edible red berry; plant bearing this; (*sl.*) vulgar sound of disapproval.

Rastafarian /-'fear-/ *n.* member of a Jamaican sect.

rat *n.* rodent like a mouse but larger; scoundrel, treacherous deserter. —*v.i.* (*p.t.* **ratted**) **rat on** desert treacherously. **rat race** fiercely competitive struggle for success.

ratafia /-'fiː.ə/ *n.* liqueur or biscuit flavoured with fruit kernels.

ratchet *n.* bar or wheel with notches in which a pawl engages to prevent backward movement.

rate[1] *n.* standard of reckoning, ratio of one quantity or amount etc. to another; rapidity; local tax formerly assessed on the value of land and buildings; (*US*) deserve; levy rates on, value for this purpose. **at any rate** no matter what happens; at least.

rate[2] *v.t.* reprimand angrily.

rateable *a.* liable to or assessed for rates (= local tax).

rather *adv.* slightly; more exactly; by preference; emphatically yes.

ratify *v.t.* confirm (an agreement etc.) formally. **ratification** *n.*

rating *n.* level at which a thing is rated; amount payable as local rates; non-commissioned sailor.

ratio /'reɪʃɪəʊ/ *n.* (*pl.* **-os**) relationship between two amounts, reckoned as the number of times one contains the other.

ratiocinate /-'ɒs-/ *v.i.* reason logically. **ratiocination** *n.*

ration *n.* fixed allowance of food etc. —*v.t.* limit to a ration.

rational *a.* able to reason; sane; based on reasoning, not unreasonable. **rationally** *adv.*, **rationality** *n.*

rationale /-'nɑːl/ *n.* fundamental reason; logical basis.

rationalism *n.* treating reason as the basis of belief and knowledge. **rationalist** *n.*, **rationalistic** *a.*

rationalize *v.t.* make logical and consistent; invent a rational explanation for; make more efficient by reorganizing. **rationalization** *n.*

rattan *n.* palm with jointed stems.

rattle *v.t./i.* make or cause to make a rapid series of short hard sounds; (*sl.*) make nervous. —*n.* rattling sound; device or toy for making this; noise. **rattle off** utter rapidly.

rattlesnake *n.* poisonous American snake with a rattling tail.

rattling *a.* that rattles; vigorous, brisk. —*adv.* (*colloq.*) very.

ratty *a.* (**-ier**, **-iest**) (*sl.*) angry.

raucous *a.* loud and harsh. **raucously** *adv.*, **raucousness** *n.*

raunchy *a.* (**-ier**, **-iest**) (*US*) slovenly, disreputable; coarsely outspoken; boisterous. **raunchily** *adv.*, **raunchiness** *n.*

ravage *v.t.* do great damage to. **ravages** *n.pl.* damage.

rave *v.i.* talk wildly or furiously; speak with rapturous enthusiasm.

ravel *v.t./i.* (*p.t.* **ravelled**) tangle.

raven[1] *n.* large black bird with a hoarse cry. —*a.* (of hair) glossy black.

raven² /'ræ/. *v.t./i.* hungrily seek prey; devour.

ravenous *a.* very hungry. **ravenously** *adv.*, **ravenousness** *n.*

ravine /-'vi:n/ *n.* deep narrow gorge.

raving *a.* frenzied (mad); notable.

ravioli *n.* Italian dish of small pasta cases containing meat.

ravish *v.t.* rape; enrapture.

raw *a.* (-er, -est) not cooked; not yet processed or manufactured; (of alcohol) undiluted; crude, lacking finish; inexperienced, untrained; stripped of skin, sensitive because of this; (of an edge of cloth) with loose threads; (of weather) damp and chilly. —*n.* raw sensitive patch of skin. **rawboned** *a.* gaunt. **raw deal** unfair treatment. **rawness** *n.*

rawhide *n.* untanned leather.

ray¹ *n.* single line or narrow beam of radiation; trace (of hope etc.); radiating line or part or thing.

ray² *n.* large sea-fish with a broad flat body.

rayon *n.* synthetic fibre or fabric, made from cellulose.

raze *v.t.* tear down (a building).

razor *n.* sharp-edged instrument used esp. for shaving hair from the skin.

razzle *n.* **on the razzle** (*sl.*) on the spree.

razzmatazz *n.* excitement; extravagant publicity etc.

RC *abbr.* Roman Catholic.

re /ri:/ *prep.* concerning.

re- *pref.* again; back again.

reach *v.t./i.* extend, be continuous; go as far as, arrive at; stretch out a hand in order to touch or take; establish communication with; achieve, attain. —*n.* distance over which a person or thing can reach; extent of abilities etc.; section of a river or canal. **reachable** *a.*

react *v.i.* cause or undergo a reaction. **reactive** *a.*

reaction *n.* response to a stimulus or act or situation etc.; chemical change produced by substances acting upon each other; occurrence of one condition after a period of the opposite.

reactionary *a.* & *n.* (person) opposed to progress and reform.

reactor *n.* apparatus for the production of nuclear energy.

read /ri:d/ *v.t./i.* (*p.t.* **read**, *pr.* red) understand the meaning of (written or printed words or symbols); speak (such words etc.) aloud; study or discover by reading; interpret mentally; have as wording; (of an instrument) indicate as a measurement; (of a computer) copy or transfer (data). —*n.* (*colloq.*) session of reading.

read-only memory etc., (in a computer) one whose contents cannot be changed by program instructions.

readable *a.* pleasant to read; legible. **readably** *adv.*, **readability** *n.*

readdress *v.t.* redirect by altering the address.

reader *n.* person who reads; senior lecturer at a university; book containing passages for reading as an exercise; device producing a readable image from a microfilm etc.

readership *n.* readers of a newspaper etc.

readily *adv.* willingly; easily.

readiness *n.* being ready.

readjust *v.t./i.* adjust again; adapt oneself again. **readjustment** *n.*

ready *a.* (-ier, -iest) fit or available for action or use; willing; about or inclined to (do something); quick. —*adv.* beforehand. **at the ready** ready for action. **ready-made** *a.* (of clothes) made in standard sizes, not to individual orders.

reafforest *v.t.* replant (former forest land) with trees.

reagent /rɪ'eɪ-/ n. substance used to produce a chemical reaction.

real a. existing as a thing or occurring as a fact; genuine, natural; (of property) immovable, as land or houses. —adv. (Sc. & US colloq.) really, very. **real estate** immovable property such as land or buildings.

realism n. representing or viewing things as they are in reality. **realist** n.

realistic a. showing realism; (of wages or prices) paying the worker or seller adequately. **realistically** adv.

reality n. quality of being real; thing or all that is real and not imagination or fantasy.

realize v.t. be or become aware of; accept as a fact; fulfil (a hope or plan); obtain money by selling (securities etc.); fetch as a price. **realization** n.

really adv. in fact; thoroughly; indeed, I assure you, I protest.

realm n. kingdom; field of activity or interest.

ream n. quantity of paper (usu. 500 sheets); (pl.) great quantity of written matter.

reap v.t. cut (grain etc.) as harvest; receive as the consequence of actions. **reaper** n.

reappear v.i. appear again.

reappraisal n. new appraisal.

rear[1] n. back part. —a. situated at the rear. **bring up the rear** be last in an advancing line. **rear admiral** naval officer next below vice admiral. **rearmost** a.

rear[2] v.t./i. bring up (children); breed and look after (animals); cultivate (crops); set up; (of a horse etc.) raise itself on its hind legs; extend to a great height.

rearguard n. troops protecting an army's rear.

rearm v.t./i. arm again. **rearmament** n.

rearrange v.t. arrange in a different way. **rearrangement** n.

rearward a., adv., & n. (towards or at) the rear. **rearwards** adv.

reason n. motive, cause, justification; ability to think and draw conclusions; sanity; good sense or judgement, what is right or practical or possible. —v.t./i. use one's ability to think and draw conclusions. **reason with** try to persuade by argument.

reasonable a. ready to use or listen to reason; in accordance with reason, logical; moderate, not expensive. **reasonably** adv.

reassemble v.t./i. assemble again.

reassure v.t. restore confidence to, remove the fears or doubts of. **reassurance** n.

rebarbative a. repellent, forbidding.

rebate[1] /'ri:-/ n. partial refund.

rebate[2] /'ri:-/ n. = rabbet.

rebel[1] /'reb-/ n. person who rebels.

rebel[2] /-'bel/ v.i. (p.t. **rebelled**) fight against or refuse allegiance to one's established government; resist control, refuse to obey. **rebellion** n., **rebellious** a.

rebound[1] /-'baʊnd/ v.i. spring back after impact.

rebound[2] /'ri:-/ n. act of rebounding. **on the rebound** while rebounding; while still reacting to a disappointment etc.

rebuff v.t. & n. snub.

rebuild v.t. (p.t. **rebuilt**) build again after destruction.

rebuke v.t. reprove. —n. reproof.

rebus /'ri:-/ n. representation of a word by pictures etc. suggesting its parts.

rebut v.t. (p.t. **rebutted**) disprove. **rebuttal** n.

recalcitrant /-'kæl-/ a. obstinately disobedient. **recalcitrance** n.

recall v.t. summon to return; remember, cause oneself to remember. —n. recalling, being recalled.

recant v.t./i. withdraw and reject (one's) former statement or belief. **recantation** n.

recap /'riː-/ v.t. (p.t. **recapped**) (colloq.) recapitulate. —n. (colloq.) recapitulation.

recapitulate v.t./i. state again the main points of (a statement or discussion). **recapitulation** n.

recapture v.t. capture or experience again. —n. recapturing.

recce /'rekɪ/ n. (sl.) reconnaissance.

recede v.i. go or shrink back; become more distant; slope backwards.

receipt /-'siːt/ n. act of receiving; written acknowledgement that something has been received or money paid. —v.t. mark (a bill) as having been paid.

receive v.t. acquire, accept, or take in (a thing offered, sent, or given); experience, be treated with; allow to enter; greet on arrival.

receiver n. person or thing that receives something; the part of a telephone that receives incoming sound; one who receives stolen goods; official who administers a bankrupt or insane person's property; apparatus that receives broadcast signals and converts them into sound or a picture.

recent a. happening or begun in a time shortly before the present. **recently** adv.

receptacle n. thing for holding what is put into it.

reception n. act, process, or way of receiving; assembly held to receive guests; place where clients etc. are received on arrival.

receptionist n. person employed to receive and direct clients etc.

receptive a. quick to receive ideas. **receptiveness** n., **receptivity** n.

recess /-'ses/ n. part or space set back from the line of a wall or room etc.; temporary cessation

from business. —v.t. make a recess in or of.

recession n. receding from a point or level; temporary decline in economic activity or prosperity.

recessive a. tending to recede.

recherché /rə'ʃeəʃeɪ/ a. devised or selected with care; far-fetched.

recidivist /-'sɪd-/ n. person who persistently relapses into crime. **recidivism** n.

recipe n. directions for preparing a dish etc. in cookery; way of achieving something.

recipient n. person who receives something.

reciprocal a. both given and received. —n. mathematical expression related to another as ⅔ is related to ⅗. **reciprocally** adv., **reciprocity** n.

reciprocate v.i. give and receive; make a return for something; move backward and forward alternately. **reciprocation** n.

recital n. reciting; long account of events; musical entertainment.

recitation n. reciting; thing recited.

recitative /-'tiːv/ n. narrative or dialogue sung in a rhythm imitating that of ordinary speech.

recite v.t. repeat aloud from memory; state (facts) in order.

reckless a. wildly impulsive. **recklessly** adv., **recklessness** n.

reckon v.t./i. count up; include in a total or class; have as one's opinion; rely. **reckon with** take into account.

reckoner n. aid to reckoning.

reclaim v.t. take action to recover possession of; make (flooded or waste land) usable. **reclamation** n.

recline v.t./i. lean (one's body), lie down.

recluse /-'kluːs/ n. person who avoids social life.

recognition n. recognizing.

recognizance /-'kɒg-/ n. pledge made to a lawcourt or magistrate; surety for this.

recognize v.t. know again from one's previous experience; realize, admit; acknowledge as genuine or valid or worthy. **recognizable** a.

recoil v.i. spring back; shrink in fear or disgust; have an adverse effect (on the originator). —n. act of recoiling.

recollect v.t. remember, call to mind. **recollection** n.

recommend v.t. advise; praise as worthy of employment or use etc.; (of qualities etc.) make acceptable or desirable. **recommendation** n.

recompense /'rek-/ v.t. make a repayment to, compensate. —n. repayment.

reconcile v.t. make friendly after an estrangement; induce to tolerate something unwelcome; make compatible. **reconciliation** n.

recondite /'rekandatt/ a. obscure, dealing with an obscure subject.

recondition v.t. overhaul, repair.

reconnaissance /-'kɒnɪs-/ n. preliminary survey, esp. exploration of an area for military purposes.

reconnoitre v.t./i. (pres.p. **reconnoitring**) make a reconnaissance (of).

reconsider v.t./i. consider again, esp. for a possible change of decision. **reconsideration** n.

reconstitute v.t. reconstruct; restore to its original form. **reconstitution** n.

reconstruct v.t. construct, build, or enact again. **reconstruction** n.

record[1] /'kɔːd/ v.t. set down in writing or other permanent form; preserve (sound) on a disc or magnetic tape for later reproduction; (of a measuring instrument) indicate, register.

record[2] /'rek-/ n. information set down in writing or other permanent form; document etc. bearing this; disc bearing recorded sound; facts known about a person's past; best performance or most remarkable event etc. of its kind. —a. best or most extreme hitherto recorded. **off the record** unofficially or not for publication. **record-player** n. apparatus for reproducing recorded sound from discs.

recorder n. person or thing that records something; judge in certain lawcourts; a kind of flute.

recordist /-'kɔː-/ n. person who records sounds.

recount v.t. narrate, tell in detail.

re-count v.t. count again. —n. second or subsequent counting.

recoup /-'kuːp/ v.t. reimburse or compensate (for).

recourse n. source of help to which one may turn. **have recourse to** turn to for help.

recover v.t./i. regain possession or use or control of; obtain as compensation; return to health or consciousness. **recovery** n.

recreation /rek-/ n. pastime; relaxation. **recreational** a.

recriminate v.i. make angry accusations in retaliation. **recrimination** n., **recriminatory** a.

recrudesce /-'des/ v.i. (of disease or discontent) break out again. **recrudescence** n., **recrudescent** a.

recruit n. new member, esp. of the armed forces. —v.t. form (an army etc.) by enlisting recruits; enlist as a recruit; refresh (one's strength etc.). **recruitment** n.

rectal a. of the rectum.

rectangle n. geometric figure with four sides and four right angles, esp. with adjacent sides unequal in length. **rectangular** a.

rectify v.t. put right; purify, refine; convert to direct current. **rectification** n., **rectifier** n.

rectilinear a. bounded by straight lines.

rectitude n. correctness of behaviour or procedure.

recto n. (pl. **-os**) right-hand page of an open book; front of a page.

rector n. member of the clergy in charge of a parish; head of certain schools, colleges, and universities.

rectory n. house of a rector.

rectum n. last section of the intestine, between colon and anus.

recumbent a. lying down, reclining.

recuperate v.t./i. recover (health, strength, or losses). **recuperation** n.

recuperative a. of recuperation.

recur v.i. (p.t. **recurred**) happen again or repeatedly. **recurrence** n.

recurrent /-'kʌ-/ a. recurring.

recurve v.t./i. bend backwards.

recusant /'rek-/ n. person who refuses to submit or comply.

recycle v.t./i. convert (waste material) for reuse.

red a. (**redder, reddest**) of or like the colour of blood; (of hair) reddish-brown; Communist, favouring Communism. —n. red colour or thing; Communist. **in the red** having a debit balance, in debt. **red carpet** privileged treatment for an important visitor. **Red Cross** international organization for the care of people wounded in war or afflicted by great natural disasters. **red-handed** a. in the act of crime. **red herring** misleading clue or diversion. **red-hot** a. glowing red from heat; (of news) completely new. **Red Indian** North American Indian, with reddish skin. **red-letter day** day of a very joyful occurrence. **red light** signal to stop; danger-signal. **red tape** excessive formalities in official transactions. **redness** n.

redbreast n. robin.

redbrick a. (of universities) founded in the 19th century or later.

redcurrant n. small round sharp-tasting red berry; bush bearing this.

redden v.t./i. make or become red.

reddish a. rather red.

redeem v.t. buy back; convert (tokens etc.) into goods or cash; reclaim; save from the consequences of sin; make up for (faults). **redemption** n., **redemptive** a.

Redeemer n. Christ, who redeemed mankind.

redeploy v.t. send to a new place or task. **redeployment** n.

redhead n. person with red hair.

rediffusion n. relaying of broadcasts, from a central receiver.

redirect v.t. direct or send to another place. **redirection** n.

redolent a. smelling strongly; reminiscent, suggestive. **redolence** n.

redouble v.t. double again.

redoubt n. outwork without flanking defences.

redoubtable /-'daut-/ a. formidable.

redound v.i. come back as an advantage or disadvantage, accrue.

redress v.i. set right. —n. reparation, amends.

redshank n. a kind of sandpiper.

redstart n. songbird with a red tail.

reduce v.t./i. make or become smaller or less; make lower in rank; slim; subdue; bring into a specified state; convert into a simpler or more general form; restore (a fractured bone) to its proper position. **reduction** n., **reducible** a.

redundant a. superfluous; no longer needed. **redundancy** n.

reduplicate v.t. repeat (a letter or syllable). **reduplication** n.

redwood n. very tall evergreen Californian tree; its reddish wood.

re-echo v.t./i. echo; echo repeatedly; resound.

reed n. water or marsh plant with tall hollow stems; its stem; vibrating part producing sound in certain wind instruments.

reedy a. (of the voice) having a thin high tone. **reediness** n.

reef n. ridge of rock or sand etc. reaching to or near the surface of water; one of the strips at the top or bottom of a sail, that can be drawn in when there is a high wind. —v.t. shorten (a sail) by drawing in a reef. **reef-knot** n. symmetrical double knot.

reefer n. thick double-breasted jacket; marijuana cigarette.

reek n. strong usu. unpleasant smell. —v.i. smell strongly.

reel n. cylinder or similar device on which something is wound; lively Scottish or folk-dance. —v.t./i. wind on or off a reel; stagger. **reel off** rattle off without effort.

re-enter v.t./i. enter again. **re-entrant** a., **re-entry** n.

reeve[1] n. (old use) chief magistrate.

reeve[2] v.t. (p.t. **rove**) thread (a rope or rod etc.) through a ring etc.; fasten thus.

refectory /-'fek-/ n. dining-room of a monastery or college etc.

refer v.t./i. (p.t. **referred**) **refer to** mention; direct to an authority or specialist; turn to for information.

referable a. able to be referred.

referee n. umpire, esp. in football and boxing; person to whom disputes are referred for decision; person willing to testify to the character or ability of one applying for a job. —v.t. (p.t. **refereed**) act as referee in (a match etc.).

reference n. act of referring; mention; relation, correspondence; direction to a source of information, this source; testimonial; person willing to testify to another's character, ability, etc. **in** or **with reference to** in

connection with, about. **reference book** book providing information for reference. **reference library** one containing books that can be consulted but not taken away.

referendum n. (pl. **-ums**) referring of a question to the people for decision by a general vote.

referral /-'fз:-/ n. referring.

refill[1] /-'fil/ v.t./i. fill again.

refill[2] /'ri:-/ n. second or later filling; material used for this.

refine v.t. remove impurities or defects from; make elegant or cultured. **refined** a.

refinement n. refining; elegance of behaviour; improvement added; fine distinction.

refiner n. one who refines crude oil or metal or sugar etc.

refinery n. establishment where crude substances are refined.

refit[1] /-'fit/ v.t. (p.t. **refitted**) renew or repair the fittings of. **refitment** n.

refit[2] /'ri:-/ n. refitment.

reflate v.t. restore (a financial system) after deflation. **reflation** n., **reflationary** a.

reflect v.t./i. throw back (light, heat, or sound), be thrown back; show an image of; correspond to in appearance or effect; bring (credit or discredit); bring discredit; think deeply, remind oneself of past events. **reflection** n.

reflective a. reflecting; thoughtful.

reflector n. thing that reflects light or heat.

reflex /'ri:-/ n. reflex action; reflex camera. —a. bent backwards. **reflex action** involuntary or instinctive movement in response to a stimulus. **reflex angle** angle of more than 180°. **reflex camera** one in which the image given by the lens is reflected to the viewfinder.

reflexive a. & n. (word or form) showing that the action of the verb is performed on its subject (e.g. *he washed himself*).

reflexology *n.* system of massage through reflex points on the feet, hands, and head. **reflexologist** *n.*

reflux *n.* flowing back.

reform *v.t./i.* improve by removing faults. —*n.* reforming. **reformer** *n.*, **reformist** *n.*

reformation *n.* reforming; **the Reformation** 16th-century movement for reform of certain practices in the Church of Rome, resulting in the establishment of Reformed or Protestant Churches.

reformative *a.* reforming.

reformatory *a.* reforming. —*n.* (US) institution to which offenders are sent to be reformed.

refract *v.t.* bend (a ray of light) where it enters water or glass etc. obliquely. **refraction** *n.*, **refractor** *n.*, **refractive** *a.*

refractory *a.* resisting control or discipline; resistant to treatment or heat. **refractoriness** *n.*

refrain[1] *n.* recurring lines of a song; music for these.

refrain[2] *v.i.* keep oneself from doing something.

refresh *v.t.* restore the vigour of by food, drink, or rest; stimulate (a person's memory) by reminding him.

refresher *n.* extra fee to counsel in a prolonged lawsuit. **refresher course** course of instruction to renew or increase a qualified person's knowledge.

refreshing *a.* restoring vigour, cooling; interesting because of its novelty. **refreshingly** *adv.*

refreshment *n.* process of refreshing; thing that refreshes, (usu. *pl.*) food and drink.

refrigerate *v.t.* make extremely cold, esp. in order to preserve and store (food). **refrigerant** *n.*, **refrigeration** *n.*

refrigerator *n.* cabinet or room in which food is stored at a very low temperature.

reft *a.* taken or torn away.

refuel *v.t.* (*p.t.* **refuelled**) replenish the fuel supply of.

refuge *n.* shelter from pursuit or danger or trouble.

refugee *n.* person who has left home and seeks refuge (e.g. from war or persecution) elsewhere.

refulgent *a.* shining. **refulgence** *n.*

refund[1] /ˈfʌnd/ *v.t.* pay back.

refund[2] /ˈriː-/ *n.* repayment, money refunded.

refurbish *v.t.* make clean or bright again, redecorate. **refurbishment** *n.*

refuse[1] /rɪˈfjuːz/ *v.t./i.* say or show that one is unwilling to accept or give or do (what is asked or required). **refusal** *n.*

refuse[2] /ˈrefjuːs/ *n.* waste material.

refute *v.t.* prove (a statement or person) to be wrong. **refutation** *n.*

regain *v.t.* obtain again after loss; reach again.

regal *a.* like or fit for a king. **regally** *adv.*, **regality** *n.*

regale *v.t.* feed or entertain well. **regalement** *n.*

regalia /-ˈɡeɪ-/ *n.pl.* emblems of royalty or rank.

regard *v.t.* look steadily at; consider to be. —*n.* steady gaze; heed; respect; (*pl.*) kindly greetings conveyed in a message. **as regards** regarding.

regarding *prep.* with reference to.

regardless *a.* & *adv.* heedless(ly).

regatta *n.* boat or yacht races organized as a sporting event.

regency *n.* rule by a regent; period of this; **the Regency** 1810–20 in England.

regenerate[1] /-eɪt/ *v.t.* give new life or vigour to. **regeneration** *n.*, **regenerative** *a.*

regenerate[2] /-ət/ *a.* regenerated.

regent *n.* person appointed to rule while the monarch is a minor or ill or absent.

reggae /'regeɪ/ *n.* West Indian style of music, with a strong beat.

regicide *n.* killing or killer of a king. **regicidal** *a.*

regime /reɪ'ʒiːm/ *n.* method or system of government or administration.

regimen *n.* prescribed course of treatment etc.; way of life.

regiment *n.* permanent unit of an army; operational unit of artillery, tanks, etc.; large array or number of things. —*v.t.* organize rigidly. **regimentation** *n.*

regimental *a.* of an army regiment.

regimentals *n.pl.* regimental uniform.

Regina /rɪ'dʒaɪ-/ *n.* reigning queen.

region *n.* continuous part of a surface, space, or body; administrative division of a country. **in the region of** approximately. **regional** *a.*

register *n.* official list; mechanical device indicating numbers or speed etc.; adjustable plate regulating the size of an opening; range of a voice or musical instrument. —*v.t./i.* enter in a register; record in writing, present for consideration; notice and remember; indicate, record; make an impression. **register office** place where records of births, marriages, and deaths are kept and civil marriages are performed. **registration** *n.*

registrar *n.* official responsible for keeping written records; judicial and administrative officer of the High Court; hospital doctor ranking just below specialist.

registry *n.* registration; place where written records are kept. **registry office** register office.

Regius professor holder of a university chair founded by the

sovereign or appointed by the Crown.

regnant *a.* reigning.

regress[1] /-'gres/ *v.i.* move backwards; relapse to an earlier or more primitive state. **regression** *n.,* **regressive** *a.*

regress[2] /'riː-/ *n.* regressive movement.

regret *n.* feeling of sorrow about a loss, or of annoyance or repentance. —*v.t.* (*p.t.* **regretted**) feel regret about. **regretful** *a.,* **regretfully** *adv.*

regrettable *a.* that is to be regretted. **regrettably** *adv.*

regular *a.* acting or occurring or done in a uniform manner or constantly at a fixed time or interval; conforming to a rule or habit; even, symmetrical; forming a country's permanent armed forces; (*colloq.*) thorough. —*n.* regular soldier etc.; (*colloq.*) regular customer or visitor etc. **regularly** *adv.,* **regularity** *n.*

regularize *v.t.* make regular; make lawful or correct. **regularization** *n.*

regulate *v.t.* control by rules; adjust to work correctly or according to one's requirements. **regulator** *n.*

regulation *n.* process of regulating; rule.

regurgitate *v.t.* bring (swallowed food) up again to the mouth; cast out again. **regurgitation** *n.*

rehabilitate *v.t.* restore to a normal life or good condition. **rehabilitation** *n.*

rehash[1] /-'hæʃ/ *v.t.* put (old material) into a new form with no great change or improvement.

rehash[2] /'riː-/ *n.* rehashing; thing made of rehashed material.

rehearse *v.t./i.* practise or train beforehand; enumerate. **rehearsal** *n.*

rehouse *v.t.* provide with new accommodation.

Reich /raix/ n. the former German State, esp. (**Third Reich**) the Nazi regime.

reign n. sovereignty, rule. —v.i. rule as king or queen; be supreme.

reimburse v.t. repay (a person), refund. **reimbursement** n.

rein n. (also pl.) long narrow strap fastened to the bit of a bridle, used to guide or check a horse; means of control. —v.t. check or control with reins.

reincarnation n. incarnation of the soul in another body after death of the first. **reincarnate** a. & v.t.

reindeer n. (pl. **reindeer**) deer of Arctic regions, with large antlers.

reinforce v.t. strengthen with additional men, material, or quantity. **reinforcement** n.

reinstate v.t. restore to a previous position. **reinstatement** n.

reiterate v.t. say or do again or repeatedly. **reiteration** n.

reject[1] /-'dʒekt/ v.t. refuse to accept; react against. **rejection** n.

reject[2] /'riː-/ n. person or thing rejected.

rejig v.t. (p.t. **rejigged**) re-equip for a new type of work; rearrange.

rejoice v.t./i. feel or show great joy; gladden.

rejoin v.t. join again; say in answer, retort.

rejoinder n. answer, retort.

rejuvenate v.t. restore youthful appearance or vigour to. **rejuvenation** n., **rejuvenator** n.

relapse v.i. fall back into a previous state; become worse after improvement. —n. relapsing.

relate v.t./i. narrate; establish a relation between; have a connection with; establish a successful relationship.

related a. having a common descent or origin.

relation n. similarity connecting persons or things; relative;

narrating; (pl.) dealings with others; (pl.) sexual intercourse. **relationship** n.

relative a. considered in relation to something else; having a connection; (in grammar) referring to an earlier noun or clause or sentence. —n. person related to another by descent or marriage; relative pronoun or adverb. **relatively** adv.

relativity n. being relative; Einstein's theory of the universe, showing that all motion is relative and treating time as a fourth dimension related to space.

relax v.t./i. make or become less tight or less tense or less strict; rest from work, indulge in recreation. **relaxation** n.

relay[1] /'riː-/ n. fresh set of people etc. to replace those who have completed a spell of work; fresh supply of material; relay race; relayed message or transmission; device relaying things or activating an electrical circuit. **relay race** race between teams in which each person in turn covers a part of the total distance.

relay[2] /-'leɪ or 'riː-/ v.t. (p.t. **relayed**) receive and pass on or retransmit (a message, broadcast, etc.).

release v.t. set free; remove from a fixed position; issue (information etc.) to the public or (a film) for general exhibition. —n. releasing; handle or catch etc. that unfastens something; information or a film or recording etc. released to the public.

relegate /'rel-/ v.t. consign to a less important place or state or group. **relegation** n.

relent v.i. become less severe or more lenient. **relentless** a., **relentlessly** adv.

relevant /'rel-/ a. related to the matter in hand. **relevance** n.

reliable a. able to be relied on; consistently good. **reliably** adv., **reliability** n.

reliance n. relying; trust, confidence. **reliant** a.

relic n. thing that survives from earlier times; (pl.) remains.

relict /'rel-/ n. person's widow; object which has survived in a primitive form.

relief n. ease given by reduction or removal of pain or anxiety etc.; thing that breaks up monotony; assistance to those in need; person replacing one who is on duty; bus etc. supplementing an ordinary service; raising of a siege; carving or moulding in which the design projects from a surface; similar effect given by colour or shading. **relief road** road by which traffic can avoid a congested area.

relieve v.t. give or bring relief to; release from a task or duty; raise the siege of. **relieve oneself** urinate or defecate.

religion n. belief in the existence of a superhuman controlling power, usu. expressed in worship; system of this; influence compared to religious faith.

religious a. of religion; believing in a religion and carrying out its practices; of a monastic order; very conscientious. **religiously** adv.

relinquish v.t. give up, cease from. **relinquishment** n.

reliquary /'rel-/ n. receptacle for relic(s) of a holy person.

relish n. great enjoyment of something; appetizing flavour; thing giving this. —v.i. enjoy greatly.

relocate v.t. move to a different place. **relocation** n.

reluctant a. unwilling, grudging one's consent. **reluctantly** adv., **reluctance** n.

rely v.i. **rely on** trust confidently, depend on for help etc.

remain v.i. be in the same place or condition during further time; be there after other parts have been used or removed.

remainder n. remaining people or things or part; quantity left after subtraction or division. —v.t. dispose of unsold copies of (a book) at a reduced price.

remains n.pl. what remains, surviving parts; dead body.

remand /'mɑː-/ v.t. send back (a prisoner) into custody while further evidence is sought. —n. remanding. **on remand** remanded.

remark n. spoken or written comment, thing said. —v.t./i. make a remark, say; notice.

remarkable a. worth noticing, unusual. **remarkably** adv.

rematch n. return match.

remedy n. thing that cures or relieves a disease or puts right a matter. —v.t. be a remedy for, put right. **remedial** /'miː-/ a.

remember v.t. keep in one's mind and recall at will; think of and make a present to; mention to sending greetings. **remember oneself** remember one's intentions or behave suitably after a lapse. **remembrance** n.

remind v.t. cause to remember.

reminder n. thing that reminds someone, letter sent as this.

reminisce v.i. think or talk about past events.

reminiscence n. reminiscing; thing reminiscent of something else; (usu. pl.) account of what one remembers.

reminiscent a. inclined to reminisce; having characteristics that remind one (of something). **reminiscently** adv.

remiss /-'mis/ a. negligent.

remission n. remitting of a debt or penalty; reduction of force or intensity.

remit[1] /-'mit/ v.t./i. (p.t. **remitted**) cancel (a debt or punishment); make or become less intense; send (money etc.); refer (a matter for decision) to an authority; postpone.

remit[2] /'riː-/ n. terms of reference.

remittance n. sending of money; money sent.

remnant n. small remaining quantity; surviving trace.

remonstrate /'rem-/ v.i. make a protest. **remonstrance** /-'mon-/ n.

remorse n. deep regret for one's wrongdoing. **remorseful** a., **remorsefully** adv.

remorseless a. relentless. **remorselessly** adv.

remote a. far away in place or time; not close; slight. **remotely** adv., **remoteness** n.

remould[1] /-'məuld/ v.t. mould again or into a new form; reconstruct the tread of (a tyre).

remould[2] /'ri:-/ n. remoulded tyre.

removable a. able to be removed.

remove v.t. take off or away from its place; dismiss from office; get rid of. —n. degree of remoteness or difference; stage; form or division in certain schools. **remover** n., **removal** n.

removed a. separated, distant. *once* or *twice* etc. **removed** (of cousins) separated by one or by two etc. generations.

remunerate v.t. pay or reward for services. **remuneration** n.

remunerative /-'mju:-/ a. giving good remuneration, profitable.

Renaissance /-'neɪsɑns/ n. revival of art and learning in Europe in the 14th–16th centuries; **renaissance** any similar revival.

renal /'ri:-/ a. of the kidneys.

rend v.t./i. (p.t. **rent**) tear.

render v.t. give, esp. in return; present or send in (a bill etc.); cause to become; give a performance of; translate; melt down (fat).

rendezvous /'rɒndeɪvuː/ n. (pl. -vous, pr. -vuːz) prearranged meeting or meeting-place. —v.i. meet at a rendezvous.

rendition n. way something is rendered or performed.

renegade /'renɪ-/ n. person who deserts from a group or cause etc.

renege /-'niːg/ v.i. fail to keep a promise or agreement.

renew v.t. restore to its original state; replace with a fresh thing or supply; get or make or give again. **renewal** n.

renewable a. able to be renewed.

rennet n. substance used to curdle milk in making cheese or junket.

renounce v.t. give up formally; refuse to abide by. **renouncement** n.

renovate /'ren-/ v.t. repair, restore to good condition. **renovation** n., **renovator** n.

renown /-'naun/ n. fame.

renowned /-'naund/ a. famous.

rent[1] *see* rend. —n. torn place.

rent[2] n. periodical payment for use of land, rooms, machinery, etc. —v.t. pay or receive rent for.

rental n. rent; renting.

renunciation n. renouncing.

reorganize v.t. organize in a new way. **reorganization** n.

rep[1] n. upholstery fabric with a corded effect.

rep[2] n. (colloq.) business firm's travelling representative.

rep[3] n. (colloq.) repertory.

repair[1] v.t. put into good condition after damage or wear; make amends for. —n. process of repairing; repaired place; condition as regards being repaired. **repairer** n.

repair[2] v.i. go.

reparation n. making amends; (pl.) compensation for war damage.

repartee n. witty reply; ability to make witty replies.

repast /-'pɑ:-/ n. (formal) a meal.

repatriate v.t. send or bring back (a person) to his own country. **repatriation** n.

repay v.t. (p.t. **repaid**) pay back. **repayment** n., **repayable** a.

repeal v.t. withdraw (a law) officially. —n. repealing of a law.

repeat v.t./i. say or do or produce or occur again; tell (a thing told to oneself) to another person. —n. repeating; thing repeated. **repeat itself** recur. **repeat oneself** say or do the same thing again. **repeatable** a.

repeatedly adv. again and again.

repeater n. device that repeats a signal.

repel v.t. (p.t. **repelled**) drive away; be impossible for (a substance) to penetrate; be repulsive or distasteful to. **repellent** a. & n.

repent v.t./i. feel regret about (what one has done or failed to do). **repentance** n., **repentant** a.

repercussion n. recoil; echo; indirect effect or reaction.

repertoire /-twa:(r)/ n. stock of songs, plays, etc., that a person or company is prepared to perform.

repertory /'rep/ n. repertoire; theatrical performances of various plays for short periods by one company (**repertory company**).

repetition n. repeating; instance of this.

repetitious a. repetitive.

repetitive a. characterized by repetition. **repetitive strain injury** injury caused by the prolonged use of particular muscles. **repetitively** adv.

repine v.i. fret, be discontented.

replace v.t. put back in its place; take the place of; provide a substitute for. **replacement** n., **replaceable** a.

replay[1] /-pleɪ/ v.t. play again.

replay[2] /'ri:-/ n. replaying.

replenish v.t. refill; renew (a supply etc.). **replenishment** n.

replete a. well stocked; full, gorged. **repletion** n.

replica n. exact reproduction.

replicate v.t. make a replica of. **replication** n.

reply v.t./i. & n. answer.

report v.t./i. give an account of;

tell as news; make a formal complaint about; present oneself. —n. spoken or written account; written statement about a pupil's or employee's work etc.; rumour; explosive sound.

reportage /-tɑ:ʒ/ n. reporting of news, style of this.

reportedly adv. according to reports.

reporter n. person employed to report news etc. for publication or broadcasting.

repose[1] n. rest, sleep; tranquillity. —v.t./i. rest, lie.

repose[2] v.t. place (trust etc.) in.

repository n. storage place.

repossess v.t. take back (goods) when hire-purchase payments have not been made. **repossession** n.

reprehend /reprɪ-/ v.t. rebuke.

reprehensible /reprɪ-/ a. deserving rebuke. **reprehensibly** adv.

represent v.t. show in a picture or play etc.; describe or declare (to be); state (facts); symbolize; be an example or embodiment of; act as deputy or agent or spokesman for. **representation** n.

representative a. typical of a group or class; based on or consisting of elected representatives. —n. sample, specimen; person's or firm's agent; person chosen to represent others.

repress v.t. suppress, keep (emotions) from finding an outlet. **repression** n., **repressive** a.

reprieve n. postponement or cancellation of punishment (esp. death sentence); temporary relief. —v.t. give a reprieve to.

reprimand v.t. & n. rebuke.

reprint[1] /-prɪ-/ v.t. print again.

reprint[2] /'ri:-/ n. reprinting; book reprinted.

reprisal n. act of retaliation.

reproach v.t. express disapproval to (a person) for a fault or offence. —n. act or instance of reproaching; thing that brings discredit.

reproachful *a.*, **reproachfully** *adv.*

reprobate /'rep-/ *n.* immoral or unprincipled person.

reprobation *n.* strong condemnation.

reproduce *v.t./i.* produce again; produce a copy or representation of; produce further members of the same species. **reproduction** *n.*

reproducible *a.* able to be reproduced.

reproductive *a.* of reproduction.

reproof *n.* expression of condemnation for a fault or offence.

reprove *v.t.* give a reproof to.

reptile *n.* member of the class of cold-blooded scaly animals with a backbone and relatively short legs or no legs. **reptilian** /-'til-/ *a.* & *n.*

republic *n.* country in which the supreme power is held by the people or their representatives.

republican *a.* of or advocating a republic. —*n.* person advocating republican government; **Republican** member of one of the two main US political parties.

repudiate *v.t.* reject or disown utterly, deny. **repudiation** *n.*

repugnant *a.* distasteful, objectionable. **repugnance** *n.*

repulse *v.t.* drive back (an attacking force); reject, rebuff. —*n.* driving back; rejection, rebuff.

repulsion *n.* repelling; strong feeling of distaste, revulsion.

repulsive *a.* arousing disgust; able to repel. **repulsively** *adv.*, **repulsiveness** *n.*

reputable /'rep-/ *a.* having a good reputation, respected.

reputation *n.* what is generally believed about a person or thing; general recognition for one's abilities or achievements.

repute /-'pju:t/ *n.* reputation.

reputed *a.* said or thought to be.

reputedly *adv.* by repute.

request *n.* asking for something; thing asked for. —*v.t.* make a request (for or of).

requiem /'rekwiem/ *n.* special Mass for the repose of the soul(s) of the dead; music for this.

require *v.t.* need, depend on for success or fulfilment; order, oblige.

requirement *n.* need.

requisite /'rek-/ *a.* required, necessary. —*n.* thing needed.

requisition *n.* formal written demand, order laying claim to use of property or materials. —*v.t.* demand or order by this.

requite *v.t.* make a return for.

reredos /'rɪədɒs/ *n.* ornamental screen covering the wall above the back of an altar.

resale *n.* sale to another person of something one has bought.

rescind /-'sɪnd/ *v.t.* repeal or cancel (a law etc.). **rescission** *n.*

rescue *v.t.* save or bring away from danger or capture etc. —*n.* rescuing. **rescuer** *n.*

research /-'sɜːtʃ/ *n.* study and investigation, esp. to discover new facts. —*v.t./i.* perform research (into). **researcher** *n.*

resemble *v.t.* be like. **resemblance** *n.*

resent *v.t.* feel displeased and indignant about. **resentment** *n.*, **resentful** *a.*, **resentfully** *adv.*

reservation *n.* reserving; reserved seat or accommodation etc.; limitation on one's agreement; strip of land between carriageways of a road; (*US*) area reserved for a special purpose, esp. Indian occupation.

reserve *v.t.* put aside for future or special use; order or set aside for a particular person; retain; postpone. —*n.* thing(s) reserved for future or special use, extra stock kept available; (also *pl.*) forces outside the regular armed services; extra player chosen in case a substitute is needed in a team; reservation between carriageways; limitation on one's agreement; reserve price; tendency to avoid showing feelings or cordiality. **in reserve** unused and available. **reserve price** lowest price acceptable for a thing to be sold at an auction etc.

reserved *a.* (of a person) showing reserve of manner.

reservist *n.* member of a reserve force.

reservoir /'rezəvwɑː(r)/ *n.* natural or artificial lake that is a source or store of water to a town etc.; container for a supply of fluid; store of information.

reshuffle *v.t.* shuffle again; interchange. —*n.* reshuffling.

reside *v.i.* dwell; (of a quality or power) be present or vested (in a person).

residence *n.* residing; dwelling. **in residence** living in a specified place to perform one's work.

residency *n.* official dwelling.

resident *a.* residing, in residence. —*n.* permanent inhabitant; (at a hotel) person staying overnight.

residential *a.* containing dwellings; of or based on residence.

residual /-'zɪd-/ *a.* left over as a residue. **residually** *adv.*

residuary /-'zɪd-/ *a.* residual; of the residue of an estate.

residue /'rez-/ *n.* what is left over.

residuum /rɪ'zɪdjʊəm/ *n.* (*pl.* -dua) residue.

resign *v.t./i.* give up (one's job or property or claim etc.). **resign oneself to** be ready to accept and endure. **resignation** *n.*

resigned *a.* having resigned oneself. **resignedly** /-'zaɪnɪd-/ *adv.*

resile *v.i.* spring back; show resilience. **resile from** withdraw from.

resilient /-'zɪl-/ *a.* springy; readily recovering from shock etc. **resiliently** *adv.*, **resilience** *n.*

resin *n.* sticky substance from plants and certain trees; similar substance made synthetically, used in plastics. **resinous** *a.*

resist *v.t./i.* oppose; use force to prevent something from happening or being successful; be undamaged or unaffected by; prevent from penetrating; refrain from accepting or yielding to. **resistance** *n.*, **resistant** *a.*

resistible *a.* able to be resisted.

resistivity *n.* resistance to the passage of electric current.

resistor *n.* device having resistance to the passage of electric current.

reskill *v.t.* teach, or equip with, new skills.

resolute *a.* showing great determination. **resolutely** *adv.*, **resoluteness** *n.*

resolution *n.* resolving; great determination; formal statement of a committee's opinion.

resolve *v.t./i.* decide firmly; solve or settle (a problem or doubts); separate into constituent parts. —*n.* thing one has decided to do; great determination.

resonant /'rez-/ *a.* resounding, echoing; reinforcing sound, esp. by vibration. **resonance** *n.*

resonate *v.i.* produce or show resonance. **resonator** *n.*

resort *v.i.* turn for help, adopt as an expedient; go customarily. —*n.* expedient, resorting to this; place resorted to; popular holiday place.

resound *v.i.* fill a place or be filled with sound; echo.

resounding *a.* notable.

resource *n.* something to which one can resort; ingenuity; (*pl.*) means available, source of wealth.

resourceful *a.* clever at finding ways of doing things. **resourcefully** *adv.*, **resourcefulness** *n.*

respect *n.* admiration felt towards a person or thing that has good qualities or achievements; politeness arising from this; attention, consideration; relation, reference; particular detail or aspect; (*pl.*) polite greetings.

—v.t. feel or show respect for. **respecter** n.

respectable a. of moderately good social standing; honest and decent; considerable. **respectably** adv., **respectability** n.

respectful a. showing respect. **respectfully** adv.

respecting prep. concerning.

respective a. belonging to each as an individual.

respectively adv. for each separately; in the order mentioned.

respiration n. breathing.

respirator n. device worn over the nose and mouth to purify air before it is inhaled; device for giving artificial respiration.

respiratory /'res-/ a. of respiration.

respire v.t./i. breathe.

respite /'respait/ n. interval of rest or relief; permitted delay.

resplendent a. brilliant with colour or decorations. **resplendently** adv.

respond v.i. make an answer. **respond to** act or react in answer to or because of.

respondent n. defendant in a lawsuit, esp. in a divorce case.

response n. answer; act, feeling, or movement produced by a stimulus or another's action.

responsibility n. being responsible; thing for which one is responsible.

responsible a. obliged to take care of something or to carry out a duty, liable to be blamed for loss or failure etc.; having to account for one's actions; capable of rational conduct; trustworthy; involving important duties; being the cause of something. **responsibly** adv.

responsive a. responding well to an influence. **responsiveness** n.

rest[1] v.t./i. be still; cease from activity or working, esp. in order to regain vigour; cause or allow to do this; (of a matter) be left without further discussion; place or

be placed for support; rely; (of a look) alight, be directed. —n. inactivity or sleep, esp. to regain vigour; prop or support for an object; interval of silence between notes in music, sign indicating this.

rest[2] v.i. remain in a specified state. —n. **the rest** the remaining part; the others. **rest with** remain in the hands or charge of.

restaurant /'restarǒ/ n. place where meals can be bought and eaten.

restaurateur /-'tз:(r)/ n. restaurant-keeper.

restful a. giving rest or a feeling of rest. **restfully** adv., **restfulness** n.

restitution n. restoring of a thing to its proper owner or original state; compensation.

restive a. restless; impatient because of delay or restraint. **restiveness** n.

restless a. unable to rest or be still. **restlessly** adv., **restlessness** n.

restoration n. restoring; restored thing; **Restoration** re-establishment of the monarchy in Britain in 1660.

restorative /-'stɒ-/ a. restoring health or strength. —n. restorative food, medicine, or treatment.

restore v.t. bring back to its original state (e.g. by repairing), or to good health or vigour; put back in a former position. **restorer** n.

restrain v.t. hold back from movement or action, keep under control. **restraint** n.

restrict v.t. put a limit on, subject to limitations. **restriction** n.

restrictive a. restricting. **restrictive practice** one preventing labour or materials from being used in the most efficient way.

result n. product of an activity or operation or calculation; score, marks, or name of the winner in

a sports event or competition.
—*v.i.* occur or have as a result.

resultant *a.* occurring as a result.

resume *v.t./i.* get or take again; begin again after stopping. **resumption** *n.*, **resumptive** *a.*

résumé /'rezjuːmeɪ/ *n.* summary.

resurface *v.t./i.* put a new surface on; return to the surface.

resurgence *n.* revival after destruction or disappearance.

resurrect *v.t.* bring back into use.

resurrection *n.* rising from the dead (**Resurrection** that of Christ); revival after disuse.

resuscitate /-'sʌsɪ-/ *v.t./i.* revive. **resuscitation** *n.*

retail /'riː-/ *n.* selling of goods to the public (not for resale). —*a. & adv.* in the retail trade. —*v.t./i.* sell or be sold in the retail trade; (*also pr.* -'teɪl) relate details of. **retailer** *n.*

retain *v.t.* keep, esp. in one's possession or memory or in use; hold in place.

retainer *n.* fee paid to retain services; (*old use*) servant, attendant.

retaliate *v.i.* repay an injury or insult etc. by inflicting one in return. **retaliation** *n.*, **retaliatory** /-'tæljə-/ *a.*

retard *v.t.* cause delay to. **retardation** *n.*

retarded *a.* backward in mental or physical development.

retch /retʃ/ *v.i.* strain one's throat as if vomiting.

retention *n.* retaining.

retentive *a.* able to retain things.

rethink *v.t.* (*p.t.* **rethought**) reconsider; plan again and differently.

reticent /'retɪ-/ *a.* not revealing one's thoughts. **reticence** *n.*

reticulate *v.t.* divide or be divided into a network. **reticulation** *n.*

reticule *n.* (*old use*) woman's handbag.

retina /'retɪ-/ *n.* (*pl.* -**as**) membrane at the back of the eyeball, sensitive to light.

retinue *n.* attendants accompanying an important person.

retire *v.t./i.* give up one's regular work because of age; cause (an employee) to do this; withdraw, retreat; go to bed. **retirement** *n.*

retiring *a.* shy, avoiding society.

retort[1] *v.t./i.* make (as) a witty or angry reply. —*n.* retorting; reply of this kind.

retort[2] *n.* vessel (usu. glass) with a long downward-bent neck, used in distilling liquids; vessel used in making gas or steel.

retouch *v.t.* touch up (a picture or photograph).

retrace *v.t.* trace back to the source. **retrace one's steps** go back the way one came.

retract *v.t./i.* withdraw. **retraction** *n.*, **retractor** *n.*, **retractable** *a.*

retractile *a.* able to be retracted.

retread *v.t.* put a new tread on (a tyre). —*n.* retreaded tyre.

retreat *v.i.* withdraw, esp. after defeat or when faced with difficulty. —*n.* retreating, withdrawal; military signal for this; place of shelter or seclusion.

retrench *v.t./i.* reduce the amount of (expenditure or operations). **retrenchment** *n.*

retrial *n.* trial of a lawsuit or defendant again.

retribution /retrɪ-/ *n.* deserved punishment. **retributive** /-'trɪb-/ *a.*

retrievable *a.* able to be retrieved.

retrieve *v.t.* regain possession of; find and extract or bring back; set right (an error etc.). —*n.* possibility of recovery. **retrieval** *n.*

retriever *n.* dog of a breed used to retrieve game.

retroactive *a.* operating retrospectively. **retroactively** *adv.*

retrograde *a.* going backwards; reverting to an inferior state.

retrogress v.i. move backwards, deteriorate. **retrogression** n., **retrogressive** a.

retro-rocket n. auxiliary rocket used for slowing a spacecraft.

retrospect. in retrospect when one looks back on a past event.

retrospection n. looking back, esp. on the past.

retrospective a. looking back on the past; (of a law etc.) made to apply to the past as well as the future. **retrospectively** adv.

retroussé /rə'tru:seɪ/ a. (of the nose) turned up at the tip.

retroverted a. turned backwards. **retroversion** n.

retrovirus n. RNA virus forming DNA during replication.

retry v.t. (p.t. **-tried**) try (a lawsuit or defendant) again.

return v.t./i. come or go back; bring, give, put, or send back; say in reply; elect as an MP. —n. returning; profit; return ticket; return match; formal report submitted by order. **return match** second match between the same opponents. **return ticket** ticket for a journey to a place and back again.

returnable a. that can or must be returned.

reunion n. social gathering of people who were formerly associated.

reunite v.t./i. bring or come together again.

reusable a. able to be used again.

rev n. (colloq.) revolution of an engine. —v.t./i. (p.t. **revved**) (colloq.) cause (an engine) to run quickly; (of an engine) revolve. **Rev.** abbr. Reverend.

revalue v.t. put a new (esp. higher) value on. **revaluation** n.

revamp v.t. renovate, give a new appearance to.

Revd. abbr. Reverend.

reveal v.t. make visible by uncovering; make known.

reveille /rɪ'vælɪ/ n. military waking-signal.

revel v.i. (p.t. **revelled**) take great delight; hold revels. **revels** n.pl. lively festivities, merrymaking. **reveller** n., **revelry** n.

revelation n. revealing; thing revealed, esp. something surprising.

revenge n. punishment, injury inflicted in return for what one has suffered; desire to inflict this; opportunity to defeat a victorious opponent. —v.t. avenge.

revengeful a. eager for revenge.

revenue n. country's income from taxes etc.; department collecting this.

reverberate v.t./i. echo, resound. **reverberant** a., **reverberation** n., **reverberator** n.

revere /-'vɪə(r)/ v.t. feel deep respect or religious veneration for.

reverence n. feeling of awe and respect or veneration. —v.t. feel or show reverence for.

reverend a. deserving to be treated with respect; **Reverend** title of a member of the clergy or (**Reverend Mother**) of the head of a convent.

reverent a. feeling or showing reverence. **reverently** adv.

reverie /'revərɪ/ n. daydream.

revers /rɪ'vɪə(r)/ n. (pl. **revers**, pr. -'vɪəz) turned-back front edge at the neck of a jacket or bodice.

reversal n. reversing.

reverse a. facing or moving in the opposite direction; opposite in character or order; upside down. —v.t./i. turn the other way round or upside down or inside out; convert to the opposite kind or effect; annul (a decree etc.); move in the opposite direction, travel backwards. —n. reverse side or effect; piece of misfortune. **reversely** adv., **reversible** a.

revert v.i. return to a former condition or habit; return to a subject in talk etc.; (of property etc.) pass to another holder when its present holder relinquishes it. **reversion** n., **reversionary** a.

revetment /-'vet-/ *n.* facing of masonry on a rampart etc.

review *n.* general survey of events or a subject; reconsideration; ceremonial inspection of troops etc.; report assessing the merits of a book or play etc. —*v.t.* make or write a review of. **reviewer** *n.*

revile *v.t.* criticize angrily in abusive language. **revilement** *n.*, **reviler** *n.*

revise *v.t.* re-examine and alter or correct; study again (work already learnt) in preparation for an examination. **reviser** *n.*, **revision** *n.*, **revisory** *a.*

revivalist *n.* person who seeks to promote religious fervour. **revivalism** *n.*, **revivalistic** *a.*

revive *v.t./i.* come or bring back to life with consciousness or vigour, or into use. **revival** *n.*

revivify *v.t.* restore to life, strength, or activity. **revivification** *n.*

revocable /'rev-/ *a.* able to be revoked.

revoke *v.t./i.* withdraw (a decree or licence etc.); fail to follow suit in a card-game when able to do so. **revocation** *n.*

revolt *v.t./i.* take part in a rebellion; be in a mood of protest or defiance; cause strong disgust in. —*n.* act or state of rebelling; sense of disgust.

revolting *a.* in revolt; causing disgust.

revolution *n.* revolving, single complete orbit or rotation; complete change of method or conditions; substitution of a new system of government, esp. by force.

revolutionary *a.* involving a great change; of political revolution. —*n.* person who begins or supports a political revolution.

revolutionize *v.t.* alter completely.

revolve *v.t./i.* turn round; move in an orbit; turn over (a problem etc.) in one's mind.

revolver *n.* a kind of pistol.

revue *n.* entertainment consisting of a series of items.

revulsion *n.* strong disgust; sudden violent change of feeling.

reward *n.* something given or received in return for a service or merit etc. —*v.t.* give a reward to.

rewind *v.t.* (*p.t.* **rewound**) wind (film, tape, etc.) back towards the beginning.

rewire *v.t.* renew the electrical wiring of.

rewrite *v.t.* (*p.t.* **rewrote**, *p.p.* **rewritten**) write again in a different form or style.

Rex *n.* reigning king.

rhapsodize *v.i.* talk or write about something ecstatically.

rhapsody *n.* ecstatic written or spoken statement; romantic musical composition. **rhapsodic, rhapsodical** *adjs.*

rheostat /'ri:ə-/ *n.* device for varying the resistance to electric current. **rheostatic** *a.*

rhesus *n.* small Indian monkey used in biological experiments. **Rhesus factor** substance usu. present in blood (**Rhesus-positive** containing this; **Rhesus-negative** not containing it).

rhetoric /'ret-/ *n.* art of using words impressively, esp. in public speaking; impressive language.

rhetorical /rɪ'tɒ-/ *a.* expressed so as to sound impressive. **rhetorical question** one phrased as a question for dramatic effect, not seeking an answer. **rhetorically** *adv.*

rheumatic *a.* of or affected with rheumatism. **rheumatics** *n.pl.* (*colloq.*) rheumatism. **rheumaticky** *a.*

rheumatism *n.* disease causing pain in the joints, muscles, or fibrous tissue.

rheumatoid *a.* having the character of rheumatism.

rhinestone *n.* imitation diamond.

rhino *n.* (*pl.* rhino *or* -os) (*sl.*) rhinoceros.

rhinoceros *n.* (*pl.* -oses) large thick-skinned animal with one horn or two horns on its nose.

rhizome /'raɪ-/ *n.* root-like stem producing roots and shoots.

rhodium *n.* metal resembling platinum.

rhododendron *n.* shrub with clusters of trumpet-shaped flowers.

rhomboid *a.* like a rhombus. —*n.* rhomboid figure.

rhombus *n.* quadrilateral with opposite sides and angles equal (and not right angles).

rhubarb *n.* garden plant with red leaf-stalks that are used like fruit.

rhyme *n.* identity of sound between words or syllables; word providing a rhyme to another; poem with line-endings that rhyme. —*v.t./i.* form a rhyme; have rhymes; treat as rhyming. **rhymer** *n.*

rhythm *n.* pattern produced by emphasis and duration of notes in music or of syllables in words, or by a regular succession of movements or events. **rhythmic** *a.*, **rhythmical** *a.*, **rhythmically** *adv.*

rib *n.* one of the curved bones round the chest; structural part resembling this; pattern of raised lines in knitting. —*v.t.* (*p.t.* ribbed) support with ribs; knit as rib; (*colloq.*) tease.

ribald /'rɪbəld/ *a.* humorous in a cheerful but vulgar or disrespectful way. **ribaldry** *n.*

riband /'rɪb-/ *n.* ribbon.

ribbed *a.* with raised ridges.

ribbon *n.* band of silky material used for decoration or tying things; strip resembling this.

ribonucleic acid substance controlling protein synthesis in cells.

rice *n.* cereal plant grown in marshes in hot countries, with seeds used as food; these seeds.

rich *a.* (-er, -est) having much wealth; made of costly materials; abundant; containing a large proportion of something (e.g. fat, fuel); (of soil) fertile; (of colour or sound or smell) pleasantly deep and strong; highly amusing. **riches** *n.pl.* much money or valuable possessions. **richness** *n.*

richly *adv.* in a rich way; fully, thoroughly.

rick[1] *n.* built stack of hay etc.

rick[2] *n.* slight sprain or strain. —*v.t.* sprain or strain slightly.

rickets *n.* children's disease with softening and deformity of the bones, caused by lack of vitamin D.

rickety *a.* shaky, insecure.

rickshaw *n.* two-wheeled hooded vehicle used in the Far East, drawn by one or more people.

ricochet /'rɪkəʃeɪ/ *n. & v.i.* (*p.t.* ricocheted, *pr.* -ʃeɪd) rebound from a surface after striking it with a glancing blow.

ricrac *n.* zigzag braid used for trimming.

rid *v.t.* (*p.t.* rid, *pres.p.* ridding) free from something unpleasant or unwanted. **get rid of** cause to go away; free oneself of.

riddance *n.* ridding. **good riddance** welcome freedom from a person or thing one is rid of.

ridden *see* ride. —*a.* full of, dominated by.

riddle[1] *n.* question etc. designed to test ingenuity or give amusement in finding its answer or meaning; something puzzling or mysterious.

riddle[2] *n.* coarse sieve. —*v.t.* pass through a riddle; pierce with many holes; permeate thoroughly.

ride *v.t./i.* (*p.t.* rode, *p.p.* ridden) sit on and be carried by (a horse or bicycle etc.) or in a car etc.; be supported on, float; yield to (a blow) to reduce its impact. —*n.* spell of riding; journey in a vehicle; track for riding on; feel of a ride. **ride up** (of a garment) work upwards when worn.

rider *n.* one who rides a horse etc.; additional statement.

ridge *n.* narrow raised strip; line where two upward slopes meet; elongated region of high barometric pressure. **ridged** *a.*

ridicule /'rɪd-/ *n.* making or being made to seem ridiculous. —*v.t.* subject to ridicule, make fun of.

ridiculous /-'dɪk-/ *a.* deserving to be laughed at, esp. in a malicious or scornful way; not worth serious consideration. **ridiculously** *adv.*

riding *n.* former division of Yorkshire.

riding-light *n.* light shown by a ship riding at anchor.

rife *a.* occurring frequently, wide-spread. **rife with** full of (rumours etc.).

riff *n.* short repeated phrase in jazz etc.

riffle *v.t./i.* flex and release (pages etc.) in quick succession.

riff-raff *n.* rabble; disreputable people.

rifle *n.* a kind of gun with a long barrel. —*v.t.* search and rob; cut spiral grooves in (a gun-barrel).

rift *n.* cleft in earth or rock; crack, split; breach in friendly relations. **rift-valley** *n.* steep-sided valley formed by subsidence.

rig[1] *v.t.* (p.t. **rigged**) provide with clothes or equipment; fit (a ship) with spars, sails, ropes, etc.; set up (a structure), esp. in a make-shift way. —*n.* way a ship's masts and sails etc. are arranged; equipment (e.g. for drilling an oil-well); (*colloq.*) outfit. **rig-out** *n.* (*colloq.*) outfit.

rig[2] *v.t.* (p.t. **rigged**) manage or control fraudulently.

rigging *n.* ropes etc. used to support a ship's masts and sails.

right *a.* morally good; in accordance with justice; proper; correct, true; in a good or normal condition; of or on the side of the body which in most people has the more-used hand. —*n.* what is just; something one is entitled to; right hand or foot; people supporting more conservative or traditional policies than others in their group. —*v.t.* restore to a proper, correct, or upright position; set right. —*adv.* on or towards the right-hand side; directly; (*colloq.*) immediately; completely; exactly; rightly; all right. **in the right** having truth or justice on one's side. **right angle** angle of 90°. **right away** immediately. **right-hand man** indispensable or chief assistant. **right-handed** *a.* using the right hand. **right of way** right to pass over another's land; path subject to this; right to proceed when another vehicle must wait. **rightly** *adv.*, **rightness** *n.*

righteous *a.* doing what is morally right, making a show of this; morally justifiable. **righteously** *adv.*, **righteousness** *n.*

rightful *a.* just, proper, legal. **rightfully** *adv.*, **rightfulness** *n.*

rightist *a. & n.* (member) of the right wing of a political party.

rigid *a.* stiff, not bending or yielding; strict, inflexible. **rigidly** *adv.*, **rigidness** *n.*, **rigidity** *n.*

rigmarole /'rɪgmərəʊl/ *n.* long rambling statement; complicated formal procedure.

rigor /'raɪ-/ *n.* **rigor mortis** stiffening of the body after death.

rigour /'rɪg-/ *n.* strictness, severity; harshness of weather or conditions. **rigorous** *a.*, **rigorously** *adv.*, **rigorousness** *n.*

rile *v.t.* (*colloq.*) annoy.

rill *n.* small stream.

rim *n.* edge or border of something more or less circular. **rimmed** *a.*

rime *n.* frost.

rimed /raɪmd/ a. coated with frost.

rimless a. (of spectacles) made without frames.

rind /raɪnd/ n. tough outer layer or skin on fruit, cheese, bacon, etc.

ring[1] n. outline of a circle; thing shaped like this; small circular metal band worn on a finger; enclosure for a circus or sports event or cattle-show etc.; combination of people acting together to control operations or policy; **the ring** bookmakers. —v.t. put a ring on or round; surround.

ring[2] v.t./i. (p.t. **rang**, p.p. **rung**) give out a loud clear resonant sound; cause (a bell) to do this; signal by ringing; be filled with sound; telephone; (colloq.) alter and sell (a stolen vehicle). —n. act or sound of ringing; specified tone or feeling of a statement etc.; (colloq.) telephone call. **ring off** end a telephone call. **ring the changes** vary things. **ring up** make a telephone call.

ringer n. person who rings bells; (US) racehorse etc. fraudulently substituted for another; person's double.

ringleader n. person who leads others in wrongdoing or riot etc.

ringlet n. long tubular curl.

ringside n. area beside a boxing ring. **ringside seat** position from which one has a clear view of the scene of action.

ringworm n. skin disease producing round scaly patches on the skin.

rink n. skating-rink.

rinse v.t. wash lightly; wash out soap etc. from. —n. process of rinsing; solution washed through hair to tint or condition it.

riot n. wild disturbance by a crowd of people; profuse display; (colloq.) very amusing person or thing. —v.i. take part in a riot or disorderly revelry. **read the**

Riot Act insist that noise or disobedience must cease. **run riot** behave in an unruly way; grow in an uncontrolled way.

riotous a. disorderly, unruly; boisterous. **riotously** adv.

RIP abbr. (Latin requiescat or requiescant) in pace) rest in peace.

rip v.t./i. (p.t. **ripped**) tear apart; remove by pulling roughly; become torn; rush along. —n. act of ripping; torn place. **let rip** (colloq.) refrain from checking the speed or progress of; speak violently. **rip-cord** n. cord for pulling to release a parachute. **rip off** (colloq.) defraud; steal. **rip-off** n., **ripper** n.

riparian a. & n. (owner) of a river-bank.

ripe a. (-er, -est) ready to be gathered and used; matured; (of age) advanced; ready. **ripeness** n.

ripen v.t./i. make or become ripe.

riposte /rɪˈpɒst/ n. quick counterstroke or retort. —v.i. deliver a riposte.

ripple n. small wave(s); gentle sound that rises and falls. —v.t./i. form ripples (in).

rip-roaring a. wildly noisy.

rise v.i. (p.t. **rose**, p.p. **risen**) come or go or extend upwards; get up from lying or sitting or kneeling, get out of bed; cease to sit for business; become upright; come to life again after death; rebel; become higher; increase; have its origin or source. —n. act or amount of rising, increase; upward slope; increase in wages. **get** or **take a rise out of** draw into a display of annoyance. **give rise to** cause.

riser n. person or thing that rises; vertical piece between treads of a staircase.

risible /ˈrɪz-/ a. laughable; inclined to laugh. **risibly** adv., **risibility** n.

rising n. revolt. —a. **rising five** etc., nearing this age. **rising**

generation young people, those who are growing up.

risk *n.* possibility of meeting danger or suffering harm; person or thing representing a source of risk. —*v.t.* expose to the chance of injury or loss; accept the risk of.

risky *a.* (-ier, -iest) full of risk. **riskily** *adv.*, **riskiness** *n.*

risotto *n.* (*pl.* -os) dish of rice containing chopped meat or fish etc.

risqué /'rɪskeɪ/ *a.* slightly indecent.

rissole *n.* fried cake of minced meat.

rite *n.* ritual.

ritual *n.* series of actions used in a religious or other ceremony. —*a.* of or done as a ritual. **ritually** *adv.*, **ritualism** *n.*, **ritualistic** *a.*

rival *n.* person or thing competing with another or that can equal another. —*a.* being a rival or rivals. —*v.t.* (*p.t.* **rivalled**) be a rival of; seem as good as. **rivalry** *n.*

riven /'rɪv-/ *a.* split, torn violently.

river *n.* large natural stream of water; great flow.

rivet /'rɪv-/ *n.* nail or bolt for holding pieces of metal together, with its end pressed down to form a head when in place. —*v.t.* (*p.t.* **riveted**) fasten with or press down as a rivet; make immovable; attract and hold (the attention of). **riveter** *n.*

Riviera /rɪvɪ'eərə/ *n.* coastal region of south-east France, Monaco, and north-west Italy.

rivulet *n.* small stream.

RNA *abbr.* ribonucleic acid.

roach *n.* (*pl.* roach) small freshwater fish of the carp family.

road *n.* way by which people or vehicles may pass between places, esp. one with a prepared surface; way of reaching something. **on the road** travelling. **road-hog** *n.* reckless or inconsiderate driver. **road-house** *n.* inn, club, or restaurant on a main road in the country. **road-metal**

n. broken stone for making the foundation of a road or railway.

roadside *n.* border of a road.

roadway *n.* road, esp. as distinct from a footpath beside it.

roadworks *n.pl.* construction or repair of roads.

roadworthy *a.* (of a vehicle) fit to be used on a road. **roadworthiness** *n.*

roam *v.t./i.* & *n.* wander.

roan *n.* horse with a dark coat sprinkled with white or grey hairs.

roar *n.* long deep sound like that made by a lion; loud laughter. —*v.t./i.* give a roar; express in this way. **roarer** *n.*

roaring *a.* noisy; briskly active.

roast *v.t./i.* cook (meat) in an oven or by exposure to great heat; expose to great heat; undergo roasting. —*n.* roast meat; joint of meat for roasting.

rob *v.t.* (*p.t.* **robbed**) steal from; take unlawfully; deprive. **robber** *n.*, **robbery** *n.*

robe *n.* long loose esp. ceremonial garment. —*v.t.* dress in a robe.

robin *n.* brown red-breasted bird.

robot /'rəʊbɒt/ *n.* machine resembling and acting like a person; piece of apparatus operated by remote control. **robotic** *a.*

robotics /-'bɒt-/ *n.* study of robots and their design, operation, etc.

robust /-'bʌst/ *a.* strong, vigorous. **robustly** *adv.*, **robustness** *n.*

roc *n.* gigantic bird of Eastern legend.

rock[1] *n.* hard part of earth's crust, below the soil; mass of this, large stone or boulder; hard sugar sweet made in cylindrical sticks. **on the rocks** (*colloq.*) short of money; (of a drink) served neat with ice cubes. **rock-bottom** *a.* (*colloq.*) very low. **rock-cake** *n.* small fruit cake with a rugged surface.

rock[2] *v.t./i.* move to and fro while supported; disturb greatly by shock. —*n.* rocking movement; a kind of modern music usu. with a strong beat. **rock and roll** form of rock music with elements of blues.

rocker n. thing that rocks; pivoting switch. **off one's rocker** (sl.) crazy.

rockery n. collection of rough stones with soil between them on which small plants are grown.

rocket n. firework that shoots into the air when ignited and then explodes; structure that flies by expelling burning gases, propelling a bomb or spacecraft; (sl.) reprimand. —v.i. (p.t. **rocketed**) move rapidly upwards or away.

rocketry n. science or practice of rocket propulsion.

rocky[1] a. (-ier, -iest) of or like rock; full of rock. **rockiness** n.

rocky[2] a. (-ier, -iest) (colloq.) unsteady. **rockily** adv., **rockiness** n.

rococo /rə'kəʊ-/ a. & n. (of or in) an ornate style of decoration in Europe in the 18th century.

rod n. slender straight round stick or metal bar; fishing-rod; measure of length (=perch[1]).

rode see **ride**.

rodent n. animal with strong front teeth for gnawing things.

rodeo /-'deɪəʊ/ n. (pl. **-os**) round-up of ranch cattle for branding etc.; exhibition of cowboys' skill in handling animals.

roe[1] n. mass of eggs in a female fish's ovary (**hard roe**) or male fish's milt (**soft roe**).

roe[2] n. (pl. **roe** or **roes**) a kind of small deer. **roebuck** n. male roe.

roentgen /'rʌntjən/ n. unit of ionizing radiation.

rogations n.pl. litany for use on **Rogation Days** the three days before Ascension Day. **Rogation Sunday** before this.

roger int. (in signalling) message received and understood.

rogue n. dishonest or unprincipled or mischievous person; wild animal living apart from the herd. **roguery** n.

roguish a. mischievous; playful. **roguishly** adv., **roguishness** n.

roister v.i. revel noisily, be uproarious. **roisterer** n.

role n. actor's part; person's or thing's function.

roll v.t./i. move (on a surface) on wheels or by turning over and over; turn on an axis or over and over; form into a cylindrical or spherical shape; flatten with a roller; rock from side to side; undulate; move or pass steadily; make a long continuous vibrating sound; (US sl.) attack and rob (a person). —n. cylinder formed by turning flexible material over and over upon itself; thing with this shape, undulation; small individual portion of bread baked in a rounded shape, this with filling; official list or register; rolling movement or sound. **be rolling (in money)** (colloq.) be wealthy. **roll-call** n. calling of a list of names to check that all are present. **rolled gold** thin coating of gold on another metal. **rolling-pin** n. roller for flattening dough.

rolling-stock n. railway engines and carriages, wagons, etc. **rolling stone** person who does not settle in one place.

roller n. cylinder rolled over things to flatten or spread them, or on which something is wound; long swelling wave. **roller-coaster** n. switchback at a fair etc. **roller-skate** n. (see **skate**[2]). **roller-skating** n. skating on roller-skates. **roller towel** towel with its ends joined to make it continuous, hung over a roller.

rollicking a. full of boisterous high spirits.

rollmop n. rolled pickled herring fillet.

roly-poly n. pudding of suet pastry spread with jam, rolled up, and boiled. —a. plump, podgy.

ROM abbr. read-only memory.

Roman a. & n. (native, inhabitant) of Rome or of the ancient Roman republic or empire; Roman Catholic. **Roman Catholic** (member) of the Church that acknowledges the Pope as its head. **Roman Catholicism** faith of the Roman Catholic Church. **Roman numerals** letters representing numbers (I = 1, V = 5, etc.).

roman n. plain upright type (not italic).

romance /-'mæns/ n. imaginative story or literature; romantic situation, event, or atmosphere; love story, love affair resembling this; picturesque exaggeration. —v.i. distort the truth or invent imaginatively. **Romance languages** those descended from Latin.

Romanesque /-'nesk/ a. & n. (of or in) a style of art and architecture in Europe after 1050–1200.

romantic a. appealing to the emotions by its imaginative or heroic or picturesque quality; involving a love affair; enjoying romantic situations etc. —n. romantic person. **romantically** adv.

romanticism n. romantic style.

romanticize v.t./i. make romantic; indulge in romance. **romanticization** n.

Romany a. & n. gypsy; (of) the gypsy language.

romp v.i. play about in a lively way; (colloq.) go along easily. —n. spell of romping.

rompers n.pl. young child's one-piece garment.

rondeau n. short poem with the opening words used as a refrain.

rondo n. (pl. -os) piece of music with a recurring theme.

rood n. crucifix, esp. on a rood-screen; quarter of an acre. **Holy Rood** (old use) Cross of Christ. **rood-screen** n. carved screen separating nave from chancel.

roof n. (pl. roofs) upper covering of a building, car, cavity, etc. —v.t. cover with a roof; be the roof of. **roofer** n.

rook[1] n. a kind of crow. —v.t. swindle, charge an extortionate price.

rook[2] n. chess piece with a top shaped like battlements.

rookery n. colony of rooks; their nesting-place; colony or breeding-place of penguins or seals.

rookie n. (sl.) recruit.

room n. space that is or could be occupied; enclosed part of a building; scope to allow something; (pl.) set of rooms as lodgings.

roomy a. able to contain much.

roost n. place where birds perch or rest. —v.i. perch, esp. for sleep.

rooster n. (US) domestic cock.

root[1] n. part of a plant that attaches it to the earth and absorbs water and nourishment from the soil; embedded part of hair, tooth, etc.; source, basis; language-element from which words have been made; number in relation to another which it produces when multiplied by itself a specified number of times; (pl.) emotional attachment to a place. —v.t./i. take root, cause to do this; cause to stand fixed and unmoving. **root out** or **up** drag or dig up by the roots; get rid of. **take root** send down roots; become established.

root[2] v.t./i. (of an animal) turn up ground with the snout or beak in search of food; rummage, extract; (US sl.) give support by applause.

rootless a. without roots. **rootlessness** n.

rope n. strong thick cord; thing resembling this. —v.t. fasten or secure with rope; fence off with rope(s). **know** or **show the ropes** know or show the procedure. **rope in** persuade to take part in an activity.

ropy a. (-ier, -iest) forming long sticky threads; (colloq.) poor in quality. **ropiness** n.

rorqual /-k(ə)l/ n. whale with a dorsal fin.

rosaceous a. of the rose family.

rosary n. set series of prayers used in the RC Church; string of beads for keeping count in this; rose-garden.

rose[1] n. ornamental usu. fragrant flower; bush or shrub bearing this; deep pink; rose-shaped object or design; sprinkling-nozzle.

rose window circular window with tracery.

rose[2] see **rise**.

rosé /'rəʊzeɪ/ n. light pink wine.

roseate /-zɪət/ a. deep pink, rosy.

rosebud n. bud of a rose.

rosemary n. shrub with fragrant leaves used to flavour food.

rosette n. rose-shaped badge or ornament.

rosewood n. fragrant close-grained wood used for making furniture.

rosin /'rɒz-/ n. a kind of resin.

roster /'rɒs-/ n. & v.t. list showing people's turns of duty etc.

rostrum /'rɒs-/ n. (pl. -tra) platform for one person.

rosy a. (-ier, -iest) deep pink; promising, hopeful. **rosily** adv., **rosiness** n.

rot v.t./i. (p.t. rotted) lose its original form by chemical action caused by bacteria or fungi etc.; cause to do this; perish through lack of use. —n. rotting, rottenness; (sl.) nonsense; series of failures.

rota n. list of duties to be done or people to do them in rotation.

rotary a. acting by rotating.

rotate v.t./i. revolve; arrange or occur or deal with in a recurrent series. **rotation** n., **rotatory** /'rəʊ-/ a.

rote n. **by rote** by memory without thought of the meaning; by a fixed procedure.

rotisserie /-'tɪs-/ n. cooking-device for roasting food on a revolving spit.

rotor n. rotating part.

rotten a. rotted, breaking easily from age or use; morally corrupt; (colloq.) worthless, unpleasant. **rottenness** n.

rotter n. (sl.) contemptible person.

Rottweiler /-vaɪ-/ n. dog of large black-and-tan breed.

rotund /-'tʌnd/ a. rounded, plump. **rotundity** n.

rotunda n. circular domed building or hall.

rouble /'ruːb(ə)l/ n. unit of money in Russia.

roué /'ruːeɪ/ n. dissolute elderly man.

rouge /ruːʒ/ n. reddish cosmetic colouring for the cheeks; fine red powder for polishing metal. —v.t. colour with rouge.

rough a. (-er, -est) having an uneven or irregular surface; coarse in texture; not gentle or careful, violent, (of weather) stormy; not perfected or detailed; approximate. —adv. roughly; in rough conditions. —n. rough thing or state; rough ground; ruffian. —v.t. make rough. **rough-and-ready** a. full of rough vigour; rough but effective. **rough-and-tumble** n. haphazard struggle. **rough diamond** diamond not yet cut; person of good nature but lacking polished manners. **rough it** do without ordinary comforts. **rough out** plan or sketch roughly. **roughly** adv., **roughness** n.

roughage n. dietary fibre.

roughcast n. plaster of lime and gravel used on buildings. —v.t. (p.t. roughcast) coat with this.

roughen v.t./i. make or become rough.

roughneck n. (colloq.) driller on an oil-rig; (US sl.) rough person.

roughshod a. (of a horse) having shoes with the nail-heads left projecting. **ride roughshod over** treat inconsiderately or arrogantly.

roulette /ruːˈlet/ n. gambling game played with a small ball on a revolving disc.

round a. (-er, -est) having a curved shape or outline; circular, spherical, or cylindrical; complete. —n. round object; slice of bread cut across a loaf; circular or recurring course or series; song for two or more voices that start at different times; shot(s) from one or more firearms, ammunition for this; one section of a competition or struggle or boxing-match. —prep. so as to circle or enclose; visiting in a series; to all points of interest in. —adv. in a circle or curve; by a circuitous route; so as to face in a different direction; round a place or group; to a person's house etc.; into consciousness after unconsciousness. —v.t./i. make or become round; make into a round figure or number; travel round. **in the round** with all sides visible. **round about** near by; approximately. **round figure** or **number** approximation without odd units. **round off** complete; make symmetrical. **round on** make an attack or retort in retaliation. **round robin** statement signed by a number of people. **round the clock** continuously through day and night. **round trip** circular tour; outward and return journey. **round up** gather into one place. **round-up** n. **roundness** n.

roundabout n. merry-go-round; road junction with a circular island round which traffic moves in one direction. —a. indirect.

roundel n. small disc; rondeau.

roundelay n. short simple song with a refrain.

rounders n. team game played with bat and ball, in which

players have to run round a circuit. **rounder** n. unit of scoring in this.

Roundhead n. supporter of the Parliamentary party in the English Civil War.

roundly adv. thoroughly, severely; in a rounded shape.

roundsman n. (pl. -men) tradesman's employee delivering goods on a regular route.

roundworm n. parasitic worm with a rounded body.

rouse v.t./i. wake; cause to become active or excited.

rousing a. vigorous, stirring.

roustabout n. labourer on an oil rig.

rout[1] n. utter defeat; disorderly retreat. —v.t. defeat completely; put to flight.

rout[2] v.t./i. fetch (out); rummage.

route n. course or way from starting-point to finishing-point. —v.t. (pres.p. **routeing**) send by a specified route. **route march** training-march for troops.

routine /ruːˈtiːn/ n. standard procedure; set sequence of movements. —a. in accordance with routine. **routinely** adv.

roux /ruː/ n. mixture of heated fat and flour as a basis for a sauce.

rove[1] v.t./i. wander. **rover** n.

rove[2] see **reeve**[2].

row[1] /rəʊ/ n. people or things in a line.

row[2] /rəʊ/ v.t./i. propel (a boat) by using oars; carry in a boat that one rows. —n. spell of rowing. **row-boat** n., **rowing-boat** n.

row[3] /raʊ/ n. (colloq.) loud noise; quarrel, angry argument; scolding. —v.t./i. (colloq.) quarrel, argue angrily; scold.

rowan /ˈrəʊ-/ n. tree bearing hanging clusters of red berries.

rowdy /ˈraʊ-/ a. (-ier, -iest) noisy and disorderly. —n. rowdy person. **rowdily** adv., **rowdiness** n.

rowel /ˈraʊəl/ n. spiked revolving disc on a spur.

rowlock /'rɒl-/ n. device on the side of a boat securing an oar.

royal a. of or suited to a king or queen; of the family or in the service or under the patronage of royalty; splendid, of exceptional size. —n. (colloq.) member of a royal family. **royal blue** bright blue. **royally** adv.

royalist n. monarchist.

Royalist n. supporter of the monarchy in the English Civil War.

royalty n. being royal; royal person(s); payment to an author etc. for each copy or performance of his work, or to a patentee for use of his patent; payment by a mining or oil company to the land-owner.

RSVP abbr. (French *répondez s'il vous plaît*) please reply.

Rt. Hon. abbr. Right Honourable.

Rt. Rev., Rt. Revd. abbrs. Right Reverend.

rub v.t./i. (p.t. **rubbed**) press against a surface and slide to and fro; polish, clean, dry, or make sore etc. by rubbing. —n. act or process of rubbing; difficulty. **rub it in** emphasize or remind a person constantly of an unpleasant fact. **rub out** remove (marks etc.) by using a rubber.

rubber[1] n. tough elastic substance made from the juice of certain plants or synthetically; piece of this for rubbing out pencil or ink marks; device for rubbing things. **rubber-stamp** v.t. approve automatically without consideration.

rubber[2] n. match of three successive games at bridge or whist.

rubberize v.t. treat or coat with rubber.

rubberneck n. & v.i. (US colloq.) (be) a gaping sightseer.

rubbery a. like rubber.

rubbish n. waste or worthless material; nonsense. —v.t. colloq. disparage. **rubbishy** a.

rubble n. waste or rough fragments of stone or brick etc.

rubella n. German measles.

rubicund /'ru:-/ a. red, ruddy.

rubric /'ru:-/ n. words put as a heading or note of explanation.

ruby n. red gem; deep red colour. —a. deep red.

RUC abbr. Royal Ulster Constabulary.

ruche /ru:ʃ/ n. fabric gathered as trimming. —v.t. gather thus.

ruck[1] v.t./i. & n. crease, wrinkle.

ruck[2] n. main body of competitors; undistinguished crowd; loose scrummage.

rucksack n. capacious bag carried on the back in hiking etc.

ructions n.pl. (colloq.) protests and noisy arguments, a row.

rudder n. vertical piece of metal or wood hinged to the stern of a boat or aircraft, used for steering.

ruddy a. (-ier, -iest) reddish. **ruddily** adv., **ruddiness** n.

rude a. (-er, -est) impolite, showing no respect; primitive, roughly made; hearty; startling. **rudely** adv., **rudeness** n.

rudiment n. rudimentary part or organ; (pl.) basic or elementary principles.

rudimentary a. incompletely developed; basic, elementary.

rue[1] n. shrub with bitter leaves formerly used in medicine.

rue[2] v.t. repent, regret.

rueful a. showing or feeling good-humoured regret. **ruefully** adv.

ruff[1] n. pleated frill worn round the neck in the 16th century; projecting or coloured ring of feathers or fur round a bird's or animal's neck; bird of the sandpiper family.

ruff[2] v.t./i. trump in a card-game. —n. trumping.

ruffian n. violent lawless person.

ruffle v.t./i. disturb the smoothness (of); upset the calmness or even temper of. —n. gathered frill.

rufous /'ru:-/ a. reddish-brown.

rug *n.* thick floor-mat; piece of thick warm fabric used as a covering.

Rugby *n.* **Rugby football** a kind of football played with an oval ball which may be kicked or carried; this ball.

rugged /-gɪd/ *a.* uneven, irregular, craggy; rough but kindly. **ruggedly** *adv.*, **ruggedness** *n.*

rugger *n.* (*colloq.*) Rugby football.

ruin *n.* severe damage or destruction; complete loss of one's fortune or prospects; broken remains of something; cause of ruin. —*v.t.* cause ruin to; reduce to ruins. **ruination** *n.*

ruinous *a.* bringing ruin; in ruins, ruined. **ruinously** *adv.*

rule *n.* statement of what can or should or must be done in certain circumstances or in a game; dominant custom; governing, control; ruler used by carpenters etc.; thin printed line, dash. —*v.t./i.* have authoritative control (over), govern; keep under control; give an authoritative decision; draw (a line) using a ruler or other straight edge, mark parallel lines on. **as a rule** usually. **rule of thumb** rough practical method of procedure. **rule out** exclude as irrelevant or ineligible.

ruler *n.* person who rules; straight strip used in measuring or for drawing straight lines.

ruling *n.* authoritative decision.

rum[1] *n.* alcoholic spirit distilled from sugar-cane or molasses.

rum[2] *a.* (*colloq.*) strange, odd.

rumba *n.* ballroom dance of Cuban origin.

rumble[1] *v.i.* make a deep heavy continuous sound; utter in a deep voice. —*n.* rumbling sound.

rumble[2] *v.t.* (*sl.*) detect the true character of; see through (a deception).

rumbustious *a.* (*colloq.*) boisterous, uproarious.

ruminant /ˈruː-/ *n.* animal that chews the cud. —*a.* ruminating.

ruminate /ˈruː-/ *v.i.* chew the cud; meditate, ponder. **rumination** *n.*, **ruminative** /ˈruː-/ *a.*

rummage *v.i. & n.* search by disarranging things. **rummage sale** jumble sale.

rummy *n.* card-game in which players try to form sets or sequences of cards.

rumour *n.* information spread by talking but not certainly true. **be rumoured** be spread as a rumour.

rump *n.* buttocks; corresponding part of a bird.

rumple *v.t./i.* make or become crumpled; make untidy.

rumpus *n.* (*colloq.*) uproar, angry dispute.

run *v.t./i.* (*p.t.* **ran**, *p.p.* **run**, *pres.p.* **running**) move with quick steps and with always at least one foot off the ground; go smoothly or swiftly; compete in a race or contest; spread; flow, exude liquid; function; travel or convey from one point to another; extend; be current or valid; be in a specified condition; cause to run; manage, organize; own and use (a vehicle etc.); (of a newspaper) print as an item; sew loosely or quickly. —*n.* spell or course of running; point scored in cricket or baseball; ladder in fabric; continuous stretch or sequence; general demand for goods etc.; general type or class of things; enclosure where domestic animals can range; track (e.g. for skiing); permission to make unrestricted use of something. **in** *or* **out of the running** with a good *or* with no chance of winning. **in the long run** in the end, over a long period. **on the run** fleeing. **run across** happen to meet or find. **run a blockade** pass through it. **run a risk** take a risk. **run a temperature** be feverish. **run away** leave quickly or secretly. **run down** stop because not rewound; reduce the numbers of; knock down with a moving vehicle or ship; discover after searching; speak of in a slighting way; **be run down** be weak or exhausted. **run-down** n. detailed analysis. **run into** collide with; happen to meet. **run off** produce (copies etc.) on a machine. **run-of-the-mill** a. ordinary. **run on** talk continually. **run out** become used up. **run out of** have used up (one's stock). **run over** knock down or crush with a vehicle. **run up** allow (a bill) to mount. **run-up** n. period leading up to an event.

runaway n. person who has run away. —a. having run away or become out of control; (of victory) won easily.

rune n. any of the letters in an early Germanic alphabet. **runic** a.

rung¹ n. crosspiece of a ladder etc.

rung² see **ring²**.

runnel n. brook, gutter.

runner n. person or animal that runs; messenger; creeping stem that roots; groove, strip, or roller etc. for a thing to move on; long narrow strip of carpet or ornamental cloth. **runner bean** climbing bean. **runner-up** n. one who finishes second in a competition.

runny a. semi-liquid; tending to flow or exude fluid.

runt n. undersized person or animal.

runway n. prepared surface on which aircraft may take off and land.

rupee /ruːˈpiː/ n. unit of money in India, Pakistan, etc.

rupture n. breaking, breach; abdominal hernia. —v.t./i. burst, break; cause hernia in.

rural a. of or in or like the countryside. **rural dean** (see **dean**).

ruse /ruːz/ n. deception, trick.

rush¹ n. marsh plant with a slender pithy stem.

rush² v.t./i. go or come or convey with great speed; act hastily; force into hasty action; attack or capture with a sudden assault. —n. rushing, instance of this; period of great activity; (colloq.) first print of a cinema film before editing. **rush hour** each of the times of day when traffic is busiest.

rusk n. a kind of biscuit.

russet a. soft reddish-brown. —n. russet colour; a kind of apple with a rough skin.

rust n. brownish corrosive coating formed on iron exposed to moisture; reddish-brown; plant disease with rust-coloured spots. —v.t./i. make or become rusty.

rustproof a. & v.t., **rustless** a.

rustic a. of or like country life or people; made of rough timber or untrimmed branches. **rusticity** n.

rusticate v.t./i. send down temporarily from a university; settle in the country. **rustication** n.

rustle v.t./i. make a sound like paper being crumpled, cause to do this; (US) steal (horses or cattle). —n. rustling sound. **rustle up** (colloq.) prepare, produce. **rustler** n.

rusty a. (-ier, -iest) affected with rust; rust-coloured; having lost quality by lack of use. **rustiness** n.

rut¹ n. deep track made by wheels; habitual usu. dull course of life. **rutted** a.

rut² n. periodic sexual excitement of a male deer, goat, etc. —v.i. (p.t. **rutted**) be affected with this.

ruthless a. having no pity. **ruthlessly** adv., **ruthlessness** n.

rye n. a kind of cereal; whisky made from rye.

S

S. abbr. south; southern.

sabbatarian n. person who observes the sabbath strictly.

sabbath *n.* day of religious services and abstinence from work (Saturday for Jews, Sunday for Christians).

sabbatical /-'bæt-/ *a.* of or like the sabbath. **sabbatical leave** leave granted at intervals to a university professor etc. for study and travel.

sable *n.* small arctic mammal with dark fur; its fur; black. —*a.* black, gloomy.

sabotage /-'tɑːʒ/ *n.* wilful damage to machinery or materials, or disruption of work. —*v.t.* commit sabotage on; make useless. **saboteur** /-'tɜː(r)/ *n.*

sabre /'seɪbə(r)/ *n.* curved sword.

sac *n.* bag-like part in an animal or plant.

saccharin /-rɪn/ *n.* very sweet substance used instead of sugar.

saccharine /-riːn/ *a.* intensely and unpleasantly sweet.

sacerdotal /-'dəʊ-/ *a.* of priests.

sachet /'sæʃeɪ/ *n.* small bag or sealed pack.

sack[1] *n.* large bag of strong coarse fabric; **the sack** (*colloq.*) dismissal from one's employment. —*v.t.* put into a sack or sacks; (*colloq.*) dismiss. **sackful** *n.* (*pl.* **-fuls**).

sack[2] *v.t.* plunder (a captured town) violently. —*n.* this act or process.

sackcloth, sacking *ns.* coarse fabric for making sacks.

sacral /'seɪ-/ *a.* of the sacrum.

sacrament *n.* any of the symbolic Christian religious ceremonies; consecrated elements in the Eucharist. **sacramental** *a.*

sacred *a.* holy; dedicated (to a person or purpose); connected with religion; sacrosanct. **sacred cow** idea etc. which its supporters will not allow to be criticized.

sacrifice *n.* slaughter of a victim or presenting of a gift to win a god's favour; this victim or gift; giving up of a valued thing for the sake of something else; thing given up, loss entailed.

—*v.t.* offer or kill or give up as a sacrifice. **sacrificial** *a.*

sacrilege /-lɪdʒ/ *n.* disrespect to a sacred thing. **sacrilegious** *a.*

sacristan *n.* person in charge of the contents of a church.

sacristy *n.* place where sacred vessels are kept in a church.

sacrosanct *a.* reverenced or respected and not to be harmed.

sacrum /'seɪ-/ *n.* composite bone forming the back of the pelvis.

sad *a.* (**sadder, saddest**) showing or causing sorrow; regrettable; (of cake etc.) dense from not having risen. **sadly** *adv.*, **sadness** *n.*

sadden *v.t./i.* make or become sad.

saddle *n.* seat for a rider; ridge of high land between two peaks; joint of meat consisting of the two loins. —*v.t.* put a saddle on (an animal); burden with a task. **in the saddle** in a controlling position.

saddler *n.* person who makes or deals in saddles and harness.

saddlery *n.* saddler's trade or goods.

sadism /'seɪ-/ *n.* enjoyment of inflicting or watching cruelty. **sadist** *n.*, **sadistic** /sə'dɪs-/ *a.*, **sadistically** *adv.*

safari /sə'fɑːrɪ/ *n.* expedition to hunt or observe wild animals. **safari park** park where exotic wild animals are kept in the open for visitors to see.

safe *a.* (**-er, -est**) free from risk or danger; providing security. —*adv.* safely. —*n.* strong lockable cupboard for valuables; ventilated cabinet for storing food. **safe conduct** immunity from arrest or harm. **safe deposit** building containing safes and strongrooms for hire. **safely** *adv.*

safeguard *n.* means of protection. —*v.t.* protect.

safety *n.* being safe, freedom from risk or danger. **safety pin** brooch-like pin with a guard protecting and securing the point. **safety-valve** *n.* valve that opens automatically to relieve excessive pressure in a steam boiler; harmless outlet for excitement etc.

saffron *n.* orange-coloured stigmas of a kind of crocus, used to colour and flavour food; colour of these; this crocus.

sag *v.i.* (*p.t.* **sagged**) droop or curve down in the middle under weight or pressure. —*n.* sagging.

saga /'sɑː-/ *n.* long story.

sagacious /-'geɪ-/ *a.* showing wisdom. **sagaciously** *adv.*, **sagacity** /-'gæ-/ *n.*

sage[1] *n.* herb with fragrant grey-green leaves used to flavour food.

sage[2] *a.* wise, esp. from experience. —*n.* wise man. **sagely** *adv.*

sago /'seɪ-/ *n.* starchy food in hard white grains, used in puddings.

sahib /'sɑːɪb/ *n.* former title of address to European men in India.

said *see* **say.**

sail *n.* piece of fabric spread to catch the wind and drive a ship or boat along; journey by ship or boat; arm of a windmill. —*v.t./i.* travel on water by use of sails or engine-power; start on a voyage; control the sailing of; move smoothly. **sailing-ship** *n.*

sailboard *n.* board with a mast and sail, used in windsurfing. **sailboarder** *n.*, **sailboarding** *n.*

sailcloth *n.* canvas for sails; strong canvas-like dress-material.

sailor *n.* member of a ship's crew; traveller considered as liable (**bad sailor**) or not liable (**good sailor**) to seasickness.

sailplane *n.* a kind of glider designed for sustained flight.

saint *n.* holy person, esp. one venerated by the RC or Orthodox Church; soul in paradise; very good or patient or unselfish person. **sainthood** *n.*, **saintly** *a.*, **saintliness** *n.*

sake[1] *n.* **for the sake of** in order to please or benefit (a person) or to get or keep (a thing).

sake[2] /'sɑːkɪ/ *n.* Japanese fermented liquor made from rice.

salaam /-'lɑːm/ *n.* oriental salutation, a low bow. —*v.t./i.* make a salaam to.

salacious /-'leɪ-/ *a.* lewd, erotic. **salaciously** *adv.*, **salaciousness** *n.*, **salacity** /-'læ-/ *n.*

salad *n.* cold dish of one or more chopped or sliced (usu. raw) vegetables.

salamander /'sæ-/ *n.* lizard-like animal.

salami /-'lɑː-/ *n.* highly-seasoned sausage sold ready to eat cold.

salaried /-rɪd/ *a.* receiving a salary.

salary *n.* fixed regular (usu. monthly or quarterly) payment by employer to employee.

sale *n.* selling, exchange of a commodity for money; event at which goods are sold; disposal of a shop's stock at reduced prices. **for** or **on sale** offered for purchase.

saleable *a.* fit to be sold, likely to find a purchaser.

saleroom *n.* room where auctions are held.

salesman, saleswoman, salesperson *ns.* (*pl.* **-men, -women**) one employed to sell goods.

salesmanship *n.* skill at selling.

salient /'seɪ-/ *a.* projecting, most noticeable. —*n.* projecting part.

saline /'seɪlaɪn/ *a.* salty, containing salt(s). **salinity** /sə'lɪn-/ *n.*

saliva /sə'laɪ-/ *n.* colourless liquid that forms in the mouth.

salivary /-'laɪ-/ *a.* of or producing saliva.

salivate /'sælɪ-/ *v.i.* produce saliva. **salivation** *n.*

sallow[1] /-ləʊ/ *a.* (**-er, -est**) (of the complexion) yellowish. **sallowness** *n.*

sallow[2] /-ləʊ/ *n.* low-growing willow.

sally *n.* sudden rush in attack; excursion; lively or witty remark. —*v.i.* **sally forth** *or* **out** make a sally (in attack) or excursion.

salmi *n.* ragout or casserole, esp. of game-birds.

salmon *n.* (*pl.* **salmon**) large fish with pinkish flesh; salmon-pink. **salmon-pink** *a.* & *n.* yellowish-pink. **salmon trout** trout resembling salmon.

salmonella *n.* a kind of bacterium causing food-poisoning.

salon /'sælɔ̃/ *n.* elegant room for receiving guests; room or establishment where a hairdresser or couturier etc. receives clients.

saloon *n.* public room for a specified purpose, or on board ship; (*US*) public bar; saloon car. **saloon car** car for a driver and passengers, with a closed body.

salsify /'sælsɪ-/ *n.* plant with a long fleshy root used as a vegetable.

salt *n.* sodium chloride obtained from mines or by evaporation from sea-water, used to season and preserve food; chemical compound of a metal and an acid; salt-cellar; (*pl.*) substance resembling salt in form, esp. a laxative. —*a.* tasting of salt; impregnated with salt. —*v.t.* season or sprinkle with salt; preserve in salt; (*sl.*) make (a mine) appear rich by fraudulently inserting precious metal before it is viewed. **old salt** experienced sailor. **salt away** (*colloq.*) put aside for the future. **salt-cellar** *n.* dish or perforated pot holding salt for use at meals. **salt-marsh** *n.* marsh flooded by the sea at high tide. **salt-pan** *n.* hollow near the sea where salt is obtained from sea-water by evaporation. **take with a grain** (*or* **pinch**) **of salt** regard sceptically. **worth one's salt** deserving one's position, competent. **salty** *a.*, **saltiness** *n.*

salting *n.* salt-marsh.

saltire /'sæ-/ *n.* a cross (×) dividing a shield into four parts.

saltpetre *n.* salty white powder used in gunpowder, in medicine, and in preserving meat.

salubrious /-'lu:-/ *a.* health-giving. **salubrity** *n.*

saluki /-'lu:-/ *n.* (*pl.* **-is**) tall swift silky-coated dog.

salutary /'sæ-/ *a.* producing a beneficial or wholesome effect.

salutation *n.* word(s) or gesture of greeting; expression of respect.

salute *n.* gesture of respect or greeting. —*v.t.* make a salute to.

salvage *n.* rescue of a ship or its cargo from loss at sea, or of property from fire etc.; saving and use of waste material; items saved thus. —*v.t.* save from loss or for use as salvage.

salvation *n.* saving from disaster, esp. from sin and its spiritual consequences.

salve[1] *n.* soothing ointment; thing that soothes. —*v.t.* soothe (conscience etc.).

salve[2] *v.t.* save from loss at sea or from a fire. **salvable** *a.*

salver *n.* a kind of small tray.

salvo *n.* (*pl.* **-oes**) firing of guns simultaneously; volley of applause.

sal volatile /və'lætɪlɪ/ flavoured solution of ammonium carbonate, sniffed as a remedy for faintness.

samba *n.* ballroom dance of Brazilian origin.

same *a.* being of one kind, not changed or different; previously mentioned; **the same** the same thing, in the same manner. **sameness** *n.*

samovar *n.* metal urn for making tea, used esp. in Russia.

sampan *n.* small boat used along coasts and rivers of China.

samphire *n.* maritime rock plant with fragrant fleshy leaves.

sample *n.* small separated part showing the quality of the whole; specimen. —*v.t.* test by taking a sample or experiencing.

sampler n. thing that takes samples; piece of embroidery worked in various stitches to show one's skill.

samurai /ˈsæmʊraɪ/ n. (pl. **samurai**) Japanese army officer; (old use) member of the military caste in Japan.

sanatorium n. (pl. **-ums**) establishment for treating chronic diseases or convalescents; room or building for sick persons in a school etc.

sanctify v.t. make holy or sacred. **sanctification** n.

sanctimonious /-ˈməʊ-/ a. making a show of righteousness or piety. **sanctimoniously** adv., **sanctimoniousness** n.

sanction n. permission, approval; penalty imposed on a country or organization.—v.t. give sanction to, authorize.

sanctity n. sacredness, holiness.

sanctuary n. sacred place; part of a chancel containing the altar; place where birds or wild animals are protected; refuge.

sanctum n. holy place; person's private room.

sand n. very fine loose fragments of crushed rock; (pl.) expanse of sand, sandbank.—v.t. sprinkle or cover with sand; smooth with sand or sandpaper.

sandal n. light shoe with straps or thongs. **sandalled** a.

sandalwood n. a kind of scented wood.

sandbag n. bag filled with sand, used to protect a wall or building.—v.t. (p.t. **-bagged**) protect with sandbags.

sandbank n. underwater deposit of sand.

sandblast v.t. treat with a jet of sand driven by compressed air or steam.

sandcastle n. structure of sand made by a child.

sandpaper n. paper with a coating of sand or other abrasive substance, used for smoothing surfaces.—v.t. smooth with this.

sandpiper n. bird inhabiting wet sandy places.

sandpit n. sand-filled hollow made for children to play in.

sandstone n. rock formed of compressed sand.

sandstorm n. desert storm of wind with blown sand.

sandwich n. two or more slices of bread with a layer of filling between; thing arranged like this. —v.t. put between two others.

sandwich-man n. man walking in the street with advertisement boards hanging in front and behind.

sandy a. like sand; covered with sand; yellowish-red.

sane a. (**-er, -est**) having a sound mind, not mad; sensible and practical. **sanely** adv.

sang see **sing**.

sang-froid /sãˈfrwɑ:/ n. calmness in danger or difficulty.

sangria n. Spanish drink of red wine and lemonade.

sanguinary /ˈsæŋgwɪn-/ a. full of bloodshed; bloodthirsty.

sanguine /-gwɪn/ a. optimistic.

sanitary a. of hygiene; hygienic; of sanitation.

sanitation n. arrangements to protect public health, esp. drainage and disposal of sewage.

sanitize v.t. make sanitary; make more acceptable by removing material.

sanity n. condition of being sane.

sank see **sink**.

Sanskrit n. ancient Indo-European language.

sap[1] n. vital liquid in plants; (sl.) foolish person.—v.t. (p.t. **sapped**) exhaust gradually. **sappy** a.

sap[2] n. trench or tunnel dug to get closer to an enemy.—v.t./i. (p.t. **sapped**) undermine with saps; weaken.

sapele /-ˈpiːlɪ/ n. mahogany-like wood; tree producing this.

sapient /'seɪ-/ a. wise; pretending wisdom. **sapiently** adv., **sapience** n.

sapling n. young tree.

sapphire n. transparent blue precious stone; its colour. —a. bright blue.

saprophyte /'sæ-/ n. fungus or related plant living on decayed matter. **saprophytic** /-'fɪt-/ a.

Saracen /'sæ-/ n. Arab or Muslim of the time of the Crusades.

sarcasm n. ironical wounding remark; use of ironical remarks. **sarcastic** a., **sarcastically** adv.

sarcophagus /-'kɒf-/ n. (pl. -gi, pr. -gaɪ) stone coffin.

sardine n. young pilchard or similar small fish.

sardonic a. humorous in a grim or sarcastic way. **sardonically** adv.

sardonyx n. onyx with white and yellow layers.

sargasso n. seaweed with berry-like air-vessels.

sari n. (pl. **-is**) length of cloth draped round the body, worn by women of the Indian subcontinent.

sarong n. strip of cloth worn round the body, esp. in Malaya and Java.

sarsaparilla n. tropical American plant; its dried root; a soft drink flavoured with this.

sarsen n. sandstone boulder.

sartorial a. of tailoring; of men's clothing.

sash[1] n. long strip of cloth worn round the body at the waist or over one shoulder.

sash[2] n. frame holding a glass pane of a window and sliding up and down in grooves. **sash-cord** n. cord attaching a balancing-weight at each end of this. **sash-window** n.

Sassenach /'sæsənæk/ n. (Sc. & Ir.) Englishman.

sat see **sit**.

Satanic /-'tæn-/ a. of Satan. **satanic** a. devilish; hellish.

Satanism n. worship of Satan.

satchel n. bag for carrying school books or other light articles, hung over the shoulder(s).

sate v.t. satiate.

sateen /-'tiːn/ n. closely woven cotton fabric resembling satin.

satellite n. heavenly or artificial body revolving round a planet; person's hanger-on; country that is subservient to another. **satellite dish** dish-shaped aerial for receiving broadcasts transmitted by satellite.

satiate /'seɪʃɪeɪt/ v.t. satisfy fully, glut. **satiation** n.

satiety /sə'taɪətɪ/ n. condition of being satiated.

satin n. silky material that is glossy on one side. —a. smooth as satin. **satiny** a.

satinette n. satin-like fabric.

satinwood n. smooth hard wood; tropical tree yielding this.

satire n. use of ridicule, irony, or sarcasm; novel or play etc. that ridicules something. **satirical** /-'tɪr-/ a., **satirically** adv.

satirize v.t. attack with satire; describe satirically. **satirist** n.

satisfactory a. satisfying an expectation or need, adequate. **satisfactorily** adv.

satisfy v.t. give (a person) what he or she wants or needs; make pleased or contented; end (a demand etc.) by giving what is required; provide with sufficient proof, convince; pay (a creditor). **satisfaction** n.

satsuma /'sæ-/ n. a kind of mandarin orange.

saturate v.t. make thoroughly wet; cause to absorb or accept as much as possible. **saturation** n.

Saturday n. day after Friday.

saturnalia /-'neɪ-/ n. wild revelry.

saturnine /-nəm/ a. having a gloomy or forbidding appearance.

satyr /-tə(r)/ n. woodland god in classical mythology, with a goat's ears, tail, and legs.

sauce *n.* liquid or semi-liquid preparation added to food to give flavour or richness; (*sl.*) impudence.

saucepan *n.* metal cooking-pot with a long handle, used for boiling things over heat.

saucer *n.* curved dish on which a cup stands.

saucy *a.* (-ier, -iest) impudent; jaunty. **saucily** *adv.*, **sauciness** *n.*

sauerkraut /'savəkraʊt/ *n.* chopped pickled cabbage.

sauna /'sɔː-/ *n.* Finnish-style steam bath.

saunter *v.i.* & *n.* stroll.

saurian /'sɔː-/ *a.* of or like a lizard. —*n.* animal of the lizard family.

sausage *n.* minced seasoned meat in a tubular case of thin skin.

sauté /'səʊteɪ/ *a.* fried quickly in little fat. —*v.t.* cook thus.

savage *a.* uncivilized; wild and fierce; cruel and hostile; (*colloq.*) very angry. —*n.* member of an uncivilized tribe. —*v.t.* maul savagely. **savagely** *adv.*, **savageness** *n.*, **savagery** *n.*

savannah /-'vænə/ *n.* grassy plain in hot regions.

savant *n.* learned person.

save *v.t./i.* rescue, keep from danger or harm or capture; avoid wasting; keep for future use, put aside money thus; relieve (a person) from (trouble etc.); prevent the scoring of (a goal etc.). —*n.* act of saving in football etc. —*prep.* saving, except. **saver** *n.*

saveloy *n.* highly seasoned sausage.

saving *prep.* except.

savings *n.pl.* money put aside for future use.

saviour *n.* person who rescues people from harm or danger; **the** *or* **our Saviour** Christ as saviour of mankind.

savoir faire /sævwa:'feə(r)/ social tact.

savory *n.* spicy herb.

savour *n.* flavour; smell. —*v.t./i.* have a certain savour; taste or smell with enjoyment.

savoury *a.* having an appetizing taste or smell; salty or piquant and not sweet in flavour. —*n.* savoury dish, esp. at the end of a meal. **savouriness** *n.*

savoy *n.* a kind of cabbage.

saw¹ *see* **see¹**.

saw² *n.* tool with a zigzag edge for cutting wood or metal. —*v.t./i.* (*p.t.* sawed, *p.p.* sawn) cut with a saw; make a to-and-fro movement.

saw³ *n.* old saying, maxim.

sawdust *n.* powdery fragments of wood, made in sawing timber.

sawfish *n.* large sea-fish with a jagged blade-like snout.

sawmill *n.* mill where timber is cut into planks etc.

sawn *see* **saw²**.

sawyer *n.* workman who saws timber.

sax *n.* (*colloq.*) saxophone.

saxe *a.* greyish-blue.

saxifrage *n.* a kind of rock plant.

Saxon *n.* & *a.* (member, language) of a Germanic people who occupied parts of England in the 5th–6th centuries.

saxophone *n.* brass wind instrument with finger-operated keys. **saxophonist** /-'ɒf-/ *n.*

say *v.t./i.* (*p.t.* **said**, pr. sed) utter, recite; express in words, state; give as an opinion or argument or excuse; suppose as a possibility etc. —*n.* power to decide. **I say!** expression of surprise or admiration, or used to call attention.

SAYE *abbr.* save-as-you-earn.

saying *n.* well-known phrase or proverb or other statement.

scab *n.* crust forming over a sore; skin-disease or plant-disease causing similar roughness; (*colloq., derog.*) blackleg. **scabby** *a.*

scabbard *n.* sheath of a sword etc.

scabies /'skeɪbiːz/ *n.* contagious skin-disease causing itching.

scabious /'skeɪbɪəs/ n. herbaceous plant with clustered flowers.

scabrous /'skeɪ-/ a. rough-surfaced; indecent.

scaffold n. wooden platform for the execution of criminals; scaffolding. —v.t. fit scaffolding to.

scaffolding n. poles and planks providing platforms for workmen building or repairing a house etc.

scalable a. able to be scaled.

scald v.t. injure or pain with hot liquid or steam; heat (milk) to near boiling-point; cleanse with boiling water. —n. injury to the skin by scalding.

scale[1] n. each of the overlapping plates of horny membrane protecting the skin of many fishes and reptiles; thing resembling this; incrustation caused by hard water or forming on teeth. —v.t./i. remove scale(s) from; come off in scales. **scaly** a.

scale[2] n. pan of a balance; (pl.) instrument for weighing things.

scale[3] n. ordered series of units or qualities etc. for measuring or classifying things; fixed series of notes in a system of music; relative size or extent. —v.t. climb; represent in measurements or extent in proportion to the size of the original.

scallop /'skɒl-/ n. shellfish with hinged fan-shaped shells; one shell of this; (pl.) semicircular curves as an ornamental edging. **scalloped** a.

scallywag n. (sl.) rascal.

scalp n. skin of the head excluding the face. —v.t. cut the scalp from.

scalpel /'skæ-/ n. surgeon's or painter's small straight knife.

scamp n. rascal. —v.t. do (work) hastily and inadequately.

scamper v.i. run hastily or in play. —n. scampering run.

scampi n.pl. large prawns.

scan v.t./i. (p.t. **scanned**) look at all parts of, esp. quickly; pass a radar or electronic beam over; analyse the rhythm of (verse); (of verse) have a regular rhythm. —n. scanning. **scanner** n.

scandal n. something disgraceful; gossip about wrongdoing. **scandalous** a., **scandalously** adv.

scandalize v.t. shock by scandal.

scandalmonger n. person who invents or spreads scandal.

Scandinavian a. & n. (native) of Scandinavia.

scansion n. scanning of verse.

scant a. scanty, insufficient.

scanty a. (-ier, -iest) small in amount or extent; barely enough. **scantily** adv., **scantiness** n.

scapegoat n. person made to bear blame that should fall on others.

scapula n. (pl. -lae) shoulder-blade.

scapular a. of the scapula. —n. monk's short cloak.

scar n. mark left by damage, esp. where a wound or sore has healed. —v.t./i. (p.t. **scarred**) mark with a scar; form scar(s).

scarab /'skæ-/ n. carving of a beetle, used in ancient Egypt as a charm.

scarce a. (-er, -est) not enough to supply a demand, rare. **make oneself scarce** (colloq.) go away.

scarcely adv. only just, almost not; not, surely not.

scarcity n. being scarce, shortage.

scare v.t./i. frighten; become frightened. —n. fright, alarm.

scarecrow n. figure dressed in old clothes and set up to scare birds away from crops.

scaremonger n. alarmist. **scaremongering** n.

scarf[1] n. (pl. **scarves**) piece or strip of material worn round the neck or tied over a woman's head.

scarf[2] n. joint made by thinning ends of timber to overlap. —v.t. join thus.

scarify[1] /'skæ-/ v.t. make slight cuts in; criticize harshly.

scarify[2] v.t. (colloq.) scare.

scarlet *a. & n.* brilliant red.
scarlet fever infectious fever producing a scarlet rash.

scarp *n.* steep slope on a hillside.

scarper *v.i.* (*sl.*) run away.

scary *a.* (-ier, -iest) frightening; easily frightened.

scat *n.* wordless jazz song using the voice as an instrument.

scathing /'skeɪð/ *a.* (of criticism) very severe.

scatter *v.t./i.* throw or put here and there; cover thus; go or send in different directions. —*n.* small scattered amount.

scatterbrain *n.* person who is frivolous or careless and unsystematic. **scatterbrained** *a.*

scatty *a.* (-ier, -iest) (*sl.*) crazy. **scattiness** *n.*

scaup /skɔ:p/ *n.* kind of duck.

scavenge *v.t./i.* search for (usable objects) among rubbish etc.; (of animals) search for decaying flesh as food. **scavenger** *n.*

scenario /-'nɑːr-/ *n.* (*pl.* -os) script or summary of a film or play; imagined sequence of events.

scene *n.* place of an event; piece of continuous action in a play or film; dramatic outburst of temper or emotion; stage scenery; landscape or view or incident as seen; (*sl.*) area of activity. **behind the scenes** hidden from public view.

scenery *n.* general (esp. picturesque) appearance of a landscape; structures used on a theatre stage to represent the scene of action.

scenic /'si:-/ *a.* picturesque.

scent *n.* pleasant smell; liquid perfume; animal's trail perceptible to a hound's sense of smell; animal's sense of smell. —*v.t.* discover by smell; suspect the presence or existence of; apply scent to, make fragrant.

sceptic /'skep-/ *n.* sceptical person.

sceptical /'skep-/ *a.* unwilling to believe things. **sceptically** *adv.*, **scepticism** *n.*

sceptre *n.* ornamental rod carried as a symbol of sovereignty.

schedule /'ʃedjuːl/ *n.* programme or timetable of events. —*v.t.* appoint in a schedule.

schematic /ski:-/ *a.* in the form of a diagram; systematic, formalized. **schematically** *adv.*

schematize *v.t.* put into schematic form. **schematization** *n.*

scheme *n.* plan of work or action. —*v.t./i.* make plans, plot. **schemer** *n.*

scherzo /'skeətsəʊ/ *n.* (*pl.* -os) lively musical composition or passage.

schism /sɪzm/ *n.* division into opposing groups through difference in belief or opinion. **schismatic** /-'mæt-/ *a. & n.*

schist /ʃɪst/ *n.* rock with components in layers.

schizoid *a.* like or suffering from schizophrenia. —*n.* schizoid person.

schizophrenia /-'fri:-/ *n.* mental disorder in which a person is unable to act or reason rationally. **schizophrenic** /-'fren-/ *a. & n.*

schmaltz *n.* sickly sentimentality.

schnitzel *n.* veal cutlet.

scholar *n.* person with great learning; academic person; holder of a scholarship. **scholarly** *a.*, **scholarliness** *n.*

scholarship *n.* grant of money towards education; great learning; scholars' methods and achievements.

scholastic /-'læs-/ *a.* of schools or education; academic.

school[1] *n.* shoal of fish or whales.

school[2] *n.* institution for educating children or giving instruction; group of philosophers, artists, etc., following the same principles. —*v.t.* train, discipline. **schoolboy** *n.*, **schoolchild** *n.* (*pl.* -children), **schoolgirl** *n.fem.*

schoolman *n.* (*pl.* -men) medieval philosopher.

schoolmaster, schoolmistress ns. male or female schoolteacher.

schoolteacher n. teacher in a school.

schooner /ˈskuː-/ n. a kind of sailing-ship; measure for sherry etc.

sciatic /saɪˈæ-/ a. of the hip or the **sciatic nerve** (nerve running from pelvis to thigh). **sciatica** n. pain in this nerve or region.

science n. branch of knowledge requiring systematic study and method, esp. dealing with substances, life, and natural laws. **scientific** a., **scientifically** adv.

scientist n. expert in science(s).

scilla /ˈsɪlə/ n. plant with small blue hanging flowers.

scimitar /ˈsɪm-/ n. short curved oriental sword.

scintillate v.i. sparkle, spark; be brilliant in wit etc. **scintillation** n.

scion /ˈsaɪən/ n. shoot, esp. cut for grafting; descendant.

scissors n.pl. cutting instrument with two pivoted blades.

sclerosis n. abnormal hardening of tissue.

scoff[1] v.i. speak contemptuously, jeer. **scoffer** n.

scoff[2] v.t. (sl.) eat quickly.

scold v.t. rebuke (esp. a child). **scolding** n.

sconce n. ornamental bracket on a wall, holding a light.

scone /skɒn or skəʊn/ n. a kind of soft flat cake baked quickly and eaten buttered.

scoop n. deep shovel-like tool; a kind of ladle; scooping movement; piece of news published by one newspaper before its rivals. —v.t. lift or hollow with (or as if with) a scoop; secure by sudden action or luck; forestall with a news scoop.

scoot v.i. run, dart.

scooter n. child's toy vehicle with a footboard and long steering-handle; a kind of lightweight motor cycle. **scooterist** n.

scope n. range of a subject etc.; opportunity, outlet.

scorch v.t./i. burn or become burnt on the surface; (sl.) travel very fast.

scorching a. (colloq.) extremely hot.

score n. number of points gained in a game or competition; set of twenty; line or mark cut into something; written or printed music showing the notes on a series of staves; record of money owing. —v.t./i. gain (points etc.) in a game or competition; keep a record of the score; achieve; cut a line or mark into; write or compose as a musical score. **on the score of** for the reason of. **score off** humiliate by a clever remark. **score out** cross out. **scorer** n.

scorn n. strong contempt. —v.t. feel or show scorn for; reject with scorn. **scornful** a., **scornfully** adv., **scornfulness** n.

scorpion n. small animal of the spider group with lobster-like claws and a sting in its long tail.

Scot n. native of Scotland.

Scotch a. Scottish. —n. form of English spoken in Scotland; Scotch whisky. **Scotch cap** man's wide beret.

scotch v.t. put an end to (a rumour).

scot-free a. unharmed, not punished; free of charge.

Scots a. Scottish. —n. Scottish dialect. **Scotsman** n. (pl. -men), **Scotswoman** n.fem. (pl. -women)

Scottish a. of Scotland or its people or their form of the English language.

scoundrel n. dishonest or unprincipled person.

scour[1] v.t. cleanse by rubbing; clear out (a channel etc.) by flowing water; purge drastically. —n. scouring; action of water on a channel etc. **scourer** n.

scour[2] v.t. search thoroughly.

scourge /skɜːdʒ/ n. whip; great affliction. —v.t. flog; afflict greatly.

Scouse a. & n. (native, dialect) of Liverpool.

Scout n. member of the Scout Association, an organization orig. established for boys.

scout[1] n. person sent to gather information, esp. about enemy movements etc. —v.i. act as scout, search.

scout[2] v.t. reject (an idea) scornfully.

scow /skaʊ/ n. a kind of flat-bottomed boat.

scowl n. sullen or angry frown. —v.i. make a scowl.

scrabble v.i. scratch with the hands or feet; grope busily.

scrag n. bony part of an animal's carcass as food.

scraggy a. (-ier, -iest) lean and bony. **scragginess** n.

scram v.imper. (sl.) go away.

scramble v.t./i. clamber; move hastily or awkwardly; struggle to do or obtain something; mix indiscriminately; cook (eggs) by mixing the contents and heating the mixture; make (a telephone conversation etc.) unintelligible except by means of a special receiver, by altering its transmission frequency; (of aircraft or crew) hurry to take off quickly. —n. scrambling walk or movement; eager struggle; motor-cycle race over rough ground. **scrambler** n.

scrap[1] n. fragment, remnant; waste material; discarded metal suitable for being reprocessed. —v.t. (p.t. **scrapped**) discard as useless.

scrap[2] n. & v.i. (colloq.) fight, quarrel.

scrapbook n. book in which to mount newspaper cuttings or similar souvenirs.

scrape v.t./i. clean, smooth, or damage by passing a hard edge across a surface; pass (an edge) across in this way; dig by scraping; make the sound of scraping; get along or through etc. with difficulty, esp. while (almost) touching; obtain or amass with difficulty; be very economical. —n. scraping movement or sound; scraped place; thinly applied layer of butter; awkward situation resulting from an escapade. **scraper** n.

scrapie n. disease of sheep.

scraping n. fragment produced by scraping.

scrappy a. (-ier, -iest) made up of scraps or disconnected elements. **scrappily** adv., **scrappiness** n.

scratch v.t./i. cut a shallow line or wound on (a surface) with something sharp; form by scratching; scrape with the fingernails; make a thin scraping sound; obtain with difficulty; withdraw from a race or competition. —n. mark, wound, or sound made by scratching; spell of scratching; line from which competitors start in a race when they receive no handicap. —a. collected from what is available; receiving no handicap. **from scratch** from the very beginning or with no advantage or preparation. **up to scratch** up to the required standard. **scratchy** a.

scratchings n.pl. crisp residue of pork fat left after rendering lard.

scrawl n. bad handwriting; something written in this. —v.t./i. write in a scrawl.

scrawny a. (-ier, -iest) scraggy.

scream v.t./i. make a long piercing cry or sound; utter in a screaming tone. —n. screaming cry or sound; (sl.) extremely amusing person or thing.

scree n. mass of loose stones on a mountain side.

screech n. harsh high-pitched scream or sound. —v.t./i. make or utter with a screech. **screech-owl** *n.* owl that makes a screeching cry.

screed *n.* tiresomely long list or letter etc.; thin layer of cement.

screen *n.* upright structure used to conceal or protect or divide something; anything serving a similar purpose; windscreen; blank surface on which pictures or cinema films or television transmissions etc. are projected; large sieve. —*v.t.* shelter, conceal; protect from discovery or deserved blame; show (images etc.) on a screen; sieve; examine for the presence or absence of a disease or quality or potential loyalty etc.

screw *n.* metal pin with a spiral ridge round its length, fastened by turning; thing twisted to tighten or press something; propeller, esp. of a ship or motor boat; act of screwing; (*sl.*) wage, salary. —*v.t./i.* fasten or tighten with screw(s); turn (a screw); twist, become twisted; oppress, extort; (*sl.*) extort money from. **screw up** summon up (one's courage etc.); (*sl.*) bungle.

screwball *n.* (*US sl.*) crazy person.

screwdriver *n.* tool for turning screws.

screwy *a.* (-ier, -iest) (*sl.*) crazy.

scribble *v.t./i.* write hurriedly or carelessly; make meaningless marks. —*n.* something scribbled.

scribe *n.* person who (before the invention of printing) made copies of writings; (in New Testament times) professional religious scholar. **scribal** *a.*

scrimmage *n.* confused struggle. —*v.i.* engage in this.

scrimp *v.t./i.* skimp.

scrimshank *v.i.* shirk work, malinger. **scrimshanker** *n.*

scrip *n.* extra share(s) (in a business) issued instead of a dividend.

script *n.* handwriting; style of printed characters resembling this; text of a play or film or broadcast talk etc.

scripture *n.* any sacred writings; **Scripture** *or* **the Scriptures** those of the Christians (Old and New Testaments) or the Jews (Old Testament). **scriptural** *a.*

scrivener /'skrɪv-/ *n.* (*old use*) person who drafts documents, clerk.

scrofula /'skrɒf-/ *n.* disease with glandular swellings. **scrofulous** *a.*

scroll *n.* roll of paper or parchment; ornamental design in this shape. —*v.t.* move (a display on a VDU screen) up or down as the screen is filled.

scrotum /'skrəʊ-/ *n.* (*pl.* -ta) pouch of skin enclosing the testicles. **scrotal** *a.*

scrounge *v.t./i.* cadge; collect by foraging. **scrounger** *n.*

scrub[1] *n.* vegetation consisting of stunted trees and shrubs; land covered with this.

scrub[2] *v.t./i.* (*p.t.* **scrubbed**) rub hard esp. with something coarse or bristly. —*n.* process of scrubbing.

scrubby *a.* (-ier, -iest) small and mean or shabby.

scruff *n.* back of the neck.

scruffy *a.* (-ier, -iest) shabby and untidy. **scruffily** *adv.*, **scruffiness** *n.*

scrum *n.* scrummage; confused struggle.

scrummage *n.* grouping of forwards in Rugby football to struggle for possession of the ball by pushing.

scrumping *n.* (*colloq.*) stealing apples from trees.

scrumptious *a.* (*colloq.*) delicious.

scrumpy *n.* (*colloq.*) rough cider.

scrunch *v.t./i.* & *n.* crunch.

scruple *n.* doubt about doing something, produced by one's conscience. —*v.t.* hesitate because of scruples.

scrupulous a. very conscientious or careful. **scrupulously** adv., **scrupulousness** n., **scrupulosity** n.

scrutineer n. person who examines ballot-papers.

scrutinize v.t. make a scrutiny of.

scrutiny n. careful look or examination.

scuba /ˈskjuː-/ n. self-contained underwater breathing apparatus. **scuba-diving** n.

scud v.i. (p.t. **scudded**) move along fast and smoothly.

scuff v.t./i. scrape or drag (one's feet) in walking; mark or scrape by doing this.

scuffle n. confused struggle or fight. —v.i. take part in a scuffle.

scull n. one of a pair of small oars; oar that rests on a boat's stern, worked with a screw-like movement. —v.t./i. row with scull(s).

scullery n. room where dishes etc. are washed.

sculpt v.t./i. (colloq.) sculpture.

sculptor n. maker of sculptures.

sculpture n. art of carving or modelling in wood or stone etc.; work made thus. —v.t./i. represent in or decorate with sculpture; be a sculptor. **sculptural** a.

scum n. layer of impurities or froth etc. on the surface of a liquid; worthless person(s). **scummy** a.

scupper n. opening in a ship's side to drain water from the deck. —v.t. (sl.) sink (a ship) deliberately, wreck.

scurf n. flakes of dry skin, esp. from the scalp; similar scaly matter. **scurfy** a.

scurrilous /ˈska-/ a. abusive and insulting; coarsely humorous. **scurrilously** adv., **scurrility** n.

scurry v.i. run hurriedly, scamper. —n. scurrying, rush.

scurvy n. disease caused by lack of vitamin C in the diet.

scut n. short tail of a rabbit, hare, or deer.

scutter v.i. & n. (colloq.) scurry.

scuttle[1] n. box or bucket for holding coal in a room; part of a car body between the windscreen and the bonnet.

scuttle[2] n. small opening with a lid, esp. in a ship's deck or side. —v.t. sink (a ship) by letting in water.

scuttle[3] v.i. & n. scurry.

scythe /saɪð/ n. implement with a curved blade on a long handle, for cutting long grass or grain.

SE abbr. south-east; south-eastern.

sea n. expanse of salt water surrounding the continents; section of this; large inland lake; waves of the sea; vast expanse. **at sea** in a ship on the sea; perplexed. **by sea** carried by ship. **sea dog** old sailor. **sea-green** a. & n. bluish-green. **sea horse** small fish with a horse-like head. **sea level** level corresponding to the mean level of the sea's surface. **sea lion** a kind of large seal. **sea-mew** n. gull. **sea urchin** sea animal with a round spiky shell.

seaboard n. coast.

seafarer n. seafaring person.

seafaring a. & n. working or travelling on the sea.

seafood n. fish or shellfish from the sea eaten as food.

seagoing a. for sea voyages; seafaring.

seagull n. gull.

seal[1] n. amphibious sea animal with thick fur or bristles.

seal[2] n. engraved piece of metal etc. used to stamp a design; its impression; action or event etc. serving to confirm or guarantee something; paper sticker resembling a postage stamp; thing used to close an opening very tightly. —v.t./i. affix a seal to; close or coat so as to prevent penetration; stick down; settle, decide (e.g. a bargain). **seal off** prevent access to (an area).

sealant n. substance for coating a surface to make it watertight or airtight.

sealing-wax n. a kind of wax used for impressing with a design.

sealskin n. seal's skin or fur used as a clothing material.

seam n. line where two edges join; layer of coal etc. in the ground. —v.t. join by a seam. **seamless** a.

seaman n. (pl. **-men**) sailor; person skilled in seafaring. **seamanship** n.

seamstress /'sem-/ n. woman whose job is sewing things.

seamy a. **seamy side** unattractive or disreputable side (of life).

seance /'seɪɑ̃s/ n. spiritualist meeting.

seaplane n. aeroplane designed to take off from and land on water.

seaport n. port on the coast.

sear v.t. scorch; burn; make callous.

search v.t./i. look, feel, or go over (a person or place etc.) in order to find something. —n. process of searching. **searcher** n.

searching a. thorough. **searchingly** adv.

searchlight n. outdoor lamp with a powerful beam; its beam.

seascape n. picture or view of the sea.

seasick a. made sick by the motion of a ship. **seasickness** n.

seaside n. coast, esp. as a place for holidays.

season n. section of the year associated with a type of weather; time when something is common or plentiful, or when an activity takes place. —v.t./i. give extra flavour to (food); dry or treat until ready for use. **season-ticket** n. ticket valid for any number of journeys or performances etc. in a specified period.

seasonable a. suitable for the season; timely. **seasonably** adv.

seasonal a. of a season or seasons; varying with the seasons. **seasonally** adv., **seasonality** n.

seasoned a. (of people) experienced.

seasoning n. substance used to season food.

seat n. thing made or used for sitting on; horizontal part of a chair etc. on which a sitter's body rests; place as member of a committee or parliament etc.; buttocks, part of a garment covering these; place where something is based; country mansion; manner of sitting on a horse etc. —v.t. cause to sit; have seats for; put (machinery etc.) on its support. **seat-belt** n. strap securing a person to a seat in a vehicle or aircraft. **be seated** sit down.

seaward a. & adv. towards the sea. **seawards** adv.

seaweed n. any plant that grows in the sea.

seaworthy a. (of ships) fit for a sea voyage. **seaworthiness** n.

sebaceous /-'beɪʃəs/ a. secreting an oily or greasy substance.

secateurs /-'tз:z or 'sek-/ n.pl. clippers for pruning plants.

secede /-'si:d/ v.i. withdraw from membership. **secession** n.

seclude v.t. keep (a person) apart from others. **secluded** a. screened from view. **seclusion** n.

second[1] /'sek-/ a. next after the first; following the first; secondary; inferior. —n. second thing, class, etc.; attendant of a person taking part in a duel or boxing-match; sixtieth part of a minute of time or (in measuring angles) degree. —v.t. assist; state one's support of (a proposal) formally. **second-best** a. next to the best in quality; inferior. **second-class** a. & adv. next or inferior to first-class in quality etc. **second cousin** (see **cousin**). **second fiddle** a subsidiary role. **at second hand** indirectly, not from the original source. **second-hand** a. bought after use by a previous owner; dealing in used goods. **second nature** habit or characteristic that has become automatic. **second-rate** *a.* inferior in quality. **second sight** supposed power to foresee future events. **second thoughts** change of mind after reconsideration. **second wind** renewed capacity for effort.

second[2] /-kɒnd/ *v.t.* transfer temporarily to another job or department. **secondment** *n.*

secondary *a.* coming after or derived from what is primary. —*n.* secondary thing. **secondary colours** those obtained by mixing two primary colours. **secondary education, secondary school** that for children who have received primary education. **secondarily** *adv.*

secondly *adv.* second.

secret *a.* kept or intended to be kept from the knowledge or view of most people; operating secretly. —*n.* something secret; mystery; thing not widely understood. **in secret** secretly. **secret police** police force operating secretly for political purposes. **secret service** government department conducting espionage. **secretly** *adv.*, **secrecy** *n.*

secretaire /sekrɪˈteə(r)/ *n.* writing-desk with drawers.

secretariat /-ˈteər-/ *n.* administrative office or department.

secretary /ˈsekrətrɪ/ *n.* person employed to help deal with correspondence and routine office-work; official in charge of an organization's correspondence; ambassador's or government minister's chief assistant. **Secretary-General** *n.* principal administrative officer. **Secretary of State** head of a major government department. **secretarial** *a.*

secrete /-ˈkriːt/ *v.t.* put into a place of concealment; produce by secretion. **secretor** *n.*

secretion /-ˈkriː-/ *n.* process of secreting; production of a substance within the body; this substance.

secretive /ˈsiːk-/ *a.* making a secret of things. **secretively** *adv.*, **secretiveness** *n.*

secretory /-ˈkriː-/ *a.* of physiological secretion.

sect *n.* group with beliefs that differ from those generally accepted.

sectarian /-ˈteər-/ *a.* of a sect or sects; narrow-mindedly promoting the interests of one's sect.

section *n.* distinct part; cross-section; subdivision; process of cutting something surgically. —*v.t.* divide into sections.

sectional *a.* of a section or sections; made in sections.

sector *n.* part of an area; branch of an activity; section of a circular area between two lines drawn from its centre to its circumference.

secular *a.* of worldly (not religious or spiritual) matters.

secure *a.* safe, esp. against attack; certain not to slip or fail. —*v.t.* make secure; fasten securely; obtain; guarantee by pledging something as security. **securely** *adv.*, **securement** *n.*

security *n.* safety; safety of a country or company against espionage, theft, or other danger; organization for ensuring this; thing serving as a pledge; certificate showing ownership of financial stocks etc.

sedan /-ˈdæn/ *n.* sedan-chair; *(US)* saloon car. **sedan chair** enclosed chair (17th–18th centuries) carried on two poles by bearers.

sedate[1] *a.* calm and dignified. **sedately** *adv.*, **sedateness** *n.*

sedate[2] *v.t.* treat with sedatives. **sedation** *n.*

sedative /ˈsed-/ *a.* having a calming effect. —*n.* sedative drug or influence.

sedentary /ˈsed-/ *a.* seated; (of work) done while sitting.

sedge *n.* grass-like plant(s) growing in marshes or by water.

sediment n. particles of solid matter in a liquid or carried by water or wind. **sedimentary** /-'ment-/ a., **sedimentation** n.

sedition /sɪ'dɪʃ(ə)n/ n. words or actions inciting people to rebellion. **seditious** a., **seditiously** adv.

seduce v.t. persuade (esp. into wrongdoing) by offering temptations; tempt immorally into sexual intercourse. **seducer** n., **seductress** n.fem., **seduction** n., **seductive** a.

sedulous /'sed-/ a. diligent and persevering. **sedulously** adv.

see[1] v.t./i. (p.t. **saw**, p.p. **seen**) perceive with the eye(s) or mind; understand; consider; be a spectator of; look at for information; meet; discover; experience, undergo; grant or obtain an interview with; escort; make sure. **see about** attend to. **seeing that** in view of the fact that, because. **see through** not be deceived by; not abandon before completion. **see-through** a. transparent. **see to** attend to.

see[2] n. position or district of a bishop or archbishop.

seed n. (pl. **seeds** or **seed**) plant's fertilized ovule; semen, milt; (old use) descendants; something from which a tendency etc. can develop; (colloq.) seeded player. —v.t./i. produce seed; sprinkle with seeds; remove seeds from; name (a strong player) as not to be matched against others named thus until the later rounds of a tournament. **go** or **run to seed** cease flowering as seed develops; become shabby or less efficient. **seed-cake** n. cake flavoured with caraway seeds. **seed-pearl** n. very small pearl.

seedless a. not containing seeds.

seedling n. very young plant growing from a seed.

seedy a. (-ier, -iest) full of seeds; looking shabby and disreputable;

(colloq.) feeling slightly ill. **seedily** adv., **seediness** n.

seek v.t. (p.t. **sought**) try to find or obtain; try (to do something). **seek out** seek specially. **seeker** n.

seem v.i. appear to be or exist or be true. **seemingly** adv.

seemly a. (-ier, -iest) in accordance with accepted standards of good taste. **seemliness** n.

seen see see[1].

seep v.i. ooze slowly out or through. **seepage** n.

seer n. prophet, person who sees visions.

seersucker n. fabric woven with a puckered surface.

see-saw n. children's amusement consisting of a long board balanced on a central support so that persons sitting on each end can make the ends go up and down alternately; constantly repeated up-and-down change. —v.i. make this movement or change; vacillate.

seethe v.i. bubble or surge as in boiling; be very agitated or excited.

segment n. part cut off or marked off or separable from others; part of a circle or sphere cut off by a straight line or plane. **segmented** a.

segregate v.t. put apart from others. **segregation** n.

seigneur /sem'jɜ:(r)/ n. feudal lord. **seigneurial** a.

seine /sem/ n. a kind of fishing-net that hangs from floats.

seismic /'saɪz-/ a. of earthquake(s).

seismograph /'saɪz-/ n. instrument for recording earthquakes.

seismology /saɪz-/ n. study of earthquakes. **seismological** a., **seismologist** n.

seize v.t./i. take hold of forcibly or suddenly or eagerly; take possession of by force or legal right; affect suddenly; seize up. **seize on** make use of eagerly. **seize up**

become stuck because of friction or undue heat.

seizure *n.* seizing; sudden attack of apoplexy or epilepsy etc.

seldom *adv.* rarely, not often.

select *v.t.* pick out as best or most suitable. —*a.* chosen, esp. for excellence; exclusive. **selector** *n.*

selection *n.* selecting; people or things selected; collection of this from which to choose.

selective *a.* chosen or choosing carefully. **selectively** *adv.*, **selectivity** *n.*

self *n.* (*pl.* **selves**) person as an individual; person's special nature; person or thing as the object of reflexive action; one's own advantage or interests; (in commerce or *colloq.*) myself, herself, himself, etc. —*a.* of the same colour or material as that used for the whole.

self- *pref.* of or to or done by oneself or itself. **self-assurance** *n.*, **self-assured** *a.* being self-confident. **self-catering** *a.* catering for oneself. **self-centred** *a.* thinking chiefly of oneself or one's own affairs. **self-command** *n.* self-control. **self-confidence** *n.*, **self-confident** *a.* being confident of one's own abilities. **self-conscious** *a.*, **self-consciousness** *n.* being embarrassed or unnatural in manner from knowing that one is observed. **self-contained** *a.* complete in itself, having all the necessary facilities; able to do without the company of others. **self-control** *n.*, **self-controlled** *a.* being able to control one's behaviour and not act emotionally. **self-denial** *n.* deliberately going without things one would like to have. **self-determination** *n.* free will; nation's own choice of its form of government or allegiance etc. **self-evident** *a.* clear without proof or explanation. **self-important** *a.* having a high opinion of one's own importance, pompous. **self-indulgent** *a.*

greatly indulging one's own desires for comfort and pleasure. **self-interest** *n.* one's own advantage. **self-made** *a.* having risen from poverty or obscurity to success by one's own efforts. **self-portrait** *n.* artist's portrait of himself or herself; writer's account of himself or herself. **self-possessed** *a.*, **self-possession** *n.* being calm and dignified. **self-raising** *a.* (of flour) containing a raising agent. **self-reliance** *n.*, **self-reliant** *a.* relying on one's own abilities and resources. **self-respect** *n.* proper regard for oneself and one's own dignity and principles etc. **self-righteous** *a.* smugly sure of one's own righteousness. **self-sacrifice** *n.*, **self-sacrificing** *a.* sacrificing one's own interests so that others may benefit. **self-satisfaction** *n.*, **self-satisfied** *a.* being pleased with oneself and one's achievements. **self-seeking** *a. & n.* seeking to promote one's own interests rather than those of others. **self-service** *a.* at which customers help themselves and pay a cashier for goods etc. taken. **self-styled** *a.* using a name or description one has adopted without right. **self-sufficient** *a.* able to provide what one needs without outside help. **self-willed** *a.* obstinately doing what one wishes.

selfish *a.* acting or done according to one's own interests and needs without regard to those of others; keeping good things for oneself. **selfishly** *adv.*, **selfishness** *n.*

selfless *a.* unselfish. **selflessly** *adv.*

selfsame *a.* the very same.

sell *v.t./i.* (*p.t.* **sold**) transfer the ownership of (goods etc.) in exchange for money; keep (goods) for sale; promote sales of; (of goods) find buyers; have a specified price; persuade into accepting (an idea etc.). —*n.* manner of selling; (*colloq.*) deception, disappointment. **sell-by date** latest recommended date of sale for perishable goods. **sell off** dispose of by selling, esp. at a reduced price. **sell out** dispose of all one's stock etc. by selling; betray. **sell-out** *n.* selling of all tickets for a show etc.; betrayal. **sell up** sell one's house or business etc. **seller** *n.*

sellable *a.* able to be sold.

Sellotape *n.* [P.] adhesive usu. transparent tape.

selvage *n.* edge of cloth woven so that it does not unravel.

selvedge *n.* = selvage.

semantic *a.* of meaning in language. **semantically** *adv.*

semantics *n.* study of meaning. —*n.pl.* meaning(s); connotation.

semaphore *n.* system of signalling by means of the arms; signalling device with mechanical arms. —*v.t./i.* signal by semaphore.

semblance *n.* outward appearance, show; resemblance.

semen /'si:-/ *n.* sperm-bearing fluid produced by male animals.

semester /i-'mes-/ *n.* half-year term in an American university.

semi- *pref.* half; partly.

semibreve *n.* note in music, equal to two minims.

semicircle *n.* half of a circle. **semicircular** *a.*

semicolon *n.* punctuation mark ; .

semiconductor *n.* substance that conducts electricity in certain conditions.

semi-detached *a.* (of a house) joined to another on one side but not on the other.

semifinal *n.* match or round preceding the final.

semifinalist *n.* competitor in a semifinal.

seminal /'sem-/ *a.* of seed or semen; giving rise to new developments. **seminally** *adv.*

seminar /'sem-/ *n.* small class for advanced discussion and research.

seminary /'sem-/ *n.* training college for priests or rabbis.

semiprecious *a.* (of gems) less valuable than those called precious.

semiquaver *n.* note in music, equal to half a quaver.

Semite /'si:ma:t/ *n.* member of the group of races that includes Jews and Arabs. **Semitic** /-'mɪt-/ *a.*

semitone *n.* half a tone in music.

semolina /-'li:-/ *n.* hard particles left when wheat is ground and sifted, used to make puddings.

Semtex *n.* [P.] very malleable odourless plastic explosive.

senate *n.* governing council in ancient Rome; upper house of certain parliaments (e.g. of the USA, of France); governing body of certain universities.

senator *n.* member of a senate.

send *v.t./i.* (*p.t.* **sent**) order or cause to go to a certain destination; send a message; cause to move or go or become. **send for** order to come or be brought. **send-off** *n.* friendly demonstration at a person's departure. **send up** (*colloq.*) make fun of by imitating. **sender** *n.*

senescent /-'nes-/ *a.* growing old. **senescence** *n.*

seneschal /'senɪʃ(ə)l/ *n.* steward of a medieval great house.

senile /'si:naɪl/ *a.* weak in body or mind because of old age; characteristic of old people. **senility** /sɪ'nɪl-/ *n.*

senior *a.* older; higher in rank or authority; for older children. —*n.* senior person; member of a senior school. **senior citizen** elderly person. **senior service** the Navy. **seniority** *n.*

senna *n.* dried pods or leaves of a tropical tree, used as a laxative.

señor /sen'jɔ:(r)/ *n.* (*pl.* **-ores**) title of a Spanish-speaking man.

señora /sen'jɔːrə/ n. title of a Spa-nish-speaking married woman.

señorita /senjə'riːtə/ n. title of a Spanish-speaking unmarried woman.

sensation n. feeling produced by stimulation of a sense-organ or of the mind; great excitement or admiration aroused in a number of people, person or thing producing this.

sensational a. causing great excitement or admiration. **sensationally** adv.

sensationalism n. use of or interest in sensational matters. **sensationalist** n.

sense n. any of the special powers (sight, hearing, smell, taste, touch) by which a living thing becomes aware of the external world; ability to perceive or be conscious of a thing; practical wisdom; meaning; (pl.) consciousness, sanity. —v.t. perceive by sense(s) or by a mental impression; (of a machine) detect. **make sense** have a meaning; be a sensible idea. **sense-organ** n. any of the organs by which the body becomes aware of the external world.

senseless a. foolish; unconscious.

sensibility n. sensitiveness.

sensible a. having or showing good sense; aware. **sensibly** adv.

sensitive a. affected by something; receiving impressions or responding to stimuli easily; easily hurt or offended; requiring tact. **sensitively** adv., **sensitivity** n.

sensitize v.t. make sensitive. **sensitization** n., **sensitizer** n.

sensor n. device that responds to a certain stimulus.

sensory a. of the senses; receiving and transmitting sensations.

sensual a. gratifying to the body; indulging oneself with physical pleasures. **sensualism** n., **sensually** adv., **sensuality** n.

sensuous a. affecting the senses pleasantly. **sensuously** adv., **sensuousness** n.

sent see **send**.

sentence n. series of words making a single complete statement; punishment awarded by a law-court; declaration of this. —v.t. pass sentence on; declare condemned (to punishment).

sententious /-'tenʃəs/ a. putting on an air of wisdom; dull and moralizing. **sententiously** adv., **sententiousness** n.

sentient /'senʃənt/ a. capable of perceiving and feeling things. **sentiently** adv., **sentience** n.

sentiment n. mental feeling; opinion; sentimentality.

sentimental a. full of romantic or nostalgic feeling. **sentimentalism** n., **sentimentality** n., **sentimentality** n.

sentinel n. sentry.

sentry n. soldier posted to keep watch and guard something.

sepal /'sep-/ n. each of the leaf-like parts forming a calyx.

separable a. able to be separated. **separability** n.

separate[1] /-ət/ a. not joined or united with others. **separates** n.pl. items of outer clothing for wearing in various combinations. **separately** adv.

separate[2] /-ert/ v.t./i. divide, keep apart; become separate; go different ways; cease to live together as a married couple. **separation** n., **separator** n.

separatist n. person who favours separation from a larger (esp. political) unit. **separatism** n.

sepia /'siː-/ n. brown colouring-matter; rich reddish-brown.

sepoy /'siːpɔɪ/ n. (old use) Indian soldier under British or European discipline.

sepsis n. septic condition.

September n. ninth month of the year.

septet n. group of seven instruments or voices; music for these.

septic *a.* infected with harmful micro-organisms. **septic tank** tank in which sewage is liquefied by bacterial activity.

septicaemia /-'si:m-/ *n.* blood-poisoning.

septuagenarian /-'neər-/ *n.* person in his or her seventies.

Septuagint *n.* Greek version of the Old Testament.

septum *n.* (*pl.* -ta) partition between two cavities (e.g. in the nose).

sepulchral /-'pʌl-/ *a.* of a tomb; dismal; (of a voice) sounding deep and hollow. **sepulchrally** *adv.*

sepulchre /'sepəlkə(r)/ *n.* tomb.

sequel *n.* what follows, esp. as a result; novel or film etc. continuing the story of an earlier one.

sequence *n.* following of one thing after another; series, set of things belonging next to each other in a particular order; section dealing with one topic in a cinema film.

sequential /-'kwenʃ(ə)l/ *a.* forming a sequence; occurring as a result; serial. **sequentially** *adv.*

sequester /-'kwes-/ *v.t.* seclude; confiscate.

sequestrate /-'kwes-/ *v.t.* confiscate; take temporary possession of. **sequestration** *n.*, **sequestrator** *n.*

sequin *n.* circular spangle. **sequinned** *a.*

sequoia /-'kwɔɪə/ *n.* Californian tree growing to a great height.

seraglio /-'rɑ:lɪəʊ/ *n.* (*pl.* -os) harem of a Muslim palace.

seraph *n.* (*pl.* -im) member of the highest order of angels in ancient Christian belief.

seraphic /-'ræf-/ *a.* like a seraph, angelic. **seraphically** *adv.*

serenade *n.* song or tune played by a lover to his lady, or suitable for this. —*v.t.* sing or play a serenade to.

serendipity /-'dɪp-/ *n.* making of pleasant discoveries by accident.

serene *a.* calm and cheerful. **Serene Highness** title of members of certain royal families. **serenely** *adv.*, **serenity** /-'ren-/ *n.*

serf *n.* medieval farm labourer forced to work for his landowner; oppressed labourer. **serfdom** *n.*

serge *n.* strong twilled fabric.

sergeant *n.* army NCO ranking just above corporal; police officer ranking just below inspector. **sergeant-major** *n.* warrant officer assisting an adjutant.

serial *n.* story presented in a series of instalments. —*a.* of or forming a series. **serially** *adv.*

serialize *v.t.* produce as a serial. **serialization** *n.*

seriatim /serɪ'er-/ *adv.* point by point in sequence.

series *n.* (*pl.* **series**) number of things of the same kind, or related to each other, occurring or arranged or produced in order.

serio-comic *a.* partly serious and partly comic.

serious *a.* solemn; sincere; important; not slight. **seriously** *adv.*, **seriousness** *n.*

serjeant-at-arms *n.* official of a court or city etc., with ceremonial duties.

sermon *n.* talk on a religious or moral subject, esp. during a religious service.

sermonize *v.i.* give a long moralizing talk. **sermonizer** *n.*

serpent *n.* snake, esp. a large one.

serpentine *a.* twisting like a snake.

serrated /-'rertɪd/ *a.* having a series of small projections. **serration** *n.*

serried /'serɪd/ *a.* arranged in a close series.

serum *n.* (*pl.* **sera**) fluid that remains when blood has clotted; this used for inoculation; watery fluid from animal tissue. **serous** *a.*

servant *n.* person employed to do domestic work in a household or as an attendant; employee.

serve *v.t./i.* perform or provide services for; be employed (in the army etc.); be suitable (for); spend due time in, undergo; present (food etc.) for others to consume; attend to (customers); (of food) be enough for; set the ball in play at tennis etc., produce thus; deliver (a legal writ etc.) to (a person); treat in a certain way; (of a male animal) copulate with. —*n.* service in tennis etc. **server** *n.*

service *n.* act of serving; being a servant; working for an employer; department of people employed by the Crown or a public organization; (*pl.*) armed forces; system that performs work for customers or supplies public needs; assistance, beneficial act; meeting for worship of God, religious ceremony; set of dishes etc. for serving a meal; game in which one serves in tennis etc.; maintenance and repair of machinery. —*v.t.* maintain and repair (machinery); supply with service(s); pay the interest on (a loan). **service area** area beside a motorway where petrol and refreshment etc. are available. **service flat** flat where domestic service is provided by the management. **service road** road giving access to houses etc. but not for use by through traffic. **service station** place where petrol etc. is available, beside a road.

serviceable *a.* usable; hard-wearing.

serviceman, servicewoman *ns.* (*pl.* -**men**, -**women**) member of the armed services.

serviette *n.* table-napkin.

servile *a.* menial; excessively submissive. **servilely** *adv.*, **servility** *n.*

servitor *n.* (*old use*) attendant, servant.

servitude *n.* condition of being forced to work for others, with no freedom.

servo- *pref.* power-assisted.

sesame /ˈsesəmɪ/ *n.* tropical plant with seeds that yield oil or are used as food; its seeds.

session *n.* meeting(s) for discussing or deciding something; period spent in an activity; academic year in certain universities; governing body of a Presbyterian church.

set[1] *v.t./i.* (*p.t.* **set**, *pres.p.* **setting**) put, place, fix in position or readiness; provide a tune for; make or become hard or firm or established; fix or appoint (a date etc.); arrange and protect (a broken bone) for healing; fix (hair) while it is damp; place (a jewel) in a framework; establish; assign as something to be done; put into a specified state; have a certain movement; be brought towards or below the horizon by earth's movement; (in dances) face another dancer and make certain steps. —*n.* way a thing sets or is set; process of setting hair; scenery or stage for a play or film; (also **sett**) badger's burrow; (also **sett**) paving-block. **be set on** be determined about. **set about** begin (a task); attack. **set-aside** *n.* policy of taking land out of production to reduce crop surpluses. **set back** halt or slow the progress of; (*sl.*) cost (a person) a specified amount. **set-back** *n.* setting back of progress. **set eyes on** catch sight of. **set fire to** cause to burn. **set forth** set out. **set in** become established. **set off** begin a journey; cause to begin; ignite, cause to explode; improve the appearance of by contrast. **set out** declare, make known; begin a journey. **set piece** formal or elaborate construction. **set sail** hoist sail(s); begin a voyage.

square right-angled triangular drawing-instrument. **set theory** study of sets of things in mathematics without regard to their individual constituents. **set to** begin doing something vigorously; begin fighting or arguing. **set-to** n. fight; argument. **set-up** n. (colloq.) structure of an organization.

set² n. people or things grouped as similar or forming a unit; games forming part of a match in tennis etc.; radio or television receiver.

sett n. (see **set¹** n.)

settee n. long seat with a back and usu. arms, for two or more people.

setter n. person or thing that sets something; dog of a long-haired breed.

setting n. way or place in which a thing is set; music for the words of a song etc.; set of cutlery or crockery for one person.

settle¹ n. wooden seat with a high back and arms.

settle² v.t./i. place so as to stay in position; establish; become established; make one's home; occupy (a previously unoccupied area); sink, come to rest; arrange as desired or conclusively; deal with; make or become calm or orderly; pay (a bill etc.); bestow legally. **settle up** pay what is owing. **settler** n.

settlement n. settling; business or financial arrangement; amount or property settled legally on a person; place occupied by settlers.

seven a. & n. one more than six (7, VII). **seventh** a. & n.

seventeen a. & n. one more than sixteen (17, XVII). **seventeenth** a. & n.

seventy a. & n. seven times ten (70, LXX). **seventieth** a. & n.

sever /'sev-/ v.t./i. cut or break off. **severance** n.

several a. a few, more than two but not many; separate, individual. —pron. several people or things.

severally adv. separately.

severe /-'vɪə(r)/ a. (-er, -est) strict; without sympathy; intense, forceful; (of style) plain, without decoration. **severely** adv., **severity** n.

sew /səʊ/ v.t./i. (p.t. **sewed**, p.p. **sewn** or **sewed**) fasten by passing thread through material, using a threaded needle or an awl etc.; make or fasten (a thing) by sewing. **sewing** n.

sewage /'sjuː-/ n. liquid waste drained from houses etc. for disposal. **sewage farm** farm where sewage is treated and used as manure. **sewage works** place where sewage is purified.

sewer¹ /'səʊ-/ n. one who sews.

sewer² /'sjuː-/ n. drain for carrying sewage. —v.t. drain with sewers.

sewerage /'sjuː-/ n. system of sewers.

sewing-machine n. machine for sewing or stitching things.

sewn see **sew**.

sex n. either of the two main groups (male and female) into which living things are placed according to their reproductive functions; fact of belonging to one of these; sexual feelings or impulses; sexual intercourse. —v.t. judge the sex of. **sexer** n.

sexagenarian /-'neər-/ n. person in his or her sixties.

sexist a. discriminating in favour of members of one sex; assuming a person's abilities and social functions are predetermined by his or her sex. —n. person who does this. **sexism** n.

sexless a. lacking sex, neuter; not involving sexual feelings.

sexology n. study of human sexual relationships. **sexological** a., **sexologist** n.

sextant *n.* instrument for finding one's position by measuring the height of the sun etc.

sextet *n.* group of six instruments or voices; music for these.

sextile /-tail/ *a.* (of stars) in the position 60° distant from each other.

sexton *n.* official in charge of a church and churchyard.

sextuplet /-'tju:-/ *n.* one of six children born at one birth.

sexual *a.* of sex or the sexes; (of reproduction) occurring by fusion of male and female cells. **sexual intercourse** copulation, insertion of the penis into the vagina. **sexually** *adv.*, **sexuality** *n.*

sexy *a.* (**-ier, -iest**) sexually attractive or stimulating. **sexily** *adv.*, **sexiness** *n.*

sez = says. **sez you** (*sl.*) that is your opinion but I disagree.

SF *abbr.* science fiction.

sh *int.* hush.

shabby *a.* (**-ier, -iest**) worn or used and not in good condition; poorly dressed; unfair, dishonourable. **shabbily** *adv.*, **shabbiness** *n.*

shack *n.* roughly built hut or shed. —*v.i.* **shack up** (*sl.*) cohabit.

shackle *n.* one of a pair of metal rings joined by a chain, for fastening a prisoner's wrists or ankles. —*v.t.* put shackles on; impede, restrict.

shad *n.* large edible fish.

shade *n.* comparative darkness; place sheltered from the sun; colour, degree or depth of this; differing variety; small amount; ghost; screen or cover used to block or moderate light; (*US*) window-blind; (*pl.*) darkness of night or evening. —*v.t./i.* block the rays of; give shade to; darken (parts of a drawing etc.); pass gradually into another colour or variety.

shadow *n.* shade; patch of this where a body blocks light-rays; person's inseparable companion;

slight trace; gloom. —*v.t.* cast shadow over; follow and watch secretly. **shadow-boxing** *n.* boxing against an imaginary opponent as a form of training. **Shadow Cabinet** members of the Opposition party acting as spokesmen on ministerial topics (so **Shadow Chancellor** etc.). **shadower** *n.*, **shadowy** *a.*

shady *a.* (**-ier, -iest**) giving shade; situated in shade; disreputable, not completely honest. **shadily** *adv.*, **shadiness** *n.*

shaft *n.* arrow, spear; long slender straight part of a thing; long bar; large axle; vertical or sloping passage or opening. —*v.t.* (*US colloq.*) treat unfairly.

shag *n.* shaggy mass; strong coarse tobacco; cormorant.

shaggy *a.* (**-ier, -iest**) having long rough hair or fibre; (of hair etc.) rough and thick. **shaggy-dog story** lengthy anecdote with a twist of humour at the end. **shagginess** *n.*

shagreen /ˈʃæ-/ *n.* untanned leather with a granulated surface; sharkskin.

shah *n.* former ruler of Iran.

shake *v.t./i.* (*p.t.* **shook**, *p.p.* **shaken**) move quickly up and down or to and fro; dislodge by doing this; shock; make less firm; (of the voice) become uneven; (*colloq.*) shake hands. —*n.* shaking, being shaken; shock; milk shake. **in a brace of shakes** (*colloq.*) very quickly. **shake down** become harmoniously adjusted; sleep in an improvised bed. **shake hands** clasp right hands in greeting or parting or agreement. **shake up** mix by shaking; rouse from lethargy, shock. **shake-up** *n.* upheaval, reorganization. **shaker** *n.*

shakedown *n.* process of shaking down; improvised bed.

Shakespearian *a.* of Shakespeare.

shako n. (*pl.* -os) military peaked cap with an upright plume or tuft.

shaky a. (-ier, -iest) shaking, unsteady; unreliable. **shakily** adv., **shakiness** n.

shale n. slate-like stone. **shaly** a.

shall v.aux. (**shalt** is used with *thou*, used with *I* and *we* to express future tense, and with other words in promises or statements of obligation.

shallot /-'lɒt/ n. onion-like plant.

shallow a. (-er, -est) of little depth; superficial. —n. shallow place. —v.t./i. make or become shallow. **shallowness** n.

shalt see **shall**.

sham n. pretence; thing that is not genuine. —a. pretended; not genuine. —v.t./i. (p.t. **shammed**) pretend; pretend to be.

shamble v.i. & n. walk or run in a shuffling or lazy way.

shambles n. scene or condition of great bloodshed or disorder.

shambolic a. (colloq.) chaotic.

shame n. painful mental feeling aroused by having done something wrong or dishonourable or ridiculous; ability to feel this; person or thing causing shame; something regrettable. —v.t. bring shame on; make ashamed; compel by arousing shame. **shameful** a., **shamefully** adv., **shameless** a., **shamelessly** adv. **shamefaced** a. looking ashamed.

shammy n. chamois leather.

shampoo n. liquid used to lather and wash hair; similar preparation for cleaning upholstery etc.; process of shampooing. —v.t. wash or clean with shampoo.

shamrock n. clover-like plant.

shandy n. mixed drink of beer and ginger-beer or lemonade.

shanghai /-'haɪ/ v.t. (pres.p. shang-haied, pres.p. **shanghaiing**) take (a person) by force or trickery and compel him or her to do something.

shank n. leg, esp. from knee to ankle; thing's shaft or stem.

shan't (colloq.) = shall not.

shantung n. soft Chinese silk.

shanty[1] n. shack. **shanty town** town consisting of shanties.

shanty[2] n. sailors' traditional song.

shape n. area or form with a definite outline; form, condition; orderly arrangement; jelly etc. shaped in a mould. —v.t. give shape to; develop into a certain condition. **shapeless** a., **shapelessness** n.

shapely a. (-ier, -iest) having a pleasant shape. **shapeliness** n.

shard n. broken piece of pottery etc.

share n. part of an amount or task etc. that one is entitled to have or do; one of the equal parts forming a business company's capital and entitling the holder to a proportion of the profits; ploughshare. —v.t./i. give or have a share (of). **share-out** n. division into shares. **shareholder** n., **sharer** n.

shark n. large voracious sea-fish; person who ruthlessly extorts money, swindler.

sharkskin n. fabric with a slightly lustrous textured weave.

sharp a. (-er, -est) having a fine edge or point capable of cutting; peaked, pointed; abrupt, not gradual; well-defined; intense, (of temper) irritable; (of tastes or smells) causing a smarting sensation; having an alert mind, intelligent; unscrupulous; vigorous, brisk; (in music) above the correct pitch, (of a note or key) a semitone above natural pitch. —adv. punctually, speedily; suddenly; at a sharp angle; above the correct pitch in music. —n. sharp note in music; symbol for this; (colloq.) swindler. **sharp practice** barely honest dealing. **sharply** adv., **sharpness** n.

sharpen v.t./i. make or become sharp or sharper. **sharpener** n.

sharper n. swindler, esp. at cards.

sharpshooter n. marksman.

shatter v.t./i. break violently into small pieces; destroy utterly; upset the calmness of.

shave v.t./i. scrape (growing hair) off the skin; clear (the chin etc.) of hair thus; cut thin slices from (wood etc.); graze gently in passing; reduce (costs etc.). —n. shaving of hair from the face. **shaver** n.

shaven a. shaved.

shaving n. thin strip of wood etc. shaved off.

shawl n. large piece of soft fabric worn round the shoulders or wrapped round a baby as a covering.

she pron. female (or thing personified as female) previously mentioned. —n. female animal.

sheaf n. (pl. **sheaves**) bundle of things laid lengthwise together; tied bundle of corn-stalks.

shear v.t./i. (p.p. **shorn** or **sheared**) cut or trim with shears or other sharp device; strip bare, deprive; break because of strain. **shearer** n.

shears n.pl. large cutting-instrument shaped like scissors.

shearwater n. sea bird with long wings.

sheath n. close-fitting cover, esp. for a blade or tool. **sheath knife** dagger-like knife carried in a sheath.

sheathe /ʃiːð/ v.t. put into a case; encase in a covering.

shebeen /-ˈbiːn/ n. (Ir.) unlicensed house selling alcoholic liquor.

shed[1] n. building for storing or sheltering things, or for use as a workshop.

shed[2] v.t. (p.t. **shed**, pres.p. **shedding**) lose by a natural falling off; take off; allow to fall or flow.

sheen n. gloss, lustre. **sheeny** a.

sheep n. (pl. **sheep**) grass-eating animal with a thick fleecy coat.

sheepdog n. dog trained to guard and herd sheep.

sheepish a. bashful, embarrassed. **sheepishly** adv., **sheepishness** n.

sheepshank n. knot used to shorten a rope without cutting it.

sheepskin n. sheep's skin with the fleece on; leather of sheep's skin.

sheer[1] a. pure, not mixed or qualified; very steep, with no slope; (of fabric) very thin, transparent. —adv. directly, straight up or down. **sheerly** adv., **sheerness** n.

sheer[2] v.i. swerve from a course.

sheet n. rectangular piece of cotton or similar fabric used in pairs as inner bedclothes; large thin piece of glass, metal, etc.; piece of paper for writing or printing on; wide expanse of water, flame, etc.; rope or chain securing the lower corner of a sail. **sheet anchor** large anchor for emergency use; thing on which one depends for security or stability.

sheikh /ʃeɪk/ n. leader of an Arab tribe or village. **sheikhdom** n. his territory.

sheila n. (Austr. & NZ sl.) young woman, girl.

shekel n. unit of money in Israel; (pl., colloq.) money, riches.

sheldrake n. (fem. & pl. **shelduck**) wild duck living on coasts.

shelf n. (pl. **shelves**) board or slab fastened horizontally for things to be placed on; thing resembling this, ledge. **shelf-life** n. time for which a stored thing remains usable. **shelf-mark** n. number marked on a book to show its place in a library.

shell n. hard outer covering of eggs, nut-kernels, and of animals such as snails and tortoises; firm framework or covering; light racing-boat; metal case filled with explosive, for firing from a large gun. —v.t. remove the shell(s) of; fire explosive shells at. **shell-**

pink *a.* & *n.* delicate pale pink.

shell-shock *n.* nervous breakdown from exposure to battle conditions.

shellac *n.* resinous substance used in varnish. —*v.t.* (*p.t.* **shellacked**) coat with this.

shellfish *n.* water animal that has a shell.

shelter *n.* structure that shields against danger, wind, rain, etc.; refuge, shielded condition. —*v.t.* provide with shelter; protect from blame, trouble, etc.; find or take shelter.

shelve *v.t./i.* arrange on a shelf; fit with shelves; put aside for later consideration or permanently; slope.

shelving *n.* shelves; material for these.

shemozzle *n.* (*sl.*) rumpus, brawl.

shenanigans *n.pl.* (*US sl.*) high-spirited behaviour; trickery.

shepherd *n.* man who tends a flock of sheep. —*v.t.* guide (people). **shepherd's pie** pie of minced meat topped with mashed potato. **shepherdess** *n.fem.*

sherbet *n.* weak sweet fruit-juice; fizzy sweet drink, powder from which this is made; flavoured water-ice.

sherd *n.* potsherd.

sheriff *n.* Crown's chief executive officer in a county; chief judge of a district in Scotland; (*US*) chief law-enforcing officer of a county.

Sherpa *n.* member of a Himalayan people of Nepal and Tibet.

sherry *n.* strong white wine orig. from southern Spain.

shibboleth *n.* old slogan or principle still considered essential by some member of a party.

shield *n.* piece of defensive armour carried on the arm to protect the body; trophy in the form of this; protective structure. —*v.t.* protect, screen; protect from discovery.

shift *v.t./i.* change or move from one position to another; change

form or character; transfer (blame etc.); (*sl.*) move quickly; manage to do something. —*n.* change of place or form etc.; set of workers who start work when another set finishes; time for which they work; evasion; scheme; woman's straight-cut dress. **make shift** (*see* **make**).

shiftless *a.* lazy and inefficient.

shifty *a.* (**-ier, -iest**) evasive, not straightforward; untrustworthy. **shiftily** *adv.*, **shiftiness** *n.*

Shiite *n.* & *a.* (member) of one of two main branches of Islam.

shillelagh /ʃrˈleɪlɪ/ *n.* Irish cudgel.

shilling *n.* former British coin (= 5p).

shilly-shally *v.i.* be unable to make up one's mind firmly.

shimmer *v.i.* & *n.* shine with a soft quivering light. **shimmery** *a.*

shin *n.* front of the leg below the knee; lower foreleg, esp. as a cut of beef. —*v.i.* (*p.t.* **shinned**) **shin up** climb.

shindy *n.* (*colloq.*) din, brawl.

shine *v.t./i.* (*p.t.* **shone**) give out or reflect light, be bright; excel; cause to shine; (*colloq.*, *p.t.* **shined**) polish. —*n.* brightness; high polish. **take a shine to** (*colloq.*) take a liking to.

shiner *n.* (*sl.*) black eye.

shingle[1] *n.* wooden roof-tile. —*v.t.* roof with shingles; cut (a woman's hair) in a short tapered style.

shingle[2] *n.* small rounded pebbles; stretch of these, esp. on a shore. **shingly** *a.*

shingles *n.* disease with a rash of small blisters.

Shinto *n.* Japanese religion revering ancestors and nature-spirits. **Shintoism** *n.*, **Shintoist** *n.*

shinty *n.* game resembling hockey.

shiny *a.* (**-ier, -iest**) shining, glossy. **shininess** *n.*

ship *n.* large sea-going vessel. —*v.t.* (*p.t.* **shipped**) put or take on board a ship; transport. **shipper** *n.*

shipbuilding *n.* business of constructing ships. **shipbuilder** *n.*

shipmate *n.* person travelling or working on the same ship as another.

shipment *n.* shipping of goods; consignment shipped.

shipping *n.* ships collectively.

shipshape *adv.* & *a.* in good order, tidy.

shipwreck *n.* destruction of a ship by storm or striking rock etc. **shipwrecked** *a.*

shipyard *n.* shipbuilding establishment.

shire *n.* county; (*Austr.*) rural area with its own elected council. **shire-horse** *n.* horse of a heavy powerful breed.

shirk *v.t./i.* avoid (duty or work etc.) selfishly. **shirker** *n.*

shirr *v.t.* gather (cloth) with parallel threads running through it.

shirt *n.* man's loose-fitting garment of cotton or silk etc. for the upper part of the body; woman's similar garment.

shirting *n.* material for shirts.

shirtwaister *n.* woman's dress with the bodice shaped like a shirt.

shirty *a.* (*sl.*) annoyed, angry.

shiver[1] *v.i.* tremble slightly esp. with cold or fear. —*n.* shivering movement. **shivery** *a.*

shiver[2] *v.t./i.* shatter.

shoal[1] *n.* great number of fish swimming together. —*v.i.* form shoals.

shoal[2] *n.* shallow place; underwater sandbank; (*pl.*) hidden dangers. —*v.i.* become shallower.

shock[1] *n.* effect of a violent impact or shake; sudden violent effect on the mind or emotions; acute weakness caused by injury, pain, or mental shock; effect of a sudden discharge of electricity through the body. —*v.t./i.* cause

to suffer shock or a shock; horrify, disgust, seem scandalous to; feel shocked.

shock[2] *n.* bushy mass of hair.

shocker *n.* (*colloq.*) shocking person or thing.

shocking *a.* causing great astonishment, indignation, or disgust; scandalous; (*colloq.*) very bad.

shod *see* **shoe**.

shoddy *n.* fibre or cloth made from old shredded cloth. —*a.* (-ier, -iest) of poor quality. **shoddily** *adv.*, **shoddiness** *n.*

shoe *n.* outer covering for a person's foot, with a fairly stiff sole; thing like this in appearance or use; horseshoe; part of a brake that presses against a wheel or its drum. —*v.t.* (*p.t.* **shod**, *pres.p.* **shoeing**) fit with a shoe or shoes. **shoe-tree** *n.* shaped block for keeping a shoe in shape.

shoehorn *n.* curved piece of stiff material for easing one's heel into the back of a shoe.

shoelace *n.* cord for fastening together the edges of a shoe's uppers.

shoemaker *n.* person whose trade is making or mending shoes.

shoeshine *n.* (*US*) polishing of shoes.

shoestring *n.* shoelace; (*colloq.*) very small and barely adequate amount of capital etc.

shone *see* **shine**.

shoo *int.* sound uttered to frighten animals away. —*v.t.* drive away by this.

shook *see* **shake**.

shoot *v.t./i.* (*p.t.* **shot**) fire (a gun etc., or a missile); kill or wound with a missile from a gun etc.; hunt with a gun for sport; send out or move swiftly; (of a plant) put forth buds or shoots; slide (a bolt) into or out of its fastening; have one's boat move swiftly over or through; take a shot at goal; photograph, film. —*n.* young branch or new growth of a plant; expedition for hunting game, land where this is held. **shoot up** rise suddenly; grow rapidly. **shooting star** small meteor seen to move quickly. **shooting-stick** n. walking-stick with a small folding seat in the handle. **shooter** n.

shop n. building or room where goods or services are sold to the public; workshop; one's own work as a subject of conversation. —v.t./i. (p.t. **shopped**) go into a shop or shops to buy things; (sl.) inform against. **shop around** look for the best bargain. **shop-floor** n. workers as distinct from management or senior union officials. **shop-soiled** a. soiled from being on display in a shop. **shop steward** trade union official elected by fellow workers as their spokesman. **shop-worn** a. shop-soiled.

shopkeeper n. person who owns or manages a shop.

shoplifter n. person who steals goods that are displayed in a shop. **shoplifting** n.

shopper n. person who shops; bag for holding shopping.

shopping n. buying goods in shops; goods bought.

shore[1] n. land along the edge of a sea or lake.

shore[2] v.t. prop or support with a length of timber.

shorn see **shear**.

short a. (-er, -est) measuring little from end to end in space or time, or from head to foot; not lasting; insufficient; having insufficient; concise, brief; curt; (of drink) small and concentrated, made with spirits; (of pastry) crisp and easily crumbled. —adv. abruptly. —n. (colloq.) short drink; short circuit; (pl.) trousers that do not reach the knee. —v.t./i. (colloq.) short-circuit. **for short** as an abbreviation. **in short** expressed briefly. **short-change** v.t. cheat, esp. by giving insufficient change. **short circuit** connection (usu. a fault) in an electrical circuit when current flows by a shorter route than the normal one. **short-circuit** v.t. cause a short circuit in; bypass. **short cut** route or method quicker than the normal one. **short drink** drink of spirits etc. **short-handed** a. having an insufficient number of workers. **short-list** v.t. put on a short list from which a final choice will be made. **short-lived** a. living or lasting for only a short time. **short odds** nearly even odds in betting. **short-sighted** a. able to see clearly only what is close; lacking foresight. **short ton** (see ton). **short wave** radio wave of frequency greater than 3 MHz.

shortage n. lack, insufficiency.

shortbread n. rich sweet biscuit.

shortcake n. shortbread.

shortcoming n. failure to reach a required standard; fault.

shorten v.t./i. make or become shorter.

shortfall n. deficit.

shorthand n. method of writing rapidly with quickly made symbols.

shortly adv. after a short time; in a few words; curtly.

shot see **shoot**. —a. (of fabric) made so that different colours show at different angles. —n. firing of a gun etc.; sound of this; person of specified skill in shooting; missile(s) for a cannon or gun etc.; heavy ball thrown as a sport; attempt to hit something or reach a target; launching of a spacecraft; stroke in tennis or cricket or billiards etc.; attempt; injection; photograph; (colloq.) dram of spirits. **like a shot** (colloq.) without hesitation.

shotgun n. gun for firing small shot at close range. **shotgun wedding** one that is enforced, esp. because the bride is pregnant.

should *v.aux.* used to express duty or obligation, possible or expected future event, or (with *I* and *we*) a polite statement or a conditional or indefinite clause.

shoulder *n.* part of the body where the arm, foreleg, or wing is attached; part of the human body between this and the neck; animal's upper foreleg as a joint of meat; projection compared to the human shoulder. —*v.t./i.* push with one's shoulder; take (a burden) on one's shoulders; take (blame or responsibility) on oneself. **shoulder arms** hold a rifle with the barrel against one's shoulder. **shoulder-blade** *n.* large flat bone of the shoulder.

shout *n.* loud cry or utterance. —*v.t./i.* utter a shout; call loudly. **shout down** silence by shouting.

shove *n.* rough push. —*v.t./i.* push roughly; (*colloq.*) put.

shovel *n.* spade-like tool for scooping earth etc.; mechanical scoop. —*v.t.* (*p.t.* **shovelled**) shift or clear with or as if with a shovel; scoop roughly.

shoveboard *n.* game in which discs are driven over a marked surface.

shoveller *n.* duck with a broad shovel-like beak.

show *v.t./i.* (*p.t.* **showed**, *p.p.* **shown**) allow or cause to be seen, offer for inspection or viewing; demonstrate, point out, prove; cause to understand; conduct; present an image of; treat with (kindness, interest, etc.); be able to be seen. —*n.* process of showing; display, public exhibition or (*colloq.*) performance; outward appearance; (*sl.*) business, undertaking. **show business** entertainment profession. **showcase** *n.* case for displaying goods or exhibits. **show off** display well or proudly or ostentatiously; try to impress people. **show of hands** raising of hands in voting.

show-piece *n.* excellent specimen used for exhibition. **show up** make or be clearly visible; reveal (a fault etc.); (*colloq.*) arrive.

showdown *n.* final test; disclosure of intentions or conditions etc.

shower *n.* brief fall of rain or of snow, bullets, stones, etc.; sudden influx of letters or gifts etc.; (also **shower-bath**) device or cabinet in which water is sprayed on a person's body; wash in this; (*US*) party for giving presents esp. to a bride-to-be. —*v.t./i.* pour down or send or come in a shower; take a shower-bath.

showerproof *a.* (of fabric) able to keep out slight rain. —*v.t.* make showerproof.

showery *a.* with showers of rain.

showjumping *n.* competitive sport of riding horses to jump over obstacles. **showjumper** *n.*

showman *n.* (pl. **-men**) organizer of circuses or similar entertainments.

showmanship *n.* skill in presenting entertainment or goods etc. well.

shown *see* **show**.

showroom *n.* room where goods are displayed for inspection.

showy *a.* (**-ier**, **-iest**) making a good display; brilliant, gaudy. **showily** *adv.*, **showiness** *n.*

shrank *see* **shrink**.

shrapnel *n.* artillery shell containing bullets or pieces of metal which it scatters on exploding; these pieces.

shred *n.* small piece torn or cut from something; small amount. —*v.t.* (*p.t.* **shredded**) tear or cut into shreds. **shredder** *n.*

shrew *n.* small mouse-like animal; shrewish woman.

shrewd *a.* (**-er**, **-est**) showing sound judgement, clever. **shrewdly** *adv.*, **shrewdness** *n.*

shrewish *a.* sharp-tempered and scolding. **shrewishly** *adv.*, **shrewishness** *n.*

shriek *n.* shrill cry or scream. —*v.t./i.* utter (with) a shriek.

shrift *n.* **short shrift** curt treatment.

shrike *n.* bird with a strong hooked beak.

shrill *a.* (**-er, -est**) piercing and high-pitched in sound. **shrilly** *adv.*, **shrillness** *n.*

shrimp *n.* small edible shellfish, pink when boiled; (*colloq.*) very small person.

shrimping *n.* catching shrimps.

shrine *n.* sacred or revered place.

shrink *v.t./i.* (*p.t.* **shrank**, *p.p.* **shrunk**) make or become smaller; draw back to avoid something. **shrink from** be unwilling to. —*n.* (*sl.*) psychiatrist.

shrinkage *n.* shrinking of textile fabric; loss by theft or wastage.

shrive *v.t* (*p.t.* **shrove**, *p.p.* **shriven**) (*old use*) give absolution to after hearing confession; submit to this.

shrivel *v.t./i.* (*p.t.* **shrivelled**) shrink and wrinkle from great heat or cold or lack of moisture.

shroud *n.* cloth wrapping a dead body for burial; thing that conceals; one of the ropes supporting a ship's mast. —*v.t.* wrap in a shroud; protect or conceal in wrappings; conceal.

Shrove Tuesday day before Ash Wednesday. **Shrovetide** *n.*

shrub *n.* woody plant smaller than a tree. **shrubby** *a.*

shrubbery *n.* area planted with shrubs.

shrug *v.t./i.* (*p.t.* **shrugged**) raise (one's shoulders) as a gesture of indifference or doubt or helplessness. —*n.* this movement.

shrunk *see* shrink.

shrunken *a.* having shrunk.

shudder *v.i.* shiver or shake violently. —*n.* this movement.

shuffle *v.t./i.* walk without lifting one's feet clear of the ground;

rearrange, jumble; keep shifting one's position; be evasive; get rid of (a burden etc.) shiftily. —*n.* shuffling movement or walk; rearrangement.

shuffleboard *n.* = shovelboard.

shun *v.t.* (*p.t.* **shunned**) avoid.

shunt *v.t./i.* move (a train) to a side track; divert. —*n.* act of shunting; (*sl.*) collision in which a vehicle knocks the back of the one in front of it.

shush *int.* & *v.t./i.* (*colloq.*) hush.

shut *v.t./i.* (*p.t.* **shut**, *pres.p.* **shutting**) move (a door or window etc.) into position to block an opening; be moved thus; prevent access to (a place); bring or fold parts of (a thing) together; trap or exclude by shutting something. —*a.* (*sl.*) rid. **shut down** cease working or business; cause to do this. **shut-down** *n.* this process. **shut-eye** *n.* (*colloq.*) sleep. **shut up** securely; (*colloq.*) stop or cease talking or making a noise, silence.

shutter *n.* screen that can be closed over a window; device that opens and closes the aperture of a camera. **shuttered** *a.*

shuttle *n.* thread-holder, esp. one carrying the weft-thread in weaving; vehicle used in a shuttle service; shuttlecock; spacecraft for repeated use. —*v.t./i.* move or travel or send to and fro. **shuttle service** transport service going to and fro.

shuttlecock *n.* small cone-shaped object struck to and fro in badminton.

shy[1] *a.* (**-er, -est**) timid and lacking self-confidence. —*v.t.* jump or move suddenly in alarm. **shyly** *adv.*, **shyness** *n.*

shy[2] *v.t.* & *n.* (*colloq.*) throw.

shyster *n.* (*colloq.*) person (esp. a lawyer) who acts without due regard for professional ethics.

SI *abbr.* Système International (French, = International System of Units).

Siamese a. & n. (native, language) of Siam (=Thailand). **Siamese cat** cat with pale fur and darker face. **Siamese twins** twins whose bodies are joined at birth.

sibilant a. sounding like a hiss. —n. sibilant speech-sound (e.g. s, sh). **sibilance** n.

sibling n. brother or sister.

sibyl n. pagan prophetess. **sibylline** a.

sic /siːk/ adv. used or spelt in the way quoted.

Sicilian a. & n. (native) of Sicily.

sick a. unwell; vomiting; likely to vomit; distressed, disgusted; finding amusement in misfortune or morbid subjects. **sick of** bored with.

sicken v.t./i. become ill; make or become distressed or disgusted. **be sickening for** be in the first stages of (a disease).

sickle n. curved blade used for cutting corn etc.; thing shaped like this.

sickly a. (-ier, -iest) unhealthy; causing sickness or distaste; weak. **sickliness** n.

sickness n. illness; vomiting.

sickroom n. room ready for or occupied by a sick person.

side n. surface of an object, esp. one that is not the top, bottom, front, back, or end; bounding line of a plane figure; either of the two halves into which something is divided; part near an edge; slope of a hill or ridge; region next to a person or thing; aspect of a problem etc.; one of two opposing groups or teams etc.; (sl.) conceit. —a. at or on the side. —v.t. join forces (with a person) in a dispute. **on the side** as a sideline; as a surreptitious activity. **side by side** close together. **side-car** n. small vehicle seating a passenger, attached to the side of a motor cycle. **side-drum** n. small double-headed drum. **side-effect** n. secondary (usu. bad) effect. **side-saddle** n. saddle on which a woman rider sits with both legs on the same side of the horse; (adv.) sitting thus. **side-stroke** n. stroke used in swimming on one's side. **side-whiskers** n.pl. whiskers on the cheek.

sideboard n. flat-topped piece of dining-room furniture with drawers and cupboards for china etc.; (pl., sl.) side-whiskers.

sideburns n.pl. short side-whiskers.

sidekick n. (US colloq.) close associate.

sidelight n. light from or on one side, esp. at side of front of vehicle; incidental information.

sideline n. thing done in addition to one's main activity; (pl.) lines bounding the sides of a football pitch etc., place for spectators; (pl.) position etc. apart from the main action. —v.t. (US) relegate to the sidelines.

sidelong a. & adv. sideways.

sidereal /saɪˈdɪər-/ a. of or measured by the stars.

sideshow n. small show forming part of a large one.

sideslip n. sideways movement, skid. —v.i. (p.t. **-slipped**) move thus.

sidesman n. (pl. **-men**) assistant churchwarden.

sidestep v.t. avoid by stepping sideways.

sidetrack v.t. divert.

sidewalk n. (US) pavement.

sideways adv. & a. to or from one side; with one side forward.

siding n. short track by the side of a railway, used in shunting.

sidle v.i. advance in a timid, furtive, or cringing way.

siege n. surrounding and blockading of a place by armed forces, in order to capture it.

sienna /sɪˈe-/ n. a kind of clay used as colouring-matter. **burnt sienna** reddish-brown. **raw sienna** brownish-yellow.

sierra /sɪ'e-/ n. chain of mountains with jagged peaks in Spain or Spanish America.

siesta /sɪ'e-/ n. afternoon nap or rest, esp. in hot countries.

sieve /sɪv/ n. utensil with a wire mesh or gauze through which liquids or fine particles can pass. —v.t. put through a sieve.

sift v.t./i. sieve; sprinkle lightly; examine carefully and select or analyse; fall as if from a sieve. **sifter** n.

sigh n. long deep breath given out audibly in sadness, tiredness, relief, etc. —v.t./i. give or express with a sigh; make a similar sound; yearn.

sight n. ability to see; seeing; being seen; thing seen or worth seeing; unsightly thing; (colloq.) great amount; device looked through to aim or observe with a gun or telescope etc.; precise aim with this. —v.t. get a sight of; aim or observe with a gun-sight etc. **at** or **on sight** as soon as seen.

sight-read v.t./i. play or sing (music) without preliminary study of the score.

sightless a. blind.

sightseeing n. visiting places of interest. **sightseer** n.

sign n. something perceived that suggests the existence of a fact, quality, or condition; symbol; signboard; notice displayed; action or gesture conveying information or a command etc.; any of the twelve divisions of the zodiac. —v.t./i. make a sign; write (one's name) on a document, convey or engage or acknowledge by this.

signal n. sign or gesture giving information or a command; object placed to give notice or warning; sequence of electrical impulses or radio waves transmitted or received. —v.t./i. (p.t. **signalled**) make a signal or signals; communicate with or announce thus. —a. noteworthy.

signal-box n. small railway building with signalling apparatus. **signaller** n., **signally** adv.

signalize v.t. make noteworthy.

signalman n. (pl. -men) person responsible for displaying naval signals or for operating railway signals.

signatory /'sɪg-/ n. each of the parties who sign an agreement.

signature n. person's name or initials written by himself in signing something; section of a book made from one sheet folded and cut; indication of key or tempo, following the clef in a musical score. **signature tune** tune used to announce a particular performer or programme.

signboard n. board bearing the name or device of a shop etc.

signet n. person's seal used with or instead of a signature. **signet-ring** n. finger-ring with an engraved design.

significance n. meaning; importance. **significant** a., **significantly** adv.

signification n. meaning.

signify v.t./i. be a sign or symbol of; have as a meaning; make known; matter.

signor /'si:njɔ:(r)/ n. (pl. -ri) title of an Italian-speaking man.

signora /si:'njɔ:rə/ n. title of an Italian-speaking married woman.

signorina /si:njɔ:'ri:nə/ n. title of an Italian-speaking unmarried woman.

signpost n. post with arms showing the direction of certain places. —v.t. provide with signpost(s).

Sikh /si:k/ n. member of a certain Indian religious sect. **Sikhism** n.

silage /'saɪ-/ n. green fodder stored and fermented in a silo.

silence n. absence of sound or of speaking. —v.t. make silent.

silencer n. device for reducing sound.

silent *a.* without sound; not speaking. **silently** *adv.*

silhouette /sɪlʊ'et/ *n.* dark shadow or outline seen against a light background. —*v.t.* show as a silhouette.

silica *n.* compound of silicon occurring as quartz and in sandstone etc. **siliceous** *a.*

silicate *n.* compound of silicon.

silicon /-kən/ *n.* chemical substance found in the earth's crust in its compound forms. **silicon chip** silicon microchip.

silicone /-kəʊn/ *n.* organic compound of silicon, used in paint, varnish, and lubricants.

silicosis /-'kəʊ-/ *n.* lung disease caused by inhaling dust that contains silica.

silk *n.* fine strong soft fibre produced by silkworms; thread or cloth made from it or resembling this; (*colloq.*) Queen's Counsel. **take silk** become a Queen's Counsel, entitled to wear a silk gown. **silky** *a.*

silken *a.* like silk.

silkworm *n.* caterpillar which feeds on mulberry leaves and spins its cocoon of silk.

sill *n.* strip of stone, wood, or metal at the base of a doorway or window opening.

silly *a.* (**-ier, -iest**) lacking good sense, foolish, unwise; feebleminded; (of a fieldsman's position in cricket) close to the batsman. —*n.* (*colloq.*) foolish person. **silly billy** (*colloq.*) foolish person. **silliness** *n.*

silo /'saɪ-/ *n.* (*pl.* **-os**) pit or airtight structure for holding silage; pit or tower for storing grain or cement or radioactive waste; underground place where a missile is kept ready for firing.

silt *n.* sediment deposited by water in a channel or harbour etc. —*v.t./i.* block or become blocked with silt.

silvan *a.* of the woods, rural.

silver *n.* shiny white precious metal; coins or articles made of this; coins made of an alloy resembling it; household cutlery; colour of silver. —*a.* made of or coloured like silver. **silver jubilee, silver wedding** 25th anniversary.

silverfish *n.* small insect with a fish-like body.

silverside *n.* joint of beef cut from the haunch, below topside.

silversmith *n.* person whose trade is making articles in silver.

silvery *a.* like silver; having a clear gentle ringing sound.

simian /'sɪm-/ *a.* monkey-like, ape-like. —*n.* monkey, ape.

similar *a.* like, alike; resembling but not the same; of the same kind or amount. **similarly** *adv.*, **similarity** *n.*

simile /'sɪmɪlɪ/ *n.* figure of speech in which one thing is compared to another.

similitude /-'mɪl-/ *n.* similarity.

simmer *v.t./i.* boil very gently; be in a state of barely suppressed anger or excitement. **simmer down** become less excited.

simnel cake rich cake covered with marzipan and decorated.

simony /'saɪ-/ *n.* wrongful buying or selling of ecclesiastical office.

simper *v.i.* smile in an affected way. —*n.* affected smile.

simple *a.* (**-er, -est**) of one element or kind; not complicated or showy or luxurious; unsophisticated, without cunning; feebleminded. **simply** *adv.*, **simplicity** *n.*

simpleton *n.* foolish or half-witted person.

simplify *v.t.* make simple; make easy to do or understand. **simplification** *n.*

simplistic *a.* over-simplified. **simplistically** *adv.*

simulate *v.t.* pretend; imitate the form or condition of. **simulation** *n.*, **simulator** *n.*

simultaneous *a.* occurring or operating at the same time. **simultaneously** *adv.*, **simultaneity** /-'neɪ-/ *n.*

sin *n.* breaking of a religious or moral law; act which does this; serious fault or offence. —*v.i.* (*p.t.* **sinned**) commit a sin.

since *prep.* after; from (a specified time) until now, within that period. —*conj.* from the time that; because. —*adv.* since that time or event.

sincere *a.* free from pretence or deceit. **sincerely** *adv.*, **sincerity** *n.*

sine /saɪn/ *n.* ratio of the length of one side of a right-angled triangle to the hypotenuse.

sinecure /'saɪ-/ *n.* position of profit or honour with no work attached.

sine die /saɪnɪ daɪɪ/ indefinitely, with no appointed date.

sinew *n.* tough fibrous tissue joining muscle to bone; tendon; (*pl.*) muscles, strength. **sinewy** *a.*

sinful *a.* full of sin, wicked. **sinfully** *adv.*, **sinfulness** *n.*

sing *v.t./i.* (*p.t.* **sang**, *p.p.* **sung**) make musical sounds with the voice; perform (a song); make a humming sound. **singer** *n.*

singe /-ndʒ/ *v.t./i.* (*pres.p.* **singeing**) burn slightly; burn the ends or edges of. —*n.* slight burn.

single *a.* one only, not double or multiple; designed for one person or thing; taken separately; unmarried; having only one circle of petals; (of a ticket) valid for an outward journey only. —*n.* one person or thing; room etc. for one person; single ticket; pop record with one piece of music on each side; (usu. *pl.*) game with one player on each side. —*v.t.* choose or distinguish from others. **single combat** duel. **single cream** thin cream. **single figures** numbers from 1 to 9. **single-handed** *a.* without help from others. **single-minded** *a.* with

one's mind set on a single purpose. **single parent** person bringing up a child or children without a partner. **singly** *adv.*

singlet *n.* sleeveless vest; athlete's shirt resembling a vest.

singleton /-ŋgəl-/ *n.* thing that occurs singly.

singsong *a.* with a monotonous rise and fall of the voice. —*n.* singsong manner; informal singing by a group of people.

singular *n.* form of a noun or verb used in referring to one person or thing. —*a.* of this form; uncommon, extraordinary. **singularly** *adv.*, **singularity** *n.*

singularize *v.t.* make different from others. **singularization** *n.*

sinister *a.* suggestive of evil; involving wickedness (in heraldry) on or of the left-hand side of a shield.

sink *v.t./i.* (*p.t.* **sank**, *p.p.* **sunk**) fall or come gradually downwards; fall below the surface of water or the sea etc.; pass into a less active condition; lose value or strength etc.; cause or allow to sink; dig (a well), bore (a shaft); engrave (a die); send (a ball) into a pocket or hole; invest (money). —*n.* fixed basin with a drainage pipe; cesspool. **sink in** become understood. **sinking fund** money set aside regularly for repayment of a debt etc.

sinker *n.* weight used to sink a fishing-line etc.

sinner *n.* person who sins.

sinter *n.* solid coalesced by heating. —*v.i.* form this.

sinuous *a.* curving, undulating.

sinus /'saɪ-/ *n.* (*pl.* **-uses**) cavity in bone or tissue, esp. that connecting with the nostrils.

sip *n.* & *v.t./i.* (*p.t.* **sipped**) drink in small mouthfuls.

siphon /'saɪ-/ *n.* bent pipe or tube used for transferring liquid by utilizing atmospheric pressure; bottle from which soda water etc. is forced out by pressure of gas.

—*v.t./i.* flow or draw out through a siphon; take from a source.

sir *n.* polite form of address to a man; **Sir** title of a knight or baronet.

sire /saɪə(r)/ *n.* polite form of address to a king; animal's male parent; (*old use*) father, male ancestor. —*v.t.* beget.

siren *n.* device that makes a loud prolonged sound as a signal; dangerously fascinating woman.

sirloin *n.* upper (best) part of loin of beef.

sirocco *n.* (*pl.* **-os**) hot wind that reaches Italy from Africa.

sisal /'saɪs-/ *n.* rope-fibre made from the leaves of a tropical plant; this plant.

siskin *n.* bird related to the goldfinch.

sissy *n.* effeminate or cowardly person. —*a.* characteristic of a sissy.

sister *n.* daughter of the same parents as another person; woman who is a fellow member of a group or Church etc.; nun; female hospital nurse in authority over others. **sister-in-law** *n.* (*pl.* **sisters-in-law**) sister of one's husband or wife; wife of one's brother. **sisterly** *a.*

sisterhood *n.* relationship of sisters; order of nuns; society of women doing religious or charitable work.

sit *v.t./i.* (*p.t.* **sat**, *pres.p.* **sitting**) take or be in a position with the body resting more or less upright on the buttocks; cause to sit; pose for a portrait; (of birds) perch, (of animals) rest with legs bent and body on the ground; (of birds) remain on the nest to hatch eggs; be situated, lie; be a candidate (for); occupy a seat as member of a committee etc.; (of a committee etc.) hold a session; have one's seat on (a horse etc.). **sit-in** *n.* occupation of a building etc. as a form of protest.

sitar /'sɪtɑː(r)/ *n.* guitar-like Indian musical instrument.

sitcom *n.* (*colloq.*) situation comedy.

site *n.* ground on which a building etc. stands or stood or is to stand, or where an event takes or took or is to take place. —*v.t.* locate, provide with a site.

sitter *n.* person sitting; sitting hen; baby-sitter; (*sl.*) easy catch or shot.

sitting *see* **sit**. —*n.* time during which a person or assembly etc. sits; clutch of eggs. **sitting-room** *n.* room used for sitting in, not a bedroom. **sitting tenant** one already in occupation of rented accommodation etc.

situate *v.t.* place or put in a certain position. **be situated** be in a certain position.

situation *n.* place (with its surroundings) occupied by something; set of circumstances; position of employment. **situation comedy** broadcast comedy involving the same characters in a series of episodes. **situational** *a.*

six *a.* & *n.* one more than five (6, VI). **at sixes and sevens** in disorder. **sixth** *a.* & *n.*

sixpence *n.* sum of 6 pence; (*old use*) coin worth this. **sixpenny** *a.*

sixteen *n.* one more than fifteen (16, XVI). **sixteenth** *a.* & *n.*

sixty *a.* & *n.* six times ten (60, LX). **sixtieth** *a.* & *n.*

size[1] *n.* relative bigness, extent; one of the series of standard measurements in which things are made and sold. —*v.t.* group according to size. **size up** estimate the size of; (*colloq.*) form a judgement of. **sized** *a.*

size[2] *n.* gluey solution used to glaze paper or stiffen textiles etc. —*v.t.* treat with size.

sizeable *a.* large; fairly large.

sizzle *v.i.* make a hissing sound like that of frying.

sjambok /'ʃæm-/ *n.* rhinoceros-hide whip.

skate[1] n. (pl. **skate**) large flat-fish.

skate[2] n. one of a pair of blades or (**roller skate**) sets of wheels attached to boots or shoes for gliding over ice or a hard surface. —v.t./i. move or perform on skates. **skate over** make only a passing reference to. **skater** n.

skateboard n. small board with wheels like those of roller-skates, for riding on while standing. —v.i. ride on a skateboard.

skedaddle v.i. (colloq.) run away.

skein /skeɪn/ n. loosely coiled bundle of yarn; flock of wild geese etc. in flight.

skeletal a. of or like a skeleton.

skeleton n. hard supporting structure of an animal body; any supporting structure; framework. **skeleton crew** or **staff** one with staff reduced to a minimum. **skeleton key** key made so as to fit many locks.

skep n. wooden or wicker basket; straw or wicker beehive.

skerry n. rocky reef or islet.

sketch n. rough drawing or painting; brief account; short usu. comic play. —v.t. make a sketch or sketches (of). **sketch map** n. roughly drawn map.

sketchy a. (-ier, -iest) rough and not detailed or substantial. **sketchily** adv., **sketchiness** n.

skew a. slanting, askew. —v.t./i. make skew; turn or twist round. **on the skew** askew.

skewbald a. (of an animal) with irregular patches of white and another colour.

skewer n. pin thrust through meat to hold it compactly in cooking. —v.t. pierce or hold in place thus.

ski /skiː/ n. (pl. **-is**) one of a pair of long narrow strips of wood etc. fixed under the feet for travelling over snow. —v.i. (p.t. **ski'd**, pres.p. **skiing**) travel on skis. **skier** n.

skid v.i. (p.t. **skidded**) (of a vehicle) slide uncontrollably. —n. skidding movement; plank etc. over which heavy objects may be dragged or rolled; helicopter's runner for use in landing; wedge acting as a brake on the wheel of a cart. **skid-pan** n. surface used for practising control of skidding vehicles.

skiff n. small light row-boat.

skilful a. having or showing great skill. **skilfully** adv.

skill n. ability to do something well. **skilled** a.

skillet n. (US) frying-pan; (old use) cooking-pot shaped like this.

skim v.t./i. (p.t. **skimmed**) take (matter) from the surface of (liquid); glide; read quickly. **skim milk** milk from which the cream has been skimmed.

skimp v.t./i. supply or use rather less than what is necessary.

skimpy a. (-ier, -iest) scanty. **skimpily** adv., **skimpiness** n.

skin n. flexible continuous covering of the human or other animal body; material made from animal skin; complexion; outer layer; skin-like film on liquid. —v.t./i. (p.t. **skinned**) strip skin from; become covered with new skin. **skin-diving** n. sport of swimming under water with flippers and breathing apparatus. **skin-diver** n.

skinflint n. miserly person.

skinny a. (-ier, -iest) very thin; miserly. **skinniness** n.

skint a. (sl.) with no money left.

skip[1] v.t./i. (p.t. **skipped**) move lightly, esp. taking two steps with each foot in turn; jump with a skipping-rope; (colloq.) omit; (colloq.) go away hastily or secretly. —n. skipping movement.

skip[2] n. cage or bucket for raising and lowering things in a quarry etc.; large container for builders' rubbish etc.

skip[3] n. skep.

skipper n. & v.t. captain.

skipping-rope *n.* rope turned over the head and under the feet while jumping in play or exercise.

skirl *n.* shrill sound characteristic of bagpipes. *—v.i.* make this sound.

skirmish *n.* minor fight or conflict. *—v.i.* take part in a skirmish.

skirt *n.* woman's garment hanging from the waist; this part of a garment; similar part; cut of beef from the lower flank. *—v.t.* go or be along the edge of.

skirting(-board) *n.* narrow board round the bottom of a room-wall.

skit *n.* short parody.

skittish *a.* frisky.

skittle *n.* one of the wooden pins set up to be bowled down with a ball or disc in the game of **skittles.** *—v.t.* **skittle out** get (batsmen) out rapidly.

skive *v.i.* (*sl.*) dodge a duty.

skivvy *n.* (*colloq.*) lowly female servant.

skua *n.* large seagull.

skulduggery *n.* (*colloq.*) trickery.

skulk *v.i.* loiter stealthily.

skull *n.* bony framework of the head; representation of this.

skullcap *n.* small cap with no peak.

skunk *n.* black bushy-tailed American animal able to spray an evil-smelling liquid; (*sl.*) contemptible person.

sky *n.* region of the clouds or upper air; weather shown by this. *—v.t.* (*p.t.* **skied**, *pres.p.* **skying**) hit (a ball) high. **sky-blue** *a.* & *n.* bright clear blue.

skydiving *n.* parachuting in which the parachute is not opened until the last moment.

skylark *n.* lark that soars while singing. *—v.i.* play mischievously.

skylight *n.* window set in the line of a roof or ceiling.

skyscraper *n.* very tall building.

slab *n.* broad flat piece of something solid.

slack[1] *a.* (**-er, -est**) not tight or tense; slow, sluggish; negligent. *—n.* slack part of a rope etc. *—v.t./i.* slacken; be lazy about work. **slacker** *n.*, **slackly** *adv.*, **slackness** *n.*

slack[2] *n.* coal-dust or fragments left when coal is screened.

slacken *v.t./i.* make or become slack.

slacks *n.pl.* trousers for casual wear.

slag *n.* solid waste matter left when metal has been separated from ore by smelting; (*sl.*) prostitute, promiscuous woman. *—v.t.* (*p.t.* **slagged**) (*sl.*) criticize, insult. **slag-heap** *n.* mound of waste matter.

slain *see* **slay.**

slake *v.t.* satisfy or make (thirst) less strong; combine (lime) with water.

slalom /ˈslɑː-/ *n.* ski-race down a zigzag course; obstacle race in canoes or cars or on water-skis etc.

slam[1] *v.t./i.* (*p.t.* **slammed**) shut forcefully and noisily; put or hit forcefully; (*sl.*) criticize severely. *—n.* slamming noise.

slam[2] *n.* winning of all tricks at cards. **grand slam** winning of 12 or 13 tricks in bridge; winning of all of a group of championships.

slander *n.* false statement uttered maliciously that damages a person's reputation; crime of uttering this. *—v.t.* utter a slander about. **slanderer** *n.*, **slanderous** *a.*

slang *n.* words or phrases or particular meanings of these used very informally for vividness or novelty. *—v.t.* use abusive language to. **slangy** *a.*

slant *v.t./i.* slope; present (news etc.) from a particular point of view. *—n.* slope; way news etc. is slanted, bias. **slantwise** *adv.*

slap *v.t./i.* (*p.t.* **slapped**) strike with the open hand or with something flat; place forcefully or carelessly. —*n.* slapping blow. —*adv.* with a slap, directly. **slap-happy** *a.* (*colloq.*) cheerfully casual. **slap-up** *a.* (*sl.*) first-class.

slapdash *a.* hasty and careless.

slapstick *n.* comedy with boisterous activities.

slash *v.t./i.* make a sweeping cutting stroke; strike thus; slit (a garment) ornamentally; reduce drastically; criticize vigorously. —*n.* slashing stroke; cut.

slat *n.* one of the thin narrow overlapping strips arranged to form a screen.

slate *n.* rock that splits easily into smooth flat blue-grey plates; piece of this used as roofing-material or (formerly) for writing on. —*v.t.* cover with slates; (*colloq.*) criticize or rebuke severely. **slaty** *a.*

slattern *n.* slovenly woman. **slatternly** *a.*

slaughter *v.t.* kill (animals) for food; kill ruthlessly or in great numbers. —*n.* this process.

slaughterhouse *n.* place where animals are killed for food.

Slav *a.* & *n.* (member) of any of the peoples of East and Central Europe who speak a Slavonic language.

slave *n.* person who is the property of another and is obliged to work for him; victim of or to a dominating influence; drudge. —*v.i.* work very hard. **slave-driver** *n.* person who makes others work very hard. **slave-driving** *n.*

slaver /ˈsleɪ-/ *v.i.* have saliva flowing from the mouth.

slavery *n.* existence or condition of slaves; very hard work.

slavish *a.* excessively submissive or imitative. **slavishly** *adv.*

Slavonic /-ˈvɒn-/ *a.* & *n.* (of) the group of languages including Russian and Polish.

slay *v.t.* (*p.t.* **slew**, *p.p.* **slain**) kill.

sleazy *a.* (-ier, -iest) (*colloq.*) dirty; disreputable. **sleaziness** *n.*

sled *n.* & *v.i.* (*p.t.* **sledded**) (*US*) sledge.

sledge *n.* narrow cart with runners instead of wheels, used on snow or for sliding. —*v.i.* travel or convey in a sledge.

sledgehammer *n.* large heavy hammer.

sleek *a.* (-er, -est) smooth and glossy; looking well fed and thriving. —*v.t.* make sleek by smoothing. **sleekness** *n.*

sleep *n.* natural condition of rest with unconsciousness and relaxation of muscles; spell of this. —*v.t./i.* (*p.t.* **slept**) be or spend (time) in a state of sleep; provide with sleeping accommodation.

sleeper *n.* one who sleeps; any of the beams on which the rails of a railway etc. rest; railway coach fitted for sleeping in; berth in this; ring worn in a pierced ear to keep the hole from closing; spy etc. who remains inactive within an organization until required.

sleeping-bag *n.* padded bag for sleeping in.

sleepless *a.* without sleep.

sleepwalk *v.i.* walk about while asleep. **sleepwalker** *n.*

sleepy *a.* (-ier, -iest) feeling or showing a desire to sleep; without stir or bustle; (of fruit) tasteless from being overripe. **sleepily** *adv.*, **sleepiness** *n.*

sleet *n.* snow and rain falling simultaneously; hail or snow that melts while falling. —*v.i.* fall as sleet. **sleety** *a.*

sleeve *n.* part of a garment covering the arm or part of it; tube-like cover; cover for a record. **up one's sleeve** concealed but available.

sleeveless *a.* without sleeves.

sleigh /sleɪ/ n. sledge, esp. as a passenger vehicle drawn by horses. —v.i. travel in a sleigh.

sleight of hand /slaɪt/ skill in using the hands to perform conjuring tricks etc.

slender a. slim and graceful; small in amount. **slenderness** n.

slept see **sleep**.

sleuth /sluːθ/ n. detective.

slew[1] v.t./i. turn or swing round.

slew[2] see **slay**.

slice n. thin broad piece (or a wedge) cut from something; portion; implement for lifting or serving fish etc.; slicing stroke. —v.t./i. cut, esp. into slices; strike (a ball in golf) badly so that it spins away from the direction intended. **slicer** n.

slick a. (colloq.) quick and cunning; smooth in manner; slippery. —n. slippery place; patch of oil on the sea. —v.t. (colloq.) make sleek.

slicker n. (US colloq.) smooth stylish townsman.

slide v.t./i. (p.t. **slid**) move or cause to move along a smooth surface touching it always with the same part; move or pass smoothly. —n. act of sliding; smooth slope down which people or things can slide; sliding part; piece of glass for holding an object under a microscope; picture for showing on a screen by means of a projector; hinged clip for holding hair in place. **slide-rule** n. ruler used for making calculations, having a sliding central strip and marked with logarithmic scales. **sliding scale** scale of fees or taxes etc. that varies according to the variation of some standard.

slight a. (-er, -est) not much, not great, not thorough; slender. —v.t. & n. insult by treating with lack of respect. **slightly** adv., **slightness** n.

slim a. (**slimmer**, **slimmest**) of small girth or thickness; small,

slight, insufficient. —v.t./i. (p.t. **slimmed**) make (oneself) slimmer by dieting, exercise, etc. **slimmer** n., **slimness** n.

slime n. unpleasant thick slippery liquid substance. **slimy** a., **slimily** adv., **sliminess** n.

sling[1] n. belt or chain or bandage etc. looped round an object to support or lift it; looped strap used to throw a stone etc. —v.t. (p.t. **slung**) suspend or lift or hurl with a sling; (colloq.) throw.

sling[2] n. sweetened drink of gin etc. and water.

slink v.i. (p.t. **slunk**) move in a stealthy or shamefaced way.

slinky a. smooth and sinuous.

slip[1] v.t./i. (p.t. **slipped**) slide accidentally; lose one's balance thus; go or put smoothly; escape hold or capture; detach, release; become detached from. —n. act of slipping; slight or casual mistake; loose covering; petticoat; slipway; fielding position in cricket; liquid containing clay for coating pottery. **give a person the slip** escape from or avoid him or her. **slip-knot** n. one that slides easily or that can be undone by pulling. **slipped disc** disc of cartilage between vertebrae that has become displaced and causes pain. **slip-road** n. road for entering or leaving a motorway or other main road. **slip up** (colloq.) make a slight or casual mistake. **slip-up** n.

slip[2] n. small piece of paper for making notes etc.

slipper n. light loose shoe for indoor wear.

slippery a. smooth or wet and difficult to hold or causing slipping; (of a person) not trustworthy. **slipperiness** n.

slippy a. (colloq.) slippery. **look slippy** (colloq.) make haste.

slipshod a. done or doing things carelessly.

slipstream *n.* current of air driven backward as something is propelled forward.

slipway *n.* sloping structure on which boats are landed or ships built or repaired.

slit *n.* narrow straight cut or opening. —*v.t.* (*p.t.* **slit**, *pres.p.* **slitting**) cut a slit in; cut into strips.

slither *v.i.* slide unsteadily.

sliver /'slɪv-/ *n.* small thin strip.

slob *n.* (*colloq.*) large and coarse or stupid person.

slobber *v.i.* slaver, dribble. **slobbery** *a.*

sloe *n.* blackthorn; its small dark plum-like fruit.

slog *v.t./i.* (*p.t.* **slogged**) hit hard; work or walk hard and steadily. —*n.* hard hit; spell of hard steady work or walking. **slogger** *n.*

slogan *n.* word or phrase adopted as a motto or in advertising.

sloop *n.* small ship with one mast.

slop *v.t./i.* (*p.t.* **slopped**) spill; splash liquid on; plod clumsily. —*n.* weak unappetizing liquid; slopped liquid; (*pl.*) liquid refuse. **slop-basin** *n.* basin for receiving dregs from teacups at the table.

slope *v.t./i.* lie or lay or turn at an angle from the horizontal or vertical. —*n.* sloping surface or ground or direction; amount by which a thing slopes. **slope off** (*sl.*) go away.

sloppy *a.* (**-ier**, **-iest**) liquid and splashing easily; slipshod; weakly sentimental. **sloppily** *adv.*, **sloppiness** *n.*

slosh *v.t./i.* (*colloq.*) splash, pour clumsily; (*sl.*) hit. —*n.* (*colloq.*) splashing sound; (*sl.*) blow.

sloshed *a.* (*sl.*) drunk.

slot *n.* narrow opening through which something is to be put; groove or slit in which something fits; position in a series or scheme. —*v.t./i.* (*p.t.* **slotted**) make slot(s) in; put or fit into a slot. **slot-machine** *n.* machine operated by inserting a coin into a slot.

sloth /sləʊθ/ *n.* laziness; slow-moving animal of tropical America.

slothful *a.* lazy. **slothfully** *adv.*

slouch *v.i.* stand, sit, or move in a lazy awkward way. —*n.* slouching movement or posture; (*sl.*) lazy or slovenly worker.

slough[1] /slaʊ/ *n.* swamp, marsh.

slough[2] /slʌf/ *n.* shed (skin); be shed in this way.

sloven /'slʌv-/ *n.* slovenly person.

slovenly /'slʌv-/ *a.* careless and untidy. **slovenliness** *n.*

slow *a.* (**-er**, **-est**) not quick or fast; showing an earlier time than the correct one; stupid. —*adv.* slowly. —*v.t./i.* reduce the speed (of). **slowly** *adv.*, **slowness** *n.*

slowcoach *n.* person who is slow in his actions or work.

slow-worm *n.* small legless lizard.

slub *n.* lump in yarn or thread.

sludge *n.* thick mud.

slug[1] *n.* small slimy animal like a snail without a shell; small lump of metal; bullet of irregular shape; (*US*) tot of liquor.

slug[2] *v.t.* (*p.t.* **slugged**) (*US*) hit hard.

sluggard *n.* slow or lazy person.

sluggish *a.* slow-moving, not lively. **sluggishly** *adv.*, **sluggishness** *n.*

sluice /sluːs/ *n.* sliding gate controlling a flow of water; this water; channel carrying off water; place where objects are rinsed; act of sluicing. —*v.t./i.* flood, scour, or rinse with a flow of water; fit with sluices.

slum *n.* squalid district. **slummy** *a.*, **slumminess** *n.*

slumber *v.i.* & *n.* sleep. **slumberer** *n.*

slumming *n.* visiting a slum; living like inhabitants of slums.

slump *n.* sudden great fall in prices or demand. —*v.i.* undergo a slump; sit or flop down slackly.

slung *see* **sling**.

slunk *see* **slink**.

slur v.t./i. (p.t. **slurred**) write, pronounce, or sound with each letter or sound running into the next; pass lightly over (a fact); (US) speak ill of. —n. slurred letter or sound; curved line marking notes to be slurred in music; discredit.

slurp v.t./i. & n. (make) a noisy sucking sound.

slurry /'slʌ-/ n. thin mud; thin liquid cement; fluid manure.

slush n. partly melted snow on the ground; silly sentimental talk or writing. **slush fund** fund for an illegal purpose, e.g. bribery. **slushy** a.

slut n. slovenly woman. **sluttish** a.

sly a. (**slyer, slyest**) unpleasantly cunning and secret; mischievous and knowing. **on the sly** secretly. **slyly** adv., **slyness** n.

smack[1] n. slap; hard hit; loud kiss. —v.t./i. slap, hit hard; close and part (lips) noisily. —adv. (colloq.) slap.

smack[2] n. & v.i. (have) a slight flavour or trace.

smack[3] n. single-masted boat.

smacker n. (sl.) loud kiss; (sl.) £1 or (US) $1.

small a. (**-er, -est**) not large or great; doing things on a small scale; petty. —n. narrowest part (of the back); (pl., colloq.) small articles of laundry, esp. underwear. —adv. in a small way. **small hours** period soon after midnight. **small-minded** a. narrow or selfish in outlook. **small talk** social conversation on unimportant subjects. **small-time** a. of an unimportant level. **smallness** n.

smallholding n. small piece of agricultural land. **smallholder** n.

smallpox n. disease with pustules that often leave bad scars.

smarmy a. (**-ier, -iest**) (colloq.) ingratiating, fulsome. **smarmily** adv., **smarminess** n.

smart a. (**-er, -est**) neat and elegant; clever; forceful, brisk. —v.i. & n. (feel) a stinging pain. **smartly** adv., **smartness** n.

smarten v.t./i. make or become smarter.

smash v.t./i. break noisily into pieces; strike forcefully; crash; overthrow; ruin, become ruined. —n. act or sound of smashing; collision; disaster; ruin.

smashing a. (colloq.) excellent.

smattering n. slight knowledge.

smear v.t./i. spread with a greasy or dirty substance; try to damage the reputation of. —n. thing smeared; mark made by this; attempt to damage a reputation. **smeary** a.

smell n. ability to perceive things by their action on the sense-organs of the nose; quality perceived thus; unpleasant quality of this kind; act of smelling. —v.t./i. (p.t. **smelt** or **smelled**) perceive the smell of; detect or test thus; give off a smell. **smelly** a.

smelling-salts n.pl. solid preparation of ammonia to be sniffed as a remedy for faintness.

smelt[1] see smell.

smelt[2] v.t. heat and melt (ore) to extract metal; obtain (metal) thus.

smelt[3] n. small fish related to the salmon.

smilax n. a kind of climbing plant.

smile n. facial expression indicating pleasure or amusement, with lips stretched and their ends upturned. —v.t./i. give a smile; express by smiling; look favourable.

smiley a. & n. (showing) a cartoon-style smiling face.

smirch v.t. smear, soil; discredit.

smirk n. self-satisfied smile. —v.i. give a smirk.

smite v.t./i. (p.t. **smote**, p.p. **smitten**) hit hard; affect suddenly.

smith *n.* person who makes things in metal; blacksmith.

smithereens *n.pl.* small fragments.

smithy *n.* blacksmith; his workshop.

smitten *see* smite.

smock *n.* loose overall. —*v.t.* ornament with close gathers stitched ornamentally. **smocking** *n.*

smog *n.* dense smoky fog.

smoke *n.* visible vapour given off by a burning substance; spell of smoking tobacco; (*sl.*) cigarette, cigar. —*v.t./i.* give out smoke or steam; (of a chimney) send smoke into a room; darken or preserve with smoke; draw smoke from (a cigarette or cigar or pipe) into the mouth; do this as a habit. **smoky** *a.*

smokeless *a.* with little or no smoke.

smoker *n.* person who smokes tobacco as a habit.

smokescreen *n.* thing intended to disguise or conceal activities.

smooth *a.* (**-er, -est**) having an even surface with no projections; not harsh in sound or taste; moving evenly without bumping; pleasantly polite but perhaps insincere. —*v.t./i.* make or become smooth. **smoothly** *adv.*, **smoothness** *n.*

smorgasbord *n.* Swedish hors d'œuvres, buffet with a variety of dishes.

smote *see* smite.

smother *v.t./i.* suffocate, stifle; cover thickly; suppress. —*n.* dense cloud of dust or smoke.

smoulder *v.i.* burn slowly with smoke but no flame; burn inwardly with concealed anger etc.

smudge *n.* dirty or blurred mark. —*v.t./i.* make a smudge on or with; become smudged; blur. **smudgy** *a.*, **smudginess** *n.*

smug *a.* (**smugger, smuggest**) self-satisfied. **smugly** *adv.*, **smugness** *n.*

smuggle *v.t.* convey secretly; bring (goods) illegally into or out of a country, esp. without paying customs duties. **smuggler** *n.*

smut *n.* small flake of soot; small black mark; indecent talk or pictures or stories. **smutty** *a.*

snack *n.* small or casual meal. **snack bar** place where snacks are sold.

snaffle *n.* horse's bit without a curb. —*v.t.* (*sl.*) take for oneself.

snag *n.* jagged projection; tear caused by this. —*v.t./i.* (*p.t.* **snagged**) catch or tear on a snag.

snail *n.* soft-bodied animal with a shell that can enclose its whole body. **snail's pace** very slow pace.

snake *n.* reptile with a long narrow body and no legs. —*v.i.* move in a winding course. **snaky** *a.*

snakeskin *n.* leather made from snakes' skins.

snap *v.t./i.* (*p.t.* **snapped**) make or cause to make a sharp cracking sound; break suddenly; bite at with a snatching movement; speak with sudden irritation; move smartly; take a snapshot of. —*n.* act or sound of snapping; fastener that closes with a snap; small crisp biscuit; sudden brief spell of cold weather; snapshot; **Snap** card-game in which players call 'snap' when two similar cards are exposed. —*adv.* with a snapping sound. —*a.* sudden, done or arranged at short notice. **snap up** take eagerly.

snapdragon *n.* garden plant with flowers that have a mouth-like opening.

snapper *n.* any of several sea-fish used as food.

snappish *a.* inclined to snap; irritable.

snappy *a.* (**-ier, -iest**) (*colloq.*) irritable; brisk; neat and elegant. **snappily** *adv.*, **snappiness** *n.*

snapshot *n.* photograph taken informally or casually.

snare *n.* trap, usu. with a noose; each of the strings stretched across a snare-drum to produce a rattling effect. —*v.t.* trap in a snare.

snarl[1] *v.t./i.* growl angrily with teeth bared; speak or utter in a bad-tempered way. —*n.* act or sound of snarling.

snarl[2] *v.t./i.* tangle. **snarl-up** *n.*

snatch *v.t./i.* seize quickly or eagerly. —*n.* act of snatching; short or brief part.

snazzy *a.* (-ier, -iest) (*sl.*) stylish.

sneak *v.t./i.* go or convey or (*sl.*) steal furtively; (*school sl.*) tell tales. —*n.* (*school sl.*) telltale.

sneakers *n.pl.* soft-soled shoes.

sneaking *a.* persistent but not openly acknowledged.

sneer *n.* scornful expression or remark. —*v.i.* show contempt by a sneer.

sneeze *n.* sudden audible involuntary expulsion of air through the nose. —*v.i.* give a sneeze.

snib *n.* fastening or catch of a window etc.

snick *v.t.* make a small cut in; hit (a ball) with a light glancing blow. —*n.* cut or blow of this kind.

snicker *v.i. & n.* snigger.

snide *a.* (*colloq.*) sneering slyly.

sniff *v.t./i.* draw air audibly through the nose; draw in as one breathes; try the smell of. —*n.* act or sound of sniffing. **sniffer** *n.*

sniffle *v.i.* sniff slightly or repeatedly. —*n.* this act or sound.

snifter *n.* (*sl.*) small drink of alcoholic liquor.

snigger *v.i. & n.* (give) a sly giggle.

snip *v.t./i.* (*p.t.* snipped) cut with scissors or shears in small quick strokes. —*n.* act or sound of snipping; piece snipped off; (*sl.*) bargain, certainty, easy task.

snipe *n.* (*pl.* snipe) wading bird with a long straight bill. —*v.i.* fire shots from a hiding-place; make sly critical remarks. **sniper** *n.*

snippet *n.* small piece.

snitch *v.t.* (*sl.*) steal.

snivel *v.i.* (*p.t.* snivelled) cry in a miserable whining way.

snob *n.* person with an exaggerated respect for social position, wealth, or certain tastes and who despises those he considers inferior. **snobbery** *n.*, **snobbish** *a.*

snood *n.* loose bag-like ornament in which a woman's hair is held at the back.

snook *n.* **cock a snook** (*colloq.*) make a contemptuous gesture.

snooker *n.* game played on a baize-covered table with 15 red and 6 other coloured balls.

snoop *v.i.* (*colloq.*) pry. **snooper** *n.*

snooty *a.* (*colloq.*) haughty and contemptuous. **snootily** *adv.*

snooze *n. & v.i.* nap.

snore *n.* snorting or grunting sound made during sleep. —*v.i.* make such sounds. **snorer** *n.*

snorkel *n.* device by which an underwater swimmer or submarine can take in and expel air. —*v.i.* (*p.t.* snorkelled) swim with a snorkel.

snort *n.* rough sound made by forcing breath through the nose, esp. in indignation. —*v.t./i.* make a snort; (*sl.*) inhale (a powdered drug).

snout *n.* animal's long projecting nose or nose and jaws; projecting front part.

snow *n.* frozen atmospheric vapour falling to earth in white flakes; fall or layer of snow. —*v.i.* fall as or like snow. **snowed under** covered with snow; overwhelmed with a mass of letters etc. **snowstorm** *n.*, **snowy** *a.*

snowball *n.* snow pressed into a compact mass for throwing in play. —*v.t./i.* throw snowballs (at); increase in size or intensity.

snowblower *n.* machine that clears snow by blowing it to the side of the road etc.

snowdrift n. mass of snow piled up by the wind.

snowdrop n. plant with small hanging white flowers blooming in spring.

snowflake n. flake of snow.

snowman n. (pl. -men) figure made of snow.

snowplough n. device for clearing roads etc. by pushing snow aside.

snub[1] v.t. (p.t. **snubbed**) reject (a person) unkindly or contemptuously. —n. treatment of this kind.

snub[2] a. (of the nose) short and stumpy. **snub-nosed** a.

snuff[1] n. powdered tobacco for sniffing up the nostrils.

snuff[2] v.t. put out (a candle) by covering or pinching the flame. **snuff it** (sl.) die. **snuffer** n.

snuffle v.i. breathe with a noisy sniff. —n. snuffling sound.

snug a. (**snugger, snuggest**) cosy; close-fitting. **snugly** a.

snuggle v.t./i. nestle, cuddle.

so adv. & conj. to the extent or in the manner or with the result indicated; very; for that reason; also. —pron. that, the same thing. **so-and-so** n. person or thing that need not be named; (colloq.) disliked person. **so-called** a. called (wrongly) by that name. **so long!** (colloq.) goodbye. **so-so** a. & adv. (colloq.) only moderately good or well. **so that** in order that.

soak v.t./i. place or lie in liquid so as to become thoroughly wet; (of liquid) penetrate; absorb; (sl.) extort money from. —n. process of soaking; (sl.) heavy drinker.

soap n. substance used in washing and cleaning things, made of fat or oil and an alkali; (colloq.) soap opera. —v.t. apply soap to. **soap opera** sentimental broadcast serial.

soapstone n. steatite.

soapsuds n.pl. froth of soapy water.

soapy a. of or like soap; containing or smeared with soap; unctuous. **soapiness** n.

soar v.i. rise high esp. in flight.

sob n. uneven drawing of breath when weeping or gasping. —v.t./i. (p.t. **sobbed**) weep, breathe, or utter with sobs.

sober a. not intoxicated; serious, not frivolous; (of colour) not bright. —v.t./i. make or become sober. **soberly** adv., **sobriety** /'brʌɪə-/ n.

sobriquet /'səʊbrɪkeɪ/ n. nickname.

soccer n. Association football.

sociable a. fond of company; characterized by friendly companionship. **sociably** adv., **sociability** n.

social a. living in an organized community; of society or its organization; sociable. —n. social gathering. **social science** study of society and social relationships. **social security** State assistance for those who lack economic security. **social services** welfare services provided by the State. **social worker** person trained to help people with social problems. **socially** adv.

socialism n. political and economic theory that resources, industries, and transport should be owned and managed by the State. **socialist** n., **socialistic** a.

socialite n. person prominent in fashionable society.

socialize v.t./i. organize in a socialistic manner; behave sociably. **socialization** n.

society n. organized community; system of living in this; people of the higher social classes; mixing with other people; group organized for a common purpose. **Society of Friends** Quakers (see **friend**). **Society of Jesus** Jesuits.

sociology n. study of human society or of social problems. **sociological** a., **sociologist** n.

sock[1] *n.* short stocking not reaching the knee; loose insole.

sock[2] *v.t.* (*sl.*) hit forcefully. —*n.* (*sl.*) forceful blow.

socket *n.* hollow into which something fits. **socketed** *a.*

sockeye *n.* a kind of salmon.

sod *n.* turf; a piece of this.

soda *n.* compound of sodium in common use, esp. sodium carbonate (**washing-soda**), bicarbonate (**baking-soda**), or hydroxide (**caustic soda**); sodawater. **soda water** water made fizzy by being charged with carbon dioxide under pressure.

sodden *a.* made very wet.

sodium *n.* soft silver-white metallic element. **sodium lamp** lamp giving a yellow light from an electrical discharge in sodium vapour.

sofa *n.* long upholstered seat with a back and raised ends.

soffit *n.* under-surface of a lintel or arch etc.

soft *a.* (**-er, -est**) not hard or firm or rough; not loud; gentle; flabby, feeble; easily influenced, tenderhearted; silly; not bright or dazzling; (*sl.*) easy; (of drinks) nonalcoholic; (of water) free from mineral salts that prevent soap from lathering; (of drugs) not likely to cause addiction; (of currency) likely to drop suddenly in value. **soft fruit** small stoneless fruit (e.g. raspberry). **soft-pedal** *v.t.* tone down, refrain from emphasizing. **soft spot** feeling of affection. **softly** *adv.*, **softness** *n.*

soften *v.t./i.* make or become soft or softer. **softener** *n.*

software *n.* computer programs or tapes containing these (as distinct from machinery or *hardware*).

softwood *n.* soft wood of coniferous trees.

soggy *a.* (**-ier, -iest**) sodden; moist and heavy. **sogginess** *n.*

soigné /ˈswɑːnjeɪ/ *a.* (*fem.* **soignée**) well-groomed and sophisticated.

soil[1] *n.* loose earth; ground as territory.

soil[2] *v.t./i.* make or become dirty.

soirée /ˈswɑːreɪ/ *n.* evening party for conversation or music.

sojourn /ˈsɒdʒɜːn/ *n.* temporary stay. —*v.i.* stay temporarily.

solace /ˈsɒl-/ *v.t. & n.* comfort in distress.

solar *a.* of or from the sun; reckoned by the sun. **solar cell** etc., device converting solar radiation into electricity. **solar plexus** network of nerves at the pit of the stomach; this area. **solar system** sun with the heavenly bodies that revolve round it.

solarium /-ˈleər-/ *n.* (*pl.* **-ia**) room fitted with glass for exposure to the sun, or with sun-lamps.

sold *see* **sell**.

solder *n.* soft alloy used to cement metal parts together. —*v.t.* join with solder. **soldering iron** tool for melting and applying solder.

soldier *n.* member of an army. —*v.i.* serve as a soldier. **soldier on** (*colloq.*) persevere doggedly. **soldierly** *a.*

soldiery *n.* soldiers collectively.

sole[1] *n.* under-surface of a foot; part of a shoe or stocking etc. covering this; lower surface, base. —*v.t.* put a sole on.

sole[2] *n.* flatfish used as food.

sole[3] *a.* one and only; belonging exclusively to one person or group. **solely** *adv.*

solecism /ˈsɒlɪs-/ *n.* mistake in the use of language; social blunder.

solemn *a.* not smiling or cheerful; formal and dignified. **solemnly** *adv.*, **solemnity** *n.*

solemnize *v.t.* celebrate (a festival etc.); perform with formal rites. **solemnization** *n.*

solenoid /ˈsəʊ-* or *ˈsɒl-/ *n.* coil of wire magnetized by electric current.

sol-fa n. system of syllables (*doh, ray, me,* etc.) representing the notes of a musical scale.

solicit v.t./i. seek to obtain by asking (for). **solicitation** n.

solicitor n. lawyer who advises clients and instructs barristers.

solicitous /-'lɪs-/ a. anxious about a person's welfare or comfort. **solicitously** adv., **solicitude** n.

solid a. keeping its shape, firm; not liquid or gas; not hollow; of the same substance throughout; continuous; of solids; with three dimensions; sound and reliable; unanimous. —n. solid substance or body or food. **solid-state** a. using transistors (which use the electronic properties of solids). **solidly** adv., **solidity** n.

solidarity n. unity resulting from common aims or interests etc.

solidify v.t./i. make or become solid. **solidification** n.

soliloquize v.i. utter a soliloquy.

soliloquy /-'lɪləkwɪ/ n. speech made aloud to oneself.

solipsism /'sɒl-/ n. theory that the self is all that exists or can be known.

solitaire n. gem set by itself; game played on a special board by one person; (*US*) card-game of patience.

solitary a. alone; single; not frequented, lonely. —n. recluse.

solitude n. being solitary.

solo n. (pl. **-os**) music for a single voice or instrument; unaccompanied performance or flight etc. —a. & adv. unaccompanied.

soloist n. performer of a solo.

solstice n. either of the times (about 21 June and 22 Dec.) or points reached when the sun is furthest from the equator.

soluble a. able to be dissolved; able to be solved. **solubility** n.

solution n. liquid containing something dissolved; process of dissolving; process of solving a problem etc.; answer found.

solvable a. able to be solved.

solve v.t. find the answer to. **solver** n.

solvent a. having enough money to pay one's debts etc.; able to dissolve another substance. —n. liquid used for dissolving something. **solvency** n.

somatic a. of the body.

sombre a. dark, gloomy. **sombrely** adv.

sombrero /-'breər-/ n. (pl. **-os**) man's hat with a very wide brim.

some a. unspecified quantity or number of; unknown, unnamed; considerable quantity; approximately; (*sl.*) remarkable. —pron. some persons or things.

somebody n. & pron. unspecified person; person of importance.

somehow adv. in an unspecified or unexplained manner; by one means or another.

someone n. & pron. somebody.

somersault /'sʌməsɔːlt/ n. & v.i. leap or roll turning one's body upside down and over.

something n. & pron. unspecified thing or extent; important or praiseworthy thing. **something like** rather like; approximately.

sometime a. & adv. former(ly); at some unspecified time.

sometimes adv. at some times but not all the time.

somewhat adv. to some extent.

somewhere adv. at, in, or to an unspecified place.

somnambulist /-'næm-/ n. sleepwalker. **somnambulism** n.

somnolent /'sɒm-/ a. sleepy; asleep. **somnolence** n.

son n. male in relation to his parents; **the Son** second person of the Trinity. **son-in-law** n. (pl. **sons-in-law**) daughter's husband.

sonar /'səʊ-/ n. device for detecting objects under water by reflection of sound-waves.

sonata /-'nɑː-/ n. musical composition for one instrument or two, usu. in several movements.

sonatina /-'tiː-/ n. simple or short sonata.

song n. singing; music for singing. **going for a song** (colloq.) being sold very cheaply.

songbird n. bird with a musical cry.

songster n. singer; songbird.

sonic a. of sound waves.

sonnet n. type of poem of 14 lines.

sonny n. (colloq.) form of address to a boy or young man.

sonorous /'sɒn-/ a. resonant. **sonorously** adv., **sonority** n.

soon adv. (-er, -est) in a short time; early; readily. **sooner or later** at some time, eventually.

soot n. black powdery substance in smoke. **sooty** a.

soothe /suːð/ v.t. calm, ease (pain etc.). **soothing** a., **soothingly** adv.

soothsayer /-θ-/ n. prophet.

sop n. piece of bread dipped in liquid before being eaten or cooked; concession to pacify a troublesome person. —v.t. (p.t. **sopped**) dip in liquid; soak up (liquid).

sophism n. sophistry. **sophist** n. person using this.

sophisticated a. characteristic of or experienced in fashionable life and its ways; complicated, elaborate. **sophistication** n.

sophistry n. clever and subtle but perhaps misleading reasoning.

sophomore /'sɒf-/ n. (US) second-year university or high-school student.

soporific a. tending to cause sleep. —n. soporific drug etc.

sopping a. very wet, drenched.

soppy a. (-ier, -iest) very wet; (colloq.) sentimental in a sickly way. **soppiness** n.

soprano n. (pl. -os) highest female or boy's singing-voice; music for this.

sorbet /-beɪ/ n. flavoured water-ice.

sorcerer n. magician. **sorceress** n.fem., **sorcery** n.

sordid a. dirty, squalid; (of motives etc.) not honourable, mercenary. **sordidly** adv., **sordidness** n.

sore a. (-er, -est) causing or suffering pain from injury or disease; (old use) serious; distressed, vexed. —n. sore place; source of distress or annoyance. **soreness** n.

sorely adv. very much, severely.

sorghum n. tropical cereal plant.

sorrel[1] /'sɒ-/ n. sharp-tasting herb.

sorrel[2] /'sɒ-/ a. light reddish-brown.

sorrow n. mental suffering caused by loss or disappointment etc.; thing causing this. —v.i. feel sorrow, grieve. **sorrowful** a., **sorrowfully** adv.

sorry a. (-ier, -iest) feeling pity or regret or sympathy; wretched.

sort n. particular kind or variety; (colloq.) person of a specified character. —v.t. arrange according to sort or size or destination etc. **out of sorts** slightly unwell or depressed.

sortie n. sally by troops from a besieged place; flight of an aircraft on a military operation.

SOS international code-signal of distress. —n. urgent appeal for help.

sot n. habitual drunkard.

sotto voce /sɒtəʊ 'vəʊtʃɪ/ in an undertone.

soufflé /'suːfleɪ/ n. light dish made with beaten egg-white.

sough /saf or saʊ/ n. & v.i. (make) a moaning or whispering sound as of wind in trees.

sought see **seek**.

souk /suːk/ n. market-place in Arab countries etc.

soul n. person's spiritual or immortal element; mental, moral, or emotional nature; personification, pattern (of honesty etc.); person; American Black culture.

soul music emotional style of jazz-playing.

soulful a. showing deep feeling, emotional. **soulfully** adv.

soulless a. lacking sensitivity or noble qualities; dull.

sound[1] n. vibrations of air detectable (at certain frequencies) by the ear; sensation produced by these; what is or may be heard. —v.t./i. produce or cause to produce sound; utter, pronounce; seem when heard; test by noting the sound produced. **sound barrier** high resistance of air to objects moving at speeds near that of sound. **sound off** (colloq.) talk or express one's opinions loudly. **sounder** n.

sound[2] a. (-er, -est) healthy; not diseased or damaged; secure; correct, well-founded; thorough. —adv. soundly. **soundly** adv., **soundness** n.

sound[3] v.t. test the depth or quality of the bottom (of a river or sea etc.), esp. by a weighted line; examine with a probe. **sounder** n.

sound[4] n. strait.

sounding-board n. board to reflect sound or increase resonance.

soundproof a. impervious to sound. —v.t. make soundproof.

soup n. liquid food made from stewed meat or vegetables etc. —v.t. **soup up** (colloq.) increase the power (of an engine etc.). **in the soup** (sl.) in difficulties. **soup-kitchen** n. place where soup etc. is supplied free to the needy. **soupy** a.

soupçon /'suːpsɔ̃/ n. trace.

sour a. (-er, -est) tasting sharp like unripe fruit; not fresh, tasting or smelling stale; (of soil) excessively acid; bad-tempered. —n. acid drink. —v.t./i. make or become sour. **sourly** adv., **sourness** n.

source n. place from which something comes or is obtained; river's starting-point; person or book etc. supplying information.

sourpuss n. (sl.) bad-tempered person.

souse v.t. steep in pickle; drench. **soused** a. (sl.) drunk.

soutane /suːˈtæn/ n. cassock of an RC priest.

south n. point or direction to the right of a person facing east; southern part. —a. in the south; (of wind) from the south. —adv. towards the south. **south-east** n. point or direction midway between south and east. (**south-easterly** a. & n., **south-eastern** a.) **south-west** n. point or direction midway between south and west. **south-westerly** a. & n., **south-western** a.

southerly /'sʌ-/ a. towards or blowing from the south.

southern a. of or in the south.

southerner n. native of the south.

southernmost a. furthest south.

southpaw n. (colloq.) left-handed person.

southward a. towards the south. **southwards** adv.

souvenir /suːvəˈnɪə(r)/ n. thing serving as a reminder of an incident or place visited.

sou'wester n. waterproof usu. oilskin hat with a broad flap at the back.

sovereign n. king or queen who is the supreme ruler of a country; British gold coin nominally worth £1. —a. supreme; (of a State) independent; very effective. **sovereignty** n.

soviet /'səʊvɪ-/ n. elected council in the USSR. **Soviet** a. & n. (person) of the Soviet Union (= USSR).

sow[1] /saʊ/ v.t. (p.t. sowed, p.p. sowed or sown) plant or scatter (seed) for growth; plant seed in; implant (ideas etc.). **sower** n.

sow[2] /saʊ/ n. adult female pig.

soy n. soya bean.

soya n. plant from whose seed (**soya bean**) an edible oil and flour are obtained.

sozzled a. (sl.) drunk.

spa n. place with a curative mineral spring.

space n. boundless expanse in which all objects exist and move; portion of this; empty area or extent; universe beyond earth's atmosphere; interval. —v.t. arrange with spaces between.

spacecraft n. (pl. -craft) vehicle for travelling in outer space.

spaceship n. spacecraft.

spacious a. providing much space, roomy. **spaciousness** n.

spade[1] n. tool for digging ground, with a broad metal blade on a handle; tool of similar shape for other purposes.

spade[2] n. playing-card of the suit marked with black figures shaped like an inverted heart with a small stem.

spadework n. hard preparatory work.

spaghetti n. pasta made in long strings.

span[1] n. extent from end to end; distance (about 9 inches or 23 cm) between the tips of the thumb and little finger when these are stretched apart; distance or part between the uprights of an arch or bridge. —v.t. (p.t. spanned) extend or reach across.

span[2] see spick and span.

spandrel n. area between an arch and its framework or between the curves of adjoining arches.

spangle n. small piece of glittering material ornamenting a dress etc. —v.t. cover with spangles or sparkling objects.

Spaniard n. native of Spain.

spaniel n. a kind of dog with drooping ears and a silky coat.

Spanish a. & n. (language) of Spain.

spank v.t. slap on the buttocks.

spanker n. fore-and-aft sail on a mizen-mast.

spanking a. (colloq.) brisk.

spanner n. tool for gripping and turning the nut on a screw etc.

spar[1] n. strong pole used as a ship's mast or yard or boom.

spar[2] n. mineral that splits easily.

spar[3] v.i. (p.t. sparred) box, esp. for practice; quarrel, argue.

spare v.t. refrain from hurting or harming; use with restraint; afford to give. —a. additional to what is usually needed or used, kept in reserve; thin, lean; small in quantity. —n. extra thing kept in reserve. **go spare** (colloq.) become very angry or upset. **spare-rib** n. cut of pork ribs. **to spare** additional to what is needed.

sparely adv., **spareness** n.

sparing /'spear-/ a. economical, not generous or wasteful.

spark n. fiery particle; flash of light produced by an electrical discharge; particle (of energy, genius, etc.). —v.t./i. give off spark(s). **spark(ing)-plug** n. device for making a spark in an internal-combustion engine. **spark off** trigger off.

sparkle v.i. shine with flashes of light; show brilliant wit or liveliness. —n. sparkling light or brightness.

sparkler n. sparkling firework.

sparkling a. (of wine) effervescent.

sparrow n. small brownish-grey bird.

sparrowhawk n. small hawk.

sparse a. thinly scattered, not dense. **sparsely** adv., **sparseness** n., **sparsity** n.

spartan a. (of conditions) simple and sometimes harsh.

spasm n. strong involuntary contraction of a muscle; sudden brief spell of activity or emotion etc.

spasmodic a. of or occurring in spasms. **spasmodically** adv.

spastic a. physically disabled by cerebral palsy which causes jerky or involuntary movements. —*n.* person suffering from this condition. **spasticity** *n.*

spat[1] *see* **spit**[1].

spat[2] *n.* short gaiter.

spate *n.* sudden flood.

spathe /speɪð/ *n.* large petal-like part of a flower, surrounding a central spike.

spatial /ˈspeɪʃ(ə)l/ *a.* of or existing in space. **spatially** *adv.*

spatter *v.t./i.* scatter or fall in small drops (on). —*n.* splash(es); sound of spattering.

spatula *n.* knife-like tool with a blunt blade; medical instrument for pressing down the tongue.

spatulate *a.* with a broad rounded end.

spavin *n.* abnormal swelling on a horse's hock. **spavined** *a.*

spawn *n.* eggs of fish or frogs or shellfish; (*derog.*) offspring; thread-like matter from which fungi grow. —*v.t./i.* deposit spawn; produce from spawn; generate.

spay *v.t.* sterilize (a female animal) by removing the ovaries.

speak *v.t.* (*p.t.* **spoke**, *p.p.* **spoken**) utter (words) in an ordinary voice; say something; converse; express by speaking; be evidence of something.

speaker *n.* person who speaks, one who makes a speech; loudspeaker; **Speaker** person presiding over the House of Commons or a similar assembly.

spear *n.* weapon for hurling, with a long shaft and pointed tip; pointed stem. —*v.t.* pierce with or as if with a spear.

spearhead *n.* foremost part of an advancing force. —*v.t.* be the spearhead of.

spearmint *n.* a kind of mint.

spec *n.* **on spec** (*colloq.*) as a speculation, without being certain.

special *a.* of a particular kind; for a particular purpose; exceptional. **specially** *adv.*

specialist *n.* expert in a particular branch of a subject, esp. of medicine.

speciality /-ˈæl-/ *n.* special quality or product or activity.

specialize *v.t./i.* be or become a specialist; adapt for a particular purpose. **specialization** *n.*

species /ˈspiːʃɪz/ *n.* (*pl.* **species**) group of similar animals or plants within a genus; kind.

specific *a.* particular, clearly distinguished from others; exact, not vague. —*n.* specific aspect or influence; remedy for a specific disease etc. **specific gravity** ratio between the weight of a substance and that of the same volume of water or air. **specifically** *adv.*

specification *n.* specifying; details describing a thing to be made or done.

specify *v.t.* mention definitely; include in specifications.

specimen *n.* part or individual taken as an example or for examination or testing.

specious /ˈspiː-/ *a.* seeming plausible or sound but lacking real merit. **speciously** *adv.*, **speciousness** *n.*

speck *n.* small spot or particle.

speckle *n.* small spot, esp. as a natural marking. **speckled** *a.*

specs *n.pl.* (*colloq.*) spectacles.

spectacle *n.* impressive sight; lavish public show; ridiculous sight; (*pl.*) pair of lenses set in a frame, worn to assist sight or protect the eyes.

spectacular *a.* impressive. —*n.* spectacular performance or production. **spectacularly** *adv.*

spectator *n.* person who watches a show or game or incident.

spectral *a.* of or like a spectre; of the spectrum.

spectre *n.* ghost; haunting fear.

spectroscope *n.* instrument for producing and examining spectra. **spectroscopic** *a.*, **spectroscopy** *n.*

spectrum *n.* (*pl.* **-tra**) bands of colour or sound forming a series according to their wavelengths; entire range of ideas etc.

speculate *v.i.* form opinions by guessing; buy in the hope of making a profit but with risk of loss. **speculation** *n.*, **speculator** *n.*, **speculative** *a.*

speculum *n.* medical instrument for looking into bodily cavities.

sped *see* speed.

speech *n.* act or power or manner of speaking; spoken communication, esp. to an audience; language, dialect.

speechify *v.i.* (*colloq.*) make speeches.

speechless *a.* unable to speak because of great emotion.

speed *n.* rate of time at which something moves or operates; rapidity. —*v.t./i.* (*p.t.* **sped**) move, pass, or send quickly; (*p.t.* **speeded**) travel at an illegal or dangerous speed. **speed up** move or operate at a greater speed. **speed-up** *n.*

speedboat *n.* fast motor boat.

speedometer /-'dɒm-/ *n.* device in a motor vehicle, showing its speed.

speedway *n.* arena for motor-cycle racing; (*US*) fast motor-road.

speedwell *n.* wild plant with small blue flowers.

speedy *a.* (**-ier**, **-iest**) rapid. **speedily** *adv.*, **speediness** *n.*

speleology /spelɪ-/ *n.* exploration and study of caves. **speleological** *a.*, **speleologist** *n.*

spell[1] *n.* words supposed to have magic power; their influence; fascination, attraction.

spell[2] *v.t./i.* (*p.t.* **spelt**) give in their correct sequence the letters that form (a word); produce as a result. **spell out** spell aloud; state explicitly. **speller** *n.*

spell[3] *n.* period of time or weather or activity. —*v.t.* take turns with (a person) in work etc.

spellbound *a.* entranced.

spelt[1] *see* spell[2].

spelt[2] *n.* a kind of wheat.

spencer *n.* woman's undergarment like a thin jumper.

spend *v.t.* (*p.t.* **spent**) pay out (money) in buying something; use for a certain purpose; use up; pass (time etc.). **spender** *n.*

spendthrift *n.* wasteful spender.

spent *see* spend.

sperm *n.* (*pl.* **sperms** or **sperm**) male reproductive cell; semen. **sperm whale** a kind of large whale.

spermatozoon /-'zəʊən/ *n.* (*pl.* **-zoa**) fertilizing cell of a male organism.

spermicidal *a.* killing sperm.

spermicide *n.*

spew *v.t./i.* vomit; cast out in a stream.

sphagnum *n.* moss growing on bogs.

sphere *n.* perfectly round solid geometric figure or object; field of action or influence etc.

spherical *a.* shaped like a sphere.

sphincter *n.* ring of muscle controlling an opening in the body.

sphinx *n.* winged monster (**the Sphinx**) in Greek mythology; stone statue with a lion's body and human or ram's head, esp. in ancient Egypt; enigmatic person.

spice *n.* flavouring-substance(s) (obtained from plants) with a strong taste or smell; thing that adds zest. —*v.t.* flavour with spice. **spicy** *a.*

spick and span neat and clean.

spider *n.* small animal (not an insect) with a segmented body and eight jointed legs, living on insects. **spidery** *a.*

spiel /spiːl/ *n.* (*sl.*) glib or lengthy speech. —*v.i.* (*sl.*) talk thus.

spigot *n.* plug stopping the vent-hole of a cask or controlling the flow of a tap.

spike n. pointed thing; pointed piece of metal. —v.t. put spikes on; pierce or fasten with a spike; (colloq.) add alcohol to (drink). **spike a person's guns** thwart him or her. **spiky** a.

spikenard /'spaik-/ n. tall fragrant plant.

spill[1] n. thin strip of wood or paper for transferring flame.

spill[2] v.t./i. (p.t. **spilt**) cause or allow to run over the edge of a container; become spilt. —n. fall. **spill the beans** (sl.) reveal information indiscreetly. **spillage** n.

spin v.t./i. (p.t. **spun**, pres.p. **spinning**) turn rapidly on its axis; draw out and twist into threads; make (yarn etc.) thus. —n. spinning movement; short drive for pleasure. **spin-drier** n. machine for drying washed articles by spinning them in a rotating drum. **spin-off** n. incidental benefit. **spin out** prolong. **spinner** n.

spina bifida /spaɪnə 'bɪf-/ congenital defect of the spine, in which membranes protrude.

spinach n. vegetable with dark-green leaves.

spinal a. of the spine.

spindle n. rod on which thread is wound in spinning; revolving pin or axis; shrub or tree with pink or red berries.

spindly a. long or tall and thin.

spindrift n. sea-spray.

spine n. backbone; needle-like projection; part of a book where the pages are hinged.

spineless a. having no backbone; lacking determination.

spinet /-'net/ n. a kind of small harpsichord.

spinnaker /'spɪn-/ n. large extra sail on a racing-yacht.

spinneret n. thread-producing organ in a spider, silkworm, etc.

spinney n. (pl. -eys) thicket.

spinning-wheel n. household device for spinning fibre into yarn.

spinster n. unmarried woman.

spiny a. full of spines, prickly.

spiral a. forming a continuous winding curve round a central point or axis. —n. spiral line or thing; continuous increase or decrease in two or more quantities alternately. —v.i. (p.t. **spiralled**) move in a spiral course. **spirally** adv.

spire n. tall pointed structure esp. on a church tower.

spirit n. mind or animating principle as distinct from body; soul; ghost; person's nature; characteristic quality; real meaning; liveliness, boldness; distilled extract; **the Spirit** the Holy Spirit; (pl.) person's feeling of cheerfulness or depression; (pl.) strong distilled alcoholic drink. —v.t. carry off swiftly and mysteriously. **spirit-lamp** n. lamp that burns methylated spirit or similar fluid. **spirit-level** n. sealed glass tube containing an air-bubble in liquid, used to test levelness.

spirited a. lively, bold; having the mental spirit(s) specified. **spiritedly** adv.

spiritual a. of the human spirit or soul; of the Church or religion. —n. religious folk-song of American Blacks. **spiritually** adv., **spirituality** n.

spiritualism n. attempted communication with spirits of the dead. **spiritualist** n., **spiritualistic** a.

spirituous a. strongly alcoholic.

spit[1] v.t./i. (p.t. **spat** or **spit**, pres.p. **spitting**) eject from the mouth; eject saliva; make a spitting sound in anger or hostility; (of rain) fall lightly. —n. spittle; act of spitting; (also **spitting image**) exact likeness.

spit[2] n. metal spike holding meat while it is roasted; narrow strip of land projecting into the sea.

—v.t. (p.t. **spitted**) pierce with or as if with a spit.

spit² n. spade's depth of earth.

spite n. malicious desire to hurt or annoy someone. —v.t. hurt or annoy from spite. **in spite of** not being prevented by. **spiteful** a., **spitefully** adv., **spitefulness** n.

spitfire n. fiery-tempered person.

spittle n. saliva.

spittoon n. receptacle for spitting into.

spiv n. (sl.) smartly dressed man who makes money shadily.

splash v.t./i. cause (liquid) to fly about in drops; move or fall or wet with such drops; decorate with irregular patches of colour etc.; display in large print; spend (money) freely. —n. act or mark or sound of splashing; (colloq.) dash of soda-water etc.; patch of colour or light; striking display. **splashy** a.

splashback n. panel behind sink to protect wall from splashes.

splatter v.t./i. & n. splash, spatter.

splay v.t./i. spread apart; slant outwards or inwards. —a. splayed.

spleen n. abdominal organ of the body, involved in maintaining the proper condition of the blood. n.

splendid a. brilliant, very impressive; excellent. **splendidly** adv.

splendour n. splendid appearance.

splenetic a. bad-tempered.

splice v.t. join by interweaving or overlapping the ends.

splint n. rigid framework preventing a limb etc. from movement, e.g. while a broken bone heals. —v.t. secure with a splint.

splinter n. thin sharp piece of broken wood etc. —v.t./i. break into splinters. **splinter group** small group that has broken away from a larger one.

split v.t./i. (p.t. **split**, pres.p. **splitting**) break or come apart, esp. lengthwise; divide, share; (sl.) reveal a secret. —n. splitting; split

thing or place; (pl.) acrobatic position with legs stretched fully apart. **split one's sides** laugh very heartily. **split second** very brief moment.

splodge v.t. & n. = splotch.

splotch v.t. & n. splash, blotch.

splurge n. ostentatious display, esp. of wealth. —v.i. make a splurge, spend money freely.

spoil v.t./i. (p.t. & p.p. **spoilt** or **spoiled**) damage, make useless or unsatisfactory; become unfit for use; harm the character of (a person) by being indulgent. —n. (also pl.) plunder; perquisites. **be spoiling for** (colloq.) desire (a fight etc.) eagerly.

spoilsport n. person who spoils others' enjoyment.

spoke¹ n. any of the bars connecting the hub to the rim of a wheel.

spoke², **spoken** see speak.

spokesman n. (pl. -men) person who speaks on behalf of a group. **spokeswoman** n. fem. (pl. women), **spokesperson** n.

spoliation n. pillaging.

sponge n. water animal with a porous structure; its skeleton, or a similar substance, esp. used for washing or cleaning or padding; sponge-cake; wash with a sponge. —v.t./i. wipe or wash with a sponge; cadge, live off the generosity of others. **sponge bag** waterproof bag for toilet articles. **sponge cake**, **sponge pudding** one with a light open texture. **spongeable** a., **spongy** a.

sponger n. person who sponges on others.

sponsor n. person who makes himself or herself responsible for a trainee etc., introduces legislation, or contributes to charity in return for another's activity; godparent; one who provides funds for a broadcast, sporting event, etc. —*v.t.* act as sponsor for. **sponsorship** *n.*

spontaneous *a.* resulting from natural impulse; not caused or suggested from outside. **spontaneously** *adv.*, **spontaneity** /-'nɪɪ-/ *n.*

spoof *n.* (*colloq.*) hoax, parody.

spook *n.* (*colloq.*) ghost. **spooky** *a.*

spool *n.* reel on which something is wound. —*v.t.* wind on a spool.

spoon *n.* utensil with a rounded bowl and a handle, used for conveying food to the mouth or for stirring things; amount it contains. —*v.t.* take or lift with a spoon; hit (a ball) feebly upwards. **spoonful** *n.* (*pl.* -**fuls**)

spoonbill *n.* wading bird with a broad flat tip to its bill.

spoonerism *n.* accidental interchange of the initial letters of two words.

spoonfeed *v.t.* (*p.t.* -**fed**) feed from a spoon; give excessive help to.

spoor *n.* track or scent left by an animal.

sporadic *a.* occurring now and then, scattered. **sporadically** *adv.*

spore *n.* one of the tiny reproductive cells of fungi, ferns, etc.

sporran *n.* pouch worn hanging in front of a kilt.

sport *n.* athletic (esp. outdoor) activity; game(s), pastime(s); amusement, fun; (*colloq.*) sportsman-like person; animal or plant that differs strikingly from its parent(s). —*v.t./i.* play, amuse oneself; wear. **sports car** open low-built fast car. **sports jacket** man's jacket for informal wear.

sporting *a.* of or interested in sport; like a sportsman. **sporting chance** reasonable chance of success.

sportive *a.* playful. **sportively** *adv.*, **sportiveness** *n.*

sportsman *n.* (*pl.* -**men**), **sportswoman** *n.fem.* (*pl.* -**women**) one who takes part in sports; one who plays fairly and generously.

sportsmanlike *a.*, **sportsmanship** *n.*

sporty *a.* (*colloq.*) sporting; dashing. **sportiness** *n.*

spot *n.* round mark or stain; pimple; place; drop; (*colloq.*) small amount; spotlight. —*v.t./i.* (*p.t.* **spotted**) mark with a spot or spots; rain slightly; (*colloq.*) notice; watch for and take note of. **in a spot** (*colloq.*) in difficulties. **on the spot** without delay or change of place; alert; (*colloq.*) compelled to take action or justify oneself. **spot check** random check. **spot on** (*colloq.*) precise, on target. **spotted dick** suet pudding containing currants. **spotter** *n.*

spotless *a.* free from stain or blemish. **spotlessly** *adv.*, **spotlessness** *n.*

spotlight *n.* lamp or its beam directed on a small area. —*v.t.* (*p.t.* -**lit** *or* -**lighted**) direct a spotlight on; draw attention to.

spotty *a.* marked with spots.

spouse *n.* person's husband or wife.

spout *n.* projecting tube through which liquid is poured or conveyed; jet of liquid. —*v.t./i.* come or send out forcefully as a jet of liquid; utter or speak lengthily. **up the spout** (*sl.*) broken, ruined, in a hopeless condition.

sprain *v.t.* injure by wrenching violently. —*n.* this injury.

sprang *see* **spring**.

sprat *n.* small herring-like fish.

sprawl *v.t./i.* sit, lie, or fall with arms and legs spread loosely; spread out irregularly. —*n.* sprawling attitude or arrangement.

spray[1] *n.* single shoot or branch with its leaves and flowers; decorative bunch of cut flowers; ornament in similar form.

spray[2] *n.* water or other liquid dispersed in very small drops; liquid for spraying; device for spraying liquid. —*v.t./i.* come or send out as spray; wet with liquid thus. **spray-gun** n. device for spraying paint etc. **sprayer** n.

spread v.t./i. (p.t. **spread**) open out; become longer or wider; cover the surface of; apply as a layer; be able to be spread; make or become widely known or felt or suffered; distribute, become distributed. —n. spreading; extent, expanse; expansion; bed-spread; (colloq.) lavish meal; thing's range; paste for spreading on bread. **spread eagle** figure of an eagle with legs and wings spread, as an emblem. **spread-eagle** v.t. spread out like this.

spreadsheet n. computer program for manipulating esp. tabulated numerical data.

spree n. (colloq.) lively outing, piece of fun.

sprig¹ n. twig, shoot.

sprig² n. small headless tack.

sprigged a. (of fabric) ornamented with sprays of flowers etc.

sprightly a. (-ier, -iest) lively, full of energy. **sprightliness** n.

spring v.t./i. (p.t. **sprang**, p.p. **sprung**) jump; move rapidly; issue, arise; become warped or split; produce or cause to operate suddenly; contrive the escape of (a prisoner). —n. act of springing, jump; device that reverts to its original position after being compressed, tightened, or stretched, used to drive clockwork or (in groups) make a seat etc. more comfortable; elasticity; place where water or oil flows naturally from the ground; season between winter and summer. **spring-clean** v.t./i. clean (one's home etc.) thoroughly. **spring tide** tide when there is the largest rise and fall of water.

springboard n. flexible board giving impetus to a gymnast or diver.

springbok n. South African gazelle.

springer n. a kind of small spaniel.

springtime n. season of spring.

springy a. (-ier, -iest) able to spring back easily after being squeezed or tightened or stretched. **springiness** n.

sprinkle v.t./i. scatter or fall in drops or particles on (a surface). —n. light shower. **sprinkler** n.

sprinkling n. something sprinkled; a few here and there.

sprint v.i. & n. run or swim etc. at full speed. **sprinter** n.

sprit n. small diagonal spar.

sprite n. elf, fairy, or goblin.

spritsail /ˈsprɪts(ə)l/ n. sail extended by a sprit.

sprocket n. projection engaging with links on a chain etc.

sprout v.t./i. begin to grow or appear; put forth. —n. plant's shoot; Brussels sprout.

spruce¹ a. neat, smart. —v.t. smarten. **sprucely** adv., **spruceness** n.

spruce² n. a kind of fir.

sprung see **spring**. —a. fitted with springs.

spry a. (**spryer**, **spryest**) active, lively. **spryly** adv., **spryness** n.

spud n. narrow spade; (sl.) potato.

spume n. froth.

spun see **spin**.

spunk n. (sl.) courage. **spunky** a.

spur n. pricking-device worn on a horseman's heel; stimulus, incentive; projection; branch road or railway. —v.t. (p.t. **spurred**) urge on (a horse) by pricking it with one's spurs; urge on, incite; stimulate. **on the spur of the moment** on impulse. **win one's spurs** prove one's ability.

spurge n. plant or bush with a bitter milky juice.

spurious a. not genuine or authentic. **spuriously** adv., **spuriousness** n.

spurn v.t. reject or treat contemptuously; repel with one's foot.

spurt *v.t./i.* gush; send out (liquid) suddenly; increase speed suddenly. —*n.* sudden gush; short burst of activity; sudden increase in speed.

sputter *v.i. & n.* splutter.

sputum *n.* expectorated matter; saliva.

spy *n.* person who secretly watches or gathers information. —*v.t./i.* catch sight of; be a spy, watch secretly. **spy out** explore secretly.

sq. *abbr.* square.

squab /-ob/ *n.* young pigeon; a kind of firmly padded cushion or seat-back.

squabble *v.i.* quarrel pettily or noisily. —*n.* quarrel of this kind.

squad *n.* small group working or being trained together.

squadron *n.* division (two troops) of a cavalry unit or armoured formation; detachment of warships; unit (10 to 18 aircraft) of the RAF.

squalid *a.* dirty and unpleasant; morally degrading. **squalidly** *adv.*, **squalor** *n.*

squall *n.* harsh cry or scream; sudden storm or wind. —*v.i.* utter a squall. **squally** *a.*

squander *v.i.* spend wastefully.

square *n.* geometric figure with four equal sides and four right angles; area or object shaped like this; L-shaped or T-shaped object for making or testing right angles; product obtained when a number is multiplied by itself; (in astrology) aspect of two planets 90° apart; (*sl.*) person considered old-fashioned or conventional. —*a.* of square shape; right-angled; of or using units expressing the measure of an area; properly arranged; equal, not owed or owing anything; straightforward; honest; (*sl.*) old-fashioned, conventional. —*adv.* squarely, directly. —*v.t./i.* make right-angled; mark with squares; place evenly; multiply by itself; settle (an

account etc.); make or be consistent; (*colloq.*) bribe. **square-bashing** *n. sl.* drill on a barrack-square. **square dance** dance in which four couples face inwards from four sides. **square meal** substantial meal. **square-rigged** *a.* having the principal sails at right angles to the ship's length. **square root** number of which a given number is the square. **square up to** face in a fighting attitude; face resolutely. **squarely** *adv.*, **squareness** *n.*

squash[1] *v.t./i.* crush, squeeze or become squeezed flat or into pulp; suppress; silence with a crushing reply. —*n.* crowd of people squashed together; fruit-flavoured soft drink; (also **squash rackets**) game played with rackets and a small ball in a closed court. **squashy** *a.*

squash[2] *n.* a kind of gourd.

squat *v.t./i.* (*p.t.* **squatted**) sit on one's heels; crouch; (*colloq.*) sit; be a squatter (in). —*n.* squatting posture; being a squatter, place occupied thus. —*a.* dumpy.

squatter *n.* person who takes unauthorized possession of unoccupied premises; (*Austr.*) sheep-farmer.

squawk *n.* loud harsh cry. —*v.t./i.* make or utter with a squawk.

squeak *n.* short high-pitched cry or sound. —*v.t./i.* make or utter with a squeak. **narrow squeak** narrow escape. **squeaky** *a.*

squeal *n.* long shrill cry or sound. —*v.t./i.* make or utter with a squeal; (*sl.*) protest sharply; (*sl.*) become an informer.

squeamish *a.* easily disgusted; over-scrupulous. **squeamishly** *adv.*, **squeamishness** *n.*

squeegee *n.* rubber tool for sweeping or squeezing away moisture. —*v.t.* treat with this.

squeeze *v.t./i.* exert pressure on; treat thus to extract moisture; force into or through, force one's way, crowd; produce by pressure or effort or compulsion; extort money etc. from. —n. squeezing; affectionate clasp or hug; drops produced by squeezing; crowd, crush, pressure of this; hardship or difficulty caused by shortage of money or time; restrictions on borrowing. **squeezer** n.

squelch v.i. & n. sound like someone treading in thick mud.

squib n. small exploding firework.

squid n. sea creature with ten arms round its mouth.

squiggle n. short curly line. **squiggly** a.

squint v.i. have one eye turned abnormally from the line of gaze of the other; look sideways or through a small opening. —n. squinting condition of an eye; sideways glance; (colloq.) look; narrow opening in the wall of a church etc. —a. askew.

squire n. country gentleman, esp. landowner; (colloq.) sir; (old use) knight's attendant.

squirearchy n. landowners collectively.

squirm v.i. wriggle; feel embarrassment. —n. wriggle.

squirrel n. small tree-climbing animal with a bushy tail.

squirt v.t./i. send out (liquid) or be sent out in a jet; wet thus. —n. syringe; jet of liquid; (colloq.) small or unimportant self-assertive fellow.

squish v.i. & n. (move with) a slight squelching sound. **squishy** a.

St abbr. Saint.

St. abbr. Street.

stab v.t. (p.t. **stabbed**) pierce, wound or kill with something pointed; poke. —n. act of stabbing; wound made thus; sensation of being stabbed; (colloq.) attempt.

stabilize /'ster-/ v.t./i. make or become stable. **stabilization** n., **stabilizer** n.

stable[1] a. (-er, -est) firmly fixed or established, not easily shaken or decomposed or destroyed. **stably** adv., **stability** n.

stable[2] n. building in which horses are kept; establishment for training racehorses; horses, people, or products etc. from the same establishment. —v.t. put or keep in a stable. **stable-boy**, **stable-lad** ns. person who works in a stable.

stabling n. accommodation for horses etc.

staccato /-'kaː-/ a. & adv. in a sharp disconnected manner.

stack n. orderly pile or heap or similar arrangement; (colloq.) large quantity; number of chimneys standing together; isolated chimney; storage section of a library. —v.t. arrange in a stack or stacks; arrange (cards) secretly for cheating; cause (aircraft) to fly at different levels while waiting to land.

stadium n. sports ground surrounded by tiers of seats for spectators.

staff n. stick or pole used as a weapon, support, measuring rod, or symbol of authority; group of assistants responsible to a manager or superior officer; people in authority within an organization, or doing administrative work; (pl. **staves**) set of five horizontal lines on which music is written. —v.t. provide with a staff of people.

stag n. fully grown male deer. **stag beetle** beetle with branched projecting mouth-parts. **stag-party** n. party of men only.

stage n. raised floor or platform; one on which plays etc. are performed; theatrical work or profession; division or point reached in a process or journey etc.; separable section of a rocket. —v.t. present on the stage; arrange and carry out. **go on the stage** become an actor or actress.

stage fright nervousness on facing an audience. **stage whisper** one meant to be overheard.

stagecoach n. (old use) horse-drawn coach running regularly between two places.

stager n. **old stager** experienced person.

stagflation n. inflation accompanied by stagnation in demand etc.

stagger v.t./i. move or go unsteadily; shock deeply; place in an alternating arrangement; arrange so as not to coincide exactly. —n. staggering movement.

staggering a. astonishing.

staging n. scaffolding; platform. **staging post** regular stopping-place on a long journey.

stagnant a. not flowing, still and stale; without activity. **stagnancy** n.

stagnate v.t. be stagnant; become dull from inactivity. **stagnation** n.

staid a. steady and serious.

stain v.t./i. discolour, become discoloured; blemish; colour with a penetrating pigment. —n. mark caused by staining; blemish; liquid for staining things.

stainless a. free from stains. **stainless steel** steel containing chromium and not liable to rust or tarnish.

stair n. one of a flight of fixed indoor steps; (pl.) a flight of these.

staircase n. stairs and their supporting structure.

stairway n. staircase.

stake n. pointed stick or post for driving into the ground; post to which a person was tied for execution by being burnt alive; money etc. wagered; share or interest in an enterprise etc. —v.t. fasten or support or mark with a stake or stakes; wager; (US colloq.) give financial or other support to. **at stake** being risked. **stake a claim** claim a right to something. **stake out** place under surveillance. **stake-out** n.

stalactite n. deposit of calcium carbonate hanging like an icicle.

stalagmite n. deposit of calcium carbonate standing like a pillar.

stale a. (-er, -est) not fresh; unpleasant or uninteresting from lack of freshness; spoilt by too much practice. —v.t./i. make or become stale. **staleness** n.

stalemate n. drawn position in chess; drawn contest; deadlock. —v.t. bring to such a state.

stalk[1] n. stem or similar supporting part.

stalk[2] v.t./i. walk in a stately or imposing manner; track or pursue stealthily. **stalker** n.

stalking-horse n. person or thing used to conceal one's intentions.

stall n. stable, cow-house; compartment in this; compartment for one person; enclosed seat in a church etc.; any of the set of seats nearest the stage in a theatre; booth or stand where goods are displayed for sale; stalling of an aircraft. —v.t./i. place or keep in a stall; (of an engine) stop suddenly from an overload or from lack of fuel; (of an aircraft) begin to drop because the speed is too low; cause to stall; stave off (a person or request) in order to gain time.

stallion n. uncastrated male horse.

stalwart /'stɔːl-/ a. sturdy; strong and faithful. —n. stalwart person.

stamen /'ster-/ n. pollen-bearing part of a flower.

stamina n. ability to withstand long physical or mental strain.

stammer v.t./i. speak with involuntary pauses or repetitions of a syllable. —n. this act or tendency.

stamp v.t./i. bring (one's foot) down heavily on the ground; press so as to cut or leave a mark or pattern, make (a mark etc.) thus; fix a postage or other stamp to; give a specified character to. —n. act or sound of stamping;

instrument for stamping a mark etc., this mark; small adhesive label for affixing to an envelope or document to show the amount paid as postage or a fee etc.; similar decorative label; characteristic indication of quality. **stamping-ground** n. usual haunt or place of action. **stamp out** extinguish by stamping; suppress by force.

stampede n. sudden rush of animals or people. —v.t./i. take part in a stampede; cause to do this or to act hurriedly.

stance n. manner of standing.

stanch v.t. restrain the flow of (blood etc.) or from (a wound).

stanchion n. upright post or support.

stand v.t./i. (p.t. **stood**) have, take, or keep a stationary upright position; be situated; place, set upright; remain; stay firm or valid; offer oneself for election; undergo; steer a specified course in sailing; endure; provide at one's own expense. —n. stationary condition; position taken up; resistance to attack; halt to give a performance; rack, pedestal; raised structure with seats at a sports ground etc.; stall for goods; standing-place for vehicles; (US) witness-box. **stand a chance** have a chance of success. **stand by** look on without interfering; stand ready for action; side with in a dispute; support in a difficulty; keep to (a promise etc.). **stand-by** & n. (person or thing) available as a substitute. **stand down** withdraw. **stand for** be present; (colloq.) tolerate. **stand in** deputize. **stand-in** n. deputy, substitute. **stand off** remain at a distance; lay off (employees) temporarily. **stand on** insist on formal observance of. **stand one's ground** not yield. **stand to reason** be logical. **stand up** come to or place in a standing position; be

valid; (colloq.) fail to keep an appointment with. **stand up for** speak in defence of. **stand up to** resist courageously; be strong enough to endure.

standard n. thing against which something may be compared for testing or measurement; average quality; required level of quality or proficiency; distinctive flag; upright support; shrub grafted on an upright stem. —a. serving as or conforming to a standard; of average or usual quality. **standard lamp** household lamp set on a tall pillar on a base.

standardize v.t. cause to conform to a standard. **standardization** n.

standing n. status; duration.

standoffish a. (colloq.) aloof.

standpipe n. vertical pipe for fluid to rise in, esp. for attachment to a water-main.

standpoint n. point of view.

standstill n. inability to proceed.

stank see **stink**.

stanza n. verse of poetry.

staphylococcus /-'kok-/ n. (pl. -ci) pus-producing bacterium. **staphylococcal** a.

staple[1] n. U-shaped spike for holding something in place; bent piece of metal or wire driven into papers and clenched to fasten them. —v.t. secure with staple(s). **stapler** n.

staple[2] a. & n. principal or standard (food or product etc.).

star n. celestial body appearing as a point of light; this regarded as influencing human affairs; figure or object with rays; asterisk; star-shaped mark indicating a category of excellence; brilliant person, famous actor or performer etc. —v.t./i. (p.t. **starred**) put an asterisk beside (an item); present or perform as a star actor. **star-gazing** n. (joc.) studying the stars.

starboard n. right-hand side of a ship or aircraft. —v.t. turn this way.

starch n. white carbohydrate; preparation of this or other substances for stiffening fabrics; stiffness of manner. —v.t. stiffen with starch. **starchy** a.

stardom n. being a star actor etc.

stare v.t./i. gaze fixedly esp. in astonishment. —n. staring gaze.

starfish n. star-shaped sea creature.

stark a. (-er, -est) desolate, bare; sharply evident; downright; naked; (old use) stiff. —adv. completely. **starkly** adv., **starkness** n.

starlight n. light from the stars.

starling n. noisy bird with glossy black speckled feathers.

starlit a. lit by starlight.

starry a. set with stars; shining like stars. **starry-eyed** a. (colloq.) romantically enthusiastic; eager but impractical.

start v.t./i. begin, cause to begin; begin operating; begin a journey; found; make a sudden movement, esp. from pain or surprise; spring suddenly; rouse (game etc.) from its covert. —n. beginning; place where a race etc. starts; advantage gained or allowed in starting; sudden movement of pain or surprise. **starter** n.

startle v.t. shock, surprise.

starve v.t./i. die or suffer acutely from lack of food; cause to do this; suffer or cause to suffer for lack (of something needed); force by starvation; (colloq.) feel very hungry or cold. **starvation** n.

starveling n. starving person or animal.

stash v.t. (sl.) stow.

state n. mode of being, with regard to characteristics or circumstances; (colloq.) excited or agitated condition of mind; grand imposing style; (often **State**) political community under one government or forming part of a federation; civil government. —a. of or involving the State; involving ceremony, for ceremonial occasions. —v.t. express in words; specify.

stateless a. not a citizen or subject of any country.

stately a. (-ier, -iest) dignified, grand. **stateliness** n.

statement n. process of stating; thing stated; formal account of facts; written report of a financial account.

stateroom n. room used on ceremonial occasions; passenger's private compartment on a ship.

statesman n. (pl. **-men**) person who is skilled or prominent in managing State affairs. **stateswoman** n.fem. (pl. **-women**), **statesmanship** n.

static a. of force acting by weight without motion; stationary; not changing. —n. atmospherics; (also **static electricity**) electricity present in a body, not flowing as current.

statics n. branch of physics dealing with bodies at rest or forces in equilibrium.

station n. place where a person or thing stands or is stationed; place where a public service or specialized activity is based; broadcasting establishment with its own frequency; stopping-place on a railway with buildings for passengers or goods or both; status; (Austr.) large farming estate, sheep-run. —v.t. put at or in a certain place for a purpose. **station-wagon** n. (US) estate car.

stationary a. not moving; not movable.

stationer n. dealer in stationery.

stationery n. writing-paper, envelopes, labels, etc.

statistic n. item of information expressed in numbers. **statistics** n. science of collecting and interpreting information based on the numbers of things. **statistical** a., **statistically** adv.

statistician *n.* expert in statistics.

statuary *n.* statues.

statue *n.* sculptured, cast, or moulded figure.

statuesque *a.* like a statue in size or dignity or stillness.

statuette *n.* small statue.

stature *n.* bodily height; greatness gained by ability or achievement.

status /'stei-/ *n.* (*pl.* **-uses**) person's position or rank in relation to others; high rank or prestige. **status quo** previous state of affairs.

statute *n.* law passed by Parliament or a similar body; one of the rules of an institution.

statutory /'stæ-/ *a.* fixed or done or required by statute.

staunch *a.* (**-er, -est**) firm in opinion or loyalty. **staunchly** *adv.*

stave *n.* one of the strips of wood forming the side of a cask or tub; staff in music. —*v.t.* (*p.t.* & *p.p.* **stove** *or* **staved**) dent, break a hole in. **stave off** (*p.t.* **staved**) ward off.

stay[1] *n.* rope or wire holding a mast or spar etc.; any prop or support; (*pl.*, *old use*) corset.

stay[2] *v.t./i.* continue in the same place or state; remain or dwell temporarily; satisfy temporarily; postpone; pause; show endurance. —*n.* period of temporary dwelling or visiting; postponement. **stay away from** not go to. **stay the course** be able to reach the end of it. **staying-power** *n.* endurance.

STD *abbr.* subscriber trunk dialling.

stead /sted/ *n.* in a person's *or* thing's place instead of him or it. **stand in good stead** be of great service to.

steadfast *a.* firm and not changing or yielding. **steadfastly** *adv.*

steady *a.* (**-ier, -iest**) firmly supported or balanced, not shaking; regular, uniform; dependable,

not excitable. —*n.* (*US colloq.*) regular boy-friend or girl-friend. —*adv.* steadily. —*v.t./i.* make or become steady. **steady state** unvarying condition. **steadily** *adv.*, **steadiness** *n.*

steak *n.* slice of meat (esp. beef) or fish, usu. grilled or fried.

steal *v.t.* (*p.t.* **stole**, *p.p.* **stolen**) take (property) dishonestly; obtain by a trick or surreptitiously; move stealthily. —*n.* (*colloq.*) stealing; bargain, easy task. **steal a march on** gain an advantage over (a person), esp. slyly. **steal the show** outshine other performers unexpectedly.

stealth *n.* stealthiness.

stealthy *a.* (**-ier, -iest**) quiet so as to avoid notice. **stealthily** *adv.*, **stealthiness** *n.*

steam *n.* gas into which water is changed by boiling; this as motive power; energy, power. —*v.t./i.* give out steam; cook or treat by steam; move by the power of steam; cover or become covered by steam; (*colloq.*) rush through a crowd robbing them. **steam engine** engine or locomotive driven by steam. **steamy** *a.*

steamboat *n.* steam-driven boat.

steamer *n.* steam-driven ship; container in which things are cooked or heated by steam.

steamroller *n.* heavy slow-moving engine with a large roller, used in road-making; crushing power. —*v.t.* crush or move (as) with a steamroller.

steamship *n.* steam-driven ship.

steatite /'stiə-/ *n.* greyish talc that feels smooth and soapy.

steed *n.* (*poetical*) horse.

steel *n.* very strong alloy of iron and carbon; tapered steel rod for sharpening knives. —*v.t.* make resolute. **steel wool** mass of fine shavings of steel used as an abrasive. **steely** *a.*, **steeliness** *n.*

steep[1] *v.t./i.* soak in liquid; permeate thoroughly.

steep² *a.* (-er, -est) sloping sharply not gradually; (*colloq.*, of price) unreasonably high. **steeply** *adv.*, **steepness** *n.*

steepen *v.t./i.* make or become steeper.

steeple *n.* tall tower with a spire, rising above a church roof.

steeplechase *n.* horse-race across country with fences to jump; race for runners with hurdles. **steeplechaser** *n.*, **steeplechasing** *n.*

steeplejack *n.* person who climbs tall chimneys etc. to do repairs.

steer¹ *n.* young male ox, esp. a bullock.

steer² *v.t./i.* direct the course of, guide by mechanism; be able to be steered. **steer clear of** avoid. **steering committee** one deciding or directing operations.

steerage *n.* steering.

steersman *n.* (*pl.* **-men**) person who steers a ship.

stein /stam/ *n.* large earthenware mug for beer etc.

stellar *a.* of a star or stars.

stem¹ *n.* supporting usu. cylindrical part, esp. of a plant, flower, leaf, or fruit; main usu. unchanging part of a noun or verb; ship's bows. —*v.i.* (*p.t.* **stemmed**) stem from have as its source.

stem² *v.t./i.* (*p.t.* **stemmed**) restrain the flow or movement of; dam.

stench *n.* foul smell.

stencil *n.* sheet of metal or card etc. with a cut-out design, painted or inked over to reproduce this on the surface below; design reproduced thus. —*v.t.* (*p.t.* **stencilled**) produce or ornament by this.

stenographer *n.* shorthand-writer.

stenography /-ˈtɔːr-/ *a.* (of a voice) extremely loud.

stentorian /-ˈtɔːr-/ *a.* (of a voice) extremely loud.

step *n.* (*p.t.* **stepped**) lift and set down a foot or alternate feet; move a short distance thus; progress. —*n.* complete movement of a foot and leg in stepping; distance covered thus; short distance; pattern of steps in dancing; sound of a step; one of a series of actions; level surface for placing the foot on in climbing; stage in a scale of promotion or precedence; (*pl.*) step-ladder. **in step** stepping in time with others; conforming. **mind** *or* **watch one's step** take care. **out of step** not in step. **step in** intervene; enter. **step on it** (*sl.*) hurry. **step up** increase.

step- *pref.* related by re-marriage of a parent, as **stepfather**, **stepmother**, **stepson**, etc. *ns.*

stephanotis /-ˈnəʊ-/ *n.* fragrant tropical climbing plant.

stepladder *n.* short ladder with a supporting framework.

steppe *n.* grassy plain, esp. in south-east Europe and Siberia.

stepping-stone *n.* raised stone for stepping on in crossing a stream etc.; means of progress.

stereo /ˈstɪə-/ *n.* (*pl.* -os) stereophonic sound or record-player etc.; stereoscopic effect.

stereophonic /sterɪəˈfɒn-/ *a.* using two transmission channels so as to give the effect of naturally distributed sound. **stereophony** *n.*

stereoscopic /ste-/ *a.* giving a three-dimensional effect.

stereotype /ˈstɪə-/ *n.* standardized conventional idea or character etc.; printing-plate cast from a mould of type. —*v.t.* standardize; cause to conform to a preconceived type. **stereotyped** *a.* standardized and hackneyed.

sterile /ˈstɪə-/ *a.* barren; free from living micro-organisms; unproductive. **sterility** *n.*

sterilize /ˈstɪə-/ *v.t.* make sterile; make unable to produce offspring, esp. by removal or obstruction of reproductive organs. **sterilization** *n.*, **sterilizer** *n.*

sterling *n.* British money. —*a.* genuine, of standard purity; excellent, of solid worth.

stern[1] *a.* (**-er, -est**) strict and severe, not kindly or cheerful. **sternly** *adv.*, **sternness** *n.*

stern[2] *n.* rear of a ship or aircraft.

sternum *n.* breastbone.

steroid /'stɪər-/ *n.* any of a group of organic compounds that includes certain hormones.

stertorous /'stɜ:-/ *a.* making a snoring or rasping sound. **stertorously** *adv.*

stet *v.imper.* let it stand as written or printed.

stethoscope *n.* instrument for listening to sounds within the body, e.g. breathing and heartbeats.

stetson *n.* hat with a wide brim and high crown.

stevedore /-vd-/ *n.* man employed in loading and unloading ships.

stew *v.t./i.* cook by simmering in a closed vessel; (*colloq.*) swelter; (*sl.*) study hard. —*n.* dish (esp. of meat) made by stewing; (*colloq.*) state of great anxiety. **stewed** *a.* (of tea) strong and bitter from infusing too long.

steward *n.* person employed to manage an estate or great house etc.; passengers' attendant and waiter on a ship, aircraft, or train; official at a race meeting or show etc. **stewardess** *n.* female steward on a ship etc.

stick[1] *n.* short relatively slender piece of wood; thing shaped like this; walking-stick; implement used to propel the ball in hockey, polo, etc.; punishment by caning or beating; criticism.

stick[2] *v.t./i.* (*p.t.* **stuck**) thrust (a thing) into something; stab; (*colloq.*) put; fix or be fixed by glue or suction etc.; jam; (*colloq.*) remain in a specified place, not progress; (*sl.*) endure. **stick at it** (*colloq.*) continue one's efforts. **stick-in-the-mud** *n.* person who will not adopt new ideas etc. **stick out** stand above the surrounding

surface; be conspicuous; (*colloq.*) persist in one's demands. **stick to** remain faithful to; keep to (a subject or position etc.). **stick together** (*colloq.*) remain united or loyal. **stick to one's guns** not yield. **stick up** (*sl.*) rob or threaten with a gun. **stick-up** *n.* (*sl.*) robbery at gunpoint. **stick up for** (*colloq.*) stand up for.

sticker *n.* adhesive label or sign.

sticking-plaster *n.* adhesive fabric for covering small cuts.

stickleback *n.* small fish with sharp spines on its back.

stickler *n.* stickler for one who insists on.

sticky *a.* (**-ier, -iest**) sticking to what is touched; humid; (*colloq.*) making objections; (*sl.*) very unpleasant. **stickily** *adv.*, **stickiness** *n.*

stiff *a.* (**-er, -est**) not bending or moving or flowing easily; difficult; formal in manner; (of wind) blowing briskly; (of a drink etc.) strong; (of a price or penalty) severe. —*n.* (*sl.*) corpse; useless or foolish person. **stiff-necked** *a.* obstinate; haughty. **stiffly** *adv.*, **stiffness** *n.*

stiffen *v.t./i.* make or become stiff. **stiffener** *n.*

stifle *v.t./i.* suffocate; feel or cause to feel unable to breathe; restrain, suppress.

stigma *n.* (*pl.* **-as**) mark of shame; part of a pistil; (*pl.* **stigmata**) mark corresponding to one of those left on Christ's crucified body.

stigmatize *v.t.* brand as something disgraceful. **stigmatization** *n.*

stile *n.* steps or bars for people to climb over a fence.

stiletto *n.* (*pl.* **-os**) dagger with a narrow blade; pointed implement. **stiletto heel** long tapering heel of a shoe.

still[1] *a.* with little or no motion or sound; (of drinks) not fizzy. —*n.* silence and calm; photograph, esp. single one from a cinema film. —*adv.* without moving; then or now as before; nevertheless; in a greater amount or degree. **still birth** birth in which the child is born dead. **still life** painting of things such as cut flowers or fruit. **stillness** *n.*

still[2] *n.* distilling apparatus. **stillroom** *n.* housekeeper's storeroom.

stillborn *a.* born dead.

stilted *a.* stiffly formal.

Stilton *n.* rich blue-veined cheese.

stilts *n.pl.* pair of poles with footrests, enabling the user to walk with feet at a distance above the ground; piles or posts on which a building stands.

stimulant *a.* stimulating. —*n.* stimulating drug or drink.

stimulate *v.t.* make more active; apply a stimulus to. **stimulation** *n.*, **stimulator** *n.*, **stimulative** *a.*

stimulus *n.* (*pl.* -**li**, *pr.* -**lar**) something that rouses a person or thing to activity or energy.

sting *n.* sharp wounding part or organ of an insect or plant etc.; wound made thus; its infliction; sharp bodily or mental pain, wounding effect. —*v.t./i.* (*p.t.* **stung**) wound or affect with a sting; feel or cause sharp pain; stimulate sharply; (*sl.*) overcharge, extort money from.

stingy /-dʒɪ/ *a.* (-**ier**, -**iest**) spending, giving, or given grudgingly or in small amounts. **stingily** *adv.*, **stinginess** *n.*

stink *n.* offensive smell; (*colloq.*) offensive fuss. —*v.t./i.* (*p.t.* & *p.p.* **stank** *or* **stunk**) give off a stink; seem very unpleasant or dishonest. **stink out** fill with or drive out by an offensive smell.

stinker *n.* (*sl.*) very objectionable person or thing; very difficult task; severe letter etc.

stinking *a.* that stinks; (*sl.*) very objectionable. —*adv.* (*sl.*) extremely.

stint *v.t.* restrict to a small allowance. —*n.* limitation of supply or effort; allotted amount of work.

stipend /'staɪ-/ *n.* salary.

stipendiary /staɪ'pen-/ *a.* receiving a stipend.

stipple *v.t.* paint, draw, or engrave in small dots; roughen the surface of. —*n.* this process or effect.

stipulate *v.t./i.* demand or insist (on) as part of an agreement. **stipulation** *n.*

stir *v.t./i.* (*p.t.* **stirred**) move; mix (a substance) by moving a spoon etc. round in it; stimulate, excite. —*n.* act or process of stirring; commotion, excitement.

stirrup *n.* support for a rider's foot, hanging from the saddle. **stirrup-cup** *n.* drink offered to a horseman etc. about to depart. **stirrup-pump** *n.* small portable pump for extinguishing small fires.

stitch *n.* single movement of a thread in and out of fabric etc. in sewing, or of a needle or hook in knitting or crochet; loop made thus; method of making a stitch; least bit of clothing; sudden pain in muscles at the side of the body. —*v.t./i.* sew; join or close with stitches. **in stitches** (*colloq.*) laughing uncontrollably.

stoat *n.* animal of the weasel family, with brown fur that turns mainly white in winter.

stock *n.* amount of something available for use or selling; livestock; lineage; money lent to a government at fixed interest; business company's capital, portion of this held by an investor; person's standing in the opinion of others; liquid made by stewing bones, meat, fish, or vegetables; garden plant with fragrant flowers; growing plant into which a graft is inserted; base, holder, or handle of an implement or machine; cravat worn as part of riding-kit; piece of black or purple fabric worn hanging from a clerical collar; (*pl.*) framework on which a ship rests during construction; (*pl.*) wooden frame with holes for a seated person's legs, used like the pillory. —*a.* stocked and regularly available; commonly used. —*v.t.* keep in stock; provide with a supply.

stock-car *n.* car used in racing where deliberate bumping is allowed. **stock exchange** place where stocks and shares are publicly bought and sold; association of dealers conducting such business. **stock-in-trade** *n.* all the requisites for carrying on a trade or business. **stock market** stock exchange; transactions there. **stock-still** *a.* motionless. **take stock** make an inventory (of stock or resources). **stock-taking** *n.* this process. **stock up** with gather a stock of.

stockade *n.* protective fence.

stockbreeder *n.* farmer who raises livestock. **stockbreeding** *n.*

stockbroker *n.* broker on the Stock Exchange.

stockinet *n.* fine machine-knitted fabric used for underwear etc.

stocking *n.* close-fitting covering for the foot and leg. **stocking-stitch** *n.* alternate rows of plain and purl in knitting.

stockist *n.* firm that stocks certain goods.

stockjobber *n.* jobber.

stockpile *n.* accumulated stock of goods etc. kept in reserve. —*v.t.* accumulate a stockpile of.

stocky *a.* (-ier, -iest) short and solidly built. **stockily** *adv.*, **stockiness** *n.*

stockyard *n.* enclosure for sorting or temporary keeping of cattle etc.

stodge *n.* (*colloq.*) stodgy food.

stodgy *a.* (-ier, -iest) (of food) heavy and filling; dull.

stoep /stu:p/ *n.* (*S. Afr.*) veranda.

stoic /'stəʊɪk/ *n.* stoical person.

stoical /'səɪ-/ *a.* calm and uncomplaining. **stoically** *adv.*, **stoicism** /-sɪz(ə)m/ *n.*

stoke *v.t.* tend and put fuel on (a fire etc.). **stoker** *n.*

stole[1] *n.* clerical vestment, a long strip of fabric hung round the neck; woman's wide scarf-like garment.

stole[2], **stolen** see **steal**.

stolid *a.* not excitable. **stolidly** *adv.*, **stolidity** *n.*

stomach *n.* internal organ in which the first part of digestion occurs; abdomen; appetite. —*v.t.* endure, tolerate. **stomach-ache** *n.* pain in the belly or bowels.

stomp *v.i.* tread heavily.

stone *n.* piece of rock; this shaped or used for a purpose; stones or rock as a substance or material; precious stone; small piece of hard substance formed in the bladder or kidney etc.; hard case round the kernel of certain fruits; grape-seed; (*pl.* **stone**) unit of weight, 14 lb. —*a.* made of stone. —*v.t.* pelt with stones; remove stones from (fruit). **Stone Age** prehistoric period when weapons and tools were made of stone.

stone- *pref.* completely (**stone-cold**).

stonemason *n.* person who cuts and shapes stone or builds in stone.

stonewall *v.i.* bat in cricket without trying to score runs; give noncommittal replies.

stoneware *n.* heavy kind of pottery.

stonework *n.* stone construction.

stony *a.* (-ier, -iest) full of stones; hard, unfeeling; unresponsive. **stony-broke** *a.* (*sl.*) = broke. **stonily** *adv.*

stood see **stand**.

stooge *n.* comedian's assistant; subordinate who does routine work; person who is another's puppet. —*v.i.* (*sl.*) act as a stooge.

stool *n.* movable seat without arms or raised back; footstool;

base of a plant, from which new stems etc. shoot; (pl.) faeces.

stool-pigeon n. decoy, esp. to trap a criminal.

stoop v.t./i. bend forwards and down; condescend; lower oneself morally. —n. stooping posture.

stop v.t./i. (p.t. **stopped**) put an end to movement, progress, or operation (of); (colloq.) stay; keep back; refuse to give or allow; close by plugging or obstructing; fill a cavity in (a tooth); press a string or block a hole in a musical instrument in order to obtain the desired pitch. —n. stopping; place where a train or bus etc. stops regularly; punctuation mark; full stop; thing that stops or prevents motion; row of organ-pipes providing tones of one quality, knob etc. controlling these; key or lever regulating a wind-instrument's pitch; each of the standard sizes of aperture in an adjustable lens. **stop down** reduce the aperture of a lens. **stop press** late news inserted in a newspaper after printing has begun.

stopcock n. valve controlling the flow in a pipe etc.; handle adjusting this.

stopgap n. temporary substitute.

stoppage n. stopping; obstruction.

stopper n. plug for closing a bottle etc. —v.t. close with a stopper.

stopwatch n. watch with mechanism for starting and stopping it at will.

storage n. storing. **storage heater** electric radiator accumulating heat in off-peak periods.

store n. supply of something available for use; large shop; storehouse; device in a computer for storing retrievable information. —v.t. collect and keep for future use; stock with something useful; deposit in a warehouse. **in store** being stored; destined to happen, imminent. **set store by** value greatly.

storehouse n. place where things are stored.

storeroom n. room used for storing things.

storey n. (pl. **-eys**) each horizontal section of a building. **storeyed** a.

stork n. large wading bird.

storm n. disturbance of the atmosphere with strong winds and usu. rain or snow; violent shower (of missiles etc.); great outbreak (of anger or abuse etc.); violent military attack. —v.t./i. rage, be violent; attack or capture by storm. **stormy** a.

story[1] n. account of an incident or series of incidents (true or invented); material for this; (colloq.) lie.

story[2] n. = storey.

stoup /stu:p/ n. stone basin for holy water; (old use) flagon, beaker.

stout a. (**-er, -est**) of considerable thickness or strength; fat; brave and resolute. —n. a kind of strong dark beer. **stoutly** adv., **stoutness** n.

stove[1] n. apparatus containing one or more ovens; closed apparatus used for heating rooms etc. **stove-enamel** n. heatproof enamel.

stove[2] see stave.

stow v.t. place in a receptacle for storage. **stow away** conceal oneself as a stowaway.

stowaway n. person who conceals himself or herself on a ship etc. so as to travel without charge or unseen.

straddle v.t./i. sit or stand (across) with legs wide apart; stand or place (things) in a line across.

strafe /-ɑ:f/ n. & v.t. bombard(ment) with gunfire.

straggle v.i. grow or spread untidily; wander separately; lag behind others. **straggler** n., **straggly** a.

straight a. (**-er, -est**) extending or moving in one direction, not curved or bent; correctly or tidily arranged; in unbroken succession; honest, frank; not modified or elaborate; without additions. —*adv.* in a straight line; direct; without delay; frankly. —*n.* straight part. **go straight** live honestly after being a criminal. **straight away** without delay. **straight face** not smiling. **straight fight** contest between only two candidates. **straight off** (*colloq.*) immediately, without hesitation. **straight out** frankly. **straightness** *n.*

straighten *v.t./i.* make or become straight.

straightforward *a.* honest, frank; without complications. **straightforwardly** *adv.*

strain[1] *n.* lineage; variety or breed of animals etc.; slight or inherited tendency in a character.

strain[2] *v.t./i.* stretch tightly, make taut; injure by excessive stretching or over-exertion; hold in a tight embrace; make an intense effort (with); pass through a sieve or similar device to separate solids from the liquid containing them. —*n.* straining, force exerted thus; injury or exhaustion caused by straining; severe demand on strength or resources; passage from a tune; tone or style of something written or spoken. **strainer** *n.*

strained *a.* (of manner etc.) produced by effort or not by genuine feeling. **strained relations** unpleasant tension between people.

strait *a.* (*old use*) narrow, restricted. —*n.* (also *pl.*) narrow stretch of water connecting two seas; (*pl.*) difficult state of affairs.

strait-jacket *n.* strong jacket-like garment put round a violent person to restrain his arms; (*v.t.*) restrict severely. **strait-laced** *a.* very prim and proper.

straitened *a.* (of conditions) poverty-stricken.

strake *n.* line of planking or metal plates from stem to stern of a boat.

strand[1] *n.* single thread; each of those twisted to form a cable or yarn etc.; lock of hair.

strand[2] *n.* shore. —*v.t./i.* run aground; leave in difficulties.

strange *a.* (**-er**, **-est**) not familiar, not well known; alien; unusual, surprising; fresh, unaccustomed. **strangely** *adv.*, **strangeness** *n.*

stranger *n.* one who is strange to a place or company or experience.

strangle *v.t./i.* kill or be killed by squeezing the throat; restrict the proper growth or operation or utterance of. **strangler** *n.*

stranglehold *n.* strangling grip.

strangulate *v.t.* compress (a vein etc.) so that nothing can pass through.

strangulation *n.* strangling; strangulating.

strap *n.* strip of leather or other flexible material for holding things together or in place, or supporting something. —*v.t.* (*p.t.* **strapped**) secure with strap(s). **strapped for** (*colloq.*) short of.

strapping *a.* tall and healthy-looking. —*n.* straps; sticking-plaster etc. used for binding injuries.

strata *see* **stratum**.

stratagem *n.* cunning method of achieving something; trick.

strategic *a.* of strategy; giving an advantage; (of weapons) very long-range. **strategical** *a.*, **strategically** *adv.*

strategist /ˈstræ-/ *n.* expert in strategy.

strategy *n.* planning and directing of the whole operation of a campaign or war; plan, policy.

strathspey /-ˈspeɪ/ *n.* slow Scottish country dance.

stratify *v.t.* arrange in strata. **stratification** *n.*

stratosphere /'stræ-/ n. layer of the atmosphere about 10–60 km above the earth's surface.

stratum /'strɑː-/ n. (pl. **strata**) one of a series of layers or levels.

straw n. dry cut stalks of grain used as material for bedding, fodder, etc.; single piece of this; narrow straw-like tube for sucking up liquid in drinking. **straw poll** unofficial poll as a test of general feeling.

strawberry n. soft juicy edible red fruit with yellow seeds on the surface. **strawberry mark** red birthmark.

stray v.i. leave one's group or proper place aimlessly; wander; deviate from a direct course or subject. —a. having strayed; isolated. —n. stray person, thing, or domestic animal.

streak n. thin line or band of a colour or substance different from its surroundings; element, trait; spell, series. —v.t./i. mark with streaks; move very rapidly; (colloq.) run naked in a public place. **streaker** n., **streaky** a.

stream n. body of water flowing in its bed; flow of liquid or things or people; current or direction of this; (in certain schools) section into which children of the same level of ability are placed. —v.t./i. flow or move as a stream; emit a stream of, run with liquid; float or wave at full length; arrange (schoolchildren) in streams. **on stream** in active operation or production.

streamer n. long narrow flag; strip of ribbon or paper etc. attached at one or both ends.

streamline v.t. give a smooth even shape that offers least resistance to movement through water or air; make more efficient by simplifying, removing superfluities, etc.

street n. public road in a town or village, with houses on one or both sides. **street credibility** familiarity with a fashionable urban subculture.

streetcar n. (US) tram.

strength n. quality of being strong; its intensity; person's or thing's strong point; number of people present or available, full number. **on the strength of** relying on as a basis or support.

strengthen v.t./i. make or become stronger.

strenuous a. making or requiring great effort. **strenuously** adv., **strenuousness** n.

streptococcus /-'kɒk-/ n. (pl. **-ci**) bacterium causing serious infections.

streptomycin n. antibiotic drug.

stress n. emphasis; extra force used on a sound in speech or music; pressure, tension, strain. —v.t. lay stress on.

stretch v.t./i. pull out tightly or into a greater extent; be able or tend to become stretched; be continuous; thrust out one's limbs and tighten the muscles; make demands on the abilities of; strain, exaggerate. —n. stretching; ability to be stretched; continuous expanse or period. —a. able to be stretched. **at a stretch** continuously. **stretch a point** agree to something not normally allowed. **stretchy** a.

stretcher n. framework for carrying a sick or injured person in a lying position; device for stretching or bracing things.

strew v.t. (p.t. **strewed**, p.p. **strewn** or **strewed**) scatter over a surface; cover with scattered things.

striation /straɪˈeɪʃ(ə)n/ n. each of a series of ridges or furrows or linear marks. **striated** a.

stricken a. affected with or overcome by an illness, shock, or grief.

strict a. (-er, -est) precisely limited or defined; without exception or deviation; requiring or giving complete obedience or exactitude. **strictly** *adv.*, **strictness** *n.*

stricture *n.* severe criticism; abnormal constriction.

stride *v.t./i.* (*p.t.* **strode**, *p.p.* **stridden**) walk with long steps; stand astride. —*n.* single long step; manner of striding; progress.

strident /'straɪ-/ *a.* loud and harsh. **stridently** *adv.*, **stridency** *n.*

strife *n.* quarrelling, conflict.

strike *v.t./i.* (*p.t.* **struck**) bring or come into sudden hard contact with; inflict (a blow), knock; attack suddenly; afflict; produce by striking or pressing something; ignite (a match) by friction; agree on (a bargain); indicate (the hour) or be indicated by a sound; reach (gold or mineral oil etc.) by digging or drilling; occur to the mind of, produce a mental impression on; lower or take down (a flag or tent etc.); stop work in protest; proceed in a certain direction; arrive at (an average or balance); assume (an attitude) dramatically. —*n.* act or instance of striking; attack; workers' refusal to work as a protest. **on strike** (of workers) striking. **strike home** deal an effective blow. **strike off** *or* **out** cross out. **strike up** begin playing or singing; start (a friendship etc.) casually.

strikebound *a.* immobilized by a workers' strike.

striker *n.* person or thing that strikes; worker who is on strike; football player whose main function is to try to score goals.

striking *a.* sure to be noticed, attractive and impressive. **strikingly** *adv.*

string *n.* narrow cord; piece of this or similar material used to fasten or pull something; stretched piece of catgut or wire etc. in a musical instrument, vibrated to produce tones; set of objects strung together; series;

(*pl.*) conditions insisted upon; (*pl.*) stringed instruments, (*sing. attrib.*) of or for these. —*v.t./i.* (*p.t.* **strung**) fit or fasten with string(s); thread on a string; trim tough fibre from (beans). **pull strings** use one's influence. **string along** (*colloq.*) deceive; go along (with). **string-course** *n.* projecting line of bricks etc. round a building. **string out** spread out in a line. **string up** hang up on strings; kill by hanging.

stringed *a.* (of musical instruments) having strings that are played by touch or with a bow or plectrum.

stringent /-ndʒ-/ *a.* strict, with firm restrictions. **stringently** *adv.*, **stringency** *n.*

stringy *a.* like string; fibrous.

strip[1] *v.t./i.* (*p.t.* **stripped**) remove (clothes, coverings, or parts etc.); pull or tear away (from); undress; deprive, e.g. of property or titles. **strip club** club where striptease performances are given. **stripper** *n.*

strip[2] *n.* long narrow piece or area. **comic strip** *or* **strip cartoon** sequence of cartoons. **strip light** tubular fluorescent lamp.

stripe *n.* long narrow band on a surface, differing in colour or texture from its surroundings; chevron on a sleeve, indicating rank. **striped** *a.*, **stripy** *a.*

stripling *n.* a youth.

striptease *n.* entertainment in which a performer gradually undresses.

strive *v.i.* (*p.t.* **strove**, *p.p.* **striven**) make great efforts; carry on a conflict.

strobe *n.* (*colloq.*) stroboscope.

stroboscope *n.* apparatus for producing a rapidly flashing bright light. **stroboscopic** *a.*

strode *see* **stride**.

stroke[1] *n.* act of striking something; single movement or action or effort; particular sequence of movements (e.g. in swimming); oarsman nearest the stern of a racing-boat; mark made by a movement of a pen or paintbrush etc.; sound made by a clock striking; attack of apoplexy or paralysis. —*v.t.* act as stroke to (a boat or crew).

stroke[2] *v.t.* pass the hand gently along the surface of. —*n.* act of stroking.

stroll *v.i. & n.* walk in a leisurely way. **stroller** *n.*

strong *a.* (**-er, -est**) capable of exerting or resisting great power; powerful through numbers, resources, or quality; concentrated; containing much alcohol; having a considerable effect; having a specified number of members; (of verbs) changing the vowel in the past tense (e.g. *strike/struck*). —*adv.* strongly. **strong-box** *n.* strongly made box for storing valuables. **strong language** forcible language, oaths or swearing. **strongminded** *a.* determined. **strong point** *n.* thing at which person excels; specially fortified position. **strongly** *adv.*

stronghold *n.* fortified place; centre of support for a cause.

strongroom *n.* room for storage and protection of valuables.

strontium *n.* silver-white metallic element. **strontium 90** its radioactive isotope.

strop *n.* device (esp. a strip of leather) for sharpening razors. —*v.t.* (*p.t.* **stropped**) sharpen on or with a strop.

stroppy *a.* (*sl.*) bad-tempered, awkward to deal with.

strove *see* **strive.**

struck *see* **strike.** —*a.* **struck on** (*colloq.*) impressed with, liking.

structuralism *n.* theory that structure rather than function is important. **structuralist** *n.*

structure *n.* way a thing is constructed or organized; thing's

supporting framework or essential parts; constructed thing, complex whole. **structural** *a.*, **structurally** *adv.*

strudel /'stru:-/ *n.* confection of thin pastry filled esp. with apple.

struggle *v.i.* move in a vigorous effort to get free; make one's way or a living etc. with difficulty; make a vigorous effort. —*n.* spell of struggling; vigorous effort; hard contest.

strum *v.t./i.* (*p.t.* **strummed**) play unskilfully or monotonously on (a musical instrument). —*n.* sound made by strumming.

strumpet *n.* (*old use*) prostitute.

strung *see* **string.** —*a.* **strung up** mentally tense or excited.

strut *n.* bar of wood or metal supporting something; strutting walk. —*v.i.* (*p.t.* **strutted**) walk in a pompous self-satisfied way.

strychnine /'strıkni:n/ *n.* bitter highly poisonous substance.

stub *n.* short stump; counterfoil of a cheque or receipt etc. —*v.t.* (*p.t.* **stubbed**) strike (one's toe) against a hard object; extinguish (a cigarette) by pressure.

stubble *n.* lower ends of cornstalks left in the ground after harvest; short stiff growth of hair or beard, esp. growing after shaving. **stubbly** *a.*

stubborn *a.* obstinate; not easy to deal with. **stubbornly** *adv.*, **stubbornness** *n.*

stubby *a.* (**-ier, -iest**) short and thick. **stubbiness** *n.*

stucco *n.* plaster or cement used for coating walls or moulding into decorations. **stuccoed** *a.*

stuck *see* **stick**[2]. —*a.* unable to move; (of an animal) that has been stabbed or had its throat cut. **stuck-up** *a.* (*colloq.*) conceited; snobbish.

stud[1] *n.* projecting nail-head or similar knob on a surface; device like a button on a shank used e.g. to fasten a detachable shirt-collar. —*v.t.* (*p.t.* **studded**) decorate with studs or precious stones; strengthen with studs.

stud[2] n. horses kept for breeding; establishment keeping these.

student n. person engaged in studying something, esp. at a college or university.

studied a. deliberate and artificial.

studio n. (pl. -os) work-room of a painter, photographer, etc.; room or premises where cinema films are made; room from which broadcasts are transmitted or where recordings are made. **studio couch** divan-like couch convertible into a bed. **studio flat** one-room flat with a kitchen and bathroom.

studious a. spending much time in study; involving study; deliberate and careful. **studiously** adv., **studiousness** n.

study n. process of studying; its subject; work presenting the results of studying a subject; musical composition designed to develop a player's skill; preliminary drawing; room used for work that involves studying. —v.t./i. give one's attention to acquiring knowledge of (a subject); examine attentively; give care and consideration to.

stuff n. material; (sl.) unnamed things, belongings, subjects, etc.; trash. —v.t./i. fill or pack tightly; fill with padding or stuffing; eat greedily.

stuffing n. padding used to fill something; savoury mixture put inside poultry, rolled meat, etc., before cooking.

stuffy a. (-ier, -iest) lacking fresh air or ventilation; dull; (colloq.) old-fashioned, prim, narrow-minded; (colloq.) showing annoyance. **stuffily** adv., **stuffiness** n.

stultify v.t. impair, make ineffective. **stultification** n.

stumble v.i. strike one's foot on something and lose one's balance; walk with frequent stumbles; make mistakes in speaking or playing music etc. —n. act of stumbling. **stumble across** or **on** discover accidentally. **stumbling-block** n. obstacle, thing causing difficulty.

stump n. base of a tree left in the ground when the rest has gone; similar remnant of something cut or broken or worn down; one of the three uprights of a wicket in cricket. —v.t./i. walk stiffly or noisily; put out (a batsman) by dislodging the bails; (colloq.) baffle. **stump up** (sl.) produce or pay over (money required).

stumpy a. (-ier, -iest) short and thick. **stumpiness** n.

stun v.t. (p.t. **stunned**) knock senseless; daze by the impact of emotion.

stung see **sting**.

stunk see **stink**.

stunner n. (colloq.) stunning person or thing.

stunning a. (colloq.) very attractive. **stunningly** adv.

stunt[1] v.t. hinder the growth or development of.

stunt[2] n. (colloq.) something unusual or difficult done as a performance or to attract attention.

stupefy v.t. dull the wits or senses of; stun with astonishment. **stupefaction** n.

stupendous a. amazing; exceedingly great. **stupendously** adv.

stupid a. not clever; slow at learning or understanding; in a state of stupor. **stupidly** adv., **stupidity** n.

stupor n. dazed almost unconscious condition.

sturdy a. (-ier, -iest) strongly built, hardy, vigorous. **sturdily** adv., **sturdiness** n.

sturgeon n. (pl. **sturgeon**) large shark-like fish yielding caviare.

stutter v.t./i. & n. stammer, esp. repeating consonants.

sty[1] n. pigsty.

sty[2] n. inflamed swelling on the edge of the eyelid.

style n. manner of writing, speaking, or doing something; shape, design; elegance; narrow extension of a plant's ovary. —v.t. design, shape, or arrange, esp. fashionably. **in style** elegantly, luxuriously.

stylish a. fashionable, elegant. **stylishly** adv., **stylishness** n.

stylist n. person who has or aims at a good style; person who styles things.

stylistic a. of literary or artistic style. **stylistically** adv.

stylized a. made to conform to a conventional style. **stylization** n.

stylus n. (pl. **-uses** or **-li**) needle-like device for cutting or following a groove in a record.

stymie /ˈstaɪmɪ/ v.t. (pres.p. **stymieing**) thwart.

styptic a. checking bleeding by causing blood-vessels to contract.

suasion n. persuasion.

suave /swɑːv/ a. smooth-mannered. **suavely** adv., **suavity** n.

sub n. (colloq.) submarine; subscription; substitute.

sub- pref. under; subordinate.

subaltern /ˈsʌb-/ n. army officer below the rank of captain.

subaqua a. (of sport etc.) taking place under water.

subatomic a. smaller than an atom; occurring in an atom.

subcommittee n. committee formed for a special purpose from some members of a main committee.

subconscious a. & n. (of) our own mental activities of which we are not aware. **subconsciously** adv.

subcontinent n. large land-mass forming part of a continent.

subcontract v.t./i. give or accept a contract to carry out all or part

of another contract. **subcontractor** n.

subculture n. culture within a larger one.

subcutaneous /-ˈteɪ-/ a. under the skin.

subdivide v.t. divide into smaller parts after a first division. **subdivision** n.

subdue v.t. overcome, bring under control; make quieter or less intense.

sub-edit v.t. act as assistant editor of; prepare material for printing. **sub-editor** n., **sub-editorial** a.

subheading n. subordinate heading.

subhuman a. less than human; not fully human.

subject[1] /ˈsʌb-/ a. not politically independent. —n. person subject to a particular political rule or ruler; person or thing being discussed, represented, or studied; word(s) in a sentence that name who or what does the action or undergoes what is stated by the verb; theme or chief phrase in a sonata etc. **subject-matter** n. matter treated in a book or speech etc. **subject to** owing obedience to; liable to; depending upon as a condition.

subject[2] /-ˈdʒekt/ v.t. bring (a country) under one's control; cause to undergo. **subjection** n.

subjective a. existing in a person's mind and not produced by things outside it; dependent on personal taste or views etc. **subjectively** adv.

subjoin v.t. add at the end.

sub judice /ˈdʒuːdɪsɪ/ under judicial consideration, not yet decided.

subjugate v.t. bring (a country) into subjection. **subjugation** n.

subjunctive a. & n. (of) the form of a verb used in expressing what is imagined, wished, or possible.

sublet v.t. (p.t. **sublet**, pres.p. **subletting**) let (rooms etc. that one holds by lease) to a tenant.

sublimate /'sʌb-/ *v.t.* divert the energy of (an emotion or impulse) into a culturally higher activity. **sublimation** *n.*

sublime *a.* most exalted; most extreme or impressive. **sublimely** *adv.*, **sublimity** *n.*

subliminal *a.* below the level of conscious awareness.

sub-machine-gun *n.* lightweight machine-gun held in the hand.

submarine *a.* under the surface of the sea. —*n.* vessel that can operate under water.

submerge *v.t./i.* put or go below the surface of water or other liquid; flood. **submergence** *n.*, **submersion** *n.*

submersible *a.* able to submerge. —*n.* submersible craft.

submicroscopic *a.* too small to be seen by an ordinary microscope.

submission *n.* submitting; theory or statement etc. submitted; being submissive, obedience.

submissive *a.* submitting to authority. **submissively** *adv.*, **submissiveness** *n.*

submit *v.t./i.* (*p.t.* **submitted**) yield to another's authority or control, surrender; subject to a process; present for consideration or decision.

subnormal *a.* below normal level.

subordinate[1] /-nət/ *a.* of lesser importance or rank; working under another's control or authority. —*n.* subordinate person.

subordinate[2] /-neɪt/ *v.t.* make subordinate; treat as of lesser importance. **subordination** *n.*

suborn *v.t.* induce by bribery to commit perjury or other unlawful act. **subornation** *n.*

subpoena /səb'pi:nə/ *n.* writ commanding a person to appear in a lawcourt. —*v.t.* (*p.t.* **subpoenaed**) summon with a subpoena.

subscribe *v.t./i.* pay (a subscription); sign. **subscribe to a**

theory etc., express agreement.

subscriber *n.*

subscription *n.* sum of money contributed; fee for membership etc.; process of subscribing.

subsection *n.* division of a section.

subsequent *a.* coming after in time or order. **subsequently** *adv.*

subservient *a.* subordinate; servile. **subserviently** *adv.*, **subservience** *n.*

subset *n.* secondary part of a set; (in mathematics) a set having all its elements contained in another set.

subside *v.i.* sink, esp. to a lower or normal level; become less intense. **subsidence** *n.*

subsidiary *a.* of secondary importance; (of a business company) controlled by another. —*n.* subsidiary thing.

subsidize *v.t.* pay a subsidy to or for. **subsidization** *n.*

subsidy *n.* money contributed to an industry or other cause needing help, or to keep prices at a desired level.

subsist *v.i.* exist; continue to exist; keep oneself alive. **subsistence** *n.*

subsoil *n.* soil lying immediately below the surface layer.

subsonic *a.* of or flying at speeds less than that of sound.

subspecies *n.* group within a species.

substance *n.* matter with more or less uniform properties; particular kind of this; essence of something spoken or written; reality, solidity.

substandard *a.* below the desired standard.

substantial *a.* of solid material or structure; of considerable amount or intensity or validity; possessing much property or wealth; in essentials. **substantially** *adv.*

substantiate *v.t.* support with evidence, prove. **substantiation** *n.*

substantive[1] /-'stæn-/ *a.* (of military rank) permanent.

substantive[2] /'sʌb-/ *n.* noun. **substantival** /-'taɪ-/ *a.*

substitute *n.* person or thing that acts or serves in place of another. —*v.t./i.* put or use or (*colloq.*) serve as a substitute. **substitution** *n.*

substratum *n.* (*pl.* **-ta**) underlying stratum; basis.

subsume *v.t.* bring or include under a particular classification.

subtenant *n.* person to whom a room etc. is sublet. **subtenancy** *n.*

subterfuge *n.* trick used to avoid blame or defeat etc.

subterranean *a.* underground.

subtitle *n.* subordinate title; caption on a cinema film. —*v.t.* provide with subtitle(s).

subtle /'sʌt(ə)l/ *a.* (**-er**, **-est**) slight and difficult to detect or identify; making fine distinctions; ingenious. **subtly** *adv.*, **subtlety** /'sʌtltɪ/ *n.*

subtopia *n.* unsightly suburbs.

subtotal *n.* total of part of a group of figures.

subtract *v.t.* remove (a part or quantity or number) from a greater one. **subtraction** *n.*

subtropical *a.* of regions bordering on the tropics.

suburb *n.* residential district lying outside the central part of a town. **suburban** *a.*, **suburbanite** *n.*

suburbia *n.* suburbs and their inhabitants.

subvention *n.* subsidy.

subvert *v.t.* overthrow the authority of, esp. by weakening people's trust. **subversion** *n.*, **subversive** *a.*

subway *n.* underground passage; (*US*) underground railway.

succeed *v.t./i.* be successful; come next to; take the place previously filled by, come by inheritance or in due order.

success *n.* favourable outcome; attainment of what was desired or attempted, or of wealth, fame, or position; successful person or thing.

successful *a.* having success. **successfully** *adv.*

succession *n.* following in order; series of people or things following each other; succeeding to a throne or other position. **in succession** one after another.

successive *a.* following in succession. **successively** *adv.*

successor *n.* person who succeeds another.

succinct /sək'sɪŋkt/ *a.* concise and clear. **succinctly** *adv.*

succour /'sʌk-/ *n.* & *n.* help.

succulent *a.* juicy; (of plants) having thick fleshy leaves or stems. —*n.* succulent plant. **succulence** *n.*

succumb *v.i.* give way to something overpowering.

such *a.* of the same or that kind or degree; so great or intense. —*pron.* that. **such-and-such** *a.* particular but not now specified.

suchlike *a.* (*colloq.*) of the same kind.

suck *v.t.* draw (liquid or air etc.) into the mouth; draw liquid from; squeeze in the mouth by using the tongue; draw in. —*n.* act or process of sucking. **suck up to** (*colloq.*) toady to.

sucker *n.* organ or device that can adhere to a surface by suction; shoot coming up from a tree's or shrub's root or underground stem; (*sl.*) person who is easily deceived.

sucking *a.* not yet weaned.

suckle *v.t./i.* feed at the breast.

suckling *n.* unweaned child or animal.

sucrose /'su:-/ *n.* sugar from cane or beet etc.

suction *n.* sucking; production of a partial vacuum so that external atmospheric pressure forces fluid etc. into the vacant space or causes adhesion.

sudden a. happening or done quickly or without warning. **all of a sudden** suddenly. **suddenly** adv., **suddenness** n.

sudorific a. & n. (drug etc.) causing sweating.

suds n.pl. soapsuds.

sue v.t./i. (pres.p. **suing**) take legal proceedings against; make an application.

suede /sweɪd/ n. leather with the flesh side rubbed into a velvety nap.

suet n. hard white fat from round an animal's kidneys, used in cooking. **suety** a.

suffer v.t./i. feel, undergo, or be subjected to (pain, loss, damage, etc.); permit; tolerate. **suffering** n.

sufferance n. **on sufferance** tolerated but only grudgingly.

suffice /ə-'fʌs/ v.t. be enough (for).

sufficient a. enough. **sufficiently** adv., **sufficiency** n.

suffix n. (pl. -ixes) letter(s) added at the end of a word to make another word.

suffocate v.t./i. kill by stopping the breathing; cause discomfort to by making breathing difficult; be suffocated. **suffocation** n.

suffragan /-gən/ n. **suffragan bishop** bishop consecrated to help another with administration; bishop in relation to an archbishop.

suffrage n. right to vote in political elections.

suffragette n. woman who (in the early 20th century) agitated for women's suffrage.

suffuse v.t. spread throughout or over. **suffusion** n.

sugar n. sweet crystalline substance obtained from the juices of various plants. **sugar beet** beet from which sugar is obtained. **sugar cane** tall tropical plant from which sugar is obtained. **sugar-daddy** n. (sl.) elderly man who lavishes gifts on a young woman. **sugar soap** abrasive compound for cleaning paint. **sugary** a.

suggest v.t. cause (an idea etc.) to be present in the mind; propose for acceptance or rejection.

suggestible a. easily influenced by people's suggestions. **suggestibility** n.

suggestion n. suggesting; thing suggested; slight trace.

suggestive a. conveying a suggestion; suggesting something indecent. **suggestively** adv.

suicidal /-'saɪ-/ a. of or involving suicide; liable to commit suicide. **suicidally** adv.

suicide n. intentional killing of oneself; person who commits suicide; act destructive to one's own interests. **commit suicide** kill oneself intentionally.

suit n. set of clothing, esp. jacket and trousers or skirt; any of the four sets (spades, hearts, diamonds, clubs) into which a pack of cards is divided; lawsuit. —v.t. meet the demands or needs of; make or be suitable or convenient for; give a pleasing appearance upon.

suitable a. right for the purpose or occasion. **suitably** adv., **suitability** n.

suitcase n. rectangular case for carrying clothes.

suite n. set of rooms or furniture; retinue; set of musical pieces.

suitor n. man who is courting a woman.

sulk v.i. be sullen because of resentment or bad temper. **sulks** n.pl. fit of sulking. **sulky** a., **sulkily** adv., **sulkiness** n.

sullen a. gloomy and unresponsive because of resentment or bad temper; dark and dismal. **sullenly** adv., **sullenness** n.

sully v.t. stain, blemish.

sulphate n. salt of sulphuric acid.

sulphide n. compound of sulphur and an element or radical.

sulphite n. salt of sulphurous acid.

sulphonamide /-'fon-/ n. a kind of antibiotic drug.

sulphur n. pale yellow non-metallic element. **sulphurous** /'sʌlfvər-/ a.

sulphuric acid strong corrosive acid.

sultan n. ruler of certain Muslim countries.

sultana n. seedless raisin; sultan's wife, mother, or daughter.

sultanate /'sʌl-/ n. sultan's territory.

sultry a. (-ier, -iest) hot and humid; (of a woman) passionate and sensual. **sultriness** n.

sum n. total; amount of money; problem in arithmetic. —v.t. (p.t. **summed**) find the sum of. **sum total** total. **sum up** give the total of; summarize; form an opinion of.

sumac /'su:-/ n. shrub whose leaves are used in tanning and dyeing; these leaves.

summarize v.t. make or be a summary of. **summarization** n.

summary n. statement giving the main points of something. —a. brief, giving the main points only; without delay; without attention to details or formalities. **summarily** adv.

summation n. adding up; summarizing.

summer n. warmest season of the year. **summer-house** n. light building in a garden or park, providing shade in summer. **summer-time** n. summer. **summer time** time shown by clocks put forward in summer to give longer light evenings. **summery** a.

summit n. highest point; top of a mountain; (also **summit conference** etc.) conference between heads of States.

summon v.t. send for (a person); order to appear in a lawcourt; gather together (one's courage etc.); call upon to do something.

summons n. command summoning a person; written order to appear in a lawcourt. —v.t. serve with a summons.

sumo n. (pl. -os) style of Japanese wrestling; wrestler in this.

sump n. reservoir of oil in a petrol engine; hole or low area into which liquid drains.

sumptuary a. regulating expenditure.

sumptuous a. splendid and costly-looking. **sumptuously** adv., **sumptuousness** n.

sun n. heavenly body round which the earth travels; light or warmth from this; any fixed star. —v.t. (p.t. **sunned**) expose to the sun. **sun-lamp** n. lamp giving ultraviolet rays for tanning or therapy.

sunbathe v.i. expose one's body to the sun. **sunbather** n.

sunbeam n. ray of sun.

sunburn n. tanning or inflammation caused by the sun. —v.i. suffer sunburn. **sunburnt** a.

sundae /-dei/ n. dish of ice cream and fruit, nuts, syrup, etc.

Sunday n. first day of the week. **Sunday school** school for religious instruction of children, held on Sundays.

sunder v.t. break or tear apart.

sundew n. bog-plant with hairs secreting moisture that traps insects.

sundial n. device that shows the time by means of a shadow on a scaled dial.

sundown n. sunset.

sundry /-drɪ/ a. various. **all and sundry** everyone. **sundries** n.pl. various small items.

sunflower n. tall garden plant bearing large yellow flowers.

sung see **sing**.

sunk see **sink**.

sunken *adj.* lying below the level of the surrounding surface.

sunken fence ditch strengthened by a wall, forming a boundary.

sunlight *n.* light from the sun.

Sunni *n.* & *a.* (*pl.* same or -**is**) (member) of one of two main branches of Islam. **Sunnite** *a.*

sunny *a.* (-**ier**, -**iest**) full of sunshine; cheerful. **sunnily** *adv.*

sunrise *n.* rising of the sun.

sunset *n.* setting of the sun; sky full of colour at sunset.

sunshade *n.* parasol; awning.

sunshine *n.* direct sunlight.

sunspot *n.* dark patch observed on the sun's surface; (*colloq.*) place with a sunny climate.

sunstroke *n.* illness caused by too much exposure to sun.

sup *v.t./i.* (*p.t.* **supped**) take (liquid) by sips or spoonfuls; eat supper. —*n.* mouthful of liquid.

super *a.* (*sl.*) excellent, superb.

superannuate *v.t.* discharge into retirement with a pension. **superannuation** *n.*

superb *a.* of the most impressive or splendid kind. **superbly** *adv.*

supercharge *v.t.* increase the power of (an engine) by a device that forces extra air or fuel into it. **supercharger** *n.*

supercilious /-'sɪl-/ *a.* haughty and superior. **superciliously** *adv.*, **superciliousness** *n.*

supererogation *n.* doing of more than is required by duty.

superficial *a.* of or on the surface, not deep or penetrating. **superficially** *adv.*, **superficiality** *n.*

superfluous *a.* more than is required. **superfluously** *adv.*, **superfluity** /-'fluː-/ *n.*

superhuman *a.* beyond ordinary human capacity or power; higher than humanity, divine.

superimpose *v.t.* place on top of something else. **superimposition** *n.*

superintend *v.t.* supervise. **superintendence** *n.*

superintendent *n.* supervisor; police officer next above inspector.

superior *a.* higher in position or rank; better, greater; showing that one feels wiser or better etc. than others. —*n.* person or thing of higher rank or ability or quality; head of a monastery etc. **superiority** *n.*

superlative *a.* of the highest degree or quality; of the grammatical form expressing 'most'. —*n.* superlative form. **superlatively** *adv.*

superman *n.* (*pl.* -**men**) man of superhuman powers.

supermarket *n.* large self-service shop.

supernatural *a.* of or involving a power above the forces of nature. **supernaturally** *adv.*

supernova *n.* (*pl.* -**ae**) star that suddenly increases very greatly in brightness.

supernumerary *a.* & *n.* extra.

superphosphate *n.* fertilizer containing phosphates.

superpower *n.* extremely powerful nation.

superscribe *v.t.* write at the top or on the outside of a document etc.

superscript *a.* written just above and to the right of a word or figure or symbol.

superscription *n.* word(s) written at the top or on the outside.

supersede *v.t.* take the place of; put or use in place of. **supersession** *n.*

supersonic *a.* of or flying at speeds greater than that of sound. **supersonically** *adv.*

superstition *n.* belief in magical and similar influences; idea or practice based on this; widely held but wrong idea. **superstitious** *a.*, **superstitiously** *adv.*

superstore *n.* supermarket.

superstructure *n.* structure that rests on something else.

supertanker *n.* very large tanker.

supervene *v.i.* occur as an interruption or a change. **supervention** *n.*

supervise *v.t.* direct and inspect. **supervision** *n.*, **supervisor** *n.*, **supervisory** /'suː-/ *a.*

supine /'suːpaɪn/ *a.* lying face upwards; indolent. **supinely** *adv.*

supper *n.* evening meal, last meal of the day.

supplant *v.t.* oust and take the place of. **supplanter** *n.*

supple *a.* bending easily. **supply** *adv.*, **suppleness** *n.*

supplement *n.* thing added as an extra part or to make up for a deficiency. —*v.t.* provide or be a supplement to. **supplementary** *a.* serving as a supplement.

suppliant /'sʌplɪ-/ *n. & a.* (person) asking humbly for something.

supplicate *v.t.* ask humbly for; beseech. **supplication** *n.*

supply *v.t.* give or provide with, make available; satisfy (a need). —*n.* supplying; stock, amount provided or available.

support *v.t.* keep from falling, sinking, or failing; bear the weight of; strengthen; supply with necessaries; help, encourage; endure, tolerate. —*n.* act of supporting; person or thing that supports. **supporter** *n.*, **supportive** *a.*

suppose *v.t.* be inclined to think; assume or accept to be true; consider as a proposal; presuppose. **be supposed to** be expected to; have as a duty.

supposedly /-zɪd-/ *adv.* according to supposition.

supposition *n.* process of supposing; what is supposed.

suppositious /-'zɪʃəs/ *a.* hypothetical.

supposititious *a.* substituted for the real thing; spurious.

suppository /-'pɒz-/ *n.* solid piece of medicinal substance placed in the rectum, vagina, or urethra and left to melt.

suppress *v.t.* put an end to the activity or existence of; keep from being known. **suppression** *n.*, **suppressor** *n.*

suppurate /-pjʊər-/ *v.i.* form pus, fester. **suppuration** *n.*

supra- *pref.* above, over.

supreme *a.* highest in authority, rank, importance, or quality. **supremely** *adv.*, **supremacy** /-'prem-/ *n.*

supremo *n.* (*pl.* **-os**) supreme leader.

surcharge *n.* additional charge; extra or excessive load. —*v.t.* make a surcharge on or to; overload.

surd *n.* mathematical quantity (esp. a root) that cannot be expressed in finite terms of whole numbers or quantities.

sure *a.* (**-er**, **-est**) having firm reasons for belief, convinced; reliable, unfailing. —*adv.* (US *colloq.*) certainly. **make sure** act so as to be certain; feel confident (perhaps mistakenly). **sure-footed** *a.* never slipping or stumbling. **sureness** *n.*

surely *adv.* in a sure manner; (used for emphasis) that must be right; (as an answer) certainly.

surety /'ʃʊətɪ/ *n.* guarantee; guarantor of a person's promise.

surf *n.* white foam of waves. **surf-riding** *or* **surfing** *ns.* sport of riding on a surfboard.

surface *n.* outside or outward appearance of something; any side of an object; uppermost area, top. —*a.* of or on the surface. —*v.t./i.* put a specified surface on; come or bring to the surface; (*colloq.*) wake. **surface mail** mail carried by sea not by air.

surfboard *n.* narrow board for riding over surf.

surfeit /'sɜːfɪt/ *n.* too much, esp. of food or drink. —*v.t.* cause to take too much of something; satiate, cloy.

surge *v.i.* move forward in or like waves; increase in volume or intensity. —*n.* wave(s); surging movement or increase.

surgeon *n.* doctor qualified to perform surgical operations.

surgery *n.* treatment by cutting or manipulation of affected parts of the body; place where or times when a doctor or dentist or an MP etc. is available for consultation. **surgical** *a.*, **surgically** *adv.*

surly *a.* (**-ier, -iest**) bad-tempered and unfriendly. **surliness** *n.*

surmise /-'maɪz/ *v.t./i. & n.* conjecture.

surmount *v.t.* overcome (a difficulty); get over (an obstacle); be on the top of. **surmountable** *a.*

surname *n.* name held by all members of a family. —*v.t.* give as a surname.

surpass *v.t.* outdo; excel.

surplice *n.* loose white vestment worn over a cassock.

surplus *n.* amount left over after what is needed has been used; excess of revenue over expenditure.

surprise *n.* emotion aroused by something sudden or unexpected; thing causing this; process of catching a person etc. unprepared. —*v.t.* cause to feel surprise; come upon or attack unexpectedly; startle thus.

surrealism *n.* style of art and literature seeking to express what is in the subconscious mind. **surrealist** *n.*, **surrealistic** *a.*

surrender *v.t./i.* hand over, give into another's power or control, esp. under compulsion; give oneself up. —*n.* surrendering.

surreptitious *a.* acting or done stealthily. **surreptitiously** *adv.*

surrogate /'sʌrəgeit/ *n.* deputy. **surrogate mother** woman who bears a child on behalf of another. **surrogacy** *n.*

surround *v.t.* come, lie, or be a round; place all round, encircle —*n.* border, edging.

surroundings *n.pl.* things or co ditions around a person or place

surveillance /-'veɪl-/ *n.* super vision; close watch.

survey[1] /-'veɪ/ *v.t.* look at and tak a general view of; make or pre sent a general examination of (subject); examine the condition of (a building); measure and map out.

survey[2] /'sɜː-/ *n.* general look at or examination of something; re port or map produced by survey ing.

surveyor *n.* person whose job is to survey land or buildings.

survival *n.* surviving; thing that has survived from an earlier time.

survive *v.t./i.* continue to live or exist; remain alive or in existence after. **survivable** *a.*, **survivabili ity** *n.*, **survivor** *n.*

susceptible /-'sep/ *a.* easily affec ted; falling in love easily. **sus ceptible of** able to undergo (proof etc.). **susceptible to** liable to be affected by. **susceptibility** *n.*

susceptive /-'sep/ *a.* susceptible.

sushi *n.* Japanese dish of fla voured garnished balls of cold rice.

suspect[1] /-'spekt/ *v.t.* have an impression of the existence or presence of; mistrust; feel to be guilty but have little or no proof.

suspect[2] /'sʌs-/ *n.* person sus pected of a crime etc. —*a.* suspected, open to suspicion.

suspend *v.t.* hang up; keep from falling or sinking in air or liquid; postpone; stop temporarily; de prive temporarily of a position or right.

suspender *n.* attachment to hold up a sock or stocking by its top.

suspense *n.* anxious uncertainty while awaiting an event etc.

suspension *n.* suspending; means by which a vehicle is supported on its axles. **suspension bridge** bridge suspended from cables that pass over supports at each end.

suspicion *n.* suspecting; partial or unconfirmed belief; slight trace.

suspicious *a.* feeling or causing suspicion. **suspiciously** *adv.*

suss *v.t.* (*sl.*) suspect of a crime. —*n.* (*sl.*) suspect; suspicion. **suss out** (*sl.*) investigate.

sustain *v.t.* support; keep alive; keep (a sound or effort) going continuously; undergo; endure without giving way; uphold the validity of.

sustenance *n.* process of sustaining life by food; food, nourishment.

suture /'su:-/ *n.* surgical stitching of a wound; stitch or thread used in this. —*v.t.* stitch (a wound).

suzerain /'su:zərem/ *n.* country or ruler with some authority over a self-governing country; overlord. **suzerainty** *n.*

svelte *a.* slender and graceful.

SW *abbr.* south-west; south-western.

swab /swɒb/ *n.* mop or pad for cleansing, drying, or absorbing things; specimen of a secretion taken with this. —*v.t.* (*p.t.* **swabbed**) cleanse or wipe with a swab.

swaddle /'swɒ-/ *v.t.* swathe in wraps or warm garments.

swag *n.* loot; carved festoon; (*Austr.*) bundle of belongings carried by a tramp etc. **swagman** *n.*

swagger *v.i.* walk or behave with aggressive pride. —*n.* this gait or manner. —*a.* (*colloq.*) smart, fashionable.

Swahili /-'hi:lɪ/ *n.* Bantu language widely used in East Africa.

swain *n.* (*old use*) country youth; (*poetical*) suitor.

swallow¹ *v.t./i.* cause or allow to go down one's throat; work

throat-muscles in doing this; take in and engulf or absorb; accept. —*n.* act of swallowing; amount swallowed.

swallow² *n.* small migratory bird with a forked tail. **swallow-dive** *n.* dive with arms outspread at the start.

swam *see* **swim.**

swamp *n.* marsh. —*v.t.* flood, drench or submerge in water; overwhelm with a mass or number of things. **swampy** *a.*

swan *n.* large usu. white waterbird with a long slender neck.

swank *n.* (*colloq.*) boastful person or behaviour; ostentation. —*v.i.* (*colloq.*) behave with swank.

swansdown *n.* swan's fine soft down, used for trimmings.

swansong *n.* person's last performance or achievement etc.

swap *v.t./i.* (*p.t.* **swapped**) & *n.* (*colloq.*) exchange.

sward *n.* expanse of short grass.

swarm¹ *n.* large cluster of people, insects (esp. bees), etc. —*v.i.* cluster, move in a swarm; be crowded or overrun.

swarm² *v.i.* **swarm up** climb by gripping with arms and legs.

swarthy /'swɔːðɪ/ *a.* (-**ier**, -**iest**) having a dark complexion. **swarthiness** *n.*

swashbuckling *a.* & *n.* swaggering boldly. **swashbuckler** *n.*

swastika /'swɒs-/ *n.* symbol formed by a cross with ends bent at right angles.

swat *v.t.* (*p.t.* **swatted**) hit hard with something flat. **swatter** *n.*

swatch /swɒtʃ/ *n.* sample(s) of cloth etc.

swath /-ɔːθ/ *n.* (*pl.* **swaths**, *pr.* -ɔːðz) strip cut in one sweep or passage by a scythe or mowing-machine; line of wheat etc. cut thus.

swathe /-eɪð/ *v.t.* wrap with layers of coverings.

sway *v.t./i.* swing gently, lean to and fro; influence the opinions of;

waver in one's opinion. —*n.* swaying movement; influence.

swear *v.t./i.* (*p.t.* **swore,** *p.p.* **sworn**) state or promise on oath; state emphatically; cause to take an oath; use curses or profane language. **swear by** appeal to as a guarantee of an oath; (*colloq.*) have great confidence in. **swear to** (*colloq.*) say that one is certain of. **swear-word** *n.* profane or indecent word used in anger etc.

sweat *n.* moisture given off by the body through the pores; state of sweating, or (*colloq.*) of great anxiety; (*colloq.*) laborious task; moisture forming in drops on a surface. —*v.t./i.* exude sweat or as sweat; be in a state of great anxiety; work long and hard. **sweat-band** *n.* band of absorbent material worn to absorb or wipe away sweat. **sweated labour** labour of workers with poor pay and conditions. **sweaty** *a.*

sweater *n.* jumper, pullover.

sweatshirt *n.* cotton sweater with sleeves.

sweatshop *n.* place employing sweated labour.

Swede *n.* native of Sweden.

swede *n.* large yellow variety of turnip.

Swedish *a. &. n.* (language) of Sweden.

sweep *v.t./i.* (*p.t.* **swept**) clear away with or as if with a broom or brush; clean or clear (a surface) thus; move or remove by pushing; go smoothly and swiftly or majestically; extend in a continuous line or slope; pass lightly or quickly over or along etc.; make (a bow or curtsy) smoothly. —*n.* sweeping movement or line or slope; act of sweeping; chimney-sweep; sweepstake. **sweep the board** win all the prizes. **sweeper** *n.*

sweeping *a.* of great scope, comprehensive; making no exceptions.

sweepstake *n.* form of gambling in which the money staked is divided among those who have drawn numbered tickets for the winners; race etc. with such betting.

sweet *a.* (**-er, -est**) tasting as of containing sugar, not bitter or savoury; fragrant; melodious; fresh, not stale; pleasant; beloved; (*colloq.*) charming. —*n.* small shaped piece of sweet substance; sweet dish forming one course of a meal; beloved person. **sweet-brier** *n.* small wild rose. **sweet pea** climbing plant with fragrant flowers. **sweet tooth** liking for sweet things. **sweetly** *adv.,* **sweetness** *n.*

sweetbread *n.* animal's thymus gland or pancreas used as food.

sweeten *v.t./i.* make or become sweet or sweeter. **sweetener** *n.*

sweetheart *n.* either of a pair of people in love with each other.

sweetmeal *a.* of sweetened wholemeal.

sweetmeat *n.* sweet; very small fancy cake.

swell *v.t./i.* (*p.t.* **swelled,** *p.p.* **swollen** *or* **swelled**) make or become larger from pressure within; curve outwards; make or become greater in amount or intensity. —*n.* act or state of swelling; heaving of the sea; gradual increase in loudness; (*colloq.*) person of high social position. —*a.* (*colloq.*) smart, excellent. **swelled head** (*sl.*) conceit.

swelling *n.* swollen place on the body.

swelter *v.i.* be uncomfortably hot.

swept *see* **sweep.**

swerve *v.t./i.* turn aside from a straight course. —*n.* swerving movement or direction.

swift *a.* (**-er, -est**) quick, rapid. —*n.* swiftly flying bird with narrow wings. **swiftly** *adv.,* **swiftness** *n.*

swig *v.t./i.* (*p.t.* **swigged**) & *n.* (*colloq.*) drink, swallow.

swill *v.t./i.* pour water over or through; wash, rinse; (of water) pour; drink greedily. —*n.* rinse; sloppy food fed to pigs.

swim *v.t./i.* (*p.t.* **swam**, *p.p.* **swum**) travel through water by movements of the body; cross by swimming; float; be covered with liquid; seem to be whirling or waving; be dizzy. —*n.* act or period of swimming. **in the swim** active in or knowing what is going on. **swimming-bath**, **swimming-pool** *ns.* artificial pool for swimming in. **swimmer** *n.*

swimmingly *adv.* with easy un-obstructed progress.

swimsuit *n.* garment worn for swimming.

swindle *v.t.* cheat in a business transaction; obtain by fraud. —*n.* piece of swindling; fraudulent person or thing. **swindler** *n.*

swine *n.pl.* pigs. —*n.* (*pl.* **swine**) (*colloq.*) hated person or thing.

swineherd *n.* (*old use*) person taking care of a number of pigs.

swing *v.t./i.* (*p.t.* **swung**) move to and fro while hanging or supported; hang by its end(s); turn in a curve; walk or run or lift etc. with an easy rhythmical movement; change from one mood or opinion to another; influence decisively; (*sl.*) be executed by hanging; play (music) with a swing rhythm. —*n.* act, movement, or extent of swinging; seat slung by ropes or chains for swinging in; jazz with the time of the melody varied. **in full swing** with activity at its greatest. **swing bridge** bridge that can be swung aside for ships to pass. **swing the lead** (see **lead**[2]). **swing-wing** *a.* aircraft wing that can be moved to slant backwards. **swinger** *n.*

swingeing /-ndʒɪŋ/ *a.* forcible; huge in amount or scope.

swinish *a.* beastly.

swipe *v.t./i.* (*colloq.*) hit with a swinging blow; snatch, steal. —*n.* (*colloq.*) swinging blow.

swirl *v.t./i.* & *n.* whirl, flow with a whirling movement.

swish *v.t./i.* move or strike with a hissing sound. —*n.* swishing sound. —*a.* (*colloq.*) smart, fashionable.

Swiss *a.* & *n.* (native) of Switzerland. **Swiss roll** thin flat sponge cake spread with jam etc. and rolled up.

switch *n.* device operated to turn electric current on or off; (*pl.*) railway points; flexible stick or rod, whip; tress of hair tied at one end; shift in opinion or method etc. —*v.t./i.* turn (on or off) by means of a switch; transfer, divert; change; whip with a switch; swing round quickly; snatch suddenly.

switchback *n.* railway used for amusement at a fair etc., with alternate steep ascents and descents; road with similar slopes.

switchboard *n.* panel of switches for making telephone connections or operating electric circuits.

swivel *n.* link or pivot enabling one part to revolve without turning another. —*v.t./i.* (*p.t.* **swivelled**) turn on or as if on a swivel.

swizzle *n.* (*colloq.*) frothy mixed alcoholic drink; (*sl.*) swindle, disappointment. **swizzle-stick** *n.* stick for stirring a drink.

swollen see **swell**.

swoon *v.i.* & *n.* faint.

swoop *v.i.* make a sudden downward rush, attack suddenly. —*n.* swooping movement or attack.

swop *v.t./i.* (*p.t.* **swopped**) & *n.* = **swap**.

sword *n.* weapon with a long blade and a hilt. **swordsman** *n.* (*pl.* **-men**).

swordfish *n.* sea fish with a long sword-like upper jaw.

swore see **swear**.

sworn *see* **swear.** —*a.* open and
determined in devotion or en-
mity.

swot *v.t./i.* (*p.t.* **swotted**) (*school
sl.*) study hard. —*n.* (*school sl.*)
hard study; person who studies
hard.

swum *see* **swim.**

swung *see* **swing.**

sybarite /'sɪbərаɪt/ *n.* person who
is excessively fond of comfort
and luxury. **sybaritic** /-'rɪt-/ *a.*

sycamore *n.* large tree of the
maple family.

sycophant /'sɪk-/ *n.* person who
tries to win favour by flattery.
sycophantic *a.*, **sycophantically** *adv.*

syllabary *n.* set of written
characters representing syllables.

syllable *n.* unit of sound in a
word. **syllabic** *a.*, **syllabically**
adv.

syllabub *n.* dish of whipped
cream flavoured with wine.

syllabus *n.* (*pl.* **-buses**) statement
of the subjects to be covered by
a course of study.

syllogism *n.* form of reasoning in
which a conclusion is reached
from two statements. **syllogistic**
a.

sylph *n.* slender girl or woman.

symbiosis *n.* (*pl.* **-oses**) relationship of different organisms living
in close association. **symbiotic** *a.*

symbol *n.* thing regarded as suggesting something; mark or sign
with a special meaning.

symbolic, symbolical *adjs.* of,
using, or used as a symbol.
symbolically *adv.*

symbolism *n.* use of symbols to
express things. **symbolist** *n.*

symbolize *v.t./i.* be a symbol of;
represent by means of a symbol.

symmetry *n.* state of having
parts that correspond in size,
shape, and position on either
side of a dividing line or round
a centre. **symmetrical** *a.*,
symmetrically *adv.*

sympathetic *a.* feeling or showing or resulting from sympathy;
likeable. **sympathetically** *adv.*

sympathize *v.i.* feel or express
sympathy. **sympathizer** *n.*

sympathy *n.* sharing or ability to
share another's emotions or sensations; pity or tenderness towards a sufferer; liking for each
other. **be in sympathy with** feel
approval of (an opinion or
desire).

symphony *n.* long elaborate
musical composition for a full
orchestra. **symphonic** *a.*

symposium *n.* (*pl.* **-ia**) meeting
for discussing a particular subject.

symptom *n.* sign of the existence
of a condition.

symptomatic *a.* serving as a
symptom.

synagogue /'sɪnəgɒg/ *n.* building
for public Jewish worship.

synchromesh *n.* device that
makes parts of a gear revolve at
the same speed while becoming
engaged.

synchronize *v.t./i.* occur, exist,
or operate at the same time;
cause to do this; cause (clocks
etc.) to show the same time.
synchronization *n.*

synchronous *a.* occurring, existing, or operating at the same
time.

syncopate *v.t.* change the beats or
accents in (music). **syncopation**
n.

syncope /'sɪŋkəpɪ/ *n.* faint, fainting.

syndicate[1] /-kət/ *n.* association of
people or firms to carry out a
business undertaking.

syndicate[2] /-keɪt/ *v.t./i.* combine
into a syndicate; publish through
an agency that supplies material
to many newspapers etc. simultaneously. **syndication** *n.*

syndrome *n.* combination of
signs, symptoms, behaviour, etc.
characteristic of a specified condition.

synod /'sɪn-/ n. council of senior clergy or church officials.

synonym n. word or phrase meaning the same as another in the same language.

synonymous /-'nɒn-/ a. equivalent in meaning.

synopsis n. (pl. **-opses**) summary, brief general survey.

syntax n. way words are arranged to form phrases and sentences. **syntactic** a., **syntactically** adv.

synthesis n. (pl. **-theses**) combining; artificial production of a substance that occurs naturally.

synthesize v.t. make by synthesis.

synthesizer n. electronic musical instrument able to produce a great variety of sounds.

synthetic a. made by synthesis, manufactured; artificial. —n. synthetic substance or fabric. **synthetically** adv.

syphilis n. a venereal disease. **syphilitic** a.

syringa /sɪ'rɪŋɡə/ n. shrub with scented flowers.

syringe /sɪ'rɪndʒ/ n. device for drawing in liquid and forcing it out in a fine stream. —v.t. wash out or spray with a syringe.

syrup n. thick sweet liquid; water sweetened with sugar. **syrupy** a.

system n. set of connected things that form a whole or work together; animal body as a whole; set of rules or practices used together; method of classification or notation or measurement; orderliness. **systems analysis** analysis of an operation in order to decide how a computer may perform it. **systems analyst** expert in this.

systematic a. methodical; according to a plan, not casually or at random. **systematically** adv.

systematize v.t. arrange according to a system. **systematization** n.

systemic /-'tem-/ a. of the body as a whole; (of a fungicide etc.) entering a plant's tissues.

systole /'sɪstəlɪ/ n. rhythmic contraction of chambers of the heart. **systolic** /-'tɒl/ a.

T

tab n. small projecting flap or strip. **keep a tab** or **tabs on** (colloq.) keep under observation. **pick up the tab** (US colloq.) be the one who pays the bill.

tabard /'tæ-/ n. short sleeveless tunic-like garment.

tabby n. cat with grey or brown fur and dark stripes.

tabernacle n. (in the Bible) portable shrine used by the Jews in the wilderness; (RC Church) receptacle for the Eucharist; Nonconformist or Mormon meeting-place for worship.

tabla n. pair of small Indian drums played with the hands.

table n. piece of furniture with a flat top supported on one or more legs; food provided at table; list of facts or figures arranged systematically, esp. in columns, (pl.) those showing the products of numbers taken in pairs. —v.t. submit (a motion or report) for discussion. **at table** while taking a meal at the table. **table tennis** game played with bats and a light hollow ball on a table.

tableau /'tæbləʊ/ n. (pl. **-eaux**, pr. -əʊz) silent motionless group arranged to represent a scene; dramatic or picturesque scene.

tablecloth n. cloth for covering a table esp. at meals.

table d'hôte /tɑː'bl 'dəʊt/ (of a meal) served at a fixed inclusive price.

tableland n. plateau of land.

tablespoon n. large spoon for serving food; amount held by this. **tablespoonful** n. (pl. **-fuls**).

tablet n. slab bearing an inscription etc.; small flat piece of a solid substance; measured amount of a drug compressed into a solid form.

tabloid n. newspaper with pages half the size of larger ones.

taboo n. ban or prohibition made by religion or social custom. —a. prohibited by a taboo.

tabor /'tei-/ n. small drum.

tabular a. arranged in a table or list.

tabulate v.t. arrange in tabular form. **tabulation** n.

tabulator n. device on a typewriter for advancing to a series of set positions in tabular work.

tachograph /'tæk-/ n. device in a motor vehicle to record speed and travel-time.

tacit /'tæs-/ a. implied or understood without being put into words. **tacitly** a.

taciturn /'tæs-/ a. saying very little. **taciturnity** n.

tack[1] n. small broad-headed nail; long temporary stitch; sailing ship's oblique course; course of action or policy. —v.t./i. nail with tack(s); stitch with tacks; add as an extra thing; sail a zigzag course.

tack[2] n. harness, saddles, etc.

tackle n. set of ropes and pulleys for lifting weights or working sails; equipment for a task or sport; act of tackling in football etc. —v.t. try to deal with or overcome (an opponent or problem etc.); intercept (an opponent who has the ball in football etc.). **tackler** n.

tacky a. (of paint etc.) sticky, not quite dry. **tackiness** n.

tact n. skill in avoiding offence or in winning goodwill. **tactful** a., **tactfully** adv.

tactic n. piece of tactics.

tactical a. of tactics; planning or planned skilfully; (of weapons) for use in a battle or at close quarters. **tactically** adv.

tactician n. expert in tactics.

tactics n. art of placing or manœuvring forces skilfully in a battle. —n.pl. manœuvring; procedure adopted to achieve something.

tactile a. of or using the sense of touch. **tactility** n.

tactless a. lacking in tact. **tactlessly** adv., **tactlessness** n.

tadpole n. larva of a frog or toad etc. at the stage when it has gills and a tail.

taffeta n. shiny silk-like fabric.

taffrail n. rail round a vessel's stern.

tag[1] n. metal or plastic point on a shoelace etc.; label; ragged end or projection; much-used phrase or quotation; (sl.) nickname. —v.t./i. (p.t. tagged) label; attach, add.

tag[2] n. children's chasing-game.

tail[1] n. animal's hindmost part, esp. when extending beyond its body; rear or hanging or inferior part; (sl.) person tailing another; (pl.) tailcoat; **tails** reverse of a coin, turned upwards after being tossed. —v.t./i. remove the stalks of; (sl.) follow closely, shadow. **tail away** = tail off. **tail-end** n. hindmost or very last part. **taillight** n. light at the back of a motor vehicle or train etc. **tail off** become fewer or smaller or slighter; end inconclusively.

tail[2] n. limitation of ownership, esp. to a person and his heirs. —a. so limited.

tailback n. long queue of traffic extending back from an obstruction.

tailboard n. hinged or removable back of a lorry etc.

tailcoat n. man's coat with the skirt tapering and divided at the back.

tailgate n. rear door in a motor vehicle.

tailless a. having no tail.

tailor n. maker of men's clothes, esp. to order. —v.t. make (clothes) as a tailor; make in a simple well-fitted design; make

or adapt for a special purpose.
tailor-made *a.*, **tailoress** *n.fem.*

tailpiece *n.* final part; decoration at the end of a book or chapter.

tailplane *n.* horizontal part of an aeroplane's tail.

tailspin *n.* aircraft's spinning dive.

taint *n.* trace of decay or infection or other bad quality. —*v.t.* affect with a taint.

take *v.t./i.* (*p.t.* **took**, *p.p.* **taken**) lay hold of; get possession of, capture; be successful or effective; make use of; indulge in; occupy (a position), esp. as one's right; obtain; buy regularly; require; cause to come or go with one; carry, remove; be affected by, catch (fire); experience or exert (a feeling or effort); find out and record; accept, endure; perform, deal with; study or teach (a subject); make a photograph (of). —*n.* amount taken or caught; instance of photographing a scene for a cinema film. **be taken by** *or* **with** find attractive. **be taken ill** become ill. **take after** resemble (a parent etc.). **take-away** *n. & a.* (cooked meal) bought at a restaurant etc. for eating elsewhere; (place) selling this. **take back** withdraw (a statement). **take in** include; make (a garment etc.) smaller; understand; deceive, cheat. **take life** kill. **take off** take (clothing etc.) from the body; mimic humorously; leave the ground and become airborne. **take-off** *n.* humorous mimicry; process of becoming airborne. **take on** acquire; undertake; engage (an employee); accept as an opponent; (*colloq.*) show great emotion. **take oneself off** depart. **take one's time** not hurry. **take out** remove; murder, destroy. **take over** take control of. (**take-over** *n.*) **take part** share in an activity. **take place** occur. **take sides** support one side or another. **take to** adopt as a habit

or custom; go to as a refuge; develop a liking or ability for. **take up** take as a hobby or business or protégé; occupy (time or space); begin (residence etc.); resume; interrupt or question (a speaker); accept (an offer). **take up with** begin to associate with. **taker** *n.*

taking *a.* attractive, captivating.

takings *n.pl.* money taken in business.

talc *n.* a kind of smooth mineral; talcum powder.

talcum *n.* talc. **talcum powder** talc powdered and usu. perfumed for use on the skin.

tale *n.* narrative, story; report spread by gossip.

talent *n.* special or very great ability; ancient unit of money.

talented *a.* having talent.

talisman *n.* (*pl.* **-mans**) object supposed to bring good luck. **talismanic** *a.*

talk *v.t./i.* convey or exchange ideas by spoken words; express in words; use (a specified language) in talking; affect or influence by talking. —*n.* talking, conversation; style of speech; informal lecture; rumour. **talk over** discuss. **talker** *n.*

talkative *a.* talking very much.

tall *a.* (**-er**, **-est**) of great or specified height; **tall order** difficult task. **tall story** (*colloq.*) one that is hard to believe. **tallness** *n.*

tallboy *n.* tall chest of drawers.

tallow *n.* animal fat used to make candles, lubricants, etc.

tally *n.* total of a debt or score. —*v.i.* correspond.

tally-ho *int.* huntsman's cry on sighting the fox.

Talmud *n.* body of Jewish law and tradition. **Talmudic** *a.*

talon *n.* bird's large claw.

tamarind *n.* tropical tree; its acid fruit.

tamarisk *n.* evergreen shrub with feathery branches.

tambour n. drum; circular frame for holding embroidery taut in working.

tambourine n. percussion instrument with jingling metal discs.

tame a. (-er, -est) (of animals) gentle and not afraid of human beings; docile; not exciting. —v.t. make tame or manageable. **tamely** adv., **tameness** n.

tamer n. person who tames and trains wild animals.

Tamil n. member or language of a people of south India and Sri Lanka.

tam-o'-shanter n. beret with a soft full top.

tamp v.t. pack down tightly.

tamper v.i. tamper with meddle or interfere with.

tampon n. plug of absorbent material inserted into the body.

tan v.t./i. (p.t. tanned) convert (hide) into leather by treating it with tannin or mineral salts; make or become brown by exposure to sun; (sl.) thrash. —n. yellowish-brown; brown colour in sun-tanned skin; tree-bark used in tanning hides. —a. yellowish-brown.

tandem n. bicycle with seats and pedals for two or more people one behind another. —adv. one behind another. **in tandem** arranged thus.

tandoor n. Indian etc. clay oven.

tandoori n. food cooked in a tandoor.

tang n. strong taste or flavour or smell; projection by which a knife-blade etc. is held in its handle. **tangy** a.

tangent n. straight line that touches the outside of a curve without intersecting it. **go off at a tangent** diverge suddenly from a line of thought etc. **tangential** a.

tangerine /-'ri:n/ n. a kind of small orange; its colour.

tangible a. able to be perceived by touch; clear and definite, real. **tangibly** adv., **tangibility** n.

tangle v.t./i. twist into a confused mass; entangle; become involved in conflict with. —n. tangled mass or condition.

tangly a. tangled.

tango n. (pl. -os) ballroom dance with gliding steps. —v.i. dance a tango.

tank n. large container for liquid or gas; armoured fighting vehicle moving on Caterpillar tracks.

tankard n. large one-handled usu. metal drinking-vessel.

tanker n. ship or aircraft or vehicle for carrying liquid in bulk.

tanner n. person who tans hides into leather.

tannery n. place where hides are tanned into leather.

tannic acid tannin.

tannin n. substance obtained from tree-barks etc. (also found in tea), used in tanning and dyeing.

tansy n. plant with yellow flowers.

tantalize v.t. torment by the sight of something desired but kept out of reach or withheld. **tantalization** n.

tantalus n. stand in which decanters of spirits are visible but locked up.

tantamount a. equivalent.

tantra n. any of a class of Hindu or Buddhist mystical or magical writings.

tantrum n. outburst of bad temper.

tap[1] n. tubular plug with a device for allowing liquid to flow through; connection for tapping a telephone. —v.t. (p.t. tapped) fit a tap into; draw off through a tap or incision; obtain supplies etc. or information from; cut a screw-thread in (a cavity); fit a listening device in (a telephone circuit). **on tap** ready to be drawn off by tap; (*colloq.*) available for use. **tap-root** *n.* plant's chief root.

tap[2] *v.t./i.* (*p.t.* **tapped**) knock gently. —*n.* light blow; sound of this. **tap-dance** *n.* dance in which the feet tap an elaborate rhythm.

tape *n.* narrow strip of woven cotton etc. for tying or fastening or labelling things; pieces of this stretched across a race-track at the finishing-line; narrow continuous strip of paper etc.; magnetic tape; tape-measure; tape recording. —*v.t.* tie or fasten with tape; record on magnetic tape. **have a thing taped** (*sl.*) understand it fully, have an organized method of dealing with it. **tape measure** *n.* strip of tape or flexible metal etc. marked for measuring length. **tape recorder** *n.* apparatus for recording and reproducing sounds or data on magnetic tape. **tape recording** *n.*

taper *n.* thin candle; wax-coated wick for conveying flame. —*v.t./i.* make or become gradually narrower. **taper off** diminish.

tapestry *n.* textile fabric woven or embroidered ornamentally.

tapeworm *n.* tape-like worm living as a parasite in intestines.

tapioca *n.* starchy grains obtained from cassava, used in making puddings.

tapir /'teɪpə(r)/ *n.* small pig-like animal with a long snout.

tappet *n.* projection used in machinery to tap against something.

taproom *n.* room where alcoholic drinks are available on tap.

tar *n.* thick dark inflammable liquid distilled from wood or coal etc.; similar substance formed by burning tobacco. —*v.t.* (*p.t.* **tarred**) coat with tar.

taradiddle *n.* (*colloq.*) petty lie; piece of nonsense.

tarantella *n.* rapid whirling dance.

tarantula /-'ræn-/ *n.* large black south European spider; large hairy tropical spider.

tarboosh *n.* cap like a fez.

tardy *a.* (-ier, -iest) slow to act or move or happen; behind time. **tardily** *adv.*, **tardiness** *n.*

tare[1] /teə(r)/ *n.* a kind of vetch.

tare[2] /teə(r)/ *n.* allowance for the weight of the container or vehicle weighed with the goods it holds.

target *n.* object or mark to be hit in shooting etc.; person or thing against which criticism is directed; objective, minimum result desired. —*v.t.* (*p.t.* **targeted**) aim at (as) a target.

tariff *n.* list of fixed charges; duty to be paid.

tarlatan *n.* stiff muslin.

Tarmac *n.* [P.] broken stone or slag mixed with tar. **tarmac** *n.* area surfaced with this. **tarmacked** *a.*

tarn *n.* small mountain lake.

tarnish *v.t./i.* lose or cause (metal) to lose lustre; blemish (a reputation). —*n.* loss of lustre; blemish.

tarot /'tærəʊ/ *n.* game played with a pack of 78 cards which are also used for fortune-telling.

tarpaulin *n.* waterproof canvas.

tarragon *n.* aromatic herb.

tarry[1] /'tɑːr-/ *a.* of or like tar.

tarry[2] /'tæ-/ *v.i.* (*old use*) delay.

tarsier *n.* small monkey-like animal of the East Indies.

tarsus *n.* (*pl.* **-si**) set of small bones forming the ankle.

tart[1] *a.* (-er, -est) acid in taste or manner. **tartly** *adv.*, **tartness** *n.*

tart[2] *n.* pie with fruit or sweet filling; piece of pastry with jam etc. on top; (*sl.*) prostitute. —*v.t.* **tart up** (*colloq.*) dress gaudily, smarten up.

tartan *n.* pattern (orig. of a Scottish clan) with coloured stripes crossing at right angles; cloth with this.

Tartar *n.* member of a group of Central Asian peoples; bad-tempered or difficult person.

tartar *n.* hard deposit forming on teeth; deposit formed by fermentation in a wine-cask.

tartare sauce sauce of mayonnaise, chopped gherkins, etc.

tartlet *n.* small tart.

task *n.* piece of work to be done. —*v.t.* make great demands upon (a person's powers); assign a task to. **to task** rebuke. **task force** group organized for a special task.

taskmaster *n.* person considered with regard to the way he imposes tasks.

tassel *n.* ornamental bunch of hanging threads; tassel-like head of maize etc. **tasselled** *a.*

taste *n.* sensation caused in the tongue by things placed upon it; ability to perceive this; small quantity (of food or drink); slight experience; liking; ability to perceive and enjoy what is beautiful or to know what is fitting. —*v.t./i.* discover or test the flavour of in one's mouth; have a certain flavour; experience. **taster** *n.*

tasteful *a.* showing good taste. **tastefully** *adv.*, **tastefulness** *n.*

tasteless *a.* having no flavour; showing poor taste. **tastelessly** *adv.*, **tastelessness** *n.*

tasty *a.* (**-ier, -iest**) having a strong flavour, appetizing.

tat[1] *v.t./i.* (*p.t.* **tatted**) do or make by tatting.

tat[2] *n.* (*colloq.*) tatty thing(s), person, or state.

tat[3] *see* **tit**[2].

tattered *a.* ragged.

tatters *n.pl.* torn pieces.

tatting *n.* a kind of lace made by hand with a small shuttle; process of making this.

tattle *v.i.* chatter idly, reveal information thus. —*n.* idle chatter.

tattoo[1] *n.* drum or bugle signal recalling soldiers to quarters in the evening; elaboration of this with music and marching, as an entertainment; tapping sound.

tattoo[2] *v.t.* mark (skin) by puncturing it and inserting pigments; make (a pattern) thus. —*n.* tattooed pattern.

tatty *a.* (**-ier, -iest**) (*colloq.*) ragged, shabby and untidy; tawdry. **tattily** *adv.*, **tattiness** *n.*

taught *see* **teach.**

taunt *v.t.* jeer at provocatively. —*n.* taunting remark.

taut *a.* stretched firmly, not slack.

tauten *v.t./i.* make or become taut.

tautology *n.* pleonasm, esp. using a word or phrase of the same grammatical function (e.g. *free, gratis, and for nothing*). **tautological** *a.*, **tautologous** *a.*

tavern *n.* (*old use*) inn, public house.

tawdry *a.* (**-ier, -iest**) showy but without real value. **tawdrily** *adv.*, **tawdriness** *n.*

tawny *a.* orange-brown.

tax *n.* money to be paid by people or firms to a government; thing that makes a heavy demand. —*v.t.* impose a tax on; require to pay tax; make heavy demands on; pay tax on. **tax-deductible** *a.* (of expenses) that may be deducted from income etc. before this is assessed for tax. **tax with** accuse of. **taxation** *n.*, **taxable** *a.*

taxi *n.* (*pl.* **-is**) car that plies for hire. —*v.i.* (*p.t.* **taxied**, *pres.p.* **taxiing**) (of an aircraft) move along ground or water under its own power. **taxi-cab** *n.* taxi.

taxidermy /'tæks-/ *n.* process of preparing, stuffing, and mounting the skins of animals in lifelike form. **taxidermist** *n.*

taxonomy *n.* scientific classification of organisms. **taxonomical** *a.*, **taxonomist** *n.*

taxpayer *n.* person who pays tax (esp. income tax).

TB *abbr.* (*colloq.*) tuberculosis.

tea *n.* dried leaves of a tropical evergreen shrub; hot drink made by infusing these (or other substances) in boiling water: afternoon or early evening meal at which tea is drunk. **tea bag** small porous bag holding a portion of tea for infusion. **tea break** interruption of work allowed for drinking tea. **tea chest** wooden box in which tea is exported. **tea cloth** cloth for a tea-table; tea towel. **tea-leaf** *n.* leaf of tea, esp. after infusion. **tea rose** rose with scent like tea. **tea towel** towel for drying washed crockery etc.

teacake *n.* bun for serving toasted and buttered.

teach *v.t./i.* (*p.t.* **taught**) impart information or skill to (a person) or about (a subject); put forward as a fact or principle; (*colloq.*) deter by punishment. **teachable** *a.*, **teacher** *n.*

teacup *n.* cup from which tea is drunk.

teak *n.* strong heavy wood of an Asian evergreen tree; this tree.

teal *n.* (*pl.* **teal**) a kind of duck.

team *n.* set of players; set of people working together; animals harnessed to draw a vehicle etc. —*v.t./i.* combine into a team or set.

teamwork *n.* organized cooperation.

teapot *n.* vessel with a spout, in which tea is made.

tear[1] /teə(r)/ *v.t./i.* (*p.t.* **tore**, *p.p.* **torn**) pull forcibly apart or away or to pieces; make (a hole etc.) thus; become torn: run, walk, or travel hurriedly. *n.* hole etc. torn.

tear[2] /tɪə(r)/ *n.* drop of liquid forming in the eye from grief or other emotion or irritation by fumes etc. **in tears** with tears flowing. **tear-gas** *n.* gas causing severe irritation of the eyes.

tearaway *n.* impetuous hooligan.

tearful *a.* shedding or ready to shed tears. **tearfully** *adv.*

tearing *a.* violent, overwhelming.

tease *v.t.* try to provoke in a playful or unkind way; pick into separate strands; brush up nap on (cloth). —*n.* person fond of teasing others.

teasel *n.* plant with bristly heads; device for brushing nap.

teaser *n.* (*colloq.*) difficult problem.

teaset *n.* set of cups and plates etc. for serving tea.

teashop *n.* shop where tea is served to the public.

teaspoon *n.* small spoon for stirring tea etc.; amount held by this. **teaspoonful** *n.* (*pl.* **-fuls**).

teat *n.* nipple on a milk-secreting organ; device of rubber etc. on a feeding-bottle, through which the contents are sucked.

tech *n.* (*colloq.*) technical college.

technical *a.* of the mechanical arts and applied sciences; of a particular subject or craft etc.; using technical terms; in a strict legal sense. **technically** *adv.*, **technicality** *n.*

technician *n.* expert in the techniques of a subject or craft; skilled mechanic.

technique /ˈtɛkniːk/ *n.* method of doing or performing something.

technocracy *n.* government or control by technical experts. **technocrat** *n.*

technology *n.* study of mechanical arts and applied sciences; these subjects; their application in industry etc. **technological** *a.*, **technologically** *adv.*, **technologist** *n.*

teddy *n.* teddy bear; garment resembling camiknickers.

teddy bear toy bear.

tedious /ˈtiːdɪəs/ *a.* tiresome because of length, slowness, or dullness. **tediously** *adv.*, **tediousness** *n.*, **tedium** *n.*

tee *n.* cleared space from which a golf ball is driven at the start of play; small heap of sand or piece of wood for supporting this ball; mark aimed at in quoits, bowls, and curling. —*v.t.* (*p.t.* **teed**) place (a ball) on a tee. **tee off** make the first stroke in golf.

teem[1] *v.i.* be full of; be present in large numbers.

teem[2] *v.i.* (of water or rain) pour.

teenager *n.* person in his or her teens.

teens *n.pl.* years of age from 13 to 19. **teenage** *a.,* **teenaged** *a.*

teeny *a.* (**-ier, -iest**) (*colloq.*) tiny.

tee-shirt *n.* = T-shirt.

teeter *v.i.* stand or move unsteadily.

teeth *see* **tooth.**

teethe *v.i.* (of a baby) have its first teeth appear through the gums. **teething troubles** problems in the early stages of an enterprise.

teetotal *a.* abstaining completely from alcohol. **teetotaller** *n.*

telecommunication *n.* communication over long distances, by telephone, radio, etc; (*pl.*) technology for this.

telegram *n.* message sent by telegraph.

telegraph *n.* system or apparatus for sending written messages, esp. by electrical impulses along wires. —*v.t.* send (a message) or communicate with (a person) thus.

telegraphist /-'leg-/ *n.* person employed in telegraphy.

telegraphy /-'leg-/ *n.* communication by telegraph. **telegraphic** *a.,* **telegraphically** *adv.*

telemeter /'tel-/ *n.* apparatus for recording and transmitting the readings of an instrument at a distance. **telemetry** /tr'lem-/ *n.*

telepathy /-'lep-/ *n.* communication between minds other than by the known senses. **telepathic** *a.,* **telepath** /'tel-/, **telepathist** /-'lep-/ *ns.*

telephone *n.* system of transmitting speech etc. by wire or radio; instrument used in this. —*v.t.* send (a message) or speak to (a person) by telephone. **telephonic** /-'fon-/ *a.,* **telephonically** *adv.,* **telephony** /-'lef-/ *n.*

telephonist /-'lef-/ *n.* operator at a telephone exchange or switchboard.

telephoto lens lens producing a large image of a distant object for photography.

teleprinter *n.* telegraph instrument for sending and receiving typewritten messages.

telerecording *n.* recorded television broadcast.

telesales *n.pl.* selling by telephone.

telescope *n.* optical instrument for making distant objects appear larger. —*v.t./i.* make or become shorter by sliding each adjacent section inside the next; compress or become compressed forcibly. **telescopic** *a.,* **telescopically** *adv.*

teletext *n.* information service transmitted from a computer source to subscribers' television screens.

televise *v.t.* transmit by television.

television *n.* system for reproducing on a screen a view of scenes etc. by radio transmission; televised programmes; (also **television set**) apparatus for receiving these. **televisual** *a.*

telex *n.* system of telegraphy using teleprinters and public transmission lines; message sent by this. —*v.t.* send (a message) or communicate with (a person) by telex.

tell *v.t./i.* (*p.t.* **told**) make known, esp. in written or spoken words; give information to; utter; reveal a secret; decide; distinguish; produce an effect; count; direct, order. **tell off** (*colloq.*) reprimand; count off or detach for duty. **tell-tale** *n.* person who tells tales; mechanical indicator. **tell tales** reveal secrets.

teller *n.* person giving an account of something; person appointed to count votes; bank cashier.

telling *a.* having a noticeable effect.

telly *n.* (*colloq.*) television.

temerity /-'me-/ *n.* audacity.

temp *n.* (*colloq.*) temporary employee.

temper *n.* state of mind as regards calmness or anger; fit of anger; calmness under provocation; condition of tempered metal. —*v.t.* bring (metal or clay) to the required hardness or consistency; moderate the effects of.

tempera *n.* method of painting (esp. on canvas) using powdered colours mixed with egg or size.

temperament *n.* person's nature as it controls his behaviour.

temperamental *a.* of or in temperament; having fits of excitable or moody behaviour. **temperamentally** *adv.*

temperance *n.* self-restraint; total abstinence from alcohol.

temperate *a.* self-restrained, moderate; (of climate) without extremes of heat and cold. **temperately** *adv.*

temperature *n.* intensity of heat or cold, esp. as shown by a thermometer; body temperature above normal.

tempest *n.* violent storm.

tempestuous *a.* stormy.

template *n.* pattern or gauge, esp. for cutting metal, stone, etc.

temple[1] *n.* building dedicated to the presence or service of god(s). **Inner Temple, Middle Temple** two Inns of Court in London.

temple[2] *n.* flat part between forehead and ear.

tempo *n.* (*pl.* -os *or* -i) time, speed, or rhythm of a piece of music; rate of motion or activity.

temporal *a.* secular; of or denoting time; of the temple(s) of the head.

temporary *a.* lasting for a limited time, not permanent. **temporarily** *adv.*

temporize *v.i.* avoid committing oneself in order to gain time. **temporization** *n.*

tempt *v.t.* persuade or try to persuade by the prospect of pleasure or advantage; arouse a desire in; risk provoking (fate) by rashness. **temptation** *n.*, **tempter** *n.*, **temptress** *n.fem.*

ten *a. & n.* one more than nine (10, X).

tenable /'ten-/ *a.* able to be defended; (of an office) able to be held. **tenability** *n.*

tenacious *a.* holding or clinging or sticking firmly. **tenaciously** *adv.*, **tenacity** *n.*

tenancy /'ten-/ *n.* use of land or a building etc. as a tenant.

tenant *n.* person who rents land or a building etc. from a landlord; (in law) occupant, owner. **tenantry** /'ten-/ *n.* tenants.

tench *n.* (*pl.* tench) fish of the carp family.

tend[1] *v.t.* take care of.

tend[2] *v.i.* have a specified tendency.

tendency *n.* way a person or thing is likely to be or behave or become; thing's direction.

tendentious *a.* aimed at helping a cause, not impartial. **tendentiously** *adv.*

tender[1] *a.* not tough or hard; easily damaged, delicate; painful when touched; easily moved to pity or sympathy; loving, gentle. **tenderly** *adv.*, **tenderness** *n.*

tender[2] *v.t./i.* offer formally; make a tender for. —*n.* formal offer to supply goods or carry out work at a stated price. **legal tender** currency that must, by law, be accepted in payment.

tender[3] *n.* vessel or vehicle conveying goods or passengers to and from a larger one; truck attached to a steam locomotive and carrying fuel and water etc.

tenderfoot *n.* inexperienced person.

tenderize *v.t.* make more tender.

tenderloin *n.* middle part of pork loin.

tendon *n.* strip of strong tissue connecting a muscle to a bone etc.

tendril *n.* thread-like part by which a climbing plant clings; slender curl of hair etc.

tenement *n.* dwelling-house; large house let in portions to tenants; rented flat or room.

tenet /'ten-/ *n.* firm belief or principle.

tenfold *a. & adv.* ten times as much or as many.

tenner *n.* (*colloq.*) £10.

tennis *n.* ball-game played with rackets over a net, with a soft ball on an open court (**lawn tennis**) or with a hard ball in a walled court (**real tennis**).

tenon *n.* projection shaped to fit into a mortise.

tenor *n.* general course or meaning; highest ordinary adult male singing-voice; music for this. —*a.* of tenor pitch.

tenpin bowling game similar to ninepins.

tense[1] *n.* any of the forms of a verb that indicate the time of the action.

tense[2] *a.* (**-er, -est**) stretched tightly; with muscles tight in anticipation; emotionally strained. —*v.t./i.* make or become tense.

tensely *adv.*, **tenseness** *n.*

tensile /-sail/ *a.* of tension; capable of being stretched. **tensility** *n.*

tension *n.* stretching; tenseness, esp. of feelings; effect produced by forces pulling against each other; electromotive force; unit of measurement in knitting.

tent *n.* portable shelter or dwelling made of canvas etc.

tentacle *n.* slender flexible part of certain animals, used for feeling or grasping things.

tentative /'ten-/ *a.* hesitant, not definite; done as a trial. **tentatively** *adv.*

tenterhooks *n.pl.* **on tenterhooks** in suspense because of uncertainty.

tenth *a. & n.* next after ninth. **tenthly** *adv.*

tenuous *a.* very thin; very slight. **tenuousness** *n.*, **tenuity** /-'nju:-/ *n.*

tenure /'ten-/ *n.* holding of office or of land or accommodation etc.

tepee /'ti:pi:/ *n.* conical tent used by North American Indians.

tepid *a.* slightly warm, lukewarm. .

tequila /-'ki:-/ *n.* Mexican liquor made from agave.

tercentenary /-'ti:n-/ *n.* 300th anniversary.

terebinth *n.* tree yielding turpentine.

tergiversation *n.* change of principles.

term *n.* time for which something lasts, fixed or limited period; period of weeks during which instruction is given in a school etc. or in which a lawcourt holds sessions; each quantity or expression in a mathematical series or ratio etc.; word or phrase; (*pl.*) stipulations, conditions offered or accepted; (*pl.*) relation between people. **come to terms with** reconcile oneself to (a difficulty etc.).

termagant *n.* bullying woman.

terminable *a.* able to be terminated.

terminal *a.* of or forming an end; of or undergoing the last stage of a fatal disease; of or done each term. —*n.* terminating point or part; terminus; building where air passengers arrive and depart; point of connection in an electric circuit or device, or of input or output to a computer etc. **terminally** *adv.*

terminate *v.t./i.* end. **termination** *n.*

terminology *n.* technical terms of a subject. **terminological** *a.*

terminus *n.* (*pl.* -i) end; last stopping-place.

termite *n.* small insect that is very destructive to timber.

tern *n.* sea bird with long wings.

ternary *a.* composed of three parts.

terrace *n.* raised level place, esp. one of a series; paved area beside a house; row of houses joined by party walls.

terracotta *n.* brownish-red unglazed pottery; its colour.

terra firma dry land, the ground.

terrain /-'rem/ *n.* land with regard to its natural features.

terrapin *n.* edible freshwater tortoise.

terrestrial /-'res-/ *a.* of the earth; of or living on land.

terrible *a.* appalling, distressing; (*colloq.*) very bad. **terribly** *adv.*

terrier *n.* small active dog.

terrific *a.* (*colloq.*) of great size; excellent. **terrifically** *adv.*

terrify *v.t.* fill with terror.

terrine /-'riːn/ *n.* pâté or similar food; earthenware dish for this.

Territorial *n.* member of the **Territorial Army**, a volunteer reserve force.

territorial *a.* of territory.

territory *n.* land under the control of a person or State or city etc.; sphere of action or thought; **Territory** area forming part of the USA, Australia, or Canada, but not ranking as a State or province.

terror *n.* extreme fear; terrifying person or thing; (*colloq.*) troublesome person or thing.

terrorism *n.* use of violence and intimidation. **terrorist** *n.*

terrorize *v.t.* fill with terror; coerce by terrorism. **terrorization** *n.*

terry *a.* looped cotton fabric used for towels etc.

terse *a.* concise, curt. **tersely** *adv.*, **terseness** *n.*

tertiary /'tɜːʃərɪ/ *a.* next after secondary.

Tessa *n.* tax exempt special savings account.

tessellated *a.* resembling mosaic.

test *n.* something done to discover a person's or thing's qualities or abilities etc.; examination (esp. in a school) on a limited subject; (*colloq.*) test match. —*v.t.* subject to a test. **test match** the last of a series of cricket or Rugby football matches between teams of certain countries. **test-tube** *n.* tube of thin glass with one end closed, used in laboratories. **tester** *n.*

testament *n.* a will; written statement of beliefs. **Old Testament** books of the Bible telling the history and beliefs of the Jews. **New Testament** those telling the life and teachings of Christ.

testamentary /-'men-/ *a.* of or given in a person's will.

testate *a.* having left a valid will at death. **testacy** *n.*

testator /-'teɪ-/ *n.* person who has made a will. **testatrix** *n.fem.*

testes see **testis**.

testicle *n.* male organ that secretes sperm-bearing fluid (in man, each of the two enclosed in the scrotum, behind the penis).

testify *v.t./i.* bear witness to; give evidence; be evidence of.

testimonial *n.* formal statement testifying to character, abilities, etc.; gift showing appreciation.

testimony *n.* declaration (esp. under oath); supporting evidence.

testis *n.* (*pl.* **testes**) testicle.

testosterone /-'tɒs-/ *n.* male sex hormone.

testy *a.* irritable. **testily** *adv.*

tetanus /'tet-/ *n.* disease in which muscles contract and stiffen, caused by bacteria.

tetchy *a.* peevish, irritable.

tête-à-tête /teɪtɑː'teɪt/ *n.* private conversation, esp. between two people. —*a.* & *adv.* together in private.

tether *n.* rope etc. fastening an animal so that it can graze. —*v.t.* fasten with a tether. **at the end of one's tether** having reached the limit of one's endurance.

tetrahedron /-'hi:-/ *n.* (*pl.* **-dra**) solid with four sides, pyramid with a triangular base.

Teutonic /tju:'tɒn-/ *a.* of Germanic peoples or their languages.

text *n.* wording; main body of a book as distinct from illustrations or notes etc.; sentence from Scripture used as the subject of a sermon; book prescribed for study. **textual** *a.*

textbook *n.* book of information for use in studying a subject.

textile *n.* woven or machine-knitted fabric. —*a.* of textiles.

texture *n.* way a fabric etc. feels to the touch. **textured** *a.* having a noticeable texture. **textural** *a.*

Thai *a. & n.* (native, language) of Thailand.

thalidomide /-'lɪd-/ *n.* sedative drug found to have caused malformation of babies' limbs.

than *conj.* used to introduce the second element in a comparison.

thank *v.t.* express gratitude to. **thank-offering** *n.* offering made as an act of thanks. **thank you** polite expression of thanks. **thanks** *n.pl.* expressions of gratitude; (*colloq.*) thank you. **thanks to** on account of, because of.

thankful *a.* feeling or expressing gratitude. **thankfully** *adv.*

thankless *a.* not likely to win thanks. **thanklessness** *n.*

thanksgiving *n.* expression of gratitude, esp. to God.

that *a. & pron.* (*pl.* **those**) the (person or thing) referred to; further or less obvious (one) of two. —*adv.* to such an extent. —*rel. pron.* used to introduce a defining clause. —*conj.* introducing a dependent clause.

thatch *n.* roof of straw etc. —*v.t.* roof with thatch. **thatcher** *n.*

thaw *v.t./i.* pass into an unfrozen state; become less cool or less formal in manner; cause to thaw. —*n.* weather that thaws ice etc.

the *a.* applied to a noun standing for a specific person or thing, or one or all of a kind, or (*pr.* ði:) used to emphasize excellence or importance; (of prices) per. —*adv.* in that degree, by that amount.

theatre *n.* building or outdoor structure for the performance of plays etc.; room or hall for lectures etc. with seats in tiers; room where surgical operations are performed; plays and acting; (of weapons) intermediate between tactical and strategic.

theatrical *a.* of or for the theatre; exaggerated for effect. **theatricals** *n.pl.* theatrical (esp. amateur) performances. **theatrically** *adv.*, **theatricality** *n.*

thee *pron.* (*old use*) objective case of *thou.*

theft *n.* stealing.

their *a.*, **theirs** *poss.pron.* belonging to them.

theism /'θi:ɪz(ə)m/ *n.* belief that the universe was created by a god, with acceptance of revelation. **theist** *n.*, **theistic** *a.*

them *pron.* objective case of *they.*

theme *n.* subject being discussed; melody which is repeated. **theme park** park with amusements organized round one theme. **thematic** /-'mæt-/ *a.*

themselves *pron.* emphatic and reflexive form of *they* and *them.*

then *adv.* at that time; next, and also; in that case. —*a. & n.* (of) that time.

thence *adv.* from that place or source.

thenceforth *adv.* from then on.

theocracy /-'ɒk-/ *n.* form of government through a divine being, either directly or through an order of priests. **theocratic** *a.*, **theocratically** *adv.*

theodolite /θɪˈɒd-/ *n.* surveying instrument for measuring angles.

theology *n.* study or system of religion. **theological** *a.*, **theologian** /-ˈləʊ-/ *n.*

theorem *n.* mathematical statement to be proved by reasoning.

theoretical *a.* based on theory only. **theoretically** *adv.*

theoretician *n.* person concerned with theory.

theorist *n.* person who theorizes.

theorize *v.i.* form theories.

theory *n.* set of ideas formulated to explain something; opinion, supposition; statement of the principles of a subject.

theosophy /-ˈɒs-/ *n.* system of philosophy that aims at direct knowledge of God by spiritual ecstasy and contemplation. **theosophical** *a.*

therapeutic /θerəˈpju:-/ *a.* curative. **therapeutically** *adv.*

therapist *n.* specialist in therapy.

therapy *n.* curative treatment; physiotherapy; psychotherapy.

there *adv.* in, at, or to that place; at that point; in that matter; introducing a sentence where the verb comes before its subject. —*n.* that place. —*int.* exclamation of satisfaction or dismay or consolation.

thereabouts *adv.* near there.

thereafter *adv.* after that.

thereby *adv.* by that means.

therefore *adv.* for that reason.

therein *adv.* in that place.

thereof *adv.* of that.

thereto *adv.* to that.

thereupon *adv.* in consequence of that, because of that.

therm *n.* unit of heat esp. in a gas supply (1.055×10^8 joules).

thermal *a.* of or using heat; warm, hot. —*n.* rising current of hot air.

thermionic valve vacuum tube in which heated electrodes emit a flow of electrons.

thermodynamics *n.* science of the relationship between heat and other forms of energy.

thermometer *n.* instrument (esp. a graduated glass tube) for measuring heat.

thermonuclear *a.* of or using nuclear reactions that occur only at very high temperatures.

thermoplastic *a.* & *n.* (substance) becoming soft when heated and hardening when cooled.

Thermos *n.* [P.] vacuum flask.

thermosetting *a.* setting permanently when heated.

thermostat *n.* device that regulates temperature automatically. **thermostatic** *a.*, **thermostatically** *adv.*

thesaurus /θɪˈsɔːr-əs/ *n.* (*pl.* **-ri**, *pr.* raɪ) comprehensive reference-book; dictionary of synonyms.

these *see* **this**.

thesis *n.* (*pl.* **theses**, *pr.* ˈθiːsiːz) theory put forward and supported by reasoning; lengthy written essay submitted for a university degree.

Thespian *a.* of tragedy or drama. —*n.* actor, actress.

thews *n.pl.* muscular strength.

they *pron.* people or things mentioned or unspecified.

thick *a.* (**-er, -est**) of great or specified distance between opposite surfaces; broad; having units that are numerous or crowded, dense; fairly stiff in consistency; stupid; hoarse; (*colloq.*) on terms of close association. —*adv.* thickly. —*n.* busiest part. **thick-skinned** *a.* not sensitive to criticism or snubs. **thickly** *adv.*, **thickness** *n.*

thicken *v.t./i.* make or become thicker.

thicket *n.* close group of shrubs and small trees etc.

thickset *a.* set or growing close together; stocky, burly.

thief n. (pl. **thieves**) one who steals. **thievish** a.

thieve v.t./i. be a thief; steal.

thievery n. thieving.

thigh n. upper part of the leg, between hip and knee.

thimble n. cap of metal etc. worn on the end of the finger to protect it in sewing. **thimbleful** n. (pl. -fuls).

thin a. (**thinner, thinnest**) of small thickness; not thick; lean, not plump; lacking substance, weak. —adv. thinly. —v.t./i. (p.t. **thinned**) make or become thinner. **thin out** make or become fewer or less crowded. **thin-skinned** a. over-sensitive to criticism or snubs. **thinly** adv., **thinness** n., **thinner** n.

thine a. & poss.pron. (old use) belonging to thee.

thing n. whatever is or may be perceived, known, or thought about; act, fact, idea, task, etc.; item; inanimate object; creature; (pl.) belongings, utensils, circumstances; **the thing** what is proper or fashionable.

think v.t./i. (p.t. **thought**) exercise the mind, form connected ideas; form or have as an idea or opinion or plan. —n. (colloq.) act of thinking. **think better of it** change one's mind after thought. **think nothing of** consider unremarkable. **think over** reach a decision by thinking. **think-tank** n. group providing ideas and advice on national or commercial problems. **thinker** n.

third a. next after second. —n. third thing, class, etc.; one of three equal parts. **third degree** (US) long severe questioning by police. **third party** another person etc. besides the two principals. **third-rate** a. very inferior in quality. **Third World** developing countries of Asia, Africa, and Latin America (orig. those

not politically aligned with Communist or Western nations). **thirdly** adv.

thirst n. feeling caused by a desire to drink; strong desire. —v.i. feel a thirst. **thirsty** a., **thirstily** adv.

thirteen a. & n. one more than twelve (13, XIII). **thirteenth** a. & n.

thirty a. three times ten (30, XXX). **thirtieth** a. & n.

this a & pron. (pl. **these**) the (person or thing) near or present or mentioned; present day or time.

thistle n. prickly plant. **thistly** a.

thistledown n. very light fluff on thistle seeds.

thither adv. (old use) to or towards that place.

thole n. peg set in a boat's gunwale to serve as a rowlock.

thong n. strip of leather used as a fastening or lash etc.

thorax n. part of the body between head or neck and abdomen. **thoracic** a.

thorn n. small sharp pointed projection on a plant; thorn-bearing tree or shrub. **thorny** a.

thorough a. complete in every way; detailed, not superficial. **thoroughly** adv., **thoroughness** n.

thoroughbred a. & n. (horse etc.) bred of pure or pedigree stock.

thoroughfare n. public way open at both ends.

thoroughgoing a. thorough.

those see **that**.

thou pron. (old use) you.

though conj. in spite of the fact that, even supposing. —adv. (colloq.) however.

thought see **think**. —n. process or power or way of thinking; idea etc. produced by thinking; intention; consideration.

thoughtful a. thinking deeply; thought out carefully; considerate. **thoughtfully** adv., **thoughtfulness** n.

thoughtless a. not alert to possible consequences; inconsiderate. **thoughtlessly** adv., **thoughtlessness** n.

thousand a. & n. ten hundred (1000, M). **thousandth** a. & n.

thrall n. bondage. **thraldom** n.

thrash v.t. beat, esp. with a stick or whip; defeat thoroughly; thresh; make flailing movements. **thrash out** discuss thoroughly.

thread n. thin length of any substance; spun cotton or wool etc. used in sewing, knitting, or making cloth; thing compared to this; spiral ridge of a screw. —v.t. pass a thread through; pass (a strip or thread etc.) through or round something; make (one's way) through a crowd or streets etc. **threader** n.

threadbare a. with nap worn and threads visible; shabbily dressed.

threadworm n. small thread-like worm, esp. found in the rectum of children.

threat n. expression of intention to punish, hurt, or harm; person or thing thought likely to bring harm or danger.

threaten v.t. make or be a threat (to).

three a. & n. one more than two (3, III). **three-dimensional** a. having or appearing to have length, breadth, and depth. **three-legged race** race between pairs of runners with the right leg of one tied to the left leg of the other. **three-quarter** n. player with a position just behind the halfbacks in Rugby football.

threefold a. & adv. three times as much or as many.

threepence /ˈθrep-/ n. sum of three pence. **threepenny** a.

threescore n. (old use) sixty.

threesome n. three together, trio.

thresh v.t./i. beat out (grain) from husks of corn; make flailing movements.

threshold n. piece of wood or stone forming the bottom of a doorway; point of entry; lowest limit at which a stimulus is perceptible; highest limit at which pain is bearable.

threw see throw.

thrice adv. (old use) three times.

thrift n. economical management of resources; plant with pink flowers. **thrifty** a., **thriftily** adv., **thriftiness** n.

thrill n. nervous tremor caused by emotion or sensation; wave of feeling or excitement. —v.t./i. feel or cause to feel a thrill.

thriller n. exciting story or play etc., esp. involving crime.

thrips n. (pl. **thrips**) insect harmful to plants.

thrive v.i. (p.t. **throve** or **thrived**, p.p. **thrived** or **thriven**) grow or develop well and vigorously; prosper.

throat n. front of the neck; passage from mouth to oesophagus or lungs; narrow passage.

throaty a. uttered deep in the throat; hoarse. **throatily** adv.

throb v.t. (p.t. **throbbed**) (of the heart or pulse) beat with more than usual force; vibrate or sound with a persistent rhythm. —n. throbbing beat or sound.

throes n.pl. severe pangs of pain. **in the throes of** struggling with the task of.

thrombosis n. formation of a clot of blood in a blood-vessel or organ of the body.

throne n. seat for a king, queen, or bishop etc. on ceremonial occasions; sovereign power.

throng n. crowded mass of people. —v.t./i. come or go or press in a throng; fill with a throng.

throstle n. song-thrush.

throttle n. valve controlling the flow of fuel or steam etc. to an engine; lever controlling this. —v.t. strangle. **throttle back or**

down reduce an engine's speed by means of the throttle.

through *prep.* & *adv.* from end to end or side to side (of), entering at one point and coming out at another; among; from beginning to end (of); so as to have finished, so as to have passed (an examination); so as to be connected by telephone (to); by the agency, means, or fault of; (*US*) up to and including. —*a.* going through; passing without stopping.

throughout *prep.* & *adv.* right through, from beginning to end (of).

throughput *n.* amount of material processed.

throve see **thrive**.

throw *v.t.* (*p.t.* **threw,** *p.p.* **thrown**) send with some force through the air in a certain direction; hurl to the ground; cause to fall; put (clothes etc.) on or off hastily; shape (pottery) on a wheel; cause to be in a certain state; (*colloq.*) disconcert; cause to extend; operate (a switch or lever); have (a fit or tantrum); (*colloq.*) give (a party). —*n.* act of throwing; distance something is thrown. **throw away** part with as useless or unwanted; fail to make use of. **throw-away** *a.* to be thrown away after use. **throwback** *n.* animal etc. showing characteristics of an ancestor that is earlier than its parents. **throw in the towel** = throw up the sponge. **throw out** discard; reject. **throw over** desert, abandon. **throw up** raise, erect; bring to notice; resign from; vomit. **throw up the sponge** admit defeat or failure. **thrower** *n.*

thrum *v.t./i.* (*p.t.* **thrummed**) strum, sound monotonously. —*n.* thrumming sound.

thrush[1] *n.* songbird, esp. one with a speckled breast.

thrush[2] *n.* fungoid infection of the throat (esp. in children); similar infection of the vagina.

thrust *v.t./t.* (*p.t.* **thrust**) push forcibly; make a forward stroke with a sword etc. —*n.* thrusting movement or force; hostile remark aimed at a person etc.

thud *n.* dull low sound like that of a blow. —*v.i.* (*p.t.* **thudded**) make or fall with a thud.

thug *n.* vicious ruffian. **thuggish** *a.*, **thuggery** *n.*

thumb *n.* short thick finger set apart from the other four. —*v.t.* wear or soil or turn (pages etc.) with the thumbs; request (a lift) by signalling with one's thumb. **thumb index** set of marked notches showing where to open a book to find a particular section. **under the thumb of** completely under the influence of.

thumbscrew *n.* former instrument of torture for squeezing the thumb; screw turned by the thumb.

thump *v.t./i.* strike or knock heavily (esp. with the fist), thud. —*n.* heavy blow; sound of thumping. **thumping** *a.* (*colloq.*) large.

thunder *n.* loud noise that accompanies lightning; similar sound. —*v.t./i.* sound with or like thunder; utter loudly; make a forceful attack in words. **steal a person's thunder** forestall him or her. **thundery** *a.*

thunderbolt *n.* imaginary missile thought of as sent to earth with a lightning-flash; startling formidable event or statement.

thunderclap *n.* clap of thunder.

thundering *a.* (*colloq.*) very big or great.

thunderous *a.* like thunder.

thunderstorm *n.* storm accompanied by thunder.

thunderstruck *a.* amazed.

thurible /'θjʊər-/ *n.* censer.

Thursday *n.* day after Wednesday.

thus *adv.* in this way; as a result of this; to this extent.

thwack *v.t./i.* strike with a heavy blow. —*n.* this blow or sound.

thwart *v.t.* prevent from doing what is intended or from being accomplished. —*n.* oarsman's bench across a boat.

thy *a.* (*old use*) belonging to thee.

thyme /taɪm/ *n.* herb with fragrant leaves.

thymol *n.* antiseptic made from oil of thyme.

thymus *n.* ductless gland near the base of the neck.

thyroid *a. & n.* **thyroid gland** large ductless gland in the neck.

thyself *pron.* emphatic and reflexive form of *thou* and *thee*.

tiara /tɪˈɑː-/ *n.* woman's jewelled crescent-shaped head-dress.

tibia *n.* (*pl.* -ae) shin-bone.

tic *n.* involuntary muscular twitch.

tick[1] *n.* regular clicking sound, esp. made by a clock or watch; (*colloq.*) moment; small mark placed against an item in a list etc., esp. to show that it is correct. —*v.t./i.* (of a clock etc.) make a series of ticks; mark with a tick. **tick off** (*sl.*) reprimand. **tick over** (of an engine) idle. **tick-tack** *n.* semaphore signalling by racecourse bookmakers. **tick-tock** *n.* ticking of a large clock.

tick[2] *n.* blood-sucking mite or parasitic insect.

tick[3] *n.* case of a mattress or pillow etc., holding the filling.

tick[4] *n.* (*colloq.*) financial credit.

ticker *n.* (*colloq.*) watch; teleprinter; (*joc.*) heart. **ticker-tape** *n.* (*US*) paper tape from a teleprinter etc.

ticket *n.* marked piece of card or paper entitling the holder to a certain right (e.g. to travel by train etc.); certificate of qualification as a ship's master or pilot etc.; label; notification of a traffic offence; list of candidates for office; **the ticket** (*sl.*) the correct or desirable thing. —*v.t.* (*p.t.* **ticketed**) put a ticket on.

ticking *n.* strong fabric for making ticks for mattresses, pillows, etc.

tickle *v.t./i.* touch or stroke lightly so as to cause a slight tingling sensation; feel this sensation; amuse, please. —*n.* act or sensation of tickling.

ticklish *a.* sensitive to tickling; (of a problem) requiring careful handling.

tidal *a.* of or affected by tides.

tidbit *n.* (*US*) titbit.

tiddler *n.* (*colloq.*) small fish, esp. stickleback or minnow; unusually small thing.

tiddly *a.* (*sl.*) slightly drunk.

tiddly-winks *n.pl.* game of flicking small counters (**tiddly-winks**) into a receptacle.

tide *n.* sea's regular rise and fall; trend of feeling or events etc.; (*old use*) season. —*v.t./i.* float with the tide. **tide over** help temporarily.

tidings *n.pl.* news.

tidy *a.* (-ier, -iest) neat and orderly; (*colloq.*) considerable. —*v.t.* make tidy. **tidily** *adv.*, **tidiness** *n.*

tie *v.t./i.* (*pres.p.* **tying**) attach or fasten with cord etc.; form into a knot or bow; unite; make the same score as another competitor; restrict, limit; unite (notes in music) by a tie. —*n.* cord etc. used for tying something; strip of material worn below the collar and knotted at the front of the neck; thing that unites or restricts; equality of score between competitors; sports match between two of a set of teams or players; (in music) curved line linking notes of the same pitch, indicating that the second is not to be sounded separately. **tie-break** *n.* means of deciding the winner when competitors have tied. **tie-clip** *n.*, **tie-pin** *n.* ornamental clip or pin for holding a necktie in place. **tie in** link or (of information etc.) be connected with something else. **tie**

up fasten with cord etc.; make (money etc.) not readily available for use; occupy fully. **tie-up** n. connection, link.

tied a. (of a public house) bound to supply only one brewer's beer; (of a house) for occupation only by a person working for its owner.

tier n. any of a series of rows or ranks or units of a structure placed one above the other.

tiff n. petty quarrel.

tiffin n. midday meal in India etc.

tiger n. large striped animal of the cat family. **tiger-cat** n. animal resembling this; large Australian marsupial cat. **tiger-lily** n. orange lily with dark spots.

tight a. (-er, -est) held or fastened firmly, fitting closely, hard to move or undo; with things or people arranged closely together; tense, strict, with nothing slack or spare; (of money etc.) severely restricted; (colloq.) stingy; (colloq.) drunk. —adv. tightly. **tight corner** difficult situation. **tight-fisted** a. stingy. **tight-lipped** a. restraining emotion. **tightly** adv., **tightness** n.

tighten v.t./i. make or become tighter.

tightrope n. tightly stretched rope on which acrobats perform.

tights n.pl. garment (esp. worn in place of stockings) covering the legs and lower part of the body.

tigress n. female tiger.

tile n. thin slab of baked clay etc. used in rows for covering roofs, walls, or floors. —v.t. cover with tiles.

till[1] v.t. prepare and use (land) for growing crops. **tillage** n.

till[2] prep. & conj. up to (a specified time).

till[3] n. receptacle for money behind the counter in a shop or bank etc.

tiller n. bar by which a rudder is turned.

tilt v.t./i. move into a sloping position; run or thrust with a lance in jousting. —n. process of tilting; sloping position. **at full tilt** at full speed or force.

tilth n. tillage; tilled soil.

timber n. wood prepared for use in building or carpentry; trees suitable for this; piece of wood or wooden beam used in constructing a house or ship.

timbered a. constructed of timber or with a timber framework; (of land) wooded.

timbre /tǽbr/ n. characteristic quality of the sound of a voice or instrument.

timbrel n. (old use) tambourine.

time n. all the years of the past, present, and future; point or portion of this; occasion, instance; allotted or available or measured time; rhythm in music; (pl.) contemporary circumstances; (pl., in multiplication or comparison) taken a number of times. —v.t. choose the time for; measure the time taken by. **behind the times** out of date. **for the time being** until another arrangement is made. **from time to time** at intervals. **in no time** very rapidly. **in time** not late; eventually. **on time** punctually. **time-and-motion** a. concerned with measuring the efficiency of effort. **time bomb** bomb that can be set to explode after an interval. **time exposure** long photographic exposure. **time-honoured** a. respected because of antiquity, traditional. **time-lag** n. interval between two connected events. **time-server** n. person who adapts his views to those of the times or of persons in power. **time-share** n. share in a property that allows use by several joint owners at agreed different times. **time-sharing** n. this system; operation of a computer system by several users for different operations simultaneously.

time-switch n. one operating automatically at a set time.

time zone region (between parallels of longitude) where a common standard time is used.

timekeeper n. person who times something or records workmen's hours of work; person in respect of punctuality; clock or watch in respect of accuracy.

timeless a. not affected by the passage of time. **timelessness** n.

timely a. occurring at just the right time. **timeliness** n.

timepiece n. clock or watch.

timer n. person or device that measures the time taken.

timetable n. list showing the times at which certain events take place.

timid a. easily alarmed, not bold, shy. **timidly** adv., **timidity** n.

timing n. way something is timed.

timorous a. timid. **timorously** adv., **timorousness** n.

timpani /'tɪmpanɪ/ n.pl. kettledrums. **timpanist** n.

tin n. silvery-white metal; (also **tin plate**) iron or steel sheets coated with tin; box or other container made of this, one in which food is sealed for preservation. —v.t. (p.t. **tinned**) coat with tin; seal (food) into a tin. **tin-pan alley** world of the composers and publishers etc. of popular music.

tin-tack n. tinned iron tack.

tinny a.

tincture n. solution of a medicinal substance in alcohol; slight tinge. —v.t. tinge.

tinder n. any dry substance that catches fire easily.

tine /taɪn/ n. prong or point of a fork, harrow, or antler.

tinge v.t. (pres.p. **tingeing**) colour slightly; give a slight trace of an element or quality to. —n. slight colouring or trace.

tingle v.i. have a slight pricking or stinging sensation. —n. this sensation.

tinker n. travelling mender of pots and pans; (Sc. & Ir.) gypsy; (colloq.) mischievous person or animal. —v.i. work at something casually trying to repair or improve it; work as a tinker.

tinkle n. series of short light ringing sounds. —v.t./i. make or cause to make a tinkle.

tinpot a. (derog.) cheap, inferior.

tinsel n. glittering decorative metallic strips or threads.

tint n. variety or slight trace of a colour. —v.t. colour slightly.

tintinnabulation n. ringing or tinkling of bells.

tiny a. (-ier, -iest) very small.

tip[1] n. end, esp. of something small or tapering. —v.t. (p.t. **tipped**) provide with a tip.

tip[2] v.t./i. (p.t. **tipped**) tilt, topple; discharge (a thing's contents) by tilting; strike lightly; name as a likely winner; make a small present of money to, esp. in acknowledgement of services. —n. small money present; private or special and useful information or advice; slight tilt or push; place where rubbish etc. is tipped. **tip off** give a warning or hint or inside information to. **tip-off** n. such a warning etc. **tip the wink** give a private signal or information to (a person). **tipper** n.

tippet n. small cape or collar of fur etc.

tipple v.t./i. drink (wine or spirits etc.) repeatedly. —n. (colloq.) alcoholic or other drink.

tipster n. person who gives tips about racehorses etc.

tipsy a. slightly drunk.

tiptoe v.i. (p.t. **tiptoeing**) walk very quietly or carefully.

tiptop a. (colloq.) first-rate.

tirade n. long angry piece of criticism or denunciation.

tire[1] v.t./i. make or become tired.

tire[2] n. (US) tyre.

tired a. feeling a desire to sleep or rest. **tired of** having had enough of and feeling impatient or bored.

tireless *a.* not tiring easily. **tirelessly** *adv.*, **tirelessness** *n.*

tiresome *a.* annoying. **tiresomeness** *n.*

tiro /'taɪ-/ *n.* (*pl.* **-os**) beginner.

tissue /'tɪʃu:/ *n.* substance forming an animal or plant body; tissue-paper; disposable piece of soft absorbent paper used as a handkerchief etc.; fine gauzy fabric; interwoven series (of lies etc.). **tissue-paper** *n.* very thin soft paper used for packing things.

tit[1] *n.* any of several small birds.

tit[2] *n.* **tit for tat** equivalent given in retaliation.

tit[3] *n.* (*vulg.*) breast, nipple.

titanic /taɪ'tæn-/ *a.* gigantic.

titanium /taɪ'teɪ-/ *n.* dark-grey metal.

titbit *n.* choice bit of food or item of information.

tithe *n.* one-tenth of the annual produce of agriculture etc., formerly paid to the Church. —*v.t.* subject to tithes.

Titian /'tɪʃ(ə)n/ *a.* (of hair) auburn.

titillate *v.t.* excite or stimulate pleasantly. **titillation** *n.*

titivate *v.t./i.* (*colloq.*) smarten up, put finishing touches to. **titivation** *n.*

title *n.* name of a book, poem, or picture etc.; word denoting rank or office, or used in speaking of or to the holder; championship in sport; legal right to ownership of property. **title-deed** *n.* legal document proving a person's title to a property. **title-page** *n.* page at the beginning of a book giving the title, the author's name, etc. **title role** part in a play etc. from which the title is taken.

titled *a.* having a title of nobility.

titmouse *n.* (*pl.* **-mice**) tit[1].

titrate /-'treɪt/ *v.t.* ascertain the amount of a constituent in (a substance) by use of a standard reagent. **titration** *n.*

titter *n.* high-pitched giggle. —*v.i.* give a titter.

tittle-tattle *v.i.* & *n.* tattle.

titular *a.* of or belonging to a title; having the title of ruler etc. but without real authority.

tizzy *n.* (*sl.*) state of nervous agitation or confusion.

TNT *abbr.* trinitrotoluene, a powerful explosive.

to *prep.* towards, so as to approach or reach or be in (a position or state etc.); as far as; as compared with, in respect of; for (a person or thing) to hold or possess or be affected by. —(with a verb) forming an infinitive, or expressing purpose or consequence etc.; used alone when the infinitive is understood. —*adv.* to a closed or almost closed position or a standstill; into a state of consciousness or activity. **to and fro** backwards and forwards. **-to-be** soon to become. **to-do** *n.* fuss.

toad *n.* frog-like animal living chiefly on land. **toad-in-the-hole** *n.* sausages baked in batter.

toadflax *n.* wild plant with yellow or purple flowers.

toadstool *n.* fungus (usu. poisonous) with a round top on a stalk.

toady *n.* sycophant. —*v.i.* behave sycophantically. **toadyism** *n.*

toast *n.* toasted bread; person or thing in whose honour a company is requested to drink; this request or instance of drinking. —*v.t./i.* brown or warm by placing before a fire etc.; honour or pledge good wishes to by drinking.

toaster *n.* electrical device for toasting bread.

toastmaster *n.* person announcing the toasts at a public dinner.

tobacco *n.* plant with leaves that are used for smoking or snuff; its prepared leaves.

tobacconist *n.* shopkeeper who sells cigarettes etc.

toboggan *n.* small sledge used for sliding downhill. **tobogganing** *n.*

toby jug mug or jug in the form of a seated old man with a three-cornered hat.

toccata /-'ka:-/ n. showy composition for a piano or organ etc.

tocsin n. bell rung as an alarm-signal; signal of disaster.

today n. & adv. (on) this present day; (at) the present time.

toddle v.i. (of a young child) walk with short unsteady steps.

toddler n. child who has only recently learnt to walk.

toddy n. sweetened drink of spirits and hot water.

toe n. any of the divisions (five in man) of the front part of the foot; part of a shoe or stocking covering the toes; lower end or tip of a tool etc. —v.t. touch with the toe(s). **be on one's toes** be alert or eager. **toe-hold** n. slight foothold. **toe the line** conform to the requirements of one's party.

toecap n. top part of the toe of a boot or shoe.

toff n. (sl.) distinguished or well-dressed person.

toffee n. sweet made with heated butter and sugar. **toffee-apple** n. toffee-coated apple on a stick.

tofu n. curd made from mashed soya beans.

tog n. unit for measuring the warmth of duvets; (pl., colloq.) clothes. —v.t. (p.t. **togged**) **tog out** or **up** (colloq.) dress up.

toga n. loose outer garment worn by men in ancient Rome.

together adv. in or into company or conjunction, towards each other; one with another; simultaneously; in unbroken succession.

toggle n. short piece of wood or metal etc. passed through a loop as a fastening device; projecting lever that operates a switch; electronic switch that turns a function on and off alternately.

toil v.i. work or move laboriously. —n. laborious work; (pl.) net, snare. **toilsome** a.

toilet n. process of dressing and grooming oneself; lavatory. **toilet water** scented lotion for the skin.

toiletries n.pl. articles used in washing and grooming oneself.

token n. sign, symbol, evidence; keepsake; voucher that can be exchanged for goods; coin-like device for operating a machine or making certain payments. —a. serving as a token or pledge but often on a small scale.

tokenism n. granting of minimal concessions.

told see **tell**. —a. **all told** counting everything or everyone.

tolerable a. endurable; passable. **tolerably** adv.

tolerance n. willingness to tolerate a person or thing; permitted variation. **tolerant** a., **tolerantly** adv.

tolerate v.t. permit without protest or interference; bear (pain etc.), not be harmed by. **toleration** n.

toll[1] /təʊl/ n. tax paid for the use of a public road or harbour etc.; loss or damage caused by a disaster etc. **toll-gate** n. barrier preventing passage until a toll is paid.

toll[2] /təʊl/ v.t./i. ring with slow strokes, esp. for a death or funeral. —n. stroke of a tolling bell.

tom n. tom-cat. **tom-cat** n. male cat.

tomahawk n. light axe used by North American Indians; (Austr.) hatchet.

tomato n. (pl. **-oes**) plant bearing glossy red or yellow fruit used as a vegetable; this fruit.

tomb /tu:m/ n. grave or other place of burial.

tombola /-'bəʊ-/ n. lottery resembling bingo.

tomboy n. girl who enjoys rough noisy recreations.

tombstone n. memorial stone set up over a grave.

tome /təʊm/ n. large book.

tomfoolery n. foolish behaviour.

tommy-gun n. portable machine-gun.

tommy-rot n. (sl.) nonsense.

tomography /-'mɒg-/ n. method of radiography displaying details of a selected plane of the body. **tomogram** n.

tomorrow n. & adv. (on) the day after today; (in) the near future.

tom-tom n. drum beaten with the hands; tall drum used in jazz bands.

ton n. measure of weight, either 2240 lb (**long ton**) or 2000 lb (**short ton**) or 1000 kg (**metric ton**); unit of volume in shipping; (colloq.) large amount; (sl.) speed of 100 m.p.h.

tone n. musical or vocal sound, esp. with reference to its pitch and quality and strength; manner of expression in speaking or writing; full interval between one note and the next in an octave; proper firmness of bodily organs and tissues; tint, shade of colour; general spirit or character. —v.t./i. give a tone of sound or colour to; harmonize in colour; give proper firmness to (muscles or skin etc.). **tone-deaf** a. unable to perceive differences of musical pitch. **tone down** make less strong or less harsh. **tonal** a., **tonally** adv., **tonality** n.

toneless a. without positive tone, not expressive. **tonelessly** adv.

tongs n.pl. instrument with two arms used for grasping things.

tongue n. muscular organ in the mouth, used in tasting and swallowing and (in humans) speaking; tongue of an ox etc. as food; ability to speak, manner of speaking; language; projecting strip; tapering jet of flame. —v.i. produce a staccato or other effect in a wind instrument by using the tongue. **tongue-tied** a. silent from shyness etc. **tongue-twister** n. sequence of words difficult to pronounce quickly and correctly. **with one's**

tongue in one's cheek speaking with sly sarcasm.

tonic n. medicine etc. with an invigorating effect; keynote in music; tonic water. —a. toning muscles etc., invigorating. **tonic sol-fa** = sol-fa. **tonic water** mineral water, esp. flavoured with quinine.

tonight n. & adv. (on) the present evening or night, or that of today.

tonnage n. ship's carrying-capacity expressed in tons; charge per ton for carrying cargo.

tonne /tʌn/ n. metric ton, 1000 kg.

tonsil n. either of two small organs near the root of the tongue.

tonsillitis n. inflammation of the tonsils.

tonsorial a. of a barber or his work.

tonsure /'tɒnʃə(r)/ n. shaving the top or all of the head as a clerical or monastic symbol; this shaven area. **tonsured** a.

too adv. to a greater extent than is desirable; (colloq.) very; also.

took see take.

tool n. thing used for working on something; person used by another for his own purposes. —v.t./i. shape or ornament with a tool; equip with tools; (sl.) drive or ride in a leisurely way.

toot n. short sound produced by a horn or whistle etc. —v.t./i. make or cause to make a toot.

tooth n. (pl. **teeth**) each of the hard white bony structures in the jaws, used in biting and chewing things; tooth-like part or projection; liking for a particular food. **in the teeth of** in spite of; in opposition to. **tooth-comb** n. comb with fine close-set teeth. **toothed** a.

toothache n. ache in a tooth.

toothbrush n. brush for cleaning the teeth.

toothless a. having no tooth.

toothpaste n. paste for cleaning the teeth.

toothpick *n.* small pointed instrument for removing bits of food from between the teeth.

toothsome *a.* delicious.

toothy *a.* having many or large teeth.

tootle *v.t./i.* toot gently or continuously.

top[1] *n.* highest point or part or position; upper surface; utmost degree or intensity; thing forming the upper part or covering; garment for the upper part of the body. —*a.* highest in position or rank etc. —*v.t.* (*p.t.* **topped**) provide or be a top for; reach the top of; be higher than; add as a final thing; remove the top of; strike (a golfball) above its centre. **on top of** in addition to. **top dog** (*sl.*) master, victor. **top-dress** *v.t.* apply fertilizer on the top of (soil). **top hat** man's stiff black or grey hat worn with formal dress. **top-heavy** *a.* overweighted at the top and liable to fall over. **top-notch** *a.* (*colloq.*) first-rate. **top secret** of the highest category of secrecy. **top up** fill up (something half empty).

top[2] *n.* toy that spins on its point when set in motion.

topaz *n.* semi-precious stone of various colours, esp. yellow.

topcoat *n.* overcoat; final coat of paint etc.

toper *n.* (*old use*) habitual drunkard.

topi /'təʊpɪ/ *n.* light pith sun-helmet.

topiary /'təʊ-/ *a. & n.* (of) the art of clipping shrubs etc. into ornamental shapes.

topic *a.* subject of a discussion or written work.

topical *a.* having reference to current events. **topically** *adv.*, **topicality** *n.*

topknot *n.* tuft, crest, or bow etc. on top of the head.

topless *a.* leaving or having the breasts bare.

topmost *a.* highest.

topography /-'pɒg-/ *n.* local geography, position of the rivers, roads, buildings, etc., of a place or district. **topographical** *a.*

topology /-'pɒl-/ *n.* study of geometrical properties unaffected by continuous change of shape or size; branch of mathematics concerned with continuity. **topological** *a.*

topper *n.* (*colloq.*) top hat.

topple *v.t./i.* be unsteady and fall; cause to do this.

topside *n.* beef from the upper part of the haunch.

topsoil *n.* top layer of the soil.

topsy-turvy *adv. & a.* upside down; in or into great disorder.

toque /təʊk/ *n.* woman's brimless hat with a high crown.

tor *n.* hill or rocky peak.

torch *n.* small hand-held electric lamp; burning piece of wood etc. carried as a light. **torchlight** *n.*

tore *see* tear[1].

toreador /'tɒ-/ *n.* fighter (esp. on horseback) in a bullfight.

torment[1] /'tɔː-/ *n.* severe suffering; cause of this.

torment[2] /-'ment/ *v.t.* subject to torment or annoyances. **tormentor** *n.*

torn *see* tear[1].

tornado /-'neɪ-/ *n.* (*pl.* -**oes**) violent destructive whirlwind.

torpedo *n.* (*pl.* -**oes**) explosive underwater missile. —*v.t.* attack or destroy with a torpedo; wreck (a plan etc.) suddenly.

torpid *a.* sluggish and inactive. **torpidly** *adv.*, **torpidity** *n.*

torpor *n.* sluggish condition.

torque /tɔːk/ *n.* force causing rotation in mechanism; ancient twisted metal necklace.

torrent *n.* rushing stream or flow; downpour. **torrential** *a.*

torrid /'tɒ-/ *a.* intensely hot.

torsion *n.* twisting, spiral twist.

torso *n.* (*pl.* -**os**) trunk of the human body.

tort *n.* any private or civil wrong (other than breach of contract) for which damages may be claimed.

tortoise /-təs/ *n.* slow-moving land or freshwater reptile with its body enclosed in a hard shell.

tortoiseshell /'tɔ:təʃel/ *n.* mottled yellowish-brown shell of certain turtles, used for making combs etc. **tortoiseshell cat** etc., one with mottled colouring.

tortuous *a.* full of twists and turns. **tortuously** *adv.*, **tortuosity** *n.*

torture *n.* severe pain; infliction of this as a punishment or means of coercion. —*v.t.* inflict torture upon; force out of its natural shape etc. **torturer** *n.*

Tory *n.* & *a.* Conservative.

tosh *n.* (*sl.*) rubbish.

toss *v.t./i.* throw lightly; send (a coin) spinning in the air to settle a question by the way it falls; throw or roll about from side to side; coat (food) by gently shaking it in dressing etc. —*n.* tossing action or movement or process. **toss off** drink rapidly; finish or compose rapidly. **toss-up** *n.* tossing of a coin; even chance.

tot[1] *n.* small child; small quantity of spirits.

tot[2] *v.t./i.* (*p.t.* totted) **tot up** (*colloq.*) add up.

total *a.* including everything or everyone; complete. —*n.* total amount. —*v.t./i.* (*p.t.* totalled) reckon the total of; amount to. **totally** *adv.*, **totality** *n.*

totalitarian /-'teər-/ *a.* of a regime in which no rival parties or loyalties are permitted. **totalitarianism** *n.*

totalizator *n.* device that automatically registers bets staked, with a view to dividing the total amount among those betting on the winner.

totalize *v.t.* find the total of.

tote[1] *n.* (*sl.*) totalizator.

tote[2] *v.t.* (*US*) carry. **tote bag** large capacious bag.

totem *n.* animal etc. adopted by North American Indians as the emblem of a clan or family; image of this. **totem-pole** *n.* pole carved or painted with totems.

totter *v.i.* walk or rock unsteadily. —*n.* tottering walk or movement. **tottery** *a.*

toucan /'tu:-/ *n.* tropical American bird with an immense beak.

touch *v.t./i.* be, come, or bring together so that there is no space between; put one's hand etc. on (a thing) lightly; press or strike lightly; reach; equal in excellence; meddle with; involve oneself in; affect slightly; rouse sympathy in; (*sl.*) persuade to give money as a loan or gift. —*n.* act, fact, or manner of touching; ability to perceive things through touching them; small thing done in producing a piece of work; style of workmanship; relationship of communication or knowledge; slight trace; part of a football field outside the touchlines; (*sl.*) act of obtaining money from a person. **touch-and-go** *a.* uncertain as regards result. **touch down** touch the ball on the ground behind the goal-line in Rugby football; (of an aircraft) land. (**touchdown** *n.*). **touchline** *n.* side limit of a football field. **touch-judge** *n.* linesman in Rugby football. **touch off** cause to explode; start (a process). **touch on** mention briefly. **touch-type** *v.i.* use a typewriter without looking at the keys. **touch up** improve by making small additions.

touché /'tu:ʃeɪ/ *int.* acknowledgement of a hit in fencing, or of a valid criticism.

touching *a.* rousing kindly feelings or pity. —*prep.* concerning.

touchstone *n.* standard or criterion by which something is judged.

touchwood *n.* wood that will catch fire easily.

touchy *a.* (-ier, -iest) easily offended. **touchiness** *n.*

tough *a.* (-er, -est) hard to break or cut or chew; hardy; unyielding. resolute; difficult; (*colloq.*, of luck) hard. —*n.* rough violent person. **toughness** *n.*

toughen *v.t./i.* make or become tough or tougher.

toupee /ˈtuːpeɪ/ *n.* wig, artificial patch of hair.

tour *n.* journey through a place, visiting things of interest or giving performances.—*v.t./i.* make a tour (of). **on tour** touring.

tour de force feat of strength or skill.

tourism *n.* organized touring or other services for tourists.

tourist *n.* person travelling or visiting a place for recreation.

tourmaline /ˈtʊəməliːn/ *n.* mineral possessing unusual electric properties and used as a gem.

tournament *n.* contest of skill involving a series of matches.

tournedos /ˈtʊənədəʊ/ *n.* (*pl.* -os) small piece of fillet of beef.

tousle /ˈtaʊ-/ *v.t.* make (hair etc.) untidy by ruffling.

tout /taʊt/ *v.t./i.* try to obtain orders (for goods or services); pester people to buy. —*n.* person who touts, tipster touting information.

tow[1] /təʊ/ *n.* coarse fibres of flax or hemp.

tow[2] /təʊ/ *v.t.* pull along behind one. —*n.* act of towing. **towing-path** *n.* path beside a canal or river, orig. for use when a horse tows a barge etc.

toward *prep.* towards.

towards *prep.* in the direction of; in relation to; as a contribution to; near, approaching.

towel *n.* piece of absorbent material for drying oneself or wiping things dry. —*v.t.* (*-ll-*, US *towelled*) rub with a towel.

towelling *n.* fabric for towels.

tower *n.* tall usu. square or circular structure, esp. as part of a church or castle etc. —*v.i.* be of great height. **tower block** tall building with many storeys. **tower of strength** source of strong reliable support.

towering *a.* (of rage) intense.

town *n.* collection of dwellings and other buildings (larger than a village); its inhabitants; central business and shopping area; London. **go to town** (*colloq.*) do something lavishly or with enthusiasm. **on the town** (*colloq.*) on a spree in town. **town hall** building containing local government offices etc. **town house** house in a town, esp. one of a terrace. **townsman** *n.* (*pl.* -men), **townswoman** *n.fem.* (*pl.* -women).

townee *n.* (*derog.*) inhabitant of a town.

township *n.* (*S. Afr.*) urban area set aside for Blacks; (esp. *Austr.* & *NZ*) small town; (*US* & *Canada*) division of a county, district six miles square.

toxaemia /-ˈsiː-/ *n.* blood-poisoning; abnormally high blood-pressure in pregnancy.

toxic *a.* of or caused by poison; poisonous. **toxicity** /-ˈɪsɪ-/ *n.*

toxicology *n.* study of poisons. **toxicological** *a.*, **toxicologist** *n.*

toxin *n.* poisonous substance, esp. formed in the body.

toy *n.* thing to play with; (*attrib.*, of a dog) of a diminutive variety. —*v.i.* **toy with** handle idly; deal with (a thing) without seriousness. **toy boy** (*colloq.*) woman's much younger male lover.

toyshop *n.* shop that sells toys.

trace[1] *n.* track or mark left behind; sign of what has existed or occurred; very small quantity. —*v.t.* follow or discover by observing marks or other evidence; mark out; copy by using tracing-paper or carbon paper. **trace element** one required only in minute amounts. **tracer** *n.*

trace[2] *n.* each of the two side-straps or ropes etc. by which a horse draws a vehicle. **kick over the traces** become insubordinate or reckless.

traceable *a.* able to be traced.

tracery *n.* openwork pattern in stone; similar decorative pattern of lines.

trachea /trə'ki:ə/ *n.* windpipe.

tracheotomy /treıkı'ɒt-/ *n.* opening made surgically into the trachea from the surface of the neck.

tracing *n.* copy of a map or drawing etc. made by tracing it. **tracing-paper** *n.* transparent paper used in this.

track *n.* mark(s) left by a moving person or thing; course; path, rough road; particular section on a record or recording-tape; continuous line of railway; continuous band round the wheels of a tank or tractor etc. —*v.t.* follow the track of, find or observe thus. **keep** *or* **lose track of** keep or fail to keep oneself informed about. **make tracks** (*sl.*) go away. **track suit** loose warm suit worn by an athlete etc. during practice. **tracker** *n.*

tract[1] *n.* stretch of land; system of connected parts of the body, along which something passes.

tract[2] *n.* pamphlet with a short essay, esp. on a religious subject.

tractable *a.* easy to deal with or control, docile. **tractability** *n.*

traction *n.* pulling. **traction-engine** *n.* engine for pulling a heavy load along a road etc.

tractor *n.* powerful motor vehicle for pulling heavy equipment.

trad *a.* & *n.* (*colloq.*) traditional (jazz).

trade *n.* exchange of goods for money or other goods; business of a particular kind, people engaged in this; trading. —*v.t./i.* engage in trade, buy and sell; exchange (goods) in trading. **trade in** give (a used article) as partial payment for another arti-cle. (**trade-in** *n.*). **trade mark** manufacturer's or trader's registered emblem or name etc. used to identify his goods. **trade off** exchange as a compromise. **trade on** use (esp. unscrupulously) for one's own advantage. **Trades Union Congress** association of representatives of British trade unions. **trade union** (*pl.* **trade unions**) organized association of employees formed to protect and promote their common interests. **trade-unionist** *n.* member of a trade union. **trade wind** constant wind blowing towards the equator from the north-east or south-east. **trader** *n.*

tradesman *n.* (*pl.* **-men**) person engaged in trade; shopkeeper; roundsman.

trading *n.* buying and selling. **trading estate** area designed to be occupied by a group of industrial and commercial firms.

tradition *n.* belief or custom handed down from one generation to another; long-established procedure; handing down of beliefs etc. **traditional** *a.*, **traditionally** *adv.*

traditionalist *n.* person who upholds traditional beliefs etc. **traditionalism** *n.*

traduce *v.t.* slander. **traducement** *n.*

traffic *n.* vehicles, ships, or aircraft moving along a route; trading. —*v.t./i.* (*p.t.* **trafficked**) trade. **traffic-lights** *n.pl.* automatic signals controlling traffic at a junction etc. by means of coloured lights. **traffic warden** official who assists police in controlling the movement and parking of road vehicles. **trafficker** *n.*

tragedian /-'dʒi:-/ *n.* writer of tragedies; actor in tragedy.

tragedienne /-'en/ *n.* actress in tragedy.

tragedy *n.* serious drama with unhappy events and a sad ending; event causing great sadness.

tragic *a.* of or in tragedy; sorrowful; causing great sadness. **tragical** *a.*, **tragically** *adv.*

tragicomedy *n.* drama of mixed tragic and comic events.

trail *v.t./i.* drag behind, esp. on the ground; hang loosely; (of a plant) grow lengthily downwards or along the ground; move wearily; lag, straggle; diminish, become fainter; track. —*n.* thing that trails; line of people or things following something; mark left, track, trace; beaten path. **trailing edge** rear edge of an aircraft's wing.

trailer *n.* truck etc. designed to be hauled by a vehicle; short extract from a film etc., shown in advance to advertise it.

train *n.* railway engine with linked carriages or trucks; people or animals moving in a line; retinue; sequence of things; part of a long robe that trails behind the wearer; line of combustible material placed to lead fire to an explosive. —*v.t./i.* bring or come to a desired standard of efficiency or condition or behaviour etc. by instruction and practice; teach to do something; aim (a gun etc.); cause (a plant) to grow in the required direction. **in train** in preparation.

trainable *a.* able to be trained.

trainee *n.* person being trained.

trainer *n.* person who trains horses or athletes etc.; (*pl.*) soft shoes as worn by athletes in training.

traipse *v.i.* (*colloq.*) trudge.

trait /tret/ *n.* characteristic.

traitor *n.* person who behaves disloyally, esp. to his country. **traitorous** *a.*

trajectory /'træ-/ *n.* path of a bullet or rocket or other body moving under certain forces.

tram *n.* public passenger vehicle running on rails laid in the road.

tramcar *n.* tram.

tramlines *n.pl.* rails on which a tram runs; (*colloq.*) pair of parallel sidelines in tennis etc.

trammel *n.* a kind of fishing-net; (*pl.*) hampering influence. —*v.t.* (*p.t.* **trammelled**) hamper.

tramp *v.t./i.* walk with heavy footsteps; go on foot across (an area); trample. —*n.* sound of heavy footsteps; long walk; vagrant; cargo boat that does not travel a regular route; (*sl.*) immoral woman.

trample *v.t./i.* tread repeatedly, crush or harm by treading.

trampoline /-li:n/ *n.* sheet attached by springs to a frame, used for jumping on in acrobatic leaps. —*v.i.* use a trampoline.

trance *n.* sleep-like or dreamy state.

tranquil *a.* calm and undisturbed. **tranquilly** *adv.*, **tranquillity** *n.*

tranquillize *v.t.* calm.

tranquillizer *n.* drug used to relieve anxiety and induce calmness.

transact *v.t.* perform or carry out (business etc.). **transaction** *n.*

transatlantic *a.* on or from the other side of the Atlantic; crossing the Atlantic.

transceiver *n.* combined radio transmitter and receiver.

transcend /-'send/ *v.t.* go beyond the range of (experience, belief, etc.); surpass. **transcendent** *a.*, **transcendence** *n.*

transcendental *a.* transcendent; abstract, obscure, visionary.

transcontinental *a.* crossing or extending across a continent.

transcribe *v.t.* copy in writing; record (sound) for reproduction; arrange (music) for a different instrument etc. **transcription** *n.*

transcript *n.* written or recorded copy.

transducer *n.* device that receives waves or other variations from one system and conveys related ones to another.

transept *n.* part lying at right angles to the nave in a church.

transfer[1] /-'fɜ:(r)/ *v.t./i.* (*p.t.* transferred) convey or move or hand over from one place or person or application etc. to another. **transference** /'træ-/ *n.*, **transferable** *a.*

transfer[2] /'træ-/ *n.* process of transferring; document transferring property or a right; design for transferring from one surface to another; paper bearing this.

transfigure *v.t.* change in appearance to something nobler or more beautiful. **transfiguration** *n.*

transfix *v.t.* pierce through, impale; make motionless with fear or astonishment.

transform *v.t./i.* change greatly in appearance or character; change the voltage of (electric current). **transformation** *n.*, **transformer** *n.*

transfuse *v.t.* give a transfusion of to; permeate; imbue.

transfusion *n.* injection of blood or other fluid into a blood vessel.

transgress *v.t./i.* break (a rule or law); go beyond (a limitation); (*old use*) sin. **transgression** *n.*, **transgressor** *n.*

transient /-zɪənt/ *a.* passing away quickly, not lasting. **transience** *n.*

transistor *n.* very small semiconductor device performing the same functions as a thermionic valve; portable radio set using transistors. **transistorized** *a.*

transit *n.* process of going or conveying across, over, or through. —*v.t.* (*p.t.* transited) make a transit across.

transition *n.* process of changing from one state or style etc. to another. **transitional** *a.*

transitive *a.* (of a verb) used with a direct object. **transitively** *adv.*

transitory *a.* lasting only briefly.

translate *v.t./i.* express in another language or other words; be able to be translated; transfer.

translation *n.*, **translator** *n.*, **translatable** *a.*

transliterate *v.t.* convert to the letters of another alphabet. **transliteration** *n.*

translucent *a.* allowing light to pass through but not transparent. **translucence** *n.*

transmigrate *v.i.* migrate; (of the soul) pass into another body after a person's death. **transmigration** *n.*

transmissible *a.* able to be transmitted.

transmission *n.* transmitting; broadcast; gear transmitting power from engine to axle.

transmit *v.t.* (*p.t.* transmitted) send or pass on from one person, place, or thing to another; send out (a signal or programme etc.) by telegraph wire or radio waves. **transmitter** *n.*

transmogrify *v.t.* (*joc.*) transform. **transmogrification** *n.*

transmute *v.t.* change in form or substance. **transmutation** *n.*

transom *n.* horizontal bar across the top of a door or window; small window above a door or another window.

transparency /-'pæ- *or* -'peər-/ *n.* being transparent; photographic slide, esp. on film not glass.

transparent /-'pæ- *or* -'peər-/ *a.* able to be seen through; easily understood, obvious. **transparently** *adv.*

transpire *v.t./i* become known; (of plants) give off (vapour) from leaves etc. **transpiration** *n.*

transplant[1] /-'plɑː-/ *v.t.* remove and replant or establish elsewhere; transfer (living tissue). **transplantation** *n.*

transplant[2] /'trɑː-/ *n.* transplanting of tissue; thing transplanted.

transport[1] /-'pɔːt/ *v.t.* convey from one place to another. **transportation** *n.*, **transporter** *n.*

transport[2] /'træ-/ *n.* process of transporting; means of conveyance; ship or aircraft for carrying troops or supplies; (*pl.*) condition of strong emotion.

transported *a.* carried away by strong emotion.

transpose *v.t.* cause (two or more things) to change places; change the position of; put (music) into a different key. **transposition** *n.*

transsexual *a. & n.* (person) having the physical characteristics of one sex and psychological characteristics of the other. **transsexualism** *n.*

transship *v.t.* transfer from one ship or conveyance to another. **transshipment** *n.*

transubstantiation *n.* conversion of the elements in the Eucharist to the body and blood of Christ.

transuranic /-ˈræn-/ *a.* belonging to a group of radioactive elements whose atoms are heavier than those of uranium.

transverse *a.* crosswise.

transvestism *n.* dressing in clothing of the opposite sex. **transvestite** *n.*

trap *n.* device for catching and holding an animal; anything by which an unsuspecting person is captured or outwitted; trapdoor; compartment with a hinged flap from which a dog is released in racing; curved section of a pipe holding liquid to prevent foul gases from coming upwards; two-wheeled horse-drawn carriage; (*sl.*) mouth. —*v.t.* (*p.t.* **trapped**) catch or hold in a trap.

trapdoor *n.* door in a floor, ceiling, or roof.

trapeze *n.* a kind of swing on which acrobatics are performed.

trapezium /-ˈpiːz-/ *n.* quadrilateral with only two opposite sides parallel; (*US*) trapezoid.

trapezoid /ˈtræp-/ *n.* quadrilateral with no sides parallel; (*US*) trapezium.

trapper *n.* person who traps animals, esp. for furs.

trappings *n.pl.* accessories; adjuncts.

Trappist *n.* member of a monastic order noted for silence.

traps *n.pl.* percussion instruments in a jazz band; (*colloq.*) baggage.

trash *n.* worthless stuff. **trashy** *a.*

trauma /ˈtrɔː-/ *n.* wound, injury; emotional shock producing a lasting effect. **traumatic** *a.*

travail *n. & v.i.* labour.

travel *v.t./i.* (*p.t.* **travelled**) go from one place to another; journey along or through; go from place to place as a salesman. —*n.* travelling, esp. abroad. **traveller** *n.*

traverse[1] /-ˈvɜːs/ *v.t.* travel or lie or extend across. **traversal** *n.*

traverse[2] /ˈtræv-/ *n.* thing that lies across another; zigzag course, each leg of this; lateral movement; steep slope that has to be crossed from side to side.

travesty /ˈtræv-/ *n.* absurd or inferior imitation. —*v.t.* make or be a travesty of.

trawl *n.* large wide-mouthed fishing-net. —*v.t./i.* fish or catch with a trawl.

trawler *n.* boat used in trawling.

tray *n.* shallow utensil on which small articles are placed for display or carrying; open receptacle for holding correspondence in an office; tray-like compartment.

treacherous *a.* showing treachery; not to be relied on, deceptive. **treacherously** *adv.*

treachery *n.* betrayal of a person or cause; act of disloyalty.

treacle *n.* thick sticky liquid produced when sugar is refined. **treacly** *a.*

tread *v.t./i.* (*p.t.* **trod**, *p.p.* **trodden**) set one's foot down; walk, step; walk on, press or crush with the feet. —*n.* manner or sound of walking; horizontal surface of a stair; part of a wheel or tyre etc. that touches the ground. **tread**

water keep upright in water by making treading movements.

treadle n. lever worked by the foot to drive a wheel. —v.i. work a treadle.

treadmill n. wide mill-wheel formerly turned by people treading on steps fixed round its edge; similar device used for exercise; tiring monotonous routine work.

treason n. treachery towards one's country or its ruler. **treasonous** a.

treasonable a. involving treason.

treasure n. collection of precious metals or gems; highly valued object or person. —v.t. value highly; store as precious. **treasure hunt** search for treasure; game of seeking a hidden object. **treasure trove** treasure of unknown ownership, found hidden; something very desirable that a person finds.

treasurer n. person in charge of the funds of an institution.

treasury n. place where treasure is kept; **the Treasury** department managing a country's revenue.

treat v.t./i. act or behave towards or deal with in a specified way; give medical treatment to; subject to a chemical or other process; buy a meal etc. for (a person) in order to give pleasure; negotiate terms. —n. something special that gives pleasure; treating of others to food etc.

treatise n. written work dealing with one subject.

treatment n. manner of dealing with a person or thing; something done to relieve illness etc.

treaty n. formal agreement made, esp. between countries.

treble a. three times as much or as many; (of a voice) high-pitched, soprano. —n. treble quantity or thing; treble voice, person with this. **trebly** adv.

tree n. perennial plant with a single thick stem; framework of

wood for various purposes. —v.t. force to take refuge up a tree.

treeless a.

trefoil /'tref-/ n. plant with three leaflets (e.g. clover); thing shaped like this.

trek n. long arduous journey. —v.i. (p.t. **trekked**) make a trek.

trellis n. light framework of crossing strips of wood etc. used to support climbing plants or as a screen.

tremble v.i. shake involuntarily, esp. from fear or cold etc.; quiver; feel very anxious. —n. trembling movement. **trembly** a.

tremendous a. immense; (colloq.) excellent. **tremendously** adv.

tremolo n. (pl. **-os**) trembling effect in music or singing.

tremor n. slight trembling movement; thrill of fear etc.

tremulous a. trembling, quivering. **tremulously** adv.

trench n. deep ditch. **trench coat** belted coat or raincoat resembling military uniform.

trenchant a. (of comments, policies, etc.) strong and effective.

trencher n. wooden platter for food. **good trencherman** hearty eater.

trend n. thing's continuing tendency. **trend-setter** n. person who leads the way in fashion etc.

trendy a. (**-ier, -iest**) (colloq.) following the latest trends of fashion. **trendily** adv., **trendiness** n.

trepan /-'pæn/ n. & v.t. trephine.

trephine /-'fi:n/ n. surgeon's cylindrical saw for removing a section of the skull. —v.t. cut with this.

trepidation n. nervousness.

trespass v.i. enter land or property unlawfully; intrude; (old use) sin. —n. act of trespassing; (old use) sin. **trespasser** n.

tress n. lock of hair.

trestle n. one of a set of supports on which a board is rested to form a table; braced framework supporting a bridge. **trestle-table** n.

trews n.pl. close-fitting usu. tartan trousers.

tri- pref. three times, triple.

triad n. group of three; Chinese usu. criminal secret society.

trial n. examination in a lawcourt by a judge to decide an issue, esp. the guilt or innocence of an accused person; process of testing qualities or performance; person or thing that tries one's patience, hardship. **on trial** undergoing a trial.

triangle n. geometric figure with three sides and three angles; thing shaped like this; triangular steel rod struck with another rod as a percussion instrument.

triangular a. shaped like a triangle; involving three people.

triangulation n. measurement or mapping of an area by means of a network of triangles.

tribe n. racial group (esp. in a primitive culture) living as a community under one or more chiefs; set or class of people. **tribal** a., **tribesman** n. (pl.**-men**).

tribulation n. great affliction.

tribunal /traɪ-/ n. board of officials appointed to adjudicate on a particular problem.

tribune[1] n. popular leader; people's official in ancient Rome.

tribune[2] n. platform, rostrum.

tributary a. & n. (stream) flowing into a larger stream or a lake.

tribute n. something said or done as a mark of respect; payment that one country or ruler was formerly obliged to pay to another.

trice n. **in a trice** in an instant.

trichology /trɪk-/ n. study of hair and its diseases. **trichologist** n.

trick n. something done to deceive or outwit someone; deception, illusion; technique, best way of doing something; feat of skill; mannerism; mischievous or discreditable act; cards played in one round of a card-game; this

round, a point gained from it; person's turn of duty (usu. for two hours) at a ship's helm. —*v.t.* deceive or persuade by a trick; deck, decorate. **do the trick** (*colloq.*) achieve what is required.

trickery n. use of tricks, deception.

trickle *v.t./i.* flow or cause to flow in a thin stream; come or go slowly or gradually. —n. trickling flow.

trickster n. person who tricks people.

tricky a. (**ier, iest**) crafty, deceitful; requiring careful handling. **trickiness** n.

tricolour /ˈtrɪk-/ n. flag with three colours in stripes.

tricot /ˈtriːkəʊ/ n. fine jersey fabric.

tricycle n. three-wheeled pedal-driven vehicle. **tricyclist** n.

trident /ˈtraɪ-/ n. three-pronged fish-spear carried as a symbol of power over the sea.

Tridentine /trɪˈdentaɪn/ a. of traditional RC orthodoxy.

triennial /traɪˈen-/ a. happening every third year; lasting three years.

trier n. person who tries hard.

trifle n. thing of only slight value or importance; very small amount, esp. of money; sweet dish of sponge cake soaked in wine or jelly etc. and topped with custard and cream. —*v.t.* behave or talk frivolously. **trifle with** toy with. **trifler** n.

trifling a. trivial.

trigger n. small lever for releasing a spring, esp. to fire a gun. —*v.t.* (also **trigger off**) set in action, cause. **trigger-happy** a. apt to shoot on slight provocation.

trigonometry /-ˈnɒm-/ n. branch of mathematics dealing with the relationship of sides and angles of triangles etc.

trike n. (*colloq.*) tricycle.

trilateral /traɪ-/ a. having three sides or three participants.

trilby n. man's soft felt hat.

trilingual /-gw(ə)l/ a. speaking or using three languages.

trill n. vibrating sound, esp. in music or singing. —v.t./i. sound or sing with a trill.

trillion n. a million million million; (US etc.) a million million.

trilobite /'traɪ-/ n. a kind of fossil crustacean.

trilogy /'trɪl-/ n. group of three related literary or operatic works.

trim a. (**trimmer, trimmest**) neat and orderly. —v.t. (p.t. **trimmed**) remove irregular parts; reduce or neaten by cutting; ornament; make (a boat or aircraft) evenly balanced by distributing its load; arrange (sails) to suit the wind. —n. condition as regards readiness or fitness; ornamentation; colour or type of upholstery etc. in a car; trimming of hair etc. **trimly** adv., **trimness** n.

trimaran /'traɪ-/ n. vessel like a catamaran, with three hulls.

trimming n. thing added as a decoration; (pl.) pieces cut off when something is trimmed.

trine n. & a. (astrological aspect) of two planets one-third of the zodiac (= 120°) apart.

trinity n. group of three; **the Trinity** the three persons of the Godhead (Father, Son, Holy Spirit) as constituting one God.

trinket n. small fancy article or piece of jewellery.

trio n. (pl. **-os**) group or set of three; music for three instruments or voices.

trip v.t./i. (p.t. **tripped**) go lightly and quickly; stumble, cause to do this; make or cause to make a blunder; release (a switch etc.) so as to operate a mechanism. —n. journey or excursion, esp. for pleasure; (colloq.) visionary experience caused by a drug;

stumble; device for tripping a mechanism. **trip-wire** n. wire stretched along the ground, operating a warning device or a mine etc. if disturbed.

tripartite /traɪ-/ a. consisting of three parts.

tripe n. stomach of an ox etc. as food; (sl.) worthless thing, nonsense.

triple a. having three parts or members; three times as much or as many. —v.t./i. increase by three times its amount. **triple time** rhythm of music with three beats to the bar.

triplet n. one of three children born at one birth; set of three.

triplex a. triple, threefold.

triplicate a. & n. existing in three examples. **in triplicate** as three identical copies.

tripod /'traɪ-/ n. three-legged stand.

tripos /'traɪpɒs/ n. final examination for the BA degree at Cambridge University.

tripper n. person who goes on a pleasure trip. **trippery** a.

triptych /'trɪptɪk/ n. picture or carving with three panels fixed or hinged side by side.

trisect v.t. divide into three equal parts. **trisection** n.

trite a. hackneyed.

triumph n. fact of being successful or victorious; joy at this; great success. —v.i. be successful or victorious, rejoice at this. **triumphant** a., **triumphantly** adv.

triumphal a. celebrating or commemorating a triumph.

triumvirate n. government or control by a board of three.

trivet /'trɪv-/ n. iron stand for a kettle etc. placed over a fire; stand for hot dish etc. on a table.

trivia n.pl. trivial things.

trivial a. of only small value or importance. **trivially** adv., **triviality** n.

trod, trodden see **tread**.

troglodyte /ˈtrɒg-/ n. cave-dweller. **troglodytic** a.

troll[1] /trəʊl/ v.t./i. sing in a care-free way; fish by drawing bait along.

troll[2] /trəʊl/ n. giant or dwarf in Scandinavian mythology.

trolley n. (pl. **-eys**) platform on wheels for transporting goods; small cart; small table on wheels for transporting food or articles. **trolley bus** bus powered by electricity from an overhead wire.

trollop n. slovenly or promiscuous woman.

trombone n. large brass wind instrument with a sliding tube.

troop n. company of people or animals; cavalry or artillery unit; Scout company. —v.t./i. assemble or go as a troop or in great numbers. **trooping the colour** ceremony of carrying the regimental flag along ranks of soldiers.

trooper n. soldier in a cavalry or armoured unit; (US) member of a State police force.

trophy n. thing taken in war or hunting etc. as a souvenir of success; object awarded as a prize.

tropic n. line of latitude 23° 27′ north or south of the equator; (pl.) region between these, with a hot climate. **tropical** a.

troposphere /ˈtrɒp-/ n. layer of the atmosphere extending from earth's surface to the stratosphere.

trot n. running action of a horse etc.; moderate running-pace. —v.t./i. (p.t. **trotted**) go or cause to go at a trot. **on the trot** (colloq.) continually busy; in succession. **trot out** (colloq.) produce.

troth /trəʊθ/ n. promise, fidelity.

Trotskyism n. principles of the Russian revolutionary leader Leon Trotsky. **Trotskyist** n.

trotter n. animal's foot as food.

troubadour /ˈtruːbədʊə(r)/ n. medieval romantic poet.

trouble n. difficulty, distress, mis-fortune; cause of this; conflict; inconvenience, exertion; unpleasantness involving punishment or rebuke; faulty functioning. —v.t./i. cause trouble to; make or be disturbed or worried; use much care and effort.

troubleshooter n. person employed to deal with faults or problems.

troublesome a. causing trouble.

troublous a. (old use) full of troubles.

trough /trɒf/ n. long narrow open receptacle, esp. for holding water or food for animals; depression between two waves or ridges; elongated region of low atmospheric pressure.

trounce v.t. thrash; defeat heavily.

troupe /truːp/ n. company of actors or other performers.

trouper /ˈtruː-/ n. member of a troupe; staunch colleague.

trousers n.pl. two-legged outer garment reaching from the waist usu. to the ankles.

trousseau /ˈtruːsəʊ/ n. (pl. **-eaux**, pr. **-əʊz**) bride's collection of clothing etc. to begin married life.

trout n. (pl. **trout**) freshwater fish valued as food and game.

trowel n. small spade-like tool with a curved blade; similar tool with a flat blade for spreading mortar etc.

troy weight system of weights used for precious metals.

truant n. person who absents himself from school or work etc. without leave. **play truant** stay away as a truant. **truancy** n.

truce n. agreement to cease hostilities temporarily.

truck[1] n. open container on wheels for transporting loads; open railway wagon; lorry.

truck[2] n. dealings.

trucker n. lorry-driver.

truckle *v.i.* submit obsequiously. **truckle-bed** *n.* low bed on wheels, kept under another.

truculent /ˈtrʌkjʊ-/ *a.* defiant and aggressive. **truculently** *adv.*, **truculence** *n.*

trudge *v.i.* walk laboriously. —*n.* laborious walk.

true *a.* (-er, -est) in accordance with fact or correct principles or an accepted standard, genuine; exact, accurate; loyal, faithful. —*adv.* truly, accurately. **true-ness** *n.*

truffle *n.* rich-flavoured underground fungus valued as a delicacy; soft chocolate sweet.

trug *n.* gardener's shallow basket.

truism *n.* statement that is obviously true, esp. a hackneyed one.

truly *adv.* truthfully; genuinely; faithfully.

trump[1] *n.* (old use) sound of a trumpet.

trump[2] *n.* playing-card of a suit temporarily ranking above others; (*colloq.*) person who behaves in a helpful or useful way. —*v.t.* **trump up** invent fraudulently. **turn up trumps** (*colloq.*) be successful or helpful.

trumpery *a.* showy but worthless.

trumpet *n.* metal wind instrument with a flared tube; thing shaped like this. —*v.t./i.* (*p.t.* **trumpeted**) blow or proclaim by a trumpet; (of an elephant) make a loud sound with its trunk. **trumpeter** *n.*

truncate *v.t.* shorten by cutting off the end. **truncation** *n.*

truncheon *n.* short thick stick carried as a weapon.

trundle *v.t./i.* roll along, move along heavily on wheels.

trunk *n.* tree's main stem; body apart from head and limbs; large box with a hinged lid, for transporting or storing clothes etc.; elephant's long flexible nose; (*US*) boot of a car; (*pl.*) shorts for swimming etc. **trunk call** long-distance inland telephone call. **trunk road** important main road.

truss *n.* bundle of hay or straw; cluster of flowers or fruit; framework of beams or bars supporting a roof etc.; padded belt or other device worn to support a hernia. —*v.t.* tie securely; support with trusses.

trust *n.* firm belief in the reliability or truth or strength etc. of a person or thing; confident expectation; responsibility arising from being entrusted with something; property legally entrusted to someone with instructions for its use; association of business firms, formed to reduce or defeat competition. —*v.t./i.* have or place trust in; entrust; hope earnestly. **in trust** held as a trust. **on trust** accepted without investigation. **trust to** rely on. **trustful** *a.*, **trustfully** *adv.*, **trustfulness** *n.*

trustee *n.* person who administers property held as a trust; one of a group managing the business affairs of an institution. **trustworthy** *a.* worthy of trust. **trustworthiness** *n.*

trusty *a.* & *n.* trustworthy (person).

truth *n.* quality of being true; something that is true.

truthful *a.* habitually telling the truth; true. **truthfully** *adv.*, **truthfulness** *n.*

try *v.t./i.* attempt; test, esp. by use; attempt to open (a door etc.); be a strain on; hold a trial of. —*n.* attempt; touchdown in Rugby football, entitling the player's side to a kick at goal. **try on** put (a garment) on to see if it fits. **try out** test by use. **try-out** *n.*

trying *a.* annoying.

tryst /trɪst/ *n.* (old use) appointed meeting, esp. of sweethearts.

tsar /zɑ:(r)/ *n.* title of the former emperor of Russia.

tsetse /'tsetsɪ, 'tet-/ n. African fly that transmits disease by its bite.

T-shirt n. simple shirt usu. of knitted cotton.

T-square n. T-shaped instrument for measuring or obtaining right angles.

tub n. open usu. round container.

tuba /'tjuː-/ n. large low-pitched brass wind instrument.

tubby a. (-ier, -iest) short and fat. **tubbiness** n.

tube n. long hollow cylinder; thing shaped like this; cathode-ray tube; (colloq.) underground railway system in London.

tuber n. short thick rounded root or underground stem from which shoots will grow.

tubercle n. small rounded swelling.

tubercular /-'bɜː-/ a. of or affected with tuberculosis.

tuberculin-tested a. (of milk) from cows shown to be free from tuberculosis.

tuberculosis n. infectious wasting disease, esp. affecting lungs.

tuberose n. tropical plant with fragrant white flowers.

tuberous a. of or like a tuber; bearing tubers.

tubing n. tubes; a length of tube.

tubular /'tjuː-/ a. tube-shaped.

TUC abbr. Trades Union Congress.

tuck n. flat fold stitched in a garment etc.; (sl.) food, esp. cakes and sweets. —v.t./i. turn into or under something so as to be concealed or held in place; cover or put away compactly; put a tuck or tucks in. **tuck in** or **into** (sl.) eat heartily. **tuck shop** shop selling cakes and sweets etc. to schoolchildren.

tucker n. (Austr. colloq.) food.

Tuesday n. day after Monday.

tufa /'tjuː-/ n. a kind of coarse rock.

tuft n. bunch of threads or grass or hair etc. held or growing together at the base. **tufted** a.

tug v.t./i. (p.t. **tugged**) pull vigorously; tow. —n. vigorous pull; small powerful boat for towing others. **tug of war** contest of strength in which two teams pull opposite ways on a rope.

tuition n. process of teaching; instruction.

tulip n. garden plant with a cup-shaped flower. **tulip-tree** n. tree with tulip-like flowers.

tulle /tjuːl/ n. fine silky net fabric used for veils and dresses.

tumble v.t./i. fall; cause to fall; roll, push, or move in a disorderly way; perform somersaults etc.; rumple. —n. fall; untidy state. **tumble-drier** n. machine for drying washing in a heated rotating drum. **tumble to** (colloq.) realize, grasp the meaning of.

tumbledown a. dilapidated.

tumbler n. drinking-glass with no handle or foot; pigeon that throws itself over backwards in flight; pivoted piece in a lock etc.; acrobat.

tumbrel n. (also **tumbril**) open cart used for carrying condemned persons to the guillotine during the French Revolution.

tumescent /-'mes-/ a. swelling. **tumescence** n.

tummy n. (colloq.) stomach.

tumour n. abnormal mass of new tissue growing in or on the body.

tumult n. uproar; conflict of emotions.

tumultuous /-'mʌl-/ a. making an uproar.

tun n. large cask; fermenting-vat.

tuna /'tjuː-/ n. (pl. **tuna**) tunny; its flesh as food.

tundra n. vast level Arctic regions where the subsoil is frozen.

tune n. melody. —v.t. put (a musical instrument) in tune; set (a radio) to the desired wavelength; adjust (an engine) to run smoothly. **in tune** playing or singing at the correct musical pitch; harmonious. **out of tune**

not in tune. **tune up** bring musical instruments to the correct or uniform pitch. **tuner** n.

tuneful a. melodious.

tuneless a. without a tune.

tungsten n. heavy grey metallic element.

tunic n. close-fitting jacket worn as part of a uniform; loose garment reaching to the hips or knees.

tuning-fork n. two-pronged steel device giving a particular note (usu. middle C) when struck.

tunnel n. underground passage. —v.t./i. (p.t. **tunnelled**) make a tunnel (through), make (one's way) thus.

tunny n. large edible sea-fish.

tup n. male sheep.

tuppence n. **tuppenny** a. = twopence, twopenny.

turban n. Muslim or Sikh man's head-dress of a scarf wound round a cap; woman's hat resembling this.

turbid a. (of liquids) muddy, not clear; disordered. **turbidity** n.

turbine /-bam/ n. machine or motor driven by a wheel that is turned by a flow of water or gas.

turbo- pref. using a turbine; driven by such engines.

turbot n. large flat sea-fish valued as food.

turbulent a. in a state of commotion or unrest; moving unevenly. **turbulently** adv., **turbulence** n.

tureen /tjʊˈriːn/ n. deep covered dish from which soup is served.

turf n. (pl. **turfs** or **turves**) short grass and the soil just below it; piece of this; slab of peat for fuel; **the turf** racecourse, horseracing. —v.t. lay (ground) with turf. **turf accountant** bookmaker. **turf out** (sl.) throw out.

turgid a. swollen and not flexible; (of language) pompous, not flowing easily. **turgidly** adv., **turgidity** n.

Turk n. native of Turkey.

turkey n. (pl. **-eys**) large bird reared for its flesh; this as food.

Turkish a. & n. (language) of Turkey. **Turkish bath** exposure of the body to hot air or steam. **Turkish delight** sweet consisting of flavoured gelatine coated in powdered sugar. **Turkish towel** towel made in terry towelling.

turmeric /ˈtɜː-/ n. plant of the ginger family; its powdered root.

turmoil n. state of great disturbance or confusion.

turn v.t./i. move round a point or axis, or so that a different side is presented; take or give a new direction (to); aim; pass round (a point); pass (a certain hour or age); send, put; change in form or appearance etc.; make or become sour or nauseated; shape in a lathe; give an elegant form to. —n. process of turning; change of direction or condition etc.; angle; bend or corner in a road; character, tendency; service of a specified kind; opportunity or obligation coming in succession; short performance in an entertainment; (colloq.) attack of illness, momentary nervous shock. **in turn** in succession. **out of turn** before or after one's proper turn; indiscreetly, presumptuously. **to a turn** so as to be cooked perfectly. **turn against** make or become hostile to. **turn down** fold down; turn a knob or tap to reduce the volume or flow of; reject. **turn in** hand in; (colloq.) go to bed; (colloq.) abandon (work etc.). **turn off** (or **on**) turn a tap or switch to stop (or start) the flow or operation of; (colloq.) cause to lose (or to feel) interest. **turn out** expel; turn off (a light etc.); equip, dress; produce by work; empty and search or clean; (colloq.) come out; summon (a military guard) for duty; prove to be the case eventually. **turn-out** n. process of turning out a room etc.; number of people attending a public or social function; thing arrayed, outfit. **turn the tables** reverse a situation and put oneself in a superior position. **turn up** discover; be found; make one's appearance; happen; turn a knob or tap to increase the volume or flow of; (*colloq.*) sicken.

turn-up *n.* turned-up part, esp. at the lower end of a trouser-leg; (*colloq.*) unexpected event.

turncoat *n.* person who changes his principles.

turner *n.* person who works with a lathe. **turnery** *n.* his work or products.

turning *n.* place where one road meets another, forming a corner. **turning-point** *n.* point at which a decisive change takes place.

turnip *n.* plant with a round white root used as a vegetable or as fodder; its root.

turnover *n.* pasty with pastry folded to enclose filling; amount of money taken in a business; rate of replacement.

turnpike *n.* (*old use & US*) road on which toll is collected at gates.

turnstile *n.* revolving barrier for admitting people to a building etc. one at a time.

turntable *n.* circular revolving platform.

turpentine *n.* oil used for thinning paint and as a solvent.

turpitude *n.* wickedness.

turps *n.* (*colloq.*) turpentine.

turquoise /-kwɔɪz/ *n.* blue-green precious stone; its colour.

turret *n.* small tower-like structure. **turreted** *a.*

turtle *n.* sea creature like a tortoise. **turn turtle** capsize. **turtledove** *n.* wild dove noted for its soft cooing. **turtle-neck** *n.* high round close-fitting neckline.

tusk *n.* one of the pair of long pointed teeth projecting outside the mouth in certain animals.

tussle *v.i. & n.* struggle, conflict.

tussock *n.* tuft or clump of grass.

tussore /'tʌs-/ *n.* strong but coarse silk.

tutelage /'tjuːtɪl-/ *n.* guardianship; tuition.

tutelary /'tjuːtɪl-/ *a.* serving as a protector or patron.

tutor *n.* private or university teacher. —*v.t./i.* act as tutor (to), teach.

tutorial /-'tɔː-/ *a.* of a tutor. —*n.* student's session with a tutor.

tut-tut *int.* exclamation of annoyance, impatience, or rebuke.

tutu /'tuːtuː/ *n.* dancer's short skirt made of layers of frills.

tuxedo /tʌk'siː-/ *n.* (*pl.* **-os**) (*US*) dinner-jacket.

TV *abbr.* television.

twaddle *n.* nonsense.

twain *a. & n.* (*old use*) two.

twang *n.* sharp ringing sound like that made by a tense wire when plucked; nasal intonation. —*v.t./i.* make or cause to make a twang.

tweak *v.t. & n.* pinch, twist, or pull with a sharp jerk.

twee *a.* affectedly dainty or quaint.

tweed *n.* twilled usu. woollen fabric; (*pl.*) clothes made of tweed. **tweedy** *a.*

tweet *n. & v.i.* chirp.

tweeter *n.* loudspeaker for reproducing high-frequency signals.

tweezers *n.pl.* small pincers for picking up or pulling very small things.

twelve *a. & n.* one more than eleven (12, XII). **twelfth** *a. & n.*

twenty *a. & n.* twice ten. **twenty-twenty** *a.* denoting normal vision; *colloq.* denoting clear perception. **twentieth** *a. & n.*

twerp *n.* (*sl.*) stupid or insignificant person.

twice *adv.* two times: in double amount or degree.

twiddle *v.t.* twist idly about. —*n.* act of twiddling. **twiddle one's thumbs** twist them idly, have nothing to do. **twiddly** *a.*

twig[1] *n.* small shoot issuing from a branch or stem.

twig[2] *v.t./i.* (*p.t.* **twigged**) (*colloq.*) realize, grasp the meaning of.

twilight *n.* light from the sky when the sun is below the horizon (esp. after sunset); period of this.

twill *n.* fabric woven so that parallel diagonal lines are produced. **twilled** *a.*

twin *n.* one of two children or animals born at one birth; one of a pair that are exactly alike. —*a.* being a twin or twins.—*v.t./i.* (*p.t.* **twinned**) combine as a pair. **twin towns** two towns that establish special social and cultural links.

twine *n.* strong thread or string. —*v.t./i.* twist; wind or coil.

twinge *n.* slight or brief pang.

twinkle *v.i.* shine with a light that flickers rapidly; move with short rapid movements. —*n.* twinkling light or look or movement.

twirl *v.t./i.* twist lightly or rapidly. —*n.* twirling movement; twirled mark. **twirly** *a.*

twist *v.t./i.* wind (strands etc.) round each other, esp. to form a single cord; make by doing this; give a spiral form to; take a spiral course, bend round; rotate, wrench out of its normal shape; distort; (*sl.*) swindle. —*n.* process of twisting; thing formed by twisting; peculiar tendency of mind or character; unexpected development etc.; (*sl.*) swindle. **twister** *n.*

twit[1] *v.t.* (*p.t.* **twitted**) taunt.

twit[2] *n.* (*sl.*) foolish or insignificant person.

twitch *v.t./i.* pull with a light jerk; quiver or contract spasmodically. —*n.* twitching movement.

twitter *v.i.* make light chirping sounds; talk rapidly in an anxious or nervous way. —*n.* twittering.

two *a. & n.* one more than one (2, II). **be in two minds** be undecided. **two-dimensional** *a.* having or appearing to have length

and breadth but no depth. **two-faced** *a.* insincere, deceitful.

two-piece *n.* suit of clothes or a woman's swimsuit consisting of two separate parts.

twofold *a. & adv.* twice as much or as many.

twopence /'tʌp-/ *n.* sum of two pence. **twopenny** *a.*

twosome *n.* two together, pair.

tycoon *n.* magnate.

tying *see* tie.

tyke *n.* objectionable fellow.

tympanum /'tɪm-/ *n.* (*pl.* **-na**) eardrum; space between the lintel and the arch above a door.

Tynwald /'tɪnwɒld/ *n.* governing assembly of the Isle of Man.

type *n.* kind, class; typical example or instance; (*colloq.*) person of specified character; (small block with a raised) letter etc. used in printing; set or kind of these. —*v.t./i.* write with a typewriter; classify according to type.

typecast *v.t.* cast (an actor) in a role appropriate to his or her nature or previous successful roles.

typescript *n.* typewritten document.

typewriter *n.* machine for producing print-like characters on paper, by pressing keys. **type-written** *a.*

typhoid *n.* **typhoid fever** serious infectious feverish disease.

typhoon *n.* violent hurricane.

typhus *n.* infectious feverish disease transmitted by parasites.

typical *a.* having the distinctive qualities of a particular type of person or thing. **typically** *adv.*

typify *v.t.* be a representative specimen of.

typist *n.* person who types.

typography *n.* art, practice, or style of printing. **typographical** *a.*

tyrannize /'tɪ-/ *v.i.* rule as or like a tyrant.

tyranny /'tɪ-/ *n.* government by a tyrant; tyrannical use of power.

tyrannical /tɪ'ræn-/ a., **tyranni-cally** adv., **tyrannous** /'tɪ-/ a.

tyrant /'taɪ-/ n. ruler or other person who uses power in a harsh, demanding, or oppressive way.

tyre n. covering round the rim of a wheel to absorb shocks.

tyro n. (pl. -os) = tiro.

U

ubiquitous /juː'bɪk-/ a. found everywhere. **ubiquity** n.

udder n. bag-like milk-secreting organ of a cow, goat, etc.

UDR abbr. Ulster Defence Regiment.

UFO n. (also ufo, pl. -os) unidentified flying object.

ugh /ʌh or ʊh/ int. exclamation of disgust.

Ugli n. [P.] mottled green and yellow citrus fruit.

ugly a. (-ier, -iest) unpleasant to look at or hear; threatening, hostile. **ugliness** n.

UHF abbr. ultra-high frequency.

UK abbr. United Kingdom.

ukulele /juːkə'leɪlɪ/ n. small four-stringed guitar.

ulcer n. open sore. **ulcerous** a.

ulcerated a. affected with ulcer(s). **ulceration** n.

ulna n. (pl. -ae) thinner long bone of the forearm. **ulnar** a.

ulster n. long loose overcoat of rough cloth.

ulterior a. beyond what is obvious or admitted.

ultimate a. last, final; fundamental. **ultimately** adv.

ultimatum n. (pl. -ums) final demand, with a threat of hostile action if this is rejected.

ultra- pref. beyond; extremely.

ultra-high a. (of frequency) between 300 and 3000 MHz.

ultramarine a. & n. deep bright blue.

ultrasonic a. above the range of normal human hearing.

ultrasound n. ultrasonic waves.

ultraviolet a. of or using radiation with a wavelength (just) beyond the violet end of the visible spectrum.

ululate /'ʌl-/ v.i. howl, wail. **ululation** n.

umbel n. flower-cluster with stalks of nearly equal length.

umber n. natural brownish colouring-matter. **burnt umber** reddish brown.

umbilical /-'bɪl-/ a. of the navel. **umbilical cord** flexible tube connecting the placenta to the navel of a foetus.

umbra n. (pl. -ae) area of total shadow cast by the moon or earth in an eclipse.

umbrage n. feeling of being offended. **take umbrage** take offence.

umbrella n. portable protection against rain, circle of fabric on a folding framework of spokes attached to a central stick.

umpire n. person appointed to supervise a game or contest etc. and see that rules are observed. —v.i. act as umpire in.

umpteen a. (sl.) very many. **umpteenth** a.

UN abbr. United Nations.

un- pref. not; reversing the action indicated by a verb, e.g. unlock.
    The number of words with this prefix is almost unlimited and many of those whose meaning is obvious are not listed below.

unable a. not able.

unaccountable a. unable to be accounted for; not having to account for one's actions etc. **unaccountably** adv.

unadopted a. (of a road) not maintained by a local authority.

unadulterated a. pure, complete.

unalloyed /-'lɔɪd/ a. pure.

unanimous a. all agreeing; agreed by all. **unanimously** adv., **unanimity** /-'nɪm-/ a.

unarmed a. without weapons.

unasked *a.* without being requested.

unassuming *a.* not arrogant, unpretentious.

unattended *a.* (of a vehicle etc.) having no person in charge of it.

unavoidable *a.* unable to be avoided. **unavoidably** *adv.*

unaware *a.* not aware.

unawares *adv.* unexpectedly; without noticing.

unbalanced *a.* not balanced; mentally unsound.

unbearable *a.* not bearable, unable to be endured.

unbeatable *a.* impossible to defeat or surpass.

unbeaten *a.* not defeated, not surpassed.

unbeknown *a.* (*colloq.*) unknown.

unbend *v.t./i.* (*p.t.* **unbent**) change from a bent position; become relaxed or affable.

unbending *a.* inflexible, refusing to alter one's demands.

unbiased *a.* not biased.

unbidden *a.* not commanded or invited.

unblock *v.t.* remove an obstruction from.

unbolt *v.t.* release (a door) by drawing back the bolt(s).

unborn *a.* not yet born.

unbosom *v.refl.* **unbosom oneself** unburden oneself.

unbounded *a.* without limits.

unbridled *a.* unrestrained.

unburden *v.refl.* **unburden oneself** reveal one's thoughts and feelings.

uncalled-for *a.* given or done impertinently or unjustifiably.

uncanny *a.* (**-ier, -iest**) strange and rather frightening; extraordinary. **uncannily** *adv.*

unceasing *a.* not ceasing.

unceremonious *a.* without proper formality or dignity.

uncertain *a.* not known or not knowing certainly; not to be depended on; changeable.

uncertainly *adv.*, **uncertainty** *n.*

unchristian *a.* contrary to Christian principles, uncharitable.

uncial /ˈʌnsɪəl/ *a.* of or used in written capital letters as found in 4th–8th-century manuscripts. —*n.* uncial letter.

uncle *n.* brother or brother-in-law of one's father or mother.

unclean *a.* not clean; ritually impure.

uncoil *v.t./i.* unwind.

uncommon *a.* not common, unusual.

uncompromising /ʌnˈkɒmprəmaɪz-/ *a.* not allowing or not seeking compromise, inflexible.

unconcern *n.* lack of concern.

unconditional *a.* not subject to conditions. **unconditionally** *adv.*

unconscionable /-ʃən-/ *a.* unscrupulous; contrary to what one's conscience feels is right.

unconscious *a.* not conscious; not aware; done without conscious intention. **unconsciously** *adv.*, **unconsciousness** *n.*

unconsidered *a.* disregarded.

uncooperative *a.* not cooperative.

uncork *v.t.* pull the cork from.

uncouple *v.t.* disconnect (things joined by a coupling).

uncouth /-ˈkuːθ/ *a.* awkward in manner, boorish.

uncover *v.t.* remove a covering from; reveal, expose.

unction *n.* anointing with oil, esp. as a religious rite; pretended earnestness, excessive politeness.

unctuous *a.* having an oily manner; smugly virtuous. **unctuously** *adv.*, **unctuousness** *n.*

uncut *a.* not cut.

undeceive *v.t.* disillusion.

undecided *a.* not yet certain; not yet having made up one's mind.

undeniable *a.* impossible to deny, undoubtedly true. **undeniably** *adv.*

under *prep.* in or to a position or rank etc. lower than; less than; governed or controlled by; subjected to; in accordance with; designated by. —*adv.* in or to a lower position or subordinate condition; in or into a state of unconsciousness; below a certain quantity, rank, or age etc. **under age** not old enough, esp. for some legal right; not yet of adult status. **under way** making progress.

under- *pref.* below; lower, subordinate; insufficiently.

underarm *a.* & *adv.* in the armpit; with the hand brought forwards and upwards.

undercarriage *n.* aircraft's landing wheels and their supports; supporting framework of a vehicle etc.

underclass *n.* social class below mainstream society.

undercliff *n.* terrace or lower cliff formed by a landslip.

underclothes *n.pl.* (also **underclothing**) underwear.

undercoat *n.* layer of paint used under a finishing coat.

undercover *a.* done or doing things secretly.

undercroft *n.* crypt.

undercurrent *n.* current flowing below a surface; underlying feeling or influence or trend.

undercut *v.t.* (*p.t.* **undercut**) cut away the part below; sell or work for a lower price than.

underdog *n.* person etc. in an inferior or subordinate position.

underdone *a.* not thoroughly cooked.

underestimate *v.t.* & *n.* (make) too low an estimate (of). **underestimation** *n.*

underfelt *n.* felt for laying under a carpet.

underfoot *adv.* on the ground; under one's feet.

undergarment *n.* piece of underwear.

undergo *v.t.* (*p.t.* **went**, *p.p.*

-**gone**) experience; be subjected to.

undergraduate *n.* university student who has not yet taken a degree.

underground[1] /-'graʊ-/ *adv.* under the surface of the ground; in secret, into secrecy or hiding.

underground[2] /'ʌn-/ *a.* under the surface of the ground; secret. —*n.* underground railway.

undergrowth *n.* shrubs and bushes growing closely, esp. under trees.

underhand[1] /'ʌn-/ *a.* done or doing things slyly or secretly; underarm.

underhand[2] /-'hæ-/ *adv.* in an underhand way.

underlay[1] /-'leɪ/ *v.t.* lay under as a support.

underlay[2] /'ʌn-/ *n.* material laid under another as a support.

underlie *v.t.* (*p.t.* -**lay**, *p.p.* -**lain**, *pres.p.* -**lying**) lie or exist beneath; be the basis of. **underlying** *a.*

underline *v.t.* draw a line under; emphasize.

underling *n.* subordinate.

undermanned *a.* having too few staff or crew etc.

undermine *v.t.* make a hollow or tunnel beneath; weaken gradually.

underneath *prep.* & *adv.* below or on the inside of (a thing).

underpaid *a.* paid too little.

underpants *n.pl.* man's undergarment covering the lower part of the body and part of the legs.

underpass *n.* road passing under another.

underpin *v.t.* (*p.t.* -**pinned**) support, strengthen from beneath.

underprivileged *a.* not having the normal standard of living or rights in a community.

underrate *v.t.* underestimate.

underripe *a.* not fully ripe.

underseal *v.t.* coat the lower surface of (a vehicle) with a protective layer. —*n.* this coating.

undersell v.t. (p.t. -**sold**) sell at a lower price than.

undershoot v.t. (p.t. -**shot**) land short of (a runway etc.).

undershot a. (of a wheel) turned by water flowing under it.

undersigned a. who has or have signed this document.

undersized a. of less than the usual size.

underskirt n. skirt for wearing beneath another; petticoat.

underslung a. supported from above.

understand v.t./i. (p.t. -**stood**) see the meaning or importance of; know the ways or workings of; know the explanation; infer; take for granted. **understandable** a.

understanding a. showing insight or sympathy. —n. ability to understand; intelligence; sympathetic insight; agreement, harmony of feeling; thing agreed.

understate v.t. express in restrained terms; represent as less than it really is. **understatement** n.

understeer v.i. (of a car) tend to turn less sharply than was intended. —n. this tendency.

understudy n. actor who learns another's part in order to be able to take his or her place if necessary. —v.t. be understudy of.

undertake v.t. (p.t. -**took**, p.p. -**taken**) agree or promise (to do something); make oneself responsible for.

undertaker n. one whose business is to organize funerals.

undertaking n. work etc. undertaken; promise, guarantee; undertaker's work.

undertone n. low or subdued tone; underlying quality or feeling.

undertow /-təʊ/ n. current below the sea's surface, moving in the opposite direction to the surface current.

undervalue v.t. put too low a value on.

underwater a. & adv. (situated, used, or done) beneath the surface of water.

underwear n. garments worn under indoor clothing.

underweight a. weighing too little.

underwent see **undergo**.

underworld n. (in mythology) abode of spirits of the dead, under the earth; part of society habitually involved in crime.

underwrite v.t. (p.t. **wrote**, p.p. -**written**) accept liability under (an insurance policy); undertake to finance. **underwriter** n.

undeserved a. not deserved. **undeservedly** /-vɪdlɪ/ adv.

undesirable a. not desirable, objectionable. **undesirably** adv.

undeveloped a. not developed.

undies n.pl. (colloq.) women's underwear.

undo v.t. (p.t. -**did**, p.p. -**done**) unfasten, unwrap; cancel the effect of, ruin.

undone a. unfastened; not done; (old use) brought to ruin.

undoubted a. not disputed. **undoubtedly** adv.

undress v.t./i. take clothes off. —n. ordinary or informal dress, not uniform or full dress.

undue a. excessive.

undulate v.t./i. have or cause to have a wavy movement or appearance. **undulation** n.

unduly adv. excessively.

undying a. everlasting.

unearth v.t. uncover or bring out from the ground; find by searching.

unearthly a. not of this earth; mysterious and frightening; (colloq.) absurdly early or inconvenient.

uneasy a. not comfortable; not confident; worrying. **uneasily** adv., **uneasiness** n.

uneatable a. not fit to be eaten.

uneconomic a. not profitable.

unemployable a. not fit for paid employment.

unemployed *a.* having no employment; without a paid job; not in use. **unemployment** *n.*

unending *a.* endless.

unequal *a.* not equal. **unequally** *adv.*

unequivocal *a.* clear and not ambiguous. **unequivocally** *adv.*

unerring /-'ɜːr-/ *a.* making no mistake.

uneven *a.* not level, not smooth; not uniform. **unevenly** *adv.*, **unevenness** *n.*

unexampled *a.* without precedent.

unexceptionable *a.* with which no fault can be found.

unexceptional *a.* not exceptional.

unexpected *a.* not expected. **unexpectedly** *adv.*

unfailing *a.* constant, reliable.

unfair *a.* not impartial, not in accordance with justice. **unfairly** *adv.*, **unfairness** *n.*

unfaithful *a.* not loyal; having committed adultery. **unfaithfully** *adv.*, **unfaithfulness** *n.*

unfasten *v.t.* open the fastening(s) of.

unfeeling *a.* lacking sensitivity; not sympathetic. **unfeelingly** *adv.*

unfit *a.* unsuitable; not in perfect health or physical condition. *—v.t. (p.t. unfitted)* make unsuitable.

unflappable *a. (colloq.)* remaining calm in a crisis.

unfold *v.t./i.* open, spread out; become known.

unforgettable *a.* impossible to forget. **unforgettably** *adv.*

unfortunate *a.* having bad luck; regrettable. **unfortunately** *adv.*

unfounded *a.* with no basis.

unfrock *v.t.* deprive (a priest) of his priesthood.

unfurl *v.t./i.* unroll; spread out.

ungainly *adv.* awkward-looking, not graceful. **ungainliness** *n.*

unget-at-able *a. (colloq.)* inaccessible.

ungodly *a.* not reverencing God; wicked; *(colloq.)* outrageous.

ungovernable *a.* uncontrollable, unruly.

ungracious *a.* not courteous or kindly. **ungraciously** *adv.*

ungrateful *a.* not grateful.

unguarded *a.* not guarded; incautious.

unguent /'ʌŋgwənt/ *n.* ointment, lubricant.

ungulate *a. & n.* hoofed (animal).

unhand *v.t.* let go of.

unhappy *a.* (**-ier, -iest**) not happy, sad; unfortunate; unsuitable. **unhappily** *adv.*, **unhappiness** *n.*

unhealthy *a.* (**-ier, -iest**) not healthy; harmful to health. **unhealthily** *adv.*

unheard-of *a.* unprecedented.

unhinge *v.t.* cause to become mentally unbalanced.

unholy *a.* (**-ier, -iest**) wicked, irreverent; *(colloq.)* very great.

unhook *v.t.* detach from hook(s); unfasten by releasing hook(s).

unhorse *v.t.* throw or drag (a rider) from a horse.

unicorn *n.* mythical horse-like animal with one straight horn on its forehead.

uniform *n.* distinctive clothing identifying the wearer as a member of an organization or group. *—a.* always the same. **uniformly** *adv.*, **uniformity** *n.*

unify *v.t.* unite. **unification** *n.*

unilateral *a.* done by or affecting one person or group etc. and not another. **unilaterally** *adv.*

unimpeachable *a.* completely trustworthy.

uninviting *a.* unattractive, repellent.

union *n.* uniting, being united; a whole formed by uniting parts; association; trade union (*see* **trade**). **Union Jack** or **flag** national flag of the UK.

unionist *n.* member of a trade union; supporter of trade unions;

one who favours union.

unionize v.t. organize into or cause to join a union. **unionization** n.

unique a. being the only one of its kind; unequalled. **uniquely** adv.

unisex a. designed in a style suitable for people of either sex.

unison n. **in unison** all together; sounding or singing together.

unit n. individual thing, person, or group, esp. as part of a complex whole; fixed quantity used as a standard in terms of which other quantities are expressed or for which a stated charge is made. **unit trust** investment company paying dividends calculated on the average return from the various securities which they hold.

Unitarian /-'tear-/ n. member of a Christian sect maintaining that God is one person not a Trinity.

unitary a. of a unit or units.

unite v.t./i. join together, make or become one; act together, co-operate.

unity n. state of being one or a unit; complex whole; number one in mathematics; agreement.

universal a. of, for, or done by all; (of a joint) able to transmit rotary power by a shaft at any selected angle. **universally** adv.

universe n. all existing things, including the earth and its creatures and all the heavenly bodies.

university n. educational institution providing facilities for advanced learning.

unjust a. not just or fair. **unjustly** adv.

unkempt a. untidy, neglected.

unkind a. not kind, harsh. **unkindly** adv., **unkindness** n.

unknown a. not known.

unleaded a. (of petrol etc.) without added lead.

unlearn v.t. cause to be no longer in one's knowledge or practises etc.

unleash v.t. release, let loose.

unless conj. if ... not, except when.

unlettered a. illiterate.

unlike a. not like. —prep. differently from.

unlikely a. not likely to happen or be true or be successful.

unlimited a. not limited, very great in number or quantity.

unlisted a. not included in a (published) list.

unload v.t./i. remove a load or cargo (from); get rid of; remove the charge from (a gun).

unlock v.t. release the lock of (a door etc.); release by unlocking.

unlooked-for a. unexpected.

unlucky a. (-ier, -iest) not lucky. **unluckily** adv.

unman v.t. (p.t. **unmanned**) weaken the self-control or courage of (a man).

unmanned a. operated without a crew.

unmarried a. not married.

unmask v.t./i. remove a mask (from); expose the true character of.

unmentionable a. not fit to be spoken of.

unmistakable a. clear, not able to be doubted or mistaken for another. **unmistakably** adv.

unmitigated a. not modified, absolute.

unmoved a. not moved, not persuaded, not affected by emotion.

unnatural a. not natural; not normal. **unnaturally** adv.

unnecessary a. not necessary; more than is necessary. **unnecessarily** adv.

unnerve v.t. cause to lose courage or determination.

unnumbered a. not marked with a number; countless.

unobtrusive a. not making oneself or itself noticed. **unobtrusively** adv.

unofficial a. not official. **unofficially** adv.

unpack *v.t./i.* open and remove the contents of (a suitcase etc.); take out from its packaging.

unparalleled *a.* never yet equalled.

unparliamentary *a.* contrary to parliamentary custom; impolite.

unpick *v.t.* undo the stitching of.

unplaced *a.* not placed as one of the first three in a race etc.

unpleasant *a.* not pleasant. **unpleasantly** *adv.*, **unpleasantness** *n.*

unpopular *a.* not liked by most people. **unpopularity** *n.*

unprecedented /-'pres-/ *a.* for which there is no precedent; unparalleled.

unpremeditated *a.* not planned beforehand.

unprepared *a.* not prepared beforehand; not ready or not equipped to do something.

unprepossessing *a.* unattractive.

unpretentious *a.* not pretentious, not showy or pompous.

unprincipled *a.* without good moral principles, unscrupulous.

unprintable *a.* too indecent or libellous etc. to be printed.

unprofessional *a.* not professional; contrary to the standards of behaviour for members of a profession. **unprofessionally** *adv.*

unprofitable *a.* not profitable; useless. **unprofitably** *adv.*

unqualified *a.* not qualified; not restricted or modified.

unquestionable *a.* too clear to be doubted. **unquestionably** *adv.*

unquote *int.* (direction in dictation etc.) mark the end of the quotation.

unravel *v.t./i.* (*p.t.* **unravelled**) disentangle; undo (knitted fabric); become unravelled.

unreasonable *a.* not reasonable; excessive, unjust. **unreasonably** *adv.*

unreel *v.t./i.* unwind from a reel.

unrelieved *a.* not relieved; without anything to give variation.

unremitting *a.* not ceasing.

unrequited /-'kwaı-/ *a.* (of love) not returned or rewarded.

unreservedly /-'vıdlı/ *adv.* without reservation, completely.

unrest *n.* restlessness, agitation.

unrivalled *a.* having no equal, incomparable.

unroll *v.t./i.* open after being rolled.

unruly *a.* not easy to control, disorderly. **unruliness** *n.*

unsaddle *v.t.* remove the saddle from.

unsaid *a.* not spoken or expressed.

unsavoury *a.* disagreeable to the taste or smell; morally disgusting.

unscathed /-'skeıðd/ *a.* without suffering any injury.

unscramble *v.t.* sort out; make (a scrambled transmission) intelligible.

unscrew *v.t.* loosen (a screw etc.); unfasten by removing screw(s).

unscripted *a.* without a prepared script.

unscrupulous *a.* not prevented by scruples of conscience.

unseat *v.t.* dislodge (a rider); remove from a parliamentary seat.

unseemly *a.* not seemly, improper.

unseen *a.* not seen. —*n.* passage for unprepared translation from a foreign language.

unselfish *a.* not selfish; considering others' needs before one's own. **unselfishly** *adv.*, **unselfishness** *n.*

unsettle *v.t.* make uneasy, disturb.

unsettled *a.* (of weather) changeable.

unshakeable *a.* firm.

unsightly *a.* not pleasant to look at, ugly. **unsightliness** *n.*

unsigned *a.* not signed.

unskilled *a.* not having or needing skill or special training.

unsociable *a.* not sociable.

unsocial *a.* not sociable; not conforming to normal social practices.

unsolicited *a.* not requested.

unsophisticated *a.* simple and natural or naïve.

unsound *a.* not sound or strong, not free from defects. **of unsound mind** insane.

unsparing *a.* giving lavishly.

unspeakable *a.* too bad to be described in words.

unstable *a.* not stable; mentally or emotionally unbalanced.

unsteady *a.* not steady. **unsteadily** *adv.*, **unsteadiness** *n.*

unstick *v.t.* (*p.t.* **-stuck**) detach (what is stuck).

unstinted *a.* given lavishly.

unstuck *a.* detached after being stuck on or together. **come unstuck** (*colloq.*) suffer disaster, fail.

unstudied *a.* natural in manner.

unsuccessful *a.* not successful. **unsuccessfully** *adv.*

unsuitable *a.* not suitable. **unsuitably** *adv.*

unsullied *a.* not sullied, pure.

unsuspecting *a.* feeling no suspicion.

unswerving *a.* not turning aside; unchanging.

unthinkable *a.* too bad or too unlikely to be thought about.

unthinking *a.* thoughtless.

untidy *a.* (**-ier**, **-iest**) not tidy. **untidily** *adv.*, **untidiness** *n.*

untie *v.t.* unfasten; release from being tied up.

until *prep. & conj.* = till[2].

untimely *a.* inopportune; premature.

untiring *a.* not becoming tired.

unto *prep.* (*old use*) to.

untold *a.* not told; too much or too many to be counted.

untouchable *a.* not able or not allowed to be touched. —*n.* member of the lowest Hindu social group in India.

untoward /-'wɔːd/ *a.* inconvenient.

untraceable *a.* unable to be traced.

untried *a.* not yet tried or tested.

untrue *a.* not true, contrary to facts; not loyal. **untruly** *adv.*

untruth *n.* untrue statement, lie; lack of truth. **untruthful** *a.*, **untruthfully** *adv.*

unused *a.* not yet used.

unusual *a.* not usual; remarkable, rare. **unusually** *adv.*

unutterable *a.* too great to be expressed in words. **unutterably** *adv.*

unvarnished *a.* not varnished; plain and straightforward.

unveil *v.t./i.* remove a veil (from); remove concealing drapery from; disclose, make publicly known.

unversed *a.* unversed in not experienced in.

unwanted *a.* not wanted.

unwarrantable *a.* unjustifiable.

unwarranted *a.* unjustified, unauthorized.

unwary *a.* not cautious.

unwell *a.* not in good health.

unwieldy *a.* awkward to move or control because of its size, shape, or weight. **unwieldiness** *n.*

unwilling *a.* not willing.

unwind *v.t./i.* (*p.t.* **unwound**) draw out or become drawn out from being wound; (*colloq.*) relax from work or tension.

unwise *a.* not wise, foolish. **unwisely** *adv.*

unwitting *a.* unaware; unintentional. **unwittingly** *adv.*

unwonted /-'wəʊ-/ *a.* not customary, not usual. **unwontedly** *adv.*

unworldly *a.* not worldly, spiritually minded. **unworldliness** *n.*

unworn *a.* not yet worn.

unworthy *a.* worthless; not deserving; unsuitable to the character (of a person or thing).

unwrap *v.t./i.* (*p.t.* **unwrapped**) open from being wrapped.

unwritten *a.* not written down; based on custom but not statute.

unzip *v.t.* (*p.t.* **unzipped**) open by the undoing of a zip-fastener.

up *adv.* to, in, or at a higher place or state etc.; to a vertical position; to a larger size; as far as a stated place, time, or amount; out of bed; into activity or efficiency; into pieces, apart; compactly; (*colloq.*) amiss, happening. —*prep.* upwards along or through or into; at a higher part of. —*a.* directed upwards; travelling towards a central place. —*v.t./i.* (*p.t.* **upped**) (*colloq.*) raise; pick up; get up (and do something). **time is up** is finished. **up in** (*colloq.*) knowledgeable about. **ups and downs** alternate good and bad fortune. **up to** occupied with, doing; required as a duty or obligation from; capable of. **up to date** in accordance with current fashion or information. **up-to-date** *a.*

upbeat *n.* unaccented beat. —*a.* (*colloq.*) optimistic, cheerful.

upbraid *v.t.* reproach.

upbringing *n.* training and education during childhood.

up-country *a.* & *adv.* inland.

update *v.t.* bring up to date. —*n.* this process; updated information etc.

up-end *v.t./i.* set or rise up on end.

upgrade *v.t.* raise to higher grade.

upheaval *n.* sudden heaving upwards; violent disturbance.

uphill *a.* & *adv.* going or doing upwards.

uphold (*v.t.* (*p.t.* **upheld**) support.

upholster *v.t.* put fabric covering, padding, etc. on (furniture).

upholstery *n.* work of upholstering furniture; material used in this.

upkeep *n.* keeping (a thing) in good condition and repair; cost of this.

upland *n.* & *a.* (of) higher or inland parts of a country.

uplift¹ /-'lı-/ *v.t.* raise.

uplift² /'ʌp-/ *n.* being raised; mentally elevating influence.

upon *prep.* on.

upper *a.* higher in place or position or rank. —*n.* part of a boot or shoe above the sole. **upper case** capital letters in printing or typing. **upper crust** (*colloq.*) aristocracy. **upper hand** mastery, dominance.

uppermost *a.* & *adv.* in, on, or to the top or most prominent position.

uppish, uppity *adjs.* (*colloq.*) self-assertive.

upright *a.* in a vertical position; (of a piano) with vertical strings; strictly honest or honourable. —*n.* post or rod etc. placed upright, esp. as a support.

uprising *n.* rebellion.

uproar *n.* outburst of noise and excitement or anger.

uproarious *a.* very noisy, with loud laughter. **uproariously** *adv.*

uproot *v.t.* pull out of the ground together with its roots; force to leave an established place.

upset¹ /-'set/ *v.t./i.* (*p.t.* **upset**, *pres.p.* **upsetting**) overturn; disrupt; distress; disturb the temper or digestion of.

upset² /'ʌp-/ *n.* upsetting.

upshot *n.* outcome.

upside down with the upper part underneath; in great disorder.

upstage *adv.* & *a.* nearer the back of a theatre stage. —*v.t.* divert attention from, outshine.

upstairs *adv.* & *a.* to or on a higher floor.

upstanding *a.* strong and healthy, well set up; standing up.

upstart *n.* person newly risen to a high position, esp. one who behaves arrogantly.

upstream *a.* & *adv.* in the direction from which a stream flows.

upsurge *n.* upward surge, rise.

upswept *a.* (of hair) combed to the top of the head.

upswing *n.* upward movement or trend.

uptake *n.* taking something up. **quick on the uptake** (*colloq.*) quick to understand what is meant.

uptight *a.* (*colloq.*) nervously tense; annoyed.

upturn[1] /-'tɜːn/ *v.t.* turn up or upwards or upside down.

upturn[2] /'ʌp-/ *n.* upheaval; upward trend, improvement.

upward *a.* moving or leading up.

upwards *adv.* towards a higher place etc.

uranium *n.* heavy grey metal used as a source of nuclear energy.

urban *a.* of a city or town.

urbane *a.* having smooth manners. **urbanely** *adv.*, **urbanity** *n.*

urbanize *v.t.* change (a place) into a town-like area. **urbanization** *n.*

urchin *n.* mischievous or raggedly dressed boy; sea-urchin.

Urdu /'uədu:, 'ɜː-/ *n.* language related to Hindi, used esp. in Pakistan.

ureter /juə'ri:-/ *n.* duct from the kidney to the bladder.

urethra /juə'ri:-/ *n.* duct by which urine is discharged from the body.

urge *v.t.* drive onward, encourage to proceed; recommend strongly or earnestly. —*n.* feeling or desire urging a person to do something.

urgent *a.* needing or calling for immediate attention or action. **urgently** *adv.*, **urgency** *n.*

urinal /juə'raɪ-/ *n.* receptacle or structure for receiving urine.

urinate /'juər-/ *v.i.* discharge urine from the body. **urination** *n.*

urine /'juərɪn/ *n.* waste liquid which collects in the bladder and is discharged from the body. **urinary** *a.*

urn *n.* a kind of vase, esp. for holding a cremated person's ashes; large metal container with a tap, for keeping water etc. hot.

ursine *a.* of or like a bear.

us *pron.* objective case of *we*.

US, USA *abbr.* United States of America.

usable *a.* able or fit to be used.

usage *n.* manner of using or treating something; customary practice.

use[1] /-z/ *v.t.* cause to act or to serve for a purpose or as an instrument or material; treat; exploit selfishly. **use up** use the whole or the remainder of; tire out.

use[2] /-s/ *n.* using, being used; power of using; purpose for which a thing is used. **make use of** use, exploit.

used[1] /-zd/ *a.* second-hand.

used[2] /-st/ *p.t.* was or were accustomed. —*a.* **used to** familiar with by practice or habit.

useful *a.* usable for a practical purpose; able to produce good results. **usefully** *adv.*, **usefulness** *n.*

useless *a.* not usable, not useful. **uselessly** *adv.*, **uselessness** *n.*

user *n.* one who uses something. **user-friendly** *a.* easy for a user to understand and operate.

usher *n.* person who shows people to their seats in a public hall etc. or into someone's presence; official acting as doorkeeper in a lawcourt. —*v.t.* lead, escort.

usherette *n.* woman who ushers people to seats in a cinema etc.

USSR *abbr.* Union of Soviet Socialist Republics.

usual *a.* such as happens or is done or used etc. in many or most instances. **usually** *adv.*

usurer /'ju:ʒ-/ *n.* person who lends money at excessively high rates.

usurp *v.t.* take (power, position, or right) wrongfully or by force. **usurpation** *n.*, **usurper** *n.*

usury /'ju:ʒ-/ *n.* lending of money at excessively high rates of interest.

utensil *n.* instrument or container, esp. for domestic use.

uterus *n.* womb. **uterine** /-ain/ *a.*

utilitarian *a.* designed to be useful rather than decorative or luxurious, severely practical.

utilitarianism *n.* theory that actions are justified if they are useful or for the benefit of the majority.

utility *n.* usefulness; useful thing. —*a.* severely practical. **utility room** room containing large fixed domestic appliances.

utilize *v.t.* use, find a use for. **utilization** *n.*

utmost *a. & n.* furthest, greatest, or extreme (point or degree etc.).

Utopia *n.* imaginary place or state where all is perfect. **Utopian** *a.*

utter[1] *a.* complete, absolute. **utterly** *adv.*

utter[2] *v.t.* make (a sound or words) with the mouth or voice; speak; put (a forged banknote or coin etc.) into circulation. **utterance** *n.*

uttermost *a. & n.* = utmost.

U-turn *n.* driving of a vehicle in a U-shaped course so as to face in the opposite direction; reversal of policy.

uvula /'juːvjʊ-/ *n.* small fleshy projection hanging at the back of the throat. **uvular** *a.*

uxorious *a.* excessively fond of one's wife.

V

V *abbr.* volt(s).

vac *n.* (*colloq.*) vacation; vacuum cleaner.

vacancy *n.* state of being vacant; vacant place or position etc.

vacant *a.* empty, not filled or occupied; showing no intelligence or interest. **vacantly** *adv.*

vacate *v.t.* cease to occupy.

vacation *n.* interval between terms in universities and lawcourts; (*US*) holiday; vacating of a place etc. —*v.i.* (*US*) spend a holiday.

vaccinate *n.* inoculate with a vaccine. **vaccination** *n.*

vaccine /'væksiːn/ *n.* preparation that gives immunity from an infection. **vaccination** *n.*

vacillate /'væs-/ *v.i.* keep changing one's mind, waver. **vacillation** *n.*

vacuous *a.* inane; expressionless. **vacuously** *adv.*, **vacuousness** *n.*, **vacuity** /-'kjuː-/ *n.*

vacuum *n.* (*pl.* -cua *or* -cuums) space from which air has been removed; absence of normal contents; (*colloq.*) vacuum cleaner. —*v.t./i.* (*colloq.*) clean with a vacuum cleaner. **vacuum cleaner** electrical apparatus that takes up dust etc. by suction. **vacuum flask** container for keeping liquids hot or cold. **vacuum-packed** *a.* sealed after partial removal of air.

vade-mecum /vɑːdɪˈmeɪ-/ *n.* handbook.

vagabond *n.* wanderer; vagrant, esp. an idle or dishonest one.

vagary /'veɪg-/ *n.* capricious act or idea or fluctuation.

vagina /-'dʒaɪnə/ *n.* passage leading from the vulva to the womb in females. **vaginal** *a.*

vagrant /'veɪ-/ *n.* person without a settled home or regular work. **vagrancy** *n.*

vague *a.* (-er, -est) not clearly expressed or perceived or identified; not expressing oneself clearly. **vaguely** *adv.*, **vagueness** *n.*

vain *a.* (-er, -est) conceited; having no value or significance; useless, futile. **in vain** uselessly. **vainly** *adv.*

vainglory *n.* great vanity. **vainglorious** *a.*

valance /'væl-/ *n.* short curtain or hanging frill.

vale *n.* valley.

valediction /væli-/ *n.* farewell. **valedictory** *a.*

valence /'veɪ-/ *n.* = valency.

valency /'veɪ-/ *n.* unit of the combining-power of atoms; this power.

valentine *n.* sweetheart chosen on St Valentine's Day (14 Feb.); greetings-card sent to one's valentine.

valerian /-'lɪər-/ *n.* strong-smelling herb with pink or white flowers.

valet /'vælɪt *or* -leɪ/ *n.* man's personal attendant who takes care of clothes etc. —*v.t.* (*p.t.* valeted) act as valet to.

valetudinarian /-'neər-/ *n.* person who excessive attention to preserving his health.

valiant *a.* brave. **valiantly** *adv.*

valid *a.* having legal force, legally usable; (of reasoning) sound, logical. **validity** *n.*

validate *v.t.* make valid, confirm. **validation** *n.*

valise /-'liːz/ *n.* travelling-bag; suitcase.

valley *n.* (*pl.* -eys) low area between hills; region drained by a river.

valour *n.* bravery, esp. in fighting.

valse *n.* = waltz.

valuable *a.* of great value or worth.

valuables *n.pl.* valuable things.

valuation *n.* estimation or estimate of a thing's worth.

value *n.* amount of money or other commodity etc. considered equivalent to something else; usefulness, importance; thing's ability to serve a purpose or cause an effect; amount etc. denoted by a symbol; (*pl.*) principles considered important. —*v.t.* estimate the value of; consider to be of great worth. **value added tax** tax on the amount by which a thing's value has been increased at each stage of its production. **value judgement** subjective estimate of quality etc.

valueless *a.* having no value.

valuer *n.* person who estimates values professionally.

valve *n.* device controlling flow through a pipe; structure allowing blood to flow in one direction only; thermionic valve; device to vary the length of the tube in a trumpet etc.; each half of the hinged shell of an oyster etc.

valvular *a.* of the valves of the heart or blood vessels; having valve(s); having the form or function of a valve.

vamoose *v.i.* (*US sl.*) depart hurriedly.

vamp[1] *n.* upper front part of a boot or shoe. —*v.t./i.* improvise (esp. a musical accompaniment).

vamp[2] *n.* (*colloq.*) woman who is an unscrupulous flirt. —*v.t./i.* (*colloq.*) behave as a vamp (to).

vampire *n.* ghost or reanimated body supposed to suck blood.

van[1] *n.* covered vehicle for transporting goods etc.; railway carriage for luggage or goods.

van[2] *n.* vanguard, forefront.

vandal *n.* person who damages things wilfully. **vandalism** *n.*

vandalize *v.t.* damage wilfully.

vane *n.* weather-vane; blade of a propeller etc.

vanguard *n.* foremost part of an advancing army etc.

vanilla *n.* a kind of flavouring, esp. obtained from the pods of a tropical orchid.

vanish *v.i.* disappear completely.

vanity *n.* conceit; worthlessness, worthless thing. **vanity bag** *or* **case** woman's small bag or case for carrying cosmetics etc. **vanity unit** wash-basin set into flat top with cupboards beneath.

vanquish *v.t.* conquer.

vantage *n.* advantage (esp. as a score in tennis). **vantage point** position giving a good view.

vapid *a.* insipid, uninteresting. **vapidly** *adv.*, **vapidity** *n.*

vaporize *v.t./i.* convert or be converted into vapour. **vaporization** *n.*

vapour *n.* moisture or other substance suspended in air; air-like substance into which certain liquids or solids are converted by heating. **vaporous** *a.*

variable *a.* varying. —*n.* thing that varies. **variability** *n.*

variance *n.* **at variance** disagreeing.

variant *a.* differing. —*n.* variant form or spelling etc.

variation *n.* varying, extent of this; variant; repetition of a melody in a different form.

varicoloured /'veər-/ *a.* variegated; of various colours.

varicose /'væ-/ *a.* (of veins) permanently swollen. **varicosity** *n.*

varied *a.* of different sorts.

variegated /'veərig-/ *a.* having irregular patches of colours. **variegation** *n.*

variety *n.* quality of not being the same; quantity of different things; class of things differing from others in their general group; member of such a class; entertainment with a series of short performances.

various *a.* of several kinds; several. **variously** *adv.*

varlet *n.* (old use) menial; rascal.

varnish *n.* liquid that dries to form a shiny transparent coating on wood etc.; paint used on the nails. —*v.t.* coat with varnish.

varsity *n.* (colloq.) university.

vary *v.t./i.* make or be or become different.

vascular *a.* of vessels or ducts for conveying blood or sap.

vase /vɑːz/ *n.* open vessel used for holding cut flowers or as an ornament.

vasectomy *n.* surgical removal of part of the ducts that carry semen from the testicles, esp. as a method of birth control.

vassal *n.* humble servant or subordinate.

vast *a.* very great in area or size. **vastly** *adv.*, **vastness** *n.*

VAT *abbr.* value added tax.

vat *n.* large tank for liquids.

vaudeville /'vɔːdə-/ *n.* variety entertainment.

vault[1] *n.* arched roof; cellar used as a storage-place; burial chamber. **vaulted** *a.*

vault[2] *v.t./i. & n.* jump, esp. while resting on the hand(s) or with the help of a pole. **vaulting-horse** *n.* padded structure for vaulting over.

vaunt *v.t./i. & n.* boast.

VDU *abbr.* visual display unit.

veal *n.* calf's flesh as food.

vector *n.* thing (e.g. velocity) that has both magnitude and direction; carrier of an infection. **vectorial** *a.*

veer *v.i.* change direction.

vegan /'viː-/ *n.* person who eats no meat or animal products.

vegetable *n.* plant grown for food. —*a.* of or from plants.

vegetarian *n.* person who eats no meat. **vegetarianism** *n.*

vegetate *v.i.* live an uneventful life.

vegetation *n.* plants collectively.

vegetative *a.* of growth and development; of vegetation.

vehement /'viːəm-/ *a.* showing strong feeling. **vehemently** *adv.*, **vehemence** *n.*

vehicle /'viːik-/ *n.* conveyance for transporting passengers or goods on land or in space; means by which something is expressed or displayed. **vehicular** /-'hik-/ *a.*

veil *n.* piece of fine net or other fabric worn as part of a headdress or to protect or conceal the face. —*v.t.* cover with or as if with a veil. **take the veil** become a nun.

vein *n.* any of the blood-vessels conveying blood towards the heart; thread-like structure; narrow streak in marble or layer in rock etc.; mood, manner. **veined** *a.*

veld /velt/ *n.* open grassland in South Africa.

vellum *n.* fine parchment; smooth writing-paper.

velocity *n.* speed.

velour /-'lʊə(r)/ *n.* plush-like fabric.

velvet *n.* woven fabric with thick short pile on one side. **on velvet** in an advantageous or prosperous position. **velvet glove** outward gentleness concealing inflexibility. **velvety** *a.*

velveteen *n.* cotton velvet.

venal /'vi:-/ *a.* able to be bribed; influenced by bribery. **venality** *n.*

vend *v.t.* sell, offer for sale.

vendetta *n.* feud.

vending-machine *n.* slot-machine where small articles are obtained.

vendor *n.* seller.

veneer *n.* thin covering layer of fine wood; superficial show of a quality. —*v.t.* cover with a veneer.

venerate *v.t.* respect deeply; honour as hallowed or sacred. **veneration** *n.*, **venerable** *a.*

venereal /-'nɪər-/ *a.* (of infections) contracted by sexual intercourse with an infected person.

Venetian *a.* & *n.* (native) of Venice. **Venetian blind** window blind of adjustable horizontal slats.

vengeance *n.* retaliation. **with a vengeance** in an extreme degree.

vengeful *a.* seeking vengeance.

venial /'vi:-/ *a.* (of a sin) pardonable, not serious. **veniality** *n.*

venison *n.* deer's flesh as food.

Venn diagram diagram using overlapping and intersecting circles etc. to show relationships between sets.

venom *n.* poisonous fluid secreted by certain snakes etc.; bitter feeling or language, hatred. **venomous** *a.*

vent[1] *n.* slit at the lower edge of the back or side of a coat.

vent[2] *n.* opening allowing air or liquid etc. to pass through. —*v.t.* make a vent in; give vent to. **give vent to** give an outlet to (feelings etc.), express freely.

ventilate *v.t.* cause air to enter or circulate freely in; express publicly. **ventilation** *n.*

ventilator *n.* device for ventilating a room etc.

ventral *a.* of or on the abdomen.

ventricle *n.* cavity, esp. in the heart or brain. **ventricular** *a.*

ventriloquist /-'trɪl-/ *n.* entertainer who can produce voice-sounds so that they seem to come from a puppet etc. **ventriloquism** *n.*

venture *n.* undertaking that involves risk. —*v.t./i.* dare; dare to go or utter. **at a venture** at random. **Venture Scout** member of the senior branch of the Scout Association.

venturesome *a.* daring.

venue /'ven-/ *n.* appointed place for a meeting etc.

veracious /-'reɪ-/ *a.* truthful; true. **veraciously** *adv.*, **veracity** /-'ræ-/ *n.*

veranda *n.* roofed terrace.

verb *n.* word indicating action or occurrence or being.

verbal *a.* of or in words; spoken; of a verb. **verbally** *adv.*

verbalize *v.t./i.* express in words; be verbose. **verbalization** *n.*

verbatim /-'beɪ-/ *adv.* & *a.* in exactly the same words.

verbena /-'bi:-/ *n.* vervain; cultivated variety of this.

verbiage /'vɜ:-/ *n.* excessive number of words.

verbose /-'bəʊs/ *a.* using more words than are needed. **verbosely** *adv.*, **verbosity** /-'bɒs-/ *n.*

verdant *a.* (of grass etc.) green. **verdancy** *n.*

verdict *n.* decision reached by a jury; decision or opinion reached after testing something.

verdigris /-grɪs/ n. green deposit forming on copper or brass.

verdure n. green vegetation; its greenness.

verge[1] n. extreme edge, brink; grass edging of a road etc.

verge[2] v.i. **verge on** border on.

verger n. person who is caretaker and attendant in a church.

verify v.t. check the truth or correctness of. **verification** n.

verily adv. (old use) in truth.

verisimilitude /-'mɪl-/ n. appearance of being true.

veritable a. real, rightly named.

verity n. (old use) truth.

vermicelli /-'sel-/ n. pasta made in slender threads.

vermicide n. substance used to kill worms.

vermiform a. worm-like in shape.

vermilion a. & n. bright red.

vermin n. (pl. **vermin**) common animal or insect regarded as a pest.

verminous a. infested with vermin.

vermouth /-məθ/ n. white wine flavoured with herbs.

vernacular n. ordinary language of a country or district.

vernal a. of or occurring in spring.

vernier n. small movable graduated scale.

veronica n. a kind of flowering herb or shrub.

verruca /-'ru:-/ n. (pl. **-ae**) wart or wart-like swelling, esp. on the foot.

versatile a. able to do or be used for many different things. **versatility** n.

verse n. metrical (not prose) composition; group of lines forming a unit in a poem or hymn; numbered division of a Bible chapter.

versed a. **versed in** experienced in.

versicle n. each of the short sentences said or sung by a member of the clergy in the liturgy.

versify v.t./i. turn into verse; express in verse; compose verse. **versification** n.

version n. particular account of a matter; translation; special or variant form.

verso n. (pl. **-os**) left-hand page of an open book; back of a page.

versus prep. against.

vertebra n. (pl. **-brae**) each segment of the backbone. **vertebral** a.

vertebrate /-brət/ a. & n. (animal) that has a backbone.

vertex n. (pl. **vertices**) highest point of a hill etc.; apex.

vertical a. perpendicular to the horizontal, upright. —n. vertical line or position. **vertically** adv., **verticality** n.

vertigo n. dizziness. **vertiginous** a.

vervain n. tall wild plant with hairy leaves and small flowers.

verve n. enthusiasm, vigour.

very adv. in a high degree, extremely; exactly. —a. actual, truly such; extreme. **very high frequency** frequency in the range 30–300 MHz. **very well** expression of consent.

vesicle /'ves-/ n. small hollow structure in a plant or animal body; blister.

vespers n.pl. RC Church service held in the evening.

vessel n. structure designed to travel on water and carry people or goods; hollow receptacle, esp. for liquid; tube-like structure conveying blood or other fluid in the body of an animal or plant.

vest n. undergarment covering the trunk of the body; (US & shop use) waistcoat. —v.t. confer or furnish with (power) as a firm or legal right. **vested interest** advantageous right securely held by a person or group.

vestibule n. entrance hall; porch.

vestige n. trace, small remaining bit; very small amount.

vestigial /-'tɪdʒ-/ a. remaining as a vestige. **vestigially** adv.

vestment n. ceremonial garment, esp. of clergy or a church choir.

vestry n. room (attached to a church) where vestments are kept and clergy etc. robe themselves.

vet n. (colloq.) veterinary surgeon. —v.t. (p.t. **vetted**) (colloq.) examine critically for faults or errors etc.

vetch n. plant of the pea family used as fodder for cattle.

veteran n. person with long experience, esp. in the armed forces. **veteran car** car made before 1916 or from 1905.

veterinarian n. veterinary surgeon.

veterinary /'vet-/ a. of or for the treatment of diseases and disorders of animals. **veterinary surgeon** person skilled in such treatment.

veto /'vi:təʊ/ n. (pl. **-oes**) authoritative rejection of something proposed; right to make this. —v.t. reject by a veto.

vex v.t. annoy. **vexed question** problem that is much discussed.

vexation n., **vexatious** a.

VHF abbr. very high frequency.

via prep. by way of, through.

viable a. capable of living or surviving; practicable. **viability** n.

viaduct n. long bridge-like structure carrying a road or railway over a valley etc.

vial n. small bottle.

viands /'vai-/ n.pl. articles of food.

viaticum n. Eucharist given to a dying person.

vibes n.pl. (colloq.) vibraphone; vibrations.

vibrant a. vibrating, resonant, thrilling with energy.

vibraphone /'vai-/ n. percussion instrument like a xylophone but with a vibrating effect.

vibrate v.t./i. move rapidly and continuously to and fro; resound, sound with rapid slight variation of pitch. **vibrator** n., **vibratory** /'vai-/ a.

vibration n. vibrating; (pl.) mental (esp. occult) emanations.

vicar n. member of the clergy in charge of a parish. **vicarial** a.

vicarage n. house of a vicar.

vicarious /-'keər-/ a. felt through sharing imaginatively in the feelings or activities etc. of another person; acting or done etc. for another. **vicariously** adv.

vice[1] n. great wickedness; a form of this; criminal and immoral practices.

vice[2] n. instrument with two jaws for holding things firmly.

vice[3] /'vaisi/ prep. in place of.

vice- pref. substitute or deputy for; next in rank to.

vice-chancellor n. deputy chancellor (esp. in a university, discharging administrative duties).

vicegerent /-'dʒe-/ a. & n. deputy.

viceroy n. person governing a colony etc. as the sovereign's representative. **viceregal** a.

vice versa /vaisi 'vɜ:-/ with terms the other way round.

vicinity /-'sɪn-/ n. surrounding district. **in the vicinity (of)** near.

vicious /'vɪʃəs/ a. brutal, strongly spiteful; savage and dangerous. **vicious circle** bad situation producing effects that produce or intensify its original cause. **viciously** adv.

vicissitude /-'sɪs-/ n. change of circumstances or luck.

victim n. person injured or killed or made to suffer; living creature killed as a religious sacrifice.

victimize v.t. single out to suffer ill treatment. **victimization** n.

victor n. winner.

Victorian a. & n. (person) of the reign of Queen Victoria (1837–1901).

victorious a. having gained victory.

victory *n.* success achieved by gaining mastery over opponent(s) or having the highest score.

victual /'vɪt(ə)l/ *v.t./i.* supply or stock with victuals; **ea**. victuals. **victuals** *n.pl.* foods.

victualler /'vɪtlə(r)/ *n.* person who supplies victuals. **licensed victualler** licensee of a public house.

vicuña /-'ku:njə/ *n.* South American animal related to the llama; soft cloth made from its wool; imitation of this.

video /'vɪdɪəʊ/ *n.* (*pl.* -**os**) recording or broadcasting of pictures; apparatus for this; videotape. —*v.t.* make a video of.

videotape *n.* magnetic tape for recording television pictures and sound.—*v.t.* record on this.

videotex *n.* (also **videotext**) electronic information system, esp. teletext or viewdata.

vie *v.i.* (*pres.p.* **vying**) carry on a rivalry, compete.

view *n.* range of vision; things within this; fine scenery; visual or mental survey; mental attitude, opinion. —*v.t./i.* survey with the eyes or mind; regard, consider; watch television. **in view of** having regard to, considering. **on view** displayed for inspection. **with a view to** with the hope or intention of. **viewer** *n.*

viewdata *n.* news and information service from a computer source to which a television screen is connected by a telephone link.

viewfinder *n.* device on a camera showing the extent of the area being photographed.

viewpoint *n.* point of view.

vigil /'vɪdʒ-/ *n.* staying awake to keep watch or pray; period of this; eve of a religious festival.

vigilant *a.* watchful. **vigilantly** *adv.*, **vigilance** *n.*

vigilante /-'lænt/ *n.* member of a self-appointed group trying to prevent crime etc. in a disorderly community.

vignette /vɪ:'njet/ *n.* portrait with the background gradually shaded off; short description.

vigour *n.* active physical or mental strength; forcefulness. **vigorous** *a.*, **vigorously** *adv.*, **vigorousness** *n.*

Viking /'vaɪ-/ *n.* ancient Scandinavian trader and pirate.

vile *a.* extremely disgusting or despicable. **vilely** *adv.*, **vileness** *n.*

vilify /'vɪl-/ *v.t.* say evil things about. **vilification** *n.*, **vilifier** *n.*

villa *n.* house in a suburban or residential district; country house in Italy or France; seaside house used for holidays.

village *n.* collection of houses etc. in a country district.

villager *n.* inhabitant of a village.

villain *n.* wicked person. **villainous** *a.*, **villainy** *n.*

villein /-lɪn/ *n.* medieval serf.

vim *n.* (*colloq.*) vigour.

vinaigrette /vɪn'gret/ *n.* small bottle for smelling-salts. **vinaigrette sauce** salad dressing of oil and vinegar.

vindicate *v.t.* clear of blame; justify. **vindication** *n.*, **vindicatory** *a.*

vindictive *a.* showing a desire for vengeance. **vindictively** *adv.*, **vindictiveness** *n.*

vine *n.* climbing or trailing woody-stemmed plant whose fruit is the grape.

vinegar *n.* sour liquid made from wine, malt, etc., by fermentation. **vinegary** *a.*

vineyard /'vɪn-/ *n.* plantation of vines for wine-making.

vintage *n.* gathering of grapes for wine-making; season of this; wine from a season's grapes, esp. when of high quality; date when something was produced or existed. —*a.* of high quality, esp.

from a past period. **vintage car** *n.* car made between 1917 and 1930.

vintner *n.* wine-merchant.

vinyl /'vaɪnl/ *n.* a kind of plastic.

viol /'vaɪəl/ *n.* medieval musical instrument resembling a violin.

viola[1] /vɪ'əʊlə/ *n.* musical instrument resembling a violin but of lower pitch.

viola[2] /'vaɪələ/ *n.* plant of the genus to which violets belong.

violate *v.t.* break (an oath or treaty etc.); treat (a sacred place) irreverently; disturb; rape. **violation** *n.*, **violator** *n.*

violent *a.* using or involving great physical force or strength or intensity; (of death) caused by external force, not natural. **violently** *adv.*, **violence** *n.*

violet *n.* small wild or garden plant, often with purple flowers; bluish-purple colour. —*a.* bluish-purple.

violin *n.* musical instrument with four strings of treble pitch, played with a bow. **violinist** *n.*

violoncello /-'tʃel-/ *n.* (*pl.* **-os**) cello.

VIP *abbr.* very important person.

viper *n.* small poisonous snake.

virago /vɪ'rɑː-/ *n.* (*pl.* **-os**) shrewish bullying woman.

viral /'vaɪ-/ *a.* of a virus.

virgin *n.* person (esp. a woman) who has never had sexual intercourse; **the Virgin** the Virgin Mary, mother of Christ. —*a.* virginal; spotless, undefiled; untouched, not yet used. **virginal** *a.*, **virginity** *n.*

virginals *n.pl.* earliest form of harpsichord.

virile /'vɪraɪl/ *a.* having masculine strength or procreative power. **virility** *n.*

virology /vaɪ'rɒl-/ *n.* study of viruses. **virologist** *n.*

virtual *a.* being so in effect though not in name. **virtually** *adv.*

virtue *n.* moral excellence, goodness; chastity; good characteristic. **by** *or* **in virtue of** because of.

virtuoso *n.* (*pl.* **-si**) expert performer. **virtuosity** /-'ɒs-/ *n.*

virtuous *a.* showing moral virtue, chaste. **virtuously** *adv.*, **virtuousness** *n.*

virulent /'vɪrʊ-/ *a.* (of poison or disease) extremely strong or violent; bitterly hostile. **virulently** *adv.*, **virulence** *n.*

virus *n.* (*pl.* **-uses**) organism (smaller than a bacterium) capable of causing disease; destructive code hidden in a computer program.

visa /'viːzə/ *n.* official mark on a passport, permitting the holder to enter a specified country. **visaed** *a.*

visage /'vɪz-/ *n.* person's face.

vis-à-vis /viːzɑː'viː/ *adv. & prep.* facing one another; as compared with.

viscera /'vɪsərə/ *n.pl.* internal organs of the body. **visceral** *a.*

viscid /'vɪsɪd/ *a.* thick and gluey. **viscidity** *n.*

viscose *n.* viscous cellulose; fabric made from this.

viscount /'vaɪk-/ *n.* nobleman ranking between earl and baron; courtesy title of earl's eldest son. **viscountess** *n.fem.*

viscous *a.* thick and gluey. **viscosity** *n.*

visibility *n.* state of being visible; range of vision as determined by conditions of light etc.

visible *a.* able to be seen or noticed. **visibly** *adv.*

vision *n.* ability to see, sight; thing seen in the imagination or a dream etc.; imaginative insight; foresight; person or sight of unusual beauty; what is seen on a television screen.

visionary *a.* fanciful; not practical. —*n.* person with visionary ideas.

visit *v.t./i.* go or come to see (a person or place) socially or as a sightseer or on business etc.; stay temporarily with or at; (in the Bible) inflict punishment for. —*n.* act of visiting. **visitor** *n.*

visitant *n.* visitor, esp. a supernatural one.

visitation *n.* official visit; trouble looked upon as punishment from God.

visor /'vaɪz-/ *n.* movable front part of a helmet, covering the face; shading device at the top of a vehicle's windscreen.

vista *n.* extensive view, esp. seen through a long opening.

visual *a.* of or from or used in seeing. **visual display unit** device displaying a computer output or input on a screen. **visually** *adv.*

visualize *v.t.* form a mental picture of. **visualization** *n.*

vital *a.* connected with or essential to life; essential to a thing's existence or success; full of vitality. **vitals** *n.pl.* vital parts of the body (e.g. heart, lungs). **vital statistics** those relating to population figures or births and deaths; (*colloq.*) measurements of a woman's bust, waist, and hips. **vitally** *adv.*

vitality *n.* liveliness, persistent energy.

vitalize *v.t.* put life or vitality into. **vitalization** *n.*

vitamin /'vɪt-/ *n.* any of the organic substances present in food and essential to nutrition. **vitaminize** *v.t.* add vitamins to.

vitiate /'vɪʃɪ-/ *v.t.* make imperfect or ineffective. **vitiation** *n.*

viticulture /'vɪt-/ *n.* vine-growing.

vitreous *a.* having a glass-like texture or finish.

vitrify *v.t./i.* change into a glassy substance, esp. by heat. **vitrifaction** *n.*

vitriol *n.* sulphuric acid or one of its salts; savagely hostile remarks. **vitriolic** *a.*

vituperate /vɪ'tju:-/ *v.i.* use abusive language. **vituperation** *n.*, **vituperative** *a.*

viva /'vaɪ-/ *n.* (*colloq.*) viva voce examination. —*v.t.* (*p.t.* **vivaed**) (*colloq.*) examine by this.

vivacious /-'veɪ-/ *a.* lively, high-spirited. **vivaciously** *adv.*, **vivacity** *n.*

vivarium *n.* (*pl.* **-ia**) place for keeping living animals etc. in natural conditions.

viva voce /vaɪvə'vəʊtʃɪ/ spoken examination; orally.

vivid *a.* bright and strong; clear; (of imagination) lively. **vividly** *adv.*, **vividness** *n.*

vivify *v.t.* put life into.

viviparous /-'vɪp-/ *a.* bringing forth young alive, not egg-laying.

vivisection *n.* performance of surgical experiments on living animals.

vixen *n.* female fox.

viz. *adv.* namely.

vizier /-'zɪə(r)/ *n.* official of high rank in certain Muslim countries.

vocabulary *n.* list of words with their meanings; words known or used by a person or group.

vocal *a.* of, for, or uttered by the voice. —*n.* piece of sung music. **vocally** *adv.*

vocalic /-'kæ-/ *a.* of vowel(s).

vocalist *n.* singer.

vocalize *v.t.* utter. **vocalization** *n.*

vocation *n.* feeling of being called by God to a certain career; natural liking for a certain type of work; trade, profession. **vocational** *a.*

vociferate *v.t./i.* say loudly, shout. **vociferation** *n.*

vociferous *a.* making a great outcry. **vociferously** *adv.*

vodka *n.* alcoholic spirit distilled chiefly from rye.

vogue /vəʊg/ *n.* current fashion; popularity. **in vogue** in fashion.

voice *n.* sounds formed in the larynx and uttered by the mouth;

ability to produce these; expressed opinion, right to express an opinion; set of verbal forms that show the relation of the subject to the action. —*v.t.* put into words, express; utter. **voice-over** *n.* narration in a film etc. without a picture of the speaker.

void *a.* empty; not valid. —*n.* empty space, emptiness. —*v.t.* make void; excrete.

voile *n.* very thin dress-fabric.

volatile /'vɒl-/ *a.* evaporating rapidly; lively, changing quickly in mood. **volatility** *n.*

volatilize *v.t./i.* turn into vapour. **volatilization** *n.*

vol-au-vent /vɒləʊ'vɑ̃/ *n.* puff pastry case filled with a savoury mixture.

volcano *n.* (*pl.* -oes) mountain or hill with openings through which lava, gases, etc., are or have been expelled. **volcanic** *a.*

vole *n.* small rat-like animal.

volition /-'lɪʃ-/ *n.* use of one's own will in making a decision etc.

volley *n.* (*pl.* -eys) simultaneous discharge of missiles etc.; outburst of questions or other words; return of the ball in tennis etc. before it touches the ground. —*v.t.* send in a volley.

volleyball *n.* game for two teams of six persons sending a large ball by hand over a net.

volt /vəʊlt/ *n.* unit of electromotive force.

voltage *n.* electromotive force expressed in volts.

volte-face /vɒlt'fɑːs/ *n.* complete change of attitude to something.

voltmeter *n.* instrument measuring electric potential in volts.

voluble *a.* speaking or spoken with a great flow of words. **volubly** *adv.*, **volubility** *n.*

volume *n.* book; amount of space occupied or contained by a three-dimensional object; size, amount; strength of sound; mass (of water, smoke, etc.).

voluminous /-'lju:-/ *a.* having great volume, bulky; copious.

voluntary *a.* done, given, or acting of one's own free will; working or done without payment; maintained by voluntary work or contributions. —*n.* organ solo at a church service. **voluntarily** *n.*

volunteer *n.* person who offers to do something; one who enrols voluntarily for military service. —*v.t./i.* undertake or offer voluntarily; be a volunteer.

voluptuary *n.* person fond of luxury etc.

voluptuous *a.* full of or fond of luxury and the pleasures of life; having a full attractive figure. **voluptuously** *adv.*, **voluptuousness** *n.*

volute /-'lju:t/ *n.* scroll ornament on a pillar etc.

vomit *v.t./i.* (*p.t.* **vomited**) eject (matter) from the stomach through the mouth. —*n.* vomited matter.

voodoo *n.* form of religion based on witchcraft, esp. in the West Indies. **voodooism** *n.*

voracious *a.* greedy in eating, ravenous; desiring much. **voraciously** *adv.*, **voracity** *n.*

vortex *n.* (*pl.* -exes *or* -ices) whirlpool; whirlwind.

vote *n.* formal expression of one's opinion or choice on a matter under discussion; choice etc. expressed thus; right to vote. —*v.t./i.* express, decide, or support etc. by a vote. **voter** *n.*

votive *a.* given in fulfilment of a vow.

vouch *v.i.* **vouch for** guarantee the accuracy or reliability etc. of.

voucher *n.* document issued for payment and exchangeable for certain goods or services; a kind of receipt.

vouchsafe *v.t.* give or grant in a gracious or condescending way.

vow *n.* solemn promise, esp. in the form of an oath to a deity or saint. —*v.t.* promise solemnly.

vowel *n.* speech-sound made without audible stopping of the breath; letter(s) representing this.

voyage *n.* journey made by water or in space. —*v.i.* make a voyage. **voyager** *n.*

voyeur /vwɑːˈjɜː(r)/ *n.* person who obtains sexual gratification by looking at the sexual acts or organs of others.

vulcanite *n.* hard black vulcanized rubber.

vulcanize *v.t.* strengthen (rubber etc.) by treating with sulphur. **vulcanization** *n.*

vulgar *a.* lacking refinement or good taste; commonly used but incorrect. **vulgar fraction** one represented by numbers above and below a line. **vulgar tongue** native or vernacular language. **vulgarly** *adv.*, **vulgarity** *n.*

vulgarian *n.* vulgar (esp. rich) person.

vulgarism *n.* vulgar word(s) etc.

vulgarize *v.t.* make vulgar; spoil by making ordinary or too well known. **vulgarization** *n.*

Vulgate *n.* 4th-century Latin version of the Bible.

vulnerable *a.* able to be hurt or injured; exposed to danger or criticism. **vulnerability** *n.*

vulture *n.* large bird of prey that lives on the flesh of dead animals.

vulva *n.* external parts of the female genital organs.

vying *see* **vie.**

W

W. *abbr.* watt(s); west; western.

wacky *a.* (-ier, -iest) (*sl.*) crazy.

wad *n.* pad of soft material; bunch of papers or banknotes. —*v.t.* (*p.t.* **wadded**) pad.

wadding *n.* padding.

waddle *v.i.* & *n.* walk with short steps and a swaying movement.

wade *v.t./i.* walk through water or mud etc., walk across (a stream); make one's way slowly and laboriously (through work etc.).

wading bird long-legged waterbird that wades. **wader** *n.*

waders *n.pl.* high waterproof boots worn in fishing etc.

wadi /ˈwɒdɪ/ *n.* (in the Middle East etc.) rocky watercourse dry except in the rainy season.

wafer *n.* thin light biscuit; small thin slice. **wafery** *a.*

waffle[1] *n.* (*colloq.*) vague wordy talk or writing. —*v.i.* (*colloq.*) talk or write waffle.

waffle[2] *n.* small cake of batter eaten hot, cooked in a **waffle-iron.**

waft *v.t./i.* carry or travel lightly through air or over water. —*n.* wafted odour.

wag *v.t./i.* (*p.t.* **wagged**) shake briskly to and fro. —*n.* wagging movement; waggish person.

wage[1] *v.t.* engage in (war).

wage[2] *n.*, **wages** *n.pl.* regular payment to an employee for his or her work.

wager *n.* & *v.t./i.* bet.

waggish *a.* joking. **waggishly** *adv.*

waggle *v.t./i.* & *n.* wag.

waggon *n.* = wagon.

wagon *n.* four-wheeled goods-vehicle pulled by horses or oxen; open railway-truck; trolley for carrying food etc.

wagoner *n.* driver of a wagon.

wagtail *n.* small bird with a long tail that wags up and down.

waif *n.* homeless helpless person, esp. an abandoned child.

wail *v.t./i.* & *n.* (utter) a long sad cry; lament.

wain *n.* (*old use*) farm wagon.

wainscot *n.* wooden panelling in a room. **wainscoting** *n.*

waist *n.* part of the human body between ribs and hips; part of a garment covering this; narrow middle part.

waistcoat *n.* close-fitting waist-length sleeveless jacket.

waistline n. outline or size of the waist.

wait v.t./i. postpone an action until a specified time or event occurs; be postponed; wait on people at a meal; pause. —n. act or period of waiting; (pl., old use) carol-singers. **wait on** hand food and drink to (persons) at a meal; fetch and carry things for; pay a respectful visit to.

waiter n. man employed to serve food and drink to customers at tables in a restaurant etc. **waitress** n.fem.

waiting-list n. list of people waiting for something. **waiting-room** n. room provided for people waiting.

waive v.t. refrain from using (a right etc.), dispense with. **waiver** n.

wake¹ v.t./i. (p.t. **woke** or **waked**, p.p. **woken** or **waked**) cease to sleep; cause to cease sleeping; evoke. —n. (Ir.) watch by a corpse before burial; attendant lamentations and merrymaking; (pl.) annual holiday in industrial northern England. **wake up** wake; make or become alert.

wake² n. track left on water's surface by a ship etc.; air-currents left behind a moving aircraft etc. **in the wake of** behind; following.

wakeful a.unable to sleep; sleepless. **wakefulness** n.

waken v.t./i. wake.

wale n. weal, ridge; broad thick timber along a ship's side.

walk v.t./i. progress by setting down one foot and then lifting the other(s) in turn; travel over in this way; cause to walk, accompany in walking; (of a ghost) appear. —n. journey on foot; manner or style of walking; place or route for walking. **walk of life** social rank; occupation. **walk out** depart suddenly and angrily; go on strike suddenly. (**walk-out** n.). **walk out on** desert. **walk-**

over n. easy victory or achievement.

walkabout n. informal stroll among a crowd by a royal person etc.; (Austr.) Aboriginal's period of wandering in the bush.

walker n. person who walks; framework to assist walking.

walkie-talkie n. small portable radio transmitter and receiver.

walking-stick n. stick carried or used as a support when walking.

walkway n. passage, wide path.

wall n. continuous upright structure forming one side of a building or room or area; thing like this in form or function. —v.t. surround or enclose with a wall. **go to the wall** suffer defeat or failure or ruin.

wallaby n. small species of kangaroo.

wallah n. (sl.) person.

wallet n. small flat folding case for banknotes or small documents.

wall-eyed a. with eyes showing white abnormally, as in a squint.

wallflower n. garden plant with fragrant flowers.

wallop v.t. (p.t. **walloped**) (sl.) thrash, hit hard. —n. (sl.) heavy blow; beer or other drink.

wallow v.i. roll in mud or water etc. —n. act of wallowing. **wallow in** take unrestrained pleasure in.

wallpaper n. paper for covering the interior walls of rooms.

wally n. (sl.) stupid person.

walnut n. nut containing a wrinkled edible kernel; tree bearing this; its wood.

walrus n. large seal-like Arctic animal with long tusks.

waltz n. ballroom dance in triple time; music for this. —v.i. dance a waltz; (colloq.) move gaily or casually.

wampum /'wom-/ n. strings of shell-beads formerly used by North American Indians for money or ornament.

wan /wɒn/ a. pallid. **wanly** adv., **wanness** n.

wand n. slender rod, esp. associated with the working of magic.

wander v.i. go from place to place with no settled route or purpose; (of a road or river) wind; stray; digress. —n. act of wandering. **wanderer** n.

wanderlust n. strong desire to travel.

wane v.i. decrease in vigour or importance; (of the moon) show a decreasing bright area after being full. **on the wane** waning.

wangle v.t. (sl.) obtain or arrange by using trickery or scheming. —n. (sl.) act of wangling.

want v.t./i. desire; need; lack; be without the necessaries of life; fall short of. —n. desire; need; lack.

wanted a. (of a suspected criminal) sought by the police.

wanting a. lacking, deficient.

wanton /'wɒn-/ a. irresponsible, lacking proper restraint.

wapiti /wɒ'pɪtɪ/ n. large North American deer.

war n. strife (esp. between countries) involving military, naval, or air attacks; open hostility; strong effort to combat crime, disease, or poverty etc. —v.i. (p.t. **warred**) make war. **at war** engaged in a war.

warble v.t./i. sing, esp. with a gentle trilling note as certain birds do. —n. warbling sound. **warbler** n.

ward n. room with beds for a group of patients in a hospital; division of a city or town, electing a councillor to represent it; person (esp. a child) under the care of a guardian or lawcourt; each of the notches or projections in a lock or its key. —v.t. **ward off** keep (a danger etc.) at a distance.

warden n. official with supervisory duties; churchwarden.

warder n. prison officer.

wardrobe n. large cupboard for storing hanging clothes; stock of clothes or costumes.

wardroom n. officers' room in a warship.

ware n. manufactured goods (esp. pottery) of the kind specified; (pl.) articles offered for sale.

warehouse n. building for storing goods or furniture.

warfare n. making war, fighting.

warhead n. explosive head of a missile etc.

warlike a. fond of making war, aggressive; of or for war.

warlock n. (old use) sorcerer.

warm a. (-er, -est) moderately hot; providing warmth; enthusiastic, hearty; kindly and affectionate. —v.t./i. make or become warm. **warm-blooded** a. having blood that remains warm permanently. **warm-hearted** a. having a kindly and affectionate disposition. **warm** to become cordial towards (a person) or more animated about (a task). **warm up** warm; reheat; prepare for exercise etc. by practice beforehand; make or become more lively. **warmly** adv., **warmness** n.

warming-pan n. covered metal pan formerly filled with hot coals and used to warm beds.

warmonger n. person who seeks to bring about war.

warmth n. warmness.

warn v.t. inform about a present or future danger or difficulty etc., advise about action in this. **warn off** tell (a person) to keep away or to avoid (a thing).

warning n. thing that serves to warn a person.

warp /wɔːp/ v.t./i. make or become bent by uneven shrinkage or expansion; distort, pervert. —n. warped condition; lengthwise threads in a loom.

warpaint n. paint applied to the body before battle; (colloq.) elaborate make-up.

warpath *n.* **on the warpath** (*colloq.*) seeking hostile confrontation or revenge.

warrant /'wɒ-/ *n.* written authorization; voucher; justification for an action etc.; proof, guarantee. —*v.t.* serve as a warrant for, justify; prove, guarantee. **warrant-officer** *n.* member of the armed services ranking between commissioned officers and NCOs.

warranty *n.* guarantee; authority or justification for an action etc.

warren *n.* piece of ground with many burrows where rabbits live and breed; building or district with many winding passages.

warring *a.* engaged in a war.

warrior *n.* person who fights in a battle.

warship *n.* ship for use in war.

wart *n.* small hard abnormal growth. **wart-hog** *n.* African pig with wart-like growths on its face. **warty** *a.*

wartime *n.* period when a war is being waged.

wary /'weəri/ *a.* (-**ier**, -**iest**) cautious, looking out for possible danger or difficulty. **warily** *adv.*, **wariness** *n.*

was see **be**.

wash *v.t./i.* cleanse with water or other liquid; wash oneself or clothes etc.; be washable; flow past or against or over; carry by flowing; coat thinly with paint; (*colloq.*, of reasoning) be valid. —*n.* process of washing or being washed; clothes etc. to be washed; disturbed water or air behind a moving ship or aircraft etc.; liquid food for pigs; thin coating of paint. **wash-basin** *n.* bowl (usu. fixed to a wall) for washing one's hands and face. **washed out** faded by washing; looking faded; pallid. **washed up** (*sl.*) defeated, having failed. **wash one's hands** of refuse to take responsibility for. **wash out** wash

(clothes etc.); make (a sport) impossible by heavy rainfall; (*colloq.*) cancel. **wash-out** *n.* (*sl.*) complete failure. **wash up** wash (dishes etc.) after use; cast up on the shore; (*US*) wash oneself.

washable *a.* able to be washed without suffering damage.

washer *n.* ring of rubber or metal etc. placed between two surfaces to give tightness; washing-machine.

washerwoman *n.* (*pl.* -**women**) woman whose occupation is washing clothes etc.

washing *n.* clothes etc. to be washed. **washing-machine** *n.* machine for washing these. **washing-up** *n.* dishes etc. for washing after use; process of washing these.

washroom *n.* (*US*) room with a lavatory.

washstand *n.* piece of furniture to hold a basin and jug of water for washing.

washtub *n.* tub for washing clothes.

washy *a.* too watery or weak; lacking vigour.

wasp *n.* stinging insect with a black-and-yellow striped body. **waspish** *a.* making sharp or irritable comments. **waspishly** *adv.*

wassail /'wɒseɪl/ *n.* (*old use*) making merry (esp. at Christmas) with drinking of spiced ale etc. —*v.i.* (*old use*) make merry thus.

wast (*old use with* thou) = was.

wastage *n.* loss or diminution by waste; loss of employees by retirement or resignation.

waste *v.t./i.* use or be used extravagantly or without adequate result; fail to use; make or become gradually weaker. —*a.* left or thrown away because not wanted; (of land) unfit for use. —*n.* process of wasting; waste material or food etc.; waste land; waste-pipe. **waste pipe** pipe carrying off used or superfluous water or steam.

wasteful *a.* wasting things. **wastefully** *adv.*, **wastefulness** *n.*

waster /'wei-/ *n.* wasteful person; (*sl.*) wastrel.

wastrel /'wei-/ *n.* good-for-nothing person.

watch *v.t./i.* look at, keep under observation; wait alertly, take heed; exercise protective care. —*n.* act of watching, constant observation or attention; sailor's period (usu. four hours) of duty, persons on duty in this; small portable device indicating the time; (*old use*) watchman, watchmen. **on the watch** waiting alertly. **watching brief** brief of a barrister who is present during a lawsuit to advise a client not directly concerned in it. **watch-night service** religious service on the last day of the year. **watch out** be on one's guard. **watchtower** *n.* tower from which observation can be kept. **watcher** *n.*

watchdog *n.* dog kept to guard property; guardian of people's rights etc.

watchful *a.* watching closely. **watchfully** *adv.*, **watchfulness** *n.*

watchmaker *n.* person who makes or repairs watches.

watchman *n.* (*pl.* **-men**) man employed to look after an empty building etc.

watchword *n.* word or phrase expressing a group's principles.

water *n.* colourless odourless tasteless liquid that is a compound of hydrogen and oxygen; this as supplied for domestic use; lake, sea; watery secretion, urine; watery preparation; level of the tide; transparency and lustre of a gem. —*v.t.* sprinkle, supply, or dilute with water; secrete tears or saliva. **by water** (of travel) in a boat etc. **in low water** short of money. **water-bed** *n.* mattress of rubber etc. filled with water. **water-biscuit** *n.* thin unsweetened biscuit. **water-butt** *n.* barrel used to catch rainwater. **water-cannon** *n.* device giving a powerful jet of water to dispel a crowd etc. **water-closet** *n.* lavatory flushed by water. **water-colour** *n.* artists' paint mixed with water (not oil); painting done with this. **water down** dilute; make less forceful. **water-glass** *n.* thick liquid used for coating eggs to preserve them. **water-ice** *n.* edible concoction of frozen flavoured water. **water lily** plant with broad floating leaves and large flowers that grows in water. **water-line** *n.* line along which the surface of water touches a ship's side. **water main** main pipe in a water-supply system. **water-meadow** *n.* meadow that is flooded periodically by a stream. **water melon** melon with red pulp and watery juice. **water-mill** *n.* mill worked by a water-wheel. **water-pistol** *n.* toy pistol that shoots a jet of water. **water polo** game played by teams of swimmers with a ball like a football. **water-power** *n.* power obtained from flowing or falling water, used to drive machinery or generate electricity. **water-rat** *n.* rat-like animal living beside a lake or stream. **water-skiing** *n.* sport of skimming over water on flat boards while towed by a motor boat. **water-splash** *n.* section of a road where vehicles must travel through a shallow stream or pool. **water-table** *n.* level below which the ground is saturated with water. **water-weed** *n.* weed growing in water. **water-wheel** *n.* wheel turned by a flow of water to work machinery. **water-wings** *n.pl.* floats worn on the shoulders by a person learning to swim.

waterbrash *n.* watery fluid brought up from the stomach.

watercourse n. stream, brook, or artificial waterway; its channel.

watercress n. a kind of cress that grows in streams and ponds.

watered a. (of silk) having an irregular wavy marking.

waterfall n. stream that falls from a height.

waterfront n. part of a town that borders on a river, lake, or sea.

watering-can n. container with a tubular spout, holding water for watering plants.

watering-place n. pool where animals drink; spa, seaside resort.

waterless a. without water.

waterlogged a. saturated with water.

waterman n. (pl. -men) boatman plying for hire.

watermark n. manufacturer's design in paper, visible when the paper is held against light.

waterproof a. unable to be penetrated by water. —n. waterproof coat or cape. —v.t. make waterproof.

watershed n. line of high land separating two river-systems; turning-point in the course of events.

waterspout n. column of water between sea and cloud, formed by a whirlwind.

watertight a. made or fastened so that water cannot get in or out; impossible to set aside or disprove.

waterway n. navigable channel.

waterworks n. establishment with machinery etc. for supplying water to a district.

watery a. of or like water; containing too much water; (of colour) pale. **wateriness** n.

watt /wɒt/ n. unit of electric power.

wattage /'wɒt-/ n. amount of electric power, expressed in watts.

wattle[1] /'wɒ-/ n. interwoven sticks used as material for fences,

walls, etc.; Australian acacia with golden flowers.

wattle[2] /'wɒ-/ n. fold of skin hanging from the neck of a turkey etc.

wave n. moving ridge of water, wave-like curve(s), e.g. in hair; advancing progress; temporary increase of an influence or condition; act of waving; wave-like motion by which heat, light, sound, or electricity etc. is spread; single curve in this. —v.t./i. move loosely to and fro or up and down; move (one's arm etc.) thus as a signal; signal or express thus; give or have a wavy course or appearance.

waveband n. range of wavelengths.

wavelength n. distance between corresponding points in a sound wave or electromagnetic wave.

wavelet n. small wave.

waver v.i. be or become unsteady; begin to give way; show hesitation or uncertainty. **waverer** n.

wavy a. (-ier, -iest) full of waves or wave-like curves.

wax[1] n. beeswax; any of various similar soft substances; polish containing this. —v.t. coat, polish, or treat with wax. **waxy** a.

wax[2] v.i. increase in vigour or importance; (of the moon) show an increasing bright area until becoming full; (old use) become.

waxen a. made of wax; like wax in paleness or smoothness.

waxwing n. small bird with red tips on some of its wing-feathers.

waxwork n. object modelled in wax, esp. lifelike model of a person.

way n. line of communication between two places; route; travelling-distance; space free of obstacles so that people etc. can pass; progress; specified direction or aspect; method, style, manner; chosen or desired course of action; difference from a specified state or condition;

(pl.) habits. —adv. (colloq.) far. **by the way** incidentally, as an irrelevant comment. **by way of** as a substitute for or a form of; by going through. **in a way** to a limited extent; in some respects. **in the way** forming an obstacle or hindrance. **on one's way** in the process of travelling or approaching. **on the way** on one's way; (of a baby) conceived but not yet born. **under way** (see **under**).

way-leave n. right of way rented to another person. **way-out** a. (colloq.) exaggeratedly unusual.

waybill n. list of the passengers or goods being carried by a vehicle.

wayfarer n. traveller, esp. on foot.

waylay v.t. (p.t. **-laid**) lie in wait for.

wayside n. side of a road or path.

wayward a. childishly self-willed, hard to control. **waywardness** n.

WC abbr. water-closet.

we pron. used by a person referring to himself and another or others; used instead of 'I' by a royal person in formal proclamations, and by the writer of an editorial article in a newspaper.

weak a. (**-er**, **-est**) lacking strength or power or number, easily broken or bent or defeated; not convincing; much diluted; (of verbs) forming the past tense by adding a suffix (e.g. walk/walked). **weak-kneed** a., **weak-minded** a. lacking determination.

weaken v.t./i. make or become weaker.

weakling n. feeble person or animal.

weakly adv. in a weak manner. —a. sickly, not robust.

weakness n. state of being weak; weak point, fault; self-indulgent liking.

weal[1] n. ridge raised on flesh esp. by the stroke of a rod or whip.

weal[2] n. (old use) welfare.

wealth n. riches; possession of these; great quantity.

wealthy a. (**-ier**, **-iest**) having wealth, rich. **wealthiness** n.

wean v.t. accustom (a baby) to take food other than milk; cause to give up something gradually.

weapon n. thing designed or used for inflicting harm or damage; means of coercing someone.

wear[1] v.t./i. (p.t. **wore**, p.p. **worn**) have on the body, e.g. as clothing or ornament; damage gradually or become damaged on the surface by rubbing, make (a hole etc.) thus; endure continued use. —n. wearing, being worn; clothing; capacity to endure being used. **wear down** exhaust or overcome (opposition etc.) by persistence. **wear off** pass off gradually. **wear on** (of time) pass gradually. **wear out** use or be used until no longer usable; tire or become tired out. **wearer** n., **wearable** a.

wear[2] v.t./i. (p.t. & p.p. **wore**) come or bring (a ship) about by turning its head away from the wind.

wearisome a. causing weariness.

weary a. (**-ier**, **-iest**) very tired; tiring, tedious. —v.t./i. make or become weary. **wearily** adv., **weariness** n.

weasel n. small wild animal with a slender body and reddish-brown fur.

weather n. state of the atmosphere with reference to sunshine, rain, wind, etc. —a. windward. —v.t./i. dry or season by exposure to the action of the weather; become dried or worn etc. thus; sail to windward of; come safely through (a storm). **under the weather** feeling unwell or depressed. **weather-beaten** a. bronzed or worn by exposure to weather. **weather-vane** n. weathercock.

weatherboard n. sloping board for keeping out rain.

weathercock n. revolving pointer (often in the form of a cockerel) mounted in a high place, turning easily to show the direction of the wind.

weave[1] v.t./i.)p.t. **wove**, p.p. **woven**) make (fabric etc.) by passing crosswise threads or strips under and over lengthwise ones; form (thread etc.) into fabric thus; compose (a story etc.). —n. style or pattern of weaving.

weave[2] v.i. move in an intricate course.

weaver n. person who weaves; tropical bird that builds an intricately woven nest.

web n. network of fine strands made by a spider etc.; skin filling the spaces between the toes of ducks, frogs, etc. **web-footed** a. having toes joined by web. **webbed** a.

webbing n. strong band(s) of woven fabric used in upholstery etc.

wed v.t./i. (p.t. **wedded**) marry; unite. **wedded to** devotedly attached to (an occupation, opinion, etc.).

wedding n. marriage ceremony and festivities.

wedge n. piece of solid substance thick at one end and tapering to a thin edge at the other, thrust between things to force them apart or prevent free movement; thing shaped like this. —v.t./i. force apart or fix firmly with a wedge; crowd tightly; be immovable.

wedlock n. married state.

Wednesday n. day after Tuesday.

wee a. (Sc.) little; (colloq.) tiny.

weed n. wild plant growing where it is not wanted; thin weak-looking person. —v.t./i. uproot and remove weeds (from). **weed-**

killer n. substance used to destroy weeds. **weed out** remove as inferior or undesirable. **weedy** a.

weeds n.pl. deep mourning formerly worn by widows.

week n. period of seven successive days, esp. from Sunday to Saturday; the six days between Sundays; the five days other than Saturday and Sunday; working-period during a week.

weekday n. day other than Sunday or Sunday and Saturday.

weekend n. Saturday and Sunday.

weekly a. & adv. (produced or occurring) once a week. —n. weekly periodical.

weeny a. (-ier, -iest) (colloq.) tiny.

weep v.t./i. (p.t. **wept**) shed (tears); shed or ooze (moisture) in drops. —n. spell of weeping. **weeper** n., **weepy** a.

weeping a. (of a tree) having drooping branches.

weevil n. small beetle that feeds on grain, nuts, tree-bark, etc.

weft n. crosswise threads in weaving.

weigh v.t. measure the weight of; have a specified weight; consider the relative importance of; have importance or influence; be burdensome. **weigh anchor** raise the anchor and start a voyage. **weigh down** bring or keep down by its weight; depress, oppress. **weigh in** be weighed (of a boxer, before a contest; of a jockey, after a race). **weigh in with** (colloq.) offer confidently as a comment etc. **weigh out** take a stated weight of; (of a jockey) be weighed before a race. **weigh up** (colloq.) form an estimate of.

weighbridge n. weighing-machine with a plate set in a road etc. for weighing vehicles.

weight n. object's mass numerically expressed using a recognized scale of units; unit or system of units used thus; piece of metal of known weight used in weighing; heavy object; heaviness; load, burden; influence; convincing effect. —v.t. attach a weight to; hold down with a weight; burden; bias. **weightless** a., **weightlessness** n.

weighting n. extra pay given in special cases.

weightlifting n. sport of lifting heavy weights.

weighty a. (-ier, -iest) heavy; showing or deserving earnest thought; influential.

weir n. small dam built so that some of a stream's water flows over it; waterfall formed thus.

weird a. (-er, -est) uncanny, bizarre. **weirdly** adv., **weirdness** n.

welcome a. received with pleasure; ungrudgingly permitted or given a right to. —int. greeting expressing pleasure at a person's coming. —n. greeting or reception, esp. a glad and kindly one. —v.t. give a welcome to; receive gladly.

weld v.t./i. unite or fuse (pieces of usu. heated metal) by hammering or pressure; make by welding; unite into a whole. —n. welded joint. **welder** n.

welfare n. well-being; organized efforts to ensure people's well-being. **Welfare State** country with highly developed social services.

welkin n. (poetic) sky.

well[1] n. shaft dug or drilled to obtain water or oil etc.; enclosed shaft-like space. —v.i. rise or spring.

well[2] adv. (better, best) in a good manner or style, rightly; thoroughly; by a considerable margin; favourably, kindly; with good reason; easily; probably. —a. in good health; in a satisfactory state or position. —int. expressing surprise, relief, or resignation etc., or said when one is hesitating. **as well** in addition; desirable; desirably. **as well as**

in addition to. **well-appointed** a. well-equipped. **well-being** n. good health, happiness, and prosperity. **well-born** a. born of good family. **well-bred** a. showing good breeding; well-mannered. **well-disposed** a. having kindly or favourable feelings. **well-heeled** a. (colloq.) wealthy. **well-knit** a. having a compact body. **well-meaning** a., **well-meant** a. acting or done with good intentions. **well off** in a satisfactory or good situation; fairly rich. **well-read** a. having read much literature. **well-spoken** a. speaking in a polite and correct way. **well-to-do** a. fairly rich. **well-wisher** n. person who wishes well to another.

wellington n. boot of rubber or other waterproof material.

wellnigh adv. almost.

Welsh a. & n. (language) of Wales. **Welsh rabbit** or **rarebit** melted or toasted cheese on toast. **Welshman** n. (pl. -men), **Welshwoman** n. (pl. -women).

welsh v.i. avoid paying one's debts; break an agreement. **welsher** n.

welt n. leather rim attaching the top of a boot or shoe to the sole; ribbed or strengthened border of a knitted garment; weal. —v.t. provide with a welt; raise weals on, thrash.

welter v.i. (of a ship etc.) be tossed to and fro on waves. —n. turmoil; disorderly mixture.

welterweight n. boxing weight (67 kg).

wen n. benign tumour on the skin.

wench n. (old use) girl, young woman.

wend v.t. **wend one's way** go.

went see **go**.

wept see **weep**.

were see **be**.

werewolf /'wɪə-/ n. (pl. -wolves) (in myths) person who at times turns into a wolf.

west n. point on the horizon where the sun sets; direction in which this lies; western part. —a. in the west; (of wind) from the west. —adv. towards the west. **go west** (sl.) be destroyed or lost or killed.

westerly a. towards or blowing from the west.

western a. of or in the west. —n. film or novel about cowboys in western North America.

westerner n. native or inhabitant of the west.

westernize v.t. make (an oriental country etc.) more like a western one in ideas and institutions. **westernization** n.

westernmost a. furthest west.

westward a. towards the west. **westwards** adv.

wet a. (**wetter, wettest**) soaked or covered with water or other liquid; rainy; not dry; allowing the sale of alcohol; (colloq.) lacking vitality; (of Conservatives) having moderate views, not strongly right-wing. —v.t. (p.t. **wetted**) make wet. —n. moisture, water; wet weather; (colloq) Conservative with moderate views. **wet blanket** gloomy person. **wet-nurse** n. woman employed to suckle another's child; (v.t.) act as wet-nurse to, coddle as if helpless. **wet suit** porous garment worn by a skin-diver etc. **wetly** adv., **wetness** n.

wether n. castrated ram.

whack v.t. & n. (colloq.) hit. **do one's whack** (sl.) do one's share.

whacked a. (colloq.) tired out.

whacking a. & adv. very (large).

whale n. very large sea animal. **a whale of a** (colloq.) an exceedingly great or good (thing).

whalebone n. horny substance from the upper jaw of whales, formerly used as stiffening.

whaler n. whaling ship; seaman hunting whales.

whaling n. hunting whales.

wham int. & n. sound of a forcible impact.

wharf n. (pl. **wharfs**) landing-stage where ships load and unload.

wharfinger /-fɪndʒ-/ n. owner or manager of a wharf.

what a. asking for a statement of amount or number or kind; how great or remarkable; the or any that. —pron. what thing(s); what did you say? —adv. to what extent or degree. —int. exclamation of surprise. **what about** what is the news or your opinion about (a subject)? **what's what** what things are useful or important etc. **what with** on account of (various causes).

whatever a. of any kind or number. —pron. anything or everything; no matter what.

whatnot n. something trivial or indefinite; stand with shelves for small objects.

whatsoever a. & pron. whatever.

wheat n. grain from which flour is made; plant producing this.

wheatear n. a kind of small bird.

wheaten a. made from wheat-flour.

wheatmeal n. wheat flour with some of the bran and germ removed.

wheedle v.t. coax.

wheel n. disc or circular frame that revolves on a shaft passing through its centre; thing resembling this; machine etc. using a wheel; wheel-like motion. —v.t./i. push or pull (a cart or bicycle etc.) along; turn; move in circles or curves. **at the wheel** driving a vehicle, directing a ship; in control of affairs. **wheel and deal** engage in scheming to exert influence. **wheel-clamp** v.t. fix a clamp on (an illegally parked car etc.).

wheelbarrow n. open container for moving small loads, with a wheel at one end.

wheelbase *n.* distance between a vehicle's front and rear axles.

wheelchair *n.* lame person's chair on wheels.

wheelie *n.* (colloq.) manœuvre on a two-wheeled vehicle etc. with one wheel off the ground.

wheeze *v.i.* breathe with a hoarse whistling sound. —*n.* this sound. **wheezy** *a.*

whelk *n.* shellfish with a spiral shell.

whelp *n.* young dog, pup. —*v.t./i.* give birth to (a whelp or whelps).

when *adv.* at what time, on what occasion; at which time. —*conj.* at the time that; whenever; as soon as; although. —*pron.* what or which time.

whence *adv.* & *conj.* from where; from which.

whenever *conj.* & *adv.* at whatever time; every time that.

where *adv.* & *conj.* at or in which place or circumstances; in what respect; from what place or source; to what place. —*pron.* what place.

whereabouts *adv.* in or near what place. —*n.* a person's or thing's approximate location.

whereas *conj.* since it is the fact that; but in contrast.

whereby *adv.* by which.

wherefore *adv.* (old use) for what reason, for this reason.

wherein *adv.* in what, in which.

whereof *adv.* of what, of which.

whereupon *adv.* after which, and then.

wherever *adv.* at or to whatever place.

wherewith *adv.* with what, with which.

wherewithal *n.* (colloq.) things (esp. money) needed for a purpose.

wherry *n.* light rowing-boat; large light barge.

whet *v.t.* (p.t. **whetted**) sharpen by rubbing against a stone etc.; stimulate (appetite or interest).

whether *conj.* introducing an alternative possibility.

whetstone *n.* shaped hard stone used for sharpening tools.

whew *int.* exclamation of surprise, dismay, or relief.

whey *n.* watery liquid left when milk forms curds.

which *a.* & *pron.* what particular one(s) of a set; and that. —*rel. pron.* thing or animal referred to.

whichever *a.* & *pron.* any which, that or those which.

whiff *n.* puff of air or odour etc.

Whig *n.* member of a former political party (succeeded by the Liberal Party). **Whiggery** *n.*

while *n.* period of time; time spent in doing something. —*conj.* during the time that, as long as; although; on the other hand. —*v.t.* **while away** pass (time) in a leisurely or interesting way.

whilst *conj.* while.

whim *n.* sudden fancy.

whimper *v.i.* make feeble crying sounds. —*n.* whimpering sound.

whimsical *a.* impulsive and playful; fanciful, quaint. **whimsically** *adv.* whimsicality *n.*

whin *n.* gorse.

whinchat *n.* small brown bird.

whine *v.t./i.* make a long high complaining cry or a similar shrill sound; complain or utter with a whine. —*n.* whining sound or complaint. **whiner** *n.*

whinge *v.i.* whine, complain.

whinny *n.* gentle or joyful neigh. —*v.i.* utter a whinny.

whip *n.* cord or strip of leather on a handle, used for striking a person or animal; official appointed to maintain discipline of his party in Parliament, party discipline and instructions given by such officials; food made with whipped cream etc. —*v.t.* (p.t. **whipped**) strike or urge on with a whip; beat into a froth; move or take suddenly; oversew. **have the whip hand** have control; (sl.) steal. **whip-round** *n.* appeal for contributions from a group. **whip up** incite.

whipcord *n.* cord of tightly twisted strands; twilled fabric with prominent ridges.

whiplash *n.* lash of a whip; jerk.

whippersnapper *n.* young insignificant presumptuous person.

whippet *n.* small dog resembling a greyhound, used for racing.

whipping-boy *n.* scapegoat.

whippy *a.* flexible, springy.

whipstock *n.* handle of a whip.

whirl *v.t./i.* swing or spin round and round; travel swiftly in a curved course; convey or go rapidly in a vehicle. —*n.* whirling movement; confused state; bustling activity.

whirligig *n.* whirling toy; merry-go-round.

whirlpool *n.* current of water whirling in a circle.

whirlwind *n.* mass of air whirling rapidly about a central point.

whirr *n.* continuous buzzing or vibrating sound. —*v.i.* make this sound.

whisk *v.t./i.* move with a quick light sweeping movement; convey or go rapidly; brush away lightly; beat into a froth. —*n.* whisking movement; instrument for beating eggs etc.; bunch of bristles etc. for brushing or flicking things.

whisker *n.* long hair-like bristle near the mouth of a cat etc.; (*pl.*) hair growing on a man's cheek. **whiskered** *a.*, **whiskery** *a.*

whiskey *n.* Irish whisky.

whisky *n.* spirit distilled from malted grain (esp. barley).

whisper *v.t./i.* speak or utter softly, not using the vocal cords; converse privately or secretly; rustle. —*n.* whispering sound or speech or remark; rumour.

whist *n.* card-game usu. for two pairs of players. **whist drive** series of games of whist for a number of players.

whistle *n.* shrill sound made by blowing through a narrow opening between the lips; similar sound; instrument for producing this. —*v.t./i.* make this sound; signal or produce (a tune) in this way. **whistle-stop** *n.* (US) brief stop (during a tour made by a politician etc.) e.g. for electioneering. **whistler** *n.*

Whit *a.* of or close to **Whit Sunday**, seventh Sunday after Easter, commemorating the descent of the Holy Spirit upon the Apostles.

whit *n.* least possible amount.

white *a.* (-er, -est) of the very lightest colour, like snow or common salt; having a light-coloured skin; pale from illness or fear etc. —*n.* white colour or thing; transparent substance (white when cooked) round egg-yolk; **White** member of the race with light-coloured skin. **white ant** termite. **white Christmas** one with snow. **white coffee** coffee with milk or cream. **white-collar worker** one not engaged in manual labour. **white elephant** useless possession. **white hope** person expected to achieve much. **white horses** white-crested waves on sea. **white-hot** *a.* (of metal) glowing white after heating. **white lie** harmless lie. **White Paper** government report giving information on a subject. **white sale** sale of household linen. **white slave** woman tricked (and usu. sent abroad) into prostitution. **white slavery** this practice or state. **white spirit** light petroleum used as a solvent. **white wine** wine of yellow colour. **whitely** *adv.*, **whiteness** *n.*

whitebait *n.* (*pl.* **whitebait**) small silvery-white fish.

Whitehall *n.* British Government or the Civil Service.

whiten *v.t./i.* make or become white or whiter.

whitewash n. liquid containing quicklime or powdered chalk, used for painting walls or ceilings etc.; means of glossing over mistakes. —v.t. paint with whitewash; gloss over mistakes in.

whitewood n. light-coloured wood, esp. prepared for staining etc.

whither adv. (old use) to what place.

whiting[1] n. (pl. **whiting**) small sea-fish used as food.

whiting[2] n. chalk prepared for use in whitewash etc.

whitlow n. small abscess under or affecting a nail.

Whitsun n. Whit Sunday and the days close to it. **Whitsuntide** n.

Whitsunday n. (Sc.) a quarter-day, 15 May.

whittle v.t. trim (wood) by cutting thin slices from the surface; reduce by removing various amounts.

whiz v.t./i. (p.t. **whizzed**) make a sound like something moving at great speed through air; move very quickly. —n. whizzing sound. **whiz-kid** n. (colloq.) brilliant or successful young person.

who pron. what or which person(s)?; the particular person(s).

whoa int. command to a horse etc. to stop or stand still.

whodunit n. (colloq.) detective or mystery story or play etc.

whoever pron. any or every person who, no matter who.

whole a. with no part removed or left out; not injured or broken. —n. full amount, all parts or members; complete system made up of parts. **on the whole** considering everything; in respect of the whole though some details form exceptions. **whole-hearted** a. without doubts or reservations. **whole number** consisting of one or more units with no fractions.

wholemeal a. made from the whole grain of wheat etc.

wholesale n. selling of goods in large quantities to be retailed by others. —a. & adv. in the wholesale trade; on a large scale. **wholesaler** n.

wholesome a. good for physical or mental health or well-being; healthy. **wholesomeness** n.

wholly adv. entirely.

whom pron. objective case of who.

whoop v.i. utter a loud cry of excitement. —n. this cry.

whoopee int. cry of exuberant joy.

whooping-cough n. infectious disease esp. of children, with a violent convulsive cough.

whoops int. (colloq.) exclamation of surprise or apology.

whop v.t. (p.t. **whopped**) (sl.) thrash, defeat.

whopper n. (sl.) something very large; great lie.

whopping a. (sl.) very large.

whore /hɔː(r)/ n. prostitute; sexually immoral woman.

whorl n. coiled form, one turn of a spiral; circle of ridges in a fingerprint; ring of leaves or petals.

whortleberry /'wɜː-/ n. bilberry.

whose pron. of whom; of which.

whosoever pron. whoever.

why adv. for what reason or purpose?; on account of which. —int. exclamation of surprised discovery or recognition.

wick n. length of thread in a candle or lamp etc., by which the flame is kept supplied with melted grease or fuel.

wicked a. morally bad, offending against what is right; formidable, severe; mischievous. **wickedly** adv., **wickedness** n.

wicker n. osiers or thin canes interwoven to make furniture or baskets etc. **wickerwork** n.

wicket n. set of three stumps and two bails used in cricket; part of a cricket ground between or near the two wickets; wicket-door, wicket-gate. **wicket-door** n., **wicket-gate** n. small door or gate for use when a larger one is closed. **wicket-keeper** n. cricket fielder stationed just behind the batsman's wicket.

wide a. (-er, -est) measuring much from side to side; having a specified width; extending far; fully opened; far from the target. —adv. widely; far from the target. —n. bowled ball that passes beyond the batsman's reach in cricket. **to the wide** completely. **wide awake** fully awake or (colloq.) alert. **widely** adv., **wideness** n.

widen v.t./i. make or become wider.

widespread a. found or distributed over a wide area.

widgeon /'wɪdʒ(ə)n/ n. wild duck.

widow n. woman whose husband has died and who has not remarried. **widowhood** n.

widowed a. made a widow or widower.

widower n. man whose wife has died and who has not remarried.

width n. wideness; distance from side to side; piece of material of full width as woven.

wield v.t. hold and use (a tool etc.); have and use (power).

wife n. (pl. **wives**) married woman in relation to her husband. **wifely** a.

wig n. covering of hair worn on the head.

wigging n. scolding.

wiggle v.t./i. & n. move repeatedly from side to side, wriggle.

wight n. (old use) person.

wigwam n. conical tent as formerly used by North American Indians.

wild a. (-er, -est) living or growing in its original or natural state, not domesticated or tame or cultivated; not civilized; disorderly; stormy; full of strong unrestrained feeling; random. —adv. in a wild manner. —n. (usu. pl.) waste place; districts far from civilization. **run wild** grow or live without being controlled. **wild-goose chase** useless quest. **wildly** adv. **wildness** n.

wildcat a. reckless; (of strikes) unofficial and irresponsible.

wildebeest /'wɪldəbi:st/ n. gnu.

wilderness n. wild uncultivated area.

wildfire n. **spread like wildfire** spread very fast.

wildfowl n. birds hunted as game.

wildlife n. wild animals.

wile n. piece of trickery. —v.t. **wile away** = while away.

wilful a. intentional, not accidental; self-willed. **wilfully** adv., **wilfulness** n.

will[1] v.aux. (wilt is used with thou) used with I and we to express promises or obligations, and with other words to express a future tense.

will[2] n. mental faculty by which a person decides upon and controls his own or others' actions; determination; that which is desired; person's attitude in wishing good or bad to others; written directions made by a person for disposal of his property after his death. —v.t. exercise one's willpower, influence by doing this; bequeath by a will. **at will** whenever one pleases. **have one's will** get what one desires. **will-power** n. control exercised by one's will. **with a will** vigorously.

willies n.pl. (sl.) nervous discomfort.

willing a. desiring to do what is required, not objecting; given or done readily. —n. **willingness**. **willingly** adv., **willingness** n.

will-o'-the-wisp n. phosphorescent light seen on marshy ground; hope or aim that lures a person on but can never be fulfilled.

willow n. tree or shrub with flexible branches; its wood.

willowy *a.* full of willows; slender and supple.

willy *n.* (*sl.*) penis.

willy-nilly *adv.* whether one desires it or not.

wilt[1] *see* **will**[1].

wilt[2] *v.t./i.* lose or cause to lose freshness and droop; become limp from exhaustion. —*n.* plant-disease that causes wilting.

wily /'wai-/ *a.* (**-ier, -iest**) full of wiles, cunning. **wiliness** *n.*

wimp *n.* (*sl.*) feeble person.

wimple *n.* medieval head-dress covering all but the face, worn by some nuns.

win *v.t./i.* (*p.t.* **won,** *pres.p.* **winning**) be victorious (in); obtain as the result of a contest or bet etc., or by effort; gain the favour or support of. —*n.* victory, esp. in a game.

wince *v.i.* make a slight movement from pain or embarrassment etc. —*n.* this movement.

winceyette *n.* cotton fabric with a soft downy surface.

winch *n.* machine for hoisting or pulling things by a cable that winds round a revolving drum. —*v.t.* hoist or pull with a winch.

wind[1] /wind/ *n.* current of air; smell carried by this; gas in the stomach or intestines; breath as needed in exertion or speech etc.; orchestra's wind instruments; useless or boastful talk. —*v.t./i.* detect by the presence of a smell; cause to be out of breath. **get** *or* **have the wind up** (*sl.*) feel frightened. **get wind of** hear a hint or rumour of. **in the wind** happening or about to happen. **like the wind** very swiftly. **put the wind up** (*sl.*) frighten. **take the wind out of a person's sails** take away an advantage, frustrate by anticipating him or her. **wind-break** *n.* protective screen shielding something from the wind. **wind-cheater** *n.* thin but wind-proof jacket. **wind-chill** *n.* cooling effect of the wind. **wind**

instrument musical instrument sounded by a current of air, esp. by the player's breath. **wind-jammer** *n.* merchant sailing-ship. **wind-sock** *n.* canvas cylinder flown at an airfield to show the direction of the wind. **wind-tunnel** *n.* enclosed tunnel in which winds can be created for testing things.

wind[2] /waind/ *v.t./i.* (*p.t.* **wound,** *pr.* waund) move or go in a curving or spiral course; wrap closely around something or round upon itself; hoist or move by turning a windlass or handle etc.; wind up (a clock etc.). **wind up** set or keep (a clock etc.) going by tightening its spring or adjusting its weights; bring or come to an end; settle the affairs of and close (a business company). **winder** *n.*

windbag *n.* (*colloq.*) person who talks lengthily.

windfall *n.* fruit blown off a tree by the wind; unexpected gain, esp. a sum of money.

winding-sheet *n.* sheet in which a corpse is wrapped for burial.

windlass *n.* winch-like device using a rope or chain that winds round a horizontal roller.

windless *a.* without wind.

windmill *n.* mill worked by the action of wind on projecting parts that radiate from a shaft.

window *n.* opening in a wall etc. to admit light and often air, usu. filled with glass; this glass; space for display of goods behind the window of a shop; opening resembling a window; section of a VDU display showing one part of the data. **window-box** *n.* trough fixed outside a window, for growing flowers etc. **window-dressing** *n.* arranging a display of goods in a shop-window; presentation of facts so as to give a favourable impression. **window-seat** *n.* seat below a window. **window-shopping** *n.* looking at displayed goods without buying.

windpipe *n.* air-passage from the throat to the bronchial tubes.

windscreen *n.* glass in the window at the front of a vehicle.

windshield *n.* (*US*) windscreen.

windsurfing *n.* sport of surfing on a board to which a sail is fixed.

windswept *a.* exposed to strong winds.

windward *a.* situated in the direction from which the wind blows. —*n.* this side or region.

windy *a.* (-ier, -iest) with much wind; exposed to wind; wordy; (*sl.*) frightened. **windiness** *n.*

wine *n.* fermented grape-juice as an alcoholic drink; fermented drink made from other fruits or plants; dark red. —*v.t./i.* drink wine; entertain with wine. **wine bar** bar or small restaurant serving wine as the main drink. **winy** *a.*

wineglass *n.* glass for drinking wine from.

winepress *n.* press in which grape-juice is extracted for wine.

wing *n.* each of a pair of projecting parts by which a bird or insect etc. is able to fly; one of the parts projecting widely from the sides of an aircraft; projecting part; bodywork just above the wheel of a car; either end of a battle array; player at either end of the forward line in football or hockey etc., side part of playing-area in these games; extreme section of a political party; air-force unit of several squadrons; (*pl.*) sides of a theatre stage. —*v.t./i.* fly, travel by wings; wound slightly in the wing or arm. **on the wing** flying. **take wing** fly away. **under one's wing** under one's protection. **wing-chair** *n.* chair with forward-projecting side pieces at the top of a high back. **wing-collar** *n.* high stiff collar with turned-down corners.

winged *a.* having wings.

winger *n.* wing player in football etc.

wingless *a.* without wings.

wink *v.i.* blink one eye as a signal; shine with a light that flashes on and off or twinkles. —*n.* act of winking. **not a wink** no sleep at all. **wink at** pretend not to notice (an illicit act etc.).

winker *n.* flashing indicator.

winkle *n.* edible sea-snail. —*v.t.* **winkle out** extract, prise out.

winner *n.* person or thing that wins; something successful.

winning *see* win. —*a.* charming, persuasive. **winning-post** *n.* post marking the end of a race. **winnings** *n.pl.* money won in betting etc.

winnow *v.t.* fan or toss (grain) to free it of chaff; separate (chaff) thus; separate from inferior elements.

winsome *a.* charming.

winter *n.* coldest season of the year. —*v.i.* spend the winter. **winter garden** garden of plants flourishing in winter. **wintry** *a.* **winy** *a.* wine-flavoured.

wipe *v.t.* clean or dry or remove by rubbing; spread thinly on a surface. —*n.* act of wiping. **wipe out** cancel; destroy completely.

wiper *n.* device that automatically wipes rain etc. from a windscreen.

wire *n.* strand of metal; length of this used for fencing, conducting electric current, etc. —*v.t.* provide or fasten or strengthen with wire(s). **wire-haired** *a.* having stiff wiry hair.

wireless *n.* radio.

wireworm *n.* destructive larva of a beetle.

wiring *n.* system of wires for conducting electricity in a building, vehicle, etc.

wiry *a.* (-ier, -iest) like wire; lean but strong. **wiriness** *n.*

wisdom *n.* being wise, soundness of judgement; wise sayings. **wisdom tooth** third and hindmost molar tooth, cut (if at all) after the age of 20.

wise[1] *a.* (**-er, -est**) showing soundness of judgement; having knowledge; (*sl.*) aware, informed. —*v.t.* (*sl.*) inform. **wisely** *adv.*

wise[2] *n.* (old use) way, manner.

wiseacre *n.* person who pretends to have great wisdom.

wisecrack *n.* (*colloq.*) witty remark. —*v.i.* (*colloq.*) make a wisecrack.

wish *n.* desire, mental aim; expression of desire. —*v.t./i.* have or express as a wish; hope or express hope about another person's welfare; foist.

wishbone *n.* forked bone between a bird's neck and breast.

wishful *a.* desiring. **wishful thinking** belief founded on wishes not facts.

wishy-washy *a.* weak in colour, character, etc.

wisp *n.* small separate bunch; small streak of smoke etc.; small thin person. **wispy** *a.*, **wispiness** *n.*

wisteria /-'teer-/ *n.* climbing shrub with hanging clusters of flowers.

wistful *a.* full of sad or vague longing. **wistfully** *adv.*, **wistfulness** *n.*

wit[1] *n.* amusing ingenuity in expressing words or ideas; person who has this; intelligence. **at one's wits' end** worried and not knowing what to do.

wit[2] *v.t./i.* (old use) **to wit** that is to say, namely.

witch *n.* person (esp. a woman) who practises witchcraft; bewitching woman. **witch-doctor** *n.* tribal magician of a primitive people. **witch-hazel** *n.* North American shrub with yellow flowers; astringent lotion made from its leaves and bark. **witch-hunt** *n.* search to find and destroy or persecute persons

thought to be witches or holders of unpopular views. **witchery** *n.*

witchcraft *n.* practice of magic.

with *prep.* in the company of, among; having, characterized by; using as an instrument or means; on the side of, of the same opinion as; in the charge of; at the same time as; in the same way or direction as; because of; under the conditions of; by addition or possession of; in regard to, towards. **be with child** (old use) be pregnant. **with it** (*colloq.*) up to date, appreciating current fashions etc.

withal *adv.* (old use) moreover; as well.

withdraw *v.t./i.* (*p.t.* **withdrew**, *p.p.* **withdrawn**) take back or away; remove (deposited money) from a bank etc.; cancel (a statement); go away from a place or from company etc. **withdrawal** *n.*

withdrawn *a.* (of a person) unsociable.

withe /wɪθ/ *n.* withy.

wither *v.t./i.* shrivel, lose freshness or vitality; subdue by scorn.

withers *n.pl.* ridge between a horse's shoulder-blades.

withhold *v.t.* (*p.t.* **withheld**) refuse to give; restrain.

within *prep.* inside; not beyond the limit or scope of; in a time no longer than. —*adv.* inside.

without *prep.* not having; in the absence of; with no action of; (old use) outside. —*adv.* outside.

withstand *v.t.* (*p.t.* **withstood**) endure successfully.

withy /'wɪðɪ/ *n.* tough flexible willow branch or osier etc., used for tying things.

witless *a.* foolish.

witness *n.* person who sees or hears something; one who gives evidence in a lawcourt; one who confirms another's signature; thing that serves as evidence. —*v.t.* be a witness of. **witness-box** *n.* enclosure from which witnesses give evidence in a lawcourt. **witness-stand** n. (US) witness-box.

witter v.i. (colloq.) talk lengthily.

witticism n. witty remark.

wittingly adv. intentionally.

witty a. (-ier, -iest) full of wit. **wittily** adv., **wittiness** n.

wives see **wife**.

wizard n. male witch, magician; person with amazing abilities. —a. (colloq.) wonderful. **wizardry** n.

wizened /'wizənd/ a. full of wrinkles, shrivelled with age.

woad n. blue dye formerly obtained from a plant; this plant.

wobble v.i. stand or move unsteadily; quiver. —n. wobbling movement; quiver. **wobbly** a.

wodge n. (colloq.) chunk, wedge.

woe n. sorrow, distress; trouble causing this, misfortune. **woeful** a., **woefully** adv., **woefulness** n.

woebegone a. looking unhappy.

wok n. bowl-shaped frying-pan used esp. in Chinese cookery.

woke, woken see **wake**[1].

wold n. (esp. in pl.) area of open upland country.

wolf n. (pl. **wolves**) fierce wild animal of the dog family; (sl.) man who aggressively seeks to attract women. —v.t. eat quickly and greedily. **cry wolf** raise false alarms. **keep the wolf from the door** ward off hunger or starvation. **wolf-whistle** n. man's admiring whistle at an attractive woman. **wolfish** a.

wolfhound n. large dog of a kind orig. used for hunting wolves.

wolfram /'wulfrəm/ n. tungsten (ore).

wolverine /'wulvəri:n/ n. North American animal of the weasel family.

woman n. (pl. **women**) adult female person; women in general; (colloq.) charwoman. **woman of the world** woman experienced in the ways of society.

womanhood n. state of being a woman.

womanize v.i. (of a man) seek women's company for sexual purposes. **womanizer** n.

womankind n. women in general.

womanly a. having qualities considered characteristic of a woman. **womanliness** n.

womb /wu:m/ n. hollow organ in female mammals in which the young develop before birth.

wombat n. small bear-like Australian animal.

women see **woman**.

womenfolk n. women in general; women of one's family.

won see **win**.

wonder n. feeling of surprise and admiration or curiosity or bewilderment; remarkable thing. —v.t./i. feel wonder or surprise; desire to know; try to decide.

wonderful a. arousing admiration. **wonderfully** adv.

wonderland n. place full of wonderful things.

wonderment n. feeling of wonder.

wondrous a. (old use) wonderful.

wonky a. (sl.) unsteady, unreliable.

wont /wəunt/ a. (old use) accustomed. —n. habitual custom.

won't (colloq.) = will not.

wonted /'wəuntid/ a. customary.

woo v.t. (old use) court; try to achieve or obtain or coax.

wood n. tough fibrous substance of a tree; this cut for use; (also pl.) trees growing fairly densely over an area of ground; ball used in bowls; golf-club with a wooden head. **out of the wood** clear of danger or difficulty.

woodbine n. wild honeysuckle.

woodcock n. a kind of game-bird.

woodcut n. engraving made on wood; picture made from this.

wooded a. covered with trees.

wooden a. made of wood; showing no expression. **woodenly** adv.

woodland n. wooded country.

woodlouse n. (pl. -lice) small wingless creature with seven pairs of legs, living in decaying wood etc.

woodpecker n. bird that taps treetrunks with its beak to discover insects.

woodpigeon n. a kind of large pigeon.

woodwind n. wind instruments made (or formerly made) of wood.

woodwork n. art or practice of making things from wood; wooden things or fittings.

woodworm n. larva of a kind of beetle that bores in wood.

woody a. like or consisting of wood; full of woods.

woof n. dog's gruff bark. —v.i. make this sound.

woofer n. loudspeaker for reproducing low-frequency signals.

wool n. fine soft hair from sheep or goats etc.; yarn or fabric made from this; thing resembling sheep's wool. **pull the wool over someone's eyes** deceive him or her. **wool-gathering** n. daydreaming.

woollen a. made of wool. **woollens** n.pl. woollen cloth or clothing.

woolly a. (-ier, -iest) covered with wool; like wool, woollen; vague. —n. (colloq.) woollen garment. **woolliness** n.

Woolsack n. large stuffed cushion on which the Lord Chancellor sits in the House of Lords.

word n. sound(s) expressing a meaning independently and forming a basic element of speech; this represented by letters or symbols; thing said; message, news; promise; command; unit of expression in a computer. —v.t. express in words. **word of honour** promise made upon one's honour. **word of mouth** spoken (not written) words. **word-perfect** a. having memorized every word perfectly.

word processor computer programmed for storing, correcting, and printing out text entered from a keyboard.

wording n. way a thing is worded.

wordy a. using too many words.

wore see **wear**[1,2].

work n. use of bodily or mental power in order to do or make something, esp. contrasted with play or recreation; thing to be undertaken; materials for use in a task; thing done or produced by work, result of action; literary or musical composition; employment; ornamentation of a certain kind, articles worked with this; made of certain materials or with certain tools; (pl.) operations of building etc., operative parts of a machine; (pl., usu. treated as sing.) factory; (usu. pl.) defensive structure; (pl., sl.) all that is available. —v.t./i. perform work; make efforts; be employed; operate, do this effectively; purchase (one's passage etc.) with one's labour; cause to work or function; bring about, accomplish; shape or knead or hammer etc. into a desired form or consistency; do or make by needlework, fretwork, etc.; excite progressively; make (a way) or pass or cause to pass gradually by effort; become (loose etc.) through repeated stress or pressure; be in motion; ferment. **work in** find a place for, insert. **work off** get rid of by activity. **work out** find or solve by calculation; plan the details of; have a specified result; take exercise. **work to rule** cause delay by over-strict observance of rules, as a form of protest. **work up** bring gradually to a more developed state; excite progressively; advance (to a climax).

workable a. able to be done or used successfully. **workability** n.

workaday a. ordinary, everyday; practical.

workaholic n. (colloq.) person addicted to working.

worker n. person who works; member of the working class; neuter bee or ant etc. that does the work of the hive or colony.

workhouse n. former public institution where people unable to support themselves were housed.

working a. engaged in work, esp. manual labour, working-class. —n. excavation(s) made in mining, tunnelling, etc. **working class** class of people who are employed for wages, esp. in manual or industrial work. **working-class** a. of this class. **working knowledge** knowledge adequate to work with.

workman n. (pl. -men) man employed to do manual labour; person who works in a specified way. **workmanlike** a. characteristic of a good workman, practical. **workmanship** n. skill in working or in a thing produced.

workout n. practice or test; exercising.

workshop n. room or building in which manual work or manufacture etc. is carried on.

workstation n. computer terminal and keyboard; desk with this; location of an individual worker or stage in manufacturing etc.

world n. universe, all that exists; earth, heavenly body like it; section of the earth; time or state or scene of human existence; people or things belonging to a certain class or sphere of activity; everything, all people; material things and occupations; very great amount.

worldly a. of or concerned with earthly life or material gains, not spiritual. **worldly-wise** a. shrewd in worldly affairs. **worldliness** n.

worldwide a. extending through the whole world.

worm n. animal with a soft rounded or flattened body and no

backbone or limbs; (pl.) internal parasites; insignificant or contemptible person; spiral part of a screw. —v.t./i. move with a twisting movement like a worm; make (one's way) thus or insidiously; obtain by crafty persistence; rid of parasitic worms. **worm-cast** n. tubular pile of earth cast up by an earthworm to the surface of the ground. **wormy** a.

wormeaten a. full of holes made by insect larvae.

wormwood n. woody plant with a bitter flavour; bitter mortification.

worn see wear¹. —a. damaged or altered by use or wear; looking exhausted. **worn-out** a.

worried a. feeling or showing worry.

worry v.t./i. be troublesome to; give way to anxiety; seize with the teeth and shake or pull about. —n. worried state, mental uneasiness; thing causing this. **worry beads** string of beads fingered to occupy or calm oneself. **worrier** n.

worse a. & adv. more bad, more badly, more evil or ill; less good, in or into less good health or condition or circumstances. —n. something worse.

worsen v.t./i. make or become worse.

worship n. reverence and respect paid to God or a god; adoration of or devotion to a person or thing; title of respect used of or to a mayor or certain magistrates. —v.t./i. (p.t. **worshipped**) honour as a deity, pay worship to; take part in an act of worship; idolize, treat with adoration. **worshipper** n.

worshipful a. (in titles) honourable.

worst a. & adv. most bad, most badly, least good. —n. worst part or feature or event etc. —v.t. defeat, outdo. **get the worst of** be defeated in.

worsted /'wustɪd/ n. a kind of smooth woollen yarn or fabric.

wort /wɜːt/ n. infusion of malt before it is fermented into beer.

worth a. having a specified value; giving a good return for, deserving; possessing as wealth. —n. value, merit, usefulness; amount that a specified sum will buy. **for all one is worth** (colloq.) with all one's energy. **worth while or worth one's while** worth the time or effort needed.

worthless a. having no value or usefulness. **worthlessness** n.

worthwhile a. worth while.

worthy a. (-ier, -iest) having great merit; deserving. —n. worthy person. **worthily** adv., **worthiness** n.

would v.aux. used in senses corresponding to *will*[1] in the past tense, conditional statements, questions, polite requests and statements, and to express probability or something that happens from time to time. **would-be** a. desiring or pretending to be.

wound[1] /wuːnd/ n. injury done to tissue by a cut or blow; injury to feelings or reputation. —v.t. inflict a wound upon.

wound[2] /waʊnd/ see **wind**[2].

wove, woven see **weave**[1].

wow int. exclamation of astonishment. —n. (sl.) sensational success.

wrack n. seaweed cast up on the shore or growing there.

wraith n. ghost, spectral apparition of a living person.

wrangle v.i. argue or quarrel noisily. —n. noisy argument or quarrel.

wrap v.t./i. (p.t. **wrapped**) enclose in a soft or flexible covering; arrange (this covering) round (a person or thing). —n. shawl or cloak etc. worn for warmth. **be wrapped up in** have one's attention deeply occupied by.

wrapper n. cover of paper etc. wrapped round something; loose dressing-gown.

wrapping n. material for wrapping things.

wrasse /ræs/ n. brightly coloured sea-fish.

wrath /rɒθ/ n. anger, indignation. **wrathful** a., **wrathfully** adv.

wreak /riːk/ v.t. inflict (vengeance etc.).

wreath /riːθ/ n. (pl. **-ths**, pr. -ðz) flowers or leaves etc. fastened into a ring, used as a decoration or placed on a grave etc.; curving line of mist or smoke.

wreathe /riːð/ v.t./i. encircle; twist into a wreath; wind, curve.

wreck n. disabling or destruction, esp. of a ship by storms or accidental damage; ship that has suffered this; remains of a greatly damaged building or vehicle etc.; person whose health has been damaged or destroyed. —v.t. cause the wreck of; involve in shipwreck.

wreckage n. remains of something wrecked; process of wrecking.

wrecker n. person who wrecks something; one employed in demolition work.

Wren n. member of the WRNS (Women's Royal Naval Service).

wren n. very small bird.

wrench v.t. twist or pull violently round; damage or pull by twisting. —n. violent twisting pull; pain caused by parting; adjustable spanner-like tool.

wrest v.t. wrench away; obtain by effort or with difficulty; twist, distort.

wrestle v.t./i. fight (esp. as a sport) by grappling with and trying to throw an opponent to the ground; struggle to deal with. —n. wrestling-match; hard struggle.

wretch n. wretched or despicable person; rascal.

wretched /-ɪd/ a. miserable, unhappy; of poor quality; contemptible, displeasing. **wretchedly** adv., **wretchedness** n.

wriggle v.t./i. move with short twisting movements; escape (out of a difficulty etc.) cunningly. —n. wriggling movement.

wring v.t. (p.t. **wrung**) twist and squeeze, esp. to remove liquid; remove (liquid) thus; squeeze firmly or forcibly; obtain with effort or difficulty. —n. wringing movement, squeeze, twist. **wringing wet** so wet that moisture can be wrung from it.

wringer n. device with rollers between which washed clothes are passed to squeeze out water.

wrinkle n. small crease; small ridge or furrow in skin; (colloq.) useful hint. —v.t./i. form wrinkles (in). **wrinkly** a.

wrist n. joint connecting hand and forearm; part of a garment covering this. **wrist-watch** n. watch worn on a strap etc. round the wrist.

wristlet n. band or bracelet etc. worn round the wrist.

writ n. formal written authoritative command. **Holy Writ** the Bible.

write v.t./i. (p.t. **wrote**, p.p. **written**, pres.p. **writing**) make letters or other symbols on a surface, esp. with a pen or pencil; form (letters etc.) thus; compose in written form, esp. for publication; be an author; write and send a letter. **write off** cancel, recognize as lost. **write-off** n. something written off as lost, vehicle too damaged to be worth repairing. **write up** write an account of; write entries in. **write-up** n. (colloq.) published account of something, review.

writer n. person who writes; author. **writer's cramp** cramp in the muscles of the hand.

writhe /raɪð/ v.i. twist one's body about, as in pain; wriggle; suffer because of shame or embarrassment.

writing n. handwriting; literary work. **in writing** in written form. **the writing on the wall** an event signifying that something is doomed. **writing-paper** n. paper for writing (esp. letters) on.

written see **write**.

wrong a. incorrect, not true; morally bad; contrary to justice; not what is required or desirable; not in a good or normal condition. —adv. in a wrong manner or direction, mistakenly. —n. what is wrong, wrong action etc.; injustice. —v.t. do a wrong to, treat unjustly. **in the wrong** not having truth or justice on one's side. **wrongly** adv., **wrongness** n.

wrongdoer n. person who acts contrary to law or moral standards. **wrongdoing** n.

wrongful a. contrary to what is right or legal. **wrongfully** adv.

wrote see **write**.

wrought /rɔːt/ (old use) = worked. —a. (of metals) shaped by hammering. **wrought iron** a tough malleable form of iron.

wrung see **wring**.

wry a. (**wryer**, **wryest**) twisted or bent out of shape; contorted in disgust or disappointment; (of humour) dry and mocking. **wryly** adv., **wryness** n.

wryneck n. small bird related to the woodpecker.

wych-elm n. elm with broad leaves and spreading branches.

wych-hazel n. = witch-hazel.

X

xenophobia /zen-/ n. strong dislike or distrust of foreigners.

Xerox /ˈzɪər-/ n. [P.] a kind of photocopying process; copy produced by this. **xerox** v.t. copy in this way.

Xmas n. (colloq.) Christmas.

X-ray n. photograph or examination made by a kind of electromagnetic radiation (**X-rays**) that can penetrate solids. —v.t. photograph, examine, or treat by X-rays.

xylophone /'zaɪ-/ n. musical instrument with flat wooden bars struck with small hammers.

Y

yacht /jɒt/ n. light sailing-vessel for racing; vessel used for private pleasure excursions. **yachting** n., **yachtsman** n. (pl. -**men**).

yak n. long-haired Asian ox.

yam n. tropical climbing plant; its edible starchy tuber; sweet potato.

Yank n. (colloq.) Yankee.

yank v.t. (colloq.) pull sharply. —n. (colloq.) sharp pull.

Yankee n. (colloq.) American; (US) inhabitants of the northern States of the USA.

yap n. shrill bark. —v.i. (p.t. **yapped**) bark shrilly.

yapp n. limp leather book-binding with overlapping edges or flaps.

yard[1] n. measure of length, = 3 feet (0.9144 metre); pole slung from a mast to support a sail. **yard-arm** n. either end of a yard supporting a sail.

yard[2] n. piece of enclosed ground, esp. attached to a building; **the Yard** (colloq.) Scotland Yard.

yardage n. length measured in yards.

yardstick n. standard of comparison.

yarmulke /'jɑː-/ n. skullcap worn by Jewish men.

yarn n. any spun thread; (colloq.) tale. —v.i. tell yarns.

yarrow n. plant with feathery leaves and strong-smelling flowers.

yashmak n. veil worn by Muslim women in certain countries.

yaw v.i. (of a ship or aircraft) fail to hold a straight course. —n. yawing.

yawl n. a kind of fishing-boat or sailing-boat.

yawn v.i. open the mouth wide and draw in breath, as when sleepy or bored; have a wide opening. —n. act of yawning.

yaws n. tropical skin-disease.

yd. abbr. yard. **yds.** abbr. yards.

ye pron. (old use) you.

yea /jeɪ/ adv. & n. (old use) yes.

year n. time taken by the earth to orbit the sun (about 365¼ days); period from 1 Jan. to 31 Dec. inclusive; consecutive period of twelve months; (pl.) age.

yearbook n. annual publication with current information about a subject.

yearling n. animal between 1 and 2 years old.

yearly a. happening, published, or payable once a year. —adv. annually.

yearn v.i. feel great longing.

yeast n. fungus used to cause fermentation in making beer and wine and as a raising agent. **yeasty** a. frothy like yeast when it is developing.

yell v.t./i. & n. shout.

yellow a. of the colour of buttercups and ripe lemons; (colloq.) cowardly. —n. yellow colour or thing. —v.t./i. turn yellow. **Yellow Pages** [P.] section of a telephone directory printed on yellow paper, listing businesses under the type of goods or services offered.

yellowhammer n. bird of the finch family with a yellow head, neck, and breast.

yellowish a. rather yellow.

yelp n. shrill yell or bark. —v.i. utter a yelp.

yen[1] *n.* (*pl.* **yen**) unit of money in Japan.

yen[2] *n.* longing, yearning.

yeoman /'jəʊ-/ *n.* (*pl.* **-men**) man who owns and farms a small estate. **Yeoman of the Guard** member of the British sovereign's bodyguard, wearing Tudor dress as uniform. **yeoman service** long useful service.

yes *adv.* & *n.* expression of agreement or consent, or of reply to a summons etc. **yes-man** *n.* person who is always ready to agree with his superiors.

yesterday *n.* & *adv.* (on) the day before today; (in) the recent past.

yet *adv.* up to this or that time, still; besides; eventually; even; nevertheless. —*conj.* nevertheless, in spite of that.

yeti /'jetɪ/ *n.* (*pl.* **-is**) large manlike or bear-like animal said to exist in the Himalayas.

yew *n.* evergreen tree with dark needle-like leaves; its wood.

Yiddish *n.* language (based on a German dialect) used by Jews of central and eastern Europe.

yield *v.t./i.* give as fruit or gain or result; surrender; do what is asked or ordered; allow (victory, right of way, etc.) to another; be able to be forced out of the natural shape. —*n.* amount yielded or produced.

yippee *int.* exclamation of delight or excitement.

yodel *v.t./i.* (*p.t.* **yodelled**) sing, or utter a musical call, with a quickly alternating change of pitch. —*n.* yodelling cry. **yodeller** *n.*

yoga /'jəʊ-/ *n.* Hindu system of meditation and self-control.

yoghurt /'jɒg-/ *n.* food made of milk that has been thickened by the action of certain bacteria.

yoiks *int.* exclamation urging hounds on in hunting.

yoke *n.* wooden cross-piece fastened over the necks of two oxen pulling a cart or plough etc.; piece

of wood shaped to fit a person's shoulders and hold a pail or other load slung from each end; top part of a garment; oppression, burdensome restraint. —*v.t.* harness with a yoke; unite.

yokel *n.* country fellow; bumpkin.

yolk /jəʊk/ *n.* round yellow internal part of an egg.

yomp *v.i.* & *n.* (*sl.*) march with heavy equipment across country.

yon *a.* & *adv.* (*dialect*) yonder.

yonder *adv.* over there. —*a.* situated or able to be seen over there.

yonks *adv.* (*sl.*) a long time.

yore *n.* of yore long ago.

yorker *n.* ball bowled to pitch just in front of the batsman.

Yorkshire pudding baked batter pudding eaten with meat.

Yorkshire terrier terrier of a long-haired toy breed.

you *pron.* person(s) addressed; one, anyone, everyone.

young *a.* (**-er**, **-est**) having lived or existed for only a short time; youthful; having little experience. —*n.* offspring (before or soon after birth) of animals.

youngster *n.* young person, child.

your *a.*, **yours** *poss.pron.* belonging to you.

you're (*colloq.*) = you are.

yourself *pron.* (*pl.* **yourselves**) emphatic and reflexive form of *you.*

youth *n.* (*pl.* **youths**, *pr.* juːðz) state or period of being young; young man; young people. **youth club** club where leisure activities are provided for young people. **youth hostel** hostel providing cheap accommodation for young travellers.

youthful *a.* young; characteristic of young people. **youthfulness** *n.*

yowl *v.i.* & *n.* howl.

Yo-yo *n.* (*pl.* **-os**) [P.] round toy that can be made to rise and fall on a string that winds in a groove round it.

yucca n. tall plant with white bell-like flowers and spiky leaves.

yule, yule-tide ns. (old use) Christmas festival.

yummy a. (colloq.) delicious.

yuppie n. (colloq.) young urban professional person.

Z

zabaglione /zɑːbɑːlˈjəʊnɪ/ n. Italian sweet of whipped egg-yolks with sugar and wine.

zany /ˈzeɪ/ a. (-ier, -iest) crazily funny. —n. zany person.

zap v.t. (p.t. **zapped**) (sl.) hit, attack, kill.

zeal n. enthusiasm, hearty and persistent effort.

zealot /ˈzel-/ n. zealous person, fanatic.

zealous /ˈzel-/ a. full of zeal. **zealously** adv.

zebra /ˈziː- or ˈzeb-/ n. African horse-like animal with black and white stripes. **zebra crossing** /ˈzeb-/ pedestrian crossing where the road is marked with broad white stripes.

zebu /ˈziːbjuː/ n. humped ox.

Zen n. form of Buddhism.

zenana /zeˈnɑː-/ n. part of a house in which women of high-caste families in India are secluded.

zenith n. the part of the sky that is directly overhead; highest point.

zephyr /ˈzefə(r)/ n. soft gentle wind.

zero n. (pl. **-os**) nought, the figure 0; nil; point marked 0 on a graduated scale, temperature corresponding to this. **zero hour** hour at which something is timed to begin. **zero in on** take aim at; focus attention on.

zest n. keen enjoyment or interest; orange or lemon peel as flavouring. **zestful** a., **zestfully** adv.

zigzag n. line or course turning right and left alternately at sharp angles. —a. & adv. as or in a zigzag. —v.i. (p.t. **zigzagged**) move in a zigzag.

zillion n. (US) indefinitely large number.

zinc n. bluish-white metal.

zing n. (colloq.) vigour. —v.i. (colloq.) move swiftly or shrilly.

zinnia n. daisy-like garden plant with bright flowers.

Zionism n. movement that sought and achieved the founding of a Jewish homeland in Palestine. **Zionist** n.

zip n. short sharp sound; vigour, liveliness; zip-fastener. —v.t./i. (p.t. **zipped**) open or close with a zip-fastener; move with the sound of 'zip' at high speed. **zip-fastener** n. fastening device with projections that interlock when brought together by a sliding tab.

Zip code (US) postal code.

zipper n. zip-fastener.

zircon n. bluish-white gem cut from a translucent mineral.

zirconium n. grey metallic element.

zither n. shallow box-like stringed instrument played with the fingers.

zodiac n. (in astrology) band of the sky divided into twelve equal parts (**signs of the zodiac**) each named from a constellation formerly situated in it. **zodiacal** /-ˈdaɪ-/ a.

zombie n. (in voodoo) corpse said to have been revived by witchcraft; (colloq.) person who seems to have no mind or will.

zone n. area with particular characteristics, purpose, or use.

—*v.t.* divide into zones; assign to a zone or zones. **zonal** *a.*

zoo *n.* place where wild animals are kept for exhibition and study.

zoology /zəʊ'ɒl- *or* zʊ'ɒl-/ *n.* study of animals. **zoological** *a.*, **zoologist** *n.*

zoom *v.i.* move quickly, esp. with a buzzing sound; rise quickly; (in photography) make a distant object appear gradually closer by means of a **zoom lens.**

zucchini /-'ki:-/ *n.* (*pl.* **-i** *or* **-is**) courgette.

Zulu *n.* (*pl.* **-us**) member or language of a Bantu people of South Africa.

zygote *n.* cell formed by the union of two gametes.

WORD-GAMES SU

Players of word-games are often at [...]
have ready access to a supply of shor[...]
regarded as valid for the purposes of [...]
larly useful are words of only two lette[...]
not followed by *u*, and words beginnin[...]
these words are excluded from a small d[...]
concentrates on current usage) because[...]
obsolete, or occur only in dialects.

All the words in the following lists are at[...]
the great historical dictionaries (such as[...]
volume *Oxford English Dictionary* and the [...]
lect Dictionary) or are included in a majo[...]
dictionary.

Words marked with an asterisk (*) are obsol[...]
subject to modern rules of inflection. Those ma[...]
a dagger (†) are obsolete and were not in use [...]
Middle English period (ending in 1500); thes[...]
cannot be assumed to form plurals and verbal inf[...]
in the modern style (for example, the plural of *ac*[...]
not 'acs').

Excluded from these lists are names of people[...]
places etc. and abbreviations (such as Dr, Mr) which[...]
not pronounced as they are spelt, and suffixes and o[...]
elements which have never been current as independ[...]
words; most word-games do not regard these as va[...]
items. An arbitrary limit of six letters has been impose[...]
throughout.

Note T[...]
the alp[...]
are no[...]

aa *n.* [...]
ab *v.* [...]
    hir[...]
†ac *n* [...]
ad *n* [...]
ae *a* [...]
af *p* [...]
ah [...]
ai [...]
ak [...]
†a[...]
a[...]
a[...]

Two-letter words

This list does not include plurals of the names of letters of [the alph]abet (*bs*, *ds*, *ms*, *ts*, etc.). These are correct formations but [are not] always regarded by word-game players as acceptable.

[...]rough cindery lava.
[...] (*dial.*) hinder. —*n.* (*dial.*)
[...]drance.
[...] *n.* (*pl.* aec) oak.
[...] (*collog.*) advertisement.
[...]. (*Sc.*) one.
[...] *prep.* (*dial.*) of; off.
[...] *int.* expressing surprise.
[...] *n.* three-toed sloth.
[...] *n.* (*dial.*) oak.
[...]l *a.* & *n.* all.
[...]m *pres. tense* of be.
[...]n *indefinite article* one.
[...]r *n.* letter r.
[...]s *adv.* & *conj.* similarly.
[...]t *prep.* having as position etc.
†au *n.* awe.
aw *n.* water-wheel board.
ax *n.* & *v.* axe.
ay *int.* ah.
ba *n.* (*Egyptian myth*) soul.
be *v.* exist.
bi *n.* & *a.* (*sl.*) bisexual
   (person).
bo *n.* a kind of fig-tree.
bu *n.* former Japanese coin.
by *prep.* & *adv.* beside.
ca *n.* (*pl.* caas or cais) (*Sc.*)
   calf.
ce *n.* letter c.
†co *n.* jackdaw.
†cu *n.* cow.
†cy *n.pl.* cows.
da *n.* Indian fibre plant.
de *prep.* of; from.
di *n.* note in music-scale.

do. *v.* perform. —*n.*
   performance.
*du *v.* (*Sc.*) do.
*dw *v.* (*Sc.*) do.
*dy *n.* (*pl.* dyce or dys)
   gaming-die.
ea *n.* (*dial.*) river; stream.
*eb *n.* ebb.
†ec *adv.* also, too.
*ed *a.* distinguished.
ee *n.* (*pl.* een) (*Sc.*) eye.
ef *n.* letter f.
*eg *n.* egg.
eh *int.* & *v.* expressing
   surprise.
†ei *a.* & *pron.* any.
*ek *adv.* & *v.* eke.
el *n.* letter l.
em *n.* unit of print measure.
en *n.* half an em.
†eo *pron.* you.
er *int.* & *v.* expressing
   hesitation.
es *n.* (*pl.* esses) letter s.
†et *prep.* at.
†eu *n.* yew.
ew *v.* (*dial.*) owe.
ex *n.* (*pl.* exes) former spouse
   etc.
ey *n.* (*dial.*) water.
fa *n.* note in music-scale.
fe *n.* (*old use*) note in
   music-scale.
fo *n.* (*dial.*) area measure.
fu *n.* (*pl.* fu) Chinese district.
fy *int.* fie.

ga *n.* (*old use*) note in music-scale.

ge *n.* (*old use*) note in music-scale.

go *v.* move. —*n.* (*pl.* **goes**) energy; turn.

gu *v.* (*dial.*) go.

gy *n.* (*Sc.*) guide-rope. *—*v.t.* guide.

ha *int. & v.* expressing surprise.

he *pron.* male mentioned.

hi *int.* attracting attention.

hm *int.* expressing doubt.

ho *int. & v.* expressing surprise.

hu *n.* Chinese liquid measure.

†**hv** *adv.* how.

†**hw** *n.* yew.

hy *v.* (*Sc.*) hie.

*****ia** *n.* (*Sc.*) jay.

†**ic** *pron.* I.

id *n.* mind's impulses.

ie *n.* Pacific islands tree.

if *conj. & n.* (on) condition (that).

†**ig** *pron.* I.

†**ih** *pron.* I.

†**ik** *pron.* I.

†**il** *n.* hedgehog.

†**im** *pron.* him.

in *prep. & adv.* within. —*n.* passage in.

io *n.* Hawaiian hawk.

*****ir** *n.* ire.

is *pres. tense* of be.

it *pron.* thing mentioned.

iv *prep.* (*dial.*) in; of.

†**iw** *n.* yew.

ja *v. & n.* (*dial.*) jaw, talk.

*****je** *adv.* yea.

jo *n.* (*pl.* **joes**) (*Sc.*) darling.

ka *n.* (*Egyptian myth*) spirit.

*****ke** *n.* (*Sc.*) jackdaw.

ki *n.* liliaceous plant.

ko *n.* (*pl.* **ko**) Chinese liquid measure.

ku *n.* (*dial.*) ulcer in the eye.

ky *n.pl.* (*Sc.*) cows.

la *n.* note in music-scale.

le *n.* = li.

li *n.* (*pl.* **li**) Chinese unit.

lo *int.* expressing surprise.

lu *v.* (*Orkney*) listen.

ly *n.* = li.

ma *n.* (*colloq.*) mother.

me *pron.* objective case of I.

mi *n.* note in music-scale.

mo *n.* (*colloq.*) moment.

mu *n.* Greek letter m.

my *a.* belonging to me.

na *adv.* (*Sc.*) no.

ne *adv. & conj.* (*old use*) not.

*****ni** *n.* = ny.

no *a.* not any.

nu *n.* Greek letter n.

†**nv** *adv. & conj.* now.

†**nw** *adv. & conj.* now.

*****ny** *n.* brood of pheasants.

*****ob** *n.* wizard.

†**oc** *conj.* but.

od *n.* hypnotic force.

oe *n.* small island.

of *prep.* belonging to.

oh *int., n., & v.* (give) cry of pain.

oi *int.* attracting attention.

†**ok** *n.* oak.

ol *n.* hydroxyl atom group.

om *n.* mantra syllable.

on *prep. & adv.* supported by; covering. —*n.* one side of a cricket field.

oo *n.* (*Sc.*) wool.

op *n.* (*colloq.*) operation.

or *conj.* as an alternative.

os^1 *n.* (*pl.* **ora**) orifice.

os^2 *n.* (*pl.* **osar** or **osars**) geological ridge.

os^3 *n.* (*pl.* **ossa**) bone.

ot *n.* (*dial.*) urchin.

ou *int.* (*Sc.*) oh.

†**ov** *pron.* you.

ow *int.* expressing pain.

ox *n.* (*pl.* **oxen** or **oxes**) a kind of animal.

oy *n.* (*Sc.*) grandchild.

pa *n.* (*colloq.*) father.

pe *n.* Hebrew letter p.

pi *n.* Greek letter p.

po *n.* (*pl.* **pos**) (*colloq.*) chamber-pot.

pu *n.* (*pl.* **pu**) Chinese measure of distance.

*__py__ *n.* pie.

qi *n.* (*Chinese philosophy*) life-force.

*__qu__ *n.* half-farthing.

ra *n.* Arabic letter r.

re *n.* note in music-scale.

ri *n.* (*pl.* **ri**) Japanese measure of distance.

*__ro__ *n.* & *v.* (*Sc.*) repose.

†**ru** *v.* rue.

*__ry__ *n.* rye.

sa *adv.* & *conj.* (*dial.*) so.

se *n.* Japanese measure of area.

sh *int.* command to silence.

si *n.* note in music-scale.

so¹ *adv.* & *conj.* therefore.

so² *n.* note in music-scale.

st *int.* attracting attention.

su *pron.* (*dial.*) she.

sy *n.* (*dial.*) scythe.

ta *n.* Arabic letter t.

te *n.* = ti.

ti *n.* note in music-scale.

to *prep.* & *adv.* towards.

tu *n.* 250 li.

*__ty__ *n.* & *v.* tie.

†**ua** *n.* woe.

ug *v.* & *n.* (*dial.*) dread.

uh *int.* inarticulate sound.

um *int.* hesitation in speech.

un *pron.* (*dial.*) one; him.

†**uo** *n.* foe.

up *adv.* & *prep.* towards. —*v.* raise. —*n.* upward direction.

us *pron.* objective case of **we**.

ut *n.* music note C.

†**uu** *n.* yew.

†**uv** *n.* yew.

uz *pron.* (*dial.*) us.

va *n.* (*Sc.*) woe.

vg *v.* = ug.

vi *n.* Polynesian fruit.

. **vo** *n.* size of book.

*__vp__ *adv.* up.

*__vs__ *pron.* us.

*__vy__ *v.* vie.

wa *n.* Siamese measure.

we *pron.* self and others.

*__wg__ *v.* (*Sc.*) = ug.

†**wi** *n.* battle; conflict.

wo *int.* recalling a hawk.

*__wp__ *adv.* (*Sc.*) up.

†**wr** *pron.* our.

*__ws__ *pron.* (*Sc.*) us.

†**wu** *adv.* how.

wy *n.* (*Sc.*) heifer.

*__xa__ *n.* shah.

xi *n.* Greek letter x.

xu *n.* (*pl.* **xu**) Vietnamese coin.

ya *n.* Arabic letter y.

†**yd** *pron.* it.

ye *pron.* (*old use*) you.

*__yf__ *conj.* if.

yi *adv.* (*dial.*) yes.

†**yk** *pron.* I.

*__yl__ *n.* isle.

†**yn** *n.* inn.

yo *int.* expressing effort.

*__yr__ *n.* ire.

*__ys__ *pron.* his.

*__yt__ *pron.* it.

yu *n.* Chinese wine-vessel.

†**yw** *pron.* you.

za *n.* Arabic letter z.

†**ze** *a.* the.

zi *adv.* & *conj.* (*dial.*) so.

zo *n.* (*pl.* **zos**) hybrid yak.

†**zy** *a.* the.

Words with a *q* not followed by *u*

The spelling *qw* was a frequent variant of *qu* and *wh* in Middle English (*c.* 1150–1500), especially in Scotland and northern England. In the words listed below, most of such forms are attested in the *Oxford English Dictionary*; several hundred others are to be found in the *Dictionary of the Older Scottish Tongue* but are excluded from the list through lack of space.

cinq *n.* number 5 on a die.

eqwal *n.* (*dial.*) green woodpecker.

faqih *n.* (*pl.* **faqihs** or **fuqaha**) fakir.

faqir *n.* fakir.

fiqh *n.* Islamic jurisprudence.

*****liqor** *n.* liquor.

miqra *n.* Hebrew biblical text.

qabab *n.* kebab.

qadhi *n.* = qadi.

qadi *n.* Muslim civil judge.

qaf *n.* letter of the Arabic alphabet.

qaid *n.* = qadi.

qanat *n.* irrigation tunnel.

qaneh *n.* ancient Hebrew measure (= 6 ells).

qanon *n.* dulcimer-like instrument.

qantar *n.* Middle Eastern unit of weight.

qasab *n.* (*pl.* **qasab**) ancient Mesopotamian measure of length.

qasaba *n.* (*pl.* **qasaba**) ancient Arabian measure of area.

qasida *n.* Arabic or Persian poem.

qat *n.* Ethiopian bush.

qazi *n.* = qadi.

qere *n.* marginal word in Hebrew Bible.

qeri *n.* = qere.

qhat *a. & pron.* what.

†**qheche** *a. & pron.* which.

†**qhete** *n.* (Sc.) wheat.

†**qhom** *pron.* whom.

†**qhwom** *pron.* whom.

qi *n.* (*Chinese philosophy*) life-force.

qibla *n.* direction towards Mecca.

qiblah *n.* = qibla.

qibli *n.* sirocco.

qindar *n.* (*pl.* **qindarka**) Albanian coin.

qintar *n.* Albanian coin.

*****qirk** *n.* quirk.

qirsh *n.* (*pl.* **qurush**) Saudi Arabian coin.

qiviut *n.* belly-wool of the musk-ox.

qiyas *n.* Islamic judgement.

qoph *n.* Hebrew letter q.

qre *n.* = qere.

*****qvair** *n.* quire.

*****qvan** *adv. & conj.* when.

†**qvare** *n.* quire.

†**qvarte** *n.* quart.

†**qvayr** *n.* quire.

†**qveise** *v.* quease (= squeeze).

†**qvele** *n.* wheel.

†**qvene** *n.* queen.

†**qverel** *n.* quarrel.

†**qveyse** v. quease
(= squeeze).

†**qvyk** n. quicken.

†**qvylte** n. quilt.

†**qwa** pron. who.

†**qwaint** a. quaint.

*****qwaire** n. quire.

†**qwal** n. (Sc.) whale.

†**qwalke** n. whelk, pimple.

†**qwall** n. (Sc.) whale.

†**qwalle** n. (Sc.) whale.

†**qwappe** v. quap (= quiver).

†**qwar** adv. & conj. (dial.)
where.

†**qware** adv. & conj. (dial.)
where.

†**qwarte** a. & n. = qwert.

†**qwarto** adv. whereto.

†**qwartt** a, & n. qwert.

†**qwasse** v. quash.

qwat v. (dial.) squash flat.

†**qwate** n. divination.

†**qwatte** v. (dial.) = qwat.

*****qway** n. whey.

†**qwaylle** n. (Sc.) whale.

†**qwayer** n. quire.

†**qwaynt** a. quaint.

†**qwe** n. (pl. **qwes**) (Sc.) musical
instrument (pipe).

†**qwech** a. & pron. which.

†**qweche** a. & pron. which.

†**qwed** a. & n. evil.

†**qwede** n. will or bequest.

†**qwedyr** n. (dial.) quiver.

†**qweed** a. & n. evil.

†**qweer** n. choir.

†**qwel** a. & pron. which.

*****qwele** n. (dial.) wheel.

†**qwelke** n. whelk.

†**qwell** n. (dial.) wheel.

†**qwelp** n. (Sc.) whelp.

†**qwelpe** n. (Sc.) whelp.

†**qwem** v. please.

†**qweme** v. please.

†**qwen** n. queen.

†**qwench** v. quench.

†**qwene** n. queen.

†**qwenne** adv. & conj. when.

†**qwens** adv. & conj. whence.

*****qwent** a. quenched.

†**qwer** n. choir.

†**qwere** n. choir.

†**qwerf** n. wharf.

qwerk n. (dial.) twist; bend.

†**qwerle** n. whirl.

*****qwern** n. quern.

†**qwerne** n. piece of ice.

†**qwert** n. health. —a.
healthy.

†**qwerte** n. & a. = qwert.

qwerty n. standard layout of
typewriter keyboard.

†**qweryn** n. piece of ice.

*****qwest** n. quest.

†**qwesye** a. queasy.

†**qwet** n. (Sc.) wheat.

†**qwete** n. (Sc.) wheat.

†**qwey** n. whey.

†**qweyll** n. (dial.) wheel.

†**qweynt** a. quaint.

*****qwha** pron. (Sc.) who.

†**qwhar** adv. & conj. where.

†**qwhare** adv. & conj. where.

†**qwheet** n. (Sc.) wheat.

†**qwheit** n. (Sc.) wheat.

†**qwhele** n. (dial.) wheel.

†**qwhen** adv. & conj. when.

†**qwhene** n. queen.

†**qwher** adv. & conj. where.

†**qwhete** n. (Sc.) wheat.

†**qwheyn** adv. & conj. (Sc.)
when.

†**qwhill** n. (Sc.) while.

†**qwhile** n. (Sc.) while.

†**qwhill** n. (Sc.) while.

†**qwhit** a. (Sc.) white.

†**qwhite** a. (Sc.) white.

†**qwhois** a. & pron. (Sc.)
which.

†**qwhom** pron. whom.

†**qwhome** *pron.* whom.
†**qwhos** *pron.* (*Sc.*) whose.
†**qwhy** *adv.* (*Sc.*) why.
†**qwhyet** *a.* (*Sc.*) white.
***qwhyl** *n.* (*Sc.*) while.
†**qwhyt** *a.* white.
†**qwhyte** *a.* (*Sc.*) white.
†**qwi** *adv.* why.
†**qwiche** *a.* & *pron.* which.
†**qwike** *a.* quick.
†**qwikk** *a.* quick.
†**qwil** *n.* quill.
†**qwile** *n.* (*Sc.*) while.
†**qwilk** *a.* & *pron.* which.
†**qwill** *n.* (*Sc.*) while.
†**qwince** *n.* quince.
qwine *n.* (*dial.*) money; corner.
qwirk *n.* (*dial.*) twist, bend.
†**qwitte** *v.* quit.
†**qwo** *n.* who.
†**qwom** *pron.* whom.
†**qwome** *pron.* whom.
†**qwon** *adv.* & *conj.* (*Sc.*) when.
qwop *v.* (*dial.*) throb with pain.
†**qworle** *n.* whorl.
†**qwose** *pron.* (*Sc.*) whose.
qwot *v.* (*dial.*) = qwat.
†**qwy** *n.* (*Sc.*) heifer.
†**qwyce** *n.* gorse.
†**qwych** *a.* & *pron.* (*Sc.*) which.

†**qwyche** *a.* & *pron.* (*Sc.*) which.
†**qwye** *n.* (*Sc.*) heifer.
†**qwyet** *n.* (*Sc.*) wheat.
†**qwyght** *a.* white.
***qwyk** *a.* quick.
†**qwyken** *v.* quicken.
†**qwykyr** *n.* wicker.
†**qwykyn** *v.* quicken.
***qwyl** *n.* (*dial.*) wheel.
†**qwyle** *n.* (*Sc.*) while.
†**qwylte** *n.* quilt.
†**qwylum** *adv.* (*Sc.*) whilom (= while).
†**qwylys** *adv.* & *n.* (*Sc.*) whiles (= while).
†**qwynce** *n.* quince.
†**qwyne** *adv.* (*dial.*) whence.
†**qwynne** *n.* whin.
†**qwynse** *n.* quinsy.
†**qwype** *n.* (*Sc.*) whip.
***qwyt** *a.* white.
***qwyte** *a.* white.
†**qwyuer** *n.* quiver.
***qwyver** *n.* quiver.
†**qwytt** *v.* quit.
shoq *n.* Indian tree.
suq *n.* Arab market-place.
tariqa *n.* Muslim ascetics' spiritual development.
tariqah *n.* = tariqa.

Words beginning with x

*xa n. shah.
†xal v. shall.
†xall v. shall.
†xalle v. shall.
*xaraf n. Oriental money-changer.
*xaroff n. = xaraf.
xebec n. sailing-boat.
xebeck n. = xebec.
†xel v. shall.
xeme n. fork-tailed gull.
xenia n. (pl. xenias) foreign pollen effect.
xenial a. of hospitality.
xenium n. (pl. xenia) gift to a guest.
xenon n. heavy inert gas.
xeque n. sheikh.
xeric a. having little moisture.
xeriff n. Muslim title.
xeroma n. abnormal bodily dryness.
xerox v. photocopy.
xi n. Greek letter x.
*xiph n. swordfish.
*xisti pl. of xystus.
xoanon n. (pl. xoana) carved image.
†xowyn v. shove.
xu n. (pl. xu) Vietnamese coin.

†xul v. shall.
†xuld v. shall.
†xulde v. shall.
†xwld v. shall.
xylan n. carbohydrate in plants.
xylary a. of xylem.
xylate n. salt of xylic acid.
xylem n. plant-tissue.
xylene n. hydrocarbon from wood-spirit.
xylic a. of a kind of acid.
xylo n. (colloq.) Xylonite (a kind of celluloid).
xylol n. xylene.
xylose n. substance obtained from xylan.
xylyl n. derivative of xylene.
xyrid n. sedge-like herb.
xyst n. xystus.
xysta pl. of xystum.
xyster n. surgeon's instrument.
xysti pl. of xystus.
xyston n. ancient Greek spear.
xystos n. xystus.
xystum n. (pl. xysta) xystus.
xystus n. (pl. xysti) covered portico.

Independent countries of the world

Country	*Adjective and Noun*
Afghanistan	Afghan
Albania	Albanian
Algeria	Algerian
Andorra	Andorran
Angola	Angolan
Antigua and Barbuda /-'tiːɡə, -'buːdə/	Antiguan, Barbudan
Argentina /-'tiːnə/	Argentinian, Argentine
Armenia	Armenian
Australia	Australian
Austria	Austrian
Azerbaijan	Azerbaijani
Bahamas /-'hɑː-/	Bahamian /-'heɪ-/
Bahrain /bɑː'reɪn/	Bahraini (*pl.* -is)
Bangladesh /-'deʃ/	Bangladeshi (*n.pl.* -is)
Barbados /-'beɪdɒs/	Barbadian
Belarus	Belarussian
Belgium	Belgian
Belize /be'liːz/	Belizian
Benin /be'niːn/	Beninese /-'niːz/
Bhutan /buː'tɑːn/	Bhutanese /-'niːz/
Bolivia	Bolivian
Bosnia and Herzegovina	Bosnian, Herzegovinian
Botswana	
Brazil	Brazilian
Brunei /'bruːnaɪ/	Bruneian
Bulgaria	Bulgarian
Burkina /-'kiː-/	Burkinan
Burma	Burmese
Burundi /bʊ'rʊndɪ/	
Cambodia	Cambodian
Cameroon	Cameroonian
Canada	Canadian

Country	Adjective and Noun
Cape Verde Islands /veəd/	Cape Verdean /'veədɪən/
Central African Republic	
Chad	Chadian /'tʃædɪən/
Chile	Chilean
China	Chinese
Colombia /-'lɒm-/	Colombian
Comoros /kə'mɒrəʊz/	Comoran
Congo	Congolese
Costa Rica /'riːkə/	Costa Rican
Croatia	Croatian (a.)
	Croat (n.)
Cuba	Cuban
Cyprus	Cypriot /'sɪp-/
Czech Republic	Czech
Denmark	Danish (a.), Dane (n.)
Djibouti /dʒɪ'buːtɪ/	Djiboutian
Dominica /dɒmɪ'niːkə/	Dominican /-'niːk-/
Dominican Republic /də'mɪɪkən/	
Ecuador /'ekwədɔː(r)/	Ecuadorean /-'dɔːr-/
Egypt	Egyptian
El Salvador /'sæl-/	Salvadorean /-'dɔːr-/
Equatorial Guinea	Equatorial Guinean
Eritrea	Eritrean
Estonia	Estonian
Ethiopia	Ethiopian
Fiji /'fiːdʒiː/	Fiji (a.), Fijian (a. & n.)
Finland	Finnish (a.), Finn (n.)
France	French (a.), Frenchman (n.), Frenchwoman (n.fem.)
Gabon /'gæbɒn/	Gabonese /-'niːz/
Gambia	Gambian
Georgia	Georgian
Germany	German
Ghana /'gɑːnə/	Ghanaian /-'neɪən/
Greece	Greek
Grenada /grə'neɪdə/	Grenadian
Guatemala /gwætɪ'mɑːlə/	Guatemalan

Country	*Adjective and Noun*
Guinea /'gɪnɪ/	Guinean /'gɪnɪən/
Guinea-Bissau /gɪnɪ bɪ'saʊ/	
Guyana /gaɪ'ænə/	Guyanese /-'niːz/
Haiti /'haɪtɪ/	Haitian /'heɪʃ(ə)n/
Honduras /hɒn'djʊərəs/	Honduran
Hungary	Hungarian
Iceland	Icelandic (*a.*), Icelander (*n.*)
India	Indian
Indonesia /-'niːʃə/	Indonesian
Iran	Iranian /-'reɪn-/
Iraq	Iraqi (*pl.* -is)
Ireland, Republic of	Irish (*a.*)
Israel	Israeli (*pl.* -is)
Italy	Italian
Ivory Coast	Ivorian
Jamaica	Jamaican
Japan	Japanese
Jordan	Jordanian /-'deɪn-/
Kazakhstan	Kazakh
Kenya /'ken- *or* 'kiːn-/	Kenyan
Kiribati /'kɪrɪbæs/	
Korea, North	North Korean
Korea, South	South Korean
Kuwait /-'weɪt/	Kuwaiti (*pl.* -is)
Kyrgyzstan	Kyrgyz
Laos /'lɑːɒs/	Laotian /lɑː'əʊʃ(ə)n/
Latvia	Latvian
Lebanon	Lebanese
Lesotho /lə'sʊtʊ/	Lesotho
Liberia	Liberian
Libya	Libyan
Liechtenstein /'lɪktənstam/	
Lithuania	Lithuanian
Luxemburg	Luxemburger (*n.*)
Madagascar	Malagasy /-'gæsɪ/ (*a.*)
Malawi /-'lɑː-/	Malawian
Malaysia	Malaysian
Maldives, The /'mɔːldɪvz/	Maldivian /-'dɪv-/
Mali /'mɑːlɪ/	Malian

Country	Adjective and Noun
Malta	Maltese
Marshall Islands	Marshall Islander (n.)
Mauritania /mɒrɪ'teɪ-/	Mauritanian
Mauritius /mə'rɪʃəs/	Mauritian
Mexico	Mexican
Micronesia	Micronesian
Moldova	Moldovan
Monaco /'mɒnəkəʊ/	Monegasque or Monacan
Mongolia	Mongolian
Morocco	Moroccan
Mozambique /-'biːk/	Mozambican /-'biːkən/
Namibia	Namibian
Nauru /naʊru/	Nauruan
Nepal /nɪ'pɔːl/	Nepalese /nepə'liːz/
Netherlands, The	Dutch (a.), Dutchman (n.), Dutchwoman (n.fem.)
New Zealand	New Zealander (n.)
Nicaragua /-'rægjʊə/	Nicaraguan
Niger /niː'dʒeə(r)/	
Nigeria	Nigerian
Norway	Norwegian
Oman /əʊ'mɑːn/	Omani (pl. -is)
Pakistan	Pakistani (pl. -is)
Panama /-'mɑː/	Panamanian /-'meɪn-/
Papua New Guinea /'pæpʊə/	Papua New Guinean
Paraguay /-'gwaɪ/	Paraguayan /-'gwaɪən/
Peru	Peruvian
Philippines, The	Philippine (a.), Filipino /-'piː-/ (n., pl. -os), Filipina (n.fem.)
Poland	Polish (a.), Pole (n.)
Portugal	Portuguese
Qatar /'kæta:(r)/	Qatari /-'tɑːrɪ/ (pl. -is)
Romania	Romanian
Russia	Russian
Rwanda /rʊ'ændə/	Rwandan
St Kitts and Nevis /'niːvɪs/	Kittitian, Nevisian
St Lucia /'luː.ʃə/	St Lucian
St Vincent /'vɪnsənt/	Vincentian

Country	Adjective and Noun
San Marino /-ˈriː-/	
São Tomé and Principe /saʊ tʊˈmeɪ, ˈprɪnsɪpɪ/	
Saudi Arabia /saʊdɪ/	Saudi Arabian
Senegal /senɪˈɡɔːl/	Senegalese /-ˈliːz/
Seychelles /seɪˈʃelz/	
Sierra Leone /lɪˈəʊn/	Sierra Leonean (n.)
Singapore	Singaporean
Slovakia	Slovak
Solomon Islands	Solomon Islander (n.)
Somalia /-ˈmɑː-/	Somali (pl. -is)
South Africa	South African
Spain	Spanish (a.), Spaniard (n.)
Sri Lanka	Sri Lankan (a.)
Sudan /suːˈdɑːn/	Sudanese /-ˈniːz/
Surinam /sʊəriˈnæm/	Surinamese /ˈmiːz/ (a.), Surinamer (n.)
Swaziland /ˈswɑː-/	Swazi
Sweden	Swedish (a.), Swede (n.)
Switzerland	Swiss
Syria	Syrian
Tajikistan	Tajik
Tanzania /-ˈnɪə/	Tanzanian
Thailand /ˈtaɪ-/	Thai
Togo /ˈtəʊɡəʊ/	Togolese /-ˈliːz/
Tonga	Tongan
Trinidad and Tobago /-ˈbeɪ-/	Trinidadian /-ˈdeɪd-/, Tobagan, Tobagonian
Tunisia	Tunisian
Turkey	Turkish (a.), Turk (n.)
Turkmenistan	Turkmen
Tuvalu /tʊˈvɑːluː/	Tuvaluan
Ukraine	Ukrainian
Uganda	Ugandan
United Arab Emirates	
United Kingdom	British (a.)
United States of America	American
Uruguay	Uruguayan

Country	Adjective and Noun
Uzbekistan	Uzbek
Vanuatu /vænwɑːˈtuː/	
Vatican City State	
Venezuela /-ˈzweɪlə/	Venezuelan
Vietnam	Vietnamese
Western Samoa /səˈməʊə/	Western Samoan
Yemen	Yemeni (*pl.* -is)
Yugoslavia	Yugoslav
Zaïre /zɑːˈɪə(r)/	Zaïrean
Zambia	Zambian
Zimbabwe	Zimbabwean

The chemical elements

The name of each element is preceded by its symbol and followed by its atomic number.

Ac	actinium	89	Gd	gadolinium	64
Al	aluminium	13	Ga	gallium	31
Am	americium	95	Ge	germanium	32
Sb	antimony	51	Au	gold	79
Ar	argon	18	Hf	hafnium	72
As	arsenic	33	Ha	hahnium	105
At	astatine	85	He	helium	2
Ba	barium	56	Ho	holmium	67
Bk	berkelium	97	H	hydrogen	1
Be	beryllium	4	In	indium	49
Bi	bismuth	83	I	iodine	53
B	boron	5	Ir	iridium	77
Br	bromine	35	Fe	iron	26
Cd	cadmium	48	Kr	krypton	36
Cs	caesium	55	La	lanthanum	57
Ca	calcium	20	Lr	lawrencium	103
Cf	californium	98	Pb	lead	82
C	carbon	6	Li	lithium	3
Ce	cerium	58	Lu	lutetium	71
Cl	chlorine	17	Mg	magnesium	12
Cr	chromium	24	Mn	manganese	25
Co	cobalt	27	Md	mendelevium	101
Cu	copper	29	Hg	mercury	80
Cm	curium	96	Mo	molybdenum	42
Dy	dysprosium	66	Nd	neodymium	60
Es	einsteinium	99	Ne	neon	10
Er	erbium	68	Np	neptunium	93
Eu	europium	63	Ni	nickel	28
Fm	fermium	100	Nb	niobium	41
F	fluorine	9	N	nitrogen	7
Fr	francium	87	No	nobelium	102

Os	osmium	76	Ag	silver	4
O	oxygen	8	Na	sodium	1
Pd	palladium	46	Sr	strontium	3.
P	phosphorus	15	S	sulphur	16
Pt	platinum	78	Ta	tantalum	7
Pu	plutonium	94	Tc	technetium	43
Po	polonium	84	Te	tellurium	52
K	potassium	19	Tb	terbium	65
Pr	praseodymium	59	Tl	thallium	81
Pm	promethium	61	Th	thorium	90
Pa	protactinium	91	Tm	thulium	69
Ra	radium	88	Sn	tin	50
Rn	radon	86	Ti	titanium	22
Re	rhenium	75	W	tungsten	74
Rh	rhodium	45	U	uranium	92
Rb	rubidium	37	V	vanadium	23
Ru	ruthenium	44	Xe	xenon	54
Rf	rutherfordium	104	Yb	ytterbium	70
Sm	samarium	62	Y	yttrium	39
Sc	scandium	21	Zn	zinc	30
Se	selenium	34	Zr	zirconium	40
Si	silicon	14			

APPENDIX III
Roman numerals

I	=	1	XX	=	20
II	=	2	XXX	=	30
III	=	3	XL	=	40
IV	=	4	L	=	50
V	=	5	LX	=	60
VI	=	6	LXX	=	70
VII	=	7	LXXX	=	80
VIII	=	8	XC	=	90
IX	=	9	C	=	100
X	=	10	CC	=	200
XI	=	11	CCC	=	300
XII	=	12	CD	=	400
XIII	=	13	D	=	500
XIV	=	14	DC	=	600
XV	=	15	DCC	=	700
XVI	=	16	DCCC	=	800
XVII	=	17	CM	=	900
XVIII	=	18	M	=	1000
XIX	=	19	MM	=	2000

MCMXCI = 1991

The metric system of weights and measures

Linear Measure

1 millimetre	= 0.039 inch
1 centimetre = 10 mm	= 0.394 inch
1 decimetre = 10 cm	= 3.94 inches
1 metre = 10 dm	= 1.094 yards
1 decametre = 10 m	= 10.94 yards
1 hectometre = 100 m	= 109.4 yards
1 kilometre = 1,000 m	= 0.6214 mile

Square Measure

1 square centimetre	= 0.155 sq. inch
1 square metre	= 1.196 sq. yards
1 are /ɑ:(r)/ = 100 sq. metres	= 119.6 sq. yards
1 hectare /ˈhekteə(r)/ = 100 ares	= 2.471 acres
1 square kilometre	= 0.386 sq. mile

Cubic Measure

1 cubic centimetre	= 0.061 cu. inch
1 cubic metre	= 1.308 cu. yards

Capacity Measure

1 millilitre	= 0.002 pint (British)
1 centilitre = 10 ml	= 0.018 pint
1 decilitre = 10 cl	= 0.176 pint
1 litre = 10 dl	= 1.76 pints
1 decalitre = 10 litres	= 2.20 gallons

Note 1 litre is almost exactly equivalent to 1,000 cubic metres.

Weight

1 milligram	= 0.015 grain
1 centigram = 10 mg	= 0.154 grain

1 decigram = 10 cg	= 1.543 grains
1 gram = 10 dg	= 15.43 grains
1 decagram = 10 g	= 5.64 drams
1 hectogram = 100 g	= 3.527 ounces
1 kilogram = 1,000 g	= 2.205 pounds
1 tonne (metric ton) = 1,000 kg	= 0.984 (long) ton

APPENDIX V

Temperatures: Celsius (centigrade) and Fahrenheit

Celsius	Fahrenheit
−17.8°	0°
−10°	14°
0°	32°
10°	50°
20°	68°
30°	86°
40°	104°
50°	122°
60°	140°
70°	158°
80°	176°
90°	194°
100°	212°

To convert Celsius into Fahrenheit: multiply by 9, divide by 5, and add 32.

To convert Fahrenheit into Celsius: subtract 32, multiply by 5, and divide by 9.

APPENDIX VI

Some points of English usage

What follows is intended as guidance on a number of uses that although widely found, are the subject of adverse comment by informed users. They should be avoided, especially in formal speech or writing. For further information see *The Oxford Miniguide to English Usage* by E. S. C. Weiner (1983).

1. Pronunciation

The following words are often mispronounced:

capitalist	/ˈkæpɪtəlɪst/	not /kəˈpɪt-/
comparable	/ˈkɒmpərəb(ə)l/	not /kəmˈpær-/
contribute	/kənˈtrɪbjuːt/	not /ˈkɒn-/
controversy	/ˈkɒntrəvəːsɪ/	is preferable to /kənˈtrɒv-/
deity	/ˈdiːɪtɪ/	not /ˈdeɪ-/
dispute	/dɪˈspjuːt/	not /ˈdɪs-/
distribute	/dɪˈstrɪbjuːt/	not /ˈdɪs-/
exquisite	/ˈekskwɪzɪt/	not /ɪksˈkwɪz-/
formidable	/ˈfɔːmɪdəb(ə)l/	not /fəˈmɪd-/
harass(ment)	/ˈhærəs/	not /həˈræs/
irreparable	/ɪˈrepərəb(ə)l/	not /ɪrɪˈpær-/
irrevocable	/ɪˈrevəkəb(ə)l/	not /ɪrɪˈvəʊk-/
kilometre	/ˈkɪləmiːtə(r)/	is preferable to /kɪˈlɒm-/
lamentable	/ˈlæmɪntəb(ə)l/	not /ləˈment-/
length	/leŋθ/	not /lenθ/
preferable	/ˈprefərəb(ə)l/	not /prɪˈfɜːrəb(ə)l/
primarily	/ˈpraɪmərɪlɪ/	not /praɪˈmeər-/
reputable	/ˈrepjʊtəb(ə)l/	not /rɪˈpjuː-/
secretary	/ˈsekrətrɪ/	not /ˈsekɪteərɪ/
strength	/streŋθ/	not /strenθ/
surveillance	/sɜːˈveɪləns/	not /səˈveɪəns/
temporarily	/ˈtempərərɪlɪ/	not /tempəˈre-/
trait	/treɪ/	not /treɪt/
vulnerable	/ˈvʌlnərəb(ə)l/	not /ˈvʌn-/

2. Spellings

Avoid these common misspellings:

alright the correct form is **all right**
barbeque the correct form is **barbecue**
onto the correct form is **on to**
til the correct form is **till** (it is not a contraction of *until*)

3. Meanings

The following words are often misused:

alibi is not a synonym for 'excuse'
anticipate is not a synonym for 'expect'
dilemma is not a synonym for 'problem'
disinterested does not mean 'uninterested'
enormity does not mean 'largeness' or 'magnitude'
fulsome is not a synonym for 'full' or 'copious'
parameter does not mean 'limit'
protagonist does not mean 'advocate' or 'champion'
refute is not a synonym for 'repudiate' or 'deny'
transpire does not mean 'happen'

Do not confuse:

alternate	*and*	alternative
comprise	*and*	compose
deprecate	*and*	depreciate
derisive	*and*	derisory
flaunt	*and*	flout
infer	*and*	imply
militate	*and*	mitigate
seasonable	*and*	seasonal

4. Plurals

Aborigines is a plural noun but there is no standard singular *Aborigine*; use **Aboriginal**.
bacteria is the plural of **bacterium**
criteria is the plural of **criterion**
data is the plural of **datum** (see below)
graffiti is the plural of **graffito**
media is the plural of **medium**

referendums is the recommended plural of **referendum**, n̶
   referenda

strata is the plural of **stratum**

None of these plurals should be used with a singular verb or wi̶
that or *this*. Correct use is *these bacteria* (the singular is *th̶*
bacterium). The word *data* is now often used (like 'information̶
with a singular verb in the context of computers, e.g. *the data*
entered here; in other contexts it should be used (like 'facts') with̶
plural verb, e.g. *these data are correct*.

5. Grammar

The following points often cause confusion:

less means 'a smaller amount or quantity of' and is used with̶
   nouns such as *money* or *porridge*, whereas

fewer means 'a smaller number of' and is used with plural nouns̶
   such as *people* or *buttons*.

shall and **will** should be used in the following way:

To express the simple future, use
   I/we **shall**
   you **will**
   he/she/it/they **will**
   as in 'I shall be at home tomorrow'; 'he will arrive later'

To express determination or a promise, use
   I/we **will**
   you **shall**
   he/she/it/they **shall**
   as in 'I *will* be heard'; 'you *shall* go to the ball'

should and **would** should be used in the following way:
   I/we **should** like to come
   I/we **should** say so
   you/he/she/they **would** like to come
   you/he/she/they **would** say so
   it **would** be correct

When the meaning is *ought to*, **should** is used in all cases:
   I/you/he/she/we/you/they **should** be able to find it
   it **should** be quite easy

Punctuation

apostrophe 1. Used to indicate the possessive case:

singular   *a boy's book; a day's work; the boss's chair*

plural with s   *a girls' school; two weeks' holiday; the bosses' chairs*

plural without s   *children's books; women's liberation*

names: singular   *Bill's book; Thomas's coat*
          Barnabas' (or Barnabas's) book; Nicholas' (or Nicholas's) coat

names ending in *-es* pronounced /-ɪz/ are treated like plurals: *Bridges' poems; Moses' mother*

before the word *sake: for God's sake; for goodness' sake; for Charles's sake*

business names often omit the apostrophe: *Debenhams; Barclays Bank*

2. Used to mark an omission of one or more letters:

e'er (= ever); *he's* (= he is or he has); *we'll* (= we shall or we will); *'88* (= 1988)

● Incorrect uses: (i) the apostrophe must not be used with a plural where there is no possessive sense, as in *tea's are served here*; (ii) there is no such word as *her's, our's, their's, your's*

● Confusions: *it's* = it is or it has (not 'belonging to it'); correct uses are *it's here* (= it is here); *it's gone* (= it has gone); but *the dog wagged its tail* (no apostrophe)
who's = who is or who has; correct uses are *who's there?; who's taken my pen?;* but *whose book is this? (whose* = belonging to whom)

colon 1. Used to introduce an example or a list:

Please send the following items: passport, two photographs, the correct fee.

2. Used to introduce an interpretation or description of what precedes it:

There is one thing we need: money.
I have news for you: we have won!

3. Used to introduce speech in a play or in a newspaper report where quotation marks are omitted:

Defence lawyer: Objection!
Judge: Objection overruled.

comma The comma marks a slight break between words or phrases etc. Among its specific uses are the following:

1. to separate items in a list:

red, white, and blue
bread, butter, jam, and cake

2. to separate main clauses:

Cars will park here, coaches will turn left.

3. after (or before and after) a vocative or a clause etc. with no finite verb:

Reader, I married him.
Well, Mr Jones, we meet again.
Having had lunch, we went back to work.

4. to separate phrases etc. in order to clarify meaning:

In the valley below, the villages looked very small.
In 1994, 1918 seems a long time ago.

5. following words that introduce direct speech, or after direct speech where there is no question mark or exclamation mark:

They answered, 'Here we are'.
'Here we are,' they answered.

6. after *Dear Sir, Dear John,* etc. in letters, and after *Yours faithfully, Yours sincerely,* etc.; after a vocative such as *My Lord.*

7. to separate a parenthetical word, phrase, or clause:

I am sure, however, that it will not happen.
Autumn, the season of mists, is here again.

● No comma is needed between month and year in dates (e.g. *in December 1992*) or between number and road in addresses (e.g. *17 Belsyre Court*).

dash 1. Used to mark the beginning and end of an interruption in the structure of a sentence:

My son—where has he gone?—would like to meet you.

In print, a line slightly longer than a hyphen is used to join pairs or groups of words where it is often equivalent to *to* or *versus*:

>the 1914–18 war; the London–Horsham–Brighton route; the Marxist–Trotskyite split

(See also **hyphen**.)

exclamation mark Used after an exclamatory word, phrase, or sentence, or an interjection:

>Well! If it isn't John!
>Order! Order!

full stop 1. Used at the end of all sentences that are not questions or exclamations.

2. Used after abbreviations:

>H. G. Wells; B.Litt.; Sun. (= Sunday); Jan. (= January); p. 7 (= page 7); e.g.; etc.; a.m.; p.m.

● A full stop should not be used with the numerical abbreviations *1st, 2nd, 3rd,* etc., nor with acronyms such as *Aslef, Naafi,* nor with words that are colloquial abbreviations (e.g. *Co-op, demo, recap, vac*).

● Full stops are not essential in abbreviations consisting entirely of capitals (e.g. *BBC, NNE, AD, BC, PLC*), nor with *C* (= Celsius), *F* (= Fahrenheit), chemical symbols, and measures of length, weight, time, etc. (except for *in.* = inch), nor for *Dr, Revd, Mr, Mrs, Ms, Mme, Mlle, St, Hants, Northants, p* (= penny or pence).

hyphen 1. Used to join two or more words so as to form a single expression:

>father-in-law; happy-go-lucky; non-stick; self-control

2. Used to join words in an attributive compound:

>a well-known man (but 'the man is well known')
>an out-of-date list (but 'the list is out of date')

3. Used to join a prefix etc. to a proper name:

>anti-Darwinian; half-Italian; non-German

4. Used to prevent misconceptions, by linking words:

>a poor-rate collection; a poor rate-collection

or by separating a prefix:

re-cover/recover; re-present/represent; re-sign/resign

5. Used to separate two similar consonant or vowel sounds, a help to understanding and pronunciation:

pre-empt; pre-exist; Ross-shire

6. Used to represent a common second element in the items of list:

two-, three-, or fourfold

7. Used at the end of a line of print to show that a word not usual hyphenated has had to be divided.

question mark 1. Used after every question that expects separate answer:

Why is he here? Who invited him?

2. Placed before a word or date etc. whose accuracy is doubted
T. Tallis ?1505–85

● It is not used in indirect questions, e.g. *We asked why he was there and who had invited him.*

quotation marks Used round a direct quotation:

'That is nonsense,' he said.

The commas stand outside the quotation marks when *he said* interrupts the quotation:

'That', he said, 'is nonsense.'

semicolon Used to separate those parts of a sentence between which there is a more distinct break than would be called for by a comma but which are too closely connected to be made into separate sentences:

To err is human; to forgive, divine.